JONATHAN BARDON was born in Dublin in 1941 and was educated at the High School Dublin, at Trinity College Dublin, and at Queen's University Belfast. He has lived in Belfast since 1963, teaching history at Orangefield Secondary School and at the College of Business Studies, now the Belfast Institute of Further and Higher Education, where he is head of the Department of Academic and Continuing Education. He has scripted various schools broadcasts series, including the much-praised *Modern Irish History* for the BBC and *Understanding Northern Ireland* for UTV/Channel 4. He was chairman of the cross-curricular working groups on *Education for Mutual Understanding* and *Cultural Heritage* which reported in 1989.

His other publications include: *The Struggle for Ireland: 400–1450 AD* (1970); *Belfast: An Illustrated History* (1982); *Dublin: One Thousand Years of Wood Quay* (1984); *Belfast: 1000 Years* (1985); *If Ever You Go To Dublin Town: A Historic Guide to the City's Street Names* (with Carol Bardon) (1988); and *Investigating Place Names in Ulster: A Teachers' Guide* (1991).

A
HISTORY
of
ULSTER

·

Jonathan Bardon

THE
BLACKSTAFF
PRESS

First published in November 1992 by
The Blackstaff Press Limited
3 Galway Park, Dundonald, Belfast BT16 0AN, Northern Ireland
with the financial assistance of the
Cultural Traditions Programme which aims to encourage
acceptance and understanding of cultural diversity.

Reprinted December 1992, 1993, 1994, 1996

Typeset by Textflow Services Limited

Printed in England by
The Bath Press

British Library Cataloguing in Publication Data
Bardon, Jonathan
History of Ulster
I. Title
941.6

ISBN 0-85640-466-7 hardback
0-85640-476-4 paperback
0-85640-498-5 limited edition

to Carol,
Jane and Daniel

CONTENTS

ACKNOWLEDGEMENTS

David Lammey, Hiram Morgan and Trevor Parkhill between them read a substantial proportion of this book in draft and I am most grateful for their constructive comments and the beneficial alterations they suggested.

I owe a particular debt of gratitude to Cynthia Wilson, who typed the final chapters, and to Robert Orr for many kindnesses.

Most sincere thanks are due to the following who lent material or drew my attention to useful sources or provided valuable advice and assistance: Tom Bartlett, Brian Barton, Henry V. Bell, Victor Blease, Martin Bowen, Beatrice Boyd, Oliver Boylan, Thérèse Brannigan, Deirdre Brown, Pat Brown, Ronnie Buchanan, Douglas Carson, Fionnuala Cook, Stephen Cook, Barry Cowan, Bill (W.H.) Crawford, Andrew Crockart, Maurna Crozier, Nessan Danaher, Marc Davis, Robson Davison, Sister Rose Devlin, John Dooher, Seamus Dunn, Kieran Fagan, Anne Gallagher, Carmel Gallagher, Brian Garrett, Charlotte Gault, Arthur and Rosemary Green, Margaret Hale, Eamon Hanna, David Hannon, Richard Hawkins, Maurice Hayes, Fred Heatley, Myrtle Hill, Pat Hill, Robert J. Hunter, Alvin Jackson, Paul Kane, Jim Kemmy, Liam Kennedy, Christine Kinealy, Brian Lambkin, John McCabe, Tim McCall, Nonie McClure, Jim McConville, Tony McCusker, Billy McGivern, Vivian McIver, Jack McKinney, Margaret McKnight, Pat MacMahon, Richard (J.R.B.) McMinn, Philip McVicker, Bill (W.A.) Maguire, John Moulden, Kay Muhr, Ray Mullan, Jim O'Hara, Maire O'Neill, Kathleen Page, Jennifer and Patricia Pauley, Philip Peattie, Joan Pettigrew, Annie Phillips, John Reaney, Chris Ryder, John Scobbie, Catherine Shannon, Sheela Speers, Ronnie Spence, Wendy Spratt, Thompson Steel, Brian Trainor, Carol Tweedale, Brian M. Walker, Patrick Walsh, Jacqueline Weir, and Barry White.

In 1989–90 the Department of Education for Northern Ireland generously seconded me to the Public Record Office of Northern Ireland, where, thanks to the hospitality and assistance provided by Anthony Malcomson, Trevor Parkhill, David Lammey, Aileen McClintock and other members of staff, much of this book was researched and written. My thanks to John Gray, John Killen, Mary Hughes, Bern Kane, Maureen Larmour and Yvonne Murphy of the Linen Hall Library, Belfast, and especially to Robert Bell and Gerry Healey who patiently and knowledgeably answered a stream of queries. Jennifer Crossland, Roger Dixon, Robert McMillen and other staff of the Belfast Central Library also were unfailingly helpful and I am particularly grateful to Michael Maultsaid for his interest and assistance. The staffs of the State Paper Office and the National Library in Dublin, and of the Ulster Museum in Belfast, were also generous with their time.

A book of this scope could not have been written without drawing heavily on the researches of many scholars and journalists: I hope that these writers will consider reference to their work in the endnotes and bibliography in part an expression of my gratitude.

I must also give my thanks to the Deputy Keeper of Records, Public Record Office of Northern Ireland, for granting me permission to quote from material deposited there; and I am indebted to the following depositors: the Earl of Gosford; the late Reverend G. Otway Woodward; the late Aiken McClelland; the late Lady Hermione Blackwood; and the late Miss Emma Duffin.

The Blackstaff Press has notably enriched the cultural life of Ulster for more than two decades. No author could ask for publishers more warmly supportive or more meticulously and professionally concerned to achieve quality.

I am deeply grateful to Carol, my wife, who typed more than two thirds of this book, gave invaluable advice, assisted with the proofreading and the compilation of the bibliography, endured a protracted disruption of domestic life and gave me vital support during the completion of a project which stretched over many years.

JONATHAN BARDON
BELFAST, 1992

1

EARLY ULSTER

c. 7000 BC–AD 800

Just south of Coleraine a great ridge of basalt lies in the path of the Bann and, after a serene passage from Lough Beg past Portglenone and Kilrea, the river is funnelled between bluffs to cascade in rapids and through weirs and sluices into a long estuary leading north-west to the Atlantic. The waters draining off nearly half the surface of Ulster pass through here, for Lough Neagh has only one outlet: at Toome where the Bann bursts out through eel traps. This lough, which the English unsuccessfully attempted to rename Lough Sidney and then Lough Chichester, is the most extensive sheet of fresh water in either Ireland or Britain; it draws to it rivers issuing from the Antrim Plateau to the north-east, the Sperrins in the west, the Mournes in the south-east and the slopes of Eshcloghfin in Monaghan where the Blackwater begins.

Here, where the Bann meets the tide, are reminders of Ulster's history: locks and sluices of nineteenth-century enterprise; quays from which Ulster Presbyterians set out to face the perils of an Atlantic voyage in the eighteenth century; fish weirs close to where sixty-two tons of salmon were netted in one day in 1632; the Cutts, where in 1611 men employed by the London Companies tried to hew a navigable passage upstream; the ruins of Castle Roe, where, a century before, the Tyrone O'Neills guarded their fishing from the O'Cahans to the west and the MacQuillans and MacDonnells in the Route; overgrown rubble of a stone castle a little upstream at Fish Loughan and hastily erected defences at Mount Sandel, from where the Normans kept a precarious hold over their manors of Twescard in the thirteenth century; and Mount Sandel fort impressively commanding the river, once perhaps the *dún* of a forgotten Gaelic king. The Norman ringwork on top of this Gaelic fort shows that here is a place where successive peoples and cultures met, clashed and blended.

The tranquil scene from Mount Sandel gives no hint of tempestuous events over the centuries: the terrified flight to Coleraine of colonists who escaped the massacre at Portna in 1641; Sir John Perrott's furious advance along the river against the MacDonnells in 1584; the running

1

battle between Edward Bruce's Scots and the Red Earl of Ulster across 'the rushing, wild, deep, Bann' in 1315; and the incursions of the Vikings in the ninth century, carrying their longships overland past the rapids to establish a raiding fleet on Lough Neagh. Mount Sandel was a favourite haunt of Victorian antiquarians; they found over a hundred Stone Age axe heads close by and the exquisite Bann disc, now the symbol of the Ulster Museum. And it was here in 1973 that archaeologists began to unearth evidence of the very first human presence in Ireland.

MOUNT SANDEL NINE THOUSAND YEARS AGO

Some worked flints were brought to the surface in 1972 close to Mount Sandel Fort when land was being prepared for a new housing estate. The following year Peter Woodman and his team of archaeologists began what seemed a routine investigation only to discover – after the carbon-14 dating of charred hazelnut shells – that human beings had dwelt here between 7000 and 6500 BC. The generally accepted date of the arrival of people in Ireland had been put back by more than a thousand years. Over five seasons the site, preserved from destruction because it was in a hollow, was meticulously excavated and its contents sieved, sifted and chemically analysed by specialists. Their findings cast a unique shaft of light back over nine millenniums on life in a Mesolithic camp in Ulster.[1]

The slope of post holes showed that saplings had been driven into the ground in a rough circle and bent over to form a domed roof by being lashed together. Lighter branches may have been interwoven to add strength and rigidity; then each hut – there were four built at different times – was covered with bark or deer hide, and reinforced against north winds with grass turfs lifted from inside. Around six metres wide, each hut gave shelter to perhaps a dozen people gathered round a bowl-shaped hearth in the centre. Charred fragments showed that this camp was perfectly sited to provide a living all year round.

The last ice sheets had retreated only about three thousand years earlier and the sea level was around five metres lower than it is today. The falls and rapids by Mount Sandel must then have made a majestic sight; below them, in early summer, salmon waited in thousands for a flood to take them upstream to spawn, and sea bass foraged at high tide in pursuit of crabs, flounder and smolts. Scale-shaped flints found in abundance almost certainly had been set into poles to harpoon these fish together with myriads of eels dropping down from Lough Neagh in autumn. Autumn, too, was the season for gathering hazelnuts: these gram for gram are seven times richer in fat, five times richer in carbohydrates, four times richer in calcium and fives richer in vitamin B_1 than eggs. These were supplemented by crab apples, goosegrass, vetches and seeds of water lilies – these last, prized by Elizabethans for cooling the passions, resemble popcorn when dropped into hot fat. In midwinter wild pigs, fattened on the abundant hazel mast, began their rutting, and male yearlings, driven out by mature boars, were vulnerable then to hunting parties armed with flint-tipped spears and arrows. This too was the time for trapping birds in the forest and overwintering wild fowl; the archaeologists found bone fragments of eagle, goshawk, capercaillie, red-throated diver, widgeon, teal, coot and some song birds. Several pieces of bone were soft, showing that carcasses had been boiled to make broth, perhaps in skins filled with water suspended over a fire – a practice observed in Ulster as late as the sixteenth century.

Flint had to be carried from as far away as the beaches of Portrush in Co. Antrim and Downhill in Co. Londonderry, and was made to give service for as long as possible. At a tool-working area to the west of the hollow, flint cores were roughed out and fashioned into axes, picks and adzes, while the smaller blades struck from them were shaped into knives, arrowheads, hide scrapers, awls and harpoon flakes. Several axe heads had been resharpened and most of the tools had been put to long use before being cast aside. One axe had traces of red ochre on its surface, which gives a hint that these people painted themselves on ceremonial occasions.

Some of the smaller implements were made from black chert, a stone only to be found in carboniferous limestone well to the south. It seems likely that this stone had been exchanged in trade with others and that the people of the Mount Sandel camp were not Ireland's first inhabitants. Where did they come from? Recent discovery of other Mesolithic sites in the Midlands and in Munster suggest that their ancestors crossed the Irish Sea by land bridges since washed away. The last land links with Britain must have been cut long before 7000 BC when the climate was much colder than today: trees, such as beech, lime and walnut; fish, such as pike, perch, tench and bream; and mammals, such as wild cattle, beaver, mole, weasel and roe deer, did not have the chance to reach Ireland before the sea engulfed the bridges.

From about 6500 BC the rains became more persistent, the temperature range narrowed, and at Mount Sandel oak, alder and elm began to tower over the hazel. Pine woods survived only on the uplands and, thus deprived of its habitat, the capercaillie became extinct in Ireland around 4000 BC.

Broken up only by loughs and broad rivers, the great forests covered all the land save for the most barren peaks. It is no surprise then that most Mesolithic sites have been found by lake margins and sea shores, especially along the Antrim coast, where workable flints were exposed in greater quantities than in any other part of the British Isles. The shift to a more oceanic climate led to an extension of wetlands, particularly in the poorly drained soils of the drumlin belt.

The last great ice sheet had torn and pulverised rock from the mountains of Ulster as it advanced south, and then as it retreated and melted it dumped this rubble as huge mounds of boulder clay in their tens of thousands. The geographer and prehistorian E. Estyn Evans has likened these to 'a necklace of beads some thirty miles wide suspended between Donegal Bay and Strangford Lough'.[2] Densely overgrown with wolf-infested thickets and separated by soft-margined loughs and treacherous fens, these low, rounded hills, known as drumlins, formed a frontier which did much to shape the future history of Ulster. This division between Ulster and the rest of Ireland should not be over-emphasised, for the barrier was never completely impenetrable; nevertheless, until the seventeenth century easy access to Ulster from the south was only by the fords of Erne in the west and the Moyry Pass in the east – the gap that is the defile in the hills south of Slieve Gullion. As the historical geographer P.J. Duffy has observed: 'There are few examples where boundaries so finely reflect a borderland as the Monaghan–Armagh–Louth county boundaries coinciding with the southern edge of the most extensive drumlin belt in western Europe.'[3] Further west, the provincial frontier was more blurred, much of Cavan and south Fermanagh not being considered part of Ulster until the fourteenth century.

Although rising sea levels had severed Ireland from Britain – the last land bridge is thought to have run from Inishowen to Islay – geologically they remain closely linked, especially in Ulster. Only thirteen miles apart at their nearest points, Scotland and Ulster share tertiary basalts in Skye, Mull and Antrim, and the massive Caledonian mountain spine runs south-west from the Cairngorms into the Sperrins, Donegal and beyond. Both Ireland and Britain are structurally attached under shallow seas to the European mainland and it was from there that profound changes followed in the fourth millennium BC.

While investigating a site at Ballynagilly, near Cookstown, in 1969, Arthur ap Simon noticed a fall in pollen from broad-leaved trees beginning around 3500 BC. Pollen is remarkably resistant to decay and is therefore invaluable in helping to explain the distant past. Alan Smith followed with a meticulous study of a bog at Fallahogy in Co. Londonderry by combining pollen counts with radiocarbon datings; in particular, he traced a sudden drop in elm tree pollen from about 3200 BC and a rise in traces of plantain, dock and nettle. In short, he was uncovering irrefutable evidence of the dramatic impact of pioneering farmers on Ulster's landscape.

THE FIRST FARMERS IN ULSTER

Some time during the first half of the fourth millennium BC intrepid family groups began to venture across the North Channel to Ulster with their domestic stock. A thirty-foot currach can take a couple of cows with their calves or, alternatively, half a dozen pigs or sheep – the perils of crossing the sea in frail craft with frightened and thirsty horned beasts, even when firmly trussed, can be imagined. If anything the journey would have been longer than today, for investigations at Ringneill Quay at Strangford Lough (where the earliest cattle, sheep and pig bones have been found in Ireland) show that the sea was then four metres higher than at present. On landing, the most urgent task was to find a stand of elm, the most reliable guide to good soil; as the men spread out through the wood girdling the trees with their stone axes, the women and children put up shelters and gathered leaves, twigs and other fodder to carry the cattle through the first critical winter. Excavations at Newferry by Lough Beg, occupied between 6240 and 3465 BC, show that for almost three thousand years Mesolithic people had made little technological advance. Now Neolithic pioneers began to transform the countryside, opening up the forest canopy and letting in sunlight to enable their animals to graze the clearings.[4]

For a long time archaeologists refused to believe that so small a population could make such a devastating impact on Ulster's woodland. It appears that trees were not laboriously felled but merely ringbarked, and extensive sweeps of forest could be killed in this way in a fairly short period. When the clearings lost their fertility, the farmers simply moved on to create new pastures. Flint was still highly prized for making arrowheads and javelin points, but it shattered easily against tree trunks; much preferred for axes was porcellanite, formed sixty million years earlier when hot Antrim lavas poured over clays to bake and compress them into this hard china-like stone. As the population rose specialist factories emerged at Tievebulliagh, Co. Antrim, and on Rathlin Island; from here polished porcellanite axe heads were traded as far away as Dorset and Inverness.

5

Naturally, timber was felled for fuel and building, and it was at Ballynagilly that the oldest known Neolithic house in either Ireland or Britain was found. This rectangular dwelling, six metres by six and a half metres, was made with radially split oak placed upright in trench foundations. Substantial posts evidently marked the position of thatched roof supports.[5] Similar houses from the same period (about 3200 BC) have been found in central Europe, illustrating the steady movement of peoples westward, bringing with them knowledge of innovations such as cereal cultivation, first developed in the Middle East. Some corn was grown in Ulster, usually on light soils capable of being worked with a stone-headed mattock. Cattle predominated, however, as they do to-day. Protecting domestic stock from the predations of bear, wolf, lynx and fox was an unending task; animals brought into a stockade every night supplied manure for spreading on corn cultivation ridges. More settled than their Mesolithic predecessors, these Neolithic peoples made and fired their own pottery; a distinctive Ulster pot shape emerged, archaeologists recognising a 'Dunmurry style' and a 'Lyles Hill style' from sites excavated near Belfast. At Goodland in Co. Antrim sherds of at least 266 pots were found, thought to be offerings to spirits or gods.

An enclosure in Scotch Street in Armagh city, revealed in 1979 by the destruction of shops during the bombing campaign,[6] seems to have been a place of ritual offerings; a circular ditch there was filled with a great quantity of pot fragments. Court cairns, the earliest megalithic monuments, were probably temples of a kind, where farming communities paid respect to departed ancestors and invoked magical help to ensure good harvests. The first to be excavated, Ballyalton in Co. Down, had a stone forecourt (where perhaps the people assembled) leading into a mound with several chambers, containing a decorated bowl, pieces of pottery, animal bones and worked flints. A court cairn at Cohaw in Co. Cavan had a youth's skull and the cremated bones of two children in its chambers, while another at Audleystown in Co. Down contained the bones of thirty-four people in its two chambers. It is likely that the dead were buried or burned elsewhere and their bones, together with other offerings, taken to the cairns at a later time. Portal tombs, or dolmens, *were* burial places and are the most splendid and striking reminders of Ulster's first farmers. Built of three or more great upright stones, with a huge capstone – requiring earth ramps and log rollers to put in place – the portal tomb is largely confined to the north. The court cairn, too, predominates in Ulster and north Connacht.

The drumlin belt seems to have cut the north off from the more sophisticated settlements in the Boyne valley, where immense and complex tumuli still remain as awesome monuments to Neolithic skill and organisation. It was on the edge of the great Newgrange tumulus by the River Boyne that hearths were found showing evidence of intense heat; dated around 2100 BC, the site gives one of the earliest signals that the skill of metalworking had arrived in Ireland.

THE BRONZE AGE IN ULSTER

Around 2000 BC Egypt's second golden age of the Middle Kingdom flourished, the Sumerians were building the great Ur ziggurat, the Chinese were cultivating tea, the Hittites were invading Anatolia, the Mycenaeans were moving into Greece, and the Minoan sea empire was approaching its zenith. Knossos in Crete had a population of some one hundred thousand, about the same as that for all Ireland. Technological advances, religious cults and artistic styles from these cradles of civilisation spread northwards and westwards. Steady immigration from the east did not necessarily mean overwhelming invasions, however, and Peter Woodman has gone so far as to conclude that the 'gene pool of the Irish was probably set by the end of the Stone Age'.[7] A bronze axe head found at Culfeightrin, near Ballycastle, fits perfectly in a stone mould discovered at Ballynahinch, showing how the skills of metalworking could be taken quickly across the country by wandering craftsmen. The heavy weight of Irish axes indicates great abundance of copper: the total weight of copper and bronze objects found dated from the early Bronze Age is around 750 kilograms – impressive enough in itself – and yet just one mine in Co. Cork is estimated to have produced no fewer than 370 tonnes in the same period. Enough tin – and sometimes arsenic and lead – could be found locally to mix with copper to make it into a stronger and more malleable bronze.[8]

Wedge-shaped graves, round-bottomed pottery beakers, V-perforated buttons, and archers' wrist guards are all tell-tale characteristics of Bronze Age sites, but most evocative of a bygone culture shining across the centuries are the rich finds of gold. Gold almost certainly was panned in the beds of streams flowing off the Sperrins and as many golden ornaments have been found in Ulster as in other provinces. Amongst the earliest, made from thin hammered sheets of gold, are sun discs, such as the one discovered at Tedavnet in Co. Monaghan, and lanulae, half-moon-shaped neck ornaments with decoration similar to that found on ceremonial bronze axes unearthed at Scrabo in Co. Down and Rosslea in Co. Fermanagh. Later objects are so heavy that they must have been used as a form of currency. Could so many beautiful and valuable ornaments have simply been lost? It is much more likely that precious goods were cast into the waters as offerings to spirits – many

7

have been found in drained loughs and bogs which were once lakes. Religion had a central role in the lives of Ulster's prehistoric peoples.

On the southern slopes of the Sperrins an intriguing group of megalithic monuments was revealed when peat was carefully removed by archaeologists from 1945 onwards. This elaborate complex of paired stone circles and alignments at Beaghmore, near Cookstown, seems to have been a ceremonial site where perhaps the aid of the gods was invoked to maintain fertility (which was falling from overgrazing at the time, about 1500 BC). As on other sites in Tyrone, several of the stone circles appear to have been placed as pointers to the horizons which saw the rising and the setting of the sun, the moon and major stars. Another place of ritual importance was the Giant's Ring, near Shaw's Bridge outside Belfast; here a great bank four metres high encircles a flat area two hundred metres across, with a portal tomb in the middle. We have only the barest hints of the ancient rituals performed in such places. In 1975 during a severe drought, preliminary investigations were made at the King's Stables, an overgrown pool artificially dug out at the base of a hill to the west of Navan in Armagh; the first finds included a spatula made from antler and some broken clay moulds for bronze swords, but deeper down the archaeologists scooped out great quantities of red deer and dog bones, and the facial part of a human skull carefully cut from the rest of the cranium. The excavator, Chris Lynn, suggests that this 'anticipates the mass of early Irish tradition which attests to veneration of sacred pools, severed head cults, animal sacrifice and votive offerings'.[9]

Overlooking the King's Stables is Haughey's Fort, an oval enclosure crowning a prominent hill clearly built for defence. This and many similar hill forts scattered across Ulster indicate an intensification of warfare during the late Bronze Age of the last millennium BC. Weapons became more sophisticated in their making: bronze spearheads with socket loops for attachment were cast from twin-valved moulds found on Inch Island in Co. Donegal; the same technique was used to cast a long bronze rapier discovered at Lissane, Co. Londonderry, and socketed axes and slashing swords inspired by models from central Europe. A tasselled belt-attachment, found at Cromaghs in Co. Antrim, was made of horsehair – this late Bronze Age ornament could have been imported but it does signal the imminent arrival of a domesticated animal that would greatly increase the tempo of Irish warfare.

An improvement in climate, which increased prosperity, helped to stimulate a remarkable flowering of artistic achievement in both bronze and gold. These include: curling bronze horns, such as that from Dromabest, Co. Antrim; a decorated bronze bucket from Capecastle

Bog in the same county; a huge but elegant cauldron from Ballyscullion, Co. Londonderry; and a bronze flesh-hook, adorned with water birds, from Dunaverney in Co. Antrim. A hoard of gold from Broighter, Co. Londonderry, includes a charming model boat with oars, a cup, necklaces, and a torc with intricate, swirling patterns – made when iron weapons were supplanting those cast from bronze, this neck ornament is a clear indication that the Celts had arrived in Ulster well before the start of the Christian era. Influences from abroad continued to generate change in Ulster; at Navan Fort the excavation of a round house and adjacent stockade (rebuilt nine times between 700 and 100 BC) yielded not only iron fragments but also the skull of a Barbary ape.[10]

The Celts were the first people north of the Alps to emerge into recorded history. Their distinctive culture evolved during the second millennium BC between Bohemia and the east bank of the Rhine and then spread north towards Denmark, south-east into the Balkans and west to France, northern Spain, Portugal, the Netherlands and Britain. By 500 BC the Celts dominated the northern half of Europe and, setting out from their hill forts, led by nobles on horseback or in chariots, they sacked Rome in 390 BC and looted the temple of the oracle at Delphi in 278 BC, crossing the Hellespont to settle Anatolia thereafter. The cult of Lugh spread across the Continent, and places as far apart as León, London, Leiden, Lyon and Legnica preserve the memory of devotion to this Celtic sun god. In contrast with the realism and natural beauty preferred by Greek and Roman artists, the imaginative art of the Celts delighted in symbols and intricate patterns. The high form of this style, known as La Tène after a site in Switzerland, made its first appearance in Ireland in the decoration of scabbards found at Lisnacroghera and Toome in Co. Antrim.[11]

When did the Celts come to Ireland? No clear answer can be given, especially for the province of Ulster. Scholars are coming increasingly to the realisation that Celtic civilisation was not the creation of a separate race but a language and a way of life spread from one people to another. Archaeological enquiry does not show evidence of formidable invasion; rather there was a steady infiltration from Britain and the European mainland over the centuries. The first Celtic speakers may have come as early as 1000 BC and in greater numbers from about 500 BC and, equipped with iron weapons and advancing on horseback, they brought the native peoples under subjugation. A constant blending of language, belief and tradition followed and the Gaelic civilisation which emerged in early Christian times – to survive independently longest in Ulster – evolved not just from the Celts but also from their predecessors to the earliest times.

9

By 133 BC the Roman conquest of Spain was complete and in 59 BC Julius Caesar began his conquest of Gaul. In 56 BC the Veneti were overwhelmed in Armorica and the Belgae were in retreat. The Celtic hegemony was collapsing before the might of Rome.

BEYOND THE ROMAN EMPIRE

In AD 82 Gnaeus Julius Agricola, governor of Britain, summoned his fleet into the Solway Firth to take aboard his waiting cohorts. Ulster was directly across the sea and this land he meant to conquer – a climax to a dazzling career the empire would not forget. Posted to Britain as military tribune twenty-one years before, Agricola had been in the thick of the desperate fighting with the Iceni and Brigantes during Boudicca's uprising. Placed in command of the XX Legion, he directed the Irish Sea flotilla for a time; perhaps it had been then that the notion that Ireland was worthy of conquest had formed in his mind. Now, returned after distinguished service as a governor in Gaul and a consul in Rome, Agricola swept all before him: in the fastnesses of Snowdonia he reduced the Ordovices to abject submission and then, pressing relentlessly northwards into Caledonia, he reached the base of the Highlands, harried the Inner Isles with his fleet and ordered the erection of a network of castella.

The Roman Empire knew little enough about this island of Hibernia on the north-western edge of its world. Sailing directions, written by a sea captain of the Greek colony of Marseille about 525 BC, referred to Ireland as 'the Sacred Isle' two days' voyage from Armorica and significantly larger than Britain. However, Himilco, the Carthaginian, journeying to the 'Tin Isles' of Scilly around 480 BC, warned of dense seaweed entanglements and threatening sea monsters beyond. It was the epic voyage of Pytheas, another Greek from Marseille, who visited Norway and circumnavigated Britain about 300 BC, which gave Mediterranean traders Ireland's correct position; this explorer's account does not survive but it seems to have formed the basis of Ptolemy's map of Ireland prepared in the second century AD. Known only from a fifteenth-century copy, this map includes some identifiable names, such as Logia (the Lagan or Belfast Lough), Isamnion (Navan Fort) and Volunti (the Ulaidh, the people of Ulster). Even after Julius Caesar invaded Britain in 55 BC, the Greek geographer and historian Strabo was asserting that the Irish 'think it decent to eat up their dead parents', but fifty years later Pomponius Mela was better informed about Ireland: 'Its climate is unfavourable for the maturing of crops, but there is such a profuse growth of grass, and this is as sweet as it is rich, that the cattle can sate themselves in a short part of the day.'[12] Tacitus was a more acute observer, and his descriptions of the Britons and continental Celts dovetail remarkably well with early Irish law tracts and heroic tales.

For information about the Celts of the British Isles, Tacitus relied on his father-in-law, Agricola; and it is from Tacitus that we learn that the invasion of Ireland was planned with a king in exile:

> Agricola received in friendly fashion an Irish petty king who had been driven out in a civil war, and kept him for use when opportunity offered. I have often heard him say that Ireland could be conquered and held by one legion and a modest force of auxiliary troops; and that it would be advantageous in dealing with Britain too if Roman forces were on all sides and the spectacle of freedom were, so to say, banished out of sight.[13]

Some scholars have made a tentative suggestion – it can be no more than that – that the Irish king was Tuathail Techtmar, forced to seek aid in Britain to recover his throne. However, Agricola's invasion was not to be: a legion of Germans stationed in Galloway mutinied and there was disturbing news of Pictish rebellion. The Emperor Domitian ordered his governor north, and later, after Agricola's recall, the Romans retired behind Hadrian's Wall. Ulster would not become part of the Roman Empire after all.

EMAIN MACHA

Ulster, too, has its defensive wall. Described on maps as the Dane's Cast, it begins in the east near Scarva on the Down–Armagh border; the next section, known as the Dorsey, stands at Drummill Bridge in south Armagh; it continues into Monaghan near Muckno Lake, where it is known either as the Worm Ditch or as the Black Pig's Dyke; and further short stretches extend through Cavan and Fermanagh to Donegal Bay. A tradition survives that it was ploughed up by the tusks of an enchanted black boar; archaeologists, however, have proved this great linear earthwork to have been a series of massive defences, not continuous, but guarding the routeways into Ulster between the bogs, loughs and drumlins. The Dorsey – from *doirse* meaning doors or gates – is double-banked and double-ditched, being a full eight metres from the top of its largest rampart to the bottom of its parallel ditch. Here a bulldozer uncovered a palisade made of hewn oak posts driven into a shallow trench across a bog and reinforced with props and horizontal boards. Michael G.L. Baillie, the paleoecologist from Queen's University Belfast who pioneered the art of dating by matching oak tree growth rings, not only demonstrated that the timber for the palisade

11

had been felled in 95 BC but also that the central post of a great ritual structure on Navan Fort had been cut down in the same year.

No one knows why a circular temple, forty-three metres in diameter, was put up inside Navan Fort. It seems to have been built quickly, perhaps by a whole community working together; held up by concentric rows of posts steadied by horizontal planks, the roof had been covered with a cairn of stones enveloped with sods. Then the whole structure had been set on fire. Had this been a ritual to invoke the aid of the gods while Ulster was under attack? The Dorsey palisade had been burned, perhaps during an assault, about the same time.[14]

Only a determined and concerted campaign by representatives of both sides of the political divide in Northern Ireland saved Navan Fort from destruction by a limestone quarry company in the 1980s. A huge circular hilltop enclosure, it is an Iron Age site of European importance and its ancient name, Emain Macha, has an Indo-European foundation myth parallel to the story of Romulus and Remus. At a fair Crunniuc mac Agnomain boasted that his wife Macha could outrun a chariot. When she protested that she was about to give birth, Conor, King of Ulster, said that she must run.

> Then she raced the chariot. As the chariot reached the end of the field, she gave birth alongside it. She bore twins, a son and a daughter. The name Emain Macha, the Twins of Macha, comes from this. As she gave birth she screamed out that all who heard that scream would suffer from the same pangs for five days and four nights in their times of greatest difficulty. This affliction, ever afterward, seized all the men of Ulster who were there that day.[15]

Translated by Thomas Kinsella, this extract is from the *Táin Bó Cuailnge*, 'The Cattle Raid of Cooley': it tells how Queen Maeve of Connacht made war on King Conor of Ulster to win possession of the Brown Bull of Cuailnge and how – when the men of Ulster were struck down by their pangs in their time of great difficulty – the champion Cuchulain single-handedly held back the men of Connacht by the ford. The earliest versions of the *Táin* were written down in the monasteries of Bangor in Co. Down and Dromsnat in Co. Monaghan in the eighth century, and some verse sections are thought to be two centuries earlier. This is the oldest vernacular epic in western European literature and it probably had a long oral existence before being committed to vellum – in 'The Voyage of Bran' King Mongan of the Ulaidh is told a story by his poets every winter night between the feasts of *Samhain* and *Bealtaine*, and this practice does not appear to have been particularly unusual.

The *Táin* and other tales in the Ulster Cycle at their best possess arresting power, vividly graphic yet stylised, in which stark reality and magic intertwine and the principal characters are ordinary mortals able on occasion to act like gods. Such characteristics are displayed in an intense form in the sorrowful tale of Deirdre in 'The Exile of the Sons of Uisliu'. In this extract the beautiful Deirdre, fostered by King Conor's command away from the eyes of other men, finds that as she reaches maturity romantic desire cannot be held back:

> One day, in winter, Deirdre's foster-father was outside, in the snow, flaying a weaned calf for her. Deirdre saw a raven drinking the blood on the snow, and she said to Leborcham, 'I could love a man with those three colours: hair like a raven, cheeks like blood and body like snow.'[16]

From these epic tales the historian gets a vivid picture of an aristocratic Iron Age society remarkably similar in many respects to Celtic Gaul described by Julius Caesar. It was a civilisation not touched by Roman conquest, major features of which survived in Ulster into the seventeenth century. Whether the *Táin* reflects life in the seventh, fifth or first centuries AD is not certain; and to what extent these stories are based on actual events is the subject of much academic controversy.

CONQUEST AND RETREAT

In the *Táin Bó Cuailnge* the men of Ulster triumph in the end over the men of Connacht but, piecing together evidence from the annals, historians know that the province was on the defensive. The over-kingdom of the Ulaidh once encompassed all of Ireland north of a line extending from the River Drowes in the west to the River Boyne in the east. By the beginning of the eighth century, when the first versions of the *Táin* were being written down, the Ulaidh held sway over little more than the modern counties of Antrim and Down. The tradition is that the Ulaidh lost Navan Fort in the fifth century to a King of Tara, Niall of the Nine Hostages, but real history is difficult to disentangle from legend and invention. And who were the Ulaidh and who were their conquerors?

Some of the most ancient tribal names end with -*raige*, meaning 'people of'; for example, the Dartraige (who gave their name to the barony of Dartry in Co. Monaghan) were the 'calf people'. Some had names beginning with *dál*, meaning 'share of'; Dál Fiatach in east Down, for example, was 'Fiatach's share'. Others are obscure in meaning, including names ending in -*ne*, such as the Eilne who lived between the River Bush and the River Bann; the Latharne who gave their name to Larne in Co. Antrim; and the Cruithne, or Cruthin, who were probably the most numerous people in Antrim and Down. Later peoples – perhaps pushed west to Ireland by the might of Rome – called themselves after gods and their tribal names have the suffix -*achta*, meaning

13

'followers of', as in the Ciannachta, 'the followers of Cian', and the Connachta, 'the followers of Conn'. Their dynasties took their name from an ancestor, real or imaginary; the Connachta ruling family Uí Néill, for example, traced their descent from Niall of the Nine Hostages, who is usually credited with the conquest of most of Ulster.

In wild country overlooking the marshland that separates the Inishowen peninsula from the rest of Donegal stands the Grianan of Aileach. This imposing circular hill fort, built massively of stone with inset stairways, wall passages and triple earthen bank defences, commands a wide view which includes Lough Foyle and much of mid-Ulster to the south-east and Lough Swilly, Muckish and the Derryveagh Mountains to the west. This for centuries was a principal stronghold of the northern Uí Néill.

The Uí Néill dynasty had emerged from their north Connacht homeland to thrust eastwards into Meath and northwards over the fords of Erne towards Inishowen. Having lost Donegal, the Ulaidh came under further assault from both Aileach and north Leinster. Navan Fort fell and the sons of Niall of the Nine Hostages set up their own dynasties in the north-west: the Cenél Conaill and the Cenél Eóghain, *cenél* meaning a wide family group embracing all great noble families of royal blood. Most of Donegal became Tír Conaill, 'the land of Conall', a name it kept until the seventeenth century; the other son gave his name first to Inishowen and then to Tír Eóghain, 'the land of Eóghan', an area of central Ulster conquered in later centuries, part of which is still known today as Co. Tyrone.[17] The Uí Néill in turn exacted tribute from peoples in southern and central Ulster known as the Airgialla, meaning 'hostage-givers'.

It is too simple to see the conquerors as Gaelic Celts and those in retreat as Ulster's aboriginal inhabitants, as some have done. Certainly the Cruthin seem to have been an ancient people – Cruthin is the Irish Celtic form of Pritani or Prydyn, from whom Britain was named. They retained an identity for many centuries to come but they do not seem to have had a language, social structure or archaeological heritage separate from the rest of the Irish. It is likely that there was a constant blending with descendants of the earliest inhabitants and later arrivals. Indeed, it could be said that in the early Middle Ages Ireland had a remarkable cultural unity and that Ulster was less distinct from other parts of the island than in some later periods.

Meanwhile, the Roman Empire, which had been so mighty in Agricola's time, was reeling under the attack of German-speaking peoples from central and northern Europe seeking new corn lands and pastures. Legion after legion was withdrawn from the outposts to defend Rome in the fourth and fifth centuries, leaving Roman Britain a prey to barbarian invaders. From the north came the Picts, from the east the English and from the west the Irish; some sought new kingdoms, some were content with loot – as torn pieces of decorated Roman silver found near Coleraine show – and others brought back slaves. One of these captives was Patrick – he was amongst those who saw to it that, as Roman Britain was falling apart, Roman civilisation most deeply affected Ireland.

THE COMING OF CHRISTIANITY

'I, Patrick, a sinner, the simplest of country men . . . was taken away into Ireland in captivity with ever so many thousands of people.' It is with these words of the Confession, inscribed in halting Latin and copied into the Book of Armagh, that written Irish history begins. For six years as a slave Patrick tended sheep 'near the western sea'; there in his extreme loneliness his faith was renewed so that 'the spirit seethed in me'. Then he walked two hundred miles to the east coast and, with the company of pirates, returned to his native Britain. There he had a vision in which a man brought him a letter and as he read he seemed to hear the voice of the Irish:

'We beg you, holy boy, to come and walk among us once again', and it completely broke my heart and I could read no more.[18]

Resolved to return, he took holy orders and – in a mission clearly co-ordinated by a British Church not yet overwhelmed by the English – he began to preach the gospel to the Irish.

Patrick's very humility frustrates the enquiry of historians: his writings give no clues about the location of his British home, or when he came back to Ireland or where he preached. Christianity had already penetrated much of the south as a result of regular trading contacts with the empire and the work of men such as Iserninus, Auxilius, Camelacus and Palladius; but Patrick is the only one to have left a written record and the authenticity of his words is still striking after more than one and a half thousand years. Most places traditionally associated with Patrick – Saul, Armagh, Downpatrick, Templepatrick, Lough Derg and Croagh Patrick, for example – are in the northern half of Ireland and it was probably in Ulster that he did most of his work, perhaps around the middle of the fifth century.

Patrick's mission was undoubtedly sustained by a vigorously evangelical British Church and the new religion was particularly successful amongst the ruling class. In his Letter to Caroticus, a British prince,

15

Patrick expresses his anger and grief that British Christians could slay his Irish converts,

> newly baptized, in their white clothing – the oil still shining on their heads – cruelly butchered and slaughtered by the sword ... Greedy wolves, they have glutted themselves with congregation of the Lord, which indeed was increasing splendidly in Ireland, with the closest care, and made up of the sons of Irish raiders and the daughters of kings who had become monks and virgins of Christ – I cannot say how many! So may the wrong done not please you! And even into Hell may it give you no pleasure![19]

Yet there is no other record of anyone being martyred for acceptance of the new religion, which in turn adapted to the old beliefs and traditions that survived for centuries after Patrick's time.

The Gaelic year began at *Samhain*, now Hallowe'en, when cattle had been brought in from their summer grazing; this was a time when spirits flew free between the real world and the other world. *Imbolg*, the first day of February, marked the start of the lambing season, and the feast of *Bealtaine*, at the start of May, was for the purification of cattle driven ceremoniously between two fires. *Lughnasa*, the first day of August, celebrated the corn harvest and paid homage to Lugh the Long-Handed, who had slain the evil Balor of the Baleful Eye. The greatest of the gods was Daghda, who had beaten off the monster Formorians when they had invaded Ireland in a magical mist. The Irish believed in the *sídhe*, the Tuatha Dé Danaann, who when conquered became invisible and lived in faery mounds. Their king, Lir, once had his palace at Finaghy in Co. Antrim and the story of his children – changed into swans by his third wife Aoife – is one of the most poignant in early western literature. Lir's son was the sea-god Manannan who, like Nuadu – powerfully portrayed in a stone figure found at Tanderagee, Co. Armagh – had his counterpart among the continental Celts. Some gods became Christianised, such as Brigantia who became Saint Brigid; her saint's day falls on *Imbolg*, 1 February. Places once important as ritual sites, such as Armagh, Tory Island and Derry, became significant centres of the Church in Ulster. Particularly favoured as locations for churches and monasteries were sacred oak groves, where druids made incantations and prophecies. The Breastplate attributed to Patrick is in effect a Christianised druidic incantation:

> I arise today
> through a mighty strength, the invocation of the Trinity,
> through belief in the threeness,
> through confession of the oneness
> of the great Creator.[20]

Derry, in Irish *doire*, means 'oak grove', and it was there that Colmcille founded his great monastery.

It was from the little kingdom of Dál Riata in the Glens of Antrim that the Gaelic colonisation of Scotland began towards the end of the fifth century. Argyle means 'eastern province of the Gael' and it was here that the first settlements were made; for more than a century territory on both sides of the North Channel formed one kingdom ruled by a dynasty tracing ancestry from Fergus Mór mac Erc. By the middle of the sixth century Bruide, King of the Picts, threatened to overwhelm the Ulster interlopers and so Dál Riata turned to the northern Uí Néill for help. The pact was sealed at Druim Ceit at Mullagh near Derry in 575; Aedán mac Gabráin, King of Dál Riata, was able to free himself from the overlordship of the Ulaidh, extend his dominions, and with his fleet raided islands as far apart as the Orkneys and the Isle of Man. The man who negotiated this alliance was a Cenél Conaill prince and a renowned churchman, Colmcille.[21]

Born at Gartan in Donegal, Colmcille studied under Finnian at Movilla in Co. Down and at Clonard on the Boyne and returned to build his own monastic settlement at Derry. Just as their pagan ancestors had cast votive offerings into the water to appease the gods, so now Gaelic rulers gave generous grants of land to the Church; the high-born Colmcille could draw on impressive resources. Not long before the meeting of Druim Ceit the Dál Riata king granted Colmcille Iona, in Scotland, for a new monastic foundation; for the next two centuries and longer Iona was to be the most famous centre of Christian learning in the Celtic world. From here missions were sent to preach to the Angles in Northumbria and to the Picts, and a network of sister houses – notably at Kells, Durrow and Swords in Leinster – drew men to study and contemplate from far afield. At Iona the Annals of Ulster, the most ancient of Irish chronicles, were first compiled, and here some of the most beautiful manuscripts – including, perhaps, the Book of Durrow and the Book of Kells – were executed. Colmcille, who had taken time to study literature and music with a Leinster poet, did much to ensure that learning and Christianity went hand in hand. The Cathach, or Psalter, of Colmcille is the oldest parchment manuscript to have survived not only in Ireland but in all of western Europe; it may have been transcribed by Colmcille himself.

Local kings vied with one another to be patrons of monasteries and their founders became saints revered for centuries to come, such as Molaise of Devenish, Eóghan of Ardstraw, Cainnech of the Roe valley,

Monenna of Killevy and Comgall of Bangor. Hundreds of monastic sites have been identified in Ulster but as most were built of wood, only traces survive. On Mahee Island in Strangford Lough, Nendrum monastery was surrounded by three concentric stone walls; inside the middle wall were round wooden huts for craftwork and a schoolhouse, and in the centre a rectangular church, a graveyard and a sundial. Some monasteries were marked by cross-carved stone pillars as at Kilnasaggart in south Armagh and at Killadeas in Fermanagh. In Donegal, at Fahan and Carndonagh in particular, finely carved stone cross slabs and pillar stones are decorated with elegant interlacing and bold figures similar to those on White Island on Lough Erne.

Sons of kings and nobles sent to be fostered or to enter the Church were expected to obey the strict rule of the monastery. 'Let the monks' food be poor and taken in the evening', Columbanus prescribed for the community of Bangor, 'vegetables, beans, flour mixed with water, together with a small loaf of bread, lest the stomach be burdened and the mind confused.' He laid down punishments when the rules were broken:

> Him who has not waited for grace at table and has not responded for grace at table and has not responded Amen, it is ordained to correct with six blows. Likewise him who has spoken while eating it is ordained to correct with six blows. Let him who has cut the table with a knife be corrected with ten blows.[22]

Under the guidance of a 'senior', the novice learned to read and studied the Scriptures and the writings of the Fathers of the Church. The Psalms had to be memorised and copied onto slates – thirty slate tablets and several styles were found at Nendrum. Only a minority of monks took holy orders and had their heads tonsured from ear to ear, and perhaps most were engaged in tilling fields and herb gardens. A large monastery, such as Bangor or Derry, was the nearest equivalent early Christian Ulster had to a town; in such a community specialised arts, such as metalworking and manuscript illumination, could flourish. Other than the church itself, the scriptorium was perhaps the monastery's most vital building. The development of a distinctive Irish script can be seen in a liturgical collection known as the Antiphonary of Bangor, written in the seventh century; here the round semi-uncial hand of the Cathach had been drawn out into hair-lines in black ink still fresh over the centuries. Some scribes relieved tedious work by scribbling in the margins. One wrote: 'Let no reader blame this writing for my arm is cramped from too much work.' Another cut himself, probably sharpening his quill, and drew a black circle round the blot of blood with the note, 'blood from the finger of Melaghlin'. 'Alas! my hand!' wrote one scribe, adding soon after, 'it is time for dinner!' Others wrote verse:

18

The little bird which has whistled
from the end of a bright-yellow bill;
it utters a note above Belfast Loch –
a blackbird from a yellow-heaped branch.[23]

As a centre of learning and Christian zeal, Bangor rivalled Iona. Its
founder Comgall seems to have worked with Colmcille and was revered by the Cruthin; in the Antiphonary it is written, 'Christ loved
Comgall. Well, too, did he the Lord.' Attached to this manuscript is
another known as the Good Rule of Bangor, including these words:

Blessed family of Bangor, founded on unerring faith, adorned with salvation's hope, perfect in charity. Ship never distressed though beaten by
waves; fully prepared for nuptials, spouse for the sovereign Lord. House
full of delicious things and built upon a rock; and no less the true vine
brought out of Egypt's land. Surely an enduring city, strong and unified,
set upon a hill. Ark shaded by Cherubim . . .[24]

Almost nothing survives of Comgall's monastery, and the Good Rule
and the Antiphonary are to be found not in Ulster but in Milan –
evidence that the great Irish mission to the mainland of Europe had
begun. Some Irish monks did penance by living apart from others in an
uninhabited place – the prefix *desert-*, as in Desertmartin, indicates the
sites of such hermitages. Others accepted voluntary exile in far-off
dangerous places, and where better to go than the European mainland?
Here, amidst the wreckage of the collapsed Roman Empire, Germanic
rulers warred with each other. Ireland, which had escaped Roman
conquest, also escaped barbarian invasion. Now Irish exiles and pilgrims began to return some of the Celtic and Roman culture to the
Continent where it had been overwhelmed. The pioneers of this remarkable exodus were monks from Bangor.

COLUMBANUS AND GALL

Towards the end of the sixth century pilgrims halted high in the French
Vosges Mountains by the ruined Roman fort of Annegray. Led by their
senior, Columbanus, these monks had come more than nine hundred
miles from Bangor and it was here they chose to build a monastery.
When the buildings were complete they continued to live and worship
as strictly as they had under the direction of their abbot Comgall in
Ulster. Soon the reputation of these men spread far, and so many
French joined the community that two sister houses were founded close
by at Luxeuil and Fontaines.

In his forthright condemnation of worldliness in the Frankish Church,
Columbanus aroused the hostility of Theoderic, King of Burgundy, and
his mother Brunhilda. Exiles this time by force, the Ulstermen, after

many journeyings, struck overland to the Rhine, where they made their way upstream; this may have inspired Columbanus to write his Boat Song:

> Lo, little bark on twin-horned Rhine
> From forests hewn to skim the brine.
> Heave, lads, and let the echoes ring.
>
> The tempests howl, the storms dismay,
> But manly strength can win the day.
> Heave, lads, and let the echoes ring . . .
>
> The King of virtues vowed a prize
> For him who wins, for him who tries.
> Think, lads, of Christ and echo him.[25]

When they reached Lake Constance they preached to Germans who had not heard the gospel before and founded a monastery at Bregenz, now in the Austrian Vorarlberg. The restless Columbanus wished to press on but Gall, one of the Bangor monks, stayed to become the local patron saint – a church, a town and a canton in Switzerland are called St Gallen to this day. Though now over seventy, Columbanus endured the perils of St Gotthard Pass to descend into northern Italy to found another monastery at Bobbio, where his tomb can still be seen.

Bangor and Iona also played a leading role in bringing Christianity to Northumbria and others from Ulster followed in the path of Columbanus to the European mainland. The Irish – known as the Scotti – were marked out not only by their asceticism but also by their reverence for learning. Many classical texts owe their survival to the diligence of scribes in foundations such as Bobbio. The Emperor Charlemagne delighted in the company of Irish scholars; for example, when there was an eclipse of the sun in 810 the astronomer Dungal of Bangor sent this explanation:

> If the moon comes afterwards, the sun blocks the sight of this heavenly body from human sight, by setting itself across it. In the event of an eclipse, nothing happens to the sun itself, it is simply hidden from our eyes.[26]

Yet the society which produced such scholars was, by the standards of thriving urban centres in Charlemagne's empire, remarkably conservative and underdeveloped.

EARLY CHRISTIAN ULSTER SOCIETY

Congal One Eye, ruler of the Cruthin kingdom of Dál nAraide and over-king of the Ulaidh, forged an alliance with Strathclyde Britons and the men of Dál Riata in a bid to make himself king of all Ireland. It was in vain; in 637 he was routed and slain at Moira by Donal mac Áedo, the Uí Néill king. These events – which lost Dál Riata control of its Scottish possessions – form the background to the epic tales 'The Banquet of Dunangay' and 'The Battle of Moira', and they are a reminder that no one in this period ever won complete mastery over the whole island. Indeed the Uí Néill themselves never conquered all of the province of Ulster.

The title *ard rí*, 'high king', had no political meaning until the eleventh century; till then provincial- or over-kings held sway. The over-kingship of the Ulaidh, for example, was drawn from one of their three strongest kingdoms: Dál Fiatach, Dál nAraide, or Uí Eachach Cobha (which gave its name to Lough Neagh and the Iveagh baronies). Subject to them were smaller kingdoms such as Latharne (Larne), Leth Cathail ('Cathal's half', now Lecale in Co. Down) and Uí Eachach Arda (from which the Ards peninsula in Co. Down is named). Beneath them in turn were numerous petty kingdoms, or *tuatha* (a word of ancient origin which is related to the English 'teutonic' and the German '*Deutsch*'). By the time of the first Viking raids the ruler of a *tuath*, which, generally, was the size of a barony, was merely described as a *tigherna*, a lord.

The Brehon laws stated that when a king died all members of his *derbhfine* – descendants in the male line of a common great-grandfather – were eligible for election to succeed him. Succession disputes were endemic and a major cause of instability, which future invaders would successfully exploit. The Gaelic ruling classes were rigidly class conscious and one of the main functions of the *filí*, the hereditary professional poets, was to recite the king's genealogy at his inauguration. The *filí* in earlier times had been druids, who now carried out a secular role as praise poets, historians, lawyers and physicians – the remarkable cultural unity of the whole of the Gaelic world was in large measure due to them. The nobles, who could all claim confidently that they were related to kings, distinguished themselves from *grád Fhéne*, the commoners, by birth and by the number of their dependants or clients. A client such as the *bó-aire*, or farmer, received land or stock from his lord and paid rent in food, labour service and free entertainment. Of the humblest tillers of the soil we know little but it is certain that slaves were integral to Gaelic society. Captured in war or purchased as children from destitute parents, slaves did much of the heavy farming work.

Ulster's landscape is thickly scattered with the remains of thousands of ring-forts, farmsteads surrounded by a circular bank and ditch. In rocky or mountainous areas, where the fort was known as a *caiseal*, the wall was made of stone and no ditch was dug; these were particularly common in Donegal, where there are at least four places called Cashel and many others incorporating the word, such as Cashelreagh, 'the grey fort'. Where the ramparts were made of soil, the ring-fort was called a *ráth*, a common element in Ulster placenames, such as Rathcoole, 'Cumhal's fort', and Rathfriland, 'Fraoile's fort'. The rath's enclosure was the *lios*, again a common prefix in northern placenames, as in Lisnaskea, 'fort of the whitethorns'. The ramparts may have done little more than prevent untended cattle from eating the thatch off houses, though sheep would be folded in the *lios* and cows milked there. In 1984 the excavation of a rath began at Deer Park Farms near Glenarm; here it was found people had lived continuously between the sixth and the tenth centuries and had simply covered their rubbish with fresh soil, thus creating a large mound. Inside this waterlogged midden one house was excavated in a remarkable state of preservation; around stout uprights, hazel rods had been tightly woven in a spiral pattern in two layers, creating a kind of cavity wall filled with moss and heather.[27]

The owner of the Deer Park ring-fort was probably a farmer of comfortable means, capable of putting together a plough team of four or more oxen in springtime. Oats, barley, rye and a little wheat were cultivated in small enclosed fields and reaped close to the ear in late summer. Small crops of onions, celery, leeks, carrots, parsnips and some peas and beans were grown in adjacent gardens, and it seems certain that the scale and variety of tillage was greatly extended by the monasteries.[28] For most people the most vital farming implement was the spade, similar to the loy widely used in modern times and capable of cutting and turning matted grassland. Apples were cultivated and the annals record that as an act of war Turlough O'Connor, King of Connacht, cut down an orchard in Tír Eóghain in 1157. Domestic stock was the mainstay of the economy, however; cattle were driven to their summer pastures, known as *buailte*, generally to uplands or dried-out fen, but no hay was saved and the animals had to eke out the winter months on reserved pastures where the grass had withered naturally. Temporary dwellings on the hillsides gave shelter to summer 'booleying' parties of women milking cows and boys guarding the herds and keeping sucking calves away from their mothers.

As cows gave no milk in winter, male yearlings were killed in autumn and the making of cheese and butter was vital to ensure a food supply during the short days. Butter was churned from sour cream, separated with the help of butterwort and carrageen moss, and *tanag*, a variety of hard cheese, was made with rennet from calves and sheep. Artificial caves or souterrains, often connected to the ring-fort, seem to have been used for storing these *bánbíd*, or white foods, though some with double chambers, such as that running off the Shaneen Park rath on the slopes of the Cave Hill, may have served as a secret refuge in time of attack. Most souterrains were lined with stone or cut from rock but one large souterrain excavated at Coolcran, near Tempo in Co. Fermanagh, in 1983 had been lined with wattlework and forty-eight sawn oak timbers. Grain was stored in strawrope granaries; oats were eaten as porridge, and barley, when not eaten as bread, was malted and brewed into ale – wine was imported by the nobility but it was probably ale that inebriated an Airgialla king during a drinking bout in 1158, which led to his murder at the hands of his servant.

The bounty of nature made a vital contribution to survival, though the nobility had hunted the wild boar to extinction by the twelfth century. Domesticated pigs fed on oak mast in the woods and good acorn and hazelnut crops were regularly recorded in the annals. The sea provided fish, seals, shellfish and *duileasc*, a seaweed still called dulse in Ulster today; freshwater fishing was jealously regulated; and a stranded whale could provide an unexpected feast – perhaps that is how a very large whale vertebra came to be incorporated in an early Christian pavement in Downpatrick. In a good year the people of Ulster were perhaps better fed than they were in the 1840s, but disaster was never far distant – a cattle raid or burning of crops; a long winter without adequate fodder for stock; a plague (that of 666 was particularly devastating); or sheep murrain, which was especially hard on the poor who depended on them for milk products as a staple food.

A king or a noble, as a member of an élite military caste, usually lived above or apart from commoners in a ring-fort built for defence on a carefully chosen site known as a *dún*, a word which is incorporated in many Ulster placenames, such as Dungiven, 'fort of the hide'; Dunseverick, 'Sobhairce's fort'; and Dungannon, 'Ceanann's fort'. The *crannóg*, or lake dwelling, was preferred in some places to the *dún*; sometimes use was made of a natural island but often a strategically placed artificial island was built up with piles, logs, woven brushwood and stones. The most striking example still to be seen is Lough-na-Cranagh on Fair Head in north Antrim. The forts of kings and their aristocratic relatives might seem to have been the greatest centres of wealth and prestige, but they were not – the monasteries were pre-eminent. Acquiring fertile and extensive tracts of land traditionally free of tribute, the monasteries by the end of the eighth century had become by far the most advanced places of economic activity, housing specialist workshops and developing the most productive farming techniques. The ruling classes, who had been the principal patrons from the outset, made sure that they kept control of the monasteries; abbots, bishops and other high clergy married and passed on ecclesiastical offices to their children – Clann Sínaich was almost a dynasty which monopolised Church posts for generations at Armagh.[29]

Armagh claimed the leading position in the Church in Ireland at the beginning of the ninth century – a claim laid out in the Book of Armagh written in 807, which contained the New Testament, a biography of Saint Martin of Tours, a cut-down version of Patrick's Confession, two Lives of Patrick (one by Muirchú and the other by Tírechán), and *Liber Angeli*, which put forward the case that Patrick had made Armagh the capital of the Irish Church. Under the patronage of the Uí Néill, Armagh flourished and became the largest urban centre not only in Ulster but in all Ireland; and in spite of all the troubles in the following centuries, growth continued, indicated by fires which destroyed a hundred houses in 1090, two streets in 1092, three streets in 1112, and five streets with large buildings in 1166.[30] As great centres of wealth, the monasteries were vulnerable to attack, particularly in times of famine, and became embroiled in dynastic wars. In 793 Armagh was attacked by the Uí Chremthainn, an Airgialla people of Fermanagh, and in another raid in 996 the Airgialla drove off two thousand cows. Between those dates, however, Armagh had been the target of many more attacks by a new people to appear in Ulster – the Vikings.

2

VIKING RAIDS AND NORMAN INVASION

c. 800–1300

OVERVIEW

> There was an astonishing and awfully great oppression over all Erinn,
> throughout its breadth, by powerful azure Norsemen, and by fierce,
> hard-hearted Danes, during a lengthened period, and for a long time, for
> the space of eight score and ten years, or, according to some authorities,
> two hundred years.[1]

So wrote the author of *Cogadh Gaedhel re Gallaibh*, 'Wars of the Irish with
the Foreigners', at the beginning of his long history of the impact of the
Viking raids on his country. Iona, and Lambay Island, off the Co.
Dublin coast, were attacked in 795 and Bangor and Downpatrick were
plundered soon afterwards; the assaults on Iona were so frequent and
devastating that the whole community moved to Meath to build a new
monastery at Kells, completed in 814. One monk wrote in the margin of
his manuscript:

> Fierce and wild is the wind tonight,
> It tosses the tresses of the sea to white;
> On such a night I take my ease;
> Fierce Northmen only course the quiet seas.[2]

At first nothing formidable stood in the way of the Northmen. Charlemagne had broken up the fleets of Frisian pirates in the North Sea,
leaving the Vikings masters of the north Atlantic, and particularly in
Ireland there could be no united opposition to the invaders while the
country was split into so many warring kingdoms. Their longships,
some over seventy feet long, were well suited to brave the hazards of
the ocean: built of well-seasoned oak planks riveted with iron to over-
lap, and bound to the ribs with tough pine roots, their hulls could not
only flex to the swell but also, with their shallow draught, negotiate
treacherous mud banks such as the bar mouth at the estuary of the
Bann. Because the Church was the main victim in the early attacks, and
as the records were written by monks, the Vikings were seen as black-
hearted barbarians by the chroniclers:

> In a word, although there were an hundred hard steeled iron heads on
> one neck, and an hundred sharp, ready, cool, never-rusting, brazen tongues
> on each head, and an hundred garrulous, loud, unceasing voices from

each tongue, they could not recount, or narrate, or enumerate, or tell, what all the Gaedhil suffered in common, both men and women, laity and clergy, old and young, noble and ignoble, of hardship and of injury, and of oppression, in every house, from these valiant, wrathful, foreign, purely pagan people.[3]

The *Cogadh Gaedhel re Gallaibh* was written in the eleventh century as a propaganda work to show that Ireland needed to be saved from the Northmen by the high-king, Brian Boru, and the events of two centuries became telescoped in the author's mind, giving the impression of constant, unrelieved pillaging. Certainly several of the raids were devastating and Ulster bore the brunt of the initial assault; there were many years of respite, however, and Ulster kings were able on several occasions to inflict overwhelming defeat on Vikings even on their own element, the sea. Though they had densely colonised adjacent Scottish Isles, the Northmen found resistance in Ulster too formidable and transferred their attentions further south. In this way Ulster failed to benefit from the commercial and town-building expertise the Vikings displayed in Dublin, Limerick and elsewhere.

Viking incursions did quicken the pace of political change in Ireland, and as provincial rulers vied with each other to make the high-kingship a reality, the northern Uí Néill had a pivotal role to play. Political unity of the whole island was near to being achieved when the Normans landed in Wexford in 1169. With their awesome military superiority, the Normans swiftly overran half the country, John de Courcy overthrowing the kingdom of the Ulaidh in Antrim and Down. The Norman invasion had a far greater impact on Ulster than the Viking raids but the northern colony was never secure, remote as it was from Dublin, the hub of the Irish lordship. By the beginning of the fourteenth century it could be said that Ulster's most distinguishing feature was that it was the most Gaelic province in Ireland.

'GREAT SEA-CAST FLOODS OF FOREIGNERS'

The first Norse raids were sporadic and not always successful; for the year 811 the Annals of Ulster have this terse entry: 'A slaughter of the heathens by the Ulaid.'[4] Then in the next decade a sustained assault got under way. Bangor was pillaged in 823 and again the following year, as the *Cogadh* records:

And they plundered Bangor of Ulad, and brake the shrine of Comgall, and killed its bishop, and its doctors, and its clergy: they devastated, also, Movilla.[5]

Ulster bore the brunt of this campaign as the Northmen moved from the coastal monasteries inland up the rivers, carrying their longships overland past rapids and falls to set up raiding fleets on Lough Erne and Lough Neagh. Their success is logged in the Annals of Ulster:

> 832: The first plundering of Armagh by the heathens three times in one month . . . 837: The churches of all Lough Erne, including Clones and Devenish, were destroyed by the heathens . . . 839: A raiding party of the foreigners were on Lough Neagh, and from there they plundered the states and churches of the north of Ireland . . . 840: Louth was plundered by the heathens from Lough Neagh and they led away captive bishops and priests and scholars, and put others to death . . . Armagh was burned with its oratories and stone church . . . [6]

Then, the *Cogadh* relates, 'there came great sea-cast floods of foreigners into Erinn' and Vikings overwintering on Lough Neagh were joined in 849 by 'seven score ships of adherents'. In 852 Armagh was laid waste yet again, this time by Dublin Norse who struck overland from Carlingford Lough. At this point, when all Ulster seemed about to be overwhelmed, the Vikings were checked; Danes, known to the Irish as 'dark foreigners', made their first appearance only to fall foul of the Norse, the 'fair foreigners'. A sea battle was fought in Carlingford Lough, and the Norse, with the help of the Ulaidh, inflicted great loss on the Danes. Ulster kings began to take advantage of Viking disunity and Dál Riata actually fought the Northmen at sea. Then in 866 Áed Finnliath, King of the northern Uí Néill, cleared the Vikings from the province, as the Annals of Ulster record:

> Aed son of Niall plundered all the strongholds of the foreigner ie in the territory of the North, both in Cenel Eogain and Dal nAraide, and took away their heads, their flocks, and their herds from camp by battle. A victory was gained over them at Lough Foyle and twelve score heads taken thereby.[7]

The Northmen did not reappear in force in Ulster for many years to come and it was further south that they built their seaport towns. Only Larne seems to have had any real permanence as a settlement and was still known as Ulfrek's fjord when the Normans arrived towards the end of the twelfth century. There are very few placenames of Norse origin in Ulster – they are: Strangford, 'strong inlet' (a reference to the powerful tide-rip at the sea lough's narrows); the Skerries, referring to the rocky island and shoals off Portrush; Carlingford, 'hag's fjord'; Olderfleet, a corruption of 'Ulfrek's fjord'; and when the Normans and English later conquered much of Antrim and Down they called the territory 'Ulster' from the Viking Uladztír, an adaptation of the Irish *tír* (land) and *Ulaidh*.

From about 860 the Annals of Ulster no longer refer to the Northmen as heathens, and Olaf, King of Dublin, was a Christian when he wed Áed Finnliath's daughter to seal his alliance with the northern Uí Néill. King Áed came close to mastering all of Ulster and posed a formidable challenge to the hegemony of the southern Uí Néill in Meath. Ireland was beginning to move towards unity under one high-king, a development hastened by the next major Viking onslaught.

By the beginning of the tenth century all the best land in Iceland had been portioned out and Vikings in Normandy and the English Danelaw had no wish to have their settlements ravaged by fresh attacks from their homeland. Thus Ireland became the principal victim of a fresh and concerted assault and, according to the *Cogadh*, the country 'became filled with immense floods, and countless sea-vomitings of ships, and boats, and fleets'.[8]

'THE WRATH OF THE BRUTAL, FEROCIOUS, UNTAMED, IMPLACABLE HORDES'

There came after that an immensely great fleet, more wonderful than all the other fleets, (for its equal or its likeness never before came to Erinn) . . . though numerous were the oft-victorious clans of the many-familied Erinn . . . yet not one of them was able to give relief, alleviation, or deliverance from that oppression and tyranny, from the numbers and multitudes, and the cruelty and the wrath of the brutal, ferocious, untamed, implacable hordes, by whom that oppression was inflicted, because of the excellence of their polished, ample, treble, heavy, trusty, glittering corslets; and their hard, strong, valiant swords; and their well-riveted long spears; and their ready, brilliant arms of valour besides.[9]

In this dire crisis, so described in the *Cogadh*, Niall Glúndubh rallied all of the northern half of Ireland known as Leth Cuinn, 'Conn's half'. Son of Áed Finnliath, Niall was accepted as ruler of both the northern and southern Uí Néill, and in 917 he led a great host deep into Munster to do battle with the Vikings. Complete victory eluded him, however, and so in 919 he advanced into Leinster with a coalition of the Uí Néill, the Airgialla and the Ulaidh only to be utterly routed on the outskirts of Dublin. Along with twelve other kings, Niall was slain and the Annals of Ulster lamented:

Mournful today is virginal Ireland
Without a mighty king in command of hostages;
It is to view the heaven and not to see the sun
To behold Niall's plain without Niall . . .[10]

Ulster itself now fell prey to invasion. In 921 the Northmen raided Tír Conaill, plundered Armagh again, and entered Lough Foyle with thirty-two ships, causing people to flee the adjacent countryside, 'except for a few who remained behind in it through sloth'. In 924 they returned to Strangford, and the Annals of Ulster record: 'A naval force of foreigners went on Lough Erne, and they ravaged the islands of the lake and the surrounding peoples, to and fro.' It was in this period that monks took refuge in tall tapered round towers with conical caps; built of stone and mortar with narrow doors raised at least ten feet from the ground, they were designed to withstand fire and attack, and to serve as belfries in time of peace. Complete towers can still be seen at Devenish and Antrim, with others in various states of decay at Drumbo, Nendrum and Maghera in Co. Down; Clones and Iniskeen in Co. Monaghan; Drumlane in Co. Cavan; Armoy in Co. Antrim; and one on Tory Island in Donegal, uniquely made of round beach stones.

The Viking tide was turned by Muircertach, Niall Glúndubh's son and successor. In a vigorous campaigning career he beat the invaders at sea on Strangford Lough in 926, took and burned Dublin in 939, ravaged the Norse settlements in the Scottish Isles with an Ulster fleet in 941 and died in combat in 943. It was not a northern dynasty but a southern one, the Dál Cais, which came closest to dominating all of Ireland in the years that followed.

In 1005 Brian Boru reached Armagh, leading the armies of Munster, Leinster, Meath, Connacht and Norse Dublin. On two previous occasions he had come north with a great host and, though he drew tribute from every other part of Ireland, the Ulster kings had stood firm. Now he paid twenty ounces of gold to the Church, recognised Armagh's claim to ecclesiastical primacy (which it has never lost since) and ordered a scribe to write in the Book of Armagh the words *Imperator Scottorum*, 'Emperor of the Irish'. It was not until the following year that he could establish his claim by making a circuit of Ulster, setting out from Sligo

and keeping his left hand to the sea, and his right hand to the land and to Benbulben, over Duff and Drowes, and into Magh-nEine, and over Ath Seanaigh at Assaroe and into Tirhugh, and over Barnesmore, and over Farsat, and into Tir Eoghain, and into Dal Riata, and into Dal nAraide, and into Ulaid, until about Lughnasa he halted at Belach Duin.[11]

Having chronicled this royal visitation, the author of the *Cogadh* paints a radiant picture of peace and prosperity flourishing through Ireland under Brian's rule. In fact it took several more punitive expeditions before the King of Tír Conaill was dragged to Kincora in Munster in 1011 to make submission. Besides, Brian's authority did not hold; Leinster and Dublin refused tribute and called in allies from across the Viking world. On Good Friday, 23 April 1014, in perhaps the greatest battle yet fought in Ireland, the Leinster–Viking host was routed and driven into the sea at Clontarf near Dublin. Sigurd, Earl of the Orkneys, the King of

Leinster, two Connacht kings, Brian's son Murchadh and many others of noble blood lay dead; then at the close of the battle, with victory within his grasp, Brian himself was slain by King Brodar of Man. In the words of the Icelandic *Saga of Burnt Njal*:

> Brian fell, but kept his kingdom
> Ere he lost one drop of blood.[12]

The bodies of Brian and his son were taken to Armagh and there buried with great ceremony. Who now would be King of Ireland?

KINGS WITH OPPOSITION

Clontarf brought neither peace nor unity to Ireland. Now that Brian Boru had ended the Uí Néill domination, any ruling family strong enough could make a bid to seize the high-kingship. If a dynasty was to have any hope of ousting rivals, it had to avoid protracted succession disputes; most families abandoned the sprawling *derbhfine* and limited choice to descendants of a single grandfather. In this way many Gaelic surnames emerged during this period, with the prefixes Ó meaning 'grandson of', and Mac, 'son of'. The O'Neills were descendants of Niall Glúndubh, for example, though they did not oust the Mac Lochlainns as rulers of Tír Eóghain until the thirteenth century. Bloody contests between rivals continued to be frequent, however.

Over one and a half centuries the provincial kings allied and clashed with each other. Some came close to success, such as Muirchertach O'Brien of Munster and Turlough O'Connor of Connacht; but all were high-kings 'with opposition', as the annalists put it. That opposition was often in Ulster, which, despite impressive fleets sent out by south- ern kings, presented a natural frontier and so was difficult to subjugate. Yet Ulster kings never had the strength to impose their will on the rest of Ireland for they had not the wealth of Viking cities such as Limerick and Dublin to draw on – indeed the province was considered the poorest in Ireland until the middle of the seventeenth century. In addi- tion, a powerful kingdom emerged in the eleventh century on the Ulster–Connacht borderlands: Bréifne, centred on the counties of Cavan and Leitrim and ruled by the O'Rourkes, effectively blocked expansion south from Tír Eóghain.

The Irish now wielded Viking axes in battle and were more prone than before to taking slaves and blinding their rivals; but it would be difficult to prove that the Northmen had increased the ferocity of warfare in the country. Besides, there were years of peace and prosperity; for example, Donal and Cellach, abbots of Armagh, were able to arrange armistices between contending kings in 1102, 1106, 1107 and 1109. Cellach took the lead in promoting reform in the Irish Church and had some success in reducing worldly abuses. His protégé, Malachy, became a powerful ally in helping to obtain support from Pope Innocent II and official papal recognition of Armagh's primacy came when Malachy was appointed archbishop of Armagh and primate in 1132. In 1142 he founded the first Cistercian monastery in Ireland on land given by the Airgialla king, Donnchadh O'Carroll, in the diocese of Clogher at Mellifont; Saint Bernard sent his architect and some of his monks to lend assistance. The political and ecclesiastical rise of Armagh did not, however, lead to a revival of learning. Bangor, Movilla, Nendrum and Derry never fully recovered from Viking attack and the Church reformers of Armagh were not respecters of tradition; thus the maintenance of Gaelic culture was left increasingly to the secular poets, bards and historians.

'THE POPE GRANTED AND DONATED IRELAND TO THE ILLUSTRIOUS
    KING OF ENGLAND, HENRY . . .'

It was a dispute between Tiernan O'Rourke, the one-eyed King of Bréifne, and Dermot MacMurrough, King of Leinster, which set in motion the events leading to the Norman invasion of Ireland. One night in 1152 hooves thundered away from the Bréifne *dún* of Dromahaire as Dermot carried off Tiernan's wife, Dervorgilla, together with a great prey of cattle. This humiliation burned in his memory and filled his heart with vengeful hatred to his dying day. O'Rourke had to wait fourteen years to have his revenge, for MacMurrough had hitched his fortunes to the rising star of Muirchertach Mac Lochlainn, the sole Cenél Eóghain high-king of the period. In 1166 Muirchertach captured and blinded the Ulaidh king, Eochaidh MacDonleavy, in defiance of solemn guarantees given by the archbishop of Armagh. The revulsion following this act of treachery caused Muirchertach's support to drop away and shortly afterwards the high-king was killed in a skirmish.

Rory O'Connor of Connacht, now rapidly establishing his claim to the high-kingship, gave his blessing to a punitive expedition against Dermot long planned by Tiernan: the men of Bréifne, supported by the Dublin Norse and the King of Meath, swept into Leinster, devastated MacMurrough's kingdom and burned his stronghold of Ferns. Instead of making a glorious last stand, Dermot sailed to Bristol and there his friend Robert fitzHarding, the city's reeve, advised him to seek support from Henry II, the Angevin king, then busy suppressing a baronial revolt in his French dominions. MacMurrough was not regarded as an unknown barbarian from the west for, more than any other Irish king, he had close ties with the Anglo-Norman world: as a supporter of ecclesiastical reform and a generous patron of the Augustinians, he was held in high esteem by English bishops; the profitable trade between Dublin and Bristol was normally under his control; and, above all, Dermot had genuine claims on Henry's gratitude. During King Stephen's reign Muirchertach Mac Lochlainn had championed Henry's claim to the English throne and Dermot's alliance with the Cenél Eóghain was fully acknowledged. In addition, Robert fitzHarding had given Henry shelter in Bristol for four years during the struggle for the Crown.[13]

Henry II, the most powerful monarch in the western world, had brought Norman sway to its zenith. A century before, William, Duke of Normandy, had gripped men's imaginations by his dramatic and sweeping conquest of England. The genius of the Normans for organisation and strong government, and their skill in warfare, made them feared and respected everywhere. Early in the twelfth century they conquered Sicily and southern Italy, extended their dominions in France, and pushed northwards into Scotland and westwards to Wales. It could be only a matter of time before they would come to Ireland. In 1155 Henry proposed the annexation of Ireland but his mother, the Empress Matilda, disapproved and the project was set aside. Influential Churchmen, however, were unwilling to let the matter drop. John of Salisbury, adviser to the archbishop of Canterbury, prevailed on Nicholas Breakspear, elected as Pope Adrian IV in 1154, to grant Ireland to Henry. John wrote later:

> In response to my petition the Pope granted and donated Ireland to the illustrious King of England, Henry, to be held by him and his successors . . . He did this in virtue of the long-established right, reputed to derive from the donation of Constantine, whereby all islands are considered to belong to the Roman Church.[14]

This was the notorious bull *Laudabiliter*.

The Church's zeal for ecclesiastical conformity in Ireland should not be underestimated. Many higher clergy in Rome considered Gaelic society incapable of promoting reform, largely as a result of reading Saint Bernard's highly popular biography of Malachy of Armagh. Saint Bernard told how Malachy, when appointed bishop of Connor (a diocese embracing much of eastern Ulster), understood

> that he had been sent not to men but to beasts. Never before had he found men so shameless in regard to morals, so dead in regard of rites, so stubborn in regard of discipline, so unclean in regard of life. They were Christians in name, in fact pagans.[15]

Beset by a kaleidoscope of troubles, Henry was not ready to help Dermot in person but otherwise he gave him full support and permission to recruit assistance. On a clear day Norman barons in south-west Wales could see the hills of Ireland across the sea, seeming to beckon them on to further conquest. Now they could go by invitation and eagerly they pledged their support to Dermot in return for promises of land. To the greatest of them, Richard fitzGilbert de Clare, Lord of Strigoil and better known as 'Strongbow', MacMurrough pledged the hand of his daughter Aoife in marriage, and the kingdom of Leinster when Dermot himself died.

The coming of the Normans to Ireland contrasted sharply with William's conquest of England in 1066. The incursion was on a smaller scale, largely organised by interrelated family groups, in particular the Geraldines – descendants of Nesta, the Welsh wife of Gerald of Windsor and mistress of Henry I – led by Raymond 'le Gros' fitzGerald and his uncle, Maurice fitzGerald. The Irish did not suspend their dynastic rivalries to present a united front and, indeed, most of their lands were left unscathed. Even the annals made only sparse references to the invasion.

The Norman achievement was striking, nevertheless: between 1169 and 1171 the Viking cities of Waterford and Dublin – offering the strongest resistance – had been taken, Rory O'Connor's host had been put to flight and the kingdoms of Leinster and Meath had been overwhelmed. Then the sudden death of Dermot in May 1171 left Strongbow master of Leinster. Though the cares of his vast domains lay heavy on his shoulders, Henry could not allow an independent Norman state to emerge across the Irish Sea. In October 1171 he came to Ireland with a force so large that no resistance was offered. All the Irish kings, except for the Cenél Eóghain and Cenél Conaill rulers, made submission to Henry. The Norman barons were confirmed in their conquests, except that Meath was granted to Hugh de Lacy as a counterweight to Strongbow. Dublin, Henry kept for himself, to be colonised by men of unwavering loyalty – who better than the citizens of Bristol who had fitted out his expedition? This city henceforth was capital of the lordship of Ireland, the latest Angevin acquisition. Here the royal governors set up a central administration, an exchequer and new courts of justice for the lordship – a dominion which in theory embraced all of Ireland but in practice included only those parts of the island under Norman control. The frontiers spread outwards as far as Limerick in the south and Bréifne in the north-west, where de Lacy killed Tiernan O'Rourke. The high-king, Rory O'Connor, sued for peace and in 1175 Henry agreed to a status quo. In his absence, however, Henry could not control the martial ardour of his vassals and at the beginning of 1177 a carefully planned invasion was being prepared for Ulster.

In early February 1177 John de Courcy, a knight from Somerset, sallied out from Dublin with twenty-two mailed horsemen and some three hundred foot soldiers. The expedition marched through Meath heading north to the plain of Muirhevna, where it was joined by Irish allies. Then de Courcy led his men beyond the furthest limits of Norman territory over the Moyry Pass into Ulster; turning east from Glen Righe, the invaders reached Lecale in fewer than four days. In front of Down, the capital of the kingdom of Dál Fiatach, the attack was prepared. 'John's followers were few in number,' the Norman chronicler Gerald of Wales recorded, 'but good, brave men, the pick of the army.'[16]

So unexpected was this Norman incursion that the local ruler, Rory MacDonleavy, fled with all his people. To seize a kingdom by surprise was one achievement but to hold it with a small force was quite another. Cardinal Vivian, the papal legate who happened to be making a pastoral visit to Ulster at the time, failed to persuade de Courcy to withdraw. MacDonleavy invoked his authority as over-king of the Ulaidh and returned a week after his flight with a great host. Defensive earthworks, hastily thrown up by de Courcy's men, were too incomplete to be effective and so it was in the open – on the ground which slopes up from the River Quoile south to Downpatrick – that a battle was fought, as Gerald relates:

> So a fierce battle commenced. To begin with they showered down a hail of arrows and spears at long range. Then they came to close quarters, lance encountered lance, sword met sword, and many were killed on either side. During this ferocious struggle while shield was rebuffed by shield, boss by boss, menacing sword by sword, foot by foot and lance by lance, only someone who was there, and who saw the blows dealt out by John's sword, how it lopped off now a head from someone's shoulders, or again arms or hands from their body, could adequately praise the powers of this valiant warrior . . . After an intense and for a long time indecisive struggle between these unevenly matched forces, John's courage at last won him the victory, and a great number of the enemy were killed along the sea shore where they had taken refuge . . . For because the surface of the shore was soft and yielding, the weight of their bodies caused men to sink deep into it, and blood pouring from their wounds remained on the surface of the slippery ground and easily came up to the knees and legs of their pursuers.[17]

An even greater Ulster coalition – including the Cenél Eóghain king, Máel Sechlainn Mac Lochlainn and the leading prelates of the province – joined King Rory for a final attempt to oust the Normans in a great assault on Down in June. Once again de Courcy triumphed, and according to the Annals of Inisfallen:

The Archbishop of Armagh, the Bishop of Down, and all the clergy were taken prisoners; and the English got possession of the croziers of St Comgall and St Dachiarog, the Canoin Phatruic [Book of Armagh], besides a bell called Ceolan an Tighearna. They afterwards, however, set the bishops at liberty and restored the Canoin Phatruic and the bell, but they killed all the inferior clergy and kept the other noble relics.[18]

A revered relic said to be the staff of Jesus, the Bachall Íosa, taken in this battle, became the prized possession of Christchurch Cathedral in Dublin until it was smashed during the sixteenth-century Reformation. The MacDonleavys were to fight de Courcy again but their kingdom was lost. In a characteristic campaign of daring the Normans had made their toe-hold in Ulster, and in their rapid overrunning of the eastern coastlands thereafter, they made a radical alteration in the province's balance of power.

'TRULY AN AMAZING ACHIEVEMENT'

For Gerald of Wales the bravery of John de Courcy – 'a man of courage and a born fighter, always in the front line, always taking upon himself the greater share of the danger' – was enough to explain the success of the Norman invasion of Ulster. It is clear, however, that de Courcy had prepared his campaign with meticulous care, acquiring the grudging approval of the royal governor in Dublin, the right of passage through Meath from the de Lacys, and information, warriors and guides from the native Irish. Nevertheless, the collapse of the Gaelic armies in Ulster has to be explained. It was not that the Irish there were lacking in courage, Gerald believed, for 'in this island, as in every country, the people of the North are always more warlike and savage'.[19] In short, the Normans in Ulster were displaying a military superiority already demonstrated in England, France and Sicily.

Irish noblemen were superb horsemen but, riding without stirrups, they could do no more than hurl their spears, before dismounting on the battlefield to fight on foot. On open ground they were no match for knights protected by kite-shaped shields and mail armour from head to toe; seated on deep high-fronted saddles and with their feet secure in stirrups, the invaders could charge their foe full tilt with lance under arm. De Courcy brought with him Flemish crossbowmen and Welsh longbowmen who could pour down a deadly rain of bolts and arrows long before the Irish could get within range to use their shortbows and hurl their lances. In his *History and Topography of Ireland* Gerald wrote that the Irish fought without armour; he continued:

They regard weapons as a burden, and they think it brave and honourable to fight unarmed. They use, however, three types of weapons – short spears, two darts, and big axes well and carefully forged, which they have taken over from the Northmen . . . They are quicker and more expert than any other people in throwing, when everything fails, stones as missiles, and such stones do great damage to the enemy in an engagement.[20]

On several occasions the Irish did win battles, for in attempting to extend his conquest, the impetuous de Courcy took many risks. In 1178, for example, the Normans camped in Glen Righe by the Newry river after a victory, only to be surprised and routed by the combined forces of Murrough O'Carroll, King of Oriel, and Rory MacDonleavy; the Annals of Ulster record that 'the Ulstermen came up with them that night and made an onset upon them. Thereupon defeat was inflicted upon the Foreigners and stark slaughter was put upon them.' Not long afterwards, Cu-maighi O'Flynn, ruler of Uí Tuirtre and Fir Lí in mid-Antrim, also defeated the Normans. John de Courcy escaped with only eleven of his knights, and Gerald tells us that

he and this tiny number of followers fought their way through to his castle, despite the fact that they had to cover a distance of thirty miles, over which they continually had to defend themselves against a large force of the enemy, without their horses, which had all been lost, wearing their armour, on foot, and having nothing to eat for two days and nights. Truly an amazing achievement and one which deserves to be remembered by posterity![21]

Perhaps the vital point in this narrative is that de Courcy and his men had a castle as a refuge of last resort. Earthen mottes and stone castles were thrown up to form a network holding the conquered lands in subjection and giving access to the sea for trade, assistance and – if necessary – escape.

MOTTES AND CASTLES

The striking feature of John de Courcy's conquest is that all parts of it had easy access to the sea. The sea was the essential Norman lifeline, made more secure when de Courcy married Affreca, daughter of Gottred, King of Man, in 1180, which gave him the use of a formidable fleet. Not all of the modern counties of Antrim and Down were overrun: at most the sub-kingdoms of Dál Fiatach, Fir Lí and portions of Uí Tuirtre succumbed. The conquest did not include the central and western Down kingdom of Uí Eachach Cobha, a watch being kept on it from the motte of Dromore. The Antrim motte was another frontier post to warn of danger threatening from Cenél Eóghain, while further south at Ballyroney, Magh Cobha motte guarded the approaches from the Airgialla kingdoms and the south.

A motte castle was a fortification erected on top of an artificial mound; the steep-sided, roughly circular mound was partly constructed with soil from its surrounding ditch but raised higher by soil brought in from further afield. In many cases, as at Dunsilly in Co. Antrim, a ring-bank was erected first and then the hollow created was filled in, the inward sloping of the soil and stone helping to stabilise the mound. Some mottes – for example, at Dunsilly and at Rathmullan and Lismahon in Co. Down – were built on earlier raths. The typical Ulster motte did not have a base court or bailey as was usual in England; an exception was Dromore, which housed a permanent garrison. Dromore and Clough mottes, also in Co. Down, had wooden palisades around their perimeters as a first line of defence. The knight in command lived in a fortified hall built on the mound's flat top; the hall was generally made of timber – as at Lismahon – but later might be replaced by a stone tower – as at Clough. In 1973 R.E. Glasscock identified 128 mottes in Ulster, but some more may yet be discovered, and others, such as Gransha, may be shown to have been structures built earlier by the native Irish. Most mottes were concentrated in south Antrim and east Down, where the Norman conquest was most permanent.[22] It was here, too, that de Courcy built the two mightiest fortresses in his domain.

De Courcy began his most important castle, Carrickfergus in Co. Antrim, on a tongue of rock jutting into Belfast Lough. Behind a surrounding wall – now the inner curtain – masons erected a massive rectangular keep with walls nine feet thick; black basalt from close by, together with some red sandstone from Whiteabbey and cream Cultra limestone shipped across the lough, were used to build this tower four storeys high, rising ninety feet above the rock. There may have been no more than a curtain wall at Carrickfergus to provide de Courcy with refuge after his disastrous defeat at the hands of the O'Flynns and it can have been only towards the end of his rule that he could direct the affairs of his lordship from the well-appointed third floor of the keep. On another defensible rock adjacent to the sea, the castle of Rath – now better known as Dundrum – stood sentinel over the land approaches to Lecale. The keep was a later addition but the great stone wall surrounding the summit was de Courcy's work.[23] These mighty bastions signalled the determination of the newcomers to stay in Ulster, as well as being intimidating fortresses against which the Gaelic Irish seemed to have no answer.

EXIT DE COURCY, ENTER DE LACY

For a quarter of a century, it seemed, John de Courcy ruled his Ulster lands with as much independence as a warlord – indeed, the chronicler

Jocelin of Furness described him as 'prince of the Ulster people' and later, in an order for his arrest, King John named him 'King of all the barons of Ulster'.[24] Certainly de Courcy minted his own halfpennies and farthings at Carrickfergus and Dundrum and administered his own justice with the assistance of his seneschal, chamberlain and constable. Information about his rule is pitifully fragmentary but the names of his principal barons appear in witness to his charters; they include Richard FitzRobert, William Savage, William Hacket, William Saracen, Richard de Dundonald, Walter de Logan and Henry de Coupland (who gave his family name to the Copeland Islands).[25] Several of these surnames remain common in Antrim and Down, but it is clear that there was no extensive colonisation, the natives remaining to till the soil.

Gerald of Wales remarked that 'the twin blemishes of excessive meanness and unreliability stained the gleaming purity of a character in other respects so worthy of praise', but he acknowledged that de Courcy 'gave the church of Christ that honour which it is due'.[26] De Courcy seems to have been eager to make amends for his initial slaughter and confiscation. An obvious site for a castle, for example, was the Dál Fiatach capital but he did not build there; instead Down – in Irish Dún-da-lethglas – was granted to the Church and renamed Downpatrick in honour of the patron saint. Lands adjacent to Dundrum Bay were assigned to give an additional income to Christchurch Cathedral in Dublin – and, no doubt, to retain the favour of the royal government there. Other substantial parts of Lecale were given to Downpatrick Cathedral, and to atone for the burning of the abbey of Erenagh during his conquest, de Courcy founded the Cistercian abbey of Inch; just north of Downpatrick, the abbey almost certainly was the first building in Gothic style raised in Ireland. De Courcy's other gifts to the Church included: the Benedictine Black Abbey in the Ards; Augustinian houses at Muckamore and Downpatrick; White Abbey near Carrickfergus; Grey Abbey, a Cistercian monastery founded by his wife Affreca; the restoration of Nendrum; and the transference to Downpatrick of what purported to be the bodies of Patrick, Brigid and Colmcille in the presence of Cardinal Vivian.

At first such attempts to gain approval were successful. In 1185 Henry II's son John, 'Lord of Ireland', named de Courcy his chief governor. In spite of an undistinguished term of office marked by inconclusive raids into Connacht, de Courcy seemed to retain the Crown's favour. Then, shortly after John became King of England in 1199, de Courcy's luck ran out – was it because he spoke out against John's ousting of Arthur of Brittany from the succession? Hugh de Lacy, younger son of the first

Lord of Meath and eager to acquire estates of his own, was authorised to wage war on de Courcy. Now Norman fought Norman, and after campaigns stretching over five years, de Courcy was driven out of Ulster. On 29 May 1205 King John created Hugh Earl of Ulster, granting him all the land of the province 'as John de Courcy held it on the day when Hugh defeated him'. De Courcy returned with one hundred vessels from Man and, landing at Strangford, laid siege to Dundrum Castle – it was in vain, for the defences he himself had made were too strong. In vain, too, was an appeal made to Pope Celestine III, and de Courcy never recovered the lands he fought so persistently to conquer. Eventually reconciled to King John as a humble knight, he lived to assist in the subsequent downfall of his tormentor Hugh de Lacy.[27]

'DREADING THE FURY OF THE KING'

William de Braose, Lord of Limerick, was King John's sworn enemy. Not only had he fallen behind in payments for his Irish lands but, worse still, his wife Matilda de Saint-Valéry had denied the king her son as hostage, saying to the royal messenger: 'I will not deliver up my son to your lord, King John, for he basely murdered his nephew Arthur, when he should have kept him in honourable custody.'[28] As John prepared a great expedition for Ireland to break the power of his overmighty subject, de Braose took refuge with his kinsman Hugh de Lacy.

On 20 June 1210 King John was in Waterford with the mightiest army yet seen in Ireland: seven thousand knights, archers, and foot soldiers. Nine days later the king was in Dublin, his force increased by feudal levies from Munster and Leinster. Unavailingly did barons from the north plead for mercy towards their lord, de Lacy. John advanced and was joined by Cathal Crobhdearg, King of Connacht, at Ardbraccan in Meath on 4 July. In desperation de Lacy levelled his castles at the approaches to Ulster, as recorded in the Annals of Inisfallen:

> When Hugh de Lacy had discovered that the King was going to the north, he burned his own castles in Machaire Conaille, and in Cuailgne, before the King's eyes . . . and he himself fled to Carrickfergus, leaving the chiefs of his people burning, levelling, and destroying the castles of the country and dreading the fury of the King . . . When the King saw this disrespect offered him, he marched from Drogheda to Carlingford.[29]

By 9 July John was in Carlingford and now loomed the problem that would face many an English army in the future – how should Ulster be entered? De Lacy moved south, preparing to make a stand, with an ambush very likely laid in the Moyry Pass. However, using his great fleet, the king transported his army over Carlingford Lough with a bridge made with boats and hundreds of pontoons brought from Dorset, Somerset and York. Then, while his men marched by the coast around the Mourne Mountains, John sailed to Ardglass and rested in Jordan de Saukeville's castle close by. Dundrum looked impregnable with its great round keep newly constructed by de Lacy in the style developed in his homeland of the Welsh Marches. John, however, brought with him an intimidating array of siege engines and the garrison fled. No detailed record of this momentous royal incursion survives except for terse entries in the exchequer rolls; there must have been a fight here, for men were paid on 14 July to make repairs to the castle:

> to Nicholas Carpenter, 10s., Ralph de Presbury, 15s., Master Osbert Quarrier, Alberic, Ditcher, 7s.6d., Master Pinell and Ernulf, miners, 1 mark . . .[30]

Two days later John was in Downpatrick, where he paid £40 to his soldiers and lost five shillings gaming with Warin FitzGerald. Soon after, siege was laid to Carrickfergus by both sea and land, and in a short time the castle surrendered. Thirty barons and knights are named as prisoners taken, including William and Luke de Audley of Strangford, Walter de Logan, and Robert de Weldebuef, owner of the Edereskel estate between Holywood and Ballyoran, Co. Down. De Braose and de Lacy escaped to France but Matilda de Braose and her son William were captured at sea by the Scottish baron, Duncan FitzGilbert, Earl of Carrick. The man given the task of bringing these unfortunates to the king was none other than John de Courcy, restored to favour though not to his lands. Matilda and her infant son were cast into prison and there, by the king's orders, both starved to death.

King John stayed at Carrickfergus for ten days making many payments, including £532 to Henry de Ver as wages for bailiffs, knights and sailors, 1,004 marks to English noblemen, and £2 12s.6d. for repairs to the castle. After ordering the bishop of Norwich to have galleys built at Antrim to place on Lough Neagh and after receiving the homage of Áed O'Neill, King of Tír Eóghain, John left Carrickfergus. At Holywood ('Apud Sanctum Boscum', in the exchequer roll) he paid sixty shillings to mariners from Bayonne on 29 July and then seized the castles of Dundonald, Ballymaghan and Ballymorran. Returning to Downpatrick early in August, King John paid Warin FitzGerald another ten shillings 'for play' and then left for the Isle of Man and England.[31]

Perhaps no king had ever had such complete power over all Ireland as John wielded by August 1210. The greatest Gaelic rulers had given their allegiance and support, and when in 1215 the English barons humiliated their king at Runnymede, there was not a murmur of rebellion from his Norman vassals across the Irish Sea. The completeness of John's success in Ireland, contrasted with his failure elsewhere, prepared the way for a further erosion of independent Ulster.

John kept the earldom of Ulster for himself and ordered the strengthening of Carrickfergus. Another curtain wall – now the middle curtain – was raised up to improve defence along the shore, especially at low tide; the royal government appointed William de Serlande as constable at £20 a year in 1217 and gave him £100 a year to pay for building work. The de Galloway Scots were rewarded for their help in 1210: Duncan of Carrick was granted the Antrim Glens from Larne to Glenarm, and his nephews – Alan, Lord of Galloway, and Thomas, Earl of Atholl – received coastlands from the Glens to Lough Foyle. These Norman Scots strove hard to win this land only partially conquered before.

De Braose died in poverty and de Lacy plotted his return to Ulster, his hopes raised by King John's death in 1216. 'If John our father of good memory truly did you wrong in any way, we should be free of that wrong', the boy-king Henry III wrote to de Lacy, who was helping to slaughter heretics in southern France at the time.[32] This conciliation was not enough: de Lacy wanted the return of the earldom of Ulster and he meant to defy Henry III to seize it.

'Hugh, as the King hears, is now plotting forcibly to invade the King's land of Ireland,' the king wrote to his governor in Dublin, 'wherefore the King commands the governor to provide against Hugh's attack by fortifying with victuals and men the King's Irish castles.' Letters from Pope Innocent III excommunicating Hugh were sent, the governor being instructed to 'use those letters at the proper time, and prepare all things for the King's security and for Hugh's injury'.[33] De Lacy slipped back to Ireland in 1223, throwing the northern half of the country into turmoil. Cathal Crobhdearg, the now aged King of Connacht, appealed to Henry III: 'Cathal is in great difficulty . . . Cathal prays the King to send a force thither to restrain Hugh's insolence.' The Annals of Connacht tell how de Lacy and his allies 'produced assaults of war and dispersion among the Foreigners of Ireland, until these rose up against them'. William the Marshal, the mightiest baron in both England and Ireland, stung by an invasion of his property in the Welsh Marches by Llywelyn, de Lacy's ally and kinsman, led a host of colonists and Irish northwards. De Lacy's Leinster castles fell one by one, including Trim after a six-week siege, and the Marshal's cousin William le Gros fought his way by sea to relieve Carrickfergus. De Lacy withdrew but returned to the fray with Áed O'Neill, King of Tír Eóghain, destroying the Earl of Atholl's castle at Coleraine, and, the annals relate, 'moved out with his Galls and Gaels, and they posted themselves in parties on the passes of Sliab Fuaid and the Dorsey of Emain and Fid Conaille, and challenged attack in these positions'.[34]

Though the Marshal took Cathal mac Annaid O'Reilly's crannog in the remote fastness of Lough Oughter in east Bréifne – where the de Lacys had secreted their womenfolk, including Llywelyn's daughter – he shrank from a protracted campaign along the Ulster borderland. An armistice was agreed and, in return for his two sons given as hostages, de Lacy got back his earldom of Ulster in 1227 save for the north Antrim coastlands given to the Scots by King John. Further Norman conquest in the north was to follow but the latent power of the Cenél Eóghain and the Cenél Conaill in central and western Ulster began to loom as a grave problem for royal government in Dublin.

TWESCARD AND BEYOND

The rapacious Hugh de Lacy lost little time in defying the terms of his reinstatement and relentlessly drove the Scots out of north Antrim. He kept most for himself but granted Duncan of Carrick's land to John Bisset, a traditional Scots enemy of the de Galloways. De Lacy strength-ened Carrickfergus Castle with a new outer curtain wall and a powerful twin-towered gatehouse, he built a new gatehouse at Dundrum, and raised another massive fortress at Greencastle to guard the narrows of Carlingford Lough – and perhaps prevent another royal bridge of boats. But because de Lacy helped to conquer the province of Connacht, large tracts of which were granted to Richard de Burgo, the English Crown indulged his defiance and they remained on good terms.[35]

It was de Lacy rather than de Courcy who was responsible for the conquest and colonisation of the northern coastland called Twescard, from the Irish *tuaisceart* meaning 'north'. Centred on Coleraine and the lower Bush valley, it had become one of the most prosperous parts of the earldom when de Lacy died in 1243. The earldom passed back to the English Crown (probably a condition of de Lacy's pardon in 1227) but it was to be a troublesome inheritance.

By the middle of the thirteenth century Gaelic Ulster had become the most extensive independent region in Ireland, the Normans penetrat-ing more deeply into the other three provinces. Yet the two great Gaelic power blocs of the north, the Cenél Eóghain and the Cenél Conaill, fell more and more on the defensive. From his castle at Sligo Maurice FitzGerald made repeated raids on Tír Conaill and in 1252 built a castle at Caol-uisce, where the waters of lower Lough Erne narrow into its outflowing river. Meanwhile, the capacity of the Cenél Eóghain to resist was weakened by a fierce dynastic dispute following the death of Áed O'Neill in 1230. Donal Mac Lochlainn, with some help from the Dublin government, dealt successfully with his O'Neill rivals until 1241, when Brian O'Neill, in alliance with the O'Donnells of Tír Conaill, killed Donal and his close kindred in a battle at Camergi – an unidentified site in Tyrone. John FitzGeoffrey, Henry III's chief governor in Ireland, exploited this weakness by building a bridge near Coleraine and a castle opposite at Killowen in 1248, and erected a castle at Magh Cobha at Ballyroney further south. From these forward positions FitzGeoffrey invaded central Ulster as far as Armagh.

Brian O'Neill counter-attacked in 1253, destroying Magh Cobha, but he felt decisive action was needed to halt the steady erosion of his territory. In 1255 Áed O'Connor, son of the King of Connacht, came to Tír Eóghain and – in return for a free hand in Bréifne – made alliance. Then in 1258 Áed O'Connor met Brian O'Neill again at Caol-uisce and there Brian was proclaimed 'King of the Gael of Erin' – a title inspired perhaps by Llywelyn's claim to be Prince of Wales. If Brian hoped to unite all the Irish of Ulster behind him – let alone the Irish of the other three provinces – then he did not come even close to success: he was opposed by the O'Donnells, the MacMahons, the O'Rahillys, the O'Rourkes, and by rival O'Neill factions. When in 1260 he joined forces with men of Connacht and made an assault on the earldom of Ulster, he was defeated and slain near Downpatrick by a levy of the town and a force led by Sir Roger des Auters. Brian's death was mourned in a lament by Gilbride MacNamee:

Death of my heart! The head of Brian
In a strange country under cold clay!
O head of Brian of Slieve Snaght,
Eire after thee is an orphan![36]

That Brian's head was sent to England indicates how serious a threat this O'Neill–O'Connor coalition was seen to be.

In 1264 Walter de Burgo, Lord of Connacht, was granted the earldom of Ulster by Edward, created Lord of Ireland by his father Henry III. The free-spending Edward was in debt to de Burgo but it also seems likely that the English Crown wearied of the defence of the earldom. With a great sweep of territory in his possession, curving round from Connacht to Twescard, the new Earl of Ulster might keep the Gaels of the north from threatening the outlying manors of the lordship of Ireland. Walter skilfully exploited the complex dynastic rivalries of Gaelic Ulster to his advantage; he won the firm alliance of Áed Buidhe O'Neill, who, with the earl's help against the O'Donnells, long held sway as King of Cenél Eóghain. In a document of 1269 'Odo Onel Rex Kenlean' – Áed O'Neill, King of Cenél Eóghain – agreed to be

> bound to the nobleman, his lord W. de Burgh as follows . . . he is bound to deliver to the said earl four hostages . . . To keep this agreement he has sworn on holy relics to the earl. If he break the agreement the earl may drive him from his kingship, which he is bound to hold of him, and give or sell it to any one else.

O'Neill was betrothed to Aleanor, the earl's cousin, and he 'promised to bind himself under pain of excommunication' to treat her honourably.[37]

When Walter de Burgo died in 1271, his son Richard was only twelve years old. During this minority a furious struggle for land in Twescard ensued between the de Mandevilles and the FitzWarins which was not brought to an end until 1280, when Richard, not quite of age, inherited his lands and castles. From the outset the new earl, popularly known as the Red Earl, ruled with a firm hand and pushed his territory deeper into Gaelic Ulster. In 1296 he joined Edward I in his devastating campaign against the Scots and gave his sister Egidia in marriage to James the Steward of Scotland; as a wedding gift, the couple received the manor of Le Roo – a clear indication that O'Cahan lands in Keenaght had been overrun, for this was Limavady on the River Roe. By the first years of the fourteenth century de Burgo had seized much of the Inishowen penin-sula, the most northerly part of Ireland disputed over by the Cenél Conaill and the Cenél Eóghain. In 1305 the earl began building the great castle of Northburgh (now confusingly known as Greencastle) to com-mand the narrows at the entrance to Lough Foyle, with a twin-towered gatehouse at one end, a polygonal tower at the other and a massive rectangular keep with walls twelve feet thick at the base.[38]

The Earl of Ulster became one of the most powerful nobles in the land. He created an impressive network of marriage alliances; his son John married a granddaughter of Edward I and his four daughters married well – Matilda to the Earl of Gloucester, Catherine to the Earl of Desmond, Joan to the Earl of Kildare, and Elizabeth to the Earl of Carrick. The Earl of Carrick was none other than Robert Bruce, and in the years that followed, this marriage in particular pulled the Red Earl's loyalties in conflicting directions in an episode which would herald the ultimate collapse of the earldom of Ulster.

THE EARLDOM OF ULSTER: KNIGHTS, FARMERS AND BETAGHS

In 1226 Geoffrey de Marisco, Henry III's chief governor in Ireland, had sent an account, which was written into the Close Roll, of rents collected by Roger de Vallibus for the Crown from the earldom of Ulster. The total sum was £939 4s.4d. from the five bailiwicks, or counties, of the earldom: Antrim, Carrickfergus, 'del Art' (Ards), 'Blathewyc' (Newtownards) and 'Ladcathel' (Lecale). Over a century later another investigation, or 'inquisition', in 1333, showed the expansion of the earldom into five 'counties': Twescard, Antrim, Carrickfergus, Blathewyc and Down. It is from this inquisition, and an assessment of Church taxation made in 1307, that most of our sparse evidence for life in the earldom derives.[39]

Each bailiwick was the responsibility of a seneschal or sheriff who was usually one of the earl's barons. He held the county court, summoning leading landholders to attend as jurors, and he arranged the settlement of minor disputes in manorial courts meeting once a fortnight. Bailiffs collected rents for the earl's treasurer. The earldom was a disturbed region at the furthest limits of the Irish lordship and it was often on a war footing. Knights were obliged to give military service, constables maintained castle defences, and able-bodied men of the towns and manors had to assemble in arms in times of danger – as when Brian O'Neill invaded Down in 1260. Mottes were concentrated on the earldom's frontiers and sometimes manned by full-time garrisons; the 1211–12 Pipe Roll shows forty men at Antrim, thirty at Dromore and ten at Magh Cobha. Native Irishmen were employed; at Antrim, for example, Irish soldiers were paid cows in compensation for their wounds and for 'losing their mantles'. Not just colonists but Irishmen too were expected to help the English king in his wars abroad. The men of Uí Tuirtre had to pay £200 to Henry III as their contribution to his war in Gascony in 1253; Cú-Uladh O'Hanlon and Aengus MacMahon are reported slain in 1297 on their return from the war in Flanders; and Richard de Burgo led natives and settlers alike in Edward I's Scottish campaigns.[40]

Next in social importance after the earl were the four great baronial families, who were, in effect, the principal landlords: the Savages, with manors mainly in Twescard; the Bissets in the Antrim Glens; the de Logans in the Six Mile Water valley; and the de Mandevilles, who first arrived with King John, with manors in north Antrim, Donegore, Comber, Killyleagh, Groomsport and Castleward. These vassals held great manors from the earl, valued in knight's fees, that is, land for which rent was due sufficient to maintain the service of a knight. In the Six Mile Water valley there were four knight's fees, each about two square miles: Twywys (Ballynure); Lyn (Ballylinny); Robertiston (Ballyrobert) and Waltirton (Ballywalter). Of lesser men we know almost nothing; a John le Masoun is mentioned as having ten acres in

Doagh and the de Sandel family acquired land in Twescard in 1300. Some tenants paid peppercorn rent only – literally in the case of the tenants of Frenestoun (Ballyfrenis, a townland in the parish of Donaghadee), who paid a pound of pepper. Nicholas Galgyl of Greyabbey gave a pair of silver spurs in rent for one farm and an otterskin for another; John de Mandeville in Greencastle paid one 'soar sparrowhawk as rent at the feast of St John Baptist'; and a tenant of Glenarm paid two pairs of white gloves for 102 acres there.[41]

At a time when the population of western Europe was rising, many settlers were attracted to Ireland, but for most the marchland of the earldom would have been too inhospitable. The ruling Gaelic families were driven out, the MacDonleavys, for example, becoming physicians in Tír Conaill. It is clear, however, that the great majority in the earldom were Irish and for the most part it was they who farmed the land. Some, such as a certain O'Hagheran in Twescard, were freemen with substantial farms, but most were villeins or 'betaghs'. 'Betagh' is an anglicisation of the Irish *biatach*, meaning 'one who gives food'; this indicates that they were freemen before the conquest, who paid rent in food. Now betaghs held pieces of land in return for unpaid labour service. An Irishman named O'Coltaran from the Cave Hill gave the services of twenty-four reapers in August in Belfast as rent for his land, the 1333 inquisition informs us.[42]

Much of the rent in the earldom was paid in corn, and landholders could increase their income by imposing charges in kind for the use of their mills. There can have been no drastic change in farming techniques in this part of Ulster except that in the most fertile areas more grain – almost certainly oats – would have been grown than before. The word 'grange', derived from Old French, meaning 'barn', is applied to manors particularly in the counties of Carrickfergus and Antrim at, for example, Dunadry, Doagh and Ballyrobert. Forbidden to build castles in stone, vassals and other substantial farmers often lived on mottes, though not in Twescard, annexed when the age of the motte had passed. Close by, on the best land, corn and perhaps some peas, beans and leeks were raised on ridges in enclosed fields of around two acres each. As in the heavily colonised manors in Leinster, there may have been large open fields cultivated in strips. Plough teams and working horses are referred to in documents of 1212 and 1282. Even on the best-run manors the yield was low by modern standards – around three crannocks after tithe deductions for every crannock of oats sown. Lack of sufficient manure was the most serious limitation and the practice of burning sods gave only a short-term gain as it reduced humus in the soil. Cattle remained at the centre of the farming economy, though the

FitzWarins complained of the loss of two thousand hogs and goats from their Twescard demesne during their war with the de Mandevilles, and sheepskins feature in the earldom's accounts for exports.

The salmon fishery of the lower Bann was the third most valuable source of income for the de Mandevilles, as well as providing for the upkeep of monks in Downpatrick. The 1333 inquisition mentions a fishery on the Roe worth twenty shillings a year, 'a fishery worth 3s 4d at Halywode', and a 'rent of 100 eels of the value of 1s' from Lough Mourne near Carrickfergus. The bishop of Down had a fishery in Lecale and herring fishermen drew up their boats on the Ards to cure their catch.[43]

THE EARLDOM OF ULSTER: TOWNS

Most Irish provincial towns were founded by the Normans and, while this is not true of Ulster, around fifteen have been identified on or close to the coastlines of Antrim and Down.

Carrickfergus, the capital of the earldom with the largest castle and parish church in the territory, had the highest valuation. The town had a representative on the Dublin guild of merchants in 1257 and traded directly with France – there is record of Thomas le Mercer's ship, bringing back Gascon wine, coming to grief in 1308. Downpatrick remained an ecclesiastical centre but it was defended by walls, the citizens being relieved of £5 in taxes to repair them after their victory over Brian O'Neill. The takings of its monthly court were worth ten shillings a year. Coulrath (Coleraine) vied with Downpatrick as the town second in importance; with its fortified bridge it was the forward position for raids to the north-west. Salmon netted at Lyn (the Cutts) were exported from here in quantity, perhaps in return for French wine – the *Grace Deu* managed to ply between Coleraine and Gascony even at the height of the Bruce invasion in 1317.[44]

Other towns, described as boroughs in the 1333 inquisition, included Le Roo (Limavady); 'The New Town of Blathewyc' (Newtownards); Dunmalys (Larne); Portkamen (Bushmills); Portros (Portrush); Grenecastell (Greencastle); Doundannald (Dundonald); Coul (Carnmoney); and Le Ford (Belfast). Le Ford, like several of these boroughs, can have been little more than a village; it had a castle, a parish church at Shankill, a chapel (on the site of the present St George's church in High Street), and a watermill (presumably at Millfield) worth 6s. 8d. a year. Antrim was the only inland town of any size, and even it was close to water. Other inland towns such as Twywys were no more than centres of manors.

The earldom of Ulster – indeed the province as a whole – was far from the centres of prosperity and trade in the south-east, such as New Ross and Waterford. It is unlikely that Ulster in this period accounted for more than one fiftieth of Ireland's overseas trade. Luxuries such as wine were paid for by modest exports of corn, hides and salt fish, and most needs were met from the immediate locality. Stone dressing and building was probably the largest industry and at Scrabo stone grave markers, decorated in a style derived from Cheshire, were taken by sea to Movilla, Holywood and other sites close to the shores of Strangford and Belfast Loughs. Glazed pottery was made in Downpatrick, where the only medieval kiln has been found in Ireland. It was from the farms and manors, however, that the great majority of the earldom's inhabitants got their living.[45]

By the start of the fourteenth century, Norman conquest in Ireland had reached its high-water mark. In the north Richard de Burgo had seized new territory as far as Inishowen, but amidst the drumlins of Down the MacCartans and the Magennises of Uí Eachach Cobha stayed free, and beyond the Bann, the Cenél Eóghain viewed the earl's latest annexations with alarm. North of Lough Neagh the Uí Tuirtre kingdom held out as a wedge between Twescard and the rest of the earldom; the fertile soils must have tempted the invaders but the Irish here fended them off with a great stone fort at Doonbought near the River Main's junction with its tributary the Clough, a stone castle at Connor near Kells, and a scattering of mottes. In short, the Irish were learning from the intruders. At the frayed fringe of the Irish lordship and with a sparse settler population, the earldom was fatally vulnerable as a great Scots army prepared an assault on Ulster.

3

PROVINCE BEYOND THE PALE

c. 1300–1558

OVERVIEW

On 26 May 1315 a formidable Scots expeditionary force disembarked near Larne with no less a mission than the complete conquest of Ireland. His triumph the previous year at Bannockburn notwithstanding, Robert Bruce had yet to force recognition that he was the rightful King of Scotland from Edward II of England. At the very least this campaign in Ireland would strike at the heart of the English colony there which had long sustained armies fighting against him in Scotland, divert the English on the Borders and give the Scots control of the Irish Sea from Man northwards. Bruce knew Ulster; he had taken refuge there in 1294 and 1306, and in 1302 he had married Elizabeth, daughter of Richard de Burgo, the Red Earl of Ulster. The prospect of Irish help made conquest seem possible: already Domnal O'Neill, King of Tír Eóghain, had pledged his support and now Bruce – ignoring his Norman ancestry and the English speech of his Lowland spearmen – called the Irish to arms, declaring that 'our people and your people, free in times past, share the same national ancestry and . . . a common language and common custom'.[1]

It was to his brother Edward, Earl of Carrick, that Robert Bruce entrusted this enterprise. Steadfast throughout all the years of failure, brave in battle and Robert's acknowledged heir, Edward Bruce sought a kingdom for himself in Ireland. The Scots invasion, however, coincided with the onset of a severe famine and, instead of conquest, the people of Ulster suffered more than three years of intense misery. Nevertheless, Norman infiltration was brought to a striking and permanent halt, and for almost two centuries the power of the English Crown declined until it was restricted to seaports and a strip of territory around Dublin known as the Pale. Following the murder of the Brown Earl of Ulster in 1333, the north in time returned almost completely to Gaelic control. Preoccupied by campaigns in France and then by the Wars of the Roses, the English government did little to arrest the decay of the Irish lordship. It was not until Henry Tudor defeated Richard III at Bosworth Field in 1485 that civil war between English barons ceased and the way was prepared for the recovery of English power in Ireland. Even then, for many years Ulster continued to be a province beyond the Pale.

Transported by the notorious pirate Thomas Dun – 'a scummer of the se', according to the poet John Barbour – Edward Bruce brought with him to Ulster, the annals record,

> the men of three hundred ships, and his warlike slaughtering army caused the whole of Ireland to tremble, both Gael and Gall. He began by harrying the choicest part of Ulster, burning Rathmore in Moylinny.[2]

Plundering the manors of the Six Mile Water, routing Sir Thomas de Mandeville, and sweeping aside the MacCartans, Edward Bruce and his O'Neill allies forced the Moyry Pass and razed Dundalk, Co. Louth, where he was inaugurated high-king. The burning of the church of Ardee, filled with men, women and children taking sanctuary, was an early sign of the ruthless and destructive character of this war. So unexpected was this Scots incursion that Edmund Butler, the newly appointed royal governor, was in Munster and Richard de Burgo was attending to his extensive possessions in Connacht. Both lords hastened northwards to meet Edward Bruce:

> When Richard de Burgh, Earl of Ulster, heard that Edward was approaching to attack him he brought together a great army from all sides to Roscommon at first, marching thence to Athlone and obliquely through Meath and Mag Breg, having with him Felim O'Connor, king of Connacht, their numbers being about twenty battalions; and this time the Galls spared not saint or shrine, however sacred, nor churchmen or laymen or sanctuary, but went wasting and ravaging across Ireland from the Shannon in the south to Coleraine and Inishowen in the north. And when this mighty column of a single host came marching together into Bregia they saw coming to meet them Edmund Butler, Justiciar of Ireland, with thirty tight battalions, but the Earl would not let him join his assembled force, for he trusted to himself and his own men to expel the Scots from Ireland.

Perhaps de Burgo feared that Butler's army would inflict on his earldom of Ulster the same devastation he himself had perpetrated; in any case, the royal governor lacked the funds to pay for further action. Advised by Domnal O'Neill, Bruce pulled back across Ulster to ravage the earl's settlements at Inishowen and the Roe valley, while de Burgo advanced down the right bank of the lower Bann only to find that the Scots

> threw down the bridge of Coleraine to hinder the Earl; and he followed them up and encamped opposite Edward and the Ulstermen on the river at Coleraine and between them they left neither wood nor lea nor corn nor crop nor stead nor barn, but fired and burnt them all.

About this time Felim O'Connor was persuaded to change sides, for the annals state that Edward Bruce 'sent men to seek him out covertly and to offer him the possession of Connacht without partition, if he would desert the earl and maintain his right to that province. And Feidlim listened tolerantly to these proposals and agreed with Edward . . .'[3] As Barbour relates:

> The Bane, that is ane arme of the se
> That with hors may nocht passit be,
> Was betuix thame and Ullister.[4]

The Bann estuary, however, was crossed with Dun's fleet and the Scots now drew close to the earl, who prepared an ambush for them:

> The Erll and all that with him war,
> Ruschit on thame with wapnys bar.

It was an inconclusive skirmish and Richard de Burgo fell back southwards towards the heart of his earldom to make a last stand by the Kellswater at Connor. There on 10 September 1315 the Scots spearmen completely overwhelmed the earl's feudal host; Sir William de Burgo, the earl's cousin, was taken prisoner and, as the annals record, 'Richard de Burgh, Earl of Ulster, was a wanderer up and down Ireland all this year, with nor power or lordship.'[5] Only Carrickfergus Castle continued to hold out.

THE SIEGE OF CARRICKFERGUS, 1315–16

After the Battle of Connor as many survivors of the earl's broken army as could make it to Carrickfergus took refuge there. In October 1315 Edward II's victuallers were ordered to supply thirty crannocks of wheat to the defenders but ships carrying the grain were scattered by a storm and the supplies were diverted to Whitehaven and Skinburness. Those within the castle would have to survive on what lay within the storehouses. Lacking heavy siege engines, the Scots settled down to starve the garrison into submission, while the main body of their army prepared to conquer the rest of Ireland.

At first Edward Bruce swept all before him. Reinforced by fresh troops brought over by the Earl of Moray in November 1315, the Scots advanced south into Leinster to defeat Roger de Mortimer and the de Lacys at Kells on 6 December, paused over Christmas at Ballymore Loughsewdy in the Midlands, and on 26 January 1316 won a great battle at Ardscull near Athy over an army led by Edmund Butler. The Scots fought a winter campaign knowing that their spearmen were at an advantage over the colonists' mounted knights at a time of the year

51

when horses were hampered by soft ground and shortage of grass. A terrible famine was sweeping Europe, however, and unable to live off the country despite their victories, the Scots were force by hunger back into Ulster.

For Henry of Thrapston, keeper of Carrickfergus Castle, the position was becoming desperate and the garrison was reduced to chewing hides. It was not until Easter 1316 that an attempt was made to bring relief; Sir Thomas de Mandeville put together a force in Drogheda and sailed to Belfast Lough. A fierce skirmish followed in the streets of Carrickfergus when the Scots were roused, but it was in vain that a desperate sally was made by the castle garrison; the Scots defeated the colonists and Sir Thomas was slain. A further relief expedition was diverted by the Earl of Ulster and the grain given to the Scots as ransom for his cousin, Sir William. It was now only a matter of time before Carrickfergus surrendered. During a parley on 24 June 1316 the garrison seized thirty Scots and held them prisoner in the dungeons; according to the Laud Annals, eight of these men were later killed and eaten by the defenders. The annals explain that this 'pitiable circumstance' came about because 'no one came up with supplies'. Finally, after a year's siege, in September 1316 Carrickfergus surrendered on condition that the garrison was spared mutilation and death.[6]

Edward Bruce's hold on Ulster was now complete. Northburgh in Inishowen and Greencastle opposite Carlingford had fallen to the Scots and Bruce was reported to have held a parliament in Ulster and hanged many of his opponents there to reinforce his authority. On 1 May 1316 Edward had himself crowned King of Ireland at Dundalk. Though many of the Gaelic Irish in Leinster and Connacht had risen against the colonists, he still had to make good his title beyond the borders of Ulster. At Christmas Robert Bruce joined his brother in Ulster, landing at Carrickfergus with an imposing force.

Early in February 1317 the two brothers broke out of Ulster to rout the Earl of Ulster in Meath and approached Dublin. The earl, who had taken refuge in the city, was imprisoned by the mayor of Dublin on suspicion that he was a secret ally of the Bruces. Though de Burgo's daughter was married to Robert, the charge was certainly false. As the citizens of Dublin repaired their walls and set fire to their suburbs, the Bruces decided against an attempt on the capital and turned aside to burn and plunder the country as far south as Limerick. The winter was even harsher than the one before and the dearth was as severe as anyone could remember: 'Great famine this year throughout Ireland', the Annals of Connacht record, and the Laud Annals assert that Bruce's men 'were so destroyed with hunger that they raised the bodies of the dead from the cemeteries . . . and their women devoured their own children from hunger'. The annalist believed this to be a punishment for eating meat during Lent, 'for they were reduced to eating one another, so that out of 10,000 there remained only about 300 who escaped the vengeance of God'.[7]

With only O'Neill and his allies still in support, the Bruces were fast failing in their great enterprise and fell back to Ulster in May 1317. Robert Bruce returned to Scotland on 22 May, leaving his brother Edward to face Roger de Mortimer, who arrived from England as Edward II's chief governor with a large army and released Richard de Burgo from custody in Dublin. For a year Edward Bruce remained with his Scots army in Ulster and neither he nor his opponents could get to grips with each other while the famine continued to rage.

John of Athy, appointed admiral of Edward II's fleet on 28 June 1318, captured Thomas Dun on 2 July and thereby cut off Edward Bruce from his supply lines to Scotland. The harvest of that year was good and action soon followed. In a final attempt Bruce invaded south once more through the Moyry Pass only to meet an English army under the command of John de Bermingham at the hill of Faughart near Dundalk. In the words of the Annals of Connacht:

> Edward Bruce, he who was the common ruin of the Galls and Gaels of Ireland, was by the Galls of Ireland killed at Dundalk by dint of fierce fighting. MacRuaidri, king of the Hebrides, and MacDomnaill, king of Argyle, and their Scots were killed with him; and never was there a better deed done for the Irish than this, since the beginning of the world and the banishing of the Formorians from Ireland. For in this Bruce's time, for three years and a half, falsehood and famine and homicide filled the country, and undoubtedly men ate each other in Ireland.[8]

THE MURDER OF THE BROWN EARL, 1333

When Richard de Burgo died in Tipperary in 1326 he was acknowledged in the annals to be 'the best of all the Galls in Ireland'.[9] As Lord of Connacht and 3rd Earl of Ulster he had title to almost half of Ireland and by the marriages of his sons and daughters he was connected with the greatest families in the island and the ruling houses of both Scotland and England. With the aid of his own Irish mercenary army he had rapidly recovered his ravaged lands in Ulster after Faughart but his death left the earldom in the hands of his fourteen-year-old grandson William. In the wake of the Bruce invasion the future of the colony in Ulster looked uncertain.

So anxious was Edward III about the stability of his Irish lordship that in 1328 he knighted William, known soon after as the Brown Earl, and gave him full possession of his lands. The earl was unequal to the task and his authority was challenged by his cousin Walter de Burgo. With royal help Walter was defeated and the Brown Earl threw his cousin into Northburgh Castle in Inishowen and there had him starved to death. In the turbulent conditions of fourteenth-century Ireland William had made too many enemies. On 6 June 1333, on his way from Newtownards to Carrickfergus, he was killed at Belfast by his own tenants, Richard and Robert de Mandeville and John de Logan. The chronicler Friar Clyn of Kilkenny blamed the murder on Gyle, Richard de Mandeville's wife and sister of Walter de Burgo. The Brown Earl's heir was his two-year-old daughter Elizabeth, taken by her mother Matilda to England, never to return. It was a disaster from which the earldom would not recover.[10]

John Darcy, newly appointed as the king's chief governor, had raised an army to go to Scotland, but now he sailed to Carrickfergus, and after some fierce fighting with de Logan and his Irish allies, which wasted the manors of Belfast and Dundonald, royal authority was reasserted. No earl would ever reside in Ulster again, however. The earldom had depended to quite an exceptional extent on the earl himself, as there was not a large class of landowners beneath him. The magnificent income of the territory came largely from the earnings of corn mills and rents paid in kind by Irish tenants who farmed the land. When the earl's power was weak or absent, then the whole structure was imperilled.[11] Immediately following William de Burgo's murder, the earldom lost its lands west of the River Bann. It took another century before most of its remaining possessions fell to the Gaelic Irish, but the process of attrition had begun and as long as the power of the English Crown in Ireland was in retreat the disintegration of the earldom could not be halted.

FAMINE AND PLAGUE

The murder of the Brown Earl had shaken the Irish lordship to its foundations. The de Burgos of Connacht threw off their allegiance to the King of England and, known thereafter as the Burkes, became thoroughly Irish. Other lords of Norman origin, who for generations had intermarried with the Irish, adopted Gaelic speech and customs. Seeming to fit the description 'more Irish than the Irish themselves', first used by Gerald of Wales, they showed scant regard for weakening royal authority and ruled great tracts of the Irish countryside as independent warlords. In 1341 leading clergy and nobility in the Irish lordship informed Edward III that 'the third part of your land of Ireland which was conquered in the time of your progenitors is now come into the hand of your Irish enemies and your English lieges are so impoverished that they can hardly live'.[12] The Government itself was impoverished as a consequence; the average annual revenue of the Irish exchequer, which had been £6,300 in 1278–99, fell to £2,512 for the years 1368–84. The royal administration concluded that the decay of the Irish lordship was due to the fact that 'many English of the land, forsaking the English language, dress, style of riding, laws, and usages, live and govern themselves according to the manners, dress and language of the Irish enemies and also had contracted marriages and alliances with them'. It was to no avail, however, that the 1366 statute of Kilkenny 'ordained and established that no alliance by marriage, gossipred, fostering of children, concubinage or sexual liaison or in any other manner be made henceforward between English and Irish on one side or the other'.[13]

In more senses than one the climate of the times accelerated the decline of the English colony in the fourteenth century. A steady deterioration of the weather across the northern hemisphere – causing the Norse to abandon Greenland, for example – brought a succession of bad harvests in its wake. The Bruce invasion had coincided with the Great European Famine of 1315–17 and the annals for the fourteenth century contain many references to bad seasons, including:

1317: Great famine this year throughout Ireland . . . 1318: Snow the like of which had not been seen for many a long year . . . 1322: Great cattle-plague throughout Ireland, the like of which had never been known before . . . 1324: The same cattle-plague was in all Ireland this year. It was called the Mael Domnaig . . . 1325: The cattle plague throughout Ireland still . . . 1328: Much thunder and lightning this year, whereby much of the fruit and produce of all Ireland was ruined, and the corn grew up white and blind . . . A great and intolerable wind this summer, with scarcity of food and clothing . . . 1335: Heavy snow in the spring, which killed most of the small birds of all Ireland . . . 1338: Nearly all the sheep in Ireland died this year . . . 1363: A great wind this year, which wrecked churches and houses and sank many ships and boats . . .[14]

This climatic deterioration is supported by dendrochronological data – that is, interpretation of oak tree rings – and seems to have been general across Europe. The colonists, depending more heavily on corn and sheep than the Gaelic Irish, suffered most and, in addition, were scourged by a succession of plagues in the fourteenth and fifteenth centuries.

The Black Death first appeared in Howth during the summer of 1348, and though in the following year the Annals of Connacht record 'A great plague in Moylurg and all Ireland this year', it seems certain that the colonists in the Irish lordship were hit hardest. The foul, congested streets of Dublin, Drogheda, Kilkenny and other English-held towns harboured populations of black rats, hosts to fleas carrying the deadly bacillus. Six further outbreaks of the Black Death before the fourteenth century closed probably reduced the population of the colony by 40 or 50 per cent, and the population slide continued into the following century. Even at the beginning of the sixteenth century, in 1515, one writer observed 'that the pestylens hathe devowrid that thEnglyshe folke, bycause they flee not therfro; and bycause the Iryshe folke abyde not ther wyth, hyt do them noo hurt'.[15]

The steady weakening of the Irish lordship had a profound influence on developments in Ulster. Even in its thirteenth-century heyday the earldom had been a troubled marchland, never as attractive to colonists as the manors of Leinster. Now the spread of disorder, the growing confidence of the Gaelic Irish and the population crash ensured that it was impossible to attract new settlers to Ulster. The sharp population fall in England made more land available there and many colonists left Ireland for good. The Gaelic Irish in Ulster were given an unrivalled opportunity to recover and extend their lands.

FOREIGN WARRIORS: 'THESE SORTE OF MEN . . . BYDE THE BRUNTE
   TO THE DEATHE'

The ability of the Gaelic lords of Ulster to strike at the Irish lordship was strengthened by their employment of mercenaries from the Highlands and Islands of Scotland; these were *galloglaigh*, meaning 'foreign warriors', anglicised as gallowglasses. Confusingly, annalists referred both to the Vikings and the English as the 'Gall'. The gallowglasses were Hebrideans of mixed Norse–Gaelic blood, who, after the Norwegian connection had been broken at the Battle of Largs in 1263, sought employment for their arms in Ulster. When Robert Bruce sailed to Ulster in 1316 the annals noted that he brought a great force of gallowglasses with him, and thereafter more and more of these fighting men came south. The O'Donnells, the ruling family of Tír Conaill, used gallowglasses to drive the O'Neills out of Cenél Moen, the fertile country around the Foyle; their leading gallowglass clan, the MacSweenys, at first were paid in kind:

> This is how the levy was made: two gallowglasses for each quarter of land, and two cows for each gallowglass deficient, that is, one cow for the man himself and one for his equipment. And Clann Sweeny say they are responsible for these as follows, that for each man equipped with a coat of mail and a breastplate, another should have a jack and a helmet: that there should be no forfeit for a helmet deficient except the gallowglass's brain (dashed out for want of it).[16]

Each gallowglass had a manservant to carry his coat of mail and a boy who looked after the food and did the cooking; he fought in traditional Viking style, wielding a battle axe or spar, 'moche like the axe of the Towre', as Sir Anthony St Leger described it. St Leger, who faced gallowglasses in battle in the sixteenth century, believed that 'these sorte of men be those that doo not lightly abandon the fielde, but byde the brunte to the deathe'. Gallowglass warriors stiffened the ranks of native Irish foot soldiers, or kerne, who, according to St Leger, fought 'bare nakyd, saving ther shurtes to hyde ther prevyties; and those have dartes and shorte bowes: which sorte of people be bothe hardy and delyver to serche woddes and maresses, in which they be harde to be beaten'.[17]

In time the MacSweenys acquired land in Tír Conaill as a more secure source of income, and divided into three clans: MacSweeny na Doe (*na d'Tuath*, 'of the Tribes') in the Rosses and around Creeslough; MacSweeny Fanad, to the west of Lough Swilly; and MacSweeny Banagh in the vicinity of Slieve League. MacCabes, MacRorys, MacDougalls and MacSheehys came from Innsi Gall – the Hebrides – to Ulster to fight there and further south; none of these, however, were as formidable as the MacDonnells, who, ensconced in the lands about Ballygawley, Co. Tyrone, became a powerful arm of the O'Neills of Tír Eóghain in their struggle to become the leading Gaelic rulers in Ireland.

THE GREAT IRISHRY

Just south-west of Newtownstewart, adjacent to the Mourne river, stand ruins of what is known as Harry Avery's Castle. Built by Henrí Aimhréidh O'Neill, this castle with its polygonal curtain wall and high D-shaped towers is evidence that the native Irish had learned much from the English. Yet this fortress faced not the English but other Gaelic Irish, the O'Donnells of Tír Eóghain. From the Outer Hebrides to the Dingle and Iveragh peninsulas in the far south-west of Ireland, the Gaelic world knew a cultural unity not yet achieved in the English-speaking regions of the British Isles – the professional learned classes ensured that there was no difference between Gaelic in Scotland and Ireland until the seventeenth century. The Straits of Moyle formed a line of communication not a barrier; the real cultural frontiers were the Highland Line, south of which lived English-speaking Scots, and the boundary of what English government called the 'Land of Peace' – the anglicised region around Dublin. The most extensive area under complete Gaelic control was centred on Ulster and known to the English – when they were not calling it the 'Land of War' – as 'The Great Irishry'.

Cultural unity did not bring with it political solidarity or patriotic feeling – the Gaels gave their allegiance to their kin, not to their country. The collapse of the English Crown's authority in Ulster in these years owed almost nothing to concerted action by Gaelic lords; that authority was brought down piecemeal by individual ruling families and their dependants acting for themselves. Inevitably this meant that Gaelic lords struggled with each other for domination. The most relentless and inconclusive contest was between the Cenél Eóghain (O'Neills) and the Cenél Conaill (O'Donnells). In this the O'Neills lost their homeland of Inishowen to the O'Dohertys, close relatives of the O'Donnells, and conceded much of Cenél Moen. The losses, however, were more than balanced by gains to Tír Eóghain of lands in the south and east of the province. Niall Mór O'Neill, King of Tír Eóghain between 1364 and 1397, inaugurated this expansion and it was continued by his son and successor Niall Óg; another son, Cú Uladh, plundered and dispossessed the Church in Armagh; and the third son, Henrí Aimhréidh, held the O'Donnells at bay in Cenél Moen. Their sons and cousins fought against each other, however, and it was rare for an O'Neill ruler to be without opposition from his own relations, in particular, the descendants of Henrí Aimhréidh – Sliocht Henri – and of Art of Omagh – Sliocht Airt. The O'Donnells tried to exploit O'Neill rivalries only to be dogged in turn by their own succession disputes. Turlough an Fiona ('of the wine'), who began his rule in 1380 by slaying his rival Shane, did nevertheless succeed in extending the frontiers of Tír Conaill into north Connacht. Turlough, indeed, was the only Irish lord of consequence who did not give his allegiance to Richard II.[18]

Richard II responded to the desperate appeal of colonists who declared that they were 'not able to . . . find or think of other remedy except the coming of the king, our lord, in his own person'. Landing at Waterford in October 1394 with the greatest army Ireland had yet seen, and after hard winter campaigning, Richard brought the Leinster Irish to heel; as a result, the chronicler Froissart records, 'the Irishmen advised themselves and came to obeissance'. Only too aware that the English were holding his grandsons hostage, Niall Mór O'Neill was amongst the eighty chieftains who made submission. Niall Mór wrote to Richard before travelling to Dublin to be knighted in Christchurch:

When I heard of your joyful coming to the land of Ireland I greatly rejoiced and now rejoice, hoping to obtain justice for many injuries done by the English marchers to me and mine.[19]

Niall Mór agreed to pay tribute to Richard's cousin, Roger de Mortimer, Earl of March, who had inherited the title to the earldom of Ulster, which had passed down to the de Mortimers from Lionel of Clarence, husband of Elizabeth, the de Burgo heiress. 'It is openly foretold that after your departure my lord the Earl of Ulster will wage war against me', Niall Mór correctly predicted in a letter to Richard. De Mortimer achieved nothing by raiding Ulster and he was killed by the Leinster Irish: this bitter blow impelled Richard to a second and disastrous expedition to Ireland in 1399. The defeated king soon returned to England to lose his throne to the Lancastrians and ultimately to lose his head.[20]

Agreements with the English quickly fell apart and great sweeps of eastern Ulster now fell to both the native Irish and the Scots of the Isles. No one Ulster lord gained unquestioned supremacy, however, and – parallel to the deadly and wasting dynastic contest between the houses of Lancaster and York – the annals for these years record succession disputes, raids and counter-raids, and maimings and murders. Only one part of the province seemed to be an exception to this rule: the kingdom of Erne.

'FERMANAGH IS THE PARADISE OF IRELAND'

I know a land whose hills should not be exchanged for any smooth plain.
Broad plains in the centre of the land, soil earliest to bear all plants, a line of fair thick woods set about the Fir Manach, protecting them.
A forest of masts is on the Erne – it makes one start with joy to see them; green banks – one could gaze on them for ever! – are on each side of it.[21]

This fifteenth-century poem, 'Do mheall an sochar Síol gColla', praised the natural defences of the kingdom of Lough Erne. Attempts to conquer Fermanagh in the thirteenth century had come to grief and Norman castles at Belleek and Lough Erne had been pulled down. The only easy invasion route was by water, but a formidable fleet on the lough waited there to fend off intruders.

The most striking feature of this Gaelic sub-kingdom was that its rulers, the Maguires, passed on the succession from father to son for more than two centuries. Brothers of the king, instead of indulging in bloody and wasteful dynastic disputes, preferred to win new lordships for themselves on the frontiers. Donn Carrach Maguire, the first to rule all the seven *tuatha* of Fir Manach, was followed on his death in 1302 by his son Flaithbheartach without contest, while another son, Amhlamh, conquered the western shores of Lough Erne, which still bear his name today as Clanawley.

The Maguire kings deftly coped with their more powerful neighbours. They paid an annual tribute of eighty cows to the earls of Ulster for their protection and, after the Brown Earl's murder, became close allies of the O'Neills of Tír Eóghain until the sixteenth century, when they fell under the power of the O'Donnells. Surveying Fermanagh in 1607, Sir John Davies observed: 'Generally the natives of this country are reputed the worst swordsmen in the north, being rather inclined to be scholars, than to be kern, or men of action.'[22] Local poets, indeed, chided their rulers for their lack of military ambition but praised them for their patronage of men of learning. Rory of the Hospitality, who became king in 1327, was described in the Annals of Clonmacnoise as 'one that bestoed most of gould, Silver, cattle & other guifts upon poets & bards & others of theire kind in Ireland'. The kingdom supported three hereditary families of poets, two families of historians, and one each of lawyers and physicians. Tadhg Dall Ó hUiginn in the sixteenth century recalled better times in his poem 'Fermanagh is the Paradise of Ireland', written in praise of Brian Maguire:

> None interfereth with any other in this pleasant earthly paradise;
> There is none bent on spoil, nor any man suffering injustice.
> There is no reaver's track in the grass . . .
> No misfortune threatening her cattle, no spoiler plundering her . . .
> It is not the properties of stones, nor is it the veil of wizardry, that guards the waters of its far-spread lands; it is not the smooth slopes, or the wood, nor is it the sorcerous arts of druids.
> They have a better protection for all boundaries – a shepherd sufficient for every one is the man – one alone is their guard.
> Brian Maguire of the bared weapons, son of Donnchadh, son of Cú Connacht; guarding buckler of Donn's land . . .
> Towards Ulster he is the ocean's surface; toward Connacht a rampart of stone . . .
> Fermanagh of the fortunate ramparts is the Adam's paradise of Inisfail . . .[23]

Earlier Church reforms had hardly touched this kingdom, which formed part of the diocese of Clogher. Hereditary clerical families had control of extensive ecclesiastical lands free from taxation and therefore had the leisure to become men of learning. In the fifteenth century Cathal MacManus, archdeacon of Clogher and a Maguire sub-chieftain, compiled one of the great treasures of medieval Ireland, the Annals of Ulster. In this chronicle he proudly recorded the birth of over a dozen children he fathered, and yet his obituary declared him to be 'a gem of purity and a turtle-dove of chastity'.[24] It was in the diocese of Clogher, in the north-western borders of the kingdom, that the place in Ireland most renowned across medieval Europe was to be found – Lough Derg.

A CATALAN VISITS LOUGH DERG

On 19 May 1396 King John of Aragon died suddenly, frightened to death, it was said, by the sight of an enormous she-wolf when he was out hunting alone. Ramon, Viscount of Perellós and of Roda, had been the king's faithful courtier and now he feared that his royal master's soul would be in torment in hell, for the king had died without confession or the rites of the Church. Perellós made up his mind to go to the remote fastness of the north-west of Ireland to Lough Derg: here a soul could be spared the pains of hell if the pilgrim could survive the dangers of Saint Patrick's Purgatory – this Perellós had read in *Tractatus de Purgatorio Sancti Patricii*, written by a twelfth-century English monk, describing the Knight Owein's journey in the underworld.

Pope Benedict III gave his blessing, but Perellós tells us, 'strongly advised me against it and he frightened me greatly, warning me that I should not do it for any reason whatsoever'.[25] Leaving Avignon on 8 September 1397, Perellós travelled through Paris to Calais, sailed to England where he was entertained by Richard II for ten days, chartered a ship in Cheshire and crossed the Irish Sea. In Dublin Roger de Mortimer urged Perellós to halt his pilgrimage for he 'would have to travel a great distance and go through the lands of savage, ungoverned people whom no man should trust'. Undeterred, Perellós obtained a letter of introduction to John Colton, archbishop of Armagh; they met at Drogheda where the archbishop

strongly advised me against such a journey . . . telling me over and above the danger involved in entering the Purgatory itself, neither he nor anyone else could ensure my safety in the lands of King O'Neill or of other lords whose territory I would have to cross before I reached the Purgatory. Unless I deliberately wished to lose my life, I should on no account attempt to go there . . . When he saw he could not change my mind, he gave me all the directions he could.[26]

Given an escort of a hundred armed men, Perellós was taken to the frontiers of Ulster where the soldiers would go no further. He rode on alone 'into the land of the savage Irish where King O'Neill reigned supreme'. Welcoming Perellós with a gift of ox meat, 'King O'Neill' – Niall Mór O'Neill of Tír Eóghain – and his retinue impressed the pilgrim:

He is the greatest king and he has forty horsemen. They ride without a saddle on a cushion and each one wears a cloak according to his rank. They are armed with coats of mail and round iron helmets like the Moors and Saracens. Some of them are like the Bernese. They have swords and very long knives and long lances, like those of that ancient country which were two fathoms in length. Their swords are like those of the Saracens, the kind we call Genoese. The pommel and the hilt are different; the pommel is almost as big as a man's hand, the knives are long, narrow and thin as one's little finger, and they are very sharp. This is how they are armed, and some use bows which are not long – only half the size of

English bows, but their range is just as good. They are very courageous. They are still at war with the English and have been for a long time. The king of England is unable to put an end to it, for they have had many great battles. Their way of fighting is like that of the Saracens who shout in the same manner.[27]

Perellós was taken by Lough Erne across wild country to Lough Derg, where there was 'so much water everywhere that a man can barely cross over the highest mountains without sinking to his waist'. There the monks warned him that he might not emerge alive from Saint Patrick's Purgatory and they sang Requiem Mass in preparation. Taken by dugout boat to Saint's Island, he entered the pit there, where 'I almost lapsed into sleep because I had been feeling so ill.'[28] Then follows his description of his journey to purgatory and the torments of men and women tortured by devils who 'were all the while shouting and howling and raising such a din . . . There I spoke at great length to my lord the king who, by God's grace, was on the road to salvation.'

Perellós returned from Lough Derg and met O'Neill again:

We were well received, with great joy and delight, and I spent the feast of Christmas with him. He held a great court in their fashion which to us seems very strange for someone of his status . . . his table was of rushes spread out on the ground while nearby they placed delicate grass for him to wipe his mouth. They used to carry the meat to him on poles.[29]

After spending New Year's Day with the Countess of March in one of her castles, Perellós made his return in time to be present at the celebrations in Rheims given in honour of the Holy Roman Emperor Wenceslas in March 1398.

LIFE IN MEDIEVAL ULSTER

The Sire de Beaujeu and Louis d'Auxerre from France, George Grissaphan and Laurence Rathold of Pászthó from Hungary, Conrad von Scharnachthal from Switzerland, Taddeo Gualandi from Italy and over a dozen other pilgrims from the European mainland left accounts of their visits to Saint Patrick's Purgatory. Only Perellós, however, made any attempt to describe the Irish they encountered; his account, *Viatge al Purgatori de Sant Patrici*, opens a unique window on the life of the people of Ulster at a time when annals were concerned almost exclusively with dynastic conflicts, military campaigns and births and deaths. It is not until the sixteenth century that this window is opened again.

Perellós did not mention that a famine was affecting Ireland at the time of his pilgrimage, which may explain his bleak impression of the people's diet. As 'a great gift', Niall Mór O'Neill sent him 'two cakes as thin as wafers and as pliable as raw dough. They were made of oats and of earth and they were black as coal, but very tasty.' He added:

> They do not eat bread, nor do they drink wine, for in that country there is none. However, the great lords drink milk as a sign of their nobility and some drink meat-broth. The common people eat meat and drink water . . . But they have plenty of butter, for oxen and cows provide all their meat.[30]

In the sixteenth century Captain Francisco de Cuellar, an Armada castaway, took refuge with the MacClancys on the shores of Lough Melvin in south-west Fermanagh; he confirms the importance of butter:

> They do not eat oftener than once a day, and this is at night; and that which they usually eat is butter with oaten bread. They drink sour milk . . . On feast days they eat some flesh half-cooked, without bread or salt.[31]

Butter was preserved in raskins, hollowed-out containers of wood, which were placed in bogs, acquiring a flavour the English disliked. On one occasion the O'Donnells fell upon Shane O'Neill's warriors while they were holding out their helmets to be served raw oatmeal with butter poured over it. Fresh milk was too precious to be drunk in quantity, but buttermilk was widely consumed and in the late sixteenth century Fynes Moryson, secretary to the lord deputy, says that the people 'esteem for a great dainty sour curds, vulgarly called Bonaclabbe'. This was *bainne clabair*, clotted milk. Blood was sometimes drawn from below the ears of living cattle or horses and mixed with butter to form a jelly. Moryson adds that 'no meat they fancy so much as pork, the fatter the better'. When on the move they stewed meat in an ox skin held above a slow fire by four stakes. This diet was supplemented by game from the woods, mushrooms, watercress and wood sorrel. By the sixteenth century wine was imported by the Gaelic lords in exchange for hides or, for example in Tír Conaill, as payment by Spaniards for the right to fish. Otherwise ale was brewed from malted oats or distilled to make *uisce beathadh*, whiskey, much favoured by English commanders for medicinal purposes. Sir Josias Bodley in 1603 found priests in Lecale pouring 'usquebaugh down their throats by day and by night'.[32]

The Ulster people, Perellós observed, 'are amongst the most beautiful men and women that I have ever seen anywhere in the world', an impression confirmed later by de Cuellar, who on more than one occasion encountered women 'beautiful in the extreme'; the men, he writes, 'are all large bodied, and of handsome features and limbs; and as active as the roe deer . . . The most of the women are very beautiful, but badly got up.' Perellós gives this description of the dress of those he met in Niall Mór O'Neill's court:

The great lords wear tunics without a lining, reaching to the knee, cut very low at the neck, almost in the style of women, and they wear great hoods which hang down to the waist, the point of which is narrow as a finger. They wear neither hose nor shoes, nor do they wear breeches, and they wear their spurs on their bare heels. The king was dressed like that on Christmas Day and so were all the clerks and knights and even the bishops and abbots and the great lords.

The common people wore what they could but 'all the principal ones wear frieze cloaks and both the women and the men show their shameful parts without any shame'. He continues:

The poor people go totally naked, although the majority wear those cloaks, good or bad. Thus were the ladies dressed. The queen, her daughter and her sister were dressed and girded, but the queen was barefoot and her handmaidens, twenty in number, were dressed as I have told you above with their shameful parts showing. And you should know that all those people were no more ashamed of this than of showing their faces.[33]

Jaroslav z Donína, a Bohemian nobleman, encountered sixteen naked women in O'Cahan's country in 1601, with 'which strange sight his eyes being dazzled, they led him into the house', according to Moryson, to converse politely in Latin in front of the fire. Joining them, the O'Cahan chief threw all his clothes off and was surprised that the baron was too bashful to do likewise. High and low alike were infested by lice, Moryson observing that 'nothing is more common among them than for the men to lie upon the women's laps on green hills till they kill their lice, with a strange nimbleness proper to that nation'.[34]

Like later English writers, Perellós assumed that the people of Gaelic Ulster were nomads:

Their dwellings are communal and most of them are set up near the oxen, for that is where they make their homes in the space of a single day and they move on through the pastures, like the swarms of Barbary in the land of the Sultan.

What he was seeing was the annual movement of cattle to and from summer pastures either on the mountains or on the bogland. Here the cows were milked and butter churned, the herdsmen putting up temporary dwellings for themselves. Below in the valleys the infield was fenced off to grow corn, generally oats but occasionally barley and wheat. Light wooden ploughs with iron shoes were attached by sally rods to horses' tails; though used only on previously ploughed land, this undoubtedly cruel practice attracted much critical English comment. The spade was the tool for breaking new ground and for raising cultivation strips (akin to American raised beds now much in vogue with organic gardeners). In autumn the fences were broken up for winter fuel and the cattle returned to graze the long stubble left by the reaping hook and to manure the infield with their droppings. There seems to have been no haymaking, though Perellós mentions a curious winter feed:

> The animals eat only grass. Instead of oats they eat holly leaves which are roasted over the fire so that the thorns of the leaves do not harm the animals' mouths.[35]

He reckoned that Niall Mór O'Neill had at least three thousand horses; these would not have been the 'garrans', or nags, for farm work, but brood mares and stallions (the only proper mount for a noble) much favoured for skirmishing in the Hundred Years War. Valued horses were fed on unthreshed oats but corn for human consumption was burned off the straw; this helped to dry the grain and gave oatcakes baked on a griddle iron a pleasantly nutty flavour, but to the English this practice was further proof of Irish barbarity. Gaelic lords had their own corn mills – small horizontal water mills without gears – as a way of raising revenue, but much grain was still ground on querns by women who stripped to prevent their clothes being ruined. Flax must have been grown extensively for the making of linen tunics, and frieze was woven from wool – pulled from the sheep's back rather than sheared – to make the *falaing*, or mantle, which found a ready export market.[36]

De Cuellar observed that the Irish 'lived in huts of straw', though these may have been temporary shelters on summer grazing grounds. There is little doubt that the majority of people in Ulster lived in post-and-wattle dwellings, usually oval or circular in shape, thatched and without chimneys. These were too flimsy to leave remains for later investigation, but in 1982 Nicholas Brannon excavated a more substantial 'coupled' house found on the south slope of Big Collin Mountain near Ballyclare in Co. Antrim. Rectangular in shape with rounded corners, it had no partitions, despite being sixteen metres long, and was built of clay and sods. Though the walls were propped up by dry-stone walling, they could not support a roof, which was held up by two pairs of long curving timbers at each end, known as couples or crucks, rising from the ground surface. Drawings of these are to be found on late-sixteenth-century maps of Ulster.[37]

The decline of the power of the great earls and the English Crown brought a halt to the building of large castles like Carrickfergus. Now the Gaelic lords erected smaller castles with such enthusiasm that Ireland became the most heavily castellated part of the British Isles. The most impressive included Fyn, Lifford and Donegal, put up by the O'Donnells; Dunseverick by the O'Cahans; Enniskillen by the Maguires;

Doe by the MacSweenys; Omagh by the O'Neills; Castlereagh by the Clandeboye O'Neills. Ireland was too disturbed to encourage the erection of undefended manor houses as in England; tower houses, at least capable of fending off marauders, were preferred.

Typically, the tower house in Ulster, such as Kilclief in Co. Down, was a single tall keep, at least twelve metres high, with two towers flanking the main entrance. The dimly lit ground floor was the storeroom, with a semi-circular barrel-vault roof, temporarily supported by woven wicker mats until the mortar had set. The upper storeys were reached by a narrow winding staircase up one of the towers, lit by arrow slits; food was cooked in braziers on the first floor and taken to the banqueting hall above; and the lord slept on the uppermost storey under a gable roof shingled with oak. Most Ulster tower houses had cells, built-in latrines, window seats, secret chambers, and a bold arch connecting the two flanking towers; here there was a 'murder hole' for shooting at – or pouring boiling water on – assailants attempting to ram the door below.[38]

Little is known about the life of the ordinary people, who no doubt suffered from labour service to build castles, the billeting of gallowglasses, and the warring of the ruling élite. They were not tied to their lords, however, and could move from one landowner to another; and the low population level put their labour at a premium so that they could bargain for better conditions.

BEYOND THE PALE

To kepen Yreland that it be not loste,
For it is a boterasse and a poste
Undre England and Wales is another.
God forbede but eche were othere brothere,
Of one ligeaunce dewe unto the kynge.

So wrote the author of *The Libelle of Englyshe Polcyce* in 1436, pointing out that 'the wylde Yrishe' had regained so much of the Irish lordship that

Our grounde there is a lytell cornere
To all Yrelande in treue comparisone.

Just the year before, the Irish Council reported in desperation to Henry VI that 'his land of Ireland is wellnigh destroyed, and inhabited with his enemies and rebels', with the consequence that the royal writ only ran in an area around Dublin 'scarcely thirty miles in length and twenty miles in breadth'. All that could be done was to construct the Pale: the Government put up fortifications, dug trenches, gave grants towards the building of tower houses, appointed guards to hold the bridges and assigned watchmen – paid by a tax called smokesilver – to light warning beacons when danger threatened.[39]

By this time the Dublin government had resigned itself to the fact that apart from Carrickfergus, Ulster was beyond the Pale. Emerging from their woody fastness of Glenconkeyne, the descendants of Áed Buidhe O'Neill – a former King of Tír Eóghain – crossed the lower Bann, overwhelmed the O'Flynns of Uí Tuirtre in mid-Antrim, and carved out a new lordship for themselves from the shattered remnants of the earldom of Ulster. Janico Savage, the earldom's seneschal, wrote a desperate appeal to Edward IV in 1467 saying that unless help was sent the Irish 'in short tyme fynally and utterly woll destroye your said Erldome'. He concluded:

> We mekely at the Reverence of almighty Jesu which by his prophete moises delyvered the children of Israel oute of the thraldome and bondage of Kyng pharoo besecheth in way of charite.

The 'charite' of £66 10s.0d. sent by the king was not enough. Janico was killed the following year and in 1481 his son, Patrick Óg, was captured, blinded and castrated by Conn O'Neill, while O'Neill's ally Glaisne Magennis, prior of Down, drove the remaining settlers from Lecale. The Whites of Dufferin (the 'Black Third', on the western shores of Strangford Lough) abandoned their inheritance for the safety of the Pale, while the Savages, driven out of the Six Mile Water valley, hung on precariously to the southern tip of the Ards. The Magennises and MacCartans engulfed central and southern Down, while Clann Aodha Buidhe emerged as the principal Gaelic lords of eastern Ulster, dominating a sweep of territory extending from Larne inland to Lough Neagh at Edenduffcarrick (now Shane's Castle, near Randalstown) and taking in the castle of Belfast and north Down, including much of the Ards. This territory the English called Clandeboye after the ruling family which had conquered it. Carrickfergus was left isolated, described in 1468 as 'a garrison of war . . . surrounded by Irish and Scots, without succour of the English for sixty miles'.[40] In north Antrim the surviving de Mandevilles had deserted their manors of Twescard, selling their interests to the MacQuillans, themselves driven out of Down. Immigrants from the south-west of Scotland who had served the earls of Ulster as mercenaries, the MacQuillans gave a new name to Twescard, the Route, named from their 'rout', the usual term then for a private army.

In contrast with Gaelic Ulster, which became almost free of interference from Dublin, another part of the Gaelic world, the lordship of the Isles, was meanwhile succumbing to the power of Edinburgh. Assisted by the Campbells, in 1476 James IV of Scotland forced the surrender of the MacDonnells, the ruling family, and absorbed the Isles into his kingdom. One branch of the MacDonnells, the Lords of Islay and Kintyre, fought a desperate rearguard action and won some victories in 1494; not long after that, however, their lord, Sir John Cahanagh MacDonnell – so called because he was fostered with the O'Cahans – was seized, convicted of high treason and executed on the Barrowmuir outside Edinburgh.

It was in the Glens of Antrim that the MacDonnells found refuge. In 1399 John Mór MacDonnell had married Margery Bisset, the last heiress of a Norman family long settled there, and thus had acquired a new territory for his people. With every reverse in Scotland a new wave of islanders brought their galleys south to Ulster. The MacDonnells made marriage alliances with all the leading families of the province, including the Savages, and brought with them MacNeills, MacAllisters, Mackays and Macrandalbanes from Kintyre and Gigha, and from the Rinns of Islay the Magees, after whom Islandmagee is named. Others ranged backwards and forwards from the Isles to serve as mercenaries for the Gaelic lords of Ulster; these men were the Redshanks, so called, as a Highland priest explained to Henry VIII, because 'wee of all people can tolerat, suffir, and away best with colde, for boithe somer and wynter (except when the froeste is most vehemante), goinge alwaies bair-leggide and bair-footide'.[41]

By the beginning of the sixteenth century the MacDonnells of the Glens, Islay and Kintyre ruled a formidable lordship in the north. Alexander MacDonnell, the son of Sir John Cahanagh and banished from Scotland, turned aside to conquer the MacQuillans of the Route, and his youngest son, Sorley Boy, was to preserve this inheritance throughout Elizabeth's Irish wars. The MacDonnells so alarmed the Irish Council in Dublin that its members sent this dispatch to the king in 1533:

> The Scottes also inhabithe now buyselley a greate parte of Ulster, which is the king's inheritance; and it is greatlie to be feared, oonles that in short tyme they be dryven from the same, that they, bringinge in more nombre daily, woll, by lyttle and lyttle soe far encroche in acquyringe and wynninge the possessions there, with the aide of the kingis disobeysant Irishe rebelles, who doo nowe ayde theym therein after soche maner, that at lengthe they will put and expel the king from his hole seignory there.[42]

THE GREAT O'NEILL

'Ulster dog from a stock of false growth': with these words the Lord of Tír Eóghain was denounced by a Welsh poet in the service of the de Mortimers.[43] Again and again the de Mortimers were frustrated in

68

their attempts to hold on to their inheritance, the earldom of Ulster. Premature deaths blighted their hope of success, one such being that of Edmund de Mortimer, who forced all the Ulster lords to submit at Trim Castle in 1425, only to die immediately afterwards from the plague. The title eventually passed to the Duke of York, who became Edward IV in 1461. Edward, with quite enough to do keeping the house of Lancaster in check, was eager to keep on good terms with the most powerful man in Ireland, Henry O'Neill.

Henry O'Neill had not yet succeeded his father when he made agreement with Henry VI's chief governor, the White Earl of Ormond, in August 1449. Henry recognised the king as his liege lord and promised to support him with armed men when required; in return the Lord of Tír Eóghain won tacit recognition as overlord of Ulster, with approval for waging war on those who refused tribute. Ormond's real objective was to put a stop to the constant depredations on the Pale and the extortion of a 'black rent' from the manors of Louth. This Henry was able to deliver and the O'Reillys, O'Hanlons, MacMahons and other south Ulster chieftains were brought to heel. In gratitude Edward IV sent presents to Henry in 1463, 'to wit, eight and forty yards of scarlet and a collar of gold'.

In that same year envoys arrived from Munster to offer O'Neill the submission of their lord, Tadhg O'Brien of Thomond. O'Brien accepted *tuarastal*, ceremonial wages from O'Neill in recognition of his subservience, but his real purpose was to persuade Henry to become high-king of Ireland and drive the English out. Henry refused, preferring the advice of his poet Tadhg Óg Ó hUiginn:

> Let the prince of Uí Néill delay in marching south – this is good advice, and let him heed my word – till he make sure of his power over his own land . . .[44]

Indeed, vigorous campaigns had to be launched against the O'Donnells and Clandeboye O'Neills. When Henry retired in 1483 all the Gaelic lords of Ulster had made their submission and endured the 'bonnacht', the billeting of O'Neill's fighting men on their lands. He had earned the title always given him in contemporary English documents, 'the Great O'Neill'. Two years later Henry Tudor defeated and killed Richard III at Bosworth. The new era dawned with the O'Donnells and O'Neills once more coming to blows, fatally exposing them to the reinvigorated power of the English Crown.

TUDOR RECOVERY

In the autumn of 1498 Henry VII's chief governor, Garret Mór Fitzgerald, 8th Earl of Kildare, led an army out of the Pale, joined forces with the

O'Donnells and Maguires, and advanced into the heart of Tír Eóghain. The Annals of Ulster record:

> The castle of Dungannon was taken this year by the Deputy of the king of the Saxons in Ireland, namely, the Earl of Kildare . . . And Donal O'Neill, with his sons and all his friends, went with a host hard to count to meet the governor to the same castle and it was taken with guns on the morrow . . . And that host of Foreigners and the Gael went from that to the castle of the Omagh and Niall, son of Art O'Neill, went to meet them and gave hostages to them in pledge for peace to save his country and his castle. And those hosts returned to their houses with triumph of victory.[45]

Henry VII had no interest in extending his Irish lordship beyond the Pale and was content to let Kildare make decisions about what should be done to protect his interests. The peace and growing prosperity of England, however, gave a new resolution to the Dublin government; this (and the ability to use artillery) put Ulster on the defensive.

Henry VIII retained the services of Garret Mór, and after his death in 1513 those of his son Garret Óg. Eventually, however, the Fitzgeralds overreached themselves; Garret Óg's son, Silken Thomas, rose in rebellion in 1534 only to be crushed in a protracted campaign. From then on Henry ruled by lord deputy, a chief governor resident in Ireland throughout his term of office. What should the king do with Ireland? In 1515, a writer signing himself 'Pandor' advised full-scale conquest and colonisation:

> Yf the king were as wise as Salamon the Sage, he shalle never subdue the wylde Iryshe to his obeysaunce, without dreadde of the swerde, and of the myght and streyghthe of his power, and of his Englyshe subgettes, orderyd as aforesayd; for aslong as they maye resyste and save their lyffes, they will never obey the Kyng.

He advised Henry to conquer Ulster and, in particular, to punish the Clandeboye O'Neills

> and to exyle, banyshe, and expulsse therfro all the captaines, growen and dyscendeyd of the blode and lynage of Hugh Boy Oneyll for ever.

If Ireland was subjected by force, he believed, 'hyt wolde be none other but a very Paradyce, delycious of all plesaunce, to respect and regard of any other land in this worlde'.[46]

The debate on policy had begun and the Tudor monarchy vacillated until almost the end of the sixteenth century between conciliation and conquest. Lord Deputy Leonard Grey believed in force and made war in Ulster several times. In 1538, for example, he attacked the MacMahons in Farney, reporting to the king that he had 'burnte all the countre, and theyr cheyff houses'.[47] The Island Scots, swarming around Lecale, brought him north again the following year; there he took Dundrum Castle – 'one of the strongyst holtes that ever I sawe in Ireland . . . Owt of whyche the sayd Scottys fled, and left mych corne, butters, and other pylfre, behinde them'. Later in the same year Grey routed the O'Neills and the O'Donnells at Bellahoe near Carrickmacross and followed this up – after an expedition to Munster – by ravaging Tír Eóghain about Dungannon, burning corn and slaying cattle, in the early months of 1540.[48] The lord deputy made too many enemies, however, and had even driven O'Neill and O'Donnell to mutual assistance; he was re-called to face charges of corruption, and on conviction, had his head chopped off by order of the king.

Sir Anthony St Leger, Grey's replacement, believed that the Gaelic lords and their people, if treated with respect, would become loyal to the Crown and abide by English law. He persuaded Henry VIII to change his title from Lord of Ireland to King of Ireland; the Irish parliament gave its approval in June 1541 and the act was translated into Irish. A show of strength was needed before O'Neill and O'Donnell – all of Ulster in fact – would submit, for St Leger wrote that these two men 'had, in effecte, all the capitaynes of the north hanginge on their slevis'.[49] When the lord deputy reached Lough Erne, Manus O'Donnell rowed ashore, sought the 'mercyfull pardone' of the king, agreed hence-forth to 'lyve in due and faythfull obedyens as his trwe and moste humblye subgete', and signed the submission 'Ego O Doñ'. A ruthless winter campaign followed, during which twenty-one days were spent destroying corn and butter in Tír Eóghain. Conn Bacach O'Neill capitu-lated and put his X mark to a formal submission, confessing 'that by ignoraunce, and for lack of knoweledge of my most bounded dieutye of allegeaunce, I have most grevouslye offended Your Majestie'.[50]

The proclamation of Henry VIII as King of Ireland was, according to St Leger, mere confirmation of what always had been the case. But in reality Henry was the first English king to lay serious claim to the whole island – the partition of Ireland between the 'Englysshe pale' and the 'Great Irishry' was to be erased, and all Gaelic lords were to hold their lands by English feudal law from the king. St Leger's scheme – known as Surrender and Regrant – was to persuade the lords to drop their traditional Gaelic titles and give up their lands, receiving them back from the king with English titles. This programme enjoyed initial suc-cess, with O'Neill leading the way in Ulster.

On Sunday 1 October 1542 Conn Bacach was in London to receive his new title of Earl of Tyrone. He put on his robes in the queen's closet at Greenwich, which 'was richly hanged with cloth of arras, and well strewed with rushes'; then he was led by two earls and a viscount

71

before Henry VIII, 'and the King girt the said sword about the said Earl baudrickwise, the foresaid Earl kneeling . . . ' The new earl 'gave his thanks in his language, and a priest made answer of his saying in English'; then to the sound of trumpets he went off to dinner carrying his letters patent before him like a prize. Having paid £10 to the office of arms and twenty angels for the hire of his gown, the 1st Earl of Tyrone tipped the trumpeters forty shillings and left for Ulster.[51] The succession of the title was now established in the English style, with Conn Bacach's illegitimate son Matthew, created Baron of Dungannon, named successor.

St Leger's policy seemed to be working well and had it been continued the Gaelic lords of Ulster might have adapted to become as much loyal agents of the English Crown as the nobility of Wales. But others at court sought subjugation not co-operation and their advice gained favour. Manus O'Donnell was offered the title Earl of Tyrconnell but it was not until the reign of James I that an O'Donnell felt able to accept it. A potent factor adding to the unease of O'Donnell, O'Neill and their dependent chiefs was Henry VIII's determination to impose his Church revolution on Ireland.

THE CHURCH IN TURMOIL

Almost 150 years before, on Wednesday 10 October 1397, John Colton, archbishop of Armagh and a former chief governor, had arrived with his retinue at Derry and was lodged in the Black Abbey of the Augustinian canons. Two days later he confirmed the election of Hugh Mac Gillibride O'Doherty as abbot and announced a series of reforms, including an order that Hugh

> dismiss and expel from your dwelling, cohabitation and care that Catherine daughter of O'Doherty whom it is said you have lately taken into concubinage and shall never afterwards take up with her again . . . and that you should make no promise nor undertake any charge concerning any other concubine whom, heaven forbid, you should take to yourself in future.

Everywhere the archbishop was welcomed with enthusiasm and on the following Sunday in the parish of Clooney he was prevailed on to celebrate Mass in the open air for 'the thousands of people who had gathered out of respect for the said father'.[52]

The Church continued to attract universal support but if Saint Malachy had been able to return to late medieval Ireland, it is certain he would have found much to reform. Church lands had fallen into the control of hereditary families of erenaghs and coarbs, and in Gaelic Ulster at any rate, the rule of celibacy was everywhere ignored. Clergy took sides in dynastic disputes and some, like Glaisne Magennis, prior of Down, were chieftains waging war on their neighbours. In 1515 the writer Pandor was convinced that Irish souls fell to hell in showers,

> for ther is no archebysshop, ne bysshop, abbot, ne pryor, parson, ne vycar, ne any other person of the Churche, highe or lowe, greate or small, Englyshe or Iryshe, that useyth to preache the worde of Godde, saveing the poore fryers beggers.[53]

The friars, particularly the Third Order of Franciscans Regular, dedicated to a simple communal life and pastoral work amongst the people, enjoyed widespread support in Gaelic Ulster in the fifteenth and sixteenth centuries. Friaries were built at Massereene, Lambeg, Larne, Bonamargy, Donegal and elsewhere. Bonamargy, built by Rory MacQuillan around 1500, is the best preserved; it was taken over by the MacDonnells and according to their historian, 'the place literally heaves with Clandonnel dust, the chieftains having found a last retreat in two very gloomy vaults under the abbey, whilst their humbler kinsmen sleep around in the sunshine of the open cemetery'.[54] Donegal friary, founded in 1474 by Nuala O'Connor, mother of Hugh Roe O'Donnell, enjoyed the patronage of the lords of Tír Conaill; friars expelled from here in the seventeenth century were to compile the Annals of the Four Masters. Because of the reverence and affection the Gaelic people had for them, the friars were thus in a strong position to take a lead in resisting the Reformation.[55]

'I entirely renounce obedience to the Roman Pontiff and his usurped authority', Conn Bacach O'Neill agreed in 1542, recognising Henry VIII as supreme head of the Church in Ireland and undertaking to 'compel all living under my rule to do the same'. Henry's break with Rome did not cause a great stir in Gaelic Ireland for the Pope's authority was feeble there; two Jesuits bearing papal letters to O'Neill and O'Donnell in 1542 waited in vain for response, for example.[56] The dissolution of Irish monasteries within the Pale in 1539 was little regretted, for these communities had long ceased to provide education, hospitality and medical services; in any case, the order had no immediate effect on Ulster outside Lecale and the Ards. Nevertheless, the destruction of relics did cause dismay, especially the smashing in Dublin of the Bachall Íosa taken from Ulster in the twelfth century. But there were no martyrs and no burnings and as yet there was little indication that religion would become a cause of division, hatred and strife in the succeeding centuries.

Protestant doctrine did not arrive until after the accession of Edward VI in 1547 and while it made some progress amongst colonists in Dublin and Galway, there was not a great deal for Mary to undo when she became queen in 1553, ordering the restoration of religious practice to that 'of old times used'.[57] Elizabeth I, coming to the throne in 1558, imposed a Protestant settlement by law but she had neither the money nor the evangelists to make the new religious regime effective. As her reign wore on, trained priests returned to Ireland, not from Oxford as in former times, but from the seminaries of Louvain, Salamanca and Rome, bearing with them the combative zeal of the Counter-Reformation. The Ulster Irish, along with the majority in the other three provinces, saw the Reformation simply as an instrument deployed by the English monarchy to bring about their subjugation. Elizabeth could do little to dispel this view, or to win hearts and minds by persuasion, for her government in Ireland was preoccupied by the objective of conquering the island from end to end.

4

THE ELIZABETHAN CONQUEST

c. 1558–1603

OVERVIEW

At the uncertain start of her reign Elizabeth could no more enforce her claim to be monarch of Ireland than her father, Henry VIII, before her. More than any other province, Ulster lay beyond the reach of the English Crown. The MacDonnells of the Isles strengthened their hold on the Antrim Glens, linking the military resources of Gaelic Scotland to those of Gaelic Ulster. Despite repeated punitive expeditions from Dublin, Ulster chieftains could still launch damaging assaults on the Pale. In addition, there were alarming reports of Ulster's conspiracy with England's continental foes; until Ireland had been subdued entirely, the queen was advised by her courtiers, there would never be security for her realm.

In 1558 Elizabeth had no plan to conquer Ulster, but its position as an independent Gaelic province was in peril, as England grew more prosperous and powerful. The populations of western European states were rising, and ambitious younger sons, inheriting nothing at home, sought their fortunes abroad. Ulster, with a sparse population and an underdeveloped economy, attracted the English just as Spaniards were drawn to Mexico and Peru. For many years the wildness of the borderlands gave Ulster effective defence and for a brief moment it seemed that the O'Neills and their allies could dislodge the English from most of Ireland; but with obsolete weaponry, inadequate sea defences and lack of political unity the Gaelic lords of the north faced an unequal struggle. A few chiefs adapted quickly to the new conditions, but most fought desperately to preserve the old Gaelic order. Elizabeth's vacillating policies prolonged Ulster's agony, and the final subjugation of the province was so terrible it left a legacy of division and hatred persisting to our own time.

SHANE THE PROUD

Brutal, vindictive and drunken, Shane O'Neill was an unlikely champion of an endangered culture. In 1559 he drove his aged father, Conn Bacach

O'Neill, Earl of Tyrone, out of Ulster and into the Pale, where he died soon after. Shane had already murdered his half-brother Matthew, heir to the earldom. By English law Matthew's eldest son, Brian, was earl, but amongst his own people Shane was unchallenged as The O'Neill.

Sir Henry Sidney, Elizabeth's lord justice, visited Shane in Tyrone and found him eager to give his allegiance provided Elizabeth acknowledged the authority he had as The O'Neill. Elizabeth was inclined to acquiesce but she took Sidney's advice to withhold recognition. To his own people O'Neill was Seáan an Diomuis, Shane the Proud. Arrogant, ruthless and wily, he was without rival in Tyrone. Despite a reputation for lack of courage in battle, he could mobilise the resources of Ulster from end to end, aspiring to dominate the O'Donnells of Tír Conaill, the Clandeboye O'Neills and the Antrim Scots. He could halt the Scottish depredations on the east coast of Ulster, and he could weld together a coalition of the Gaelic world and link it with Catholic powers hostile to England. Indeed by 1560 so many Scots warriors had entered Shane's service that Lord Justice Sir William Fitzwilliam sent this desperate appeal to the queen's secretary, Sir William Cecil: 'Send us over men that we may fight ere we die.'[1]

Shane swept south, plundering the O'Reillys and raiding the Pale, and then in May 1561 he moved west against Calvagh O'Donnell, Lord of Tír Conaill. Calvagh's wife Catherine, widow of the 4th Earl of Argyll, was said to be infatuated with Shane; certainly she led Calvagh into a trap while he was besieging a rebellious kinsman at Glenveagh. It was sweet revenge, for Calvagh had overwhelmed Shane in a night attack four years before. The O'Donnell chief was bound in chains and Catherine became Shane's mistress only to be abused cruelly and set aside soon after.

Shane O'Neill had made war not only on a neighbour but on an ally of the English Crown. Elizabeth sent the Earl of Sussex as her lord lieutenant and in Dublin had Shane proclaimed a traitor – the proclamation noted how little the queen's 'gentle, favourable and merciful dealing with him hath wrought in his cankered and traitorous stomach'.[2] Fiercely intent on humbling this northern rebel, Sussex set out from Dublin on 2 June 1561; he reached Armagh three weeks later only to find that O'Neill had pulled back with his cattle to the borders of Tír Conaill. Heavy rain in July made the River Blackwater impassable and, soon after, supplies ran out, forcing a humiliating English retreat to Newry. In desperation Sussex concocted a plan to poison Shane, with a contingency scheme – as he frankly explained to Elizabeth – to murder the poisoner, Neill Grey, should he fail. Nothing came of this plan; instead a more ambitious incursion was prepared for the autumn.

The queen sent her lord lieutenant an additional £2,000, reinforcements from Berwick and ships pressed from along the Lancashire coast. With some seven hundred English soldiers, a levy of kerne from the Pale, and hired Scots, Sussex advanced from Dundalk to the hard-pressed garrison in Armagh. From there he pushed on north-west to Omagh, rounding up a great herd of Shane's brood mares and cattle en route. Again Shane disengaged. Unable to manage the captured herd, Sussex slaughtered the animals and moved on down the Mourne valley to Derry to join the O'Donnells and be revictualled by the queen's fleet. The ships did not appear though they had been at sea for forty days and Sussex was forced to make an ignominious retreat back the way he had come. The lord lieutenant's boast that he had broken Shane's power was belied by a devastating raid on Meath launched from Ulster. The queen felt she had no recourse but conciliation.

SHANE IN THE COURT OF ELIZABETH

On 2 January 1562 Shane O'Neill entered London, accompanied by the Earls of Kildare and Ormond, and with an escort of fifty gallowglasses. The warriors – bare-headed, with hair flowing on to their shoulders, short tunics, heavy cloaks, and linen vests dyed saffron with urine – drew crowds of onlookers as large as those that had turned out to gape at native Americans and Chinese in the city a short time before. Only the enticement of £2,000 for expenses and guarantees from five Irish earls had persuaded Shane to cross the Irish Sea. Kildare, his cousin, and Ormond, kinsman of the queen, were not allowed to leave his side. Next day at Greenwich, in the presence of the ambassadors of Sweden, Savoy, Spain and Venice and all the court, O'Neill threw himself to the floor before Elizabeth; then rising to his knees, he made a passionate speech in Irish, punctuated by howls which caused great astonishment. 'For lack of education and civility I have offended,' the Earl of Kildare began, translating Shane's words.[3] When Sussex arrived in London, Shane was less servile and neither man disguised his hatred of the other. Would Shane be given recognition as The O'Neill and the title of Earl of Tyrone? Weeks of indecision followed until the queen summoned Brian O'Neill to London to help her make up her mind. On his way, at Carlingford, Brian was slain. Had he been murdered by Shane's order? No proof could be established and so Elizabeth hastened to make an agreement. O'Neill was recognised as 'captain' of Tyrone, O'Cahan's country and much of Antrim; the English garrison was to stay at Armagh; and Shane promised to be at peace with his Irish neighbours for six months. Brian's brother Hugh was brought to

England for safekeeping, and Calvagh O'Donnell, in chains in Tyrone, was still to have his future decided.

For both Elizabeth and Shane this was an unsatisfactory compromise. It demanded trust on both sides – trust that was almost entirely lacking.

'ULSTER WAS THEIRS, AND SHALL BE MINE . . .'

'I am upon my keeping every day since his coming to Ireland.'[4] So wrote Hugh Maguire, Lord of Fermanagh, in a despairing letter to Sussex soon after Shane O'Neill's return. Rapidly and violently Shane reasserted his power across Ulster. In two devastating raids some thirty thousand O'Donnell cattle were seized, leaving the people of Tír Conaill starving on the highways. The O'Reillys and O'Hanlons were plundered, and then Shane launched a fierce attack on Maguire. Crossing the Erne at Belleek, Shane ravaged the country southwards, destroying the harvest and cutting down over three hundred men, women and children. Hugh Maguire attempted a last stand on the islands of Lough Erne, and as O'Neill's assault was prepared, Maguire penned a final frantic appeal to Sussex:

> I cannot scape neither by land nor by water, except God and your Lordship do help me at this need; all my country are against me because of their great losses and for fear, and all my men's pleasure is that I should yield myself to Shane.[5]

It was to no avail, and the O'Hanlon chief observed bitterly that it would be better to serve the worst Irishman of Ulster than to trust the queen.

Not until early in 1563 was Sussex ready for a new offensive in Ulster; a muster of the Pale was called up and five hundred labourers were sent from there to hew a passage through woods impeding the route from Dundalk to Armagh. Continuous rain slowed Sussex's advance, and Shane's men, poised on the edges of bogs, made galling attacks on the lord lieutenant's army. The exhausted English reached Armagh only to have three hundred pack horses stolen by O'Neill's warriors during a tempestuous downpour at night. Forced by shortage of food to pull back to the Pale after three weeks, Sussex returned a fortnight later, this time penetrating as far as Clogher. Again Shane – ready enough to make a frontal assault on his Irish neighbours – avoided direct battle with the English, and kept down his losses by driving his herds into Fermanagh.

Ignoring Sussex's protests, Elizabeth authorised an interim agreement with Shane in the autumn of 1563. She abandoned Armagh but obtained Calvagh O'Donnell's release. For over two years Calvagh had been in bonds, his neck in a collar chained to fetters on his ankles so that he could neither sit nor stand. Calvagh wept when he reached the Pale, recalling that Shane's irons had been 'so sore that the very blood did run down on every side of mine irons, insomuch that I did wish after death a thousand times'.[6]

It was Robert Dudley, Earl of Leicester, who advised Shane to win the queen's favour by driving the Scots from the Antrim Glens. O'Neill had long laid claim to this territory and in 1564 he obtained tacit approval from Dublin Castle to strike at the MacDonnells. After fierce but inconclusive skirmishing that year, he held back until Easter 1565. Shane advanced from the Fews, in south Armagh, to Dromore, in Down, and then waited for the Clandeboye O'Neills to join him at Edenduffcarrick. As Shane drew near, the Scots set their warning fires ablaze on Fair Head and the high ground behind Torr Point. The men of Kintyre seized their weapons and manned their galleys, and on May eve James MacDonnell led them across the North Channel, his brother Alexander Oge staying to muster another force to follow. James MacDonnell was too late: as his vessels approached Cushendun, flames leaped from his castle at Red Bay. Sorley Boy MacDonnell, who had been leading the defence of the Glens, fell back to join his brother James and together they made a desperate last stand by the slopes of Knocklayd. Shane overwhelmed the Scots, as he reported in a letter written in Latin and sent to Dublin Castle:

> Early next morning, we advanced upon them drawn up in battle array, and the fight was furiously maintained on both sides. But God, best and greatest, of his mere grace, and for the welfare of her Majesty the Queen, gave us the victory against them. James and his brother Sorley were taken prisoners, and a third brother, Angus, surnamed the 'Contentious', and John Roe, were slain ... besides many of the Scottish nobility were captured, and great numbers of their men killed, amounting in all to six or seven hundred. Few escaped who were not taken or slain. Glory be to God, such was the result of these my services undertaken for her Majesty.[7]

Refusing appeals from both Elizabeth and Mary Queen of Scots to accept a ransom, Shane let James MacDonnell die of his wounds and ill-treatment. Dunseverick fell, Ballycastle was taken, and – after Shane threatened to starve Sorley Boy to death – Dunluce capitulated. O'Neill had all Ulster in thrall, as he exultantly declared in a letter to Sir Henry Sidney:

> I am in blood and power better than the best of them ... my ancestors were Kings of Ulster, Ulster was theirs, and shall be mine. And for O'Donnell, he shall never come into his country if I can keep him out of it, nor Bagenal into the Newry, nor the Earl of Kildare into Dundrum or Lecale. They are mine; with this sword I won them, with this sword I will keep them. This is my answer.[8]

Sidney, Sussex's kinsman and protégé, was that year appointed the queen's lord deputy; he regarded Shane as being as arrogant and evil as Lucifer. As for Elizabeth, in March 1566 she wrote to ask Sidney how 'such a cankred dangerous rebel' might be 'utterly extirped'.[9]

THE FALL OF SHANE O'NEILL

In the summer of 1566, while Shane was plundering Dundalk, campaigning in Fermanagh and burning Armagh Cathedral, an English naval squadron steered into Lough Foyle with three hundred Berwick arquebusiers, six hundred levies from the West Country, one hundred London foot soldiers, and a small force of cavalry. In command was the queen's lieutenant of the ordnance, Edward Randolph. Meanwhile, Sidney advanced north from the Pale with a large army, accompanied by Calvagh O'Donnell and Shane Maguire, successor to Hugh.

At first all went well. Shane O'Neill launched stinging blows on stragglers from bogs and woods, but he dared not risk open battle. Sidney concentrated on destruction: Benburb was left a ruin; corn was burned; cattle were rounded up and slaughtered. Fermanagh was recovered, though Shane Maguire died just before reaching his homeland. Randolph and Sidney rendezvoused at Lifford and the lord deputy left supplies and reinforcements for a new fort being built at Derry. After restoring Calvagh to power in Tír Conaill, Sidney turned south-west through the Barnesmore Gap to Donegal town and Ballyshannon.

Then in November 1566 Shane made an assault on the Derry garrison but as he had no means of replying to concentrated gunfire, the Tyrone men were driven back with heavy losses. Randolph, however, was killed, and as the young sea captain, Humphrey Gilbert, sailed back to keep the queen informed, the English ran out of food and fell prey to disease. Finally, on 21 April 1567, a spark from the garrison's forge blew up the magazine; the English survivors sailed away soon after.

Meanwhile, Calvagh had been thrown from his horse and killed. Led now by Sir Hugh O'Donnell, Shane's nephew, the men of Tír Conaill prepared to resist Shane who was advancing against them. As the O'Neills crossed the River Swilly at Farsetmore they met a furious onslaught of O'Donnells and MacSweenys, as the Annals of the Four Masters record:

> They proceeded to strike, mangle, slaughter, and cut down one another for a long time, so that men were soon laid low, heroes wounded, youths slain, and robust heroes mangled in the slaughter.[10]

Shane's warriors retreated into the advancing tide, there to be drowned or cut down. His army destroyed not by the English but by the O'Donnells, Shane fled eastwards to take refuge with the MacDonnells in the Glens. It was an extraordinary decision but perhaps Shane hoped that by bringing Sorley Boy and Lady Agnes, widow of James MacDonnell, he could buy protection. The MacDonnells prepared a feast at Glenshesk in an apparent mood of reconciliation. They 'fell to quaffing', a quarrel broke out, and Shane was hacked to death. It is likely that he was assassinated by the MacDonnells after Sidney, through the intermediacy of Captain William Piers, promised them that he would let them stay in Ulster – the promise was not kept.

Had they but known, the MacDonnells could have claimed a thousand marks as reward for Shane's head. Captain Piers of Carrickfergus dug up the body, cut off the head and sent it 'pickled in a pipkin' to Sidney, who placed it on a spike over Dublin Castle's gate arch – the historian Edmund Campion found it still there four years later. It was an ignominious end for Shane the Proud.[11]

DISASTER IN THE ARDS

Sidney had no intention of rewarding the MacDonnells; instead he schemed to drive the Scots from the Glens, push the Irish west of the Bann river and settle Englishmen on the coastlands of Antrim and Down. His 'Ulster Project' caused quite a stir at court. Sir William Cecil looked forward to merchants 'intrenchyng themselves' to create 'haven townes' and recommended the settling in Ulster of retired soldiers, especially 'good husband men, plow wryghtes, kart wryghtes and smythes . . . eyther to take habitation yf they be hable, or els to staye and serve there under sotche gentlemen as shall inhabyte there'.[12] Valentine Browne, who had transported Randolph's Berwick soldiers in 1566, asked Sidney to petition the queen on his behalf for 'the fyshing of the Ban and other waters in that provynce'.[13]

Finally persuaded by the Earl of Leicester, Elizabeth's favourite and Sidney's brother-in-law, she gave her approval for the project and the lord deputy set out for Carrickfergus to make preparations. Without adequate military protection, however, prospective settlers found the risks too great. 'None will come from home,' Sidney reported in 1570, 'but uppon some certen gaine and assurance to them and their successors.'[14] Besides, the fall of Shane O'Neill had done little to increase English power in Ulster. The Tyrone O'Neills had a new chief, Turlough Luineach (so named because he had been fostered by the O'Luneys) who assumed the traditional title of The O'Neill. To the alarm of the

English he established good terms with the O'Donnells and hired great numbers of Redshank mercenaries from them. Turlough burned the towns of those who rejected his authority and it was said his armed forces equalled those once led by Shane. Finally, the outbreak of widespread rebellion in Munster in 1568 left few English troops available for service to protect colonists in Ulster.

One English gentleman was not to be discouraged. Sir Thomas Smith, provost of Eton, vice-chancellor at Cambridge and queen's privy councillor, obtained letters patent entitling him and his son Thomas to the lands of Clandeboye. In a pamphlet outlining his plans, Smith made it clear that he intended to sweep away the native Irish except for 'churls' to plough the soil: 'Every Irishman shall be forbidden to wear English apparel or weapon upon pain of death. That no Irishman, born of Irish race and brought up Irish, shall purchase land, bear office, be chosen of any jury.'[15] This was a private enterprise and Cecil was so confident of its success that he invested £333 6s.8d. in it.

Sir William Fitzwilliam, newly appointed as lord deputy, was furious. Had not Brian MacPhelim O'Neill, Lord of Lower Clandeboye, been knighted for his service against Shane O'Neill? Might not this ill-considered scheme set Ulster aflame at a time when Munster was in full insurrection? Smith's enterprise was doomed from the outset. Only around one hundred colonists disembarked at Strangford village in August 1572, led not by Sir Thomas but by his even more inexperienced son. As the expedition moved north towards Newtownards, Sir Brian swept through north Down burning abbeys and other buildings which might give shelter to the English. Smith had to seek refuge in Ringhaddy Castle and it was in vain that he appealed to Dublin for help. When Smith was slain by his Irish servants in Comber the following year, a more grandiose enterprise was already under way.

ESSEX IN ULSTER

On 16 August 1573 a second expedition set out from Liverpool. Its leader Walter Devereux, Earl of Essex, was so certain of success that he had mortgaged most of his extensive English and Welsh estates for £10,000 to finance the project. The queen – grateful for Essex's service in crushing Northumberland's rebellion and in foiling the escape attempt of Mary Queen of Scots from Tutbury – agreed to grant him most of Antrim and pay half the cost of the one thousand soldiers he had with him.

Dispersed by a northerly wind, the expedition had an uncertain beginning. Essex took refuge on the Copeland Islands until he could sail for Carrickfergus. Sir Brian made cautious submission, and Essex reported, 'I took him by the hand, as a sign of his restitution to her Highness's service.'[16] The chief of Clandeboye was not impressed, however, when Essex took ten thousand head of his cattle into custody and after a fortnight he bribed the guards at Carrickfergus to release them. Essex pursued Sir Brian in vain and the cattle were secreted at Massereene.

The gentlemen colonists soon lost enthusiasm and little was achieved. In November 1573 Essex wrote in complaint to the queen:

> Two great disadvantages I find in this little time of my continuance here. The first by the adventurers, of whom the most part, not having forgotten the delicacies of England, and wanting the resolute minds to endure the travail of a year or two in this waste country, having forsaken me, feigning excuses to repair home where I hear they give forth speeches in dislike of the enterprise to the discouragement of others. The second, that the common hired soldiers, both horsemen and footmen, mislike of their pay.[17]

The enterprise fared no better the following year when Essex was given the title of governor of Ulster; the earl did little more with his new position than display deceit and cold-blooded cruelty. He hanged some Devon men for attempted desertion; imprisoned Captain Piers for showing friendship to Sir Brian; and then set out to wreak havoc on the followers, crops and cattle of Turlough Luineach. Having slaughtered a band of O'Neills taking refuge on a river island at Banbridge, Essex burned corn all down the Blackwater and Clogher valleys, reaching Derry without engaging Turlough in battle. In a further incursion 1,200 cattle were taken, and the building of a fort for two hundred men was begun at the Blackwater. Peace was restored with Sir Brian but this was to occasion a unique act of treachery. When the agreement was made, Essex and his principal followers were invited to a feast in Belfast Castle in October 1574, as the Annals of the Four Masters record:

> They passed three nights and days together pleasantly and cheerfully. At the expiration of this time, as they were agreeably drinking and making merry, Brian, his brother, and his wife, were seized upon by the Earl, and all his people put unsparingly to the sword – men, women, youths, and maidens – in Brian's own presence. Brian was afterwards sent to Dublin, together with his wife and brother, where they were cut in quarters. Such was the end of their feast.[18]

An act of equal barbarity was carried out the following summer. Sorley Boy MacDonnell was one of the most astute politicians in the Gaelic world. In the Isles he made peace with the Campbells and in 1569 arranged the marriage of Lady Agnes, his brother's widow, to Turlough Luineach. Fiona MacDonnell, the daughter of Lady Agnes, was married in turn to Hugh O'Donnell, Lord of Tír Conaill – she became the celebrated Ineen Dubh, the dark daughter. These arrangements formed the basis of an impressive coalition and had Elizabeth been prepared to recognise the MacDonnell rights to the Glens she too might have had a valued ally. By the summer of 1575, however, Essex was determined to break Sorley Boy's power. Two men later to become renowned Elizabethans were put in command of Essex's army: Captain John Norris, constable of Belfast and son of a Groom of the Stole executed for adultery with Anne Boleyn, and Francis Drake, already famous for his seizure of a Spanish treasure convoy at Nombre de Dios the year before, now in command of three frigates and other vessels from Carrickfergus.

The assault fleet reached Arkill Bay on the east side of Rathlin Island on the morning of 22 July 1575. The Scots fought to prevent a landing, but under Captain Norris, the English, Essex reported to the queen, 'did with valiant minds leap to land, and charged them so hotly, as they drave them to retire with speed, chasing them to a castle which they had of very great strength'.[19] For four days the castle, containing many women and children, was pounded by ship's cannon; without a well, its wooden ramparts destroyed by red-hot cannon balls, and its gate breached, it could not hold out for long. The garrison surrendered at dawn on 26 July on condition their lives were spared, but as Sidney reported:

> The soldiers, being moved and much stirred with the loss of their fellows that were slain, and desirous of revenge, made request, or rather pressed, to have the killing of them, which they did all ... There were slain that came out of the castle of all sorts 200 ... They be occupied still in killing, and have slain that they have found hidden in caves and in the cliffs of the sea to the number of 300 or 400 more.[20]

Essex relayed to the queen information received from his spy, that Sorley had 'stood upon the mainland of the Glynnes and saw the taking of the island, and was like to run mad for sorrow (as the spy saith), turning and tormenting himself, and saying that he had then lost all that ever he had'.[21] Elizabeth did not reprove Essex for the cruelty he had authorised; on the contrary, he was told to inform Captain Norris 'that we will not be unmindful of his good services', and she added in her own hand:

> If lines could value life; or thanks could answer praise, I should esteen my pen's labour the best employed time that many years had lent me ... your most loving cousin and sovereign E.R.[22]

'For my part I will not leave the enterprise as long as I have any foot of land in England unsold,' Essex declared to the queen, but there was no disguising his failure.[23] Sidney, serving another term as lord deputy, came north in September 1575 and found the Blackwater fort incomplete and not worth the upkeep; Rathlin Island 'veri easy to be wonne at any tyme but very chardgious and hard to be held'; and Clandeboye 'utterly disinhabited'.[24] The only consolation was that Turlough Luineach, because of his 'ill diet, and continual surfeit' was likely to die soon, a prediction which proved false.[25] Turlough made submission to Sidney at Armagh. As for Sorley Boy, Sidney believed, he should be given recognition as ruler of the Glens – even though he had ravaged Carrickfergus in revenge for the Rathlin massacre.

Elizabeth withdrew her support for Essex, though he continued to dream of what might have been:

> I resolve not to build but at one place; namelie, at Belfast; and that of littel charge; a small towne there will keep the passage, relieve Knockfergus with wood, and horsemen being laid there shall command the plains of Clandeboye.[26]

Granted the title of Earl Marshal of Ireland, Essex retired to Dublin, where he died of dysentery in September 1576 at the age of thirty-six. That a favoured nobleman could ruin himself in such a way showed how the English still underestimated the difficulty of subjugating Ulster. Sidney felt certain a better man could have succeeded and urged the queen to promote 'the introduction of collonys of English and other loyal subjects, whereby a perpetuall inhabitation would have ensued to be recompense as well of that which was spent, as for a yerely and continuall profitt by rent and services, and strength of the country against all forreyne invasion'.[27] The Essex fiasco, however, led Sidney to conclude that such a scheme was 'no subject's enterprise, a prince's purse and power must do it'.[28] Elizabeth was not yet ready for such an expensive project and in 1575 disbanded one third of her army in Ireland. Partly as a result, Ulster enjoyed comparative peace for the next decade.

'RASH, UNADVISED JOURNEYS'

> Here is a great bruit of 2000 Scots landed in Clandeboye. Tyrlagh Lenagh's marriage with the Scot is cause of all this, and if her Majesty does not provide against her devices, this Scottish woman will make a new Scotland of Ulster. She hath already planted a good foundation; for she in Tyrone, and her daughter in Tyrconnell, do carry all the sway in the North.[29]

So wrote Sir Nicholas Malby in 1580. Malby, sent north while he was governor of Connacht, had the recurring nightmare of Elizabethan administrators – a coalition of Catholic warriors of the Isles, Mary Queen of Scots, the French and the Irish. In retrospect the ambitions of the Gaelic Scots and Irish were too localised then to represent such a threat but the constant influx of Highlanders and Islanders to obtain paid military service with Ulster chiefs was genuine cause for anxiety. Malby got no support but in 1584 the new lord deputy, Sir John Perrott, assembled two thousand veterans at Newry and was joined by the Earls of Thomond and Ormond. Perrott had previously dismissed Ulster 'as a fit receptacle for all the savage beasts of the land',[30] but now he was determined to drive the Scots from the province altogether.

As Perrott's army advanced down both banks of the lower Bann, most of the Scots retreated in their galleys to the Isles. Randal MacDonnell, however, held out in Dunluce Castle with forty men. Perched on a high, sea-tunnelled rock near Portballintrae, with a strong gatehouse and bristling with turrets, Dunluce seemed impregnable; but pounded for two days in September by the lord deputy's cannon, including a culverin considered the largest in the realm, the garrison surrendered. Appalled by the expense of this and further expeditions into Ulster, considering most of the Scots had departed, Elizabeth sent Perrott this stinging reproof in her own hand:

> Let us have no more such rash, unadvised journeys without good ground as your last journey in the North. We marvel that you hanged not such saucy an advertiser as he that made you believe so great a company was coming . . . take heed ere you use us so again.[31]

Meanwhile Sorley Boy held a meeting of Island chiefs on Bute and there won support for the recovery of his Antrim lands. Sir Henry Bagenal's camp was overrun at Red Bay, Rathlin was recovered and on the night of 1 January 1585 Sir William Stanley's men at Bonamargy Abbey came under attack. Stanley reported to Bagenal:

> About 11 of the clok the same nyght, came certayne troupes of Skottes on foote, and about VI horsemen with them, who had upon their staves wadds lyghted, wherewith they sodaynly sett the roufe of the churche, being thatched, on fyer. They gave us a brave canvasado, and entered our campe. The alarme beinge geven, I came forth in my shert . . . I had twelve choys men hurte, and myselfe with arowes, in the raynes of my bak, as I called forwarde my men; in the arme, and in the flanke, and through the thigh; of which wounds I am verie sore.[32]

The MacDonnells offered to parley but Perrott refused and so the Scots fought on. On Hallowe'en night 1585 eighty Scots landed at Dunluce and (possibly with the help of the constable's Scots mistress) scaled the cliffs and ramparts with the aid of ropes twisted from withies. Peter Carey, the constable, refused quarter and fought to the last of his men; he himself was hanged from the walls by a withy rope. 'I do not weigh the loss,' Perrott remarked when the news was brought to him, 'but can hardly endure the discredit.'[33] It was some consolation to him that his men succeeded in slaying Sorley Boy's son, Alasdair, who had taken refuge in a grave in a later engagement. A Captain Price opened the coffin and found 'a quick corse therein, and in memory of Dunluce we cried quittance with him, and sent his head to be set on Dublin Castle'.[34]

Perrott agreed to make peace with the MacDonnells and Sorley Boy came to Dublin in 1586. Shown Alasdair's head on a spike he said, 'My son hath many heads.'[35] Sorley prostrated himself before a portrait of Elizabeth, a small price to pay for recognition of his family's right to the Glens and the Route. Now over eighty years old, he planned to repair Dunluce – an undertaking completed with the help of Armada treasure salvaged from the *Girona*.

Throughout the spring of 1588 the invincible Armada, 130 vessels in all, massed before Lisbon, took on stores and made ready for the invasion of England. After years of vacillation Philip II of Spain, who had married Mary Tudor without ever setting eyes on her, embarked finally on war against her half-sister Elizabeth. Now with one daring blow he would end the galling raids on his treasure fleets, cut off Elizabeth's aid to the Protestant Dutch and achieve victory for the Counter-Reformation. The Duke of Parma had fifty thousand seasoned campaigners in the Spanish Netherlands ready for transportation across the Channel to do battle with the heretics.

During the morning of 9 May the first ships weighed anchor in the Tagus, dropped below Belem and steered into the open Atlantic. From the time the Armada entered the Narrow Seas, however, Philip's grandiose enterprise began to fail: harried by English culverins and scattered by fireships, the Spanish fleet sailed up the North Sea, around the Shetlands and westwards deep into the Atlantic and then south in a long sweep home. In the mountainous seas stirred up by autumn gales some vessels foundered and others were driven towards the rocky headlands of Ireland.

TREACHERY AT GALLAGH

On 14 September 1588 *La Trinidad Valencera* sought shelter in the lee of the Inishowen peninsula. Despite being one of the greatest ships of the Spanish Armada, the vessel was dangerously overloaded (having rescued the entire crew of *Barca de Amburg* in mid-ocean) and had been shipping water in the wild southwesterly storm. Limping down the eastern shore, the ship cast anchor in Kinnagoe Bay and the Maestre de Campo and Commander of the Regiment of Naples, Don Alonso de Luzon, sent a cockboat ashore. As a survivor related to Philip II:

> They landed with rapiers in their hands whereupon they found four or five savages who bade them welcome and used them well until twenty more wild men came unto them, after which time they took away a bag of money.[36]

The 'wild men' were O'Dohertys of Inishowen who, though nominally in alliance with the English, did what they could for the stricken Spanish. For two days boats and currachs plied back and forth with supplies until suddenly *La Trinidad Valencera* sank; forty men still below were drowned. The poor country of Inishowen, Don Alonso saw, could not for long support his company of 350 men; he resolved to cross the Foyle and seek the help of Sorley Boy to reach neutral Scotland. Pounded by English warships in the Narrow Seas and scattered at Gravelines, enduring the terror of mountainous waves round Scotland and in the North Atlantic, subsisting on mouldy biscuit and putrid salt meat, and until now desperately short of drinking water, the survivors had barely the strength to make the journey. Still, this mixed band of Spaniards, Neapolitans, Greeks and Dalmatians set out with banners flying and drums beating.

Sir William Fitzwilliam, sworn in as lord deputy for a second term just a few days earlier, had only two thousand soldiers in the Irish army. Even a modest Spanish landing could occasion a major uprising. His orders were clear: kill without delay any Spaniard cast ashore. Don Alonso's men had got as far as Gallagh, just north of Derry, when they were confronted by a force of Irish soldiers in English pay led by Major John Kelly, perhaps on the orders of Hugh O'Neill, created the Earl of Tyrone in 1585. After a brisk skirmish in the dark, the exhausted Spaniards surrendered on condition that they would be escorted as prisoners of war to Dublin. As soon as they had given up their swords and pistols, however, they were stripped naked and at first light taken into a field. There almost two hundred of them were butchered by arquebusiers on one side and cavalry on the other.[37] About one hundred escaped, most of whom died of exposure, though some were given refuge by Catholic clergy, and a few reached Scotland with the aid of the O'Cahans and MacDonnells. Some officers were kept alive for ransom though many died in Drogheda; Don Alonso was released in London in 1591.

THE VOYAGE OF THE *GIRONA*

Don Alonso Martinez de Leiva de Rioja, Knight of Santiago, Commander of Alcuescar, was general-in-chief of the land forces of the

Armada entrusted with the conquest of England in joint action with the Duke of Parma. By September 1588 his only concern was to survive. Buffeted by the storm, de Leiva's ship, *Sancta Maria Rata Encoronada*, foundered in Blacksod Bay in Mayo. The survivors transferred to *Duquesa Santa Ana*, a transport vessel; to reach Spain in such an overladen ship was impossible and so de Leiva set out for Scotland.

A strong southwesterly pushed the *Duquesa* past Erris, across Donegal Bay, to skirt Slieve League and the island of Rathlin O'Beirne. Then at night a squall drove her by Slievetooey into the treacherous shallows of Loughros More Bay, 'where falling to anchor,' an Irishman on board recalled, 'there fell a great storm which brake in sunder all their cables and struck them upon ground'.[38] Though his leg had been broken against the capstan, de Leiva rallied the survivors to entrench themselves on an island in Kiltooris Lough. A heavy iron gun mounted there was found in 1968 – the first iron cannon to be recovered from the Armada in modern times. In Kerry, Clare and Sligo Fitzwilliam's officials saw to it that the Spaniards were stripped and slaughtered. Here in Donegal, the corner of Ireland most remote from English power, the MacSweenys gave food and help to the Armada castaways.

It was more than a week before de Leiva heard that other Spaniards were sheltered just across the mountains at Killybegs. Perhaps a thousand men accompanied the commander in his litter over the slopes of Mulmosog. Three ships had come into Killybegs but only one remained afloat, the *Girona*, a three-masted galleass with 36 oars pulled by 244 rowers. De Leiva resolved to repair the ship and sail for Scotland. Patrick Eulane, a spy in English pay, dashed off a message to Sir Henry Bagenal:

MacSweeny's fear to hunger his country. The Spaniards are buying garrons and mares for food. The best of the Spaniards in MacSweeny's country are going away and will leave the rest to shift for themselves because the ship cannot receive them all.[39]

About 1,300 Spaniards crowded aboard the *Girona*, leaving around 200 of their compatriots behind, as another spy reported:

The 26th of this instant October the said galley departed from the said harbour with as many Spaniards as she could carry . . . the Spaniards gave MacSweeny, at their departure, twelve butts of sack wine . . . The MacSweenys and their followers have gotten great store of the Spanish calivers and muskets.[40]

The *Girona* negotiated the wild waters off Bloody Foreland and Inishowen only to have her rudder smashed by a northerly gale which blew the vessel on to the north Antrim coast. Just east of Dunluce at

Lacada Point the ship struck a long basalt reef and split apart, the poop being swept along, leaving a trail of stone arquebus balls as far as Spanish Cave. That terrible night the disaster at sea was so great that the death toll was only two hundred short of the number lost in the *Titanic* in 1912; in the pitch blackness close to midnight, with a strong tide sweeping away from the reef, only nine men survived. Three hundred and eighty years later the Belgian archaeologist, Robert Sténuit, discovered the wreck and after careful underwater excavation brought the *Girona*'s treasures to the surface – the most complete piece of Armada archaeological evidence and a permanent reminder of the flower of the Spanish nobility who died with Don Alonso de Leiva, and the nameless sailors, conscripts and galley slaves who perished in these cold northern waters of Ulster. A survivor of the Armada, commenting on this loss of life, wrote: 'The gentlemen were so many that a list of their names would fill a quire of paper.'[41]

'SUCH A THING WAS NEVER SEEN'

Unable to make headway against the wind on 20 September 1588, three Armada ships anchored in Sligo Bay, half a league from the shore. After five days at anchor, Captain Francisco de Cuellar related afterwards:

> There sprang up so great a storm on our beam, with a sea up to the heavens, so that the cables could not hold nor the sails serve us ... We were driven ashore, with all three ships upon a beach covered with very fine sand, shut in on one side and the other by great rocks. Such a thing was never seen; for within the space of an hour all three ships were broken to pieces, so that there did not escape three hundred men, and more than one thousand were drowned.[42]

Driven on to the storm beach of Streedagh, just south of Bundoran, these vessels – the *San Juan*, the *Lavia*, and the *Santa Maria de Vision* – foundered so quickly that the disaster was on the same scale as the wreck of the *Girona*. Sir Geoffrey Fenton, secretary to the Irish Council, reported to Sir William Cecil:

> At my late being at Sligo I numbered in one strand of less than five miles in length above 1,100 dead corpses of men which the sea had driven upon the shore.

His legs crushed, de Cuellar came ashore on a floating hatchway cover:

> Supplicating Our Lady of Ontanar there came four waves one after the other and without knowing how, or how to swim, they cast me upon the shore where I emerged unable to stand, all covered with blood.[43]

Most of the survivors were cut down or hanged but de Cuellar, after being stripped and beaten, and enslaved for a time by a blacksmith, reached the territory of 'an important savage' – probably Sir Brian O'Rourke of Bréifne, then at war with the English. Here the Spaniard was taken in by the resourceful chief of the MacClancys in the vicinity of Lough Melvin. Then in November 1588, Lord Deputy Fitzwilliam made a forced march from Dublin to the north-west with all the troops he could muster. Inexorably the English closed in on the MacClancy chief:

> This savage, taking into consideration the great force that was coming against him, and that he could not resist it, decided to fly to the mountains, which was his only remedy . . . we decided to say to the savage that we wished to hold the castle and defend it to the death.[44]

Soon after MacClancy had left with his people and his cattle, about eight hundred of Fitzwilliam's troops appeared on the shore of Melvin and called on de Cuellar and his fellow survivors to surrender. Standing on a crannog, the castle held out even when the English hanged two Spanish captives before the defenders' eyes. Without boats the lord deputy's men could do no more than wait, and eventually – beset by snowstorms – they withdrew. The delighted MacClancy offered his sister in marriage but de Cuellar preferred to leave in the dead of night at the beginning of January 1589.

After three weeks de Cuellar reached Dunluce but the English were there in search of survivors. He took refuge in a mountain hut near Castleroe for six weeks, after which: 'I was now able to show myself in the town, which was of thatched houses, and there were some very pretty girls, with whom I struck up a great friendship.'[45] With their help he found Redmond O'Gallagher, Catholic bishop of Derry, who got him a passage to Scotland and from there to Flanders (where again he was shipwrecked and narrowly escaped being run through by the Dutch). De Cuellar's account, written from the Spanish Netherlands for a friend in Spain, includes this observation:

> The savages are well affected to us Spaniards, because they realise that we are attacking the heretics and are their great enemies. If it was not for those natives who kept us as if belonging to themselves, not one of our people would have escaped. We owe them a good turn for that, though they were the first to rob and strip us when we were cast on shore.[46]

At one point there were perhaps three thousand Spaniards in Ulster. By 1589 nearly all had departed or been slain, though a handful remained to instruct the Irish in modern military techniques. If 1588 was a moment for action against the intrusion of English power in Ulster, that moment soon passed. Sir Brian O'Rourke was executed at Tyburn; Bishop O'Gallagher, who had brought tears of emotion to de Cuellar's eyes, was killed later by the English; Sorley Boy did not wish to undo his recent agreement with the English Crown; Sir Hugh O'Donnell did not dare to help the Spaniards in Tír Conaill, as his son, Red Hugh, was held hostage in Dublin Castle; and Hugh O'Neill helped to transfer some Spanish prisoners to the Pale.

THE NATIVE PLANTATION OF MONAGHAN

The fate of the Spaniards and those who harboured them showed the extent to which English power had advanced in Ulster since Elizabeth had come to the throne. Ulster chieftains and their people kept their lands, but they had been wary of showing defiance, displaying little inclination to pull together in opposition to the Crown. It was with comparative ease, for example, that Lord Deputy Fitzwilliam broke up the ruling family in Monaghan, the MacMahons.

Sir Ross MacMahon, considered a 'good subject', died in 1589 without an heir by English feudal law. Hugh Roe, his brother, won recognition as heir but used troops lent to him by the lord deputy to burn corn on the lands of his rival Heber MacCooley MacMahon and to raid cattle in the barony of Farney, the property of the Earl of Essex. In 1590 Fitzwilliam took an expedition to Monaghan and hanged Hugh Roe. This severe punishment was followed by a partition of all Monaghan – with the exception of Essex's estate in Farney – amongst five leading MacMahons, the chieftain of the MacKennas, and other native freeholders who paid rent both to the queen and their native lords. It was a skilful application of the principle of divide and rule, which brought about a permanent reduction in the MacMahon power and an extension of English control.[47]

The independence and strength of native and Anglo-Irish lords in Connacht had been sapped steadily and effectively by Elizabeth's agents using methods similar to those employed by Fitzwilliam in Monaghan. There seemed every reason to believe that English royal power would extend piecemeal over all Ulster as it had over all Connacht. The Clandeboye O'Neills were weakened by internal dissension; the MacDonnells did not want to jeopardise Sorley Boy's agreement with the Crown; Sir Hugh O'Donnell of Tír Conaill was plagued by threats to his authority by Hugh Dubh and the nine sons of Conn, son of Calvagh; and in Tyrone power was uneasily shared by Turlough Luineach, The O'Neill, and Hugh O'Neill, Earl of Tyrone, both harassed in turn by the McShanes – the seven sons of Shane O'Neill. If English officials felt confident about the progress of the queen's peace in Ulster, they reckoned without the queen's own protégé, Hugh O'Neill.

Hugh O'Neill seemed to owe all he had to the English. It had been an English king who had given an earldom to his grandfather, Conn Bacach and, after the murder first of his father Matthew and then of his brother Brian, it had been Elizabeth who had affirmed Hugh as Baron of Dungannon in 1568. Carefully nurtured by the Crown and given a good English education, Hugh had been proclaimed Earl of Tyrone in 1585. For several years it seemed that the English had been right to give Hugh their support – he had campaigned with Essex, had given no aid to the Spaniards, and often lent military aid to the lord deputy of the day. Yet O'Neill was to become the most dangerous and astute of Elizabeth's opponents not only in Ulster but in all Ireland. Just when and for what reasons Tyrone turned against the queen is still veiled in mystery: the great weight of surviving evidence for the remaining years of the sixteenth century is on the English side and only a few sparse documents cast a dim light on the epic struggle from the Irish point of view.

It is certain that O'Neill wanted power in Ulster and for a long time English help was essential in assisting him towards that objective. Patience and diplomacy were equally important. It took skill to settle in at Dungannon while Turlough Luineach remained alive and while Shane O'Neill's sons were at large. It took vision to assuage the age-old enmity between the O'Neills and the O'Donnells and make a firm alliance to his own advantage.

In 1587 Perrott, then lord deputy, sent a ship laden with wine to Lough Swilly and it took little to persuade Red Hugh O'Donnell, then the guest of the MacSweenys at Rathmullan, to come aboard. Red Hugh was taken hostage and kept captive thereafter in Dublin Castle. The favoured heir to Tír Conaill, son of the indomitable Ineen Dubh, grandson of Lady Agnes, nephew of Turlough Luineach and son-in-law (though he was only sixteen years old) of Hugh O'Neill, Red Hugh was an effective surety for O'Donnell's good behaviour. According to the Annals of the Four Masters, Red Hugh

> was constantly revolving in his mind the manner in which he might make his escape. This was not an easy matter for him, for he was confined in a closely-secured apartment every night in the castle until sunrise next day. This castle was surrounded by a wide and very deep ditch, full of water.[48]

During Christmas 1590 rope was smuggled in and Red Hugh escaped to take refuge with Phelim O'Toole in the Wicklow Mountains; but O'Toole, fearing government retribution, returned him to the English. A year later, on Christmas night 1591, O'Donnell escaped with two fellow prisoners, Art and Henry O'Neill, sons of Shane O'Neill; slipping out through the castle sewer, they headed south through the snow to Glenmalure, the O'Byrne stronghold. The O'Byrnes found them 'covered over with white-bordered shrouds of hailstones freezing around them, and their light clothes and fine-threaded shirts adhered to their skin'.[49] Art died in their arms but the other two returned safely to Ulster, escorted by Hugh O'Neill's ally, Turlough O'Hagan. Henry was held by Tyrone but Red Hugh was sent down Lough Erne to his father's castle at Ballyshannon; here the physicians amputated Hugh's frost-bitten toes. In May 1592 Red Hugh was proclaimed The O'Donnell, his aged father agreeing to step down. Turlough Luineach resigned his authority as The O'Neill the following year, leaving the Earl of Tyrone without rival in mid-Ulster; when Turlough died in 1595, Hugh was duly inaugurated as The O'Neill at Tullahogue. The way was now clear for a coalition of the two most powerful rulers in Ulster.

Had he remained a servant of the queen, Tyrone could have continued to wield great authority in Ulster. He would exercise greater power, however, if he became Gaelic king of the province. His ambition was undoubtedly fed by the growing anxiety of the Gaelic Irish in Ulster: they knew well the recent treachery and slaughter in Connacht and, though not averse to sporadic mayhem themselves, they seem genuinely to have been appalled by the massacre of the Scots on Rathlin, Essex's bloodshed in Belfast Castle, and the treacherous seizure of hostages. The division of Monaghan and the encroachment of the queen's officials seemed to be pushing the Gaelic lords of Ulster to the end of the line. Armed resistance was their time-honoured reaction – not a national revolt in the modern sense but a struggle by an aristocratic caste to preserve an ancient way of life.

Tyrone's dispute with Sir Henry Bagenal, marshal of the queen's army, should not be discounted as a cause of the approaching war. In 1591 O'Neill, now fifty years old, eloped with Sir Henry's twenty-year-old sister Mabel. Their marriage did not last long, Mabel dying five years later. Bagenal never forgave Tyrone and vented his feelings to Cecil:

> I can but accurse myself and fortune that my blood, which in my father and myself hath often been spilled in repressing this rebellious race, should now be mingled with so traitorous a stock and kindred.[50]

Bagenal was a natural leader of those who were urging Elizabeth to clip Tyrone's wings.

Bagenal and Tyrone campaigned together for the last time in 1593. Hugh Maguire, fearing an imposed redivision of lands in Fermanagh, had risen in rebellion against the queen. Facing the combined forces of O'Neill and the marshal, Maguire could make no headway, and he was routed at the ford of the Erne at Belleek. O'Neill, wounded in the thigh, complained that the marshal gave him no credit for his help, while Bagenal, unable to conceal his loathing for his brother-in-law, suspected him of treasonable intentions.

Maguire refused to give in and for many months his castle on the island of Enniskillen was besieged by the English. Then on 2 February 1594 the castle fell: from one side, boats – shielded by hides stretched over wooden rods – carried men to undermine the barbican with picks, while a direct assault was being made from the other. Maguire fought on, however, now with the support of Red Hugh O'Donnell. Tyrone made his first open act of defiance and refused to give any further help – Maguire, indeed, was his son-in-law. The English garrison in Enniskillen was dangerously exposed and at the ford of Drumane over the Arney river a relief force led by Sir Henry Duke was overwhelmed. The Annals of the Four Masters record:

> A fierce and vehement conflict and a spirited and hard-contested battle was fought between the two parties, till at length Maguire and his forces routed the others by dint of fighting . . . Many steeds, weapons, and other spoils were left behind in that place, besides the steeds and horses that were loaded with provisions on their way to Enniskillen . . . The name of the ford at which this great victory was gained was changed to the Ford of the Biscuits, from the number of biscuits and small cakes left there to the victors on that day.[51]

Maguire recovered Enniskillen the following year, by which time O'Neill was at war with the queen.

The skirmishing for Enniskillen showed how vulnerable were English garrisons planted in hostile territory. Retaining and provisioning forward positions proved far more difficult than setting them up in the first place; and yet Elizabeth's government could see no other way of taming the Ulster lords than by maintaining fortified posts in their territories.

In February 1595 O'Neill carried out his first direct act of war against the queen: he destroyed the Blackwater Fort, pulling down the bridge he had helped Essex to build nearly twenty years earlier. This, together with Maguire's recovery of Enniskillen, put the more southerly Monaghan garrison in peril. When dissident MacMahons surrounded the fort, Sir Henry Bagenal agreed to lead north a relief column towards the end of May. O'Neill prepared an ambush four miles from Monaghan at Crossdall, forcing Bagenal to expend much of his powder before breaking through to the beleaguered garrison.

On 13 June Bagenal's troop moved out of Monaghan, marching more rapidly now that they were not loaded with supplies and taking a new route south-east by Lough Muckno. O'Neill followed closely, harrying the column through the rough country. Then at Crossaghy Hill, half a mile east of Clontibret church, Tyrone made an all-out attempt to stop the English crossing a stream. When the earl was seen 'surveying the battle thence and giving his orders', a knight from the Pale named Seagrave charged across the ford with forty troopers, and both he and O'Neill splintered their lances against the corselet of the other.[52] Seagrave threw O'Neill to the ground but as they wrestled O'Cahan's son cut off the knight's arm, giving Tyrone time to stab his assailant to death. The assault on the English was pressed home for more than eight hours and at dusk Captain Merriman had to send out 'a sleeve of pikes for lack of munition to charge upon Tyrone's shot'.[53] That night the English made camp at Ballycowan, melting down Bagenal's pewter dishes to make bullets. Dawn revealed that O'Neill had withdrawn, probably because his men had no powder left, and when Bagenal's men reached Newry that evening his losses were seen to be severe; there were, it was admitted, 'more hurt men in the late service than was convenient to declare'.[54]

Clontibret showed that Tyrone commanded a force more formidable and professional than Elizabeth's commanders had encountered in Ireland before. Sir Edward York, who had been in command of Bagenal's cavalry, observed how the Irish came up 'within half caliver shot of the main stand of our pikes' to throw their spears and 'that in no place whatsoever he had served in all his life he never saw more readier or perfecter shot'.[55] The close co-operation between Irish horse and foot impressed York particularly.

The rise of the Campbells and the caution of James VI in Scotland, together with the vigilance of English pinnaces in the North Channel, cut down the supply of Scots Redshank mercenaries to the Ulster lords. Instead Hugh O'Neill raised a great Gaelic host in his own lands. Proclamations were read in churches and public places, and recruits were called up each year early in the spring. Shane O'Neill had armed not only his landowning freemen but also his common peasantry, being, in Sidney's view, 'the first ever that did so of an Irishman'. Tyrone perfected this mass conscription, giving his men training, discipline and modern firearms. These levies, known as *buannadha* or 'bonaghts', became as formidable as gallowglass professionals and marched in companies carrying colours to the beat of drums and the skirl of war pipes. Taught by 'butter captains' (English-trained officers given to O'Neill while still in the queen's service) and a few remaining Spanish survivors, O'Neill's troops mastered the caliver or arquebus, and the heavier musket that fired bullets weighing between one and two ounces, some cast from lead originally intended for O'Neill's castle at Dungannon. Even Tyrone's own gallowglass MacDonnells from the Blackwater valley gave up their traditional battle-axe. All down to the poorest servants could be called up, including the *ceatharnaigh* or kerne, light foot soldiers who could muster from any part of Ulster within three days. O'Neill, his allied chiefs and their kinsmen, who formed the traditional aristocratic warrior caste, made up the cavalry of this Ulster army. It was estimated that by 1595 Tyrone commanded one thousand horse, one thousand pikemen and four thousand foot carrying firearms. The English in Ireland – let alone Ulster – had not before met such an adversary: O'Neill had brought the squabbling septs of his province under his command, had proved himself a skilled tactician in battle and now he was leading his people into their bloodiest struggle so far, which would leave shock waves reverberating down the centuries.[56]

'FREEING THE COUNTRY FROM THE ROD OF TYRANNICAL EVIL'

One by one, routes into Ulster seemed to be closing for the English. In June 1595 Ulick Burke of Connacht killed the governor of Sligo, George Bingham, and presented the town and its arsenal of cannon to Red Hugh. All that remained open was the precarious passage to Armagh. Sir William Russell, appointed lord deputy the year before, came north with Sir John Norris, general of her majesty's forces in Ulster, to proclaim O'Neill a traitor in Dundalk and Newry. Then closely shadowed by Tyrone, he advanced to Armagh and reinforced the cathedral there at the end of June. O'Neill demolished Dungannon Castle before the eyes of the English,

> in so great a haste [that one night it was] stately and high in the sight of all our army, the next day by noon it was so low that it could scarcely be discerned.[57]

O'Neill knew his castle could not withstand the force of cannon that his spies had seen in Newry. The stone was carried off to crannogs and other defensible and remote storehouses. Tyrone agreed to a truce to last until the following year, probably not because he believed it would lead to peace but because it gave him time.

O'Neill and O'Donnell knew that outside help was essential to ensure total victory – the help not only of disaffected lords in the other three provinces but also of overseas enemies of England. The fate of the Catholic Church was a constant theme in the letters sent to Spain. Philip II – hard-pressed in France and his government veering towards bankruptcy – was eager, nevertheless, to do what he could. In May 1596 the Spanish king's emissary, Alonso Cobos, sailed into Killybegs with munitions from Philip and indulgences and relics from Pope Clement VIII. Cobos walked forty miles to meet O'Neill for he would speak only with him, O'Donnell, O'Doherty and their secretaries. The Ulster lords asked for immediate assistance and wrote also to Philip's son, the Prince of the Asturias, asking him to

> aid in his clemency this most excellent and just cause, that of asserting Catholic liberty and of freeing the country from the rod of tyrannical evil, and that, with the help of the Divine Majesty, he may win for Christ an infinite number of souls, snatching them from the jaws of hell.[58]

This was elegantly signed by both O'Neill and O'Donnell (the former also impressing it with his seal of the Red Hand of Ulster) at Lifford, dated 16 May 1596.

Two other Spanish officers, Luis de Cisneros and de Medinilla, assessed what might be required and suggested Carlingford, Sligo, Teelin, Killybegs and Limerick as possible landing places. Then in June 1596 a joint Anglo-Dutch fleet wreaked havoc on Cadiz, burning the city and capturing or destroying fifty-seven ships. Philip was eager for revenge and prepared an armada for Ulster, while O'Donnell stockpiled food to sustain the Spaniards. It was late October when eighty-one vessels left Lisbon and were joined by nineteen more from Seville under the command of Don Martín de Padilla; but before this fleet could join up with other ships from El Ferrol and Vigo, it was overwhelmed by a terrible storm – more than two thousand men perished and at least thirty-two ships were lost. A year later another armada sailed with 136 vessels and over 12,600 men but it too was dispersed by storms. Philip could not summon enough strength for a third attempt.[59]

O'Neill and O'Donnell would have to fight on, depending on their own resources.

'Branches will sprout as long as the root is untouched', Lord Thomas Burgh, appointed lord deputy in 1597, wrote to Sir Robert Cecil, the queen's secretary. He continued:

Bring the axe thither, and they do wither; lop, others spring; cut that, all decays . . . I will encamp by him, force him, follow, omit no opportunity by night or day . . . I will, God willing, stick to him and if need be lie on the ground and drink water ten weeks.

Burgh was sure that if O'Neill 'be well pressed, all is got'.[60] He set out to cross Ulster in July, planning a rendezvous with the new governor of Connacht, Sir Conyers Clifford, who was to invade Tír Conaill. The lord deputy had not the resources for such an ambitious scheme; he blundered as far as the Blackwater but could get no further. Clifford, meanwhile, defeated the Irish at Belleek but was then driven back over the Erne at Ballyshannon, many of his men swept to their deaths over the salmon leap; his force was saved from annihilation only by a downpour that extinguished the matches of the Irish calivers.

Burgh built a new fort on the Blackwater to replace the one O'Neill destroyed in 1595; it was, he wrote, 'my first child . . . an eyesore in the heart of O'Neill's country'. In fact he had left a hostage to fortune and abandoned Armagh to sustain it. The war continued to take its toll. Maurice Kyffin, Cecil's Irish agent, reported: 'Between the rebels on the one side and our own soldiers (being for the most part Irish and living altogether on the spoil) all is devoured and destroyed.'[61] Burgh saw misery

woeful to behold to Christian eyes. I see soldiers, citizens, villagers, and all sorts of people daily perish through famine; meat failing the man of war makes him savage, so as the end is both spoiler and spoiled are in like calamity.[62]

Burgh himself fell victim to famine fever: he was carried on a litter to Newry, where he died on 13 October 1597.

Ulster was by no means in ruins as yet and it is possible that, so far, the Pale had suffered most from the exactions of the Government and the depredations of the soldiery. Tyrone, it was thought, could raise £80,000 a year in Ulster and the war cost him £500 a day when on campaign. It is an indication of the strength of the Gaelic economy in the province that such warfare could be so long sustained. Not until the end of the war, when scorched-earth policies created widespread famine, was there destitution throughout Ulster.

Burgh had hoped to bring supplies to the Blackwater Fort from Belfast Lough via Antrim and from there across Lough Neagh. His plan was spoiled by Shane MacBrian O'Neill, Lord of Clandeboye, who took Belfast Castle and hanged and disembowelled all the English garrison. Sir John Chichester, governor of Carrickfergus and a veteran of Clontibret, saw that 'boats may be landed within a butte shot of the said castle; for the recovery whereof I made choice that it should be one of my first works'. On 11 July 1597 he disembarked with a hundred men and it was 'no long time before we took the place, without any loss to us, and put those we found in it to the sword'.[63]

The fall of Edenduffcarrick on the shores of Lough Neagh followed soon after, but Chichester failed to ensure good relations with the Antrim Scots. Sir James MacDonnell, who had succeeded his father Sorley Boy, visited Edinburgh that year to ensure James VI of Scotland's good will. MacDonnell is described in the *Chronicle of the Scottis Kingis* as 'ane man of Scottis bluid, albeit his landis lye in Ireland. He was ane bra man of person and behaviour, but he had not the Scots tongue, nor nae language but Erse.'[64] Sir James refused to give Chichester a cannon retrieved from the wreck of the *Girona* and held out in Dunluce:

> They have likewise broken down two of their castells, the one called Glinarme, and the other Red Bawne, forteffeinge themselves only in Dunluse, where they have planted three peeces of ordnaunce, demicannon, and culvering, which were had out of one of the Spanish ships coming upon that coast after our fight with them.[65]

When Captain Maunsell, one of Chichester's officers, drove off a large herd of MacDonnell cattle, Sir James and his brother Randal swept south. 'What say you?' Chichester called to his officers during a parley outside Carrickfergus. 'Shall we charge them?' In the rash attack that followed Chichester was shot through the head and 180 of his men were killed. Recent English gains in this area were lost at a stroke, and for little reason: Sir James protested to the queen that he merely wished to negotiate concerning 'stealthes', that is, thieving, or in this case rustling:

> My commynge from hance was to have parlitt vithe the governor concerninge stealthes that was committit be capten mansells hoers in absence of Shir Jhonne Chichester.[66]

Now the MacDonnells had become formidable allies of O'Neill and O'Donnell and the isolation of the Blackwater Fort was complete.

'I protest to God the state of the scurvy fort of Blackwater,' the Earl of Ormond remarked in his dispatch to Cecil, 'which cannot be long held, doth more touch my heart than all the spoils that ever were made by traitors of mine own lands. The fort was always falling, and never victualled but once (by myself) without an army.'[67] Ormond, acting as the queen's lord general in the absence of a deputy, preferred the fort to be 'razed, or yielded upon composition, than the soldiers to be left to the uttermost danger'.[68] The position of the garrison of 150 men in the heart of Ulster was becoming desperate: an Irish attack had been repelled only by firing cannon, crammed with musket balls, through embrasures in the parapet; desperate sallies had to be made to bring in wood and water; and the soldiers were reduced to eating grass growing on the ramparts.

The Irish Council in Dublin did not agree with Ormond, and on the arrival of fresh troops in July 1598, Sir Henry Bagenal's offer to lead an expedition to relieve the fort was accepted. The marshal, with three hundred horse and four thousand foot, arrived in Armagh without incident on 13 August, leading one of the largest forces to have entered Ulster for many years. From the moment he left Armagh early next morning Bagenal faced disaster. O'Neill had long prepared for this opportunity: he himself was in command on the left, O'Donnell on the right, Randal MacDonnell close by and Sir Hugh Maguire leading the horse. As Bagenal thrust across country his army was assailed by caliver and musket shot fired from the woods, where the Irish were safe from Sir Calisthenes Brooke's cavalry. Pack horses and four cannon dragged by bullocks impeded regiments marching behind, while under Sir Richard Percy's command, the van advanced to near annihilation. O'Neill had a deep trench running almost a mile between two bogs. Behind, a heavy saker stuck in the bed of a stream oozing from a bog – the yellow ford which gave the battle its name. Bagenal rode back to help extricate the gun but when he raised his visor he was shot in the face and fell dying. The Irish closed in as Percy's men threw down their calivers and fled back wildly into the mêlée at the ford, and the débâcle was complete when a soldier, refilling his powder horn, exploded two barrels with his match. Finally the Irish 'came on amain with a full cry after their manner'.[69]

Neither for the first nor the last time O'Neill stayed his hand. He made no attempt to halt the retreat of the survivors and even allowed the men of the Blackwater Fort to march south to the Pale. Perhaps he hoped to ease negotiations for another truce. As it was, 800 men and 25 officers in the invading force had been killed, together with 400 wounded and some 300 deserting to O'Neill's side. It was the greatest victory Gaelic Ulster ever achieved over the Crown. Many, indeed, regard the Yellow Ford as the most disastrous defeat the English ever suffered at the hands of the Irish.

'BY GOD I WILL BEAT TYRONE IN THE FIELD'

In every part of Ulster, save Carrickfergus and Newry, the Crown was defeated. Within weeks of the Yellow Ford, Connacht was overrun by O'Donnell, the O'Mores furiously attacked the English settlement in the Midlands, and the plantation in Munster disintegrated, the colonists being driven out, mutilated or killed. English rule, not only in the extremities but over the whole island, was in peril. While Ireland was almost bereft of English troops, O'Neill again hesitated and the opportunity soon passed – his ambition was to be the unchallenged ruler of Ulster not of Ireland, and to win the queen's acceptance of his rule.

Elizabeth had no longer any wish to talk: the Yellow Ford convinced her that she must unstintingly use her treasure to defeat Tyrone. Over the winter of 1598–9, troops were levied on an unprecedented scale across England, and rich contracts for food, munitions, camp equipment and medical supplies were made with London merchants. And who would lead the new army? Opposing factions at court vied for the queen's favour and the victor emerged with the exalted title of lord lieutenant: Robert Devereux, 2nd Earl of Essex. 'I have beaten Knollys and Mountjoy in the Council,' he exulted, 'and by God I will beat Tyrone in the field.'[70]

Storms delayed Essex until mid-April 1599 and the same winds engulfed a vessel that had sailed out of Dublin to greet him; it took down with it the Earl of Kildare and eighteen Leinster lords. This was an ill-omened start to a disastrous viceroyalty, at a time when as many as twenty thousand Irish may have been in arms against the queen, with the further prospect of Spanish aid. Essex had with him the greatest English army yet seen in Ireland but he did not, as he pledged, meet Tyrone in the field. The summer was spent in an attempt to detach Munster and Leinster allies from O'Neill. Elizabeth fretted that her lord lieutenant was costing her £1,000 a day and urged him to put the axe 'to the root of that tree which hath been the treasonable stock from which so many poisoned plants and grafts have been derived'.[71] As reports of aimless expeditions and inconsequential sieges were brought to her, Sir John Harington observed: 'She walks much in her privy chamber, and stamps with her feet at ill news, and thrusts her rusty sword at times into the arras in great rage.'[72]

The news got worse. Sir Conyers Clifford and his army were over-whelmed by the O'Rourkes in the Curlieu Mountains and his head was sent to Red Hugh. Then, when Essex at last set out for Ulster at the end of August, troops began to desert. O'Neill and the lord lieutenant confronted each other at Ardee, but instead of fighting, a curious parley followed by the Lagan, a stream entering the River Glyde near Dundalk. Tyrone rode deep into the stream and talked alone with Essex for half an hour. They met again with witnesses and agreed a six-week truce. The Ulster Irish retired having made no concessions whatever.

'To trust this traitor upon oath is to trust a devil upon his religion,' Elizabeth said in despair, scathingly describing the truce as a 'quick end made of a slow proceeding'.[73] Essex then suddenly deserted his post, returned to London, and burst into the queen's bedchamber to beg forgiveness; he was committed to the custody of Lord Keeper Egerton. Essex's truce was extended in December 1599 but, while O'Neill wanted to maintain it, the English were preparing to renew the fight. In January 1600 Tyrone moved out of Cavan to punish those who had not re-mained faithful to his alliance. He left the O'Carrolls' land with 'ashes instead of its corn and embers instead of its mansions', and then he swept south to camp in west Cork, where he accepted allegiance and hostages from the lords of Munster and burned the lands of the Barrys to encourage the faint-hearted.[74] Very soon, however, O'Neill was to meet an opponent as tenacious and resourceful as himself – Mountjoy.

MOUNTJOY

Charles Blount, Lord Mountjoy, though only thirty-six years old when he was appointed lord deputy in January 1600, believed himself to be in constant bad health. He smoked heavily as a preventative against dis-ease, took an afternoon sleep in his tent when on campaign, and to keep warm he wore three pairs of silk stockings with woollen stockings over them under his high linen boot hose and swaddled himself with three waistcoats under his coat. Plagued by acute headaches, he nevertheless inspired his men with greater success than any of his predecessors and he appeared to be fearless in battle – at different times his horse was shot under him, his greyhound running beside him was shot dead, and his chaplain, one of his secretaries and a gentleman of his chamber were killed close by him.[75]

The new lord deputy had an army of 1,200 horse, many of them experienced soldiers, and the supply of munitions, provisions and fodder was better organised than before. With this force Mountjoy planned to break O'Neill's rebellion by an unceasing war of attrition; he preferred to fight in winter when it was more difficult for the Irish to hide in the leafless woods, their stores of grain could be burned, and their cattle quickly exhausted by hunger when stampeded, so that they could more easily be captured or cut down. Less inclined than his predecessors to show mercy, Mountjoy intended to break Ulster's resistance by slaughtering the fighting men and starving the people.

Just two days after Mountjoy's arrival in Dublin, O'Neill had a brush with the English outside Cork city. In a chance encounter Sir Warham St Leger fired his pistol at an Irishman charging at him with a spear; St Leger was killed but so was his assailant, Hugh Maguire, commander of Tyrone's horse. On hearing this bitter news, O'Neill returned rapidly to Ulster. Meanwhile Mountjoy put into effect the plan Essex had failed to carry out – an amphibious operation to place a garrison at the head of Lough Foyle to drive a wedge between the territories of O'Donnell and O'Neill.

DOCWRA AT DERRY: 'A FITT PLACE TO MAKE OUR MAINE PLANTATION IN'

On 7 May 1600 an impressive fleet sailed out of Carrickfergus harbour with some four thousand foot soldiers and two hundred cavalry on board under the command of Sir Henry Docwra. It took a full week to reach Lough Foyle, 'the windes often fayling, & sometimes full against us', and then a further two days were lost stranded on sandbanks. On 16 May the English finally disembarked at Culmore on the south-western shore of the sea lough and threw up a fort there on the site of a ruined castle. Irishmen watching the invaders from a hill were pursued, but, according to Docwra, 'by ignorance of the wayes our horses were presentlie boggt'.[76] Then Docwra advanced up the Foyle and, as he relates in his *Narration*, he laid the foundations of the modern city of Derry:

> On the 22nd of May wee put the Army in order to marche, & leaving Captain Lancellott Atford at Culmore with 600 men, to make up the workes, wee went to the Derry 4 myles of upon the River side, a place in manner of an Iland Comprehending within it 40 acres of Ground, wherein were the Ruines of an old Abbay, of a Bishopp's houses, of two churches, & at one of the ends of it an old Castle, the River called loughfoyle encompassing it all on one side, & a bogg most commonlie wett, & not easilie passable except in two or three places dividing it from the maine land.
>
> This peece of Ground we possest our selves of without Resistaunce, & iudging it a fitt place to make our maine plantation in, being somewhat hie, & therefore dry, & healthie to dwell upon, att that end where the old Castle stood, being closer to the water side, I presentlie resolved to raise a fforte to keep our stoore of Munition & victuells in, & in the other a little

above, where the walls of an old Cathedral church were yet standing, to evert another for our future safetie & retreate unto upon all occasions.[77]

Docwra, an experienced campaigner from the wars in Connacht, avoided the temptation to march directly towards O'Neill's strongholds and instead concentrated on making Derry secure enough to 'sitt it out all winter'. Two warships were sent out to forage for timber across the estuary in O'Cahan's territory and 'there was not a sticke of it brought home, but was first well fought for'.[78] With nearby quarries and rubble from old buildings bound by mortar made from cockle shells, it was possible to complete the fortifications before the end of summer. While this work was in progress, the presence of such a large army produced the first hair cracks in the coalition of Ulster lords O'Neill had held together for so long. In June Art O'Neill, son of Turlough Luineach, joined Docwra with some forty men and led the English to make a surprise assault on O'Cahan's herdsmen:

These men marching all night put over at Greene-castle, & by breake of day, on the 10th day of June, fell in the middest of their Creagtes unexpected, Ceazed a greate pray, & brought it to the Waterside; but for want of meanes to bring it all away, they hackt & mangled as many as they could, & with Some 100 Cowes, which they put abord theire Boats, besids what the Souldiers brought away kild, they retourned.[79]

There followed skirmishes with O'Doherty of Inishowen, during one of which Docwra's 'horse was shott in two places & fell deade under mee'.[80] In another clash Red Hugh O'Donnell captured two hundred English horses grazing outside the Derry fort; during a vain pursuit to recover his mounts, Docwra was struck by an Irishman's spear 'in the Foreheade, in soe much as I fell for deade, & was a good while deprived of my sences'.[81] For three weeks the commander lay recovering, and for some time his position deteriorated:

And now the winter beganne to be feirce upon us, our men wasted with continuall laboures, the Iland scattered with Cabbins full of sicke men, our Biskitt all spent, our other provisions of nothing but Meale, Butter, & a little Wine, & that by Computation to hould out but 6 dayes longer.[82]

In fact, it was only September but the condition of the English soldiers became so acute that O'Donnell offered men who deserted a free passage unmolested. O'Neill now joined Red Hugh and made a midnight attack from the bog next to the island. Irish muskets that were fired too soon gave the defenders time enough to rally and drive off the attackers, who 'takeing a fright, confusedly retyred as fast as they could'. 'The very next day', Docwra wrote, 'came in a supplie of victuells, very shortly after 50 newe horse, & shortlie after that againe 600 foote.'[83]

105

The tide of war was now turning against the Ulster lords: their Munster allies were being cowed by Sir George Carew; Mountjoy's advance forced Tyrone to return to the Moyry Pass; Red Hugh had to leave for Connacht to reassert his authority there; and the patient Docwra continued to detach Irishmen to his own side. On 3 October Niall Garbh O'Donnell rode in to Derry to offer his services to the English. Placed in command of Tír Conaill during Red Hugh's absence, Niall Garbh, as grandson of Calvagh, now claimed the right to be The O'Donnell. His crossing of the lines was a coup for Docwra, who sent him upstream to capture Lifford. Only O'Neill himself could hope to evict Docwra and that he could not do without defeating Mountjoy. He now battled with the fierce desperation of a commander forced to fight on two fronts.

IN THE MOYRY PASS

The wild autumn storms that had assailed Docwra were meanwhile buffeting Mountjoy, 'his Lordship's Tent being continually wet', his secretary Fynes Moryson wrote, 'and often blown down'.[84] O'Neill had long prepared to make a stand in the Moyry Pass and on viewing Tyrone's elaborate defences, Mountjoy observed: 'These barbarous people had far exceeded their custom and our expectation.'[85] In a letter to the queen's government in London he described the pass as

> being naturally one of the most Difficult Passages of *Ireland*, fortified with good Art, and with admirable Industry, (the Enemy having raised from Mountain to Mountain, from Wood to Wood, and from Bog to Bog, long Traverses, with huge and high Flanckers of great Stones, mingled with Turf, and staked in both Sides with Pallisadoes watled,) and possessed with one of the greatest Armies that ever they were able to make. But that which was our main Impediment, was the Extremity of the Weather, and great Rain, which made the Rivers unpassable.[86]

On the afternoon of Thursday 2 October 1600 the Irish advanced with pike and handgun in formidable array. Mountjoy threw five regiments against them but after three hours of close fighting the English fell back in confusion. An English counter-attack the following Sunday also failed. 'We are now but where we were in the beginning', Sir Geoffrey Fenton observed.[87] A spy reported to Mountjoy that Tyrone was building 'sconces', digging trenches, and having the thickets 'plashed' (intertwining branches to impede cavalry) in Monaghan and Bréifne; he found O'Neill urging his people 'with great earnestness to work lustily and patiently', for if the lord deputy broke through, then it was 'farewell Ulster and all the north'.[88] Meanwhile dysentery spread amongst the English troops and one of their captains remarked on

O'Neill's defences that he never saw 'a more villainous piece of work, and an impossible thing for an army to pass without an intolerable loss'.[89]

Then, unaccountably, O'Neill withdrew from the pass on 13 October and four days later Mountjoy marched through without opposition. Why did Tyrone abandon such a strong defensive position? Was it because he never ceased to hope the English would make terms? Or was the decision made in response to Red Hugh's frantic calls for assistance against Docwra? Whatever the reason, O'Neill's retreat was probably the gravest strategic error made by the Ulster Irish in nine years of war against the English. After resting in Newry, Mountjoy advanced towards Armagh, stopping to erect a fort he named Mountnorris eight miles from the city. Tyrone's men attempted to impede the work, as Moryson records:

> There began between our Foot and theirs, a very good Skirmish, till our Men did beat them off, and brought with them great Store of Corn and Wood, and killed divers of them. The next Day we began to work, in the building of the Fort, and to impeach our Work, the Rogues began to skirmish with us on both Sides, which was excellently maintained by some few of our Men, that we sent out: We saw many of them killed, and after understood they lost a great Number, whereof many were Horsemen, of the best sort, that had lighted to incourage their Men to fight.[90]

Before leaving, Mountjoy put a garrison of four hundred foot under the command of Captain Edward Blaney and proclaimed a reward for O'Neill dead or alive:

> The weather grew so extream, as it blew down all our Tents, and tore them in Pieces, and killed many of our Horses, so that the 10th Day his Lordship putting all the Army in Arms, with all the Drums and Trumpets, and a great Volley of Shot, proclaimed *Tyrone's* head, (with Promise of £2000 to him that brought him alive, and £1000 to him that brought him dead).[91]

On his return by way of Carlingford, Mountjoy sustained severe losses by 'a Barricado reaching a good Way into the Wood and down to the Sea' from which O'Neill 'poured upon us great Vollies of Shot'. The strength of the Ulster lords remained formidable but they were now on the defensive and English mastery of the seas – cutting off Scottish aid and bringing in, without resistance, reinforcements and provisions – was telling against them. Mountjoy's tenacious winter campaigning, together with Docwra's steady success, wore down the Ulster Irish. Only timely and significant Spanish aid could change the course of the war.

He who would England win
Must with Ireland begin.

In the Catholic courts of Europe O'Neill strove to drive home the message of this popular contemporary proverb.[92] Having refused to join the Munster rebels twenty years earlier in a crusade to save Irish Catholicism, Tyrone knew now that it was as a defender of the faith that he was most likely to gain support. Father Edmund MacDonnell, dean of Armagh, and Peter Lombard, bishop of Waterford and later archbishop of Armagh, were his most energetic representatives. They in turn won the support of Fray Mateo de Oviedo and Don Martin de la Cerda.

In the spring of 1600, just when Docwra was entering the Foyle, de Ovieda and de la Cerda sailed into Donegal Bay, bringing with them one thousand arquebuses with powder, lead and fuse. No fewer than sixty Irish commanders assembled in Donegal Abbey to meet the Spanish envoys; help must come soon, they declared, for they could only afford to pay their fighting men for five months longer. On his return, de la Cerda gained an audience with Philip III at Segovia in June, presenting him with a detailed memorial seeking immediate aid, which may in part have been dictated by Tyrone.[93]

'The expedition must go this year', Philip ordered; 'to that end the council will put all in order with the utmost speed.' To the Duke of Lerma's protests that the king was all but bankrupt, Philip responded: 'I myself will see that the money is provided.'[94] De la Cerda returned to Tír Conaill in December and landed at Teelin with 20,000 ducats, 2,000 arquebuses and 150 quintals each of powder, lead and fuse. But there was no news that the Spanish had sailed and, indeed, the vacillating Philip deployed the assembled force elsewhere instead. By the time another expedition was ready the resistance of the Gaelic lords of Ulster was close to being broken.

'WE SPARE NONE OF WHAT QUALITY OR SEX SOEVER'

Neither Mountjoy nor Docwra relaxed their campaigns of attrition during the winter of 1600–1601. The men of Docwra's garrison 'sett divers Preys of Cattle, & did many other services all the winter longe' with the help of Niall Garbh, 'without whose intelligence and guidance little or nothing could have beene done of our selves'.[95] Sir Art O'Neill died following a drinking bout but this was more than offset by the support of Cahir O'Doherty. Rescued by MacDavitt foster-brothers from Red Hugh, Cahir was proclaimed successor to the Inishowen lordship on the death of his father Sir John in January 1601. From that day forward, Docwra states in his *Narration*, 'wee had many faithfull & singuler services' from the O'Dohertys.[96]

Control of the Inishowen peninsula, so far not ravaged by war, gave Docwra the chance to move against the MacSweenys of Fanad. In March 1601 MacSweeny submitted and gave hostages, but encouraged by Red Hugh, renewed the fight. Docwra retaliated:

> in revenge whereof I presentlie hunge up his Pledges, & in September following made annother journey upon him, burnt & destroyed his houses & corne, whereupon Winter approaching insued the death of most of his People.[97]

O'Donnell had narrowly escaped being trapped against trenches Docwra cut across the narrow base of Inishowen, while his rival, Niall Garbh, came close to capturing O'Neill in O'Cahan's country and took Donegal Abbey in August. The driving of the wedge between O'Donnell and O'Neill was all but complete.

'When the plough and breeding of cattle shall cease,' a government agent reported in 1600, 'then will the rebellion end.' This certainly was Mountjoy's belief as he 'spoiled all the Farney' in Monaghan and 'wasted the Fuse' (the Fews of south Armagh) at the end of 1600.[98] Early in 1601 he felled the woods about the Moyry Pass to remove cover for the Irish, seized castles in Lecale and placed a garrison in Armagh. At the beginning of April Captain Edward Blaney and Captain Josias Bodley (brother of Sir Thomas, founder of the Bodleian Library) took one of Tyrone's greatest strongholds, the crannog fortress of Lough Lurcan. Moryson records that Bodley,

> carrying certain Fire-works provided in case the Boat should fail, went to the Fort, and joining with Captain *Blany*, marched towards that Island where they arrived by Eight of the Clock in the Morning, and leaving their Forces behind a Wood, they both went together to discover the Island, which done Captain *Bodley* made ready 30 Arrows with Wild-fire, and so they both fell down with 100 Shot close to the Water, where the Shot playing incessantly upon the Island, while the other delivered their Arrows, suddenly the Houses fired, and burnt so vehemently, as the Rebels lodging there, forsook the Island, and swam to the further Shoar.

Out of thirty on the crannog only four escaped alive and 'great Store of Butter, Corn, Meal, and Powder, was burned and spoiled in the Island, which all the Rebels of that Country made their Magazine'.[99]

Sir Arthur Chichester, using Carrickfergus as his base, had ravaged Clandeboye, kept the MacDonnells at bay, and crossed Lough Neagh to create havoc on the western shores. In May 1601 he reported to Mountjoy:

> We have killed, burnt, and spoiled all along the lough within four miles of Dungannon, from whence we returned hither yesterday; in which

journeys we have killed above one hundred people of all sorts, besides such as were burnt, how many I know not. We spare none of what quality or sex soever, and it hath bred much terror in the people . . . and Tyrone himself lay within a mile of this place, but kept himself safe.[100]

Mountjoy urged Docwra to 'burn all the Dwellings, and destroy the Corn on the ground, which might be done by encamping upon, and cutting it down with Swords' – a suggestion early implemented in the vicinity of Lough Erne. The lord deputy himself, Moryson records, 'destroyed the Rebels Corn about *Armagh* (whereof he found great Abundance) and would destroy the rest, this Course causing Famine, being the only sure Way to reduce or root out the Rebels'.[101] He recovered the Blackwater Fort and beat off an attack on Armagh by some three thousand of O'Neill's musketeers on the night of 4 August.

Four days later Mountjoy received letters from Cecil that the Spanish were approaching Ireland.

KINSALE

On 21 September 1601 a fleet of Spanish vessels entered the Bandon estuary without opposition and seized the port of Kinsale. The naval commander, Don Diego de Brochero y Añaya, was so eager to return to Spain with his vessels and mutinous crews, that he cast the supplies onto the tidal mud, destroying much of the biscuit. Don Juan del Águila, released from gaol (where he had been imprisoned for mistreating his soldiers) to command the expeditionary force, would have preferred to disembark in Tír Conaill, but had been overruled by de Oviedo. With only 3,500 men in a province recovered by the English, and with all their ships sent home, the Spaniards could do little else but appeal to O'Neill and O'Donnell to march south.[102]

A week later the Ulster lords were faced with an agonising decision – should they risk all to reach the Spaniards? If they stayed, the two Hughs could recover their position while Mountjoy marched south, but in the end O'Donnell persuaded the others to march to Munster. Mountjoy reached Kinsale before them with over 11,000 foot and 850 horse, camping before the walled town and ravaging the country in the vicinity to deprive the Spaniards of supplies. As the Four Masters record:

They allowed the garrison there neither quiet, rest, sleep, nor repose for a long time; and they gave each other violent conflicts and onsets.[103]

O'Donnell had set out from Ballymote on 2 November and gave Carew the slip by crossing a frozen defile over the Slieve Felim Mountains. O'Neill made Lough Ramor in Cavan his rallying point and moved out cautiously on 9 November, ravaging the Pale on the way south to weaken the lord deputy's supply lines. The Ulster Irish had covered over three hundred miles, wading river after river, often up to the chest, and drew up to Kinsale in good order, camping to the north and east of the English, severing Mountjoy's supply lines with Cork. As the English slightly outnumbered the combined forces of the Irish and the Spanish, O'Neill believed the best hope was to sit tight and starve the English into surrender. Indeed, the harsh weather and lack of provisions inflicted horrifying losses throughout December, as the lord deputy reported: 'In shorter time than is almost credible our new men were wholly wasted, and either by death, sickness, or running away those companies and supplies grown altogether unserviceable.'[104] 'And it was most true,' Moryson wrote, 'that our men daily died by dozens.' In a letter written to Cecil on Christmas Eve Carew confided: 'I assure your honour . . . that a more miserable siege hath not been seen, or so great a mortality without a plague.'[105]

The first hours of Christmas Eve 1601 were violently stormy, with lightning seen to strike some spears. The Irish army advanced in preparation for attack. Águila had made a desperate plea for help: 'I was confident your Excellencies would have come. I beseech you to do so, with as much speed, and as well furnished as you possibly may . . . I will give them their hands full from the town.'[106] Red Hugh implored O'Neill to attack, for he 'was oppressed at heart and ashamed to hear the complaint and distress of the Spaniards'. The lord deputy had not gone to bed that night and, according to Moryson, had been forewarned of the impending attack by Brian MacHugh Oge MacMahon of the Irish Army in return 'for a bottle of Usquebagh' – perhaps a propagandist invention. In any case, the English could see the Irish lighting their matches in the dark. Some of the Ulstermen lost their way and, as the Gaelic host hesitated to regroup, Mountjoy launched a furious cavalry charge on the Irish infantry, knocking them off balance and then scattering them.

For the first time in this war O'Neill exposed his troops in the open and with fatal consequences. In a couple of hours after dawn it was all over, and Águila's sally from the walls of Kinsale came too late. The Annals of the Four Masters recognised this rout as the passing of an era:

> Manifest was the displeasure of God, and misfortune to the Irish of fine Fodhla . . . Immense and countless was the loss in that place; for the prowess and valour, prosperity and affluence, nobleness and chivalry, dignity and renown, bravery and protection, devotion and pure religion, of the Island, were lost in this engagement.[107]

Kinsale was Gaelic Ireland's Culloden: all of O'Neill's previous triumphs were now wiped out at a stroke and, though the war continued for more than another year, the complete conquest of all Ireland was only a matter of time. The battle was even a greater disaster for Spain than the defeat of her Armada in 1588. With France paralysed by religious civil war, the European conflict was largely confined to the Lowlands. Kinsale tipped the balance in favour of England and the Netherlands, forcing Philip III to make terms by 1604. Before that could happen, the final subjugation of Ulster had to be executed.

ULSTER'S AGONY

The remnant of the Ulster army retreated north with O'Neill and Red Hugh sailed for Spain; the Tír Conaill chief was twice given an audience with Philip III but further aid was not forthcoming. O'Donnell fell ill at Simancas and died at the end of August 1602, being buried at Valladolid. O'Neill sued for terms but Elizabeth wrote to her lord deputy:

> We do require you very earnestly to be very wary in taking the Submissions of these Rebels . . . Next We do require you, even whilst the Iron is hot, so to strike, as this may not only prove a good Summer's Journey, but may deserve the Title of that Action which is the War's Conclusion. For furtherance whereof We have spared no Charge.[108]

In her own hand the queen wrote in the margin: 'We con you many Lauds for having so nearly approached the villainous Rebel, and see no Reason why so great Forces should not end his Days.'[109]

In 1602 Mountjoy did have a good summer's journey. He reached the Blackwater in June and built a new fort, named Charlemont from a combination of his Christian name and title, with a garrison under the command of Captain Toby Caulfield. Docwra extended his authority south to Ballyshannon, rounding up and killing those still in arms, including those who 'came into my hands alive, whome I caused the Souldiers to hewe in peeces with theire swordes',[110] and in July Donal O'Cahan, Tyrone's principal vassal, made submission. Summoned with Chichester to join Mountjoy, Docwra observed: 'The axe was nowe at the roote of the tree, & I may well say, the Necke of the Rebellion as good as utterlie broken.'[111] O'Neill, with only a few hundred men still by him, held out first in the fastness of Glenconkeyne and then in the woodlands of Fermanagh. The lord deputy entered the smoking ruins of Dungannon without resistance and destroyed the ancient coronation site of the O'Neills at Tullahogue:

> The Lord Deputy spent some five Days about *Tullagh Oge*, where the ô Neals were of old Custom created, and there he spoiled the Corn of all the

Country, and *Tyrone's* own Corn, and brake down the Chair wherein the ô Neals were wont to be created, being of Stone, planted in the open Field.[112]

Mountjoy concentrated on seizing cattle and destroying corn as harvest approached, and ordered Docwra and Chichester to do likewise, reporting to London that 'for all Events we have spoiled and mean to spoil their Corn'.[113] The inevitable consequence was a famine of great severity, as Moryson records:

Now because I have often made mention formerly of our destroying the Rebels Corn, and using all Means to famish them, let me by two or three Examples shew the miserable Estate to which the Rebels were thereby brought. *Sir Arthur Chichester, Sir Richard Moryson,* and the other Commanders . . . saw a most horrible Spectacle of three Children (whereof the eldest was not above ten Years old,) all eating and gnawing with their Teeth the Entrails of their Mother, upon whose Flesh they had fed 20 Days past, and having eaten all from the Feet upward to the bare Bones, roasting it continually by a slow Fire, were now come to the eating of her said Entrails in like sort roasted, yet not divided from the Body, being as yet raw.[114]

Captain Trevor, Moryson continues, found women in the Newry district lighting fires in the fields

and divers little children driving out the Cattle in the cold Mornings, and coming thither to warm them, were by them surprized, killed, and eaten, which at last was discovered by a great Girl breaking from them by Strength of her Body, and Captain *Trevor* sending out Soldiers to know the Truth, they found the Childrens Skulls and Bones, and apprehended the old Women, who were executed for the Fact.[115]

Moryson describes 'Carcasses scattered in many Places, all dead of Famine'; common people surviving on 'Hawks, Kites, and unsavory Birds of Prey'; Irish prisoners thrusting 'long Needles into the Horses of our *English* Troops, and they dying thereupon, to be ready to tear out one another's Throat for a Share of them'; and he concludes that 'no Spectacle was more frequent in the Ditches of Towns, and especially in wasted Countries, than to see Multitudes of these poor People dead with their Mouths all coloured green by eating Nettles, Docks, and all things they could rend up above Ground'.[116]

Mountjoy looked forward to the end of O'Neill, 'the most ungrateful Viper to us that raised him', but as the English closed in the queen cancelled her previous instructions to her lord deputy and instructed him to offer a pardon.[117] Tyrone eagerly accepted the offer of a safe-conduct taken to him by Sir Garret Moore, who took him to his estate of Mellifont Abbey in March 1603. The terms were more lenient than Tyrone could have dared to hope for: provided he renounced the title

The O'Neill, he retained his lordship over most of his traditional territory and this was formally recognised in English law as his personal possession; in addition O'Neill maintained his traditional authority over O'Cahan country. Mountjoy was eager for agreement, for he knew, and O'Neill did not, that Elizabeth had died six days earlier – the lord deputy could not be certain that James I would support him as the queen had done.

The peace agreed at Mellifont had a poor chance of surviving intact. Too many had died and too many nursed bitter memories of suffering, betrayal and loss. The Gaelic lords of Ulster, fearing treachery in any case, would not easily accept English government and law against which they had fought so hard. The conquest of Ireland had cost the Crown £2 million and many merchants were ruined by the disastrous debasement of the Irish currency. War veterans, adventurers, merchant contractors, and government officials, alarmed by the great debts left by the war, were dismayed to find that the lands of Ulster were not available for dismembering. English Churchmen and statesmen feared the survival of Catholic leaders who had strong ties with England's continental enemies. Great changes were certain to follow the Nine Years War but it took the collapse of Mountjoy's treaty with O'Neill to effect a transformation of Ulster in the reign of the Stuarts.

5

THE PLANTATION OF ULSTER
1603–1685

OVERVIEW

On 2 June 1603 Mountjoy left Ireland for the last time in company with Hugh O'Neill and Rory O'Donnell. In the pinnace *Tramontana* they narrowly missed shipwreck and on the road from Beaumaris, in north Wales, the Earl of Tyrone was pelted with stones and mud by women who had lost their menfolk in the Irish wars.[1] In London the Gaelic lords were well received by James I, and O'Donnell was created Earl of Tyrconnell. The generous royal pardon infuriated the servitors, those who had fought for the Crown in the long wars in Ulster; one of them observed:

> I have lived to see that damnable rebel Tyrone brought to England, honoured, and well liked . . . I adventured perils by sea and land, was near starving, ate horse flesh in Munster, and all to quell that man, who now smileth in peace at those who did hazard their lives to destroy him.[2]

Mountjoy, created Earl of Devonshire and made a privy councillor, persuaded the king to uphold the Treaty of Mellifont. Crown officers in Ireland, however, were appalled to see Tyrone hold sway over almost three counties. Appointed lord deputy in 1605, Sir Arthur Chichester wanted a greater share of the lands he had helped to conquer, setting a low value on his grant: 'I wyll gladly sell the whole landes for the wch others sell, five pounds in fee simple.'[3] Sir John Davies, who survived being disbarred for breaking a cudgel over a fellow lawyer's head to become Irish attorney-general in 1606, yearned to impose English law on 'the Irishry in the Province of Ulster . . . the most rude and unreformed part of Ireland, and the seat and nest of the last great rebellion'.[4] Together they set out to undermine the overweening power of the northern Gaelic lords. Their scheme was more successful than they dared to hope but even they were mystified at the sudden Flight of the Earls in the autumn of 1607.

Elizabethan conquest was therefore followed by Jacobean plantation, a colonising enterprise matching in scale and character the contemporary English migrations to the New World. Unlike native Americans, who were all but wiped out by disease and slaughter, the Ulster Irish survived; when the settlement faltered they wreaked vengeance on the planters in 1641. As Ireland was sucked into the vortex of the English Civil War, the province once more was reduced to destitution by protracted warfare. The calm following the Restoration encouraged a revival of colonial enterprise and showed how Ulster could prosper given a period of peace. Fear and resentment had been etched into the folk memory, however, reinforced by a further bout of political instability across the Irish Sea.

THE FLIGHT OF THE EARLS

Towards the end of August 1607 a Breton vessel steered into Lough Swilly and cast anchor off Rathmullan. Though it carried nets and a good supply of salt, the ship had not come to fish and at nightfall a messenger came ashore with gold and silver from the King of Spain.

Cuchonnacht Maguire, Lord of Fermanagh, had planned this enterprise for more than a year; a master of disguise and described by the Four Masters as a 'rapid-marching adventurous man, endowed with wisdom and beauty of person', he was certain the Gaelic lords would be beggared by the Crown.[5] A commission appointed in 1605 'for division and bounding of the lords' and gentlemen's livings' had partitioned the lordship of Fermanagh between two hundred freeholders, leaving Cuchonnacht with only half of the Maguire demesne lands.[6] The Earl of Tyrconnell eagerly awaited Cuchonnacht's messenger. His position had become desperate: Inishowen had been granted to Sir Cahir O'Doherty; the Crown commission ruled that neither the O'Boyles nor the MacSweenys need pay tribute to the earl; Niall Garbh O'Donnell had acquired the fertile lands about Lifford, described by Rory as 'the only jewel' of his earldom; and the Church lands had been taken over completely by George Montgomery, the new bishop of the united dioceses of Derry, Clogher and Raphoe.[7] Davies observed that the earl was 'very meanly followed' and with only mountainous infertile land to provide an income, Tyrconnell preferred the prospect of a military career in the service of Philip III.

O'Neill had no thought of flight; on the contrary he strengthened his direct control over sub-chieftains and tenants within his vast earldom. However, Chichester and Davies whittled away at Tyrone's authority – a task eased by Mountjoy's death in 1606 – to the extent that, in the lord deputy's words, 'now the law of England, and the Ministers thereof, were shackles and handlocks unto him, and the garrisons planted in his country were as pricks in his side'.[8] Bishop Montgomery not only

116

challenged O'Neill over the extent and control of Church lands but also encouraged Donal O'Cahan to deny Tyrone's traditional overlordship in his territory. Relations between the two chiefs were embittered when O'Cahan cast aside his wife, O'Neill's daughter, and eventually James I summoned both men to his court to hear a final judgement. O'Neill seemed confident of a decision in his favour.

O'Neill was in Meath helping the lord deputy in court sessions when a messenger arrived from Lough Swilly. This was an unexpected shock – if Tyrconnell and Maguire fled to Spain, might not he be accused of staying behind to rouse the country against the king? The French ambassador was not alone in thinking that O'Neill would be thrown in the Tower if he went to London. 'I know that they wish to kill him by poison or by any possible means', the Spanish ambassador wrote to Philip.[9]

With a heavy heart Tyrone decided he had no choice but to leave his native province. At Slane 'he took his leave of the Lord Deputy in a more sad and passionate manner than he used at other times' and returned in haste to Dungannon. According to Davies, over the Sperrins

> he travelled all night with his impediments, that is, his women and children; and it is likewise reported that the Countess, his wife, being exceedingly weary, slipped down from her horse, and weeping, said she could go no farther; whereupon the Earl drew his sword, and swore a great oath that he would kill her in the place, if she would not pass on with him, and put on a more cheerful countenance withal.[10]

At Rathmullan a child with six toes on one foot (considered very lucky) was sent for and they 'took the infant violently . . . which terrified the foster-father'. They crowded aboard the vessel, the cream of Ulster's aristocracy, but in the haste of leaving, many, including Tyrone's son Conn, were left behind. They later reported to Philip that at noon on Friday 4 September,

> leaving their horses on the shore with no one to hold their bridles, they went aboard a ship to the number of about one hundred persons, including soldiers, women and principal gentlemen.

As they passed the Mayo coast a pair of merlins alighted and these were fed and cared for. Contrary winds drove them to the Seine estuary; disembarking at Quillebeuf, they presented the hawks to the governor of Rouen and eventually got permission to go to Spanish Flanders. There followed barren years of exile, a stream of letters to Philip, and the gradual realisation that Spain would not help them recover their lands. When the Earl of Tyrone died in July 1616 in Rome, the Gaelic order in Ulster, which had flourished for a thousand years, was being swept away. The Annals of the Four Masters lamented:

Woe to the heart that meditated, woe to the mind that conceived, woe to the council that decided on, the project of their setting out on this voyage, without knowing whether they should ever return to their native principalities or patrimonies to the end of the world.[11]

THE REVOLT OF SIR CAHIR O'DOHERTY

'The undutiful departure of the Earls of Tirone, Tirconell, and McGwyre offers good occasion for a plantation,' an Irish Crown official observed to Robert Cecil, now Lord Salisbury.[12] Chichester quickly grasped the opportunity presented, though he knew of no plan to seize or poison O'Neill and thought 'it were strange that he should quit an Earldom, and so large and beneficial a territory for smoke and castles in the air'.[13] The lord deputy wrote to James I in September 1607:

> If His Majesty will, during their absence, assume the countries into his possession, divide the lands amongst the inhabitants . . . and will bestow the rest upon servitors and men of worth here, and withal bring in colonies of civil people of England and Scotland . . . the country will ever after be happily settled.

There was no time like the present, for 'the whole realm, and especially the fugitives countries, are more utterly depopulated and poor than ever before for many hundred years'.[14]

Inheriting an immense debt from Elizabeth's Irish wars, James found much to attract him in his lord deputy's proposal. However, England had been at peace with Spain since 1604 and to confiscate lands simply for leaving them, the king reflected, 'might blemish the reputation of that friendship which ought to be mutually observed between us and other princes'. Nevertheless James decided that the earls were 'baseborn contemptible creatures' and Davies had them 'attainted by outlawry' on the flimsy charge that when they gathered at Rathmullan they were levying war against the king.[15] In December 1607 lands of the departed lords were confiscated and preparations for a plantation began. Events the following spring were greatly to extend the scope of the project.

Sir Cahir O'Doherty of Inishowen had been foreman of the grand jury that had found a true bill for treason against the earls. O'Doherty quarrelled with Sir George Paulet, who had replaced Docwra as governor of Derry in 1607. Possessing none of his predecessor's diplomatic finesse, Paulet was contemptuous of the native Irish and punched O'Doherty in the face. O'Doherty, the Four Masters record, 'would rather have suffered death than live to brook such insult and dishonour'. He invited Captain Henry Hart, governor of Culmore Fort, and his wife to dinner at his new castle at Burt; there he 'seized' them, threatening 'that if she or he did not take some present course for the delivery of Culmore into his hands, both they and their children should die'. Culmore fell by this ruse and the following night, 19 April 1608, O'Doherty attacked Derry with about seventy men. As the watchmen were asleep, Sir Cahir took the lower fort without a fight, but his ally, Phelim Reagh MacDavitt, encountered resistance in the higher fort after he shot Paulet dead. John Baker, a surviving defender, recalled

> Lieutenant Gordon, lying within his chamber within the higher fort, and hearing the shot, issued forth naked upon the rampier toward the court of guard, with his rapier and dagger, where, with one soldier in his company, he set upon the enemy and killed two of them, using most comfortable words of courage to the soldiers to stand to it and fight for their lives; but the enemy being far more in number, one struck him on the forehead with a stone, whereat, being somewhat amazed, they rushed upon him and killed him and the soldiers also.

As dawn broke the surviving townspeople barricaded themselves in the Bishop's House and adjacent dwellings but, Baker records,

> destitute of victuals and munition, and seeing a piece brought by the enemy from Culmore, and ready mounted to batter the said houses, and being out of all hope of relief at that time and wearied with the lamentable outcry of women and children, after much parley and messages to and fro, yielded the said houses.[16]

The bishop's wife, Susan Montgomery, was held prisoner for a time and her husband's library of three hundred books was destroyed as Derry was set aflame. Strabane was burned soon after and the revolt threatened to spread across Ulster as factions of the O'Cahans and O'Hanlons came out in rebellion and O'Doherty invaded mid-Ulster. From Coleraine Sir Thomas Phillips wrote a frantic appeal for help, concluding with the words 'haist haist haist'. Sir Richard Wingfield, the marshal, counterattacked and recovered the burnt shell of Derry; and on 5 July Sir Cahir was killed at the Rock of Doon, near Kilmacrennan. Meanwhile, Chichester put down the O'Hanlons, hanging many he captured, and moved from Mountnorris to Dungannon, executing dozens more by hanging, 'a death which they contemn more, he thinks, than any other nation living; they are generally so stupid by nature, or so tough or disposed by their priests, that they show no remorse of conscience, or fear of death'. The last O'Cahan rebels were pursued into the woods of Glenconkeyne, where, Chichester reported, 'the wild inhabitants wondered as much to see the King's Deputy, as the ghosts in Virgil wondered to see Aeneas alive in Hell'.[17]

Notwithstanding Sir Cahir's death, the revolt continued. Sir Oliver Lambert besieged Doe Castle, 'the strongest hold in all the province

119

which endured 100 blows of the demi-cannon before it yielded'.[18] Shane MacManus Óg O'Donnell retreated to the islands, pursued by Sir Henry Folliot, governor of Ballyshannon, with a hundred men and five vessels. The chase extended from Aranmore north to Inishbofin and Tory, Shane and his followers escaping at night in their currachs, 'which are boats they may make of hides'.[19] In these wild exposed waters the first English attempts to land on Tory failed, 'the weather growing foul and the night drawing on'. Finally Folliot took the island castle by treachery, cutting down the warders after promising them their lives; the governor explained the escape of Shane MacManus himself as due to 'the continual foul weather and contrary winds'.[20] The rebellion concluded when Marshal Wingfield crossed the mountains to Glenveagh, where the O'Gallaghers, the O'Donnell fosterers, made a last but futile stand in their island castle. The English were getting to know the province they had conquered from end to end, parts of which Chichester admitted had been only recently as inaccessible as 'the kingdom of China'. The highlands from Errigal to Muckish and Glenveagh repelled the lord deputy, being 'one of the most barren, uncouth, and desolate countries that could be seen, fit only to confine rebels and ill spirits into'.[21] This distaste, however, did not prevent Chichester from seeking and obtaining a grant of O'Doherty's lordship of Inishowen for himself almost immediately afterwards.

Sir John Davies was already planning ahead while the campaigns still raged in Donegal. From the army camp near Coleraine on 5 August the attorney-general wrote to the king that he had six counties 'now in demesne and actual possession in this province; which is a greater extent of land than any prince in Europe has to dispose of'. He urged James to colonise the whole area thoroughly, for the enterprise would be jeopardised 'if the number of civil persons who are to be planted do not exceed the number of the natives, who will quickly overgrow them as weeds overgrow the good corn'.[22]

The king was more than ready to agree to a full-scale plantation, for his enthusiasm had already been kindled by the success of pioneering settlements in Antrim and Down.

'CIVILIZINGE OF THOSE RUDE PARTES': ANTRIM AND DOWN

At the close of the Nine Years War Conn Mac Néill O'Neill, Lord of Upper Clandeboye and the Great Ards, had languished in a Carrickfergus dungeon, convicted of levying war against Elizabeth. Not long afterwards Hugh Montgomery, 6th Laird of Braidstane, came to his aid, sending his agent from Ayr to win the heart of the gaoler's daughter. The agent 'ply'd his oar so well that in a few nights he had certain proofs of the bride's cordial love'. She opened the cell and Conn lowered himself down the rope to a waiting boat to be taken to Largs and freedom. According to another account of the escape, Conn's wife assisted by smuggling in rope in two big cheeses, 'the meat being neatly taken out, and filled with cords, well packed in, and the holes handsomely made up again'. In Scotland Conn readily agreed to divide his estate with Montgomery if a pardon could be got from the king.[23]

In London the Reverend George Montgomery, Hugh's brother, obtained the royal pardon but only on condition that James Hamilton was given a third share of the O'Neill lordship. Hamilton and the Montgomery brothers had long served James as his secret agents in what were now his three kingdoms; all three Scots were to reap rich rewards in Ulster for their service. It was they who began the plantation of Protestant British settlers in Ulster. With the king's approval the triple division was made at the end of April 1605; Conn O'Neill got half of Upper Clandeboye centred on Castlereagh, while Hugh Montgomery and James Hamilton shared the rest of the estates between them. Hamilton, a Glasgow schoolmaster who had become bursar of Trinity College in Dublin, acquired further vast territories (partly by buying up a grant made to a London merchant) in Antrim and Down. Hamilton silenced the outraged Chichester by giving him Massereene and pacified Hugh Montgomery, if only for a time, by selling him Newtownards, Movilla, Greyabbey and adjacent lands for £106 5s.0d. George Montgomery, meanwhile, enjoyed rapid promotion from a Somerset parish to become dean of Norwich and then bishop of the combined sees of Derry, Clogher and Raphoe.

Conn O'Neill was perhaps fortunate to emerge from these tortuous dealings with an estate of sixty townlands – after all, he was only one of several claimants to Upper Clandeboye. In the dramatically changed political climate, other Gaelic lords in Antrim and Down made room for servitors and colonisers in return for a secure title in English law to their lands.[24] Chichester believed it foolhardy to try to dispossess all the Irish and advised James to allow newcomers and natives to live side by side. Sir Shane MacBrian O'Neill – who gave his name to the castle at Edenduffcarrick on the north shore of Lough Neagh – had more land than Chichester in Lower Clandeboye, and his neighbours, the O'Haras and MacQuillans, got substantial land grants. Phelim MacCartan got Kinelearty in south Down on condition that he passed 'the thirde part of all that his countrie' to the servitor Sir Edmund Cromwell.[25] Brian Óg Magennis held Kilwarlin and Sir Arthur Magennis secured his title to 120 townlands in Iveagh. Almost all of these estates were fertile farmland and only the most substantial Gaelic lord in the region, Sir Randal MacDonnell, owned large tracts of mountain and bog.[26] Chichester begrudged Sir Randal his three hundred thousand acres in the Route and the Antrim Glens and declared that 'a more cancred and malicious person' could not be found.[27] Though the MacDonnell chief had fought with Tyrone at Kinsale, James remembered his help in crushing the MacDonnells of Dunyveg. Sir Randal for his part pleased the king by inviting Lowland Scots to settle in the Route; James firmly reminded his lord deputy that MacDonnell 'allwaies both by his dutifull behaviour to our state and the example of his civill orderly life indevored very much of the Reformation and civilizinge of those rude partes of the countrie wheare he dwells'.[28] Sir Randal was created 1st Earl of Antrim in 1620.

'The whole region of the county Antrim', a patent of 1604 began, was 'wasted by rebellion' and James Hamilton's lands in Down were described as 'depopulated and wasted'.[29] When Hugh Montgomery and Conn O'Neill returned from raising 'recruits of money' in Scotland to their estates in Down in 1606, they found

> those parishes were now more wasted than America (when the Spaniards landed there) . . . 30 cabins could not be found, nor any stone walls, but ruined roofless churches, and a few vaults at Grey Abbey, and a stump of an old castle in Newtown, in each of which some Gentlemen sheltered themselves at their first coming over.
>
> But Sir Hugh in the said spring brought with him divers artificers, as smiths, masons, carpenters, &c . . . They soon made cottages and booths for themselves, because sods and saplins of ashes, alders, and birch trees (above 30 years old) with rushes for thatch, and bushes for wattles, were at hand. And also they made a shelter of the said stump of the castle for Sir Hugh, whose residence was mostly there.[30]

Timber was hewn and drawn by Irish labourers from the woods, some felled in Slut Neal by the River Lagan and floated downstream to Belfast, to be taken from there by sea to Donaghadee and Newtownards. Sir Hugh built a harbour at Donaghadee, only three hours' sailing from Portpatrick in a fair wind. Here arrived 'a constant flux of passengers coming daily over', ignoring 'evil report of wolves and woodkerns'. Manured with sea wrack, the soil was ploughed to give bountiful harvests in 1606 and 1607; and Lady Montgomery had a watermill put up in every parish to grind the corn. Poor men from Scotland, each arriving with a cow and a few sheep, were let grazing land and some were persuaded to make cloth. After only two years, according to the Montgomery manuscripts, the colony was flourishing:

Now every body minded their trades, and the plough, and the spade, building and setting fruit trees, &c, in orchards and gardens, and by ditching in their grounds. The old women spun, and the young girls plyed their nimble fingers at knitting – and every body was innocently busy. Now the Golden peaceable age renewed, no strife, contention, querulous lawyers, or Scottish or Irish feuds, between clanns and families, and sirnames, disturbing the tranquillity of those times; and the towns and temples were erected, with other great works done (even in troublesome years).[31]

This is a highly romantic picture, but the success of the Scottish settlement in north Down could not be denied.

The plantation commissioners in 1611 reported that 'Sir Hughe Montgomery knight hath repayred parte of the Abbey of Neowtowne for his owne dwellinge, and made a good towne of a hundred houses or thereaboutes all peopled with Scottes.' Later a school was founded in Newtownards, the principal master paid £20 a year 'to teach Latin, Greek and Logycks, allowing the scholars a green for recreation at goff, football, and archery'. Sir James Hamilton's colony is not so well documented as Montgomery's but it clearly was at least as successful. The plantation commissioners reported:

Sir James Hamylton knight hath buylded a fayre stone house at the Towne of Bangor in the Upper Clandeboye . . . The Towne consistes of 80 neowe houses all inhabited with Scotishmen and Englishmen. And hath brought out of England 20 artifficers, who are makinge materialles of tymber, bricke and stone for another house there.

The said Sir James Hamylton is preparinge to buyld another house in Hollywoode three mylles from Bangor and two hundred thousand of brickes with other materialles ready at the place, where there are some 20 houses inhabited with English and Scottes.

As the man with chief responsibility for directing the plantation of Ulster, Chichester was eager to set a good example to others on his own grant of lands in and around Belfast. He was assisted by several army officers who had fought with him in the recent Irish wars and now rented land from him on favourable terms. Foremost of these was Moses Hill, a former lieutenant of Chichester's horse troop and now provost marshal; where Shaw's Bridge today crosses the Lagan he had erected 'a stronge Forte buylte upon a passadge on the playnes of Moylon with a stronge palisado and a drawbridge', and further downstream he had built a fortified house 'where the sea ebbes and flowes in a place called Strondmellis'. At Belfast the commissioners found 'many masons, bricklayers and other laborers a worke' erecting a large brick castle which 'will defend the passage over the foorde at Bealefast between the Upper and Lower Clandeboye, and likewise the bridge over the Ryver of Owynvarra [the Blackstaff], between Malon and Bealfast'. They continued:

> The Towne of Bealfast is plotted out in a good forme, wherein are many famelyes of English Scotish and some Manksmen already inhabitinge of which some are artificers who have buylte good tymber houses with chimneyes after the fashion of the English palle, and one Inn with very good lodginges which is a great comforte to the Travellers in those partes.

All along the road to Carrickfergus the colony flourished, with English cagework and stone houses either completed or being built, and in the town itself '4 oxeteemes, 2 horseteems and many garrons and carres drawinge of stones and of other Materialles' and 'we founde 4 lyme kills on fyre employed in burninge of lymestone' brought from Whitehead.[32] Other busy settlers included John Dobbs, Ensign John Dalway, Captain Hugh Clotworthy at Massereene, Captain Roger Langford at Muckamore, Sir Thomas Phillips at Toome, and Sir Fulke Conway in Killultagh. Several of these men had hope of acquiring more land west of the River Bann as the plantation of Ulster got under way.

THE PRINTED BOOK: THE PLANTATION OF ULSTER BEGINS

'You have not gone unregarded of the best', Chichester wrote in 1608 to Sir Niall Garbh O'Donnell. 'You may expect recompense.'[33] Sir Niall, however, was accused of delaying twenty-four hours before informing Dublin of O'Doherty's revolt and he and his son were arrested. Donal O'Cahan, protesting his loyalty, was seized also and all three were committed to the Tower of London, where they died in their cells, accused but not convicted of treason.[34] That only some had been disloyal was not to prevent the almost complete confiscation of territory of the lords of Ulster west of the Bann: the summer assizes of 1608 judged that almost all of Tyrconnell, Coleraine, Tyrone, Armagh, Fermanagh and Cavan were in the king's hands. The so-called 'native plantation' of Monaghan in 1593 was allowed to stand and the lord deputy's grant of Inishowen was confirmed.

James I could not turn down this unique opportunity to reward at little cost the many who had claims on his patronage. Besides, a plantation would quieten Ulster and free the province from the risk of further native rebellion and foreign invasion. The project would be, the king observed to Chichester, a civilising enterprise which would 'establish the true religion of Christ among men . . . almost lost in superstition'. This was the era of colonial expansion when England sought to catch up with Spain, Portugal and Holland; just a few months before the Flight of the Earls the first successful band of English settlers had embarked for

Virginia. As for Chichester, he declared that he would rather 'labour with his hands in the plantation of Ulster than dance or play in that of Virginia'.[35]

Attorney-General Sir John Davies and Chief Justice Sir James Ley travelled to London in the autumn of 1608 with a recommended scheme to which Chichester added his 'Notes of Remembrance' – he feared that Davies would encourage the king to disregard the claims of the loyal natives. When a comprehensive plan was published in January 1609, the lord deputy's fears seemed confirmed; Chichester persuaded the Government to allow him to head a more detailed survey of the confiscated lands. Though maps were produced, this was an inquiry rather than a survey of measurement and much confusion arose from different Irish divisions: ballybetaghs subdivided into townland units, known as tates in Fermanagh, polls in Cavan and ballyboes elsewhere. The work was finished in September 1609, Chichester rounding up nearly a thousand Ulster 'swordsmen' from the woods for forcible export to Sweden's army, remarking that these were 'but an unprofitable burden of the earth, cruel, wild, malefactors, thieves'.[36]

The 'Printed Book' of conditions for successful applicants for Ulster land was published in London in April 1610. Separation was the essence of the scheme, in which the largest group of colonists, known as undertakers, had to clear their estates completely of native Irish inhabitants. The confiscated land of each county was divided into baronies or 'precincts', and each precinct subdivided into large, middle and small estates or 'proportions', with a rent-free allowance of woodland and bog. Undertakers had to be English or Scots who had taken the Oath of Supremacy – that is, Protestants – and who were to pay rent of £5 6s.8d. to the king for every thousand acres. Servitors and favoured native Irish (who did not have to take the oath) were to have their estates in the same precincts, the theory being that ex-officers would be in a good position to keep a watchful eye on discontented or rebellious Irish. Undertakers had to undertake to plant twenty-four Protestant English or 'inland' Scots from at least ten families on every thousand acres, while servitors were not required to plant (if they did not plant they paid £8 per thousand acres, and £5 6s.8d. if they did). Those Irish granted proportions were to adopt English farming methods and pay £10 13s. 4d. per thousand acres. All classes of planters had obligations to build stone houses and defensive works, graded according to whether they had three thousand, or two thousand, or one thousand acres in their proportions. Deadlines were set for arriving, colonising, building and rent payment, and conditions were laid down for building towns, bringing in craftsmen, founding schools and erecting parish churches.[37]

Some native Irish were exempt from the plantation, the most prominent being Conor Roe Maguire in east Fermanagh, Sir Turlough MacHenry O'Neill of the Fews and, in Armagh and Tyrone, the heirs of Sir Henry Óg O'Neill, who had been killed in the campaign to suppress O'Doherty's revolt. The lord deputy was filled with a deep sense of foreboding; on reading the Printed Book he saw that the attorney-general's counsels had prevailed. The undertakers, numbering around one hundred, had more than one quarter of the confiscated territory; Chichester doubted if they had the resources to carry out their obligations. The most experienced English and Scots – the servitors – had not been given enough; numbering about fifty, they got around one fifth of the land, not sufficient to carry out the defensive role expected of them. The 'deserving' Irish favoured with grants were left in possession of between one quarter and one fifth of the confiscated lands and some had these estates only during their lifetimes. Ruthless commander though he had been, Chichester believed the Ulster Irish were harshly treated. His attempts to win the confidence of selected chieftains had come to nothing and his dream of creating a large class of anglicised and contented Irish landholders had now to be abandoned. Twenty years would pass before the lord deputy's anxieties would be shown to be justified. Eochaid O'Hussey, the most renowned bard in Fermanagh, did get a small estate but he mourned the condition of his country, Innisfail, the Island of Fate:

Now is Innisfail taken at disadvantage,
Nurse of the sons of Milesius of Spain;
Her strength is reft, she is caught unrewarded;
Denizens of all strange countries flock to her.

No friend falls now for her sake,
For her no fight is procured;
Woe is me for the light in which she is today.
No utterance is heard from her.[38]

'FROM SCOTLAND CAME MANY, AND FROM ENGLAND NOT A FEW . . .'

Thomas Blenerhasset, arriving from Norfolk during the summer of 1610 to take possession of his grant in Fermanagh, wrote a pamphlet before the end of the year exhorting his fellow Englishmen to join him:

Fayre England, thy flourishing sister, brave Hibernia; (with most respective termes) commendeth unto thy due consideration her yongest daughter, depopulated Ulster . . . Dispoyled, she presents her-selfe (as it were) in a ragged sad sabled robe, ragged (indeed) there remayneth nothing but ruynes and desolation, with a very little showe of any humanitie: of her selfe she aboundeth with many the best blessings of God . . . Fayre

126

England, she hath more people than she can well sustaine: goodly Ulster for want of people unmanured, her pleasant fieldes and riche groundes, they remaine if not desolate, worsse . . .[39]

That England was overpopulated was widely held; in 1619 another English writer urged the transport to Ulster 'of the superfluous multitudes of poor people which overspill the realm of England to the weal of both kingdoms'.[40] Underpopulated and underdeveloped Ulster offered prospective colonists a secure title to cheap land, bountiful fisheries and great tracts of valuable woodland. Apart from Iceland, England and Scotland were the first countries in Europe to have their forests seriously depleted; in 1633 the Scot William Lithgow wrote:

Ah! what makes now, my Countrey looke so bare?
Thus voyd of planting, Woods and Forests fayre.[41]

Stands of sessile oak, ash, elm, willow and alder in Glenconkeyne, Lough Erne, Killetra, Killultagh and the Dufferin offered a quick return on investment when converted into barrel staves, ship timber, rafters and charcoal for iron smelting.

The great migration to Ulster began, drawn from every class of British society: servitors who had long sought a share in the province they conquered; younger sons of gentlemen – such as Chichester himself and his neighbours, Fulke Conway and Sir Faithful Fortescue – eager for lands to call their own; Scottish nobles like the Earl of Abercorn and Lord Ochiltree, induced to plant Tyrone 'for a countenance and strength to the rest';[42] relatives, neighbours, artisans and dependants of undertakers; rack-rented and evicted Lowland Scots farmers; and horse thieves and other fugitives from justice. The English had more capital but the Scots were the most determined planters, as Sir William Alexander observed:

Scotland by reason of her populousnesse being constrained to disburden her selfe (like the painfull Bees) did every yeere send forth swarmes.[43]

Most came from south-west Scotland, Lanark, Renfrew and Sterlingshire: here land was hard to come by and lairds evicted tenants unable to make the down payments required under the 'feuing' land-letting system. Some came from the Borders: here in the 'middle shires' the Earl of Dunbar's joint commission of English and Scots harried the cattle reavers and enforced the king's law by the gallows – the Johnston family alone faced seventy-seven charges of slaughter in 1609. Those who had lived by plunder now had no work, the king being assured that in every Border parish there was 'ane grit number fund of ydle people without any calling, industrie, or lauthfull means to leif by'.[44] Later in the century the Reverend Andrew Stewart of Donaghadee claimed that from Scotland came many, and from England not a few, yet all of them generally the scum of both nations, who, for debt or breaking and fleeing from justice, or seeking shelter, came thither.[45]

There was some truth in this, the king remarking in 1615 that 'it almost became ane ordinerie trade to transport goods into Ireland stollen in the middle shires'. In 1622 the Irish Council ordered the imprisonment of vagrant and criminal Scots 'pestring and disturbing the Northern plantations of this kingdome', but most men from the Borders headed straight for the remotest settlements to escape arrest, and their surnames – Johnston, Armstrong, Elliott and Beattie, in that order – dominated the muster rolls of Co. Fermanagh.[46]

'Make speede, get thee to Ulster, serve God, be sober', Blenerhasset urged his readers, but even he was aware that all was not well. Everywhere the native Irish were waiting to be moved or dispossessed and in the forests lurked the woodkerne, landless men and former soldiers of O'Neill, who threatened the settlements. At Charlemont Sir Toby Caulfield was forced 'every night to lay up all his cattle as it were in warde, and doe hee and his what they can, the woolfe and the woodkerne (within caliver shot of his forte) have often times a share'.[47] And all this time rumours of O'Neill's return with Spanish help caused anxiety both in Ulster and in London. James I feared that not enough men of wealth had applied for land in Ulster; to strengthen the plantation, therefore, he turned to the City of London.

THE LONDONDERRY PLANTATION

In April 1609 Sir Thomas Phillips travelled to London to propose that the City merchants should plant the county of Coleraine, 'conceiving the Londoners to be the ablest body to undergo so brave and great a work as the plantation of that country'.[48] Phillips, an experienced servitor known to be 'a very discreete & vallient comander at all tymes',[49] had energetically developed his grant of abbey lands in Coleraine and his lease of Toome; others, however, had not imitated his enterprise and he was sure his colony was dangerously exposed to the Irish. King James and his principal advisor, Lord Salisbury, were delighted with the proposal – few undertakers had been attracted to this part of Ulster, inhabited by resentful O'Cahans in the lowlands and woodkerne in the forests.

The response of a special court of aldermen on 1 July 1609 was less than enthusiastic, the Fishmongers concluding that 'it were best never to entermeddle at al in this busyness . . . for that it is thought it wil be exceeding chargeable'.[50] Nevertheless, a deputation was sent to tour the county in the autumn and, impressed by valuable woodland there, recommended plantation. The Livery Companies, descended from the medieval guilds, could afford to dictate terms to the king: the City had underwritten much of the cost of conquering Ulster and was the most reliable source of ready money for the Government. Fretting at the slow progress of his Ulster enterprise, James granted to the London Companies not only all of Co. Coleraine but also the barony of Loughinsholin, detached from Tyrone, together with Culmore and the towns of Coleraine and Derry. Derry acquired 12,615 acres adjoining from Tyrconnell, which was renamed Co. Donegal. Coleraine was given nearly eighteen thousand acres detached from Co. Antrim, both Sir Randal MacDonnell and Phillips being paid compensation.[51] By an agreement made in January 1610 the supervision of this huge area – thought to be forty thousand acres but in reality more than half a million acres – was placed in the hands of 'The Society of the Governor and Assistants, London, of the New Plantation in Ulster, within the Realm of Ireland', better known as The Honourable The Irish Society.[52] The enterprise to colonise this vast region, named Co. Londonderry, had much in common with other joint-stock ventures in London, such as the Virginia Company and the East India Company; unlike those schemes, however, this plantation yielded only endless expense and conflict with the monarchy.

An immediate start was made by sending two agents, John Rowley and Tristram Beresford, to Ulster along with 130 masons, carpenters and other workmen supervised by Rowley's brother-in-law, William Gage. These men turned out to be unscrupulous asset-strippers, who lined their own pockets and plundered the woods of Loughinsholin, exporting tens of thousands of pipe staves 'contrary to o[r] order and o[r] Articles of Agreement, w[ch] is very displeasing to us'.[53] The workmen, paid three months in arrears, became demoralised and drunken; the progress in building houses and walls at Coleraine and Derry was compared unfavourably with Captain Edward Doddington's reconstruction of O'Cahan's castle at Dungiven and Sir Thomas Phillips's new settlement at Limavady.[54] Most progress was made at Coleraine, which was surrounded by a 'rampier', a massive clay and sod wall. In his survey of 1611, Lord Carew found nearly a hundred men in Loughinsholin squaring timber and making poles, laths, prefabricated sections of ships and partly finished frames for houses; fifty men with oxen drew this wood to the Bann, where it was taken by barge downstream to the Salmon Leap and from there to Coleraine and Derry.[55] Sent out by the Irish Society in the autumn of 1613, Alderman George Smithes and Matthias Springham stamped on corruption and inefficiency, and 'trod out' the ground for the walls of Derry, arranging piecework rates with the masons who were to build them. On their return to London and the submission of their report, a letter of dismissal was sent out to Rowley.[56]

On 17 December 1613 at a court of Common Council, with great pomp and ceremony, a draw was held for the twelve proportions of the Londonderry plantation. Captain Doddington and Thomas Raven, the surveyor of the City of London, had been hired to survey and divide the grant into sections, which were supposed to vary in size according to the value of the land. The fifty-five London Companies, regularly levied for contributions to the enterprise, arranged themselves into twelve associations, the Goldsmiths, for example, joining with the Cordwainers, Paint-stainers and Armourers.[57] By the luck of the draw, taken by the City swordbearer, the Grocers, the Fishmongers and the Goldsmiths got fertile proportions, while the Drapers and the Skinners were left with land that was poorer and more inaccessible.

In 1614 Sir Josias Bodley, director-general of fortifications in Ireland, surveyed the London lands for the king. He was appalled by the lack of progress:

> Haveing taken an exact survey of y[e] workes and plantacon performed by the Cittie of London, I cannot find that either in the one or other they ever intended his Ma[ties] satisfacc'on and regarded the true end and drifte of his favourable graunte soe that whatsoever they talke of great masses of wealth by them expended, nameing what sommes they please, yett of anie reall plantacon or fortificacon to y[e] purpose (y[e] onlie meanes of setting and secureing these partes which they have undertaken) they have little or nothing to say.[58]

In particular the native Irish were still in the proportions. When James read the report he was furious: the clearing of natives was 'the fundamental reason' for the plantation. According to Rowley, who had bounced back as the Drapers' agent, royal anger 'stirred upp' the 'companies to be planting & buildinge'.

Meanwhile Sir Toby Caulfield reported that a Franciscan friar had preached a seditious sermon to over one thousand Irish and fourteen priests in the woods of Loughinsholin, urging them 'to stand on their keeping and go into plain rebellion'.[59] In 1615 a conspiracy of O'Cahans, O'Neills and O'Mullans was scotched and the confiscations that followed further reduced the lands in Londonderry that had been assigned to the natives. Erratic government policies thereafter did nothing to appease the resentment of the Gaelic Irish in the north which threatened the very survival of the Ulster plantation.

John Rowley, the mayor of Derry, informed the Drapers' Company in 1615 that his men were building Moneymore 'as it were wth the Sworde in one hande and the Axe in thother'.[60] The following year the Ironmongers' agent, George Canning, reported to London that his labourers were 'fearful to work in the wooddes except they be 10 or 12 in a companie'. Again and again woodkerne emerged from their forest and mountain retreats to plunder and harry the settlers, despite Chichester's drive to 'take up the lewd Kerns or such as have bin Rebells or are idle Livers' and ship them for military service in Sweden.[61]

It was in vain that James raged against the undertakers for failing to remove the natives from their proportions; the Gaelic Irish were too useful to the colonists as labourers and as tenants prepared to pay high rent to avoid eviction. The failure to attempt a measured survey of the confiscated lands resulted in proportions vastly greater in acreage than that stated in the grants. Planters could not find cash to colonise such extensive lands and so most natives stayed on. In despair the king, in September 1619, announced the forfeit of undertakers' estates for breaking the conditions laid down in the Printed Book; however, the planters could have their lands back if they paid double rents and fines. The colonists willingly paid up and so the grand plan to separate natives and newcomers had come to nothing.

The Gaelic Irish in the north had, in most cases, simply changed their landlords, but that did not mean they were content. With no security of tenure, their burdensome rents set by informal arrangements from year to year, and their status severely reduced, the natives yearned for a return of the old order. The change was felt most acutely by the former Gaelic élite, especially those not classed as 'deserving'. Fear Flatha Ó Gnímh, the Antrim poet, regretted that he had not been taught a practical trade:

Alas that the fosterer in lore did not teach the breaking of steeds
or the steering of ships, or the yoking of ploughs behind oxen,
to the men who compose lays.
Woe to the scholar who knows not some craft that would be
no cause to censure, that he might join timbers, or shape a vat,
ere he attained the service of learning.
The honour of poesy is departed;
The credit of guardianship is gone,
So that the school of Ireland's land were better
As husbandmen of the ploughland.[62]

These Gaelic Irish were confronted by alien planters adhering to a variety of Protestantism far distant from their own Catholicism. The

Puritan beliefs of the colonists were held not only by the Calvinist Presbyterians but also by the leading Churchmen of the Established Church in Ulster. Measures taken against the Catholic Church were sporadic and often ineffective. In September 1632, for example, Saint Patrick's Purgatory in Lough Derg was ordered to be destroyed and its community dispersed, but such action was merely irritating and the Church rapidly reorganised itself in these years. The Franciscans increased their numbers threefold in Ireland between 1623 and 1639 and reoccupied many of the Ulster friaries.[63] Together with priests returning from seminaries on the European mainland, they instilled a new zeal amongst Old English and native Irish Catholics alike: in Ulster, therefore, the uncompromising spirit of the Counter-Reformation faced the inflexible determination of the Puritan settlers. Hostility, suspicion and uncertainty created a dangerously unstable atmosphere of fear in the province.

On the lonely settlements by the Sperrins or Glenveagh the baying of a wolf at the moon must have sent a chill down the spine of many a colonist who had never heard the sound before. The fear of woodkerne lurking in the thickets was better founded. The greatest threat, however, was the smouldering resentment of the native Irish who worked and farmed with the settlers. In 1628 Sir Thomas Phillips warned the Government that 'it is fered that they will Rise upon a Sudden and Cutt the Throts of the poore dispersed Brittish'.[64] In the parish of Donegore in Antrim a Presbyterian preacher had a vision on his deathbed: ' "The dead bodies of many thousands, who this day despise the glorious gospel, shall lie upon the earth as dung unburied." And whilst one said "Is there no remedy?" he cried thrice, "No remedy, no remedy, no remedy!" '[65] That was in 1634; the blundering policies of Charles I seemed almost to be willing the prophecy to come true.

WENTWORTH, LESLIE AND THE BLACK OATH

Charles I, who succeeded to the throne in 1625, did not share his father's enthusiasm for the Ulster plantation and no further surveys were authorised. Instead the king sought to increase his personal power and for this he needed money which did not have to be sanctioned by parliament. In the summer of 1633 Thomas Wentworth was sent to Ireland as the king's trusted lord deputy to raise funds for the royal coffers and to enforce High Church conformity on the Protestants.

Imperious and indefatigable, Wentworth soon alienated every interest group in the country. A Commission for Defective Titles sent ripples of alarm through the landed classes: natives, Old English and planters alike paid heavy fines to retain their estates. For failing to evict the Irish from their lands the London Companies and the Irish Society were hounded until the Court of Star Chamber condemned them to pay a fine of £70,000 and surrender their grant in 1635; the fine was reduced on appeal. The only objective was to raise cash; the royal commission managing the Londoners' proportions simply rack-rented the tenants great and small. Then Wentworth turned on the Presbyterians of the north.

Henry Leslie, the newly appointed bishop of Down, made a special visitation to his diocese in the summer of 1636, and summoned his clergy to a meeting in Belfast on 10 August. He chose as his text Matthew 18:17, 'but if he neglect to hear the church, let him be unto thee as an heathen man and a publican'. Then he vilified those ministers who had succumbed to Presbyterianism:

> They think by their puff of preaching to blowe downe the goodly orders of our church, as the walls of Jericho were beaten downe with sheepes hornes. Good God! is not this the sinne of Uzziah, who intruded himselfe into the office of priesthood? . . . They have cryed downe the most wholesome orders of the church as popish superstitions.[66]

A lively disputation followed until it was silenced by the bishop of Derry, John Bramhall; the following day those clergy who refused to recant were deprived of their offices. The excommunicated ministers sailed off in the *Eagle Wing* with about 140 followers to make a new start in America but they were forced back by storms. Many took refuge in Scotland, to be joined by others as the persecution continued.

Nowhere had plantation been more successful than in Antrim and Down: the towns of Belfast, Carrickfergus, Bangor and Newry became flourishing commercial centres; the barony of Lecale twice in the 1620s exported the greatest volume of oats from Ireland; and round one third of all cattle sent abroad came from eastern Ulster. Decline set in, however, in the 1630s. In part this was due to a succession of harvest failures but it was seriously aggravated by Wentworth's determination to stamp out Protestant nonconformity.[67]

In Scotland Puritan opposition to Charles I was coming to a head. There opposition to the new Prayer Book was led by Robert Blair, former minister of Bangor, and John Livingstone, former minister of Killinchy – both had been excommunicated by Bishop Leslie and both played their part in rallying support for the Covenant, a bond of union among the king's Scottish opponents.[68]

Many Scots in Ulster needed no encouragement to sign the Covenant and Bishop Leslie, at Wentworth's behest, lost no time in taking action against them. 'They do threaten me for my life,' the bishop told the lord deputy, 'but, by the grace of God, all their brags shall never make me faint in doing service to God and the King!' As Charles prepared to wage war on the Covenanters, Wentworth drafted a command that all Scots in Ulster over the age of sixteen, male and female, must take an 'oath of abjuration of their abominable covenant' – better known as the Black Oath.[69]

Wentworth had raised an army of three thousand in Ireland to fight for the king and in the summer of 1639 half this force was sent north to Carrickfergus under the command of Sir George Radcliffe to assist Bishop Leslie. The oath had to be taken kneeling and if it was refused Leslie's commission had the power to fine, imprison and excommunicate. One family was fined a total of £13,000 and imprisoned at their own expense in Dublin, while many others, like Robert Adair with extensive lands around Ballymena, fled back to their native Scotland. So many left Antrim and Down that in places not enough were left to bring in the harvest. The Reverend Patrick Adair concluded that for Irish Presbyterians this 'proved the hottest piece of persecution this poor infant church did meet with, and the strongest wind to separate between the wheat and chaff'.[70]

The king's military reverses in Scotland and the growing power of the Commons at Westminster led to Wentworth's impeachment and execution in 1641 – the treatment of the London Companies and the Presbyterians contributed powerfully to his downfall. Sir John Clotworthy presented a long petition to parliament on behalf of the Ulster Puritans. They had 'translated themselves out of several parts of his Majesties kingdomes of England and Scotland, to promote the infant Plantation of Ireland' and when they expected to reap the fruit of their labours they were oppressed by 'the unblest way of the Prelacy with their faction', with the result that very many were

> reviled, threatned, imprisoned, fettered together by threes and foures in iron yoakes, some in chaines carried up to Dublin, in Starre chamber fined in thousands beyond abilitie, and condemned to perpetuall imprisonment; Divers poore women but two dayes before delivery of children were apprehended, threatnd, and terrified . . . They therefore most humbly pray that this unlawfull hierarchicall government with all their appendices may bee utterly extirpate.[71]

This government in time would be extirpated and was already so weakened that the king restored the Irish Society their land in Londonderry. More worrying to the Commons, however, was the raising of an Irish Catholic army and royal intrigues with the Catholic Earl of Antrim.

Sir Randal MacDonnell, 2nd Earl of Antrim, lost £2,000 at court during one game of ninepins in 1635 and by 1640 he had debts of £39,377; only by mortgaging the entire barony of Carey did he save himself from ruin. The Gaelic lords of Ulster found it hard to adapt to British methods of estate management and most were in dire financial straits by 1641. Sir Conn O'Neill of Clandeboye was the first to lose everything, selling his townlands one by one and leaving his son Daniel to live by his wits at court. Sir Phelim O'Neill, Lord of Kinard in south Tyrone, mortgaged his estates for more than £13,000, while Lord Maguire of Fermanagh declared that he was 'overwhelmed in debt and the smallness of my nowe estate'.[72]

These descendants of 'deserving natives' loathed Wentworth's regime; at a time when they had been impoverished by the harvest failures of 1629–32, the lord deputy levied 'recusancy' fines to the letter of the law for non-attendance at Established Church services and drastically lowered the value of their estates by questioning their land titles. The O'Reillys of Cavan told the Dublin administration that they were oppressed with

> grievous vexations, either to the captivating of oure consciences, our looseinge of our lawfull liberties, or utter expulsion from our native seates, without any just grounds given.[73]

Rory O'More, with lands in Armagh, led the conspiracy of the Ulster lords, which matured fitfully from February 1641. Returned émigré officers, brought back by Charles I from Spanish service to organise an Irish army, instilled Counter-Reformation zeal into the plot. Final arrangements were made on 5 October in the house of Turlough O'Neill at Lough Ross in Co. Monaghan: Dublin Castle would be seized on 23 October while Sir Phelim O'Neill would lead a simultaneous revolt in Ulster.

On the night of 22 October Owen O'Connolly sat drinking with his foster brother Hugh MacMahon in Winetavern Street in Dublin. There O'Connolly learned of the plot and, having been instructed in Protestant doctrine by Sir John Clotworthy, he had no hesitation in informing the lords justice. Sir William Cole from Enniskillen also attempted to send warning but his messenger was waylaid. Dublin Castle rallied its defences and MacMahon, Lord Maguire and other conspirators were imprisoned in the fortress they had planned to capture. The plot had been foiled but that same night the rebellion in Ulster had begun.

Just before eight o'clock on the evening of Friday 22 October Sir Phelim O'Neill called on his neighbour Lord Caulfield at Charlemont and invited himself to dinner. Once inside Sir Phelim and his men seized the fort and imprisoned the garrison and its commander; then they galloped to Dungannon, which had fallen by a similar ruse, reaching it by midnight. Just before dawn next day O'Neill surprised Mountjoy with the help of the O'Quinns and at the same time the O'Donnellys took Castlecaulfield.[74] Before nightfall that Saturday Sir Conn Magennis, uncle of the 2nd Viscount Iveagh, had led a successful assault on Newry, and Lurgan was in flames, Sir William Brownlow surrendering the castle there next day. On Sunday Sir Phelim issued a proclamation from Dungannon, declaring that the rising

> is noe wayes intended against our Soveraine Lord the King, nor the hurt of any of his subiets, eyther of the Inglish or Schotish nation, but onely for the defence and liberty of our selves and the Irish natives of this kingdome.[75]

So far the rebellion had limited objectives and no appeal had been made to foreign powers. So far under the direction of native Irish gentry the insurgents had shed comparatively little blood. 'I protest that no Scottsman should be touched,' Sir Phelim's brother declared, while Philip O'Reilly in capturing Cavan ordered his men 'not to meddle with anie of the Scotishe natioun, except they give cause'.[76] Within days the insurgents were striking south to Dundalk, north to Moneymore, which had been seized by the O'Hagans, and west towards Fermanagh where the Maguires had risen.

At 9 p.m. on Saturday 23 October Bishop Leslie wrote in haste from Lisburn (then known as Lisnagarvey) to the 2nd Viscount Montgomery of the Ards warning him that Sir Phelim was in revolt 'with a huge multitude of Irish souldiers, and that this day they are advanced as farre as Tonregee'. This was followed by another message that

> the newes which I sent unto your Lordship about 4 houres agoe are too true, and a great dale worse than I then understood. For the Newry is taken and we expect them here this night . . .[77]

Robert Lawson, a merchant and sheriff of Londonderry, returned from doing business with Lord Hamilton at Killyleagh to call on his wife at the New Forge ironworks near Belfast. He found most of the townspeople 'fled and flying, and carrying their goods to Carrickfergus', the elderly Viscount Edward Chichester already on board ship. He beat a drum through the streets, raised about 160 men, and reached Lisburn at four o'clock on Monday afternoon, 25 October. Sir Conn Magennis, having burned Dromore, approached Lisburn that night but 'making show of six or seven lighted matches for every piece, to astonish the enemy', Lawson's men forced him back.[78] It was to no avail that the Irish drove four hundred head of cattle at the gates next day, and on Wednesday Lord Montgomery and Lord Hamilton brought up reinforcements. Three times the rebels attacked Lisburn and three times they were thrown back, the last assault being led by Sir Phelim himself on 28 November. Belfast and Carrickfergus were thus saved and Colonel James Clotworthy had time to secure Antrim, the Agnews to defend Larne, James Shaw to fortify Ballygally, and Archibald Stewart, Lord Antrim's agent, to place garrisons in north Antrim.

Elsewhere in the province the insurgents seemed to sweep all before them. Portadown fell, all Cavan was overwhelmed and on 28 October, after holding out for some days, Armagh capitulated. In Fermanagh Rory Maguire, Lord Enniskillen's brother, had given the signal when he burned the village of Lisnarick and all the planter castles came under siege. The McCaffreys took Archdalestown, the McMurrays captured Garrison and, after seizing Irvinestown, Rory forced the capitulation of Lisnaskea on 25 October. Sir William Cole, however, held out at Enniskillen.[79]

Everywhere the Catholic gentry depended on an uprising of the Gaelic peasantry and after the first fortnight they lost control. Hungered by harvest failures, and listening to wild prophecies and rumours of a Puritan plot to massacre them, they threw themselves with merciless ferocity on the settlers.

THE 1641 MASSACRES

In the library of Trinity College in Dublin there are over thirty manuscript volumes filled with the sworn statements of survivors of 1641, gathered to justify a massive confiscation of land held by Catholics. Ever since W.H. Lecky debated the issue at length, Irish historians have been reluctant to accept these depositions as having any value. Certainly much of the evidence is fantastic, grossly exaggerated and even salacious, but M. Perceval-Maxwell, in a trenchant analysis, shows that some of the statements are supported by other documents. Many of the incidents described would have been run-of-the-mill in the Thirty Years War, then still raging in Germany. Anyone familiar, for example, with the savage atrocities perpetrated by both sides in the first fortnight of the Spanish Civil War in 1936 is aware what man can do to man when all authority collapses in a climate of fear and want, when people are inflamed by rumour, religious passion and a lust for revenge. Besides, in 1642 the English and Scots wreaked a bloody revenge – 'nits make lice' was a popular cry of those who justified the killing of Catholic Irish children.

The Irish victories were so rapid in the first few days that the leaders did not know what to do with those who surrendered. After they had robbed and stripped the settlers in Cavan, the O'Reillys simply released them, 'turned naked, without respect of age or sex, upon the wild, barren mountains, in the cold air, exposed to all the severity of the winter; from whence in such posture and state they wandered towards Dublin'. Perhaps two thirds of the twelve thousand or so who perished before the end of the year died of exposure and hunger.[80] Others, like Viscount Caulfield, were simply shot dead. The massacre at Portadown is well authenticated; there Manus Roe O'Cahan drove about eighty men, women and children

> off the bridge into the water and then and there instantly and most barbarously drowned the most of them. And those that could not swim and came to the shore they knocked on the head, and so after drowned them, or else shot them to death in the water.

Elizabeth Price, who put her X mark to this deposition, said she was kept alive because they thought she was hiding money and she 'had the soles of her feet fried and burnt at the fire, and was often scourged or whipped'.[81] Anne Blenerhasset, whose husband Francis was shot dead in Ballyshannon, saw colonists hanged from tenterhooks in Fermanagh. Ellen Matchett gave one of several accounts of settlers burned to death in houses where they had taken refuge; she herself was 'miraculously preserved by a mastiff dog that set upon these slaughtering and bloody rebels' and survived with others in hiding, emerging 'sometimes to get the brains of a cow, dead of disease, boiled with nettles, which they accounted good fare'.[82]

Neither side gave quarter in this war. In Fermanagh the Maguires killed the garrison of Tully Castle after promising mercy, while Sir William Cole killed some two hundred Irish captured in a sally from Enniskillen. Nearly four hundred Scots who surrendered in south Tyrone were put to the sword, Turlough O'Neill admitting 'that ill favored massaker neere Augher'.[83] As the native Irish swept south they took Dundalk, besieged Drogheda and overwhelmed a government army at Julianstown on 29 November. The following month the Catholic Old English made alliance with Sir Phelim's Ulster Irish and the rebellion now became national. In the far north refugees crowded into Derry, and in Coleraine, where some were killed when the parish church was struck by lightning, one hundred died each day from disease. In north

Antrim some Catholic Scots joined the rebellion, slaughtering settlers at Portna, while at Movanagher survivors took shelter in 'little Hutts, pestered and packed with poore people'.[84] Over five hundred Ulster colonists took refuge on the Isle of Bute alone and in the presbyteries of Ayr and Irvine some four thousand others were in danger of starving. The Scottish privy council ordered a special collection explaining that 'by famine they will miserablie perish if they are not tymouslie supplied'.[85] At the same time the Scots were cautiously considering an urgent plea from London to send a relief army to Ulster.

'THE LORD OF HOSTS HAD A CONTROVERSIE WITH US . . .': BENBURB, 1646

Major-General Robert Monro, after landing at Carrickfergus on 3 April 1642, set out southwards with his Scots army in pursuit of the Irish. A hardened veteran of the Thirty Years War, he simply slaughtered his captives, first at Kilwarlin Wood, then at Loughbrickland, and finally at Newry, where, after shooting and hanging sixty men, he did stop his soldiers throwing women in the river and using them as targets, though only after several had been killed. The rebels hid in the woods, so in marching north again he seized their cattle and slaughtered any Irish men, women and children that he found.[86] Along the lower Bann thirty or forty Irish making for the river were 'cutt downe, with sume wyves and chyldrene for I promis,' reported Adjutant-General Peter Leslie, 'such gallants gotis but small mercie if they come in your comone sogeris handis'.[87] Mountjoy and Dungannon were recovered, and in desperation the Ulster Irish prepared to capitulate. Just then, at the end of July 1642, Owen Roe O'Neill disembarked at Doe Castle in Donegal. Nephew of the Great O'Neill, Owen Roe had been brooding in Spanish service in Flanders since 1641, and now used his prestige and military experience to stiffen the ranks of the Ulster Irish. The task was not easy, for Ulster, the province he had left forty years before, 'not only looks like a desert, but like Hell . . .'[88]

The English Civil War began in August 1642 and Irish politics, already confused, became labyrinthine in its complexity in the years that followed. Ulster Catholics and Protestants were each, at various times and for different reasons, opponents and allies of the king, but almost always opposed to each other. Edmund O'Reilly, archbishop of Armagh, had given the formal approval of the Catholic Church to the rebellion at the Synod of Kells in March 1642. This in turn led the Old English, native Irish and clergy to pool their resources and form 'the Confederate Catholics of Ireland' at Kilkenny in October. As the English Civil War gathered pace, however, the Catholic Old English were eager for a deal with Charles I and a 'cessation' or truce was agreed in 1643. The native Irish, particularly in Ulster, wanted to fight on to recover their lands, but without resources they could do little more than skirmish with Monro. Then in 1645 Giovanni Battista Rinuccini arrived as papal nuncio with impressive supplies of arms, thus giving Owen Roe a chance to put the Ulster army he had trained into action. At the beginning of June 1646 Monro moved out of winter quarters with some six thousand men and six field pieces drawn by oxen; his plan was to strike southwards through the Midlands to Kilkenny, the base of the Confederacy. Halting near Armagh, he learned that Owen Roe threatened his rear just north of the Blackwater at Benburb. Force-marching his men almost twenty miles, Monro crossed the river at Caledon on 5 June and began with a brisk cannonade. Owen Roe harangued his men:

> Let your manhood be seen by your push of pike. Your word is *Sancta Maria*, and so in the name of the Father, Son, and Holy Ghost advance! – and give not fire till you are within pike-length![89]

With no guns but with an equal number of men, the Irish army steadily pressed the exhausted Scots back to the river, slaughtering them. Hugh Montgomery, 3rd Viscount of the Ards, fell captive; Monro escaped only after he had cast away his coat, hat and wig; and between one third and one half of all the Scots were killed, the Irish sustaining only trifling losses. When the news reached Rome Pope Innocent X himself attended a Te Deum in Santa Maria Maggiore: it was the greatest and most annihilating victory in arms the Irish ever won over the British. 'For ought I can understand,' Monro ruefully observed, 'the Lord of Hosts had a controversie with us to rub shame in our faces.'[90]

The victory was thrown away. Though all Ulster was now at his mercy, Owen Roe instead turned south to help Rinuccini take control of the Catholic Confederacy in Kilkenny. In September 1646, having locked up the Confederacy supreme council with O'Neill's help, Rinuccini appointed himself president, broke the three-year truce and resumed the war against the Protestants, Royalist and Parliamentarian alike. A bewildering period of inconclusive negotiation, internal disputation and indecisive campaigning was brought to an abrupt end by the execution of Charles I in January 1649 and Cromwell's arrival in August. After taking Drogheda on 11 September, Cromwell put all but thirty of the garrison to the sword (around 2,600), and captured priests, by his own account, 'were knocked on the head promiscuously'. This, he observed, was retribution for the Ulster massacres of 1641: 'I am persuaded that this is the righteous judgement of God upon those barbarous wretches who have imbrued their hands with so much innocent blood.'[91] In fact most of the slaughtered garrison were either English or Old English and a second massacre was carried out in Wexford a month later when around two thousand were killed, but opponents of any kind could expect little mercy as the firm hand of the Commonwealth began to come down on Ulster.

CROMWELLIAN ULSTER

The subjugation of Ulster was bloody and protracted. When Cromwell sent Colonel Robert Venables to recover the north he had the support only of Sir Charles Coote, commander of the Derry garrison. These were seasoned veterans of Naseby, however, and Venables took Newry and Belfast without difficulty, laying siege thereafter to Carrickfergus. The Lords Hamilton and Montgomery declared for Charles II, as had nearly all Scots, and summoned their men to Newtownards and Comber; meanwhile Coote sped southwards to meet them and made camp at Lisburn. Early in December 1649 Venables and Coote cut the settlers' army to pieces near Lisburn, killing one thousand men, many hacked down in a relentless cavalry pursuit. General Tam Dalyell then surrendered Carrickfergus.[92]

Owen Roe O'Neill died in November and Bishop Heber MacMahon of Clogher was elected to lead Catholic resistance. When MacMahon took Dungiven and put all the men there to the sword next spring, the colonists realised their best interests were served by supporting Venables. The Parliamentarians routed the Irish at Scarrifhollis near Letterkenny in June 1650 and soon afterwards Bishop MacMahon was captured in Enniskillen and hanged. Charlemont Fort, the last Confederate stronghold in the north, surrendered on 14 August, though sporadic guerrilla fighting lasted until Philip O'Reilly formally capitulated in April 1653, after a successful assault on Lough Oughter.

Commonwealth commander Colonel Richard Lawrence found starving wretches picking carrion out of a ditch and wrote that 'the plague and the famine had swept away whole countries that a man might travel twenty or thirty miles and not see a living creature, either man, beast, or bird'.[93] Wolves so increased that they had a price on their heads and it was said they fed upon orphan children wandering the roads. Hundreds, including Sir Phelim O'Neill, were executed; around 12,000 were transported to West Indian islands; 3,400 soldiers were exiled to the European mainland; and millions of acres were confiscated. Only those landowners who could prove 'constant good affection' to the parliamentary cause were not punished. In practice Protestants were absolved if they paid fines, but almost all Catholic landowners disappeared in Ulster, many obtaining smaller estates in Leitrim as compensation. In Ulster the biggest confiscations were in the east and south of the province: 41 per cent of the land of Antrim; 26 per cent of Down; 34 per cent of Armagh; and 38 per cent of Monaghan. Only 4 per cent of Tyrone was confiscated and Cromwell's charter restored Derry property to the City of London, showing that the Ulster plantation was largely undisturbed.[94] Land was granted to soldiers and 'adventurers' – those who had advanced money to parliament – but many sold their interests. A fresh set of landowners and jobbers arrived in Ulster, but this time there was no real attempt to remove the native cultivators. The Gaelic aristocracy, already shattered by the Ulster plantation, was all but wiped out and the foundations of the Protestant Ascendancy had been firmly laid.

RESTORATION AND PEACE

General George Monck, who for a time had held Belfast with Parliamentarian troops against Scots royalists, proclaimed the restoration of Charles II in 1660; in gratitude the citizens of Belfast presented him with this verse:

Advance George Monck & Monck St George shall be
Englands Restorer to Its Liberty
Scotlands Protector Irelands President
Reduceing all to a ffree Parliam[t]
And if thou dost intend the other thinge
Goe on and all shall Crye God save y[e] Kinge.[95]

The colonists in Ulster were pleased to see an end to political uncertainty, provided the king did not restore all the Catholics to their lands. Charles II, for his part, had no wish to go on his travels again; however, something would have to be done for Catholics who had remained loyal to the Crown through all its troubles and the court was inundated with petitions. The king's charter replaced Cromwell's Charter of Londonderry and formally restored to the Londoners all the lands and rights taken away by his father and appointed a thirty-six-member commission to sort out conflicting claims. The Act of Settlement in 1662 declared that land had to be found for 'innocent Papists'. But who was innocent? Charles did not wish to dislodge planters and adventurers, but he was persuaded that there was much free land for the taking. The commissioners' task was made immensely difficult when the king insisted that the Earl of Antrim should be restored to his lands and declared innocent. The earl had been imprisoned in the Tower after the Restoration, mainly to protect him from his creditors it seems, but his case had been pressed by the dowager Queen Henrietta Maria. The Court of Claims, under heavy pressure from the Crown, voted the earl innocent by four votes to three; the Duke of Ormond, the viceroy, observed that 'it is very frequently & too plausibly said this breakeing in upon the prescribed methode of the Act cutts of all present & future security'.[96] Protestants in Ireland and Britain alike were outraged and were only appeased to some extent by a further Act of Explanation in 1665: Lord Antrim was to be restored to his estates but was no longer to be classed as 'innocent'; and soldiers and adventurers granted land had to give up one-third of their estates to make land available for those Protestants who had had to give way to Catholics.

The overall result was that Cromwell's settlement was not overturned. Of the Gaelic landlords in Ulster only Lord Antrim was restored, and by 1688 less than 4 per cent of counties in the province, other than Antrim, was owned by Catholics. Once more men who had lost everything withdrew to the woods and the hills and stood 'upon their keeping'. The name given to a landless outlaw in this period was 'tory', an anglicised version of an Irish word meaning 'pursuer' or 'raider' – a word of abuse subsequently applied by the Whigs to their political opponents in the Westminster parliament. Draconian legislation by the Commonwealth failed to extirpate the tories who continued to terrorise much of Ulster during the reign of Charles II, and the most notorious of all was Redmond O'Hanlon.

REDMOND O'HANLON: 'THE INCOMPARABLE AND INDEFATIGABLE TORY'

A proclamation of 1674 offered rewards to anyone who could bring in tories, dead or alive; one of those named with £10 on his head was 'Redmond O'Hanlon of Tanderagee, in the county of Armagh, yeoman'. Born in 1640 near Poyntzpass, O'Hanlon was drawn from the class of Gaelic landowners who had lost everything in the Cromwellian cataclysm. His career began as a footboy to Sir George Acheson of Markethill and, after a brief period of employment as a poll tax collector, he joined a band of tories led by his kinsman, Laughlin O'Hanlon. Imprisoned for stealing horses, he bribed his way out of Armagh gaol and – according to the author of a popular biography published in 1681 of this 'Incomparable and Indefatigable Tory' – 'despairing of mercy or pardon, he resolved to abandon himself to all Lewdness and to become a perfect bird of Prey'.[97]

In 1679 Edmund Murphy, a Franciscan, faced a charge of criminal connection with tories in south Armagh and – to save his own skin – he agreed to help hunt down Redmond O'Hanlon. Murphy concocted a scheme to ambush O'Hanlon with the aid of a rival tory leader, Cormack Raver O'Murphy. O'Hanlon heard of the plot, however, and had O'Murphy murdered. Landowners now took joint action; they cut down the Glen Woods, O'Hanlon's hideout just south of Poyntzpass, and paid a force of thirty men ninepence a day each for three months to track down the outlaw. O'Hanlon was wounded in a close encounter and had to lie up for a time on Ram's Island on Lough Neagh, but he soon resumed his brigandage. In August he was robbing in Fermanagh and then on 4 September 1679 he slew Henry St John, grand-nephew of a former lord deputy, at Knockbridge near Tanderagee. At St John's funeral the Reverend Laurence Power denounced O'Hanlon as

> a cunning and dangerous fellow who though Proclaimed as Outlaw with the rest of his Crew and summs of Money upon their heads, yet he raigns still and keeps all in subjection so far that 'tis credibly reported he raises more in a year by contribution à la mode de France, than the King's Land-Taxes and Chimney Money come to.

This 'pack of insolent bloudy outlaws,' Power said, had 'so riveted themselves in these parts ... that they exercise a kind of separate Sovereignty in three or four Counties'.[98]

Reports of O'Hanlon's daring now appeared in London newspapers as he plundered Down, Leitrim and Roscommon in October 1679. Magistrates of those three counties met that month in Hillsborough and organised the guarding of all passes between Armagh and Down. Seven tories were killed and, though O'Hanlon escaped, he knew his opponents were closing in on him. Deborah Annesley of Castlewellan, daughter of Henry Jones, bishop of Meath, warned him that he could expect no pardon. It was the viceroy himself who brought about O'Hanlon's fall; William Lucas of Drumintyan, Co. Down, was authorised to go beyond the law to slay the tory leader. On 25 April 1681, by previous arrangement with Lucas, Art O'Hanlon shot dead his foster brother Redmond at Eight Mile Bridge near Hilltown. Ormond made Lucas an army lieutenant and gave Art O'Hanlon a pardon and £200. The following month Lieutenant Lucas sent a jubilant report that he was shooting tories about Newry. Laughlin O'Hanlon was killed in December and soon the last of the Ulster tories were being rounded up. On 17 March 1683 Sir William Stewart, of Newtownstewart in Co. Tyrone, wrote to Ormond:

> There was never such a winter for country sports as the last and I have enjoyed them in much perfection. I had very good hawks and hounds but we have not had more success in any sport than Tory hunting. The gentlemen of the country have been so hearty in that chase that of thirteen in the county where I live in November, the last was killed two days before I left home.[99]

In the same year that Redmond O'Hanlon was killed the Catholic primate of all Ireland was executed. This judicial murder was the climax of the so-called Popish Plot, in which Catholics were supposed to be planning to assassinate the king. In this notorious intrigue Father Edmund Murphy and Bishop Henry Jones had central roles to play in fabricating the evidence.

Under Cromwell's regime Catholics endured much persecution: those who sheltered priests were imprisoned; around one thousand priests were banished; and outlawed worship was confined to a 'Mass rock' in a remote place. Edmund O'Reilly, archbishop of Armagh, wrote that he 'made for myself a small hut in a mountainous district, one here, another there, so that no one else should suffer for my sake'. He managed to retain twenty-two priests in the county of Armagh but they lived

> in much endurance and misery as to worldly things; they visit the sick by night; they celebrate mass before and round about dawn, and that in hiding places and recesses, having appointed scouts to look around and with eyes and ears agog to keep watch lest the soldiers come by surprise.[100]

The accession of Charles II ushered in a new era of toleration for all. After ejecting over sixty ministers for refusing to accept the Book of Common Prayer, the Government ceased to interfere with the Presbyterians who accepted the *regium donum*, a grant from the king for the upkeep of their ministers. Catholic worship became public again, Mass houses were built, and religious orders began to return. Some Protestants did not relish this revival, however. Bishop Henry Jones conspired with Lord Shaftesbury to accuse Archbishop Oliver Plunkett, O'Reilly's successor as primate, of plotting a French invasion. Even a Protestant jury in Dundalk had no difficulty in throwing out these trumped-up charges; it was English rather than Irish Protestant frenzy that sealed the primate's fate. Edmund Murphy – a Franciscan hostile to metropolitan interference – concocted the evidence Shaftesbury needed; and condemned in London, the archbishop was hanged, drawn and quartered at Tyburn in 1681. He was canonised on 12 October 1975.

The Popish Plot did not have an Irish counterpart and, taken as a whole, these were years when religious tensions eased perceptibly, peace prevailed and striking economic progress was achieved.

RECOVERY

'I dare not tell your Lordship of the misery and distraction the country here is in', Sir George Rawdon wrote to Lord Conway in 1657. 'You cannot believe it. No money stirring.'[101] The province was in a wretched economic condition on the accession of Charles II and recovery was not helped by restrictions imposed on Ireland by the Westminster parliament: in an attempt to protect English farmers the export of cattle to Britain was prohibited from 1663 and by 1681 the ban had been extended to sheep, pigs, beef, pork, bacon, butter and cheese. Yet rapid recovery did take place – the rising prosperity of England and her colonies, together with growing trade opportunities on the European mainland, kept up the momentum. The proportion of Irish exports going to England fell from 74 per cent in 1665 to 30 per cent by 1683, but the volume kept increasing and new markets were found.[102]

By 1683 Belfast was exporting more butter than any other port in Ireland and was soon to bypass Limerick to become the fourth largest town in Ireland. This explosive growth is all the more remarkable in that a census of 1659 had placed Belfast fourth in the following rank order of returns for Ulster: Derry (population, 1,052); Carrickfergus (962); Coleraine (633); Belfast (589); Armagh (409); Lisburn (357); Downpatrick (308); and Enniskillen (210).[103] The figures for Cavan and Tyrone have been lost. By 1685 the surveyor Thomas Phillips was writing that Belfast 'is one of the most considerable places in the Kingdom, having never less than 40 or 50 sail before it'. A shipping list of 1682 names sixty-seven Belfast-owned ships. 'The quantities of Butter and Beef which it sends into Foreign Parts are almost incredible', Dr William Sacheverell observed. 'I have seen the Barrels pil'd up in the very Streets.' France was the destination for one third of the corn, half of the beef, and three quarters of the butter exported from the town.[104]

The City of London suffered huge losses during the Plague of 1665 and the Great Fire of 1666, and Derry had its own serious fire in 1668; the Irish Society had little money to spare, therefore, to reinvigorate its plantation. In the early years Coleraine and Derry had depended heavily on exports of timber, but now the woods had almost all gone. Captain William Jackson was dismissed as wood ranger to the Irish Society in 1672 for illicitly exporting wood staves, but orders to prevent further felling came too late. Ironworks closed down for lack of charcoal to fire them. The salmon fisheries were self-sustaining and remained profitable; salted salmon was exported as far as Venice and Bilbao, and in 1684 Spain imported 1,885 barrels of salmon from Derry alone.[105]

By the 1680s Connacht, not Ulster, was the poorest province in Ireland. Immigrants from Britain – this time a majority was English – were arriving in great numbers again. The plantation, then, could be judged a success, though many of the original aims had not been achieved. The colonists clustered most thickly in the fertile valleys, where the Irish had been most numerous in the previous century. Only a few parts of the province – areas of east Down, south Antrim and north Armagh – were exclusively settled by the newcomers. Elsewhere the planters and natives mingled, and to a greater extent than is often acknowledged. In Antrim and Down Gaelic families often dropped the 'O' and the 'Mac' from their names and became Protestants. In western Ulster many Protestant planters married local women and after a generation or two became Catholic and Gaelic speaking. Religion, rather than blood, was the badge of ethnic division – a division which yawned wide again on the accession of James II.

KING WILLIAM'S WAR AND PEACE
1685–1750

In 1682 Dr William Molyneux in Dublin was commissioned to collect statistical accounts of Irish districts for inclusion in Moses Pitt's 'Grand Atlas'. The publication fell through before it got to Ireland but a few manuscript descriptions survive and they paint a picture of a province which was settled and growing in prosperity. In his account of Oneilland barony in north Armagh, William Brooke observed:

> The soile of this Barony of O'Nealand is very deep and fertile, being productive of all Sorts of grain, as wheat, Rye, Barly, Oats, &c. The vast quantity of wheat that is yearly carried hence into the County of Antrim, besides the maintenance of above two thousand Familys with bread, which Number I find to Inhabit this Small Barony, most whereof being English, do plainly demonstrate it to be the granary of Ulster, and one of Ceres's chiefest barns for Corn; and as it Excells all the rest for Corn, so it challenges the preference for fruit trees, good sider being sold here for 30 shillings the hogshead.[1]

As under the terms of their leases tenants were made to plant apple trees, Brooke predicted that 'this County twenty or thirty years hence will be little inferiour to the best sider county in England'. In and about Lurgan 'is managed the greatest Linnen manufacture in Ireland', and he concludes, 'the fertility of the Soile, the curious inclosures, the shady Groves and delicate seats, that are everywhere dispersed over this Barony doe all concur to make it a Paradise of pleasure'.

William Montgomery described the Ards peninsula, giving an impression of a peaceful and flourishing settlement, where from

> the Northeast coast of the whole barroney lett us note that All along: from hence to the barr of Strongford river the Inhabitants doe Manure & Dung the land with sea oar by them called Tangle which being spread on it and plowed down makes winter grain & summer Barly grow in aboundance & clean without weeds cocle or tares; the roads are pleasant & smooth in depth of winter.

He is very knowledgeable about the abundant wild fowl and fish in Strangford Lough but observes the shortage of timber – the gentry had to send to Scotland for coal while their tenants found 'abundance of fewel cut by the Spade (and dryed in the sunn)'. Oysters could be got in the lough, then as now, and a salt marsh near Newtownards was so valued for its medicinal herbs that 'the Netherland Duch' offered to lease it for £2,000 but were refused by Lord Montgomery.[2]

Richard Dobbs of Carrickfergus, in his eccentric and chaotic description of Co. Antrim submitted to Dr Molyneux, remarks that the timber bridge over the Bann at Portglenone is one of the best 'in the three kingdoms; there are seats upon it to rest and view the Pleasures of the Band water', while another at Coleraine was 'able to vie with Port Glenoyne Bridge'. He estimated Islandmagee to be 5,500 acres, 'whereof 5000 I am sure is fit for fork and scythe, nor did I ever see better ground for so much together, whether for grain or cattle', and at Brown's Bay the land was

> sandy, dry, and fit for rabbits; but the people here think that no profit can be made but by ploughing, in which the men spend their whole time, except the summer quarter in providing and bringing home fireing; and the women theirs, in spinning and making linen cloth, and some ordinary woollen for their family's use.

He discusses the excellent fox hunting there, the value of the Gobbins caves for hiding stolen horses before they were smuggled to Scotland, and the collection of sea birds and their eggs from the cliffs, where he could not 'look down from the top to the bottom, without some horror, and yet I have been shown a boy of about 16, that would take the Leather of a horse, drying the Leather, stake it into the Ground, would for eggs, or a sea Gull go down as far as the leather reached'.[3]

These are descriptions of Protestant Ulster: Brooke observes that the 'few Irish we have amongst us are very much reclaimed of their barbarous customs, the most of them speaking English'; and Dobbs writes that there were no Irish in Ballycarry, while in his home parish of Kilroot – apart from his own Anglican family and servants – the people were 'all presbiterians and Scotch, not one natural Irish in the Parish, nor papist'.[4] The plantation in Ulster had flourished for most of Charles II's reign and, despite the growing attractions of English colonies in America, the province drew in a steady flow of English and Scots.

The accession of a Catholic king, James II, in 1685 sent tremors of alarm not only through the length and breadth of England but also through the Protestant settlement in Ireland. His actions correspondingly raised the hopes of Catholic gentry who had lost so much in Cromwell's land settlement. Again the country was thrown into conflict and, for a time, the fate of Britain and much of Europe seemed to hinge on the outcome of the contest in Ulster. In the end the triumph of William of Orange was so complete that it was followed by the longest peace the province had ever known. From being the poorest of the four provinces, Ulster became the most prosperous: the population rose; the province acquired an extensive road network and its first canal; market towns flourished; and above all, the striking success of the linen industry spread a new prosperity over a wide region. All classes profited but, while Catholics chafed under the erratic enforcement of the Penal Laws, members of the Established Church were the chief beneficiaries. Yet the eighteenth century was a time of rising expectations and great numbers of Ulster Presbyterians left to make a new life for themselves in North America.

'WE DETERMINED TO MAINTAIN THE CITY AT ALL HAZARDS'

Ho, brother Teig, dost hear de decree,
Lillibulero Bullen a la!
Dat we shall have a new Deputy?
Lillibulero Bullen a la!
Ho, by my Soul, it is a Talbot,
And he shall cut all de Protestant t'roat.

Thomas Wharton, the Englishman who composed this mocking ballad to a tune by Purcell, claimed later that it whistled a king out of three kingdoms.[5] One of the few Catholics to survive Cromwell's massacre at Drogheda, Richard Talbot had risen from being the sixteenth child of an impoverished Kildare gentleman to become James II's principal agent in promoting the revival of Catholic fortunes in Ireland. Created the Earl of Tyrconnell in 1685, Talbot arrived in Dublin as lord deputy in February 1687. Tyrconnell did not delay in his mission: most privy councillors and judges appointed were Catholics; all counties save Donegal acquired Catholic sheriffs; boroughs were presented with new charters giving Catholic majorities to all corporations except Belfast; and the army was purged of Protestant officers.[6] One comfort for Protestants was that James II seemed unwilling to overturn previous land settlements. Some dismissed officers left Ireland to serve William of Orange, but for the present, Ulster Protestants were content to sit tight and await developments.

On 10 October 1688 William of Orange published his Declaration explaining why he was about to invade England and no fewer than fifty thousand copies were sent across the Channel. Sixteen years earlier the kings of France and England had together almost overwhelmed the Dutch Republic and now they threatened to do so again. William had good reason to believe that Louis XIV aimed at nothing short of European domination and intended the invasion of Holland: in 1682 the king had seized William's own principality of Orange in south-eastern

France; in 1685 he had revoked the rights and freedoms guaranteed to Huguenots by the 1598 Edict of Nantes, thus making a bid to be the champion of the Catholic powers; and on 22 September 1688 the French entered the Rhineland and laid siege to the fort of Phillipsburg with the obvious intention of clearing a path into Holland without violating the neutrality of the Spanish Netherlands.[7] On 28 October 1688 the Dutch States-General explained why it would support William's expedition:

> The French king having often, yea, upon all occasions, showed the ill-will he bore to this Republick, it is to be feared that if the King of Great Britain reach his mark, to wit, ane absolute power over his people, then will both these kings, partly out of maxime of state, and partly out of hatred and zeale against the Protestant religion, endeavour to ruine, and, if possible extirpate this Republick.[8]

In fact William had no wish to lead a coalition of Protestant powers, and not only did he restrain zealots in Holland from turning on the Catholic minority there but he also drew Catholic princes into his alliance against France, including the Emperor Leopold I of Austria and the Elector Maximilian of Bavaria.

In England James II also sought religious toleration but his blundering policies soon brought him into conflict with Whigs and Tories alike. He attempted to reduce parliament to a cipher and, having promoted Catholics to all positions of importance in Ireland, now seemed to threaten English Protestant liberties by importing an army of Irish Papists. The nobility of England could no longer field an army capable of halting James's quest for absolute power and a disastrous alliance with Louis XIV, and so they turned to William of Orange for aid. English aristocrats were mainly concerned to preserve their own powers and privileges, but William's overriding aim in sailing for England was to save the Dutch Republic from imminent destruction and to ensure European stability – that was still to be his aim when he came to Ulster two years later.

An imposing Dutch army disembarked at Brixham on 5 November 1688 and, when a few days later Louis XIV ordered the invasion of Holland, the German princes rallied to its defence. After fatal vacillation James fled to France just before Christmas and the following February William and his wife Mary, James's eldest daughter, were declared joint sovereigns of England, Scotland and Ireland. This bloodless revolution gave the English parliament new constitutional powers but members were not stirred to action until news came in March that James had arrived in Ireland with a formidable French army. 'If Ireland be lost,' one MP observed, 'England will follow', and another declared: ''Tis more than an Irish war, I think 'tis a French war.'[9] For a brief moment in history the fate of much of Europe turned on events in Ireland.

In Ulster Protestants had already begun to organise. On 3 December 1688 an anonymous letter addressed to Lord Mount-Alexander had been found lying in a street in Comber, Co. Down; it began:

> Good my Lord, I have written to you to let you know that all our Irishmen through Ireland is sworn that on the ninth day of this month they are to fall on to kill and murder man, wife and child; and I desire your Lordship to take care of yourself.[10]

Whether it was genuine or bogus, the letter raised the spectre of 1641 and galvanised the Protestant gentry to action as copies passed to Belfast and from there to George Canning in Garvagh, who sent further transcriptions to Limavady and Derry. Alderman Alexander Tomkins was reading out the Comber letter to citizens in Derry when a messenger arrived from George Phillips – grandson of Sir Thomas – warning that Lord Antrim was approaching with 1,200 Catholic Redshanks. Tyrconnell – or 'Lying Dick Talbot' as Protestants called him – had ordered Antrim's regiment to replace the largely Protestant garrison he had unwisely left in Derry.

Ezekial Hopkins, bishop of Derry, advised citizens to admit Lord Antrim's troops, but when the Redshanks entered the Waterside and began to cross the Foyle, thirteen apprentice boys seized the keys from the main guard, raised the drawbridge at Ferryquay Gate and closed the gates. The resolution of the apprentice boys, Captain Thomas Ash recalled,

> acted like magic and roused an unanimous spirit of defence; and now with one voice we determined to maintain the city at all hazards, and each age and sex conjoined in the important cause.[11]

John Campsie, mayor of Derry until ousted by Tyrconnell, resumed office, expelled remaining Catholics and issued this proclamation:

> We have resolved to stand upon our guard and to defend our walls, and not to admit of any Papists whatsoever to quarter amongst us.[12]

THE BREAK OF DROMORE

Early in 1689 a Council of Protestant Gentlemen – representing Monaghan, Armagh, Down and Antrim – met at Loughbrickland under the leadership of Lord Mount-Alexander to organise resistance to Tyrconnell. An assault was made on the Catholic garrison in Carrickfergus but it failed completely; a friar named O'Haggerty reported the besiegers were 'the most part without arms and, such as had them, their arms were unfixt and unfit for service'.[13] Mount-Alexander's efforts were too dilatory; under the command of Richard Hamilton, the Jacobites – those who remained loyal to King James – swept northwards and overwhelmed the Protestants led by Arthur Rawdon at Dromore on 14 March 1689. After this 'break of Dromore' all of eastern Ulster fell to Hamilton's men, who plundered Hillsborough, Lisburn and Antrim, and occupied Belfast without meeting resistance there. During a snowstorm on 28 March a Jacobite attack on Coleraine was beaten off; however, the garrison commander there, Gustavus Hamilton, ordered a tactical retreat to Derry. On the other side of Ulster another Gustavus Hamilton, the nephew of Lord Glenawley elected governor the previous year, organised the defence of Enniskillen; though he had no artillery, his long-range fowling pieces kept Lord Galmoy and his Jacobites at a respectful distance. James had not delayed on arrival at Kinsale on 12 March and his progress to Dublin was a triumph. 'Now or Never! Now and for Ever!' proclaimed Tyrconnell's banner flying at Dublin Castle. And indeed it looked as if all Ireland would fall under James's control. For William III everything now depended on whether or not the Protestants in Ulster could hold out long enough until he could send aid.

David Cairns, a Tyrone lawyer whose son was one of the thirteen apprentice boys, had sailed to London to seek aid from the Irish Society. That help arrived in the form of HMS *Deliverance*, brought into the Foyle by yet another Hamilton, Captain James, nephew of the Jacobite commander and later the Earl of Abercorn. The 8,000 muskets, 480 barrels of powder and £9,000 brought ashore meant that Derry could resist the Jacobites – but had its commander the will to resist? Lieutenant-Colonel Robert Lundy, military governor of Derry, ordered a general withdrawal of northern garrisons to the city. The consequence was that valuable supplies fell to the Jacobites, particularly in Charlemont, though the garrisons of Cavan and Monaghan, 'lest the enemy should possess themselves of their stronghouses, goods and provisions, set fire to all and marcht away to the light of it'.[14] Confidence in Lundy was ebbing rapidly and Cairns, returned from London on 10 April, found the governor speaking to his officers in such a way 'concerning the indefensibleness of the place that they could see little hope and were unwilling to stay'.[15] Whether or not Lundy was hedging his bets between James and William, or secretly supported James, or was simply incompetent, he was no man to command the defence of a beleaguered city.

From all over Ulster, Protestants poured into Derry carrying what they could and leaving only Enniskillen as an alternative refuge. In addition to a garrison of over seven thousand men, perhaps thirty thousand Protestants sought sanctuary in the city. In a very real sense, therefore, the fate of the Protestant settlement in Ulster depended on Derry's ability to hold out. If Derry fell then James would be ready to use Ireland as a base from which he could make an assault on England to recover his throne, and Louis XIV would be one step nearer neutralising England and overrunning Holland.

On Saturday 13 April 1689 Richard Hamilton and his Jacobite troops chased stragglers from the Coleraine garrison across the Foyle and into the city. As a symbolic gesture a single shot was fired from the Waterside, the cannon ball striking the bastion by the Ferryquay Gate. Upstream on the west bank, men from the Derry garrison were overwhelmed by the French and Irish troops led by Lieutenant-General Conrad von Rosen, a Livonian soldier of fortune in the pay of Louis XIV. Driven out of their trenches at Lifford, Long Causey and Cladyford, the Protestant foot soldiers were hacked down, while their cavalry support ignominiously galloped in retreat to Derry. The Williamites had been beaten 'although we were five to one against them,' Thomas Ash recorded in his diary, 'which caused suspicion that Colonel Lundy was a traitor to our cause.'[16] When Lundy refused the support of two regiments sent out from Liverpool, that suspicion became a certainty.

Adam Murray, a farmer from the Faughan valley who had been in the fight at the fords, led a citizens' revolt and overthrew Lundy. Joint governors were appointed in his place: Major Henry Baker, a professional soldier from Co. Louth, and the Reverend George Walker, Church of Ireland rector of Donoughmore. Both were to provide inspired leadership and, indeed, humaneness when they allowed Lundy to slip away over the walls disguised as a common soldier carrying a bundle of match. The garrison was reorganised, and food – much of it abandoned by fleeing merchants and deserting officers – was brought into a common store. But what were the prospects of successful resistance? In his *True Account of the Siege of Londonderry* Walker recalled:

> We had but few horse to sally out with and no forage; no Engineers to instruct us in our works; no Fireworks, not so much as a hand-grenado to annoy the enemy; nor a gun well mounted in the town.[17]

Well-mounted or not, some of the guns were impressive enough, the largest being 'Roaring Meg', given to the city in 1642 by the Fishmongers' Company. Thanks to the *Deliverance* there was no shortage of powder and handguns.

King James, exhilarated by news of the victory at the fords, joined his besieging army. On 18 April he advanced towards the walls and offered terms; he was greeted with cries of 'No surrender!' and a fierce and sustained barrage of shot and ball. Just out of range, James sat motionless on his horse for several hours in the pouring rain. Then at the entreaty of his French advisers the king returned to Dublin where Louis XIV's ambassador, Comte d'Avaux, observed that James 'appears to me to be very mortified over his latest proceeding'.[18]

The Jacobites were ill-equipped for a long siege. One French supply officer reported that 'most of the soldiers in front of Derry have still only pointed sticks, without iron tips', and a regiment inspected by James had only one matchlock in a hundred fit for service.[19] A single mortar was the only artillery piece the besiegers possessed; more heavy guns arrived later but they were not sufficient to attempt a breach of the walls except at very close quarters. The need to get near to the walls was underlined by the success of audacious sallies from the city towards the end of April, in which the French generals Maumont and Pusignan were mortally wounded. In particular, the defenders had entrenched themselves on a knoll to the west of the city, where a windmill stood. The anonymous Jacobite author of *A Light to the Blind* observed:

This work they well manned with firelocks, and planted two or three small pieces of cannon on the windmill. General Hamilton, observing that the rebels made a walking place of this entrenched ground for the preservation of their health, and that they gave annoyance with their cannon from the said mill and with their long fowling-pieces, which carried by several yards farther than muskets, and they made much use of the water which they found in a spring within the aforesaid ground, he took up a resolution to attempt the regaining of that land, to prevent further mischief to his own, and to straiten the enemy. Whereupon he commanded, on the sixth of May, an attack to be made upon the entrenchment.[20]

The Jacobite assault was a complete failure and several leading Old English gentlemen were either killed or taken prisoner. Amongst those captured were Lord Netterville and Lieutenant-Colonel William Talbot (cousin of Lying Dick and promptly nicknamed 'Wicked Will' by his captors). As an alternative strategy, General Richard Hamilton drew the net tighter by moving the main Jacobite camp forward from St Johnston to Balloughry Hill, cutting the city off from much of its water supply and severing its communication with the outside world – the defenders did not know, for example, that Culmore Fort at the entrance to Lough Foyle had fallen to the Jacobites without a fight. At the end of May a siege train of heavy guns sent by James arrived to intensify the bombardment of the city, which had not ceased since the beginning of the siege. The shells that the mortar, there from the start, lobbed into Derry weighed 270 pounds each, Walker recalled,

> and contained several pounds of powder in the shell; they plowed up our streets and broke down our houses, so that there was no passing the streets or staying within doors, but all flock to the Walls and the remotest parts of the Town, where we continued very safe, while many of our sick were killed, not being able to leave their houses.[21]

The rain of shells, bombs and cannon balls never threatened to breach the walls, but it did exact a heavy toll of life from the densely packed defenders. Captain George Holmes recalled that 'one bomb slew seventeen persons. I was in the next room one night at my supper (which was but mean) and seven men were thrown out of the third room next to that we were in, all killed and some of them in pieces.'[22]

General Richard Hamilton ordered another major attack on Windmill Hill on 4 June, but after fierce hand-to-hand fighting the Jacobites were again forced back. A Presbyterian minister, the Reverend John Mackenzie, wrote afterwards:

> Our women also did good service carrying ammunition, match, bread and drink to our men, and assisted to very good purpose at the bogside in beating off with stones the granadeers who came next to our lines. These were taken up from the streets to deaden the fall of shells.[23]

'Blessed be God!' Captain Thomas Ash – the hero of this action – recorded in his diary. 'We had a notable victory over them, to their great discouragement.'[24] The French general, the Marquis de Pointis, ruefully concluded that 'the state of affairs is such that attacking must be no longer thought of and it will be well if without raising the siege we shall have to wait on hunger'.

After months of siege the defenders were starving. Walker provides a price list for July: 'Horse-flesh 1/8d a lb; quarter of a dog 5/6 (fattened by eating the bodies of the slain Irish); a dog's head 2/6; a cat 4/6; a rat 1/0; a mouse 6d; a small flook [flounder] taken in the river; not to be bought for money . . .'[25] George Holmes observed:

> I believe there died 15,000 men, women and children, many of which died for want of meat. But we had a great fever amongst us and all the children died, almost whole families not one left alive.[26]

Because of the fever, another survivor wrote, people 'died so fast at length as could scarce be found room to interr them, even the backsides and gardens were filled up with graves, and some thrown in cellars; some whole families were entirely extinct'.[27]

General Hamilton's very humanity may have cost him the siege. Some ten thousand unarmed civilians had been allowed to leave Derry, thus enabling those who remained to hold out longer. General Rosen, who had returned after accompanying James to Dublin, found Hamilton's weakness contemptible; he rounded up Protestants over a wide area and then drove them against the walls at the beginning of July, leaving them to be fed by the defenders. In response, the garrison erected a gallows on the Double Bastion and threatened to hang the Jacobite prisoners. Rosen was then overruled by his fellow officers and recalled soon after, James observing that 'none but a barbarous Muscovite could have thought of so cruel a contrivance'.[28]

'WHAT SHOUTS OF JOY': THE RELIEF OF DERRY

Major-General Percy Kirke, infamous for his cruelties after the Battle of Sedgemoor, sailed into Lough Foyle on 11 June with thirty vessels. For the next six weeks he refused to risk the guns of Culmore to bring relief to Derry. Another deterrent was a floating boom across the Foyle at Brookhall, completed under the direction of the Marquis de Pointis just a week before Kirke's arrival; made of fir beams fastened with chains, it seemed an insuperable barrier below the city. A young boy carried messages between Derry and the fleet on papers concealed in his rectum. 'Be good husbands to your victuals,' Kirke ordered and sailed round to Lough Swilly to land troops at Inch in a vain attempt to draw the Jacobites from the siege.[29] Duke Friedrich Schomberg, King William's general whose son was serving behind the walls in Derry, sent a stiff note from London ordering Kirke to attempt the relief of the city forthwith.

At 7 p.m. on Sunday 28 July 1689, while the *Dartmouth* engaged Culmore, a longboat and three small vessels – the *Mountjoy* of Derry, the *Phoenix* of Coleraine and the *Jerusalem* – sailed up the Foyle. The wind dropped completely but the flowing tide pushed the *Mountjoy* against the boom, snapping its chains. Micaiah Browning, the ship's captain and a native of Derry, died as he ordered his men to respond to the Jacobite guns with a volley of partridge shot, and the ship, stuck fast in the mud, was freed in the recoil to drift up to the city. The shore gunners were drunk with brandy and fired wildly, the author of *A Light to the Blind* observed bitterly; he continued:

What shouts of joy the town gave hereat you may easily imagine, and what pangs of heart it gave to the loyal army you may as easily conceive . . . Lord, who seest the hearts of people, we leave the judgement of this affair to Thy mercy. In the interim those gunners lost Ireland through their neglect of duty.[30]

Derry was the last walled city to be built in western Europe. The siege of 105 days was the last great siege in British history, and the most

157

renowned. 'Oh! to hear the loud acclamations of the garrison soldiers round the Walls when the ships came to the Quay', Ash wrote in his diary. '. . . The Lord, who has preserved this City from the Enemy, I hope will always keep it to the Protestants.'[31] For the Protestants of Ulster this epic defence gave inspiration for more than three centuries to come. For King William the steadfast refusal of Derry to surrender provided a vital breathing space in his war with Louis XIV and gave him a base in Ireland to drive out King James in a campaign that had just begun.

ENNISKILLEN: 1689

Now that the boom across the Foyle had been broken, General Hamilton realised that Derry could be provisioned regularly from Kirke's fleet and on Wednesday 31 July he decided to raise the siege. That very same day the Williamites based in Enniskillen won a notable victory over the Jacobites at the southern end of upper Lough Erne. The armed civilians in Enniskillen had not felt bound by Lundy's order in April that they should fall back to Derry and their defiance had done much to enable the city to hold out. It was observed soon after

> that during the whole time of that long siege the men of Enniskillen kept at least one half of the Irish army from coming to Derry, and kept them in so great fear of their coming to relieve the town that they durst never make a regular attack upon the place.[32]

Two troops of horse and six companies of foot, from the garrison that had abandoned Sligo on Lundy's orders, joined the defenders of Enniskillen in April. Gustavus Hamilton now felt his garrison strong enough to strike out at the Jacobites before they could lay siege to his island town. It was difficult to catch the Jacobites unawares as the local Irish maintained an effective intelligence network. Nevertheless, military parties from Enniskillen plundered the camp at Trillick to the north-east on 24 April; burned Augher Castle to the east on 28 April; raided Clones and much of Monaghan and Cavan to the south-east at the end of April; and routed the Jacobites at the 'break of Belleek' to the west on 8 May, thus ending the siege of Ballyshannon. Enniskillen was kept well supplied with food by these raids, its garrison bringing back three thousand cattle, two thousand sheep and many tons of grain in its most daring expedition as far south as Kells in Meath towards the end of May. The only serious reverse was on 13 July when the Duke of Berwick – James II's natural son by Arabella Churchill – left Derry, crossed the Barnesmore Gap into Donegal and caught the Williamites unawares near Trillick, inflicting severe casualties. This was more than offset, however, when General Kirke sent experienced officers and munitions by sea to Ballyshannon and from there upstream to Enniskillen.

Lieutenant-General Justin MacCarthy, recently created Viscount Mountcashel by James II, meanwhile advanced north from Dublin with a formidable army, and on the evening of 28 July – when the *Mountjoy* was breaking the boom at Derry – a desperate appeal arrived from Colonel Crichton that Mountcashel was bombarding Crom Castle with his cannon. Led by English officers sent by Kirke, the Enniskillen army hurried south along the heavily indented eastern shores of upper Lough Erne towards the castle. After routing some Jacobites near Lisnaskea, the Enniskillen garrison advanced on Mountcashel at Newtownbutler, adopting as their battle cry 'No Popery!' With over three thousand men facing an army of two thousand, Mountcashel should have won, but a confused order to his cavalry caused them to turn tail and the Jacobite foot was driven to the lough shore. Of five hundred men who tried to swim across the lough, only one survived and the rest of the foot were hunted down and slain; quarter was given only to around four hundred officers and almost two thousand other Jacobites were put to the sword. This ruthless annihilation was by far the greatest victory yet won by the Williamites and the Comte d'Avaux wrote to Louis XIV in disgust that Mountcashel had been taken prisoner and his troops

> put to flight in a manner to make one despair of such soldiers . . . the cavalry and dragoons fled without firing a pistol, and after some of them had burst their horses with the force of flight, they took to their feet and threw away their weapons, their swords, and jackets, that they might run more swiftly.[33]

West of the Bann, Ulster was soon cleared of Jacobites as General Hamilton's troops at Derry, Lifford and Strabane marched south, burning Omagh en route. In eastern Ulster the forces of King James were thrown on the defensive and the Duke of Schomberg's Williamite army met no opposition as it came ashore at Ballyholme Bay on 13 August 1689.

SCHOMBERG'S SUCCESS AND FAILURE

When the Duke of Schomberg arrived, 'the shore was all crowded with Protestants – men, women, and children – old and young', a contemporary news sheet reported, 'falling on their knees with tears in their eyes thanking God and the English for their deliverance'.[34] The Williamite commander expected an immediate Jacobite assault, observing 'if they have one dram of courage or wit they will attack us this night since they will never expect the like opportunity';[35] but General Thomas Maxwell withdrew his cavalry without molesting the twelve regiments of foot brought ashore. Schomberg then closed in on Carrickfergus, where, according to *A Full and True Account*, the Jacobites 'thought fit, in some measure, to retrieve their Credit and Reputation'; it continued:

> But when our Frigats at Sea, and Land Forces at Land had appeared before it, and made such Breaches in the Walls, and Destruction in the Town, by their Guns and Bombs, they judged it safest for them to Capitulate and Surrender; which they did on Wednesday last . . . The Town has been so miserably defaced, by the continual playing of the Bombs for five Days together, that it looks like a dismal heape of ruine.[36]

The Jacobites were fortunate not to have been lynched as they marched out, the Williamite chaplain George Story observed, for 'the Countrey people were so inveterate against them . . . that they stript most part of the Women, and forced a great many Arms from the Men . . . and so rude were the *Irish Scots*, that the Duke was forced to ride in among them, with his Pistol in his hand, to keep the *Irish* from being murdered'.[37] His army augmented by fresh arrivals to nearly twenty thousand – including two battalions of Dutch infantry and four Huguenot regiments – Schomberg marched south to Newry early in September as the Jacobites pulled out of Ulster, the Duke of Berwick ravaging the borderlands to delay him.

General Rosen advised James to burn Dublin and retreat behind the Shannon to await French reinforcements; but Tyrconnell, energetically raising new armies, urged making a stand north of Drogheda, and his counsel prevailed. Almost certainly Schomberg now lost the opportunity for a quick victory; but the duke – a seventy-four-year-old veteran with service in the Dutch, French and Brandenburg armies – was loath to take risks. Having crossed the Moyry Pass, Schomberg camped north of Dundalk and refused action. Tyrconnell wrote to James's queen, Mary of Modena, that 'wee bearded Monsieur de Schomberg these three weakes togeather, and burnt all his forrage to his very camp, to provoke him, but all would not doe'.[38] With their tents pitched by a marsh, the Williamite soldiers were ravaged by fever. As Story wrote in his *Impartial History*, around 1,700 died at Dundalk and another 1,000 in vessels taking the sick back to Belfast Lough:

> Nay, so great was the Mortality, that several ships had all the Men in them dead, and no Body to look after them whilst they lay in the Bay at *Carickfergus*. As for the Great Hospital at *Belfast*, there were 3762 that died in it from the first of *November* to the first of *May*, as appears by the Tallies given in by the Men that buried them; There were several that had their Limbs so mortified in the Camp, and afterwards, that some had their Toes, and some their whole Feet that fell off as the Surgeons were dressing them; so that upon the whole matter, we lost nigh one half of the Men that we took over with us.[39]

In the meantime Tyrconnell was rebuilding his armies and success-fully appealing to the French for supplies and reinforcements. Schomberg retired to winter quarters at Lisburn and, as his men continued to die, he busied himself with their moral welfare, which included issuing an order punishing 'the Horrid and Detestable Crimes of Prophane Curs-ing, Swearing, and taking God's Holy Name in vain'.[40]

'HIS MAJ[TY] WAS HERE IN THE CROWD OF ALL': THE BOYNE

With a heavy heart William realised that he had no choice but to go to Ireland himself and, hearing of this, Tyrconnell confided to Mary of Modena, 'I fear this confounded Prince of Orange's comeing over to us with such a power this spring to invade us anew, will sett us hard.'[41] In preparation William greatly reinforced Schomberg, including a force of Danish mercenaries hired from Christian V in March 1690; according to Story these were 'lusty Fellows, and well Clothed and Armed' but their correspondence shows that they did not relish their billet at Galgorm near Ballymena.[42]

Sir Cloudesley Shovell's squadron of warships escorted William's fleet of about three hundred vessels across the Irish Sea into Belfast Lough on 14 June 1690. The king stepped ashore at Carrickfergus, mounted his horse and, as the author of *An Exact Account* records, 'rode through the main streets of the town, where almost numberless crowds received him with continued shouts and acclamations on till the Whitehouse'.[43] Constantijn Huygens, a Dutch captain, noticed that William received Schomberg coldly, but they drove together in a coach along the lough shore to Belfast; here they were met, Story recalled,

> by a great concourse of People who at first could do nothing but Stare, never having seen a King before in that part of the World, but after a while some of them began to Huzzah, the rest took it up (as Hounds follow a Scent).[44]

Never before had Belfast greeted so many men of distinction – Godard van Reede, Baron de Ginkel of Utrecht; Hans Willem Bentinck, the king's close adviser; the Duke of Würtemberg-Neustadt, the German commander of the Danish force; Count Henry Nassau; Prince Georg of Daamstadt, brother of Christian V of Denmark; the Duke of Ormond; and many others. Close to the North Gate William met the hero of the siege of Derry, the Reverend George Walker, and accepted a verse address from the Belfast Corporation urging him to 'Pull the stiff kneck of every Papist down'. This pale asthmatic monarch, his face lined with the constant pain of fighting ill health, told the people in halting English that he had come to see that the people of Ireland would 'be settled in a lasting peace', and he was heard to remark that he had not come to let the grass grow under his feet.[45] Meanwhile, an army of continental size was disembarking; the author of *An Exact Account* described the scene:

> The Lough between this and Carrickfergus seems like a wood, there being no less than seven hundred sail of ships in it, mostly laden with provisions and ammunition . . . The great numbers of coaches, waggons, baggage horses and the like is almost incredible to be supplied from England, or any of the biggest nations of Europe. I cannot think that any army of Christendom hath the like.[46]

There were over forty pieces of artillery – six- and twelve-pounder demi-culverins, nineteen- and twenty-four-pounder cannon and mortars. Some of the Dutch guns required sixteen horses to pull them, and altogether William had more than one thousand horses to draw his artillery and gun equipment. James II's spies reported back to Dublin that the Prince of Orange had £25,000 and several tons of tin halfpence and farthings: in fact William had brought £200,000 in cash to pay his men.

On 19 June King William received a deputation of Presbyterian ministers and awarded them an annual subsidy, the *regium donum*, of £1,200. Though he had been promised the bishopric of Derry, the Reverend George Walker objected vigorously; but as Sir Robert Southwell explained to Lord Nottingham, the king 'has convinced me that as King James works by his priests so these men will do like service to his Majesty and uniting the people unto him and making a good report of things in Scotland'.[47]

That evening William set out for Lisburn and the advance south began. Though there was a brief skirmish there, the Moyry Pass was not seriously contested by James, who, at the urging of the Comte de Lauzun, Rosen's replacement as the French commander, pulled out of Dundalk to take up battle positions on the south bank of the Boyne. The Danes marched to Armagh – described by one of them as 'a miserable place with poor inhabitants' – but then moved east again to join William at Dundalk. On 28 June the Duke of Würtemberg-Neustadt, after having one of his men shot for attempted mutiny, wrote to Denmark from Dundalk: 'The enemy yield everywhere; if they go on like this we shall soon be in Dublin.'[48]

On Monday 30 June William deployed his troops on the north side of the Boyne, just west of Drogheda. He did not know that that very day the English navy was being badly beaten by the French off Beachy Head – there was much at stake in the coming battle. The international composition of his army underlined the fact that it represented the Grand Alliance against France, the world's greatest power: here were regiments of English, Dutch, Danes, French Huguenots, Germans, and Ulster Protestant skirmishers ('half-naked with sabre and pistols hanging from their belts,' Story remarked, '... like a Horde of Tartars').[49] Numbering some 36,000 and with modern artillery and handguns (the Danes were equipped with flintlocks), the Williamites were at least 10,000 stronger than the Jacobites. Although recently re-equipped by a French fleet – a striking feature of this war is the failure of navies on both sides to cut supply lines – James's army was also greatly inferior in firepower. William was superstitiously opposed to doing anything important on a Monday, but according to Southwell:

> His Majesty at his arrival yesterday near the river about 12 of the Clock, rode in full view of the Irish army, which are ranged upwards on the other side. The enemy even discovered it must be his Majesty ... They began to fire and presently one of the balls past so close to his Majesty's back upon the blade of his right shoulder as to take away his outward coat, his chamois waistcoat, shirt and all to draw near half a spoonful of blood.[50]

Next morning, Tuesday 1 July, the battle began with an artillery barrage and William decided on a frontal assault across the river at Oldbridge, while he sent his right wing upstream in a feint which most successfully drew the French away. The Dutch Blue Guards had to wade up to their armpits at Oldbridge, opposed fiercely by Tyrconnell's cavalry, but in the end the Williamites triumphed by superior firepower and weight of numbers. Schomberg was killed by mistake by a French Huguenot who 'shot him into the throat, and down he dropt quite dead', according to Southwell;[51] however, Danish and Irish accounts say that the duke was slain by one of Tyrconnell's Life Guards. The Reverend George Walker was killed also. To Southwell's alarm William 'weares his Star and Garter and will not disguise who he is ...' He continued:

> His Maj[ty] was here in the crowd of all, drawing his sword & animating those that fled to follow him, His danger was great among the enemyes guns which killed 30 of the Iniskillingers on the spott. Nay one of the Inniskillingers came with a Pistol cockt to his Maj[ty] till he called out; What are you angry with your friends! The truth is the cloaths of friends and foes are soe much alike.[52]

The Battle of the Boyne was not a rout, as Southwell acknowledged: "'Tis agreed their foot did not performe over well, but the horse are comended for doeing severall bold things in many particulars & in generall for makeing an admirable retreat, which was they say conducted by Count Lozune.'[53] The Irish and French retired in good order to fight doggedly behind the Shannon for another year. Yet the battle was decisive; it was a severe blow to Louis XIV's pretensions to European hegemony and was celebrated by the singing of the Te Deum in Vienna; James, who made a precipitate flight to France, could no longer think of Ireland as a springboard for recovering his throne; for the English the Glorious Revolution and parliamentary rule were made secure; for the Old English in Ireland the defeat dashed hopes of recovering their estates; and for Ulster Protestants the battle ensured the survival of their plantation and a victory for their liberty to be celebrated from year to year:

Let man with man, let kin with kin
  Contend through fields of slaughter –
Whoever fights, may freedom win,
  As then, at the Boyne Water.[54]

FROM THE BOYNE TO AUGHRIM, 1690–1

It is the coming of King James that took Ireland from us,
With his one shoe English and his one shoe Irish,
He would neither strike a blow nor would he come to terms,
And that has left, so long as they shall exist, misfortune upon the Gaels.

This was the bitter comment of a poet writing in Irish on James II's ignominious flight.[55] Tyrconnell wanted to make immediate terms with William III but the Jacobite army preferred the advice to fight on given by Patrick Sarsfield, a dashing cavalry commander and grandson of the 1641 leader Rory O'More. As the Jacobites prepared to hold a line along the Shannon, William followed and laid siege to Limerick early in August 1690. Sarsfield led a daring and successful raid on William's siege train as it came through the mountains at Ballyneety; deprived of his heavy guns, the king failed in his assault on the city and returned to direct affairs from London. Ginkel now commanded the Williamite army; he was eager to offer terms and return to the war on the European mainland but, heartened by their recent successes, the Jacobites determined to continue the war.

'The enemy are burning all before us', Ginkel wrote on 27 December, 'and the Rapparees are in so great a number that we can neither find forage nor cover, which hinders much our march.'[56] Named from their principal weapon, a half-pike known as a *rapaire*, the rapparees were Irish skirmishers who did much to frustrate Ginkel's attempts to bring the war in Ireland to a rapid conclusion. In May 1691 the Jacobites acquired a new commander, Charles Chalmont, the Marquis de Saint-Ruth; his considerable reputation was severely shaken, however, when in June he failed to stop Ginkel's men fording the Shannon near Athlone. Sixteen miles to the south-west, near the village of Aughrim,

Saint-Ruth prepared a set-piece battle on the limestone Galway plain; his plan was to lure the Williamites into a treacherous bog in front of his line. At first these tactics seemed to work: thick mist enveloped Ginkel's army as it moved out of Ballinasloe on Sunday 12 July; the Huguenots were drawn into the bog, cut off and slaughtered, while the Danes strove in vain to relieve them; the Irish pikemen stood firm even when 'the blood flowed into their shewse';[57] and Ulster Jacobites, led by Gordon O'Neill, spiked a battery of Williamite guns. 'They are beaten, *mes enfants*,' Saint-Ruth cried out, but a cannon ball, fired at extreme range, took off his head.[58] As Ginkel made a devastating flanking assault over a narrow stretch of dry ground, the Jacobite horse – the flower of the Old English gentry – turned tail and abandoned their foot to their fate.

Aughrim was the bloodiest battle ever fought on Irish soil. One general, three major-generals, seven brigadiers, twenty-two colonels, seventeen lieutenant-colonels and over seven thousand other ranks were killed. When news of the victory spread north, the Protestants of Ulster set bonfires ablazing, as they would do every year thereafter; over time the Williamite triumphs of 1 July 1690 and 12 July 1691 – partly as a result of the eighteenth-century shift from the Julian to the Gregorian calendar – fused into one celebration. Aughrim was also the last decisive battle in Irish history. As Ginkel renewed the siege of Limerick even Sarsfield knew he would have to sue for peace, and on 3 October 1691 the Treaty of Limerick was signed: fifteen thousand Irish soldiers were allowed to sail away to serve Louis XIV; those who stayed and gave their allegiance to William and Mary were to keep their lands; Catholics were to have such freedom of worship 'as they did enjoy in the reign of King Charles II'; and only Protestants were to live inside the walls of Limerick and Galway.[59] English and Irish Protestants were not slow to condemn this Dutch generosity:

Hard fate that still attends our Irish war,
The conquerors lose, the conquered gainers are;
Their pen's the symbol of our sword's defeat,
We fight like heroes but like fools we treat.[60]

RAPPAREES 'LATELY GROWING SO INSOLENT'

The Protestant gentry vented their fury at the Treaty of Limerick when William III summoned his first Irish parliament in 1692. The king's viceroy, Lord Sidney, found the Irish Commons 'a company of mad-men; they talk of freeing themselves from the yoke of England'; neither he nor his successor Lord Capel could get them to ratify Ginkel's treaty.[61] Williamite victory in Ireland had done much to frustrate Louis XIV's dreams of European hegemony, but it had also secured constitutional rule in the Three Kingdoms and the ascendancy of Protestant landowners in Ireland.

William did what he could to limit the scope of land confiscation, but if the Glorious Revolution meant anything, it meant that the monarch had to bow to the wishes of parliament. In Ulster the Catholics did not have much more to lose, except, that is, for the Earl of Antrim. 'I feare hee will be restoured,' observed an agent of Londonderry Corporation, 'for wee have no evidence against him.'[62] The luck of the MacDonnells held out and the earl was duly restored. When the king's grants to his favourites had been firmly revoked at Westminster, and all Jacobite claims had been met or denied, nearly half a million acres were available for sale. By then the bottom had dropped out of the market for land which had been won with so much blood, especially as only Protestants could buy. Half the land was bought at a knockdown price by a consortium of London merchants calling themselves the 'Company for Making Hollow Sword-Blades in England'. The merchants sold out six years later and, indeed, many estates changed hands. William Conolly was one of those with ready cash and a good business head who made a fortune from land jobbing; the son of a native Irish innkeeper in Ballyshannon, he became a Protestant and ultimately the Speaker of the Irish House of Commons and the richest man in Ireland.

Land confiscation never promised to come near to covering the cost of the campaign against the Jacobites in Ireland, an island of little more than strategic interest to William III. The peace that followed Aughrim, nevertheless, did allow the king to concentrate on the war against Louis XIV in the Low Countries. At first victory eluded him and in 1692 the allied armies were badly mauled at Steenkirk, and the fortress of Namur fell to the French. In the same year, however, the tide of the war turned when in a six-day battle at La Hogue the combined Dutch and English fleets all but destroyed French naval power. Then in 1695 William achieved his greatest triumph by recovering Namur, and by 1697 Louis agreed to terms. The Peace of Rijswijk concluded nine years of international conflict, forcing Louis to recognise William as king by the grace of God and to withdraw support from James. England and Holland would fight France again but the Williamite settlement in Ireland was completely secure for at least a century to come. The dispossessed had no hope of recovering their lands and were forced either to become tenants of the new proprietors or to eke out a living as hunted men in the hills.

Many Jacobites – the Wild Geese – had gone into exile to serve in the French army but some of the dispossessed and dozens of discharged soldiers stayed behind to live as outlaws. Ulster's wild southern border-lands had once been a refuge for woodkerne and tories; now they harboured rapparees. Patrick O'Connelly, better known as Parra Glas, periodically emerged from his cave at Tullygillen to terrorise the coun-tryside around Monaghan town until, proclaimed by a grand jury in 1711, he was captured and hanged. Seán Bearnach, a toothless rapparee said to be able to bite gold and silver coins with his gums, had his refuge at Minyamer, where the borders of Tyrone, Fermanagh and Monaghan join together; he held up coaches, rustled landlords' cattle and robbed the homes of the rich until he was betrayed and beheaded. In 1717 the Protestants of Carrickmacross petitioned the lord lieutenant unsuccess-fully for a troop of dragoons, as the rapparees were 'lately growing so insolent as to appear publicly, well-armed, and mounted'.[63] The follow-ing year there was a pitched battle with rapparees near the town. The best known outlaw in that area was Patrick Fleming; he and his band were eventually captured after a drinking bout in a shebeen when Caitlín Gearr MacMahon, the woman of the house, poured water in their pistols and summoned the soldiery. They were executed at the Rock of Miskish nearby and as their heads were being taken to Dundalk blood seeped out of the creels carrying them, causing a drover to collapse with fright. The last of the Monaghan rapparees was captured in 1722. Thereafter outlaws were simply common thieves and highway-men, such as Collier the Robber, who had the reputation of robbing the rich to help the poor; for long after, when a family prospered, neigh-bours would say, 'They must have got Collier's money.'[64]

At a time when Scots and English were coming to settle in Ulster in great numbers this lawlessness discouraged colonisation of such bor-derlands. In 1702 a tenant in Co. Monaghan wrote to Lord Weymouth:

> My family is in danger of being ruined, and the calamity of the present time by the low rates of goods is such that I am not able to sell them any longer, and, moreover the Natives of the County make altogether a prey of me being a stranger and remote.[65]

Over most of the province, however, peace returned with remarkable speed – indeed, it could be said that the Treaty of Limerick inaugurated the longest peace Ulster has ever known. It was the completeness of the Williamite victory, however, which ensured the century of calm that followed it. Most of the Gaelic aristocracy in Ulster had been swept away earlier in the seventeenth century and now the Catholic Old English – never strong in the north – were either in exile or held in check by a host of legal restrictions. Catholics had retained 22 per cent of the country in 1688 but the confiscations following the broken Treaty of

Limerick reduced the proportion to 14 per cent. By 1776 Arthur Young, the agricultural improver, was estimating that Catholics had only 5 per cent of the land of Ireland, even though they formed three quarters of the population. This further decline was due almost entirely to the Penal Laws.

PREVENTING THE FURTHER GROWTH OF POPERY

> Whereas, it is Notoriously known, that the late Rebellions in this Kingdom have been Contrived, Promoted and Carried on by Popish Archbishops, Bishops, Jesuits, and other Ecclesiastical Persons of the Romish Clergy. And forasmuch as the Peace and Publick Safety of this Kingdom is in Danger . . . which said Romish Clergy do, not only endeavour to withdraw his Majesty's Subjects from their Obedience but do daily stir up, and move Sedition, and Rebellion, to the great hazard of the Ruine and Desolation of this Kingdom . . .

So began a penal law which exiled the Catholic hierarchy and regular clergy; its language reflects the insecurity of Protestants who twice in the seventeenth century had faced ruin at the hands of the Catholic Irish.[66] The Irish parliament, almost exclusively representing the landed gentry of the Established Church, was convinced that the victories of Derry, Enniskillen, the Boyne and Aughrim could only be maintained by keeping Catholics in subjection. William King, the bishop of Derry, believed the Catholics themselves were responsible for their own repression, 'since it is apparent that the necessity was brought about by them, that either they or we must be ruined'.[67]

The Irish parliament began the Penal Code in 1695 by preventing Catholics from bearing arms, educating their children and owning any horse above £5 in value. This was a defiant rejection of the Treaty of Limerick and William – anxious not to alienate Leopold I, his Catholic ally against Louis XIV – viewed the strident demand for further legislation with some distaste. Indeed, the king was able to stave off the banishment of monks and friars, but his death in 1702 removed the final constraints. Queen Anne's government found parts of the bill to Prevent the Further Growth of Popery unnecessarily vindictive; but it had no wish to quarrel with the Irish parliament and the proposals became law in 1704. Westminster did stifle more extreme propositions such as that made in 1719 to castrate unregistered priests. The Irish privy council explained:

> The Commons proposed the marking of every priest who shall be convicted of being an unregistered priest . . . remaining in this Kingdom after 1st May 1720 with a large 'P' to be made with a red hot iron on the cheek. The council generally disliked that punishment, and have altered it into

that of castration which they are persuaded will be the most effectual remedy.[68]

The final penal law, depriving Catholics of the vote, did not enter the statute book until 1728.

The Penal Laws were directed principally at Catholic men of property; the most effective legislation deprived them of political and economic power. Catholics could not buy land, and estates had to be divided equally amongst sons; Catholics could not have leases running for more than thirty-one years and the rent was to be at least two thirds of the holding's yearly value; the lucrative legal profession, the army and all public offices were closed to Catholics; and Catholics could not vote, be members of parliament or of municipal corporations, or sit on grand juries. The enforcement of these measures helped to create a highly privileged élite aptly described in the 1790s as the Protestant Ascendancy. By assuming that land was the source of wealth, however, the Irish parliament failed to stop the rise of a Catholic middle class during the eighteenth century; unable to buy land, Catholics were forced to invest their capital in commercial ventures, which, despite the risk, usually brought a better return than farming.

The most unworkable clauses of the Penal Laws were those concerned with worship. At first there seemed to be some success: over four hundred Jesuits, monks and friars were exiled in 1698; there was no Catholic archbishop of Armagh between 1692 and 1714; and the bishop of Dromore, Patrick Donnelly, was gaoled and only able to continue his ministry thereafter from his refuge on the slopes of Slieve Gullion – disguised as a harper, he was later immortalised as 'The Bard of Armagh'. Yet even after the most determined period of persecution there were fourteen bishops in Ireland at the close of Queen Anne's reign. Pilgrimages – including that to Lough Derg specifically outlawed in the 1704 act – continued without interference (the Protestant Leslie family charged sixpence to each pilgrim going over to Saint Patrick's Purgatory). Priests were not prevented from saying Mass provided they registered with the authorities. Only thirty-three priests out of around one thousand took an oath, imposed in 1710, abjuring the authority of the pope; and for a time most priests were therefore unregistered and forced to resort once again to Mass rocks. Hugh MacMahon, Catholic bishop of Clogher and later archbishop of Armagh, records:

Over the countryside people might be seen signalling to each other on their fingers the hour that Mass was to begin in order that people might be able to kneel down and follow mentally the Mass being celebrated at a distance.[69]

The Government had neither the staff nor the stomach to enforce the oath for any length of time and religious restrictions fell into abeyance as the century advanced. Only a few Protestants showed any enthusiasm for attempting to convert Catholics. One such was the Co. Cavan rector, John Richardson, who preached and published sermons and liturgy in Irish. His *Proposal for the Conversion of the Popish Natives of Ireland*, printed in 1712, won the approval of Bishop King, who had imported Gaelic-speaking clergy to minister to Island Scots settled in Inishowen and Co. Antrim. Only 5,500 Catholics officially converted to the Established Church between 1703 and 1789, however, and these were drawn from the gentry eager to avoid subdivision of their estates and to find careers for younger sons in the legal profession. These conversions significantly reduced the percentage of land held by Catholics, especially when Alexander MacDonnell, the 5th Earl of Antrim, 'turned' on reaching his majority in 1734. Such converts soon blended in with members of the Ascendancy, who were not eager to widen greatly their circle of privilege; their view was put with brutal clarity by Lord Drogheda:

> I shall be very glad to see the Protestant religion strengthened; but what will we do for hewers of wood and drawers of water, for labouring men to plough our lands, thresh our corn, etc?[70]

Catholic labouring men, unable to buy land or obtain any but the shortest of leases, were hardly touched by the Penal Laws; but even if this code was widely ineffective it kept vivid the memory of defeat and confiscation. Chief Justice Robinson went too far when he declared: 'The Law does not suppose any such person to exist as an Irish Roman Catholic'; but the majority of the country's inhabitants – and around half the people of Ulster – were at the very least second-class citizens. Unlike similar laws imposed on Huguenots in France and Protestants in Silesia, the Penal Code was applied by a minority to a majority, as Samuel Johnson – who paid a brief visit to the Giant's Causeway – observed:

> The Irish are in a most unnatural state, for we see there the minority prevailing over the majority. There is no instance even in the Ten Persecutions, of such severity as that which the Protestants of Ireland have exercised against the Catholics.[71]

Later in the century Edmund Burke described the Penal Code as a machine of elaborate contrivance 'as well fitted for the oppression, impoverishment, and degradation of a people, and the debasement in them of human nature itself, as ever proceeded from the perverted ingenuity of Man'.[72] Burke was a product of the Enlightenment, but earlier in the century all major Christian sects sought not toleration but victory. Even in Ireland the fear of Catholic resurgence did not prevent the Established Church from imposing penal laws on the Presbyterians.

Though they might avoid parts of the province most persistently scourged by the rapparees, Presbyterian Scots poured into Ulster even before the Williamite War was at an end. It was observed that 'vast numbers of them followed the Army as Victuallers . . . and purchased most of the vast preys which were taken by the Army in the Campaign and drove incredible numbers of cattel into Ulster'.[73] A string of harvest failures in the 1690s brought about such a terrible famine in Scotland that perhaps one quarter of the population died; many survivors sought to make a new start for themselves on the far side of the North Channel. Edward Synge, bishop of Tuam, estimated that fifty thousand Scots families came to Ulster between 1689 and 1715; this figure is probably too high but the Presbyterians were able to record a doubling of their congregations between 1660 and 1715.[74] Bishop MacMahon wrote in 1714:

> Although all Ireland is suffering, this province is worse off than the others, because of the fact that from the neighbouring country of Scotland, Calvinists are coming over here daily in large groups of families, occupying the town and villages, seizing the farms in the richer parts of the country and expelling the natives.[75]

Members of the Established Church were also alarmed by this influx, for in several parts of Ulster Presbyterians formed overwhelming majorities – Jonathan Swift was unhappy at Kilroot not just because he was thwarted in love but also because he had almost no Anglicans living in his parish. With powerful allies nearby in Scotland, where the Episcopal Church was soon to be overthrown, Ulster Presbyterians threatened the privileges of the Established Church and made inroads on Anglican congregations too often neglected by worldly or absentee clergy. 'They openly hold their sessions and provincial synods for regulating of all matters of ecclesiastical concern', Dr Edward Walkington, the bishop of Down and Connor, indignantly complained, as he and other Anglican clergy called for action to curb what they saw as arrogant pretensions.[76]

Presbyterians resented having to pay tithes to a Church to which they did not belong, but at least their ministers were paid out of a royal bounty of £1,200 a year. During William's reign their only serious complaint was that Presbyterian marriage was not recognised; in an address sent from Belfast to the lord lieutenant in 1701 they sought the repeal of the law which obliged persons so married publickly to confess themselves guilty of the damnable sin of fornication, to the no small grief of your petitioners who are hereby made infamous, their children incapable of succeeding to their effects, and of divers other privileges as being bastards.[77]

Then in 1704 the English privy council added a clause to the Irish parliament's draft bill to Prevent the Further Growth of Popery: it stated that any person holding public office must produce a certificate proving that he had received the sacrament of the Lord's Supper 'according to the usage of the Church of Ireland ... immediately after divine service and sermon'.[78] Since Catholics were already disqualified by previous penal laws, this sacramental test was really directed at the Presbyterians, who, when the bill received royal assent, could no longer be members of municipal corporations or hold commissions in the army or the militia.

Ulster Presbyterians were outraged by the test but at the same time they were amongst the most eager supporters of the Popery Bill; their protests were muted therefore. Nevertheless, from his cell in Newgate Prison, Daniel Defoe launched into a fierce attack on the test. In his pamphlet, *The Parallel; or Persecution the Shortest Way to Prevent the Growth of Popery in Ireland*, Defoe declared that since the Williamite War Ulster Presbyterians 'instead of being remembered to their honour ... have been ranked amongst the worst enemies of the Church, and chained to a Bill to prevent the further growth of Popery'. He continued:

> Will any man in the world tell us that to divide the Protestants is a way to prevent the further growth of Popery, when their united force is little enough to keep it down? This is like sinking the ship to drown the rats, or cutting off the foot to cure the corns.[79]

Sure in the knowledge that Presbyterians would always rally to the Protestant cause in time of danger, the Established Church continued to harry dissenters who defied its authority. Dr William Tisdall, vicar of Belfast, shared the view of Jonathan Swift that Presbyterians were more to be feared than the Catholics themselves. Swift may have helped Tisdall to compose a pamphlet attacking the Presbyterians, ironically titled *A Sample of True-Blew Presbyterian Loyalty in all Changes and Turns of Government*. The citizens of Belfast, now overwhelmingly Presbyterian, reacted by obstructing the vicar's collection of 'house-money' in the town and by bringing back John McBride – their Presbyterian minister forced to flee to Scotland in 1708 when Tisdall accused him of being a Jacobite. Tisdall was quite unable to enforce warrants he issued to suppress pamphlets he condemned as scurrilous, including McBride's denunciation of the vicar, entitled *A Sample of Jet-black Prelatic Calumny*.[80]

172

In the countryside, too, the state Church attempted to thwart the advance of Protestant dissent. In Co. Cavan the Established Church was indignant when Presbyterians competed with it for the souls of Ulster Protestants. On 10 December 1712 Presbyterian ministers drawn from all over Ulster gathered at Belturbet to set up a new congregation. They had been encouraged by the frequent absence of the local rector, the Reverend John Richardson, famous for his campaign to end the Lough Derg pilgrimage; as the bishop of Kilmore explained to the lord lieutenant, Richardson 'notwithstanding my repeated Commands, has absented himself from his Cure, which has given encouragement to those schismatics to make so bold an attempt . . .'[81] Hearing of the meeting, the dean of Kilmore, Dr Jeremiah Marsh, rallied the local Anglicans:

> We thought it our duty to use our best endeavours to stop these pernicious designs and practices which were carrying on to the endangering the unity and peace of the church . . . when we came to Belturbet, we found no less than 10 Presbyterian Preachers (which had held as they call it, a Presbytery there) and two young men, Probationers, one of whom they were to settle at Belturbet to pervert the people, for as yet there are in the town but 2 Presbyterian Inhabitants *of any note* namely Hansard the Apothecary & Cummin the small merchant.

The ministers were arrested and a county grand jury was empannelled to bring in the unanimous verdict that the Presbyterians were guilty of endeavouring to disturb the peace. The jury also called for a weekday sermon 'that the People might have no excuse to run from the Church to follow Meetings'.[82] A couple of months later Robert Wodrow, an agent of the Scottish Presbyterians visiting Ulster congregations, reported: 'I find our brethren there are in very ill circumstances. High church is rampant and flaming.'[83] In 1714 the *regium donum* was suspended but the accession of George I ushered in a new era of toleration. Ulster Presbyterians showed their loyalty when they flocked to join the militia during the Jacobite invasion scare of 1715 and in 1719 the Toleration Act gave Presbyterians in Ireland official recognition.

The Test Act remained on the statute book but it was never enforced to the letter. Its main effect was to force Presbyterians to withdraw from municipal corporations but as Bishop King observed in a letter to Swift in April 1708: 'I do not know any officer that has on account of the Test parted with his command and I do not believe there will';[84] and, indeed, there were no fewer than twenty-four Indemnity Acts between 1719 and 1778 allowing Presbyterians to hold public offices and commands in the militia. From 1719 it cannot be said that Presbyterians suffered serious discrimination and, had they been united, they probably could have forced parliament to repeal the test. As in Scotland, they were divided between 'subscribers' who adhered to the Westminster Confession of Faith and 'non-subscribers' who did not. In the 1740s Scottish 'seceders' began their missionary activities in Ulster and there were further divisions between traditional Calvinist 'Old Light' Presbyterians and 'New Light' Presbyterians who left the interpretation of the Scriptures to individual conscience. By then there were at least five Presbyterian sects and out of 107 publications by Irish Presbyterian ministers between 1731 and 1775, 49 concerned internal disputes. This was offset, however, by steadily improving relations between Presbyterians and the Church of Ireland.

Because they offered no threat to the Established Church, other dissenting Protestants were not seriously persecuted. The Society of Friends was at first stronger in the south than in the north, but they were locally important in Lisburn and in the vicinity of Lurgan. One Quaker did have his house in Lisburn burned because he failed to light a bonfire to welcome the arrival of William of Orange in 1690, but generally their pacifist beliefs were respected. An act of 1692 For the Encouragement of Protestant Strangers in Ireland allowed foreign Protestants to use their own rites. Louis Crommelin received a large subsidy in 1698 to bring a colony of Huguenots to Lisburn, though most were scattered when the town was consumed by fire in 1707. The position of other dissenters was greatly improved by the Toleration Act of 1719 and as the eighteenth century progressed the essential religious distinction in Ulster, as in the rest of Ireland, was between Catholics and Protestants.

If full toleration had been given earlier and the sacramental test removed, it is doubtful whether Presbyterians would have been wealthy enough to be eligible for many offices in local and central government. Writing in 1716, Henry Maxwell of Finneybrogue, who had been MP for Bangor in Queen Anne's reign, observed:

> The body of our dissenters consist of the middling and meaner sort of people, chiefly in the north, and in the north there are not many of them estated men when compared with those of the established church, so that when their disabilities shall be taken off their want of fortune and interest will always hinder them from coming into the militia in any invidious or dangerous numbers.[85]

Primate Hugh Boulter noted that their 'strength is principally in the north, where indeed they are numerous, but not the proprietors of much land or wealth. I have been assured that if the test were taken off there are not twenty persons amongst them qualified for substance to be justices of the peace.'[86] The most prominent Presbyterian landowner was Colonel Upton of Templepatrick. Indeed many Presbyterians, in

174

addition to Catholics, were finding it difficult to make ends meet in the harsh economic climate of the early eighteenth century.

In 1703 Richard Fitch, agent of Lord Bath's estate in Co. Monaghan, wrote from Ballymackney to Lord Weymouth:

> I never had the like trouble with cattle as I have had of late with your Lordship's. We had 34 – took the distemper, some died with their bodies swelled as much as their hides would hold, others swelling in their heads and throats, and some died. I used all the money I could . . . Several men have had great losses. Still the distemper is in the country.[87]

Cattle disease and harvest failure caused great distress in Ulster during the early decades of the eighteenth century. Arriving in Derry in the summer of 1718, Bishop William Nicolson found 'dismal marks of hunger and want' on the faces of the people in his diocese, and a few years later, when one of his coach horses was accidentally killed, some fifty people fell on the carcass, hacking off pieces with choppers and axes to take home for their families. 'We seem to be brought to the brink of a famine', he wrote. 'God defend us from the pestilence.'[88] Hugh Boulter described the results of food scarcity in a letter to the archbishop of Canterbury in February 1727:

> Oatmeal (which is the bread of the north) sold for twice or thrice the usual price: and we met all the roads full of whole families that had left their homes to beg abroad, since their neighbours had nothing to relieve them with. And as the winter subsistance of the poor is chiefly potatoes, this scarcity drove the poor to begin with their potatoes before they were full grown . . . so that this summer must be more fatal to us than the last; when I fear many hundreds perished by famine.[89]

This scarcity of 1726–7 was followed by a severe famine in 1728–9. Then at the end of 1739 a sharp frost set in and lasted for seven weeks: potatoes in store and in clamps in the fields were destroyed; cattle died; water-powered cornmills could not operate; and an ox was roasted on the ice on the frozen River Foyle. Shortage of seed and further bad weather led to a terrible famine in 1741; in the words of the author of *The Groans of Ireland*, a pamphlet written in that year:

> Want and misery in every face; the rich unable, almost, as they were willing, to relieve the poor; the roads spread with dead and dying bodies; mankind the colour of the docks and nettles which they fed on; two or three, sometimes more, in a car going to the grave for want of bearers to carry them, and many buried only in the fields and ditches where they perished.[90]

175

In the wake of this famine, at its most severe in Ulster, fever exacted a fearful toll during the hot summer of 1741:

The universal scarcity was ensued by fluxes and malignant fevers which swept off multitudes of all sorts; whole villages were laid waste by want and sickness and death in various shapes; and scarce a house in the whole island escaped from tears and mourning.[91]

The Irish called this *bliadhain an áir*, year of the slaughter; perhaps around three hundred thousand died, a death toll in proportion as terrible as the Great Famine of the 1840s. The meagre documentary record of this calamity is an indication that such acts of God were still considered a normal feature of the human condition in north-western Europe in the early eighteenth century. The people in Ulster who suffered most and who died first were the poorest of the Catholic Irish; but the English and Scottish settlers had come to the north of Ireland to find a better life and when the expectations of many had not been fulfilled they moved on across the Atlantic to the New World.

'A VAST NUMBER OF PEOPLE SHIPPING OFF FOR PENNSYLVANIA AND BOSTON . . .'

There is a hundred families gone through this towne this week past for New England and all the fforsters as I gave your honour account. Mr Bellsore of Lisinskey has set up fifty tates of land on the Cross of Clownis this day that is all waste, the tenants having all gone to New England. I believe that we shall have nothing left but Irish at last; but I hope your honour's estate will be safe enough, for they complayne most of the hardshipps of the tythes makes them all goe, which is true, for the Clergy is unreasonable.[92]

Dacre Barrett, owner of a large estate at Clones in Co. Monaghan, received this news from his agent in 1719.

The view that emigration would drain Ireland of its Protestant settlers was shared by William King, archbishop of Dublin and a commissioner for the Irish government, who wrote in 1718: 'No papists stir . . . The papists being already five or six to one, and being a breeding people, you may imagine in what condition we are like to be in.'[93] Small numbers of Ulster Presbyterians had emigrated to America in the late seventeenth century, mainly from the Laggan in north-east Donegal, but it was not until 1718 that the exodus began in earnest. In that year eleven Presbyterian ministers and nearly three hundred members of their congregations petitioned the governor of New England, Samuel Shute, for a grant of land. Shute gave every encouragement and in the summer of the same year five ships left Derry quay for Boston. James McGregor, minister of the Aghadowey congregation

176

and leader of the expedition, got a grant of land on the frontier north of the Merrimac river in what is now New Hampshire, which he named Londonderry in honour, he said, of Ulster Protestants' 'finest hour'.[94] Another ship, the *Maccullum*, followed soon after from Derry and its passengers settled at Casco Bay in Maine, where they were soon locked in conflict with local native Americans – from the outset the Ulster Presbyterians were to prove themselves pugnacious frontiersmen.

This migration across the Atlantic got under way just at the time that the coming of Scots into Ulster had almost completely ceased. Catholics had neither the resources nor the inclination to go to colonies, which were in any case still overwhelmingly Protestant. The momentum of Presbyterian emigration gathered pace – around 3,500 left Ulster between 1725 and 1727 – to reach a peak in 1728–9. Thomas Whitney, a seaman waiting to sail from Larne Lough, wrote in July 1728:

> Here are a vast number of people shipping off for Pennsylvania and Boston, here are three ships at Larne, 5 at Derry two at Coleraine 3 at Belfast and 4 at Sligo, I'm assured within these eight years there are gone above forty thousand people out of Ulster and the low part of Connacht.[95]

This was a wild overestimate but certainly the outflow was enough to alarm the Government; in November 1728 Primate Hugh Boulter, deputising for the viceroy as lord justice, informed the Duke of Newcastle:

> The humour has spread like a contagious distemper, and the people will hardly hear any body that tries to cure them of their madness. The worst is that it affects only protestants, and reigns chiefly in the north, which is the seat of our linen manufacture.[96]

Boulter contributed £500 to an appeal sponsored by the Merchant Taylors to relieve distress in Ulster and he hoped that 'this will put some stop to the great desertion we have been threatened with there . . . As bad as things have been here, I am satisfied the bulk of these adventurers worst themselves by removing to *America*, and hope the frenzy will gradually abate.'[97] He was mistaken – the following year the exodus continued unabated.

As Boulter recognised, poverty was perhaps the most important reason why Ulster Protestants decided to move on to America in this period. An *Address of Protestant Dissenting Ministers to the King* of 1729 argued that the sacramental test was found by Ulster Presbyterians to be 'so very grievous that they have in great numbers transported themselves to the American Plantations for the sake of that liberty and ease which they are denied in their native country'.[98] Almost certainly this was not the main cause, though Presbyterian ministers had a key part to play in organising the first sailings across the Atlantic; Ezekiel Stewart of Portstewart observed in 1729:

> The Presbiteirin ministers have taken their shear of pains to seduce their poor Ignorant heerers, by Bellowing from their pulpits against the Landlords and the Clargey, calling them Rackers of Rents and Scruers of Tythes . . . There are two of these Preachers caryed this affair to such a length that they went themselves to New England and caryed numbers with them . . .[99]

Some clergy themselves were in dire straits, and in 1720 the synod sent out a circular letter asking for money to help needy ministers.

Contemporaries agreed that rents were rising fast and that this was a significant factor in encouraging emigration. Immediately after the Williamite War, landowners had been anxious to attract reliable Protestant tenants, and had given out long leases at low rents. Now in more settled conditions demand for land rose sharply and as leases expired rents were jacked up; leases were generally issued to Protestants for three named lives (extending until the last of the three persons named had died) and many of these 'fell in' during the 1720s and 1730s. Repeated harvest failures made it impossible for many who renewed their tenancies to pay their rents. On the Southwell estate near Downpatrick the total rents rose from £1,244 in 1713 to £2,254 in 1731; the income from rents of thirty-four farms on the Hertford estate near Lisburn increased by more than 100 per cent from £90 5s.6d. in 1719 to £222 16s.7d. in 1728; and between 1716 and 1736 the total rental of the Clothworkers proportion in Co. Londonderry nearly doubled from £528 7s.0d. to £1,002 16s.6d.[100] These increased rents were still comparatively low by the standards of the day, but Protestants who had built up their farms often from overgrown unfenced land deeply resented higher rents when times were so hard. Tenants were therefore tempted to sell their interest in their holdings (a right accepted by most landlords and later known as the Ulster Custom) to raise a little capital to help them reach America. In 1729 Justices of Assize for the North West Circuit of Ulster reported that those preparing to emigrate

> complain that several gentlemen have lately raised their rents above the value of their lands . . . The Protestant tenants complain that many landlords turn them out of their farms and give them to Papists for the sake of a little increase in rent . . . They likewise complain of vigorous methods in payment of their tithes, the clergy generally setting their parishes to lay farmers, who they allege demand more than the value for their tithes.[101]

The same report remarked on the lure of the New World for such Protestants, noting the success of agents sent around the province by ships' masters, who 'assure them that in America they may get good land to them and their posterity for little or no rent, without either paying tithes or taxes, and amuse them with such accounts of those countries as they know will be most agreeable to them'. Primate Boulter also referred to the activities of these agents 'who deluded the people with stories of great plenty and estates to be had for going for in those parts of the world: and they have been the better able to seduce people, by reason of the necessities of the poor of late.'[102]

In the eighteenth century Ulster was an unpromising province for farming compared with other extensive regions in Ireland. Not only is it the coldest province but half its area is above three hundred feet; an underlay of carboniferous limestone extends only a little way into southern Ulster; and even there its sweetening effect is offset by poor drainage, leaving the soil cold and sticky even where it is not covered by tracts of bog and lakeland. Yet from the 1740s onwards the population of Ulster began to rise rapidly, living standards improved, and visitors frequently remarked on the many signs of prosperity to be seen everywhere. Even the most advanced agricultural improvements of the day could not have brought about such a striking advance. It was the success of the linen industry that made Ulster the most prosperous part of Ireland for the remainder of the century and beyond.

THE DOMESTIC LINEN INDUSTRY

On 30 October 1747 an advertisement appeared in the *Belfast News-Letter* offering land for leasing at Tullyvallen, Alexander Hamilton's estate in south Armagh:

> On each of the said farms there is plenty of good meadow and turf; a large river runs through the middle of said lands that never wants water sufficient to turn many mills, with many places very proper for bleaching greens, and a fall of 180 feet in less than two miles, and places where mill ponds may easily be made. By the great plenty of turf, water, bog, timber for building and meadow, the linen manufacture may be carried on as cheap as in any part of Ireland.[103]

Within easy reach of Armagh, Dundalk and Castleblayney – all good market towns – Tullyvallen soon prospered under the name it retains to this day, Newtownhamilton, and its development illustrates the intimate relationship between family farming and the emergence of the domestic linen industry. The advertisement also shows that it was very much in the landlord's interest to promote an activity that would help to make the payment of rent more certain.

From very early times the Irish had grown their own flax and made their own 'bandle linen'; it gets scant attention in Gaelic records, however, for it was woven up by people who were low born. Bandle linen was still made for local sale in the eighteenth century, but its width was too narrow for the export market. Some of the leading planters, such as the Clotworthys of south Antrim, encouraged their tenants to grow and spin flax to give them extra income to help tide them over hard times. Lancashire weavers were eager to buy Ulster yarn, but some of the colonists were weavers themselves, who knew what sold best in the English market, and by the 1680s 'Ulsters' were being recorded as a distinct variety of linen cloth. The Government, too, was keen to foster an industry that did not conflict with English commercial interests; in 1696 Irish linen, in its 'brown' or unbleached form, was freed of all English import duties and this, together with the comparatively low rents and cheap food then prevailing in Ulster keeping production costs down, at once gave northern Irish linen a distinct edge over German and Dutch cloth on the English market. Only the import duty on dyed Irish linens proved prohibitive, and though the customs charge on 'white' or bleached linen was not removed until 1782, it did not prevent a dramatic growth of exports for most of the eighteenth century.[104] Total linen exports rose from two and a half million yards in the 1720s to eight million yards in the 1740s and seventeen million yards by the 1800s.

The Irish parliament, keenly aware of the need to promote economic development, devoted much of its time to the linen industry. For example, it paid the Huguenot Louis Crommelin to establish a colony of skilled weavers in Lisburn in 1698. Though the enterprise was only partly successful and the craftsmen were scattered by a terrible fire which destroyed the town in 1707, information on the latest continental techniques was spread widely across Ulster. Then an act of 1710 set aside funds raised from import duties on calico and linen (and later on, tea, coffee, chocolate and cocoa nuts) for 'the use of hempen and flaxen manufactures in this kingdom and to no other use whatsoever'.[105] The seventy-two trustees of this fund, known as the Irish Linen Board, were almost all members of the Irish parliament. What they lacked in expertise they made up for in the influence they could wield, particularly over the many Irishmen who sat for British constituencies in the Westminster House of Commons. The board gave grants to inventors, subsidies to bleachers, bounties on the export of sailcloth, spinning wheels to the poor, tuition fees to spinning schools, and at different times supported every branch of the trade. Though it was frequently and sometimes outrageously defrauded, the board unquestionably gave invaluable support in the first decades of its life.[106]

Ulster weavers had neither the capital nor the contacts to export directly to England, and English merchants preferred to come to Dublin three or four times a year to buy Irish linen. The linen board built a

Linen Hall on the north side of the city in 1728 and the Ulster origin of most of the cloth brought there is underlined by the names of the streets adjoining it: Coleraine Street, Lurgan Street and Lisburn Street. Here linen brought from the north in solid-wheeled carts was sold to Dublin 'factors', who in turn struck deals with English merchants, and it was not until the 1780s that the capital ceased to be the main point of export for Ulster cloth.

The making of linen in Ulster was essentially a domestic industry carried on for the most part by people who divided their time between farming and the making of yarn and cloth. Flax is a greedy crop, requiring good soil and heavy manuring, but if it could be included in the farm's rotation, it was a good cash crop which went a long way towards paying the rent. Planted in the spring and producing a delicate blue flower in early summer, flax was ready for harvesting around the middle of August. To ensure as long a fibre as possible, it was pulled, not cut, and then tied in sheaves, or beets, and allowed to dry in stooks for a few days. The beets were weighed down in a pond or dammed stream, known as a lint hole, and allowed to rot for about a fortnight, when they were raised and spread on fields to dry. Only after the flax was 'broken', 'scutched' and 'hackled' – each process in itself intensely laborious – could the fibres be made into yarn: long fibres produced fine linen yarn, while short fibres were suitable for coarse cloth.

The native Irish had spun yarn from a distaff with a weighted stone, or whorl, but this was being rapidly replaced by a treadle-operated spinning wheel. The linen board distributed thousands of these, mostly of the Dutch or Castle design. By the end of the century a spinning wheel was given to anyone 'who should sow between the 10th Day of March and the 1st Day of June 1796, with a sufficient Quantity of good sound Flax-seed, any Quantity of Land, well prepared and fit for the purpose'.[107] In that year the parish of Clontibret, in Co. Monaghan, alone received 312 wheels.

The yarn, wound on a clock reel, was ready for the weaver – usually a man, for weaving was heavy work. Preparing the loom was time-consuming, often taking more than a week:

> There is considerable skill and knowledge required for putting up a loom properly, mounting her, and giving her a complete rig. Sometimes the weaver can do this for himself, but often he possesses not the necessary knowledge, nor the way to carry it into practice. And hence, in almost every country district, there are some of clearer heads and readier hands who become a sort of professors in this line.[108]

When the loom was tackled, the warp threads had to be dressed with flour and water, fanned dry with a wing, and then rubbed with tallow.

Only then was the weft ready to be placed in the hand shuttle – the 'flying shuttle' was not adopted for linen weaving until the beginning of the nineteenth century. Linen cloth was usually woven into a web, a roll of cloth a yard wide and twenty-five yards in length. The web of unbleached linen then had to be cleaned of its tallow and flour and whitened before it was ready for the tailor.

Early in the eighteenth century weavers bleached their own webs but this process was almost as labour intensive as the making of the cloth itself and took around six months. The linen had to be boiled and rinsed between seven and twelve times, and then laid out on the grass for a week or so between each boiling to be whitened by the sun and the rain.[109] Even then linen was not ready for sale until the weave had been closed and given a sheen by being hammered on a flat stone with a wooden club, or beetle. Not only was this exhausting but it long delayed the time when a family could get hard cash for its webs. These finishing processes were the first to become mechanised, drapers raising capital in Dublin to harness the streams to drive engines by water power.

Even during the last decade of the seventeenth century Ulster had remained the poorest province in Ireland, and this poverty had been aggravated by the destruction and dislocation of the Williamite War. The early part of the eighteenth century had been characterised by privation arising out of endemic harvest failure. Now, in the 1740s, the application of a new sophisticated technology to the making of linen gave a dramatic impulse to the region's economy. This, together with the cultivation of an exotic crop, the potato, the opening up of fresh colonial markets, and improved international trading conditions, would make Ulster the most prosperous of the four provinces and ultimately Europe's leading producer of fine linen.

7

PROSPERITY, REVOLUTION AND REACTION

c. 1750–1800

OVERVIEW

In east Tyrone small amounts of coal had been dug out of the ground from the middle of the seventeenth century, but the sinking of deep shafts in the 1720s revealed deposits on a scale not yet found anywhere in Ireland. This discovery, observed the county historian Walter Harris in 1744,

> was a natural Benefit thought very worthy of publick Record: And accordingly a Plan was laid for bringing this Coal by Sea to Dublin, where the Consumption of that sort of Fuel is computed to cost £70,000 per Annum . . . This noble Undertaking was carried on by Parliamentary Encouragement.[1]

This ambitious project was to construct a man-made waterway from Lough Neagh, thrusting through the drumlins, over Poyntz Pass to the sea at Newry. In 1742 the work was complete and that year, after negotiating fifteen locks and sailing down the Irish Sea, the *Dublin Newsletter* reported, the *Cope* 'came into this Harbour laden with Coals and being the first vessel that has come through the Canal had a flag at her topmost head and fired guns as she came up the Channel'.[2]

The hope that Co. Tyrone would provide Ireland's capital city with all its fuel needs proved illusory, but Harris was right to predict that the 'Benefit arising to the Kingdom from the Execution of this scheme will be very considerable, as a thorough Trade will be carried on by inland Navigation between Dublin and the Counties of Armagh, Down, Antrim and Tirone, for all kinds of Goods and Manufactures'.[3] Improved communications helped to ensure that when harvests failed, distress and higher prices were usually the result, rather than thousands dying of starvation as in earlier times. Ulster became the most prosperous province in Ireland – the evangelist John Wesley wrote in his *Journal* in 1756: 'No sooner did we enter Ulster than we observed the difference. The ground was cultivated just as in England, and the cottages not only neat, but with doors, chimneys and windows.'[4] Three years later a circuit judge, Edward Willes, observed:

From Monaghan quite to Carrickfergus, which is about fifty miles, is the very picture of industry, nor did I ever see in England or Ireland a finer cultivated country. The whole road for the space of fifty miles is, as it were, one continued village of neat cottages . . . 'Tis a fine sight to behold the great number of bleach yards: they look like white patches of unmelted snow in the winter time.[5]

The long peace was the bedrock of Ulster's eighteenth-century prosperity. Yet growth and change created new tensions. The history of this period can be seen as a race between productivity and population explosion. Productivity was generally ahead, but the province was more exposed than before to international fluctuations and the downturn of the 1770s stimulated rural unrest and intense political excitement. The route to America provided an invaluable safety valve, but the landlords' monopoly of power and wealth was increasingly challenged by a rising Presbyterian middle class inspired by subversive ideas accompanying incoming cargoes of American flaxseed and French brandy. For a time the north-east became the most radical centre in Ireland and some democrats there, inspired by revolution in France, threw themselves into conspiracy. Ruthless repression, sectarian violence in mid-Ulster and the decisive defeat of rebellion in 1798 shattered the fiery idealism of the radicals. The Union of 1801 was greeted neither by enthusiastic support nor by strong hostility – most people in Ulster were simply thankful they had survived.

LINEN ON THE GREEN

In 1776 Arthur Young visited the linen market at Lurgan, Co. Armagh:

The cambricks are sold early, and through the whole morning; but when the clock strikes eleven the drapers jump upon stone standings, and the weavers instantly flock about them with their pieces . . . The draper's clerk stands by him, and writes his master's name on the pieces he buys, with the price . . . At twelve it ends; then there is an hour for measuring the pieces, and paying the money; for nothing but ready money is taken; and this is the way the business is carried on at all the markets. Three thousand pieces a week are sold here, at 35s each on an average, or £5,250, and per annum £273,000 and this is all made in a circumference of not many miles.[6]

Landlords vied with each other to get patents to run markets, for though linen was exempt from tolls, weavers bought oatmeal, meat, butter, candles and other essentials with their earnings. Drapers bought cloth unbleached, thus giving weavers a quicker return for their work. In effect these linen merchants became Ulster's first capitalists, investing their profits in bleach greens, where, with the aid of water power, they finished the cloth to the high standard required by the English market.

With much hilly ground, steady rainfall and poor evaporation, Ulster abounds in streams suited to water power. In the seventeenth century cornmills turned by horizontal wheels transferred to more efficient vertical wheels. The power transmitted from the wheel down the axle could be harnessed to an impressive array of labour-saving machines by the linen drapers. The drapers, in short, made sure that Ulster had an important and early role to play in Europe's first industrial revolution.

The heart of the industry was the 'linen triangle', extending from Dungannon, east to Lisburn, and south to Armagh; then, as output increased, Newry was drawn in. Within this area and later beyond it, drapers sought out suitable sites for their bleach yards along the rivers, particularly the upper Bann, from Balleevy to Gilford; the Lagan, from Lambeg to Donaghcloney; the Callan, from Milford south to Keady; and the Claudy, the Agivey, the Aghadowey, the Main, the Braid, and the Sixmilewater.[7] On the Callan there were no bleach works until 1743, and yet by 1771 there were thirty-six bleach yards along its banks and its tributaries, finishing 108,500 pieces totalling 2,712,500 yards. By 1795 it was reckoned there were fifty-one bleach yards in Co. Armagh, finishing 162,500 pieces of linen, for which the drapers had paid £270,000.[8] A typical concern might cover three acres and have two or three water wheels.

The linen was first steeped in a great wooden tank with a bottom of stone flags, then put on grass for three or four days before being 'bucked' or boiled, in an alkaline lye for twelve hours – a process repeated ten times.[9] Thereafter it was steeped in an acid solution before being washed again. Rub boards – corrugated wooden boards which were pushed backwards and forwards by water power while wet soaped cloth was drawn between them – came into use as early as 1705 and were a local invention.[10] Some drapers agreed with Young, who remarked that 'the rubbing appears to me an operation for giving the cloth beauty at the expence of strength . . . This is a very fine invention for wearing out a manufacture as soon as made.'[11] The wash mill, introduced in the 1720s, was an adaptation from the English fulling mill: two massive feet, or stocks, each weighing around a quarter of a ton, were suspended from a great wooden frame and swung to swirl and squeeze the cloth. In between these repeated operations the linen pieces were laid on spread fields to bleach in the sun, wind and rain, carefully guarded from watch houses.[12] That a vigilant eye had to be kept on the bleaching webs is clear from this *Belfast News-Letter* report of 11 April 1783:

At the assizes for the county of Down, which ended on Wednesday last, the following persons were capitally convicted, and received sentence as follows . . . Stephen Gordon, otherwise McGurnaghan (to be executed at Castlewellan on Monday next the 14th inst.) for stealing linen out of the bleachgreen of George and Walter Crawford of Balleivy; George Brown (to be executed at Downpatrick 1st June next) for stealing linen out of the bleachgreen of Samuel McAlester of Lisnamore; John Wright (to be executed at Banbridge on Monday 21st inst.) for stealing linen cloth out of the bleachgreen of James Clibborn at Banbridge, and John Holmes (to be executed at Downpatrick on the 1st June next) for receiving said linen knowing it to be stolen.[13]

In the middle of the century few bleach greens could finish more than a thousand pieces in a year, but by the beginning of the nineteenth century some could process as many as ten thousand. In part this was due to better chemical treatment: in the 1750s dilute sulphuric acid replaced buttermilk sour; and then in 1785 the bleaching power of chlorine was discovered, which greatly speeded up finishing and allowed it to take place all year round.[14]

The first beetling engine seems to have been set up at Drum Bridge on the Lagan in 1725, with a Dutchman as manager. A striking improvement on hand beating, this technology was soon adopted by all the drapers. A row of heavy beams (usually of beech and each five feet long) dropped in turn onto the cloth, the stamping process bringing out the natural lustre of the fibres, and giving the necessary sheen to high-quality ducks, hollands, hucks, buckrams, interlinings, and umbrella and book-binding cloth.[15] As pounding one piece could last up to a fortnight and beat out a thunderous tattoo reminiscent of a huge Lambeg drum, the beetling mill had to be placed some distance from the main works. Wallace Clark, whose ancestor erected the first beetling mill in Co. Londonderry at Upperlands, describes this deafening new machinery in *Linen on the Green*:

The sound, orchestrated by the squeak and creak of the wheel, and the splash of water, was like forty wooden wheeled drays being galloped over a cobbled bridge.[16]

Water power was also harnessed in scutch mills to break flax between pairs of revolving grooved rollers and to beat off unwanted pith and skin by fast-turning wooden blades. Even by the twentieth century, this method had changed little and the work was unpleasant and dangerous:

I remember people losing fingers. It was cold work as we scutched in the winter-time and there was no heating inside the mill because of the danger of fire. It was unhealthy work too as the air was full of dust from the shoves, sometimes so thick you could hardly see to the other side of the room. It certainly did not suit people with weak chests or asthma.[17]

The health of workers was of no concern to the linen board in its regulation of the trade to maintain standards. On the whole, its intervention was beneficial to the merchants: it persuaded the Irish parliament to pass laws in 1733 to enforce the inspection of cloth and in 1745 to ensure that linen was lapped in open folds so that any part could easily be examined by the buyer.[18] The return of a large consignment of linen from Chester market, due to faults in weaving, led the board, in 1762, to command the sealing of webs for quality before being sold. In May of that year weavers in Lisburn rose in revolt, surging through the market belabouring drapers with blackthorn sticks and destroying their property. The military had to be called in to disperse them, but the weavers had overreached themselves – Lord Hillsborough insisted on the new seals in Lisburn and parliament enforced them two years later. Within a few weeks of the new law, 1,300 sealmasters were appointed. The linen board had the good sense to appoint weavers and to trust that they would only mark good-quality cloth for fear of giving their own work a bad name. In 1782 it was the turn of the board to go too far when it called on sealmasters to take an oath including the words: 'I will not knowingly seal or stamp ... any linen that is mildewed, rotten, unmerchantable, or fraudulently made up.'[19] Drapers and weavers alike were insulted, forced the board to withdraw its scheme, and – blaming the Dublin merchants – decided to market their own cloth in Ulster. White linen halls were built in Newry and Belfast in 1783; Dublin lost its role but the halls were not a success for by this time drapers had both the contacts and the funds to deal directly with English merchants.

In the late eighteenth century there was a rough balance of power between drapers and weavers. After visiting the linen market in Armagh city, Arthur Young noted: 'There are many drapers, so that the man tries whom he pleases: there is no combination against the seller, but rather a competition.'[20] He also noticed that drapers 'find here that when provisions are very cheap the poor spend much of their time in whiskey-houses. All the drapers wish that oatmeal was never under 1d a pound.'[21] When trade was brisk drapers often sent 'jobbers' to the homes of weavers and to distant markets to make sure they had enough webs to finish. The extent of competition is illustrated by the market book of Thomas Greer of Dungannon in 1748–59: it shows that even in his home town he bought 559 pieces from 329 weavers, of whom 233 sold to him on only one occasion, and 64 on only two occasions.[22] Drapers themselves competed vigorously with one another, though rivalry could be softened by commercial interdependence, family connection and friendship. In 1795 these lines of verse were enclosed with a pack of linen sent from Thomas Stott and Company, Dromore, to James Gilmour, Garvagh:

This morn, Frien' James, we sent a wheen
Of good thick lawns and cambrics thin
To Maister Mirries at Belfast
(As we've been wont this sometime past).
The hail are packed in ae stout kist
That nothing hurtful might maelist.

The lawns we fear ye'll no think cheap
Though we by them smal' profit reap.
The cambrics, tho' they luk but lean
Will make a shift to haud their ain.
On baith to this bit paper joined
The bill o' parcels ye will find.
An' we hae placed the fair amount
Right cannily to your account,
Which, if we cast the figures straight,
Is just of pounds four score and eight,
Five Irish siller shillins smug
And six bawbees – to buy a mug.[23]

This flourishing industry not only brought prosperity to those directly engaged in it but also stimulated the whole economy of the north by providing a ready market for the produce of farms across the province.

THE EXPANSION OF FARMING

'I am now got into the linen country, and the worst husbandry I have met with', Young noted in his journal as he made his way from Ravensdale by an 'abominably bad' turnpike road into Co. Armagh. Yet at the same time he saw that the local people were more prosperous than in any other part of Ireland and later realised that linen, not farming, was their main source of income. At Kilmore, near Lurgan, he observed: 'They are in general very bad farmers, being but the second attention', and that flax growing had 'a bad effect on them, stiffening their fingers and hands, so that they do not return to their work so well as they left it'. On the road between Belfast and Antrim Young acidly remarked that the farmer-weavers did no more with their land than turn some cows on it: 'Pity they do not improve . . . The linen manufacture spreads over the whole country, consequently the farms are very small, being nothing but patches for the convenience of weavers.' However, as he continued his tour of 1776 he was to find that much of the land in Ulster was intensively and efficiently farmed. Arriving at Shane's Castle, for example, he was 'most agreeably saluted with four men hoeing a field of turneps round it, as a preparation for grass. These were the first turnep hoers I have seen in Ireland, and I was more pleased than if I had seen four emperors.'[24]

For farmer-weavers the first priority was to rent land as close as possible to the main linen markets and for this they were prepared to pay exceptionally high rents. Expenses could be reduced by taking in a journeyman weaver as a lodger and by subletting to labourers for a year at a time. These labourers, or cottiers, grew flax and potatoes, and earned a few shillings by spinning yarn. In this way farming provided an important buffer if there was a sudden downturn in the market for linen.[25] The only prolonged slump was in the 1770s and the steady rise in the population of the linen triangle provided an immense market for food – the incentive to increase the yield of the soil and to bring waterlogged lands, scrub and mountain sides into full cultivation was therefore strong.

The great forests of Glenconkeyne, Killultagh and the Dufferin had been swept away and the oakwoods south of Lough Neagh had only partly been replaced by orchards. When the woodland of the Roe valley was felled in 1770, Co. Londonderry was left more bereft of trees than any other county in Ireland, and only the margins and islands of Lough Erne, some slopes of the Sperrins and Glenveagh mountains, and a couple of the Glens of Antrim were left with woods of any respectable size.[26] Losing their habitat, the native red deer became extinct in the north, and the last wolf was killed in the Sperrins in the 1760s. No attempt was made to coppice trees and settlers recklessly squandered the woodlands not only to build their homes and towns but also to export barrel staves, boards and ship timber. For a time ironworks and tanneries had flourished. Sir Charles Coote of Cavan once employed 2,500 men in his ironfounding concern and it, along with other similar enterprises, had been the most prodigal consumer of wood – it took two and a half tons of charcoal to make one ton of bar iron. Thomas Waring, five times sovereign of Belfast between 1652 and 1666, had a large tannery between North Street and Waring Street and he and his family had other tanneries at Toome, Derriaghy and Lurgan. Tanners preferred to strip bark from living oak and eventually their depredations deprived them of their raw material, though small pits survived at Cootehill, Killeshandra, Ballycastle, Enniskillen and Belfast.[27]

In the eighteenth century the scarcity of local wood had become acute: as early as 1718 it was noted that wood was 'extraordinary dear' in Ballyclare and in 1735 that in Carrickfergus 'timber is so dear . . . that it is better to sell the ground than to build'.[28] In 1780 a mighty tree forty-two feet in girth, known as the Royal Oak, was felled on the Conway estate near Antrim. Part of it was sawn up to build a fifty-ton vessel for Lough Neagh but – as a striking illustration of the soaring price of wood products – the bark alone of this single oak was sold for £40. Belfast depended heavily on wood imported from eastern Europe and by 1751 timber imports for the whole island were valued at £56,000. Too late the Irish parliament made the felling of trees at night a felony, and grand juries, not only courts but until 1898 the local government of the Irish countryside, were instructed to plant woods; 132,000 acres were planted by 1801, but as Young observed, 'the greatest part of the kingdom exhibits a naked, bleak, dreary view for want of wood'.[29]

Forest clearance did nevertheless increase land available for farming. Together with the maintenance of peace, two vital ingredients were available to make possible the intensive exploitation of wetlands, scrub and mountain: potatoes and turf. The earliest authenticated reference to potatoes in Ireland dates from 1606 when Hugh Montgomery's wife gave Scots land for this crop at Comber, still the best known centre for potatoes in Ulster.[30] The potato, which tolerates a wide range of soils, was considered the best crop for clearing land and provided an abundant staple diet – it was reckoned that one Irish acre could feed eight people for a year. The most characteristic implement for preparing and cultivating new land was the loy, from the Irish *láighe*, a spade with a long shaft, one foot rest and a narrow iron blade; this was ideal for cutting and turning the sod. Heath and coarse grass sods were lifted, dried and burned, and the ashes spread to fertilise the soil beneath. The Irish parliament passed an act in 1743 outlawing this 'paring and burning' but it could not be enforced and later it was recognised that provided manure was dug in, this was a good way to bring scrub land into cultivation. Potatoes were grown on raised ridges known, inappropriately, as lazy beds: sods were carefully turned over (with elaborate local variations in technique), ashes spread over these, potatoes planted on top and then covered with mould from the adjacent furrow. The broad foliage of the growing haulms then helped to suppress weeds by blocking out the sunlight. Potatoes became part of the rotation with barley and, if the soil could be made fertile enough, flax.[31]

Turf from the bog (known as 'peats from the moss' in areas of dense Lowland Scots settlement) not only provided hard-won but abundant firing and building material (in the form of sods and bog oak) but also found a ready market in the valleys to heat the bleachers' boilers. Cash earned in this way could buy limestone or marl to be taken back up to the hills, there to be burned in kilns to sweeten acid soils. Liming increased the fertility of the soil for perhaps a dozen years after application but, as Walter Harris, author of *The Antient and Present State of the County of Down*, pointed out in 1744 when describing marling in Lecale:

It may be worth considering, whether the Injudicious Use of this unctu-
ous Earth may not in time impoverish, and render the Soil unprolifick, by
giving the Earth too great a Fermentation; and skilful Husbandmen
already begin to complain of it upon this Account.[32]

Liming had to be balanced by adequate dunging. Animal manures
were so precious that cottiers usually kept their heaps in clear view in
front of their cabins, while in Gweedore byre dwellings were mucked
out only once a year to produce between ten and fifteen tons of manure
from each house.[33]

The opening up of new land yielded rewards slowly enough and the
labour of cultivation and the prising out of rocks or stumps was unremitting, as Harris acknowledged when describing farming at Dromara
on the slopes of Slieve Croob:

The face of the Country hereabouts is rough, bleak and unimproved; yet
produces the Necessaries of Life sufficient to support a large Number of
Inhabitants, who have little other Bread Corn but Oats, of which they
make great Quantities of Meal to supply not only themselves, but the
neighbouring Markets. They are an industrious hardy People, and may
be properly said *to eat their Bread in the Sweat of their Face*, the Courseness
of the Land obliging them to great Labour. The Coldness of the Soil
occasions their Harvests to be late; yet by due Care and Culture it yields
Rye and great Quantities of Flax. The Plenty of cheap firing got out of
Bogs and Mosses throughout this whole Country does not a little contribute to the Service of the Linen Trade.[34]

Coastal farms could draw on the bounty of the sea and even today
shell sand is still highly prized for spreading on peaty, acid soils. Harris
found the lands about Tyrella, in Co. Down, so enriched by 'Sea-shells,
of which there is a vast plenty at Hand, that they yield 15s to 20s *per*
Acre. The Shells lie within two Foot of the Surface of the Earth, and
ought to remain spread on the Land for three Years before they are
plowed in, and then it will produce all sorts of Grain for 10 Years at
least.'[35] Young counted thirty-five kilns on the road between Newtownards and Portaferry burning limestone shipped from Carlingford, and
along the shore of Strangford Lough he

observed heaps of white shells; and upon enquiry, found that they dig
them at low water in the Loch in any quantities . . . Shells are some time
before they work, but they last longer than lime, directly contrary to what
I was told before, from whence one may suppose the point disputable.[36]

Sea weed was rightly seen as an excellent manure and was gathered along every shore; native Irish speakers in Donegal carefully
distinguished between the various species while English speakers
referred to seaweed as wrack, sea bar and kelp. Knotted, bladder and

191

saw wrack were carefully cultivated around the Co. Down shoreline, particularly in Mill Bay and around the Ards peninsula, in rectangular plots or 'cuts' marked out with boulders, which also gave anchorage for the weed.[37] Elsewhere wrack was used almost exclusively for manuring potatoes, particularly in Co. Donegal, where it was cut and gathered into currachs. Storms blew in kelp and other weed from the deeps, also eagerly harvested; 'kelp', however, was a word then used for seaweed of any kind burned to ash for bleaching and fertiliser. Harris observed:

> But this Vegetable is too precious to be used much as a Manure; for they turn it to a better Account by burning it into Kelp, which they do in such great Quantities, that they not only supply the Linen Manufacturers in this and neighbouring Counties, but export it in Abundance for the Use of the Glass-Houses in *Dublin* and *Bristol*, as appears from the Custom-House Books of *Portaferry*.[38]

Young noted that some gentlemen rented stretches of shoreline and that kelp ashes sold for forty or fifty shillings a ton.

RABBITS, GEESE, WHISKEY, WHALES AND FISH

The remarkable expansion of western Europe's commercial wealth, overseas trade, industrial enterprise and population – particularly in Britain – was responsible ultimately for Ulster's rapid development in the eighteenth century. In England especially the ability of the market to take increasing quantities of linen provided a vital stimulus to the province's economy. It would be wrong, however, to regard all in the north as engaged either in making linen or in making food available for the linen triangle.

The north-west of Ulster could be seen as a distinct economic region; even with the inclusion of Coleraine, the area contributed only around 15 per cent of the annual total of brown linen sales in the north. Farming was the main activity but much of the land was poor and unyielding. In Magilligan, a flat sandy headland in north Co. Londonderry, salt spray damaged grass and crops, and to prosper the people had to supplement their income in other ways.[39] Here the sand dunes and marram grass were home to the most extensive rabbit warren in Ulster; the local people – trapping the animals with ferrets and nets – sold the carcasses in the region for about 4d. each, or ate the meat themselves and found buyers eager to take the skins for Dublin's large hatting trade. The Gage family, leasing the land from the Church, tripled the rent to 120 dozen rabbit skins in the 1750s and instituted a restricted killing season from November to February. By the beginning of the nineteenth century the annual take was around 2,500 dozen animals, selling at thirteen shillings a dozen.[40] In winter barnacle geese flying in from the north could be trapped at night, as Dean Henry observed in 1739:

> In the Months of October, November and December there come into it vast flights of Barnacles, which as they fly low along the Southern Shore, are taken on Nets Erected on long poles.[41]

Lough Foyle was famous for its oysters and Magilligan farms often paid part of their rent in honey, for, as it was noted in 1725, the 'abundance of and great variety of flowers rendered Magilligan honey so delicious that the produce of Tircreven commanded a higher price than any other brought to the Dublin market'. This coastline was already attracting summer visitors seeking good health, as is seen in a *Belfast News-Letter* advertisement of March 1771:

> The Goat's Whey here far exceeds that of any other part of the Kingdom, owing to the Nature of their browsing, which abounds with wild Thyme and many other salubrious Herbs; and as to Salt Water Bathing Places, they are excelled by none.[42]

Nearly all the barley in the north-west was grown for making whiskey and by the 1780s there were no fewer than forty legal distillers in Co. Londonderry, with Coleraine second only to Dublin in importance. After 1779 the Irish parliament – in an attempt to boost sales of beer and stout – jacked up the excise duty on spirits, leaving only Newry and Belfast with legal distilleries by the beginning of the nineteenth century. Nevertheless, the making of illegal poteen flourished in the north-west, particularly on the Inishowen peninsula and at Magilligan, where stills could be hidden behind the dunes from gaugers' eyes. The Ordnance Survey of 1835 reckoned that thirty years earlier there were no fewer than four hundred illicit stills operating in Magilligan alone, and in 1791 a correspondent of the *Londonderry Journal* wrote that no legal distilleries had survived in the area 'and yet whiskey is as plenty and pernicious as ever. Thus we have a drunken commonalty without a farthing of revenue.'[43] Barley for poteen-making generally sold for three times the usual price and its cultivation spread wealth so widely that it encouraged landlords to raise rents. It was stated in 1808 that 'Loch Foyle was generally covered with boats, transporting illicit spirits from Inishowen to the County of Londonderry, from whence their cargoes were smuggled over a great part of Ireland'.[44]

The Irish have been notoriously unwilling to eat fish except on fast days and the consumption of shellfish was a mark of extreme poverty. Yet the planters prized the oysters of Strangford and Lough Foyle, and in times of harvest failure the prolific coastal and inland waters helped to save people from starvation. Harris wrote in 1744:

The Coast affords plenty and variety of Sea Fish, and such Quantities of Sand Eels have sometimes been taken on it, particularly in the late Season of scarcity, that the Poor carried them away in Sack fulls . . . On the Shores about *Hollywood* are found vast Quantities of Muscles, (but not of the sort that breed Pearls) on which the poor Inhabitants feed much without feeling any Inconvenience, dressing them when shelled with Butter, Pepper and Onions.[45]

Young observed that 'the whole barony of Ards are fishermen, sailors, and farmers, by turns' and that Portaferry alone had 110 fishing boats.[46] There the herring fishery began on 12 July in Strangford Lough and finished in September, each boat netting about six maze (three thousand) herring every night in season. The fishery in Co. Donegal was on a much larger scale. Robert Alexander, a Derry merchant, founded a major concern on Lough Swilly in 1773 and built a large salt house, capable of holding two hundred tons, for preserving herring for export to feed slaves in the West Indies. Between mid-October and Christmas the shoals were immense; Young learned that the herring 'swarmed so, that a boat which went out at 7 in the evening, returned at 11 full, and went out on a second trip. The fellows said it was difficult to row through them.'[47] In south Donegal another great enterprise was run by Alexander Montgomery, Lord Conyngham's agent, who had his own salt works and made his own nets from imported Baltic hemp, tanning them with bark and waterproofing them with a mixture of tar and fish oil. Young regretted the absence of 'smoak houses' for kippers, remarking that 'it is a strange neglect, that the landlords do not plant some of the monstrous wastes in this country with a quick growing copse wood'. Conyngham, with government help, invested some £50,000 in the fishery; but the Chevalier de Latocnaye found it in difficulties in 1796: 'The herrings were, with reason, frightened by these immense preparations which seemed to menace their entire destruction, and took themselves off and have not reappeared since.'[48]

Co. Donegal was also the centre of Ireland's whaling industry; sperm whales were present between November and February, followed in the spring by baleen whales. Thomas Nesbit of Kilmacrennan claimed to have invented the harpoon gun in 1759, taking whales with it when Dutch, Danish and British vessels failed to get any, along with forty-two basking sharks in a week, extracting up to a ton of oil from each fish. When a whale was killed, Nesbit let it sink to the bottom for two days, 'where he leaves a boat, or a cask, as a buoy to mark the place, to be ready there when the whale rises, that they may tow it into harbour'.[49]

Lough Neagh had its own species of white fish, known as pollan, then considered a freshwater herring. It also had trout known as dollaghan, which still run the feeder streams to spawn, the largest,

Harris informs us, 'called the *Buddagh*, some of which have been taken that amounted to 30 Pounds weight', and he adds: 'Of later Years great Numbers of *Pikes* have got into it, and have increased prodigiously.'[50] Salmon from Lough Erne only cost 1½d. a pound, but Young observed 'trout, perch, pike, and bream, so plentiful as to have no price. Sir James Caldwell has taken 17 cwt of fish, bream and pike, in one day.' At Coleraine Young just missed seeing 1,452 salmon taken at one drag of one net, but 'I had the pleasure of seeing 370 drawn in at once', and at the leap he noted straw ropes hung in the water to give elvers coming from the sea a route past the falls on their way to Lough Neagh; on their return the eels were trapped at Toome to the value of £1,000 a year. The Ballyshannon salmon fishery was let annually for £400 and there Young was 'delighted to see the salmon jump, to me an unusual sight: the water was perfectly alive with them'.[51]

'The Irish gentry are an expensive people, they live in the most open hospitable manner continually feasting with one another', the English antiquary John Loveday remarked during a tour made in 1732.[52] Certainly there is ample evidence that the great landowners in Ulster in the eighteenth century could afford an extravagant lifestyle. Sarah Siddons, the celebrated actress, visited her friend Lady O'Neill at Shane's Castle in 1783:

It is scarce possible to conceive the splendour of this almost Royal Establishment, except by recollecting the circumstances of an Arabian Night's entertainment. Six or eight carriages with a numerous throung of Lords and Ladies and gentlemen on Horseback began the day by making excursions about this terrestrial paradise, returning home but just in time to dress for dinner. The table was served with a profusion and elegance to which I have never seen anything comparable . . . A fine band of musicians played during the repast. They were stationed on the Corridor, which led from the dining room into a fine Conservatory, where we plucked our dessert from numerous trees of the most exquisite fruits, and where the waves of the superb Lake wash'd its feet while its delicious murmurs were accompanied with strains of celestial harmony from the Corridor.[53]

The uncertainty and turbulence of the seventeenth century had made it difficult for grantees to realise the full potential of their estates; now in the eighteenth century they reaped the material rewards of victorious peace. Except in Antrim and Down, estates were compact and fairly easily managed, and to promote the plantation the Crown had given landlords exceptional authority: an act of 1747 confirmed their right to pack town corporations with their agents, friends and relations; unlike most of their English counterparts they controlled manor courts, giving them swift and cheap regulation of their arrangements with tenants; and by applying for royal patents they could promote lucrative weekly markets and annual fairs on their lands. The county grand juries were entirely controlled by the local gentry, who could vote much of the county 'cess' to the building of roads and other projects of direct benefit to their estates. The plantation and later confiscations ensured that virtually all the farmland of Ulster was enclosed and so proprietors avoided the expense and delay so many English landlords had in getting rid of the scattered holdings of the open-field system. In return for long leases and compact farms, tenants agreed to erect their own farm buildings and fence all the outbounds of their lands. The great influx of colonists in the closing years of the seventeenth century meant there was no need to tout for Protestant tenants on the best lands, and Catholic natives, if they did not become undertenants, were compelled to move out to open up more marginal land.

'Long leases are the ruin of Ireland and of every man in it and the great obstruction to improvement,' grumbled Lord Abercorn in 1770 – arrangements that had been so convenient earlier in the century now led to fixed rents at a time of fast-rising land values, allowing tenants to sublet very profitably. Leases end eventually, however, and when they fell in landlords were able to raise rents and make direct arrangements with subtenants to their own profit; this was especially true in the linen triangle, where weavers would pay high rents to stay close to the markets. The rise in prosperity and in population – between 1753 and 1791 the number of houses paying hearth tax in Ulster almost doubled – gave northern landlords a unique opportunity to 'set', or lease, their estates to give them a much higher income. Henry Cavendish wrote in 1784:

I am just returned from the North where I have been setting between three and four thousand acres. The populousness of that county owing to the linen manufacture enabled me to set the lands to much better advantage than I can set lands of the same quality of Munster, I may reasonably say twenty-five per cent better.[54]

It is true that rents received by the great landowners failed on average to keep up with land values, and that several were guilty of gross mismanagement. In return for cash payments some owners gave out very long leases or even leases in perpetuity, often with low rents. For example, in Co. Monaghan the Massereene family got only £1,082 a year for their 21,755 statute acres of land; almost half of Lord Macartney's estate at Ballymoney was let in perpetuity at 1¹/₂d. an acre; over a quarter of Lord Erne's land at Lifford brought in just over a shilling an acre; and in Co. Londonderry the Haberdashers, Goldsmiths, Vintners and Merchant Taylors had let all of their property on perpetuity leases by the end of the eighteenth century.[55] Nevertheless, most of the great landed proprietors in Ulster – even those badly in debt – lived as lavishly as German princes, building sumptuous mansions and laying out extensive gardens.

CASTLES, MANSIONS AND PALACES: 'THE SPOILED CHILDREN OF FORTUNE'

Until after the close of the Williamite War the gentry of Ulster had to build with defence as well as comfort and beauty in mind. The Rowan Hamilton family at Killyleagh and Lord O'Neill at Edenduffcarrick both included portions of old castles in their mansions, but most eighteenth-century landowners preferred to make a fresh start. Without exception, all looked east across the Irish Sea for inspiration. The classical style became the vogue when Sir Gustavus Hume, high sheriff of Co. Fermanagh, invited the Huguenot architect Richard Cassels to build his country seat on the western peninsula of lower Lough Erne in 1728; Cassels also designed Ballyhaise House for Colonel Newburgh in Co. Cavan before moving on to build for richer patrons further south. Robert Adam sent over plans for the rebuilding of Castle Upton in Co. Antrim, and James Wyatt, after designing Baronscourt in Co. Tyrone, was engaged to oversee the erection of Castle Coole, his neo-classical masterpiece.[56]

It cost Armar Lowry-Corry, the 1st Earl of Belmore, some £90,000 to build Castle Coole. He chartered a brig to bring Portland stone from the Isle of Wight to a specially constructed quay at Ballyshannon; from there the blocks were carted ten miles to Lough Erne to be taken by barge to Enniskillen, and more bullock carts were used for the last two miles to complete the delivery. In 1791 there were 25 stone cutters, 26 stone masons, 10 stone sawyers, 17 carpenters, and 83 labourers at work on the site. Visiting in 1796, de Latocnaye found the interior 'full of rare marbles, and the walls of several rooms are covered with rare stucco work produced at great cost, and by workers brought from Italy'. He thought it was a palace too fine for a rural landowner, adding, 'temples should be left to the gods'. When the earl died in 1802 his estate had debts of £70,000.[57]

Lord Belmore's extravagance was exceeded by that of the 'Earl-Bishop', Frederick Augustus Hervey, who after being appointed bishop of Derry succeeded his brother as Earl of Bristol. Like several of his Ulster contemporaries, the bishop rejected the serene landscaping of Capability Brown in favour of wild romantic settings.[58] First he built at Downhill on the rugged Londonderry coast, a huge, rather forbidding, palace – 'Never seen so bad a house occupy as much ground', Edward Wakefield noted in 1812. Mr Justice Day wrote the following after his visit in 1801:

> It is impossible not to regret the misapplication of so much treasure upon a spot where no suitable Demesne can be created, where Trees will not grow . . . where the salt spray begins to corrode this sumptuous Pile of Grecian Architecture, and the imagination anticipating the distant period weeps over the splendid Ruin, a sad monument of human folly.[59]

The bishop had spent around £80,000 on Downhill – and a Grecian-style temple dedicated to his pretty cousin Frideswide Mussenden close by, perched on top of a 180-foot cliff – when he threw himself into a new project to build another great house by Lough Beg at Ballyscullion, as he told his daughter, ' in a situation, beautiful and salubrious beyond all description'. He had a canal cut to surround the demesne, and the Drapers' Company, he wrote,

> have in the most obliging & flattering manner given me unanimously £100 towards building a steeple & spire at Ballynascreen, so that before the end of the year I hope to have 4 or 5 spires in the sight of Ballyscullion built chiefly at the expense of other people to beautify my prospect.[60]

Well might de Latocnaye conclude: 'Oh, what a lovely thing it is to be an Anglican bishop or minister! These are the spoiled children of fortune, rich as bankers, enjoying good wine, good cheer, and pretty women, and all that for their benediction. God bless them!'[61] In 1791 Hervey left Ireland for ever to collect art treasures for his houses; he was arrested by Napoleon on suspicion of being a spy and had £18,000 worth of art purchases confiscated – which was just as well, as Downhill was destroyed by fire in 1851 and paintings by Rubens, Dürer, Correggio, Tintoretto and Murillo were lost. Ballyscullion was never finished and its columns now form the façade of St George's parish church in High Street, Belfast.

Other lavish mansions of the period include: Lord Macartney's Lissanoure at Ballymoney; the 1st Earl of Clanbrassil's Tollymore, north of Slieve Donard; Lady Antrim's Glenarm Castle; Lord Orrery's Caledon House; Florence Court completed for the Earl of Enniskillen; Lord O'Neill's Shane's Castle; and Castle Caldwell on an eastern peninsula of lower Lough Erne. Great sums were spent on gardens and demesnes. Sir Arthur Rawdon built the first hothouse in Ireland at Moira and sent a ship to Jamaica to get plants to fill it.[62] John Boyle, the 5th Earl of Orrery, had been inspired to romantic-poetic gardening by his friends Pope and Swift; he put up statues and made a root house and a house of bones, still partly intact, at Caledon. As he wrote to a friend:

> We intend to strike the Caledonians with wonder and amazement, by affixing an ivory palace before their view. We have already gathered together great numbers of bones. Our friends the butchers and tanners of Tyrone have promised to increase the number . . . Caledon has changed me into a Hibernian. It is a charming place indeed.[63]

However, in January 1747 he was 'going on in Mottos', putting Latin inscriptions on statues, when his tenants got the notion

> that I am atheistically inclined by putting up heathen statues and writing upon them certain words in an unknown language. They immediately suspected me for a papist, and my statues had been demolished, my woods burnt and my throat cut had not I suddenly placed a seat under a holly bush with this plain inscription, SIT DOWN AND WELCOME.[64]

The beautiful wild demesnes of Fermanagh inspired Arthur Young to break off from his fact-filled and generally pedestrian narrative. 'Nothing can be more beautiful than the approach to Castle Caldwell,' he wrote, 'the promontories of thick wood, which shoot into Loch Earne, under the shade of a great ridge of mountains, have the finest effect imaginable . . . the whole unites to form one of the most glorious scenes I ever beheld.' When he left, Sir James Caldwell sent him 'with colours flying, and his band of music playing, on board his six-oared barge for Inniskilling'; as he passed Lord Ely's Gully Island he asked 'what more can be wished for in a retreat?' and admired 'the hanging grounds' of Castle Hume.[65]

Such luxury and beauty could be enjoyed only with the acquiescence of the tenantry, who had little to spare for expensive entertainment – though Young saw a ragged weaver put twenty guineas on a horse at the Maze races and he observed that Lurgan weavers kept

> packs of hounds, every man and joining; they hunt hares: a pack of hounds is never heard, but all the weavers leave their looms, and away they go after them by hundreds. This much amazed me.[66]

Young was also responsible for making the most celebrated denunciation of Irish landlords:

> A landlord in Ireland can scarcely invent an order which a servant, labourer or cottar dares to refuse to execute. Nothing satisfies him but an unlimited submission. Disrespect or anything tending towards sauciness he may punish with his cane or his horsewhip with the most perfect security, a poor man would have his bones broke if he offered to lift his

hand in his own defence. Knocking down is spoken of in the country in a manner that makes an Englishman stare. Landlords of consequence have assured me that many of their cottars would think themselves honoured by having their wives and daughters sent for to the bed of their masters.[67]

THE GROWTH OF ULSTER'S TOWNS

'The pay of the army is the only thing that I can hear of which keeps a little ready money amongst us', Bishop Nicolson wrote of Derry city in the 1720s, 'and this can be neither a lasting nor sufficient support.' A good many houses in Armagh city were still 'ruined in wars' in 1704, as in several other Ulster towns, and famine, epidemics and emigration arrested urban growth until almost the middle of the eighteenth century. Thereafter, the expansion of the domestic linen industry, the revival of trade, and the Newry canal's success in opening up the interior stimulated town development until by 1800 there were about fifty market towns in the province with a population of five hundred or more.[68]

Still possessing more capital and credit than merchants, the gentry and nobility were the principal developers. William Stewart, the Tyrone MP, laid out Cookstown in 1736, giving it a splendid tree-lined main street 136 feet wide and a mile and one quarter long.[69] Downpatrick, with only twenty-five stone houses at the start of the century, was restored by the Southwell family and by 1744 had a large market house, a courthouse, a diocesan school, and – Harris observed – 'Mr Southwell hath a few years ago founded and endowed an Hospital for the Reception of decayed Tenants of the Family, and other pious Uses.'[70] Lord Hillsborough rebuilt Banbridge on a cruciform plan and, obtaining a patent to hold markets and fairs in 1767, attracted leading drapers to conduct their business there; and an English brickmaker was contracted to help make the town of Hillsborough one of the most elegant in the north. Harris praised Newtownards and its market house, 'a handsome Structure, on the West End of which is erected a Cupola with a publick Clock; before it stands a neat Octagon Building of hewn Stone', and in 1770 the town acquired a fine town hall. The designs of eighteenth-century landlords have left their mark on a great many Ulster towns, some attractively eccentric like Castlewellan with two large open 'places', the lower oval and the upper six-sided.[71]

Not all plans succeeded. Warrenpoint had the largest square of any town in Ulster, but while its growth was respectable enough, it did not live up to expectations. Towns laid out by London Companies were slow in growing and some, such as Salterstown, failed completely. Others suffered from neglect, such as Dromore, described by Young as 'a miserable nest of dirty mud cabins', and Carrickfergus, dismissed by Edward Willes as 'a sorry old town'.[72] The successes outweighed the failures, however. The 1802 Tyrone county survey observed that 'when the new town will be completed, Dungannon altogether will have no equal in the North'.[73] Just a year after the fire of 1707 which completely destroyed Lisburn, William Molyneux was able to make this report:

> If the story of the Phoenix be ever true, sure 'tis in this town. For here you see one of the beautifullest towns perhaps in the three kingdoms – all brick houses, slated, of one bigness, all new and almost finished, rising from the most terrible rubbish that can be imagined.[74]

In 1759 Willes compared Lisburn to Stratford, and when the Lagan canal reached the town in 1763, rapid development followed. Enniskillen and Monaghan acquired handsome public buildings, but the most striking improvements in an inland town were made in Armagh city. Richard Robinson, who became Baron Rokeby in 1777, was the first primate of the Established Church to make Armagh his permanent residence. When appointed in 1765 he found the city with fewer than two thousand inhabitants and only three buildings with slate roofs. Robinson threw himself into an ambitious programme to make Armagh a centre of elegance and learning: he restored the cathedral, built a splendid archbishop's palace, founded an infirmary and a classical school, cut freshwater channels, sank wells, made sewers, and paved and lit the streets. John Wesley considered that in lieu of preparing for heaven Robinson gave too much time to works of temporal utility.[75] Armagh became a great linen market, with thirty-nine cloth mills inside a six-mile radius, and Churchmen, lawyers, teachers and builders brought money into the city, raising its population to over six thousand by the end of the century. In 1790 Robinson endowed an observatory on the north-east of the city, appointing the Reverend James Hamilton as its first director. Hamilton, using a simple telescope in Cookstown, had recorded the transit of Mercury in 1783 with greater accuracy than Greenwich Observatory.[76]

Ulster's largest towns were still its ports. According to Molyneux's description of 1708, Derry was 'a good, large, compact, well-built town', but he added: 'Since the siege . . . it does not seem to be a place of much business, riches, or trade.'[77] Cut off from much of its natural hinterland by the Foyle, Derry did not alter its shape over a century after the siege, except for the growth of a modest Catholic suburb outside Bishop's Gate. Visitors, nevertheless, found the city attractive. The English travel writer, Charles Bowden, noted that the 'houses in general are remarkably well built, and the public buildings are very handsome structures . . . The church is one of the handsomest I beheld since I left the metropolis.'[78] Willes thought Derry very pretty and similar to Warwick, though he felt it was 'rather inconvenient for coaches for the streets are rather too steep to go up or down with safety', and his ague was inflamed because for the citizens 'There is no land between them and the North Pole.' And the author of *Hibernia Curiosa* came to the unreserved conclusion that Derry was 'the cleanest, best-built and most beautifully situated of any town in Ireland'.[79] In 1791 a wooden bridge was erected by Cox and Thompson of Boston, which brought immediate economic benefits; five years later de Latocnaye wrote:

> Londonderry has not the air of an Irish town. There is there an activity and an industry which are not generally to be found in other parts of the country.[80]

In 1689 the Duke of Berwick, retreating before Schomberg's army, had put Newry to the torch, leaving only the castle and half a dozen houses still standing. Early in the seventeenth century the port had been the largest in Ulster and now Nicholas Bagenal planned to restore Newry to that position. Bagenal died in 1712 but his heir, Robert Needham, continued the work with energy, deepening the Clanrye river and building quays. The opening of the canal to Lough Neagh made Newry the most flourishing town in the north, classed in 1777 as the fourth busiest port in Ireland. Though the yield of coal from Tyrone proved disappointing, traffic on the canal was heavy; Young observed that it was 'indeed a noble work. I was amazed to see ships of 150 tons and more lying in it.'[81] Until the 1780s Newry was the principal place of export for finished linens and through its channel and canal twelve thousand tons of cargo passed each year, including bleachers' potash, provisions and colonial luxuries, such as sugar, coffee and tea. It had a tannery, iron and brass foundries, a sugar refinery, saltworks, a spade mill, and glassworks with a regular export trade to the Carolinas. The town was grand enough to invite Handel to conduct his *Alexander's Feast* in 1742 and to build a theatre in High Street, opening with George Farquhar's *The Inconstant* in 1769.[82] Yet in the final decades of the eighteenth century Newry had to relinquish its premier position in Ulster to Belfast.

On 24 April 1708 Belfast Castle was gutted by fire; in the blaze three of the 4th Earl of Donegall's sisters were burned to death. The Chichester family had lost its principal home and remained absentee for the rest of the century, leaving Belfast without its central focus. 'I live in the neighbourhood of Belfast', Lord Massereene wrote in 1752, 'and know it to be in a ruinous condition.'[83] Above all, development of the town was stifled by short leases and tenancies which contained no obligation to carry out improvements; and it was left to the 5th earl, who succeeded his imbecile uncle in 1757, to grant the long leases without which the rapid growth of Belfast in the late eighteenth century would not have been possible.

In spite of a steep increase in rents, the new leases launched a major rebuilding of the town to strictly specified standards. The Farset river was covered over in the 1770s, making High Street a wide thoroughfare; new quays were constructed; a handsome Poor House was built at North Queen Street; and Lord Donegall put up a new parish church, an Exchange and Assembly Rooms, and donated ground for the White Linen Hall, opened in 1784.

In 1777 Robert Joy formed a partnership to build the town's first cotton mill in Francis Street, and though Ireland's first steam-driven mill was founded at Lisburn in 1789, Belfast was to become the centre of Ireland's cotton industry. The Joy family also owned the Cromac paper works and the *Belfast News-Letter*, the province's most forthright and influential newspaper. By 1791 Belfast had a population of eighteen thousand, with a prosperous, confident and largely Presbyterian middle class giving a radical lead to the rest of the country.[84] The town by then had become the most successful port in Ulster and the third largest in Ireland and, though Belfast was not an important centre for flax weaving, it was surrounded by bleachworks harnessing every available stream and was neck and neck with Newry as the leading place of linen export. Both these towns owed their prosperity not only to overseas trade but also to their ability to draw in business from the heart of Ulster by inland waterways.

INLAND NAVIGATIONS AND ROADS

During the 1654 Civil Survey it was noted that coal was being mined at Tullyniskan in east Tyrone. More coal deposits were found nearby at Drumglass in 1692 and these were being exploited by somewhat crude techniques for a Dublin consortium soon afterwards. Then in 1723 Francis Seymour, an entrepreneur, leased land from the archbishop of Armagh and began mining by more sophisticated methods at Brackaville, soon to be known as Coalisland. Seymour sank a shaft 156 feet deep at his 'Engine Pit' and a few years later a 'cut' was begun to connect Coalisland to the Blackwater to take the coal to Lough Neagh.[85]

General George Monck, who restored Charles II to the throne, had suggested constructing a navigation between Lough Neagh and Newry, but it was not till 1703 that Francis Nevil, collector of Her Majesty's

Revenues in Ireland, was asked by the Irish parliament to carry out a survey 'with a designe of drawing a Canal or making a Passage for Boats from the said Lough to the Sea'.[86] No further action was taken until 1729 when parliament set up the Commissioners of Inland Navigation for Ireland and levied duties on luxury goods to provide the new body with funds. The population of Dublin had increased sevenfold since 1660 and it was fast becoming the second city of the empire – a mushroom growth not possible without massive importation of British coal each year. Colliers had to face prevailing westerlies, and supplies of coal were expensive and unreliable. With the optimistic prospect that the Tyrone coalfield could supply the capital's needs, the Newry Navigation was begun in 1731. Under the direction first of Sir Edward Lovett Pearce and then of his deputy, the Huguenot Richard Cassels, and finally of the English engineer Thomas Steers, the canal was completed in 1742 and on 28 March in the same year the *Cope* and the *Boulter* of Lough Neagh sailed into the port of Dublin with cargoes of Tyrone coal.

The making of the Newry Navigation was a great engineering feat. A canal of fifteen locks, including the first stone lock chamber in Ireland, it crossed eighteen miles of rough country to a height of seventy-eight feet above sea level to connect Lough Neagh with the sea – the earliest true summit-level canal, pre-dating both the Sankey Cut at St Helens and the Bridgewater Canal to Manchester. Never before in peacetime had so many men been put to work on a single project in Ireland, for it was excavated without machinery at 7d. a day for each man 'provided with one good working tool, such as spade, pick, stubbing axe or shovel'. Between 1759 and 1769 a ship canal was made at Newry so that larger vessels could take the coal to Dublin.[87]

The Tyrone coalfield never achieved what was expected of it. Severe faulting made mining difficult – not to speak of the dangers run by the men working below, blasting seams with gunpowder and lighting their way with candles stuck in lumps of clay on their caps. A partnership formed in 1749, headed by Primate George Stone, was characterised by gross incompetence and corruption, and another created in 1756 squandered £12,000 of its government grant to little effect.[88] Yet the Newry canal prospered; it was both a cause and a consequence of eighteenth-century prosperity in Ulster. Without the steadily improving economic prospects of the province's hinterland the navigation would not have been built, and the new waterway stimulated the domestic linen industry in central Ulster by providing an inexpensive route for imported bleachers' potash and exported cloth. The Lagan Navigation, begun in 1756, became equally important, the first lighter reaching Lisburn on 9 September 1763, as the *Belfast News-Letter* reported:

The day was indeed a happy one . . . A band of music played the whole way to over one thousand persons who accompanied the lighter on the banks of the waterway as far as Lisburn where the inhabitants expressed their unfeigned satisfaction at the completion of this great and truly useful work up to their town.[89]

Thomas Greg and Waddell Cunningham, two Belfast entrepreneurs, set up a sulphuric acid works on Vitriol Island at Lisburn the next year and used the navigation to take bottles and phials upstream from the Belfast glassworks; by December 1793 the canal had reached Lough Neagh, joining it at Ellis's Gut.

Until the coming of the railways, canals provided the best and most inexpensive transport for bulky and fragile goods. For most people in Ulster, however, roads remained the principal means of communication. Inland navigations required huge injections of capital and the support of central government. Roads on the other hand were a local responsibility and a source of mounting friction. A major grievance shared by merchants, weavers and farmers was that all decisions on the levying of local taxes and how they were spent were made by the gentry and aristocracy of the Established Church. The principal concern of local government was the improvement of roads and bridges. From 1615 it was the duty of parishes to repair roads; every farmer owning a plough had to contribute a cart and horses, together with four men, and poorer tenants and labourers were bound to attend in person for six days.[90] From 1710 county grand juries could levy a cess, or local rate, to make new roads, but the money raised was rarely enough to do anything worth while. Turnpike trusts could be set up from 1733; the two most important turnpike roads ran from Armagh to Lisburn, and from Belfast to Dundalk. These suited cattle drovers, pack horses and light 'truckle carrs' taking linen to Dublin, but the tolls were too high for heavy vehicles.

In an attempt to raise enough money to make good roads, the Armagh Grand Jury imposed a heavier cess in 1763 to the fury, in particular, of the weavers. Parliament approved, however, and passed over full responsibility for road building to all grand juries in 1765, ending unpaid six-day labour and subsidies to turnpikes. The grand juries used three quarters of their substantial income from cess to extend the road system and build bridges, such as those over the lower Bann at Toome and Portneil (the one at Portglenone had collapsed in 1733). From 1772 minor roads were funded by parishes levying a penny cess. There was much jobbery, corruption and inefficiency, but the legacy of the eighteenth century is that Ulster still has one of the best secondary road networks available anywhere.

Compulsory labour and a burdensome cess brought social tensions to the surface. In 1761 bands of weavers and farmers, calling themselves 'The Hearts of Oak', tore down most of the toll gates on the turnpikes, and when the cess was increased in 1763, the disorder spread out from Armagh to Monaghan, Cavan, Fermanagh, Tyrone and Londonderry. For more than five years constables were quite unable to collect any cess from the north Armagh barony of Oneilland and in the end the turbulence had to be quelled by the army in 1772. Eighteenth-century progress subjected the social fabric of Ulster to severe strain and was accompanied by violent fluctuations – the trade downturn of the 1770s was especially acute, triggering popular revolt.[91]

'SUCH GRIEVOUS OPPRESSIONS THAT THE POOR IS TURNED BLACK IN THE FACE': THE HEARTS OF STEEL

On the morning of Sunday 23 December 1770 angry farmers gathered at Templepatrick Meeting House and, armed with firelocks, pistols and pitchforks, set out for Belfast. Led by a man on horseback named Crawford, who carried crowbars wrapped in straw rope, they numbered 1,200 as they advanced on the town's North Gate. Calling themselves 'The Hearts of Steel', they surged round the barrack intent on forcing the release of a comrade held on the charge of maiming cattle belonging to a Belfast merchant. Dr Alexander Haliday, a leading citizen, was captured while pleading with them not to destroy the house of Waddell Cunningham, a shipowner; he was sent to try to negotiate the prisoner's release. A contemporary letter describes the sequel:

> The Doctor had just reached the Barrack on this embassy, passing through an immense multitude consisting of the people from the country intermixed with those of the town, when the gate was thrown open by the military, who fired upon the assailants, killed five persons and wounded nine others.[92]

In the meantime Cunningham's house in Hercules Lane was burning fiercely, putting the whole town in danger. At one o'clock in the morning the sovereign saw no alternative but to give up the prisoner to prevent the destruction of Belfast.

The immediate cause of this assault was the eviction of tenants by the Upton family from their Templepatrick estate; poor tenants had been ejected and replaced by speculators, including Waddell Cunningham, who had been able to outbid them when leases expired. In the same year the leases of Lord Donegall's Co. Antrim estate expired; farms were relet at the old rents but with heavy fines for lease renewal to give the 5th earl immediate cash to pay for his extravagant spending on

Fisherwick Park in Staffordshire. The *Public Journal* castigated Lord Donegall who

> either set a great scope to one man, or he took fines, by which means the poor industrious tenants, who occupied the land, unable to pay the demand of their landlord . . . Nay, they were often turned off their farms, and those fertile fields, which produced bread for their inhabitants, were converted into pasturage, and the country, once populous wore, and still wears, the face of depopulation and misery.[93]

The 'houghing' of cattle – deliberately laming the animals by cutting their leg tendons – became so prevalent that the *Belfast News-Letter* reported it to be carried on 'even at noonday undisguised'.[94] The revolt spilled over into the counties of Londonderry, Tyrone and Down, merging with the Hearts of Oak resistance to the cess in Armagh. These troubles continued through 1771 and into 1772. 'The Hearts of Steel and Hearts of Oak are giving us abundance of news', began a letter from Armagh in March 1772. It told how they forced farmers to sell potatoes and meal at prices they fixed themselves, called on landlords 'denouncing threats of burning their houses in case there should be any attempt to levy the cess', and if those with land to rent refused to grant leases at twelve shillings an acre, 'they pulled down or burned their houses'.[95] When Sir Richard Johnston of Gilford captured 'the ring-leader of this banditti', his house was besieged next day:

> They began to fire at the windows and set the offices on fire. The fire was returned from the house and three as they say of their men killed, upon which Mr Morell a dissenting minister, neighbour to Mr Johnston, desirous to prevent further bloodshed, drew up a window in order to speak out to them, but was saluted by four musket balls in his head and breast. He fell dead out of the windows.

Johnston hung out a flag of truce and escaped through a back window 'but was so closely pursued that he was obliged to swim the Bann and had several shots fired at him in the water'. Johnston gathered together a posse of 150 men, but hearing that four thousand were preparing to face him near Loughbrickland, he decided to await the arrival of regular troops.[96]

The army arrived soon afterwards for this had been only one episode in a series of disturbances causing the Irish parliament to rush through 'An Act for the more effectual punishment of wicked and disorderly persons in Antrim, Down, Armagh, the city and county of Londonderry, and county Tyrone'. As soldiers spread through the province they crushed the uncoordinated uprisings, men were tried and hanged, and it was reported that many insurgents were drowned while attempting to escape to Scotland in open boats. Lord Townshend, the viceroy, ordered a general pardon in November 1772 and privately condemned the landlords whose rents were 'stretched to the utmost'. In their Proclamation of March 1772 the Hearts of Steel blamed the 'heavy rents which are become so great a burden to us that we are not scarcely able to bear', and continued:

> Betwixt landlord and rectors, the very marrow is screwed out of our bones . . . they have reduced us to such a deplorable state by such grievous oppressions that the poor is turned black in the face, and the skin parched on their back, that they are rendered incapable to support their starving families, that nature is but scarcely supported, that they have not even food, nor yet raiment to secure them from the extremities of the weather wither by day or night.[97]

Townshend's successor, Lord Harcourt, agreed that 'the unreasonable rise of lands' was the cause of the disturbances. Rent increases coincided with a succession of acute harvest failures in 1770, 1771 and 1772, and by 1773 bread prices were close to those during the famine of 1741. Townshend had concluded that the people he governed were 'in a state of poverty not to be described'.[98] Then, when the harvests improved, the linen trade was hit by a catastrophic slump; merchants were left with £900,000 worth of linen unsold in April 1773, leading the *Londonderry Journal* to report: 'Trade was never more stagnant in the memory of living man.' This was a crisis that rippled through the western world and the Hearts of Steel troubles are mirrored, for example, in popular disturbances in France. English merchants who normally advanced credit to Ulster drapers could not do so in 1772–3. Thomas Waite, undersecretary of state, described the crisis to Sir George Macartney in 1773:

> In this kingdom such a want of money was hardly ever known; linens to the value of £200,000 of last year's stock unsold at this time in Dublin, besides great quantities in the hands of different dealers in different parts of the kingdom, and no demand at all for them in London where I am told there is upwards of the value of £300,000 on hand. The bankers will neither discount nor lend one shilling upon any security.[99]

It is little wonder, then, that thousands turned to America for refuge. In May 1773 Lord Donegall's Co. Antrim agent wrote the following to his employer:

> The Linen Trade seems totally at a stand . . . This cannot last long, for if it does this Country must be ruined. The Imigration to America seems rather to increase than diminish. Some of the People might be spared but the Money taken with them is what makes this Country Wretched. The Sums gone & going out is inconceivable.[100]

'The good Bargins of yar lands in that country doe greatly encourage me to pluck up my spirits and make redie for the journey, for we are now oppressed with our lands at 8s. an acre,' David Lindsay explained to his Pennsylvanian cousins in 1758.[101] Increasing rents, subdivision of farms and growing population pressure on the land kept up a steady annual outflow of Ulster people prepared to face the hazards of an Atlantic crossing. The journey could be perilous: in 1729, 175 people died on board two vessels from Belfast during the crossing; in 1741 the *Seaflower* sprang her mast en route to Philadelphia and 46 passengers died, 6 of their corpses being eaten in desperation by the survivors; and in 1762 a fortnight of storms drove the *Sally* off her course from Belfast to Philadelphia and 64 passengers perished.[102] John Smilie of Greyabbey survived this last voyage and wrote an account of it for his father:

> Nothing was now to be heard aboard our Ship but the Cries of distressed children, and of their distressed Mothers, unable to relieve them. Our Ship was now truly a real Spectacle of Horror! Never a Day passed without one or two of our Crew put over Board; many kill'd themselves by drinking Salt Water; and their own Urine was a common Drink; yet in the midst of all our Miseries, our Captain shewed not the least Remorse or Pity.[103]

The captain and officers of the *Providence*, which left Portrush for New York in August 1768, abandoned ship as it filled with water during a storm and rowed away in a longboat, leaving twenty-three passengers to their fate, including a woman and her two children. Despite such dangers, some five thousand people, nearly all Protestants, left Ulster each year for America. As Thomas Wright wrote to his fellow Quaker, Thomas Greer of Dungannon, in 1773, advising him to allow his nephew to come to Pennsylvania: 'I believe with thy approbation I might venture to think he or any young man may have ten chances to one to make a fortune here than in Ireland.'[104]

When the economic crisis struck in 1770, emigration to America reached a new peak of about ten thousand a year. Some forty thousand tons of emigrant shipping left Ulster ports between 1771 and 1774, and the estimate made by a linen board inspector that each ton represented one emigrant is supported by other contemporary evidence. Those who could not pay their passage became indentured servants, that is, they agreed to work for only their keep in America for several years in lieu of the fare of about £3 5s.0d. A very high proportion of those leaving were linen weavers, many of them tenant farmers who sold their interest in their holdings to have some capital to make a new start.[105] In April 1773 the *Londonderry Journal* reported 'that one ship, last year, had no less than £4000 in specie on board'. It continued:

> Their removal is sensibly felt in this country – This prevalent humour of industrious Protestants withdrawing from this once flourishing corner of the kingdom seems to be increasing . . . Till now, it was chiefly the very meanest of the people that went off, mostly in the station of indentured servants and such as had become obnoxious to their mother country. In short it is computed from many concurrent circumstances, that the North of Ireland has in the last five or six years been drained of one fourth of its trading cash, and the like proportion of the manufacturing people – Where the evil will end, remains only in the womb of time to determine.[106]

Shipping companies sent their agents into all the leading market towns with enticing stories of cheap land and prosperity. Vessels carrying casks of flaxseed to Ulster from the colonies were eager to take on passengers for the return journeys. The governor of North Carolina, Arthur Dobbs of Carrickfergus, was only one of many colonial land developers anxious to attract Ulster families to the American back country. Ulster Presbyterians – known as the 'Scotch-Irish' – were already accustomed to being on the move and clearing and defending their land; woodkerne, tories and rapparees at home had prepared them for frontier skirmishing with Pontiac and other native Americans. 'Get some guns for us,' James Magraw urged his brother in Paxtang. 'There's a good wheen of ingens about here.'[107] Magraw was writing from the Cumberland valley, where the fertile soil attracted many Scotch-Irish pioneers; from there they pushed south into Virginia to the Appalachians and fanned out over the South Carolina Piedmont, and then on to West Virginia and through the Cumberland Gap into Kentucky and Tennessee. In 1776 Benjamin Franklin reckoned that the Scotch-Irish and their descendants formed one third of Pennsylvania's 350,000 inhabitants. By that year perhaps one quarter of a million Ulster people had emigrated to the American colonies. The peak of the emigration was reached in the first half of 1773. Then, as Thomas Wright informed Thomas Greer in a letter written from Bucks County on 14 June 1774:

> The Colonies at present is in a very dissatisfied position by reason of the impositions of Great Britain; Boston is entirely blocked up since the first of this month that no vessel is to pass or repass . . . some here is apprehensive the event will be attended with much bloodshed.[108]

Emigration abruptly ceased as the American revolution began.

'THE ENEMY WAS AT OUR DOORS': THE FORMATION OF THE VOLUNTEERS

On 13 April 1778 Paul Jones, the American privateer, sailed his ship *Ranger* into Belfast Lough and engaged *Drake*, a Royal Navy sloop stationed there. After an obstinate fight of forty-three minutes off the Copeland Islands, the British vessel struck its colours and was seized. The American Revoluntionary War, now more than two years old, had been brought to the very shores of Ulster. Stewart Banks, sovereign of Belfast, applied to Dublin Castle for help. In reply, Chief Secretary Richard Heron admitted that 'there is reason to apprehend three or four privateers in company, may in a few days make attempts on the Northern Coasts of this Kingdom' but that all he could spare were half a company of invalids and a troop or two of dismounted horse.[109] 'Abandoned by the Government in the hour of Danger,' Lord Charlemont wrote, 'the inhabitants of Belfast were left to their own defence, and boldly and instantly undertook it.' A Volunteer company formed on Saint Patrick's Day now took on an urgent role and recruitment was brisk.[110] In June, the Belfast News-Letter reported, they 'marched to church in their uniform, which is scarlet turned up with black velvet, white waistcoat and breeches ... The clothing of the majority of the Company was of IRISH MANUFACTURE; and the whole made a brilliant and pleasing appearance.'[111]

When the American revolution broke, the sympathy of the northern Protestants was with the colonists, for as William Steel Dickson said in a sermon he gave in Belfast, 'There is scarcely a Protestant family of the middle classes amongst us who does not reckon kindred with the inhabitants of that extensive continent.'[112] Lord Harcourt informed London that Ulster Presbyterians were Americans 'in their hearts' and 'talking in all companies in such a way that if they are not rebels, it is hard to find a name for them'. Early in 1778, however, France had joined the war on the side of the colonists and Ulster Protestants had no difficulty in recognising the traditional enemy. As recently as 1760, during the Seven Years War, the French had made a descent on Carrickfergus under the command of General François Thurot, and held it for a week. Now, determined to defend the country from invasion, Volunteer companies formed rapidly across Ulster and in the rest of the island.

The Government's position was fast becoming desperate. The lord lieutenant, the Earl of Buckinghamshire, was forced to suspend 'all salaries and pensions, civil and military, Parliamentary grants, clothing arrears, etc', but even then only an advance of £50,000 from the Bank of England saved the Irish treasury from bankruptcy.[113] Tax receipts were sharply down, for the country was in crisis. The depression begun in the early 1770s was now aggravated by the dislocation of war and government trade embargoes. Linen sales continued to plummet, as William Brownlow, MP for Co. Armagh, told the Irish Commons in

211

February 1778: 'The last September market was bad, this is worse. This may be seen at the Linen Hall: a great quantity of linens are unsold.' Harvests had been light in the mid-1770s. John Moore, agent of the Annesley estates in Co. Down, tried to collect the rents in the spring of 1778 but 'this was not to be done', and he added bleakly a few months later, 'universal poverty and distress now stare us in the face'.[114]

The Government could find no money to finance a militia when Ireland was all but stripped of regular troops to fight in America. Lord Charlemont, elected commander-in-chief of the Volunteers, summed up the Government's plight:

> Ireland was hourly threatened with Invasion – The Enemy was at our Doors, and Administration had no possible Means of Assistance – Unsupported by England and destitute both of Men and of Money they shuddered at the Idea of the most trifling Incursion – They feared and consequently hated the Volunteers, yet to them alone They looked for Assistance, for Safety – and They saw, with a Mixture of Grief and Joy, the Country, which They were unable to defend, compleatly protected by its own Efforts, without that Expense to which they were wholly unequal.[115]

Charlemont was right to point out that the defence of Ireland depended on the Volunteers and in May 1779 the viceroy admitted this in a letter to the British home secretary, the Earl of Hillsborough: 'Unpleasing as the Institution of those Corps may be in many respects, there can be no doubt, in case of a French invasion, that most material utility might be derived from them.'[116]

Until now recruitment to the Volunteers was patchy and in June a letter in the *Londonderry Journal* seemed to indicate a decline of enthusiasm even in Belfast:

> The Volunteers of this place are as tired of military exercise as children are of a rattle . . . Our cloud cap'd grenadiers and our gorgeous infantry are dissolving apace as the summer approaches . . . After the amusement of a year our Volunteers rest satisfied with a fine coat and a firelock.[117]

In that same month, however, Buckinghamshire, after much heart-searching, agreed to give out to the Volunteers the sixteen thousand militia muskets he had in store. By handing out so many weapons to a force with no legal status, the lord lieutenant had advertised his government's acute financial embarrassment and greatly strengthened the Volunteers over whom he had no control. There were more rumours of French invasion and in a few weeks the number of Volunteers leaped from twelve thousand to forty thousand, half of them in Ulster. Such a large independent army was certain in such a crisis to wield formidable political influence. A momentous phase in the country's history had begun.

Ulster grandees who were not absentee landlords looked on Dublin, rather than Belfast or Newry, as their capital. Several built sumptuous town mansions there, such as Moira House, Tyrone House, Northland House (built for the Knox family of Dungannon), and Charlemont House (this was in addition to Marino in the suburbs, where the Casino alone cost the earl £60,000), and the Fermanagh lords Ely and Hume were leading developers in the city. Here they spent their winters, especially when the Irish parliament was in session. They unhesitatingly saw themselves as Irishmen, not as Ulstermen, and it did not occur to them to form a distinct political grouping; yet these peers and their protégés were particularly well represented in the Patriot opposition and, more recently, in the Volunteers. Charlemont not only led the Patriots in the Lords but he had obtained Ulster seats for the opposition's most outstanding spokesmen, Henry Flood and Henry Grattan. It was Grattan who said that England's difficulty was Ireland's opportunity – the American war gave the Patriots and the Volunteers a unique chance to force the pace of political reform.

Ireland's constitutional position closely resembled that of some of the American colonies now in revolt. Westminster alone controlled imperial and foreign affairs, and the viceroy (by now always given the title of lord lieutenant) and other members of the Irish executive were appointed, not by the parliament in Dublin, but by the government of the day in London. The Irish parliament – utterly unrepresentative except of the leading landed interests – met only every other year and had its powers emasculated; Poyning's Law allowed for the alteration or suppression of Irish bills by the English privy council; and the 1720 Declaratory Act gave Westminster authority to legislate for Ireland, a right most frequently used to regulate trade. The loose interest groups opposed to the Government and calling themselves Patriots had no thought of severing the British connection, but they did want to obtain more genuine power for their parliament.

Grattan once referred to the Volunteers as 'the armed property of the nation'. Only landlords, substantial farmers, merchants and professional men could afford to pay around £1 15s.0d. for a musket, buy a uniform and suffer loss of earnings while drilling and on manoeuvre. According to Patrick Morgan of Hilltown, the Volunteers of Rathfriland, led by the Presbyterian minister the Reverend Samuel Barber even on Sundays (he ignored a woman who exclaimed, 'Good Lord, sure this must be a breach of the holy Sabbath!'), 'are all men in business who lose at least half their time in learning the use of arms'.[118] Nevertheless, the

Volunteers were democratically organised: officers were elected by the ranks and, for example, a man who had just paid £25,000 for an estate in Larne was content to serve as a private in his local company. Some landlords were alarmed by the radicalism of fellow Volunteers but for the moment they all pulled together not only to defend their country but also to throw their weight behind the Patriots. No one was better qualified to forge this alliance than the Earl of Charlemont; he was the Patriot leader and it was he who had rallied Volunteers in 1760 with such energy that Thurot had no choice but to abandon Carrickfergus.

'Talk not to me of peace; Ireland is not in a state of peace; it is smothered war,' the Patriot Hussey Burgh proclaimed in the Irish Commons; 'England has sown her laws like dragon's teeth, and they have sprung up in armed men.'[119] By November 1779 the Government was helpless before menacing demonstrations of Volunteers, a vigorous campaign against British goods, and a united Patriot majority. At the end of the year the beleaguered Tory ministry at Westminster, reeling from news of disastrous defeat in America, responded to Buckinghamshire's frantic appeals for immediate concessions. Laws imposed by England on Ireland, forbidding the export of wool, glass, leather and other goods, were completely removed. Volunteers in Ulster had been nervous about the campaign for 'free trade', fearing that linen might lose its protected position in the British market. They rejoiced, however, in the successful challenge to England's right to make laws for Ireland and they now threw themselves into a campaign to change Poyning's Law and to get rid of the Declaratory Act.

'WE SEEK FOR OUR RIGHTS, AND NO MORE THAN OUR RIGHTS':
THE DUNGANNON CONVENTION, 1782

The Westminster government stood firm against the demand for legislative independence. Indeed, most of the Patriots thought the Volunteer campaign too extreme. Denouncing them as 'Venal Senators', the Earl-Bishop urged timely concession in a letter of April 1780 written from Derry to his son-in-law:

> Do not flatter yourself that the minds of the people are quieted by the late concessions. Three new companies of Volunteers are raised this instant within ten miles of me . . . an inhabitant of Dublin or of the county of Louth can have no idea of that elastic, incontrollable spirit that pervades the six northern counties. For God's sake do not call it forth, lest you find its name *Legion*. Why should not England at this instant treat Ireland as a prudent husband would treat a frantic wife: indulge her during the frenzy – it can have no fatal, no irremediable consequences . . .[120]

When Hervey closed the letter with a warning that Ireland could go the way of the American colonies, he did not draw the parallel that his own wife had walked out on him.

Martial reviews at Belfast, Derry, Newry, Enniskillen and Downpatrick over the summer of 1780 kept up the pressure. 'If the resolute defence of national rights and liberties be sedition,' the Belfast battalion declared in August, 'we will not then scruple to denominate the Volunteers of Ireland traitors.'[121] The following summer the three-day manoeuvres in Belfast were the largest in the country, attracting one hundred thousand spectators. However, both the Government and the Irish parliament continued to ignore the Volunteer demands, and new tactics were approved at a meeting in Armagh in December – delegates from every Volunteer company in Ulster were summoned to Dungannon.

On the morning of 15 February 1782, 242 delegates, representing 143 companies, marched two by two down the streets of Dungannon lined by the local light infantry company to the parish church. William Irvine, colonel of the Lowtherstown Company in Fermanagh, took the chair and between noon and eight that evening propositions were debated and voted on. The motions passed were a clarion call for legislative independence:

> Resolved unanimously, That a claim of any body of men, other than the King, Lords and Commons of Ireland, to make laws to bind this kingdom, is unconstitutional, illegal, and a Grievance.
>
> Resolved (with one dissenting voice only), That the powers exercised by the Privy Councils of both kingdoms, under, or under colour or pretence of, the Law of Poyning's, are unconstitutional and a Grievance.

These were but two of twenty resolutions approved, including agreement to send an address of support to the Patriots:

> In a free country, the voice of the People must prevail. We know our duty to our Sovereign, and are loyal. We know our duty to ourselves, and are resolved to be Free. We seek for our Rights, and no more than our Rights; and, in so just a pursuit, we should doubt the Being of a Providence, if we doubted of success.[122]

Charlemont, Grattan and Flood had vetted the resolutions and were ready in Dublin to carry the campaign again to parliament. There they could not break the government majority, but the motions passed at Dungannon won the approval of grand juries, corporations, town meetings and Volunteer corps up and down the country. 'Your cursed Volunteers, and Patriots have alarmed us here very much', Lord Hillsborough wrote from London, but a dangerous confrontation was prevented when Lord North's government fell a few weeks later.[123] The new Whig government granted all that was demanded even before it attempted to extricate Britain from the American war. From now on the Irish parliament could make its own laws, but for some Ulster radicals legislative independence was only the first victory.

'You represent property not numbers,' Thomas Conolly, the Londonderry MP, interposed during the debate in which Hussey Burgh made his famous declamation. He was right: the parliament in Dublin, better known after 1782 as 'Grattan's Parliament', did not represent the people of Ireland. In county elections Protestant freeholders were so dependent on their landlords that contests, if they took place at all, were usually between aristocratic factions. In the north only Carrickfergus and Derry had genuinely free elections; all the rest of the towns with representation were 'close' boroughs controlled by patrons, with electorates as small as thirty-six in Coleraine and thirteen in Belfast. Boroughs could be bought and sold: for example, Augher was purchased by the 1st Marquess of Abercorn, and Lifford by a Dublin merchant. Catholics had no part to play whatsoever.[124]

Flushed with their recent victories, northern Volunteers pressed strongly for parliamentary reform in 1783. Lisburn led the way by writing to English radicals for advice and another Volunteer convention met at Dungannon on 8 September. There it was agreed to hold a national convention in Dublin in November. The Government and even most of the Patriots were alarmed – were the Volunteers about to overawe parliament with force? There was no need for anxiety: Charlemont was deeply embarrassed to have to chair the proceedings; weeks of confused debate followed on what in practice was meant by 'a more equal representation of the people'; the Earl-Bishop shocked moderates with wild speeches; and, above all, there was deep division on whether or not Catholics should be given the vote. When a programme was agreed, Henry Flood and William Brownlow, still in Volunteer uniform, presented their demands to the Commons in College Green. Barry Yelverton, a leading Patriot and now attorney-general, said he admired the Volunteers but

> when they form themselves into a debating society, and with that rude instrument the bayonet probe and explore a constitution which requires the nicest hand to touch, I own my respect and veneration for them is destroyed.[125]

An overwhelming majority of MPs agreed with him and the reform proposals were thrown out. The Volunteers had no intention of resorting to arms and drifted home; in any case, the American war was over, a militia had been formed and regular troops returned in force to Ireland. The movement rapidly declined, except in Ulster.

Catholics were simply bystanders in this campaign and as yet their leaders did not have the confidence to seek their rights except in the most respectful terms. Relief acts in 1778 and 1782 removed restrictions on their education, their right to buy land and the hated provision that they must divide their land between their sons. This easing of the Penal Laws was to a considerable extent due to pressure from both the Patriots and the Volunteers. At Dungannon in 1782 the Volunteers passed a resolution 'that, as men and as Irishmen, as Christians and as Protestants, we rejoice in the relaxation of the penal laws against our Roman Catholic fellow subjects', but this did not mean Catholics should be completely freed from restrictions.[126] In a sermon to Volunteers at Ballybay, Co. Monaghan, the Reverend John Rodgers urged Volunteers

> not to consent to the repeal of the penal laws, or to allow of a legal toleration of the Popish religion . . . Popery is of a persecuting spirit and has always marked her steps, wherever she trod, with blood. Protestants must not expect to have any security for their religious liberty from her.[127]

John Wesley confided to his *Journal* that the Volunteers 'if they answer no other end, at least keep the Papists in order'; and many would have agreed with his letter to the *Freeman's Journal* in 1780 in favour of keeping the remaining Penal Laws:

> I would not have the Roman Catholics persecuted at all. I would only have them hindered from doing hurt: I would not put it in their power to cut the throats of their quiet neighbours.[128]

Catholics found their most ardent champions in Belfast and its surrounding districts. Over most of Ireland, Protestants were in a small minority, concerned to defend their privileges; over much of Ulster, Protestants and Catholics were roughly equal in number, and the old rivalries were still strong; only east of the Bann did Protestants have such an overwhelming majority that they had no fears of a Catholic resurgence. Here the Presbyterians of Antrim and Down had a long tradition of defending their rights against tithe collectors, clergy and landlords of the Established Church, and many of the more prosperous farmers and businessmen were 'New Light' or Nonsubscribing Presbyterians who cherished independent thought and refused to have doctrine imposed on them. Denied access to Trinity College Dublin, Presbyterians took degrees in medicine and divinity at Edinburgh and Glasgow, then perhaps the most open-minded universities in Europe. The Enlightenment had taken deep root in Belfast, still barely one tenth the size of Dublin but growing fast. Here an energetic and confident middle class showed their dedication to improvement not only by founding a chamber of commerce, a harbour board and a linen hall but also by passionate debating of new political ideas coming in with their cargoes from Scotland, America and France. Eager to demonstrate their opposition to 'the rankest bigotry and ignorance', in March 1784 they entertained two escaped Turks and paid their passage back to Istanbul; the *Belfast News-Letter* commented:

> How grateful to the liberal mind, to perceive the distinction of *Turk* and *Christian*, in short, all local and religious prejudices, sunk in the more sublime affection which, as the offspring of one common parent, we all owe to one another.[129]

The Belfast delegates to the national convention were bitterly disappointed that they had failed to convince their fellow Volunteers that Catholics should be given the vote. The following year the Belfast 1st Volunteer Company defiantly invited Catholics to enlist in their ranks, the first in Ireland formally to do so. Then in May 1784 they attended Mass at St Mary's chapel, which they had largely paid for, since the several hundred Catholics in the town were too poor to meet the cost.

The Presbyterian liberals had challenged the exclusiveness of the Ascendancy – a term coined in the 1790s to describe the Anglican landowning and professional élite. For the present they had failed and it was not until the French Revolution broke that they got another opportunity to puncture the complacency of the Ascendancy's monopoly of power.[130]

'FOURTEENTH JULY, 1789; SACRED TO LIBERTY'

Describing the French Revolution as 'the greatest event in human annals', the *Belfast News-Letter* was doing no more than reflecting the widely held opinion of leading citizens in the town and its neighbourhood. It continued:

> Twenty-six Millions of our fellow creatures (near one sixth of the inhabitants of Europe) bursting their chains, and throwing off in an instant, the degrading yoke of slavery – it is a scene so new, interesting, and sublime, that the heart which cannot participate in the triumph, must either have been vitiated by illiberal politics, or be naturally depraved.[131]

The example of France spurred the Presbyterians of Belfast to campaign anew for the reform of parliament – they contemptuously rejected Edmund Burke's prediction that the revolution must end in the tyrannical rule of 'the swinish multitude', and in *Freedom Triumphant* gave new words to 'The Boyne Water':

From France now see LIBERTY'S TREE,
Its branches wide extending;
The Swine to it for shelter run –
Full fast they are assembling;
They grunt and groan, with hideous tone,
Against all base connivers;
They now unite, and swear they'll bite
Their unrelenting drivers.[132]

On the afternoon of 14 July 1791 the Belfast Volunteers, including a troop of light dragoons and the artillery corps trailing four brass six-pounders, set out from the Exchange 'together with such a multitude of our unarmed inhabitants as no former event ever was the means of assembling'. Before them they held aloft portraits of Franklin and Mirabeau, and a great banner showing on one side 'a very animated representation of *The Releasement of the Prisoners from the Bastile . . .* Motto at the bottom of the painting – *Fourteenth July, 1789; Sacred to Liberty*. The reverse contained a large figure of Hibernia in reclining posture, one hand and foot in shackles, a Volunteer presenting to her a figure of Liberty.' On their arrival at the White Linen Hall three volleys were fired into the air, answered between each by salvoes from the artillery; then Volunteers and citizens formed a circle and solemnly agreed to send their declaration to the national assembly of France:

If we be asked, what is the French revolution to us? we answer; – MUCH. Much as MEN – It is good for human nature that the grass grows where the Bastile stood . . . As IRISHMEN. We too have a country, and we hold it very dear . . . so dear to us its *Freedom*, that we wish for nothing so much as a real representative of the national will, the surest guide and guardian of national happiness.

Go on then – Great and Gallant People! . . . you are, in very truth the Hope of this World.

A month later Belfast got back rapturous replies, including this one from Nantes:

LIBERTY OR DEATH! . . . Citizens of Belfast! you have celebrated that Triumph of the human kind, and you have done it with such splendour, as renders you truly worthy to partake of the hatred with which we are *honoured* by crowned tyrants . . . we swear to preserve it in our archives.[133]

This exuberant commemoration of the second anniversary of the fall of the Bastille had been organised by the reviving Volunteers and the Northern Whig Club, formed in the town the previous year at the request of Lord Charlemont. Though it was more outspoken than its

Dublin parent, the club did not go far enough for some Belfast radicals. It failed to do more than support the Patriot Party and refused to recommend the admittance of Catholics to the rights of citizenship. The 1st Belfast Volunteer Company duly passed its own resolution in favour of Catholic emancipation and a small group of men met regularly to prepare the ground for a new radical organisation in the town.

UNITED IRISHMEN

On 10 October 1791 Theobald Wolfe Tone caught the mail coach at Capel Street in Dublin and set out for Belfast, arriving on the evening of the following day.[134] This Dublin lawyer had deeply impressed northern reformers by his recently published *Argument on Behalf of the Catholics of Ireland*, and now his advice was sought on how best to press for rapid political reform. On Friday 14 October the Society of United Irishmen of Belfast was founded in Peggy Barclay's tavern in Crown Entry, off High Street. Tone gave the new organisation its title and helped to draft some of its resolutions but the society was really the brainchild of Dr William Drennan, son of the New Light minister of the 1st Presbyterian Church in Rosemary Street. Much of the initial planning was done by Drennan's brother-in-law, Samuel McTier, and its first secretary was Robert Simms, owner of the Ballyclare paper mill. The society's Declaration stated:

> In the present great aera of reform, when unjust governments are falling in every quarter of Europe . . . WE HAVE NO NATIONAL GOVERNMENT –
> we are ruled by Englishmen, and the servants of Englishmen . . . Satisfied, as we are, that the intestine divisions among Irishmen have too often given encouragement and impunity to profligate, audacious and corrupt administrations . . . we do call on and most earnestly exhort our country-men in general to follow our example.[135]

The United Irishmen sought 'a cordial union among *all the people of Ireland*', and a complete reform of the Irish parliament, which must 'include *Irishmen* of every religious persuasion'. In January 1792 they launched the *Northern Star* to promote the radical cause, with Samuel Neilson, owner of Belfast's largest woollen drapery business, as editor. The new organisation spread rapidly to neighbouring towns, amongst Presbyterian farmers in Antrim and Down, and to the capital. Archibald Hamilton Rowan was the only northern landlord of consequence to join; Jemmy Hope of Templepatrick, apprenticed as a weaver, was the only leader who could claim to be a working man; and the great majority of members were young articulate middle-class businessmen and professionals determined to break the power of the Ascendancy.

They had no real programme of social reform and, for example, turned out in 1792 to suppress 'idle and wicked' Antrim weavers demonstrating for better wages.[136] Unlike Tone, most United Irishmen were not yet republicans, and even he was not, in any modern sense, a democrat. They were not yet revolutionaries but believed that the 'extrinsic power' of England could be 'resisted with effect solely by *unanimity, decision and spirit in the people'.*[137] Tone found that Belfast radicals were remarkably ignorant of their fellow Catholic Irish men and women, yet what kept them together and drove them forward was a fervent determination to win political rights for Catholics. The reformers of Belfast – moderates and radicals alike – were enthusiastic patriots and in 1792 were responsible for organising the first great revival of Irish traditional music. The Belfast Harp Festival, arranged to coincide with the Bastille commemoration that summer, marks the beginning of a long association between northern Protestants and the Gaelic revival. 'Strum and be hanged', Tone scribbled in his journal after attending a performance of harpers in the Assembly Rooms; but Edward Bunting, organist at St Anne's parish church, was captivated and spent the rest of his life travelling the country, putting down on paper the songs and airs he heard. Bunting's first collection of 1797 got an enthusiastic reception and was drawn on heavily by Thomas Moore in his *Melodies*; Martha McTier wrote to her brother: 'to me they are sounds might make Pitt melt for the poor Irish'.

'I am turned, quite turned against the French', Mrs McTier observed on reading of the prison massacres in Paris during September 1792.[138] Revolutionary France, which had achieved so much in the first two years with comparatively little loss of life, had now lapsed into blood-letting and war. Then in February 1793, when Britain was drawn into this conflict, northern radicals seemed little better than traitors to Dublin Castle. The lord lieutenant suppressed the Volunteers in March, troops were let run amok in Belfast, and the Government began raising a militia to defend the country from a possible French invasion.

However, the United Irishmen, too, had achieved much in its first two years. William Pitt's government at Westminster, becoming ever more anxious as the French armies swept from victory to victory, was eager to make concessions in Ireland in case the ties between northern Presbyterian radicals and Catholics should become dangerously strong. In 1792 Catholics won the right to enter the legal profession and in January of the following year the lord lieutenant, perhaps more out of duty than conviction, announced to the Irish parliament: 'His Majesty trusts that the situation of His Majesty's Catholic subjects will engage your serious attention.' With the aid of strong pressure from Pitt and lavish use of patronage, the Irish legislature was cajoled into giving Catholics the vote. Reformers now believed that full Catholic emancipation would follow.

Lord Fitzwilliam took office as lord lieutenant in 1795 with the intention of overseeing the removal of the last major penal law, that which prevented Catholics sitting in parliament, and he had the dedicated support of Henry Grattan. The Catholic Committee, in presenting a petition signed by half a million, made plain its loyalty to the Crown. 'It is upon the large principle of leaving not a point of distinction in rights and capacities between Protestants and Catholics', Fitzwilliam wrote back to London, 'that I propose, as I do, that no reserve should be made.'[139] Pitt's government lost its nerve and permission was denied. Fitzwilliam made public his deep disappointment and was recalled. Dublin was at a standstill and the people lined the shores, the *Belfast News-Letter* reported, as Fitzwilliam sailed down the Liffey: 'They saw his Lordship, ashamed to betray the most amiable weakness, and with his handkerchief, endeavouring to conceal pure tears springing from an undefiled heart.'[140] In Belfast, the *Northern Star* observed, 'There was not a Shop or Counting-house open during the whole day – all was one scene of sullen indignation.'[141] Grattan put forward his bill to remove the last of the Penal Laws and in its favour George Knox, the Tyrone MP and friend of Tone, delivered a passionate speech:

> Much of the real, and no small share of the personal, property of the country is in Catholic hands. The lower class, ignorant and turbulent, are fit instruments in the hands of irritated and unsubdued ambition ... If we drive the rich Catholic from the Legislature and from our own society, we force him to attach himself to the needy and disaffected ... Take, then, your choice; re-enact your penal laws, risk a rebellion, a separation or an Union, or pass this Bill.[142]

Without government support the bill was certain to fail. This was one of the most fateful moments in Irish history. Pitt pulled back from attempting to appease Irish Catholics and put all his trust in the ability of the Ascendancy to stay in control. Middle-class Presbyterians and Catholics, confident of emancipation, were shattered by the turn of events; they were 'upon the recall of Lord Fitzwilliam', the chief secretary remarked, 'led to despair of anything effectual without the assistance of the French'.[143] Tone was caught negotiating with a French spy and exiled; in May 1795, just before he left Belfast for America, he climbed the Cave Hill overlooking the town, as he records in his diary:

> Russell, Neilson, Simms, McCracken, and one or two more of us, on the summit of McArt's fort took a solemn obligation – which I think I may say

I have on my part endeavoured to fulfil – never to desist in our efforts until we had subverted the authority of England over our country and asserted her independence.[144]

Such idealists represented only a small proportion of Ulster Protestants. Over much of the province the defeat of Catholic emancipation was warmly welcomed, and the turbulence of which Knox warned was reaching boiling point in Co. Armagh.

PEEP O' DAY BOYS AND DEFENDERS

In 1791 John Byrne, a Catholic dyer from Armagh city, looked back wistfully to the tolerant spirit of the 1782 Dungannon Convention; then 'nothing but joy seemed to beam in the hearts of each party, until faction that damned fiend of hell, soon envied that dawning sun'.[145] Drunken affrays in the vicinity of Markethill, between gangs calling themselves the Nappach Fleet, the Bawn Fleet and the Bunkerhill Defenders, had become openly sectarian by 1786. The combatants regrouped, Protestants becoming the Peep o' Day Boys and Catholics the Defenders, and for the next decade and more sectarian warfare raged in Co. Armagh. Better armed, the Peep o' Day Boys at first swept all before them – a 'low set of fellows,' Lord Gosford observed, '. . . who with Guns and Bayonets, and Other Weapons Break Open the Houses of the Roman Catholicks, and as I am informed treat many of them with Cruelty'.[146] According to Byrne, some Protestant gentlemen lent arms to Catholics

> to protect themselves from depredations of these fanatick madmen; and many poor creatures were obliged to abandon their houses at night, and sleep in turf-bogs, in little huts made of sods; so great was the zeal of our holy crusados this year.[147]

Many local Volunteers were frankly partisan, however. In November 1788 when a Catholic mob near Blackwatertown taunted the Benburb Volunteers for marching to 'The Protestant Boys' and 'The Boyne Water', it was fired on; two were killed and three were mortally wounded. The following July more lives were lost when Volunteers made a successful assault on Defenders assembled on Lisnaglade Fort near Tandragee.[148]

'For heavens sake dont forget the Powder & Ball with all Expedition', John Moore wrote in haste to Lord Charlemont in July 1789. Moore, a Drumbanagher magistrate, had no hesitation in giving out arms to 'the Protestant Boys that have none' because the Catholics 'are now begin[g] their Night Depredations and Lye in Wait behind Ditches, to murder and Destroy Every protestant that appears'.[149] The sectarian violence fanned out from the 'Low Country' to the uplands of south Armagh;

here the Catholics – still speaking Gaelic and wearing mantles – had the advantage of numbers and turned on the Protestants with a ferocity not seen for more than a century. A horrific climax was reached when Defenders attacked a schoolmaster's home in Forkhill on 28 January 1791, described by the Reverend Edward Hudson, Presbyterian minister of Jonesborough:

> With a trembling hand and a heart bursting with grief and impotent indignation, I sit down to give you some account of the dreadful transactions of last night at Forkil – You know Barkeley who was stabbed by Donnelly – He is one of the Schoolmasters of Forkil . . . in rushed a Body of Hellhounds – not content with cutting & stabbing him in several places, they drew a cord round his neck until his Tongue was forced out – It they cut off and three fingers of his right hand – They then cut out his wife's tongue and some of the villains held her whilst another with a case knife cut off her Thumb and four of her fingers one after another – They cut and battered her in different places – She I fear cannot recover – There was in the house a Brother of hers about fourteen years old on a visit to his Sister – his Tongue those merciless Villains cut out and cut off the calf of his leg with a sword.[150]

'The Whole country for Ten Mile Round is in absolute Rebellion & Confusion', Moore wrote. 'Where it will end God only knows.' Ancient hatreds gushed to the surface as the violence spilled over into neighbouring counties – in the words of Hudson, 'the same hereditary Enmities handed down from generation to generation'.[151] In a detailed analysis written for the 1st Marquess of Abercorn in 1797, Dr William Richardson put the troubles down to the excitement caused by Volunteering during the American war giving 'the people high confidence in their own strength' and, he continued,

> much offence had lately been taken because the catholics in the general increase in wealth had raised the price of land by bidding high when it became vacant. This was the real cause of our ill-humour: the relaxation of the popery laws but the pretence.[152]

Certainly competition to rent patches of land near the markets became fierce with the rapid recovery of the linen industry and Armagh became the most populous county in Ireland. Few Catholics were drapers but many were weavers competing with their Protestant neighbours and trade rivalry easily became sectarian rivalry. At the best of times linen was subject to alarming fluctuations but the outbreak of war – the longest in modern European history – upset the delicate balance between food and linen prices.

The war signalled a new intensity in the Armagh disturbances. In 1793 the Government set about raising a militia, causing much unrest. In theory recruits were chosen by ballot but in practice local sheriffs tended to pick Catholics first; this conscription of breadwinners could cause great distress, as the men were not allowed to serve in their own counties. The Defenders now set up a co-ordinated network of oath-bound clubs, and the movement was spread by newly recruited militiamen. Both the Government and United Irishmen tended to dismiss the Defenders as ignorant and poverty-stricken houghers and rick-burners, but for the most part these Catholics were literate, English-speaking tradesmen, living in or near the towns and socially midway between the drapers and the cottier class. Frankly sectarian though they were, the Defenders were influenced to some degree by American and French revolutionary thinking and, for the first time in a hundred years, they sought to overturn the seventeenth-century land settlements. To create an atmosphere of awe and mystery to bond new members, the Defenders adopted messianic signs and catechisms. This is an extract from a paper found on a prisoner in Cavan gaol in 1795:

> I am afraid. So am I. O do not. Why so? The duke of York will save us. I am in love. So am I. Who baptized you? St. John. Where? At the river. What river? Jordan. What did he baptize you for? To be loyal. To whom? To God and my brethern . . . Where is your signs? I carry them about my body. Let us see them. Hold your left wrist with your two right forefingers and drop your hand with a smart air.[153]

Defenderism spread southwards and in 1794 there was a furious uprising in Co. Cavan. In north Armagh, however, General William Dalrymple found many Catholics 'preparing for flight the moment their little harvests are brought in, some are gone to America, others to Connaught – Their houses are placarded, and their fears excessive.'[154] It was here, in the vicinity of Loughgall, that the Peep o' Day Boys were to win a great victory.

'I WILL BLOW YOUR SOUL TO THE LOW HILS OF HELL':
THE DIAMOND AND AFTER

In September 1795 Defenders assembled near Loughgall at a crossroads known as The Diamond to face the Peep o' Day Boys in battle. When the Protestants were reinforced by a Co. Down contingent called the Bleary Boys, however, the Defenders took their priest's advice and agreed to a truce. Both sides withdrew but on 21 September a fresh body of Defenders arrived from Co. Tyrone determined to fight. The Peep o' Day Boys, on home ground, quickly reassembled and took position on the brow of a hill overlooking The Diamond; then, according to William Blacker, they opened fire with cool and steady aim at the swarms of Defenders, who were in a manner cooped up in the valley and presented an excellent mark for their shots. The affair was of brief duration . . . from the bodies found afterwards by the reapers in the cornfields, I am inclined to think that not less than thirty lost their lives.[155]

The victorious Peep o' Day boys then marched into Loughgall and there, in the house of James Sloan, the Orange Order was founded. This was a defensive association of lodges pledged to defend 'the King and his heirs so long as he or they support the Protestant Ascendancy'.

At first the order was a parallel organisation to the Defenders – it was oath bound, used passwords and signs, was confined to one sect, and its membership comprised mainly weaver-farmers. William Blacker was one of the very few of the landed gentry who joined the order at the outset. He later described the inaugural meeting of his lodge in a dark damp house:

> It was a scene not unworthy of the pen of a Scott or the pencil of Salvator Rosa to view the assemblage of men, young and old, some seated on heaps of sods or rude blocks of wood, some standing in various attitudes, most of them armed with guns of every age and calibre . . . in as much as rust and antiquity had blighted the spring of their days into utter incapacity to strike fire. There was a stern solemnity in the reading of the lesson from Scripture and administering the oath to the newly admitted brethren.

Blacker did not approve, however, of the immediate outcome of the Battle of The Diamond:

> Unhappily . . . A determination was expressed of driving from this quarter of the county the entire of its Roman Catholic population . . . A written notice was thrown into or posted upon the door of a house warning the inmates, in the words of Oliver Cromwell, to betake themselves 'to Hell or Connaught'.[156]

Another sample of 'placarding' was sent by General Dalrymple to Dublin. It warned a woman of Keady and her brother that they must not inform on local Orangemen,

> otherwise Be all the Secruts of hell your house Shall Be Burned to the Ground. Both his Soul & your Shall be Blwed To the Blue flames of hell. Now Teak this for Warnig, For if you Bee in this Contry Wednesday Night I will Blow your Soul to the Low hils of hell And Burn the House you are in.[157]

The 'wreckers' smashed looms, tore up webs and destroyed great numbers of homes. This not only reduced competition during a brief slump in the linen industry but also drove some seven thousand Catholics out of Co. Armagh in just two months. Many did flee to Connacht.

Lord Altamont reckoned that four thousand had taken refuge in Co. Mayo alone and his brother concluded:

> Be assured that no circumstance that has happened in Ireland for a hundred years past, has gone so decidedly to separate the mind of this country from the Government . . . The Emigration from the North continues; every day families arrive here with the wreck of their properties.

Local magistrates were either unable or unwilling to uphold the rule of law. They were addressed by Lord Gosford, governor of Armagh, on 28 December 1795:

> It is no secret, that a persecution . . . is now raging in this county; neither age nor sex, etc, is sufficient to excite mercy, much less to afford protection. The only crime which the wretched objects of this ruthless persecution are charged with, is a crime of easy proof; it is simply a profession of the Roman Catholic faith, or an intimate connection with a person professing this faith. A lawless banditti have constituted themselves judges of this new species of delinquency, and the sentence they have denounced is equally concise and terrible – it is nothing less than a confiscation of all property, and an immediate banishment.[158]

Gosford concluded by saying that 'the supineness of the magistracy of Armagh is become a common topic of conversation in every corner of the kingdom', and added that he was 'as true a Protestant as any gentleman in this room'.

'To the ARMAGH PERSECUTION is the Union of Irishmen most exceedingly indebted', leading state prisoners were to claim in 1798.[159] Following the recall of Fitzwilliam, the United Irishmen had become a secret oathbound revolutionary body, organised in thirty-six-man cells, pledged to fight for an Irish republic with the assistance of the French. Now tens of thousands of Defenders clamoured to be part of the coming revolution for, far from shattering the movement, the Orangemen seem to have hastened recruitment by scattering highly political Catholics far to the west and south. Executed in dozens and transported in hundreds in the 1795 autumn assizes, the Defenders did not flinch, not even when the Catholic archbishop of Dublin, John Troy, declared them excommunicate.[160] The United Irish leaders could not spurn such a vast field army for, until now, their organisation was confined to bourgeois radicals in Belfast, Lisburn and Dublin, and Presbyterian farmers in Antrim and Down. Hopes for success were high – news was reaching Ulster that the French were ready to bring aid.

> They come, they come, see myriads come,
>   Of Frenchmen to relieve us,
> Seize, seize the pike, beat, beat the drum,
>   They come, my friends, to save us.[161]

227

For Britain and the Irish government news from the European mainland was thoroughly depressing: Belgium and the Rhineland had been overrun; Prussia, Russia and Spain had been knocked out of the war; and in the harsh winter of 1794–5 the French advanced over the ice into Holland, overwhelming the British expeditionary force and seizing the frozen-in Dutch fleet with their cavalry. Pitt's efficient secret service reported that the French Directory would attempt an assault on Ireland.

A desperate situation required draconian measures, Lord Camden concluded. The lord lieutenant had little difficulty persuading a frightened parliament to rush through an Indemnity Bill (to exonerate the many magistrates who had exceeded their powers) and an Insurrection Bill (giving the lord lieutenant power to impose martial law and send suspects to serve in the navy, and the courts the authority to order the execution of those found guilty of administering unlawful oaths). Then in June 1796 the yeomanry was set up. Almost completely Protestant, this force was allowed to serve in its home counties, and in mid-Ulster men from Orange lodges were amongst the earliest recruits. Samuel Neilson, Robert Simms, Thomas Russell and Charles Teeling were arrested in September and charged with treason; but the United Irishmen were growing stronger not weaker. Arms were stockpiled in caves near Cushendall; kegs of gunpowder were looted from army stores in Belfast; and de Latocnaye was astonished to see a Scottish regiment at Ballycastle 'very well received by the inhabitants, who, during the night, may it please you, stole the whole of the ammunition and half the arms of the soldiers! Just imagine . . .'[162] It was reported that ash trees were being felled for pike shafts in the counties of Londonderry, Tyrone, Antrim and Down; Samuel Murphy of Newry wrote:

> The vile mob have begun to cut down and carry all the ash timber for shafts to their pikes; at Kinghill Cabra, and Lord Clanbrassil's, many hundreds assemble in the early part of the night, exult and huza on the fall of each tree.[163]

Bernard MacSheehy, an Irish officer in the French army, arrived in November 1796 to gauge the level of likely support for a French invasion. He believed there were 50,000 ready to join the French in the north, with 20 cannon, 15,000 arms, 8,000 horses, and able leaders. Thus encouraged, a formidable fleet – with 14,450 soldiers and 41,644 muskets – sailed out of Brest on 16 December 1796 and steered north-west to Ireland.[164]

> The French are in the Bay! they'll be here without delay,
> And the Orange will decay, says the Shan Van Vocht.[165]

On 22 December the French entered Bantry Bay, but their commander was missing and as a result of mismanagement and storms no landing was made. 'Well, England has not had such an escape since the Spanish Armada', Wolfe Tone truthfully wrote in his *Journal* on Saint Stephen's Day.[166] Tone himself had sailed with the invasion fleet, on board the *Indomptable*. French naval losses were so severe that another expedition was not possible the following year; but news of the appearance of the French electrified the United Irishmen and their Defender allies. In Ulster, United Irish membership doubled in the first four months of 1797. Joseph Lees, secretary to the post office, got a letter at the end of January from Rostrevor, Co. Down, telling him that the village 'swarms with United Irishmen as does Hilltown four miles distant . . . in truth the Inhabitants in general in this county are not better disposed' than those of the County of Antrim'.[167] A powerful revolutionary coalition was now arrayed against the Government; all wanted to sever the connection with England, but in the event of success, it would be difficult to keep them together. The Defenders, west of the Bann and spreading southwards, sought wholesale land confiscation. The bourgeois leaders had in mind a government similar to the French Directory with themselves in charge – major social upheaval was not part of their agenda. The Presbyterian farmers east of the Bann called themselves, simply, the People. They were the true democrats seeking popular parliamentary government, freedom of conscience and expression, and equality before the law. Like the Defenders, however, they mingled local grievances with national demands, as can be seen in these extracts from a paper seized in Ballynahinch in 1795:

1st Tithes will be abolished . . . 2nd Hearth-money – that abominable badge of slavery and oppression to the poor – will cease; 3rd . . . tobacco for which we now pay 10d per 1 lb will be then had for 4d – Aye for 4d . . . 6th County cesses would not be squandered in jobs among the parasites of agents . . . 9th . . . every man would have an opportunity of knowing his rights for a newspaper which now costs 2d would then be sold for a half-penny. 10th The honest farmer would be protected in the enjoyment of all his appurtenances against the intrusions of moss-bailiffs and bog-trotters.[168]

Early 1797 may well have been the best moment for insurrection but, believing another French expedition was imminent, the United leaders held back their men. It was left to the Government to seize the initiative. When prominent United Irishmen had been arrested in the autumn of 1796, the authorities were left in no doubt as to the solidarity of Presbyterian radicals in Antrim and Down. On 14 October the *Belfast News-*

Letter reported mass turnouts to harvest the crops of prisoners and their families:

Elred Pottinger Esq. of Mount-pottinger had 12 acres of oats cut down in 13 ¹/₂ minutes. A poor man in the same neighbourhood had two acres cut by the same reapers, during the time he was lighting his pipe. Mr William Orr, near Antrim (*at present in Carrickfergus gaol,*) had his entire harvest cut down by near 600 of his neighbours, in a few hours . . . Mr William Weir, of Dunmurry, (*now in prison,*) had 2,360 stooks of grain, and 38 ricks of hay, carried in, and completely stacked and thatched, in three hours.[169]

Six days later the *Northern Star* added: 'About 1500 people assembled and in *seven minutes*, dug a field of potatoes belonging to Mr Samuel Neilson of this town, (now in *Kilmainham*).'

Only the most rigorous methods swiftly applied, Dublin Castle decided, could stifle the coming rebellion in the north.

'THE FLAME IS SMOTHERED': 1797

'Nothing but terror will keep them in order', Lieutenant-General Gerard Lake wrote on taking up his post in Belfast. 'It is plain every act of sedition originates in this town.'[170] On 13 March 1797 he proclaimed martial law, ordering the immediate surrender of all arms and ammunition. Military searches began at once in Belfast and Carrickfergus, spreading out to Loughbrickland next day, Rathfriland on 23 March, and Armagh the week following. In the first ten days alone 5,462 firearms were seized, together with an immense number of pikes. Nicholas Mageean, a Saintfield farmer, and Edward Newell, a miniaturist from Downpatrick, had penetrated the inner counsels of the United Irishmen and, thanks to their information, Lake was able to take almost all the leading revolutionaries. Seven tumbrils left Belfast in April laden with prisoners to be escorted by a troop of dragoons to Dublin; others were held on board a hulk anchored in the Garmoyle Pool.

'The flame is smothered, but not extinguished,' Lake declared as he applied harsher regulations in May.[171] The Monaghan Militia silenced the *Northern Star* for ever by demolishing its premises in Belfast, and in the countryside the yeomanry were let loose, striking terror by burning houses and flogging suspects. The Reverend Robert Magill watched men flogged at Broughshane:

I saw Samuel Bones of Lower Broughshane receive 500 lashes – 250 on the back and 250 on the buttocks. I saw Samuel Crawford of Ballymena receive 500 lashes. The only words he spoke during the time were 'Gentlemen, be pleased to shoot me'; I heard him utter them. I saw Hood Haslett of Ballymena receive 500 lashes. I believe he was only about nineteen years of age. Before he had received the 500 lashes I heard him exclaiming, 'I am cutting through' . . . [172]

John Gifford, captain of the Dublin Militia, was courtmartialled for protesting at the burning of Kilkeel by the yeomanry and a Welsh fencible regiment known as the Ancient Britons; he described the scene to Undersecretary Edward Cooke:

> I was directed by the smoke and flames of burning houses and by the dead bodies of boys and old men slain by the Britons though no opposition whatever had been given by them and I shall answer to Almighty God, I believe a single gun was not fired but by Britons or Yeomanry.[173]

When seventy men of the Monaghan Militia were found to be sworn members of the United Irishmen, Lake made a public example of four privates who refused to inform on their fellows. In full military procession the condemned were taken from Belfast to Lisburn, where at Blaris Camp they were executed beside their coffins. All the troops then had to file past the corpses.

The United Irishmen still at large exhausted their funds in legal fees but almost fifty prisoners were executed, nevertheless, including several Presbyterian ministers. The most notorious conviction was that of William Orr, a farmer of Farranshane near Antrim. Held at Carrickfergus for a year, Orr was charged with administering unlawful oaths. The prosecution was led by the attorney-general and the defence by John Philpot Curran, the distinguished Patriot; his solicitor was James McGuckin, soon to become a paid government informer. Even the packed jury found the evidence conflicting and recommended the prisoner to mercy, but Orr was executed on 14 October 1797 on the Gallows Green outside the town. His 'Dying Declaration' was printed and distributed in thousands:

> If to have loved my Country, to have known its Wrongs, to have felt the Injuries of the persecuted Catholics and to have united with them and all other Religious Persuasions in the most orderly and least sanguinery Means of procuring Redress; – If these be Felonies I am a Felon, but not otherwise.[174]

By the end of 1797 Lake's ruthless campaign had almost obliterated the United Irishmen in Ulster, where previously they had been strongest. No attempt was made to disarm the Orangemen – if there had been, Brigadier-General Knox concluded, 'the whole of Ulster would be as bad as Antrim and Down'.[175] Indeed, as recruits for the yeomanry, the Orangemen provided an invaluable addition to government forces.

Far from snuffing out rebellion in the south, however, Lake helped to provoke it there in 1798. When the storm broke in the province of

231

Leinster towards the end of May, the United Irishmen in Ulster were still in a state of confused impotence.

As darkness fell on Wednesday 6 June 1798 armed United Irishmen met at the Cold Well near Larne and in the small hours moved into the town, driving a party of Tay Fencibles back to their barrack. Then as dawn came they drew off to join their comrades on Donegore Hill. They had fired the first shots of the rebellion in Ulster.

The northern revolutionaries were utterly disorganised when the insurrection began in the south on the night of 23 May. Even when the peasantry of Kildare, Carlow and Wexford swept to victory, the Ulster leaders could not agree to act; and it was only when Henry Joy McCracken arrived from Dublin that the most determined decided to rise on 7 June. McCracken had no intention of attempting an assault on his home town of Belfast, now the second largest garrison in the country. Instead he ordered his men to seize their local towns and then join him in an attack on Antrim.[176]

As the United men of Crebilly, wearing green cockades, marched north through Broughshane they were cheered by children bearing green branches representing the Tree of Liberty. The Ballymoney contingent gathered at Kilraghts and then, with other parties from mid-Antrim, advanced on Ballymena. The toll exacted by Lake the year before was now revealed: only the men of the Braid valley were well equipped with firelocks; 150 had no weapons at all; and according to Samuel McSkimin, the yeoman and historian, the rest only had 'pitchforks, peat spades, scythes, bayonets, sharpened harrow-pins fixed on poles, old rusty sword blades and reaping hooks'.[177] Entering by Church Street they nevertheless forced the surrender of Ballymena by placing burning tar barrels against the Market House after a brisk battle. Meanwhile Randalstown fell to the insurgents by a similar device – the yeomanry there were smoked into submission when straw was set on fire underneath the Market House. One party was sent to break down the bridge at Toome to prevent the military further west from crossing the Bann; this task took fourteen hours of hard manual labour. The main contingent at Randalstown then hastened to reach Antrim.

McCracken had set out from Craigarogan Fort near Roughfort with a small band of followers and, as they advanced north through Dunadry and Muckamore singing 'La Marseillaise', they were joined by United men from all over south Antrim. But barely half of those pledged to rise turned up and they had only one cannon, a brass six-pounder long hidden under the floor of Templepatrick Meeting House and now mounted on the wheels of an old chaise. According to McSkimin this 'piece was under the direction of deserters, chiefly from the artillery, but they had neither slow match nor portfires – peat, carried by one of the gunners, in an iron pot, serving for both'.[178] As the rebels approached Antrim by the Scotch Quarter they not only found houses of suspects set ablaze but that the town garrison had been reinforced by the 22nd Dragoons force-marched from Blaris. The defenders fired two cannon so inaccurately that the grapeshot merely cast up gravel in the faces of the attackers; the Templepatrick gun fired two deadly rounds and then fell off its mounting; making a cavalry charge, the dragoons merely transfixed themselves on the insurgent pikes; and men from Ballyclare were fighting their way forward down Bow Lane. It was in this last action that Lord O'Neill – once the darling of the Presbyterian freeholders now in combat against him – was killed near the Market House. The main Blaris force, under Colonel James Durham of the Fife Fencibles, now bombarded the town from Sentry Hill and then poured into the streets scattering insurgents.

As a matter of course, the soldiery finished off any wounded rebels they found and summarily executed thirty others captured in arms. It was only three days later that the streets were cleared and the bodies thrown into sandpits on the shore of Lough Neagh. Samuel Skelton, Lord Massereene's agent, recalled:

> As a cart-load of dead and dying arrived at the sand pit a yeoman officer asked the driver 'Where the devil did these rascals come from?' A poor wretch raised his gory head from the cart and feebly answered 'I come frae Ballyboley.' He was buried with the rest.[179]

McCracken, Jemmy Hope and a few others attempted to rally the fleeing insurgents, but to no avail. Randalstown and Ballymena were abandoned. After hiding out on Slemish and the Cave Hill, McCracken from the slopes of Collin Mountain watched Saintfield burn and heard the distant guns at Ballynahinch. The Co. Down uprising had begun.

INSURRECTION IN DOWN

On Friday 8 June men from Killinchy bearing arms came to Saintfield and laid siege to a farmstead owned by the McKee family, thought to be informers. Next morning they set fire to the building and the entire household perished in the flames – a deed for which eleven were subsequently hanged. Later that Saturday Colonel Chetwynd Stapylton approached with the Newtownards Yeoman cavalry, volunteers led by three Church of Ireland clergy, and 270 York Fencibles. About 4.30 p.m.

the insurgents ambushed this force, Richard Frazer of Ravarna leading a charge of pikemen from the demesne woods on the Comber Road. Before he was driven off, Stapylton lost 3 officers, 5 sergeants, 1 clergyman, 2 drummers and 45 other ranks; a York Fencible veteran of the French wars later recalled that 'for danger and desperation this skirmish exceeded anything he had before witnessed'.[180]

Other actions that day were not so successful. Men from Bangor and Donaghadee were driven out of Newtownards by volleys from the Market House and survivors were forced to spend the night on Scrabo Hill. An attack on Portaferry Market House was beaten back when insurgents came under flanking fire from a revenue vessel anchored near the quay. News of the victory at Saintfield spread rapidly, however, and United Irishmen hurried to join the rebel camp there at the Creevy Rocks.

'Cause them that have charge over the city to draw near, even every man with his destroying weapon in his hand': the Reverend Thomas Ledlie Birch took his text from Ezekiel 9:1, when he preached at the Creevy Rocks on Sunday 10 June.[181] But several crucial days were lost here for the insurgents had no leader – their commander, the Reverend William Steel Dickson, had been arrested at Ballynahinch on 5 June. Eventually Henry Monro, a Scottish merchant from Lisburn, agreed to head the Down insurrection. Monro ordered his rebel army south to Ballynahinch, where a new camp was made at Montalto on Ednavady, with an entrenched forward position on Windmill Hill.

On 11 June Major-General George Nugent, commander of the government forces, issued a proclamation warning that unless the rebels laid down their arms and released their prisoners he would 'proceed to set fire to and totally destroy the towns of Killinchy, Killyleagh, Ballynahinch, Saintfield and every cottage and farmhouse in the vicinity of those places, carry off the stock and cattle and put everyone to the sword who may be found in arms'.[182] Nugent was as good as his word: the following day the Ballynahinch insurgents could see columns of smoke rising into the still air as the troops set fire to farmhouses and haggards and burned Saintfield to the ground. Nugent stopped to await reinforcements from Downpatrick. The weather was perfect that day, as it had been for weeks. James Thomson, then a boy of twelve and later the father of the scientist Lord Kelvin, accompanied women carrying food to the rebel encampment, where he found

a considerable number sheltering themselves from the scorching rays of a burning sun under the shade of the trees . . . They wore no uniforms; yet they presented a tolerably decent appearance being dressed, no doubt, in their 'Sunday clothes' . . . The only thing in which they all concurred was the wearing of green: almost every individual having a knot of ribbons of that colour, sometimes mixed with yellow in his hat . . . and many . . . bore ornaments of various descriptions and of different degrees of taste and execution; the most of which had been presented as tributes of regard and affection and as incentives to heroic deeds, by females whose breasts beat as high in patriotic ardour as those of their husbands, their sweethearts and their brothers . . . on a sudden an alarm was given . . . In a moment all was bustle through the field.[183]

The reinforcements had arrived from Downpatrick and Nugent began pounding the rebel positions with his eight guns, which included two howitzers firing exploding shells. The insurgents on Windmill Hill were overwhelmed and Hugh McCulloch, a grocer from Bangor, was captured and hanged on the summit from one of the mill's sails.

Until dark, Ballynahinch was bombarded and then it was occupied by the Monaghan Militia, who were soon drunk and out of control. Monro was urged to attack them from Ednavady but he is reputed to have replied: 'We scorn to avail ourselves of the ungenerous advantage which night affords; we will meet them in the blush of open day.'[184] Awed by Nugent's artillery, many insurgents deserted the field of battle that night. Those remaining launched a dawn attack on the militia, which, a survivor recalled,

did not fail to salute us with a brisk fire. We ran up like bloodhounds and the Monaghans fled into the town where they kept up a kind of broken fire which we returned, although only about twenty of us were armed with muskets.[185]

At around 7 a.m. rebel ammunition ran out and Nugent's army, numbering close to three thousand, overwhelmed the United Irish on Ednavady Hill. No quarter was given as the cavalry in relentless pursuit hacked down those in flight through lanes and byways. Elizabeth Gray of Gransha, who had stayed on the field of battle, was overtaken and killed with her brother George and her lover Willie Boal; she was the first to die, shot through the eye by a yeoman, Thomas Neilson of Annahilt. Monro evaded capture for two days, but then, according to a broadside ballad:

Monro being weary, and wanting to sleep,
He gave a woman ten guineas his secrets to keep;
When she got the money the devil tempted her so,
That she sent for the army who surrounded Monro.[186]

Condemned to death, Monro was taken to the market place in Lisburn; an officer present recalled: 'I stood very near him when at the foot of the gallows, and he settled his accounts as coolly as if he had been in his own office, a free man . . . This done, he said a short prayer . . .'[187]

235

On 20 June Colonel Atherton reported from Newtownards:

We have burned Johnston's house at Crawford's-Bourn-Mills – at Bangor, destroyed the furniture of Pat. Agnew; James Francis and Gibbison and Campbell's *not finished yet* – At Ballyholme, burned the house of Johnston – at the Demesnes near Bangor, the houses of Jas Richardson and John Scott – at Ballymaconnell Mills, burned the house of McConnell, Miller and James Martin, a Capt. and friend of McCullock's, hanged at Ballynahinch . . . We hope you will think we have done *tolerably* well. Tomorrow we go to Portaferry . . .[188]

The reprisals following the Battle of Ballynahinch were fearful, yet Nugent behaved with more humanity than Lake in Wexford. Indeed, news of atrocities against Protestants at Scullabogue and on Wexford Bridge did much to dampen swiftly the embers of revolt in the north. An army officer recorded in his journal:

A few executions more ended the outbreak in Ulster; for the accounts of the bloody goings-on in Wexford had their full share in bringing the Northerns to their senses, as many of them made no scruple of declaring at the place of execution.[189]

One of the last to be executed was Henry Joy McCracken, taken at Carrickfergus and hanged in Belfast's Cornmarket on 17 July 1798. The Crown attorney offered him his life if he would name his co-conspirators, but he refused, whispering to his sister Mary Ann: 'You must be prepared for my conviction.'

Some twenty thousand had died in the rebellion, principally in Leinster, but the year's fighting was not yet done: the French had at last made a landing.

THE END OF THE REBELLION

Although General Jean Humbert came ashore at Killala, Co. Mayo, on 22 August 1798, it had been his intention to make for Killybegs, Co. Donegal, but storms had driven him back. Thereafter he disregarded his instructions to stay in a remote part of Ulster until a larger French expedition arrived; instead he routed Lake at Castlebar and roused the Defenders of Roscommon and Longford until all were overwhelmed at Ballinamuck. Napper Tandy, the veteran patriot, sailed into Rutland Bay in Donegal on 17 September on board the corvette *Anacreon* with two hundred men, artillery and several thousand stands of arms. The Rutland postmaster was an old friend and from him he learned of Humbert's defeat. Local people were eager to join in rebellion, but Tandy resisted the urgings of his fellow officers, spent a pleasant evening with the postmaster, was carried insensible back on board, and sailed away.

I met with Napper Tandy, and he took me by the hand,
Saying, how is old Ireland? and how does she stand?[190]

Napoleon Bonaparte had once expressed his lack of faith in a levée en masse of potatoes, but after his defeat in Egypt the Directory made new attempts to send aid to Ireland. The overwhelming superiority of British naval power again and again frustrated these intentions, but an expedition of ten warships, led by Contre-Amiral Jean Bompard, managed to reach the coast of Ulster, only to be caught by Sir John Warren's squadron off Lough Swilly in a storm. The badly damaged *Hoche* struck its colours and was towed to Buncrana. The first to step ashore on 3 November was Wolfe Tone, who, Sir George Hill recalled, 'recognised and addressed me instantly with as much sang-froid as you might expect from his character'. Sent by Lord Cavan to Dublin, condemned and denied military execution, Tone slit his throat in prison and died seven days later.[191]

The French had been acting on stale information: the spirit of insurrection was dead in Ulster by the autumn of 1798, whatever it might be in the rest of the country. Presbyterians who had turned out in Antrim and Down felt betrayed by bourgeois leaders who had spurred them to revolt only to hesitate when the rebellion began or, like Robert Simms, to resign from their posts at the eleventh hour. The insurrection in the south had been a peasant jacquerie characterised by sectarian killings. Partly as a result, the Orange Order spread outwards and upwards; the experience of serving in the yeomanry brought large numbers of the northern gentry into the movement. Such Protestants could congratulate themselves for one of the most striking features of the 1798 Rebellion – the complete failure of mid-Ulster, the home of Defenderism, to take part in the uprising. Catholics here were cowed, surrounded by Protestant neighbours armed by the Government, and suffering a new wave of sectarian attacks so severe that Orange grand masters met in August to discuss ways of reducing them. For Catholics the scheme to unite the kingdoms of Great Britain and Ireland the following year was of little or no consequence.[192]

'JOBBING WITH THE MOST CORRUPT PEOPLE UNDER HEAVEN':
THE UNION, 1800

In December 1779 Sir George Macartney, an Ulsterman and a former chief secretary, was sent to Ireland on a secret mission to ascertain what the reaction might be to a proposal to unite the Dublin and Westminster parliaments. After assuring Prime Minister William Pitt that even the lord lieutenant 'has not the smallest suspicion of my real errand in this

237

kingdom', he reported bluntly: 'The idea of a union at present would excite a rebellion.'[193] Twenty years later the self-confidence of the Ascendancy was reeling in the wake of the Ninety-eight insurrection, and the government of Ireland had become utterly dependent on British military and financial support. While the rebellion still raged, Lord Cornwallis was sent over as lord lieutenant and commander-in-chief not only to crush the uprising but also to force through legislation bringing the life of the Dublin parliament to an end. The first vote on the Union Bill, in January 1799, was discouraging; it was rejected by a margin of two votes and for such a crucial measure a large majority was essential. From Ulster, the Abercorn, Tyrone, Hertford and Roden interests had voted for the Union, but others, normally loyal to the Government, had either abstained or voted against; they included the Enniskillen, Belmore, Downshire and Donegall interests, controlling between them around twenty-eight MPs in the Irish Commons.

'My occupation is now of the most unpleasant nature, negotiating and jobbing with the most corrupt people under heaven', Cornwallis wrote; 'I despise and hate myself every hour for engaging in such dirty work.'[194] He wrote letter after letter cajoling and urging borough own-ers to change their minds; for example, he asked Lord Gosford to get his son, Major Acheson MP, to moderate his stand against the Union and not to be harried into 'measures that must prove highly prejudicial to this distracted country'.[195] Cornwallis delegated the main task of build-ing up a majority to Robert Stewart, Lord Castlereagh. Originally elected as a radical by the freeholders of Co. Down, Castlereagh had become the first Presbyterian for a long time to reach high office in Ireland. Appointed chief secretary in 1798, he now worked on the abstainers, in particular, with consummate skill. Lord Donegall, for instance, was won over by being given high command in the yeomanry, and in contrast to the emotional appeals of anti-unionists, Castlereagh made closely argued speeches to demonstrate the economic advantages of union. Ulster linen drapers needed no persuasion – complete free trade between the two kingdoms was to their advantage. The cotton manu-facturers of Belfast were contented when an additional clause was inserted, keeping protective duties on their product in place for the next twenty years.

Both Cornwallis and Castlereagh hoped that full Catholic emancipa-tion could be included in the Union Bill, but hardliners in the Irish government, fearful of a 'Popish democracy', persuaded Pitt to drop this proposal. Pitt did, however, promise to carry emancipation after the Union and for this reason Catholic men of property supported the bill. For the same reason most members of the Orange Order campaigned to preserve the 'Protestant constitution'; in the counties of Armagh and Monaghan alone, thirty-six lodges passed declarations opposing the Union. On the whole, however, the Union was a burning issue only within the narrow élite of the Ascendancy. John Galt of Coleraine kept a diary which is full of references to Lake's repression of 1797 and the bloodshed the following year, but there is not a single mention of the Union even though Cornwallis visited his town in October 1799.

Early in 1800 the Union Bill passed the Irish Commons by a majority of sixty-five, and the Irish Lords by a margin of twenty-five. Westminster gave its approval and on 1 January 1801 the new Union Jack, incorporating Saint Patrick's cross, was run up flagpoles in all the principal towns. For the great majority of the people of Ulster it was an event of no consequence – far more important were the hardships brought about by wartime inflation and harvest failures. John Galt's entry for 26 October 1799 declared that God 'now threatens us with cleaness of teeth; a great part of our crops are yet green, and rotting under the rain, and what is reaped mostly spoiled by the constant wet', and on 2 April 1800 he added: 'How easy it is for God to punish a world, provisions are now got to a melancholy price for the poor.'[196]

In years to come hunger would often be, as it had been in the past, the most vital concern; but the Union would move steadily centre stage in the theatre of Ulster politics.

8

PROGRESS AND POVERTY

c. 1800–1850

OVERVIEW

Early in July 1803 two United Irish envoys, Thomas Russell and William Hamilton, returned from France with disappointing news that Napoleon was not yet ready to send an expedition to Ireland. Determined all the same to make a new attempt, they joined Jemmy Hope and Robert Emmet in the Dublin Liberties. Russell and Hope then travelled north. Russell was reported to have told United Irish delegates at Castlereagh that 'if fifty or an hundred would assemble, they would encrease rapidly ... Dublin and the South were compleatly ready'. Men drilled at Carnmoney, Newry, Ballynahinch and Knockbracken but although 'in many parts anxious for a rising,' a spy informed Dublin Castle, 'yet they cannot see how it is to be effected, having no system amongst them. Arms they have but few.'[1] Emmet's Dublin insurrection was a fiasco, and in the north there was a miserable turnout as Russell raised the standard of revolt by the Buck's Head dolmen near Loughinisland. When in October Russell was hanged at Downpatrick gaol, he joined the swelling ranks of Irish revolutionary martyrs and became the subject of one of Ulster's best-known recitations, 'The Man from God-knows-where'.

The 1835 Ordnance Survey Memoir for the district of Connor in Co. Antrim observed that the people there almost to a man had been 'engaged in the rebellion of 1798 ... However, since that time their politics have changed, and now they seem indifferent and careless on the subject.'[2] Presbyterian radicalism wilted before the mounting self-confidence of organised Irish Catholicism. Sectarian antagonism – almost certainly aggravated by a new devotional and evangelical fervour in Catholic and Protestant Churches alike – was drawn into eastern Ulster by thousands of migrants from west of the Bann in search of work in the Lagan valley mills. Belfast became the most industrial corner of Ireland, but much of its success depended on an abundant supply of cheap labour emerging from an impoverished Ulster countryside. Here agricultural prices sank as the Napoleonic Wars drew to a close and at the same time the domestic linen industry was being slowly but inexorably driven to the wall by an unequal competition with steam-powered mills in Belfast, Leeds and Manchester. In 1821 Ulster's population of two million was almost equal to that of the whole of Scotland, but too much of the dangerously crowded countryside was left utterly dependent on what the overworked soil could still yield. When the potato blight destroyed the food of the poor in the 1840s, great sections of Ulster's population faced disaster.

That Ulster's suffering was somewhat less than that experienced by Munster and Connacht did not prevent the Great Famine from being a catastrophe over large regions of the north. For many Catholics, however, it was the Union, not the fungus *Phytophthora infestans*, which was to blame; but it was an Ulster Protestant, John Mitchel, who gave the most simplistic and extreme explanation: 'That million and a half men, women and children, were carefully, prudently, and peacefully *slain* by the English government.'[3] Mitchel did not speak for the majority of northern Protestants: for them the Union had become the essential bulwark of their liberties.

AFTER THE UNION

'The most Jacobinical thing I ever heard of!' George III shouted out during his levee at Windsor on 28 January 1801.[4] The secretary of war had just reminded him of the Government's pledge to emancipate the Catholics, and the king continued: 'I shall reckon any man my personal enemy who proposes any such measure.' The Act of Union had been in force for less than a month and now, at a dangerous moment in the war against Napoleon, the king had made it impossible for his prime minister to carry on. Unable to keep his promise or unite his cabinet behind him, William Pitt resigned on 3 February. Later, when George III was in his straitjacket impotently gnashing his gums, the Prince Regent made clear his view that if Catholics were allowed to sit in parliament, the British constitution would be in peril.

'As long as we exclude Catholics from natural liberty, and the common rights of man,' Grattan declared at Westminster, 'we are not a *people*.'[5] This was not a matter of great concern for the hundred Irish members now sitting in the Commons, though most owed their seats to Catholic votes (sixty-four were county MPs and fourteen were from 'open' boroughs). Two thirds of the Irish MPs were drawn from substantial Ascendancy landowning families and one half of those who sat in the Commons between 1801 and 1820 never made a single speech there. The support they gave to Grattan and the Whigs for Catholic relief proposals can best be described as tepid. Concentrating on winning the war and fearful of 'Jacobinism', Westminster saw no need for emancipation. Two Ulstermen played a notable role in welding together the coalitions responsible for bringing France to defeat, Lord Castlereagh, now against emancipation, and the pro-emancipationist, George Canning. Great rivals, their hatred of each other was so intense they even risked open scandal in a duel, when Canning wounded Castlereagh in the thigh.

Irish Catholics of education and property felt cheated; as in 1795, their hopes had been raised and then dashed. The Union, which had been in effect a no-confidence vote in the ability of the Protestant Ascendancy to govern Ireland, now seemed to shore up that élite. Apart from moving Protestant representation from one capital to another, the Union had changed little. Protestant landowners still controlled the grand juries; Protestant burgesses made no effort to invite Catholics to join them in their corporations; the law was still enforced by Protestant sheriffs; the tithe was still levied for the Church of Ireland; the new Irish Constabulary, launched in 1822, was officered by Protestants; and most lucrative posts were monopolised by Protestants. Catholics could be appointed to most legal offices but in 1828 they held only 39 out of a total of 1,314 in Ireland; and jobs and offices paid or subsidised by the Crown numbered 3,033 but Catholics had only 134 of them.[6] The Union had been an emergency measure, considered a strategic necessity during the war, but Pitt had hoped the Irish would come to accept it as the Scots in time had adjusted to theirs. The failure to obtain emancipation straight away dashed Pitt's not unjustifiable hope, and the growing Irish Catholic middle class turned steadily against the Union and joined in concerted action with the peasantry.

'Union or no Union seems equally disregarded in Belfast', Martha McTier had written to her brother Dr William Drennan in December 1798. Within a few years, however, Protestants in every part of Ulster – radical and conservative – were fully won over to the Union.[7] Inevitably issues such as emancipation and the Union were drawn into the traditional sectarian rivalries of the Ulster countryside.

RIBBONMEN AND ORANGEMEN

The day came out, they did repair
In multitudes to Garvagh fair;
Some travelled thirty miles and mair
To burn the town of Garvagh.[8]

On Monday 26 July 1813 some four hundred Catholic 'Ribbonmen', armed with bludgeons and intent on destroying the tavern where the Orange lodge met, converged on Garvagh. They sought to avenge a

242

defeat at the previous fair. The town was packed, for it was the Lammas Fair, the biggest market of the year. As trading was drawing to a close a whistle was blown; the Ribbonmen tied long white handkerchiefs round their waists, and then began stoning the King's Arms. Alexander Purviance, the local magistrate, had only four constables to assist him and dared not call out the yeomanry for fear it would support the Orangemen; indeed, yeomanry muskets were being primed and cocked inside the tavern thronged with Protestants rallying to its defence. When 'the crowd called upon the Protestant Orange rascals and masons to shew their yellow faces,' a witness named Maybury recalled, it was answered by a volley of gunfire. William Doey, a 'mountainy man' from Foreglen, fell dead, several others were desperately wounded, and the rest of the Ribbonmen, lacking the firearms needed for a counter-attack, fled through the Canning estate to the open countryside.

Had it not been celebrated in an Orange ballad, 'The Battle of Garvagh' might be long forgotten. It was merely one of several sectarian clashes showing that the turbulence of the 1790s continued into the new century, though on a reduced scale. Simply a new name for Defenderism, Ribbonism was strongest in Ulster and flourished despite the vehement denunciations of the clergy. Drawn mainly from the towns and the linen triangle, the Ribbonmen were both revolutionary and sectarian and – like many English industrial workers at the time – were strongly influenced by millennial prophecies. In 1822 a spy reported:

> I have heard different discourses concerning prophecies, respecting the destruction of the Protestant religion and the British government . . . They spoke of a prophecy to be fulfilled in the year 1825, for the overthrow of the tyranny of Orangemen and government, and that there will be but one religion.[9]

The prophecies of Pastorini, the pseudonym of an eighteenth-century English Catholic bishop, foretold the violent destruction of Protestant Churches in 1825. Cheap editions circulated freely as the year of doom approached, and when it passed quietly, 1844 was fixed as the new date when the 'locusts from the bottomless pit' – the Protestants – would meet their end. Ribbonmen pledged themselves to help the prophecy come to pass, as their oath in Ulster shows:

> I, A.B., Do Swear in the presence of My Brethren and by the † of St Peter and of Our Blessed Lady that I will Aid and Support Our holy Religion by Destroying the Heriticks and as far as my power & property will Go not one Shall be excepted . . . I Do further Swear that I will be Ready in twelve Hours Warning to put Our Glorious Design in Execution Against the Heriticks of Every Sect So Help me God By the † of St Peter.[10]

Meanwhile, the Orange movement increased in strength. At the height of the Napoleonic Wars 25,000 regular troops and 31,000 yeomen were on active service in Ireland; 20,000 of the yeomanry were stationed in Ulster and nearly all were Orangemen. The order gained respectability as more and more of the Protestant gentry were persuaded to enrol, particularly by Thomas Verner, an Armagh landowner and Lord Donegall's brother-in-law who became the first Irish grand master. This left the Government in a quandary: it had been alarmed by Orange excesses during the rebellion but it could not but be grateful for the services rendered. The authorities did not interfere with the great parades on 12 July 1801 in Downpatrick, Coleraine and The Diamond. Continued reports of intimidation and the blatant partiality of Orange magistrates, however, encouraged the Government to take some action. Robert Peel, appointed Irish chief secretary in 1812, soon proved that he was not 'Orange Peel', as Daniel O'Connell described him. He set up a mobile constabulary (certain to be more impartial than the yeomanry in dealing with disturbances) and began appointing stipendiary magistrates, independent of local politics, to improve the prospects for justice. Then from 1821 the lord lieutenants consistently attempted to stop Orange demonstrations. Soon after, the Government was faced with a mass movement for emancipation, and in taking rigorous action against Catholic organisation, it tried to be even-handed by moving strongly against the Orange Order. The Orange movement was threatened with extinction.[11]

'I care no more for a Catholic than I care for a Chinese,' one MP remarked. If Westminster remained indifferent then the Catholic bourgeoisie would force Ireland to the top of the agenda.[12] The intense excitement of the twenty years prior to the Union meant that the people were already highly politicised, but it was the striking achievement of Daniel O'Connell, the Kerry landowner and lawyer, to bring together priests, the middle class and peasantry into one formidable agitation. The Catholic Association, formed in 1823, created a mass membership the following year by enrolling associate members for a contribution of a penny a month. With the assistance of priests, the movement acquired a sophisticated local administrative network never before achieved by an Irish political organisation. Though O'Connell's language was often violent, the movement was law-abiding – when the Catholic Association was banned in 1825, it duly dissolved itself and set up a new organisation.

The Unlawful Societies Act which put down the Catholic Association also suppressed the Orange Order. In both Britain and Ireland the upper classes, finding themselves shunned in official circles, had already been dissociating themselves rapidly from the movement; now the banning of the order was accepted with calm resignation by its leaders. The organisation remained intact in Ulster, however, and militant Protestantism mobilised as the drive for emancipation reached its climax.

The turning point was the election of 1826: what Wolfe Tone had described as the 'wretched tribe of forty shilling freeholders, whom we see driven to their octennial market, by their landlords, as much their property as the sheep or the bullochs', now defied those landlords in half a dozen constituencies.[13] Two of those constituencies were in Ulster: in the face of open threats of eviction, Co. Monaghan voters went against their landlords to elect Henry Westenra and defeat the anti-emancipationist Charles Leslie; and in Co. Cavan some eight hundred tenants voted against their proprietors' instructions in an unsuccessful bid to oust the sitting members. Yet Ulster was far from giving the lead in the drive for emancipation.

THE 'INVASION OF ULSTER' AND EMANCIPATION

In the autumn of 1828, Jack Lawless, the Belfast journalist who was one of O'Connell's most energetic lieutenants, announced the 'invasion of Ulster' – he and his supporters would advance from town to town in the province, holding public meetings, rallying support for emancipation, and collecting the 'Catholic Rent'. Ulster's contribution to the Catholic Rent – a fighting fund mainly for protecting tenants who voted against their landlords' wishes – was pitiful: a mere £204 out of a total of £2,899 for the whole country that year.

On 17 September Lawless arrived in Carrickmacross, the frontier town of Co. Monaghan, and declared that he would enter Ballybay six days later with fifty thousand followers. Ballybay was then almost exclusively Presbyterian and an alarm call went out to all the Protestants in the county. Some eight thousand Orangemen rallied in the town, the *Northern Whig* reported:

> They were in general armed with muskets; but failing these, swords, bayonets, pitch-forks, scythes, &c. &c. were in requisition. A set of more determined men, perhaps, never appeared in any cause. It is well known that many of them made their wills, and settled their affairs before they left their houses in the morning.[14]

General Thornton, in command of foot soldiers, all the county police, and a troop of lancers, galloped towards Carrickmacross and persuaded Lawless to go instead to Rockcorry chapel by a circuitous route. A bloody conflict, it seemed, was thus prevented (one correspondent

245

reckoned one hundred thousand followed Lawless), but as supporters from both sides were going home they met on the Rockcorry Road:

A conflict ensued immediately. How it commenced is not well known; but the termination was awfully fatal. One Catholic was run through the body with a sword or bayonet, and died on the spot. Another had his leg shattered by a musket ball, and is lying, with little hopes of recovery. Several, it is supposed, must have been slightly wounded, as they were fired upon for nearly a mile during their retreat.

Armagh was to be Lawless's next venue. On Tuesday 30 September, market day, armed Protestants poured in only to hear that local Catholics had successfully pleaded with their leader to stay away. In celebration the Orangemen 'marched through the city, beating drums, huzzaing, and now and then firing shots. In Scotch-street, upwards of thirty shots were fired . . . *Several of the guns were bright, and were evidently yeomanry arms, and the cavalry swords were of the same description.'*

The *Northern Whig*, a journal which had replaced the *Belfast News-Letter* as the voice of Protestant liberalism in Ulster, warmly supported Catholic emancipation but considered that 'Mr Lawless's procedure was impolitic in the highest degree', and continued:

The state of the country at the present crisis is truly awful. In the North a desperate and armed faction, released from a temporary check, exasperated by a partial rebuff, and thirsting for blood, are daily excited against their Catholic countrymen by the inflammatory harangues of men, whose conduct more resembles that of Priests of Malock, than Ministers of Jesus.[15]

One of the inflammatory clergy was the Reverend Mr Horner who, before an enthusiastic audience in Omagh courthouse on 2 October 1828, urged

resistance to all who would subvert the Constitution . . . resistance by an appeal to the sword – (The speaker was here interrupted by a burst of applause which lasted for several minutes) . . . even the *alternative* of Connaught may no longer be left as a refuge for the fugitives – (cheers) – but than an indignant nation, giving a loose to its resentment, and measuring punishment only by provocation, may rid the country of them altogether, and rescue itself from the cruel necessity of chastising them again – (cheering).

The meeting in Omagh was to found a Brunswick Club – a club set up as an alternative to the banned Orange Order. Lawless's 'invasion' prompted the calling of meetings all over Ulster to establish these Protestant clubs; over a ten-day period clubs were founded at Omagh, Tandragee, Lifford, Portadown, Carrickfergus, Downpatrick, Lisburn and the Moy. Most of these meetings were accompanied by great demonstrations, band playing, the shouldering of arms and the open support of the yeomanry wearing party badges and insignia. The *Newry Telegraph* estimated that forty thousand had met at Tandragee, and after the Moy demonstration a group went to a nearby townland, where all but two families were Catholics. Their approach 'was announced by drums, fifes, bugles, and by playing party tunes, such as "Holy Water", "Croppies lie down", and "Kick the Pope before Us" . . . till two in the morning, when they marched back, playing the same tunes, huzzaing, and firing shots'.[16]

Daniel O'Connell had been elected for Co. Clare in June of that year, though he could not take his seat. He had mobilised such a formidable display of Catholic power, however, that Wellington's government felt it had no choice but to give way. In 1829 Catholics won their emancipation. Contrary to the general view, Irish Protestants, especially in the north, did not accept emancipation as inevitable and henceforth most saw themselves as a beleaguered people. Ulster was turbulent that summer. When the 12 July parade was banned in Belfast, Orange masters told the magistrates, 'The Orangemen of Belfast cannot be prevented from walking.' A demonstration in Sandy Row was followed next day by rioting at Millfield and Brown Street. The Larne coach was smashed and many were injured, one man 'had his skull fractured by the blow of a stone-hammer, and when on the ground was stabbed in three places, apparently with a pen-knife'. Over the next few days 'broken heads and broken windows are of hourly occurrence'. There was fierce rioting in Armagh; stone-throwing at Greyabbey; a 'fatal recountre' near Enniskillen; Orangemen shot three men in Strabane; at least four were killed at Coalisland; and other lives were lost at Stewartstown, the Moy and Portglenone (where in that district alone some twenty deaths were reported).

The *Northern Whig* had observed about Lawless: 'As to his reconciling the Catholics and Orangemen – the idea is Quixotic.'[17] A fervent religious revival was sweeping much of Europe and its impact on Ireland, both Protestant and Catholic, was such that an apparently insuperable barrier had been put up to impede lasting reconciliation.

CATHOLICS IN ULSTER: 'THEY ARE GREATLY INFERIOR . . .'

Even when Napoleon's empire was still extending its sway, the Catholic revival in Europe had begun. The Jesuit Order was restored and the Church, with a fresh roll of martyrs scythed down by the guillotine, set about winning back souls lost to the deism of the Enlightenment and the atheism of the revolution. It was not long before this new devotional fervour and drive against laxity reached Ireland.

In 1808 Edward Wakefield, writing about Donegal, observed that there 'are few chapels in this county . . . The priest and his congregation must sometimes meet under a rock, or take advantage of any other shelter they can.'[18] Open-air Masses were still being held in Portrush and in several Tyrone and Londonderry parishes in the 1830s. The poverty of parishioners was the main reason and it was poverty which largely explained the low contributions to the Catholic Rent. The Catholics of Ulster made up over one fifth of Ireland's population and at least half the inhabitants of the province, but they were overwhelmingly confined to the lowest rungs of the social ladder. Only in Newry were propertied and educated Catholics well represented, and the vast majority of Catholics were cottiers, labourers and poor tenants, the most prosperous being the farmer-weavers of the linen triangle. In 1825 the Reverend Henry Cooke, champion of Presbyterian orthodoxy, declared that Catholics 'are greatly inferior in point of education; they are greatly inferior, generally, in point of farming . . . they put up with far less comfort, both in point of dress and food'.[19] The census of 1861 was to show that only 29 per cent of Catholics in Ulster could read and write, compared with 59 per cent of Presbyterians and 50 per cent of members of the Church of Ireland.

Catholic bishops found church attendance at the turn of the century disturbingly low in Ulster: only 43 per cent in Belfast and under 40 per cent in the wilder parts of Cavan, Donegal and Tyrone. This did not mean the people were unbelievers and, for example, the Ordnance Survey could find only one atheist in the parish of Clones, a man 'who believes the Devil is a bugbear got up by the clergy to make money'.[20] The laxity of the clergy had been exposed in 1775 when Pope Pius VI suspended the archbishop of Armagh, Anthony Blake, for spending all his time in his Co. Galway home. A new generation of bishops, such as Edward Kernan of Clogher, suppressed unseemly quarrels between the clergy, who in future were forbidden to hunt, drink in public and attend theatres. To make up for past neglect, great numbers of adults were confirmed in the diocese of Derry in 1841 and there was a fresh insistence on regular attendance, religious instruction and devout behaviour.

The Catholic Church made only slow progress in curbing traditional practices and customs surviving, in some cases, from pagan times. Again and again, strictures were issued against unruly behaviour at wakes, which in Donegal, for example, were 'attended with unbounded mirth and festivity'. From Armagh it was reported that there were 'tricks and pastimes quite unbecoming' of a sexually suggestive nature and that in some cases the corpse was dealt a hand of cards, had a pipe stuck in his mouth, or was taken on to the floor for a dance.[21] Attempts were made to substitute hymns for 'the savage custom of howling and bawling at funerals'; this was the 'keen', in Irish *caoineadh*, described by John Wesley as 'a dismal inarticulate yell' but admired by the Church of Ireland curate of Dungiven in 1814: 'Its affecting cadences will continue to find admirers whenever what is truly sad and plaintive can be relished or understood.'[22] The pilgrimage to Lough Derg was attracting between ten thousand and fifteen thousand a year in the 1830s; steps were taken to curb commercial exploitation here, and other pilgrimages across the province were put down – priests were ordered to stay away from the Saint John's Eve gatherings in Cavan and at Struell Wells in Co. Down, for example. The Ordnance Survey memoirs of the 1830s record the advent of a new Catholic puritanism in Ulster: dancing and cockfighting at Duneane, Co. Antrim, 'are denounced by their clergy and partially given up'; the hire of pipers for dancing at Cushendall had been usual 'but their priest put a total stop to it'; and in Rostrevor, gatherings 'for the purpose of amusement do not take place as formerly, such meetings being opposed by the Roman Catholic clergy'.[23]

PROTESTANT ULSTER AND THE SECOND REFORMATION

At present we attend evangelical meetings every evening from 6 till 9 . . . these meetings are held to hundreds in mute attention to a variety of well gifted men of a superior order and manner to any itinerants I ever heard, extremely zealous and *loyal*.

So wrote Martha McTier from Belfast in September 1801; the sister of Dr Drennan and friend of Thomas Russell, she had no liking for the preachers' attitude to political dissent.[24] But she is recording a phenomenon that swept over Protestant Ireland in the nineteenth century and had a powerful impact on developments in Ulster. The evangelical revival seized the imagination of peoples throughout northern Europe as Napoleon's armies retreated before the victorious armies of the dynastic powers – indeed Tsar Alexander I put down his own conversion to 'the judgement of the Lord in the snowfields'. Horrified by the realities of violence and disillusioned by failure, many United Irish Presbyterians found solace in the certainties of evangelical religion. The way had been prepared by John Wesley, who had visited Ireland twenty-one times and had enlisted some twenty thousand followers. The evangelical emphasis on faith, the literal truth of the Bible, personal conversion and a new enthusiasm proved attractive to more and more Protestants and created strong reaction against both liberal New Light principles and the worldliness of the Established Church.

I speak openly before the world and I declare the doctrines held and taught by the Arian ministers and professors in Belfast are in direct opposition to the scripture.[25]

Henry Cooke launched this virulent attack on the Belfast Academical Institution at the Presbyterian Synod in Newry in 1822, declaring that the teachers there held 'Arian' beliefs, that is, heretical opinions including a rejection of the doctrine of the Trinity. Cooke, originally Henry Macook of Maghera, had won notoriety by his powerful, emotional preaching and an attack on his colleagues for their lenient treatment of a minister who had confessed to 'ante-nuptial fornication'.[26] Dr Henry Montgomery, a professor at the Academical Institution, led a successful campaign to prevent the expulsion of New Light teachers; but in the larger struggle against orthodoxy he was the loser. At the synods held in Coleraine in 1825 and in Strabane in 1827 he failed to convince his fellow ministers that a range of beliefs could be tolerated within Presbyterianism. As a result, he and other liberals felt they had no choice but to withdraw and form their own rump synod in 1830, which eventually became the Nonsubscribing Presbyterian Church. The triumphant Cooke, meanwhile, won over the strictly orthodox Seceders and the great majority of Ulster Presbyterians united in 1840 to form the General Assembly of the Presbyterian Church in Ireland.

Cooke was burned in effigy in Ballycarry and his inquisitorial visitations caused much resentment, but it was in vain that Montgomery looked back to the time when amidst 'a recognised variety of creeds there was a perfect unity of spirit, for every man, while rejoicing in his own liberty, respected the right of his brother'.[27] Cooke once asserted that he was 'as pure of political feeling as the virgin snow', but the controversy – which for more than a decade dominated the columns of northern newspapers – was highly political. Montgomery, whose Antrim home had been burned by government forces in 1798, supported reform and Catholic relief, while Cooke, remembering with disgust the revolutionary turbulence of the 1790s in Co. Londonderry, declared that he contemplated Catholic emancipation with 'horror, disapprobation and dismay'.[28] He was to forge a new conservative alliance between the majority of Ulster Presbyterians and the Ascendancy.

In 1811 Percy Jocelyn, bishop of Clogher and son of the 1st Earl of Roden, was caught in a compromising position with a guardsman in the White Hart public house in Westminster. The scandal was all the greater because some years earlier the bishop had had his servant flogged through the streets of Dublin and imprisoned for two years for the 'libel' of accusing Jocelyn of making an improper proposal.[29] The whole embarrassing episode did much to impel the Church of Ireland to enforce higher standards amongst its clergy. Lord George Beresford, primate of Armagh for forty years, tightened up discipline and ensured that gone were the days when an Earl-Bishop could desert his diocese for twenty-one years.

With reform came a resurgence of puritanism amongst both Anglicans and Presbyterians. When Cooke announced in 1829 that he had given up strong drink, he was merely following the lead given by several flourishing temperance organisations. The Ordnance Survey memoirs indicate a general increase in sobriety; in Tamlaght O'Crilly in Co. Londonderry the Drumbolg Temperance Society had 240 members, and horse racing at Greenlough had ceased in 1814 'in consequence of drunkenness, quarrelling and party fighting'. 'The taste for amusement has here,' the memoir for Doagh observed, 'as throughout the neighbourhood, greatly declined . . . Since the more general introduction of book clubs, cock-fighting has almost disappeared.' There the prosperous farmers did play for small stakes in card games called 'Spoil Fives'; the author of the memoir found them 'strictly Scottish . . . cold, stiff and disagreeable' and as for lower-class Protestants they were 'riotous, quarrelsome and obstinate, without possessing 1 particle of humour, fun or good nature'. In nearby Donegore 'wakes, which formerly had been scenes of amusement, are now observed with decorum and propriety, the evening being spent in reading aloud the scriptures'; here the people were well known for their 'idioms and old saws, which are very quaint'. Shane's Castle park had been 'open to the public on Sundays, but on a remonstrance being made to Lord O'Neill by some of the respectable inhabitants of the neighbourhood of Antrim . . . he very properly withdrew the lease for admission to it'. Nevertheless, in that area an 'implicit belief exists in ghosts, fairies and banshees, in enchantments and in the power which the fairies so wantonly exercise in depriving cows of their milk, nor are these notions confined to any particular sect or denomination'.[30]

The people living in Islandmagee, also 'inveterately superstitious', resolutely resisted the temperance movement, though Lord Dungannon had smashed up all fourteen public houses on the peninsula. The author of the memoir for this parish reported:

The inhabitants of all sexes and classes are perhaps a more immoral race than is to be found in any other rural district in Antrim. Their drunkenness and intemperance is everywhere proverbial . . . What makes their immorality the more disgusting is the openness and want of shame with which it is exhibited. The women whenever from home, or indeed whenever they can procure the means, drink raw spirits in such quantities as

251

would astonish any but a native . . . the number of sudden, violent and premature deaths among them, solely from the effects of intemperance, is appalling . . . Some have fallen off carts or staggered into a hole on their way home. Others have been smothered, 2 have committed suicide, several have lost their reason, and many still remain as examples and warnings, in their paralysed bodies and shattered intellects, to those who are treading in their footsteps.[31]

In time, however, the temperance movement triumphed even here and today no part of Ulster is more bereft of public houses than Islandmagee. The memoir also remarked that there 'is not the slightest tinge of party or sectarian feeling in the parish' – an observation which could not be made about many other parts of the province.

From the beginning of the nineteenth century many of the lower clergy in the Established Church were inspired with evangelical zeal and for the first time in over a hundred years Protestants launched a drive to convert Catholics. This 'Second Reformation' began in 1799 when the Methodists sent three Irish-speaking missionaries to work among Catholics. The Presbyterians and Baptists followed suit, but the lead was taken by Anglicans, backed by wealthy bodies in London – the Religious Tract and Book Society alone gave out nearly four and a half million tracts over ten years, for example. Catholics were offered free or cheap schooling provided they accepted Protestant religious instruction; this was particularly successful in Ulster, where Catholics from the province formed 40 per cent of pupils in schools in Ireland run by the proselytising London Hibernian Society. Public debating duels between Protestant and Catholic clergy became popular in the south, but were condemned by Presbyterians. Nevertheless, a three-day contest at Ballymena in July 1827 between the Reverend Robert Stewart and the Reverend Bernard McAuley PP attracted wide attention. Inevitably these developments did nothing to improve relations between Catholics and Protestants. Lord Farnham, founder of the Association for Promoting the Second Reformation, was an example of how tactless and provocative proselytising could be: week by week the earl proclaimed the numbers of souls fresh won over from Popery on wall posters or on placards hung from the backs of people walking the town of Cavan.[32]

Lord Farnham was responsible for major evictions of Catholics on his estate south-east of Lough Ramor in order to bring in more politically compatible Protestant tenants. Other clearances of this kind in Co. Cavan followed on the property of Sir George Hodson, on the Headfort estates and on the lands of the Reverend Marcus Beresford.

Such evictions usually provoked serious rioting. Both Farnham and Beresford were prominent members of the Orange Order, now thrown on the defensive.[33]

'THIS CLOSE-COMPACTED PHALANX OF INFIDELITY AND POPERY'

In July 1830 blood flowed in the streets of Paris once more as the hated Bourbons were driven out; the following month the people of Brussels fought Dutch royal troops from their barricades; and as the fire of revolution spread into central and southern Europe the Whigs took office at Westminster for the first time in over twenty years, only to face an alarming English agricultural labourers' revolt and a bloody campaign against the tithe in Leinster. Ulster was turbulent too, as companies of the 64th Regiment stationed at Maghera and Castledawson attempted to disperse parties of Orangemen and Ribbonmen during the 12 July parades. A couple of dozen Orangemen were arrested after Catholic homes had been burned, only to be 'rescued' in a courtroom riot at the Derry assizes; some were later recaptured and transported to Botany Bay. Then in November the Catholic village of Maghery was burned to the ground in revenge for a Ribbon attack on an Orange band in which drums had been punctured. The following year regular troops were pulled out of Ulster to suppress the Tithe War in the south. The local yeomanry, called out to maintain order in the north and re-equipped with modern arms, proved violent and partisan. On 18 June 1831, for example, after being taunted by a large crowd in Newtownbarry, Co. Cavan, the yeomen opened fire, killing seventeen people and wounding twenty.

In August 1832 the Party Processions Act outlawed Orange demonstrations. Though the legislation making it an illegal organisation had lapsed and though it proved beyond the capacity of the authorities to suppress its parades in Ulster, the Orange Order faced the mounting hostility of the governing classes. The Great Reform Act had just become law and the Whig government was grateful for O'Connell's support. In return it produced legislation which chipped away at the privileges of the Ascendancy, extending the constabulary, appointing Catholic magistrates, and reducing the tithe and the Church of Ireland establishment. O'Connell called for repeal of the Union – the return of a Dublin parliament – but for the present, support even from Irish Catholics was disappointing. The Whigs adamantly rejected repeal but continued an informal parliamentary alliance with O'Connell.[34]

Henry Cooke – dubbed the 'American doctor' by the *Northern Whig* after he had been awarded an honorary degree by Jefferson College – raged against 'this close-compacted phalanx of infidelity and Popery'. He was the principal speaker at a great Conservative demonstration at Hillsborough on 30 October 1834, called by Lord Roden to unite Protestants of all sects, for their privileges, as in 1688, were in 'imminent peril'. After declaring that repeal was 'just a discreet word for Romish ascendancy and Protestant extermination', Cooke 'published' the banns of marriage between Presbyterianism and the Establishment, 'a sacred marriage of Christian forbearance where they differ, of Christian love where they agree, and of Christian co-operation in all matters where their common safety is concerned'. While many liberal Presbyterians denounced Cooke's proposed union – for example, in a series of letters to the *Londonderry Standard* the Reverend D.G. Brown condemned this 'monstrous union of Presbytery and Prelacy' – more and more believed the time had come to make common cause against the rising tide of Irish nationalism.[35] Despite government protests that high sheriffs and magistrates should not have allowed them to be called, other large demonstrations followed, notably at Cavan, where thirty thousand Orangemen assembled, some shouldering arms, and at Dungannon, where on 12 November 1834 Lords Caledon, Belmore, Abercorn, Hamilton and Alexander watched some seventy-five thousand Orangemen file past their platform.[36]

The Whigs were unmoved and formalised their alliance with O'Connell in 1835. In the same year a parliamentary select committee produced a 4,500-page report on the Orange Order. For MPs the most alarming conclusion was not only that the yeomanry was controlled by Orangemen but also that the army was full of lodges – especially worrying, as the British grand master, the Duke of Cumberland, was William IV's brother and a field marshal. To prevent stern action by parliament, Cumberland dissolved the army lodges in February 1836, and the Grand Orange Lodge of Ireland was dissolved the following April. The order continued in Ulster but was largely deserted by the upper classes and almost another fifty years were to pass before the movement recovered its prestige and influence.[37]

Conservative Protestants watched with dismay as the Whigs produced a succession of reforms for Ireland including: National Schools (Cooke led a campaign against their interdenominational make-up); the abolition of sixty-eight corporations largely controlled by landlords and their replacement by ten corporations elected by ratepayers (including Belfast and Derry); and the introduction of workhouses to be financed by a new poor rate. But for O'Connell this was a miserable crop of reforms and in 1840 he broke with the Whigs and launched a new mass movement for repeal of the Act of Union.

O'Connell had once toasted the 'Immortal Memory' of William III by drinking a tumbler-full of Boyne water at Drogheda, and he never ceased to hope that Ulster Presbyterians would join him in his great campaign for repeal. On 2 January 1841 he accepted the invitation of the Loyal National Repeal Association in Belfast to speak in the town. Cooke promptly challenged O'Connell to a public debate:

> When you *invade* Ulster, and unfurl the flag of *Repeal*, you will find yourself in a new climate . . . I believe you are a great bad man, engaged in a great bad cause – and as easily foiled by a weak man, armed with a good cause, as Goliath, the Giant of Gath, was discomfited by the stripling, with no weapon but a sling and two pebbles from the brook . . . *You cannot avoid this discussion.* I am the man you have so often reviled *behind his back* – can you do less than meet him *face-to-face*?[38]

'My friend Bully Cooke, the cock of the North,' O'Connell told his supporters in Dublin, 'has written the most insulting letter he could pen' – but he did not accept the challenge. The original plan for a procession into Ulster was dropped; had it not been, a loyalist pamphleteer observed, 'a counter array would inevitably have been formed to stop the invading cortege . . . no human foresight can calculate the terrible consequences which might have ensued . . .'

The Government took no chances and engaged two steamers to take detachments of the 99th Regiment from Dublin to the north; the Enniskillen Dragoons were marched from Dundalk to Belfast; and the artillery arrived with four pieces of cannon – a body of more than two thousand men, not including special reinforcements of mounted and foot police. 'O'Connell's Insult to the North!' placards proclaimed, calling on loyalists to greet 'the great defamer of the glorious character of Protestant Ulster' in force as he passed through. Immense crowds met in Dromore, Hillsborough and Lisburn but they had to be satisfied with burning O'Connell in effigy, for on Saturday 16 January he slipped through incognito and 'literally stole into our town "as a thief in the night"'.[39] O'Connell did indeed find himself in a new climate in Belfast. He did not even dare leave the safety of Kern's Hotel in Donegall Place to attend Mass at St Patrick's the following morning.

On Monday O'Connell met a deputation of tradesmen, the *Northern Whig* remarking on 'the blunt cordiality of their greetings such as "give me your hand Dan"; "here's a hand Dan, my boy, with a heart in it", &c., &c.'. Only a handful of liberal Protestants turned up that evening to join a host of Catholic supporters for the repeal dinner at the Victoria Theatre in Chichester Street, an event at which O'Connell scoffed at the 'boxing buffoon of a Divine'. It was not until Tuesday 19 January that the Liberator faced the public in the open. On the balcony of Kern's Hotel he threw off his green cloak, and displayed 'a surtout of Repeal frieze, with a white velvet collar, and Repeal buttons'. 'The fraternal force of liberty, presaging prosperity,' he bellowed, 'will rise from Connemara to the Hill of Howth – will pass from Cape Clear to the Giant's Causeway; and the men of Belfast will gladden, in pleasing gratitude, as the joyous sound passes them.' But he could not be heard, save by reporters next to him:

> Yells, hisses, groans, cheers, and exclamations of all descriptions were blended together in the most strange confusion imaginable . . . 'Ha, Dan, there's Dr Cooke coming' – 'No Pope' – 'No Surrender' – 'Come down out of that ye big beggerman, till we shake hands with ye' – 'Put out the Ballymacarrett weavers; go home to your sowens, ye scarecrows' – 'Dan O'Connell for ever' – 'Hurrah for Repeal', etc.[40]

That evening, as O'Connell attended a soiree in the May Street Music Hall, a stone-throwing battle raged outside, while a 'still larger body of people traversed the town, shouting and yelling . . . they smashed the windows of several houses, confining their rage, principally, to the residences of those persons who had been accessory to the late Repeal'. A well-aimed stone broke through a window and sliced through a blind to shatter the grand chandelier in Kern's Hotel, and in the office of the Belfast repeal journal, the *Vindicator*, this report was being compiled: 'While we write, they are after being repulsed by the police, in the fifth attempt to break open the door; and there is scarcely a whole pane in the front of the office.'[41]

Next morning, escorted by four cars full of police and a body of police cavalry, O'Connell left Belfast for Donaghadee. When he arrived his appearance, the *Northern Whig* reported, 'was that of a man altogether afraid of his own shadow', and he was much alarmed when a pane was broken, but this was caused only by a little boy

> in anxiety to see the great Liberator . . . A gentleman present assured him this was no danger, as this was a Presbyterian country, where crime was unknown.

Nevertheless, there was hissing and groaning as he approached the cross-channel vessel and a woman threw a tea cup at him. At the gangplank O'Connell approached an old fisherman and said, 'You have very pretty girls here.' 'Yes,' the old man replied, 'but none of them are Repealers.'[42]

On 21 and 22 January two 'Grand Conservative Demonstrations' were held in Belfast. The first, in the Circus, was requisitioned by no fewer than forty-one peers and noblemen, and here Cooke proposed a motion that 'looking to the numerous and solid advantages which have accrued to Ireland' from the Union, the meeting saw 'with indignation and alarm, the recently renewed efforts to effect its Repeal'. Cooke concluded his long peroration by attributing Belfast's recent rapid growth to legislative union with Britain and to Protestantism:

> Look at the town of Belfast. When I was myself a youth I remember it almost a village. But what a glorious sight does it now present – the masted grove within our harbour – (cheers) – our mighty warehouses teeming with the wealth of every climate – (cheers) – our giant manufactories lifting themselves on every side – (cheers) – our streets marching on . . . And all this we owe to the Union. (Loud cheers.) No, not all – for throned above our fair town, and looking serenely from our mountain's brow, I behold the genii of Protestantism and Liberty, sitting inseparable in their power, while the genius of Industry which nightly reclines at their feet, starts with every morning in renovated might, and puts forth his energies, and showers down his blessings, in the fair and smiling lands of a Chichester, a Conway, or a Hill. (Vehement cheers.) Yes Mr. O'Connell, we will guard the Union as we will guard our liberties, and advance and secure the prosperity of our country . . . Look at Belfast, and be a Repealer – if you can. (The Rev. Doctor then retired amid the most enthusiastic cheering, and loud shouts of approbation, which continued for several minutes.)[43]

Cooke made a similar speech at a massive open-air demonstration the following day, putting forward what would be the unionist case for decades to come – Protestant liberties would be imperilled by a Catholic ascendancy in a Dublin parliament; Ulster's prosperity and industrial growth were due to Protestant enterprise; and Ulster's future lay in serving the markets of Britain's expanding empire.

Despite impressive displays of strength at 'monster meetings' in the south, O'Connell's drive for repeal came to grief in 1843. When Peel banned a great demonstration due to take place at Clontarf, O'Connell agreed to remain within the law and the movement lost its momentum thereafter. By then the state of the economy was of far more immediate concern than the political future of the country.

THE RISE AND FALL OF COTTON

In February 1802 the Belfast Chamber of Commerce met for the first time in eight years; in 1794 it had been shattered by the first round of government arrests and now former United Irishmen and yeomen pulled together to look after the commercial and industrial welfare of their town. Indeed, to a far greater extent than the landlord MPs and the indolent corporations, the chamber of commerce represented the economic interests of Ulster. It obtained a marked improvement in the postal services; offered a low-interest loan to the first person to run a regular coach to Enniskillen; campaigned for a string of lighthouses from St John's Point north to the Isle of Barra; bought up the bankrupt Lord Donegall's interests in the Lagan Navigation in 1809; pressed successfully for a canal from Lough Neagh to Lough Erne; won approval for a Belfast base for the East Indies trade in 1824; and resolved to support the building of railways 'by every means in their power'. The same entrepreneurs gave Ulster a sound banking system, finally ending Dublin's long domination as the economic centre of gravity for northern farmers and traders. In 1824, the Bank of Ireland's monopoly was brought to an end when the Northern Bank was reconstituted on a joint-stock basis; in 1825 and 1836, respectively, the Belfast Bank and the Ulster Bank were set up as joint-stock concerns. All three had their headquarters in Belfast, which by then had nine insurance companies, including the Sun, the Norwich Union and the Royal Exchange.[44]

Viable banks and reliable insurance were vital in helping firms ride out the violent fluctuations in Ulster's economy in the early nineteenth century. In 1809, for example, two thousand cotton looms in the Belfast area were idle for five weeks, but, overall, almost every sector of the province's economy was stimulated by the long wars against Napoleon. Not only was there an unprecedented demand for linen sailcloth, material for uniforms and provisions for the army and navy but also the commercial blockades of the war created acute shortages in the rapidly expanding English market. Ulster was Britain's principal overseas supplier of cattle; animals reared on hill farms and fattened in the lowlands were driven in their thousands to Donaghadee for transport across the Irish Sea. Nowhere was hectic growth more evident than in Belfast: its population increased by almost 47 per cent between 1801, when it was 19,000, and 1811, when it was nearly 28,000; its customs yield rose from £182,000 in 1802 to just under £321,000 in 1808; and in 1810 its exports included over 15 million yards of linen, 63,561 hundredweight of bacon, 51,547 firkins of butter and 1,884 kegs of ox tongues.[45] Yet it was the manufacture of an exotic import – cotton – for sale to the home market that was the most arresting feature of Belfast's expansion in these years.

Clustering round Belfast Lough for the most part, to be close to seaborne supplies of fuel and raw material, factories spun cotton by steam or water power; this mill yarn was then 'put out' to hand-loom weavers to be made into cloth. John Milford's mill in Winetavern Street was five storeys high and its 5,364 spindles and 24 carding machines were turned by a ten-horsepower steam engine. McCrum, Leppers and Company, behind the Artillery Barracks, had a factory two hundred feet long and five storeys high, which for a time was the largest in Ireland. Destroyed by a great fire in February 1813, it was rebuilt in the same year. Thomas Mulholland moved his business from Winetavern Street to Henry Street in 1822 and when his mill there was completed it bypassed McCrum's in capacity to become the biggest in the country.[46] In 1811 the Reverend John Dubourdieu calculated that in the Belfast area there were 150,000 power-driven spindles making over 70 million hanks of cotton yarn, and concluded 'that not less than 30,000 individuals derive a good support from the muslin and calico branches of this trade, taking in all the different departments'. Ten one-hundred-ton vessels plied the North Channel to bring over the six thousand tons of Cumbrian and Ayr coal needed each year to raise steam in the mills. By the end of the Napoleonic Wars in 1815 Belfast was taking half of Ireland's cotton wool and yarn.[47]

The close of hostilities precipitated a severe trade depression; the cotton manufacturer, Hugh McCall, remembered that 'terrible disasters spread through every avenue of industry, but no department suffered more than the cotton manufacture'. He continued:

Goods fell in value 30 to 40 per cent . . . Production for a time was partially suspended, and when weavers did get work, the scale of wages was lowered to a point which, at the high rates current for the necessities of life, left the most diligent weavers the barest means of subsistence.

Desperate weavers attacked the home of Francis Johnson, a hated employer living on Peter's Hill in Belfast in the summer of 1815; the hall door and window shutters were daubed with tar and set alight. Early next year there was a further armed attack in which a bomb was thrown that would have wrecked the house if it had not been tossed with a pitchfork to the back door just before it exploded; 'Mr Johnson defended himself with great heroism, and, until assistance arrived, he kept the enemy at bay by the incessant firing of his blunderbuss.' Three men were capitally convicted as a result – the last public hanging in Belfast. However, no one was convicted when the workers' leader, Gordon Maxwell, was mortally wounded at Malone even though, as he lay dying in Lisburn Infirmary, he obtained 'sworn informations against a local manufacturer'.[48]

The condition of cotton hand-loom weavers did not improve. Writing in 1802, Dubourdieu observed that a good cotton weaver could earn 'from eighteen shillings to a guinea per week, more than double the wages of a linen weaver . . . and a smart young cotton weaver became no slight attraction in the eyes of a country belle'. By the 1820s wages paid to a cotton weaver had sunk to seven shillings a week and they continued to fall. In the trade slump of 1825–6 one third of the cotton weavers in Belfast and its neighbourhood were unemployed, while the remainder endured grim conditions; the weavers of Ballymacarrett worked from 4 a.m. to midnight, seven days a week, for a wage of 4s.6d. Wives served as winders unpaid, rent cost one shilling, and another shilling was needed for fuel and candles. The *Belfast News-Letter* reported in February 1830 that Ballymacarrett weavers were forced to live on Indian meal unfit for cattle and that they were reduced to skeletons from overwork and lack of sleep.

The real problem was that the Ulster cotton industry was losing its competitive edge. Though Belfast concerns were comparatively large and labour was cheaper than in England, Lancashire calico, muslin and cord – cheaper and finer than Ulster cotton, and woven by steam – swept into Ireland capturing the market. As weavers' wages were so low, Ulster manufacturers did not see the need for power looms until it was too late; protective duties were removed in 1824 and by 1836 parliamentary commissioners declared that the cotton industry in Ireland was almost extinct. Once a luxury material, cotton had become the cheapest of all textiles and thus threatened the very survival of the Ulster linen industry.

'THE FAR SEEING MERCHANTS OF THE NORTHERN ATHENS':
THE POWER-SPINNING OF FLAX

In 1805 the linen board offered a subsidy to anyone who could erect machinery 'for spinning hemp or flax for sail-cloth . . . to be worked by steam or water, ten shillings per spindle'.[49] The urgent needs of war prompted this offer and the first to take it was Samuel Crookshank of Rademon, near Crossgar, who was paid £78. By 1809 eleven more mills had been set up: Buncrana, Milford and Ramelton in Co. Donegal; Broughshane, Balnamore, Crumlin and Cushendall in Co. Antrim; Templegowran and Comber in Co. Down; Bessbrook in Co. Armagh; and Derryvale in Co. Tyrone. The experiment, however, was not a success – the machinery could only make the coarsest yarn and frequently broke down, wasting a great deal of flax in the process. Attempts to spin flax in cotton mills – for example, at Hillsborough, Bangor, Larne and Ballynure – were also a failure. Linen, in short, cannot be spun like cotton; flax fibres are bound together by a gummy substance which makes the strands to be spun slightly greasy. The hand-spinner could coax the strands into yarn with her fingers, but the fibres either stuck together or snapped in power-driven roving machinery. Then in 1825 James Kay of Preston discovered that a six-hour soaking in cold water made the flax slippery enough to be drawn by power-spinning machines into fine yarn without dissolving out the gum. Soon after, it was found that drawing the flax through a trough of hot water achieved the same result as the cold soaking. It looked as if the north of England was ready to supplant Ulster as the centre of the linen industry.

Small water-powered concerns were the first to try the new wet-spinning process in Ulster; during 1826–7 they included James Nicholson and James McKean of Keady, William Hudson of Mountcaulfield, and G. and F.W. Hayes of Seapatrick. The first commercially successful application, however, was by James and William Murland at Annsborough, near Castlewellan, in 1828. This was the year the linen board was wound up and McCall noted that Murland's 'without the aid of bounties or premiums, soon proved that private enterprise requires only a fair field to ensure its success'.[50] Then, in the same year, on Sunday 10 June, Mulholland's York Street cotton factory in Belfast went on fire and burned so fiercely for several hours that the flames could be seen from several miles away. Mulholland's was rebuilt not for cotton-spinning but for the power-spinning of flax. It was a decision of vital importance in the history of Ulster's industrial development – a decision carefully based on experiments with wet-spinning in their Francis Street premises. It was the scale of the new York Street mill that was so striking: a five-storey factory with 3 steam engines, putting out 115 horsepower, driving 15,300 spindles, and with a 186-foot-tall chimney (which had to be rebuilt after the night of the Big Wind in January 1839). Thereafter, some seven hundred tons of flax were converted into yarn each year and, McCall observed, 'it was not unusual to spin a single pound of flax into a thread of sixty or seventy thousand yards long'. He continued:

The profits of the York Street concern exceeded the dreamiest imaginings of the proprietors . . . Several of the far seeing merchants of the Northern Athens began to surmise the truth respecting the new El Dorado that had been discovered in York Street, and no long time elapsed until other tall chimneys began to rise in different parts of the town.[51]

The threatened collapse of Ulster's linen industry was thus averted by the enterprise of firms capable of competing with Manchester on its own terms by mass-producing linen of ever-improving quality at a steadily falling cost – for example, Mulholland's forty-lea line yarn, second quality, dropped in price from eleven shillings a bundle in 1834 to five shillings by 1847. The capital, business skills and technical exper-tise earlier acquired by drapers and cotton manufacturers were now redeployed to make eastern Ulster the one part of Ireland where the industrial revolution made spectacular progress in the nineteenth century. In 1834 around a dozen wet-spinning mills were in operation in Ulster and by 1850 this number had reached sixty-two, with a total horsepower of 19,000. The steam-powered mills clustered in Belfast with easy access to the docks for imported coal and supplies of flax brought in principally from Russia. Over 40 per cent of horsepower was generated by water; this was used by rural wet-spinning mills, buying in locally grown flax, and prospering only if they were large. Several proprietors imitated the Barbours – who had built Plantation near Lisburn in 1784 – by laying out purpose-built mill villages: the most notable were Sion Mills, founded by the Herdmans in 1835; Dunbarton at Gilford erected by Dunbar McMaster and Company in the late 1830s; and Bessbrook laid out by the Richardsons in the 1840s. For such concerns cheap and rapid access to overseas markets was essential and they pressed strongly for an improvement in the province's internal communications.[52]

'THE MOST NOBLE AND GALLANT WORKS OF ART':
CANALS, RAILWAYS AND ROADS

In 1814 the engineer John Killaly was commissioned by the Directors-General of Inland Navigation to assess the value of a canal linking Lough Neagh with Lough Erne. The following year he reported:

> Great benefits would result to the province of Ulster from the execution of this canal by its affording a cheap mode of transporting the redundant produce of the Counties of Cavan, Monaghan, Fermanagh, Tyrone etc. to the markets of Belfast, Newry and Armagh . . . a door would be opened to the English market from the north western parts of Ireland; agriculture would be encouraged; the comforts of the poor increased.[53]

The Government hesitated to commit itself to such a great undertaking but a vigorous campaign, headed by the Belfast Chamber of Commerce, persuaded it to give its approval in 1825. Subscribers included the Marquess of Donegall, Lord Rossmore and the Marquess of Downshire, but the main cost was to be borne by the state.

Overcoming severe technical difficulties at the Blackwater gorge at Benburb, the canal reached Monaghan town in 1838; ascending from there by nineteen locks, it reached Wattle Bridge and opened to commercial traffic in 1842. To obtain the full benefit of this waterway, Ulster business interests argued, the connection from upper Lough Erne to the Shannon had to be made. The Government agreed to the project partly because it looked as if it might improve the drainage of the region and partly to provide relief work for those made destitute by the potato harvest failures. Over thirty-eight miles long and making use of the many loughs in its path, the Ballinamore and Ballyconnell Navigation eventually opened in 1860. Seldom was so much good money so obviously thrown after bad, for without massive industrial development in the west, it was never likely to yield a return – a problem compounded by the failure to ensure that the system had a standard width throughout. Another scheme prompted by the need to provide relief during the Great Famine was the canalisation of the lower Bann, which, if nothing else, ended the annual inundation of some twenty-five thousand acres on the margins of Lough Neagh.

In general, waterways in Ulster – as in Ireland as a whole – proved disappointing; too much of the hinterland was too impoverished to provide the canals with the regular traffic needed to make them profitable even before railways began to revolutionise transport across the country.

Towards the end of July 1837 *Express* and *Fury*, two 2-2-2 locomotives built by Sharp, Roberts and Company of Manchester, were drawn up from the Belfast quays by ten horses to Glengall Place, the *Belfast News-Letter* reported, 'attended by immense crowds of spectators, who incessantly cheered their progress through the streets'.[54] For the past two years a line had been laid between Belfast and Lisburn. Nearly 1,600 people gathered a couple of days later, even though it was 4.30 in the morning, to watch the first experimental run, and 'cheered very heartily', the *Commercial Chronicle* observed, as it 'proceeded in a gallant style towards Lisburn'. Then on 12 August the line was formally opened, and the *Belfast News-Letter* gave this account:

> The crowds assembled in the neighbourhood of the Railway were immense, and universal enthusiasm prevailed at the success with which this truly national undertaking has been hitherto prosecuted. The number of passengers during the day amounted upwards of *three thousand*, while hundreds were disappointed in obtaining places. This is a flattering commencement, and we hope that it is only a prophetic omen of the reward to which the Company may reasonably look forward.[55]

There were some who alleged that smoke from the engines would frighten cows into refusing milk and the Belfast Presbytery condemned the running of trains on the Sabbath; one minister told his congregation he 'would rather join a company for theft and murder than the Ulster Railway Company, since its business is sending souls to the devil at the rate of 6d a piece' and that every blast of the railway whistle was 'answered by a shout in Hell'.[56]

The Ulster Railway Company was not to be halted by such objections and by 1842 the line had reached Portadown via Lurgan and Seagoe, the treasury providing £20,000 because of the difficulty of raising sufficient private capital. Third-class passengers paid a shilling to reach Portadown and stood in open carriages without seats or roofs. On 1 March 1848 the first train arrived at Armagh 'amid the acclamations of many of the townspeople', after crossing the upper Bann by a great wooden viaduct of five thirty-nine-foot spans. 'The elegant lightness of the proportions', glowed the *Ulster Railway Handbook*, 'conveys but an inadequate idea of extreme solidity and strength, which can best be understood by the fact of its sustaining unshaken the huge weight of its engines and trains which daily test its powers of endurance'.[57]

On 16 November 1845 the 10th Viscount Massereene had cut the first sod of the Belfast and Ballymena Railway near Whitehouse. The consortium, composed principally of textile manufacturers including the Mulhollands, Grimshaws and Herdmans, employed Charles Lanyon as engineer to supervise the thirty-eight miles of track to Ballymena, reached in April 1848. Another group, led by John Andrews, the Comber linen millowner, launched the Belfast and County Down Railway in June 1846; it moved forward gingerly 'in view of the bad effects which the late mania for railway speculations has had on the money market'. In August 1848 Holywood was reached, the *Belfast News-Letter* correctly predicting:

> There can be little doubt that when the facilities for access to the excellent sea bathing of the southern shore of Belfast bay afforded to the inhabitants of this great town by this short line of railway come to be duly appreciated, the traffic on it will go on steadily increasing.[58]

Meanwhile, the main line thrust through Knock, Dundonald and Comber to reach Newtownards in May 1850.

Work was already under way on joining the Dublin to Drogheda line with the Ulster Railway, connecting at Portadown. Though the first railway in Ireland had been built between Dublin and Kingstown in 1834, eastern Ulster was better equipped with railroads than any other part of the country by the middle of the century. Opening up the interior was more important to Ulster businessmen than establishing links with the south, and the result was to draw more and more of the province's commerce towards Belfast. Single track cost around £10,000 a mile to build and it is remarkable that so much capital could be raised in eastern Ulster for so many railway projects during the years when the Great Famine was raging.

For a time the advent of the railways stimulated mail and coach services. For example, the Enniskillen Day, the Omagh Day and the

Portadown Fair Trader brought in passengers from the countryside to the main stations, while the Belfast Night Mail picked up travellers from Drogheda on the arrival of the Dublin train at 7 p.m. and drove through Dundalk, Newry and Banbridge to pull into Lisburn station to catch the Belfast train at five o'clock next morning.[59] Grand juries continued to extend the network of roads, being subsidised by the Board of Works, set up in 1831, for major projects. The most spectacular undertaking in these years was the opening up of the Glens by the Antrim Coast Road. A mail-coach road running along the western side of the Antrim Plateau had been completed in 1838, much of it crossing extensive bog; but as the commissioners for public works had pointed out when approval was given in 1832, the coast road 'being necessarily carried in some parts under high perpendicular rocks, and at the verge of an exposed sea, bears some remarkable features of construction, and requires very great skill and attentive consideration in its execution in detail'. This great enterprise was just being completed when William Makepeace Thackeray travelled it in 1842:

> The 'Antrim coast road', which we now, after a few miles, begin to follow, besides being one of the most noble and gallant works of art that is to be seen in any country, is likewise a route highly picturesque and romantic; the sea spreading wide before the spectator's eyes upon one side of the route, the tall cliffs of limestone rising abruptly above him on the other . . . except peerless Westport, I have seen nothing in Ireland so picturesque as this noble line of coast-scenery . . . The road, which almost always skirts the hill-side, has been torn sheer through the rock here and there; and immense work of levelling, shovelling, picking, blasting, filling, is going on along the whole line.[60]

This road opened up the Glens, which until now had found contact with Scottish Isles as usual as that with the rest of Ireland, and did much to integrate the region into the province.

On the other side of Ulster, the wilder coast of Donegal was less well served and most of the mountainous interior was completely inaccessible. The Board of Works made an eleven-mile road round the north coast to Gweedore in 1834 but failed to build a bridge across the Clady river. Lord George Hill wrote in 1845:

> The continual occurrence of providential escapes in crossing the river, made the passage of it quite a dreadful ordeal in the time of rains, when the river would suddenly become swollen to a frightful degree . . . On one occasion, an English traveller arrived at the east bank of the river; having to choose between two evils, he determined to attempt the passage. After a succession of desperate jumps from one rock or stone to another, he at last – in about the middle of the river – came to a full stand! . . . The people became very uneasy, seeing that his situation was every moment

becoming more critical, as the floods were rising rapidly. One of them, at last, with all the energy of an excited and kind-hearted Irishman, screamed out mightily, *'jump*, yer sowl, if there's life in you.'

It was all in vain – he could not stir – and the people ultimately saved him, only with much difficulty, they having been actually obliged, in the dearth of timber of a more suitable scantling, *to break up one of their bed-steads*, in order to make a bridge of its sides.[61]

In the summer of 1837 the lord lieutenant made a tour of Donegal but found the county road from Dunfanaghy so boggy that, Hill informs us,

> his Excellency might not have been able to proceed along a part of it, had it not been for the ingenuity of a country fellow, who, observing the difficulty, with all the quickness and spirit of a rustic Raleigh, ran to his cabin, *whipt* off the door, and hurrying to his Excellency's relief, laid it down before his horse's feet; by this device his Lordship and staff were enabled to proceed in comfort. As soon as they had passed, the man immediately hoisted the door on his shoulders, tripped on merrily before his Excellency, until he saw it necessary to lower it again.[62]

Improvements followed soon after, however, and in carrying them out, the Board of Works was motivated more and more by the need to provide seasonal employment in a countryside becoming ever more impoverished.

'THE MACHINERY HAS THROWN OUR FAMILIES IDLE'

> Health to Mr Orr as each fortnight goes round,
> Is toasted with joy where his workmen abound,
> Praise to him is due for exerting his skill,
> And relieving the poor by his great Spinning Mill.[63]

This doggerel in praise of Jacob Orr's Laurelhill factory on the Callan river in Co. Armagh reflects the gratitude of only a privileged minority who obtained regular employment in the linen mills. For the great majority in the Ulster countryside mechanisation spelled disaster.

The power-spinning of flax destroyed a vital supplement to the family incomes of labourers, cottiers and small farmers. As early as 1812, the employer Joseph Nicholson of Bessbrook observed about the extension of machinery that

> its worst effects are felt by the poor women, who must sell at the prices of the day or remain unemployed, and it frequently happens that they dispose of the worked article for less than the raw material cost them. To one unacquainted with Ireland the small earnings of the poorer females – frequently not more than two pence per day, working diligently from morning till night, for months together – must appear very extraordinary.[64]

Lieutenant P. Taylor, in his memoir for the parish of Currin in Co. Monaghan in 1835, noted that the 'most industrious and active spinner cannot earn more than 2d. a day'; the memoir for Drummaul in Co. Antrim states that 'the females and younger members of the family are thrown out of employment by the introduction of mill-spun yarn'; and a weaver giving evidence in 1840 said that hand-spinners 'now have about 1½d. or 2d., at the outside, a hank where they got it to do, but that is seldom the case now . . . The machinery has thrown our families idle.'[65] As Thomas Beggs, a weaver who died in the Famine wrote:

> But the guid auld times are gane out o' sight,
> An' it mak's the saut tear aften start to mine e'e;
> For lords o' the Mill and Machine ha'e decreed
> That bodies like me maun beg their bread.[66]

By the 1830s the whole domestic linen industry was in a state of near collapse and yet tens of thousands of people in Ulster continued to be dependent on it for survival. The real problem was the mass production of cheap cotton cloth in Britain, which depressed the price that could be asked for the competing textile, linen. It is unlikely that repeal of the Union could have stayed or reversed this trend; a Dublin parliament would hardly have adopted the draconian measures required to provide adequate protection for the domestic production of linen, especially as most of the cloth was destined for export. Even swingeing import duties in the German states could not stop English cotton driving local textile industries to the wall. In Ulster the wet-spinning mills certainly hastened the death of the cottage industry, but had they not done so, factories in Leeds, Dundee and elsewhere would have taken over the lead in the power production of linen yarn.

As hand-spinners lost their work, the status and income of linen weavers were steadily pushed down. The desperation of the poor prepared to work for barest subsistence, combined with competition from cotton woven by power, depressed earnings to between three and eight shillings a week by the 1840s. In 1821 a statistical report on the barony of Raphoe noted that 'twenty years ago there was scarcely a common weaver who had not ten pounds to lend whereas an equal sum would at this day purchase almost any individual of that class out of a habitation'.[67] Weavers became employees, getting their yarn 'put out' by the flax-spinning mills; no longer their own masters, they had to abide by the conditions laid down by factory owners taking advantage of the vast numbers desperate for employment, as this weaver's ticket shows:

> No wages promised. Weaving paid according to the manner the work is executed. Four weeks allowed for working; if more, 2d. per day will be

taken off the wages. Tallow must not be used in dressing; and if candle grease, or oil from spindle, be on the linen, there will be a heavy fine.

August 21, 1838. J. Murland[68]

The belated introduction of the flying shuttle speeded up the weaving and made it easier for women to work the loom: this de-skilling of what was once a proud and independent craft resulted in weavers finding themselves on a par with the poorest cottiers and labourers, forced to work almost every waking hour to survive. The following extracts from the Ordnance Survey memoirs show the impact of mechanisation on the Ulster countryside:

> The great bulk of the adult male population of this parish . . . took the land at a high rent when trade was prosperous, they paid no attention to agriculture, and consequently were unprepared to meet the very great reverse which has latterly befallen them [Drummaul, Co. Antrim] . . . The manufacture of coarse linen has almost ceased within the parish . . . the flying shuttle seldom resounds [Laragh, Co. Cavan] . . . The weaving of linen cloth . . . has fallen off so much in consequence of the great reduction in prices that at present there is scarcely a loom at work [Dunsfort, Co. Down] . . . Not profitable; a good weaver can only earn about 5s. a week and a spinner must work hard to earn 2d. a day [Pomeroy, Co. Tyrone] . . . The ruins of the extensive bleachfields, which are observable around the district, testifying by their magnitude the outlay of vast capital in their erection, very few of which unfortunately are now in operation [Currin, Co. Monaghan].[69]

Only the largest and most efficient linen firms survived and over much of Ulster the industry all but disappeared. Where it held out, even the miserable earnings gave significant protection from the disasters which were to strike those now utterly dependent on what the land could yield.

'THE GREATER PART OF THE WILDEST COUNTRY IS VERY THICKLY INHABITED'

'Till men of property set some plans on foot to alleviate the condition of the poor, there can be no chance of improving their situations', James McEvoy wrote in 1802, drawing attention to the plight of cottiers and labourers in Co. Tyrone.[70] McEvoy was one of several authors commissioned by the Dublin Society to compile county statistical surveys during the Napoleonic Wars, volumes of which reveal much about the impact of the population explosion on the Ulster countryside. The rising demand for Irish corn in Britain – which increased in value by one quarter during the conflict – brought unprecedented prosperity to many landlords and farmers. Owners of estates raised rents and shortened leases as soon as they expired. In Co. Cavan, for example, on the Garvagh estate leases granted in the eighteenth century for 'the life of the Prince of Wales', which averaged forty years, were renewed in 1806 for only twenty-one years, and rents rose from seven shillings to twenty-five shillings an acre; on the Groome property, near Bailieborough, leases which had been set for three lives or thirty-one years were renewed in 1809 for one life or twenty-one years and rents were put up to thirty-four shillings per Irish acre; and on the Crofton estate the prewar average of thirteen shillings per Irish acre was replaced by a wartime average of twenty-four shillings. The rent roll of the Downshire estate went up from £30,000 a year in 1801 to £55,000 a year by 1815, though to a considerable extent the value was eroded by wartime inflation and many leaseholders were able to keep their income ahead of rent increases.[71] The rapid increase in the numbers of cottiers and labourers, however, intensified competition for land sublet from farmers – without the protection of leases these wretched people bid against each other from year to year. In his survey of Co. Londonderry in 1802, the Reverend Vaughan Sampson gave many examples of annual rents paid for scraps of land, known over much of Ulster as 'cot-takes' or 'tacks'.

> Near Cross, in the vale of the Fahan, at Gortnessay, the cottier gets half an acre of second crop for flax. Again, in the same district, half an acre of oats, one rood of flax, and a miserable pasture for a cow ... This sort of *tack* has been raised from three to five guineas.
> In the freeholds of Tully, the half tack, that is, without land, consists of a house, garden, and a rood of lint, with bad grass for a cow. This now pays five guineas ... On the west bank of the Roe, approaching to Dungiven, where the soil is coarse, the cottier has a bad cabin, and worse grass, for two guineas.[72]

'Armagh is indisputably, in proportion to its size, the most populous county in Ireland', Sir Charles Coote wrote in his survey of 1804, adding: 'Although much of the surface is covered with mountains, yet the greater part of the wildest country is very thickly inhabited.' So dense was the population here that the turf bogs 'are very much exhausted ... we cannot conceive there is a sufficiency of bog for the demand'. In Co. Londonderry the 'peat-mosses, most conveniently situated, are, in some places, totally, and in others, nearly run out'; in such locations loose peat 'is collected into heaps of wet mire, baked, shaped by the hand, and afterwards spread to harden. These are called baked turf, and form but very bad fires. In Myroe, even this substitute for fuel is almost exhausted.' Coal could be got from the Ballycastle mines, 'but the quality is not good; some veins are full of martial pyrites, and, of course, stink of sulpher; others doze away after a blaze, into a white slate, being of too argillaceous a nature'.[73]

269

At least shortage of turf was not a problem in the wilder and more mountainous parts of Ulster. Here only the potato made possible the cultivation of such marginal land; in Co. Tyrone, McEvoy observed, 'we meet with innumerable small patches throughout the country, in many parts almost up to the summits of the highest mountains'.[74] 'Paring and burning' was no longer condemned; it was, the Reverend John Dubourdieu remarked in his 1812 survey of Co. Antrim, 'a speedy and effectual mode of bringing strong soils, or even land of a thinner kind, into good order', and Dr James McParlan, in his survey of Co. Donegal in 1802, regretted that 'paring and burning are almost totally neglected in this county'. In almost every part of Ulster potatoes formed an essential part of the usual rotation of crops and won the unanimous approval of experts. A progressive gentleman farmer in Co. Donegal, McParlan informed his readers, 'has put his face directly against the introduction of green crops, because they interfered, he thought, with the culture of potatoes; and any thing to check them, as the staple support of Ireland, he would not countenance'.[75] In Co. Antrim, Dubourdieu noted that manure

> is mostly appropriated to the potatoe crop, and to a better purpose it could not be applied; in the first instance, affording an ample supply of the most wholesome food, and, in the second, being one of the very best preparations for a succeeding crop of grain . . . The very general use of potatoes gives a species of plentiful appearance to the repasts of the lower orders.

Around half the annual crop of potatoes was set aside as fodder, particularly for pigs.[76] McEvoy observed:

> A country may be overstocked with barley . . . the case is different with respect to potatoes; there cannot be too many of them. As long as Britain retains a navy, there will be a demand for pork. Potatoes are not only the food of man but are also that of horses, cattle, pigs, and poultry; sheep, also, are easily taught to eat them.[77]

A typical rotation on good land, for example on the Fanad peninsula, was '1. potatoes, 2. barley, 3. oats, 4. flax, 5. oats, 6. peas, 7. oats', and on poor land, such as the 'wretched country' at Glenfin, 'two abortive crops are their only course, 1. potatoes, 2. oats, their soil refusing totally both barley and flax. Their own oats never answer for seed; they must get it from the Laggan.'[78] Regardless of the rotation, cottiers and labourers depended ever more heavily for subsistence on the potato, selling other crops and pigs to pay the rent. As potatoes in this period failed no more often than oats or barley, there were no warnings as yet that the dependence of the poor on this one crop was in any way dangerous for the future.

A family could eke out an existence on little more than half an acre of potatoes, which was certainly not possible with any other crop; and, if potatoes could be supplemented with buttermilk, they very nearly provided a balanced though monotonous diet. In the absence of terrible epidemics or ruinous war, the population rose to the limit the land could bear. Density of population, however, did not necessarily mean destitution. A surgeon remarked in a letter of August 1805 that the prosperity of Co. Armagh could be seen 'even in the countenances of the dogs and cats'.[79] Coote reckoned that the average size of a farm in that county was less than five acres; here weavers married as early as cottiers elsewhere but this was not a cause of anxiety as long as a living could still be got from the hand loom. Coote explained:

A scrap of land is now the great desideratum of a cow's grass, and a garden, nor does the indulgent parent often refuse a portion of his own scanty plot, to ensure the comforts of the young people. Marriages are therefore encouraged, and take place very early; this is by no means a secondary cause of subdivision of farms, or of the great value of land.
Proprietors find it in their account to let land in small parcels, as the weaver will pay for just what suits his own convenience, in the vicinity of a good market town, much more than could be afforded for a large farm, the rent of which is to be made by the business of agriculture.[80]

Such relentless subdivision of land was to prove disastrous, however, when earnings from the domestic linen industry crashed in the years following Waterloo.

'THEIR VERY APPEARANCE BESPEAKS THEM VICTIMS OF RAPACITY
AND RACKRENT'

It was an Ulsterman, Lord Castlereagh, who was largely responsible for negotiating the 1815 Treaty of Vienna which ushered in the longest era of peace Europe had hitherto enjoyed. The close of almost one quarter of a century of continuous warfare, however, was followed by a severe slump aggravated by the return of so many discharged and unemployed soldiers. In Ulster this coincided with atrocious weather conditions, as Hugh McCall remembered:

The deficient harvests of 1816 and '17 had caused almost universal dearth and scarcity of food ... This calamity was rendered doubly severe because of the exceeding dulness which had fallen on the trade and commerce ... Vast numbers of weavers in the principal centres of trade were unable to find employment, and, as the farm labourers gradually fell into the same position, an almost general state of compulsory idleness spread over the country during the winter of 1816. Towards the spring of the following year, fever of a very virulent type set in, and amid its ravages the rich and the poor alike fell victims.[81]

The memoir for the parish of Cumber, Co. Londonderry, recorded: 'The year 1816 was felt very severely. So impoverished were the people that the levying of the money assessed upon them at vestry was postponed.'[82] 'In the memorable summer of 1817,' a schoolmaster wrote in Co. Londonderry, 'many lowland farmers were obliged to bring home their cattle from the mountain pastures, lest they should be bled to death by the herds, who boiled and ate the blood!!'[83]

When the harvests recovered, people living in the countryside discovered that peace was bringing with it permanent changes, many of them threatening their livelihood. Not only did the output of steam-powered mills slash earnings in the domestic linen industry, but agricultural prices suffered a sharp and prolonged fall. In addition, stock-rearing became more profitable than the growing of grain, thus curtailing the demand in some areas for labourers to plough the soil and to reap, bind, thresh and winnow the corn. Furthermore, in spite of Belfast's dramatic growth, there was not yet enough urban employment to draw in all the destitute from the countryside. Ulster remained more rural than either Leinster or Munster: in 1841 fewer than 10 per cent of its people lived in towns of two thousand inhabitants or more. The census of that year showed, for example, that almost one quarter of a million lived in Co. Cavan, yet the populations of the six largest towns were: Cavan 3,749; Cootehill 2,425; Kingscourt 1,614; Belturbet 1,620; Bailieborough 1,203; and Killashandra 1,085. The birth rate slackened somewhat, but with the momentum of previous decades, the number of people in Ulster reached 2.4 million by 1841. Perhaps half of this population was made up of cottiers, labourers and impoverished weavers and their families desperately struggling to survive.[84]

The Corn Law, enacted by Westminster in 1815, failed to stop the fall in prices, and in the protracted depression almost everyone getting a living from the land was in difficulties. As Kevin O'Neill observes in his study of pre-Famine Killashandra: 'Tenants were forced to endure the scissors effect created by their recently increased rents, cutting against rapidly falling prices.' Far from being subsistence farmers, leaseholders and cottiers alike were extremely sensitive to the British market and were forced to sell greater quantities of farm produce to raise cash for their rents. Some landlords reduced rents but never as much as they had raised them during the Napoleonic Wars. In Co. Cavan, for example, the Hodson estate lowered rents by between 30 per cent and 60 per cent, but this was after an increase of 257 per cent in 1806–12; on the Garvagh property there were no permanent reductions until 1826; and in 1843 some tenants on the Royal School estates were still paying rents set during the war. Canals, better roads, railways and cheap steamship services helped better-off farmers to benefit from the recovery of butter prices and to get live pigs and cattle and perishable eggs to the British market. Oats, the main cash crop of the undertenant and cottier, nevertheless remained depressed in price. For the rack-rented rural poor the only Irish question of any significance was whether or not they could gain access to a piece of land to pull themselves through another year.[85]

In the early 1820s John MacCloskey, tutor to the Clark family of Upperlands who ran a celebrated classical school at Tirgarvel, wrote a statistical account of the parishes of Ballinascreen, Kilcronaghan and Desertmartin for the North West Farming Society. He reckoned that there were only about thirty substantial farmers in this whole district, 'wanting few of the real luxuries and none of the comforts of life'; but, he continued, the 'lower and more numerous class of farmers present a sad contrast to the men above mentioned':

> Their very appearance bespeaks them victims of rapacity and rackrent. They are indeed ground down by an insupportable burden, and all labour under a deficiency of capital. Their numerous families are quite adequate to the consumption of the farm's produce; yet the crops must be hurried to market to meet the November rent, and the summer's provisions purchased at an advanced rate. In short, their lives are a continued struggle for existence.[86]

These poor farmers were better off, nevertheless, than the cottiers whose 'perennial fare is potatoes and buttermilk; the supply of the latter fails in the spring months'. He continued:

> Towards August even the potato fails: they are then constrained to make a meal of cabbage leaves . . . From butcher's meat, their abstinence is more rigid than that of the most austere eastern ascetic. Their voluntary lent is perennial . . . the easy prey of oppression, of fever, of famine, this unhappy being passes his toilsome years, rising however, with gaiety and elasticity of spirit, above the gloomy despondency.[87]

In 1820 Mr Twogood wrote a report for the Fishmongers' Company on the condition of tenants living in the foothills of the Sperrins. Perhaps half the population of Ulster lived thus:

> In the course of the day we entered . . . many very wretched hovels, called cabins. The following picture will apply with variations to most of them. On entering the cabin by a door thro' which smoke is perhaps issuing at the time, you observed a bog-peat fire, around which is a group of boys and girls, as ragged as possible, and all without shoes and stockings, sometimes a large pig crosses the cabin without ceremony, or a small one is lying by the fire, with its nose close to the toes of the children. Perhaps an old man is seen or woman, the grandfather or grandmother of the family with a baby in her lap; two or three stout girls spinning flax, the spinning wheels making a whirring noise, like the humming of bees, a

dog lying at his length in the chimney corner; perhaps a goose hatching her eggs under the dresser; and all this in a small cabin, full of smoke, an earth floor, a heap of potatoes in one corner, and a heap of turf in another, sometimes a cow, sometimes a horse occupies a corner. In an inner room there are two or three wretched beds.[88]

Ten years later the sharp decline in earnings from the domestic linen industry silenced the spinning wheels, impoverishing such families still further.

'STRUGGLING THROUGH LIFE IN POVERTY AND WRETCHEDNESS'

In the autumn of 1824 the Ordnance Survey staff arrived at Phoenix Park in Dublin to begin mapping the whole of Ireland on a scale of six inches to one statute mile. It was a great undertaking carried out with dedication; for example, a senior officer of the Royal Engineers, Joseph Portlock, lived under canvas at two thousand feet in the depths of winter, while working on the local triangulation in Co. Donegal. A detailed memoir was ordered for every parish but alarm at the costs involved caused the abandonment of this part of the project.[89] These unpublished memoirs survive for much of Ulster and paint a vivid picture of rural life in the middle and late 1830s. In particular, they provide striking evidence of the increasing misery of those living at the bottom of the social pyramid. In 1835 Lieutenant P. Taylor described the level to which the people had been reduced in his memoir for the parish of Currin in south-west Monaghan:

The wretched hovels, scantily covered with straw, surrounded and almost entombed with mire, which everywhere present themselves throughout the parish, sufficiently testify that the total absence of all activity in industry is one source of the wretchedness and misery which almost overwhelms the land. In no kingdom in the universe does so general an appearance of poverty and destitution prevail as in the persons and domiciles of this intelligent, lively but thoughtless community.

Subdivision, he believed, was the main cause of this poverty,

the *ne plus ultra* of experience, through a series of many generations, a system not arising from the hydraheaded monster absenteeism nor the high rent of land, but emanating from a practice of sub-dividing farms into small tenures, and subletting the same to insolvent tenantry . . . Not 1 in 20 possess the means of paying up their rent, and their cabans, almost universally built in a combination of mud and straw, present a most wretched appearance.

Lieutenant J. Greatorex, in his memoir for Aghalurcher in Co. Fermanagh, also observed the prevalence of subdivision and early improvident marriages in the cottier and labouring classes:

It is customary as soon as the children of a family grow up for them to marry, usually at an early age, and begin the work on their own account, building mud huts wherever a few acres of land are to be obtained, and struggling through life in poverty and wretchedness, but apparently contented and cheerful.[90]

The author of the memoir for the parish of Drummaul in Co. Antrim commented that in the labouring classes marriages 'of women under 17 and of men under 21 are not unusual'. While he acknowledged the collapse in earnings from linen, he castigated the manner in which Lord O'Neill treated his tenantry. O'Neill had not been in Randalstown three times over the previous fifteen years, though he lived only four miles from the town and extracted £30,000 annually in rent from the parish. In granting tenancies he was guided not by the solvency of families but by the rents they were prepared to pay. The memoir described a typical tenant on the O'Neill estate:

In the very first year he is in arrears of rent, and also in debt for provisions for his family. The second year leaves him still in arrears, and in the third year he is ejected . . . The number of ejectments annually served on his estate are almost incredible, and in the depth of winter many a family is annually turned adrift . . . He takes no other interest in his tenantry, either in alleviating their annual distress (in spring) nor in contributing to their mental or social improvement in any respect.[91]

No doubt such reports influenced the Government in its decision not to publish the Ordnance Survey memoirs. Actually, evictions for failure to pay the rent were comparatively rare before the Famine but notices to quit were often issued as a threat. Over much of Ulster it was the custom to allow tenants to be six months in arrears – known as the 'hanging gale' – but this deprived them of any legal protection their leases might contain. Longer delays in paying the rent were often punished by fines (which in Killashandra parish added some 5 per cent to the overall rent roll), or by bailiffs seizing crops or driving off stock.[92]

Despite the striking advance of industrialisation, all over Europe landlords continued to monopolise economic and political power; and at least the rural poor of Ulster were not subjected to mass clearances, as in Scotland, and they were not serfs as were most of the peasantry in the Austrian and Russian empires. Even the serfs of Russia, however, had community rights, village elders with a say in the rotation of crops and the distribution of land, and common land for the grazing of stock. In Ireland the cottiers and labourers were given no long-term interest in the holdings and potato gardens they tilled. With no guarantee that they could remain on their scraps of land for another year, with no

275

property of any consequence to pass on to their children, and with no marketable commodity other than the strength of their bodies, they had no incentive to build more comfortable and permanent dwellings and no inducement to delay marriage. As in many parts of Asia and Africa today, the labour of children from an early age was an economic asset and a large family gave some hope of support in old age.

One result of the congestion was a pressure on the land so intense that little room was left for wild life. 'Foxes, badgers and hedgehogs are very rare', it was remarked of the parish of Ballybay, and in neighbouring Aghabog it was reported that 'the extermination of partridges and hares is almost complete . . . the otter and the badger have become entirely extinct'.[93] In 1802 the Reverend Vaughan Sampson observed a few sea eagles in Co. Londonderry: 'They prey on rabbits and young lambs, and build in high and solitary rocks, near the sea.' Golden eagles only survived on the Donegal side of Lough Foyle and hunted for rabbits at Magilligan, but 'these are growing scarce', and the memoir for Aghalurcher in 1835 remarked that they had deserted their nest site on Belmore Mountain.

Outside the walled demesnes the land had become almost bereft of trees. Cabins could only be made of sods, mud or stone, for timber was beyond the means of the cottier; according to McEvoy, ash cost 3s.3d. per cubic foot, between twelve shillings and sixteen shillings had to be paid for wood to make a plough, and the poor man had to make couples and other roof timbers from the bog. 'I have been often an eye-witness to scenes of struggling and great fatigue in getting out logs of timber to the hard land', he wrote. Bog fir, he continued, 'when beaten out into small filaments, is found to answer for ropes, which are principally used for cording of beds . . . it is a kind of trade with many poor people in the vicinities of bogs'.[94]

Wage labourers rented even smaller pieces of land than the cottiers and for higher rents. Partly to tide them over periods of unemployment, labourers usually held the ground for their cabin and potato garden under a system known as conacre: the farmer offered land for potato planting for a period of eleven months only, usually a rood or half-rood, and the labourer had to pay the rent in full before lifting the potato crop in the autumn. Rents for these plots were exceptionally high; the Poor Law Commission put the average in Co. Cavan at £8–9 per acre on land for which the farmer paid twenty-five to thirty shillings.[95] Sometimes the labourer could pay the rent in kind by working for the farmer, but usually he sought wages of 8d. or 9d. a day on the open market. As it could be difficult to get enough work locally, labourers often became migrant workers after planting their potatoes, while their families took to the roads to beg. Many crossed the Irish Sea to make hay and reap the harvest, returning with their wages sewn into their coats to pay their rent and lift their potatoes in the autumn. Several memoirs refer to this seasonal work:

> Their wives and children are left at home . . . Some have very small farms, and pay their rents by what they earn in Scotland and England. Others purchase goods and bring them home to retail them, such as umbrellas and handkerchiefs [Bovevagh, Co. Londonderry] . . . Many cottiers go to the county of Meath for harvest work. They do not take their families [Galloon, Co. Fermanagh] . . . They leave behind them their families, who in many cases, close their cabins and beg for the season [Trory, Co. Fermanagh] . . . They leave their wives and families behind who generally support themselves during their absence by begging. They rent conacre and sow potatoes for their winter support [Drumlomman, Co. Cavan].[96]

Labourers and their families lived on the edge of subsistence, wearing clothes cast off by the farmers. 'The clothing of the labouring classes is of such nature,' said the parish priest of Killashandra, 'that to my knowledge many of them are kept from prayers on Sunday'; and the Church of Ireland register in the same parish shows that Protestant labourers had their children baptised at home because they could not attend church in their rags.[97]

Potatoes and oatmeal formed the staple diet of farmers who, as in Drumachose in Co. Londonderry, could supplement this with 'smoked or salt beef, bacon, eggs, fowl and in summer and autumn with the addition of lamb and fish'. 'Potatoes and thin buttermilk constitute their chief and almost only source of subsistence'; this memoir for Currin in Co. Monaghan could be applied to cottiers and labourers over most of the province. In Drumlomman 'they substitute a drink made of onions boiled in water' when buttermilk could not be had. Boxty, 'made with potatoes and potato starch', was eaten in Co. Tyrone and another dish popular across Ulster had oat chaff as its main constituent; this – according to the memoir for Aghaderg in Co. Down – was known as 'flummery also called "sowins" made of the husky part of the oat, sifted from the meal called seeds, steeped until soured and then boiled'. By summer the potatoes had either given out or gone rotten (early varieties do not seem to have been available). These were the 'hungry months' when those unable to buy meal crowded the roads to beg.[98]

The English Poor Law system was applied to Ireland in 1838 but most of the rates levied on property owners seem to have been spent on buildings in the first few years. Outdoor relief was refused to the able-bodied and only a tiny proportion of the destitute were accepted indoors, where work was hard and families were split up. The concentration of the linen industry had left the outer fringes of Ulster in greatest destitution, particularly Co. Cavan and Co. Monaghan, but perhaps the poorest region was west Donegal.

In 1837 a National School teacher, Patrick McKye, wrote a memorial to the lord lieutenant on behalf of the inhabitants of West Tullaghobegley in Co. Donegal, who 'are in the most needy, hungry, and naked condition of any people that ever came within the precincts of my knowledge'. There the population of some nine thousand possessed between all of them only one cart, one plough, sixteen harrows, eight saddles, twenty shovels, seven table-forks, twenty-seven geese, eight turkeys, three watches and two feather beds. In the whole parish there was not a single wheel car, not a pig, not a clock, and not a pair of boots; and there were no fruit trees nor crops of turnips, parsnips, carrots or clover. He continued:

> None of their either married or unmarried women can afford more than one shift, and the fewest number cannot afford any . . . nor can many of them afford a second bed, but whole families of sons and daughters of mature age indiscriminately lieing together with their parents, and all in the bare buff. Their beds are straw – green and dried rushes or mountain bent: their bed cloathes are either coarse sheets, or no sheets, and ragged filthy blankets . . . if any unprejudiced gentleman should be sent here to investigate . . . I can show him about one hundred and forty children bare naked, and was so during winter, and some hundreds only covered with filthy rags, most disgustful to look at.[99]

Long storms had ruined their crops and now they faced starvation; many could afford only one meal every three days and McKye found

> their children crying and fainting with hunger, and their parents weeping, being full of grief, hunger, debility and dejection, with glooming aspect, looking at their children likely to expire in the jaws of starvation.

An English gentleman, 'whose name has never transpired', read this appeal and sent a large supply of clothes and bed ticks. It seems likely that this barren coastland, known as Gweedore, and its adjacent islands had only acquired a dense population towards the end of the eighteenth century. The thin and leached soil in its natural state was most unyielding, but by unremitting labour the people had made the coastland fertile by spreading shell sand and seaweed on the ground. In addition, like the people of Rathlin, they could burn kelp and sell the ashes for the production of iodine. In summer cattle were taken to the mountains, moors and islands to be grazed and milked, which meant that some families needed three cabins to live in at different times of the year. On good land, as part of the rotation, barley was grown, as Dr McParlan noted:

> The interstices of those mountains are a great barley country, which is all converted into whiskey . . . It is by running their barley into this beverage they provide for one half year's rent. This is therefore a tax raised by the rich on the morals and industry of the poor.[100]

Living mainly on potatoes, the people of Gweedore supplemented their diet with buttermilk, and shellfish and dulse gathered from the shore. The herring fishery fluctuated from season to season and was hampered by the very high cost of salt and by fishermen from Co. Dublin, who, according to Lord George Hill,

> molest the poor natives, cutting their nets and otherwise annoying them . . . therefore, contrary to what should be the practice, they cast their nets by *day light*, leave them there all night, and return in the morning to *look for them*. By such means, if a storm arises, the nets break adrift, get mixed together, and floating about full of dead fish, scare the shoals from the coast.

An accident at the beginning of the century had put an end to whaling: 'One of the whales, angry at this invasion of their empire of the ocean,' McParlan wrote, 'gave Mr. Nisbett's boat a whisk of its tail, and shattered it in pieces; two men were lost.' In this district the ancient paddle currach, only nine feet from stem to stern, was used to carry turf, seaweed and stock between the islands and the mainland.[101] According to Hill, one could be made in four days from 'seven score of sallows', the flexible frame then being 'skinned' with hide or tarred canvas, 'But they are very "*ticklish*" things, and great skill and caution is required for their safe management.'[102]

Lord George Hill, the fifth son of the 2nd Marquess of Downshire, bought twenty-three thousand acres of Gweedore from 1838 onwards. He was convinced the poverty and wretchedness of the area was the result 'of a system, which for ages has held its sway, and which no one proprietor could grapple with, or obviate, unless he was prepared, resolutely, patiently, and expensively, to introduce and work out, a *counter*-system'. The old Irish practice of dividing out the land into small scattered patches, known to the English as 'rundale', aimed to apportion out as fairly as possible the infield, the outfield and mountain pasture. It also survived in parts of Co. Londonderry, being denounced in the memoir for Tamlaght O'Crilly as the 'greatest obstruction to improvement . . . to be seen in the absurdly small size of the fields'.[103] The rise in population had reduced these rundale fields to minute patches, as Hill described in his account of the changes he made in *Facts From Gweedore*:

> Under such circumstances as these, could any one wonder at the desperation of a poor man, who having his inheritance in *thirty-two* different places, abandoned them in utter despair of ever being able *to make them out*! . . . One instance of sub-division may be mentioned; a small field of about *half an acre*, was held by *twenty-six* people!![104]

Hill lived on his estate, learned to speak Irish fluently, ploughed back all his profits and was, according to Thomas Carlyle, the historian, who met him at Kilmacrennan in 1849, 'a man you love at first sight, handsome, gravely smiling; thick grizzled hair, military composure'. He enclosed his great property, consolidating the rundale holdings into rectangular farms; yet he encountered bitter opposition. The problem was that rents before his arrival had been, on his own admission, trifling and irregularly collected, some tenants being as many as twenty years in arrears. He also underestimated the importance of summer grazing on the mountains and, together with the revenue police, put down illicit distillation, which up to then had been a crucial source of ready cash for the community.

In reality the population of Gweedore had become so dense by the 1840s that the people, reduced to a low subsistence level, could not afford to pay rent at all. The survival of such a large number of inhabitants on such poor land was made possible only by the successful cultivation of the potato. When that crop failed mass starvation could be the only outcome.

THE FAMINE: 1845–6

In the middle of September 1845 the maturing potato crop began to rot over much of Ireland. 'We had a field of potatoes that year in the back lane,' James Brown of Donaghmore, Co. Tyrone, recalled, 'and in one night they were struck with the blight and both tops and roots were blackened.' As he acknowledged, however, the damage was only partial and some of the tubers were sound.[105] Much of Ulster escaped – losses in the counties of Fermanagh, Tyrone and Londonderry being the lowest in the country – and, to compensate, the oat harvest was, according to the *Northern Whig*, 'the best crop, in quality and quantity, we have had for ten years past'. Nevertheless, the medical officer for Coleraine workhouse reported, 'Nothing else is heard of, nothing else is spoken of . . . Famine must be looked forward to . . .' The potato crop had failed before: in Co. Donegal in 1830 and 1831; over all of Ulster in 1835; and there had been widespread losses in 1836 and 1837. But this was a new disease, *Phytophthora infestans*, a microscopic fungus for which there was then no remedy and which struck again with virulent force in the summer of 1846.[106]

'I remember driving to Bundoran through Co. Fermanagh with my sister Bella on August 3rd,' Brown wrote, 'and as we went seeing the fine crops of potatoes in the fields. We spent three days in Bundoran and, returning, found these same crops blackened and useless.' The Reverend Samuel Montgomery, rector of Ballinascreen in Co. Londonderry, made this entry in the parish register:

> On the three last days of July and the first six days of August 1846 the potatoes were suddenly attacked, when in their full growth, with a sudden blight. The tops were first observed to wither and then, on looking to the roots, the tubers were found hastening to Decomposition. The entire crop that in the Month of July appeared so luxuriant, about the 15th of August manifested only blackened and withered stems. The whole atmosphere in the Month of September was tainted with the odour of the decaying potatoes.[107]

Underneath his signature he wrote, 'Increase the fruits of the earth by Thy heavenly benediction.'

'Rotten potatoes have done it all,' the Duke of Wellington remarked to the diarist Charles Greville, 'they put Peel in his d—d fright.'[108] Sir Robert Peel, the prime minister, had repealed the Corn Laws in June of that year in an attempt to free the market and encourage the importation of cheap grain into Ireland. It was an act of political suicide: the Tory grandees rounded on this jumped-up cotton magnate and made it impossible for him to continue, and in July Lord John Russell headed a new Whig government. Peel, who knew more about Ireland than most of his colleagues, had acted promptly by the standards of the day: he advanced loans of £134,000 to grand juries to give the destitute employment in building harbours, piers and roads; and finding corn almost unobtainable on the European mainland, bought cargoes of American maize for sale in Ireland at cost price. Now the new Whig government turned for advice to Charles Trevelyan, permanent head of the treasury. Trevelyan recommended a drastic reduction in the distribution of subsidised food and a major extension of public works. Free-market forces must not be disrupted by government interference and the poor must work for their food – views which accorded well with Whig *laissez-faire* doctrine. In his memorandum to the cabinet on 1 August Trevelyan observed that 'the supply of the home market may safely be left to the foresight of private merchants', but even he realised that this could not be true of the remote parts of Ireland. On his recommendation, therefore, the Government agreed to corn depots along the Atlantic seaboard north to Donegal to be managed by the army commissariat.[109]

On 29 August 1846 the Glenties Board of Guardians wrote to Commissary-General Sir Randolph Routh to inform him 'of the melancholy distress which at present exists in this Union . . . a famine, with all its baneful consequences, presses, if the people be not immediately relieved by the speedy and benevolent intervention of Government in affording them provision at first cost price'.[110] Routh, however, had his orders to hold back what he had in store to encourage farmers to bring their oats to market; his stocks were low in any case and cargoes of Indian corn were not expected to arrive until December. Meanwhile, his junior officers reported that 'Irish stones are ill adapted to the grinding of Indian corn' and that there were only two flour mills, at Rathmelton and Coxtown, in the whole county of Donegal fitted with French stones with this capability.[111] Few places had sufficient storage, and distribution along these wild coasts would have to be by steamer in winter, otherwise 'it will be impossible to carry on the service without fearful consequences resulting at times from the inadequacy of sailing vessels'.[112]

In the middle of September the coastguard officer at Loughros Point, Mr Moore, could endure no longer the heart-rending sight of the famished vainly seeking food at nearby Ardara; he sailed to Sligo, the biggest commissariat depot in Ireland, to obtain supplies. He reported after he returned:

> I never saw anything like it, and I hope I never will. People came 18 miles for a little meal, which I could not give. 14 tons, all but one bag, went in a day.[113]

From nearby Inniskeel, an island at the mouth of Gweebarra Bay, the Reverend James Ovens sent this plea to Deputy Commissary-General Dobree on 3 October:

> I have not words to describe the state of destitution of this quarter of the country from want of a supply of food for sale . . . The poor farmers are now compelled, at a ruinous expense of time and money, to go 45 miles to Derry market, and then pay an exorbitant price for Indian meal . . . The Relief Committee most earnestly desire me to call your humane and immediate attention to the situation and utter destitution of the people.[114]

Dobree knew that *Warrior* was in Mulroy Bay but, as he gloomily informed Trevelyan, 'there is every probability of her consuming a whole month in carrying 15 tons of meal from hence to the coast of Donegal . . . There are no markets.' At the end of October he gave 'a little relief occasionally to the poor people' but, he hastened to assure

Trevelyan, 'I have reduced my sales to the lowest ebb.'[115]

By November the price of Indian corn had reached £18 a ton and depots were actually making considerable profits. Oatmeal now cost half a crown a stone – should not the Irish ports be closed to stop the export of corn to Britain? When Routh made this proposal it was firmly rejected by Trevelyan and Lord Russell agreed with him. At last, on 28 November 1846 *Bossidar* of Trieste sailed in to Killybegs with 501 tons of Indian corn, and though the local commissary clerk protested he had store only for 200 tons, the price began to fall. It was hoped the destitute would be able to buy food with wages earned on the public works.[116]

The new system of public works had been devised by Trevelyan back in August 1846. The works could not be 'reproductive' – that is, they must not profit individuals or compete with capitalist enterprise – and were therefore largely confined to building walls, roads, bridges, causeways and fences. Unlike Peel's scheme, where the Government accepted much of the cost, the new relief works were to be financed entirely out of the county cess, though the treasury would advance loans. Irish property must pay for Irish poverty. The administration of the scheme was transferred from grand juries to the Board of Works, which was intended to reduce delays, but it was not until October that this cumbersome bureaucracy (eventually numbering twelve thousand officials) could issue tickets giving employment to those considered sufficiently destitute.[117]

'I fear the pressure on the Public Works in this county is likely to be greater than was anticipated,' Captain W. Flude reported from Monaghan, 'in spite of all I can do to keep lists of the destitute as small as possible . . . this necessarily occupies a great deal of my time.'[118] The scale of the Famine in much of Ulster was far greater than officials expected, and during agonising delays before relief work began, there were alarming signs of disorder. At Ballyconnell a mob locked up the grand jury to force the magistrates to vote a high level of cess for relief work, but 'a messenger was sent for troops, on whose appearance the *boys* unlocked the door and dispersed'. Around Newry the people 'have constantly nightly meetings' to discuss withholding rent; in Co. Armagh 'there has recently sprung up a considerable trade in fire-arms'; sacks of biscuit were pillaged in Killybegs; and poultry houses, turnip fields and flour carts had been robbed on the Inishowen peninsula.[119] A threatening letter had been posted to the Culdaff Relief Committee, in Inishowen, 'to the purpose that the people were in a state of desperation, and that if they did not shortly get work, they would proceed to help themselves'. The committee was sympathetic, for relief works there had not begun as late as 24 November:

The destitution in this district is so great that the people are losing their accustomed patience . . . in order to preserve a large part of the population from actual starvation, it is of the utmost importance that all works should be at once commenced.[120]

Four days later Lieutenant Griffith reported from Co. Armagh that people in the uplands were 'in a state approaching starvation and famine . . . numbers are likely to perish of hunger unless immediate instantaneous relief be provided for them'.[121]

The relief works were hampered by a shortage of wheel and hand barrows, a lack of engineers to direct operations, and heavy falls of snow from the middle of November. Only by getting work could the hungry earn money to buy food, but not all who sought employment could get it. Lieutenant J.W. Milward travelled west from Donegal town, along the post road being built, to issue work tickets on 30 November:

As I call out each man's name I inquire his circumstances; and should I not consider him destitute, I strike him out of the list . . . I am very careful about the numbering of the tickets, so that should one be lost or forged I can detect it immediately.[122]

He was besieged by men clamouring for work; at Killybegs an 'immense crowd assembled; but very orderly and quiet' and at Carrick a 'tremendous crowd assembled here also . . . a good deal of shouting, etc., but no harm done'. Almost all the Board of Works officials reported that no winter ploughing was being done, smallholders preferring instead to seek employment. An order that relief payments could be made to men tilling their own land was brusquely countermanded by Trevelyan.

By early December the snow lay between six and eight inches deep, making 'communication with the mountain districts impossible, which will render the amount of distress really alarming'. Yet the 'people continued to work during the whole time, but could do nothing but break stones'. The officials' reports became more urgent: in Co. Armagh 'the misery and destitution of the people is extreme'; in Co. Donegal 'the people most wretched, as their appearance fully showed'; in Co. Fermanagh the 'distress is, I am sorry to say on the increase'; and in Co. Monaghan 'the destitution is awful, and, I fear, increasing . . . The clergy of all denominations are pressing for employment for their followers . . . in short, I am beset, morning, noon and night.'[123] As the appalling weather made labour on the roads a misery for people clad in rags and emaciated by hunger, would it not be more humane and inexpensive simply to distribute food? On 16 December Deputy-Assistant Commissary-General Gem sent this plea from Burtonport:

I have the honour to inform you that the distress of the wretched people here is heart-rending. Something ought to be done for them; they can get nothing to purchase . . . The people in Arranmore Island are living on seaweed . . . The roads through the mountains are nearly impassable . . . It strikes the people as being very unfeeling on our part to keep corn in the store without issuing it . . . I hope I may soon get authority to issue. I would think little of my trouble if, by issuing from morning until night, I could relieve their distress.[124]

The Religious Society of Friends did not, like many British charities, simply send contributions to committees in Ireland for use by the Board of Works. Acting with a directness which would not shame the most modern relief agency, the Quakers set out to feed the people: 'Strictest instructions were given . . . that no preference should be made in the distribution of relief on the ground of religious persuasion.'[125] Their scheme was first to establish a network of boilers for making soup, and in December they sent William Forster and James Hack Tuke to begin this task. At Stranorlar, on 12 December, Forster found that many of the people were 'scarcely able to crawl' and that public works there had not even begun. Conditions were no better at Dunfanaghy, where again there were no relief works and fishermen could not go to sea because of the weather – 'constant storms of snow and hail', which forced the visitors to abandon their baggage in a snowdrift for a time. Most to be pitied were 'the miserable and neglected tenantry of the Marquis of Conyngham, an absentee proprietor who holds an immense tract of land here'; they had been given no aid and no public works had been proposed. Every place visited by the Quakers received a soup boiler and money to buy ingredients.[126]

Relief committees were especially active in Antrim and Down. At a meeting in Belfast Town Hall, called on 17 November to set up soup kitchens, the Reverend William Johnston thanked the provision merchants of Dock Ward for subscribing £196 'to grant a wholesome meal to those who were starving. A calamity unprecedented had befallen the country, and that, combined with the shortening of hours in the mills, had reduced hundreds of their fellow-townsmen to a state of wretchedness and misery that could scarcely be described.'[127] The following month labourers laid off by the Belfast and Ballymena Railway became so desperate that they attacked several bakeries in the town. The Lisburn soup kitchen regularly fed 1,286 people; between thirty and fifty women in Killyleagh gave meals to the poor every day; Killough relief committee bought a boiler on 23 December; the Kircubbin committee gave out coarse bread with soup; and £287 10s.0d. was raised for the Ballymoney soup kitchen.[128]

'They were aware how heavily the hand of Providence had visited the island,' Alexander Adair was reported to have said to a meeting in Ballymena courthouse, but they also 'knew that this particular portion of it had suffered far less than other parts of it'. In contrast, one of the worst affected counties was Monaghan, where relief committees could feed only a tiny proportion of the dense population, where public works failed to provide employment for all those in distress, and where the commissariat had no depots.[129] The *Fermanagh Reporter* described conditions there in December 1846:

> It would be impossible to exaggerate the awful destitution that exists in the town of Clones and neighbourhood . . . no day passes but some victims of this frightful calamity are committed to the grave. The number of deaths in Clones workhouse, during the last week, has been twenty-five, at the lowest . . . The workhouse contains upwards of a hundred over the regulated number; and most of them were all but starved before they obtained admission. Their exhausted frames were then unable to bear the food doled out to them; and hence they are, at this moment, dying in dozens.[130]

Some landlords did take vigorous action to help the people. The Stronge family of Tynan Abbey gave 'employment to all who apply for it; and large quantities of strong soup are daily made in this house, and retailed in the village of Tynan at a halfpenny the quart, and in the cases of the most destitute the soup is *given* to them'.[131] On Christmas Day 1846 the Marquess of Waterford wrote to his agent in Co. Londonderry, where he owned eight thousand acres, sending £300 because he had 'many melancholy reports from many clergymen stating the necessity of immediate relief'. The money was for the free distribution of soup (he supplied a recipe with a generous proportion of meat) and one hundred pounds of bread each week. The marquess concluded: 'set the pot a-boiling as soon as you can . . . Of course you will stop the breaking of stones at Aghadowey . . . Many happy Christmas's to you.'[132]

There is some evidence to show that landlords in Ulster were more generous in waiving part of their rents than those in other parts of Ireland. Ahoghill tenants were given a 10 per cent reduction and free seed for spring planting, while the proprietors of Knockaneigh estate at Killylea in Co. Armagh 'ordered their agent to give every tenant, who paid the November rent of 1845, a clear receipt to May 1846, being a half-year's rent wiped off'. Other landowners were not so generous. Tenants in Co. Antrim demanded a 50 per cent reduction because they had been 'visited by a great national calamity, which has entirely, and at once, extinguished the greater proportion of our agricultural pro-duce' and many depended on weaving linen, which 'continues in a state of deep depression'.[133] Their memorial, reprinted in *The Times* on 16 November, concluded with this clarion call:

> Landlords of Antrim! will you – can you, in the face of all these facts, compel us to sell our cows, or part with the only portion of bread which remains for the support of our families, in order to satisfy your claims? . . . Landlords, ye are men, and think, and feel, and pity, and love as men.[134]

Some landlords objected to paying high rates for 'lavish and wasteful expenditure on public works'. The *Northern Whig* was disgusted to find some journals applauding these protests, remarking: 'It is really sickening to read the trash with which those vehicles endeavour to debauch the public mind.'[135] The Marquess of Downshire, whose estates enjoyed a 5 per cent increase in rent income in the difficult years between 1815 and 1845, issued a handbill on 30 December objecting to baronial sessions called to levy a new rate to provide urgent relief; it was, he declared, 'a pretext for voting away other people's money for useless jobs . . . for the purpose of carrying on *useless* or *injurious Works*'.[136] When the sessions met a few days later, some six thousand people, many starving and ragged, crowded outside Castlewellan courthouse, fearful that Downshire would prevent a rate being struck. Inside, Captain Brereton, the Board of Works inspecting officer, only persuaded the men of property to vote for relief with difficulty:

> I am sorry to say there was a great desire evinced by the landed proprietors to hide the poverty of the people. I was, therefore, most urgently attacked by many of them for performing my duty in bringing the destitution of the barony before their notice. When the famishing people found there was a sum of money presented for their relief they departed quietly to their homes.[137]

Meanwhile there was every sign, as the atrocious weather continued, that the whole system of relief by public works was collapsing.

THE PUBLIC WORKS BREAK DOWN: 1847

The winter 1846–7 was as cold and as long as any in living memory. From the north-east blew 'perfect hurricanes of snow, hail and sleet', which, when they did not bring the relief works to a standstill, caused ill-clad and famished labourers to drop from exposure.[138] In the middle of January the Glenties workhouse was 'very much damaged by the hurricane of the 17th ultimo as great quantities of slates, tiles, lead and metal pipes have been blown off which gives free access to the down rain in many places'.[139] Men returned from hill-cutting at Ballinaleck, Captain Handcock reported from Fermanagh, 'are so weak and infirm that they could not do a day's work so must be put to break stones . . .

287

and the general cry when they are put to stone breaking is, that the cold of sitting on stones kills them'.[140] Yet more people were applying to the public works than could be taken on; on 5 January a crowd of men at Carrigart, angry that their names were not on the lists, locked officials into the schoolhouse and fought a stone-throwing battle with the revenue police called out to disperse them. Captain O'Neill wrote:

> I beg further to add that, from the excited state of the people in that part of the country, and the great poverty, wretchedness and destitution that exist, it would not be advisable to stop any of the works now in progress, as it might drive the people to desperation.[141]

From all over Ulster came reports of a deteriorating situation. Captain Brereton wrote on 16 January that the worst-affected areas in Co. Down were Rathfriland, Ballymacarrett and the Mournes; that three hundred men at Kilkeel were 'in a very excited state' when not accepted for work; and, he continued:

> *The very small farmers*, I am sorry to say, are *now compelled* to *commence* consuming the small stock of corn they had intended for *seed* for this year's crop, and, in most instances, their *stack-yards* will be *completely empty* in a month hence.[142]

The following day George Dawson, brother-in-law of Sir Robert Peel, wrote from Castledawson to Sir Thomas Fremantle, a former Irish chief secretary:

> My dear Fremantle,
> I really have not had heart to write to you before, for I had nothing to communicate except the heart rending scenes of misery which I daily witness. I wish I had never come here. If I had known what I was to encounter in this hitherto happy district, I should have spared myself the pain of witnessing a misery which, with every feeling of compassion and every expenditure within my means, I can do no more than most inadequately and feebly relieve.
>   I can think of nothing else than the wretched condition of this wretched people. We are comparatively well off in this neighbourhood – there is no want of food, but it is at such a price, as to make it totally impossible for a poor man to support a family with the wages he receives. I do not exaggerate when I tell you that from the moment I open my hall door in the morning until dark, I have a crowd of women and children crying out for something to save them from starving. The men, except the old and infirm, stay away and show the greatest patience and resignation. I have been obliged to turn my kitchen into a bakery and soup shop to enable me to feed the miserable children and mothers that cannot be sent away empty. So great is their distress that they actually faint on getting food into their stomachs . . . We are also visited by hordes of wandering poor, who come from the mountains or other districts less favoured by a

resident gentry; and worst of all, death is dealing severely and consigning many to an untimely tomb . . . I see enough to make the heart sick . . . hundreds will die of starvation.[143]

From early February 1847 there were fresh and heavy falls of snow, and in the vicinity of Omagh 'the weaker and worse clad, and perhaps badly fed workmen, were not able to endure it', and when the snow on the roads became three feet deep, the relief works had to be stopped. At Belturbet, where the works stayed open, the men 'were so emaciated and debilitated, they were unable, during the inclement weather, to work so as to keep up the natural warmth of the body, and fatal disease has been the consequence'.[144] At Carrickmacross relief operations were closed down with the result that

the people thrown out of work have no resource whatsoever; hundreds spend days without food, and in the absence of proper subsistence have recourse to most unwholesome diet. Their deserted and wretched cabins, their forlorn and distressing look, with pain and sickness so dreadfully depicted in every countenance, is horribly painful to look at; and with all this human misery, there is no person putting his shoulder to the burthen – no proper efforts are being made to relieve the people. How it will end, God only knows.[145]

Workhouses were the refuges of last resort and most were now overflowing. The death rate in Lurgan workhouse was so appalling that at the end of January the Poor Law commissioners demanded an explanation. Dr Bell, the medical officer, wrote in reply:

Many diseases are now prevalent in the country, and the great majority of new admissions are, when brought into the house, at the point of death, in a moribund state. Many have been known to die on the road, and others on being raised from their beds to come to the workhouse have died before they could be put into the cart, and numbers have died in less than 24 hours subsequent to their admission . . . many dying persons are sent for admission merely that coffins may be obtained for them at the expense of the Union.[146]

The workhouse was grossly overcrowded, with the result that 'it has been impossible to provide dry beds in many instances in cases of those wetted by weakly ill children and by persons in a sickly state. This sleeping upon damp beds has increased fever and bowel complaints which have in many instances proved fatal.'[147] The numbers of deaths in the workhouse were 36 for the week ending 9 January 1847, 55 on 16 January, 58 on 23 January, 68 on 30 January and 95 on 6 February. The Reverend W.P. Oulton, the chaplain, blamed the 'dreadful mortality which has swept our workhouse' on sour bread and putrid broth made of rotten beef: 'the ward master Lutton whom I questioned about it said "it was so offensive when cutting it up after being boiled he could hardly stand over it" . . . like the flesh of an animal that had died of disease'.[148]

By 26 February Glenties workhouse was bursting with 1,485 inmates, and because absentee landlords would not pay their rates, the union was bankrupt – the Letterkenny branch of the Belfast Bank wrote that 'it will not allow any cash advances to any Poor Law Union' and the commissioners were asked to institute proceedings against the Marquess of Conyngham because he 'refuses to pay the arrears of poor rate'.[149] At Letterkenny Mr R. Harvey of Leik Glebe found it 'revolting to every right and sacred feeling' that the workhouse had kept corpses for six days before burial. He discovered bodies being buried in moonlight and there 'was neither friend nor clergyman along with the coffins, nor had the lad any line from any person to certify that the deceased parties had died in the poor house'.[150] Joseph Rowntree, the noted Yorkshire Quaker, reproved the Letterkenny guardians for refusing admission to three destitute children even though the house was not full. At Ballyshannon workhouse an employee about to give out bowls of boiled Indian meal told Rowntree bluntly: 'It will kill them; the system of old infirm persons cannot do with it.' Rowntree was horrified at the condition of labourers employed by J.P. Boyd JP, a north Donegal landowner:

> It almost paralysed me to know on what principle of humanity or in doing as he would be done by, to account for his giving 9d. a day during the last four months to his labourers. Those I saw were six in family existing on 9d. per head when the father was in full work in favourable weather. It is to be regretted that any Justice of the Peace should with ample means at his command pay . . . a pittance so mean whilst oatmeal is about 3s.6d. per stone.[151]

The rates of pay on the relief works were often lower than those paid by Boyd. 'The Inspectors of Drainage have remarked to me that in *hard stony ground,*' the inspecting officer for Co. Tyrone reported on 6 February, 'or where *large stones frequently* occur in the line of a drain, it is *impossible* for the men to earn enough for the support of their families at the rate of 4d. per perch.' As men were paid piece rates, those weakened by hunger earned less and less; and when bad weather stopped work, labourers were put on half-pay breaking stones.[152] In Co. Monaghan 'the works in aid of relief were not commenced until the people were almost starving' and the labourers there were too weak to earn more than 8d. a day. At Ballinamallard the men and boys were so feeble that they 'are not able to do half a-day's work. At Lisnaskea it is much the same.'[153] From Killybegs came this report from Mr Kennan on 22 February:

The destitution is frightful; two or three funerals pass by my windows every morning, arising of course from want of food, which produces, first, diarrhoea, then prostration, low typhus fever, and death . . . I attend the sick and dying, and see the people in their own homes; and I assure you my heart bleeds to see the miserable state in which the *poor, honest* and *industrious* man is placed.

He condemned the relief works as pointless: smallholders had no energy left to attend to their farms after a day's labour on poorly made roads *'that will never be finished'*.[154] Indeed, by now, the Government was agreed that public works had failed and that a fresh solution was required.

SOUP KITCHENS, FEVER AND THE END OF RELIEF: 1847–8

An Act for the Temporary Relief of Destitute Persons in Ireland, passed in February 1847, was, in effect, an open admission by the Government that its policies had failed. Henceforth relief would be provided by the free distribution of soup, Lord John Russell explained to parliament, 'so that labouring men should be allowed to work on their own plots of ground, or for the farmers, and thus tend to produce food for the next harvest'. No more corn would be bought by the Government and the ports would stay open: 'We think it far better,' Russell continued, 'to leave the supplying of the people to private enterprise and to the ordinary trade.'[155] Charitable subscriptions were invited, the Government would make a donation, but the main cost was to be borne by the ratepayers.

A formidable new bureaucracy had to be created, headed by the Relief Commission, drawing on commissariat and Board of Works staff, and co-operating with local relief committees. Some 10,000 account books, 80,000 sheets and 3 million ration tickets had to be printed and distributed, and relief committees formed or reconstituted, before the machinery could be set in motion. Meanwhile, the public works were run down; 20 per cent of labourers were laid off on 20 March, a further 10 per cent on 24 April, and then the whole system was wound up in May and June 1847.[156] Now the destitute formed orderly lines, with cans, pots or bowls in their hands, to be given stirabout made of boiled Indian corn, with the addition of some rice when it could be had.

By the spring of 1847, people, weakened by starvation, were falling victim to fever and dying in their thousands. Deaths resulted principally from 'famine fever', typhus and relapsing fever transmitted by lice; the 'bloody flux' or bacillary dysentery, often aggravated by contaminated soup; 'famine dropsy' or hunger oedema; and scurvy caused by a switch from a diet of potatoes to a staple of Indian corn, which contains no vitamin C. A Quaker philanthropist was warned that he was putting himself at risk by standing in a crowd of 'about 200 wretched looking objects' waiting to be given food at Rutland Island, Co. Donegal. Fever was most likely to seize hold in the emaciated frames of the starving, but it was highly contagious, especially to those who ministered to the sick and dying; in one year seven doctors died in Cavan, for example.[157] Hordes of the poor brought disease into eastern Ulster, the part of Ireland so far least affected by the Famine, and a great many impoverished weavers fell victim. Dr Andrew Malcolm, who worked day and night to treat those stricken by fever, recalled the influx of the starving into Belfast:

> Famine was depicted in the look, in the hue, in the voice, and the gait. The food of a nation had been cut off; the physical strength of a whole people was reduced; and this condition, highly favourable to the impression of the plague-breath, resulted in the most terrible epidemic that this Island ever experienced.[158]

In March 1847 the *Swatara*, a vessel carrying emigrants, was twice forced by contrary winds to put into Belfast. Typhus fever, which had spread rapidly in the cramped conditions below decks, now swept from the port throughout the town, creating a plague, Dr Malcolm wrote, 'in comparison with which all previous epidemics were trivial and insignificant'. In addition, fever victims poured into the town from the countryside, the Belfast Board of Guardians noted in their minutes, 'attracted by the reputation of the local charities, and have thus become the means of importing disease and demoralisation, adding very considerably to the local taxation'. Leading citizens set up a Board of Health in May, sheds were put up beside the Frederick Street Hospital when it overflowed, the workhouse infirmary was enlarged, and a temporary hospital was erected in the grounds of the Belfast Academical Institution. 'This great movement well became the capital of the North', Dr Malcolm remembered: 'It was the crowning act in her History, and made her, for a time, an example for the world.'[159] Yet still the epidemic raged, as the *Belfast News-Letter* reported on 30 April 1847:

> We stated in our last, that on Sunday, the 25th inst., the number of patients in the fever wards of our workhouse was 514: but we have since been given to understand that the number of patients has diminished to 476. This is really an alarming amount, and yet it is only one of the numerous tests by which we estimate the spread of the pestilence. Among our gentry and merchants also, the deaths are more numerous than they have been at the same period in former years, and we are sorry to add that several of our most respected townsmen are at this moment dangerously ill.[160]

In an interdenominational representation to the Belfast Poor Law Union in June, Dr William Bruce and Dr Cornelius Denvir declared that all the cemeteries in the town would be full by 1 July and 'that after the period above-mentioned the bodies of the poor must lie unburied unless a burying ground can be provided by the Board of Guardians'.[161] In July the epidemic reached its peak; the hospitals were overflowing, the *Belfast News-Letter* reported,

> Yet hundreds – for whom there remains no provision – are daily exposed in the delirium of this frightful malady, on the streets, or left to die in their filthy and ill-ventilated hovels . . . It is now a thing of daily occurrence to see haggard, sallow and emaciated beings, stricken down by fever or debility from actual want, stretched prostrate upon the footways of our streets and bridges.[162]

As fever penetrated every part of Ulster, save for a stretch of coastline from Warrenpoint to Rostrevor, the public works were closed down. In many places the soup kitchens were not operating fully, as at Kilnaleck, Co. Cavan, where all men were so equally destitute that lots were drawn to decide who would be discharged; 'the wretched creatures on whom the lot fell raised a dreadful cry', an official reported.[163] Impatient at the dilatory Relief Commission, the Leslie family gave stirabout and turnips to all comers, dished out from a great cauldron set up in the courtyard of Castle Leslie, Co. Monaghan. Yet the government soup kitchens saved more lives than any other measure taken during the Famine to provide relief. By 3 July 1847, 3,020,712 people in Ireland were being fed every day, though it is reckoned that some 15 per cent of those discharged from the public works were not able to get ration tickets for themselves and their families.[164]

The fine summer of 1847 ensured that the grain harvest was excellent and kept the blight at bay, but the acreage planted with what few tubers had survived two years of famine was so small that the poor still faced mass starvation. Yet the Government stopped the distribution of soup in almost all districts in September. From now on, under the Poor Law Extension Bill which became law in June, the burden of relief was to fall entirely on the workhouses financed by rates to be paid by Irish property owners. This was unquestionably the harshest decision made by Westminster during the Famine.[165] Landlords, many of them already bankrupt, defaulted on the rates and, particularly in the poorer districts, it was difficult to find enough men of education and property ready to give their time to serve as guardians. Earlier in the year a Board of Works inspector described Glenties Union as being 'in a most deplorable state'; he continued:

The chairman is a *tinker*; there is no doctor, and some idea of the class of the Guardians may be formed by the fact that two of them got tickets for the work, one of whom is still working, and a perfect object of charity.[166]

On 24 July Dr Phelan of Ballymena sent a damning report of his inspection of Lowtherstown workhouse in Co. Fermanagh. It was 'in great disorder . . . and the condition of a considerable number of sick and infirm, compel me to remark it as the worst I have visited in the north of Ireland'; he described how

> a male idiot boy, whose limbs are greatly crippled, and who is quite incapable of helping himself . . . was lying on the floor, outside the cell's door – a more pitiable or wretched object I never beheld. He lay on about as much straw as barely covered the floor . . . His thighs and legs were on the bare floor, the straw not extending far enough. He was as filthy as imagination can conceive.[167]

Over the past year 20.5 per cent of inmates, 432 out of 2,110 admissions, had died. On 14 September the Poor Law commissioners, exasperated by the failure to strike a rate capable of repaying its government loan, dissolved the Lowtherstown Board of Guardians.

In November Cavan Union was described as being 'unfortunate and truly neglected . . . whilst the people are dying from destitution'.[168] The property of the principal landlord was in the court of chancery, there was no resident gentry, and the union was completely bankrupt. 'A spirit of the utmost apathy and indifference appears to exist at this Board', an inspector reported, and he himself had to 'commence at once to relieve the wretched objects who presented themselves as recipients for relief unavailing'.[169] Another inspector in the same month described Ballyshannon workhouse as 'very much neglected for a considerable period', finding

> the sewers leading from it without a sufficient discharging power: the smell arising from this cause is most offensive, and distinctly to be perceived through the house itself, so much so, that I, yesterday, noticed it to the doctor as calculated to induce disease.[170]

There is little doubt, however, that conditions over most of Ulster had greatly improved by the autumn of 1847. The fever epidemic had largely run its course and, as George Dawson wrote from Co. Londonderry in November:

> In the first place we have been blessed with a most superabundant harvest in everything but potatoes . . . I never saw the farms' stackyards in Ireland so full as at present. I am in hopes that employment will continue, at least in this part of the country. This district is particularly famous for its weavers, and strange to say, whilst the manufacturers are working short time or dismissing their people in Lancashire and Carlisle,

the same men are sending their yarn here to be woven in greater quantities than ever . . . they have actually doubled the price for weaving a web which they have hitherto given.[171]

A significant minority, however, had been left with no means to support themselves and could not buy grain or bread at any price. Many had sold their looms long since and in 1848 more and more turned for help to the workhouse.

'I HAVE FREQUENTLY HEARD THE HORRORS OF SKIBBEREEN QUOTED, BUT THEY CAN HARDLY HAVE EXCEEDED THESE'

The spring of 1848 was bitterly cold, with heavy falls of snow in February, but there was a widespread confident belief that the frost would kill the blight in the ground. Everywhere cottiers and labourers did all they could to buy enough to plant their plots. At the end of March the Glenties Union reported 'that there is a great anxiety to obtain seed potatoes, but, from the great scarcity of them in this Union, it is feared that the small farmers will not be able to procure a sufficiency to crop their land. I have known some of them to send 20 and 30 miles for a few stone, and to pay the rate of 10d. per stone for them.'[172]

In normal times the spring usually saw an increase in the privations of the poor and, particularly in the counties of Donegal, Fermanagh, Cavan and Monaghan, where dependence on potatoes was greatest, workhouses were under acute strain. Here it was becoming impossible to collect enough rates to cover the expense of feeding and housing the inmates. From Ballyshannon a Poor Law inspector wrote:

The collection the last week was smaller than it should have been, had due exertion been used; and I have spoken to some and written to others of the collectors, to warn them that they will be subject to dismissal if it does not progress more rapidly; and I trust that next week this may produce a larger sum.[173]

For a time he was able to squeeze more rates out of landholders, especially in Belleek, where 'the collector is an energetic, fearless man', but by April he was reporting to the Poor Law commissioners 'that unless assistance is given at once, the collection of the rate may be considered at an end'.[174] The whole administration of the workhouses was breaking down and yet more and more people were seeking them out as their last refuge.

'We, the Protestant and Roman Catholic clergymen of the parish of Killashandra', began an impassioned appeal written on 8 January 1848 by the Reverend Samuel Roberts and the Reverend M. McQuaid PP to the Poor Law commissioners:

As the poorhouse of Cootehill *is full* – as there is *no employment* in drainage or otherwise, going on in the parish – as typhus fever is very prevalent indeed, owing in a great degree to the destitution – and as the number of destitute persons is daily increasing by the eviction of small farmers for non-payment of rent or otherwise – we earnestly request that you will, as soon as possible, afford relief to the above classes, lest the consequences of starvation, namely, *pestilence and death*, disgrace the Cootehill Union, as it did that of Cavan recently . . . many of the aged and infirm have, at this inclement season of the year, to walk five or six miles for their scanty relief, and very many of them are nearly naked.[175]

Roberts wrote several times again over the next few weeks giving numerous examples to underline 'the fearful and melancholy state of things in the Union of Cootehill'. 'In fact, gentlemen,' he wrote on 1 February, 'the state of the poor in this parish and in the neighbouring parishes is heart-rending in the extreme. Why has not the 3s. rate that was applotted in October, now three months ago – why has it not been collected yet? Will it become easier of collection as the season advances? No.' He concluded:

I trust you will excuse me for this letter, nothing but stern duty compels me, but it is the duty of my office, firmly, calmly, and perseveringly, to advocate the cause of my poor, poor people; and I will do so.[176]

The commissioners eventually dissolved the Cootehill Board of Guardians, having found a debt of £3,000, 'considerable jobbing' by contractors, and collectors 'totally regardless of their duty', one of whom had absconded with £300.[177]

The early months of 1848 saw a resurgence of fever which spread with fearful speed through the densely packed poorhouses. The Enniskillen workhouse, accessible only by boat in the winter, had to erect a 'recovery house' in the grounds and rent extra accommodation at Hall's Lane in the town. Still there was not enough room for the sick, as Dr Nixon, the medical officer, made clear in his notes:

Tuesday, January 4th – Had to order plank down to the recovery-house, as there is not a portion of the floor dry in the male side . . . Have to report that the roof of one half of the temporary fever hospital in Hall's-lane fell in yesterday . . . Would wish to know how the cases of fever now arising over 100 are to be provided for, as I am ordered not to admit more than that number.

Tuesday, 11th – Have to report that the roof of the temporary fever hospital further gave way on the 7th instant; in consequence was obliged to have most of the patients brought across the lake, in the rain, at 11 o'clock at night, to their great injury.

The roof still had not been fixed when Temporary Inspector d'Arcy reported on 2 March. D'Arcy found 242 inmates under medical treatment in Enniskillen workhouse and 'of these 107 were in fever and small-pox, which cannot now be stayed by vaccination, as the doctor told me he has been obliged to give that practice up, from the reduced condition of the children from want of food and sufficient diet, as the incision made in the arm to receive the infection becomes a sloughing gangrene, which produces almost certain death'. He came upon twenty-nine patients sharing beds in one room, eighteen feet long by sixteen feet wide, and, he continued:

> Immediately previous to my visit there had been *five children in one bed, three of whom were in fever and two in small-pox* . . . No statement of mine can convey an idea of the wretched condition the inmates of this house were in; I have frequently heard the horrors of Skibbereen quoted, but they can hardly have exceeded these.[178]

As early as March 1847, the Newtownards Union recognised that the Poor Law was too inflexible to deal with the crisis facing the country, and under the chairmanship of the popular landlord William Sharman Crawford, the guardians agreed to petition parliament to amend the legislation so that 'Boards of Guardians should have the power of giving temporary out-door relief, *in food*, to the able-bodied poor'.[179] Even though indoor relief was at least four times as expensive as outdoor relief, the Government insisted on the 'test' – the 'able-bodied' could only get relief if they agreed to stay in the workhouse. There was some easing of this regulation in 1848, though doctrinaire refusal to give hand-outs to the destitute unemployed continued in England, where it was partly responsible for the massive resurgence of Chartism, culminating in the great demonstration at Kennington Common in April. The relaxation in Ireland was prompted by the alarming mortality in the congested workhouses – between 11 and 12 per 1,000 inmates per week in January and February 1848.[180]

Much of the outdoor relief was paid for by charities, in particular the British Association, which was feeding four thousand in the Bally-shannon Union and over eight thousand children in the Glenties Union each week by February 1848. There was no large-scale transfer to outdoor relief, however. In the Donegal Union the test was less rigorously applied, 'but an erroneous impression having been thereby produced that the out-door relief was to come into general operation', it was reported on 21 February, 'a crush of applicants for relief presented themselves'.[181] Even those who were prepared to submit themselves to the rigours of the workhouse regime often found they were refused entry. An amending clause to the Poor Law of 1847 excluded from relief cottiers and their families who rented or owned one quarter of an acre or more. The result was that tens of thousands had no choice but to abandon their holdings. A few held on grimly without relief, as d'Arcy reported from Ballyshannon:

> A man named Keenan . . . had died of destitution and want of food . . . I found, on examination, that the wife had previously died, and that five children were left in a state of the most melancholy misery; the father, it was evident, had fallen a sacrifice to the determination to hold his land (2¹/₂ acres) sooner than come with his family to the workhouse for relief.[182]

The opinion of many ratepayers, however, was that relief was too generously applied. William Archdale, a Fermanagh landlord, wrote several cantankerous protests in 1848: 'I object to the scale of out-door relief adopted . . . the Vice-Guardians do not sufficiently study economy . . . and men are put on with more than quarter of an acre . . . All the farmers and ratepayers in the country are enraged.'[183] In June the Letterkenny guardians gave out two hundred handbills 'to earnestly request the rate-payers of this Union to refuse alms to all travelling vagrants'.[184] By then the question being asked all over the country was, what would the harvest be like?

THE CONTINUING CRISIS: 1848–50

Hunger was the main driving force behind the revolutions which convulsed much of Europe in 1848. The first barricades were thrown up in Palermo and in the weeks that followed the fire of revolt flared out from Sicily up the Italian peninsula; on 22 February King Louis Philippe was overthrown in Paris; in March Vienna, Budapest and Berlin were paralysed by insurrection; and by the early summer in central Europe there was not a city with a population of one hundred thousand or more which had not experienced revolution. 'Ireland's opportunity, thank God and France, has come at last!' Charles Gavan Duffy announced on 4 March: 'We must die rather than let this providential hour pass over us unliberated.'[185]

Duffy, son of a Catholic bleacher in Monaghan, had edited the *Vindicator* for northern repealers but, impatient with O'Connell's parliamentary approach, had helped to found Young Ireland in 1842 to promote the new racial and romantic nationalism sweeping much of continental Europe. As editor of the *Nation*, Duffy employed the Banbridge solicitor, John Mitchel, as a leading contributor. Born in Co. Londonderry the son of a Presbyterian minister, Mitchel published the *United Irishman* in 1848, appealing to the spirit of Ninety-eight and calling for an immediate mass uprising. A starving people, however, had no interest in insurrection. The lord lieutenant sent his children home to England and troops poured into Ireland as the Whig administration watched the fall of government after government on the European mainland. But there was no need for alarm: Mitchel was arrested without difficulty and sentenced to fourteen years' transportation, and Ireland's sole contribution to the 'Year of Revolutions' was the 'Battle of Widow McCormack's Cabbage Patch', in which a small force of police, firing their carbines from a farmhouse in Co. Tipperary, dispersed some fifty insurgents at the end of July.

The harvests were good in central Europe, and as the peasants left the barricades to reap their corn, the forces of reaction began to recover. But in Ireland constant rain produced the worst grain harvest for many years and hastened the spread of blight, once more destroying the potato crop.[186] Officially the Famine was over but the workhouses were still overflowing and the destitute were still dying. The only government concession in this continuing crisis was to allow an extension of outdoor relief, but the burden was still to fall on Irish ratepayers. Early in 1849 the prime minister announced that a special 'rate-in-aid' of sixpence in the pound would be levied on all Irish unions to make funds available for the most distressed districts in the south and west. This produced howls of protest from several Ulster Boards of Guardians. On 24 February the Newry Union recorded its resolution: 'We emphatically deny that the industrious population of this province are under any moral obligation to sustain the burden of the poverty of any other province of Ireland.'[187] A few days later the Letterkenny guardians added their objection to the proposed rate, as it 'entitles the idle to be fed at the cost of the industrious; and they respectfully but earnestly protest against the injustice of placing rates wrung from the industrious Northerners at the disposal of Western and Southern Guardians'.[188]

The Government imposed the 'rate-in-aid' in June of that year, nevertheless, and ran down outdoor relief, thus increasing the number of workhouse inmates to a peak of 264,000 by the third week of June 1850, and a year later the number was only 1,000 less than that figure.[189] Private charitable contributions fell away after news of Young Ireland's rebellious activities and some English took the view expressed by Thomas Carlyle: 'Ireland is like a half-starved rat, that crosses the path of an elephant. What must the elephant do? Squelch it – by heavens – squelch it.'[190] Across the land almost one million had died and around one million had emigrated.

Altogether the British government contributed less than half the cost of famine relief, the rest being raised from Ireland itself. The biggest grants were to the public works, around £2.4 million, and the cancellation of workhouse debts in 1853. Overall the balance of Westminster's

299

contribution was some £7 million: from one point of view, no European state had ever taken such vigorous action to cope with a natural disaster; but another view is that this sum was paltry when it is considered that landlords were able to collect around 75 per cent of their rents, that the ports were not closed, that the United Kingdom's annual tax revenue in the late 1840s was around £53 million, and that £69.3 million were expended on fighting the Crimean War.[191] Neither Ireland nor Britain was ruled by representatives of the people. As in every other European state, political power was wielded by a narrow caste of landed and moneyed families, in spite of the Great Reform Act, and the British élite treated their own poor and disadvantaged with as much neglect as they did the Irish victims of famine and disease.

During the first half of the nineteenth century the European continent had undergone impressive if uneven economic growth but, particularly in Ireland, the Austrian Empire, and in the German and Italian states, it had been overwhelmed by the population explosion. Yet at the same time as the streets of central European cities were being filled by the destitute pouring in from the countryside and fighting raged round the barricades, solid foundations of future prosperity in which all could share were being laid by inventors and men of capital. Drawing unprecedented quantities of coal to the surface and applying new techniques of mass production, entrepreneurs built railways and set up ironworks, textile mills and engineering shops. Britain was the industrial giant, leading the way, but on the European mainland Belgium followed closely and in Lorraine, Nord, the Rhineland, Silesia and Bohemia tall chimneys were beginning to dominate the skyline. Simultaneously the European powers were ruthlessly extending their domination in other continents and as new resources were drawn in from overseas, the ports burgeoned. Ulster had been an important cradle of the first industrial revolution and even now – while famine still stalked the land and cholera reaped a fearsome harvest – men of property in Belfast prepared to celebrate the completion of a major engineering enterprise which would make their town a great imperial port: the Victoria Channel.

'DESERVING OF RECORD IN THE BRIGHTEST PAGES OF THE HISTORY OF THE PROGRESS OF BELFAST'

At 1.30 p.m. on Tuesday 10 July 1849 the Belfast Harbour Commissioners, members of the Town Council, the Council of the Chamber of Commerce, the principal gentry and merchants of Belfast, Major-General Bainbrigge and officers and men of the 13th Regiment stepped on board the royal mail steamer *Prince of Wales*. They had come to open the new channel running from the Garmoyle Pool in Belfast Lough to the quays, which would enable large vessels to come up the Lagan at any state of the tide. Then, at the signal of a ship's bell, the tug *Superb* set off, the *Belfast News-Letter* reported, followed by the *Prince of Wales*, which,

> with the Commissioners and their party, the band striking up an inspiriting air, moved majestically into the centre of the river; into her wake fell the *Whitehaven*, crowded with pleasure-seekers, from her mooring at Queen's-quay; and in the rere of the flotilla, the *Erin's Queen*, graceful as a Nereid, glided into the channel, with the *Fawn* and the *Gannet* in tow, rainbowed with their lines of bunting . . . Along the whole line of the opposite quay, loud huzzas from a dense multitude of spectators rent the air. To those on board the fleet the spectacle was truly enchanting as the noble shores of the Lough began to open on their view, heightened in effect by the exhilarating influence of the crowds, the acclamations, the strains of martial music, the roar of cannon, and the summer sweetness of air, earth, and water.

William Pirrie, chairman of the commissioners, made a short speech, poured a libation of champagne into the river 'as the rite of inauguration', and named the new cut the Victoria Channel. Immediately afterwards, the *Belfast News-Letter* continued:

> A scarlet flag, inscribed with the words 'The New Channel Opened', was then unfurled from the mizen-mast head, amidst the huzzas of her living freight. The booming of cannon announced the completion of the auspicious event, and 'Rule Britannia' resounded from the deck, the Paean of a peaceful victory, by the arms of enterprise and skill, over the last natural obstacle which retarded the prosperity of the Port.[192]

The Harbour Commissioners, previously the Ballast Board, had conducted a tenacious and energetic campaign to win parliamentary approval and to raise funds for this great enterprise. Work on the channel had begun in 1839 and the cut through the great banks of slob was now 'sufficiently deep to admit the passage of vessels of the heaviest tonnage, nearly in a line with the newly-constructed quays, about half a mile below them, all protected on either side with a well-finished embankment'. The *Belfast News-Letter* continued:

> The New Cut now affords a safe, short, and easy entrance to our harbour, avoiding henceforth and for ever the delay and risk of the old, tortuous, and difficult channel, which except at high tides, few vessels of large tonnage could pass through without the certainty of getting aground.

The completion of the channel was a vital step in the continuing rapid development of Belfast and a remarkable achievement carried out during the last great famine in western Europe. The opening was a day when 'the busy mart of Northern traffic seemed for a time, to bask in the poetical atmosphere of a Venetian regatta or a Neapolitan carnival,' the *Belfast News-Letter* observed, 'deserving of record in the brightest pages of the history of the progress of Belfast towards the enviable rank she is hastening to attain among the commercial *entrepots* of the British empire'.[193]

A month later Queen Victoria, Prince Albert and the Prince of Wales sailed up the new channel to be rapturously received by the citizens of Belfast. They drove up High Street in Lord Londonderry's carriage past 'thousands of gaily-dressed and animated spectators, whose acclamations, as the cortege passed by, rose like the roar of the wind in the forest'. The queen viewed an exhibition of the province's principal industry, 'from flax in the growth to the splendid damask', in the White Linen Hall. As she drove through the streets a poor woman ran beside the carriage crying 'Och, the Lord love her purty face . . . God save your Majesty and the whole of yez – hurra!'; on the Lisburn Road the workhouse children gave three shrill cheers; and, after inspecting Mulholland's mill, the royal party re-embarked as the staff of the Donegall Arms prepared a banquet to be given by the mayor 'of the most *recherche* kind', including 'all the delicacies of the season'.[194] Dargan's Island, called after the contractor who had engineered the new channel and created from the dredged spoil, was promptly renamed Queen's Island. There was as yet no sign that this addition to east Belfast would shortly become Ulster's industrial heartland.

At this time Belfast was recovering from an epidemic of cholera, which had moved across Europe like a dark cloud as the last embers of the revolutions were being ruthlessly extinguished. The disease reached peaks in March and July of 1849 and at the dispensary station alone 997 victims had died. Over much of the rest of the province the Famine still raged but even this did not suppress traditional sectarian enmities. On 12 July 1849, two days after the opening of the Victoria Channel, there occurred near Castlewellan one of the most violent affrays of the nineteenth century in Ireland, the party fight at Dolly's Brae.

DOLLY'S BRAE

'Twas on the 12th day of July, in the year of '49,
Ten hundreds of our Orangemen together did combine,
In memory of King William, on that bright and glorious day,
To walk all round Lord Roden's park, and right over Dolly's Brae.[195]

When members of the Orange Order announced that they would march from Rathfriland through Lord Annesley's estate at Castlewellan to

Tollymore Park, the Government was alarmed. The route chosen was a long one, veering north through the townland of Magheramayo, inhabited almost exclusively by Catholics; Major Arthur Wilkinson believed the Protestants were 'epicures to choose it instead of keeping on a good road'.[196] Clearly the intention was to provoke the Catholic Ribbonmen, but as the Party Processions Act had lapsed, the authorities hoped that if enough troops and police were sent, a clash could be prevented. On Tuesday 10 July Major Wilkinson was therefore sent to Castlewellan in command of a troop of 13th Light Dragoons, a company of 19th Foot and a body of constabulary, with Captain Skinner JP and two resident magistrates representing the civil power since martial law had not been imposed.

Early on Thursday 12 July Wilkinson's men took up position at Dolly's Brae, a defile on the route where there had been trouble the previous year. Soon after, several hundred Ribbonmen arrived, who 'appeared very much astonished at finding the pass pre-occupied'. The Orange procession wound out of Rathfriland, bands playing, numbering between 1,200 and 1,400 'all armed to the teeth' and escorted by a force of dragoons and some anxious magistrates. They marched peacefully through Magheramayo, over Dolly's Brae, through Castlewellan and south to Lord Roden's demesne at Tollymore.

During the afternoon the number of Ribbonmen built up to more than a thousand, armed with pitchforks, pikes and muskets. Quite undeterred by the close proximity of the troops, they kept watch over the pass and carried out manoeuvres – as Major Wilkinson remarked laconically, 'the Ribbon party were constantly "blazing away" with their arms; but no breach of the peace occurred . . . in fact, they had a regular field day'. At 5 p.m. the Orangemen marched out of Tollymore and army officers were surprised that magistrates made no attempt to induce them to take the good road back to Rathfriland. On the return journey the dragoons followed the procession, while the Ribbonmen moved away from Wilkinson's troops at Dolly's Brae to take position on a hill overlooking the road about a mile beyond the pass.

'Now, my boys, not a shot is to be fired,' a man at the head of the Orange procession called out to those behind him. James Ponsonby Hill, sub-inspector of constabulary, stood at Dolly's Brae, as he later told the inquest: 'I addressed every file of the procession as it passed, asking them, for God's sake, to pass on quietly, and not to fire a shot, even for fun.' Then 'there went bang a shot in front,' Wilkinson recalled, 'but I don't know where it came from no more than the man in the moon.' Major Henry White thought it was 'more like a squib . . . my impression is that it came from the head of the Orange party'. There followed 'a succession of shots from both sides ... a regular blazing away, helter-skelter'.

'For God's sake, shall we take the hill?' the sub-inspector called out to a magistrate as Ribbon bullets flew in amongst the police and troops. Getting approval, Hill led his constables

> up the hill in double quick time. Shots were tearing up the ground where the men were ... I ordered a few of the police for God's sake to fire and they did. When they did so the people ran. I then at once said, 'Not another shot – we have conquered, and have mercy.'

Hill's appeal to the Orangemen was to no avail, for 'at that time the gun balls were flying, I should say in hundreds, from the Protestant party'. 'The general encounter was then over,' added White, 'but the Orangemen continued firing.' George Fitzmaurice RM rode along the line of Orangemen urging them to stop shooting for fear of hitting the police on the hill, but to no effect. Then at the end of the procession he found Catholic homes being attacked and one of their owners wounded:

> I said to them, there's a man lying on the road. Go back, perhaps he's not dead, and afford him some assistance. They roared out – 'He's not one of our party.'[197]

'The houses appeared to have been fired by stragglers of the Orange party,' Wilkinson recalled; 'We did the best we could to put out the fires, which were all about.'

At the top of the hill the police found eighteen pitchforks, seven pikes and ten muskets, and half a dozen bodies. Not a single Orangeman was wounded. The forces of law and order were also unscathed, except for a constable accidentally bayoneted in the arm by a fellow policeman when charging Ribbonmen on the hill. The Catholics took away most of their dead and wounded, but the *Newry Telegraph*, which gave the most detailed report of the affray, reckoned 'that no fewer than fifty of the Ribbonmen were either killed or wounded'. The government inquiry estimated that at least thirty Catholics had been killed; its report, the *Battle of Magheramayo*, led Westminster to place a new Party Processions Act on the statute book in 1850.[198]

During that summer of 1849 the revolutions in central Europe were finally put down by the dynastic powers: the frightened petty princes of the German states called in Prussian troops to restore order; after a furious resistance the Roman Republic fell on 3 July and Pope Pius IX returned protected by French bayonets; in August the Hungarian revolutionaries, caught between Prince Felix Schwarzenberg in the west and two hundred thousand Russians pouring in from the east, capitulated to the tsar at Világos; and after an epic struggle the republicans of

Venice, ravaged by cholera and pounded from the mainland by modern artillery from the Skoda works, surrendered to the Austrian Emperor Franz Josef on 22 August. These events seem remote from the sectarian clash at Dolly's Brae – but were they so distant?

The nationalist zeal that raced eastwards across the European continent in the 1840s along the new-built network of railway track awakened ethnic passions of ancient origin. Not all the defeated revolutionary leaders who took refuge in England were carriers of the torch of liberty. Those who lionised Lajos Kossuth in London were not aware that during his rule as governor of Hungary he had instigated horrific massacres of Slav peoples who refused the domination of the Magyar master race, describing the Croats as 'not enough for a single meal' and saying to the Serbs, 'the sword shall decide between us'.[199] The continuing sectarian tensions in Ulster had much in common with the emerging ethnic rivalries of central and eastern Europe. In the second half of the nineteenth century, improving communications, the spread of literacy, and economic progress heightened and democratised nationalism all over Europe to join with or conflict with ancient loyalties and imperialist ambitions. So it was in Ulster: in the face of the rising tide of Irish nationalism loyalists cherished their ties with the British Empire, which, during its rapid expansion, brought unprecedented prosperity to the province.

9
IMPERIAL BASTION
c. 1850–1890

On the afternoon of Sunday 12 July 1857 Orangemen in the pews of Christ Church in Belfast listened as the Reverend Thomas Drew brought his sermon to a climax:

> The cells of the Pope's prisons were paved with the calcined bones of men and cemented with human gore and human hair. . .The Word of God makes all plain; puts to eternal shame the practices of persecutors, and stigmatises with enduring reprobation the arrogant pretences of Popes and the outrageous dogmata of their blood-stained religion.[1]

Outside on the frontiers of the Catholic Pound the presence of Town Police attracted a hostile crowd, and when the Orangemen emerged they were reinforced by Protestants from the adjacent Sandy Row. Fierce rioting ensued. The police blatantly joined the Protestant side and it was left to a small force of the constabulary to attempt to contain the violence. Ten days of intense sectarian rioting followed.

The 1857 riots showed that traditional fears and rivalries, far from wilting when transferred from the countryside, found new strength in the narrow streets of working-class Belfast, especially along the frontier zone between the main Protestant and Catholic enclaves, described by Frankfort Moore as the 'seismic area of the city – that part in which streaks of disagreement lie in parallel lines'.[2] There were riots also in Derry, Portadown and Lurgan, but these were minor by comparison with those in Belfast in 1864, 1872 and 1886, which resulted in more deaths than all the nationalist uprisings of the nineteenth century put together. In part, mounting sectarian violence reflected the very success of Belfast's linen mills and factories, engineering works and shipbuilding yards; the population they drew in from the countryside was not only volatile and unstable but also densely concentrated and very large. By 1891 Belfast was the biggest city in Ireland. Its industrial and commercial progress was without parallel and the Lagan valley formed the vital and closely integrated western corner of an area encompassing the manufacturing regions of Scotland and the north of England, then one of the most advanced economic regions on earth and the industrial heartland of an expanding empire.

Rural Ulster was remarkably tranquil in these years. The vigilant supervision of the widely respected constabulary was in part responsible, but nothing promoted the peace of the countryside more than a marked rise in living standards in the quarter-century following the Famine. Tenant farmers found the confidence and resources to campaign with considerable success to reduce the power their landlords had over them. Catholics and Protestants co-operated closely in this movement and the small coterie of Liberal MP's all owed their seats to cross-community support. The steady growth of national feeling amongst Catholics, however, reawakened Protestant fears and the political polarisation of the province was complete when the Liberal government made its first attempt to give Ireland a parliament of her own in 1886.

The Famine brought a halt to population expansion and the number of inhabitants in Ulster continued to fall for the rest of the century. This drop, from 2,386,000 in 1841 to 1,620,000 by 1891, was less severe than in the rest of Ireland and in the same period Ulster's population as a percentage of that of the whole country rose from 29.4 to 34.4. Nevertheless, the Famine had marked the onset of a decline in population against the trend in all of the rest of Europe.[3]

THE FAMINE'S TOLL

It was not until the publication of the census returns of 1851 that the full impact of the Famine on the population was revealed. The number of Ulster's inhabitants fell by 374,000 between 1841 and 1851, a drop of 15.7 per cent compared with 19.9 per cent for the whole of Ireland. The north had fared better than the south and west but not as well as Leinster, and the effect of the Famine varied greatly in different parts of the province. To obtain a true picture, historians now attempt to calculate 'excess deaths', that is, the number over and above those who would have died from the usual causes. Ulster suffered around 224,000 excess deaths, or 8.6 per cent. The dreadful losses for the southern parts of the province largely account for this high figure; the average annual rates per thousand of excess mortality between 1846 and 1851 were 42.7 for Co. Cavan, 29.2 for Co. Fermanagh, and 28.6 for Co. Monaghan.

Armagh, Tyrone and Antrim were close to the national average with rates of 15.3, 15.2 and 15.0 respectively.[4] The rates for the remaining counties were: 10.7 for Donegal; 6.7 for Down; and 5.7 for Londonderry. The figures for Donegal and Londonderry seem surprising; it is likely that the well-established pattern of seasonal migration and emigration allowed a great many of the destitute to escape just before the Famine or during its early stages.

Such statistics do not include the very great numbers who died soon after arrival in Britain or en route to America. Where whole communities were wiped out by starvation and fever – for example, on islands off the Donegal coast – enumeration must have been difficult. Donegal was the only Ulster county to have army commissariat depots, and officers' reports give detailed descriptions of a kind not available for the rest of the province. Also, this was a county of sharp contrasts, where the Atlantic coastlands suffered much more than the fertile Laggan district. Economic historian L.A. Clarkson calculates that in addition to excess deaths in Ulster about a further two hundred thousand 'loss of births' must be accounted for, resulting from the death of marriage partners and amenorrhoea among women brought on by hunger and disease. He also estimates that famine deaths in the province were almost exactly equalled by the number of emigrants.[5]

THE TIDE OF EMIGRATION

Many saw emigration as the only hope of staying alive during the Famine. One such was Michael Rush of Ardglass, Co. Down, who wrote to his parents in America:

> Now my dear father and mother, if you knew what hunger we and our fellow-countrymen are suffering, you would take us out of this poverty Isle . . . if you don't endeavour to take us out of it, it will be the first news you will hear by some friend of me and my little family to be lost by hunger, and there are thousands dread they will share the same fate.[6]

Had there not been unique opportunities for flight overseas the effects of the potato harvest failures would have been even more horrific – opportunities rarely available today to victims of destitution, disease and natural disaster across the world. In eleven years during and after the Famine Ireland sent abroad over two million people, more than had emigrated over the preceding two and a half centuries. Around 1.2 million left the country between 1846 and 1851. Though the proportion of emigrants from Connacht doubled during the Famine, Ulster was still in the lead, providing 40.6 per cent of those leaving in 1847–8.[7] Against the trend in some other parts of Ireland, emigration from the north was heaviest where starvation had reaped its most fearful harvest: Cavan and Monaghan lost up to one fifth of their 1841 populations from emigration alone. The outflow from Fermanagh and Tyrone was also high.[8] Donegal and Londonderry, leading emigrant counties before the Famine, had slipped slightly lower down the scale, though the former provided a remarkably high proportion of emigration ballads. The rapid growth of Belfast did much to stem the tide from rural Antrim and Down, and the emergence of Portadown and Lurgan as important manufacturing and railway towns absorbed many who abandoned their smallholdings in Armagh, the most populous county in 1841; the emigration from there was considerable nevertheless.

Statistics are notoriously treacherous partly because of the difficulty of distinguishing between migrant labourers and permanent emigrants, and also because some were almost constantly on the move. For example, Owen Mangan, born 1839 at Billy Hill in Co. Cavan the son of a drover and illicit distiller, lived in Monaghan, Cootehill, Bailieborough and Drogheda at various times; he left for England in 1853, where he lived in Liverpool, Preston and St Helen's; he emigrated to America in 1867, where he moved from Philadelphia to Fall River, Massachusetts, and to Rhode Island; he was variously employed as a policeman, grocer, cooper, loom fixer, shoemaker, storekeeper, factory hand and insurance salesman. One of his brothers emigrated to New Orleans, another went to sea, the third joined the Papal army, while the fourth fled Durham for Philadelphia to escape arrest as a member of the Fenian Brotherhood.[9]

America was the preferred ultimate destination amongst emigrants from every county. While the Famine was at its worst, flight from starvation was the primary aim. Strict controls imposed by the United States government on its passenger vessels pushed fares up, but lax standards on British ships kept fares to Canada as low as £3 per person, one third of the cost of going to New York. Vessels carrying salt fish, oil, timber and flaxseed from the St Lawrence and Newfoundland to British ports had not enough cargo to take back even to serve as ballast; owners therefore gladly accepted destitute Irish into their holds, usually at Liverpool, the cheapest point of departure. These were the infamous 'coffin ships', grossly overcrowded and inadequately provided with food and clean water, where louse-borne famine fever flourished. Stephen de Vere noted in his diary what he saw when vessels anchored at the quarantine station at Grosse Isle in the St Lawrence: '. . . water covered with beds cooking vessels etc. of the dead. Ghastly appearance of boats full of sick going ashore never to return. Several died between ship and shore. Wives separated from husbands, children from parents, etc.' A medical officer on Grosse Isle saw 'a stream of foul air issuing from the hatches as dense and as palpable as seen on a foggy day from a dung heap'.[10] Amongst those going to Canada in 1847 over 5 per cent died at sea; 3.5 per cent in quarantine on Grosse Isle; and over 8 per cent in Canadian hospitals. Many better-off Protestants stayed in British North America, but the great majority of Catholics pressed on southwards to the United States.

Though now greatly outnumbered by Catholics, the Scotch-Irish from Ulster still formed a significant proportion of European immigrants arriving in the United States. One of these was Andrew Greenlees who came from a fairly prosperous farming family with a holding near Larne. Arriving at Plattsburgh, New York, in 1852, he found himself at first 'in the midst of strangers, buffeting my way through the dangers and difficulties of this world alone, without an earthly counsellor and guide'.[11] Six months later, having got a job as a moulder, he was delighted with his new life, as he wrote to his brother John, a Presbyterian minister:

> This is a free country. Jack's as good as his master. If he don't like one of them, go to another. Plenty of work and plenty of wages, plenty to eat and no landlords. That's enough. What more does a man want . . . I had a letter from John Temple a few days ago. He is well. He says if you knew the rights of man in Magheramorne you would stay in it no longer than you could get a ship to take you off.[12]

The following year Greenlees moved on to Troy, New York, and by March 1856 he was in Ottawa, Illinois. He looked down on the destitute Catholic Irish pouring in:

> I would much rather live with the red men of the forest than with the Irish where you are. I never saw genuine Irish until I came to this country. And I assure you I don't think it strange that they are everywhere spoken against . . . All men are respected that will respect themselves, live at least morally and improve their minds by study and reading . . . Of course this does not include the low catholic Irish and Dutch, for to a man they are addicted to drinking and loafing round rum shops.[13]

The price of a fare to America could be had for less than could be raised from the sale of a heifer or from a summer's earnings in the fields. Yet for many this was more than could be saved. Great numbers poured into ports and industrial towns on the British mainland, and Glasgow in particular was the destination of many Ulster emigrants. Under the heading 'The Irish Invasion', the *Glasgow Herald* reported on 11 June 1847:

> The streets of Glasgow are at present literally swarming with vagrants from the sister kingdom, and the misery which many of these poor creatures endure can scarcely be less than what they have fled or been

driven from at home. Many of them are absolutely without procuring lodging of even the meanest description, and are obliged consequently to make their bed frequently with a stone for a pillow.[14]

The *Edinburgh Medical Journal* reported in 1848 that many 'poor, starved, destitute, and diseased creatures were brought and laid down before the doors' of the Glasgow Infirmary and 'in numerous instances it was destitution and starvation more than fever which was their chief affliction'.[15] By 1849 the Glasgow parochial authorities were sending paupers back to Ireland, generally to Belfast, at the rate of one thousand a month, but Poor Law officials often attempted to return them. One woman with a baby was shipped back to Belfast, kept in the workhouse there for twelve hours without a morsel to eat, and then returned to Glasgow on SS *Aurora* with a sixpenny loaf to share with four others. Three Donegal orphans were dispatched from Campsie to Glenties only to be sent back to Derry and from there to Glasgow with a few pence and a handful of biscuits.[16]

After the Famine, the attractions of greater opportunity and prosperity abroad, rather than destitution at home, drew people from their homeland. In Ulster the potato harvest failures merely intensified and broadened a pattern of emigration long established, and when recovery followed, the outflow continued. Most emigrants left for good, tending in Britain to concentrate in London, Manchester, Liverpool and Glasgow, gradually diffusing to smaller towns thereafter. In Glasgow and Liverpool, where for a time the immigrant Irish formed one fifth of the population, Orange and Green divisions were firmly implanted, leading at times to violent clashes. After severe disorder on 12 July 1851 (known as Carpenters' Day because of Protestant domination of that trade), Liverpool banished processions beyond the borough limits. On 12 July 1859 Protestant and Catholic miners confronted each other at Linwood Bridge in Paisley: shots were fired; 'stones were thrown by both parties and knives and sticks with spears were used as well as bludgeons and other legal weapons'; and a Catholic was stabbed to death.[17]

Most emigrants paid their own way, a minority being subsidised by landlords who considered that assisted passages provided a humane and rapid way of reducing poor rates and clearing scrapholders from their estates. William Stewart Trench, agent on the Bath estate in Co. Monaghan, became notorious for his robust approach to removing unwanted tenants: he arranged the emigration of 2,500 to the United States, serving ejectment orders on those who refused to co-operate.[18] Emigration to Australia was quite beyond the means of the ordinary tenant or labourer, and financial assistance was essential. Some Ulstermen were to travel to the southern hemisphere as convicts in chains:

He brought me back to Omagh Jail, in the County of Tyrone,
From that I was transported from Erin's lovely home . . .
There are seven links upon my chain, and every link a year,
Before I can return again to the arms of my dear.[19]

Many of the pioneers from Ulster in Australia and New Zealand were from prosperous bourgeois families and, as emigration increased later in the century, they and their descendants were to play a notable role in the shaping of these dominions. Irish immigrants integrated more rapidly into their host Anglophone societies than is generally recognised, but a significant minority kept up a keen interest in their homeland, eager to help redress injustices which had sent them into exile.

The immense outflow steadily reduced population pressure on the land, thus ensuring a rise in living standards in the countryside. Those who had survived the horrors of the Famine, however, were determined that never again would landlords have such total control over their destiny.

EVICTION

In his fiercely partisan tract *The Last Conquest of Ireland* John Mitchel looked back on his years spent as a solicitor in Ulster:

> At every quarter sessions, in every county, there were always many ejectments; and I have seen them signed by assistant barristers by hundreds in one sheaf. They were then placed in the hands of bailiffs and police, and came down upon some devoted townland with more terrible destruction than an enemy's sword and torch. Whole neighbourhoods were often thrown out upon the highways in winter.[20]

This is propagandist exaggeration: in the years before the Famine ejectment orders were largely used as threats by landlords and only rarely carried through to eviction. Nevertheless, Mitchel's description could be applied accurately to the six-year period between 1849 and 1854 when forty-nine thousand families – amounting to almost one quarter of a million persons throughout Ireland – were permanently dispossessed in the post-Famine clearances. These figures do not include the evictions between 1846 and 1848, before the constabulary began making returns, when dispossession seems to have been particularly relentless in the counties of Armagh, Antrim and Monaghan.

Most landlords did not have to resort to legal ejectment; the payment of small sums in compensation was often all that was required. In any case, many smallholders abandoned their plots during the Famine to comply with the 1847 Poor Law Act excluding them from workhouse relief if they held a quarter-acre or more. Not all unwanted tenants were prepared to go, however, and landlords were anxious to rid themselves of those with holdings of £4 or less for whom they were liable to pay rates.[21] 'Sir, I send herewith a list of Tenants from which Notices to Quit can be filled', an agent wrote from Markethill in March 1847 to his employer William Cotter Kyle, requesting that evictions be carried out 'as easily as convenient'.[22] Those tenants who had fallen behind in rent payments were naturally most vulnerable but prompt payment was no protection if a landlord (often close to bankruptcy himself) was determined to consolidate the farms on his estate. Patrick Murphy, a tenant on the Wingfield estate near Monaghan town, wrote in protest to his agent:

> I have lived on this land for forty years and have worked hard. I was never behind with my rent. I do not know why I was ejected.[23]

Ulster does not seem to have suffered the wholesale clearances carried out in the west and south-west. Captain Arthur Kennedy, a Poor Law inspector in Co. Clare not noted for his generosity to the destitute, recalled times 'when I came back from some scene of eviction so maddened by the sights of hunger and misery I had seen in the day's work that I felt disposed to take the gun from behind my door and shoot the first landlord I met'.[24] There was little shooting and, indeed, the whole country was remarkably calm. A rare exception was the murder of Thomas Bateson, agent for the Templetown estate in Co. Monaghan, battered to death by three men as he walked down the Keady Road leading out of Castleblayney on the afternoon of 4 December 1851. Bateson was loathed because he had refused rent reductions during the Famine, had struck a farmer during an ejectment (for which he was fined), had confiscated stock and crops in lieu of rent, and had evicted 34 families totalling 222 people to create a model farm. When the murderers were eventually condemned in 1854, five thousand gathered outside Monaghan gaol to watch them hang – 'Hell cannot scare us,' one cried out from the scaffold.[25]

Concerted action against landlord power began not with wretched evicted smallholders but amongst more substantial tenants, many of whom had come through the potato harvest failures largely unscathed. Their aim was to defend the Ulster tenant right – a custom long accepted in the north that there would be no eviction if the rent was paid and that a tenant giving up his holding could demand a lump-sum payment (often as high as £10 an acre) from the incoming tenant. The 1845 Devon Commission had criticised this practice, which seems to have prevailed over most of Ulster, and several northern landlords had recently disregarded it. The problem was that tenant right was merely a custom, variously interpreted in different areas (in some places it gave no protection from eviction), but it was a valuable form of insurance, providing the outgoing tenant, for example, with enough cash to take his family to America. Such a right was worth defending.[26]

> Let the people know the fate of their neighbours on the property of Mr Shirley of Carrickmacross where you could ascend a hill and count tens and fifties and hundreds of ruined homesteads whose blackened walls and silent desolation tell to God and man that the merciless destroyer has been there; where there are thirteen auxiliary workhouses and more sought for, as all are crammed in suffocation.

So the Reverend Dr David Bell, minister of the Derryvalley Presbyterian congregation near Ballybay, declared to a packed audience in the Belfast Music Hall early in June 1850. He had travelled up from Co. Monaghan to win support for a new association of tenant farmers seeking to defend their customary rights. Bell finished with this clarion call:

> In the name of justice, in the name of humanity, in the name of mercy, in the awful name of God, I call upon Lord John Russell; I call upon the Government; I call upon the Imperial Legislature to render the poor man's property as sacred as that of the rich.[27]

In 1847 the Ulster Tenant Right Association was launched while the Famine was still at its worst by William Sharman Crawford of Crawfordsburn, the Radical MP for Rochdale who had helped to draft the People's Charter in 1838 and who had striven indefatigably but unsuccessfully to persuade Westminster to give legal force to the Ulster Custom. Now Presbyterian ministers and their congregations – always eager to challenge Anglican landlord power – joined the new movement in force; their spokesman was Dr James McKnight, editor of the *Londonderry Standard* and, for a time, of the Presbyterian journal, *Banner of Ulster*. McKnight argued that Ulster landlords were trustees rather than full owners, because their undertaker forebears had been granted uncultivated wastes during the plantation and it had been the tenants and their descendants – Protestant and Catholic alike – who had carved out fertile farms from this wilderness by the sweat of their brows. Landlords, therefore, had no right to evict and were only entitled to rent for the 'raw earth'.[28]

Tenant-right associations had been founded by Catholic curates in Co. Kilkenny and then in August 1850 a national organisation, the Irish Tenant League, was launched by three journalists: Frederick Lucas, editor of the Catholic *Tablet*; Sir John Grey, of the *Freeman's Journal*; and Charles Gavan Duffy, the Monaghan Young Irelander who had founded and revived the *Nation*.[29] Sharman Crawford took the chair and Dr McKnight was elected president. It seemed a unique moment in Irish history when north and south, and Protestant and Catholic, were working together in one movement. The *Fermanagh Mail* certainly thought so:

> It was a grand ennobling sight to see the children of the Covenant from the far North, the Elizabethan settlers from the Ards of Ulster, the Cromwellians of the centre, the Normans of the Pale, the Milesians of Connaught . . . and the Williamites of Fermanagh and Meath, all, all, united in harmonious concert for this dear old land.[30]

For Duffy this was 'The League of North and South', bonding Catholic and Protestant farmers in a common cause, and for a time his passionate hope seemed justified. Monster meetings were planned, including one at Ballybay for 1 October 1850; the *Dundalk Democrat* urged a full attendance, declaring:

> Never did a race of human beings need glad tidings as much at this time as the people of County Monaghan . . . The character of the landlords is such not only to make the angels weep but even to hate the very form and shape of men.[31]

At Ballybay, on the top of a hill close to the Monaghan road, a platform to take five hundred was put up, together with a flagstaff flying a banner of blue, white, green and orange, designed to represent all creeds. Some thirty thousand assembled on the day, the Cootehill contingent led by a band playing 'We're Paddies Ever More'. The climax of the meeting was a resolution proposed by the Reverend Philip Brennan PP and seconded by Dr Bell:

> That in this locality every engine which earth and hell could set in motion has been mustered to prevent this meeting. Many have been kept away whose hearts are with us, who had not sufficient resolution to overcome the unlimited and ruthless powers of our merciless oppressors.[32]

That evening a soirée, attended by several priests and Presbyterian ministers, was held on the platform, while bands played a medley of tunes including 'Saint Patrick's Day', 'The Protestant Boys', and 'The Boyne Water'.

McKnight was largely responsible for crystallising the aims of the league into the 'three Fs': fair rent (in effect, a reduction of rent set by tribunals); free sale (the extension of the Ulster Custom to the whole island); and fixity of tenure (no eviction if rent had been paid). Crawford, a landlord in receipt of £8,000 a year in rent, found fixity of tenure difficult to swallow but the programme was agreed – a programme that was to guide the Irish land reform movement for the next thirty years.

315

How could the league now bring enough pressure to bear on a parliament still largely composed of landlords? It was Pope Pius IX's decision in September 1850 to give England a hierarchy of bishops and archbishops that seemed to give the tenants' movement just the opportunity it was seeking.[33] The indignant Liberal government rushed through a bill confirming the illegality of Catholic prelates assuming territorial titles; Irish Liberal MPs, dependent on Catholic votes, were outraged and formed their own independent Irish party, and the league, against Duffy's advice, threw in its lot with the new party, popularly known as the Irish Brigade. These independent MPs, most of them supporting tenant right, played a key role in forcing a general election in 1852. In the south the election was a triumph, returning around forty-eight MPs pledged to the independent party. In Ulster, however, not a single independent candidate was elected, even though Sharman Crawford gave up Rochdale to stand in Co. Down. Only one northern MP, William Kirk of Newry, openly supported tenant right. 'The League of North and South' now seemed an extravagant title.

Then followed disaster: breaking their pledge to remain independent, William Keogh and John Sadleir accepted office in Lord Aberdeen's new government and the unity of the Irish Brigade began to disintegrate, especially when it engaged in a long quarrel with the formidable archbishop of Dublin, Paul Cullen. Sharman Crawford retired to Crawfordsburn in 1852 and Duffy emigrated to Australia in 1855, becoming prime minister of Victoria in 1871 and receiving a knighthood in 1873.[34]

Fear of militant Catholicism does not seem to have been the main reason for the failure of Ulster tenants to get MPs elected. Simply, northern landlords had a more effective control over their tenant voters than their counterparts in the south – indeed, they could threaten to disregard the Ulster Custom if their candidates were not supported. The tenant-right movement was to have its day again in the north but only after the political grip of Conservative landlords had been loosened by secret voting and extensions of the franchise. Fellow feeling with southern tenants was not yet lost but for the present the agitation died down because farmers were now enjoying a prosperity they had never known before.

PROGRESS IN FARMING

The Famine ruined several great landowners, though none of them died of starvation. In the hope that English investors would be attracted to buy Irish estates and transform Irish agriculture, Westminster placed the Encumbered Estates Act on the Statute Book in 1849. It was designed to cut through the tangled web of legal obligations that had held up the sale of landed property weighed down by debt and it operated with impressive speed.

The most spectacular sale at the encumbered estates court was the property of the 3rd Marquess of Donegall, which owed nothing whatever to the Famine but everything to the wild extravagance of his father. George Augustus Chichester, the 2nd marquess, had already been imprisoned for debt before succeeding to the title in 1799; the contents of his house in Belfast's Donegall Square had been put under the hammer in 1806; the sheriff of Down seized the contents of Ormeau House in 1817; and in 1822 a new settlement aimed to raise £217,000 by dispensing perpetual leases in return for cash payments. All this new income was squandered and when he died in 1844 he left his heir with debts of nearly £400,000, fourteen times the annual rental. The 3rd marquess had no choice but to let the encumbered estates court arrange the sale of thirty thousand acres, all that was left of a once vast and lucrative property.[35]

The fall of the house of Chichester was an early sign that the great landed proprietors were entering the last phase of their domination, but it was not seen as such at the time. Landlords were being given a new opportunity to show that they deserved their position at the apex of Irish society by reviving Irish agriculture. The task was not to be accomplished by English entrepreneurs, as Westminster hoped. Looking back in 1877, A.M. Sullivan, editor of the *Nation*, rightly observed:

> The anticipations and prophecies about 'English capital' have all proved illusory ... Up to August 1857, out of 7489 purchases, 7180 were Irish; only 309 were 'English, Scotch or foreigners' ... English capital has preferred Turkish bonds and Honduras loans. [36]

Sullivan was wrong to conclude that the Irish purchasers were 'chiefly mercantile men who have saved money in trade'. Most were members of the Irish landed and professional élite, such as John George Adair, heir of a noted improving landlord in Queen's County and nephew of William Stewart Trench, who was to buy twenty-eight thousand acres in Co. Donegal with unexpected consequences for the future. The Ascendancy, at least in its ownership of land, remained firmly in position, but it was the farmers themselves who were largely responsible for the modernisation that followed.

Typical of a prosperous tenant farmer in south Antrim, Thomas George McKinney was able to take advantage of Lord Donegall's financial plight by buying, in 1826, a lease in perpetuity for his farm at Sentry Hill for £90 16s.5d. – a similar farm was valued at nearly £1,000 in 1840.

Like many other leaseholders with substantial holdings, he was able to offset potato losses during the Famine by profitable sales of grain and dairy produce.[37] From 1853 agricultural prices began to rise and received a further fillip the following year with the outbreak of the Crimean War. The strong demand for provisions for Britain's expeditionary forces, which included several Ulster regiments, helped the McKinneys to add another 31 acres to their holding of 45 acres in 1861 and a further 16 soon after. The only serious downturn was during the early 1860s, when bad weather damaged crops; otherwise farmers, rich and poor, enjoyed a sustained rise in their incomes lasting a quarter of a century.

Despite the inglorious incompetence of her Crimean campaign, Britain was now at her zenith as the world's greatest naval, trading and industrial power, and the burgeoning urban population of the manufacturing regions provided a ready market for farm produce carried regularly and speedily across the Irish Sea. The rapid extension of the railways – only Co. Donegal lacked a through main line by 1860 – brought perishable eggs, fresh meat and dairy produce reliably and inexpensively to the ports, and the growth of manufacturing centres in Ulster after the Famine provided a ready market closer to home.

Sentry Hill, close to Belfast, was particularly well placed. Butter had to be churned as early as two or three in the morning so that the Belfast market could be reached in time. The McKinneys installed a horse-driven churning machine in May 1850 but most Ulster farms continued to depend on hand plunge churns well into the twentieth century. Cows were in the fields between April and September and, while the McKinneys bought in 'slummage' (residue grain from distilleries) as a supplement, meadow hay was the main winter feed. After the Famine, hay-making became the most characteristic farming activity and, by the end of the century, hay was Ireland's main crop. Mowing machines were being made from the 1850s, but on most Ulster farms grass was cut with the scythe. In fine weather grass could be cut, shaken, turned and built into the typical Ulster lap-cocks shaped like ladies' muffs all in one day. Later in the century horse-drawn hay sweeps known as Tumblin' Paddies came into general use.[38]

Scythes were not widely used for harvesting corn until towards the end of the century for fear that too much ripe grain would be shaken off during cutting. In any case, much corn was still grown on ridges not suited to the scythe. Reaping hooks and sickles were preferred, the reapers followed by binders who bound up the cut corn into sheaves, or 'straps'. At Sentry Hill William McKinney recorded for 1 September 1873: 'Margt Crawford lifted. John made straps. Thos held back the corn with a rod. I tyed and stooked. Got 89 stooks cut today.'[39] Ten sheaves made a stook. Even on such a prosperous farm, which specialised in growing seed oats, it was not until 1884 that a mechanical reaper-binder was purchased. A threshing machine had replaced flails in 1871. Portable machines, which could be hired, were well-suited to small Ulster farms. Towards the end of the century many of these were steam-powered, the farmer supplying the coal and giving board and lodging to the operator, and banding together neighbours to help with the work. Nothing was wasted: at Sentry Hill the worst oats were crushed for cow feed; straw was sold to the local brickworks; and the chaff was put into bags for stuffing mattresses.

The spade remained the principal implement for cultivation on small-holdings, but a steady rise in the cost of hiring labour led to it being replaced by the plough on larger farms. Light wooden ploughs were favoured on sloping ground. In the lowlands the old Irish long-beamed plough – which required a ploughman, a driver to control the horses, and a boy to steady the beam – was being replaced by all-metal swing ploughs and wheel ploughs, requiring less skill and manpower but only suitable for flat ground. Horse-drawn harrows and rollers speeded up the preparation of ground, but even on large estates seed drills only slowly replaced broadcast sowing.[40]

Despite the terrible losses of the 1840s, and again in 1861, potato cultivation still had a central role in Ulster agriculture. Lazy beds were preferred on newly broken land, but otherwise, drills, increasingly made with the aid of horsepower, were gaining favour.[41] On small farms the children were kept off school to lift and sort the tubers. Larger farms hired labour to lift the crop, and filthy and exhausting work it was, as described by Patrick MacGill of Co. Donegal:

> Nine of the older men dug the potatoes from the ground with short three-pronged graips. The women followed behind, crawling on their knees and dragging two baskets a-piece along with them . . . The first day was wet . . . The job, bad enough for men, was killing for women. All day long, on their hands and knees, they dragged through the slush and rubble of the field. The baskets which they hauled after them were cased in a clay to a depth of several inches, and sometimes when emptied of potatoes a basket weighed over two stone. Pools of water gathered in the hollows of the dress that covered the calves of their legs. [42]

The first successful potato-digging machine was patented by J. Hanson of Doagh, Co. Antrim, in 1855, but on most farms hand-lifting was preferred to ensure that all tubers were saved and with the minimum of damage. Blight remained a constant threat and it was not until 1882 that it was discovered that copper sulphate would kill the fungus.

In spite of much assertion to the contrary, farming in Ulster was no more efficient than in the rest of Ireland – in a survey of 1854 only Connacht had a worse record for weed control, for example. Northern farmers, however, benefited from readier access to growing industrial markets and an ever-rising demand for flax in the mills. This labour-intensive cash crop was well-suited to small family farms since it gave a high gross income per acre. Sir George Hodson's agent in Co. Cavan reckoned that flax grown on one eleventh of the area of the estate paid all the rents and left some profit over for the tenants.[43] This was during the great linen boom of the 1860s when the McKinneys got ten shillings a stone for their flax, and though the price dropped to 6s.9d. by 1883, it was worth while maintaining seven dams at Sentry Hill, fed by streams from Carnmoney bog and Colinward.[44]

The efficiency of Irish agriculture compared favourably with that of other western European states. A steady rise in agricultural prices, however, was probably more important than an improvement in techniques in raising living standards on the farm. Between the 1850s and the 1870s prices rose by 14 per cent for pork, 40 per cent for butter, over 50 per cent for beef and over 100 per cent for store cattle. Overall the value of Irish agricultural output rose by 47 per cent in the quarter-century following the Famine. In addition tenants were paying rents which were falling in real terms. Rackrenting – that is, increasing rents with every price rise – was no longer common. A detailed survey of fifty estates shows that though some landlords increased rents by over 50 per cent, the average increase in this period was only 20 per cent. In short, a growing share of agricultural profit was going to the tenant farmer. The Ulster Custom demonstrates how the relative position of landlords was slipping. Lump-sum payments made by incoming tenants show that they went far beyond compensating outgoing tenants for improvements; in 1868, for example, £563 15s.0d. was paid for a farm on the Abercorn estate in Co. Donegal, where the annual rental was £15. Lump-sum payments, made both to leaseholders and yearly tenants, indicated a dramatically increased share of agricultural income to farmers at the expense of landowners. Tenants were determined not to lose this advantage.[45]

Landlords, who also benefited from rising prices, seem to have been largely unaware of this slip in their relative position and, indeed, landlord power, particularly in the north, was still formidable. As late as 1876 almost 80 per cent of Ulster was held by 804 owners, though there were

190,973 occupiers of land of whom only 18 per cent had leases. Amongst the leading proprietors were: the Marquess of Downshire with 70,143 acres bringing in an annual rent of £67,708; the Duke of Abercorn with 76,000 acres in the counties of Donegal and Tyrone; the Marquess of Hertford with 66,000 acres in south Antrim bringing in an annual rent of £58,000; the Marquess of Conyngham with 122,300 acres of mostly mountainous country in Co. Donegal with a rateable valuation of £15,166; and Lord O'Neill with 64,163 acres in mid-Antrim. These men were as rich as many German princes and even the typical Irish landlord was more prosperous than leading Prussian junkers. As a class, Irish proprietors had a collective income more than the public revenue of Ireland and more than the cost of maintaining the Royal Navy. Together they formed a mighty vested interest. However much tenants had increased their share of the country's agricultural income, they still felt deeply insecure, and on subsistence holdings to pay any rent at all was to pay too much. The Ulster Custom depended on the grace and favour of the landlord and there was nothing the law could do to restrain a proprietor from imposing swingeing rent increases or clearing his estate of unwanted tenants. No event in this period gave farmers a sharper reminder of the legal power of the landlord than the Derryveagh evictions of 1861.[46]

'THE POLICE OFFICERS THEMSELVES COULD NOT REFRAIN FROM WEEPING': THE DERRYVEAGH EVICTIONS, 1861

On a wild mountain slope near Lough Veagh a man's body was found on Thursday 15 November 1860, the skull crushed by a heavy stone lying close by, still matted with hair and blood. The murder victim was James Murray, steward to John George Adair, the Queen's County landowner who had bought the north Donegal estates of Gartan, Glenveagh and Derryveagh in stages from 1857 onwards. There is no reason to doubt Adair when he wrote later that he made these purchases because he was 'enchanted by the surpassing beauty of the scenery'.[47] Adair, however, was a highly successful speculator who had borrowed profitably to buy encumbered estates and he expected a return from his Ulster property. Scottish sheep and shepherds were brought in clearly with the intention of supplanting the native peasantry – a cause of great alarm as some years before Lord George Hill had overriden customary grazing rights with his sheep on the neighbouring Gweedore estate.

From the outset Adair had been high-handed: he impounded straying animals, raising £368 in fines for their release over two years; he quarrelled with almost everyone, including another landlord and the police, and was prosecuted for assault; he had four tenants arrested without a warrant, who had to petition the lord lieutenant for their release; and he evicted two tenants without paying them the full value of their tenant right. Adair's shepherds were violent and disreputable: they claimed compensation for the malicious slaughter of their sheep, but the police found sixty-five dead 'from *exposure, want* and *neglect* on the part of the shepherds', and sixteen sheep skins drying in Murray's house; and not long after Murray's murder shepherd Dugald Rankin shot a constable through the hand in a Strabane public house and another, Adam Grierson, was imprisoned for assault.[48]

Only a month after buying Derryveagh in December 1859 Adair had served notices to quit on his tenantry. Now he was convinced that local people were responsible for Murray's murder, though after a thorough inquiry the police could produce no evidence that this was the case. Adair determined to evict all his Derryveagh tenants and nothing in law could prevent him from doing so. Arguing that he and his men were endangered by a Ribbon conspiracy, Adair persuaded a reluctant Dublin Castle to send up a large force of police. It was in vain that the Reverend Henry Maturin, the rector of Gartan, joined with the local parish priest, the Reverend Daniel Kair, to appeal for mercy in an open letter to Adair, begging him to 'reconsider his resolution and not to visit so many of God's creatures with dire destruction'.[49]

On Monday 8 April 1861 Sub-Sheriff Samuel Crookshank, accompanied by two hundred police commanded by Sub-Inspector William Henry and a party of Adair's men shouldering crowbars, left Letterkenny barracks and moved up into the high country at Lough Barra by the foot of Slieve Snaght. Then, as the *Londonderry Standard* reported, 'the terrible reality of the law suddenly burst with surprise on the spectators', and it continued:

> The police were halted, and the sheriff, with a small escort, proceeded to the house of a widow woman, named McAward, aged 60 years, living with whom were six daughters and a son ... Forced to discharge an unpleasant duty, the sheriff entered the house and delivered up possession to Mr Adair's steward, whereupon six men, who had been brought from a distance, immediately fell to level the house to the ground. The scene then became indescribable. The bereaved widow and her daughters were frantic with despair. Throwing themselves on the ground they became almost insensible, and bursting out in the old Irish wail – then heard by many for the first time – their terrifying cries resounded along the mountain side for many miles ... with bleak poverty before them, and only the blue sky to shelter them, they naturally lost all hope, and those who witnessed their agony will never forget the sight. No one could

stand by unmoved. Every heart was touched, and tears of sympathy flowed from many . . . the sobs of helpless children took hold of every heart.[50]

Moving from house to house across country down to the shores of Lough Gartan, the sub-sheriff and Adair's men took three days to evict 244 people from 46 households and to unroof or level 28 homes over an area of 11,602 acres. The constabulary was not called upon, for there was no resistance of any kind, and it was observed, 'the police officers themselves could not refrain from weeping'. The stunned tenantry refused at first to make their way to the Letterkenny workhouse, as the *Londonderry Standard* reported:

> As night set in the scene became fearfully sad. Passing along the base of the mountain the spectator might have observed near to each house its former inmates crouching round a turf fire, convenient to a hedge, and as a drizzling rain poured upon them they found no cover . . . There these poor starving people remain on the cold bleak mountains, no one caring for them whether they live or die. 'Tis horrible to think of, but more horrible to behold.[51]

A few days later the Poor Law inspector, Robert Hamilton, arrived at Derryveagh to find that the elderly relieving officer at Letterkenny had made no arrangements to take the evicted families to the workhouse. He was appalled. He had 'seen nothing like it since the Evictions in Mayo in 1847'. A week later, on 27 April, he pencilled a confidential report to Dublin listing all those evicted, with these annotations:

> Widow Ward – 4 family – house down – This woman is described as being in very miserable circumstances . . .
>
> Owen Ward – 6 family – house down – A very touching story was told by the Constable respecting his case on the day of eviction, after being repeatedly warned by the Sheriff to leave the premises – the old man in doing so Kissed the walls of his house – and each member of his family did the same . . .
>
> William Ward – 3 family – house down – Still remains in the neighbourhood at the ruins of his former dwelling. Appears to be a very bad case . . .

Hamilton arranged for most of the evicted to be admitted to the workhouse. One man died there soon after 'and I am sorry to say another man who was represented as having been a very respectable farmer has become melancholy mad'.[52]

In the months that followed the Derryveagh evictions became international news and were debated three times at Westminster, William Scully, MP for Cork, reading out the newspaper accounts when the Irish chief secretary said that he had no official report on the affair. A fund was opened and one contribution of £80 arrived from as far away as

Marseille. Michael O'Grady founded the Australian Donegal Relief Committee in Melbourne to bring out many of the evicted families to make a new life in the southern hemisphere. After prostrating themselves on their family graves, they left to the sound of keening from their neighbours to take the train from Letterkenny to Dublin. There, at a farewell dinner in Fleming's Hotel in Mary's Abbey, the Reverend James McFadden, curate of Falcarragh, addressed them in Irish; this, in translation, is how he concluded:

> Friends have reached out their hands to you; these friends await you on the shore of that better land . . . And boys, don't forget poor Old Ireland (intense emotion, and cries of 'Never – never God knows') – don't forget the old people at home, boys. Sure they will be counting the days till a letter comes from you.[53]

And who murdered James Murray? On 30 May 1861 Theobald Dillon RM wrote to Undersecretary Sir Thomas Larcom expressing his belief that Murray's wife 'and Dugald Rankin conspired to get Murray murdered, and I believe the actual murderer was Archibald Campbell . . . her husband was not three days buried when she had Rankin sleeping in the same room with her'. W.E. Vaughan, in *Sin, Sheep and Scotsmen*, concludes that the evictions could 'plausibly be used to demonstrate the evil consequences of illicit love in a cold, wet climate'.[54] Adair completed Glenveagh Castle in 1870 and died peacefully in St Louis, Missouri, in 1885. His widow imported Scottish red deer and made Glenveagh Ireland's most celebrated hunting lodge; she entertained the Duke of Connaught and his party there in 1902. In 1937 a United States citizen, Henry McIlhenny, bought the estate. The grandson of a tenant farmer from Milford who had made his fortune by inventing the gas meter in Columbus, Georgia, he made a gift of Glenveagh to the Irish people and it is now a national park.

The Derryveagh evictions showed that, in spite of a general rise in living standards, there could still be suffering and oppression in the Ulster countryside. Meanwhile, on the other side of the province, Belfast was experiencing another spectacular surge of expansion but here, too, economic success did not eliminate misery and acute deprivation.

WALKS AMONG THE POOR OF BELFAST

The Reverend W.M. O'Hanlon, who had come from Lancashire to be minister of the Congregationalist Church in Upper Donegall Street, wrote a series of letters to the *Northern Whig* in 1852 calling 'the earnest attention of the more affluent, respectable, and especially the Christian public of Belfast, to the deplorable condition of the poor who inhabit the back-streets, courts, and alleys, of our rapidly extending and populous town'. The sight of seven people living in one room in Brady's Row in the dock area he found 'revolting, disgusting, and heart-rending . . . It haunts one like a loathsome and odious spectacle, from which the eye and the thoughts cannot escape.' In his next letter, dated 15 September 1852, O'Hanlon began:

> Let me first direct your eyes to some of the purlieus of North Queen-street . . . plunging into the alleys and entries of this neighbourhood, what indescribable scenes of poverty, filth, and wretchedness everywhere meet the eye! Barrack-lane was surely built when it was imagined the world would soon prove too strait for the number of its inhabitants . . . no pure breath of heaven ever enters here; it is tainted and loaded by the most noisome, reeking feculance, as it struggles to reach these loathsome hovels.

Here he found that seven out of nine houses were 'abodes of guilt', where counterfeiters, thieves and prostitutes 'all herd together in this place as in a common hell, and sounds of blasphemy, shouts of mad debauch, and cries of quarrel and blood, are frequently heard here through the livelong night'. Moving south to Carrick Hill he observed in Drummond's-court as many as three families living in each of its tiny four-roomed houses; in Round-entry 'the most loathsome corruptions' were being harboured; in Peel's-court 'the air is such that we could not stand a moment without a sense of deadly sickness and loathing warning us to flee the foul spot'; and he could give no description of Stewart's-court 'because of the effluvium which met us on the very threshold'. Pepperhill-court was characterised by

> whiskey-drinking and lewd singing . . . and the lazy and laden atmosphere is duly stirred at times by the frantic shouts of low bacchanalian orgies . . . the fever-car had just departed on our arrival, bearing away to the hospital some wretched victim of miasma and foulness.

As he crossed the Blackstaff river, 'I felt as though actually pursued by grim Pestilence and Death'. 'After returning from some of these explorations,' O'Hanlon reflected, 'and seating myself alone, I have really felt as though all were only an ugly dream – as if I had really been the victim of nightmare . . . my soul has been sickened and oppressed, beyond the power of words to tell, by what I have seen.'[55]

O'Hanlon believed that strong drink was the principal scourge of the poor, but unlike many of his contemporaries, he did not blame alcohol for all the social ills of his day. He quoted Thomas Drummond's celebrated words that 'property has its duties as well as its rights', and condemning the slum landlords, he observed that 'the principle seems to be lost sight of in such squalid nooks'. Such forthright views possibly explain why the Irish Evangelical Society withdrew its grant to him. The Reverend A. McIntyre blamed low wages for much of the wretchedness he found. In his diary for 8 December 1853 he records a visit to a family living at number twelve Little Donegall Street; there a widow and her daughter embroidered cloth as piecework and her little boy cut stone. Margaret Lyons, the widow, he described as

> an old skeleton, having the appearance of one lately risen from the grave, seated on a stone and surrounded by slates, pieces of old mortar, the floor flooded with water and no fire . . . The entire top of the house had fallen in . . . She complained that she had got her death from the rain and frost that came down upon her in bed. I asked her why she did not go to the Workhouse. She said she did not like to be separated from her children.[56]

In a paper read before the British Association in September 1852, Dr Andrew Malcolm gave statistical proof of the close connection between filth and fever. In the 1847 epidemic 70 per cent of houses 'deficient in sewerage' had fever, but only 19 per cent of houses in the better-drained districts suffered; and Drummond's-court, with only 41 houses, had 113 fever cases between 1837 and 1847. Recent research by Peter Froggatt, the medical historian, shows that Belfast had the worst death rate in Ireland, over twice that for the island as a whole, and possibly the worst in the United Kingdom.[57] Malcolm calculated that in 1852 – a year without famine or cholera epidemics – the average age of death in Belfast was nine years, because the 'infant mortality is absolutely excessive'. Yet he was not wrong to point out that the 'main streets, for width and regularity of outline, are proverbially a model' and that 'where nought but vice, death, and poverty, held their fearful orgies, has risen, as if by enchantment, a splendid array of marts and emporia of trade and commerce'.[58]

Driven from the countryside by hunger, eviction and the collapse of the domestic linen industry, the destitute poured into Belfast. Many continued on across the sea to settle in the British mainland, and some pressed on further to America. Those who remained in Belfast often had neither the strength nor the resources to go further. Besides, more than any other town in Ireland, Belfast offered plentiful opportunities for employment and the population doubled in twenty years: in 1851 it was 87,062; in 1861, 121,602; and in 1871, 174,412. The principal cause of this hectic urban growth was the massive expansion of the factory-based linen industry, an industry presented unexpectedly with unique opportunities by events across the Atlantic.

'You will see by the papers that we have rather exciting times here now', Andrew Greenlees wrote to his brother from the state of Illinois in March 1856. He continued:

Slavery and freedom seem ready for a fight . . . A civil war would not be anything unnatural to look for, and if it be the means by which slavery is to be done away with, the sooner it comes the better.[59]

Five years later his predictions were proved correct and Greenlees kept his Ulster relations informed. In September 1863 when the tide had turned against the Confederacy he wrote that 'the father of waters, the Mississippi, is again open. The gordion knot at Vicksburg has been untied, or rather cut, by the gallant Grant.'[60] Union commander Grant was one of around a score of generals and senior officers of Ulster Presbyterian origin prominent in the American Civil War, including Confederates 'Jeb' Stuart and 'Stonewall' Jackson. John Mitchel, having escaped from Australia in 1853, made his way to America where he espoused the Southern cause.

The Union fleet imposed an effective blockade on cotton exports from the Confederate States across the Atlantic and then in 1864 – as the Prussians invaded Denmark and sectarian riots raged in Belfast – Union troops advanced south, devastating the cotton plantations. Starved of their raw material, the Lancashire cotton mills fell silent. Linen was the nearest substitute for cotton and thus Ulster faced the challenge of making up the shortfall in the British market.

Had the war broken out just a few years earlier the challenge could not have been met. Power looms for linen were being developed in the north of England and 3,600 were in operation there in 1850, when all Ireland could only muster 58. As William Charley observed in *Flax and Its Products in Ireland*, published in 1862: 'So long as a man's labour could be had at the handloom in Ireland for a shilling a day, it was felt no power loom could work much, if at all cheaper.' English power looms at first could only weave the coarsest cloth but in time specialist firms in Preston, Blackburn and Bury mastered the problems caused by linen yarn's lack of elasticity and by 1857, 1,691 power looms were in operation in Ireland.[61]

Gloomy forecasts accompanied reports of war in the Belfast newspapers, for the United States had been taking more than 40 per cent of Irish linen exports. A financial collapse in America in 1857 had very quickly been followed by most mills in the Belfast region putting their workers on short time. Recovery thereafter had been slow, though spirits were raised by the lowering of French tariffs in the Cobden–Chevalier Treaty of 1860, in which John Mulholland, proprietor of the York Street mill, played a leading part. At first the pessimistic predictions seemed verified, for in 1861 the United States took only 18 per cent of Ireland's linen exports. At the same time, however, the price of cotton was rocketing from around 9d. an ounce in 1861 to £1 4s.0¹/₂d. in 1863. A boom followed in the Ulster linen industry quite without equal in the nineteenth century. In June 1865 the *Northern Whig* reported:

> New mills and factories are springing up on all sides, while as fast as they can be got started, orders flow in and such a thing as manufacturing for stock is almost unknown.[62]

The linen boom continued beyond the Union victory in 1865, the United Kingdom exporting 255 million yards the following year, most of it from Ulster. In 1867 the province's mills and factories reached a remarkable capacity of nine hundred thousand spindles and over twelve thousand power looms. In that year, however, the carpetbaggers restored the ruined cotton plantations and cheap cotton wool reappeared on the world markets. This led to 'a cataclysmic reversal of fortune', the *Linen Trade Circular* reported, and continued: 'The sinews of industry had become paralysed, as the partially silent spindle and noiseless loom only too clearly testify.' By 1868 sixty thousand spindles and four thousand power looms were idle.[63] Partial recovery followed in 1870 but hopes that linen would permanently supplant cotton were completely dashed. Nevertheless, Ulster was now firmly established as the greatest centre of linen production in the world.

Contrasting with the tall spinning mills, the new single-storey weaving factories covered extensive ground. The vibration caused by a heavy shuttle thundering across each power loom 160 times a minute made it unsafe to place such machinery on upper storeys. Their characteristic saw-edged roofs were designed to catch the north light, considered best for the close inspection of cloth.

From the outset most weaving factories were powered by steam; thus a great many clustered in Belfast with easy access to cross-channel coal landing at the docks. Some great firms prospered in a rural setting, provided coal could be brought in by rail. Clark's of Upperlands, for example, had the Northern Counties Railway Company build a siding right up to the bleach green after it had been found that a stationmaster had defrauded the linen firm of some £3,000. Outside of Belfast the towns of Coleraine, Ballymena, Lisburn, Lurgan, Portadown and Newry all benefited from the presence of large mills and factories served by rail. Some towns and villages such as Bessbrook, Gilford, Sion Mills, Drumaness, Hilden and Shrigley virtually owed their existence to the linen industry: and others, including Castlewellan, Killyleagh and Comber, were heavily dependent on one or two linen firms in the locality. The firm of Dunbar, McMaster and Company had largely built Gilford in Co. Down before the Famine; in 1870 it gave work to 2,000, owned 180 houses and the co-operative shop in High Street, ran the fire-fighting service and had its own fever hospital, lithographic works and gas supply. In addition, the company had built three schools and several reading rooms, and had paid most of the cost of erecting a church each for the Presbyterians, Anglicans and Catholics. Rents for houses were 2s.6d., 2s.0d., or 1s.6d. a week, depending on size, and the firm provided allotments regularly manured with the contents of dry privies and the rakings of pig sties. New arrivals were given coal and a week's supply of groceries on credit, though this encouraged the occasional midnight flit. At the end of the century all but eight of the eighty-seven male heads of households in Hill Street, High Street and Ann Street were employed by the firm. Sport was encouraged by the mill owners and Bessbrook became noted for its international football and rugby players, and Donaghcloney and Sion Mills for cricket. Bessbrook, in particular, was regarded as an ideal community by several British industrialists and served as a model for Bourneville and Port Sunlight. Even in the best-regulated mills and factories, however, the manufacture of linen posed a constant threat to the health of workers.[64]

'THE DEATH RATE FROM CHEST AFFECTIONS IS VERY HIGH . . .'

Writing an account of the influence of flax-spinning on the health of mill workers in 1867, Dr John Moore concluded that 'the employment will be found, if not one of the most lucrative, at least one of the most healthy in the whole range of our manufactures'. Nevertheless, he was concerned about the spinning rooms where 'little girls are engaged, and here it is that the tender form of childhood is often in danger of being taxed beyond what it is able to bear'.[65] Ten years later damning reports by Dr C.D. Purdon, certifying surgeon of the Belfast factory district, exposed the complacency of Moore's conclusion and, in particular, drew attention to the damaging effect of flax dust on the lungs of mill workers.

On first arriving at the spinning mill, scutched flax had to be hackled, a process by which men cleaned and squared up handfuls of fibre by drawing them through boards fitted with iron pins. Hacklers, as part of the workforce élite, were comparatively well paid but their work was carried out in an atmosphere loaded with particles of flax, known as pouce, and Dr Purdon found that their 'mortality from Phthisis, etc., is very high . . . this affection of the lungs, that flax dressers suffer so much from, is so well known to the army surgeons that they have forbidden the recruiting sergeants to enlist any from this department'. Next the flax was sent to the machine room for combing to separate the 'tow', or short fibre, from the 'line', the best long fibre. The pouce here was so dense that it quickly entered the lungs of the machine boys. 'In severe and well marked attacks', Dr Purdon wrote, 'the paroxysm of cough and dyspnoea lasts for a considerable time, and does not pass off until the contents of the stomach are ejected, and often blood is spat up'. He continued:

> In a great number of instances the lad is obliged to leave the mill, and seek for employment in healthier trades. But still in cold weather he suffers from cough and shortness of breath, and in many cases his life is termi- nated by Phthisis . . . numbers linger out a diseased existence, in other callings, only to terminate in death.

The sorters then arranged the different qualities of flax; by the time they reached 'about thirty years of age their appearance begins to alter, the face gets an anxious look, shoulders begin to get rounded – in fact, they become prematurely aged, and the greatest number die before 45 years'. The next process was 'preparing' and 'carding', which Dr Moore looked on as 'the dustiest, most disagreeable, as well as the most unwholesome and most dangerous of all the departments'. The girls who worked there, Dr Purdon wrote, 'suffer in the same manner as the males, but in a far more aggravated degree . . . in this department the death rate from chest affections is very high'.[66]

After preparing, the flax passed through a frame in the 'roving room', where it was twisted on to bobbins and taken to the spinning room. The young girls here were known as doffers, because they saw to it that full bobbins of spun yarn were doffed from each spinning frame and re- placed with empty bobbins to be filled; they were supervised by an adult who decided the moment to doff a particular frame. If necessary the flyers were oiled, and then the doffers sped to the next frame, 'singing all the time', ready to doff in response to the whistle of their doffing mistress.

According to Dr Purdon, spinners suffered not from pouce 'but from the moisture and heat of the rooms, which often causes them to faint, and accidents have occurred by their falling on the machinery . . . The temperature is sometimes excessive.' He continued:

A good deal of disease is generated by their garments being wetted by the spray from the spindles . . . the Doffer, in departing from the country mill with her clothes wet from the spray, and having to go a greater distance before she arrives at home, her clothes become quite cold, and Bronchial affections being constantly produced, causes greater mortality.

New recruits to the spinning room often suffered from 'mill fever', apparently brought on by the odour of oil and flax, the symptoms being 'rigors, nausea, vomiting, quickly followed by pain in the head, thirst, heat of skin, etc.'[67]

The yellow belly doffers,
Dirty wipers down,
The nasty, stinking spinning room,
The stink will knock you down.

'There is also a form of papular eruption to which the spinners are liable upon the face and arms', Dr Moore wrote, in addition to 'the deformity of the foot – a species of talapsis', and 'onychia' caused by contaminated water washing round barefoot doffers, which 'requires for its remedy a most painful operation, either the dissecting out or wrenching out the entire roots of the great toe-nail'.

The spun yarn was prepared for the weavers by the 'reelers' and 'winders' taking if off the bobbins and forming it into hanks. 'From the peculiar exertion necessary to keep the reels in motion,' Dr Moore concluded, 'I believe that hernia will be found to exist in this class to a considerable extent.'[68] Before being woven, the yarn had to be dressed with a mixture of carrageen moss, flour and tallow. 'The room in which the Dressing is carried on', Dr Purdon reported, 'requires to be kept at a very high temperature, varying from 90 to 120, or 125°.' Only men over eighteen were employed there and 'as it is considered that their lives were shortened by several years they are paid very high wages'.[69]

In the 1890s McCrum, Mercer and Company of Milford, Co. Armagh, estimated that it took between two and three months to train a power-loom weaver and cost the firm not less than £25 in wages and defective cloth. Under the supervision of a 'tenter', the weaver learned to change a shuttle, how to draw in broken ends of warp, and how to tie a weaver's knot. Particularly where fine yarn was woven, the temperature and humidity were kept very high by steam and hundreds of gas jets. In consequence, Dr Purdon noted, the weavers 'suffer greatly from chest affections', explaining:

This is caused not only by inhaling the damp air . . . but also from young persons under 18 years of age being employed at either one heavy or two looms. The constant stooping over these, combined with the other causes, renders the death rate very high.[70]

No mention was made of the damaging effect of deafening noise caused by whirling power belts, clashing Jacquard cards, flying shuttles and banging sleys, nor of the danger of passing on tuberculosis by 'kissing the shuttle' to suck out the end of the yarn.[71]

Few attempts were made to reduce these dangers to health until the twentieth century. Powered fans were not made compulsory until 1906; 'kissing the shuttle' was not stopped by law until 1958; an alternative dressing yarn not needing a high temperature, devised by Professor Hodges, does not seem to have been widely adopted; and the Baker Respirator, a mask for filtering out pouce, was not generally issued.

Linen workers also ran the risk of being maimed or killed by exposed machinery. Certainly the *Belfast News-Letter*, in its issue of 1 May 1854, did not expect an employee of Messrs Rowan of York Street to recover: 'She was engaged at the carding part of the machinery and her hair by some means got entangled in the machinery in which the greater part of the scalp was removed from the head.' In the same year a thirteen-year-old boy was injured when a belt on a revolving drum broke at Sion Mills. Herdman's appealed successfully against a fine of £10 and the *Belfast News-Letter* observed:

> It is but a false, mawkish and mongrel humanity which cares not though trade should go to the dogs lest an impudent little larking scamp . . . should fail to get his cut fingers salved with a ten pound note.[72]

In March 1855 Ulster linen manufacturers joined the National Association of Factory Occupiers (Charles Dickens called it the 'Association for the Mangling of Operatives'), which opposed legislation to fence off dangerous machines. An act in 1856 to make owners place guards on their machinery was largely evaded and further legislation was required in 1876. Even so, at the end of the century inspectors complained that it was difficult to obtain convictions for breaches of the regulations. In any case, a likely cause of accidents was exhaustion from long hours of work. Employers got round the 1847 Factory Act, limiting hours of work for women and children to ten a day, by introducing a relay system. It was not until 1874 that hours were successfully cut down to ten every weekday and six on Saturdays and, even then, employers added an extra duty of cleaning machines after hours. Until 1874 the usual working day began at 5 a.m. and ended at 7 or 8 p.m. Thereafter, until the beginning of the twentieth century, the working day began at 6.30 a.m. and finished at 6 p.m., with two three-quarter-hour breaks. The minimum age for starting at the spinning mill or weaving factory was eight years until 1874, when it was raised to ten years, eleven years in 1891 and twelve years in 1901. These juveniles or 'half-timers' attended school either in the mornings or afternoons, or on alternate days.

'Our country is not in a position to bear this legislation. It will ruin our trade, and perhaps leave Belfast a forest of smokeless chimneys': this was the *Belfast News-Letter*'s comment on the 1874 act and five years later the linen merchant Robert Lloyd-Patterson said in a speech to the Belfast Chamber of Commerce that any 'more of this paternal legislation will have the tendency to legislate the trade out of the country'.[73] In a report of 31 October 1875, the Factory Inspectorate concluded that the introduction of the Saturday half-holiday 'in place of being a boon is a curse', because it encouraged drunkenness, which was also promoted by 'the high rate of wages and shorter hours of work, which enables the worker to spend more money and time in the public house'.[74] In fact only skilled men and overseers could earn enough to support a family of four at 'a minimum comfort level' and wages in the linen industry were consistently lower than in other textile factories in the United Kingdom. A Board of Trade inquiry listed average earnings of linen operatives working full time in the last pay week of September 1906: men £1 2s.4d., lads 7s.8d., women 10s.9d., and girls 6s.7d. Adelaide Anderson, one of the first female factory inspectors, added that the wages 'of an immense number of women . . . did not rise above 7 or 8s out of which came deductions for disciplinary fines, charges for damage or purchase of damaged articles, so that for many young women 5–6s per week was nearer the mark'.[75] W. Liddell and Company produced a conditions of service document in 1890 for workers in its Donaghcloney power-loom factory. The longest section – taking up sixty-six lines – was on fines, including:

Fines: Class 1: Being absent from work without leave for more than 2 hours; . . . using improper language to anyone; . . . refusing to obey the orders of the employers or overseer; smoking tobacco . . . For each such act one shilling.

. . . neglecting to keep the machinery under the worker's charge clean and properly oiled; allowing pirns, bobbins, yarn or waste to lie about the floor; . . . widening gas burners or neglecting to shut off the gas – For each such act sixpence.[76]

Mill workers and factory operatives were subjected to a great deal of patronising advice, much of which could not be applied without an increase in wages. Even Dr Robert Newett, the humane and conscientious medical officer at Ligoniel near Belfast, concluded an address to employees in June 1875 with these words:

As opportunity offers, read good and profitable books: banish from your houses the villainous trash issued in cheaper numbers which sets forth as heroes, the highwaymen, and other vile characters of a past age. Be sure such reading will deprave the moral perceptions of your young people.[77]

A linen mill required up to four times as many operatives as a cotton mill with the same number of spindles. It was therefore the united opinion of employers that wages must be kept down, especially as mills in Russia, Austria-Hungary, Belgium and France were becoming more competitive partly owing to even cheaper labour costs. In all European states, however, linen-spinning retreated to some degree before cotton, which was cheaper and could be finished in a greater variety of ways. The spinning capacity of Irish mills fell from 925,000 to 828,000 spindles between 1875 and 1900. Several firms went to the wall in the 1890s, including the Belfast Flax Spinning Company, which owed more than £20,000 to the Ulster Bank. Meanwhile, foreign yarn imported into Belfast rose from one hundred tons in 1880 to six thousand tons in 1895 to be woven up in the steadily expanding power-loom factories. This more than offset the fall in employment in the mills, and the numbers engaged in the Irish linen industry – almost exclusively based in Ulster – climbed from fifty-six thousand in 1875 to sixty-nine thousand in 1896.[78]

Characterised as they were by low rates of pay, the linen mills and factories could not alone have given Belfast the prosperity it enjoyed in the late nineteenth century. For this the higher wages of the engineering industry were vital, in particular those earned in the spectacularly successful shipyard on Queen's Island.

HARLAND AND WOLFF: IRON SHIPBUILDING IN BELFAST

On 22 October 1851 the *Belfast News-Letter* reported that 'the attentive observer of the manufacturing progress of our town must have been struck with the gradual growth of a huge establishment in Eliza Street'. This great ironworks, which included 'four steam engines and boilers, puddled iron mill and squeezer, plate and angle iron mills, a tilt hammer, roll turning lathes . . . and many tools', had been set up just north of the Lagan at Cromac at the cost of £25,000 by two Liverpool businessmen, Robert Pace and Thomas Gladstone.[79] Hopes that coal would be found on the Downshire estate were not realised, and the enterprise soon found it difficult to compete with English and Scottish ironmasters with ample supplies of fuel close at hand. The Harbour Commissioners eagerly accepted a proposal to transfer the operation to Queen's Island with the purpose of building iron ships, though by the time the commissioners had completed a yard there, Pace and Gladstone had leased their debt-laden concern to a Liverpool engineer, Robert Hickson. Recognising his lack of experience, Hickson engaged a manager for the shipyard, Edward J. Harland. This appointment was of momentous importance for the industrial future of Ulster.

Harland had learned his trade with George Stephenson and Son on the Tyne and then, as a journeyman employed by J. and G. Thomson at Govan on the upper Clyde, had helped to design and build eleven iron steamers. On arriving in Belfast, the new twenty-three-year-old manager at once showed the ruthless determination he was to display all his life: he cut wages, banned smoking, and brought in shipwrights from the Clyde when the men went on strike. On 1 October 1855 Harland successfully completed the *Khersonese*, and in 1856 launched the 1,387-ton *Circassian*, the largest ship ever to have been built in Ireland. He soon planned to set up on his own and in 1857 applied to Liverpool City Council for ground at Garstang to build a shipyard there, but he was turned down because of his 'youth and inexperience'. Further applications at Birkenhead and elsewhere on the Mersey were also rejected. It cannot be doubted that the history of the north of Ireland would have been very different if Harland had been accepted. The Ulster Bank had already foreclosed on the ironworks and in September 1858 Hickson offered Harland the Queen's Island yard for £5,000.[80]

Harland was able to accept Hickson's offer only because he had the full financial backing of Gustav C. Schwabe, a partner in John Bibby and Sons of Liverpool who had been deeply impressed by the young man's engineering prowess. Schwabe's nephew, Gustav Wolff, had already joined Harland as personal assistant in 1857. The Bibby line immediately placed orders for three 1,500-ton barque-rigged steamers, the *Venetian* and *Sicilian* completed in 1859, and the *Syrian* in 1860, all fitted with engines supplied by MacNab of Greenock and screws which could be raised when the ships could catch a following wind. A high proportion of ocean-going vessels built by Harland and Wolff, as the company was named from 1861, were to orders from the Bibby line. Disparagingly called 'Bibby Coffins', these craft caused a sensation in the shipping world because of their revolutionary design 'of increased length, without any increase in the beam'. As Harland explained: 'The hull of the ship was converted into a box girder of immensely increased strength.'[81] The characteristic square bilge and flat underside of the hull soon became known in the trade as the 'Belfast bottom'. Business was brisk during the American Civil War when the Confederate States were eager to buy fast steamers capable of running the Union blockade. The Harbour Commissioners greatly improved facilities on Queen's Island during this time by building the Hamilton graving dock and the Abercorn basin, nearing completion as the *Istrian, Iberian* and *Illyrian* – the finest of this Bibby series – were being launched in 1867.[82]

The shipyard on Queen's Island was now of international importance and its success was the outcome of international expertise and enterprise. Harland combined a head for business with imaginative and innovative engineering genius; Wolff brought to Belfast the financial and technical prowess he had acquired in Hamburg and Liverpool; and Schwabe supplied the venture capital and market, obtaining in turn ships from his nephew's firm that exactly met his specifications. Local design talent was added by Walter and Alexander Wilson, brothers brought in as 'gentlemen apprentices' in 1857, and William J. Pirrie, grandson of the celebrated Harbour Board chairman, who became not only an accomplished draughtsman but also a flamboyant and persuasive salesman.

Belfast appeared to have few of the assets needed to become a great shipbuilding centre, and credit must first be given to the Harbour Commissioners for making the most of what advantages it did have. Only after the excavation of the Victoria Channel and the creation of ample space at Queen's Island could shipbuilders make full use of the shelter and depth of water available in the lough. The commissioners concentrated the trading docks on the Co. Antrim side of the Lagan, leaving the Co. Down side free for shipbuilding and laying out small yards in anticipation. Just across the sea, Scotland and the north-west of England supplied inexpensive coal and iron; the Clyde provided indispensable specialist engine-making and metal-working; and Liverpool beckoned as the gateway of the fast-growing empire.

A severe slump followed the ending of the American Civil War and several vessels were built at a loss, including a shortfall of £5,000 on the gun boat HMS *Lynx*, Harland and Wolff's first Admiralty order, launched in 1868. Nevertheless, the population time bomb, which it could be argued had first exploded in Ireland and Britain in the eighteenth century, continued to send its shock waves eastwards, now reaching the Russian Empire and the Balkans. Tens of thousands sought a better life in America – not to speak of the added impulse given by the suppression of Poland in 1863, Bismarck's wars, Bulgarian horrors and tsarist pogroms – thus creating a market of unprecedented size in the transport of emigrants across the ocean.

BELFAST AND THE WHITE STAR LINE

During an after-dinner game of billiards in Broughton Hall, Schwabe's Liverpool home, a proposal was made to create a new shipping line capable of competing with the well-established Cunard and Inman lines on the profitable North Atlantic run. Present was Thomas Ismay who had just bought the White Star line, bankrupted in an over-eager attempt to cash in on the passenger traffic created by the Australian gold rush. On 6 September 1869 the Oceanic Steam Navigation Company, still known as the White Star line, was duly registered.[83] Only those lines which ensured speed, safety, low fares for emigrants, and luxury for the rich could survive the intense competition for transatlantic passengers. It was a time of rapid technological advance in shipbuilding, and Harland and Wolff, vital to White Star's plans, was in the van.

To meet an immediate order for five 420-foot vessels at over £110,000 each, with the novel feature of financial penalty for late delivery, Harland and Wolff had to re-equip the yard completely at a cost of £30,000, building four new berths and a special steamship, *Camel*, to carry heavy machinery and plating from Britain to Belfast. The Harbour Commissioners helped by erecting a pair of 50-ton masting shears on the east side of the Abercorn quay for lifting in masts and engines. The *Oceanic*, the first White Star ship launched at Queen's Island, can be regarded as the first modern liner. For the first time accommodation was extended to the full width of the vessel and first-class passengers were placed amidships away from the vibration and roll experienced aft. The *Oceanic* made her maiden voyage to New York in March 1871 and her three sisters – *Atlantic, Baltic,* and *Republic* – were all in service the following year. The slightly larger *Adriatic* left the slips in 1872; 3,868 tons gross, she was the first ship to be lit by gas generated on board. Powered by vertical overhead compound engines ordered from firms in London and Liverpool, these vessels with their record-breaking speeds and elegant design made all other North Atlantic liners obsolete. Even Cunard commissioned Harland and Wolff to lengthen four of their steamers.[84]

Cunard and Inman lost no time in replying to the White Star challenge and this in turn led the White Star to order two larger ships from Harland and Wolff, the *Britannic* and *Germanic*, launched in 1874. These slim vessels, each 5,000 tons and 455 feet long, cut the Atlantic crossing by a day. The *Germanic* won back the Blue Riband from the Inman line by reaching America in seven and a half days. The White Star line won international fame for Harland and Wolff, but, equally, it was Harland and Wolff which made the White Star line.

In 1874 the partnership was reconstructed to include William J. Pirrie as chief draughtsman, Walter Wilson as yard manager, and Alexander Wilson in charge of engine design and installation. Edward Harland was beginning to involve himself in public affairs and Gustav Wolff became an active partner in the Belfast Ropework Company, formed in 1872 by W.H. Smiles – eldest son of Samuel Smiles, the celebrated prophet of Victorian enterprise culture – and a consortium of local businessmen. Wolff ensured large orders for the new concern, strategically placed adjacent to Queen's Island in east Belfast. Shipowners in turn appreciated the convenient supply of competitively priced, high-quality ropes, particularly those made from Manila hemp bathed in oil. Also producing binder twine, window-blind cord, trawl nets and fishing lines, the ropeworks grew until they became the biggest in the world. Harland became mayor of Belfast in 1885 and 1886, and Conservative MP for North Belfast between 1887 and his death in 1895. Wolff sat as Conservative MP for East Belfast between 1892 and 1910. 'I had no idea when I came to Belfast in 1858 I would be a permanent citizen,' he said on being made an honorary burgess in 1911, adding, 'I have no regrets I stayed.'[85]

William J. Pirrie presided over Harland and Wolff during its greatest years. Ebullient and daring, he set out with dazzling skill and energy to win new orders for the firm at a time of acute depression in the industry. 'What is the matter?' a friend asked a shipowner one day in the Liverpool Exchange; 'Pirrie,' he replied, 'has just persuaded me to order a ship and I don't know what the deuce I'll do with it.'[86] Some business could only be won by offering credit; the African Steamship Company, for example, was loaned £30,000 to finance a ship under construction. Walter Wilson, who preferred to avoid the public gaze, concentrated on the technical innovation that was vital for survival.

Previously too brittle, steel was now superseding iron, making hulls lighter and stronger; and the development of high-pressure, triple-expansion steam engines increased ship space for passengers and crew by reducing the hold space for coal. A major reorganisation of the company was essential. More land was acquired from the Harbour Commissioners to increase the extent of the yard to forty acres; open-hearth steel-making plant and new bending equipment had to be bought; and the firm constructed its own engine works in 1880. Harland and Wolff was therefore ready to take advantage of the shipping boom which began in 1882 and, thanks to Pirrie's persuasive salesmanship as well as the firm's reputation for quality, business came from a much wider range of companies than before. White Star, nevertheless, continued as the most valued customer, particularly when orders came in for two great liners, the *Teutonic* and the *Majestic*. During their construction the Institute of Mechanical Engineers visited Belfast in 1888 and the journal *Engineering* provided the first detailed description of the yard:

The workshops are situated between the two ranges of slips . . . The machine tools . . . are necessarily of great size and power in order to deal with the big work and notably the extra long plates used in the construction of the two big vessels . . . The most notable features in this part of the works, however, are the very massive plate rolls.

The whole shipyard had a telephone system linking all departments and offices, and was fitted with electric light generated by twelve dynamos driven by a pair of horizontal engines. In the engine works there was 'a large horizontal slotting and planing machine by Smith, Beacock and Tannett, which will plane 21 feet and slot $15^1/_2$ feet' and in the engine works' smithy were 'three steam hammers by David and Primrose and twenty-two fires'.[87] This sober technical report in a national journal underlines the integration of Belfast in the mainstream of British industry.

With the launching of the *Teutonic* and the *Majestic* in 1889, Harland and Wolff ushered in a new era, and the two vessels were acclaimed immediately as the most advanced on the Atlantic run. The *Majestic* was the slightly larger of the two; just under 10,000 gross tons, she could accommodate 300 first-class, 175 second-class and 855 steerage passengers.[88] The *Teutonic* achieved the record maiden Atlantic passage time of 6 days, 17 hours and 25 minutes.

Harland and Wolff's success encouraged the growth of other shipbuilding firms in Belfast. MacIlwaine and Lewis, owners of the Ulster Iron Works, moved to the Abercorn basin in 1868 and established a reputation for high-quality ship construction on a small scale. A more serious rival was Workman Clark and Company, set up near the Milewater on the north side of the Lagan and employing 150 men. It began building in 1880 and quickly established a close working relationship with J.P. Corry and Company and the City line of Glasgow. Known familiarly as the 'wee yard', its growth was nevertheless impressive and by 1902 it had a workforce of seven thousand on a fifty-acre site. Harland and Wolff kept ahead, with seven thousand employees in 1890 rising to nine thousand by the end of the century – the most important single employer of male labour in Ulster.[89] Between the financial years 1890–1 and 1893–4 Harland and Wolff headed the list for the largest number of vessels built by any shipyard in the United Kingdom and output averaged one hundred thousand tons a year throughout the 1890s.

The shipyards' success demonstrated that Ulster was in the forefront of international economic advance, with an industry dependent on the outside world both for raw materials and sales. The very vessels launched from Queen's Island drew the north of Ireland into closer contact with ideas and movements overseas. Not all of these were concerned with material progress: the great campaign for Christian spiritual renewal launched in America in 1858 surged across the Atlantic and reached the shores of Ulster early in the following year. Here it struck a chord deep in the hearts of many Protestants who had remained faithful to the beliefs of their forefathers when so many of their co-religionists across the Irish Sea had long since abandoned theirs.

'THE MIGHTY WAVE OF MERCY SWELLED GLORIOUSLY HIGH': THE 1859 REVIVAL

'A revival is now passing over the churches of America such as has not been known since Apostolic times', the *Irish Presbyterian* reported on 1 June 1858,[90] and soon after, the General Assembly held a special session which agreed to send out a circular letter commending the new movement. Ulster Protestant immigrants played a leading role in the revival sweeping the eastern states of America, often setting aside sober Presbyterianism for the stronger emotional appeal of the Baptist Church. With tireless zeal, the Reverend S.J. Jones got the revival under way in mid-Antrim, holding as many as a hundred prayer meetings a week in Connor and Ballymena. From there the movement spread rapidly to neighbouring counties and as far south as Cavan and Monaghan over the winter of 1858–9. The Reverend David Adams of Ahoghill, Co. Antrim, remembered:

> In the end of April and the beginning of May the wind of the Spirit calmed, but about the middle of May it blew a heavenly hurricane, and the mighty wave of mercy swelled gloriously mountain high, sweeping across the dead sea of our rural population, and washing the rocky hearts of formal worshippers.[91]

Presbyterian, Methodist and Church of Ireland clergy combined to organise a series of prayer and praise meetings in Ballymena at the town hall, outside the linen hall and in Springwell Street. The reporter for the *Ballymena Observer* found the houses in Springwell Street 'besieged by a throng of *all* classes', explaining:

> These were the homes of the 'stricken' parties, some of whom were in a state of very great weakness, and partial stupor; some were dreadfully excited, calling upon God for mercy with an earnestness which no intelligent investigator could doubt.

The revival, the editor remarked, 'is advancing wave after wave, like some resistless tide upon the strand; each surging swell marking its onward progress to a predestined limit, but no human eye can see the boundary'.[92]

Thousands gathered on Fair Hill on Tuesday 7 June 1859 for the first great revival meeting in Coleraine. The impact was so dramatic that it merited reports in the *Glasgow Guardian*, and the *Coleraine Chronicle* observed that trade 'except in Bibles and Testaments, if not suspended, has been partially paralysed – those who conducted it having for the present given it up or become incapable of transacting it'. The newspaper was late that week because the compositors were for a time unable to work. At the Irish Society school one boy cried out in the classroom, 'O sir, I am so happy I have the Lord Jesus in my heart!' and the rest of the boys, hearing this,

> cast themselves upon their knees and began to cry for mercy. The girls' school was above, and the cry no sooner penetrated to their room, than, hearing in it a call to themselves they, too, fell upon their knees and wept.

Parents later joined their children and stayed praying with them until 11 p.m. – 'a more affecting or impressive sight could not be witnessed this side of the grave than witnessing these young children crying for mercy', the *Chronicle* concluded.[93] A ball planned by the town commissioners to mark the completion of the new town hall was abandoned in favour of a prayer meeting; at the petty sessions on 17 June not a single case of riot or drunkenness was brought and one public house sold nothing until 3 p.m.; and in a single house sixteen apprentices were 'saved'.

Meanwhile, meetings were being held at Portrush and every evening in Victoria Market in Derry, where the number of streetwalkers was reduced by conversion from fifty to twenty. In Belfast Dr Henry Cooke, the Earl of Roden and the Anglican bishop of Down and Connor presided over a United Prayer Meeting on Thursday 19 June and preparations were well in hand for the greatest meeting of all. On Sunday 29 June 1859 between thirty-five thousand and forty thousand crowded into the Botanic Gardens, a private park on the south side of Belfast. The Reverend John Johnston of Tullylish, moderator of the Presbyterian General Assembly, presided. Since not all could hear him, about twenty other meetings sprang up before people left the gardens at 3.30 p.m. to catch their special trains.

Some twenty thousand assembled again in the Botanic Gardens on 17 August, though it was harvest time, and other great meetings followed at Randalstown, Lurgan, Portadown and Armagh. An English writer reckoned that twenty thousand were present at Armagh on 16 September, and he observed:

> What struck me most of all was, not the case of those who were prostrated and forced to cry for mercy, but the case of those who were manifestly

struggling to conceal their convictions and to suppress the rising emotions of their hearts. In many cases I saw the big tear roll down the man or woman's cheek; and I saw strong men seeking to conceal their feelings by hiding their faces in their caps and hats, and leaning upon one another, as hardly able to stand before the preacher's words and appeals.[94]

In the short term the revival brought about dramatic changes to the life style of Ulster Protestants. Church attendance rose sharply and at Holy Trinity Church in Belfast, for example, the Reverend Theophilus Campbell confirmed 150 compared with 20 the year before. At the licensing sessions in Crumlin, where there were sixteen public houses, 'no fewer than ten publicans declined to seek renewals', the *Banner of Ulster* reported, ' . . . six others applied for, and obtained renewals, solely in order to obtain time to dispose of their remaining stock'.

The drive against alcohol, led by Protestant and Catholic clergy alike, had some curious results in the Ulster countryside. Methylated spirits, a sixth of the price of whiskey, were clandestinely swigged away from the disapproving eyes of neighbours by men of the Braid valley on the slopes of Slemish, and hardened drinkers in Ballynahinch mixed this industrial alcohol with sweetened tea or with cheap red wine to produce a brew known as 'hard blow'. Even stranger was the epidemic of ether-drinking which flourished in Co. Tyrone and south Co. Londonderry between about 1860 and the end of the century. The addict would begin by 'renching his gums' with cold water, then hold his nose and take about a tablespoonful of ether. After fighting the urge to vomit he would experience 'violent eructations' by the 'great dissipation of wind', and for ten minutes or so he would be hopelessly drunk. One consumer described the effect: 'You always heard music, and you'd be cocking your ears at it . . . others would see men climbing up the walls.' Since the effects of ether lasted no more than half an hour, ether-drinking had the advantage that those arrested for being drunk and disorderly would be completely sober when being charged in the police barracks.

'Smell a man's breath and tell his religion,' Protestants said of etherdrinkers, but an English surgeon, H.N. Draper, reckoned that nothing 'could be more unwarrantable or unfair', since in Tobermore 'there are enough and to spare of Protestant ether-drinkers '. In 1890 the *British Medical Journal* estimated that there were fifty thousand 'etheromaniacs' in mid-Ulster consuming seventeen thousand gallons annually, and in Cookstown alone the railway brought in two tons a year.[95] Etherdrinking had been fashionable in America amongst the upper classes earlier in the century, but now tended to flourish in places where restrictions on alcohol were severe, such as Norway, East Prussia and Russia. In Ulster the towns most affected were Cookstown, Draperstown,

Maghera, Magherafelt, Pomeroy and Dungannon. Publicans generally avoided ether, which was sold instead by grocers, druggists, bakers, hawkers, and doctors short of patients. A Catholic who had taken the total abstinence pledge when Father Mathew's temperance campaign was at its height described ether as a 'liquor on which one might get drunk with an easy conscience'. The Royal Irish Constabulary's success in closing down illicit poteen stills did much to encourage ether-drinking, but the most important factor was price: 'two-pennyworth, twice repeated, gave the hardened drinker a blissful fair-day'.[96]

'The aythur is putting the people astray, an' desthroyin' their heads,' an employee at Tyrone asylum told the *Lancet*, and Draper described one man in his early forties as already 'a wizened, beat, decrepit and tottering old man; a battered and lonely hulk cast up on the shores of existence – a hopeless and despairing human wreck'.[97] Ether may have been no more dangerous than alcohol, but the odd drop going 'the wrong way' could bring death by spasm or suffocation, and even going the right way 'would kill or bust you if you didn't rift'. The greatest danger was fire: a farmer at Bellaghy 'won day after a dose uv it, he wint to light his pipe and the fire cot his breath, and tuk fire inside, and only for a man that was carryin' in a jug of wather wud some whiskey to the kitchen, he'd a lost his life. He just held him down at wanst, as quick as he could, and poured the wather down his throat.'[98]

'Et's the threemenj'essest stuff offered, but it's near bet down, for none of the clargy iv any profession'll allow it,' a labourer said to Draper in 1876, but it took an order by the chancellor of the exchequer, in 1890, to have ether 'scheduled' under the 1870 Poisons Act to bring about a rapid decline of this addiction.[99]

The evangelical revival had its critics even amongst devout Protestants. 'Conviction! Convulsions! Epilepsy! Insanity!' proclaimed a placard carried by a group hostile to Ballymena revivalists. The Reverend Isaac Nelson, a Presbyterian minister in Belfast, described 1859 as 'the Year of Delusion', which was 'from the first but a huge juggle, a giant imposture, having really no more to do with Christianity than the phenomena of electro-biology', and, indeed, fraudulent stigmata were exposed by the Reverend William Breakey of the First Lisburn Presbyterian Church. Some were appalled by the expressions of intense religious emotion, condemned by the *Lancet* as 'insane and indecent follies . . . evidence of a temporary unsettling of reason among the duped'. The Reverend S.J. Moore approvingly described the impact of his own preaching:

They fall as nerveless and paralysed, and powerless, as if killed instantly by a gun-shot. They fall with a deep groan – some with a wild cry of

horror . . . The whole frame trembles like an aspen leaf, an intolerable
weight is felt upon the chest, a choking sensation is experienced.[100]

Church attendance did fall back after 1859–60 (the Tobermore Baptists,
for example, after a leap in numbers declined to the levels of 1849–50 by
1874), but further revivals and four visits by the American evangelists,
Moody and Sankey, between 1867 and 1892, increased churchgoing
again.[101]

A Catholic judge at the Downpatrick assizes, Chief-Baron Pigott,
concluded in 1859 that the 'revival now proceeding has extinguished
party animosities, and produced the most wholesome moral results'.[102]
In the short term there is no evidence that the movement increased
sectarian tension. A minister who led his boys through Belfast after the
Botanic Gardens meeting on 29 June stopped hymn-singing as they
passed through the Pound 'in case it would needlessly annoy their
Roman Catholic neighbours, but they resumed again as soon as they
reached Townsend Street'.[103] The 12 July parades of 1859 were remarkably quiet; in Ballymena there were no uniforms, drums or music and
one observer in Belfast 'saw detachments of police seated on forms at
the corners of the streets, as idle as a painted ship on a painted ocean'.[104]
Some of the leading preachers, however, reviled 'Romanism' and claimed
substantial numbers of Catholic converts. The Reverend Hugh Hanna
in Belfast said that, as a result, 'their sturdiest adherents are exceedingly
mad against us. Their Press teems with the vilest productions with the
purpose of disparaging the Revival', and the Reverend J. McAllister of
Armagh believed the 'opposition from Roman Catholics, Arians,
Puseyites, infidels, and profane formal Protestants is violent, bitter and
unceasing'.[105] The revival emphasised the differences between the two
broad streams of Christianity, particularly veneration of the Sabbath,
which, for example, put an end to Sunday pleasure cruises on Strangford
Lough. The Catholic Church, too, was stressing its distinctiveness in a
vigorous drive for reform and renewal.

THE CATHOLIC RENEWAL

Between 22 August and 10 September 1850 a Catholic synod was held at
Thurles, Co. Tipperary. There the bishops agreed to strengthen their
collective authority and the supremacy of the Pope; to regularise devotional practice and root out religious customs of doubtful Christian
origin; to launch a counter-attack on Second Reformation missionary
activity; to insist that Protestant partners marrying Catholics guarantee
that all their children be brought up as Catholics; and to campaign for
denominational education at every level, though the decision to oppose

the non-denominational Queen's Colleges funded by the Government was arrived at only with difficulty.

Presiding at the synod was Paul Cullen, archbishop of Armagh. Though he was translated to Dublin in 1852, Cullen remained firmly at the helm until his death in 1878 – a position recognised by Pope Pius IX in 1866 when he made the archbishop Ireland's first cardinal. No man was to make such a deep and lasting impression on the modern Catholic Church in Ireland. Cullen had been rector of the Irish College in Rome for eighteen years and he used his personal contacts in the Vatican to forge stronger links between Ireland and the Papacy than had ever existed before. Cullen's return to Ireland marked a new phase in the recovery of Catholic self-confidence and added a new element of combativeness. At his behest Redemptorists and other missionary orders swept into the small pockets of recent converts to Protestantism and swiftly won them back to Mother Church.[106] Cullen declared that he had never dined with a Protestant and said on one occasion 'the devil who animates Protestantism does not hold himself obliged to observe any promise'.[107] The cardinal did mellow with age and was eventually to dine with the Prince of Wales in 1868; nevertheless, Cullen's long reign was viewed with mounting alarm by Ulster Protestants, themselves encouraged by clergy and politicians to regard Catholicism as a 'blood-stained religion' threatening their liberties.[108]

Nowhere did the Catholic Church seem in more urgent need of regeneration than in Ulster, even though Catholics still formed a majority of the population – 50.5 per cent in the 1861 census. Regular church attendance was lower than in the rest of Ireland; illegitimacy rates were higher amongst Ulster Catholics as well as Ulster Protestants than in the other three provinces; and folk religion was prevalent. In part this was due to the fact that Catholics in the province were overwhelmingly confined to the lower rungs of the social ladder, literally unable to afford to participate in institutional devotion. In 1871, when their share of a population of 879,805 had slipped to 48.9 per cent, Catholics made up the following percentages of these occupations: magistrates 7.6; lawyers 14.1; commercial clerks 15.9; shipbuilding workers 16.9; domestic servants 46.3; agricultural labourers 57.3; and indoor farm servants 63.1. In the Clogher valley, for example, Catholics formed about half the population, but in 1860, of thirty-seven farmers with a rateable value of £60 or above, only one was Catholic.

Protestants in Ulster formed a relatively compact community, with distinct majorities in the counties of Antrim, Down and Londonderry (where their most numerous denomination was Presbyterian), around half the people in Armagh, Fermanagh and Tyrone (where Anglicans

345

outnumbered Presbyterians), and about one fifth of the populations of Donegal, Cavan and Monaghan – around the same proportion, then, as in the counties of Wicklow and Dublin.[109] Even outlying Protestant areas were usually linked by corridors of co-religionists to larger settlements. By contrast, Catholics in Ulster were more scattered, with isolated enclaves in north Antrim, the Sperrins, the Mournes, the Bogside suburb of Derry, and at least three distinct quarters in Belfast, where the rapid growth of a large underclass presented special problems.[110]

In May 1865 Patrick Dorrian, a former parish priest of Loughinisland, succeeded to the bishopric of Down and Connor, a diocese including east Co. Down, all of Co. Antrim, and Belfast. Though not Cullen's first choice, Dorrian proved a more dynamic standard-bearer of Catholic renewal than the archbishop had dared to hope. Belfast had been an almost exclusively Protestant town, but from the beginning of the nineteenth century burgeoning industrial development drew in the landless poor of all sects from the Ulster countryside and, as the traveller John Barrow observed, 'within a few years some four or five thousand raw, uneducated Catholic labourers from the South and West had poured into the city'.[111] By 1834 there were 19,712 Catholics in Belfast, 32 per cent of the town's population. For the next thirty years the proportion hovered around the one-third mark, and though the percentage dropped to 24.3 in 1901, the numbers kept rising. By 1871 there were more Catholics in Belfast than in the whole of Co. Fermanagh, where they formed a majority.[112] Cornelius Denvir, bishop of Down and Connor between 1835 and 1865, had been quite unequal to the task of providing adequate pastoral care for his new urban flock, who, in any case, were often too poor to pay for the upkeep of their Church.

Soon after his consecration in 1865, Dorrian launched a general mission in Belfast. Twelve additional priests were brought in to help the eight parish clergy of the town hear confessions for ten hours a day over a month beginning 21 October. The delighted bishop reported to the Vatican that 'persons who have not been at confession for years are coming in crowds and waiting for several sittings', and his final estimate was that thirty thousand had been to confession and holy communion. Thereafter, missions were held in Belfast about every three years and, in between, ordinary missions were conducted by members of religious orders. Parochial societies sprang up to maintain devotional zeal; confraternities of Christian doctrine evangelised children and young adults; the Rosarian Society ran lending libraries of religious books; confraternities of the Blessed Sacrament promoted Eucharistic devotion; and by 1877 the St Vincent de Paul Society alone recorded over two thousand boys attending its Sunday schools. Adults who had missed confirmation as children were now confirmed in great numbers, and some, it was claimed, were converts from Protestantism. When he visited Rome in 1882, Dorrian reported that there were 70,000 Catholics in Belfast served by 28 priests, assisted by 70 nuns and 12 Christian Brothers, and that confessions were heard daily in seven chapels.[113]

When an Austrian Redemptorist held a mission in Enniskillen in 1852, he found that Catholics in the town 'had never even witnessed benediction of the Blessed Sacrament, never seen incense rise from a thurible'.[114] Within a few years such a discovery became more and more unlikely. Regular attendance at Mass had previously been limited to a pious minority of educated and prosperous Catholics; now, probably for the first time in Irish history, it became universal. Before the Famine the population had been rising faster than the Church could supply priests to minister to them; now – in spite of the growth of Belfast and many provincial towns – the population was falling all over the country and yet the number of clergy increased. In the diocese of Down and Connor, for example, the number of priests rose from 80 in 1865 to 130 by 1885.

Not only did Catholics make confession and attend Mass more frequently but they also supplemented these with additional services such as novenas, stations of the cross, benediction and retreats. Italian forms of piety spread widely, including devotion to the Virgin Mary, Saint Joseph and Saint Anthony; adoration of the Blessed Eucharist and the Sacred Heart; participation in religious processions; and the adoption of aids to private devotion such as rosary beads, scapulars, medals, and religious pictures and sculptures.[115] Church building was well under way in the early nineteenth century – twenty-five chapels were put up in Co. Monaghan between 1783 and 1842 – but many of these were humble structures. After the Famine many chapels, such as St Mary's and St Patrick's in Belfast, were replaced by larger, more flamboyant, buildings.

In 1850 Charles McNally, bishop of Clogher, made Monaghan town his episcopal seat and launched a scheme to build a cathedral there. It proved a long, arduous task. On 18 June 1861 the archbishop of Cashel, ten bishops, fifty priests and about ten thousand people assembled in Monaghan for the blessing and laying of the foundation stone. Lord Rossmore allowed limestone to be quarried from Tirkeenan, and without pay, men from surrounding parishes carted in stone, lime and sand to the site. Then, objecting to the independent stand taken by the Church in local elections, Rossmore closed off his quarry and demanded compensation. The walls were not finished until 1874; priests were sent to Australia and New Zealand to raise funds, Charles Gavan Duffy contributing £2,000; a three-ton bell was erected in 1885; and finally, after thirty-one years, the completed Monaghan cathedral was dedicated on 21 August 1892.[116] St Patrick's Catholic Cathedral in Armagh was even longer in the building: the foundation stone was laid by Archbishop Crolly in 1840; the main fabric was completed in 1873; but the sumptuous interior was not ready until 1904.[117] In Belfast, St Peter's church – soon to be the town's procathedral – was erected with greater speed. Designed by Father Jeremiah McAuley, it was dedicated in the presence of Cardinal Cullen in 1866 and acquired splendid twin spires twenty years later.[118]

The Irish Church had a unity rare in the rest of Catholic Europe. Cullen was an ultramontane, that is, he upheld the Pope's claim to hold sway over a universal Church; but, unlike French and English ultramontanes, he did not align himself with the political far right. His pastorals and letters display a deep-felt concern for the plight of the poor and the need to take action to right social injustice. As in the Presbyterian Church, class tension between clergy and laity hardly existed, and while ministers of religion were rarely drawn from the ranks of the poor, they were not part of the ruling élite. The support for Pius IX's 'Syllabus of Errors' – a catalogue published in 1864 denouncing modern 'errors', including the separation of Church and state – can best be described as tepid.[119] Cullen had no desire for a theocratic state and, indeed, it would not be wrong to describe the Church in Ireland as the most liberal European wing of the Catholic Church. Catholic bishops were not true liberals, however, as their unswerving campaign for denominational education demonstrated and, in any case, the subtle distinctions within Catholicism were lost on most Protestants.

The Catholic and Protestant revivals were remarkably similar in character. Both displayed intense religious fervour and a triumphalist assertiveness. Both made faith the cornerstone of their beliefs and laid new emphasis on regular prayer, private devotions, participation in church services and Sunday instruction for children. Both embraced a fervent puritanism and were opposed to sexual permissiveness, strong drink and 'pernicious' literature. Both accepted infallibility, one of the Pope and the other of the literal truth of the Bible as God's word, and both – with the help of rising living standards – adopted 'Victorian morality' with a greater enthusiasm than the English themselves. And yet most Catholics and Protestants were acutely aware of what divided them, particularly in the sectarian enclaves of Belfast where the frontiers were kept unstable by the massive influx of newcomers from the countryside. The working classes packed into such warrens as the Pound and Sandy Row were for the most part comparatively recent immigrants. They had chosen where they had settled with care. Belfast has been described as a collection of villages; certainly, almost self-contained communities clustered round the mills but the invisible dividing lines running through these districts were primarily a reflection of sectarianism imported from rural Ulster. Here, where the low-paid majority eked out a wretched existence, religious hatreds had ample opportunity to fester in brutalising conditions. Sectarian clashes were frequent and in 1857 they reached a new peak of intensity.

'NEITHER LIFE OR PROPERTY IS SAFE HERE': THE 1857 RIOTS

On Monday night, 12 July 1857, while mobs hurled stones and insults at each other across wasteland by Albert Street, Catholics at Millfield wrecked a spirit grocer's store and beat two Methodist ministers with sticks. On Tuesday night Sandy Row Protestants made a determined attack on the Pound, smashing windows with long poles and setting houses on fire. Meanwhile, Catholics destroyed a Methodist church on the Falls Road, and the hussars arrived only to be pelted by 'kidney pavers' dug up from the streets. The violence was particularly severe on Saturday 18 July, when the mills stopped work at two o'clock. Walls running behind houses had been demolished to provide ammunition, which was heaped in piles along the roads; the police were swept aside as the mobs clashed in ferocious combat in front of the Pound; and for hours the fighting continued until the constabulary advanced in formation with loaded carbines. Sporadic gunfire continued through the night and resumed in earnest on Sunday afternoon. Head-Constable Henderson from Quadrant Street saw a ditch 'closely lined with men, having guns levelled, firing without intermission'.[120] Numerically inferior and less well-armed, Catholics now fought an unequal battle. That evening Dr Cornelius Denvir, Catholic bishop of Down and Connor, sent a hastily written appeal to the authorities:

> On last night four Catholics were shot in their own cath. district by the Orangemen who came down from Sandy Row. At this moment they are burning some houses in the Pound Loaning. All this district is Catholic and the Orangemen tonight are making new attacks – neither life or property is safe here. We are afraid to move out at all . . . excuse haste and fear.[121]

After a Catholic mill girl had been shot dead on 1 August there was an uneasy truce until sectarian passions were again inflamed by street preaching from the Custom House steps. Here, Frankfort Moore remembered, there was a 'warm interchange of opinion on a basis of basalt' and a Town policeman ordered his nurse:

> Take them childer out o' this or I'll not be tellin' ye. Don't ye see he's read the Riot Act. Heth! you're a gierl bringin' them wee'uns intill a crowd like thon![122]

It was well into September before the violence ceased. On the eleventh of that month the London *Daily News* marvelled at this upsurge of ancient hatreds:

Geologists are much divided upon the question whether a volcano, whose eruptive powers have been fully developed, has ever been known to die out. Observers of social phenomena are equally at fault as to whether the destructive agency of religious fanaticism, having once been long established, can ever be safely regarded as extinct. Long lulls occur in the mischievous action of both ... But ever and anon men are startled by unlooked-for and unaccountable tremblings of the earth beneath their feet; and the premonitory signs of mad commotion fill the air, and before they have time to inquire or reason about the cause of the long-latent and almost forgotten evil it has burst over their heads and filled the tranquil home with sorrow and dismay.[123]

After a few years of calm, intercommunal warfare periodically flared up again, its scale magnified by the very size of Belfast, now rapidly becoming a major industrial port. Notwithstanding rising living standards in the countryside, people from rural Ulster continued to pour into the town, attracted by job opportunities in the mills, factories, the shipyard, the building trade and harbour developments. In Frankfort Moore's opinion the riots of 1864

were due to the importation the previous year of some hundreds – perhaps thousands – of navvies to dig a new dock, and it was found out that a large proportion of these men were Roman Catholics. The balance of the fighting power among the belligerent classes was thereby disturbed.[124]

'THE GUNS FIRED CONTINUOUSLY, THE BULLETS PIERCED THE AIR':
THE 1864 RIOTS

Throughout the month of August 1864 the fighting was so severe and continuous in Belfast that many mills and factories were forced to close. The destruction by the mobs was so widespread on Friday 12 August that the *Belfast News-Letter* commented: 'The whole thing seemed like a burlesque on an invasion by a Gothic horde on a Roman province.'[125] The following Monday Catholic navvies rampaged through the town centre and savagely attacked the Protestant National School at the foot of the Shankill Road. That afternoon Protestants made an assault on St Malachy's Catholic Church with concentrated gunfire until they were dispersed by a cavalry charge down Ormeau Avenue. And that night Dublin Castle sent up a special train of twenty-seven wagons carrying two field guns and substantial reinforcements of constabulary, cavalry and infantry. Next morning gun battles raged on the borders of the Pound, wedged between the Shankill district to the north and Sandy Row on the south. Sub-Inspector John Caulfield, only just arrived with his constables from Meath, faced people from Sandy Row ferociously determined to press home their attack on the Pound. Three times waves of attackers pelted his force with cobblestones and shots were fired by the rioters during the last wave. Struck on the chest by a spent bullet, Caulfield raised his constabulary sword and ordered his men to take aim. Amongst those who fell in the subsequent volley was John McConnell, a Sandy Row father of five, mortally wounded in the skull. One Town policeman had been seen inciting the mob and another was subsequently arrested for throwing stones at the constabulary.[126]

Next day, Wednesday 17 August, the shipwrights of the Shankill converged on the Catholic navvies at work excavating the docks. The navvies had no line of retreat but the mud and the water. Neal Fagan was fatally wounded by the blow of a ship adze, and others fled before sustained gunfire.

The funeral of John McConnell on Thursday 18 August was turned into a massive parade of loyalist strength. The hearse set out from Sandy Row shortly after 3 p.m., followed by thirty cabs and jaunting cars and at least five thousand men. 'I think every man had a pistol', James Kennedy JP recalled, and others brandished fearsome bludgeons studded with nails and scimitars fashioned from barrel hoops. When the procession turned unexpectedly into Donegall Place, Belfast's most fashionable street, the forces of the Crown could do little more than hold back Catholics massing in Hercules Street. Shots were exchanged in Castle Place and a *Northern Whig* reporter saw

a relative of the deceased, taking out a rifled pistol of large size and firing shots rapidly and continuously, as fast as he could reload, in the direction of Hercules Place corner. The guns fired continuously, the bullets pierced the air, whirr after whirr, in a continuous volley.[127]

Astonishingly, no one was killed. That evening about one hundred houses were wrecked in Stanhope Street and off the Lodge Road. The Reverend Isaac Nelson, a Presbyterian minister, said later in evidence:

The mobs in my neighbourhood not only hunted poor Roman Catholic neighbours out of their houses, but I had to go and beseech them to grant so many hours to these poor people to take their furniture out . . . I could have sat down and wept when a poor little girl came with a pet canary bird in a cage, when the poor people had been driven from the houses, the children in one direction and the father and mother in another.[128]

By nightfall there were almost 1,000 constables, 150 Town Police, 600 special constables, 6 troops of the 4th Hussars, infantry of the 84th

Regiment and half a battery of artillery in Belfast. This great force, together with what Frankfort Moore called 'the usual autumn monsoon', at last brought the riots to an end.[129] The official figure of twelve dead was almost certainly too low, for, as in all sectarian clashes of the nineteenth century, both sides attempted to bury some of their dead without the knowledge of the authorities. Loyalists could, on the whole, preen themselves for trouncing their rivals, but developments elsewhere in Ireland caused mounting anxiety; in particular, the emergence of a new form of militant nationalism – Fenianism.

'SORDID APOSTLES OF A FALSE AND ODIOUS LIBERTY': THE FENIANS

Amidst the splendour of the imperial court in Vienna, Franz Josef could find comfort in the stirring strains of Strauss's *Radetzky March*, reminding him of the Habsburg dynasty's triumphs over the revolutionaries in 1849. Nationalism, however, refused to be cowed and was beginning to acquire powerful backing. In the first generation after Waterloo, hereditary rulers thought only of resisting liberalism and nationalism – forces viewed as 'moral gangrene', in the words of Prince Metternich, to be surgically removed. Some of the second generation of monarchs saw advantages in going part of the distance with national zeal; they included Victor Emmanuel II of Sardinia and Napoleon III of France, who conspired to wage war on Austria in 1859 to liberate Italy. That summer at Solferino, the bloodiest battle since Leipzig in 1813, the victorious Napoleon was sickened by the slaughter and hastily pulled back. But the mould set in 1815 had been broken and Italian nationalists, determined to unite their country, began to overrun the Papal States.

'*Robber take your hand from the throat of the Vicar of Christ*,' proclaimed the archbishop of Armagh, Joseph Dixon, endorsing Cullen's campaign to rally Irish Catholic help for Pius IX.[130] Monster meetings were held up and down the country, one of the largest being at Clones on 7 February 1860: £80,000 were raised (never before had Irish Catholics contributed such a large sum for a single cause); and Count Charles McDonnell, an Austrian of Irish extraction, mobilised an Irish brigade to defend the Pope. It was all in vain: some of the Irish volunteers went on a mutinous drunken spree in Macerata; five hundred fell prisoner at Spoleto and Perugia; and the Papal States, except for an enclave around Rome, were engulfed to become part of the new kingdom of Italy. Besides, nationalist passion was spreading outwards and downwards in Ireland itself.[131]

In January 1861 Terence Bellew MacManus, a Fermanagh-born veteran of the 1848 rising who had escaped from penal servitude in Australia, died in poverty in California. Exiles determined to take him back to his native land for burial and make his last journey a grand propaganda drive for Irish freedom. Cullen was horrified by the lying-in-state in St Patrick's Cathedral, New York, and refused a similar ceremony in Dublin. Nevertheless, some thirty thousand Dubliners followed the hearse to Glasnevin and listened to James Stephens make an oration by torchlight. Irish Catholics were not always ready to follow the guidance given to them by the princes of the Church.[132]

James Stephens, another veteran of 1848, had returned from Paris, where he had been perfecting his conspiratorial prowess, to found a revolutionary organisation in Dublin in 1858 dedicated to the establishment of an Irish republic by force of arms. Early the following year Stephens galvanised militant exiles in New York and set up the Fenian Brotherhood. The movement in Ireland, now officially called the Irish Republican Brotherhood but better known as the Fenians, spread rapidly amongst labourers, shopkeepers and others hard hit by the successive harvest failures of the early 1860s. It is difficult to assess the support for a secret oath-bound organisation, but it seems that Fenianism was at its weakest in Ulster, where it had trouble supplanting the more traditional sectarian Ribbonism. Constabulary reports failed to confirm Conservative claims that Ulster Catholics were joining the brotherhood in droves, but none the less, 'Fenian' joined 'taig' at the top of the list of hostile epithets Protestants used for their Catholic neighbours.

When the American Civil War ended in the summer of 1865 a quarter of a million dollars was raised to finance the long-planned Fenian rising in Ireland but arrangements for insurrection were disrupted by fatal indecision, internal disputes, informers, arrests and the petulance of Stephens. Excitement was intense, however, when news came through of a Fenian raid on Canada and that the 'wolves' (mostly Union ex-servicemen) had set sail for Ireland in January 1867. In the same month nine Fenian suspects were arrested in Belfast, in possession of lead, bullets and bullet moulds, and more were held after twenty rifles were seized by police in the Pound.[133] When leading Fenians proclaimed the Irish Republic on 4 March 1867, Bishop Dorrian responded the next day in his Lenten pastoral:

Is it not then the blindest folly to listen to the arguments of the selfish and sordid apostles of a false and odious liberty, who would seduce . . . well-disposed countrymen from an allegiance which is of divine obligation?[134]

That night several thousand Fenians assembled in the snow with what arms they could muster, but the well-informed authorities had arrested their principal leaders. A few volleys fired by fourteen constables dispersed the largest force of insurgents at Tallaght, outside Dublin, and after some skirmishes in the counties of Limerick, Cork, Tipperary and Sligo, it was all over by March. Queen Victoria was so pleased with the efficiency of the police, who had not needed military support, that she renamed them the Royal Irish Constabulary.

The Fenian rising did not touch Ulster directly. Catholics in the province did join the movement for the better treatment of political prisoners and when one of them, William Harbinson, died in Belfast gaol in September over thirty thousand attended his funeral. Sympathy for prisoners did not mean support for the Fenian programme, however, but it did lead to a recognition amongst liberal opinion in Britain that the Irish problem needed to be addressed; the prominent English Liberal John Bright, for example, called for an amnesty. In September 1867 a police sergeant was killed in Manchester during the rescue of two prominent Fenians and three men were publicly executed at Salford for the deed. Then in December an attempt to free another Fenian leader by blowing in the wall of Clerkenwell prison in London killed twelve people and fearfully injured many others.[135] These two incidents made a deep impression on William Ewart Gladstone, leader of the Liberal Party.

A true follower of Peel, Gladstone was convinced that long-term solutions to Irish problems were vital for the stability of the United Kingdom. The Fenian outrages in England gave a fresh urgency to the task and Gladstone declared that, should the Liberals come to power, they would disestablish the Church of Ireland and legislate to protect the rights of tenants on the land. This programme at once divided Irish Protestants: some were appalled that a key part of the Act of Union – state support for the Anglican Church – would be removed; while Presbyterians, with no interest in upholding the privileges of the Church of Ireland, relished the prospect of tenant right being given the force of law.

Meanwhile Benjamin Disraeli hoped he had 'dished the Whigs' by stealing the principal plank of the Liberal programme – parliamentary reform. The 1867 Representation of the People Act gave artisans the vote and in the following year the property qualification in Irish boroughs was halved. The first Ulster politician to recognise the importance of this change was William Johnston of Ballykilbeg.

CONSERVATIVES, LIBERALS AND PARTY PROCESSIONS

Against the advice of the Irish Grand Lodge of the Orange Order, William Johnston announced that he would lead a great parade from Newtownards to Bangor on 12 July 1867 in open defiance of the Party Processions Act. Johnston, owner of a small Co. Down estate and publisher of loyalist ballads, novels and tracts, believed that if Catholics could turn funerals and unveilings into political demonstrations, Orangemen should be able to march unmolested by the law.[136]

At 9 a.m. on Friday 12 July a train packed with Orangemen left the Belfast station of the Holywood and Bangor Railway. Only after the train pulled out were Orange flags and scarves unfurled from every carriage window. The *Belfast News-Letter* reported: 'A procession of gaily-decorated yachts or barges could scarcely have presented a finer sight', and when the Orangemen disembarked at Bangor, they walked on to Newtownards 'without interruption save the *cead mille failthes* of hosts of sympathisers'. A special train with 36 carriages carried demonstrators from Lecale, the Downpatrick contingent alone carrying 49 stand of colours and 67 drums. Johnston, after being given a 'perfect ovation', led the Orangemen over the neck of the Ards peninsula towards Bangor, with the Amateur Conservative Band of Belfast, bearing 130 stand of colours, in the van. Augmented by passengers carried from Belfast by the paddle steamship *Erin*, the Orangemen filled an eight-acre field. The *Belfast News-Letter* commended 'the well-conducted, well-dressed and well-to-do multitude who assembled at Bangor to commemorate once more the glorious, pious, and immortal memory of William III'. At least thirty thousand Orangemen were present: 'After this we shall perhaps hear no more about Orangemen being practically defunct.' Other demonstrations were held the same day all over the province, notably at the Maze, Dunadry, Derry, Armagh, and Enniskillen, where Orangemen finished the day by taking a pleasure trip across Lough Erne to Belleek in the paddle steamboats *Devenish* and *Rossclare*. In Belfast demonstrators discreetly assembled in the southern suburb of Malone before marching up to Ballylesson.[137]

Johnston defiantly refused an apology to the authorities and in February 1868 he was sentenced to serve a short spell in prison, a judgment upheld by the Duke of Abercorn, the Conservative lord lieutenant. Seen now as a martyr, 'fearless' and 'indomitable', on his release he was given a rapturous reception in Belfast's Ulster Hall at an 'Indignation' meeting called by the Orange and Protestant Working Men's Association. Soon after, Johnston declared:

> We will have an Orange Party, please God, after a while in the House of Commons . . . For all the good some of the Ulster members do the Orange cause they might as well have been selected from the Deaf and Dumb Institute.[138]

A general election was called soon afterwards and when the Conservatives failed to nominate Johnston for Belfast, he put himself forward in any case. The Liberals, too, made a strong bid in Belfast by nominating Thomas McClure, a Presbyterian tobacco manufacturer. Completely routing the two official Conservatives, Johnston and McClure won the two borough seats. In Londonderry City the Liberals, with their candidate Richard Dowse QC, ousted the sitting Conservative Lord Claud Hamilton, second son of the Duke of Abercorn. Otherwise Gladstone reaped a miserable crop in Ulster: the Liberals won only four seats while the Conservatives retained twenty-five.[139]

At first sight the domination of the Conservatives, fiercely opposed to disestablishment, seems to indicate the triumph of sectarianism in Ulster politics. In fact it merely demonstrates the enormous power still wielded by landed proprietors in the north. The ballot was public and a tenant who voted against his landlord's candidate faced the threat of harassment or eviction. Only in one county, Monaghan, did the Liberals attempt a contest and there they were badly beaten by a Shirley and a Leslie.[140] Most of the towns eligible to return members were 'pocket boroughs', where landlords controlled the vote. The MP for Lisburn, for example, was Rear-Admiral G.H. Seymour, a close relative of the 4th Marquess of Hertford who owned sixty-six thousand acres in south Antrim. His election agent was Dean J.W. Stannus, who was also agent for the Hertford estate. One voter said in court:

> At the last County Antrim election I voted for Seymour, and I would rather not have gone, for I was not fit. I have got some notices to quit. I would have voted for a Liberal man if I durst, but I was afraid to do it, for fear Mr Stannus would throw me out of my wee place.[141]

The triumph of Johnston in Belfast did warn the Conservatives that they could not rely on deference where landlord influence was weak and that a populist appeal to traditional loyalism might well be the way to win the support of the newly enfranchised artisans. The election of McClure and Dowse showed that the Liberal Party in Ulster truly crossed the sectarian divide, for an analysis of the results makes it clear that they owed their victory to a combination of Catholic and Presbyterian votes. The results would have been very different if all working men had possessed the vote: both in Derry and Belfast sectarian animosity resolutely refused to die down. In the summer of 1872, for example, a nationalist demonstration of some thirty thousand at Hannahstown, seeking the release of Fenian prisoners, set off another round of fierce rioting in Belfast. On Friday 10 August at least two men were killed as Protestants drove Catholics out of Malvern Street. Another Catholic was found shot dead on the Falls Road early next morning and that afternoon mobs fought a deadly sectarian battle on brickfields lying between the Shankill and the Pound. The *Daily Telegraph* reported that Belfast 'presented the appearance of a place that had been sacked by an infuriated army . . . the feathers from a hundred mattresses strew the roadway, and piles of embers here and there show the spots in which the furniture of the victims of one side or the other has been reduced to ashes'.[142]

Sectarian feeling was not intense everywhere. In Fermanagh when the first Catholic high sheriff met the solidly Protestant grand jury there was 'a strife of courtesy and Christian kindness'; the Reverend William Magee, rector of Enniskillen and later bishop of Peterborough, persuaded parishioners to take down loyalist flags in case they caused offence to their Catholic neighbours; and an examination of tenant-right sales in Magheracross in the same county shows that Protestants and Catholics freely sold farms to each other.[143] In the countryside, where there was a well-founded tradition of neighbourliness and mutual assistance, farmers of all creeds had a common interest in defending tenant right and in challenging the Ascendancy. Not until Gladstone had pushed Westminster further down the road towards democracy could an effective challenge be made in Ulster.

PACIFYING IRELAND?

'My mission is to pacify Ireland,' Gladstone remarked in 1868 as he set off for Windsor to be accepted by Queen Victoria as her prime minister. Ulster notwithstanding, Ireland had elected sixty-six Liberals and Gladstone felt a strong moral obligation to take immediate action. On 1 March 1869 he introduced his bill to disestablish the Irish Church and spoke for three hours. 'So long as that Establishment lives,' he warned, 'painful and bitter memories of Ascendancy can never be effaced.'[144] It was a blow to the Ascendancy that deeply alarmed many landlords, including Lord Cole, eldest son of the Earl of Erne, who declared it to be 'the first step of an onward march of communistic and socialistic ideas'.[145] Despite a generous compensation of £8 million for the Church of Ireland and £764,688 to the Presbyterians in lieu of the *regium donum*, the state grant, northern Protestants had to face the fact that Westminster had bowed to the wishes of the majority in Ireland by lopping off an important branch of the Union.

The seals on the Church Bill had scarcely time to harden before Gladstone was busy preparing a Land Bill to legalise the Ulster Custom. It was not an easy task, as he confided to his diary in September 1869:

I have puzzled & puzzled over it & cannot for the life of me see how it is to be legalised without being essentially changed. It is like trying in algebra to solve a problem of two unknown quantities with only one equation.[146]

Proposing the bill on 15 February 1870, the prime minister alluded to 'the great mischief' of insecurity of tenure and referred darkly to 'the lavish and pitiless use of notices to quit' – here he was probably thinking not so much of Derryveagh as of John George Adair's neighbour in Co. Donegal, the pitiless Lord Leitrim.[147] Not only William Johnston but also the Conservative landlords Lieutenant-Colonel W.B. Forde of Co. Down and William Verner of Co. Armagh voted for the bill. Other proprietors were worried: time-honoured and previously sacrosanct rights of property were being tampered with. For all its importance for the future, however, the 1870 Land Act was a bitter disappointment to the tenants: it proved a solicitor's nightmare attempting to interpret the terms 'in all essential particulars', 'exorbitant', and 'disturbance'; and while 'free sale' had largely been conceded, it only went a little way towards 'fair rent' and 'fixity of tenure'.

To the delight of his adherents, Johnston of Ballykilbeg got the Party Processions Act repealed by private member's bill in 1870. The act had become completely unenforceable and was in danger of bringing the law into contempt owing to ludicrous decisions such as those handed down in the Belfast Police Court in 1870 just before repeal: it seemed barely reasonable to impose fines of forty shillings each on John Kerr, for cursing the Pope, and on George Murray, for cursing the Pope and the Pope's granny; but it was plainly silly to levy the same fine on Teresa Brown for the even-handed naming of her two cats, 'Orange Bill' and 'Papist Kate'.[148]

More important for the future was the introduction of secret voting in 1872. At a stroke the grip of the landlords on the electorate had been weakened. Gladstone, who had still much to learn about Ireland, found that his land legislation merely gave added impetus to the tenant-right movement and now the secret ballot gave farmers a freer hand in deciding who should represent them, especially in Ulster. The Belleek Pottery in Co. Fermanagh found a ready local sale for its chamber pots decorated on each inside bottom with a portrait of Gladstone.[149]

'HOME RULE IS SIMPLE ROME RULE'

Gladstone was no democrat but during his long career, Westminster, with his help, steadily became more representative of the people it governed. The election of 1868 seemed to show that this could only strengthen the Liberals in Ireland as the ground was cut from beneath the Ascendancy, but that was not to be. On 19 May 1870, at Bilton's Hotel in Dublin, the Home Government Association was formed to demand, in the words of Isaac Butt, 'full control over our domestic affairs'. The son of a Donegal clergyman, Butt, who had become a Dublin University professor and then a Conservative MP between 1852 and 1865, seemed an unlikely leader of a new movement seeking the restoration of a Dublin parliament. However, his brilliant legal defence of Young Irelander and Fenian prisoners had won the respect of a wide range of Irish nationalists. For nearly a quarter of a century the issue of repeal of the Union had been all but dead; now it was revived by an uneasy alliance of Conservatives disgusted at the disestablishment of their Church, Irish Liberals disappointed by the Land Act, former repealers, and Fenians searching for an alternative to futile revolution.[150]

Butt was returned as a Home Rule MP for Limerick in 1871 and soon gathered round him a loose coalition of about two dozen Irish members in the Commons. Disappointed by Gladstone's higher education proposals, the Catholic bishops transferred their support to the association, relaunched in 1873 as the Home Rule League. Members of the league in parliament in their turn helped to precipitate Gladstone's fall and the general election of 1874 – the first to be carried out by secret ballot. The results had dramatic consequences for both British and Irish politics. A deadly and irreversible blow was delivered to Liberal representation in Ireland with the election of fifty-nine Home Rulers and only in Ulster was something of the previous pattern of representation retained.

'Never, we believe, within the recollection of living men were so many seats contested in this province', the *Ulster Examiner* correctly observed. Only in two boroughs was no challenge thrown down. 'This country, in my opinion,' Joseph Biggar declared, 'can never rise from her present state of stagnation until she has once again a native parliament.'[151] Biggar, a Presbyterian pork merchant from Belfast, was one of two Home Rulers standing in Co. Cavan, but he knew the movement to restore a Dublin parliament was so far weak in the north, and there, the bogey of Home Rule proved invaluable to the Conservatives, especially in the volatile urban constituencies. On 5 February 1874 the *Belfast News-Letter* declared:

Home rule is simple Rome rule, and, if home rule were accomplished tomorrow, before that day week Rome rule would be evident.[152]

In Co. Tyrone Captain H.W.L. Corry, Conservative MP, appealed to traditional loyalism:

As a Conservative, I shall always seek to maintain the integrity of this great Empire; and, as a Protestant, I shall use my utmost endeavours to uphold our glorious constitution, granting at the same time to every man the fullest civil and religious liberty.[153]

Nevertheless, as one of Corry's supporters pointed out to the Earl of Belmore, the 'democratic Orange tenant right vote, under the ballot, is much more potent for mischief than I anticipated'.[154] Corry was opposed by Ellison-Macartney, standing as an independent Conservative for tenant right and supported, like most Liberal candidates, by Presbyterian and Catholic farmers working together in tenants' associations. Both Liberal tenant-right candidates won in Co. Londonderry; Ellison-Macartney was elected in Co. Tyrone; both Home Rulers took Co. Cavan; and the Conservatives were fortunate to retain twenty-one seats, leaving the Liberals an increased total of six MPs in the province.

The 1874 election brought no advantage to Home Rulers, Liberals and tenant-right MPs. Disraeli's Conservative government, largely absorbed by foreign crises and imperial adventures, almost completely ignored Irish affairs. Butt and his supporters played the parliamentary game to no effect. Joseph Biggar, for a time a member of the IRB and recently elected for Cavan, had no qualms about breaking the unwritten rules of the world's most exclusive gentlemen's club: from 1874 he began obstructing the business of the Commons to force the House to pay attention to Ireland. With a harsh grating voice and in a Belfast accent few could follow, Biggar read interminable extracts from Statutes of the Realm in a tedious monotone. On the evening of 22 April 1875 he spoke for four hours, with extended boring readings, concluding with the remark that he was 'unwilling to detain the House any longer'.[155] As he sat down a member newly returned in a by-election in Co. Meath entered the chamber: his name was Charles Stewart Parnell. Soon Parnell was joining Biggar in parliamentary obstruction and gaining the support of a growing number of Irish MPs. Butt strongly disapproved of this tactic; he was, however, an infrequent attender and, plagued by financial difficulties and criticised for his dissolute life style, he was gently pushed aside.

There was every reason why Westminster should give Ireland more of its attention: from 1877 the country was assailed by an agricultural crisis of such dimensions that it evoked vivid reminders of the Great Famine. Once more the dreaded blight returned but this time the distress on the land was caused in part by bountiful harvests won from the virgin soils of the American prairies.

CRISIS ON THE LAND

In a letter from Kansas in 1874 Andrew Greenlees wrote:

The government gives to each settler a homestead of 160 acres of land outside railroad limits, inside railroad limits 80 acres . . . The prairie is beautiful. It is fairly a forest of flowers . . . 'wherefore if God so clotheth the grass, shall he not much more clothe you, O ye of little faith'.

That autumn, however, a plague of grasshoppers destroyed two thirds of the corn in the state:

Here we are . . . our means exhausted. An abundance almost within our grasp, but in a moment destroyed . . . Meantime, we trust that He who permitted the scourge will also open up a way for us.

Over the following seasons the yield was indeed magnificent and by October 1876 Greenlees 'had upwards of two thousand bushels of wheat for market'. He was only one of an advancing army of sod-busters and nesters sending their corn by rail to the Atlantic ports for transport to Europe.[156] At the same time, following the ruthless extermination of the Plains Indians, the open range was being tamed by barbed wire, making unprecedented quantities of inexpensive meat available to the Old World. Steel-hulled vessels powered by efficient compound or triple-expansion engines, which increased hold capacity by reducing the fuel required, made it economic to carry food in bulk across the ocean for the first time. Belfast shipbuilding firms were well to the fore in this revolution: Harland and Wolff launched two 4,400-ton ships in 1881, the *Arabic* and the *Coptic*, specifically designed for carrying live cattle across the Atlantic; and from the outset Workman Clark specialised in food transport vessels, particularly for refrigerated meat.[157] The urban working classes appreciated the consequent fall in the cost of their groceries, but for small farmers in Ireland this vast flow of cheap produce was disastrous. Above all, food prices failed to rise in compensation – as they had always done in the past – when ruinous weather and disease decimated their crops.

Unremitting rain throughout August 1877 destroyed the oats and rotted the potatoes in the ground, especially in the west and north-west. For a time emigrants' remittances, credit from the 'gombeen men' and earnings brought back by migrant labourers helped to alleviate distress. Nevertheless, many smallholders could not pay their rents, and evictions, negligible in the good years, leaped to 406 in 1877 and to 843 in 1878. Then the indifferent harvest of 1878 was followed by a disastrous season, the worst since the Famine. The year 1879 was the wettest and coldest since records began. Between March and September rain fell on 125 days out of a six-month total of 183, that is, two days out of every three. While cereal production fell only by one fifth, turnips and green crops dropped by one half and, above all, the potato crop was ravaged by blight, reducing its yield by more than two thirds. Smallholders in the west, still dependent on the potato for their staple diet, faced

361

starvation. To make matters worse, prices for all agricultural output slid down relentlessly; evictions for failure to pay rent jumped to 1,098; the onset of an international depression dried up alternative sources of employment; and the winter of 1879–80 was extremely severe.[158]

The Government refused to give special aid on the grounds that it would be unfair since no special action had been taken to help Lancashire cotton workers during the American Civil War. For people in the far west, particularly in the counties of Mayo and Donegal, the charity provided by the Mansion House Committee in Dublin and the Central Relief Committee of the Society of Friends was the only hope of avoiding death from hunger, cold and disease.

JAMES HACK TUKE VISITS DONEGAL: FEBRUARY–MARCH 1880

On behalf of the Society of Friends James Hack Tuke returned to Ireland in February 1880, retracing his steps in Co. Donegal and battling through blizzards of snow and sleet as he had done in 1847. On this occasion the people were not dying of starvation but there was great want and misery especially in the Glenties Union, a region stretching north from Killybegs to Dungloe where, against the national trend, the population had been rising. At Killybegs he found that 'the fish have nearly all left the Bay . . . so that combined loss of fish and potatoes really leaves them destitute'. Here a man told him he had worked for seven years in the United States to earn £125 to buy the tenant right on a twenty-two acre farm:

> 'But,' he added, with emotion, 'this is my last year here; it's no use, a man may as well lie down and die – we are beaten . . . I shall take my wife and family away to Ameriky again . . . *Nature binds a man to his own counthrey* – but I can't stand it any longer.'[159]

Most of the farmers had sold off all their stock, save for a few hens. Near Kilcar, where the 'faces of the people are more like "Famine" faces than those in any other place', Tuke spoke to Patrick Burns who owed three years' rent and his county cess; he had 'neither cow, nor calf, nor ewe, nor lamb, nor baste that treads the earth . . . only ten fowls which left a few eggs'. Another family with a similar story added 'we must not grumble', even though all they had left was the cat – 'Yes, we must keep that.'[160]

On 1 March Tuke left Bunbeg by Derrybeg for the townland of Meenacladdy. 'Imagine, over this wild waste,' he wrote, 'little dwellings scattered at wide intervals, some of rough stone and some of mere peat sods, scarcely distinguishable from the surrounding surface; add to this the blinding squalls of sleet or snow which swept over it.' He continued:

It is not merely the unusual distress of to-day, arising from the causes which I have enumerated, but the every-day life, the normal condition of hundreds, nay thousands, of families on the west coast of Donegal.

He gave example after example of families who could not possibly survive without the oatmeal given out by the relief committees. Many lived in turf dwellings with no windows, a low gap for a door, and a hole in the roof for some of the smoke to escape by; one was only ten feet by twelve feet and with 'barely room to stand upright', which his English companions 'could not believe was a human habitation'.[161] Stock in the area had largely been sold: out of 920 sheep and 248 cattle some years earlier, only 127 sheep and 69 cattle remained.

The problems arising from the potato failure had been compounded by the early return of migrant labourers from Scotland in 1879, where no 'tatie hoking', or potato-lifting work, could be had. Gweedore normally sent off two men per household, each bringing back £4, or £8,000 for the region. Now the families were in debt for the fares there and back. Another £8,000 was normally earned by sending boys and girls as farm servants in the Laggan, but now the farmers of east Donegal could not afford to hire them. Half the population of Killybegs was destitute; six hundred out of eight hundred families in Glencolumbkille were on relief; and Tuke reckoned eight thousand families in the Glenties Union needed help until the next harvest. He was scathing about the failure of the Poor Law to provide real help; it was 'in fact inoperative as regards out-door relief. The guardians do not incline to tax themselves, it seems.' He found the landlords of Donegal a singularly unprepossessing lot who regularly refused to vote money for public works or relief. Dunfanaghy Union, for example, had funds only to keep thirty-nine inmates during the terrible winter of 1879–80.[162] The constabulary inspector in Gweedore 'spoke in the highest terms of the conduct of the people in his district. There is little or no crime, very little drunkenness, and great chastity among the women.' Tuke found 'simple well-bred courtesy' everywhere and remarked: 'It is touching to see how patiently they bear their want.'[163] However, the smallholders of the west determined not to submit tamely as they had done in the Famine of the 1840s: there was widespread intimidation of bailiffs; and some resorted to murder.

THE MURDER OF LORD LEITRIM

'Lord Leitrim must surely know that not even a nobleman can do what *he likes* with impunity', the *Londonderry Standard* observed in 1857, '. . . evil passions will be inflamed and many families, now comparatively comfortable, will be reduced to total destitution.'[164] Three years earlier William Clements, 3rd Earl of Leitrim, had inherited property amounting to 94,535 acres, including an estate of 54,352 acres in north Donegal. No man in Ireland so perfectly matched the nationalist caricature of the predatory landlord: he swept away rundale with such ruthless vigour that his Donegal demesne became known as 'The Straight Lined Estate'; he ejected Protestants and Catholics with equal enthusiasm; he removed all the tenants of Rawros to build his castle at Manorvaughan and those at Cratlagh to plant a vista of trees; he forced a farmer keeping goats against his rules to kill them on the spot before his eyes; he forced himself on his tenants' daughters, causing one girl, it was said, to drown herself in sorrow in a nearby lough; and, according to the *Freeman's Journal*, he 'set himself, avowedly and deliberately, to destroy' the Ulster Custom, describing the Land Act of 1870, which thereafter enforced compensation, as 'only another step in the process of spoliation which had been commenced by the Irish Church Act'.[165] Like his neighbour John George Adair, he quarrelled with almost everybody, including: the Presbyterian minister of Milford, who unsuccessfully took Lord Leitrim to court for sharply increasing his rent; the Catholics in Mohill, where he pulled down their chapel with the aid of crowbar men; the constabulary, one of whom was awarded £100 compensation after being libelled by the earl; the owner of Doe Castle over the rights of the Lacagh Fishery; and the lord lieutenant, the Earl of Carlisle, who stripped him of his post as justice of the peace for the counties of Donegal, Leitrim and Galway. This last incident made Leitrim a pariah even within his own class; when a man was arrested for firing a blunderbuss at the earl, the lord lieutenant had him committed to an asylum rather than see him hang.

Indeed, there were several attempts to kill Lord Leitrim and his employees – one bailiff survived an armed attack only because the bullet struck a gold sovereign in his top pocket. The men of Fanad launched no fewer than three attempts on Leitrim's life, one failing because the assailant due to fire the blunderbuss fainted at the crucial moment. Late in 1877 Ribbonmen and Fenians met at Killyorial and agreed that the Ribbonman Mickey Rua McElwee and two Fenian tailors 'An Táilliúir Rua' Neil Shiels and Michael Heraghty should make a fresh assault. Armed with five muzzle-loaders, the three men lay in wait at Woodquarter as dawn broke on 2 April 1878. They had been tipped off that the earl would be travelling that way to Milford from Manorvaughan. The first shot killed Leitrim's driver, two more shots mortally wounded his clerk and further rounds gravely wounded the earl, preventing him from firing either his pistol or his revolver.

With no time to reload, the men overpowered the seventy-two-year-old Lord Leitrim and clubbed him to death with a musket butt. McElwee had to cut his red beard to free himself from the victim's dying grip.[166]

With £1,000 the Duke of Abercorn headed a list of those offering a reward to find the murderers. The 4th earl later offered the huge sum of £10,000, yet the money was never collected. The police knew who the assailants were, but could find no one prepared to give sufficient evidence for a conviction. There is more than a suggestion that the constabulary did not try hard enough.

Neither bloody murder nor armed revolution brought down landlordism in Ireland. During the years of prosperity an alliance of Presbyterian and Catholic farmers in Ulster kept alive the peaceful agitation for tenant right. Now, as the agricultural crisis struck hard, the lead was taken over by a remarkable mass movement of smallholders in the west. Certainly there was an upsurge in intimidation and 'outrage', but peaceful cooperation – mainly solidarity in refusing to rent farms where tenants had been evicted – was the principal weapon deployed. Home Rule MPs had no choice but to ally themselves with the farmers and assist in the formation of the Irish National Land League in 1879. American Fenians, organised in Clan na Gael led by John Devoy, gave enthusiastic backing to the new movement, while in Ulster the Liberals rallied the tenant farmers in preparation for the general election of April 1880.

ULSTER LABOURERS RELIEVE CAPTAIN BOYCOTT, 1880

In January 1880 the Marquess of Hamilton, MP for Donegal and later 2nd Duke of Abercorn, wrote to Disraeli's secretary:

> There is only one subject that these tenant farmers in the north of Ireland at the present time care about – and that is the land question. It is all-absorbing to them. They care little about general policies or foreign policies.[167]

This certainly proved the case in the Ulster countryside as the election campaign got under way, J.A. Pomeroy writing from Co. Tyrone on 3 April that 'nobody here I am afraid cares a button for anything except the three Fs'. As those qualified for the vote went to the polls the *Fermanagh Times* declared:

> The question of the hour is a sad one – destitution. It is echoed from the Giant's Causeway to the Cove of Cork. Go where we may, throughout Ireland to-day, we hear the wail of distress for food.[168]

The Liberals reached their high tide mark by winning nine seats. The Marquess of Hamilton, grumbling that the Presbyterians were not as fearful of Popery as they had been, was ousted in Co. Donegal by a Liberal Presbyterian minister from Letterkenny. The Conservative vote held up in the boroughs, where the election was closer to a sectarian head count, but the number of MPs with a landlord background returned from the province dropped to fifteen compared with twenty-five in 1868.[169]

Across the Irish Sea Gladstone was swept back to power but he failed to take decisive action to calm the land agitation. In Connacht the movement reached a new peak of intensity in the autumn of 1880 as the people took Parnell's advice to shun the offending landlord 'as if he were a leper of old'. Captain Charles Boycott, agent for Lord Erne's Mayo estate, became a celebrated victim when he described his plight in a letter to *The Times*. Ulster Conservatives, fervently supported by the *Belfast News-Letter*, determined to lead an armed expedition of Orangemen to Connacht to lift Boycott's potato crop and thrash his corn. The alarmed Chief Secretary William E. Forster rushed seven thousand troops to Mayo, including the Hospital Corps under the command of Surgeon-Major Reynolds VC (hero of Rorke's Drift the year before in the Zulu Wars), and limited the Orange labourers to fifty. Twenty-five Protestant labourers from Co. Monaghan joined twenty-five Protestant labourers from Co. Cavan at Clones station on Thursday 11 November 1880, where for fear of 'the bludgeon men of Mayo' they were each given a revolver.[170]

Before the eyes of the world's press the expedition's special train drew in to Claremorris station and the Orangemen trudged through the driving rain to Ballinrobe and on to Lough Mask House. Here they slept in army tents, and sang loyalist songs round campfires as they cooked potatoes, for which Captain Boycott, the *Belfast News-Letter* admitted, meanly charged them 9d. a stone. Then in driving rain the work began.

The relief of Captain Boycott was a pyrrhic victory for it had cost £10,000 to save his crops. To rescue every beleaguered landlord in this way would be quite impossible. 'The bright Irish have invented a new word', *Le Figaro* reported, 'they are currently saying to *boycott* somebody, meaning to ostracise him.'[171] Boycotting proved an extremely effective tactic and the Land League went from strength to strength, now rallying support in Ulster.

'THE FLAG OF THE LAND LEAGUE IS NOW UNFURLED IN THE VERY HEART OF THE PROTESTANT NORTH'

As Clifford Lloyd made his way down to Saintfield from Belfast early on the morning of 23 October 1880, he was an anxious man. The Land League had permission to hold a meeting there, in the heart of loyalist

Co. Down. Lloyd loathed the league for its 'dissemination of treason, plunder and crime', but called back from his command in the Burma Police to serve as a special resident magistrate, he must obey his instructions from the lord lieutenant to 'assist in preserving the peace'. He had already sent down six hundred RIC men and when he himself arrived in Saintfield he closed the public houses and informed local leaders that 'it would naturally be impossible to allow a counter-demonstration ... the loyal population being extremely exasperated'.[172]

The Land League meeting began in a field outside the town, the platform party including Joseph Biggar MP, John Dillon MP and Michael Davitt. Lloyd recorded his impressions: Michael Davitt, a Fenian prisoner released two years before and now the leading figure in the Land League, 'struck me as being a very effective speaker, and to a sentimental nature I should imagine he was especially convincing. He has but one arm, and I could not help feeling a certain amount of sympathy for him personally.' None the less, he was sure Davitt was 'ought else but an ardent and uncompromising rebel'[173] when he heard him propose this motion:

> That, as the Ulster custom has utterly failed to protect the property of tenants against the rapacity of landlords, the land question can be definitely settled only by making the cultivators of the soil proprietors.[174]

Thus the goalposts for Gladstone had been shifted. No longer would the '3 Fs' be enough. The landlords themselves must go.

As Davitt was speaking a messenger dashed over to tell Lloyd 'that a special train, conveying several hundreds of Orangemen, had arrived, and that many of the loyalists were armed with revolvers'. Lloyd called out three hundred constables and persuaded the Orangemen to withdraw, whereupon they went off to hold their own 'indignation' meeting. Later, however, they took to the fields 'with further designs upon the Land Leaguers', advancing

> down the hillsides towards the meeting, flourishing sticks and making a noise, and it became necessary to cause a charge to be executed by a small party of police. Thirty or forty loyalists succeeded in getting through the lines of armed men into the ground reserved for the meeting ... A few prisoners were taken, and retained as hostages.[175]

At least no blood had been spilled as at Dungannon the previous August when Orangemen shot two people dead. The danger of sectarian conflict was always there, but during most of 1880 and 1881 northern Protestants as well as Catholics thronged to attend league meetings and there was little violence. The Liberals, who had not won a single borough in Ulster the previous April, swiftly adopted a programme almost as radical as that of the league in order to retain support from farmers. On 21 November 1880, for example, the Liberal landlord, William Anketell, joined with the Orange leader of Carrickmacross, Henry Overend, and Canon Patrick Smollen of Clones to co-ordinate the tenants' campaign in Co. Monaghan. Now the Land League could operate across the province and Orangemen and other Protestants were in a majority at meetings in Cookstown and Ballycastle. On 3 December the Presbyterian journal *Witness* observed:

> The flag of the Land League is now unfurled in the very heart of the Protestant north, and the standard bearers are now busy beating up recruits amongst the loyal men of Down and Antrim . . . The invasion of Ulster by these enemies of landlordism and all its works was to be the signal for civil war. But these sanguine and sanguinary prophecies remain unfulfilled predictions. The Land League is with us, yet Ulster is at peace.[176]

A meeting at Brookeborough, Co. Fermanagh, was banned by Conservative magistrates on 9 December, yet farmers gathered in force to listen to James Little and James Thomas, both masters of Orange lodges. Conservatives and Ulster landlords in general were alarmed. The Reverend D.C. Abbot observed: 'Most of the Presbyterians, the younger Methodists, and I may say all the Romanists go in the "whole length of the unclean animal" with the Land League.'[177] Sir Thomas Bateson, later Lord Deramore, at the end of the year sent this account to the leader of the opposition, Lord Salisbury:

> A few weeks since, the Land League invaded Ulster . . . men who voted for the Conservatives last April are now openly fraternising with democrats whom six weeks ago they would not have touched with a long pole, and the wave of communism has spread like wildfire.[178]

The start of 1881 saw no falling off in the popular campaign. Davitt returned for a tour of Ulster, addressing ten thousand at Downpatrick on 6 January, where Clifford Lloyd did not enjoy being cheered for his handling of the 'bludgeon men' at Saintfield. At Letterkenny, Co. Donegal, on 19 January Davitt declared that the Boyne no longer divided Ireland and, despite a bad fall from his car in a snowstorm, he was at Kinnegoe in Co. Armagh on 21 January addressing two thousand Protestant farmers,with James Weir, master of the local Orange lodge, in the chair. Davitt said:

> You are no longer the tame and superstitious fools who fought for their amusement and profit with your equally foolish and superstitious Catholic fellow workers . . . No, my friends, the landlords of Ireland are all of one religion – their God is Mammon and rackrents, and evictions their

only morality, while the toilers of the fields, whether Orangemen, Catholics, Presbyterians, or Methodists are the victims whom they desire to see fling themselves beneath the juggernaut of landlordism.[179]

Twelve days later Davitt was arrested, taken to England, and gaoled. On 2 February 1881 the Irish members in the Commons brought their obstructive tactics to a climax as the Government prepared repressive legislation in a desperate attempt to curb mounting rural disorder and violence in the west.

'WHAT THE BREWERS WOULD CALL TREBLE X' : THE 1881 LAND ACT

'The Government wants war and they shall have it,' Parnell told the press on 24 January 1881.[180] That day Irish Chief Secretary Forster sought to introduce his Protection for Person and Property Bill which would empower the authorities to imprison any 'reasonably suspected' person. Next day Irish MPs kept the Commons in session for twenty-two hours by continuous obstruction and this filibuster dragged on for the next week. 'Such work is all very well for coal heavers who rely on physical strength,' sighed a Conservative MP.[181] Queen Victoria was appalled and sent a note to the Liberal peer, Lord Hartington:

> The Queen trusts that measures will be found to prevent the dreadful Irish people from succeeding in the attempt to delay the passing of the important measures of coercion.[182]

Measures were found: at 9 a.m. on 2 February, while Biggar was on his feet, the Speaker refused to allow any more members to speak. The long tradition of unlimited debate was brought to an end. Next day the Irish MPs, after deliberately flouting the rules of the House, were expelled en masse. Obstruction was at an end, and over the next couple of months Forster successfully steered coercive legislation through parliament.

Forster at the same time urgently pressed Gladstone to make his Land Bill as far-reaching as possible. For much of 1880 the prime minister thought that only minor adjustments to the 1870 act were needed but by the spring of 1881 he was convinced the bill had to be 'what the brewers would call treble X'.[183] The 'three Fs' were granted in full: fair rent, if it could not be amicably agreed, would be set by land courts to last fifteen years; free sale enforced compensation for improvements; and fixity of tenure gave protection against eviction provided the rent was paid. 'I must make one admission,' Gladstone said the following year, 'and that is that without the Land League, the Act of 1881 would not be on the statute books.'[184]

During the final debate on the Land Bill, electric light was turned on in the House of Commons for the first time. It could have been symbolic of the dawn of a new age when the governing classes voted to tamper with the principle of *laissez-faire* and deliver a body blow to the unfettered rights of property. Certainly in Ulster, where the agitation had not been marked by the violence experienced in much of the rest of Ireland, tenants associations and Liberals greeted the act with acclaim. The Land League was considered to have done its work as farmers rushed to have their rents judicially fixed by the new Land Commission. Typical of the fair rents set by the land courts are the following samples from Co. Monaghan: Peter Callaghan on the Shirley estate reduced from £18 16s.0d. to £15; William Wright on the Anketell estate from £33 to £22; and Owen Smyth on the Rossmore estate from £25 19s.0d. to £21. Some landlords agreed on reductions without judicial haggling: the Rathdonnell estate granted a rent cut of 25 per cent; and when the agent of the Carrickatee property announced reductions of up to 40 per cent his car was pulled from Ballybay station to his hotel and his bailiff was carried shoulder high.[185]

In the rest of Ireland the response to the act was mixed. Most farmers were keen to apply to the courts, but the legislation fell far short of the league's aim to abolish landlordism. Parnell had to walk a tightrope to stop the splitting of his movement: he advised the testing of the act by sending a selection of cases to the courts while at the same time he threw himself into a vehement campaign against coercion. His extreme speeches landed him in gaol in October 1881, where he joined other leading 'suspects' – in some respects this solved his dilemma. Thereafter, violence raged over much of the south and during Parnell's imprisonment there were fourteen murders and sixty-one cases of 'firing at the person'.

Ulster farmers, particularly Presbyterian members of tenants associations who had joined hands with the Land League, were deeply dismayed. Parnell and his associates were released in the spring of 1882 following an unwritten understanding with Gladstone known as the Kilmainham Treaty: the Liberals would provide help for tenants hopelessly in arrears if the Irish nationalist MPs would discountenance violence and support Gladstone's reform programme. This did not halt the steady drifting apart of Protestant and Catholic farmers in the north, especially when Parnell launched a new movement to concentrate on winning Home Rule for Ireland.

ULSTER POLITICS POLARISED, 1881–5

The 1881 Land Act led directly to a by-election because E.C. Litton, MP for Co.Tyrone, was appointed a commissioner of the new court to adjudicate fair rents. The Unitarian minister of Moneymore, the Reverend Harold Rylett, stood as a nationalist candidate in favour of Home Rule and Parnell came north at the end of August to campaign on his behalf, saying: 'We can never hope for really just laws until we obtain a representative assembly, making its laws on Irish soil.'[186] The popular and radical Liberal, T.A. Dickson, won the seat, narrowly beating the Conservative, Colonel W.S. Knox, an Orange grand master. James Crossle, who had campaigned for Knox, wrote in disgust:

> That low fellow Dickson was returned by Protestants and I believe numbers of Orangemen voted against their Grand Master. The fact is the Protestants as well as the Roman Catholics do not want an Orangeman or even a Fenian if he is a gentleman or a landlord. I look upon the event of this election as a death blow to Protestantism.[187]

Crossle need not have been so despondent. Rylett won only 907 votes but Protestants who had been co-operating with the Land League were deeply offended that he and Parnell had nearly allowed the Conservative to win. Thereafter, Protestant and Catholic co-operation in rural politics rapidly declined. Protestants were alienated by the extreme policies of the Land League during Parnell's imprisonment – when tenants were advised to 'hold the harvest' and pay no rent – and were aghast when the new Irish chief secretary, Lord Frederick Cavendish, and Undersecretary Thomas Burke were knifed to death outside the Viceregal Lodge in Dublin's Phoenix Park on 6 May 1882. Catholic farmers who had followed the advice of their clergy to vote for Liberals in the north much preferred to have the opportunity to vote for nationalist candidates. The drawing back of rural Protestants from Parnell's movement was noted with satisfaction by Sir Thomas Bateson in a letter to Lord Salisbury in June 1882:

> I have just come back from the north of Ireland. There has been a considerable change in the feelings of the better class of Liberal Presbyterians since the Kilmainham Treaty and the Dublin assassinations. The same applies to the democratic Presbyterian farmers ... there seems to be a growing feeling that the policy of the National party is to stamp out the English garrison and make Ireland a purely R. Catholic country. There is throughout Ulster a growing distrust of the R. Catholics on the part of the Protestant farmers.[188]

Butt had died in 1879 and Parnell had been elected leader of the Home Rulers the following year. Now Parnell was creating a modern, highly disciplined party, known as the Irish Parliamentary Party, with its MPs generally referred to as Nationalists, with a capital N. Home Rule, not land reform, was made the first objective. 'What we have wanted for two hundred years in Ireland was an honest dictator,' Tim

Healy told an audience in Liverpool, 'and we have at last got one in the person of Mr. Parnell.'[189] Certainly Parnell, setting his movement firmly back on the constitutional track, exercised undisputed control.

Healy put himself forward as a Nationalist candidate in a by-election in Co. Monaghan in the summer of 1883 and won the seat. The Liberal vote all but collapsed and it was quite clear that all the Catholics had voted for Healy and nearly all the Protestants for the Conservative candidate. In Belfast and the other principal towns of Ulster, politics had been polarised on sectarian lines for years. Now the polarisation of the northern countryside was well under way, especially when the Nationalists – excited by their victory in Monaghan – announced a new drive to extend their party all over Ulster in the autumn of 1883. 'All Ulster is ours' was the Nationalist cry, but the Dungannon Volunteer Committee of Watchfulness, thinking no doubt of O'Connell's incursion forty years earlier, called it 'The Invasion of Ulster'.

When Parnell announced that he would speak in Dungannon in September, William Copeland Trimble, editor of the *Impartial Reporter*, who for a time welcomed the Land League, wrote: 'What brings Mr. Parnell to Tyrone is not clear: what good he can hope to effect we do not know; but it is evident that he has roused the Orange blood of the county.' [190] In the same issue he quoted this Orange appeal:

Are you prepared to allow Parnell, the leader of the enemies of our united empire, the champion of the principle, Ireland for the Irish . . . meaning Ireland for the Romanists . . . Are you prepared to accept the doctrine of the English radicals that the Protestants of Ireland are aliens in their land and should be swept out of it by fair means or foul?[191]

Nationalists assumed that, because so many Ulster Protestant farmers had joined them in the Land League, they would now back their campaign for a parliament in Dublin. Indeed, most southern Nationalists knew remarkably little about the deep political and religious tensions in Ulster society – Parnell, for example, when speaking in Enniskillen assumed that it was exclusively a Protestant town and he, a Protestant landlord who did not attend church, underestimated the vital role of religion in the north.

In October 1883 Nationalists called a public meeting at Rosslea, a small town in south-east Fermanagh. The poster advertising the demonstration was hardly likely to attract Protestant support:

Men of Fermanagh and Monaghan, prove by your presence at the meeting your unalterable devotion to the cause that your fathers fought and bled and died for – the cause of Irish nationality; prove to the hydra-headed monster of landlordism and your English taskmasters that you will never rest contented until the land of Ireland is the property of the whole people of Ireland, to be administered by government existing for and by the will of the Irish nation.[192]

The 5th Baron Rossmore, grand master of the Orange Order in Monaghan, immediately called on his brethren to rally in a counter-demonstration and issued free tickets on special trains to bring in supporters from all over Cavan, Monaghan and Fermanagh. The authorities rushed troops and police to Rosslea, where fortunately the River Finn, swollen by a flood, kept some five thousand nationalists separated from about seven thousand Orangemen. Thomas MacKnight, editor of the liberal unionist *Northern Whig*, reported:

> Lord Rossmore . . . was represented as saying, that the Nationalists on the hill were rebels and scavengers, whom the Orangemen could easily vanquish, and that the Brethren could also, if they thought fit, eat up the handful of soldiers in a few seconds.[193]

When the resident magistrate threatened to arrest Rossmore, his lord-ship responded:

> Then I invite you to arrest me at once, and on you and you alone will rest the blame of having transformed this orderly body of men into a leaderless mob.[194]

Rossmore refused to follow the route recommended by the resident magistrate and the result was, MacKnight continued, that the 'parties were with the utmost difficulty prevented from coming into collision. Revolver shots were fired, and angry defiances exchanged.'[195] No one was hurt but Rossmore was dismissed from his post as a magistrate. Further demonstrations were banned but that did not prevent an im-posing assembly of nationalists at Dromore, Co. Tyrone, confronted by a counter-demonstration led by Colonel Knox, the defeated Conserva-tive candidate and lord lieutenant of the county. Sectarian tension, ever present in the towns, revived over much of Ulster's countryside. Evi-dence that the polarisation of politics in the province was all but com-plete was amply revealed in the general election of 1885.

'THE DAY OF THE PEOPLE'S POWER HAS COME': THE ELECTION OF 1885

On 8 June 1885 there was to be a division in the Commons on an additional tax on wines and spirits. Parnell summoned all absent Nation-alists to Westminster by telegram and all thirty-nine Irish Parliamentary Party MPs trooped through the lobby to vote against the Government. Gladstone's administration lost by 263 votes to 252. On the Conservative benches 'a collection of bores and the bored became a mass of screaming, waving, gesticulating lunatics', Lord Randolph Churchill emitting hysterical yells 'like a wild animal fastening its teeth on the prey', while the Nationalists cried out with vehemence, 'Remember Coercion'.[196] The Liberals could not carry on and over the next few months Lord Salisbury's caretaker government in gratitude dropped coercion and produced a Land Act with the purpose of lending £5 million to tenants to buy the ownership of their farms. Then, as the year drew to a close, the voters of the United Kingdom went to the polls.

No one could predict the outcome. Gladstone's parliamentary reforms had tripled the Irish electorate by giving labourers the vote; election expenses were severely restricted, further reducing landlord influence; and a redistribution of parliamentary divisions gave Ulster twenty-seven county seats and reduced the borough constituencies to six, four of them in Belfast. There had been little time to adjust to these changes. With remarkable speed the Nationalists set up an effective machine in the north, concentrating on constituencies where they had a chance. In a secret deal they agreed not to oppose the Conservatives in Mid Armagh to spoil the Liberal's hope of election there, while the Conservatives left the Nationalists alone in South Armagh. While the Conservatives set out to woo Orange labourers, the Liberals experienced great difficulty in adapting to the new circumstances. Home Rule seemed the only issue: on 13 November *Witness* concluded:

> It seems to us that the great question before Irish, and especially Ulster, constituencies in the present electioneering contest is the maintenance of the legislative union between Great Britain and Ireland.[197]

Passions, fears and hopes ran high. At a rally in Glenties William O'Brien, the Co. Cork Nationalist MP, declared:

> Here in Donegal you and your fathers before you lived in perpetual terror of your lives, terror of eviction, terror of starvation . . . You had no body to speak for you, no body to fight for you . . . Well, these days are gone – thank God for it, and the day of the people's power has come.[198]

A sign of the times was the new Protestant solidarity. Major Edward J. Saunderson, once a Liberal MP for Co. Cavan, was now the Conservative candidate for North Armagh and darling of the Orangemen of Portadown, who, according to the county chaplain, 'are determined to have you . . . The Orange spirit is aroused, and now it is victory or death with them . . . '[199] Party scrutineers were fiercely vigilant during the extraordinarily high turnout reaching over 93 per cent in some divisions.

Liberal representation was completely wiped out. The Conservatives held sixteen of their seats and the Nationalists won seventeen, failing to take West Belfast and Londonderry City by only a few dozen votes. All the Conservative MPs were Protestant, voted in overwhelmingly by Protestants. All the Nationalist MPs in the north were Catholic, one elected in Co. Donegal declaring that only five Protestants had voted for him. It was the most significant election in Ulster's history. Henceforth all elections would be fought on the issue of the Union, for or against. Liberal sentiment remained strong in the Protestant heartlands, but the tenant farmer vote was swamped by that of farm labourers who had no interest in tenant right and often got better wages and conditions when employed directly by landlords. Support for the Orange Order was always strongest amongst Protestant labourers who now relished the return of the upper classes in force to the movement. Catholic 'mountainy men', eking out a living on the marginal soils, had never wanted to support Protestant Liberals and were now uplifted by Parnell's spectacular victory.

The Irish Parliamentary Party won eighty-six seats if T.P. O'Connor, who took the Scotland Road Division in Liverpool as a Nationalist, is included. 'Ireland has been knocking long enough on the English door with kid gloves,' Parnell announced after the election, '. . . now it will knock with the mailed fist.'[200] His party held the balance of power in the governing assembly of the world's greatest trading power, the world's most extensive empire. His advice to the Irish in Britain to vote Conservative may have cost the Liberals up to twenty-five seats there. The Liberals in Britain won eighty-six seats more than the Conservatives, a margin exactly equalled by the size of the Irish Parliamentary Party. The Conservatives would not offer Home Rule – what would the Liberals do? Parnell seemed to have an unassailable mandate from Ireland for a parliament in Dublin. Even a majority of MPs in Ulster, the most Protestant province, had pledged themselves to Home Rule.

'ULSTER WILL FIGHT, AND ULSTER WILL BE RIGHT':
THE FIRST HOME RULE BILL, 1886

Towards the end of 1885 Thomas MacKnight visited the leading Ulster Liberal, Sir Edward Cowan, at Craigavad in north Down. There he startled his host by saying abruptly: 'Gladstone has gone over to the Home Rulers.' His record of Cowan's incredulous reply and their heated exchange continues:

'Impossible! Absurd! I have received a letter from my friend Mr. Campbell-Bannerman assuring me that there is no truth in those rumours.'
'But I wrote to Mr. Gladstone himself about those rumours, and this is his reply.'
I put Mr. Gladstone's letter in Sir Edward's hands. He read it slowly and then hesitated to speak.

'What do you think of it?' I asked.
'I must candidly say that I do not like it.'
'Nor I. It means to us utter ruin.'[201]

The great majority of Ulster Liberals greeted the news of Gladstone's new-found support for Home Rule with similar consternation. They assumed he had changed his mind for narrow party advantage in order to return to power, which he was able to do after joining with the Nationalists to defeat Lord Salisbury's government on 27 January 1886. Exhaustive modern research has largely confirmed that Gladstone was possessed by a genuine feeling of high moral purpose. After all, he had already demonstrated his distaste for imperial oppression of emergent nationalities in the Balkans. His policy of coercion blended with conciliation had proved a bitter disappointment: Britain now had a duty to right past wrongs. Home Rule, he felt sure, was the only real way to pacify Ireland.

With some distaste Queen Victoria accepted Gladstone as her prime minister for the third time on 30 January, disinclined as she was to 'take this half-crazy and in many ways ridiculous old man for the sake of the country'.[202] She encouraged influential Liberals to detach themselves, and five peers, who had been members of Gladstone's previous government, now refused to serve in this new one. At Dungannon only two days later, on 1 February, the Conservatives in Ulster launched their campaign against Home Rule. There the 5th Earl of Ranfurly gave England this advice:

Let me recommend a change of treatment. Let her drop for a time the remedial plan, and try instead a good thrashing. It will have a surprising effect. The unruly child will become quiet, peaceful and industrious.[203]

Binding themselves more closely to the Orange Order, the Conservatives brought their demonstrations across Ulster to a climax with a 'Monster Meeting of Conservatives and Orangemen' in the Ulster Hall in Belfast on 22 February. The principal speaker was to be the wayward Lord Randolph Churchill, son of the Duke of Marlborough. Not long before, Churchill had told Lord Salisbury that 'these foul Ulster Tories have always ruined our party', but by 16 February he had decided that if Gladstone 'went for Home Rule, the Orange card would be the one to play. Please God it may turn out the ace of trumps and not the two.'[204]

'Ulster will fight, and Ulster will be right,' Churchill proclaimed to cheering supporters at Larne and greater numbers turned out to greet him in Belfast as he made his way to the Ulster Hall. 'The hall was crowded to excess', the *Belfast News-Letter* reported and for one and a half hours Churchill held the rapt attention of his audience, saying:

On you it primarily rests whether Ireland shall remain an integral portion of this great empire sharing in its glory, partaking of all its strength, benefiting by all its wealth . . . or whether, on the other hand, Ireland shall become the focus and the centre of foreign intrigue and deadly conspiracy.[205]

Churchill had urged loyalists to organise so that Home Rule might not come upon them 'as a thief in the night'. Some took him at his word and reports came in from parts of the province that Orangemen were drilling with and without arms. While there was no evidence of large-scale paramilitary preparation, both Gladstone and the Irish National-ists gravely underestimated the strength of northern Protestant feeling against a Dublin parliament. Ulster Liberals, meanwhile, had been thrown into confusion by Gladstone's announcement. Their candidate, T.A. Dickson, had been decisively beaten in the Mid Armagh by-election on 1 February, his brother-in-law concluding:

The Home Rule scare carried the election, and every other consideration will be regarded as of secondary importance in every Protestant home-stead in Ulster until this bogey is laid.[206]

Six hundred Liberal delegates met in Belfast on 19 March only to display bitter division on the issue. They did agree to send a deputation to interview leading politicians in London. Adam Duffin, writing to this wife, found that John Bright

loathes the 86 Parnellites even more than we do, but is quite hopeless or very nearly so. He says they *must* get rid of these scoundrels in the House & what then is the alternative to Home Rule . . . The probability is that Mr Gladstone's prestige & wonderful power of persuading himself & other people will carry his scheme through the house of Commons.[207]

In fact Bright soon after threw his formidable influence against Home Rule, and when Joseph Chamberlain, the talented spokesman for the left wing of the Liberal Party, deserted Gladstone, the fate of the bill was in doubt.

'THE EXCITEMENT WAS AT ITS HIGHEST PITCH': HOME RULE DEFEATED

Not since the second reading of the Great Reform Bill in 1832 was the Commons so packed and so tense as when Gladstone introduced the Home Rule Bill on 8 April 1886. The Marquis de Breteuil and the German chancellor's son were amongst those in the visitors' gallery; the journalist Frank Harris recorded the occasion:

The House was so thronged that members sat about on the steps leading from the floor and even on the arms of the benches and on each other's knees . . . every diplomat in London seemed to be present; and cheek by jowl with the black uniforms of bishops, Indian princes by the dozen blazing with diamonds lent a rich Oriental flavour to the scene.

Gladstone spoke for two and half hours:

His head was like that of an old eagle – luminous eyes, rapacious beak and bony jaws . . . His voice was a high, clear tenor; his gestures rare but well chosen; his utterance as fluid as water . . . he seemed so passionately sincere and earnest that time and again you might have thought he was expounding God's law conveyed to him on Sinai.[208]

In Ulster, too, as Thomas MacKnight remembered, 'the excitement was at its highest pitch . . . even the morning papers published editions containing Mr. Gladstone's speech at intervals as it was transmitted through the telegraph wires, and large crowds assembled round the newspaper offices eagerly buying copies'.[209]

The prime minister's Home Rule proposals, officially referred to as the Government of Ireland Bill, were complex. The Dublin parliament was to consist of two 'orders' which would normally sit together as one chamber: the lower order would be elected on the franchise of the day; and the upper order, intended to give special representation to Irish Protestants, was to be made up of twenty-eight Irish peers, and seventy-five members elected by voters with a high property qualification. Irish representation at Westminster was to cease, responsibility for defence, foreign policy, trade, navigation and taxation being retained by the imperial parliament. By later standards Gladstone was offering Ireland a very limited form of devolution – little more than control over the police, civil service and judiciary – but, whatever their private reservations, Nationalists gave Gladstone their unreserved backing. Parnell knew that all his party's disciplined energy would be needed to secure the passage of the bill. A few nights after the prime minister's epic speech, Parnell rose to speak in a House not half so full as on the previous occasion. Harris recalled:

Yet the scene to me was more impressive . . . I soon noticed that the hands holding his coat were so tense that the knuckles went white; he hadn't a single oratorical trick; he spoke quite naturally but slowly . . . I felt very much as I had felt when drinking in Bismarck's great speech in the Reichstag five years before, that a great man was talking and the words were prophetic and the place sacred.[210]

In his speech Gladstone had hinted that special arrangements could be made for Ulster, but at Parnell's behest the suggestion was not raised again. Northern Protestants were not impressed by the safeguards intended in the second order; 'on examination', MacKnight wrote, 'the guarantees were found by those to whom they were of vital importance to be utterly illusory', for when the orders voted together Protestants 'would still be hopelessly outnumbered'.[211] The great majority of Liberals in Ulster turned against Gladstone and organised a large demonstration in the Ulster Hall on 30 April. There it was resolved that the Home Rule Bill was 'fraught with danger to the industrial, social, and moral welfare of the country'.[212] The Route Tenants' Defence Association led by Samuel C. McElroy declared its continued confidence in Gladstone, and towards the end of May the Portadown Liberal Thomas Shillington formed the Irish Protestant Home Rule Association. Nevertheless, most Liberals – henceforth known as Liberal Unionists – collaborated with erstwhile Conservative opponents to present a united front against the bill.

As early as 14 January 1886, Edward Saunderson had brought together Irish Conservatives to form a parliamentary Ulster party with the purpose of ensuring that their colleagues across the Irish Sea kept their interests at heart. Saunderson was pushing at an open door. At St James's Hall on 15 May a Conservative demonstration gave three cheers for Ulster, and their leader, Lord Salisbury, remarked: 'You would not confide free representative institutions to the Hottentots, for example', explaining to his audience that the Celtic Irish were unsuited to self-government and that democracy 'works admirably when it is confined to people who are of Teutonic race'.[213] He concluded by observing that Irish loyalists would be justified in using violence in defence of their political faith.

The fate of the Home Rule Bill was sealed by the defection of substantial numbers of Liberal MPs. The hostility of the Whig right wing was expected; like the Conservatives they feared the dismemberment of the empire. Sir George Trevelyan, a leading member of this group and son of the man who administered relief during the Famine, said to Thomas MacKnight: 'It is not the Home Rule question as it affects Ireland that so much concerns me: it is the precedent set for India.'[214] More dangerous for Gladstone was the mass desertion of fifty-five left-wing Liberal MPs led by Joseph Chamberlain at a conference held on 31 May. 'Think, I beseech you,' Gladstone implored in vain during the final debate, 'think well, think wisely, think not for the moment but for the years that are to come before you reject this Bill.'[215]

During the first hours of 8 June 1886 the division was taken: ninety-three Liberal MPs voted with the Conservatives against the bill, which was defeated by a margin of thirty votes. Thomas MacKnight remembered:

In Belfast the first people to be aware of the defeat of the Bill, independently of the newspaper officials, were the police on duty in the streets. Several of them were seen embracing one another for joy at having escaped being left, after two years, to an Irish Government.[216]

379

Frankfort Moore was one of the journalists who got the news by electric telegraph. As he walked home at 4 a.m. he was met by scores of workmen

> who had left their homes in the side streets, and especially in the ultra-Protestant Sandy Row, the scene of many a fierce encounter between two religious factions, to put to me in their own idiom and staccato pronunciation the burning question:
> 'Is them 'uns bate?'
> And when I assured them that the unspeakable Nationalists had been beaten by a good majority, once more cheers were raised.[217]

However, that fine morning was just a calm interlude in a conflict started four days before and which, as it intensified, was to be the worst violence experienced anywhere in Ireland in the nineteenth century. As in previous Belfast riots, the main battle zone was to the west of the town centre. In its massive two-volume report the Commission of Inquiry explained:

> The extremity to which party and religious feeling has grown in Belfast is shown strikingly by the fact that the people of the artisan and labouring class, disregarding the ordinary considerations of convenience, dwell to a large extent in separate quarters, each of which is almost entirely given up to persons of one particular faith, and the boundaries of which are sharply defined ... The month of June, 1886, opened in Belfast upon a condition of great excitement and high party feeling. The Home Rule Bill was then before Parliament; and the measure evoked strong feeling in Belfast ... this apparently political question evoked the spirit of sectarian animosity.[218]

'THE SANGUINARY SLAUGHTER OF A PEOPLE RESOLVED TO RESIST A WICKED POLICY': THE 1886 RIOTS

The Catholic navvies at work on the Alexandra dock attacked and drove out a Protestant on 3 June 1886, warning him that 'neither he nor any of his sort should get leave to work there, or earn a loaf there or any other place'. The following day at 'dinner hour' up to a thousand shipwrights descended on the navvies. A few who stood their ground were severely beaten and the inquiry reported:

> The majority of them, however, sought refuge in the Lagan which runs by the dock. About twenty got on a raft. Others tried to escape by swimming. Some of the fugitives, who had either slipped off the raft or got tired from swimming, were soon in danger of drowning. One man returned to the shore and was badly beaten by the Island men, who also continued throwing stones at the men in the water. In the result one lad named Curran was drowned.[219]

As rioting got under way in the brickfields Sir Edward Harland, the mayor, telegraphed Dublin Castle on 7 June requesting reinforcements to assist the 525 men of the RIC based in Belfast – the partisan Town Police had been disbanded in 1865. As news spread the following day of the defeat of the Home Rule Bill, Protestants left their work early and while Orange bands played loyalist airs, they lit bonfires and tar barrels in jubilation. To lament the bill's failure, Catholics set fire to their chimneys. The combined result, the *Belfast News-Letter* noted, was a pall over the town 'as thick as a London fog'.[220] That evening Protestants in the Shankill began attacking public houses owned by Catholics, and rural constables disembarking at the railway stations were led through a maze of unfamiliar streets by Town-Inspector Thomas Carr.

Carr arrived in Percy Street only to find he was too late to save Duffy's public house from being completely wrecked. The inquiry report continues:

Mr. Carr and his party, as they advanced up the street, were furiously attacked by the mob, which numbered some hundreds of people. They poured on the police heavy showers of stones and bottles. The police – a number of whom had firearms – charged, by Mr. Carr's orders, three times; once with fixed bayonets; but the mob kept up the attack with unabated fierceness. Some of the streets of Belfast are paved with small paving stones, popularly called 'kidneys', and these formidable missiles were rooted from the street by the women and handed to the men.

Almost every policeman in Mr. Carr's party was struck with stones, by the tremendous fusillade of these weapons which was kept up by the mob. In the third charge Mr. Carr received some injuries of great severity; almost at the same moment one stone striking him on the leg, a second splitting his thumb, while the third struck him on the forehead, knocking him down.[221]

When Carr got to his feet he read the Riot Act and ordered his men to fire buckshot over the heads of the rioters, who at last dispersed.

Next day, Wednesday 9 June, some of the bloodiest fighting took place. While most of the police were attempting to restore order in Donegall Street, other constables were engaged in a losing battle on the Shankill. There trouble began when the police tried to prevent the looting of a liquor store; then the police infuriated the Protestants by batoning men returning from work; and finally, after they had been driven back by a mob of some two thousand, three civil magistrates, seventy-two constables, several police officers and a reporter took refuge in the small two-storey Bower's Hill barracks. The besieged came under ferocious and prolonged attack. According to the *Belfast News-Letter*, kidney pavers had been

strewn over the road by a number of vicious young women who carried them in their aprons ... and when the stone-throwing waned for a moment girls and women came to the front and uttered the most desperate threats to the men who desisted.[222]

A salvo of paving stones destroyed the telegraph apparatus, and in desperation the defenders opened fire on the mob. The shooting was indiscriminate: of the seven killed only two were rioting. At 10 p.m. the Highland Light Infantry came to the rescue and found several children unconscious from the drinking of looted alcohol.

Many Protestants became convinced that Gladstone's government was intent on punishing them for opposing Home Rule. The following Sunday the Reverend Hugh Hanna said from his pulpit in St Enoch's Presbyterian Church:

> It was right that the loyalty of the land should celebrate as it did the victory that God has given us . . . But that celebration has cost us dear. It incurred the wrath of a Government that has been traitorous to its trusts . . . The armed servants of that Government are sent to suppress rejoicing loyalty by the sanguinary slaughter of a people resolved to resist a wicked policy.[223]

The fact that most of the police were southern Catholics, officered though they were by Protestants, only reinforced this conviction. Battles between loyalists and the constabulary continued to rage. Sectarian mobs renewed their engagements at the brickfields on the night of 13 July: the police killed two rioters with buckshot; a soldier was shot dead on the Shankill; and a head-constable was mortally wounded. The return of a Sunday school excursion accompanied by an Orange band attracted a stone-throwing mob in Donegall Street on 31 July. In retaliation Protestants attacked Catholic children returning from their outing the next day. Frankfort Moore was in York Street that night, witnessing 'dense crowds surging in every direction, and shot after shot I heard above shouts that suggested something very like Pandemonium . . . I felt I had learned something of the impotence of every arm except artillery in the case of street fighting.'[224]

Thirteen died violently that weekend. The following Saturday almost all Catholics were driven from the shipyards, and the police, trapped in Dover Street, killed three people as they shot their way to safety. Another twelve were killed that weekend and when at last the riots subsided in mid-September the official death toll was thirty-one, though the actual number killed, according to George Foy who made surgical reports on the riots, was probably around fifty.

'KILLING HOME RULE WITH KINDNESS'

'There can be no doubt that the Loyalists are arming,' the Conservative MP for West Belfast, James Haslett, had said to the correspondent of the *Birmingham Gazette* just before the vote on the Home Rule Bill.[225]

Nevertheless, the only Ulster Protestants who had resorted to violence were artisans and labourers of Belfast during the riots of 1886. The danger of rule by a Dublin parliament had passed with the defeat of the bill, and the defection of so many Liberals made it impossible for Gladstone to carry on. A general election followed in July 1886 with results providing further reassurance for opponents of Home Rule. Chamberlain's and Lord Hartington's Liberals joined with Conservatives to form the Conservative and Unionist Party – known as Unionists until 1922 – and won a handsome majority, enabling Lord Salisbury to become prime minister once more. The outcome in Ulster was not very different from that of seven months before: sixteen Nationalists, fifteen Unionists and two Liberal Unionists were elected. The contests in Londonderry City and West Belfast were decided by a handful of votes. Justin MacCarthy won Derry only after an electoral petition and Haslett lost to Thomas Sexton who declared: 'Let us not forget how much we are indebted to our Protestant friends for our victory.'[226] It is unlikely, however, that more than a couple of dozen Protestants had voted for Sexton. The Gladstonian Liberal candidate in North Antrim, Samuel C. McElroy, did get 1,910 votes but perhaps the majority were cast by Catholics of the Glens. It was clear that nearly all Protestants had voted against Home Rule and nearly all Catholics for candidates supporting Home Rule. Only when the constitutional issue was not to the fore would this pattern show any significant change.

How close had Ulster come to a general upheaval? On the eve of the Home Rule Bill being put to the vote William Johnston of Ballykilbeg had told the Commons that resistance would be offered 'at the point of the bayonet', and D.P. Barton, MP for Mid Armagh, informed the House during the second reading that he had joined a paramilitary force which 'might lead to his spending his life in penal servitude'. Henry Labouchere MP mocked these 'cock and bull stories' and the embarrassed Conservative member for North Tyrone, Lord Ernest Hamilton, dismissed talk of civil war as 'absurd and childish nonsense'.[227] But Thomas MacKnight recalled:

> The word 'Resist! Resist!' was on the lips not merely of Orangemen, but of Liberals, of those who by their profession were men of peace, merchants, manufacturers, bankers, medical men, and even clergymen.[228]

That some military preparation was being made by loyalists is clear from Johnston's entry in his diary three days after the defeat of the Home Rule Bill: 'We decided to stop drilling for the present.'[229]

Lord Salisbury stated firmly that what Ireland needed was twenty years of resolute government. His nephew Arthur Balfour, replacing the distraught Sir Michael Hicks Beach as Irish chief secretary in March 1887, soon proved that he could administer Ireland with a firm hand. Nationalists had launched a new land agitation, known as the Plan of Campaign, to force landlords to reduce rents below those fixed under the 1881 act. Balfour responded with a new dose of coercion. It was Joseph Chamberlain who persuaded the Government to mitigate repression with some concession. Due to further American food imports farmers were once again in difficulties, and as the likelihood of Home Rule receded, Presbyterian tenants might renew their co-operation with a southern land movement. Chamberlain came to Ireland in October 1887 and when he was billed to speak in the Ulster Hall soon 'no tickets could be had for love or money'.[230] He made his biggest impression, however, at Coleraine. There in a great tent on Fair Hill, 'which had been supplied with 210 gas jets', he told eight thousand people that he had persuaded the Government to adopt a new and radical approach to the land question.[231] He spoke true: the Conservatives were coming round to the view that the only long-term answer was to buy out the landlords. Land purchase, together with other reforms, might also have the effect of 'killing Home Rule with kindness'.

Even in Ulster, where they remained strongest, landlords were losing their central role. Conservative and Liberal governments alike had undermined their ascendancy. Resident magistrates and the constabulary largely replaced them in administering the law and yet they continued to depend on the law to ensure their rents were paid. The landowners' share of income from the land kept falling and not only did they fail to invest significantly in agricultural improvement but they also missed the opportunity to put their money into banks, railways and the retail trade. Landlords remained important figures in the Unionist Party, but the real drive, money and organisation came from the Protestant business classes. The impressive commercial and industrial strength of Ulster, especially in and around Belfast, as the Victorian age was succeeded by the Edwardian, provided Unionists with formidable powers of resistance when Home Rule once more became the central issue at Westminster.

10

THE ULSTER CRISIS

1890–1920

Two minutes before noon on Saturday 13 October 1888 the discharge of fog signals on the Great Northern Railway line warned of the imminent arrival of a special train from Dublin. As the locomotive steamed into Belfast's Great Victoria Street terminus, 'gaily decked with flags and banners', one hundred men of the Gordon Highlanders presented arms and the band of the Black Watch played 'God Save the Queen'. Then Charles Vane-Tempest-Stewart, 6th Marquess of Londonderry and lord lieutenant of Ireland, stepped out of the viceregal saloon carriage onto red carpet to be greeted by the mayor of Belfast, Sir James Haslett. Mounted constabulary took up the van as the state carriage took their excellencies down Glengall Place, Wellington Place, Donegall Place and into Royal Avenue, recently completed along the line of Hercules Lane to become Belfast's main thoroughfare. 'The windows of the houses were filled with heads and faces', the *Belfast Evening Telegraph* reported, 'and every available point for witnessing the procession was occupied.'

The lord lieutenant was certain of a warm reception here in the heart of the loyalist north, particularly as he was one of many Ulstermen in these years who occupied high office in the British Empire. Belfast had become a thriving imperial city and it was to give formal recognition to this status that the marquess was making his state visit.[1] At a sumptuous feast in the town hall in Victoria Street, where 'an immense number of people who awaited their arrival manifested their loyalty by repeated acclamations', Lord Londonderry said that

> her Majesty the Queen has been graciously pleased to confer on your town the dignity, the honour and the title of city (Loud cheers). And that honour is enhanced by the fact that on no other occasion has this title been conferred except the town was the seat of a bishopric.[2]

The charter arrived on 5 November but it was not until four years later that the head of Belfast Corporation was entitled to call himself lord mayor.

Londonderry's speech concentrated on the success of Unionist coercion, which in time suppressed the land agitation in the south and west. Nationalist disarray was complete in 1890: the Irish Parliamentary Party split disastrously when Parnell was cited as co-respondent in a divorce case. In a brief return to power the Liberals made a new attempt to give Ireland a parliament of her own, but the certainty that the House of Lords would throw out the 1893 Home Rule Bill kept the Union secure. Until 1906 Unionist governments dominated at Westminster. In an attempt to draw the remaining teeth of the Home Rule movement, Unionist ministers added concession to coercion: local government was democratised; economic assistance was given to 'Congested Districts', including Co. Donegal; and, above all, landlords were first persuaded and then forced to sell out to their tenants – a process which, when complete, would effect a bloodless revolution in the countryside quite without parallel in any other European state.[3]

Such concessions did not kill Irish nationalist feeling, strengthened as it was by the Gaelic revival which had its origins in Ulster. By 1910 the reunited Irish Parliamentary Party once more held the balance of power at Westminster and as the third Home Rule Bill made its slow but seemingly inexorable journey towards the Statute Book the loyalists of Ulster mounted a massive campaign of resistance. Ireland seemed on the brink of civil conflict when the First World War broke in Europe. Cataclysmic events abroad, however, did nothing to alter the polarised political views of the people of Ulster. Ireland got Home Rule and more, but only at the price of partitioning Ulster and leaving the six northeastern counties within the Union. This partial victory for the loyalists could not have been achieved but for the economic vitality of their stronghold, Belfast.

'A GREAT, WIDE, VIGOROUS, PROSPEROUS, GROWING CITY': BELFAST

In its editorial on the lord lieutenant's visit, the *Belfast News-Letter* remarked that if Belfast's 'founders could now revisit the city they might witness conditions which their liveliest imagination could never have contemplated'. The *Pictorial World* the following year observed that Belfast, with 'some 1,600 streets, the aggregate length of which is close upon 200 miles', had become 'a great, wide, vigorous, prosperous, growing city, already covering no less than 6,805 acres, and at present throwing out its arms eagerly asking for more broad stretches of both Antrim and Down'.[4] In 1891, the year in which the census confirmed that Belfast had bypassed Dublin to become the largest city in Ireland, *The Industries of Ireland* found that the

business-like aspect of the city is particularly impressive . . . Here in these crowded rushing thoroughfares, we find the pulsing heart of a mighty commercial organisation, whose vitality is ever augmenting, and whose influence is already world-wide.[5]

Belfast had become one of the great cities of western Europe and a random perusal of the city directory reveals a rich diversity: 192 linen manufacturers; 34 bleachers and finishers; 37 shipowners; 16 ships' brokers; 32 civil engineers; 24 building contractors; 33 architects; 12 estate agents; 32 bakers; 58 pawnbrokers; 4 gun and pistol manufacturers; 2 clog makers; 25 private schools; 17 publishers; 35 booksellers; 3 feather dressers; and 18 consulates, including one for Hawaii. The city had a dynamic chamber of commerce and was the centre for three large and progressive banking companies: the Ulster Bank, with its headquarters in Waring Street; the Northern Banking Company in Victoria Street; and the Belfast Banking Company, also in Waring Street. Belfast produced the cheapest gas in the United Kingdom from its vast works at Cromac recently taken over by the corporation, itself the most democratic in Ireland, having obtained household suffrage in 1887, twelve years before the rest of Ireland. The city's fire brigade was shortly to be the first in the United Kingdom to have an ambulance service.

Thanks in part to the achievement of its eighty-two National Schools, Belfast had become the centre of the most literate corner of Ireland. The city's leading newspapers were read all over Ulster: the *Belfast Morning News*, the country's first penny newspaper, Nationalist in politics; the *Belfast Evening Telegraph*, Ireland's first halfpenny newspaper, describing itself as Protestant and constitutional; the Liberal Unionist *Northern Whig* and the Conservative Unionist *Belfast News-Letter*, forced by competition to reduce their prices to a penny each; and the Presbyterian weekly, *Witness*, a champion of tenants' rights. Steeples and spires competed with mill chimneys to break the city's skyline: citizens could choose to worship in one of thirty-five Presbyterian, eighteen Methodist, seven Catholic and three Baptist churches. The Plymouth Brethren had five mission halls; open-air sermons could be heard at the Custom House steps; and there were two synagogues, thanks to Daniel Jaffe, a linen merchant originally from Hamburg and father of Sir Otto Jaffe, lord mayor of Belfast 1899–1900 and 1904–5. The Irish Temperance League ran twenty-two coffee houses in the city: the one at the Donegall Quay ferry steps was open day and night, and another, at 108½ Ann Street, served chops for sixpence. While the quiet of a Belfast Sunday became legendary, in this city, where the percentage of Catholics had fallen to 26.3 by 1891, Calvinist principles had not achieved complete acceptance. The city had over four hundred public houses, not including 'spirit groceries', and several flourishing music halls and theatres. For example, on the night of Lord Londonderry's visit in October 1888, the Alhambra Theatre in North Street included in its programme David, Wood and Hone, 'the great negro burlesque trio'; Professor Leozedt, the famous illusionist; and the Sisters Flexmore. On the same evening a new show opened in the New Theatre Royal in Arthur Square:

> Important: Any persons, male or female, gentle or simple, who may be Martyrs to that fiendish atrocity, A LAZY, SNEAKING, SLUGGISH LIVER, can be Cured in One Night by sitting out a Performance of The Arabian Nights and laughing themselves Upside Down and Inside Out.

To match its new status as Ireland's largest city, Belfast acquired a splendid theatre in December 1895, the Grand Opera House, which opened with the pantomime *Blue Beard*. Frank Matcham's lavish interior, the *Belfast News-Letter* observed, created 'a most brilliant and charming Eastern effect'.

Belfast had a remarkable array of charitable organisations – vitally necessary, though the corporation had a good record for promoting improvements and the Government was more interventionist in Ireland than it was on the British mainland.[6] In addition to its Union Workhouse and Clifton Street Poor House, the city had a Deaf and Dumb Institute on the Lisburn Road, a Lunatic Asylum on the Falls Road, a Hospital for Sick Children in Queen Street, a Hospital for Skin Diseases in Glenravel Street, an Eye and Ear Dispensary in Great Victoria Street, the Mater Hospital on the Crumlin Road and a Royal Hospital in Frederick Street. This last became the Royal Victoria Hospital and, with the special patronage of Lady Margaret Pirrie, acquired new premises at the junction of the Grosvenor and Falls Roads, opened in 1903 by Edward VII and fitted with an advanced ventilation system pioneered in Harland and Wolff ocean liners. The city's charities included: the Convent of Nazareth, Ballynafeigh, for the aged, infirm and infantile poor of all creeds; the Protestant Female Industrial School for homeless or unprotected girls; the Elim Home for Destitute Boys and Girls on the Crumlin Road, 'to rescue orphan, homeless and destitute street arabs'; the Provident Home for Friendless Females of Good Character 'who would otherwise be exposed to temptation'; and the Ulster

Female Penitentiary, Brunswick Street, 'to receive penitent victims of seduction . . . without distinction of sect or party'.[7]

Though Belfast was pre-eminently an industrial city, it was still of major importance as a market and a place of export for agricultural produce, despite falling prices and a succession of bad seasons. The Turnley Street Hay and Straw Market was open every day to supply the needs of the city's six hundred jaunting cars, in addition to horse-drawn trams and omnibuses, traders' carts and private carriages. May's Market also met daily to sell corn, grass seed and flaxseed, and cattle and horse fairs were held there. The Butter Market operated six days a week in Great Patrick Street, where heavily salted butter could be bought in firkins, crocks, lumps and prints. Friday saw great herds of cattle – steaming, lowing and butting – urged on by drovers, shouting and waving ashplants, down the city thoroughfares for sale in Oxford Street; and in nearby George's Market, meat, poultry, eggs and fish were sold by vociferous traders from innumerable stalls.

Several professional families remained in Great Victoria Street and there were nine medical doctors in College Square East; but the introduction in 1881 of tuppenny fares on the trams for any journey and the extension of track to Malone Park, Newtownbreda, Sydenham and Fortwilliam during the remaining years of the decade hastened the departure of the middle classes from the city centre. McLaughlin and Harvey at their Laganvale Works on the Ormeau Road and H. and J. Martin nearby made the cheapest bricks in Ireland – half the cost of those in Dublin – and built comfortable suburban dwellings for developers, such as R.J. McConnell and Baron Templemore, at Rosetta, Mountpottinger, the Antrim Road and along the Malone ridge. The landscape artist Paul Henry, brought up in Ulsterville Avenue in the 1880s, recalled: 'In my childhood there was no more familiar sight than the unending procession of carts of bricks with which Belfast was feverishly built.'[8] Appalling conditions still prevailed in inner-city courts and entries but stringent requirements laid down by the corporation ensured that the new rows of 'kitchen' and 'parlour' houses provided some of the best accommodation for workers in Ireland, certainly superior to the draughty tenements of Dublin.

The most splendid buildings in Belfast were neither municipal nor ecclesiastical, but commercial. Richardson, Sons and Owden's massive and ornate warehouse, famous for its linen dress foundations, towered over the White Linen Hall and was admired by Oscar Wilde. It was upstaged in 1888 by Robinson and Cleaver's taller but less attractive Irish Linen Warehouse, which posted more than one third of parcels sent from Belfast. But the real commercial heart of the province's principal employer of industrial labour was in and around Bedford Street – it was here that many deals were struck for the sale of more than one hundred thousand miles of linen cloth made each year in Ulster by the 1880s.

BELFAST'S INDUSTRIAL MIGHT

In 1894, when there were nine hundred thousand spindles in use in Ulster's linen industry, the president of the Belfast Chamber of Commerce, H.O. Lanyon, made this estimation:

> I find the length of yarn produced in the year amounts to about 644,000,000 miles, making a thread which would encircle the world 25,000 times. If it could be used for a telephone wire it would give us six lines to the sun, and about 380 besides to the moon. The exports of linen in 1894 measured about 156,000,000 yards, which would make a girdle for the earth at the Equator three yards wide, or cover an area of 32,000 acres, or it would reach from end to end of the County of Down, one mile wide.[9]

The lion's share of this remarkable productive capacity was based in Belfast. The York Street Flax Spinning and Weaving Company, the largest of its kind in the world, had 55,000 spindles and 1,000 looms, and employed 4,000 workers, not including embroiderers and other outworkers. Through its branches and agencies as far apart as New York, Riga, St Petersburg and Melbourne, the firm sold fronting linens, interlinings, sheets, printed dress linens and lawns, damask tablecloths and napkins, glass cloths, elastic canvas, drills, ducks, hollands, cambrics, a great range of handkerchiefs, and clothing for Latin America described as 'Creas, Platillas, Bretanas, Silesias, Irlandas etc.'. Ewart's Mill on the Crumlin Road was almost as large with 32,000 spindles, 1,900 looms and 3,500 employees; other great concerns included the Brookfield Mill, the Wolfhill mills and factories at Ligoniel, the Linfield Mill at Sandy Row and John Shaw Brown of Edenderry. Brown's had the largest contracts in the United Kingdom for table and bed linens, and Harden's of Amelia Street claimed to have the largest handkerchief manufactory in the world, fancy stitching and embroidery being carried out 'in the cottages of the Irish peasantry, whose work of this class is absolutely unrivalled'.[10]

The emergence of a successful engineering industry in Belfast was fostered by the growing needs of the linen and shipbuilding firms. Many of the entrepreneurs were outsiders: the Clonard Foundry, making Duplex machines to hackle both ends of the flax, was set up by George Horner from Leeds; James Scrimgeour from Scotland began making textile machinery in Albert Street; he was bought out by James

Mackie, also a Scot, and by 1892 the firm was making one hundred spinning frames a year, in addition to spindles, fluting rollers, flax cutters, bundling presses and twisting frames. Belfast also became the main centre in Ireland for manufacturing steam engines: John Rowan and Sons invented piston rings still in use; McAdam Brothers made steam pumps for irrigating the Nile; and Combe Barbour – together with Mackie's the largest engineering firm outside the shipyards – built quadruple-expansion engines for cotton mills in India. Musgrave Brothers won an international reputation for their patent stable and house fittings, and by the end of the century Davidson's Sirocco Works had become the world leader in the manufacture of ventilation, fan and tea-drying machinery.[11]

Belfast was rapidly becoming a world centre for the production of aerated waters – an extraordinary achievement considering the water was obtained by boring artesian wells through the foul sleech of Cromac. Ross's of Victoria Square specialised in Royal Ginger Ale, 'a delicious aromatic and refreshing beverage, utterly free from any intoxicating tendency', much prized in the United States; Evans's Cromac Works was noted for its Sarsparilla; but the largest concern was Cantrell and Cochrane, sending out to 'all civilised portions of the known world' its Aromatic Ginger Ale, Fruit Flavoured Lemonade, Sparkling Montserrat, Club Soda, and Refreshing Seltzer, Kali and Lithia waters, which were described in an advertisement in the 1887 directory as

> sparkling like champagne, agreeable to the taste as that much lauded and very costly wine, but not leaving as champagne does so often, repentance and self reproach as a heritage of the morrow.[12]

Hangovers notwithstanding, the city had four large distilleries and by the end of the century Belfast exported 60 per cent of Ireland's whiskey. Thomas Gallaher had transferred his tobacco firm from Derry to Belfast in 1867 and, growing his own leaf on extensive estates in North Carolina, he was importing raw tobacco to the value of £480,000 by 1889 and employing six hundred people. According to *The Industries of Ireland*, Gallaher's 'delicious and fragrant' flake tobacco in use 'is attended with unmingled satisfaction'. 'The visitor to this model establishment', it continued,

> if he be of the mighty army of smokers he will find pleasure in the reflection that he is one of the many millions whose devotion to the *celestial fume* has brought into existence such a wondrous and unique industry as that which receives such excellent exemplification under Messrs. Gallaher & Company's influential auspices.[13]

Marcus Ward had the distinction of being awarded the Cross of the Legion of Honour in 1878 by the president of France, Marshal

MacMahon, whose family was of Ulster stock. Ward had, in Belfast, one of the largest printing and paper-making firms in the British Isles and claimed to have pioneered the mass production of Christmas cards. At every turn a visitor would be reminded of the remarkable diversity of Belfast's industrial enterprise, ranging from Carmichael's Hat Manufactory in North Street, with sales as far away as 'France, Switzerland, Africa and other countries', to Frederick King and Company of Waring Street, pioneering makers of desiccated soups sold worldwide, particularly to shipping firms and navies.

By far the most striking evidence of Belfast's economic power, setting the city apart from any other in Ireland, were the huge shipbuilding yards on Queen's Island. 'Messrs. Harland & Wolff, Limited', *The Industries of Ireland* enthused,

> stand to-day among the very largest ship-builders in the British Isles, and their achievements in all the most conspicuous modern phases of this important national industry have not been surpassed by any of their numerous contemporaries on the coasts of Albion . . . the firm here under notice have earned for the once obscure and almost untravelled river Lagan an international reputation as one of the great shipbuilding rivers of the world.[14]

These words could have been written with even greater emphasis ten years later, for the decade of the 1890s was one of spectacular growth, pushing Harland and Wolff forward to become the greatest shipyard in the world launching the world's largest ships.

'THE GREATEST EVENT OF ITS KIND THE WORLD HAS EVER WITNESSED':
THE LAUNCH OF THE *OCEANIC*, 1899

From early morning on Saturday 14 January 1899 special excursion trains drew in at Belfast's three railway termini bringing sightseers from all over Ulster to view the launch of the *Oceanic*, the largest ship in the world. According to the *Belfast News-Letter*, there were also visitors 'from London, Liverpool, Glasgow and all other great British ports, from the United States – whose people venerate enterprise and esteem affectionately everything which is big – and from almost every European country'. The weather was bright and sharp as immense crowds made their way to the riverside. A large pavilion had been put up on Victoria wharf for ticket-holders, providing seating for two thousand and a promenade for another three thousand.[15]

The ship's construction was the climax of a remarkable decade for Harland and Wolff. In the financial years 1890–1 and 1893–4 the company headed the list for the largest number of vessels built by any shipyard in the United Kingdom, more than fifty ships in all. Gustav Wolff was an active Unionist at Westminster, where he was known as 'Teutonic'; Edward Harland, also an MP and dubbed 'Majestic', died in 1895; Gustav Schwabe died in 1898; Thomas Ismay was to die soon after the *Oceanic*'s launch; and this left William Pirrie in supreme control of a firm of international importance rapidly acquiring for itself a pivotal position in a great shipping cartel.[16] The company survived an immense fire in July 1896 and carried out a massive reorganisation programme, including the erection of a gigantic gantry, carrying mobile cranes to lift the hydraulic riveting machines. By 1899 the yard extended over eighty acres and employed ten thousand men.[17] A correspondent of the *Windsor Magazine* described work in progress on the Island:

> Men rush about with great plates of steel on handcarts; there is the creaking of cranes as the plates are swung through the air into place, the clang of hammers reverberating again and again. Every vessel is surrounded by a network of scaffolding, and inclined wooden ways are built to the top of the ship. Chains, pieces of iron, heaps of bolts and blocks of wood litter the ground, and you shudder as the casual remark is made to keep out of the way of falling bolts . . . on the average a baker's dozen of men are killed in the course of a year.[18]

The *Oceanic* – the second ship of that name built for the White Star line – had been ordered as a competitor to rival North German Lloyd's *Kaiser Wilhelm der Grosse* and Cunard's *Campania* and *Lucania* in the lucrative transatlantic passenger market. With a gross tonnage of 17,274, a length of 685.7 feet, a breadth of 68.3 feet, a hold of 44.5 feet, and fitted with four-cyclinder, triple-expansion engines, the *Oceanic* would outdistance all rivals. Thirteen feet longer and eight feet deeper than Brunel's *Great Eastern*, she would be the largest ship afloat and the longest ever launched. As the launch became imminent, the *Belfast Evening Telegraph* reporter noticed that

> a dead silence of suppressed excitement permeated the people on the shore and on the top. A rocket went up . . . And they stared with every optical nerve strained at the leviathan. No movement yet! The excitement became deeper! Then a man said in an awestricken voice: 'Isn't it like an execution?'[19]

Two guns were fired to signal the shipwrights to stand aside, the general manager waved the launch flag, and – released by a hydraulic trigger – at twenty-seven minutes past eleven the *Oceanic* began to move. As the great vessel slid down, the *Freeman's Journal* reported: 'Pieces of timber as large almost as forest trees rose into the air like chips in a wind and fell in showers on the water. Presently the great hawsers, which held the two immense bow chains in sections, began to break and fly into the air.' The ship settled, the *Belfast News-Letter* observed, 'like a gull alighting with graceful curve on the water', though the displacement wave soaked many, including William Pirrie. The *Freeman's Journal*, often scathing about Belfast's pretensions, described the launch as

> the greatest event of its kind the world has ever witnessed, and in a certain sense, perhaps the most epoch-making incident of the century.[20]

Belfast's emergence as a leading industrial port owed much to the dramatic growth of the European economy during the second half of the nineteenth century. While much of Ulster west of the Bann benefited but little, this quickening reached out to the north-west of the province to bring about a remarkable revitalisation of Derry.

DERRY: INDUSTRIAL AND COMMERCIAL PROGRESS

'That the spirit of progress has taken up its abode in modern Londonderry will not be doubted by anyone who knows anything about the "Maiden City" and its great advancement during recent years.' So wrote a contributor to the 1891 *Industries of Ireland*, introducing his entry on John Brewster, bread and biscuit manufacturer in James Street, 'a notable illustration of the prevailing local energy'.[21] The Honourable the Irish Society had been disappointed by the feeble growth of Derry, only the twelfth largest urban centre in Ireland by 1821. The later nineteenth century, however, saw a surge in the city's development: between 1881 and 1911 the population doubled to over forty thousand, making Derry the fourth largest city in the country. This expansion was largely generated by the success there of the shirt-making industry.

Cotton shirts, with linen fronts and cuffs, were supplanting those made of flannel. In Derry William Scott of Balloughry was the first to exploit the commercial possibilities of these new garments by securing orders in Glasgow for shirts cut out in city workshops and embroidered and sewn up in the countryside. The invention of steam-driven machines for both cutting and sewing brought shirt-making into factories, the most impressive being a five-storey block covering almost an acre in Foyle Road, erected in 1857 by two Scots, William Tillie and John Henderson. By 1891 the firm had added a steam laundry to its premises, exported its products – the 'Celtic' shirt in particular – across the empire and in Latin America, and employed 1,500 at its Foyle Road factory and another 3,000 rural workers.[22] In *Das Kapital* Karl Marx referred to the role of outworkers in this industry:

> Capital also sets in motion, by means of invisible threads, another army: that of the workers in the domestic industries, who dwell in the large towns and are also scattered over the face of the country. An example: The shirt factory of Messrs. Tillie at Londonderry, which employs 1,000

operatives in the factory itself, and 9,000 people spread up and down the country and working in their houses.[23]

In fact Tillie and Henderson did not employ as many as 9,000 outworkers, but by 1902 there were 38 factories in Derry, with 113 rural branches or 'stations', paying out more than £300,000 a year in wages to some 18,000 employees, more than half of whom were outworkers in rural Co. Londonderry and Co. Donegal, Inishowen in particular.

While a welcome additional income to a smallholding family, the rates of pay were poor – to earn nine shillings in a week a woman had to sew up between twenty-four and thirty shirts. Indeed shirt-making as a whole was a low-wage industry, at least 80 per cent of employees being female. Even in its industrial heyday Derry had great difficulty in providing sufficient work for its male citizens.

Derry had for long been one of the most important emigrant ports in Ireland and for a time the principal one. Earlier in the nineteenth century the trade was dominated by Americans who brought over flaxseed and timber and returned across the Atlantic with Irish emigrants. Some Derry merchants, buying Canadian-built sailing vessels, set up in competition and after the Famine two firms dominated – J. and J.L. Cooke and William McCorkell and Company. Business was good during the American Civil War and the great linen boom, but contracted thereafter. Cooke's survived for a time by shipping over pitch pine and McCorkell's imported American grain in its fine fleet of sailing ships, landing twenty thousand tons at Derry Quay in 1881. As steam vessels became more efficient, however, these firms were driven to the wall, McCorkell's winding up in 1896. The transport of some 3,500 migrant labourers each year to Scotland was largely in the hands of Glasgow shipowners.

Attempts were made to make Derry a shipbuilding centre. Captain William Coppin had built sailing vessels in the 1830s and launched the world's largest screw-propulsion vessel, the *Great Northern*, in 1843; but his steamships were not a commercial success. In 1882 a second attempt was made when W.F. Biggar set up the Foyle Shipyard at Pennyburn. He built twenty-six sailing vessels and six steamers before his company was forced to close down in 1892. In 1899 the Londonderry Shipbuilding and Engineering Company resumed operations at the Foyle yard and, taken over by Swan and Hunter in 1912, it prospered in a small way with good prospects as the First World War broke.[24]

Derry had become a thriving commercial and industrial centre by the beginning of the twentieth century. Its economy was diversified by busy corn and saw mills, foundries, tanneries, tobacco manufacture, salmon netting, oyster fishing and whiskey distillation – A.A. Watt's Abbey Street distillery was for a time the largest in Ireland. The city had its own centre for training Presbyterian ministers, Magee College; two of the most renowned schools in the north-west, St Columb's and Foyle College; a magnificent double-decked bridge across the river; a fine new Guildhall opened in 1890 and rebuilt after a fire in 1908; the most splendid department store outside of Belfast, Austin's, rebuilt in 1906; and four railway termini.

Celebrated across the world by the ever-popular 'Londonderry Air' (also the brand name of a perfume made by Glendenning's Medical Hall in Strand Road), Derry had nevertheless acquired urban sectarian problems similar to those of Belfast, though on a smaller scale.[25] The city had been almost exclusively Protestant until the early nineteenth century. Economic expansion thereafter drew in the rural poor, particularly from Inishowen and Magilligan, hard hit by the suppression of illicit distillation. Protestants settled to the north of the city, immediately south of the walls in and around Fountain Street, and across the Foyle in the Waterside. Catholics clustered and spread out from the Bogside west of the walls and by 1891 they formed a majority of 4,500 over Protestants living in Derry. Knife-edge parliamentary contests and fierce disputation in the registration courts, together with traditional festivals, helped to heighten sectarian passions. Factory owners staggered closing times in an attempt to stem almost daily taunting by both sides and severe rioting was a frequent occurrence, notably in 1868–70 and in 1899.

The city reached an economic plateau in the first years of the twentieth century, partly because great liners ceased to call regularly at the port and partly owing to mounting competition facing the shirt-making industry. Derry was at the very edge of Ulster's industrial region centred on Belfast and it was beginning to share some of the economic decline experienced by much of the province west of the River Bann.

ULSTER'S TOWNS

During the second half of the nineteenth century and for much of the twentieth century, Ireland was unique in being the only country in Europe to experience a fall in population. Between 1841 and 1911 there was a decrease of 46 per cent. Apart from the Famine, emigration was the principal cause and, while it did slow down after the Famine, the outward flow was encouraged by the severe fall in agricultural prices after 1877. Death rates were highest in Belfast and the industrial towns but in rural areas the number of births per marriage fell, with the exception of Donegal where it rose by 23 per cent between 1871 and 1891, possibly owing to the decline in seasonal migration to Scotland.

Ulster's population fell 34 per cent, from 2.4 million to 1.6 million, between 1841 and 1911. Because this decline was less severe than in the other three provinces, Ulster's share of the inhabitants of Ireland rose in this period from 29 to 36 per cent.[26] Emigration in the north was partly stemmed by the burgeoning of Belfast, a city which by 1911 was home to almost one quarter of Ulster's population. West of the Bann, population decline was similar to that in the rest of the island and was most sharply felt in the counties of Cavan, Monaghan, Tyrone and Fermanagh. Enniskillen, Cavan, Belturbet, Cootehill, Clones, Castleblayney, Armagh and Limavady lost between a quarter and a third of their populations over this seventy-year period, even though the proportion of people living in towns in the north rose from less than 10 per cent to almost 40 per cent. Carrickmacross, Newry, Monaghan, Dungannon and Letterkenny experienced no change, leaving only five growing towns in the western half of Ulster: Cookstown, Omagh, Derry, Strabane and Bundoran.[27]

In some towns local industries wilted before the onslaught of more competitive goods made in Belfast and brought in by rail. This happened in Armagh, which was overtaken in size by Lurgan in 1871 and also by Portadown in the 1890s. Portadown, little more than a village at the beginning of the nineteenth century, flourished by being the junction for four busy railway lines, becoming an important market for all of southern Ulster.[28] The railway also stimulated growth in Cookstown, Omagh, Ballymoney and Ballymena. 'In Ballymena,' Hugh McCall remarked, ' ... the dignity of labour stamps on the countenance of its children a certain sturdiness of character and a degree of honest independence which at once proclaim the glory and power of industry.' Contemporaries attributed Ballymena's success to the Protestant work ethic and its inhabitants' legendary care with money, but the town's growth to nine thousand people by 1891 was due at least as much to its rail connection and its position well within Belfast's industrialising influence. By the end of the century the Braidwater Spinning Mill, employing one thousand people, was only one of several flourishing linen firms; at Hillmount twenty thousand yards were processed each working day; twenty-five thousand webs a year were finished at Lisnafallen; three large firms made embroidered handkerchiefs; and the town was an important agricultural market, selling sixty thousand pigs each year, most of them slaughtered and cured locally.[29]

Ballymoney and Coleraine also enjoyed diversified economies and made modest growth. Extensive canalisation of the lower Bann failed to make Coleraine a great port, but salmon netting and linen manufacture remained important. Kennedy's Coleraine Foundry was one of Ireland's leading makers of agricultural implements and water turbines.

In addition, *The Industries of Ireland* observed: '"Old Coleraine" whiskey has become a household word among *connoisseurs* of "the crayther" and its name is accepted in many quarters of the highest authority as a synonym for perfection in malt spirit.'[30] The same guide commended Lisburn for 'its attractive appearance, handsome buildings, and general air of thrift and progress'.[31] Like Holywood, Lisburn was close enough to Belfast to become a dormitory town but its population of twelve thousand by the end of the century was largely sustained by its own commercial and industrial success. The Hilden Mills, owned by William Barbour and Sons, by the 1890s had become the largest linen thread manufacturers in the world. Extending over 34 acres – not including ground for 500 workers' cottages – the works had 30,000 spindles spinning thread and 8,000 twisting it, using more than 100 tons of flax, tow and hemp in a week. Together with additional mills at Sprucefield and Dunmurry, the firm employed five thousand in Ulster and had set up an extensive plant at Paterson, New Jersey, producing over two thousand US dollars worth of finished goods every month.[32]

Not all towns in eastern Ulster enjoyed growth. Downpatrick, Portaferry and Donaghadee declined because their port facilities were not suited to modern trading and passenger vessels. They were superseded not only by Belfast but also by Larne, stimulated by a regular steamship service to Stranraer and transatlantic liners calling in to its deep, safe harbour. Rathfriland, once an important market town, failed to compete with Banbridge, Gilford, Dromore, Comber and Newtownards further north – all growing textile towns – and with Newry further south.

Though a bustling, prosperous town, Newry did not fulfil the promise of the eighteenth century and by the 1890s it had ceased to grow. The extension of railways undermined the competitiveness of the Newry canal and drew the bulk of linen exports instead to Belfast. Newry was connected only by a branch line to the Great Northern Railway from Belfast to Dublin and, in any case, the clearing out of obstructions at Narrow Water, the construction of the Victoria locks between 1842 and 1850, and the deepening of Carlingford Lough completed in 1894, failed to turn the port into a viable rival to Belfast. Warrenpoint, close by, disappointed its commercial promoters, but instead became a seaside resort much favoured for a time by Lancashire holiday-makers. Economic progress created a prosperous middle class which became accustomed to taking summer holidays by the sea. Bangor, with a population of 7,800 by 1911, was the largest resort; Portrush grew rapidly from the 1880s to over 2,000; and Bundoran in south Donegal made spectacular growth in the first years of the twentieth century.[33]

Cheap and rapid transport hastened the penetration of mass-produced goods from across the Irish Sea and from Belfast into rural Ulster. As a result, many traditional crafts expired, though a few survived to find a wider market. One striking success was the porcelain works of D. McBirney and Company which drew on the water power of the Erne at Belleek to create a high-lustre, elaborately ornate and extremely delicate china, 'now known over the whole world to millions of people who do not know where Beleek is', *Lowe's 1880 Directory* observed.[34] Lace-making was started in Carrickmacross in the 1820s by Mrs Grey Porter and was energetically promoted by Tristram Kennedy, agent of the Marquess of Bath, who imported samples of Brussels lace during the Famine. By 1887, 154 girls were employed in Crossmaglen guipure and appliqué lace schools, but a successful export industry was really established by the Sisters of the Order of St Louis in Carrickmacross in the 1890s, which earned £20,000 in its first ten years. Lady Aberdeen, wife of the 7th earl who was twice lord lieutenant, was a faithful patroness, and when she brought forty lace workers to the Chicago World Fair in 1893, they returned with profits of £50,000. By 1907, earnings from the industry were worth £100,000 a year. The work was low-paid, however, and hard on the eyes, especially at night when the lacemaker had to intensify the light from an oil lamp through a glass globe filled with water. This industrial craft declined rapidly after the First World War.[35]

The sea-fishing industry never fulfilled the hopeful predictions of economists, partly because Cornish and Scots boat owners were usually better equipped. However, the seasonal appearance of mackerel and herring shoals did provide a modest prosperity to Kilkeel, Ardglass and Annalong, in Co. Down, and Killybegs, in Co. Donegal. The heyday was in the 1870s when at Kilkeel, according to the *Downpatrick Recorder*, 'fifty luggers are constantly employed, eighteen or twenty of the boats belonging to the immediate neighbourhood'.[36] Since it cost £4 a week to victual a lugger, merchants in the town did well in season. Drift nets were shot at dusk, each boat carrying a train of 50 to 60 nets, each 15 fathoms long. The importation of cheap refrigerated meat cut the price of fresh fish from Ulster in British markets and the province was no match for the Isle of Man when it came to curing herrings. Nevertheless, Kilkeel in 1890 had 35 per cent of the total value of herrings landed in Ireland, and several fishing ports, Ardglass in particular, built up a brisk export market in salt mackerel for sale in the West Indies.[37]

With its mix of modern industry, family farms, traditional crafts and efficient communications, Ulster in many respects looked like several provincial regions of the British mainland. In the peculiar nature of its divided society, however, it seemed to have more in common with provinces of the Austro-Hungarian, Russian and Turkish empires.

More clearly now than at any time since the seventeenth century the inhabitants of Ulster seemed divided sharply into two ethnic groups with profoundly divergent aspirations. Some, indeed, were convinced that Protestants and Catholics there formed two separate nations. During the second half of the nineteenth century Ulster had joined in the developing European debates on racial typifications and national traits. The *Ulster Journal of Archaeology*, founded in 1852, in its first issues ran a series of articles entitled 'The origin and characteristics of the population in the counties of Down and Antrim', which informed readers that Protestants in eastern Ulster were Anglo-Saxon in race, possessing the inherited virtues of thrift, capacity for hard work and respect for law and order. Using such words as 'staunch' and 'stalwart' to describe themselves, northern Protestants had no difficulty in accepting this theory – Colonel Thomas Waring, for example, assuring an audience at Magheralin, Co. Down, in 1886 that the English and Scots would not desert 'their own flesh and blood'.[38] Nationalists, though they might add adjectives such as 'dour' and 'mean', largely accepted Protestants' assumption of their racial separateness, for they at the same time were emphasising their Gaelic origins and laying claim to inherent characteristics such as hospitality, passion and love of poetry. This mutual acceptance of racial separation can be seen when Michael Davitt made a speech in May 1886 claiming that Ulster unionists were but alien settlers in Ulster, Celtic neither by race nor habit; this drew the following retort from the *Belfast News-Letter* on 14 May:

> We have every reason to be thankful . . . that Ulstermen are not Celts and not being so, why should they be subject to a government of the worst class of Celts?[39]

This view is still widely accepted today – was this theory of racial separation justified?

There is growing scholarly evidence that seventeenth-century planters and their descendants did not separate themselves from the native Irish population as much as was formerly believed. Lowland Scots and English settlers in western Ulster, particularly those of low status, sometimes married local women and within a generation their descendants could well be speaking Irish. On the other side of the province the incoming flood of British colonists encouraged many native Irish to embrace Protestantism, speak English and drop the prefix 'O' or 'Mac' from their surnames. A cursory glance at registers in segregated schools past and present will show many 'British' surnames, such as Hume, in Catholic roll books and 'Irish' surnames, such as Magennis, in Protestant ones. Genealogists have uncovered a far greater degree of religious conversion and native–planter, Catholic–Protestant intermarriage than might be expected.

The nineteenth century saw a dramatic fall in the number of people in Ireland who could speak Irish and, as surnames were anglicised, translated or given pseudo-translations, the memory of ancestral connection was often lost. Many Donnellys (originally Ó Donnghaile) in the Coleraine district became Donaldsons; Laverys (Ó Labhradha) on the eastern shore of Lough Neagh became Armstrongs; the Johnston and Johnson surnames, of Scots and English origin, were borrowed by MacKeowns, MacShanes and Bissetts; the Co. Cavan sept of Mac Cathail Riabhaigh (a name usually anglicised Culreavy) became Gray (*riabhach* means 'grey' in Irish); and many of the MacBrin family of Co. Down changed their name to Burns, an Argyll surname which had already incorporated the Gaelic clan of MacBurney from Dumfriesshire. Some names were easily confused and amalgamated, such as the Scottish Border surname Kerr and the Irish surname Carr, an anglicisation either of the Co. Donegal Mac Giolla Chathair, 'son of the devotee of (St) Cathair' or the Co. Monaghan Mac Giolla Cheara, 'son of the devotee of (St) Ceara'. The Carrolls or O'Carrolls of Dromore almost all changed their surname to Cardwell. Most of the Ulster sept of Ó Dreáin anglicised to Adrain but some, in a pseudo-translation, converted to Hawthorne, *droighean* in Gaelic meaning 'blackthorn' or 'hawthorn'. Many members of the MacAree family in Co. Monaghan changed their name to King, assuming their surname derived from Mac an Ríogh, 'son of a king', though it is more likely to come from Mac Fhearadhaigh, 'son of the manly one'. Even the dropping of a prefix could invalidate conclusions on regional origin, in the absence of other evidence: the common Ulster surname Neill is borne by people who could descend from the Scots Neilsons or MacNeillies; from the MacNeills of the Isles; from any branch of the Ulster O'Neills; or from Mac an Fhilidh, 'son of the poet', which had also been anglicised as MacNeilly, Neely, MacAnelly, MacAnilly and MacNeely.[40]

In short, by the late nineteenth century descendants of natives and planters had become so intermingled that it would be quite wrong to conclude – as so many do – that the great majority of Catholics are of Gaelic origin and that most Protestants are of British colonial stock. However, detailed investigation would surely reveal a similar lack of clarity in the ethnic distinctions then so passionately espoused in the

Austro-Hungarian, Turkish and Russian empires. What mattered was that Serbs, Croats, Slovenes, Czechs, Bulgars, Poles and others *felt* themselves to be separate nations. Similarly, the vast majority of Ulster Catholics thought of themselves as part of an Irish nation, worthy of self-government; and Ulster Protestants, with a few notable exceptions drawn largely from the intelligentsia, saw themselves as Britons (though, perhaps, with their own regional characteristics), who should not be cut loose from the United Kingdom. These clashing aspirations continued to generate eddies of turbulence, sometimes becoming dangerous cyclones, for many years to come. Politicians, however, often displayed a striking inability to recognise the portents of storm.

'YOU WOULD NOT HAVE ONE BUT TWO OPPRESSED MINORITIES':
NATIONALISTS AND LIBERALS

In a speech to Portsmouth Liberals in 1886, Parnell held up a map of Ireland with Ulster Unionist constituencies coloured in yellow. 'This little yellow patch,' he said in mocking tones, 'covered by my forefinger represents Protestant Ulster – (loud laughter) – and now they say they want a separate parliament for this little yellow patch up in the north-east!'[41] He and other Irish Parliamentary Party politicians consistently underestimated how formidable was the obstacle thrown up by Ulster Protestant opposition on the road to their promised land of Home Rule. Parnell still seemed to think that northern Unionists comprised only landlords, carpenters and 'the artisans of towns such as Portadown'.[42] Talk of armed resistance to a Dublin parliament was lightly dismissed, for example by the *Connaught People* as 'empty fire and brimstone talk' and by the nationalist songwriter, Timothy O'Sullivan, as 'mere Saundersonian slap-dash, with about as much substance in it as a soap-bubble'. Certainly Edward Saunderson, the Ulster Unionist leader until his death in 1906, reinforced this view by his affability. John Dillon wrote:

> He is in the habit of talking about civil war in Ulster, and at the same time he cracks so many jokes that . . . the impression he makes is that he does not care a half-crown whether Home Rule is granted or not.[43]

Most Nationalists, taking comfort from the fact that their party held around half the seats in the province, assumed that they would make further electoral inroads in the north and that the problem of Protestant hostility would simply ebb away – a view reinforced by a misinterpretation of events in Ulster in the 1790s. John Redmond, who was to lead the Irish Parliamentary Party from 1900 to 1918, argued that if Belfast was left out, Catholics were '55 per cent of the whole population' of

Ulster. Many regarded Belfast as an un-Irish aberration, the Gaelic revival encouraging them to see industrialisation as corrupting. No serious thought was given to attempting to work out constitutional formulae or to win the hearts and minds of northern Protestants. Only Thomas Sexton, the Cork lawyer representing West Belfast, made a closely argued case to show that the political partition of Ireland could create as many problems as it might solve:

> You would not have one but two oppressed minorities. You would have the 200,000 Catholics and 500,000 Protestants of the north of Ireland, and the 3,000,000 Catholics and 300,000 Protestants of the south in the other provinces, so that in order to please 500,000, or the men who are supposed to represent them, you will outrage the feelings of 200,000 Catholics and 300,000 Protestants . . . the Catholic population so interpenetrates every portion of Ulster that even if you have a parliament in every parish, you would still have a minority in each.[44]

Even if Sexton meant the exclusion of only part of Ulster, he nevertheless showed a woeful ignorance of population distribution, readily available in the 1881 census returns as 865,856 Protestants and 833,560 Catholics in Ulster. The 1887 report on the Belfast riots of the previous year seemed to confirm the fear of oppression of Catholics in a separately ruled Ulster: Catholics had received most of the compensation for property destroyed and an appendix showed that of eighty-nine men employed by the Belfast Corporation only two were Catholics, and they were in low-paid positions. Separate constitutional arrangements for the north seemed so unlikely to the Nationalists that they gave little further thought to this Ulster Catholic minority. Ultimate success for their cause over the whole island seemed certain; when the Nationalist Justin MacCarthy unseated the Unionist in Londonderry City on petition in October 1886, the *United Ireland* exulted:

> 'No surrender' has got a new meaning. It is a national watchword now. The nation holds the inviolate city and means to keep it for all time . . . Today the territory occupied by the West Britons who won't become Irishmen is growing narrower and narrower.[45]

Gladstonian Liberals shared this belief that Ulster Protestant hostility to Home Rule would disappear. Henry Labouchere said:

> The area over which the Orangemen hold sway is growing smaller and smaller every year. Many of the Presbyterians of Ulster have already thrown in their lot with the Home Rulers. There is now but one single northern Irish county which does not return a Parnellite – viz. Antrim.[46]

Sir Charles Russell, the Liberal MP of Ulster Catholic extraction, believed that once the land problem was resolved and once Protestants 'understand that they have no right to be regarded in any exceptional way, and must cast in their lot on equal terms with their Catholic brethren, that the repugnance they now feel would be greatly lessened, and in time altogether cease'. A Liberal deputation to Ulster in 1887 had returned with this confident report:

> In Ulster the great majority of the people who are opposed to Home Rule will, when Home Rule is granted, forget past differences . . . Considerations of common interests will make them join with their fellow-countrymen in carrying on the government of Ireland . . . They themselves even now are aware that this will be the case.[47]

Gladstone was immersing himself in reading Irish history and had been deeply impressed by the leading role taken by Volunteers in Ulster in obtaining reform and legislative independence in the eighteenth century. In time, he was sure, Ulster Protestants would become nationalists. He was also moved by accounts of past English oppression (obtained largely from the works of the Unionist historian W.E.H. Lecky), and agreed with Sir William Harcourt who said: 'We hold Ireland by force and by force alone as much as in the days of Cromwell.'[48] Lord Rosebery recalled that while he was visiting the Liberal leader in 1891 Gladstone watched a play at his home and then

> came back chilled and tired, and lost control of himself (for the third time in my experience) in speaking of the Irish rebellion of 1798. In vain did I try to keep him off and turn the subject.[49]

Yet Gladstone's knowledge of Ulster remained vague. For example, he made an observation in 1890 that Protestants in the province were 'possibly near half a million in number'. He agreed with his colleague Lord Spencer that Protestant bigotry was the only serious problem, as it antagonised Catholics:

> Bitter religious animosity has been shown, but where? In Ulster, where, I believe, the Protestants have been the chief cause of keeping up their [Catholic] animosity.[50]

'ALL OUR PROGRESS HAS BEEN MADE UNDER THE UNION'

On the evening of 2 August 1886, while the Belfast riots still raged, Thomas MacKnight dined with leading businessmen. He asked the chairman of Harland and Wolff, William Pirrie, 'whether it were true . . . that if the Home Rule Bill ever became law, his firm would withdraw their great shipbuilding works from Belfast, and take them to the Clyde. "Most certainly," he said, "this would be done."' A similar question was put to the other men round the table:

They all said that under an Irish Parliament and Government there would be no security for life nor property, no fair play to the Loyalists in the North of Ireland, and that utter want of commercial confidence without which Belfast could not continue to prosper. They all agreed with their host that the great manufacturing and industrial enterprises of their town would have to seek a new home on the other side of the Irish Sea.[51]

This was not empty talk: nearly a century later Michael Moss and John R. Hume found evidence in the Harland and Wolff papers that by the time Pirrie was being questioned at the dinner table, preparations were well under way to find a haven on the Mersey. The defeat of Gladstone put these plans into cold storage until he returned to power and put forward another Home Rule Bill in 1893. On 10 November of that year Harland and Wolff answered an advertisement for vacant shipyards owned by the Mersey Dock and Harbour Board, requesting 'information as to the situation, accommodation and rent of the premises in question'. Once again the danger of Home Rule passed away and on 1 January 1894, having 'carefully considered the question of becoming tenants of one of the vacant yards on the Mersey', the directors dropped the matter.[52]

Protestants may have had only a small majority over Catholics in the province but they dominated its economic life. Most of the land and all but a small proportion of businesses were owned by Protestants. Only 3 per cent of the Belfast Chamber of Commerce in 1893 were Catholics;[53] in 1886 the chamber had voted unanimously for a resolution rejecting any dilution of the Union and, in an address presented to Gladstone in 1893, declared:

All our progress has been made under the Union. We were a small, insignificant town at the end of the last century, deeply disaffected and hostile to the British Empire. Since the Union and equal laws, we have been wedded to the Empire and made a progress second to none . . . Why should we be driven by force to abandon the conditions which have led to that success?[54]

Northern Protestant businessmen feared that a Dublin parliament would be dominated by farmers neither competent to administer industrial Ulster nor concerned about its welfare. They were sure that Nationalists would tax the north too heavily and damage its industries by protective tariffs designed to promote southern self-sufficiency, which, in turn, would subject Ulster's raw materials to ruinous import duties, possibly provoking foreign retaliation. Skilled Protestant artisans also feared that Home Rule could threaten their privileged position in the industrial workforce. There were as many low-paid unskilled workers in Belfast who were Protestant as were Catholic but the great majority of better-paid skilled workers in the city were Protestant. In 1901 this 'aristocracy of labour' formed 24 per cent of the city's workers and though about one quarter of the citizens were Catholics they held only 6 per cent of jobs as shipwrights, 10 per cent as boilermakers, 10 per cent as engine and machine workers, 12 per cent as plumbers and 15 per cent as carpenters. By contrast, 41 per cent of low-paid dockers and 50 per cent of female linen-spinners in Belfast were Catholic. A Dublin parliament might contemplate an attempt to redress this state of affairs.[55]

For nearly everyone in Ulster religion was the badge of distinction. Though Belfast's town clerk, Samuel Black, had told Riots commissioners that he could recognise a Catholic by his face, it could not seriously be considered that Protestants and Catholics were physically different from each other. A century earlier most Catholics could be distinguished by their Irish speech but now, in all but the remote uplands and western districts, English had become the language of all in the north. The rich diversity of Ulster dialects – much relished at the time by writers such as Wesley Lyttle ('Rabin Gordon') and Adam Lynn, the Cullybackey rhymester – reflected regional and district difference only, not distinguishing Protestant and Catholic. Religion, then, remained the sole ethnic divider. Just as Catholics often felt themselves to be an exploited subject people in Ulster, so northern Protestants regarded themselves as a beleaguered minority in the whole of Ireland. Fear was, and continues to be, an underlying feature of tensions in the north. For all the bravado of their 12 July celebrations, Ulster Protestants feared Catholics, tending to place their Orange halls close to invisible frontiers with Catholic districts.

International Catholicism was seen as a dark conspiracy, perpetually endangering Protestant liberties – a view reinforced by the intransigence of Pope Pius X, who issued the *Ne Temere* decree in 1907 which laid down that Catholics marrying Protestants must bring up their children as Catholics. In Ireland the growth of Catholic power seemed to be inexorable, putting Protestant Ulster on the defensive. Catholics were becoming a majority in Derry, 'leaving the political fortunes of the city at the mercy of the casual labourer who drifted in from the wilds of Donegal', as Ronald McNeill MP put it.[56] Like the Nationalists, Protestants wrongly expected the Unionist Party to lose electoral ground with the passage of time. Their Catholic neighbours might form a local minority, but because they gave their allegiance to the Irish Parliamentary Party and Dublin rule, they were not to be trusted and they might well seek vengeance for past wrongs. The writer Lynn C. Doyle was seventeen years old in 1890; he recalled:

Home Rulers to my childish mind were a dark, subtle, and dangerous race, outwardly genial and friendly, but inwardly meditating fearful things . . . and one could never tell the moment they were ready to rise, murder my uncle, possess themselves of his farm, and drive out my aunt and myself to perish on the mountains . . . in my aunt's stories it was on the mountains we always died.[57]

Individually known Catholics could be faithful friends, he continued:

As for my aunt, I know that in matters demanding honesty and fidelity she would have trusted Tom Brogan, her thirty years' retainer, sooner than the worshipful master of an Orange lodge. Nevertheless, the unknown Home Ruler remained to me an object of fear and suspicion.[58]

Protestants, like many settler communities in their attitude to natives, saw Catholics as feckless and dangerous en masse. In 1887 Mabel Sharman Crawford, daughter of the tenant-right leader, recalled:

The widespread belief that Irish poverty and turbulence originate in the baleful influences of creed and race is very generally held as an unquestionable truth in north-east Ulster, where I lived.[59]

Catholicism was regarded as an oppressive backward religion and the fear that Home Rule would result in Rome rule was genuine. Protestants visualised a Dublin government putting education entirely in the hands of the Church and forcing their children to attend Catholic schools and reserving public employment exclusively for Catholics. Such fears, together with a widely held belief in their own moral and racial superiority, made Protestants unwilling to accept the rule of Catholics who, though they might make 'excellent soldiers and servants when under strict discipline', were judged utterly incapable of protecting hard-won prosperity and Protestant liberties in the north.[60]

Gladstone was still at the helm of the Liberal Party, with Home Rule remaining at the top of his agenda. Unionists were watchful but, with Lord Salisbury in power, their determination was not yet put to the test. Besides, the Irish Parliamentary Party was riven by a bitter quarrel when the details of Parnell's liaison with Katharine O'Shea were revealed to the world in 1890. The *Methodist Times* observed that if the Nationalists kept Parnell as their leader, the Irish would be branded as 'an obscene race utterly unfit for anything except a militant despotism'.[61] With English Nonconformist conscience roused, Gladstone issued a statement that, if Parnell did not retire, his own leadership of the Liberal Party would be rendered 'almost a nullity'.[62] The Irish Catholic hierarchy held its hand until the fateful meeting of the Irish Party in Committee Room 15 of the House of Commons at the beginning of December 1890; there, by forty-five votes to twenty-nine, the Nationalists ousted Parnell. By refusing to accept this verdict Parnell split the party he had so skilfully put together. Davitt denounced him as a 'cold-blooded sensualist' and the Catholic Church threw its formidable weight against him.[63] In Ulster Patrick MacAllister, bishop of Down and Connor, campaigned relentlessly against the *Belfast Morning News*, which remained faithful to Parnell, and set up the anti-Parnellite *Irish News* in opposition. The clergy were so successful that within eighteen months the *Belfast Morning News* had been taken over by its new rival.

Parnell himself toured the country in all weathers and spoke in the Ulster Hall on 29 May 1891, when he declared, somewhat uncharacteristically, 'that until the religious prejudices of the minority, whether reasonable or unreasonable, are conciliated . . . Ireland can never enjoy perfect freedom, Ireland can never be united'.[64] However, in Ulster the clergy had almost taken control of the Nationalists, providing 29 members of the local executive of 80 in Belfast, 32 out of 98 in Armagh, and 25 out of 66 in Antrim. Exhausted, Parnell died in Katharine's arms at Brighton on 6 October 1891. The split in the Irish Parliamentary Party survived his death for almost a decade: in the north there were fewer than one thousand Parnellites, while the triumphant anti-Parnellites enrolled over thirty-one thousand members, won over, an RIC memorandum of 1892 concluded, 'by the R.C. clergy who completely control the Nationalist electorate in Ulster'.[65]

If Nationalist quarrels brought comfort to Unionists, it was short-lived. The electorate in Britain was impatient for change and Gladstone was justifiably confident of victory in the general election called for the summer of 1892. The prospect of another Home Rule Bill galvanised Ulster Unionists, and at a series of meetings in Lord Downshire's London house plans were laid for an orderly and dignified convention in Belfast to demonstrate to the world the strength of loyalist feeling in the north. In the words of the *Belfast News-Letter*:

> There was an impression abroad in England and in Scotland to the effect that Ulster Unionists after protesting against Home Rule would ultimately submit to it if it were forced upon them, and that this mistaken impression must be driven from the minds of the British electorate.[66]

'ONE WITH BRITAIN HEART AND SOUL': THE ULSTER UNIONIST CONVENTION,1892

'What the city itself looked like is impossible to describe adequately', *The Times* reporter wrote from Belfast on Friday 17 June 1892. He continued:

> From an early hour it was literally en fête. Flags and banners floated from every point of vantage, and the leading thoroughfares were alive with colours. Many thousands of delegates and visitors from England and

Scotland arrived on Thursday . . . Tens of thousands more arrived from all parts of Ulster by the morning trains to-day.[67]

The *Freeman's Journal* was grateful 'that there were no bands, and we were therefore spared the ear-splitting sounds which are so inseparably associated with Orange and other demonstrations in Ulster'.[68] Unionist leaders were determined to erase the memory of the vicious rioting that had so besmirched the opposition to Home Rule in 1886. This time twelve thousand delegates had been elected by Unionist associations across the province and they were to meet indoors on the plains of Stranmillis in a specially constructed convention hall, described by the *Northern Whig*:

> The building covers one acre, the glass in the roof being about one third of an acre in extent . . . the largest which has ever been erected in Great Britain or Ireland for political purposes, being 224 feet in the front and running back for about 150 feet.[69]

The Times reporter watched the delegates 'all orderly, all moving, scant of speech but with an air of quiet resolution, in one direction to the hall'.[70] As the men approached they saw above the entrance the arms of Ulster and a shield eight feet square, on which were the arms of England, Ireland and Scotland, surmounted by a trophy of Union flags and across the panel the words 'Ulster Unionist Convention 1892' and 'God Save the Queen'. Delegates had a choice of twenty-four doors and eight aisles by which they could reach their numbered seats; there they could read mottoes around the hall, including the 1798 slogan 'Erin-go-Bragh', 'Defence not Defiance', 'Quis separabit?', 'In union is our strength and freedom', 'Keep our noble Kingdom whole', and the words of the poet laureate:

> One with Britain heart and soul:
> One life, one flag, one fleet, one throne.[71]

'As far as sight could reach, sat row upon row of sturdy men packed closely together', an English visitor wrote the following day to *The Times*; 'There was no singing of patriotic songs; these hard-featured Ulstermen were come together for business, not for noise.'[72] 'There were the rugged strength and energy of the North,' the *Northern Whig* declared, 'still Liberal, still Conservative, on this occasion and in this cause they know but one name – that of Unionist.' The Church of Ireland archbishop of Armagh began the proceedings by asking God to send down 'Thy Holy Spirit to guide our deliberations for the advancement of Thy Glory, the safety of the Throne, and the integrity of the Empire'. Then, led by a male-voice choir, all sang the versified Psalm 46:

> God is our refuge and our strength,
> In straits a present aid;

Therefore, although the earth remove,
We will not be afraid . . .[73]

Even the *Freeman's Journal* commented that 'considering the number of people who joined in it, they kept wonderful time, and sang in excellent tune'; however, it found the Duke of Abercorn's 'laboured and set' oration rather flat until he concluded with energy: 'Men of the North – I say – We will not have Home Rule!' The most effective speech was given by the Liberal Unionist, Thomas Sinclair:

> We are children of the Revolution of 1688, and cost what it may, we will have nothing to do with a Dublin Parliament (Loud cheers). If it be ever set up, we shall simply ignore its existence (Tremendous cheering). Its acts will be but as waste paper – (cheers) – the police will find our barracks preoccupied with our own constabulary, its judges will sit in empty courthouses (cheers) . . . If Mr. Gladstone, in mad wantonness, can induce Parliament to pass it into law, Ulstermen will be idiots and worse than idiots, if they do not utterly repudiate it (Loud applause).[74]

When the meeting broke up at 2.45 p.m. the nearby Botanic Gardens filled with great crowds of supporters, estimated by the *Londonderry Standard* to total three hundred thousand. Speakers addressed audiences from three platforms, one on the principal lawn, the second on the rosary slope, and the third on the oak lawn. The *Northern Whig* regretted that no 'blandishments of Flora had the slightest effect' upon the vast assembly which 'recked little that this meant death to a poor floral victim'.[75] Hostile references to Catholics had been carefully avoided and the highly organised, sober respectability of the convention was clearly designed to impress public opinion in Britain.

'WE SHALL DEFEAT THIS CONSPIRACY': THE SECOND HOME RULE BILL, 1893

Just before the 1892 convention the Liberal Sir William Harcourt addressed himself sardonically to the Ulster Unionists: 'I assure you that I shall watch your strategy with interest, and try to alarm myself as much as I can manage.'[76] As it turned out, the speeches in Belfast had been more moderate than those made by Lord Salisbury and Arthur Balfour, most threatening no more than non-cooperation. In an important address at Clapham the following day, Gladstone congratulated the Ulstermen for their restraint but he was unmoved by their arguments. Reminding Ulster Protestants of their role in Grattan's Parliament, he urged them to consult 'the deeds of their ancestors' which would show them that Irish freedom would 'unite Protestants and Catholics into one indissoluble mass'. He was grateful to the Ulster Unionist leaders for dropping the idea of seeking a separate assembly 'for the small proportion of Ulster in which the Protestants are so concentrated'.[77] This, indeed, Saunderson and his colleagues had done, partly to retain the influential support of southern landlords; however, it exposed them to the charge that they were refusing to accept the democratic will of the Irish people. Moreover, the results of the general election showed that Unionists did not even have the support of the majority of voters in the United Kingdom as a whole.

With the backing of both Nationalist factions, Gladstone was able to form a government in August 1892 with a majority of forty MPs. Almost at once he set about preparing his second Home Rule Bill. Ulster Unionists at least had the consolation that they had won a decisive majority in their province. The Nationalists lost North Fermanagh, Londonderry City and West Belfast, reducing their representation in the north to fourteen. The Unionists, now with eighteen seats, had been helped by Nationalist disarray following the fall of Parnell; the disinclination of Protestant Home Rulers to vote for candidates so openly backed by the Catholic Church; and careful registration of Unionists in the marginal constituencies. Mary Arnold-Foster, wife of the new Unionist MP for West Belfast, attributed her husband's success to

working men . . . who quietly took the matter into their own hands, and, at any cost to themselves, moved into each house that fell vacant in our debatable land, and at last by their determination converted the minority of 1886 into the solid Unionist majority of 1892.[78]

Gladstone presented his Home Rule Bill to the Commons on 13 February 1893. The financial provisions were more carefully thought through than in 1886 but otherwise the bill's main differences to its predecessor were that Ireland would send eighty MPs to Westminster and that of the two chambers sitting in Dublin, the upper order would be composed entirely of representatives elected by voters with high property qualifications. No bill in the nineteenth century occupied so much parliamentary time. Fighting the provisions clause by clause, Unionists spoke 938 times for a total of almost 153 hours over 82 days; the Liberals and Nationalists made 459 speeches, lasting over 57 hours in all. In the protracted debates the Parnellites and anti-Parnellites were quite unable to prevent their bitter quarrel breaking out in public. 'It is all a conflict of jealousies and hates and the national cause is forgotten', Justin MacCarthy wrote, '. . . I feel terribly depressed.'[79] Ulster Unionists meanwhile carried out a vigorous campaign to publicise their cause in England and at last succeeded in getting an audience with Gladstone on 28 March 1893. The prime minister gave the Belfast Chamber of Commerce twenty minutes and when its representatives said the chamber was non-political, he interjected: 'Almost entirely Protestant, I think.'

'Largely, but not entirely so,' said the president, and Gladstone snapped in reply: 'Only eight Catholics to 260 Protestants.'[80] Another spokesman was interrupted ten times in fewer than ten minutes. Practically no time was allowed to the Belfast Harbour Commissioners and the Linen Merchants Association. Next day Adam Duffin, the Liberal Unionist, wrote to his wife:

> Dearest – As I expected we did not get much change out of Gladstone yesterday . . . I bowled him over the first shot on the customs figures. He gently insinuated that our zeal to magnify the importance of our City had led us into egregious error . . . the old man was jumping with impatience & we have at least got it clearly brought out that he closured us . . .
> Love & kisses to the chicks.
> We shall defeat this conspiracy . . . Geo. Clark says the old man is *mad* & we ought to publish the fact & give no other answer! I say he is bad. He has the look of a bird of prey and the smile of a hyena. It was positively shocking to see the hideous mechanical grin with which he took leave of us.[81]

On 4 April 1893 Arthur Balfour, the former Irish chief secretary, stood for four hours on a great platform in front of Belfast's Linen Hall to watch a march-past of one hundred thousand loyalists. Thomas MacKnight remembered:

> Such a display the city had never before seen . . . there was one vast sea of heads . . . the late Irish Chief Secretary was, with uncovered head, loudly applauded as the various bodies, most of them with bands and banners, filed past. A copy of the Home Rule Bill was burnt publicly and stamped upon amid great cheering.[82]

Amongst those campaigning in England was the 4th Viscount Templetown who spoke to several Conservative associations in London. In June a large parcel accompanied his report to a meeting of the Unionist Clubs Council in Belfast:

> And now I have the honour and great pleasure of reporting to this meeting that the magnificent Union Jack you see before you was entrusted to me to bring over to you as a token of sympathy from the Unionists of Stepney, in public meeting assembled, as you see by the streamer. The kind reference to the Irish Loyalists by Mr. Wootton-Isaacson when presenting the flag was received, gentlemen, by that magnificent meeting, with cheer and cheer, and bodes well to the Unionist Cause in that East End constituency.[83]

All this effort notwithstanding, the House of Commons passed the bill. The House of Lords was packed when it gave its verdict on 9 September 1893, and it was said that only two Unionist peers were absent without valid excuse – one shooting lions in Somaliland, the other killing rats at Reigate.[84] A constitutional crisis should have followed when the Lords threw out the bill by 419 votes to 41, rejecting the will of the elected representatives of the people. Gladstone wanted to call a general election on the issue but his cabinet refused to support him. As Irish Chief Secretary John Morley observed: 'The temperature of feeling for the Irish task was not by any means uniform or equable.' Henry Ponsonby, a Liberal with property in Ulster, remarked: 'I am anxious to find a hearty Home Ruler but, except Mr. Gladstone, he is not easy to find.'[85] The Nationalists in turn were too demoralised by their bitter internal squabbles to conduct an effective campaign outside Westminster; Davitt wrote to Dillon: 'I feel almost ashamed to go before an educated English audience while we are showing ourselves so unworthy of Home Rule.'[86]

'HOME RULE SLEEPING THE SLEEP OF THE UNJUST'

Exhausted and dispirited after his second failure to get Home Rule for Ireland, Gladstone retired in March 1894. The Liberals were fast losing their appetite for a concession which had become distasteful to the English electorate; Lord Rosebery, the new prime minister, remarked that 'as there were many roads to Rome, there were many ways to Home Rule', adding, 'there has been for a long time no enthusiasm for any measure'.[87] In any case, the Conservatives returned to power the following year and were to stay in office for the ensuing decade without a break. Lord Salisbury had no doubt that his government should leave 'Home Rule sleeping the sleep of the unjust'.[88]

Parnell was dead, Gladstone was out of the political arena, the Liberals had shelved Home Rule, the Irish Parliamentary Party remained bitterly divided, and Ireland was calm. The Conservative policy of killing Home Rule with kindness was renewed, but since there did not seem to be much to kill, the kindness could be rationed to no more than what the British electorate considered just. Arthur Balfour had once observed that Irish nationalism was 'born in the peasant's cot, where men forgive if the belly gain'; his brother Gerald, now Irish chief secretary, agreed.[89] The Congested Districts Board subsidised local crafts, amalgamated smallholdings, promoted agricultural improvement and built harbours, including that at Killybegs which still displays the letters CDB. Originally confined to the overpopulated Atlantic seaboard, the Congested Districts Board's area of operation was steadily extended, though in Ulster it operated only in Co. Donegal and small stretches of Fermanagh and Tyrone. In spite of the considerable sums expended no impressive results flowed from these efforts – even the rapid adoption of an effective potato spray and of disease-resistant tubers was due mainly to the farmers' own initiative.

413

The Government was reluctant to promote measures which were controversial and which could not command support of Unionists and Nationalists alike. One of the most significant measures of the administration, the Local Government Act of 1898, was the outcome of crisis management and not of forward planning. A royal commission had reported that Ireland was being overtaxed to the tune of £2,750,000 a year and, briefly, Irish Unionists and Nationalists united in common indignation. The Government's alarmed response to an all-Ireland committee – which included Saunderson, Redmond, Healy and Dillon – was to sweep away grand juries and give democracy to rural Ireland. Nationalists swiftly won control of the new county councils, elected by all male ratepayers, except in the Protestant-dominated areas of the north-east. Unionists were appeased by generous support for the rates from the exchequer. Unfortunately new local government jobs thus created were not thrown open to public competitive examinations and the result was the rapid entrenchment of petty local patronage, with baleful consequences for Ulster in the decades to come.

Ulster Unionists had mixed feelings about this 'constructive Unionism', such as it was, particularly as the Government seemed to take its advice from progressive southern Unionists with scant regard for traditional northern loyalism. As the danger of Home Rule receded discipline was difficult to maintain and Ulster Unionist MPs rarely spoke with one voice. Until his death in 1906 Saunderson, nicknamed 'The Dancing Dervish', remained leader of the Irish Unionist coterie of generally around twenty MPs. Witty and charming, he was nevertheless 'absolutely devoid of business capacity', according to his friend J. Mackay Wilson. 'Saunderson . . . is sure to be wrong, if there is a chance,' observed H.O. Arnold-Forster, MP for West Belfast.[90] 'Was that all right?' Saunderson asked a colleague after a speech in the Commons on the 1896 Land Bill:

> 'Excellent,' was the answer, 'but you might have said something about the Bill.' 'How could I? I never read it.'[91]

Fortunately for the party the number of lawyers in the group capable of drafting amendments increased as landlord representation declined. Some, however, were openly motivated by self-interest, such as William Moore, who, according to his daughter, 'never made any secret or mystery of why he went into parliament, it was the way to get promotion at the bar'.[92] Others, notably 'Jemmy' McCalmont and Henry Liddell, made but a feeble contribution in the Commons and were usually to be found at the Members' Bar. At a time when the loyalist cause was being promoted constitutionally, with little extra-parliamentary pressure, these shortcomings were noticed by the Ulster Unionist electorate. In the early years of the twentieth century Unionist solidarity in Ulster came close to being riven by disputes as dangerous as those which had split the Irish Parliamentary Party.

RECONCILIATIONS AND ESTRANGEMENTS

Parnell's creation, the formidable and disciplined Irish Parliamentary Party, remained shattered and demoralised in the years following the defeat of the second Home Rule Bill. John Dillon, elected leader of the anti-Parnellites in 1896, described the behaviour of two of his fellow MPs in February 1898: one 'appeared yesterday in a horrible state of intoxication and voted in the wrong lobby' and another 'has been drunk for several days and was in a most beastly condition while I was moving the adjournment yesterday'. 'I am very sorry to say,' Dillon remarked to his friend William O'Brien later that summer, 'that an increasing number of them are prepared to throw themselves into oceans of whiskey and into nothing else.'[93] To make matters worse, Tim Healy's clericalist faction within the anti-Parnellites provoked much public acrimony. Nationalist Ulster remained solidly anti-Parnellite but even here the return of two Healyites, Arthur O'Connor and T.D. Sullivan, for East and West Donegal, was followed by unedifying wrangling within the party. Patrick O'Donnell, bishop of Raphoe and a supporter of Dillon's, vainly urged reconciliation:

> Good intentions, splendid services in the past and strong love of the old land should outweigh with us the intense dissatisfaction with which we have viewed all abetting of the various attempts made on the discipline of the Irish party and its credit with the people.[94]

Early in 1898 William O'Brien launched the United Irish League in Co. Mayo. He had been appalled by the widespread distress he had witnessed following potato harvest failures the previous year and he was impatient with the Nationalist policy of waiting for Home Rule to solve all problems. O'Brien called on the Congested Districts Board to speed up the redistribution of land to give impoverished scrapholders a share of large farms owned by prosperous graziers. By August 1899, the police reported to the undersecretary in Dublin Castle, the league had over thirty-three thousand members and it was spreading into Ulster despite the opposition of Healyite priests there, and Belfast was the first city to have a branch. The movement threatened to upstage both the Parnellite and anti-Parnellite factions and, following much intricate negotiation, the Irish Parliamentary Party agreed to reunite in 1900 under the leadership of the Parnellite MP for Waterford, John Redmond. Discontent on the land challenged the complacency not only of the Nationalists but also of the Unionist MPs in Ulster. Thomas W. Russell, a successful hotelier and son of a Scottish stonemason, had as Unionist MP for South Tyrone at first championed the rights of landlords. Soon he became aware of the continued discontent of Presbyterian farmers, still resentful of Anglican monopoly and finding rents difficult to pay as agricultural prices moved steadily downwards. With tireless energy he built up his own party in the Unionist heartlands, pledged to get rid of the landlords altogether by compulsory land purchase. In 1902 and 1903 Russellite candidates defeated official Unionists in East Down and North Fermanagh – victories made possible by what Edward Carson, Unionist MP for Dublin University, called an 'unholy alliance' of Liberal Unionist Presbyterians and Methodists, and Catholics who normally had no opportunity to vote for a Nationalist candidate. Joshua Peel, Unionist agent for Mid Armagh, grumbled that 'it makes one indignant to think that those Presbyterians, for the sake of getting a Presbyterian into Parliament, would join hands with the enemies of the Union and their country'.[95] Official Unionist confidence was badly shaken, particularly as there were also signs of loyalist disaffection in urban constituencies.

In the segregated working-class enclaves of Belfast sectarian bitterness was probably more intense than in any other part of Ulster. Here Lindsay Crawford's denunciation of 'ritualistic practices' and other 'Romanist' tendencies in the Church of England struck a chord in loyalist streets. Born in Lisburn, a member of the Orange Order in Dublin and the editor of the *Irish Protestant*, Crawford vilified constructive Unionism and the Conservative policy of placating Catholic Ireland:

> Right along the line of the Unionist alliance every Protestant landmark has been obliterated and in return for the support of Roman Catholic unionist and ritualist, official Unionism has effaced Protestantism from its programme . . . although Home Rule was defeated Rome Rule still survives under the guise of Unionism.[96]

Crawford gave his full backing to Tom Sloan, leader of the Belfast Protestant Association, when he stood as an independent against the official Unionist in the South Belfast by-election in 1902, caused by the death of William Johnston of Ballykilbeg. Sloan won the seat and was duly suspended from the Orange Order. In retaliation he and Crawford founded the Independent Orange Order in July 1903, which soon had fifty-five lodges, twenty of them in Belfast.

The new order was sympathetic to the labour movement and Sloan was the only Unionist MP to vote for the Miners' Eight Hour Bill. Sectarian differences made urban Ulster unpromising soil for the cultivation of socialism. Nevertheless, Belfast was giving a lead in Ireland in

416

the organisation of labour. The Irish Trade Union Congress had been set up in 1894, and by 1899 half the affiliated trade unionists for the whole island were working in the city and its environs. In 1903 delegates of thirty-six trade-union branches, members of the Independent Labour Party, the Belfast Ethical Society and the Clarion Fellowship met to establish the Belfast Labour Representation Committee. Keir Hardie urged the meeting to prepare at once to win a seat for Labour. When Sir James Haslett, the sitting member for North Belfast, died in 1905, William Walker was selected to throw down the challenge.

Circumstances appeared favourable for Walker, a talented speaker and a socialist who had done much to organise linen workers: the Unionist candidate, Sir Daniel Dixon, was so hostile to the claims of labour that even the *Belfast News-Letter* had opposed his nomination; a severe recession was increasing working-class discontent; Sloan and the Independent Orange Order signalled their support; and there was a chance that Joseph Devlin, the Nationalist MP for West Belfast known to be a champion of the underdog, would call on Catholic voters to poll for Walker.[97] Then, fatally, Walker agreed to answer a questionnaire presented to him by the Protestant Imperial Federation and his controversial replies – calculated to reassure Sloan and the Independent Orange Order – were anonymously printed on handbills and distributed in Catholic streets. Ramsay MacDonald, Walker's election agent, was in despair:

> I was never more sick of an election than that at North Belfast and then the religious replies coming at the end of it knocked everything out of me. I am afraid that those answers of his will make it impossible to win the constituency.[98]

MacDonald was right. A meeting of the Belfast executive of the United Irish League refused to call on nationalists to vote for Walker and an estimated one thousand Catholic votes were lost. Walker got 3,966 votes but Dixon, with 4,440 votes, won the seat.

Nevertheless, the Unionists had been given a fright at a time when the socialist tide in Europe was rising, when militant trade unionists were paralysing whole industries in Britain, France and Spain, and when armed revolutionaries were raising barricades in St Petersburg. Party activists saw the urgent need to return to traditional values, to reinvigorate constituency support and to find an issue capable of reuniting all loyalists. That issue was to be presented by the flamboyant new chief secretary in Dublin Castle.

THE END OF CONSTRUCTIVE UNIONISM

Great grandson of Lord Edward FitzGerald, George Wyndham seemed to have inherited some of his forebear's revolutionary zeal on taking office as Irish chief secretary in November 1900. Mafeking had been relieved, the Khaki Election had been won and the time seemed right to demonstrate to all the benefits of the imperial connection to Ireland – an island, Wyndham felt certain, best governed in the manner of a Crown Colony. There was mounting alarm in the treasury as he outlined his plans to wipe out poverty, rehouse a third of the population, settle the university question and get rid of landlordism. Financial objections were swept aside by public support on both sides of the Irish Sea. On 2 September 1902 the landowner Captain John Shawe-Taylor wrote to the press inviting landlord and tenant representatives to seek a final solution to the Irish land question. Lord Abercorn and Saunderson were amongst those who attended a conference under the chairmanship of Lord Dunraven which recommended that a massive scheme of land purchase be undertaken at once by the Government.

To Wyndham's delight the Government's hand was forced by a unanimous paean of praise for Dunraven's report from Nationalists, Unionists and the British press. In 1903 Westminster passed Wyndham's Land Bill, which encouraged landlords to sell entire estates, the money being advanced to tenants by the treasury to be repaid over sixty-eight and a half years by annuities at the rate of 3.25 per cent. The Presbyterian farmers of the north had always been in the van of the movement for land purchase and Unionist MPs, such as W.G. Ellison-Macartney and Edward Carson, who thought the measure too sweeping kept their reservations to themselves. The act was an immediate success, though it took further legislation in 1909 to compel all landlords to sell.[99] The land issue virtually dropped out of the Irish Question. Landlords, generally eager to sell, either retained only their demesnes or cleared off altogether: such a revolution was to be accomplished in many other European states only by violence and bloodshed.

Having triumphantly stampeded his government over land purchase, Wyndham now eagerly set out to resolve the university question. He was, however, incautious, imperious and overconfident: Margot Asquith noted in her diary that 'they found him in Ireland rather an intriguer ... the only two faults I should find in him are want of judgement and want of nerve'.[100] When Wyndham proposed to implement a royal commission recommendation to set up a Catholic-controlled university in Dublin, Unionist MPs from Ulster openly rebelled. Saunderson threatened to resign the Conservative whip, and at a meeting in Dublin in January 1904 Lord Londonderry announced bluntly that the Government had no intention of reforming university education. Wyndham was forced into a humiliating retreat and Arthur Balfour, now prime minister, was deeply affronted by this northern hostility, though he did not challenge Lord London-derry's claim.

In times of crisis Ulster Unionists and Conservative governments were firm allies but in intervening years relations were often severely strained. Cabinet ministers seemed bored by northern loyalist anxieties and only rarely could be persuaded to visit Ulster. They were shocked by the frank sectarianism of some MPs, doubted their commitment to empire and were alarmed by the conditions they placed on their loyalty: 'Are you sure all Ulstermen are *loyal* in the best and most unselfish sense of the word?' the Earl of Cadogan asked the Irish Unionist leader Walter Long, 'I will not write what I think . . . ' W.H. Smith was exasperated by the recalcitrance of Irish landlords, many of them from the north, remarking to Arthur Balfour: 'How is it possible to help them – and I sometimes think – is it worthwhile to try?'[101]

For northern Unionists the chief-secretaryship of Wyndham was the last straw. Certainly they welcomed the way he cut the ground from under Thomas W. Russell's feet by land purchase, but they resented his refusal to put patronage their way and the radical progressive policy he seemed set on implementing. Wyndham for his part disliked 'Orange uncouthness' and found 'the parochialism of the Ulster right-wing . . . beyond belief'. By 1904 he was remarking: 'My contact with the Ulster members is like catching an "itch" from park pests.'[102] The open estrangement of northern Unionists began in September 1902 with the appointment as undersecretary in Dublin Castle of Sir Antony MacDonnell, a Catholic Irishman with a distinguished career in India behind him. Ulster MPs were deeply suspicious of this 'crypto-Nationalist' at the chief secretary's right hand and their fears were confirmed when in the autumn of 1904 it was revealed that MacDonnell and Dunraven were drafting proposals for devolution in Ireland. As T.P. O'Connor, Nationalist MP for Liverpool's Scotland Road Division, glee-fully pointed out, devolution was simply the Latin word for Home Rule. Ulster Unionists angrily called for MacDonnell's dismissal, and Nationalist MPs, frustrated by the lack of concessions to them, joined in the hue and cry. Wyndham denied having seen MacDonnell's proposals but he was not convincing and recent research has shown that he was lying. He resigned in the spring of 1905, to dissolve rapidly in alcohol thereafter.

Constructive unionism was in ruins.

THE GAELIC REVIVAL

In 1986 Ardrigh, a large house on the Antrim Road in Belfast, was demolished to make way for a block of flats. With its name (meaning 'high king') intended to evoke a heroic Celtic past, this for many years had been the home of Francis Joseph Bigger, a well-to-do Presbyterian solicitor and freemason, and an ardent patron of the Gaelic cultural renaissance at the turn of the century. Here Bigger put together a remarkable collection of books of Irish interest, subsequently bequeathed to the Belfast Central Library, and kept open house for those concerned to preserve and revive Ireland's Gaelic heritage, holding a 'firelight' school on Sundays for literary and political discussion and music, including Francis 'Da' McPeake playing his *uilleann* pipes. Ardrigh was the northern focal point for those who turned their backs on their urban, industrial environment and took instead a romantic, almost mystical, view of the Gaelic past and sought to promote what they believed to be the noble virtues of a simple, unspoiled rural people not yet corrupted by an alien, commercialised culture.[103]

Bigger was only one in a long line of Ulster Protestants fascinated by Ireland's remote past and surviving Gaelic traditions. In 1840 Edward Bunting completed his long life's work of collection by publishing *The Ancient Music of Ireland*. Samuel Ferguson, born in Belfast's High Street in 1810, taught himself Irish and turned for inspiration to the epics of ancient Ireland; his somewhat overblown verse translations – including *The Tain-Quest, Deirdre, Lays of the Western Gael*, and *Congal* – stimulated keen interest in his country's cultural heritage. Dr William Reeves, successively Church of Ireland curate in Lisburn, rector in Ballymena and bishop of Down, became the most distinguished Gaelic scholar of his day. He translated Adamnan's biography of Colmcille, wrote a host of academic works on ecclesiastical antiquities and on medieval Irish history, and used a legacy of £300 to save the Book of Armagh for the nation. George Sigerson, a medical doctor from Strabane who gave the inaugural lecture to the Irish National Literary Society in 1892, combined elegance with accuracy in his translations published in *Bards of the Gael and Gall* in 1897. These men were unionist in politics, but the Protestants who were regular guests at Ardrigh were nationalists attempting to swim against the strong local tide. They included: Sir Shane Leslie, cousin of Winston Churchill, subsequently disinherited by his father because of his prolific anti-unionist writing; Roger Casement, the colonial administrator and future revolutionary from Ballycastle who organised a *feis* at Cushendall in 1904, largely paid for by Bigger; Canon James Owen Hannay (George A. Birmingham), the novelist who became an executive member of the Gaelic League; the landscape artist Paul Henry and his brother Professor Robert M. Henry, who persuaded Queen's University Belfast to teach Gaelic; the Presbyterian journalists Robert Lynd and James Winder Good; the novelist Forrest Reid; Bulmer

Hobson, the Lisburn Quaker, who with Bigger founded the Ulster Literary Theatre in 1902 and subsequently became a republican organiser; Harry Morrow, author of the ever-popular play *Thompson in Tír na nÓg;* the actor–playwright Samuel Waddell (Rutherford Mayne), and his sister Helen, later a celebrated medievalist; Alice Milligan, poet and daughter of a Protestant businessman in Omagh; and the Methodist musicologist Herbert Hughes.[104]

Ardrigh was one of the very few places in Ulster where Protestants, Catholics and sceptics met regularly for social as well as business purposes. Alice Milligan joined with the daughter of a veteran Belfast Fenian, Anna Johnston (Ethna Carbery), to edit the short-lived journal *Shan Van Vocht,* which celebrated national heroes and encouraged the revival of Irish. In August 1903 Bigger and Hughes toured north Donegal to collect traditional melodies. On their return they combined with the Catholic brothers John and Joseph Campbell to produce the *Songs of Uladh,* published at Bigger's expense in 1904. John Campbell was the illustrator and Joseph, who wrote words in English to the collected music, recalled later that Hughes, looking 'like Schubert in some foreign lithographs', would sit at the piano and

> play over the airs, improvising an accompaniment as he proceeded – first, in their natural tempo, and then more slowly so that I could catch and absorb the peculiar quality of each. In this way such pieces as 'My Lagan Love' and the 'Gartan Mother's Lullaby' came before the world.[105]

Another frequent visitor to Ardrigh was Eoin MacNeill. A Catholic brought up in Glenarm and educated at St Malachy's College in Belfast, he joined with Douglas Hyde in 1893 to found the Gaelic League, dedicated to promoting the revival of the Irish language. By the beginning of the new century some one hundred thousand had joined the movement. When Hyde visited Ardrigh, Bigger and his friends became members, but with only around five hundred joining over the whole province, Ulster was far behind the rest of the island. The province was usually regarded as the most anglicised in Ireland but the 1901 census shows that there were more Gaelic speakers there than in Leinster, even when Co. Donegal was not included. The Sperrins, south Monaghan, north-west Cavan, the Mournes and the Antrim Glens had significant numbers of Gaelic speakers; Belfast had 3,587, most of them recent immigrants from remote districts; and Co. Donegal, with 60,677, had nearly two thirds of the north's native speakers. Yet barely 6 per cent of Ulster's population could speak Irish and the rate of decline was rapid, hastened by emigration and the tendency for native speakers to regard the language as a badge of poverty and social inferiority. The Gaelic

League did much to restore dignity to the Irish language – denounced by the *Morning Post* as 'kitchen kaffir' and by the *Daily Mail* as a 'barbarous tongue' – but apart from some success in urban districts, the organisation was unable to halt this decline. The league, however, was part of a movement making a profound impact on Ireland's politics.[106]

'THE FOUL BREATH OF PAGANISED SOCIETY'

Protestants, north and south, had done much to launch the Gaelic revival and the Irish-Ireland movement which flowered in the doldrum years following the fall of Parnell. Bigger and his friends, however, were utterly unrepresentative of the mass of Ulster Protestants who were repelled by these new interpretations of cultural identity. Even Hyde and MacNeill became increasingly alarmed by the widespread tendency to refuse to accept Protestants as true Irishmen. D.P. Moran, the acerbic editor of the *Leader*, bluntly stated what many in the island believed when he wrote that the Irish nation was Catholic and that if Protestants refused to accept the majority culture then the only solution was partition, leaving the 'Orangemen and their friends in the north-east corner'.[107] An essential part of the nurturing of Irish self-reliance, Moran believed, was the blending of the Gaelic revival with renascent Catholicism. The spread northwards of the Gaelic Athletic Association, founded in 1884 and taking root in rural areas, also tended to be divisive as it excluded from membership soldiers, police and anyone associated with 'Britishness', including those who played cricket, rugby and other 'foreign games'. Little wonder that the convention of 1892 was the last occasion on which Ulster Unionists were to display the slogan of 1798, 'Erin-go-Bragh'. In addition, local branches of the Gaelic Athletic Association and the Gaelic League – particularly in Ulster where Catholic middle-class leaders were few and far between – fell easily under the control of Catholic clergy.

Visiting Ireland in the first years of the twentieth century, the Italian Father Buonaiuti noticed 'the curious fact that the language revival is accompanied by an intensification of missionary zeal, a re-awakening of that ardour for winning converts to the Faith'.[108] Certainly the Gaelic revivalists roundly condemned what they saw as the corrupting influence of the urban, materialistic, secularist and liberal culture emanating from Britain. The movement therefore blended easily with the continuing Catholic revival, which now combined a proselytising puritanism with romantic zeal. To the discomfort of the Irish Parliamentary Party, dependent on brewers and distillers, the revival had become deeply ascetic: the Pioneer Total Abstinence Association, founded in 1901, won numerous adherents and the new slogan 'Ireland sober, Ireland free' was often to be heard. The *Messenger of the Sacred Heart*, with a circulation of seventy-three thousand by 1904, constantly denounced intemperance and immorality, and in 1907 Cardinal Logue listed the two greatest threats to Irish Catholicism as, first, 'unsavoury' literature from Britain and, second, an atheistic spirit. The hierarchy's journal, the *Catholic Bulletin*, claimed in 1913:

> For the last twenty years the Gael has been crying – oftentimes a voice in the wilderness – for help to beat back the Anglicisation he saw dragging its slimy length along – the immoral literature, the smutty postcards, the lewd and the suggestive songs were bad, yet they were mere puffs from the foul breath of paganised society. The full sewerage from the *cloaca maxima* of Anglicisation is now discharged upon us. The black devil of Socialism, hoof and horns is amongst us . . . [109]

John O'Doherty, bishop of Derry, had no liking for Healy's clericalist faction in the Irish Parliamentary Party; nevertheless, he remarked to a fellow bishop in 1897: 'So vile a set of bigots does not exist in creation as the Protestants of Ulster.'[110] If one of their leaders felt this way, how might the rest of Ulster Catholics feel? And the worst fears of northern Protestants were confirmed when in March 1912, on the eve of the third Home Rule Bill, the *Catholic Bulletin* declared:

> The time has arrived for action. The day of Ireland's missionary heroism is at hand . . . To bring into the bosom of Holy Church the million of our separated brethren is a most attractive programme.[111]

HIBERNIANS AND REPUBLICANS

Joseph Devlin did succeed in wresting the control of the Irish Parliamentary Party machine in Belfast from Bishop Henry and his Catholic Representation Association. 'Wee Joe', who began his career as a bartender and then won West Belfast for the Nationalists by a margin of sixteen votes in 1907, was welcomed by Redmond and Dillon as the man who could deliver the northern Catholic vote. Known as the 'pocket Demosthenes', Devlin was a colourful figure in the Commons and for thirty years he was to be the undisputed ruler of the Falls and Smithfield wards, which, after the reorganisation of boundaries in 1896, could be counted on to return eight Catholic councillors.

The politics of this ghetto fiefdom was narrow and sectarian. Devlin revived the ancient Order of Hibernians and became the grand master of its ruling body, the Board of Erin. Formed in 1838 as an organisation for Ribbonmen, the Hibernians had sixty thousand members by 1909 and many more besides overseas. It was a Catholic mirror image of the Orange Order. Devlin's own newspaper, the *Northern Star*, was openly anti-Protestant, each week carrying an article entitled 'Why I became a Catholic'. The issue of 3 August 1907, for example, included a feature with the following headlines: 'THE RELIGION OF THE MUCK-RAKE – PROTESTANTISM FEEDS GREEDILY ON GARBAGE – CHRISTIAN (?) LITERATURE DOING THE DEVIL'S WORK'.[112] In this city where politics was more intensely polarised than anywhere else in Ireland it is not surprising that here were to be found not only the most inflexible loyalists but also the most determined republican militants.

In the early years of the century Belfast had the most active cells of the IRB in Ireland. At a time when the brotherhood was moribund in Dublin, the piano-tuner Denis McCullough revitalised the separatist movement in the heart of Unionist territory. Disgusted by the slovenly manner in which he had been sworn into the organisation at the side door of Donnelly's public house in 1901, McCullough weeded out the faint-hearted – including his own father – and worked with unremitting zeal to enrol in the brotherhood young men determined to fight for a republic. He was joined by the journalist Bulmer Hobson – born in Holywood and educated at Friends School, Lisburn – and together they launched the Dungannon Club in 1905 to revive republican feeling. Hobson later recalled:

> This club composed of about fifty young men and boys was the most vital political organism I have ever known . . . without the influence of a single well-known name or any asset save the faith and enthusiasm of its members, it set itself the task of uniting Protestant and Catholic Irishmen to achieve the independence of Ireland.[113]

Named to evoke memories of the Dungannon Convention in 1782 and the winning of legislative independence, the club rejected the narrow sectarianism of older men in the Hibernians. In 1907 it merged with Arthur Griffith's separatist but non-violent Sinn Féin (meaning 'ourselves', a name suggested by Edward Carson's Gaelic Leaguer cousin, Maire Butler). The dedication of these northern republicans attracted the attention of John Devoy, head of the IRB's American counterpart, Clan na Gael. Rejecting constitutional nationalism after the fall of Parnell, Devoy had despaired of revitalising physical-force republicanism in Ireland until these young Ulstermen came to his notice. Four other northerners were to become Devoy's faithful lieutenants: Sean MacDermott, for a time a bartender and tram driver in Belfast; Thomas Clarke, born on the Isle of Wight but brought up in Dungannon, who had served fifteen years in prison for his part in the dynamiting campaign of the 1880s; the medical student Patrick McCartan from Carrickmore, who had joined Clan na Gael in Philadelphia after running away from home; and Roger Casement who was drawn into the republican conspiracy following his retirement from public service. Devoy sent money and instructions to prepare for armed rebellion. On the eve of the First World War his northern zealots had seized complete control of the brotherhood, toppling the Dublin leadership opposed to insurrection – a task made easier by the massive campaign of resistance conducted by Ulster Unionists against the third Home Rule Bill.

'A LITTLE, MODEST, SHY, HUMBLE EFFORT': THE LIBERALS RETURN

The momentous general election of January 1906 dashed the Irish Parliamentary Party's rising expectation that Home Rule would soon be clearly on the horizon. The Conservative and Unionist vote crashed so dramatically that Sir Henry Campbell-Bannerman, the new Liberal prime minister, had no need of Nationalist support. Besides, the Liberals were nervously reluctant to put Home Rule near the top of their agenda. 'Things must advance towards Home Rule,' Sir Edward Grey, now the foreign secretary, had said in 1901, 'but I think it must be step-by-step.'[114] This step-by-step approach was adopted as party policy and on the eve of the election Herbert H. Asquith had written that 'it will be no part of the policy of the new Liberal government to introduce a Home Rule Bill in a new parliament'.[115]

Never before had so many men of humble origins been returned to the Commons and at once they set about implementing a packed programme of reform designed to sweep aside the complacency and neglect of a decade and more. One measure alone – Asquith's Old Age Pensions Act of 1908 – at a stroke reversed the fiscal imbalance between Ireland and the rest of the United Kingdom. The Government tripped badly, however, in making its first tentative step towards Home Rule: a bill was put forward to create an Irish Council, two-thirds elected and one-third appointed, with administrative control over such matters as local government, congested districts, public works, education and agriculture. Augustine Birrell, the Irish chief secretary, explained to the Commons that the council would leave the powers of Westminster 'majestically unaffected' and Campbell-Bannerman described the bill to a Manchester audience as a 'little, modest, shy, humble effort to give administrative powers to the Irish people'.[116] Little wonder that the rank and file of the Irish Parliamentary Party turned on Redmond for even considering such a paltry measure. Undeterred, the ebullient Birrell cultivated good relations with the Nationalists and steered through a Universities Bill (creating the National University and the Queen's University in 1908), completed the compulsory land purchase legislation and made more money available for education, housing and the congested districts. Nevertheless, the Nationalist leaders were uneasy: 'An effort must be made to put some life into the movement', Dillon wrote to Redmond. 'At present it is very much asleep, and Sinn Feiners, Gaelic League, etc., etc., are making great play.'[117]

Even a 'humble' step towards Home Rule sent a *frisson* of alarm through loyalist ranks in Ulster. At Westminster Ulster Unionists were like gadflies, John Lonsdale, MP for Mid Armagh, setting a record by addressing no fewer than 370 questions to ministers. To Birrell these MPs were 'carrion crows', directing questions 'for the sole purpose of maligning and misrepresenting their native country'.[118] These men felt increasingly isolated and fearful that their British colleagues would desert them. 'Belfast is out of the question,' Arthur Balfour snapped when invited to address the Ulster Unionist Council, still resenting the Ulstermen's recriminations over devolution proposals.[119] Indeed the energetic Welsh radical David Lloyd George, visiting Belfast as a government minister in 1907, exultantly pointed out that the only leading opposition MPs who had bothered to speak to Ulster Unionists on their home ground were 'Mr. Walter Long, an amiable Wiltshire Orangeman, Lord Londonderry, a wild Durham Orangeman – and Captain Craig'.[120] Defeated in Bristol and elected in November 1906 for South County Dublin, Long attended a golfing dinner at Portrush and agreed to lead the Irish Unionists. He proved a bitter disappointment: he failed to attend the annual Ulster Unionist Council meetings in 1908 and 1909; and, perhaps taking heed of a friend's warning against 'sinking yourself in the Irish stew', he announced his intention of standing for a London seat at the next election.[121]

Ulster Unionists had already decided they must depend on themselves. The Unionist council had been formed in December 1904 'for bringing into line all Local Unionist Associations in the Province of Ulster, with a view to consistent and continuous political action'.[122] From now on southern Unionists would have to fend for themselves and the council swiftly reinvigorated and co-ordinated loyalism across the province. Party machinery was streamlined and Unionist associations were formed or re-formed in East Donegal, North Monaghan and Newry. Shaken by the rapid rise of the Independent Orange Order, the Ulster party forged new links with the official Orange Order, Captain James Craig, the new MP for East Down, tirelessly addressing one lodge meeting after another. The need to hold together urban supporters of the loyalist cause was even greater – Unionists shared with Nationalists a conservative horror of socialism – and was underlined dramatically when Belfast was convulsed by a great labour dispute in 1907.

On the morning of 9 May 1907 Belfast dockers who had been agitating for better conditions found themselves locked out by their employers and their places taken by drafts of imported blacklegs. The dockers then converged on a ship unloading at Kelly's coal quay, sweeping aside the harbour police and hurling stones and lumps of coal at the strikebreakers. The *Belfast Evening Telegraph* reported:

> Many of the missiles fell with ominous thuds on the bridge of the vessel and others thrown with unerring aim, found their way into the holds, and fell among the labourers, causing them to scatter in all directions.[123]

The non-union men soon capitulated but more were brought into the port, billeted each night on SS *Calorific* moored in Belfast Lough and assailed each morning by salvoes of rivets, nuts and bolts as the ship steamed past Queen's Island to the quays.

Employers belonging to the Shipping Federation in the city were led by Thomas Gallaher, chairman of the Belfast Steamship Company and owner of the great tobacco works in York Street. He was determined to resist the new militancy of the low paid now beginning to join trade unions for the first time. The man Gallaher most feared was Jim Larkin, who had arrived from Liverpool at the beginning of the year as organiser for the National Union of Dock Labourers. Tall, restless and charismatic, Larkin had achieved conspicuous success in recruiting the unskilled men, rousing them at street corners: 'Half a dozen words from Jim Larkin,' Joseph Cooper recalled, 'and you were all together.'[124] Having brought together Catholics working at the deep-sea docks and Protestant dockers on the cross-channel quays, Larkin now strove to bond the working classes of both sects to establish their right to be members of a trade union.

As summer approached the dispute spread. Shipyard iron-moulders struck on 31 May and their action led to the laying off of nearly four thousand men; by 18 June firemen and sailors on Head Line ships were on strike; on 26 June all the dockers at the Heysham, Barrow and Fleetwood berths came out; and the following day the carters began to join the struggle. The employers stood firm: the Master Carriers declared that unless the carters returned to work all would be locked out; the railway companies announced that they would 'not re-employ the men who left work'; and the shipping firms made it clear that they were 'determined to fight to a finish'.[125] From the Custom House steps the trade-union leader Alex Boyd told strikers it was 'now war to the knife', while the *Northern Whig* warned its readers: 'We are on the eve of an experience something akin to that which paralysed Russian cities during the last couple of years.'[126]

When on 11 July employers locked out the coal-heavers, paralysis began to spread through the city's industries. Next day the Independent Orange Order, during its 12 July demonstration at Shaw's Bridge, pledged its support for the men, the Reverend J. Calvin saying that they were 'a democracy fighting for mere existence against an aristocratic and selfish monied class'. Larkin denounced Gallaher as 'an obscene scoundrel', adding later that the man they were fighting 'would not be hanged for no honest rope would do it'. Huge strike meetings spread out from Corporation Square to the Custom House and into the working-class districts, though in the Shankill speakers were 'somewhat interrupted by a drumming party'. Lindsay Crawford from a platform in Queen's Square declared: 'Stand firm, out of this movement will spring not only the strength of organised labour but also . . . the unity of all Irishmen.'[127] Larkin read out an extract from a letter written by the Reverend S. Simms, minister of Agnes Street Presbyterian Church:

> The insane actions of the coal merchants have brought the matter to a crisis. The battle is now between the classes and the masses, and the masses will ultimately win. Not one pound of coal shall I purchase from the federated employers any longer.[128]

By 18 July Combe Barbour's in North Howard Street and several large linen firms had closed for lack of coal and the *Belfast News-Letter* predicted that at least seven thousand would be laid off by early August. The dispute widened when the Power-Loom Manufacturers' Association and the Corporation Tramway Committee locked out their workers. 'You will notice deadlock is due to refusal of employers to consult Trades Union leaders', Sir Antony MacDonnell scribbled in the margin of a police report he was passing on to the chief secretary; nevertheless, he agreed to send more troops to Belfast.[129]

The employers were confident they could starve their workers into submission. When the general secretary of the National Union of Dock Labourers, James Sexton, arrived in Belfast on 19 July he applauded the workers' solidarity but caused consternation by producing a mere £200 in strike pay. Concerned to protect the finances of his union, he swiftly settled the coal dispute after a meeting with the lord mayor on 25 July. A great victory demonstration passed through the main working-class districts and converged on the city hall to be addressed from four separate platforms: and yet nothing had been won which had not been offered by employers weeks earlier and there was still no official recognition of the union. In addition, the way was now open for piecemeal settlements with other groups of strikers.

Meanwhile, a police mutiny was under way. Larkin had no expectation of this when on 17 July he said that the constabulary 'were working eighteen hours a day, and they would go on strike too – only they dared not'. Then two days later by the Heysham shed Constable William Barrett refused to sit beside a blackleg driver on a motor wagon. Barrett was suspended but succeeded in getting nearly three hundred men together in a protest meeting at Musgrave Street barracks. Acting Commissioner Henry Morrell, after being knocked to the floor, rose up and punched a constable, and then, the *Constabulary Gazette* reported, 'tables and forms were overturned and the police cheered defiance to all authority'.[130] Soon after, around eight hundred of the Belfast force of one thousand men were disobeying orders. In Dublin Castle, Undersecretary Sir Antony MacDonnell acted swiftly: Barrett was dismissed, 6 constables were suspended and by 2 August 203 others had been transferred to country districts. At first light on 1 August nine warships from the second division of the Atlantic Fleet anchored off Bangor at the mouth of Belfast Lough and 2,550 troops – Cameron Highlanders, Berkshires and battalions of the Middlesex and Essex Regiments – were rushed to the city to join the 2nd Battalion of the Royal Sussex Regiment, the 1st Battalion of the Rifle Brigade and a squadron of the 3rd Dragoon Guards already there. The mutiny quickly collapsed.

'Catholics cannot be socialists,' Joseph Devlin once declared.[131] But the blanketing of the city with English and Scottish troops – Irish regiments were deliberately not sent – brought him to the strike platforms for the first time, despite his loathing of Larkinism. His bitter oratory and the growing numbers of blacklegs sparked off a riot in the lower Falls on the evening of Sunday 11 August. After a police van had been attacked, 2,600 troops, 80 cavalry and 500 police were sent up the Grosvenor Road. The first cavalry charge was launched at 8 p.m. and the *Belfast News-Letter* reported:

> In one of the bye streets a squadron of cavalry were subjected to a terrific storm of paviors, which were rained on them from the upper windows, and the men to save their faces had to lie down on their saddles.

In this maze of streets the problem for the military was, the *Northern Whig* observed, that 'while the rioters knew every hole, the forces of the law were hopelessly ignorant of the ramifications'.[132] The following night the troops fared no better and the 'singular sight was witnessed of the Tommies digging up kidneys for all they were worth'.[133] The Riot Act was read and seven soldiers fired up the Falls Road: Maggie Lennon, looking for her child, and Charles McMullan, on his way home from work, were shot dead.

Sectarian fighting did not ensue. Order was restored next day when Catholic clergy, William Walker and other strike leaders posted up handbills reading:

Not as Catholics or Protestants, as Nationalists or Unionists, but as Belfast men and workers stand together and don't be misled by the employers' game of dividing Catholic and Protestant.[134]

By now carters and dockers were streaming back to work and with the assistance of George Askwith, the Board of Trade's most skilled arbitrator, a settlement was made. The employers had won an almost complete victory, several of them never again employing union men they had locked out. During that dispute three colliers were diverted from Belfast to Newry where the dockers had been organised by James Fearon with Larkin's assistance. On reaching Newry port the ships were 'blacked' and the strike extended when importers subsequently attempted to use Warrenpoint. By February 1908, however, the men had drifted back to work without any of their demands having been met. Another strike by coal men, dockers and cranemen in November was swiftly crushed. Larkin moved on to Dublin, there to leave the National Union of Dock Labourers and found his own Irish Transport and General Workers' Union.

For a time Catholics and Protestants had campaigned shoulder to shoulder, but another quarter of a century would pass before poverty would again bring them together in a common cause. It would take more than trade-union loyalty to detach them from their traditional political allegiances. Besides, events at Westminster were shortly to arouse the people of Ulster to passionate defence of, or opposition to, Home Rule.

HOME RULE PROMISED AND LOYALIST RESISTANCE PREPARED

When Campbell-Bannerman died in 1908 and Asquith took his place as prime minister, Britain was entering the most dangerous constitutional crisis since the Glorious Revolution. For three years the House of Lords had been emasculating bills sent up from the Commons. David Lloyd George, who had replaced Asquith as chancellor of the exchequer, now threw down a gauntlet which was readily picked up by the peers. The 'People's Budget' introduced in April 1909 to wage, in Lloyd George's words, 'implacable warfare against poverty and squalidness', was haughtily rejected by the Lords.[135] Asquith had no choice but to take the issue to the people, and a general election followed in January 1910.

Now was the moment for Redmond to exact the price of his support. Setting aside their conservative distaste for a budget that Dillon

430

believed would 'hit Ireland with intolerable injustice',[136] the National-ists had voted in division after division with the Government. On the eve of the election Asquith announced that the Irish Question could be solved only 'by a policy which, while safeguarding the supremacy and indefeasible authority of the imperial Parliament, will set up in Ireland a system of full self-government in regard to purely Irish affairs'.[137] The Liberals won the election but with such a reduced majority that they were now dependent on the forty Labour and eighty-two Nationalist MPs to stay in power. The Lords gave way and accepted the budget only to face a Parliament Bill designed to deny peers the right to reject bills from the Commons for more than three successive sessions. When the Lords threw out this bill, once again there was a constitutional impasse which could only be resolved by another election. For the people of Britain the issue was whether or not the hereditary peers should be allowed to reject the will of the people's representatives. For the people of Ireland the issue was whether or not the Lords' veto, the last constitu-tional barrier to Home Rule, would be removed.

Despite occasional dark threats of popular resistance, since 1886 the Ulster Unionists had put their faith in parliamentary action. Now – still uncertain of Tory resolve at Westminster and disgusted by the apparent indifference of the British electorate – northern loyalist leaders firmly embarked on an unconstitutional course. This fateful decision was taken earlier than is generally acknowledged: in November 1910, a month before the second election of that year, the Ulster Unionist Council formed a secret committee to oversee the buying of weapons from arms dealers and the formation of an Ulster army to resist the imposition of Home Rule. The council's agent was Major Fred Crawford, secretary of the Ulster Reform Club, a veteran of the Boer War, a former engineer with the White Star line and the founder of Young Ulster in 1892, an armed secret society which had seriously considered kidnap-ping Gladstone on Brighton promenade.[138] On 22 November 1910, act-ing under instructions of the council committee and using an alias, Crawford wrote to five arms manufacturers, including Steyr, and Deutsche Waffen und Munitionsfabriken, seeking a quotation for twenty thousand rifles and a million rounds of ammunition, adding: 'The rifles need not be very latest pattern – second hand ones in good order preferred.'[139] Further requests for tenders were made in continental newspapers in December, and later that month Colonel R.H. Wallace, secretary to the Grand Orange Lodge of Ulster, confided to a Canadian supporter:

At the present we are quietly organising. The various lodges have re-ceived enrolment forms and will be taught simple movements.[140]

In the December 1910 general election the Conservative and Unionist Party won exactly the same number of seats as the Liberals, but Asquith remained as prime minister with the support of forty-two Labour MPs and eighty-four Nationalists. Redmond again held the balance of power. On 23 December Sir Edward Carson told Lady Londonderry that he felt 'seedy and depressed since the elections', and he had good cause, for the passage of the Parliament Bill was now inevitable, thus depriving the Unionists of their last parliamentary weapon with which to resist the verdict of the Commons on Home Rule.[141] Even before the Parliament Act had been entered in the Statute Book in August 1911, the Ulster Unionist Council voted its first cash allocation for the buying of rifles in March and on 20 April Captain James Craig wrote to Crawford: 'I am convinced that unless a steady supply is started, we will be caught like rats in a trap.'[142] Carson in turn made his position clear to Craig at the end of July 1911:

> I am not for a game of bluff, and unless men are prepared to make great sacrifices which they clearly understand, the talk of resistance is no use.[143]

Carson had agreed to become the new leader of the Ulster Unionists and with his customary attention to detail Craig prepared a great demonstration to introduce him to his followers.

CARSON AND CRAIG

> I know the responsibility you are putting on me to-day. In your presence I cheerfully accept it, grave as it is, and I now enter into a compact with you, and every one of you, and with the help of God you and I joined together . . . will yet defeat the most nefarious conspiracy that has ever been hatched against a free people.

From a platform overlooking Belfast Lough at Craigavon, Craig's estate at Strandtown, Carson addressed these words to fifty thousand men from Unionist Clubs and Orange lodges drawn from all parts of Ulster on Saturday 23 September 1911. Simple rejection of Home Rule was not enough. 'We must be prepared,' he warned, ' . . . the morning Home Rule passes, ourselves to become responsible for the government of the Protestant Province of Ulster.'[144] Three days later Carson explained to another audience at Portrush that a provisional government of Ulster must be formed to take over all areas of the province that loyalists would be able to control.

Sir Edward Carson seemed an unlikely leader to be chosen by the Ulster Unionists but he brought undoubted prestige to their movement, being one of the most brilliant lawyers of his day. He had become a household name in 1895 when he brought down Oscar Wilde and again

in 1909 when he cleared the name of George Archer-Shee (a case drama-
tised by Terence Rattigan in *The Winslow Boy*). Returned as a Liberal
Unionist for Trinity College, he served as Balfour's solicitor-general
and could have expected high office in a future Tory government. 'It is
only for Ireland that I'm in politics,' he told Asquith and, as a southern
Unionist, he was certain that the welfare of the island as a whole
depended on the maintenance of the Union. He agreed to lead Ulster
loyalists in the belief that if he could prevent Home Rule being applied
to Ulster then Home Rule could not be applied to the rest of Ireland, for
Redmond would never accept a divided island. No man in Ireland,
with the possible exception of Jim Larkin, could sway an audience with
such skill. In private he was something of a temperamental hypochon-
driac and he could express grave doubts about the unconstitutional
course he was taking; but in public Carson's tall frame commanded
respect and the grim set of his lower jaw seemed to show northern
loyalists that he would not yield in championing their cause.

'James Craig did all the work and I got all the credit', Carson later
observed with much truth. The seventh child of a self-made whiskey
distiller, Captain James Craig – the man who masterminded Ulster
loyalist resistance to Home Rule – was Carson's partner rather than his
second-in-command. He had already demonstrated his courage, solidarity with the rank and file, and organisational flair as an officer in the
Boer War. Returned for East Down in 1906, he proved to be a diligent if
undistinguished MP, *Punch* describing him in 1909 as follows:

> This tall, broad-shouldered, florid-faced stonewaller is at once the delight
> and despair of the House of Commons . . . Scores of motions in the
> Captain's name were down on the paper . . . Taunts are flung at him
> across the gangway by the Nationalists. No matter. The brogue-tongued
> Captain plods along, swamping Ministerial time and patience by the
> dreary drip of words.[145]

To a greater extent than Carson, Craig shared the prejudices and fears
of the Ulster Protestants he represented. His concern was loyalist
Ulster. Carson wanted to maintain the Union for all of Ireland; Craig
wanted to maintain the Union in order to save Protestant Ulster. Events
were to prove that Craig's objective was the more realistic of the two.
For the moment, the abilities of Carson and Craig complemented each
other as they led their devoted followers into uncharted waters.

'ONCE AGAIN YOU HOLD THE PASS, THE PASS FOR THE EMPIRE'

'We must not attach too much importance to these frothings of Sir
Edward Carson,' Winston Churchill said in a speech made at Dundee in
October 1911; 'I daresay when the worst comes to the worst we shall find

that civil war evaporates in uncivil words.'[146] He was convinced, as were most Liberals and Nationalists, that Ulster Unionists were only engaged in what Redmond described as a 'gigantic game of bluff and blackmail'. Redmond's complacency survived into 1913 when he assured Asquith that 'nobody denies that a riot may be attempted in Belfast and one or two other towns, but nobody in Ulster, outside a certain number of fanatics and leaders, believes in any organised rebellion, active or passive'.[147] As for Churchill, who as home secretary had promised that the Government would introduce a Home Rule Bill in the next session 'and press it forward with all their strength', he was soon to experience the strength of loyalist feeling at first hand.[148]

Invited to speak in Belfast by the Ulster Liberal Association headed by Lord Pirrie, Churchill faced a hostile crowd singing the national anthem as he came ashore at Larne on the morning of 8 February 1912. Larger and more menacing throngs of demonstrators met him in Belfast and shipwrights threatened to overturn his motorcar.[149] Denied the use of the Ulster Hall where a quarter of a century before his father had warned that Home Rule could come upon them 'as a thief in the night', the home secretary was forced to speak in Celtic Park. There he addressed a Home Rule audience in a rain-sodden marquee. Though the city was now packed with troops, Churchill left for the docks by a circuitous route and loyalist wits were not slow to say that *he* had left Belfast like a thief in the night.

> The dark eleventh hour
> Draws on and sees us sold . . .[150]

So Kipling began an indignant poem, 'Ulster 1912', published in the *Morning Post*, showing that British Conservatives were rallying to the Ulster Unionist cause. Damaged bridges between the Ulster and British sections of the party were rapidly repaired, a task greatly eased by the accession of Andrew Bonar Law to the leadership on the resignation of Balfour in November 1911. Bonar Law once said to Austen Chamberlain that until the First World War he cared only for two things in politics, Ulster and tariff reform. His father had been born in Coleraine and had been Presbyterian minister in the town before answering a call to New Brunswick. The new opposition leader's determination to save Protestant Ulster was reinforced by his close friendship with the 6th Marquess of Londonderry and his wife Lady Theresa, who had arranged his social engagements ever since his own wife's death in 1908.

On Easter Tuesday 1912 Bonar Law and seventy other English, Scottish and Welsh MPs made their way to the Agricultural Society's show grounds at Balmoral in south Belfast. Seventy special trains brought in one hundred thousand loyalist demonstrators who, after marching past the platforms, listened to opening prayers by the Church of Ireland primate and the moderator of the Presbyterian Church and joined in singing Psalm 90. As a resolution against Home Rule was passed the largest union flag ever woven was unfurled from a ninety-foot flagstaff. Bonar Law assured them they were not just campaigning for themselves:

> Once again you hold the pass, the pass for the Empire. You are a besieged city. The timid have left you; your Lundys have betrayed you; but you have closed your gates. The Government have erected by their Parliament Act a boom against you to shut you off from the help of the British people. You will burst that boom. That help will come . . .[151]

Essentially Bonar Law gave the same message as Kipling's concluding lines:

> If England drive us forth
> We shall not fall alone.[152]

Out of office now for seven years, the longest consecutive period in half a century, the Conservatives were convinced that it was only the Home Rule issue that had prevented their return to power. Despite the fact that in 1910 the Unionist Associations of Ireland had sent 342 propagandists in January and 381 in December to inform voters of the imminent danger of Home Rule, Bonar Law argued that Asquith had not warned the British people of his 'corrupt parliamentary bargain' with the Irish Parliamentary Party.[153] The extreme reaction of the Conservatives was partly the response of a traditional ruling caste not yet ready to face the consequences of parliamentary democracy. To some extent the Ulster cause was espoused because, unlike tariff reform, it could reunite the party. Yet there was more here than a desire to be revenged on the Liberals for recent humiliations: a formidable body of British opinion saw Home Rule as a deadly threat to the empire. Seen by many as a great civilising force, the empire and its peoples could be torn asunder by any measure of Irish independence. The Home Rule Bill about to be introduced might well be a modest measure of devolution, but as Nationalist leaders themselves suggested, it could be extended at a later date – this was just what was feared on both sides of the Irish Sea.

'I CAN IMAGINE NO LENGTH OF RESISTANCE TO WHICH ULSTER CAN GO . . .'

'If I may say so reverently,' Redmond said to the House of Commons with evident emotion, 'I personally thank God that I have lived to see this day.'[154] That day, 11 April 1912, the Home Rule Bill was introduced,

Asquith explaining that it would maintain 'unimpaired, and beyond the reach of challenge or question, the supremacy, absolute and sovereign, of the Imperial Parliament'.[155] Cardinal Logue dismissed the measure as 'a skeleton on which to hang restrictions', and Arthur Griffith of Sinn Féin commented: 'If this is liberty, the lexicographers have deceived us.'[156] The mass of Irish nationalists, however, sought devolution and not complete separation, and this bill – modelled on that of 1893 but providing better financial terms and immediate control of the judiciary – seemed to bring members of the Irish Parliamentary Party to their promised land.

Bonar Law spoke with exceptional bitterness in the protracted debates that followed, warning that Ulster would 'resist by force' and if troops were ordered to take action against the province, it was not likely they would obey. At a great Unionist rally at Blenheim Palace in July he echoed Bismarck's 'blood and iron' speech to the Reichstag when he said 'there are things stronger than parliamentary majorities'. If Ulster loyalists resorted to force, they would have his backing:

> I repeat now with a full sense of the responsibility which attaches to my position, that, in my opinion, if such an attempt is made, I can imagine no length of resistance to which Ulster can go in which I should not be prepared to support them.[157]

Passions were running high in Ulster. On Saturday 29 June a Sunday school outing, with bands, banners with Bible texts, and union flags, was attacked at Castledawson, Co. Londonderry, by members of an Ancient Order of Hibernians procession. Several children were badly hurt and some were found much later hiding in terror a mile away from the affray. 'Remember Castledawson' became a fresh loyalist watchword and the following Monday Protestant shipwrights rounded on Catholic workmen in the Belfast yards, assaulting them, pelting them with rivet ends, and driving them out. On 14 September at Celtic Park, at a match between the home team and their Protestant rivals, Linfield Football Club, furious fighting broke out between the spectators who used both knives and revolvers. Sixty injured were treated in the Royal Victoria Hospital. The danger of outright sectarian warfare loomed large. Only by a series of massive displays of loyalist solidarity, the Ulster Unionist Council believed, could British sympathy be won and violence be avoided.

On 18 September 1912 Carson arrived in Enniskillen, the first official visit made by a leading national figure to Co. Fermanagh for a very long time. Here, in contrast to neighbouring Tyrone and the eastern part of Ulster, the response of Protestants to the Home Rule threat had been distinctly lethargic. W.C. Trimble, who had constantly upbraided fellow loyalists for their inaction, now led a volunteer unit of two hundred cavalry to escort the Unionist leader to Portora Hill. There forty thousand members of Unionist Clubs paraded and Carson launched the campaign to sweep from the west of loyalist Ulster eastwards to Belfast. He spoke at six meetings and leading British Conservatives addressed demonstrations in the rural loyalist heartlands, including the brilliant advocate Frederick Edwin Smith and notable aristocratic diehards such as Lord Willoughby de Broke, Lord Salisbury, Lord Hugh Cecil and Lord Charles Beresford. Already, on 19 September, Carson had made public Ulster's Solemn League and Covenant. This was to be signed all over the province in the climax to the campaign on 28 September – Ulster Day.

ULSTER DAY: SATURDAY 28 SEPTEMBER 1912

'There was a Sabbatical appearance about the streets in the early morning', the *Belfast News-Letter* reporter observed in Belfast; 'The clang of the hammer, the throbbing of machinery, and the whirr of the loom were no longer heard.' Instead, 'the artisans, dressed in their best attire, joined their employers in the services at the various Churches, where Providence was supplicated to avert the very grave and real danger that threatens the country'.[158]

In the Ulster Hall, Craig, taking his place beside Carson, reminded everyone that there should be no applause as this was a religious service. The packed congregation sang 'O God, our help in ages past', and after prayers and lessons had been read, the former Presbyterian moderator, Dr William McKean, rose to deliver his sermon, taking as his text 1 Timothy 6:20: 'Keep that which is committed to thy trust.' In it he declared:

> We are plain, blunt men who love peace and industry. The Irish question is at bottom a war against Protestantism; it is an attempt to establish a Roman Catholic ascendancy in Ireland to begin the disintegration of the Empire by securing a second parliament in Dublin.[159]

All over Ulster the Protestant people emerged from churches and meeting halls to sign the Covenant, pledging themselves 'to stand by one another in defending for ourselves and our children our cherished position of equal citizenship in the United Kingdom and in using all means which may be found necessary to defeat the present conspiracy to set up a Home Rule Parliament in Ireland'.[160] At Castle Upton in Co. Antrim, Lord Templetown, the man who had done most to create the Unionist Clubs, signed the Covenant on an old drum of the

437

Templepatrick Infantry. At Baronscourt in Co. Tyrone the Duke of Abercorn inscribed his signature under an old oak tree.

In Belfast the Portland stone of the city hall gleamed in the sun. Formally opened six years before, this was one of the most sumptuous municipal buildings in the United Kingdom, a fitting heart of resistance to Home Rule. Loyalists were proud of Belfast's pre-eminence as the city with the world's largest shipyard, ropeworks, tobacco factory, linen-spinning mill, tea machinery works, aerated water factory and dry dock. With the launch of the *Olympic* in 1910, Harland and Wolff was again constructing the world's biggest ships, though the tragic sinking of the sister liner *Titanic* in April 1912 with the loss of 1,490 passengers and crew (the figure established by the British inquiry), cast a shadow over the reputation of Belfast and, in particular, over that of the White Star line, the firm's most valuable customer. As a guard of honour stood to attention – splendid with military medals, specially embroidered sashes, and white staves – Carson entered the vestibule of the city hall and advanced towards a circular table directly under the dome rising 173 feet above him. There he signed the Covenant with a silver square-sided pen presented to him and when he re-emerged the reverential hum of the vast crowd changed to tempestuous cheering.

At 2.30 p.m. a procession of bands from every Protestant quarter of Belfast converged on the city hall, each contingent halting at a prear-ranged position and continuing to play different loyalist airs, creating, in the opinion of the *Northern Whig*, 'a fine post-impressionist effect about it that should have pleased admirers of the new style of music'. Reporting for the *Pall Mall Gazette*, J.L. Garvin wrote: 'Seen from the topmost outside gallery of the dome, the square below and the streets striking away from it were black with people. Through all the mass, with drums and fifes, the clubs marched all day.'[161] Bowler-hatted stewards struggled to regulate the flow of men eager to sign. A double row of desks stretching right round the building made it possible for 550 to sign simultaneously. Signatures were still being affixed after 11 p.m. Women signed their own separate declaration. Altogether 471,414 men and women who could prove Ulster birth signed either the Cov-enant or the declaration, over thirty thousand more women, in fact, than men.

At 8.30 p.m. a brass band advanced towards the Ulster Club in Castle Place playing 'See the Conquering Hero Comes', its staff major and spear carriers almost having to carve a way through the surging mass to accompany Carson in a waiting motor brake to the docks. The vehicle was pulled down High Street by hundreds of willing hands. 'With a roaring hurricane of cheers punctuated on every side by the steady rattle of revolver shots,' Garvin wrote, 'onward swept this whole city in motion with a tumult that was mad.' At Donegall Quay Sir Edward was saluted by a fusillade of shots as Captain John Paisley welcomed him aboard *Patriotic*. 'Keep the old flag flying and No Surrender!' Carson urged from the upper deck and as the vessel steamed into the Victoria Channel bonfires in Great Patrick Street sprang to life, a huge fire on the Cave Hill threw a brilliant glare over the sky, fifty other bonfires blazed from hills and headlands round Belfast Lough, and salvoes of rockets shot up into the air.[162]

Ulster Day was denounced as 'a silly masquerade' by the *Irish News* and as 'an impressive farce' by the *Freeman's Journal*, while the *Manchester Guardian* contrasted 'the anarchic hectoring of the ascendancy party and the loyal patient reliance of the Ulster Nationalists upon English justice and firmness'. Garvin, however, now knew this was no game of bluff and blackmail: 'No-one for a moment could have mistaken the concentrated will and courage of those people.' The next two years seemed to reveal the truth of his judgement.[163]

THE ULSTER VOLUNTEER FORCE

'Traitor!' Sir William Bull roared at Asquith when it was made clear that Home Rule would be pushed through the Commons by the guillotine. That day in the House, 13 November 1912, tempers flared as opposition MPs chanted 'resign, resign', and 'civil war, civil war', and Ulsterman Ronald McNeill, MP for East Kent, hurled a bound copy of the standing orders at Churchill, striking him on the head.[164] Nevertheless, early in 1913 the bill passed the Commons only to be rejected by the Lords by 326 votes to 69. Soon after, the Nationalists recovered Londonderry City, tipping the balance of MPs in Ulster in their favour, seventeen to sixteen. Undeterred, the Ulster Unionist Council at its annual meeting in January had already decided to use 'all means which may be found necessary' to stop Home Rule: the scheme for setting up the provisional government of Ulster was ready and the Ulster Volunteer Force, to be recruited from men who had signed the Covenant, was formally instituted.

Wooden batons and dummy rifles made of pine were used to train men who flocked to join the UVF. Lieutenant-General Sir George Richardson, veteran of the Afghan Wars who had also led the final assault on Peking during the Boxer Rising, agreed to command this loyalist army. Making Belfast's Old Town Hall its headquarters, the UVF grew to ninety thousand men by the end of the year, not including the Motor Car Corps, the Signalling and Dispatch Rider Corps, the

Ballymena Horse, the Medical Corps and the Nursing Corps. In west Belfast Captain Frank Percy Crozier paraded his regiment four nights a week at Forth River Football Ground while in Ballymacarrett one company drilled on waste ground just outside Ye Olde Princess Picture Palace. In rural Ulster the UVF took on much of the character of the eighteenth-century Volunteers, training on demesnes including Donard Park, Castle Hume, Springhill, Shane's Castle and Killyleagh Castle. The Tyrone Regiment encamped at Baronscourt for a weekend in October 1913, consuming a ton of potatoes and 1,470 pounds of beef, and were given squad, battalion and musketry drill, and a lantern-slide lecture on the South African War. Enthusiasm was weakest in western Ulster; in the Laggan, for example, Presbyterian farmers seem to have resented the prominent role of Church of Ireland clergy and landlords.[165] In July 1913 the RIC county inspector for Donegal reported to Dublin Castle that while Protestants there bitterly opposed Home Rule,

> they would not be capable of doing anything to prevent it being operative and owing to the friendly feelings that genuinely exist between the Roman Catholics and the Protestants, the latter would not turn on their Roman Catholic neighbours for revenge.[166]

Even as late as the summer of 1914 the Donegal UVF had not attracted a majority of adult Protestant males in the county.

Northern Protestants opposed to the tactics being adopted by the Ulster Unionist Council were not confined to the tiny minority, such as Casement and Hobson, who committed themselves to the nationalist cause. The old liberal hostility to landlord power survived amongst many Presbyterian farmers, particularly in Co. Antrim. The Reverend James B. Armour of Ballymoney had won notoriety in May 1893 by declaring that the 'principle of Home Rule is a Presbyterian principle' and denouncing his fellow ministers' 'senseless fear of Romanism'.[167] In 1911 he re-emerged to scoff at loyalist threats of resistance as 'the result of a bad attack of *delirium tremens*'. When the threats began to materialise, Armour described Carson as 'a sheer mountebank, the greatest enemy of Protestantism in my opinion existing, inflaming men to violence'.[168] On 24 October 1913 some four hundred Protestants attended a meeting in Ballymoney Town Hall organised by Armour and Captain Jack White of Whitehall, Ballymena. 'No provisional or provincial government for us' proclaimed a banner at the meeting where Sir Roger Casement made his first public speech.[169] Most of those who attended were not Irish-Irelanders, being anti-*Unionist* rather than anti-*unionist*: the Independent Orange Order was strong in the Route and the election of a Liberal, R.G. Glendinning, in

1906 seems to have been due largely to his support for compulsory land purchase. Liberal support in the area was rapidly declining and the Unionists held the seat comfortably from 1910 onwards: a demonstration addressed by Captain James Craig in Ballymoney on 21 November 1913 drew far greater support than Armour's meeting the month before.

Recruitment to and the organisation of the UVF had been impressive by any standards, but could it stop Home Rule unless it was fully armed? Could Ulster Unionist resistance force Asquith to modify his bill?

'WAIT TILL THEY GET THEIR FIST CLUTCHING THE STEEL BARREL
OF A BUSINESS RIFLE'

'I have never heard that orange bitters will mix with Irish whiskey,' an English Liberal MP had observed at an early stage in the Home Rule debate.[170] Then his amendment to exclude the four most Protestant counties of Ulster from the bill's operation had been decisively rejected. When in September 1913 Lord Loreburn, who had helped to draft the bill, called for a compromise on Ulster to avoid a civil war, the Government was forced to reconsider. Asquith and Bonar Law met several times in secret during the final months of 1913, both men clearly eager for a settlement but both hamstrung by their Irish allies. In October Redmond declared that 'Irish nationalists can never be assenting parties to the mutilation of the Irish nation . . . The two nation theory is to us an abomination and a blasphemy.'[171] All hopes of a compromise disappeared when Carson told Asquith on 22 January 1914 that he could not agree to 'anything short of the exclusion of Ulster'.[172] With Redmond's very reluctant assent, the Government introduced a complicated amendment allowing each Ulster county to opt out of Home Rule for six years. 'We do not want sentence of death with a stay of execution for six years,' Carson told the Commons on 9 March 1914 and ten days later he challenged the Government to 'come and try conclusions with us in Ulster', saying as he left the House, 'I am off to Belfast.' As he boarded his train at Euston less than an hour later he told a reporter: 'I go to my people.'[173]

Unknown to Asquith, Carson had learned from high-ranking army officers that the Government intended decisive action to prevent the UVF seizing Ulster and the Ulster Unionist Council setting up its provisional government. Colonel John Seely, the war minister, asked the commander-in-chief in Ireland to strengthen the approaches to Ulster at Enniskillen, Dundalk and Newry, and to take special precautions to safeguard arms depots. Winston Churchill, now first lord of the Admiralty, ordered a naval cordon into position: two light cruisers from Bantry Bay to Belfast Lough; seven battleships from the Third Battle Squadron anchored off Spain to Lamlash in the Firth of Clyde; eight destroyers from Plymouth to the same destination; and two warships from Plymouth to take troops to Dundalk. Uncertain of its next step, the Liberal government quickly lost the initiative. Sixty cavalry officers at the Curragh army camp in Co. Kildare announced that they would prefer to be dismissed rather than lead their men against Ulster loyalists. Seely yielded to senior army pressure and gave the cavalry a written assurance that the Government did not intend to crush political opposition in the north. The war minister was dismissed but it was too late. Fully alerted, the UVF moved its headquarters to a heavily sandbagged Craigavon at Craig's Strandtown estate; Balfour and Carson addressed a huge protest meeting in Hyde Park on 4 April; Lord Milner rallied support for the Unionists across the empire and announced that a British Covenant to support Ulster was receiving signatures at the rate of thirty thousand a day; and the Duchess of Somerset wrote to Carson:

> This is to assure you of our *unfailing support* and to *implore* you to take all care of yourself . . . The *day* that the first shot is fired in Ireland – I shall have my complete ambulance started and ready – 2 medical men, 2 surgeons, 6 trained nurses and 32 orderlies – I have also undertaken to house 100 women and children from Ulster.[174]

'Trust in the old party – and Home Rule next year,' Redmond had promised at a great rally in Dublin's Sackville Street in March 1912. Now it looked as if the Unionist threat of violence was about to thwart the wishes of the great majority of the Irish people. Still, the Irish Parliamentary Party leader steadfastly resisted demands for a Nationalist volunteer force and Joseph Devlin swiftly quashed proposals to found a Catholic military corps in Belfast. Then in August 1913 a titanic labour struggle began in Dublin, marked by incidents of police brutality. On the first evening of the strike Jim Larkin declared:

> If it is right and legal for the men of Ulster to arm, why should it not be right and legal for the men of Dublin to arm to protect themselves?[175]

Soon after, the Irish Citizen Army was formed, armed almost exclusively with hurley sticks. From the outset James Connolly nursed hopes of putting this army to socialist and revolutionary purposes.

'Personally I think the Orangeman with a rifle is a much less ridiculous figure than the nationalist without a rifle,' the separatist schoolmaster Patrick Pearse said in 1913 and already the IRB had leased a shooting gallery for training its members on Sunday mornings.[176] The key figure in the IRB was now Bulmer Hobson and his opportunity came when Eoin MacNeill published an article on 1 November 1913 entitled 'The North began', a reference to Thomas Davis's poem 'The Song of the Volunteers of 1782'. MacNeill argued that nationalists should defend legislative independence as the eighteenth-century Volunteers had done. Bulmer Hobson persuaded MacNeill to preside at a meeting in the Rotunda's large concert hall in Dublin on 25 November. Some three thousand men joined the Irish Volunteers at once and by January 1914 the number had risen to ten thousand. Northern nationalists were quick to join the movement and, even though 57.3 per cent of Ulster was Protestant in population, six months later nearly one third of the Irish Volunteers were enrolled in the north. Eight battalions, for example, were formed in Co. Fermanagh in January 1914 and were allowed the use of the old county gaol by the council which had previously refused permission to the UVF.[177] The object of the Irish Volunteers was vaguely defined as being 'to secure and maintain the rights and liberties common to all the people of Ireland' and their duties 'will be defensive and protective, and they will not contemplate either aggression or domination'.[178]

Of the 30 members on the Irish Volunteers' executive, 4 were members of the Irish Parliamentary Party, 4 were from the Ancient Order of Hibernians, 12 were secret members of the IRB and of the remaining 10, 5 were to take part with the brotherhood in the Easter Rising of 1916. Thomas Clarke wrote enthusiastically to Joe McGarrity, the Tyrone-born Clan na Gael leader in Philadelphia:

> Joe, it is worth living in Ireland these times – there is an awakening . . .
> Wait till they get their fist clutching the steel barrel of a business rifle and then Irish instincts and Irish manhood can be relied upon.[179]

At the beginning of December 1913 the funds of the Irish Volunteers stood at £8 7s.6d., most of it indirectly subscribed by Clan na Gael, and there were few weapons for the thousands recruited. The UVF already had over £1 million pledged to it and £70,000 invested in a hazardous enterprise to bring guns to Ulster. Throughout 1913 Major Fred Crawford, using false names and disguises, had been able to purchase small quantities of weapons in Britain and Germany but customs officials were vigilant. Arms had been seized at the docks and Lord Leitrim's gun-running to Carrigart in north Donegal came to an abrupt end after his private steamer had been arrested by patrol boats. Only by one daring stroke, Crawford persuaded the Ulster Unionist Council, could enough modern weapons and ammunition be run into Ulster to equip the entire UVF. 'Crawford,' Carson said in a steady, determined voice, 'I'll see you through this business, if I should have to go to prison for it.'[180]

During the afternoon of 30 March 1914 Danish customs officers seized the papers of SS *Fanny* taking on cargo off the Baltic island of Langeland. The mysterious bundles, the officials suspected, might well contain arms for militant home rulers in Iceland, a Danish possession. The weapons, as *The Times* correctly informed its readers on 1 April, were destined not for Iceland but for Ulster. By then the *Fanny* had cut and run into a gale out of territorial waters. On board was Major Crawford with 216 tons of arms bought from the dealer Benny Spiro: 11,000 Männlicher rifles brought by special freight train from the Steyr works in Austria; 9,000 ex-German Army Mausers; 4,600 Italian Vetterli-Vitali rifles; and 5 million rounds of ammunition in clips of five, all taken by lighters from Hamburg through the Kiel Canal. As *Fanny* was sure to be recognised as she approached Irish waters, Crawford bought the SS *Clydevalley* in Glasgow and on the night of 19–20 April the guns were transferred off the Tuskar Rock – both vessels with their lights out were almost swamped by the wake from one of the battleships making her way from Spain to Lamlash on Churchill's orders.[181] That same night instructions had been issued for a full test mobilisation of the UVF. General Sir William Adair, commander in Co. Antrim, summoned members of the Motor Corps:

> It is absolutely necessary that your car should arrive at Larne in the night of Friday–Saturday 24th–25th instant *at 1 a.m. punctually but not before that hour* for a very secret and important duty . . .[182]

Only twelve men knew for certain the elaborate plan for landing and distributing the arms. Arrangements were meticulous, as Captain F. Hall, military secretary to the UVF, recorded in a memorandum which includes the following:

> Arrangements were made to 'short circuit' (*not* to cut or damage) all telegraph & 'phone wires to Larne at Magheramorne, at 9.15 p.m. after last train had gone down. All lines on Bangor Road & rail to be 'shorted' at midnight except the Glasgow Trunk Lines.
> The private telephone connecting H'wood Barracks to Exchange was tapped & a man sat at it from 10 p.m. till 3 a.m.[183]

That night while the authorities investigated SS *Balmerino*, a decoy ship sent into Belfast Lough, the arms were brought in without interference at Larne, Bangor and Donaghadee, and loaded on to motorcars, which then sped through the small hours distributing them to prepared dumps all over the province. Probably for the first time in history motor vehicles had been used on a large scale for a military purpose, and with striking success. Captain Wilfrid Spender, a member of the UVF headquarters staff, was a key figure in the operation; his wife Lilian recorded in her diary for 24–5 April:

> W. had told me he would have to be away that night with the General, seeing after the big Test Mobilisation which was to take place then, but which was being kept a profound secret until the last moment . . . His post was to be at Musgrave Channel, assisting at the Hoax which took in all the Customs officers, & kept them occupied all night, watching the 'Balmerino' which of course contained nothing but coal! . . .
> I was anxious, & we occupied ourselves as best we could, by catechising one another in First Aid & Home Nursing . . . The whole proceedings are almost incredible, and nothing but the most perfect organisation, combined with the most perfect and loyal co-operation on the part of all concerned, could have carried it through without a single case of bloodshed. Need I say that for the organisation W. himself was mainly responsible, the scheme having been originally drawn up by him?[184]

TO THE BRINK OF CIVIL WAR

For almost half a century the gun had been largely absent from Irish politics and representatives had pursued their objectives by constitutional means. Now the gun had returned centre stage. The Irish tradition of armed defiance, which had seemed all but extinct, in a few short years had sprung back to vigorous life. The UVF, now impressively armed, revitalised militant separatism. The IRB, almost defunct at the beginning of the century, now recruited a new generation of young men and acquired key positions on the Irish Volunteers' executive. Redmond, Dillon and Devlin watched the rise of the Irish Volunteers, numbering 129,000 by May 1914, with the deepest misgivings but they could not ignore a movement so popular with their electorate. In an attempt to prevent civil war by bringing the organisation under his control, Redmond issued a press statement on 9 June explaining that the Irish Parliamentary Party must control the Volunteers or else it would launch a new movement of its own. MacNeill reluctantly agreed and twenty-five Irish Parliamentary Party nominees were accepted on to the executive. Nationalist opinion seemed to approve Redmond's action and by the end of June, membership of the Volunteers had risen to 130,000.

Though Asquith might refer to his own 'masterly inactivity' and the merits of his policy of 'wait-and-see', he had long since lost the initiative. The Curragh incident made it clear that the Government could not depend on the regular army to quell rebellion in Ulster. The importation of German rifles now made such a rebellion a distinct possibility. The UVF made elaborate plans to prevent the seizure of their arms, Colonel G. Hacket Pain issuing a memorandum as chief staff officer: 'In the event of any attempt being made to seize arms, etc. . . . intimation will be given to the officers in charge of the Constabulary that their armed attempt will be promptly and firmly resisted.'[185] In fact the Government had no intention of trying to recover the weapons – indeed, Redmond advised them not to attempt it.

By now Asquith was reconciled to partition in some form, Redmond ruefully observing that he had been less influenced by the Irish Parliamentary Party's unswerving support than by Carson's pugnacious threat of force. The Nationalist MP T.P. O'Connor nevertheless concluded that the Liberals 'would be more than human if they did not want to get Home Rule out of the way' by these means. Bonar Law, too, began to see partition as a solution and George V urged the prime minister to exclude permanently the six north-eastern counties. Such talk caused alarm amongst loyalists on the fringes of Ulster: while Carson seemed to want nothing less than the exclusion of all nine counties, other Unionists were not certain that he would get his way. At a meeting of the Monaghan branch of the Ulster Women's Unionist Council, held in the town's assembly rooms on 26 February 1914, Miss Murray-Ker offered her house as a UVF hospital and then concluded the evening by saying:

> If Ulster is excluded from Home Rule, it seems that Monaghan will not be included in Ulster. The prospect before us Loyalist and Ulster Protestants is that ... of being placed under a Dublin Roman Catholic Parliament which will be under priestly influence and dominated – and this I fear most – by Mr Devlin's anti-Protestant Ancient Order of Hibernians.[186]

For many Catholics in Ulster the prospect of exclusion seemed more depressing than that of getting no Home Rule at all. At a mass meeting of nationalists at Donaghmore in Co. Tyrone on Sunday 9 November 1913, the United Irish League organiser J.P. Convery was reported by the *Irish News* as saying: 'Under no circumstances would they allow Ulster or any portion of it to be taken from the map of Ireland (Cheers).' The next speaker said that

> if a vote of Nationalist Ulster was taken, they would fight on sooner than accept any form of Home Rule which would make the government of Ulster different in any respect from that which would obtain in the rest of Ireland.[187]

The Reverend Canon McCartan PP, who presided at this meeting, was to repeat this threat the following June when he promised violent resistance should there be an attempt to exclude any part of Co. Tyrone.[188]

By the early summer of 1914 Asquith's government seemed beset by crises. The assassination of the heir-apparent to the Austro-Hungarian throne at Sarajevo on 28 June seemed less critical than turbulent labour disputes in Britain and the threat of a general strike in the autumn. The suffragettes, too, were bringing their campaign to a crescendo: in Ulster, Major-General Sir Hugh McCalmont's home in Whiteabbey was burned, the cost of destruction being £11,000; Orlands House, once the palace of the Catholic bishop of Down and Connor, was also burned down by female activists; and in Belfast women set fire to the Tea House at Bellevue, Annadale Hall and the pavilion of the Cavehill Bowling and Tennis Club.[189] Above all, Ireland lurched closer to the brink of civil war and in Ulster the danger was most acute where Irish Volunteers – 41,000 in the province out of a national total of 129,000, according to a count made in May 1914 – and Ulster Volunteers could be seen drilling in adjacent streets.

The Home Rule Bill had passed the Commons for the third time on 25 May 1914 and now only required the royal signature to become law. Tedious and inconclusive negotiations continued. Finally George V called an all-party conference at Buckingham Palace on 21 July, saying in his opening address:

> For months we have watched with deep misgivings the course of events in Ireland . . . and today the cry of civil war is on the lips of the most responsible and sober-minded of my people . . . to me it is unthinkable, as it must be to you, that we should be brought to the brink of fratricidal strife upon issues apparently so capable of adjustment as those you are now asked to consider, if handled in a spirit of generous compromise.[190]

The conference, according to Churchill, 'toiled round the muddy byways of Fermanagh and Tyrone', but there was no spirit of generous compromise and the talks broke down on 24 July.[191] 'I see no hopes of peace,' Carson gloomily observed, 'I see nothing at present but darkness and shadows . . . we shall have once more to assert the manhood of our race.'[192]

On Sunday 26 July a consignment of obsolete single-shot Mausers was bought in Hamburg and taken by yacht to Howth near Dublin: dozens were openly paraded in the streets by Irish Volunteers. Soldiers, who had attempted to take some of the rifles, opened fire on a taunting crowd, killing four people and wounding a further thirty-seven. Nationalists were intensely bitter when they compared their treatment with that of the UVF. Asquith ordered a public inquiry and on 30 July, now thoroughly alarmed by the European crisis, he decided on the permanent exclusion of the counties of Antrim, Down, Armagh and Londonderry from the jurisdiction of Home Rule. General von Bernhardt in Berlin was certain that the critical situation in Ireland would paralyse Britain 'if it ever comes to war with England'. The American ambassador to the German Empire reported that it was 'believed by the Germans that Ireland would rise in rebellion the moment war was

447

declared'.[193] Field Marshal Conrad von Hötzendorff was sure that the Ulster crisis would give him a free hand in Serbia.

Hötzendorff's punitive expedition against Serbia began to escalate. On 1 August Germany declared war on Russia and on the same day arms were landed on a Co. Wicklow beach for the Irish Volunteers – Hamburg had supplied weapons to both contending parties in Ireland. On 3 August 1914 German troops began to pour across the Belgian frontier. The following day the United Kingdom was at war. It was not to be in Ulster but in France that the manhood of Carson's race would be asserted.

'FAITHFUL TO ERIN, WE ANSWER HER CALL!'

'All officers, non-commissioned officers and men who are in the Ulster Volunteer Force . . . are requested to answer immediately his Majesty's call, as our first duty as loyal subjects is to the King': with this telegram Carson pulled his followers back from the brink of civil war. 'I say to the Government that they may tomorrow withdraw every one of their troops from Ireland,' Redmond had said on that emotional night of 3 August in the Commons, ' . . . the armed Catholics in the South will only be too glad to join arms with the armed Protestant Ulstermen.' With evident relief Sir Edward Grey, the foreign secretary, said that 'the one bright spot in the very dreadful situation is Ireland'.[194] No doubt Asquith privately shared this sentiment as, in Churchill's words, 'the parishes of Fermanagh and Tyrone faded back into the mists and squalls of Ireland'.[195] The war also released Bonar Law, Carson and Craig from their predicament since being offered the permanent exclusion of four counties – could they really have led a successful rebellion to hold on to Derry city, Fermanagh and Tyrone, all with Catholic majorities?

The martial fever that gripped so many parts of Europe was not slow in infecting Ulster. The *Irish News* reported that as early as 5 August, 'about six hundred men attached to the Irish Volunteers in Belfast were called up, and there was a great gathering to wish them God-speed . . . while at the same time a quota of the Ulster Volunteers were being "seen off" by a cheering crowd with a band and pipers'.[196] In the euphoria, traditional enmities were suspended, and the following day this verse – composed jointly by a Belfast member of the UVF and an Irish Volunteer from the Glens of Antrim – was published in the same newspaper:

Bless the good fortune which brings us together,
Rich men and poor men, short men and tall;
Some from the seaside and some from the heather,

448

Townsmen and countrymen, Irishmen all;
Ulstermen, Munstermen, Connachtmen, Leinstermen,
Faithful to Erin, we answer her call![197]

This did not achieve the fame of Rupert Brooke's 'Now God be thanked who has matched us with His hour', but it was written in the same spirit. On Monday 10 August, under the headline 'TYRONE'S FINE EXAMPLE. NATIONAL AND ULSTER VOLUNTEERS MARCH TOGETHER. ROUSING SCENES', the *Irish News* carried this report from Omagh:

> The Ulster Volunteers and Irish National Volunteers united at Omagh on Friday night in giving a most hearty send-off to the final draft of the Army Reserve of the Royal Inniskillings, who left the town about half-past nine o'clock, and a scene of an unparalleled description was witnessed when the procession of both bodies of Volunteers and military marched through the town together . . . Subsequently, as both bodies of Volunteers paraded the town, they met one another and respectfully saluted.

There was a similar scene in Strabane next day at the end of which Captain Roderick Gallaher of the Irish Volunteers 'called for three cheers for the Ulster Volunteers, the call being responded to in a most spirited manner'. Captain William Smyth of the Ulster Volunteers in turn called for a rousing three cheers for the Irish Volunteers.[198]

'I want the Ulster Volunteers,' Lord Kitchener said to Colonel T.E. Hickman MP, president of the British League for the Defence of Ulster. The new war secretary certainly had changed his view since he had testily remarked that he did not trust 'one single Irishman with a rifle in his hands one single yard'.[199] Carson and Craig called at the War Office soon afterwards. The Ulster Unionist leader never liked Kitchener – 'that great stuffed oaf,' he was once heard to say – and the interview began badly. 'Surely you are not going to hold out for Tyrone and Fermanagh?' the war secretary opened, to which Carson snapped back, 'You're a damned clever fellow telling me what I ought to be doing.'[200] Having so often proclaimed the loyalty of Protestant Ulster, however, the Unionist leaders could not stand back. They returned to Kitchener and offered him thirty-five thousand men without conditions and to their surprise he agreed to keep the UVF together in one Ulster Division. The elated Craig immediately jumped into a taxi to Moss Brothers and ordered ten thousand complete uniforms. 'Don't say another word,' Oliver Locker-Lampson said when Craig confessed he had not made arrangements to pay for the uniforms; 'There's a thousand pounds to go on with, and nine more will follow in a day or two.' Warm approval was obtained from the Ulster Unionist Council in Belfast, where Carson declared: 'England's difficulty is not Ulster's opportunity . . . We do not seek to purchase terms by selling our patriotism.'[201]

The Irish Parliamentary Party leaders were taking great political risks in committing the Irish Volunteers to the service of king and empire. Redmond at first only pledged their support in the defence of Ireland but on 20 September, in a speech given in Co. Wicklow, he called on the Volunteers to fight 'wherever the firing-line extends'.[202] This was too much for Eoin MacNeill and other separatists: about 11,000 broke away and retained the original title of Irish Volunteers but the great majority, around 170,000, stayed with the Irish Parliamentary Party to form the National Volunteers. The Nationalist leaders threw themselves eagerly into the recruiting drive, Joseph Devlin well to the fore in Ulster. Lord Basil Blackwood, third son of the 1st Marquess of Dufferin and Ava, wrote to his mother:

> In one respect *you* would find Devlin congenial company. In spite of stories about his drunkenness, he is a rigid teetotaller. He is also very keen about recruiting and General Parsons wrote to him the other day to say he was the only man who got them recruits, so you see every Devil has a silver lining.[203]

There was to be much recrimination later about levels of recruitment. T.J. Campbell, Devlin's associate, calculated that by the end of 1915, twenty-eight thousand Ulster Volunteers and twenty-seven thousand National Volunteers had joined up. The 1921 parliamentary paper *Recruiting in Ireland* reported an enlistment of thirty-two thousand by January 1916 from Belfast and the counties of Antrim and Down. It seems that nationalists joined up as eagerly as unionists in the early months of the conflict but that a rapid shift in the climate of opinion and several disappointments caused recruitment to drop away thereafter. One early blow was Kitchener's absolute refusal to treat the National Volunteers on the same basis as the Ulster Volunteers, who had their own 36th (Ulster) Division and cap badge, while nationalists were to be scattered in many different regiments and divisions. Another disappointment which steadily sapped the Irish Parliamentary Party's power base was the continued postponement of Home Rule.

HOME RULE ENACTED AND POSTPONED

'The Irish on both sides are giving me a lot of trouble just at a difficult moment', Asquith confided to his diary, adding: 'I sometimes wish we could submerge the whole lot of them and their island for say, ten years, under the waves of the Atlantic.'[204] Once more he was attempting to find a formula acceptable in the interim to all parties. On 15 September he told the Commons that the UVF's patriotic spirit made the coercion of Ulster 'unthinkable', but that in three days' time the Home Rule Bill would become law. Nevertheless, he continued, Home Rule would not be implemented until the end of the war and amending legislation later on would make special provision for Ulster. Bonar Law, arguing that mean advantage had been taken of loyalist patriotism, made a speech so vitriolic that Liberal ministers left the House, Asquith explained, 'lest they should be unable to overcome their impulse to throw books, paper knives, and other handy missiles at his head'.[205] Soon after, Carson stumped out and the entire opposition followed him.

On 18 September someone in the Commons waved a green flag emblazoned with a harp and there was much rejoicing in Nationalist ranks. Redmond, however, had as much reason for anxiety as the Unionists. In September 1914 it was still possible to believe the fighting would be over by Christmas but as the months rolled by the war of movement was replaced by a bloody and inconclusive slogging match in the trenches. As the Irish Parliamentary Party leaders gloomily surveyed newspaper columns listing names of their volunteers who had died at Gallipoli or on the Western Front, they saw Home Rule receding into an uncertain future. Recruitment from Catholic Ireland was reduced to a trickle and already there were signs that what had been the firm rock of Nationalist electoral support was turning to sand.

In spite of the speed with which it had formed the 36th (Ulster) Division, the War Office was slow in committing it to the front. Only dimly aware of the carnage ahead of them, the men underwent extensive training in camps at Clandeboye and Ballykinler in Co. Down and at Finner near Ballyshannon in Co. Donegal. Then, on 8 May 1915, after being inspected by Major-General Sir Hugh McCalmont at Malone, the division marched through the centre of Belfast. Special trains brought loved-ones to the city and photographs of that day show crowds densely packed around the city hall, with some boys perilously perched on tram standards, watching the men march away, followed by motor ambulances, each marked with the name of the town or association which had donated it. After further preparations in Sussex, the division disembarked at Le Havre and Boulogne in the first days of October 1915.

Protected by the Royal Navy and far out of range of Zeppelins, the farms, mills, workshops and shipyards of Ulster strove to meet the insatiable demands of the Allied war effort. Never had the people been so prosperous and rarely had the island known such domestic peace. News that a rebellion had broken out in Dublin on Easter Monday, 1916, came, therefore, as a complete surprise. Even Dr Patrick McCartan, a member of the IRB supreme council, wrote from Co. Tyrone that the 'whole business was like a thunderbolt to me'.[206]

Sir Roger Casement would still have secured a place in history had he carried through his original plan to retire to South Africa. During a distinguished career in the consular service, he had won international acclaim for his reports on ruthless cruelty and enslavement in the Belgian Congo and in Peru. Then, appalled by the threat of fellow Protestant Ulstermen to resist Home Rule by force, he had become an ardent militant separatist. Casement was in America raising money for the Irish Volunteers when war broke out and John Devoy of Clan na Gael arranged for him to see the German ambassador there to seek military aid for an Irish rebellion. Soon after, Casement travelled in secret to Berlin and eventually secured a German promise to send a shipment of arms to Ireland in 1916.

In Belfast, Denis McCullough was commandant of the Irish Volunteers but unknown to all but a very few of his men he was also president of the supreme council of the IRB. Like Father James O'Daly of Clogher and Father Eugene Coyle, both members of the brotherhood but exempted from taking its oath, McCullough awaited news of German help and the call to arms. Patrick McCartan, dispensary doctor at Gortin in Co. Tyrone and co-opted on to the supreme council in 1914, travelled to America at his own expense in 1915. There he reassured Clan na Gael that Casement was not a British spy and in Philadelphia Joe McGarrity – like McCartan born in the parish of Termonmaguirk near Carrickmore in the 1870s – gave him £2,000 in gold. McCartan was to lead the men of Tyrone to Belcoo in Co. Fermanagh to join with the men of Co. Mayo: only the signal was awaited.

This was the conspiracy of a tiny minority. Eoin MacNeill, in charge of the Irish Volunteers, issued a countermanding order when he got wind of the plan. Bulmer Hobson, now out of favour with the supreme council, was held prisoner by the brotherhood in Dublin lest he reveal its secrets. Casement was arrested in Co. Kerry, the German arms ship was intercepted and the decision to go ahead with the rising was taken solely by two Ulstermen, Thomas Clarke and, the real organiser, Sean MacDermott. So obsessed was MacDermott by the need for secrecy that McCullough never got an order to take action. McCartan only got the signal on Easter Monday, 24 April, the day the insurrection began in Dublin. In the only letter written by a member of the supreme council during the rising, McCartan described to McGarrity what happened:

> We have failed in Tyrone – miserably failed – but it is not the fault of Tyrone but of Dublin. They did not let me know till the last minute . . . Carrickmore however did turn out, and were ready about eleven o'clock to march. It was pouring rain and naturally damped their ardour.

452

Donaghmore and Coalisland who got word first waited orders from me and hence did not start till 11 o'clock Tuesday. I started to meet them but missed them, so that, all round the trial was a failure. Father O'Daly arrived about eleven . . .
After this attempt to mobilize there were 6000 rounds of ammunition left at my fathers . . . the enemy swooped down on the house yesterday with 200 soldiers and police and carried it off in triumph. It is a terrible blow to us as it deprives Sixmilecross and Carrickmore men of stuff.[207]

Swift action by the police brought any attempt at republican rebellion in Ulster to an abrupt end.[208] McCartan was forced into hiding in a barn in the Sperrins and it was there on Friday of Easter week, 28 April, that he wrote his letter on the back of fourteen blank cheques, concluding: 'I hope only that for the honour of Tyrone we will get a chance yet to show the rest of Ireland that there is still red blood here.'[209] On Saturday 29 April Patrick Pearse, head of 'The Provisional Government of the Irish Republic', surrendered, and James Connolly, the republican socialist now gravely wounded, signed separately on behalf of the Irish Citizen Army.

The Liberal Unionist Adam Duffin likened the rebellion to a 'comic opera founded on the Wolfe Tone fiasco a hundred years ago', but this uprising by scarcely 2,000 had cost 450 lives, 2,614 wounded, and £3 million worth of damage in Dublin.[210] The cost in other respects was incalculable. 'My first feeling on hearing of this insane movement', Redmond wrote, 'was one of horror, discouragement, almost despair.'[211] As military tribunals in Dublin condemned insurgent leaders to execution by firing squad, the power base of the Irish Parliamentary Party was being eroded away. The *Irish News* in Belfast was the first nationalist newspaper to call for a halt to the executions, but in Dublin the *Irish Independent* and the *Freeman's Journal* waited until MacDermott and Connolly were safely dead before adding their voices.[212] 'No true Irishman calls for vengeance,' Carson said, recognising the disastrous effect the shootings were having on nationalist opinion and when the toll reached fifteen the Government finally intervened to stop them.[213] The number rose to sixteen when Roger Casement was hanged at Pentonville prison on 3 August.

The Irish Parliamentary Party's only hope now was the immediate implementation of Home Rule. Redmond's position had already been weakened the year before when those who had led the resistance to a Dublin government were brought into a new wartime coalition government. Now Asquith sent Lloyd George to Ireland to negotiate a settlement. Carson spent an hour and a half persuading the Ulster Unionist Council to accept Lloyd George's offer of the exclusion of six northeastern counties and this was agreed for the first time. Unionists in the counties of Donegal, Cavan and Monaghan accepted their fate with heavy hearts and, according to Ronald McNeill: 'Men not prone to emotion shed tears.'[214] Hugh de Fellenberg Montgomery, a Fivemiletown landlord and member of the council, recognised that Unionists might be more secure in a six-county rather than a nine-county Ulster:

> To begin fighting here at the end of the great war would be hopeless and we could not hope for any support . . . we could not possibly hope to get more than we were now offered without fighting, viz. the exclusion of six counties, we should probably get less: We should be in a better position to hold our own and help our friends with only six counties excluded returning 16 Unionists and 9 Nationalists than we should be with 9 counties excluded returning 17 Nationalists and 16 Unionists . . . of course if the Home Rulers themselves refused the offer that is a different pair of shoes . . . [215]

Redmond held out for temporary rather than permanent exclusion of the north-east but, in any case, Lloyd George's negotiations were wrecked by the implacable opposition to compromise by Walter Long and Lord Lansdowne. Asquith had not the strength to force a settlement, thus seeming to justify Dillon's earlier observation that his government seemed bent on 'manufacturing Sinn Feiners'.

When the Easter Rising broke there seemed no hope of victory for the Allies: Gallipoli had just been ignominiously evacuated; the Italians had made eleven futile assaults along the Isonzo; the Russians were reaching the point of exhaustion; after enduring the heaviest bombardment the world had yet seen, the French were losing the flower of their armies in a stubborn defence of Verdun; and just a week before the Dublin rebellion, the Royal Navy had come off worst in the titanic clash of the dreadnoughts off Jutland. Now all hopes were pinned on a massive offensive being prepared for the early summer along the River Somme.

SACRIFICE AT THE SOMME

At 7.10 a.m. on 1 July 1916, concealed by a smoke barrage and lingering mist, troops of the Ulster Division climbed out of their trenches and formed up in no-man's-land. It was the anniversary of the Battle of the Boyne; some men wore orange lilies and at least one sergeant draped his sash over his uniform. Here, in front of Thiepval Wood and astride the River Ancre, the six-day Allied artillery barrage reached a horrific climax. 'As the shells passed over our heads', John Stewart-Moore observed, 'the air hummed like a swarm of a 100 million hornets.'[216] At 7.30 a.m. the guns suddenly stopped firing, officers blew their whistles, and the men advanced at a steady marching pace towards the German first line.

The massive bombardment had neither cut the wire nor knocked out the enemy machine-gun nests. North of the Ancre the attack was a disastrous failure as troops were caught by crossfire in a deep ravine – according to a survivor the bullets 'came like water from an immense hose with a perforated top'.[217] Opposite Thiepval Wood the Ulster Division advanced in formation with astonishing speed, capturing the Schwaben Redoubt and reaching the German fourth line where the fighting was like 'a Belfast riot on the top of Mount Vesuvius'.[218] Dangerously overextended, exposed to relentless fire and mistakenly shelled from their own side, whole companies were wiped out and by nightfall all gains had been lost. Blacker's Boys – men from the Armagh, Monaghan and Cavan Ulster Volunteers – returned with only sixty-four men out of six hundred who had gone over the parapet. Soon after, seventeen-year-old Private Herbert Beattie wrote home to Belfast:

Dear Mother . . . tell them that ther is not another grosvenor Rd fellow left but myself. Mother wee were tramping over the dead i think there is onley about 4 hundred left out of about 13 hundered . . . Mother if God spers me to get home safe i will have something ufal to tell you if hell is any wores i would not like to go to it.[219]

Adam Duffin's daughter, Emma, was a nurse waiting to treat the wounded at Le Havre. She wrote in her diary:

I had not been on night duty very long when the big push began and the trains came and came, and the boats did not come fast enough, and we worked all night and came on duty again after breakfast and prayed and looked for the boats, especially the Asturias as she was the biggest. I was sent on duty on the station platform; if the hospital had not made me realize the war I realized it that night; under the big arc lights in the station lay stretchers 4 deep . . . at the end of the station were the walking cases; they were past walking, and the majority had lain down huddled together, their arms in slings, and their heads bound up, the mud from the trenches sticking to their clothes and the blood still caked on them. I was up and down all night feeling I was in a bad dream . . . attempting the hopeless task of trying to make men with their legs in splints a little more comfortable, feeling the pulses of the men who felt faint, rearranging a bandage that had slipped and watching for haemorrhages.[220]

In just the first two days of the Battle of the Somme 5,500 men of the Ulster Division had been killed or wounded. Four men – Private William McFadzean, Private Robert Quigg, Lieutenant Geoffrey Cather and Captain Eric Bell – were awarded posthumous Victoria Crosses. In Ulster, on 12 July 1916, when the clocks struck noon all work was suspended, trams stopped in their tracks, trains pulled up and the Twelfth celebrations were abandoned as the province remembered the fallen in deep silence. Ulster's tightknit Protestant community would never forget the terrible sacrifice that had been made.

No end to the fighting was in sight. It was now a war of attrition in which victory could go only to the side mobilising more men and harnessing the greater share of economic power. Lloyd George, proving his ability to get things done as minister of munitions, had been able to oust Asquith as prime minister in December 1916 and all his qualities were required when Germany launched a campaign of unrestricted submarine warfare in February 1917. Early in that year SS *Laurentic*, after calling briefly at the Buncrana Royal Navy base, was sunk on leaving Lough Swilly off Fanad Head, with a loss of 354 lives. Completed at Queen's Island in 1909 as Harland and Wolff's first large passenger liner powered by marine turbines, the ship had been converted into an auxiliary cruiser. Most of the forty-three tons of gold and silver on board was recovered after the war.[221] In April the U-boats sank 555,056 tons of British merchant vessels, while in the same month United Kingdom yards launched only 69,711 tons. More than ever the skills and capacity of the Belfast shipbuilding industry were urgently required.

Belfast had been the fastest-growing shipbuilding region ever since 1878, with an average annual growth rate of 7.8 per cent, more than twice the rate of Clydeside, and in 1914 Harland and Wolff was responsible for almost 8 per cent of world output. Since neither of the Belfast yards had any Admiralty work on hand, and the Government gave priority to naval vessels, they were forced to cut back on their labour force – depleted by enlistment in any case – owing to shortage of materials. In 1914 the workforce at Harland and Wolff fell from 24,425 to 18,412 between July and the end of October. Then, realising that this would not be a short war, Churchill ensured that orders flowed in. Skilled labour became so scarce that in the week ending 27 April 1915, 1,239 shipwrights and boilermakers worked between sixty and eighty-five hours. Harland and Wolff built monitors for shelling coastal defences; two cruisers, one adapted as a seaplane carrier; and from 1917 'standard' ships, simplified cargo vessels urgently needed to replace losses on the high seas. The firm invested £1 million in 1917 primarily to build a new forty-one-acre yard on the east side of the Musgrave Channel. In March 1918 Lloyd George appointed Lord Pirrie controller-general of merchant shipbuilding and under his direction output was raised by nearly 50 per cent by the time of the armistice.

During 1918 alone, Harland and Wolff launched 201,070 tons of merchant shipping, 120,000 tons more than the firm's nearest United Kingdom rival. Workman Clark built boom defence vessels, patrol boats, sloops and cargo ships totalling 260,000 tons during the war. Harland and Wolff broke all records in completing standard ships; one was launched from Queen's Island on the morning of Tuesday 10 September 1918; by nightfall the engines and boilers were on board, and by 9 p.m. on Saturday it was ready for sea.[222]

The importation of colonial produce during the U-boat campaign became so hazardous that the population of the United Kingdom became heavily dependent on food produced at home. The numerous small farmers of Ireland successfully defied government attempts to regulate prices in a seller's market and enjoyed a prosperity they had never experienced before. In addition, inflation reduced the real value of land purchase annuity repayments. Exhortations to plough grassland were largely unnecessary especially in Ulster. In the six northeastern counties arable land increased by more than two hundred thousand acres, much of it to grow flax no longer obtainable from German-occupied Belgium. Linen had been making a strong recovery before the war and now – to meet the demand for uniforms, tents, knapsacks, stretchers, sheets and aeroplane fabric – mills and factories worked at full stretch, raising the workforce from seventy-six thousand in 1913 to ninety thousand by the end of the war. The Derry shirt-making trade also enjoyed a welcome revival, War Office contracts alone averaging nearly £830,000 each year of the war. In the first years of the hostilities workers raised their living standards mainly by overtime payments, but by 1917 wages caught up with and then bypassed prices.[223]

All the traditional export industries prospered, the Belfast Ropeworks, for example, producing 50 per cent of the Royal Navy's cordage requirements. There were new industries too. In 1917 Lord Pirrie volunteered to open an aeroplane works, starting with six de Havilland machines, followed by one hundred Handley Page V/1500 heavy bombers for raiding Berlin, and three hundred Avros. He built an aerodrome on the site of a 170-acre farm he bought at Aldergrove in Co. Antrim. 'There is no pleasure like work,' the seventy-one-year-old entrepreneur said to a reporter in 1918. 'I am never idle. I work all day.'[224]

Lord Pirrie, one of the most powerful tycoons in Europe, had great confidence in the future prosperity of Ireland's industrial north-east. He supported Home Rule until the shock of the Easter Rising changed his mind. Now he was in favour of partition, a constitutional arrangement becoming ever more likely as the war drew to a close.

Soon after becoming prime minister in December 1916, Lloyd George announced an amnesty for suspects interned after the Easter Rising. Several of those released threw themselves into the North Roscommon by-election in February 1917 and helped to ensure the victory of Count George Plunkett, a separatist and father of one of the leaders executed by firing squad. This severe blow to the Irish Parliamentary Party was followed by the formation of a new coalition of advanced nationalists in April, called Sinn Féin. Arthur Griffith's original Sinn Féin had all but expired by 1916, but partly because journalists had insisted on calling the insurrection the 'Sinn Féin rebellion', the name was now applied to this broad organisation serving as an umbrella for all those seeking Irish independence, ranging from Home Rulers dissatisfied with Redmond's performance to militant republicans, some of them survivors of the rising. Over the next year Sinn Féin won five out of eight by-elections, its MPs pledged not to take their seats at Westminster. Though the new party was a good deal more conservative and constitutional than seemed apparent from its rhetoric, Ulster Unionists saw this development as certain proof that Home Rule was never more than a staging post to complete separation.

Lloyd George, anxious to placate the Irish Parliamentary Party and Irish-American opinion now that the United States was in the war, called an Irish Convention, which met in Trinity College Dublin from 25 July 1917. Twenty Ulster Unionists attended, led by Hugh Thom Barrie, MP for North Londonderry. Having agreed that 'nothing in any way binding would be done without consultation with the Ulster people', which in effect meant that they would be guided by the Ulster Unionist Council, these northern delegates had little room for manoeuvre.[225] To their consternation they found southern Unionists prepared to make major concessions to the Nationalists in order to avoid the partition of the island. In disgust Adam Duffin wrote to his wife on 28 November:

> We had a very interesting pow-wow with the Southern Unionist lot . . .
> They want to capitulate & make terms with the enemy lest a worse thing
> befall them. They are a cowardly crew & stupid to boot. We shall do all
> we can to stiffen them & keep them in our ranks.[226]

Duffin did not succeed and southern Unionists appealed to Lloyd George who wrote to Bonar Law, now his chancellor of the exchequer, urging Unionist compromise, otherwise

> the Irish in AMERICA would be more rampageous than ever . . . The
> Irish are now paralysing the war activities of AMERICA . . . This is the

opportunity for ULSTER to show that it places the Empire above every-thing . . . if America goes wrong we are lost. I wish Ulster would fully realise what that means. I am afraid they don't.[227]

The Ulster Unionist delegation held firm against the Nationalists and the southern Unionists and thus prevented agreement. Any compromise would have been unreal in any case: Sinn Féin had refused to attend the convention.

Ulster Nationalists for a time were able to stem the rising tide of Sinn Féin. Their constituency organisations were vigorous and given new life by the formation of the Irish Nation League in 1916 at Omagh to campaign against partition.[228] Eamon de Valera, the sole surviving male commandant of the Easter Rising and now leader of Sinn Féin and president of the Irish Volunteers, came north to support Dr Patrick McCartan in the February 1918 by-election in South Armagh. Speaking at Bessbrook, he described Unionists as 'a rock in the road' to an Irish settlement and told his audience they 'must if necessary blast it out of their path'.[229] Clearly Sinn Féin had a more militant approach to union-ism than the Irish Parliamentary Party. Despite the assistance of twenty motorcars of constituency workers from the south, Sinn Féin was de-feated in both South Armagh and East Tyrone in straight contests with the Nationalists.

In March 1918, just before the convention broke up, John Redmond died. His son, campaigning in his British Army uniform, defeated Sinn Féin in the ensuing Waterford by-election but the final destruc-tion of the party Redmond had reunited was about to be accomplished by Lloyd George's coalition government. In the spring of 1918 Ludendorff launched Germany's last great offensive towards Paris and in April London decided to impose conscription in Ireland in a desperate search for more men. The reaction was immediate and Na-tionalists, Sinn Féin and the Catholic hierarchy united to oppose the conscription order, described by Cardinal Logue as 'an oppressive and inhuman law'. John Dillon, now leading the Irish Parliamentary Party, bitterly observed that the Government was conspiring to leave nothing in Ireland but 'Republican separatists and Ulster loyalists' and he withdrew his MPs from Westminster in protest. An effective one-day general strike against conscription on 23 April in all but one province of Ireland – Ulster did not participate – reflected the solidar-ity generated by this issue. The following month Lord French, the new lord lieutenant, announced the existence of a 'German Plot' – for which no real evidence was produced – and had seventy-three of the leading Sinn Féin activists, including de Valera, arrested and imprisoned. 'Put him in to get him out: Vote for Griffith the Man in Jail for Ireland' announced posters in East Cavan during a by-election there in June and Griffith won by a majority of 1,204.[230] 'We had the worst of both worlds,' Churchill ruefully observed, 'all the resentment against compulsion and in the end no law and no men.' Sinn Féin was to reap its reward for leading the campaign against conscription in the general election which followed the armistice.

'THE GLADNESS OF THIS HOUR IS CHASTENED BY THE THOUGHT OF THE VACANT CHAIR'

Enniskillen may have been the first town in the United Kingdom to hear of the armistice. Having picked up a faint radio message at 6.30 a.m., troops in the military barracks there spread the news by launching rockets and soon church bells rang out to greet crowds gathering for the hiring fair.[231]

On 11 November 1918 the Spanish influenza epidemic, which killed more people than had been slain on all the battlefields of the First World War, was sweeping across Ulster. Schools, Sunday schools and public libraries had been closed in Belfast, though most picture houses stayed open, including the Panopticon in High Street, 'kept "Flu" Proof by frequent spraying with a mixture of Phenol and Lavender, the finest Germ-killer in the world'. Irish time was then half an hour later than in Britain and news of the armistice arrived in the city at mid-morning. 'At 11 a.m.', the *Belfast News-Letter* reported, 'the local postal telegraph staff stood to attention and sang with great fervour the first verse of the National Anthem, followed by three rousing cheers.' The sounding of ships' sirens and the firing of fog detonators at the railway termini signalled the ending of the war across Belfast and, in the account given in the *Irish News*, people poured out of the mills, city-centre stores and workshops, producing 'a display of enthusiasm, amounting almost to emotionalism, on the part of the public such as has never been witnessed in this city'. Mill girls swept down the Falls Road 'to the accompaniment of lively choruses while Irish flags of green and gold mingled with the Stars and Stripes and flags of the Allies'. At Dunmurry Joseph Waring told a great crowd of loyalists that they had every reason to thank God that they could still re-echo the old Derry watchword 'No Surrender!', and then accompanied by Orange bands the revellers streamed north to Belfast.

Trams were forced to halt as women linked arms with soldiers from the Victoria barracks, and waving flags and blouses, and holding aloft turnips on pointed sticks, pillaged a pony cart of its load of scantlings to build a bonfire in Royal Avenue. After raiding several shops, ship-wrights broke into the Panopticon around 1 p.m. and, according to the *Irish News*,

> they proceeded to wreck everything they could lay their hands on. Pictures were smashed; several arc lamps were shattered, scores of seats were pulled up from the floors and thrown through the windows on to the street. Gas brackets were torn from the walls, so that the gas was allowed to escape in great volume.

The men were not to return to work for a week. At nightfall the 'extraordinary spectacle was also to be witnessed of an immense game of ring o'roses, proceeding right in the middle of Castle Place, while bands of all descriptions, many accompanied by torch lights, added to the general din'. In some places 'more boisterous elements got out of hand, and in excess of spirits over-stepped the limits of discretion'; rockets were fired; and great crowds were still outside the city hall, around the statue of Queen Victoria draped with bunting, long after midnight. 'In the hour of triumph', the *Belfast Telegraph* reminded its readers, 'it would be ungenerous not to think of . . . the greater army which mourns at home, wives for husbands and mothers for sons, who are to-day beneath the sod in France, and Flanders. For those lonely ones, the gladness of this hour is chastened by the thought of the vacant chair.'[232]

Around 170,000 Irishmen enlisted during the war – some 41 per cent of the male population between the ages of 10 and 44 in the 1911 census – and about half of them were from Ulster. Of the forty thousand to fifty thousand who had given their lives in the fighting, at least half were Catholics. By comparison only a couple of hundred republicans had been killed in the Easter insurrection, yet these men, Professor Tom Kettle observed, 'will go down in history as heroes and martyrs, and I will go down – if I go down at all – as a bloody British officer'.[233] Kettle, a Catholic and a National Volunteer, was killed in 1916 on the Western Front. Now the Irish Volunteers reorganised and gained recruits rapidly amongst landless young men unable to emigrate during the war. Alarming reports of successful raids for arms were coming in as the country prepared for a general election called for 14 December 1918. Eight years had passed since the previous poll including more than four years of tumultuous change during a world war, and few could predict the outcome, all the more so since the latest parliamentary Reform Act more than doubled the Irish electorate from 701,475 in 1910 to 1,936,673 in 1918. For the first time tens of thousands of agricultural labourers and urban workers could vote, together with women over the age of thirty who were ratepayers or married to ratepayers. In addition, there was a long overdue redistribution of seats. Belfast, for example, now had seven constituencies instead of the previous four and an electorate of 170,901 compared with only 57,174 entitled to vote in 1910.

The Irish Parliamentary Party was annihilated, retaining only six seats out of the sixty-eight they held on the eve of the poll. Four of these were in Ulster, three of them partly as the result of an electoral pact with Sinn Féin, arranged by Cardinal Logue, in constituencies where Unionists were certain to win if there had been three-way contests. In South Fermanagh, where the primate chose a Sinn Féin candidate, local police reported confidentially that they were certain Catholics there would have preferred a Nationalist nominee.[234] In West Belfast Devlin successfully fended off a Sinn Féin challenge from de Valera, who was still held in an English prison, and Carson won in the new division of Duncairn with a huge majority. The Ulster Unionist representation leaped from eighteen to twenty-three, to which could be added two from Trinity College and one from Co. Dublin. In the rest of Ireland Sinn Féin had captured seventy-three seats – including Countess Markievicz's victory, the first woman elected to the Commons – and now claimed to be 'the great representative organisation of the Irish people in Ireland and throughout the world'.[235]

John Dillon's prediction that there would be only republican separatists and Ulster loyalists representing Ireland had all but come true.

POLITICAL UNCERTAINTY AND ECONOMIC PROSPERITY

Early in 1919 Carson received a summons in Irish to attend Dáil Éireann, an assembly of the elected representatives of the Irish nation, in Dublin's Mansion House on 21 January. The amused Ulster Unionist leader kept it as a souvenir and there was laughter in the Dáil when the reading out of his name at roll call was greeted by silence. Thirty-four Sinn Féin deputies were not present either, as they were still being detained at His Majesty's pleasure. Nevertheless, nationalist Ireland had voted overwhelmingly for Sinn Féin and the Dáil felt justified in making its Declaration of Irish Independence, stating that 'the Irish Republic was proclaimed in Dublin on Easter Monday 1916'.[236] There was no suggestion that the Dáil would resort to force either to compel Westminster to give way or to ensure a unified thirty-two-county state. The Dáil put all its faith in its 'Message to the Free Nations of the World', an appeal to the Paris Peace Conference which had opened the previous day.

Sinn Féin had no policy on Ulster, no plan for conciliating or compromising with the Protestant majority in the north-east. Dáil deputies seem to have assumed that the whole island of Ireland would be the unit chosen for the application of the self-determination principle espoused by the American president, Woodrow Wilson. A casual glance at the 1918 election results seemed at first to support the Sinn Féin case: Ulster Unionists had won a majority in only four of Ulster's nine counties. This showed that a large geographical area of the province could be claimed for the nationalist cause and be duly coloured green in Sinn Féin propagandist publications. A closer examination of the results, however, revealed that where Ulster's population was most concentrated, in the five north-eastern counties, the Unionists captured twenty-two constituencies, leaving the Irish Parliamentary Party and Sinn Féin with only seven seats here between them.

Agreed that partition was the most practical political solution, Ulster Unionists felt exceptionally confident in 1919. In Britain, too, the general election had been a landmark, for although Lloyd George was still prime minister, he now led a coalition consisting of 520 MPs, 400 of whom were Conservative and Unionist possessing an absolute majority in the Commons. Such men were unlikely, it was thought, to betray their allies in Ulster. Besides, the Sinn Féin MPs refused to sit at Westminster; the Irish Parliamentary Party had all but disappeared; and Carson, Craig and Lord Londonderry all had places in the Government, and were therefore in a strong position to influence legislation for Ireland.

The republican argument that a partitioned Ulster could not survive economically seemed ridiculous in 1919. The province thrived in the postwar boom fuelled by the need to replace what had been destroyed, by pent-up consumer demand, and by desperate food shortages in central and eastern Europe. The cost of living had doubled but prices for farm produce more than kept pace: £1 5s.6½d. worth of eggs in 1915 cost £3 8s.2d. by 1919; £1 4s.10d. worth of pork in 1915 cost £3 2s.10d. by 1920; and a bundle of flax worth £1 18s.2d. in 1915 fetched £4 4s.10d. by 1920. No wonder the *Northern Whig* observed in 1919 that over the previous five years 'the price of land had soared to a remarkable degree'. In the same year the *Belfast News-Letter* concluded that 'in the long history of the linen industry, 1919 may in future be called the *annus mirabilis'*. Never before and never again were there so many spindles and looms at work in Ulster.[237]

At the end of armistice week in 1918, Lord Pirrie issued this manifesto to his marine engineers and shipyard workers:

The War is over in the Fields, but not in the Shipyards, Germany is beaten but she cannot give us back all the shipping she has destroyed . . . there must be no slackening of effort in shipbuilding as ships are as vitally necessary today as at any period in the history of this country.[238]

The skilled engineers responded early in the new year by downing tools and demanding a forty-four-hour week and soon they were joined by all the shipyard men, the gas workers and the electricity station workers. On 25 January 1919 a formidable struggle began as strikers smashed the windows of shops still using gas light and electricity. The trams could not run, picture houses closed, the yards and engineering shops were silent, thousands of linen workers were laid off, the Belfast Ropeworks was closed down, the *Irish News* could not roll its presses, and by the end of the first week bread was running short in Belfast. The *Belfast News-Letter* fulminated that the strike was the work of 'Bolshevik agitators whose aim is to smash all the institutions of the country' and that the dispute 'will rejoice the heart of Sinn Fein'.[239] The employers demanded military intervention and Joseph Devlin supported them, but Unionist politicians were loathe to alienate workers who had given them such a convincing vote in the general election. However, the army occupied the gasworks and electricity station at 6 a.m. on Saturday 14 February and by the following Thursday the strike had collapsed. The workers lost that particular battle but in the boom conditions their wages kept up with prices, often surpassing them, and differentials between skilled and unskilled earnings were narrowed.

Work resumed on Queen's Island on 20 February, and though unemployment was already severe on Clydeside, Belfast's high reputation for quality and Pirrie's business acumen kept the shipyards busy, raising the workforce to a historic peak of almost thirty thousand. Unlike most other shipbuilders, Harland and Wolff completed all the standard ships which were under construction in the yard at the time of the armistice. By July 1919 the firm had orders for seventy-two vessels totalling nearly half a million tons and contracts for twenty-three sets of marine machinery. The keel was laid for a sister ship to the *Britannic*, sunk in the Aegean in 1916. In the order placed before the war it was to have been named the *Germanic* but now it was to be the *Homeric*. The company opened its east yard in November 1919: its six berths, with more capacity than the north and south yards put together, were fitted with portable cofferdams to create dry docks while vessels were being built. The firm was in the forefront of diesel marine engine-making and Pirrie invested £1 million in the Clyde Foundry to make the necessary precision castings. Harland and Wolff and Workman Clark were respectively first and second of all United Kingdom yards in terms of tonnage launched that year.[240]

'THE DREARY STEEPLES OF FERMANAGH AND TYRONE EMERGING ONCE AGAIN'

An early decision made at the Paris Peace Conference was the confirmation of Luxemburg's independence. Since that state was smaller than Co. Antrim and possessed a thriving economy, the future looked bright for a partitioned Ulster in 1919–20 as Lloyd George's government readdressed the problem of sorting out Ireland's constitutional future. The exclusion of all nine counties of the province was no longer seriously contemplated. Should the excluded territory include all of the counties of Fermanagh and Tyrone, both with large tracts of country inhabited overwhelmingly by Catholics? The problem was essentially the same as it had been in 1912–14, as Churchill reminded the House of Commons in his most celebrated speech on Ireland:

> Then came the Great War. Every institution, almost, in the world was strained. Great Empires have been overturned. The whole map of Europe has been changed. The position of countries has been violently altered. The modes of thought of men, the whole outlook on affairs, the grouping of parties, all have encountered violent and tremendous changes in the deluge of the world. But as the deluge subsides and the waters fall short we see the dreary steeples of Fermanagh and Tyrone emerging once again. The integrity of their quarrel is one of the few institutions that has been unaltered in the cataclysm which has swept the world.[241]

As Lloyd George laboured on the details of the Bill for the Better Government of Ireland through the year 1920 that quarrel became openly violent. At the Paris Peace Conference, Gavan Duffy, grandson of the Young Ireland leader, and Sean T. O'Kelly were again and again rebuffed in their attempt to get international recognition for an all-Ireland republic. The conference was swamped by dozens of delegations – including one led by Ho Chi Minh seeking independence for the Vietnamese in French Indo-China – all lobbying for self-determination of their nationalities. President Woodrow Wilson, himself of Ulster Presbyterian extraction, was baffled by Europe's ethnic complexity and had no wish to embarrass Britain, the United States' closest wartime ally, by agreeing to the Dáil's demands.

On 21 January 1919, the day the Dáil had first met, two RIC constables escorting a cart of gelignite to a quarry in Co. Tipperary were overpowered and shot dead by masked Volunteers who made off with the police weapons and explosives. As the Dáil delegation in Paris failed to send home positive news of progress, violent incidents of this kind multiplied. Irish Volunteers, now calling themselves the Irish Republican Army, grew ever more restless, and when Lloyd George declared the Dáil illegal in September 1919, the restraining hand of constitutional politicians was removed. By 1920 full-scale guerrilla warfare had developed over much of the south and as the year advanced it spread northwards, inflaming ancient hatreds, plunging Ulster into the most terrible period of violence the province had experienced since the eighteenth century.

The civil war, postponed by a general European war in 1914, had begun.

11

PARTITIONED PROVINCE: THE EARLY YEARS

1920–1939

OVERVIEW

The sustained slaughter and destruction of the First World War seemed to accustom men to the regular use of violence to advance a cause, redress grievances and enforce the will of government. After the armistice, blood continued to flow on the European mainland: British, French and Polish troops intervened unsuccessfully against the Bolsheviks in Russia only to intensify the miseries of a civil war there which left millions dying of typhus and starvation; squads of Fascist ex-servicemen and revolutionary socialists fought each other for supremacy in the streets of northern Italian cities; Spartacists and disbanded soldiers of the Freikorps threatened to stifle the infant Weimar Republic in its cradle; Admiral Horthy crushed the Communists in Budapest with an army invading from Transylvania; and in the new states emerging from the wreck of the Austro-Hungarian, German and Russian empires, ethnic rivalries flared into violent struggles. The economist, John Maynard Keynes, captured the atmosphere of the time when he wrote:

> We have been moved almost beyond endurance, and need rest. Never in the lifetime of men now living has the universal element in the soul of man burnt so dimly.[1]

The cult of violence in Ireland thrived in fertile soil before the war: it had been fostered either by stirring tales of imperial adventure or by romantic nationalist writing, such as the popular novels of Canon P.A. Sheehan; and then it had been boosted by the exhilaration of gun-running and drilling in rival volunteer armies. Now men returned from the front, many inured to violence by the horrors of trench warfare, to renew their fighting in Ireland. Robert Lynd, by then the correspondent of the *Daily News*, reported that 'soldiers who fought for the Allies as they return home are becoming converted by the thousand into Sinn Feiners', some, like Tom Barry, to become leading men in the IRA.

Returning soldiers played a crucial role in reviving the UVF, particularly in Derry.[2] 'I had thought my soldiering days were over', wrote Captain Sir Basil Brooke, the Fermanagh landlord awarded the Military Cross during the war; ' . . . I was to become a soldier of a very different sort . . . but I had the added stimulant of defending my own birthplace.'[3] As IRA attacks spread northwards Brooke took a lead in organising Protestant resistance, while, at the same time, Lloyd George recruited ex-servicemen to revive the demoralised RIC and thus unleashed the notorious Black and Tans, and the Auxiliaries, on the southern Irish countryside.

As the Anglo-Irish War edged into Ulster it triggered off a sectarian conflict there more vicious and lethal than all the northern riots of the previous century put together. This killing and destruction intensified as Westminster applied its elaborate constitutional solutions in 1921, giving dominion status to the Irish Free State and Home Rule to the six northeastern counties, henceforth called Northern Ireland. In doing so it partitioned the historic province of Ulster. Donegal, Cavan and Monaghan became peripheral counties of a state which, after a ruinous civil war, steadily loosened its last ties with the British Empire. That same civil war did much to enable the Unionist government to establish its authority over Northern Ireland. As peace returned British governments began to feel they really had – at last – solved the Irish Question and they did not allow themselves to be troubled by the North's petty affairs. During the interwar years, the economy of the whole region languished in profoundly altered world trading conditions. Northern Ireland was given less help than other depressed areas of the United Kingdom and, partly as a result, per capita incomes there fell even further behind those in Britain. Only very briefly, in Belfast in 1932, did the common experience of deprivation draw together people of both religions in common protest. Though Northern Ireland after 1922 enjoyed a remarkable calm, with perhaps the lowest 'ordinary' crime rate in Europe, intercommunal tensions had not been significantly reduced, and, while neither Craig nor his colleagues had created these divisions, they did little to assuage them.

'A DEADLY FIRE FROM THE CITY WALLS': SECTARIAN WARFARE IN DERRY, 1920

'"No Surrender" – Citadel Conquered After Centuries of Oppression – Overthrow of Ascendancy': this is how the *Derry Journal* trumpeted the Unionists' first ever loss of control over the Londonderry Corporation in January 1920. Alderman Hugh O'Doherty, the city's first Catholic mayor put in office by the combined vote of Irish Parliamentary Party and Sinn Féin councillors, in his inaugural speech had few words of comfort for local loyalists:

Rest assured that mighty changes are coming in Ireland. Do you Protestants wish to play a part in them? The Unionist position is no longer tenable; your leaders are abandoning it . . . do you not see that Englishmen are prepared to sacrifice you if they can secure the goodwill of the rest of Ireland? . . . Ireland's right to determine her own destiny will come about whether the Protestants of Ulster like it or not.[4]

Lloyd George had hoped these local government elections, the first in the United Kingdom to be conducted under a system of proportional representation, would demonstrate the limitations of Sinn Féin's support, and to some extent this hope was justified: Unionists, Nationalists, Labour and others won 1,256 seats compared with 550 taken by Sinn Féin. There was Unionist consternation, however, when ten urban councils, including Derry, Strabane, Enniskillen, Armagh and Omagh, fell under joint Nationalist–Sinn Féin control in the six north-eastern counties due to be excluded from Home Rule. A further thirteen rural councils were lost in June. Even in Belfast the number of Unionist councillors had been cut from fifty-two to twenty-nine, largely as a result of victories by the Belfast Labour Party. Could these Unionist losses encourage Westminster to reconsider the exclusion of the entire six-county area? Loyalist fears of abandonment were particularly acute on the edge of this region – in Derry.

In the middle of April 1920 some republican prisoners were brought to Bishop Street gaol, which straddled the Catholic Bogside and the Protestant Fountain Street area. After much taunting by both sides at the corner of Long Tower Street, 'a great storm centre in party fights in the city', the *Derry Journal* reported,

the rival parties became more aggressive and blows were exchanged, the Unionist crowd being rushed up Albert Street by the opposing crowd. Stones were thrown freely, and the crash of glass was heard continuously . . . For fully an hour a desperate conflict raged.

Shots were fired into the Bogside on 18 April and police made a bayonet charge against Catholic rioters in the city centre. Trouble flared up again on 14 May and the following day in a four-hour gun battle between the police and the IRA the local head of the RIC special branch was shot dead. The UVF reorganised and, wearing masks and carrying arms, its men mounted road blocks. According to the *Derry Journal*:

They took possession of Carlisle Bridge and held it for almost two hours. Every pedestrian crossing the Bridge during that period was stopped, challenged, and had to declare his religion, and if it were found he was a Catholic he was maltreated . . . Some of these ruffians had their faces blackened, others wore black masks, and a few had handkerchiefs on their faces with holes for the eyes. Armed with revolvers they took possession of Carlisle Road and indulged in indiscriminate revolver firing.[5]

A Catholic, returned from the trenches gassed and wounded, was killed.

Worse violence followed next month, starting with an attack on Catholics walking at Prehen Wood on 13 June. Fierce rioting at the junction of Long Tower Street and Bishop Street spread into the Waterside, where Catholic homes were set on fire on Saturday 18 June. Led by ex-servicemen, the UVF seized control of the Diamond and Guildhall Square, and began firing down from the old city walls. The *Derry Journal* reported:

> The Long Tower, an exclusively Catholic district, was kept for hours under a deadly fire from the City Walls and Unionist strongholds of Fountain Street and Albert Street. At least three men were shot dead and many persons including a baby in arms were wounded. In the Diamond and at Butcher Street men were also killed.[6]

The IRA counter-attacked only to be driven back from the walls by superior firepower, but republicans did dislodge the UVF from St Columb's College on Windmill Hill – the site of a Protestant victory during the siege of 1689. Catholics burned Protestants out of the Bogside and shot dead two Protestants. By the time 1,500 troops had arrived on 23 June, eight Catholics and four Protestants had been killed. The army imposed a curfew and directed heavy machine-gun fire into the Bogside, killing six more Catholics; and as shootings, assassinations and reprisals continued, despite the presence of soldiers, the death toll for the city eventually reached forty.[7]

A striking feature of the army's intervention in Derry was its close co-operation with the local UVF, thereby aligning itself with one side in a sectarian conflict generations old. The temptation to draw on the strength of the UVF was strong at a time when Britain's armed forces were stretched to the limit and facing disturbances in India and new commitments in the Middle East. The Dáil had been suppressed and Sinn Féin proscribed as a political organisation in November 1919, yet the king's writ was not running over large tracts of the south: in 1920 Sinn Féin courts and Irish Volunteer police patrols operated in 22 counties; the Dáil continued to meet in secret session; Michael Collins, as the Dáil's finance minister, raised £358,000 in a national loan and directed IRA operations at the same time; and, after the RIC had withdrawn to central posts, 150 barracks and numerous tax offices were burned down on the night of 3–4 April and, by the end of the year, 510 unoccupied barracks had been destroyed

The evacuation of outlying barracks caused consternation amongst loyalists in rural Ulster. Confidential police reports showed a deteriorating situation: in Co. Donegal 'quiet law-abiding people live in constant dread ... Sinn Fein entirely dominate the community'; in Co. Tyrone Irish Parliamentary Party supporters had 'become more extreme ... throwing in their lot with Sinn Fein as they see the activities of this party unchecked'; and Co. Fermanagh was being 'infected by the general spread of lawlessness in the country', with Sinn Féin 'working secretly, with a fairly large following' in Lisnaskea, Newtownbutler and Maguiresbridge, holding courts and carrying out raids for arms.[8] Loyalists began to organise themselves. In Armagh, John Webster, a local merchant, 'called a number of responsible men together and we decided to form a type of security or protective patrol to operate at night in the city'. He got 174 rifles from the UVF's headquarters in Belfast, smuggled in another 50 carbines from Scotland, and 'visited most of the Orange Halls in the south end of County Armagh in an effort to re-form the old UVF. We were very successful ... '[9] A vigilante patrol had been formed at Lisbellaw in Co. Fermanagh by Lieutenant-Colonel George Liddle when the RIC had abandoned the local barracks. On the night of 8–9 June loyalists there knew an attack was coming when the telegraph wires to the railway station were cut; the IRA was allowed to set fire to the courthouse, and then the church bell rang out as a signal to ambush the raiders. In the heavy firing that followed, two were wounded on each side and the IRA scattered towards Tempo and Enniskillen. When the army arrived and attempted to disarm the patrol, the vigilantes 'pointed out that they were fighting under the Union Jack and eventually after considerable discussion they were allowed to keep their arms'.[10]

After this incident the RIC county inspector feared that 'a very serious encounter may be expected involving considerable loss of life and very bitter party feeling if further attack is made by Irish Volunteers'. Sir Basil Brooke took out UVF rifles from their hiding place in Colebrooke House and formed a vigilante patrol, beginning with fourteen men on his demesne. The Protestant enclave in this part of Fermanagh was particularly vulnerable to IRA raids from the adjacent counties of Cavan, Monaghan and Tyrone. In July 1920 Brooke wrote to General Sir Nevil Macready, the commander-in-chief in Ireland, urging recognition of his loyalist vigilantes, otherwise the 'hotheads will take matters into their own hands and threaten retaliation'.[11]

Meanwhile, outright sectarian warfare had broken out in Belfast.

VIOLENCE IN LISBURN, BANBRIDGE, DROMORE AND BELFAST:
JULY–AUGUST 1920

'We in Ulster will tolerate no Sinn Fein,' Carson said at the 'Field' at Finaghy in Belfast on 12 July 1920. He warned the Government: 'But we tell you this – that if, having offered you our help, you are yourselves unable to protect us from the machinations of Sinn Fein, and you won't take our help; well then, we tell you that we will take the matter into our own hands. We will reorganise.'[12] Loyalists in the city were soon carrying out their threat.

On 21 July, the first full day back at work after the Twelfth holiday, notices were posted in the shipyards calling 'Protestant and Unionist' workers to meet at lunch time outside the gates of Workman Clark's south yard. It was the day of the funeral of Colonel G.F. Smyth, an RIC divisional commissioner from Banbridge, shot dead in Cork four days previously. The call to drive out 'disloyal' workers was enthusiastically supported. At the end of the meeting hundreds of apprentices and rivet boys from Workman Clark marched into Harland and Wolff's yard and ordered out Catholics and socialists. Some were kicked and beaten, others were pelted with rivets, and some were forced to swim for their lives, as one Catholic remembered:

> The gates were smashed down with sledges, the vests and shirts of those at work were torn open to see if the men were wearing any Catholic emblems, and woe betide the man who was. One man was set upon, thrown into the dock, had to swim the Musgrave Channel, and having been pelted with rivets, had to swim two or three miles, to emerge in streams of blood and rush to the police office in a nude state.[13]

Following Smyth's funeral, loyalists in Banbridge attacked Catholic-owned businesses and homes, and the trouble spread to neighbouring Dromore. After being driven out of local mills and factories, virtually the entire Catholic populations of both towns were forced to flee. Catholics were attacked in Bangor also, but it was in Belfast that the most ferocious fighting ensued. Trams carrying shipyard workers home that evening were stoned as they passed the Catholic enclave of Short Strand, and for the next three days and nights there was outright intercommunal warfare, as loyalists attempted to burn Catholics out. Protestants closed in on St Matthew's Church and set ablaze its convent; fierce fighting followed. Troops restored order by firing on both sides. After three days seven Catholics and six Protestants had died violently but the killing in the city had only begun.

Though Catholics counter-attacked, they formed only a quarter of Belfast's population and they had few firearms. They were driven from the Sirocco Works, Mackie's, McLaughlin and Harvey's, Musgrave's and Combe Barbour's – during the First World War Catholics had acquired jobs in these firms which traditionally employed Protestants. A committee headed by the Catholic bishop, Dr Joseph MacRory, estimated that ten thousand men and one thousand women had been expelled from their work; and, as the postwar boom collapsed soon afterwards, very few got their jobs back. With only brief periods of intermission, Belfast was to be convulsed by violence for the next two years.

On Sunday 22 August District Inspector Oswald Swanzy was shot dead in the centre of Lisburn and in the next three days Protestants attacked and burned sixty Catholic-owned public houses and business premises, set fire to the priest's house and some Catholic houses, and finally drove out almost all the Catholic residents, many of whom took refuge in Dundalk. Fred Crawford, now a lieutenant-colonel, visited Lisburn soon afterwards but he had little sympathy for the victims:

> Lisburn is like a bombarded town in France ... All this is done by Unionists as a protest against these cold blooded murders & the victims are Rebels or their Sympathisers ... We visited the ruins of the Priest's house on chapel hill it was burnt or gutted & the furniture all destroyed ... It has been stated that there are only four or five R.C. families left in Lisburn others say this is wrong that there are far more. Be that as it may there certainly are practically no shops or places of business left to the R.Cs.

He mentioned that he heard 'of some very hard cases of where Unionists had lost practically all they had by the fire of the house of a catholic spreading to theirs' – a particularly monocular view of the tragedy that had struck Lisburn. Crawford was active in reorganising the UVF and when asked for help in Belfast he 'filled two grenades with dynamite fuze & detonator ... I am using these hand grenades & lending some of them to reliable men who reside in danger zones & where they may be murdered any night.'[14] He also had half a million rounds of prewar ammunition hidden in his bleach works near Brown Square.

Intense violence erupted again in Belfast. An isolated Catholic district north of the Crumlin Road, known as the Bone or Marrowbone because of its shape, came under Protestant assault. A Catholic counter-attack came to grief in Ewart's Row. All the usual sectarian flash points in the city were engulfed in protracted rioting, particularly Cupar Street, Kashmir Road, Albert Street and Durham Street in west Belfast, and the lower Newtownards Road in Ballymacarrett. In east Belfast the people of Short Strand saw themselves marooned on a Catholic island in the midst of a hostile Protestant sea. Protestants saw such Catholics as supporters of the widening IRA guerrilla campaign. Here Protestants made repeated attempts to drive Catholics from their homes and singled out spirit grocery stores for looting and destruction. The Reverend John Redmond, Church of Ireland vicar of Ballymacarrett, was not sorry to see the closing of spirit groceries, which were 'the ruination of

472

many women and homes', the owners being 'nearly all Roman Catholics who were regarded, not without some reason, as Sinn Feiners'.[15] He was against anarchy and wanton destruction, however, and enrolled ex-servicemen as special constables on Thursday 26 August at St Patrick's School attached to his church.

That day began, in the very confined area between St Patrick's Church and St Matthew's, with firemen vainly attempting to extinguish no fewer than twenty-four malicious fires and troops mortally wounding two looting youths. There was trouble when shipyard men came home at lunch time and from 2 p.m. onwards fierce stone-throwing battles raged between Catholics in Seaforde Street and Protestants making forays from the railway embankment. The lower end of the Newtownards Road was littered with kidney pavers, 'of which tons were dug up from side streets as ammunition', the *Northern Whig* reported. While an armoured car opened fire, troops attempted, with limited success, to separate the combatants with a bayonet charge. The crowds were back in force at 6 p.m. when the shipyard men poured out of Harland and Wolff. Taunted and stoned, the workers swept aside the barbed-wire entanglement at the corner of Seaforde Street, using the troops' armoured car as a screen. 'They seemed to have petrol in plenty', the *Irish News* reported, 'and all the materials necessary for carrying out systematic incendiarism, and they were also evidently well-armed with revolvers.' Five more spirit groceries were set ablaze and, soon afterwards, O'Kane's funeral parlour at the corner of Seaforde Street and Lennon's spirit grocery on the opposite corner blazed up in the biggest conflagration so far. 'In Dee Street a spirit grocery was fired,' the *Belfast Telegraph* reported, 'while in Pitt Street a huge pile of furniture taken from one of the residences was set on fire and burned furiously for several hours.' The *Belfast News-Letter* observed that around these fires 'crowds of young people gathered, singing and dancing'.[16] Armed only with batons, Redmond's vigilante patrol could do little and when it left at 11 p.m., Murray's public house on the corner of Templemore Avenue was looted and fired. At the same time the nearby military post at Bridge End was attacked by the IRA, and troops, returning fire, killed one man and wounded another. The turmoil ceased finally at midnight when, the *Irish News* reported in heavy type, 'the Newtownards Road was absolutely swept by machine gun and rifle fire in both directions'.[17]

All these incidents occurred in just one district during one day in one week of protracted rioting, in which there had been 180 major fires, causing nearly £1 million worth of damage. The Conservative *Birmingham Post* warned Unionists in Ulster that the ill-treatment of Catholics would 'alienate the sympathies of the great masses of people who desire to help her'. The *Westminster Gazette* published a cartoon of Carson 'watching the Orange glow in Belfast', while the opposition press was more outspoken: 'The bloody harvest of Carsonism is being reaped in Belfast', remarked the *Daily Herald*, and the *Daily News* commented that virtually 'the whole of this damage has been done to the property of Catholics', and that this persecution was 'probably unmatched outside the area of Russian or Polish pogroms'.[18]

Ulster Unionist leaders themselves were alarmed that their cause would be ruined by further unconstrained assaults on the Catholic population. Craig simultaneously threatened and warned the Government of this in a memorandum on 1 September 1920:

> The Loyalists in Ulster believe that the Rebel plans are definitely directed towards the establishment of a Republic hostile to the British Empire, and that they are working in conjunction with Bolshevik Forces elsewhere towards that end.
>   . . . the situation is becoming so desperate that unless the Government will take immediate action, it may be advisable for them to see what steps can be taken towards a system of *organised* reprisals . . . partly to restrain their own followers . . . unless urgent action is taken, civil war on a very large scale is inevitable.[19]

'THERE WOULD BE UNCEASING AND UNENDING CIVIL WAR':
THE ULSTER SPECIAL CONSTABULARY

Shortly after its formation, Brooke had asked Dublin Castle to recognise his Fermanagh vigilante force as an official special constabulary. In the reply he received refusing sanction, the suggestion was made that he provide his men with caps and whistles for summoning the RIC. 'When I produced this letter to my boys they shook with laughter', Brooke recalled. 'Dublin can go to hell, they said, we'll look after ourselves.'[20]

As early as 25 June 1920 the Ulster Unionist Council had decided to revive the UVF and on 16 July Carson asked Wilfrid Spender, now a lieutenant-colonel, to take charge. Spender left his job at the Ministry of Pensions and within four days he was back in Ulster. Lloyd George and his Irish chief secretary, Sir Hamar Greenwood, made no attempt to stop this development – indeed Greenwood gave his approval, though he added, 'it would be politically unwise to announce this publicly'.[21] Cabinet approval had not been given and Dublin Castle officials remained hostile. Nevertheless, army commanders worked hand in glove with the rapidly re-emerging UVF. Spender sent Colonel George Moore Irvine as a full-time organiser to Derry and Lieutenant-Colonel Fred Crawford was delighted:

Colonel Moore Irvine . . . so impressed the GOC (Derry) with the object and aims of the UVF that the latter now refers everything to him . . . Irvine says he is virtually the Governor of Derry . . . The GOC recognises that the UVF are for King and country and that the rebels are simply for all the British enemy and to kick free from the British empire.[22]

Even the constabulary, because of its predominantly Catholic rank and file, was no longer considered trustworthy, Spender reporting: 'All Intelligence work in Londonderry and Tyrone and, I think, Fermanagh, is now done by the UVF in direct communication with the military, the RIC being eliminated completely.'[23] General Macready was furious, however: he wanted all civilians of every persuasion disarmed and Greenwood had not kept him informed.

'What would happen if the Protestants of the six counties were given weapons,' Churchill asked, ' . . . and charged with . . . maintaining law and order and policing the country?' Churchill put this question at a joint meeting between the cabinet and the Irish administration on 23 July 1920. Castle officials were aghast: W.E. Wylie, legal adviser to the Irish executive, predicted that 'Sinn Fein would arm a more numerous and equally efficient force . . . In Belfast the Protestants would reduce the Catholics to a state of terror. In Tyrone there would be unceasing and unending civil war.' Even the diehard Lord Curzon described Churchill's proposal as 'a most fatal suggestion'. Though Thomas Jones, assistant secretary to the cabinet, warned that one of 'the most deeply held beliefs in the South is that Ulster has the government by the throat', Lloyd George was not able to prove his own assertion that he had 'murder by the throat' as IRA attacks in the south became more daring and frequent.[24] Lloyd George overlooked the record of Lisburn town council's special constables, some of whom had been charged by the RIC and convicted of riot and looting; of three Belfast special constables with armbands and batons caught robbing a Catholic-owned public house in Ballymacarrett on 28 August; and of members of the Dromore UVF, who supervised the expulsion of Catholic families from the town. The prime minister decided to form the Ulster Special Constabulary in September, though details were not made public until 22 October 1920.

The new constabulary was divided into three categories. A Specials, numbering two thousand, were to be full-time and mobile, uniformed and paid like the RIC. B Specials, by far the largest section, numbering 19,500, would be part-time, uniformed and unpaid, serving only in their own areas principally on patrol duty, and armed with weapons kept in police barracks. No final figure was placed on the number of C Specials, an unpaid reserve force identified by caps and armlets to be called out only in dire emergencies and issued with some weapons and firearms licences. The Ulster Special Constabulary was to be responsible to Lieutenant-Colonel Charles Wickham, the new RIC divisional commissioner in the north, freshly returned from fighting the Bolsheviks in the Russian civil war. The structure of the force was similar to that proposed by Craig – closely modelled on the UVF. Whole units of the Ulster Volunteers joined the new constabulary and their commanders – such as Sir Basil Brooke in Fermanagh, General Ambrose Ricardo in Tyrone, and John Webster in Armagh – were given senior positions. All 'well-disposed citizens' were invited to join but no determined effort was made to get Catholics to apply. General Ricardo complained that Colonel J.K. McClintock, county commandant in Tyrone, refused to accept any Catholics, and a proposal that Catholic units could patrol Catholic areas, made by Lurgan justices of the peace, got no support. In effect, the Westminster government had created an officially sanctioned Protestant paramilitary force and the RIC county inspector for Londonderry feared 'serious trouble' between the Specials and the regular police, 'especially the Catholic members'.[25]

In the House of Commons Joseph Devlin was furious in his denunciation:

> The Chief Secretary is going to arm pogromists to murder the Catholics ... we would not touch your special constabulary with a 40-foot pole. Their pogrom is to be made less difficult. Instead of paving stones and sticks they are to be given rifles.

The *Westminster Gazette* concluded that this 'is quite the most inhuman expedient the government could have devised' because 'all the eager spirits who have driven nationalist workmen from the docks or have demonstrated their loyalty by looting Catholic shops will be eligible'.[26] By now, however, the Anglo-Irish War in the south had reached a new level of intensity and most MPs were grateful that the special constabulary would release more police and troops to combat the IRA. Though Greenwood denied this at Westminster, it was clear that the special constabulary would operate only in the six north-eastern counties – an indication that the Better Government of Ireland Act was about to partition Ulster.

THE CREATION OF NORTHERN IRELAND

During the years 1919–21 the map of Europe was redrawn in a series of peace treaties. In 1920 the United Kingdom also acquired a new frontier running through the province of Ulster, though by the decision of parliament rather than by international accord. The Treaty of Versailles allowed the exact positioning of Germany's borders in Upper Silesia,

Schleswig, Marienwerder and Allenstein to be agreed after holding plebiscites. Should Westminster also apply President Wilson's principle of self-determination by holding a referendum in Ulster? This proposition was hastily rejected by a cabinet committee set up in October 1919 – somewhat tardily, in view of Asquith's promise in 1914 – to draft what would in effect be a fourth Home Rule Bill for Ireland. Balfour argued that plebiscites were only suited to vanquished enemies: 'Ireland is not like a conquered state, which we can carve up as in Central Europe.'[27]

The British government could not ignore the prevailing spirit of the times, however, and this in part explains the complexity of the solution proposed. The cabinet committee was headed by Walter Long, former leader of the Irish Unionists – an example of how the balance of power had tilted away from southern Nationalists since 1914 and especially since, in Balfour's words, 'the blessed refusal of Sinn Feiners to take the Oath of Allegiance in 1918'.[28] With only a half-dozen demoralised Irish Parliamentary Party MPs in the Commons, Ulster Unionists essentially got the constitutional arrangement they desired.

The Government of Ireland Bill, introduced on 25 February 1920, proposed two Irish parliaments, one for the six north-eastern counties to be called Northern Ireland and another for the other twenty-six counties to be known as Southern Ireland. Since ultimate sovereignty was to be reserved to Westminster, both parts of Ireland were to continue to send representatives there. Why then not simply allow Northern Ireland to be ruled directly from London? For British politicians the setting up of a parliament in Belfast responsible for all local affairs had the strong attraction of shifting the constant burden of managing day-to-day Irish matters firmly across the Irish Sea. There was also the vague assumption – not tested by consultation – that Nationalists would find two Home Rule parliaments less repellent than a straightforward exclusion of the north-east. As a gesture towards the self-determination principle, the bill proposed a Council of Ireland, made up of twenty representatives each from the Dublin and Belfast parliaments, 'with a view to the eventual establishment of a parliament for the whole of Ireland, and to bring about harmonious action between the parliaments and governments of Southern Ireland and Northern Ireland'.[29]

The Ulster Unionist Council was somewhat unconvincing in asserting that loyalists would be making a 'supreme sacrifice' by accepting a parliament in Belfast. Captain Charles Craig, brother of James and MP for South Antrim, said in the Commons on 29 March that 'without a parliament of our own constant attacks would be made upon us, and constant attempts would be made . . . to draw us into a Dublin parliament'. He said that he profoundly distrusted the Labour Party and

477

Asquith's Liberal opposition: 'We believe that if either of those parties, or the two in combination, were once more in power our chances of remaining a part of the United Kingdom would be very small indeed.'[30]

Getting the council to agree to a six-county Northern Ireland was much more difficult. The Co. Cavan landlord, the 11th Baron Farnham, and Michael Knight, a solicitor from Clones, put forward an amendment to partition off the entire province at a meeting on 10 March 1920. Unionist delegates from the counties of Donegal, Cavan and Monaghan argued that: a province with a majority of two hundred thousand Protestants should have no trouble voting a majority of loyalists to a Belfast parliament; Ulster was a geographical entity and all 'our trade, business and railways are connected with it'; and 'the ridiculous boundary' would cut off Co. Donegal. They considered it 'unwise that the northern parliament should have too great a Unionist majority'. Delegates from the rest of Ulster did not agree and rejected the amendment so brusquely that Sir James Stronge, the Co. Armagh landowner, felt that 'the three counties have been thrown to the wolves with very little compunction'. Essentially most delegates were not convinced that a nine-county parliament would have a sufficiently secure Unionist majority: 'A couple of members sick, or two or three members absent for some accidental reason, might in one evening hand over the entire Ulster parliament and the entire Ulster position.'[31]

Did Northern Ireland have to engulf the six north-eastern counties intact? This question was hardly considered in 1920. Nationalists of every variety found partition so repugnant that they did not revive proposals for county plebiscites made by Asquith and others before the war. There was no reason why units other than counties, such as Poor Law Unions, could not have been used as a guide to drawing the frontier. Carson had argued before the war that the four most Protestant counties – Antrim, Down, Londonderry and Armagh – could make a perfectly viable unit, possessing together a population greater than that of New Zealand or Newfoundland. He was silent on the issue now. James Craig suggested a boundary commission in 1919 but then thought better of it; yet the drawing of a frontier to enclose the most Protestant areas would have been no more difficult than the task facing boundary commissioners negotiating a line between Poles and Germans in Upper Silesia. Essentially the Ulster Unionists – in power at Westminster and facing negligible opposition from the rump of the Irish Parliamentary Party – set out to get as much territory as they could without endangering their majority in order to bring as many outlying Protestants as they could into their fold. Their behaviour was similar to that of other postwar winners, such as the Italians in Istria, the Greeks in Thrace, the

Romanians in Transylvania and the Poles east of the Vistula, when negotiating their political borders.

Carson was not in favour of devolution for Northern Ireland: 'You cannot knock Parliaments up and down as you do a ball, and, once you have planted them there, you cannot get rid of them.'[32] He had failed in his ultimate objective of preventing *any* part of Ireland from getting Home Rule and it was time, he felt, to bow out. Sir James Craig – he had been knighted in 1917 – was Carson's natural successor; appointed financial secretary to the Admiralty, he had expectations, justified or not, of high office at Westminster and it was with hesitation that he resigned from Lloyd George's government in March 1921 to lead the Ulster Unionists. Lady Craig recorded in her diary:

> J. has his last day at the Admiralty, taking leave of the staff, and his last day at the House, giving up the keys of his locker, etc . . . When he joins us in the evening, we feel very mournful, and I have never seen him so
> . depressed, as he is always so philosophical, and says one should never dwell on what is done with, but concentrate on the present and the future.[33]

Sinn Féin rejected the 'Partition Act' out of hand and carried on the struggle to make the Dáil the parliament of a thirty-two-county Irish republic. Nevertheless, the Better Government of Ireland Act, receiving the royal assent on 23 December and due to come into force on 1 May 1921, was to become, in effect, the constitution of Northern Ireland for the next fifty years. Thus it was that the part of Ulster that had fought hardest against Home Rule was the only part of Ireland to get Home Rule.

'STRETCH OUT THE HAND OF FORBEARANCE AND CONCILIATION'

> The cause is sacred and worthy of every personal sacrifice. Rally round me that I may shatter our enemies and their hopes of a republic flag. The Union Jack must sweep the polls. Vote early, work late . . .

With this message Craig urged loyalists to give his party total support in the Northern Ireland elections called for Empire Day, 24 May 1921. The Nationalists, led by Joseph Devlin, condemned partition as likely to sink 'this fair and fertile island, set in the western seas' into 'irretrievable chaos, a mass of blackened ruins and bleaching bones'. De Valera, a Sinn Féin candidate in Co. Down, asked the 'men and women of northeast Ulster' to vote 'so that there may be an end to boycott and retaliation, to partition, disunion and ruin'.[34] Craig's principal anxiety was that Labour in Belfast would draw off the loyalist vote. He need not have worried: when Labour candidates booked the Ulster Hall for a final rally on 17 May, loyalist shipwrights prevented them from getting in. 'Mass meeting of loyal shipyard workers who have captured Ulster Hall from Bolsheviks Baird, Midgley and Hanna request that you address them for a few minutes tonight', telegraphed the men to Craig in London, who replied: 'I am with them in spirit. Know they will do their part. I will do mine. Well done big and wee yards.'[35] Not one Labour candidate was elected. The Unionist fear that the single transferable voting system of proportional representation – prescribed in the Government of Ireland Act – would not be to their advantage proved unfounded. In an 89 per cent poll, 40 Unionists, 6 Sinn Féiners, and 6 Nationalists were returned. The election had been, as most elections were to be in Northern Ireland in the future, little more than a sectarian head count. In the South Sinn Féin won 124 seats out of 128, all unopposed.

Shortly before the election, on 5 May, Craig had made an extraordinary journey to Dublin and had been driven from there by 'three of the worst looking toughs I have ever seen' via a devious route to a suburban villa.[36] There he met de Valera, elected president of the Dáil, who recalled:

> I said after the first few moments' silence 'Well?' He looked at me and he said 'Well?' I then said, 'I'm too old at this political business to have nonsense of this kind: each waiting for the other to begin' and I started putting our case to him. He spoke of the Union as if it were a sacred thing.

Craig's recollection was that after half an hour de Valera 'had reached the era of Brian Boru. After another half hour he had advanced to the period of some king a century or two later. By this time, I was getting tired . . . fortunately, a fine Kerry Blue entered the room and enabled me to change the conversation.' 'I must say I liked him', de Valera observed, but neither man even began to appreciate the other's point of view and, after politely agreeing to differ, they parted.[37]

It is possible that this secret meeting between the two leaders had been set up indirectly by the British government, now desperately seeking an end to hostilities in Ireland. Since the beginning of the year British armed forces had made significant progress against the IRA, but Lloyd George blenched when he was told that ultimate victory would require the service of one hundred thousand men at a cost of £100 million. Besides, British public opinion was impatient for a settlement and many agreed with Asquith when he said: 'Things are being done in Ireland which would disgrace the blackest annals of the lowest despotism in Europe.'[38] The IRA flying columns, despite some spectacular successes in west Cork, were now hard-pressed and lost key activists and a sizeable proportion of their arms in a disastrous attack on Dublin's Custom House in May.

Collins later told Greenwood: 'You had us dead beat. We could not have lasted another three weeks.'[39] When George V offered to go to Belfast to open the Northern Ireland parliament, Lloyd George seized the opportunity to offer an olive branch to Sinn Féin.

> I could not have allowed myself to give to Ireland by deputy alone my earnest prayers and good wishes in the new era which opens with this ceremony, and I have therefore come in person . . .[40]

With these words the king began his crucial speech in Belfast City Hall at the state opening of the Northern Ireland parliament on 22 June 1921. Lady Craig had heard from Buckingham Palace 'that many letters have been received there begging that their Majesties should not go over to Ulster'. Indeed, only ten days before, seven people had died in renewed rioting in Belfast. In her diary Lady Craig recorded how the demonstration of loyalty was combined with strict security:

> Jun. 22. The great day . . . the King and Queen have the most wonderful reception. The decorations everywhere are extremely well done and even the little side streets that they will never be within miles of are draped with bunting and flags, and the pavement and lampposts painted red, white and blue, really most touching . . . J. goes to the docks of course to meet them . . . precautions had been taken of every description, trusted men stationed in each house, and on every roof top . . . The actual Opening was the first part of the functions.[41]

George V addressed only the Unionist MPs, for the Nationalists and Sinn Féiners held to their pledge 'not to enter this north-eastern parliament' and Cardinal Logue had also refused an invitation to attend. Nevertheless, the king's speech was intended to reach far beyond the walls of the city hall:

> This is a great and critical occasion in the history of the Six Counties, but not for the Six Counties alone, for everything which interests them touches Ireland . . . I speak from a full heart when I pray that my coming to Ireland to-day may prove to be the first step towards an end of strife amongst her people, whatever their race or creed.
> In that hope, I appeal to all Irishmen to pause, to stretch out the hand of forbearance and conciliation, to forgive and forget, and to join in making for the land which they love a new era of peace, contentment, and good will.[42]

Then Queen Mary was taken to the Ulster Hall, where, according to Lady Craig, the scenes 'were unforgettable, as the people could not contain themselves, and cheered for several minutes, and broke into singing the National Anthem at a moment when it was not on the official programme'. 'I can't tell you how glad I am I came,' the king said to Craig, 'but you know my entourage were very much against it.'[43]

George V's entourage had reason to be anxious. While the king was opening the northern parliament, elected Sinn Féin members were taking their seats in the Dáil and refusing to operate the act. The following day the IRA blew up the train carrying the king's cavalry escort from Belfast back to Dublin, killing four men and eighty horses. June had been a violent month in Northern Ireland: RIC men had been killed in Swatragh, Co. Londonderry, and Belfast; Special constables had been shot dead in Newry and Belfast and ten Catholics had been killed, apparently in reprisal by Specials; and in the York Street area of Belfast intercommunal warfare had erupted, leading to the driving out of families from the mixed streets between the New Lodge Road and Tiger Bay. The month of July was more violent still: the fighting was at its worst when Special constables joined Protestant mobs in Belfast over the Twelfth holiday. Sixteen Catholics and seven Protestants were killed and over two hundred Catholic homes were destroyed.[44]

The king's appeal, however, had been heard. A truce between the IRA and the British government came into force on 11 July 1921, de Valera went to London for talks, and a cautious peace settled on Northern Ireland. As far as Craig was concerned, Sinn Féin and the Westminster government could make what arrangements they wanted for the twenty-six counties, provided Northern Ireland was left alone. Anticipating better times, he said on 20 September:

> We here are prepared to work in friendly rivalry with our fellow country-men in the South and West . . . We are prepared to work for the better-ment of the people of Ireland, not to quarrel, not to continue political strife.[45]

Northern Ireland, however, could not be sealed hermetically from developments elsewhere, as Craig soon discovered.

'CRAIG WILL NOT BUDGE ONE INCH': THE ANGLO-IRISH TREATY, 1921

'I found it almost impossible to make any of them admit the reality of the Ulster difficulty,' Thomas Jones remarked after talking to a Sinn Féin deputation in July 1921; ' . . . if we left Irishmen alone they would quickly settle their squabbles. You know the sort of stuff.'[46] Fearful that concessions would be required of him, Craig had turned down Lloyd George's entreaties to join the discussions and 'explore to the utmost the possibility of a settlement'.[47] He also refused to join the formal negotiations that began in London on 11 October between the British government and plenipotentiaries sent over by the Dáil. Arthur Griffith, head of the delegation, put Irish independence above Irish unity, but he made the northern state his central tactical weapon: if Ireland was let go from the empire, then he was prepared to accept the existence of Northern Ireland, but if not, then he would insist on a united Ireland.

There followed weeks of deadlock. At different times the prime minister fumed that he wanted 'a complete smash-up of the revolutionists'; Churchill was spotted 'breathing fire and slaughter'; and Bonar Law was heard muttering down the corridor that 'the Irish were an inferior race.'[48] George Gavan Duffy, grandson of the Monaghan Young Irelander, raised the question of detaching nationalist areas from Northern Ireland and Lloyd George slipped Jones this note: '17 Oct. Tyrone and Fermanagh. This is going to wreck settlement.'[49] Dependent on Conservative support, the prime minister could not concede an independent republic, so he applied strong pressure on Northern Ireland to accept an all-Ireland parliament. As Austen Chamberlain, leader of the Unionists in the Commons, explained to his wife: 'The six counties was a compromise, and, like all compromises, is illogical and indefensible, and you could not raise an army in England to fight for *that* as we could for Crown and empire.'[50]

The Northern Ireland premier was soon in London to protest. 'Craig will not budge one inch,' Lloyd George observed on 7 November, and Lord Curzon heard Craig speak 'of being betrayed, surprised, dismayed, turned out of the British system'.[51] In the end Bonar Law came to the rescue, saying that Ulster Unionists were being asked for 'the surrender of everything for which they have been fighting for thirty-five years'.[52] Craig's sense of isolation was almost complete, nevertheless: the British public's sympathy for Ulster loyalists had been declining steadily since their refusal to bend at the Irish Convention in 1917, and now even the *Daily Express* assured its readers: 'ULSTER WILL BE WRONG . . . unless the Ulster cabinet abandons its uncompromising attitude it will be guilty of the greatest political crime in history.'[53]

'A dreary December evening in 10 Downing Street', Lloyd George recalled, '. . . and now came the final treaty of peace. Would it be signed?' Here, according to Churchill, 'unutterably wearied Ministers faced the Irish delegation themselves in actual desperation, and knowing well that death stood at their elbows'.[54] The prime minister melodramatically held up two letters, both addressed to Craig: one said that agreement had been reached; and the other that it had not, and that the Anglo-Irish War would resume in three days. A special train was at Euston with steam up ready to take one of the letters to Holyhead and from there by destroyer to Belfast. 'Michael Collins rose looking as if he was going to shoot somebody, preferably himself', Churchill recalled, as he and the rest of the Dáil plenipotentiaries signed the Anglo-Irish Treaty at 2.10 a.m. on 6 December 1921.[55]

The treaty set aside the Government of Ireland Act for the twenty-six counties, now to be known as the Irish Free State and having a constitutional relationship with Britain very similar to that of the dominion of Canada. How had Lloyd George been able to get Sinn Féin to agree to remain within the empire? The answer lay in Article XII, which provided for a boundary commission. Convinced that this could tear great lumps out of Northern Ireland, Craig went immediately to London to protest. In a letter to Sir Maurice Hankey, Jones wrote:

> Sir James Craig was closeted with the P.M. .... He then went off to his Doctor to be inoculated – I suppose against a Sinn Fein germ. Anyhow, yesterday he charged the P.M. with a breach of faith . . . Carson . . . wrote a nasty letter.[56]

Craig himself wrote an extremely bitter letter to Austen Chamberlain on his return to Belfast:

> What attitude will the British Government adopt if the government of Northern Ireland finds it necessary to call upon their friends and supporters – more especially the members of the Loyal Orange Institution – to come to their assistance by means of arms, ammunition and money from Great Britain, the Dominions and other parts of the world where people of Ulster descent are in strength and desirous of helping?
> ... contemporaneously with the functioning of the Treaty, Loyalists may declare independence on their own behalf, seize the Customs and other Government Departments and set up an authority of their own. Many already believe that violence is the only language understood by Mr Lloyd George and his Ministers.[57]

THE KILLING GOES ON

Article XII of the treaty may well have been a diplomatic masterstroke in London, but in Ulster it immediately magnified uncertainty and unrest. Loyalists living near the border were now gripped with apprehension that soon they would fall under the jurisdiction of the Free State. Suddenly nationalists of every variety had their expectations raised and many believed so much territory would be transferred that Northern Ireland could not possibly survive – a view shared for a time even by Lloyd George. In fact, the main outcome of the treaty in Northern Ireland was intense disorder and bloodshed.

For all its success in the South, the truce of July 1921 had not stopped the killing in the North. In Belfast one horrific incident followed another: twenty were left dead after three days of fighting north of the city centre in August; on 18 September troops opened fire on loyalist rioters and killed two women near York Street; on 24 September a youth was shot dead as he left St Matthew's Church in Short Strand; next day a bomb thrown by Catholics in Seaforde Street killed two people and a bomb thrown by Protestants into Weaver Street left one man dead and four children under the age of six seriously injured; and a few days later Catholics opened fire on a Protestant funeral, killing one person. Altogether 27 people were killed in sectarian fighting between 19 and 25 November and by the end of the year the death toll in the city for the previous twelve months had reached 109.[58] To make matters worse the Dáil kept up its 'Belfast Boycott' of goods exported to the South, originally imposed in protest at the shipyard expulsions. In Churchill's view:

> It recognised and established real partition, spiritual and voluntary partition, before physical partition had been established . . . it did not secure the reinstatement of a single expelled Nationalist, nor the conversion of a single Unionist. It was merely a blind suicidal contribution to the general hate.[59]

The IRA used the truce to send southern commandants north to stiffen northern units, particularly in urban enclaves. One was the notorious Dan Breen, who had killed the first policemen at Soloheadbeg, and another was the future Fascist leader Eoin O'Duffy, who declared at a rally outside Armagh in September that if loyalists insisted on partition, Sinn Féin members 'would have to put on the screw – the boycott. They would have to tighten the screw and, if necessary, they would have to use the lead against them.'[60] With the acceptance of the truce, B Special patrols were suspended, but Protestants seeking action continued to join the UVF now under Crawford's command. In London, Michael Collins caused acute embarrassment in the British government negotiating team when he produced a secret circular issued by Colonel Wickham on 9 November, revealing that the Northern Ireland government intended 'obtaining the services of the best elements' in the 'unauthorised Loyalist defence forces' – and this at a time when Westminster still had full responsibility for all categories of police.[61]

The new year saw the unleashing of pent-up forces in Northern Ireland as the terms of the treaty were being hotly debated inside the Dáil and by the general public all over the island.

'THE CROSS-FIRING THAT WAS KEPT UP DAY AND NIGHT'

Rising in the Dáil to second the motion to approve the treaty, Deputy Sean MacEoin said: 'To me symbols, recognitions, shadows, have very little meaning. What I want, what the people of Ireland want, is not shadows but real substances . . . ' Yet in fifteen days of debate symbols seemed to be the central issue. For both sides the position of the Irish

Free State within the empire and, in particular, the oath of fidelity to the Crown, were of far greater concern than the fate of Ulster. Whether for or against the treaty, deputies were complacent about the vague terms of reference for the Boundary Commission and the lack of provision for plebiscites even in border areas, even though the commission that divided Upper Silesia had just completed its work. In his 'Document No. 2' – an alternative to the treaty – de Valera included Article XII verbatim.[62] On 7 January 1922 the Dáil approved the treaty by the uncomfortably narrow margin of sixty-four votes to fifty-seven. De Valera flounced out of the chamber with his supporters and thus it was that Collins became chairman of the Provisional Government of the Irish Free State.

Collins met Craig in London and on 21 January it was agreed that the Belfast boycott should 'be discontinued immediately' and that the northern government 'facilitate in every way the return of Catholic workmen to the shipyards, as and when trade revival enables the firms concerned to absorb the present unemployed'.[63] There was no agreement on the Boundary Commission, however, and within a few weeks the two governments were perilously close to outright war with each other.

The IRA was augmented by the British government's decision to release political prisoners, some from Ballykinler, Co. Down, in December and January. Restless from lack of action, IRA units were united in their determination to destabilise Northern Ireland whatever their views on the treaty. Their new campaign in 1922 was prompted by the arrest in the middle of January of eleven men from Co. Monaghan. The men claimed to be going to a football match in Derry but, since they were carrying revolvers and included Dan Hogan, the officer commanding the 5th northern division of the IRA, they almost certainly were planning to rescue three IRA prisoners due to be hanged in the city for killing two warders with chloroform. In retaliation for the arrests, the IRA captured three RIC men in Co. Tyrone and held them hostage. This was followed by a major IRA incursion across the border into the counties of Tyrone and Fermanagh on the night of 7–8 February: some forty prominent loyalists were seized and taken south. They included the eighty-year-old Anketell Moutray, Orange county grand master in Tyrone, who was to exasperate his captors by singing metrical psalms and 'God Save the King' without ceasing.

The *Belfast News-Letter* described the kidnappings as 'an act of war against the British Crown of the most offensive and heinous sort, an act which if perpetrated by an alien people, would be visited with retaliatory violence'. In fact the British government tried to calm the situation by persuading Craig to release the 'Monaghan footballers' and the IRA then returned their loyalist captives.[64] The situation was inflamed further by an incident in Co. Monaghan on 11 February: a patrol of sixteen A Specials travelled by rail from Newtownards en route for Enniskillen; the line ran through Co. Monaghan, and the local IRA clearly had advance information that the constables would be on board. The young Patrick Shea watched volunteers in Clones

> race through the centre of the town, their klaxon horns screaming continuously. The men in the cars were all carrying arms; some of them had Thompson machine-guns with circular drums of ammunition shining beneath their short barrels.

Then the train drew in to Clones station:

> As soon as the train stopped Commandant Fitzpatrick, who was in charge of the Army contingent, walked, revolver in hand, to the compartment in which the Specials were. He called on them to surrender and come out and was immediately shot dead. Hell was then let loose. Bullets poured into the carriage containing the Specials, passengers cried out in terror, jumped from the train and ran in all directions. It was all over in a few minutes. In the shattered carriage the sergeant and three of the constables lay dead.

Shea's father, an RIC sergeant who had earlier saved Fitzpatrick from being shot out of hand by the Black and Tans, helped one of the surviving Specials back over the border hidden in a delivery van.[65] A riot ensued in Lisbellaw when the train arrived with the dead, and news of the episode sparked off a fresh bout of violence in Belfast. Loyalists attacked Catholic districts now reinforced by IRA units and so intense was the fighting that the death toll for the city was forty-four, the highest monthly total so far. Shipyard trams were bombed, but the most horrific incident was the killing of six Catholic children in Weaver Street in a bomb attack.

The situation deteriorated further in March: troops used machine guns against snipers in the Falls; men laying tramlines on the Antrim Road came under fire; bombs were thrown onto a tram passing the New Lodge Road; a B Special was shot by British soldiers; and both sides perpetrated assassinations and reprisals of frightful barbarity. In the early hours of 24 March uniformed men, thought to have been RIC, broke into the home of Owen MacMahon, a Catholic publican who lived in Austin Road. Five members of the family were shot dead; only the youngest child, who crept under a table, survived. On 31 March a bomb was thrown into the kitchen of a home in Brown Street. Francis Donnelly, a Protestant, had been reading his evening newspaper by the fire; he and his two daughters were severely wounded and his two boys – aged twelve and two years ten months – died from their injuries. As they left the attackers fired revolver shots at Donnelly's wife, who was nursing a baby.

Altogether sixty-one people died in Belfast in the violence of March 1922. Isolated Catholic and Protestant families were particularly vulnerable and intimidation, house-burning, rioting and assassination drew the lines between the two communities in the city more tautly than ever. Atrocity followed atrocity, counter-assassination followed almost every death, and large areas of Belfast were virtually at war. Robert McElborough, a gas worker, described what conditions were like in east Belfast:

> I was taken off the meter work and was told by the superintendent to keep the lamps in Seaforde Street and the Short Strand in repair . . . This was in 1922, and anyone who lived in the area remembers the cross-firing that was kept up day and night. No-one would venture out and trams passed this area at full empty, or with passengers lying flat on the floor . . .
> I can't tell how I got the cart into this area. I ran with it and got safely into Madrid Street and into Seaforde Street with rifles cracking overhead . . . there was times when I had to clear out, when someone who lived in the district had been shot by a sniper. It was the snipers on the roofs and back windows who were the danger. Anyone seen on the streets within the range of their gun was their target, and they found out later through the press what side he belonged to. I had seen men who were going to work shot dead as a reprisal for some other victim. My only dread was when I was standing on the ladder putting up a lamp, bullets that I suppose were meant for me went through the lamp reflector . . . [66]

'They were bad times,' a B Special from Co. Londonderry recalled. 'No one would have opened the door at night unless he was sure who was knocking or gone out alone after dark even if in bad need of the doctor.'[67] In rural areas the IRA was able to go on the offensive during March when, over a ten-day period, activists killed five Special constables and one RIC man; burned flax mills in Co. Londonderry; and seized RIC barracks in Pomeroy, Maghera and Belcoo. At Belcoo, on the Fermanagh–Leitrim border, all arms and ammunition were taken, houses were raided, and four civilians and sixteen policemen were captured.[68]

The very survival of Northern Ireland now seemed to be at stake. Craig met the new threat by expanding the B class of Special constables. Arms were distributed to them in convoys of furniture vans and, in country districts, the men were allowed to keep their weapons at home. Each constable was equipped with a rifle, one hundred rounds of ammunition and a bayonet, and ex-army uniforms dyed dark green were issued. Protestant farmers and workers for the most part, on duty in their spare time and with no pay, the B Specials were in effect a militia who bore the main brunt of the campaign. The expansion of the force made it possible to seal off long stretches of the three-hundred-mile border. Only main roads, policed by road blocks, were kept open and minor roads were closed by blowing up bridges, by trenching or by covering them with constabulary posts. In some places, sniping from across the border was so heavy that farmers were forced to evacuate, leaving Specials to feed cattle and poultry.

Craig was prepared to attempt conciliation as well as force, and Collins, finding the anti-treaty IRA restive and virtually a law unto itself, was eager to try negotiation again. Another pact was signed between the two premiers in London on 30 March 1922. 'Peace is today declared', the document began and the Westminster government gave a grant of £500,000 towards unemployment relief in Northern Ireland. The agreement aimed to draw Catholics into the Special constabulary and almost from the outset it began to break down. Field Marshal Sir Henry Wilson – former chief of the imperial staff, military adviser to the Northern Ireland government and Unionist MP for North Down – virulently opposed the pact, saying sharply at a meeting with northern ministers: 'Who is governing Ulster, you or Collins?' 'If you do not want to lose all your police force you will cancel that agreement,' James Cooper, Unionist MP for Fermanagh, warned Craig in parliament.[69]

On 1 April an RIC constable from Brown Square barracks in Belfast was shot dead. Less than an hour later uniformed police broke into Catholic homes in Arnon Street and Stanhope Street and in reprisal beat a man to death with a sledgehammer, mortally wounded a child, shot three men dead and injured two other children. Though some police came forward to identify the perpetrators, and though Collins telegraphed Craig that an inquiry was 'imperatively necessary', the Northern Ireland government refused an investigation.[70] Collins soon became convinced that a pogrom was being directed at Belfast Catholics, a belief reinforced by the burning of about fifty Catholic homes in Antigua Street and Saunderson Street and the arrival of hundreds of refugees in Dublin. He now began to supply weapons to northern units of the IRA, exchanging rifles intended for the Irish Free State Army for older guns provided by Cork brigades and these in turn were sent to Ulster, where the serial numbers could not be traced. By now, disagreement over the treaty had split the IRA down the middle and it is significant that most northern units stayed loyal to Collins. This extraordinary action by Collins also reveals his desperation as the Free State drifted steadily towards civil war – anti-treaty forces, known as 'Irregulars', had already seized barracks and public buildings in

Dublin, and perhaps he felt that open warfare could be delayed in a combined campaign against Northern Ireland.

As IRA action intensified the Northern Ireland government was adopting exceptional measures to deal with the crisis.

'I say to the Government, "Take whatever powers you require and we will give them to you",' Captain Mulholland declared in the northern parliament, at this time meeting in the Presbyterian Assembly College in Belfast. On 5 April 1922 the Royal Ulster Constabulary was formed. It was closely modelled on 'the old RIC that every Irishman was proud of', as Lloyd Campbell described the force to the applause of fellow Unionists, 'and which physically, mentally, and morally was the finest body of disciplined men that ever walked this earth'.[71] To this gendarmerie could be added the augmented Special constabulary – now controlled by the Northern Ireland government but still financed by Westminster – until by the early summer there were fifty thousand regular and part-time policemen, that is, one policeman for every six families in the region, or put another way, one policeman for every two Catholic families.

On 7 April 1922 the Civil Authorities (Special Powers) Bill became law, giving the minister of home affairs authority to detain suspects and to set up courts of summary jurisdiction. George Hanna MP protested that the bill was too complicated: there were, he said, 'nine sections of the bill and thirty regulations. One section would have been sufficient: "The Home Secretary shall have the power to do whatever he likes, or let somebody else do whatever he likes for him." That is the whole Bill.'[72] The special courts could detain suspects without trial for unspecified periods, impose sentences of penal servitude or death, and 'in addition to any other punishment which may lawfully be imposed, order such person, if a male, to be at once privately whipped'. The *Manchester Guardian* found this legislation more draconian than Lloyd George's Restoration of Order in Ireland Act which it replaced:

> Whilst envenomed politicians in the Ulster parliament are voting themselves power to use torture and capital punishment against citizens whom they forbid to defend themselves while they scarcely attempt to protect them from massacre, some of their own partisans in Belfast carry wholesale murder to refinements of barbarity hardly surpassed in Armenia and Constantinople.[73]

The Northern Ireland government countered that 'an exceptional time ... requires exceptional measures'. Robert Lynn, MP for Belfast Central and editor of the *Northern Whig*, argued that 'the Government has not gone far enough . . . This is no time for indulging in legal hair-splitting.' The question at issue was simple, he said: 'Is civilisation going to be allowed to exist, or is there going to be anarchy?'[74]

Northern Ireland seemed to be teetering on the brink of anarchy in the late spring of 1922. Signing himself 'One who thinks we have taken enough lying down', an ex-serviceman from Co. Londonderry wrote a letter on 6 May to the *Belfast News-Letter* describing conditions there:

> On Tuesday night last I viewed the whole situation from midnight till 4 a.m. from a high hilltop, and it reminded me of what one was accustomed to see during the Great War in France. Signals were being exchanged by the Sinn Feiners all along the Sperrins with their friends who were murdering the police in Bellaghy, etc. Verey lights were going up from the barracks that were being attacked, and the same game was being played by the Sinn Feiners to try to draw the Crossleys in the wrong direction.[75]

In an attempt to relieve the pressure on Catholic enclaves in Belfast, the IRA launched a campaign of 'consigning to the flames the manu-factories and businesses of the powers behind the murders', in the words of the anti-treaty newspaper the *Plain People*.[76] In a fifteen-day assault in May, forty-one serious fires in Belfast caused damage esti-mated at £500,000, and then followed the burning of 'big houses', including Shane's Castle by the shores of Lough Neagh; Crebilly Castle, near Ballymena; Glenmona House in Cushendun; Garron Tower on the Antrim coast; Kilclief House at Strangford; and Hawethorne Hill, Armagh. Railway stations and flax mills in rural areas were set on fire. After the IRA had killed three policemen and burned a mill in Desertmartin, seven Catholics were murdered in reprisal and following the burning of some of their businesses and homes, all the Catholic residents of this Co. Londonderry town were driven out.[77]

The tempo of killing in Belfast increased. On 18 May three Catholics were shot dead in the city and the following day three Protestants were murdered in a cooperage in Little Patrick Street. On 22 May, W.J. Twaddell, MP for Woodvale, was shot dead on the way to his outfitter's shop – the only MP to be assassinated in Northern Ireland until the murder of the Reverend Robert Bradford in 1981. Twaddell had an enthusiastic following on the Shankill Road and his murder led to the immediate imposition of internment. All the two hundred men arrested in the first sweep were Catholics, who, after being held in Belfast, Larne and Newtownards, were transferred to an old ship moored in Larne Lough. Though a curfew was imposed, the killing and destruction continued. Altogether forty-four Catholics and twenty-two Protestants met with violent deaths in Belfast during the month of May.

Soon after, a frontier incident put Anglo-Irish relations under intense strain. Joe Sweeney, commander of the pro-treaty forces in Co. Donegal, had reinforced his garrison in Pettigo, a largely Protestant village that straddled the border. The neighbouring portion of Fermanagh, a tongue of territory cut off from the rest of the county by lower Lough Erne and the river issuing from it, seemed dangerously exposed. Fifty A Specials arrived by boat and commandeered Magherameenagh Castle within this area. Reinforcements were ambushed near Belleek and their Lancia car was taken, and after a siege, the Specials abandoned the castle and evacuated by pleasure steamer. 'INVASION OF ULSTER. Northern territory was invaded by huge forces of IRA men on Sunday', began an alarmist report in the *Belfast News-Letter* on 30 May, and Craig demanded military retaliation.[78] Though General Macready insisted that 'in military opinion an invasion as reported in London is a farce and exaggerated', Churchill in his capacity as colonial secretary ordered several hundred troops, with artillery and armoured cars, to converge by land and water on Belleek and Pettigo.[79] Thomas Jones at Chequers 'could not sleep for hours as I feared that the troops were moving towards Belleek and that we might have some bloody business on the following day'.[80] The two villages were surrounded and shelled by howitzers, three IRA men and one Special constable were killed, and British soldiers now occupied a portion of Free State territory. Lloyd George was so relieved that large-scale bloodshed had been avoided and so amused by Churchill's overreaction that he ordered champagne. According to Jones: 'We began innocently enough with Welsh hymns but the P.M.'s desire to celebrate the victory of Belleek led him to sing "Scots wha hae" putting in Winston's name wherever he could.'[81]

The impression that both factions of the IRA were attempting to force border revision by violence was reinforced soon after by the murder of six Presbyterians on a roadway just west of Newry on 17 June. Reprisal killings followed in south Down and Cushendall, in Co. Antrim, leaving seven Catholics dead. Collins did not question British military presence in Co. Donegal as expected, for he was making his last desperate attempts to prevent civil war. The Free State electorate voted decisively for the treaty that month, strengthening the Provisional Government's hand. Then the whole situation was transformed, north and south, by another murder: Field Marshal Sir Henry Wilson was shot dead in London on 22 June, almost certainly on the 'stale' order of Michael Collins. Now the Provisional Government's hand was forced: Churchill insisted that Collins take action against the anti-treaty IRA or the British would intervene and use their own army. At 4.29 a.m. on Wednesday 28 June a field gun fired across the River Liffey at the Irregular garrison in the Four Courts and moments later a torrent of bullets poured from both sides. The Irish Civil War had begun.

After fierce fighting in the centre of Dublin, the Irregulars took their campaign into the countryside in a guerrilla war more bitter and deadly than the recent conflict against the British government. What should the IRA in Ulster do? On 2 August 1922 Collins called a meeting with the northern leaders of the pro-treaty IRA and, according to Seamus Woods, the officer commanding the 3rd northern battalion in Belfast, Collins 'outlined the policy we were to adopt – the non-recognition of the Northern government and passive resistance to its functioning. At the same time, from the military point of view, we were to avoid as far as possible coming into direct conflict with the armed forces of the Northern government.'[82] As the war in the South intensified, however, the Provisional Government had no desire to divert any of its resources northwards and resolved formally on 19 August that 'a peace policy should be adopted in regard to future dealings with North-East Ulster'. Three days later, Collins was killed in an ambush in his native Co. Cork. Of all the Dublin government ministers, Collins had been most deeply concerned about the fate of northern Catholics. Now his place was taken by William Thomas Cosgrave, who encouraged the pro-treaty northern IRA to come south and join the National Army – indeed, Woods became an assistant to the chief of staff. In response to the Irregulars' tactics of arson, ambush and assassination, Cosgrave showed ruthless determination. Using legislation more sweeping than the Special Powers Act in the North, the Provisional Government had seventy-seven republicans condemned to death by military courts. Joe McKelvey, commander of the anti-treaty IRA in eastern Ulster and captured after the fall of the Four Courts in Dublin, was one of four men executed in reprisal for the murder of a Dáil deputy.

The great majority of the IRA in the North stayed loyal to the Provisional Government, which paid salaries to seventy-two full-time officers and men in Belfast. As these men were under orders not to confront security forces in Northern Ireland and as most of the fighting was far to the south, Ulster now became the most peaceful province in the country. Its most disturbed county was Donegal, where Commandant-General Charles Daly opposed the treaty and he and his Irregulars held out for some time in the mountains. After several running fights, they were rounded up in groups of between twenty and forty by National Army troops led by Commandant-General Joe Sweeney, who had led the pro-treaty IRA in the county during the Anglo-Irish War.

Sean Larkin, from Co. Londonderry, and Daly were shot by firing squad in Drumboe Castle on 14 March 1923, eight months after their capture.[83] Eight weeks later, on 24 May, de Valera issued this message to the Irregulars: 'Soldiers of the Republic, Legion of the Rearguard . . . Military victory must be allowed to rest for the moment with those who have destroyed the Republic.'[84]

The civil war was a remarkable stroke of good fortune for the Northern Ireland government. As IRA activists disengaged or withdrew to fight each other across the frontier incidents of violence – horrific though many of them were – steadily declined and by 1923 it could be said that the region was at peace. The price in blood had been heavy: between July 1920 and July 1922 the death toll in the six counties was 557 – 303 Catholics, 172 Protestants and 82 members of the security forces.[85] In Belfast, 236 people had been killed in the first months of 1922, more than in the widespread troubles in Germany in the same period. In Belfast there had been a vicious sectarian war at a time of political turmoil, and yet the statistics speak for themselves: Catholics formed only a quarter of the city's population but had suffered 257 civilian deaths out of 416 in a two-year period. Catholic relief organisations estimated that in Belfast between 8,700 and 11,000 Catholics had been driven out of their jobs, that 23,000 Catholics had been forced out of their homes, and that about 500 Catholic-owned businesses had been destroyed. Protestants believed that Catholics were aiming for nothing less than the destruction of the state, but they formed one third of the population of Northern Ireland and the Government was now faced with the problem of what policy to adopt towards such a substantial alienated minority.

The Irish Free State had also paid a heavy price: perhaps as many as four thousand killed; a debt of £17 million; the cost of destruction estimated at a further £30 million; and a legacy of bitterness for decades to come. Kevin O'Higgins described the government of which he was a member as

> simply eight young men . . . standing amidst the ruins of one administration, with the foundations of another not yet laid, and with wild men screaming through the key-hole. No police was functioning through the country, no system of justice was operating, the wheels of the administration hung idle, battered out of recognition by the clash of rival jurisdictions.[86]

Such a government, facing the awesome task of reconstruction in the twenty-six counties, could not put the implementation of the Boundary Commission at the top of its agenda. This was another stroke of luck for Craig. Yet another had been the fall of Lloyd George in October 1922, and his replacement by the man he once described as 'meekly ambitious', Bonar Law, the Ulster Unionists' most unwavering friend at Westminster. As a result, Craig had now a period of remarkable calm in which to shape the future of Northern Ireland.

'CZECHO-SLOVAKIA AND ULSTER ARE BORN TO TROUBLE AS THE SPARKS FLY UPWARDS'

'The existing state of central and south-eastern Europe is a terrible example of the evils which spring from the creation of new frontiers', Lloyd George had once written to Craig in a vain attempt to get him to agree to an all-Ireland parliament. No doubt it had been in reaction to a similar lecture that Craig had emerged from Downing Street just after the signing of the treaty saying, 'There's a verse in the Bible which says Czecho-Slovakia and Ulster are born to trouble as the sparks fly upwards.'[87] Whether or not the Northern Ireland premier understood the full implications of his remark is difficult to say.

In these years parallels could be drawn between Northern Ireland and states emerging from collapsed empires in central Europe. Of these only Austria had a fairly homogeneous ethnic composition and it has been estimated that more than 25 million found themselves as national minorities after 1919. Only two thirds of the inhabitants of Poland spoke Polish, for example, and there were 4.6 million Germans, Poles, Ruthenes and Magyars in Czechoslovakia out of a total population of 14.3 million. Here language was the badge of distinction, unlike Ulster. Yet closer similarities with Northern Ireland's divided society can be found. Czechs and Slovaks spoke the same language, though in different dialects, but, in spite of appalling dangers threatening them, relations were severely strained between the devout Catholic peasants of Slovakia and the urbanised sceptics of Bohemia and Moravia. Perhaps an even closer parallel could be sought in Yugoslavia, where ethnic tensions constantly threatened to destroy the new state. Here Serbs and Croats shared the same tongue but were bitterly divided by cultural traditions and religion. Catholic Croats could be compared with Ulster Protestants, regarding themselves as more civilised and prosperous than the more numerous Greek Orthodox Serbs, and fearful that they would be dominated in a united South Slav state – as indeed they were for a time. Ethnic groups in Yugoslavia claimed to be able to distinguish each other by smell just as people in Ulster had their own equally bogus means of identifying 'the other sort'.

Northern Ireland, however, did set out with assets several central European states did not possess. The evils of landlordism, which had largely been swept away in Ireland by land purchase, remained as virulently as before in Hungary, Poland and Romania. Like Czechoslovakia, but unlike most of the other successor states, Northern Ireland had a developed industrial base, experience of participation in representative institutions, and a substantial middle class from which competent public servants could be recruited; and, unlike Czechoslovakia, Northern Ireland had a powerful neighbour ready to provide support in times of crisis.

'We have nothing in our view except the welfare of the people,' Craig had said in the Northern Ireland Commons in September 1921, '. . . every person inside our particular boundary may rest assured that there will be nothing meted out to them but the strictest justice. None need be afraid.'[88] A year later such magnanimity had been severely eroded by the IRA campaign and mounting criticism from the British press. The fact that a third of the population was so hostile to the six-county state that it hoped for its downfall would have taxed the ingenuity of any government of the region. Now Ulster Unionists felt embattled and isolated. Few were disposed to conciliation and yet the restoration of peace in 1923 gave the Northern Ireland government a unique opportunity to attempt a healing of wounds and to woo at least some of the minority into an acceptance of the new regime.

THE FAILURE TO CONCILIATE

James Lichfield, a senior civil servant seconded to Northern Ireland, confided to Thomas Jones that 'the only Cabinet Minister of real value was Craig himself'.[89] This condemnation is too sweeping but there is much evidence that the horizon was limited for most members of the Northern Ireland government. In part this was because Ulster unionism was by its nature defensive, tending to throw up leaders who were dogged, reliable and conservative, rather than imaginative and innovative. The average age of fifty-four was rather high for members of a new government of Britain's first devolved region and owing to Craig's reluctance to change his team it tended to rise until it was sixty-two by 1938. Indeed, only twelve individuals had served in government by the outbreak of the Second World War. Members of the first government all had roots deep in Ulster but without exception they were drawn from the upper layers of provincial society: Craig, the son of a millionaire, had substantial independent means; Lord Londonderry, minister of education, and Edward Archdale, minister of agriculture and commerce, owned large landed estates; John Andrews, minister of labour, was chairman of his family's linen firm and a director in two other companies; Hugh Pollock, minister of finance, was managing director of a firm of flour importers, a director of the Belfast Ropeworks and chairman of the Belfast Harbour Commissioners; Richard Dawson Bates, minister of home affairs, was a prosperous solicitor who had been the paid secretary of the Ulster Unionist Council; and James Milne Barbour, who joined the cabinet in 1925 as minister of commerce when Archdale's responsibilities were split, was head of a linen firm of international importance. Milne Barbour, Londonderry and Pollock had been, and Archdale and Andrews were later to be, presidents of the Belfast Chamber of Commerce.[90] Stephen George Tallents, the civil servant sent to find out why the Craig–Collins pact had broken down, regarded Pollock as 'better informed and more intellectual than his colleagues', and Sir Laming Worthington-Evans, the war minister, was impressed by his competence, remarking, 'I admit he looks after every half-crown.'[91] Pollock, Londonderry and Milne Barbour, though deeply conservative on social and financial matters, were easily the most broad-minded and outward-looking members of the Government; they were unable, however, to win acceptance of their views from the rest of their colleagues.

Milne Barbour was in favour of engaging substantial numbers of Catholics in the civil service, 'though it may be a risky thing politically to say'.[92] Civil servants previously employed by Dublin Castle were invited to apply for transfer to Belfast but only forty-two did so. Some of these were Catholic but the only one to reach the rank of permanent secretary was Bonaparte Wyse. An unusual man in every way, he was descended from Napoleon I's brother, Lucien, he treated his staff to readings in Greek at the start of each working day, and he travelled home to Dublin every weekend. In 1924 Craig received a deputation from the Ulster Protestant Voters' Defence Association, which protested that Catholics were getting preference in public appointments. The prime minister took this complaint seriously and instituted a detailed investigation, causing the RUC inspector-general to express his concern that this would 'bring unfair influence to bear on the detriment of R.C. members of the Force'.[93]

Craig continued to receive such deputations in spite of incontrovertible evidence that civil servants were drawn overwhelmingly from the Protestant section of the community. Some early appointments were blatantly political – Wilfrid Spender, for example, was made cabinet secretary – but thereafter a selection board demanded good educational qualifications. Corruption seems to have been kept out of the service but political interference was constant. In 1934 Spender was exasperated by the 'vile persecution' of a Catholic gardener employed on the Stormont estate, even though he had a distinguished war record and a personal reference from the Prince of Wales. Asked to investigate by Craig, who had listened to complaints about this man from the Orange Order, Spender responded bluntly:

> I think the only course would be for the Government to come out in the open and say that only Protestants are admitted to our Service. I should greatly regret such a course.[94]

Some government ministers made it quite clear that they would not regret such a course, however. The *Northern Whig* reported a speech by Archdale in 1925:

> A man in Fintona asked him how it was that he had over 50 percent Roman Catholics in his ministry. He thought that that was too funny. He had 109 on his staff and so far as he knew there were four Roman Catholics. Three of these were Civil Servants turned over to him, whom he had to take when he began.[95]

Andrews answered an allegation that twenty-eight out of thirty-one porters in the parliament buildings were Catholic by saying in the Commons: 'I have investigated the matter, and I find that there are 30 Protestants, and only one Roman Catholic there temporarily.' On returning from holiday in 1926, Andrews found two 'Free Staters' in his ministry and straight away ordered that such men be disqualified immediately, even though they had impeccable British Army records.[96] G.C. Duggan, a senior civil servant, recalled that Dawson Bates 'made it clear to his Permanent Secretary that he did not want his most juvenile clerk or typist, if a Papist, assigned for duty to his ministry'. After hearing, 'with a great deal of surprise, that a Roman Catholic Telephonist has been appointed', Bates refused to use the telephone for important business until he had succeeded in getting this employee transferred.[97]

There is little doubt that Craig's appointment of Bates to such a crucial ministry as Home Affairs made it exceedingly difficult to conciliate the Catholic minority. Bates openly regarded Catholics as enemies to be kept in check and he set a low standard in public life by timidity in dealing with corruption, notably in the Belfast Corporation, and by his blatant disregard for impartial procedures in, for example, the granting of contracts. Even his reputation for organisational efficiency was undeserved: Sir Wilson Hungerford had been employed from 1912 in the Ulster Unionist Council office, then under Bates's direction, and he found that the 'finances of the organisation were in something of a mess . . . seeing a large pile of angry letters from every newspaper office in Ireland protesting at the receipt of a mere 5/- postal order to pay for the insertion of a large advertisement'.[98]

It could be shown that Catholics were reluctant to seek employment in the service of a government they did not want. Patrick Shea, one of a number of successful Catholic applicants to the civil service, observed that the view of their co-religionists was that 'we had joined the enemy; we were lost souls'.[99] Nevertheless, Craig and his colleagues lacked the vision to make a special effort to win allies in the minority by attracting them into public service, particularly at a time when the Special constabulary was exclusively Protestant in composition. One third of places in the RUC was reserved for Catholics but they comprised only around one sixth of the force, most of them former members of the RIC. Again, no attempt was made to increase this proportion and by 1936 there were only 488 Catholics out of 2,849 in the RUC and only 9 Catholics among the 55 officers holding the rank of district inspector and above.[100]

Discrimination in public employment was not yet at the top of nationalists' list of grievances. A much more likely item was the Northern Ireland government's reorganisation of local government.

'MOST UNFORTUNATE AND ILL-TIMED': THE ABOLITION OF
PROPORTIONAL REPRESENTATION

On 22 June 1921, the day George V opened the Northern Ireland parliament, Thomas Corrigan – the secretary of Fermanagh County Council and a leading member of Sinn Féin imprisoned in 1918–19 – pulled down the Union flag from Enniskillen courthouse. Police promptly rehoisted the flag while the council voted to place this notice on the door:

> Notice to ratepayers. Owing to the invasion and commandeering, by Crown forces, of the offices of the Fermanagh County Council ... the business of the county council has been suspended for the day.

The police remained, telling officials 'to have a few days' holiday'.[101] Then the following December the council resolved: 'We ... do not recognise the partition parliament in Belfast and do hereby direct our secretary to hold no further communications with either Belfast or British local government departments, and we pledge our allegiance to Dail Eireann.'[102] The Northern Ireland parliament had just put through a bill empowering the Government to dissolve local authorities refusing to carry out their functions, and at once the police took over the council headquarters and impounded all its records. Though Derry had been dissuaded from doing so by Church leaders, many other local councils controlled by Nationalist–Sinn Féin coalitions had given their allegiance to the Dáil and now they paid the penalty: by April 1922 twenty-one local authorities – including those of Newry, Armagh,

Strabane, Cookstown, Downpatrick, Magherafelt and Keady, and the county councils of Tyrone and Fermanagh – had been dissolved and their functions taken over by government-appointed commissioners.

Unionists west of the Bann demanded further punishment. Mrs Dehra Chichester, MP for Londonderry, spoke of the tyranny with which nationalist councils 'ground the minority under their heel', and continued:

> We have had to sit there and listen to our King being insulted, to our Government being derided. We have been told that killing was no murder unless committed by the foreign invader.[103]

Dawson Bates was only too ready to comply with the growing campaign in outlying areas for the immediate abolition of proportional representation. Like all members of the Government, he had the liveliest fear of socialism and had been concerned at the success of Labour candidates in 1920 who had won control of Lurgan, got representation for the first time in Lisburn and Bangor, and greatly reduced the Unionist majority in Belfast. The decision to put forward a bill was taken lightly and the issue was barely discussed in cabinet. With no opposition present to delay its progress, the bill was ready to become law by 5 July 1922. 'Do you not see . . . the true meaning of all this?' Collins had asked Churchill. He argued that the bill's purpose was 'to oust the Catholic and Nationalist people of the Six Counties from their rightful share in local administration' and, in anticipation of the Boundary Commission's work, 'to paint the Counties of Tyrone and Fermanagh with a deep Orange tint'.[104] Churchill agreed and, believing the treaty to be imperilled, he persuaded the lord lieutenant to withhold royal assent. Craig and his colleagues then threatened to resign. Lloyd George's coalition, already coming apart at the seams, faced the fact that there was no alternative government in Northern Ireland and it had not the stomach to resume direct Westminster rule there. After Collins's death, Cosgrave did not press the issue with the same vehemence. While admitting that the bill was 'most unfortunate and ill-timed', the coalition government backed down and, after a two-month delay, royal assent was given on 11 September 1922.[105]

The Unionists could argue that they had acted justifiably during what amounted to wartime conditions. The same excuse could not be given the following year when the abolition of proportional representation was followed by the rearrangement of local government boundaries. Judge John Leech, the deputy recorder of Belfast, agreed to head a commission to hold inquiries in controversial areas. Except in

Irvinestown and Ballycastle, Nationalists and Sinn Féin refused to meet the Leech commission. The result was that local Unionist parties, with the enthusiastic co-operation of Dawson Bates, were able to dictate the positioning of boundaries with meticulous care to their own complete satisfaction. The results speak for themselves. Since many Catholics abstained in 1924, the best comparison is between the local election results of 1920 and 1927. In 1920 opposition parties won control of twenty-four local authorities out of twenty-seven, but by 1927 Unionists had a majority in all but twelve councils. Unionists recovered Londonderry Corporation and the county councils of Fermanagh and Tyrone. Westminster made no attempt to intervene in what had been a blatant exercise in gerrymandering. In Omagh Rural District Council, for example, Catholics outnumbered Protestants by 8,179 and though nationalists cast 5,381 more votes than unionists, the new electoral boundaries gave Unionists a majority of eighteen representatives there. Again, Catholics made up 56 per cent of Fermanagh's population but their representation on local bodies in the county fell from 52.5 per cent to 36.75 per cent.[106]

Unionists countered criticism by pointing to the failure of Nationalists and Sinn Féin to make submissions to the Leech commission. Certainly by refusing to take their seats in the Northern Ireland parliament, Nationalists and Sinn Féin not only reinforced the Unionist view that they were intent on bringing down the state but also denied themselves a wider audience and a chance to obtain some redress from Westminster. A striking feature of the interwar period is the low calibre of leadership in the Catholic community, perhaps reflecting the small size of its educated middle class. Craig and his colleagues certainly did not exhibit any leadership qualities in this episode. The deep divisions in Ulster society ensured that a return to the X-system of voting meant that in most seats there were no contests because the outcome was so predictable. Bates had succeeded all too well in his objective of eliminating or reducing Labour representation and thus contributed to the ossification of Northern Ireland's political life.

'PROTESTANT TEACHERS TO TEACH PROTESTANT CHILDREN'

Charles S.H. Vane-Tempest-Stewart, the 7th Marquess of Londonderry, had made considerable personal sacrifices by joining the Northern Ireland government. One of the richest men in the kingdom at the dazzling centre of London society, he turned down the offer to become air minister to join Craig and his colleagues as minister of education. Back in Ulster he looked oddly out of place and out of time, Lady Spender remarking that 'he apes his ancestor the great Lord Castlereagh, wears a high black stock over his collar and a very tightly fitting frock coat, and doesn't look as if he belongs to this century at all'.[107] Determined to uphold the Union his forebear had forged, he threw himself enthusiastically into the task, and won the devoted support of his civil servants, in spite of his tendency to address them like domestics and to emphasise points by striking his ministerial table with his riding crop.

'Religious instruction in a denominational sense during the hours of compulsory attendance there will not be,' Londonderry declared in 1923, overruling one of the main recommendations of a committee he had appointed under the chairmanship of Robert Lynn.[108] The marquess, like the architects of the National Schools the previous century, set out to create a system of elementary schools drawing pupils from all parts of the community. He now faced the intense hostility of both the Catholic and Protestant Churches. The managers of Catholic schools had stated their opinion in 1921 that 'the only satisfactory system of education for Catholics is one wherein Catholic children are taught in Catholic schools by Catholic teachers under Catholic auspices'.[109] Catholics refused to serve on the Lynn committee and Catholic teachers, meeting at Strabane and Omagh in February 1922, pledged themselves not to accept salaries from the Northern Ireland government and recognised only the authority of the Department of Education in Dublin. Around one third of Catholic schools refused co-operation and for several months the Provisional Government paid the salaries of their teachers; as the civil war extended, however, the Cosgrave government stopped payments by October 1922 and the campaign of non-cooperation ended soon after. By then the Catholic Church had lost the opportunity to protect its interests.

Protestant opposition was slower in coming. In part this was due to the complexity of the Education Bill, which Londonderry steered through parliament in 1923 with remarkable ease considering the outcome. The act incorporated most of the Lynn committee's recommendations that the state pay all teachers' salaries in elementary schools, which were to be in three categories: first, those fully maintained by local authorities and the state; second, 'four-and-two' schools (where the management committee was made up of four persons nominated by the managers or trustees, and two by the local education authority) were eligible for capital grants and got half the cost of repairs, equipment, heating, lighting and cleaning; but the voluntary schools, the third category, got only a contribution towards heating, lighting and cleaning. Londonderry spoke hopefully of having schools where children of different faiths might study and play together, and allowed denominational religious instruction only outside hours of compulsory attendance. He pointed to Section 5 of the Government of Ireland Act which made it illegal 'either directly or indirectly to establish or endow any religion', or to set religious tests for teachers maintained out of public funds.[110]

'Protestant teachers to teach Protestant children' was the watchword of clergy who resented their loss of control over teaching appointments and campaigned for compulsory Bible instruction in the state schools.[111] Alderman James Duff, chairman of the Belfast Education Committee, countered that 'any clergyman who says that under the new education act the Bible is thrown out of the schools is a man who has no right to wear the cloth'. The Ulster Teachers' Union, composed of Protestants, carried a resolution denouncing these 'discontented divines who were misleading people', but led by the Reverend Dr William Corkey, manager of nine schools in the Shankill area, the campaign gathered strength. The United Education Committee of the Protestant Churches, founded in 1924, saw its opportunity as a general election approached early in 1925: the committee met the Belfast County Grand Orange Lodge and leading politicians on 27 February; a provincial conference was called for 5 March; and a stirring handbill was distributed. With the title 'PROTESTANTS AWAKE' in large red letters, the handbill denounced the Londonderry act, arguing, for example, that 'the door is thrown open for a Bolshevist or an Atheist or a Roman Catholic to become a teacher in a Protestant school'.[112]

On 3 March 1925 Londonderry gave a press conference reaffirming that his Education Act would not be changed. The United Education Committee's meeting on 5 March in the Presbyterian Assembly Hall in Belfast was impressively attended and – while the education minister was in England – Craig capitulated and an amending bill was rushed through parliament with such indecent speed that it had received royal assent by 13 March. Henceforth clergy could advise on the appointment of teachers; education authorities could take a candidate's religion into account when making a teaching appointment; and teachers were compelled to give 'simple Bible instruction' as part of their contractual duties. Not surprisingly, Londonderry resigned the following year to take on what were for him more congenial opponents – his mining employees in the Durham coalfield.

Dr Corkey and his 'discontented divines' were not yet satisfied and such was the vehemence of their campaign that the principal Protestant and Catholic teachers' unions jointly opposed it. Once again an impending general election, in 1929, gave the United Education Committee its opportunity. James Caulfield, 5th Viscount Charlemont and Lord Londonderry's more compliant successor, hastily prepared a new bill. This time the Catholic Church did not stand aside: Joseph Devlin, now leading ten Nationalists in the Northern Ireland Commons, argued that Catholic schools were worse off than before partition; Catholic bishops threatened to invoke Section 5 of the 1920 act; the Ancient Order of Hibernians held monster protest meetings across the six counties on Saint Patrick's Day, with ten thousand attending at Omagh; and the *Irish News* published a letter, surrounded by a funereal black band, from the bishop of Down and Connor, Dr Daniel Mageean:

> In view of the attack on Catholic interests in education by the bill now before the parliament of the Six Counties, I would ask the clergy of this diocese to say in the mass the prayer Pro qua-conque Necessitate . . . and I would request the laity to join with the priest in praying that God may guide and help us in this hour of danger.[113]

The bishops' threat was enough and on 8 May 1930 the prime minister announced at an Orange luncheon in Warrenpoint that an additional clause in the Education Bill would provide 50 per cent grants for building and extension of privately managed elementary schools.

The Reformed Churches, which had asserted that 'the Protestant cause was in grave peril', had triumphed, nevertheless.[114] They were able to ensure that only Protestant teachers would be appointed to schools wholly funded by the state and local authorities and that in such schools it was the duty of education authorities to provide Bible instruction in compulsory attendance hours as long as the parents of at least ten children demanded it. The act's additional clause greatly improved the position of Catholic schools but it was clear the provisions of the 1920 act had been flouted. The 1930 Education Act allowed two school systems to operate, the Catholic one only partly funded from local and central government sources, and the fully funded one attended almost exclusively by Protestants because 'simple Bible instruction' was in effect mandatory. The reading of any version of the Bible without denominational comment was unacceptable to Catholics, and Dr Mageean explained further:

> We cannot transfer our schools. We cannot accept simple Bible teaching. I wish to emphasize this point. Simple Bible teaching is based on the fundamental principle of Protestantism, the interpretation of sacred Scriptures by private judgement.[115]

The Westminster government was deeply unhappy and when the bill was in draft, Charlemont and his senior officials were summoned to the Home Office in London. There the permanent secretary, Sir John Anderson, considered that obligatory simple Bible teaching 'would certainly be regarded by Roman Catholics as unacceptable and constituting a preference in violation of Section 5'.[116] Once again, however, Westminster could not face withholding assent and it was left to a

Northern Ireland attorney-general, John MacDermott, to declare in 1945 that the 1930 legislation broke the terms of the 1920 Government of Ireland Act. Had Nationalist politicians and the Catholic Church complained to London the matter almost certainly would have been referred to the judicial committee of the privy council. In fact, the Catholic hierarchy felt that it had done well in the circumstances, retaining complete control over Catholic schools. Bishops could have chosen to opt for 'four-and-two' status, as some Protestant schools had done, but this would have meant sharing management with Catholic laity, which they were not then prepared to do. The result of this insistence on total clerical control was that a generation of Catholic children suffered from inadequate and outmoded facilities by comparison with their Protestant peers. But even if Catholic schools had accepted 'four-and-two' management, as did some Christian Brothers schools, they still would have been disadvantaged. There is no doubt that Westminster had allowed the Unionist government with its unassailable majority to discriminate against Catholics in education provision.

'NOT AN INCH': THE BOUNDARY COMMISSION, 1924-5

In October 1922 Cosgrave appointed Kevin O'Shiel, a Co. Tyrone lawyer, to gather evidence and seek out witnesses to go before the Boundary Commission. O'Shiel set up the North-East Boundary Bureau and compiled a handbook, impressively illustrated with maps, bar charts and statistical data. The Irish Civil War was still raging, however, and Cosgrave was in no position to press for the immediate implementation of Article XII of the treaty. Besides, the Conservative government had no desire to raise the issue – 'a very dangerous topic', as Bonar Law described it to Thomas Jones, who recommended 'that we ought to play for its indefinite postponement'.[117] Then the formation of the first Labour government of 22 January 1924 raised the spectre of Dublin rule described by Craig's brother Charles in 1920, particularly when Ramsay MacDonald summoned a conference on the Boundary Commission on 1 February. At the same time Cosgrave was impelled to action by a mutiny of senior army officers, partly caused by discontent over the fruits of the treaty. On 10 March 1924, Jones recorded in his diary:

> Having been weak in handling the mutiny, the Free State Government are determined to show themselves strong on the Boundary issue, and have sent a stiff letter to us asking that the Commission shall be set up forthwith.[118]

Jones, indeed, was surprised Cosgrave had not taken the matter to the League of Nations.

Having temporised as long as he could, Craig flatly refused to appoint a commissioner when pressed on 10 May. Could Britain appoint a commissioner for Northern Ireland? After months of deliberation the judicial committee of the privy council said it could not. Two government ministers, J.H. Thomas and Arthur Henderson, rushed across to Dublin and promised an amending bill, duly passed just before the Labour government's fall in October 1924. Justice Richard Feetham of the South African Supreme Court had already agreed to become Westminster's representative and chairman, and now MacDonald appointed J.R. Fisher, a Unionist and former editor of the *Northern Whig*, to represent Northern Ireland.

Spender warned Britain of the likelihood of 'a rising of the Protestant workmen with the object of evicting Roman Catholics'; Bates drafted a memorandum listing the forces at the Northern Ireland government's disposal should it be necessary to confront either the British Army or Free State troops; full test mobilisations of B and C Specials were held in the counties of Fermanagh, Tyrone and Armagh; and Craig's cabinet agreed to order 156 Vickers and Lewis machine guns and 14 million rounds of ammunition – enough for 'a small war', Assistant Undersecretary Sir Ernest Clark observed in alarm. Captain Herbert Dixon, the chief whip organised rallies in border counties; Robert McBride MP said British bayonets would be required to transfer any part of Co. Down; J.F. Gordon MP, calling on Specials to resist any transfer, said he had raised three UVF battalions in Liverpool to oppose the commission; and Andrews told a Black Preceptory branch of the Orange Order in Newry that the Government would not give up the town, even if the commission recommended it.[119] All this bluster could not prevent the first meeting of the commission and Craig did not attempt to obstruct it – after all, MacDonald had assured him in September that only 'moderate adjustments' were intended; Stanley Baldwin, the new prime minister, was opposed to major change and observed about southern nationalists that it was 'difficult to forgive assassination and to forget their behaviour in the war'; and at Westminster an amendment seeking only minor rectification, though defeated, had the support of a signatory of the treaty, Sir Laming Worthington-Evans.[120] The Free State government appointed Eoin MacNeill, now minister for education, as their commissioner and he, Fisher and Feetham had their first meeting on 6 November 1924. There all three commissioners decided on strict secrecy.

In Newry, Patrick Shea remembered, 'the Boundary Commission was an unending topic of conversation . . . if the declared intention of adjusting the Border "in accordance with the wishes of the inhabitants" meant anything, Newry's future in the Free State was assured'.[121] One of the town's leading Unionists exchanged his Newry house for one in Warrenpoint owned by a republican businessman so that each man could live in his preferred state. Shea joined people lining Newry's streets to watch the boundary commissioners and their assistants drive slowly through in a fleet of large cars. At the end of 1924 the commissioners spent a fortnight touring the border and on one occasion, after getting completely lost on a minor road, they were put back on course by an RUC patrol.

Much of 1925 was spent in receiving deputations and legal submissions. The wording of Article XII was extraordinarily vague: it set the commission the task of determining, 'in accordance with the wishes of the inhabitants, so far as may be compatible with economic and geographic conditions, the boundaries between Northern Ireland and the rest of Ireland'.[122] Upright and conscientious, Feetham nevertheless interpreted this article in a narrow, legalistic way and placed economic and geographic conditions well to the fore. He accepted, for example, the Unionist argument that the Mournes should stay in Northern Ireland since that area supplied Belfast's water and that Newry was within that city's commercial orbit. MacNeill was at a disadvantage being the only commissioner without legal training and expected to continue his duties as a government minister while Feetham and Fisher were paid to devote themselves full time. Nevertheless, MacNeill was remarkably inept in representing his government: he failed to press for the appointment of O'Shiel to the secretariat, while Feetham brought in experienced Britons, including one who had served on the Upper Silesian commission; and he indicated early on that even if he disagreed with his two colleagues he would sign the report in the interest of a peaceful settlement.[123] This last concession would give Fisher and Feetham a free hand to work on a mere rectification of the frontier.

Seeking 'a pronouncement by the people while the Commission is sitting in their midst', Craig called an election in April 1925. 'He will be a courageous man,' he said, 'who will attempt to divide the loyalist party when that very stern and grim problem is facing the people.'[124] Devlin announced his decision 'to enter the Northern parliament and apply myself to the task of fighting for those National and democratic interests to which I have given a lifelong devotion . . . Permanent abstention means permanent disfranchisement.'[125] The Catholic Church had urged this step and eight of the eleven Nationalist candidates were proposed by priests. Catholic voters clearly approved, returning ten Nationalists and only two abstaining Sinn Féiners. Craig did not get the overwhelming mandate from Protestants he had hoped for, particularly in constituencies not likely to be affected by the Boundary Commission: two Independent Unionists topped the poll in North and South Belfast; three Labour candidates, all Protestants, were returned for East, North and West Belfast; and an Unbought Tenants' Association candidate was elected in Co. Antrim. The only comfort for the prime minister was that the Unionist vote was up in the constituencies touching the border. There loyalists had heeded Craig's election cry, 'Not an inch' – would the Boundary Commission do the same?

Having sifted through more than a hundred written submissions, the commission toured the border areas again. At the hearings Nationalists were getting hints that their expectations might not be realised: at Newry Feetham observed that 'Carlingford Lough might be regarded as a good natural boundary'; and at Derry the local Nationalist MP was asked, the minutes record, 'whether he did not think that the transference of Derry to the Free State would be a serious surgical operation, a question which the witnesses seemed to take as indicating a reluctance to make any changes'.[126] As the commission continued its work, right-wing imperialists in the Conservative government became jittery and pressed for talks with Craig. 'The Report ought to be applied automatically, whatever it is', Jones advised. ' . . . Once you begin to discuss, and negotiate and adjust you are in the Irish bog again.'[127] Baldwin agreed and promised to implement the full report, the first draft of which was completed on 5 November 1925.

On 7 November the *Morning Post* published a 'forecast' of the Boundary Commission's report with a map which was a remarkably accurate indication of the forthcoming award.[128] How had this 'unfortunate and unaccountable . . . premature and unauthorised publication,' as Baldwin described it to the South African premier, occurred?[129] The answer is that Fisher had broken his pledge of secrecy: in June he informed the wife of D.D. Reid, the Ulster Unionist leader at Westminster, that 'it will now be a matter of border townlands for the most part', and on 18 October Fisher had written to Carson:

> I think there is no harm in letting you know confidentially that I am well satisfied with the result which will not shift a stone or tile of your enduring work for Ulster. It will remain a solid and close-knit unit with five counties intact and the sixth somewhat trimmed on the outer edge. It will control the gates to its own waters at Beleek and Newry and the Derry navigation to the open sea. No centre of even secondary importance goes over, and with Derry, Strabane, Enniskillen, Newtownbutler, Keady and Newry in safe keeping your handiwork will survive.[130]

The Free State was to gain part of south Armagh, a strip of south-west Fermanagh and the salient of Tyrone jutting into Donegal west of

Castlederg. Northern Ireland was to acquire part of the Laggan in east Donegal, Pettigo, and a small slice of Co. Monaghan. These recommendations would have reduced Northern Ireland's population by a mere 1.8 per cent, its area by 3.7 per cent, and the length of its frontier by fifty-one miles. Feetham had taken the view that Northern Ireland should remain 'the same provincial entity . . . capable of maintaining a Parliament and Government'.[131] His belief was that the Catholic majorities in Derry, Strabane, Newry and other border towns were not overwhelming enough to justify transfer – only Crossmaglen was so qualified.

The press leak caused an immediate crisis in Dublin. There was a tense debate in the Dáil on Thursday 19 November when Denis McCullough, now a deputy supporting the Government, questioned the right to take territory from the Free State, which was being asked to give up rich farmland and 'good grouse shooting' in east Donegal in return for 'mountain tracts with uneconomic holders, and they would simply swell the Old Age Pensions list'.[132] MacNeill resigned from the commission the same day and, after a confused explanation in the Dáil, from the Government as well. Fearing defeat in the Dáil, Cosgrave hastily arranged a meeting in London with Baldwin and Craig. There it was agreed to suppress the Boundary Commission report, to revoke the powers of the commission, to maintain the existing border, and to transfer the functions of the Council of Ireland to the Belfast and Dublin parliaments. To sweeten a very bitter pill, the Free State was released from its obligation under Article V of the treaty to contribute to the reduction of the United Kingdom's national debt – this, according to Churchill, was worth between £6.25 million and £8.25 million a year to the Dublin government. The newspapers were full of the Locarno Pact recently signed in Germany and perhaps it was in the prevailing spirit of the times that on 3 December 1925 the three governments declared that they were 'united in amity . . . and resolved to aid one another in a spirit of neighbourly comradeship'.[133]

When Craig returned to Belfast on 5 December he was given an enthusiastic reception and shipyard workers gave him a gold mounted portion of a foot rule – the inch he had not surrendered. A few days later the Northern Ireland parliament presented him with a silver cup, on which members' signatures were engraved in facsimile, and with the words 'Not an inch' inscribed on the plinth. Cosgrave was glad to have escaped from 'this barren question of the Boundary' and he frankly admitted the 'half-truth' of the 'taunt of having sold the Roman Catholics in Northern Ireland'.[134] He sought no guarantees or financial support for northern Catholics and did not take up Baldwin's offer to appoint Joseph Devlin as liaison agent on their behalf.

The suppression of the Boundary Commission forced the Catholic minority to accept, whether they liked it or not, that they were citizens of Northern Ireland. Joseph Devlin, representing West Belfast, and Thomas McAllister, MP for Co. Antrim, entered the Commons: three more Nationalists took their seats in 1926; and by 1928 there were ten Nationalists, three Labour MPs and a couple of Independents sitting on the opposition benches. Meanwhile de Valera led Fianna Fáil, the newly formed anti-treaty party, into the Dáil. North and south, the spirit of the Locarno and Kellogg pacts seemed to settle on Ireland as parliamentary debates took on an air of reality they had not possessed before, and on both sides of the border abstentionist Sinn Féin found itself cold-shouldered by electorates almost wholly won back to constitutional politics. Reconciliation, however, was as fragile in the North as it was on the European mainland. The Nationalists refused to become an official opposition, Cahir Healy telling the Commons:

> We will only intervene when we feel that we can expose injustice. But we reserve the right to come in or stay outside as and when our people may decide.[135]

They were constantly aware that if they were too conciliatory they could easily forfeit their support. Unionists for their part remained deeply distrustful of representatives, no matter how conservative and constitutional they might be, whose ultimate aim was to bring about the dissolution of Northern Ireland. The Unionist MP William Grant told the Northern Ireland Commons in 1927 that he was one of those

> who never cared whether there was any Opposition in the House or not. I am glad to see them here, but if they went out of the House to-day I would have no regrets. I would not care if they never came back again.[136]

The prime minister was about to show that he, too, did not seem to care if the Nationalists never came back.

Craig had laid his plans to get rid of proportional representation in parliamentary elections as early as 1924 but he stayed his hand while the Boundary Commission was at work. The 1925 election, which reduced the Unionist vote and created a small Labour opposition, reinforced the prime minister's determination. He sought a clear-cut division between loyalism and nationalism so that in every election 'the real question' would be 'whether we are going to remain part and parcel of Great Britain and the Empire or whether on the other hand we are going to submerge ourselves in a Dublin Parliament'.[137] Ulster unionism was by no means as monolithic as it seemed to outsiders. The three Labour MPs were all Protestants, and Local Optionists – seeking the prohibition of alcohol sales – tormented Craig like gadflies and seemed to be gaining widespread support in rural areas. The bill to abolish proportional representation was eventually presented in February 1929, just three months before the next election because, the chief whip explained, 'of course the Nationalist and Labour people will bitterly oppose it'.[138]

They did. Sam Kyle, leader of the Northern Ireland Labour Party, declared that the bill was 'deliberately designed to favour the Unionist Party in that it will make it the more difficult for minorities to secure representation'. Devlin told Craig that 'you are going to perpetuate the old party divisions of Protestant and Catholic, Orange and Green', and described the bill as 'a mean, contemptible and callous attempt' to rob the minority of safeguards in the 1920 act.[139] Undeterred, the Government pressed ahead and, after a swift redrawing of electoral boundaries, increased its representation to thirty-eight in the general election. The nationalists were reduced by one seat to eleven; Labour by two seats to one; and two Independent Unionists were also returned. Manipulation of constituency boundaries was not so blatant as in the reorganisation of local government in 1922–3, but the abolition of proportional representation largely produced the result Craig desired. More clearly than before the Northern Ireland Commons was divided into Orange and Green, and an effective wedge had been driven between Labour and Nationalists in Belfast constituencies where previously they had co-operated. The distribution of Protestants and Catholics in the region made the outcome of elections in single-seat constituencies highly predictable. There had been only eight uncontested seats in 1925 but by 1933 there were thirty-three – 70 per cent. Westminster was even less concerned to intervene in 1929 than it had been in 1922.

Though Labour suffered most, the Nationalists expressed themselves most bitterly. Devlin said in the northern Commons in March 1932:

> You had opponents willing to co-operate. We did not seek office. We sought service. We were willing to help. But you rejected all friendly offers ... You went on on the old political lines, fostering hatreds, keeping one third of the population as if they were pariahs in the community.[140]

Two months later Devlin led all of the Nationalists out of the chamber and for the rest of the decade they pursued a policy, if it can be called that, of intermittent and erratic abstentionism. When Devlin died in January 1934 loyalists stood in silent tribute, nevertheless, when Andrews moved a vote of condolence, saying: 'Ulster has lost one of her distinguished sons and a great Parliamentarian ... he was an

511

honourable opponent who loved his country and the welfare of its inhabitants.' 'I never consented to be the leader of a Catholic Party and I never will consent,' Devlin had said and yet that was just what he had been. He had much in common with the Unionists he opposed: like them he fostered an organisation, the Ancient Order of Hibernians, which helped to keep sectarian passion alive; like them he worked closely with religious leaders; and like them he was hostile to Labour organisations he could not lead. The Nationalist newspaper, the *Irish News*, was as narrowly partisan as the three Unionist dailies; in his novel, *The Emperor of Ice-Cream*, Brian Moore refers to characteristic items to be found there:

> A Jewish name discovered in an account of a financial transaction, a Franco victory over the godless Reds, a hint of British perfidy in international affairs, an Irish triumph on the sports field, an evidence of Protestant bigotry, a discovery of Ulster governmental corruption.[141]

T.J. Campbell, a former editor of the *Irish News*, succeeded Devlin but entirely lacked his predecessor's abilities. Even when the Nationalists were prepared to co-operate as a constitutional opposition, they proved to be ill-informed, uncoordinated and ineffective. None the less, the long-term consequences of the Unionists' reluctance to foster constructive opposition are still being felt to this day.

Traditional sectarian divisions made it extremely difficult to create an effective Labour opposition. The Irish Labour Party had avoided election contests until the national question was settled in 1922 and Independent Labour candidates in Belfast failed to win a single seat. It was not until 1924 that the Northern Ireland Labour Party was formed and Craig was severely shaken by the victory of all three of its candidates the following year. The abolition of proportional representation was a severe blow, and Craig was far more skilful than Cosgrave, his southern counterpart, at wooing working-class voters. The 'step-by-step' policy meant that the Unionists – by keeping pace with British social legislation – constantly stole the Northern Ireland Labour Party's clothes; the Ulster Unionist Labour Association, formed by Carson in 1918, gave the illusion of working-class participation and put up working-class candidates; and Craig adroitly exploited the Northern Ireland Labour Party's refusal to decide where it stood on the constitutional issue. Labour could only make headway in Belfast, for Northern Ireland – like the rest of Ulster and, indeed, all of Ireland – was a profoundly conservative region, where radicalism had been siphoned off by decades of emigration. Labour MPs, joined occasionally by Independent Unionists, had to contend with an overwhelming distrust of state intervention and of state spending – unless the bills were paid out of pockets on the other side of the Irish Sea.

Craig enjoyed majorities more secure than those to be found in any other democratic state in Europe. He was able, therefore, to rule in a presidential style which suited his cheerful and friendly disposition. Above all, he liked to make himself accessible to his own supporters, which ensured that, in a region with such a small population, he was often dealing with questions of a very petty nature indeed. He liked to tour the counties receiving deputations, listening to demands and appeals, and handing out promises of help. In 1927, for example, Craig met sixty-five deputations, spoke to twenty individuals, and made so many promises of financial aid (some of them overturning cabinet decisions) that both Pollock and the inappropriately named Spender made frantic but impotent protests. He defended a Stewartstown potato inspector against complaints made by local farmers and, at Cookstown, he intervened to ensure the repair of a road. That year the *Mid-Ulster Mail* expressed its gratitude to the prime minister, created 1st Viscount Craigavon just a few weeks before:

> He came as the Premier, prepared to hear anything that the people had to say, and to judge on the spot. It is particularly gratifying to the ratepayers of the Rural and Urban districts to know that when his attention had been called to the injustice which existed in regard to the upkeep of the road from Orritor quarry to Cookstown railway station . . . his Lordship . . . swept the red tape aside in a regal fashion and uttered his fiat – let it be done from this very day.[142]

The fact that 'the people' were invariably Protestant, together with the prime minister's willingness to receive deputation after deputation complaining about the growing influence of 'disloyalist elements', only helped to strengthen the alienation of the Catholic minority.

Nationalists ignored the celebrations in November 1932 when the Prince of Wales opened the Northern Ireland parliament's permanent home at Stormont in east Belfast. According to St John Ervine, the playwright and Craigavon's biographer, the prince performed the ceremony 'with an unsmiling face and glum and sulky looks', though he enjoyed playing a Lambeg drum in Hillsborough later in the day.[143] This fine neo-classical structure in a magnificent setting was, in Pollock's words, 'the outward and visible proof of the permanence of our institutions; that for all time we are bound indissolubly to the British crown'.[144] This very permanence left northern Catholics feeling more abandoned than ever, particularly when the Special Powers Act, directed almost exclusively against the minority, was made permanent in the following year.

The quality of debate at Stormont never even began to match the grand surroundings: MPs were often embarrassingly inarticulate, badly informed, and concerned only with petty local matters. Even Devlin, considered by Lord Haldane to have been the finest orator of his day at Westminster, was long past his best. Unionist MPs only rarely put forward private member's bills and only very few of those were of regional concern. Much parliamentary time was spent duplicating legislation initiated at Westminster and periods of recess were extraordinarily long. Craig himself seemed largely concerned to preserve the status quo and the impression of uncoordinated drift became more evident in the 1930s. In part this was due to his advancing years but much must have arisen from frustration at the limitations imposed by the 1920 act.

'A FORM OF HOME RULE THE DEVIL HIMSELF COULD NEVER HAVE IMAGINED'

The Reverend James B. Armour observed that Ulster Unionists had no choice but to accept devolution 'because they had yelled about "No Home Rule" for a generation and then they were compelled to take a form of Home Rule that the Devil himself could never have imagined'.[145] It was indeed an irony that the byzantine constitutional relationship between Belfast and London had largely been of Gladstone's devising. Outsiders who pointed to the special powers and forces adopted by the Northern Ireland cabinet generally were not aware how severely the 1920 act circumscribed its authority and freedom of action.

Northern Ireland's executive and legislature had been given responsibility but little real power, at least in theory. Only Westminster had the right to amend the local constitution and Section 75 of the act stated that 'the supreme authority of the Parliament of the United Kingdom shall remain unaffected and undiminished over all persons, matters, and things' in Northern Ireland.[146] Because they were of imperial concern, certain legislative powers, described as 'excepted services', were retained by Westminster: these included the army and navy, trade agreements, the currency, and the making of war and peace. 'Reserved services' – including most taxation, the postal services and the supreme court of Northern Ireland – were to be kept by Westminster until the whole of Ireland had a single parliament. In addition, all laws passed in the mother parliament applied to Northern Ireland unless the region was specifically excluded.

If in practice Westminster did not exert its full authority until direct rule in 1972, during the interwar years the regional government discovered the financial provisions of the 1920 act acutely constraining. Not only did the imperial government deduct from reserved taxation the cost of reserved services but it also required Northern Ireland to make an 'imperial contribution' towards the cost of the armed forces and other excepted services. In theory, but often not in practice, the devolved government controlled most of its expenditure, but it had charge over less than 20 per cent of Northern Ireland's revenues. Customs dues, income tax, surtax, taxes on capital and profits, and most excise duties were imposed and collected at uniform rates throughout the United Kingdom and thus the regional government could not adjust them to meet its own needs. To make matters more difficult, local government spending was relatively insignificant for historic reasons. In the financial year 1927–8 rates in Britain covered 42 per cent of total public 'domestic' expenditure but the rates in Northern Ireland shouldered only 19 per cent of the burden. In Victorian and Edwardian Ireland the cost of the police and education services had been centrally financed and this practice was only marginally altered in Northern Ireland. Teachers' salaries were paid by the Ministry of Education and not by local authorities as in Britain. In 1930–1 the net cost of education in the region was over £2 million but local councils contributed only £92,000. In the same financial year, Belfast gave £25,000 and Derry £120 towards £1,079,000 needed to pay for policing, while other local councils provided nothing at all. Such a deeply conservative province as Ulster, whether the territory fell within Northern Ireland or the Free State, was uniformly hostile to high rates – here there were no thrusting high-spending councils eager to eradicate past neglect.[147]

The Better Government of Ireland Act was a bizarre amalgam of untried fillets cut from the three previous Home Rule Bills and desperate constitutional expedients designed to extricate Lloyd George's government from its Irish quagmire. Yet the United Kingdom's first experiment in devolution might well have worked more successfully had not the financial provisions been drafted during the high point of an uninterrupted ten-year economic boom. Then it seemed that with a buoyant economy, the new regional government would have no difficulty paying its way. When Northern Ireland came to birth, however, Ulster was assailed by an unremitting depression lasting two decades.

'DOZENS OF MEN AWAITING A NOD OR A SIGNAL'

The deep scars left by the Troubles might have healed in time had Northern Ireland enjoyed a long period of prosperity after 1922. The boom years, however, did not return: nearly 23 per cent were unemployed in 1922 and for the rest of the decade on average around one fifth of all insured workers had no jobs. The slump developed into a protracted depression as the region's traditional staple industries continued to contract. Here, in the most economically disadvantaged part of the United Kingdom, the Depression began early. Hugh Finnegan, a cattle dealer and butcher, recalled taking his horse and dray to collect bags of feed at the Belfast docks:

> In the days of the great depression of the 1920s . . . I used to go down Pilot Street, a long narrow street to dockland, and lolling against the walls were dozens of men awaiting a nod or a signal to come and assist. They would load the fourteen bags on my cart and when the job was completed they received the princely sum of one shilling – there was no quibbling, only competition for who would get the call.[148]

The region's economic difficulties had little to do with political turmoil, the creation of a new land frontier, or the inaction of the government in Belfast. The real problem was that the First World War had brought about traumatic changes in world trading conditions: in these years Northern Ireland was producing and attempting to sell goods of which there was a surplus abroad. The six-county region was overwhelmingly dependent on linen, shipbuilding, and agriculture, and all three industries faced severe hardship after the collapse of the postwar boom in the middle of 1920. Northern Ireland was by no means alone: Lancashire, the Tyne, and Clydeside suffered industrial decline for much the same reasons and in a similar way to Belfast and its immediate hinterland; and the steep drop in prices hit Ulster farms and those across the Irish Sea equally hard.

LINEN'S DIFFICULTIES

As Britain prepared to equip a hundred divisions in 1914, the Government placed orders with Clark's of Upperlands for a million yards of hollands and the firm's entire stock of heavy linen for tents and kitbags. In these days before synthetics, Wallace Clark observed, linen was the fighting fibre:

> Its strength, resistance to rot and abrasion, low stretch combined with the ability of individual fibres to swell and create a watertight surface made it the best fabric for almost every use – linen canvas for ships' awnings and sails, tents, lorry covers, water bags, hoses, slings and chutes for ammunition handling, protective clothing; lighter fabrics for shirts, linings and interlinings for uniforms, outer fabrics for tropical wear where linen's absorbency gave maximum wearer comfort; linen gauze for surgical bandages where it would sterilise better than any other fibre.[149]

But was linen to be the fibre for peacetime? After a brief nervous slump, prices began to pick up in March 1919 and over the next year rose by 300 per cent to, for example, £3 12s.6d. per bundle of standard tow weft – a level not surpassed until 1974; then prices began to tumble: falling to

£2 8s.0d. in September 1920; 19s.0d. in 1921; and 13s.0d. by 1924. A strong recovery in 1925 was then killed in April when Churchill returned the pound sterling to the gold standard, overvaluing the currency by around 10 per cent. Linen exports were severely overpriced abroad, unemployment in the industry rose to 32 per cent, and piece goods bringing in £100 in 1913 could fetch only £40 by 1927. In short, this industry was not merely adjusting after overexpansion during the war: through a confused pattern of fluctuations, a steady and permanent decline could be detected, with baleful consequences for a great many people in Northern Ireland.

Contemporaries were too ready to assume that the linen industry's troubles were brought on by inefficiency, cut-throat competition, poor marketing, and – as the report of a government inquiry put it in 1928 – 'the present disjointed organisation of the industry'.[150] Modern investigation seems to indicate high levels of efficiency, ready adaptability, no severe shortage of capital, a greater degree of integration than was apparent, and an ability to fend off international competition most effectively.[151] Ulster did not lose its share of the world market. The real problem was that across the world the demand for linen was suffering inexorable decline. In part this was due to a narrowing of the gaps between classes: there were fewer house maids to undertake the laborious tasks of laundering and ironing a material so liable to crease and absorb dirt. Fashion changes were more rapid now than before the war and the argument that linen would last a lifetime held no appeal for the flapper generation. Skirts and dresses were shorter in any case, and layers of linen underwear were no longer needed in such quantity. Even the upper classes preferred to entertain in restaurants – where polished wood surfaces became an acceptable alternative to linen tablecloths – rather than employ cooks for dinner parties at home. Rayon and other synthetic fibres did not pose a serious threat until after the Second World War but the cotton challenge became ever more formidable. Cotton was grown in economically depressed tropical regions, where labour was cheap; its harvesting and processing was much more easily mechanised than those of flax; and the introduction of the ring spindle further reduced production costs.

In a census of production, taken in 1924, 81,198, or 51.77 per cent, of Northern Ireland's total labour force was employed making linen. It retained its central position in the North's economy but such a labour-intensive industry could only survive by keeping wages down to a wretchedly low level. Wages were far higher in shipbuilding and engineering but workers in these industries too now faced an uncertain future.

Lord Pirrie exuded confidence when he addressed a meeting at Harland and Wolff on 12 February 1924. In spite of his admission the previous year that there was 'a grave shortage of work', twenty-two vessels had left the ways at Queen's Island and he expressed the feeling, the minutes record, 'that in two or three months' time we shall be in a better position as regards work'. Soon after, he left to investigate holiday cruise facilities in Latin America but died in Panama on 7 June at the age of seventy-eight. On hearing the news, Hugh Pollock, the finance minister, declared:

> A great Ulsterman has fallen today! . . . Lord Pirrie was not only a mighty architect, whose vast designs embraced the globe; he was the great master builder who carried these designs into execution, a veritable Napoleon of industry in the greatness and splendour of the schemes which had even then taken form in his mind.[152]

Pirrie's successor was Sir Owen Cosby Philipps, chairman of the Royal Mail Group and recently created Baron Kylsant of Carmarthen. When he looked at the firm's books, Kylsant was appalled. No one knew anything of the prospective contracts Pirrie had spoken of the previous February; work in progress that year had been financed by discounting bills valued at more than £12 million; overdrafts, mostly with the Midland Bank, totalled £3 million; interest payments on loans had been deferred; and every vessel under construction was being built at a loss. The company was on the edge of bankruptcy and all Kylsant's artistry was required to hide the truth from the business world.

Once the postwar boom had collapsed in 1920, Belfast shipbuilders found their commercial scene drastically altered. Replacement demand was reduced now that the world stock of vessels was newer than before the war. The United States, Japan, the Netherlands, Sweden and other states subsidised and protected firms which had sprung up during the conflict rather than let them go under during a time of overcapacity. The demand for shipping across the globe, which had increased by 6 per cent each year between 1900 and 1914, dropped to 1.7 per cent per annum between 1919 and 1938. Still operating in a free-market economy, United Kingdom shipbuilding companies were all in difficulties as prices fell: for example, the market value of a 7,500-ton steamer drifted down from £230,000 in 1919 to £60,000 by 1939. Northern Ireland firms were particularly vulnerable as they sold their product almost exclusively in a shrinking market, the United Kingdom – Britain lost her commercial pre-eminence as her share of the world merchant fleet declined from 43 per cent in 1914 to 26 per cent in 1938. The North of

Ireland Shipbuilding and Engineering Company, the Swan and Hunter subsidiary in Derry which had prospered during the war, was forced to close its yard in 1924.[153] Before 1914 Workman Clark had on two occasions launched more tonnage in a year than any other shipbuilder in the world. Then in 1920 the firm was bought over by the Northumberland Shipping Company, which had borrowed £3 million at a high fixed interest to repay a bank loan. Not only was the company crippled by repayments but in 1927 it was successfully prosecuted for issuing a fraudulent prospectus in 1920. Though Workman Clark was financially revamped in 1928, in that year it launched only a 360-ton sludge vessel for Belfast Corporation.[154]

Harland and Wolff was dangerously exposed in this changed climate. Saddled with enormous debts – a consequence of Pirrie's reckless investments in plant never fully used and of his pricing policy – Kylsant found the Queen's Island production costs higher than elsewhere and the senior management sapped of initiative by years of dictatorial and secretive direction under their chairman. Kylsant hid the firm's financial plight from the public eye by methods which eventually earned him a year in prison for fraud in 1931. The survival of Harland and Wolff in these difficult years owed much to direct intervention by the Northern Ireland government. Westminster guaranteed loans to shipbuilding concerns under the Trade Facilities Act of 1921 and Harland and Wolff – with operations on the Clyde, at Southampton and on the Thames – benefited to some degree. This was not enough for Pirrie, who persuaded Pollock to put forward the Northern Ireland Loans Guarantee Bill, which became law in December 1922. Unlike the Westminster legislation, this act allowed the importation of cheaper foreign steel and remained in force after Churchill withdrew loan guarantees in Britain in 1927. Without the support of the Government in Belfast, Harland and Wolff might well have foundered before the end of the decade.

Harland and Wolff gave every public appearance of recovery in the late 1920s. The company's reputation for design and technical excellence remained as high as ever and, in collaboration with the Danish firm of Burmeister and Wain, Queen's Island was in the forefront of marine diesel engine development. Harland and Wolff completed forty-nine vessels in 1927 – the sixth year running the company headed the list of output from United Kingdom firms. Pride of place went to the White Star *Laurentic*, described as follows by the *Shipbuilding and Shipping Record*:

The amenities provided for passengers are, probably, unexcelled by any steamer afloat . . . Thus from the Louis Seize dining saloon, which seats 30 passengers, one may pass either to the lounge, a reproduction of Italian

Renaissance work – and here is a parquet floor for dancing – or to the Empire drawing room, or the oak panelled smoking room designed on Jacobean lines.[155]

The following year the Royal Mail Group ordered three large liners for the Union-Castle line, and the Pacific Steam Navigation Company's contract for the 17,700-ton *Reina del Pacifico* reaffirmed Belfast's reputation for high-quality passenger liners. In 1929, despite an ever-worsening financial position, Harland and Wolff launched both the largest tonnage in the world and the biggest ship, the *Britannic*. That same year, however, the Wall Street Crash delivered the *coup de grâce* to the Roaring Twenties and shipbuilding in Belfast was soon facing the most severe crisis in its history.

AGRICULTURE AND CROSS-BORDER TRADE

Depressed industrial wages were mitigated to some degree by falling food prices but this was no comfort to Northern Ireland's farmers. During the war, producers across the world had increased their output and when peace returned Ulster farmers faced intense competition in the British market, still completely open.

Northern farms were exceptionally small: only 4.4 per cent in the region exceeded one hundred acres, compared with 8.8 per cent in the Irish Free State and 20.9 per cent in England and Wales; and a census of 1937 showed that 37.9 per cent of holdings were below fifteen acres and 82.7 below fifty acres. The picturesque pattern of rectangular fields surrounded by hedges – known in Ulster as ditches – indicated the prevalence of mixed farming which not only spread income over the year but also gave some protection against violent market fluctuations. Legislation promoted at Westminster in 1925 completed land purchase and ensured that almost all the region's 105,215 holdings were owner-occupied. Only a very few farms could afford to employ an agricultural labourer and a decent living could only be got by setting all members of the family to work for long hours. Flax was no longer a profitable cash crop and, together with apple-growing in Co. Armagh, accounted for only 2 per cent of Northern Ireland's acreage.

Agriculture was the largest single industry, engaging 26 per cent of the workforce compared with 6.2 per cent in the United Kingdom as a whole. Farmers formed such a powerful lobby that Tommy Henderson, the colourful Independent Unionist MP for Shankill, once declared in frustration:

If a farmer wanted someone to blow his nose some Hon. Member would get up and raise the question in this House, and a man would be appointed not only to blow the farmer's nose but to wipe it for him.[156]

520

In contrast with Westminster's *laissez-faire* approach, the Northern Ireland government – within the constraints of the Government of Ireland Act – was effectively interventionist. The act precluded tariff protection and export subsidy and instead the Ministry of Agriculture set out to improve the quality of farm produce for the British market. The 1922 Livestock Breeding Act made the licensing of bulls compulsory to eliminate inferior sires, a typical specimen being described by Archdale as being 'more like a goat than a bull'.[157] Ulster eggs had commanded the top price across the Irish Sea in 1921, but two years later they had slipped to fourth place, dropped sharply in price and more than twenty-five million fewer were being sold there. The 1924 Eggs Marketing Act did much to reverse this trend by making sure that only clean, graded and fresh eggs were exported.

Farmers were most immediately affected by the creation of the border, which ran across the fields of so many and even down the middle of some of their houses. Yet the smallholders did not allow themselves to be discommoded for long by the new frontier and the customs posts, which became operational in April 1923. The governments north and south recognised the impossibility of rigid control: dealers were restricted to approved roads during certain hours but farmers and cattle drovers could use any road at any time. Cosgrave's governments did not attempt to create the siege economy advocated by Sinn Féin mainly because they did not see how smuggling could be controlled.

It was observed at the time and often subsequently that the land boundary dislocated Ulster's economy and, in particular, damaged the prospects of both Newry and Derry. During the 1920s, at least, there was little evidence of this and the apparent fall in North–South trade may largely be accounted for by faulty record-keeping. Real harm had been done before this by the Belfast Boycott, which drastically reduced the business of northern banks in the South, lost Belfast about £5 million worth of sales in 1921, and took most northern commercial travellers off southern roads. Michael Gallaher admitted in 1923 that his firm's trade in the Irish Free State 'had never recovered from the Boycott' and the imposition of a tobacco tariff did not affect Belfast's tobacco exports for there was no more trade in the South left to be lost.[158] Derry's trade with its Co. Donegal hinterland was hardly affected at all – the city's exports as a percentage of all-Ireland exports actually rose from 3.31 in 1924 to 3.98 in 1931, and while the value of imports declined slightly, the quantity increased over the same period. Newry's exports to the Irish Free State did fall considerably but this was not brought about by partition: coal and grain were not affected by duties and the real problem was that the ship canal could not be used by large vessels.

The most irksome Free State impost was the payment of sixpence on every item, other than 'household supplies' and 'personal effects', specified in the customs manifest. This was not onerous except for small traders and individuals but, together with a duty on imported apparel imposed by the Dublin government, it did encourage smuggling. In particular, southerners crossed into Northern Ireland wearing old clothes and returned wearing what they had bought there. In 1930 the *Irish Times* surveyed the border and a Derry shopkeeper told its reporter that 'on some days of the week, particularly after market day, the principal refuse which the Corporation carts collect consists of the worn out boots and shoes of Donegal'.[159] 'All the women entering Derry from this district go in as lean kine and return resembling fatted calves', the *Irish Times* reporter observed in Co. Donegal,[160] and on the south Armagh border he was told that two crossing points were impossible to supervise: at Cullyhanna where the road switchbacked into Northern Ireland and then into the Free State; and at Jonesborough where the border ran through the middle of a shop.

Cross-border trade was far less significant than cross-channel and overseas commerce and this made Northern Ireland exceptionally vulnerable to worldwide cyclical fluctuations. The Ministry of Commerce was understandably excited therefore by a development commission's report that the region had coal deposits to the value of some £100 million. As Archdale explained in a memorandum:

> There is no doubt that the whole economic situation in Ulster will be changed, and from being a country necessarily importing all her raw material she will become self-contained in that respect, will be the home of many new industries, and will be in a position to give employment on a very large scale.[161]

Sir Samuel Kelly, the province's leading coal merchant and a noted UVF gun-runner, sank two circular shafts to the depth of 1,072 feet at Annagher, north-east of Coalisland, in 1923–4. Some of the seams were found to be thirteen feet thick and prospects seemed so good that at the cost of £200,000 the most modern equipment was installed, railway sidings were laid to the pit heads, and more than two hundred miners were brought over from Cumberland and Scotland. The Northern Ireland government gave grants and guaranteed loans but it was all in vain. Between July 1924 and December 1926 some thirty-six thousand tons of coal were raised but production costs were three times higher than in British coalfields and at £1 2s.11d. per ton the government subsidy was eleven times higher than the average subsidy in Britain.

Then the mining engineers met insuperable obstacles which forced the closure of the whole operation – inadequate preliminary surveys had failed to detect severe faulting, making commercial exploitation impossible.[162]

Having burned its fingers badly in this project, the Northern Ireland government – other than assisting the shipyards and the marketing of farm produce – was reluctant to be drawn into further economic intervention. In any case, its powers were limited under the Government of Ireland Act and, above all, its resources were stretched to the very limit in an attempt to keep in step with Westminster in making provision for the unemployed.

'CUT OFF GRANTS TO PARASITES': THE GUARDIANS AND POOR RELIEF

Belfast, which contained half the region's number of unemployed, saw very little of the world boom in the late 1920s – the Roaring Twenties were experienced elsewhere and had no meaning for its citizens. New industries, such as electrical engineering and motorcar manufacture, helped to offset the decline of staple export industries in Britain, particularly in the south-east. In Northern Ireland political turmoil and uncertainty may have discouraged them from coming to the region. Even in the mildest years of the Depression, between 1923 and 1930, unemployment averaged 19 per cent of the insured workforce. Craig was determined that citizens under his jurisdiction would enjoy the same protection as those in the rest of the United Kingdom. He told the Northern Ireland Commons in March 1922: 'It will never be said that the workers in our midst worked under conditions worse than those across the water.' Referring to Andrews, his minister of labour, he continued: 'Where employment and benefits are concerned it will be his duty to see, and he will see, that a man is treated as well on this side of the water as he is across the water.'[163] Andrews, indeed, was the most enthusiastic supporter of the step-by-step policy, but he, Craig and Bates encountered strong opposition from Pollock, Milne Barbour and Spender. Pollock was opposed to taxation to pay for benefits which would impose burdens on industry 'at a moment when foreign competition (of an unfair character) is rendering trade conditions so difficult'. He would have agreed with William Strachan, head of Workman Clark, who said in 1925:

Not until more factory gates are closed and no money is forthcoming with which to pay rates out of which sheltered men and dole lifters receive their demands, will authorities and men believe that there is a limit to what employers can stand.[164]

Craig's view prevailed, nevertheless, but so many were out of work that it proved financially impossible to keep abreast in other branches of the social services. In addition, the benefit rules were narrowly and rigidly applied. Patrick Shea, working for the Ministry of Labour, records that claimants could be disallowed the dole unless they proved they were genuinely seeking work, and this 'sent the unemployed walking the streets to call at offices, shops, factories, warehouses and building sites asking for notes certifying that they had applied for employment but that there were no vacancies'. He remembered interviewing a widow whose claim for benefit he had to reject:

> I felt I had handled a difficult situation rather well. She walked silently to the door, opened it and turning to the rows of silent men, now poring over their papers, she addressed the whole company. She spoke calmly and purposefully. 'During the war my husband made bombs. He spent four years making bombs. I wish to Jaysus I had one of them now.'[165]

As many were out of work for extended periods they lost their eligibility for unemployment benefit and were forced to turn to the Poor Law as the only official alternative to starvation. Some Boards of Guardians, notably in Newry, treated the long-term unemployed with a fair degree of generosity. The Belfast guardians, however, still applied the old workhouse test with rigour: applicants were carefully questioned by relieving officers; nothing would be given until savings had been exhausted; relief was in the form of groceries obtained by 'chits' from named shops; and the names of successful applicants were posted on gable walls. Quite apart from the public humiliation involved, such a system gave ample opportunity for excluding political opponents and rewarding supporters. The guardians' niggardly attitude towards the provision of outdoor relief provoked several demonstrations, including one on 19 January 1924 when four thousand unemployed held a meeting outside the board's headquarters in Glengall Street. Unrest mounted when the return to the gold standard delivered damaging blows to Belfast's economy.

On 14 June 1926 hungry unemployed men gathered on the Shankill Road. There were now thirty thousand out of work in Belfast and police drew their batons as Samuel Patterson, on behalf of the recently formed Unemployed Workers' Organisation, began to address the crowd:

> Comrades and unemployed, we read in the Scriptures that the earth is the Lord's and the fullness thereof . . . you were heroes when you were in the trenches. If you were still the same heroes, 300 of you could still go up to the workhouse, even though you have not the privilege of having a six-pounder behind you and take possession for a day . . . Here are the police

coming. They are always on the alert when revolution is spoken of. Run like hell![166]

Convicted of making a seditious speech, Patterson was sentenced to six months' imprisonment. The following day, led by bands, the unemployed marched from the city hall to the Union Workhouse on the Lisburn Road. Only Jack Beattie and William McMullen, both Labour MPs and members of the board, were allowed to enter. When they obstructed the guardians' meeting the MPs were seized by the police and thrown out onto the pavement.

For fear of alienating its supporters, the Government refused to put pressure on the Belfast guardians, though Andrews wrote in exasperation to Craig on 9 August 1928:

How they can call themselves the guardians of the poor I do not know as they approach the whole problem from one viewpoint alone, namely saving the ratepayers.[167]

Andrews made his protest after an unrewarding meeting with the guardians the day before. The minutes record the views of the chairman: 'Faced with such sloth, fecklessness and iniquity, the Guardians' duty was to discourage idleness and to create a spirit of independence since much of the money given to the poor was wasted.' His successor, Lily Coleman, became celebrated for her notorious remark, about outdoor-relief applicants, that there was 'no poverty under the blankets'.[168] Some two hundred charities gave what relief they could. These included the Shankill Road Mission and Toc H, but the most important was the St Vincent de Paul Society which spent over £12,000 a year and helped twelve times as many as received assistance from the guardians.

In 1928 Neville Chamberlain swept away Boards of Guardians and introduced cash payments as of right. The Northern Ireland government did not follow suit but it did put through a bill forcing the guardians to extend relief. Still the Belfast board resisted, being congratulated for its stand against this 'wastrel class' by a delegation of four Protestant clergymen who called on the guardians 'to cut off grants to parasites'.[169] This was in November 1929 when the whole industrialised world was reeling from the news of the Wall Street Crash.

'SUCH POVERTY AND NEED': THE ONSET OF THE DEPRESSION

'The fundamental business of the country,' said President Hoover, 'is on a sound and prosperous basis.' He was wrong: on 23 October 1929 security prices on the Wall Street stock market crumbled in a wave of frenzied selling and in less than a month the securities lost twenty-six

525

billion US dollars – more than 40 per cent – of their face value. 'We have now passed the worst,' Hoover announced in May 1930. America had not passed the worst, and by 1933 the total production of the economy had fallen by a third and nearly thirteen million were unemployed. The collapse of business confidence after the great speculative orgy of 1928–9 was followed by an unrelieved world depression lasting ten years. The shock waves surged east over the Atlantic as American finance houses recalled short-term loans; financial panic swept across Europe when Credit-Anstalt, Austria's principal bank, collapsed in June 1931; by August 1931 even the Bank of England was forced to close its doors; six million were out of work in Germany and three million in the United Kingdom in 1933; and in just four years the volume of international trade was barely one third of what it had been on the eve of the crash.

Heavily dependent on a limited range of exports, Northern Ireland was particularly vulnerable. As world trade contracted and foreign governments raised prohibitive tariffs to protect their ailing industries the numbers out of work rose alarmingly: by 1932 the official unemployment rate was 28 per cent, or seventy-two thousand registered out of work to which could be added another thirty thousand unregistered unemployed. Orders generated in earlier confident years delayed the impact of the slump on Queen's Island, which was busier in 1930 than at any time since the postwar boom. In that year work on the *Britannic* was completed and vessels launched or delivered totalled 130,537 tons, including *Warwick Castle*, *Winchester Castle*, *Highland Hope* and *Highland Princess*. Meanwhile, shipping rates sagged down catastrophically, the Union-Castle line cancelled its repair contracts with Harland and Wolff, and the company's accounts were so appalling for 1931 that they were not published until September 1932. Not a single ship was launched at Queen's Island between 10 December 1931 and 1 May 1934, and the number of employees in Belfast was reduced from 10,428 in 1930 to 1,554 in 1932. The world crisis was too much for Workman Clark: after the delivery of the tanker *Acavus*, ship number 536, in January 1935, the 'wee yard' had no more orders and was forced to close down.[170]

The impact of the Depression was most severe on states exporting food and raw materials, and these included some of the principal markets for linen – a luxury material that was all too easily replaced with cotton. As countries across the world took refuge behind high tariff barriers a near collapse of linen output followed in 1930. Smaller firms went to the wall and around one third of workers in the industry became unemployed. In its editorial on 2 October 1932 the *Belfast News-Letter* commented:

Winter approaches, the church clergy, heads of church missions, lay social workers and others state that at no time within their experience were there such poverty and need as exist at present. We are told that those on Outdoor Relief are on the verge of starvation; unless something is done and done quickly, conditions will become tragically worse.[171]

'BATONS WERE USELESS AND THE POLICE WERE COMPELLED
TO FIRE': THE OUTDOOR RELIEF RIOTS, 1932

On Friday 30 September 1932 Lord Craigavon rose to speak to a motion thanking the Belfast Corporation for the use of the city hall for meetings of the Northern Ireland Parliament, shortly to move to new premises at Stormont. This was too much for Jack Beattie: he seized the mace and shouted out that his motion had been unaccountably refused, a motion to bring 'to your notice the serious position of the unemployment in Northern Ireland'. Uproar followed as Beattie refused to withdraw and Tommy Henderson joined in, declaring: 'I condemn the way the Government have treated the unemployed; it is a disgrace to civilisation.' Ignoring the Speaker's pleas for order, Beattie again shouted out: 'I am going to put this out of action . . . The House indulges in hypocrisy while there are starving thousands outside.' He then wrested the mace from the sergeant-at-arms, threw it upon the floor, and walked out. Henderson roared out above the tumult, 'What about the 78,000 unemployed who are starving?'; to a cry from the Government benches of 'God Save the King', he responded 'God Save the People'; and then he withdrew, leaving only ex-District Inspector J.W. Nixon, Independent Unionist MP for Woodvale, on the opposition benches.[172]

The Presbyterian Church declared that 'the grants that are being made to those who are entirely dependent on outdoor relief are inadequate to provide the barest necessities of life'. According to the Reverend John N. Spence of the Methodist Church's Belfast Central Mission, the assistance being given was lower 'per head of population than any British city of comparable size'. For a time the prevailing distress in the city brought together working-class people of both religions in common protest. The lead was taken by men resurfacing the streets in task work, without which the unemployed could not qualify for relief payments. Over the summer the Unemployed Workers' Committee had organised an impressive series of public meetings and marches, causing Dawson Bates to give this warning to the cabinet:

There can be no doubt that unless some ameliorative measures are adopted there will be a large body of the population driven to desperation by poverty and hunger . . . the situation is rapidly approaching a crisis.[173]

The evening before Beattie's mace-throwing in the Commons, the outdoor-relief workers agreed to strike to force their demands for an increase in levels of assistance and for an end to task work and payments in kind. The strike began on Monday 3 October and that evening sixty thousand from all over Belfast – led by bands playing 'Yes, We Have No Bananas' – marched from Frederick Street Labour Exchange to a torch-lit rally at the Custom House. Next day seven thousand people accompanied a deputation to the Union Workhouse, where the guardians were meeting, and men lay down on the tramlines to stop traffic on the Lisburn Road. The following Wednesday a larger demonstration defied a police ban to accompany three hundred men who demanded admission to the workhouse. The RUC launched baton charges again and again, pushing the demonstrators back to Sandy Row, where they broke windows and looted shops. The guardians, meanwhile, refused to concede the strikers' demands.

The Government banned all marches when the Unemployed Workers' Committee planned a great protest demonstration for Tuesday 11 October. That day the police converged on the five assembly points, starting in east Belfast. Here, *The Times* correspondent watched 'dense crowds of strikers' congregating:

An attempt was made to form up in procession . . . At Templemore Avenue an attack was made by a crowd armed with stones on an isolated party of police. They drew their batons, but things were looking very ugly when police reinforcements in a caged car appeared on the scene.[174]

The *Belfast Telegraph* described what followed:

Templemore Avenue filled with men as if by magic from various side streets. They formed up in marching order, whilst at their lead rushed a man wearing a cap, shouting wildly, 'Fall in and follow me' . . . As the crowd continued to advance an order was given: 'Draw-Ready-Charge!' Men in the crowd went down like nine-pins, and the rest fled helter skelter.

There were further baton charges as Catholics from Seaforde Street attempted to rescue largely Protestant strikers being driven away in police 'cages'.

The worst violence was in the lower Falls, where the people put up barricades in an attempt to impede the police who used their firearms freely. According to the *Belfast Telegraph*:

For more than 300 yards there was an angry mob in action . . . Albert Street itself was the cockpit. The crowd fired the watchmen's huts, and the barricades also went up in flames . . . The screams of the women who were trapped in the streets and could not reach home were heard above the din. Police reinforcements were summoned. Constables wearing bandoliers filled with bullets and with rifles at the ready were speedily jumping out of caged cars. Other constables with revolvers in hand peered cautiously round the street corner as the hail of stones came out of Albert Street. Batons were useless and the police were compelled to fire.[175]

It was here that Samuel Baxter, a Protestant flower-seller, was shot dead; John Geegan, a Catholic from Smithfield, was mortally wounded in the stomach; and fourteen others suffered gunshot wounds. John Campbell, secretary of the Northern Ireland Labour Party and a guardian, thought it 'noteworthy that although the recent trouble was spread all over the city, only in a Roman Catholic area did the police use their guns'.[176] News of the fighting soon reached the Shankill where James Kelly had been sent by the *Irish Press* to cover the march from Tennent Street:

> I remember a woman with a shawl come running to the people I was talking to. She shouted: 'They're kicking the shite out of the peelers up the Falls. Are you going to let them down?' And that seemed to be the flashpoint for the riot . . . I took refuge in a shirt factory in Agnes Street and we saw some of the Protestant workers actually shooting at the police.[177]

Order was restored by nightfall when a curfew came into force. The last major eruption was in the York Street area the following evening when police armed with rifles opened fire on crowds of looters. John Kennan, of Leeson Street, was shot dead and the list of wounded filled newspaper columns. By now the thoroughly alarmed government was forcing the guardians to relent and on 14 October substantial increases in relief were announced. 'A glorious victory has been achieved,' one strike leader declared.[178] Next day the British trade-union leader, Tom Mann, led the funeral procession of Samuel Baxter in the most impressive demonstration of working-class solidarity Belfast has ever seen.

'EVERY POSSIBLE ECONOMY BECAME THE WAY OF LIFE'

The Depression was unrelenting – this was no temporary downswing in the economy. Between 1931 and 1939, 27 per cent of the insured workforce was unemployed. The lowest point was reached in July 1935 when 101,967 in the region were out of work, but Northern Ireland's relative position was at its worst in 1938: in February of that year 29.5 per cent of insured industrial workers were unemployed as compared with 23.8 per cent in Wales, the highest figure for any region in Britain.[179]

Dr James Deeny, in an investigation of the health and financial circumstances of 205 women in Lurgan in 1938, reported what would seem obvious today: that there was a very close relationship between unemployment, sickness and poverty. Those from families dependent on state

529

benefits, in his view, simply did not have enough income to pay for the bare necessities of life, though they 'were not the poorest in Lurgan by any means; in fact, they could be regarded as industrial aristocrats'.[180] The Presbyterian Church in Ireland Social Services Committee engaged A. Beacham of the Department of Economics at Queen's University Belfast to survey a working-class housing estate in the city in the winter of 1937–8. Beacham drew a poverty line based on guidelines set by the British Medical Association and Seebohm Rowntree, and he found that one third of 436 households investigated were below this line:

> At least 33 per cent of the families ... are in considerable economic distress, whilst a further 29 per cent are living under conditions which may be termed as 'barely sufficient' and probably intolerable for any length of time.[181]

He found one quarter of these households to be completely dependent on state benefits, and of these, 70 per cent were in extreme poverty. Another survey in Belfast carried out during the same winter by the Methodist Church's Temperance and Social Welfare Committee showed that: 76 per cent of 705 households investigated were below Rowntree's 1936 poverty line; 40 per cent of these households were totally reliant on state benefits, and of these, 89 per cent fell below the poverty line.

The Government did not carry out its own surveys and it was left to the Methodists and Presbyterians to reveal that those dependent on state benefits had not enough to survive. As Winifred Campbell recalled:

> Short time employment was common enough. It simply meant a tightening of the belt for a while ... As months stretched into years, people began to despair. Every possible economy became the way of life.[182]

The poor were endlessly resourceful to make ends meet. Sam McAughtry remembered that in Belfast

> money for food was so scarce that kids like myself were sent down to John McCollum's bakery off York Street on a Monday morning to queue up for the bread and buns kept in the shop over the weekend. Stales, we used to call them, and in my case they were collected in a clean pillow-case, half filled for about a tanner.[183]

Leo Boyle remembered that a bowl of cracked eggs could be got from Gracey's of York Street for sixpence. He used to see 'people going down to Sawer's on Christmas Eve and waiting on the remnants of the turkeys, buying gizzards and turkeys' necks' to make soup because they could not buy a fowl for the next day. Others bought food in very small quantities.[184] Bella O'Hara remembered:

> You could have got a halfpenny of tea, and you got a halfpenny of sugar, up in McCroan's, up Lancaster Street, 6 o'clock in the morning ... And

you'd have got lovely bacon cuttings – I'd have called them 'kilties' garters' – 4d a pound . . . Over in the wee chemist I used to say 'Give us tuppence of the treacle.' We put treacle on the bread and ate it like jam. It was lovely. It kept you all right too, it kept your bowels right.[185]

Fresh sweet milk was a luxury and the working class had condensed milk or buttermilk as alternatives – 'a penny in the gas and the gas tube in the buttermilk really made a nice intoxicating drink,' Charlie Hull observed.[186] Harold Binks remembered seeing barefooted children waiting at the Albert Bridge pens to get unwanted, unsterilised milk from cows about to be shipped to England. Such disregard for hygiene was not uncommon and, indeed, contaminated milk was a potent cause of early death in these years.

'THERE WERE WHOLE FAMILIES WIPED OUT': ILLNESS AND POVERTY

Paddy Scott remembered walking through north Belfast on his way to the university and seeing

> young children with deformed legs, gaunt looking; I subsequently discovered it was rickets due to malnutrition. I also noticed the women were gaunt, lifeless, and particularly the young men . . . their eyes were lifeless, expressionless, which gave me the impression that they were people who had lost all hope . . . if you were sensitive at all, you couldn't help but have a reaction.[187]

In 1931 life expectancy at birth in Northern Ireland was 57.1 years, a statistic similar to that for the rest of the United Kingdom. But for generations past, people had lived longer in the countryside than in urban areas and Belfast's health record during the interwar years is particularly bleak. When compared with six British cities, Belfast had the lowest infant mortality rate in 1901 but in 1938 it had the highest rate, ninety-six per one thousand live births compared with, for example, fifty-nine in Sheffield. Anne Boyle recollected:

> There was so much infant mortality that it seemed as if every week blue baby-coffins were coming out of every street. I had three brothers and a sister dead before they were two years old, out of eleven of us.[188]

'Maternity is a more dangerous occupation in Northern Ireland than in the Free State or in England', Professor R.J. Johnstone MP accurately observed, for maternal mortality actually *rose* by one fifth between 1922 and 1938.[189] Malnutrition arising out of poverty was the principal cause of this increase, aggravated by the working-class tradition of feeding the man of the house, then the children and finally the mother. In Lurgan Dr Deeny found that the women in his survey, whether employed or unemployed, were anaemic, shorter than they should have been, and had poor skin colour. Bryce Miller remembered that his mother would take only three days off work when she had a child, for the family could not do without her wages.[190]

Lack of hygiene, poverty and utterly inadequate medical care largely explain why in Belfast 51 per cent of all deaths under fifteen years of age were caused by infectious diseases – 25 per cent higher than in English county boroughs. Whooping cough, influenza and measles killed around three times as many in Belfast in the late 1930s than in similar cities across the Irish Sea. Pneumonia was the deadliest disease but the main killer of young adults was tuberculosis, responsible for 49 per cent of all deaths in the age group fifteen to twenty-five and for 38 per cent of those between twenty-five and thirty-five. Much had been achieved since the beginning of the century but the mortality rate from tuberculosis was 20 per cent higher in Northern Ireland than in the rest of the United Kingdom. Anne Boyle remembered:

> There were twenty-eight in my class at school and when I was about twenty-five, I would say that more than half of those girls were dead, mostly from tuberculosis. There were whole families wiped out with tuberculosis. I remember the sexton of Sacred Heart chapel, Paddy McKernan; all he had was four daughters, and those four daughters died within a couple of years. They were teenage girls.[191]

Of the many causes of the high death rate from this disease, cramped and poor-quality housing was very high on the list.

'PEOPLE LIVING IN INDESCRIBABLE FILTH AND SQUALOR'

'It has been estimated that 96 per cent of all the houses in Fermanagh have no running water', John Mogey observed in the 1940s, and he continued:

> The water-borne disposal of sewage is impossible without this service . . .
> Whole townlands were found in which there was not a single well . . .
> Many farmers objected that, if the byre was reconstructed as ordered by the Ministry's inspectors it would be better than the dwelling house. This was often a true observation.[192]

Despite the availability of generous assistance from the Government, not a single labourer's cottage was built by the public authorities in Co. Fermanagh during the interwar years. This is merely the worst example of Northern Ireland's dismal housing record in this period. Belfast Corporation, on the other hand, seemed well satisfied with its achievement: in 1929 the city surveyor claimed that 'Belfast can justly claim to be a city without slums'; three years later the medical officer of health reasoned that the expansion of the suburbs 'prevents the formation of slums as I understand the term'; and in 1937 the town clerk commented in the bicentenary edition of the *Belfast News-Letter* that 'the outstanding enterprise of the Corporation since the Great War was in connection with housing'.[193] In fact the corporation's record was woefully bad and its complacency was exposed in Dr Carnwath's damning health report on Belfast in 1941, which included this description of working-class dwellings surveyed:

> Damp, mouldering walls, many of them bulging, rickety stairs, broken floors, crumbling ceilings were common defects. Some of the 'houses' were mere hovels, with people living in indescribable filth and squalor . . . In a group of three of the worst houses, each sublet to three tenants . . . rents were 1/9d a week for a small attic which it was an adventure to approach.[194]

An independent study found 190 people living in twelve houses in Lonsdale Street off the Crumlin Road and health officers from 1936 onwards warned Belfast Corporation that ten thousand houses for which it was responsible were 'inimical to health' and 'unfit for human habitation' – warnings which produced no active response.[195] A big fish in a small pond, the corporation had an overweening and baleful influence on the Government's housing policy.

At first it looked as if Northern Ireland would be able to follow Westminster's housing policy and the Housing Act of 1923 closely mirrored Neville Chamberlain's legislation giving subsidies to private builders. In 1924, however, Wheatley's Housing Act revolutionised housing provision in Britain by virtually making it a social service: councils were to build houses for renting and an upper limit was to be placed on those rents. Belfast Corporation found the Wheatley solution quite unacceptable, because an intolerable burden would be placed on the ratepayers and Pollock, the finance minister, was only too happy to agree. Northern Ireland, therefore, went its own way: state subsidies were offered to local authorities and private builders; and local authorities were given the power to supplement government grants to private builders. No fewer than thirteen Housing Acts regulated the subsidies, which rose to £100 per house by 1927 but were reduced to £25 in 1932 and finally withdrawn altogether in 1937.[196]

Some opposition MPs – notably Joseph Devlin, Cahir Healy and Jack Beattie – did demand that housing become a social service but their efforts were amateurish and uncoordinated, and their speeches rambling and ill-informed. The deeply conservative population of the region ensured the return of councillors intensely hostile to rate increases. Local authorities generally did their best to evade their responsibilities and Belfast Corporation proved it was barely fit to undertake them. A report of 1926 revealed gross corruption in Belfast's housing committee, but Dawson Bates timidly refused to take punitive action. The corporation put up a mere 16 houses under direct contract and only subsidised the building of 2,600 more in the whole interwar period. For its size and resources Newry was rather more adventurous: the council granted £1,700 from the profits of its gas service towards the building of forty-two houses in O'Neill Avenue; and at a cost of £20,000 bought and converted the linen hall into dwelling units for nearly four hundred people. Elsewhere, local authority inaction was the result not only of conservatism but also of political fear – particularly west of the Bann – that knife-edge majorities would be imperilled by the erection of even a handful of dwellings. In any case, the Government was distinctly tepid in encouraging local council initiative. Downpatrick council put up forty houses between 1927 and 1933 but, though there were no rent arrears or additional charges on the rates, the Ministry of Home Affairs refused another scheme in 1936 to build 'parlour' houses on the grounds that 'kitchen' houses of six hundred square feet each were quite large enough 'for the poorer members of the working classes'.[197] The following year the Government withdrew subsidies altogether, largely because its financial position was becoming desperate.

'MENDICANTS ON BRITAIN'S BOUNTY'

The tortuous financial relationship between Westminster and Belfast was worked out when the postwar boom was at its height in 1919–20. Then it was considered that the provisions were 'generous, and sufficient to enable the two Parliaments to enter upon their duties without fear that their efforts will be stultified by want of money'.[198] In 1922–3, however, Northern Ireland's revenue had dropped £3 million under the estimate and it remained well below until 1938–9. The regional government's income, over which the parliament in Belfast had almost no control, was steadily eroded by impoverishment arising out of industrial decline; tax cuts imposed by Conservative governments; the de-rating of agricultural land in 1929; and 'the fact that the consumption of alcoholic drink in Northern Ireland is diminishing to a marked extent', the political scientist Nicholas Mansergh observed in 1936, ' . . . due partly to social distress but more largely to the strength of the temperance movement'.[199]

Pollock firmly believed that Northern Ireland should learn to stand on its own two feet and either tighten its belt accordingly or impose special additional taxation in the region, which he said was 'preferable to appearing as mendicants on Britain's bounty'.[200] Andrews railed against Pollock's orthodoxy, pointing out that Northern Ireland was not 'an autonomous State, but simply a subordinate legislature' and arguing that it 'is inequitable that our people should be put in a worse position than their fellow-subjects in any other area of the United Kingdom as a consequence of the devolution of social services'.[201] Fortunately, Craig agreed and cheerfully embarked on what Andrews called 'repeated begging expeditions' to London. He got Bonar Law's government to appoint an arbitration committee under Lord Frederick Colwyn in 1923, which two years later recommended that the imperial contribution would not be a first charge but the residue left over after 'necessary' domestic expenditure. This was accepted and led to the steady reduction of the contribution. By the 1930s the imperial contribution all but disappeared as the economic blizzard struck Ulster. Westminster still refused new arrangements and budgets were balanced only by what one treasury official described as 'fudges', 'wangles', and 'dodges and devices'.[202] One result was that the Northern Ireland government was paralysed into virtual inaction. Another was that Westminster was saved a great deal of money because it was not obliged to treat the region with the same generosity as other unemployment blackspots, such as south Wales and Clydeside.

FIANNA FÁIL AND THE ECONOMIC WAR

On Wednesday 9 March 1932 Eamon de Valera entered Leinster House in Dublin to take up office as premier of the Irish Free State. It was a tense moment. Cumann na nGaedheal, the pro-treaty party, had been in power for ten years without a break. Now Cosgrave and his supporters feared that de Valera's republicans of Fianna Fáil – described by Sean Lemass in 1928 as 'a slightly constitutional party' – would bring about economic ruin, a revival of the IRA with official approval, and a dangerous confrontation with Britain. Apprehensive that army and police leaders would attempt a coup to prevent them taking office, some Fianna Fáil deputies carried revolvers into the Dáil and, just outside the chamber, one was found putting together a Thompson sub-machine-gun in a telephone box. 'We heard of frightful things that would happen the moment the Fianna Fáil government came to power,' de Valera said soon afterwards. 'We have seen no evidence of these things.'[203] For the moment he was right, but over the next few years parliamentary rule in the Free State was imperilled by the quasi-fascist Blueshirts on the right and IRA activists of both the radical right and the militant left.

There was a severe riot in Enniskillen when local nationalists held a rally to celebrate Fianna Fáil's victory. Sectarian passions welled up to the surface over the Ulster countryside at a time when the Depression brought a near collapse of agricultural prices. John Maynard Keynes described the deprivation being endured by Northern Ireland's small farmers as 'almost unbelievable'.[204] Far from bringing together the rural poor of both religions in common action, hardship seems rather to have inflamed ancient enmities. At Orange rallies on both sides of the border on 12 July 1931 a resolution, warning 'in the most emphatic manner, all Protestants to beware of the insidious propaganda of the Roman Catholic Church', was carried with acclamation and trouble broke out at parades in Co. Monaghan.[205] In August 1931 a mob prevented an Orange gathering in Cavan and an Orange hall was attacked, and there were anti-Catholic riots in Portadown, Armagh and Lisburn. In December of that year Cardinal MacRory publicly declared: 'The Protestant Church in Ireland – and the same is true of the Protestant Church anywhere else – is not only not the rightful representative of the early Irish Church, but it is not even a part of the Church of Christ.'[206] Particularly along the border, Fianna Fáil's accession to power aroused intense feelings of fear and anticipation.

De Valera informed the Westminster government that he would remove the oath of fidelity to the Crown from the Irish constitution and withhold payment of the land annuities to Britain. There was little the British government could do about the removal of the oath, as under the 1931 Statute of Westminster, legislation from the mother parliament only applied to dominions at their request and with their consent. Refusal to remit the annuities – repayments under the Land Purchase Acts – was a breach of an international agreement and Ramsay MacDonald's government lost no time in retaliating. The economic war had begun.

On 12 July 1932 Westminster imposed a 20 per cent duty on livestock, dead meat and dairy produce from the Irish Free State. Ten days later the Fianna Fáil government retaliated with a 20 per cent tariff on British electrical goods, cement, machinery, iron and steel, sugar and molasses, and a duty of five shillings a ton on British coal and coke. The impact was immediate. The Irish Free State's adverse balance of trade for August 1932 was £1,433,204 as against £316,875 for August 1931; the cattle trade suffered a loss of almost £1 million for the month; and one half of the market for butter, two thirds of the market for bacon and ham, and four fifths of the market for poultry had been lost. Though a massive increase in smuggling renders the figures suspect, exports from north to south, according to official statistics, had dropped by 1936 to one third of the 1931 level.[207]

At the close of the 1932 election campaign de Valera had told a *News Chronicle* reporter that Fianna Fáil could 'only protest' about partition and that there were 'no effective steps that we can take to abolish the Boundary. Force is out of the question.'[208] He took the view that Britain had deliberately fomented religious tensions in Ulster to divide and weaken Irishmen and that partition was the culmination of this policy. Pressure had to be applied, therefore, not on Belfast but on London to reunify Ireland and, once achieved, this would ensure a stable friendly power on Britain's western flank. It would take time to restore Irish unity and in the meantime de Valera's confrontation with Britain gave Fianna Fáil the opportunity to put into operation the old Sinn Féin policy of economic self-sufficiency. Fianna Fáil gave little thought to the effect their actions would have on Catholics in Northern Ireland: a Nationalist wrote to Cahir Healy complaining of de Valera's 'mad policy' and concluded that 'what is a border today will be a frontier tomorrow'.[209] In the short term deteriorating relations between Dublin and London seem mainly to have aggravated religious tensions in Northern Ireland.

'OURS IS A PROTESTANT GOVERNMENT'

Thousands of northern Catholics travelled to Dublin for the thirty-first International Eucharistic Congress in June 1932. According to T.J. Campbell, the scenes 'were the most impressive and joyful ever witnessed among the Irish nation'. He continued:

> Particularly so was the concluding spectacle of the mighty battalions on the march from the Phoenix Park, where Pontifical High Mass was celebrated by his Grace Most Rev. Dr. Curley, Archbishop of Baltimore, before a congregation of about 1,000,000, to O'Connell Bridge for the Solemn Benediction and the Papal Blessing by the Cardinal Legate, Cardinal Lauri. The procession was like a swiftly-flowing, never-ending stream of humanity . . . Amid a deep hush the crowds fell on their knees awaiting in awe and homage the passing-by of the King of Kings. Torchbearers and thurifers were unobserved. All eyes were fixed on the moving canopy, in which his Eminence the Papal Legate knelt, holding the monstrance enshrining the Blessed Sacrament. All heads bent low as the Lord of Hosts passed by. Rapt adoration, amid breathless stillness, was around.[210]

During the congress Campbell noted that the 'Catholic quarters of Belfast, Derry, Newry, and other Northern towns looked their brightest and bravest'.[211]

Cardinal Lauri visited Newry and, as he drove to the cathedral through streets decorated with bunting, children sang hymns and waved Papal flags. The Northern Ireland cabinet concluded that the congress had created 'excitement amounting almost to frenzy . . . along the border'.[212] Special trains and buses returning with pilgrims were attacked at Loughbrickland, Banbridge, Lurgan, Portadown, Kilkeel and Lisburn. During the summer marching season resolutions were carried denouncing 'the unchanging bigotry of Rome' and, in particular, 'the arrogant, intolerant and un-Christian pretensions fulminated by Cardinal MacRory'.[213] At the Poyntzpass 12 July demonstration the prime minister declared defiantly: 'Ours is a Protestant government and I am an Orangeman.'[214] A more notorious speech by a member of the Government, Sir Basil Brooke, was given exactly a year later at Newtownbutler. As reported in the *Fermanagh Times*, Brooke said:

> There were a great number of Protestants and Orangemen who employed Roman Catholics. He felt he could speak freely on this subject as he had not a Roman Catholic about his place . . . He would point out that the Roman Catholics were endeavouring to get in everywhere and were out with all their force and might to destroy the power and constitution of Ulster. There was a definite plot to overpower the vote of Unionists in the north. He would appeal to Loyalists, therefore, wherever possible, to employ Protestant lads and lassies (cheers).[215]

The Unionists had just lost control of Lisnaskea and this undoubtedly prompted Brooke's remarks. In fact the proportion of Protestants in Co. Fermanagh was rising and it is more likely that dissatisfaction at the Government's response to rural distress was responsible for the Unionist reverse.

Brooke's speech attracted widespread attention because a Church of Ireland clergyman from Co. Cavan protested that Protestants in the Free State were repelled by his excited tone and because it was condemned in public by a prominent Co. Fermanagh landlord, Captain T.T. Verschoyle, who said:

> He who sows the wind shall reap the whirlwind . . . it remains to be seen whether the Colebrooke Hitler will receive a well-merited rebuke from a responsible member of the government.[216]

There was no rebuke. When Cahir Healy raised the issue at Stormont, Craigavon replied that 'there is not one of my colleagues who does not entirely agree with him, and I would not ask him to withdraw one word'.[217] Brooke himself was unrepentant and repeated the substance of his Newtownbutler speech several times. In October at Enniskillen he said 'he believed from the bottom of his heart all he said' and in Derry he spoke of the infiltration of Catholics, which, if not checked, 'would result in their becoming in a few years so numerous that they would be able to vote Ulster into the Free State'.[218] As for the prime minister, after inconsistently urging his colleagues in private to moderate their tone, he responded to criticism of the Orange Order by saying:

> I have always said I am an Orangeman first and a politician and Member of this Parliament afterwards . . . The Hon. Member must remember that in the South they boasted of a Catholic State. They still boast of Southern

Ireland being a Catholic State. All I boast is that we are a Protestant Parliament and a Protestant State.[219]

Southern politicians often assumed that leaders in the North were responsible for dividing the people there but the roots of sectarianism ran deep in Northern Ireland society. While they can be condemned for failing to give a positive lead in promoting reconciliation, such men were merely reflecting views very widely held. Historian David Kennedy recalled the words of a socialist speaker near the Central Library in Belfast:

> If you took all the Orange sashes and all the Green sashes in Belfast and tied them round a ticket of loaves and threw them in the Lagan, the gulls, the common ordinary sea-gulls, they'd go for the bread, but the other gulls – yous ones – yous'd go for the sashes every time.[220]

'BATTLE RAGED BETWEEN THE OPPOSING FORCES': THE 1935 BELFAST RIOTS

In November 1933 a Catholic publican, Dan O'Boyle, was shot dead in York Street in Belfast. This was the first sectarian murder since 1922. As the bitter quest for work continued religious hatreds were easily brought to the surface. The extent of co-operation between the poor of both religions during the outdoor-relief riots of 1932 has been exaggerated and romanticised, and there is no evidence that intercommunal tensions were eased for more than a few days. Violent incidents in Belfast became more frequent in 1934: in May Protestants attacked Catholic homes just north of the city centre; in July shots were fired at Catholics in North Thomas Street; and on 16 September loyalists wrecked forty Catholic homes in Marine Street and New Dock Street and a kerbstone thrown through one window mortally wounded a crippled man unable to move to safety.

In 1935 feelings ran high when Protestants triumphantly celebrated George V's jubilee. A Catholic was shot dead in his shop in Great George's Street and rioting flared up in east Belfast as the Catholic church in Willowfield neared completion. During May and June twenty-six people were injured in the disturbances and at least forty homes were damaged. Fearing trouble on 12 July, the Ministry of Home Affairs banned all parades from 18 June. 'You may be perfectly certain that on the Twelfth of July Orangemen will be marching throughout Northern Ireland' was the defiant response of Sir Joseph Davison, the Orange grand master, and Dawson Bates – in the absence of the prime minister who was on one of his numerous leisurely tours of the Commonwealth – decided to lift the ban.[221] Dr John MacNeice, Church of

Ireland bishop of Down and father of the poet Louis MacNeice, made this appeal on the eve of the celebrations:

> Forget the things that are behind. Forget the unhappy past. Forget the story of the old feuds, the old triumphs, the old humiliations.

There were no disturbances as the Orangemen paraded on 12 July but at the Belmont 'Field' Davison referred directly to the bishop's appeal:

> Are we to forget that the flag of Empire is described as a foreign flag and our beloved King insulted by Mr. De Valera? Are we to forget that the aim of these people is to establish an all-Ireland Roman Catholic State, in which Protestantism will be crushed out of existence? But, above all, are we to forget the heroic achievements of our forefathers?

Only towards the end of the day, as the Orangemen paraded home down Royal Avenue into York Street, did violence break out. 'Unprovoked Attack on the Orange Procession', ran one headline in the *Belfast Telegraph*'s account, but neither side planned to make an attack on the other, concluded Henry S. Kennedy, an *Irish News* reporter who saw the riot begin. A trivial incident led the Orangemen to assume a major attack had begun and to vent their fury, according to the *Irish News*, they rushed 'up into Lancaster Street smashing windows on both sides as far as Pentland Street, deacon poles and stones being the weapons used. The Catholics rallied, and seizing stones drove the invading mob back into York Street.' Kennedy recalled:

> I remember a man out in front firing a revolver repeatedly in the direction of Lancaster Street. It looked so harmless in action, the reports of the shots so faint, the small puffs of smoke so innocent that it was incredible that this was an instrument of death ... At another stage when an attacking party had again entered Lancaster Street and again been driven out there came over the roof tops a shower of heavy stones ... I marked one particularly big one falling, as I thought, just past the head of a man running along the middle of York Street. But he fell and lay crumpled up and quite still.[222]

There followed what the *Northern Whig* described as 'the worst night of disorder since 1921–2'.[223] According to the *Belfast News-Letter*, policemen who attempted to hold back the Orangemen 'were thrust forcibly to one side, and were threatened by deacon poles'.[224] Later that evening, the *Irish News* reported:

> For over two hours battle raged between the opposing forces, and scenes that almost beggar description were enacted. Armoured cars, firing machine-guns, while police, armed with rifles or revolvers, fired upon gunmen and stone-throwers at all points, but from the corner of Donegall Street to the middle of York Street the fighting raged uninterruptedly for two hours.[225]

That night 2 civilians were killed, 35 civilians and 3 policemen were wounded, 14 houses were set on fire and 47 other dwellings were wrecked. Troops were called in and a curfew was imposed, but the rioting continued unabated the next evening. *The Times* correspondent described how loyalists following the funeral of a Protestant victim

> got completely out of hand. They rushed into North Ann Street, and before the police could prevent them they smashed all the windows of houses occupied by Roman Catholics. They also invaded Earl Street and North Thomas Street and continued their orgy of destruction.[226]

Night after night the violence continued. Soldiers with fixed bayonets were posted at collapsible barbed-wire entanglements designed to separate the mobs; police patrolled the whole York Street area on foot, in tenders, and in caged cars; and Whippet cars, with their Vickers guns at the ready, were stationed at strategic points throughout the city. It was nearly the end of August before the rioting ceased, by which time eight Protestants and five Catholics had been killed. At an inquest on riot victims the city coroner placed much of the blame on political leaders:

> It is all so wanton and meaningless . . . Party passion is a very inflammable commodity. Bigotry is the curse of peace and goodwill. The poor people who commit these riots are easily led and influenced . . . there would be less bigotry if there was less public speechmaking of a kind by so called leaders of public opinion . . . It is not good Protestantism to preach a gospel of hate and enmity towards those who differ from us in religion and politics.[227]

There had been more deaths in the Protestant community but Catholics had suffered most in other respects. The great majority of the wounded were Catholic; over two thousand Catholics and only a handful of Protestants had been driven from their homes; and 95 per cent of the £21,669 compensation for destruction to property was paid out to Catholics. At the request of Dr Mageean and the Nationalists, fifty-nine MPs at Westminster called for an inquiry, but Stanley Baldwin, the prime minister, replied that 'the matter is entirely within the discretion and responsibility of the government of Northern Ireland' and that an inquiry was completely ruled out 'for fundamental constitutional reasons'. Leaders of the minority had put the 1920 Government of Ireland Act to the test and found it wanting.[228] In the South de Valera had successfully neutralised the anti-democratic challenges from the Blueshirts and the IRA. In 1933 O'Duffy had been widely expected to lead a Fascist coup during the annual commemoration of Griffith, Collins and O'Higgins, but he backed down in face of de Valera's security measures; thereafter, legislation from the Cosgrave era, intended for use against the IRA, was used effectively to break up the movement. Fianna Fáil found it more difficult to deal with the IRA, so recently its political and military ally. However, the IRA's defiance of the law, together with a number of squalid assassinations, forced de Valera's hand: from May 1934 members of the organisation, including the legendary Tom Barry, were sentenced to terms of imprisonment with hard labour, and on 18 June 1936 the IRA was proclaimed an illegal organisation. At the end of 1936, as the *Round Table* pointed out, the Spanish Civil War enabled Ireland to get rid of some of her wild men of both varieties, some Blueshirts joining Franco's National Front and many members of the IRA volunteering for the International Brigade – along with a significant number of Belfast Protestants (mostly Communists) – to fight for the Spanish Republic. The decks thus cleared, northern Catholics entertained the hope that de Valera would now see his way to taking a more active interest in their plight. Indeed, improved relations between Dublin and London, signalled by a partial retreat in the economic war, reinforced this hope by opening the possibility of de Valera enlisting Westminster's help. De Valera's constitution two years later did much to dash those aspirations.

'DO THE PEOPLE OF ULSTER WISH TO REMAIN CITIZENS
OF THE UNITED KINGDOM?'

'What about the Six Counties?' someone shouted at de Valera when he was speaking at Monaghan on Sunday 27 June 1937. 'My reply is get a copy of the new Constitution,' the southern premier responded. 'There is in it an assertion that the national territory is the whole of Ireland not part of it.'[229]

Ever since the abdication of Edward VIII in December 1936, de Valera had been working strenuously to deliver the *coup de grâce* to the 1921 treaty. His External Relations Act ended the Free State's standing as a dominion and made it no more than 'externally associated' with the Commonwealth. He drafted a new constitution which provided for an elected president, with duties that were to be largely ceremonial, and a vocational senate inspired by Mussolini's corporate state. The most controversial sections included: Article 2, which claimed for the Irish nation jurisdiction over the whole island; Article 3, which accepted that the laws of the state could apply only in the twenty-six counties, 'pending reintegration of the national territory'; Article 4, which described the state as 'Éire, or in English, Ireland'; and articles acknowledging 'the special position of the Holy Catholic Apostolic and Roman Church'.

542

J.J. McElligott, secretary to the Department of Finance in the Free State, was sharply critical of the controversial articles. He argued that they would 'not contribute anything to effecting the unity of Ireland, but rather the reverse'; and he believed Article 2 gave a

permanent place in the Constitution to a claim to 'Hiberia Irredenta'. The parallel with Italy's historical attitude to the Adriatic seaboard beyond its recognised territory is striking and in that case it is likely to have lasting ill-effects on our political relations with our nearest neighbours.[230]

McElligott's protests were ignored. Frank MacDermot – the historian who had done as much as anyone to create the new conservative party of Fine Gael – opposed the constitution in the Dáil, since it 'offers no basis for union with the North and contains various provisions tending to prolong partition'.[231] Even within his own party, however, MacDermot failed to get substantial support for the creation of a society sufficiently pluralist to encourage northern Protestants to join with the South sometime in the future.

A referendum on 1 July 1937 – held the same day as the general election which confirmed de Valera as *taoiseach*, or premier, of Éire – approved the new constitution by 685,105 votes to 526,945, a majority less overwhelming than Fianna Fáil expected. Unionists in Northern Ireland were not at all displeased. Craigavon said that he had no objection to the special position given to the Catholic Church for

while the Government of the South is carried on along lines which I presume are very suitable to the majority of Roman Catholics in that part . . . surely the Hon. Member will admit that the Government of the North, with a majority of Protestants, should carry on the administration according to Protestant ideas and Protestant desires.[232]

The *Northern Whig* observed that the 1937 constitution proved that 'the South possesses a Catholic Parliament for a Catholic people' and that northerners were repelled by 'the narrow and fanatical type of Nationalism which Southern Republicans have fostered . . . hardly distinguishable from the tribalism of the most primitive peoples'.[233] Northern Catholics felt isolated and abandoned, for de Valera, in spite of his irredentist claims, had chosen to create a twenty-six-county state that seemed to close off the few remaining routes to reunification – a state verging on the theocratic, with rigid censorship and a constitutional prohibition on divorce and family planning; a state compelling every child to learn Irish and turning its back, like Northern Ireland, on the cultural diversity of its people; and a state with one of the most highly protected economies in the world.

543

The Westminster government accepted the new constitution philosophically enough and was relieved that at least de Valera, having 'delivered the goods' to his own supporters, for his part was now eager 'for a closer *rapprochement*' with Britain and Northern Ireland.[234] Mounting anxiety about the growing strength and pugnacity of the Third Reich encouraged the British government to ensure the friendship of Éire on its western flank in the event of a war. Alarmed by the taoiseach's placing of partition firmly on the agenda, Craigavon called a general election in February 1938. 'He is the one politician who can win an election without leaving his fireside', the *Daily Express* observed and, indeed, a severe bout of flu did confine the prime minister to his fireside throughout the campaign.[235]

Both de Valera and the Nationalists were caught off guard by Craigavon's announcement. De Valera created confusion by urging Nationalists to boycott the election and the opposition was further divided, particularly in Belfast, by clashing allegiances in the Spanish Civil War. In the Belfast Dock constituency the sitting Labour MP, Harry Midgley, was outspoken in his support for the beleaguered Spanish Republic and described Franco as a 'monstrosity' and 'a killer of babies'. He was opposed not only by a Unionist but also by the Nationalist James Collins, who openly backed Franco's armed rebellion and during a tempestuous meeting in St Mary's Hall on 7 February declared: 'The Central–Falls–Dock Nationalist Axis athwart Belfast will be something to set before Mr Chamberlain at his next talks with Mr. De Valera.' On that occasion, Collins's main opponents were republicans. The *Irish News* reported:

> Republicans sang 'The Soldier's Song' and Nationalist supporters, rising from their chairs sang 'A Nation Once Again', while children screamed with fright. In the confusion chairs were overturned and added to the general turmoil. The scenes continued for nearly an hour, when the police, who were summoned, arrived.

Night after night there were violent clashes in the Dock constituency as Midgley faced hostile crowds shouting 'Up Franco', 'Remember Spain', and 'We want Franco'.[236]

Within the loyalist camp, Craigavon was challenged by the newly formed Progressive Unionist Party led by the millionaire Westminster MP for South Belfast, W.J. Stewart. The new party criticised the traditional sectarianism of government ministers and sought a more adventurous economic policy to reduce the total of ninety thousand now out of work in the region. Apart from some ugly scenes in East Tyrone, where Nationalist cars were wrecked and agents were assaulted at Tullyhogue, the election was a quiet one in rural constituencies. In parts of Belfast, however, it was a violent day: in Oldpark armed men burned a Unionist car; republican and nationalist women fought in the streets and tore each other's hair; cars were wrecked in the Falls, where windows were broken and five people were injured after a police baton charge in Slate Street; and for the B Specials it was a day of full alert.

Craigavon brought off a Unionist triumph equalled only by that of 1921. Not a single Progressive Unionist was elected. Midgley lost his seat to a Unionist. Only two Labour candidates were returned: Paddy Agnew, the party's first Catholic MP, elected unopposed in South Armagh; and Jack Beattie, expelled from the party for his anti-partitionist stand. 'Do the people of Ulster wish to remain citizens of the United Kingdom or to become citizens of an All-Ireland Republic?' was the 'Vital Question which People Must Answer', according to the *Belfast News-Letter*. Now the voters had given their answer. *The Times* commented on the Unionists' success:

> A snap election on an unreal issue has given them complete victory . . . Whether it was worthwhile to advance the date of the election in order to prove what has been self-evident since Parnell's day is another matter.[237]

De Valera was quite unable to move Neville Chamberlain's government on the issue of partition. Otherwise he was the chief beneficiary in the Anglo-Éire Agreement signed on 25 April 1938: Britain handed over the 'Treaty ports' of Lough Swilly, Berehaven and Cobh, thus demonstrating that Éire was in practice a sovereign independent state and making neutrality in a European war a practical possibility; Westminster abandoned £100 million of land annuities still owing for a lump-sum payment of £10 million; and though punitive and retaliatory duties were dropped by both sides, Éire retained the right to protect newly established industries while Britain reopened her markets. For Chamberlain the vast improvement in Anglo-Irish relations was a triumphant demonstration of the success of appeasement. Disappointed at his failure to extract a British promise to reconsider partition, de Valera nevertheless was satisfied that his experiment in economic self-sufficiency could continue. In the Dáil the taoiseach frankly admitted that a sudden ending of partition would present insuperable problems in absorbing ninety thousand unemployed in the North and 'that a number of industrialists down here would be shivering if we had the whole country in now'.[238] Actually de Valera's self-sufficiency had done much to help Northern Ireland's economy to survive these bleak years.

545

At a time when world food prices were tumbling, Britain's punitive duties on Free State produce during the economic war at least gave Northern Ireland farmers the chance to make up the shortfall. In addition, the British government set aside the policy of free and unrestricted access for foreign agricultural produce, thus giving the region a competitive edge over outsiders in the lucrative market in England's south-east. Prices had dropped most severely in cereals and Northern Ireland, concentrating on beef, dairy produce and pigs, was able to ride out the agricultural depression rather better than some other British regions. Nevertheless, on average, farms in Northern Ireland were only one third the size of British farms and they were acutely short of capital and machinery.

Sir Basil Brooke, who succeeded Archdale as minister of agriculture in 1933, declared that the staff in his department were 'not to be beaten in any country of the world'.[239] Certainly the experience, ability and enthusiasm of his civil servants did much to improve the region's agricultural performance in these years and provided a rare example of the advantages devolved government could yield. Above all, Archdale and Brooke presided over marketing legislation, mounting to twenty-one statutes up to 1939, which was flexible and responsive to the region's interests. Supply was regulated, stringent minimum standards were set, processing was modernised, and the product was altered to meet changing market demands.

The most striking achievement was the trebling of the number of pigs in Northern Ireland, giving it the highest density in any region in Britain or Ireland. The traditional market for roll bacon – boned but not skinned – in Scotland and the north of England was depressed, whereas the demand for lean bacon, first created by the Danes, was growing in London and the south-east. Protesting farmers were steered away from the Large Ulster White towards the Wiltshire breed, a leaner animal that travelled well. Small farms in the counties of Antrim and Down benefited most from the four Wiltshire factories set up by 1939 and capable of processing 450,000 pigs each year, and from the increase in sales from £1,140,000 in 1931–2 to £4,423,000 by 1937–8. Writing in the bicentenary edition of the *Belfast News-Letter* in 1937, Brooke was probably right to comment that the Marketing of Potatoes Act (1928) 'put for the first time graded quality potatoes on the British market and despite glutted markets and depressed prices, enabled Northern Ireland to maintain shipments when potatoes were rotting in the clamps in England'; that the Marketing of Fruit Act (1931) 'has enabled four times as many apples to be shipped prior to the Act'; that the Milk and Milk Products Act (1934) 'brought considerable relief to the creamery industry, threatened as it was with complete collapse'; and that as a result of eggs marketing legislation, 'the output of the poultry industry of the six counties of Northern Ireland exceeds that of the whole of Ireland in 1906'.[240] Brooke liked to compare the prosperity of northern farmers with the backwardness and poverty of southern counterparts but it is unlikely that this would bear close examination. Certainly the region's farmers remained very poor by British standards and most had incomes no higher than industrial wage-earners, while agricultural labourers were paid from £1 5s.0d. to £1 7s.6d. in the 1930s, less than the £1 10s.0d. dole given to a married man with two children. Nevertheless, the condition of those getting their living from the land would have been worse still but for energetic action by the Northern Ireland government.

Only low wages and long hours made possible the continued predominance of linen in the region. In September 1937 the writer Alfred S. Moore indicated the extent of the industry's production:

Visualise a great white highway one quarter mile broad extending down Ireland from the Giant's Causeway to Mizen Head in Cork – 300 miles – and you can grasp the magnitude of the Ulster linen annual output. In fact, its extent would cover Belfast's whole city area (21 square miles) thrice over.[241]

In that year William Ewart and Son advertised that it produced from its looms two million yards of cloth a month and enough thread from its spindles to go 'round the globe in 90 minutes'. The British government's decision to abandon the gold standard and to take protective measures against dumping on the home market did much to help the industry survive. Profit margins were perilously narrow and survival required expertise, 'flair and strong nerves', Wallace Clark of Upperlands recalled:

Much of the business was transacted on a Friday morning in Belfast where Bedford Street was the equivalent of the Cotton Exchange in Manchester. There flax merchants sought out spinners, weavers dickered with the commission houses who dealt in yarn, while merchants button-holed converters . . . They talked on the pavements and in adjacent offices. Victorian and dark most of them were, with an excess of frosted glass and brown paint. Young Harry had to squint at a bit of cloth with a counting glass, make up a price, and accept or reject the business on the spot. One sixteenth of a penny a yard was the difference between profit and loss.[242]

Other industrial firms retained their reputation and trade. The Belfast Ropeworks employed four thousand people and exported thirteen thousand tons of rope, cordage and twine in 1936. Some businesses defied economic trends and increased their sales. Both tea and tobacco help to depress the appetite and it is not surprising therefore that Davidsons and Gallahers prospered during the hungry thirties. Davidson's Sirocco Works continued to supply 70 per cent of the world's tea machinery and Gallahers raised its exports from four thousand tons of tobacco and cigarettes in 1930 to ten thousand tons in 1936. Still the largest independent tobacco factory in the world, Gallahers owed its success to the efficient application of modern technology. With the exception of Short and Harland's aircraft factory, the Government was almost completely unsuccessful in attracting new industries to Northern Ireland and the New Industries (Development) Acts of 1932 and 1937 provided financial inducements so modest that only 279 jobs were otherwise created. In fairness, several other regions of the United Kingdom – including Wales with its abundant domestic supplies of coal and steel – were just as unsuccessful. What industrial success Northern Ireland did enjoy was provided by firms well established before the end of the nineteenth century.

Early in 1934 the Northern Ireland Ministry of Finance negotiated a vital financial co-operative deal with the Midland Bank to make it possible for Harland and Wolff to accept an order for four Union-Castle liners. For two years the company had not launched a single ship; now this crucial pump priming by the Government made it possible for Belfast to take immediate advantage of a mild recovery in shipping rates. By the middle of the year Harland and Wolff had orders for twenty-four vessels, was employing ten thousand men and it launched a greater tonnage than any other yard in the world in both 1935 and 1936. Amongst the ships leaving the ways was *Stirling Castle*, the 25,594-ton liner, powered by ten-cylinder, double-acting, two-stroke airless injection diesel engines, which beat the record for the Southampton to Capetown route set forty-three years earlier. In addition, the company increased Belfast's share of the British market from an average 9.7 per cent in the 1920s to 12.8 per cent by 1935, and attempted to diversify by building stationary land engines and diesel-electric locomotives, grain silos and steelwork for cinemas. Frederick Rebbeck, the energetic and dictatorial head of Harland and Wolff, complained with some justice that Belfast did not get its fair share of Admiralty orders and by 1938 only one cruiser and one aircraft carrier were being constructed on Queen's Island. Nevertheless, he ignored his creditors' protests to modernise facilities in order to cope with naval contracts, and persuaded the

Belfast Harbour Commissioners to deepen the Victoria Channel, create the Herdman Channel, and construct the Pollock Dock and Basin.

Rebbeck steered his firm with consummate skill through the most difficult decade in British shipbuilding history but he would not have succeeded without the unwavering support of the Northern Ireland government. In December 1936 the chairman of the Midland Bank summoned Rebbeck to head office and charged him with

> living in a wrong atmosphere, and that the Northern Ireland Government was so obsessed with the idea of providing employment that they were exercising considerate pressure on Harland & Wolff to take ships at any sort of price if only they would provide employment and take the men at Belfast off the 'dole'.

It was fortunate for Northern Ireland that both Rebbeck and the Government chose to ignore him and take pride in the fact that the company was 'making no small contribution to the solution of the country's unemployment problem' and that 'the alternative was to take no work at all'.[243]

The extension of Belfast's port facilities reclaimed four hundred acres of slob land from the lough and it was soon realised that this would make a highly suitable airport for both conventional and amphibious aeroplanes. In March 1938 Annie Chamberlain, the prime minister's wife, performed the opening ceremony for Sydenham aerodrome alongside the Musgrave yard. By then work was well advanced close by on a new aircraft factory.[244] This had little to do with the Northern Ireland government's meagre financial inducements but was due to the growing threat of a general European war. 'The bomber will always get through,' Baldwin had once remarked gloomily at Westminster and, instead of ordering fighter aircraft, the Government signed contracts for aeroplanes capable of launching counter-attacks. Short Brothers of Rochester ran out of space and sought a new site well away from the threat of German assault. Belfast had a large pool of unemployed skilled workers, sheltered water ideal for flying boats, a deep-water dock and an aerodrome with exceptionally long runways. A business marriage was arranged to create Short and Harland Limited in June 1936 and, even while the factory was still under construction, work was well under way to meet the first orders for Sunderlands, Bristol Bombays and Hereford bombers. Nearby, HMS *Belfast* was launched in March 1938 and completed her sea trials in August 1939. Between those dates, profound changes being wrought on the European mainland caused the British government to raise the tempo of the rearmament programme. While this crisis promised to revitalise Northern Ireland's economy, it put others in peril. On 12 March 1938 the Wehrmacht crossed the Austrian frontier and Hitler drove through Vienna soon afterwards to complete the Anschluss, the union of his homeland with the Third Reich. This first step towards the making of a Greater Germany not only put Czechoslovakia – the sole surviving democracy in central Europe – in mortal danger, but also spread Nazi oppression to new frontiers. The autumn of 1938 saw both the Munich agreement and a new onslaught on the Jews, culminating in Kristallnacht – a night of concerted attacks on synagogues throughout the Reich. For many desperate people in Vienna it was already becoming too late to get out.

'NO REPLY. REGRET. NO OPENING. NOT WRITTEN TO.'

During the autumn of 1938 letters from Austria began to land on desks in the Northern Ireland Ministry of Commerce. When civil servants opened them they were made vividly aware of the tragedy unfolding in central Europe. As Dorothea Both, a maker of artificial flowers in Vienna, explained in her letter of 8 September, an article had appeared on 29 August in the *Zionistische Rundschau* indicating that the Northern Ireland government 'would be disposed to receive emigrants from Austria which would establish manufactures or trades and offer work and gain to workless people'. As a result, nearly three hundred letters – some posted mistakenly to Dublin and redirected – arrived in Belfast from Jews appealing for permission to settle in Northern Ireland. Some sent elaborate brochures and prospectuses of their businesses which had been or were about to be confiscated by the Nazi authorities.

Many wrote in halting, broken English. Applicants included: Alfred Bornstein, a distiller of liquors and essences; Marianne and Thomas Israel Bein, 'Christian religion', silk fabric designers; Dr Edmund Berliner, manufacturer of leather belts from Bratislava; Alfred Bermann on behalf of his son Otto, a weaver who had spent six months in a concentration camp; and Fritz and Paul Furnburg, textile chemists. Paul Braun, leader of a concert and jazz band, scribbled at the bottom of his typed letter: 'I will still mention that my comrades and I are Jews.' Henriette Wollisch desperately sought an entry permit for her son imprisoned in Dachau – she was certain he would be released if he could be found a job in Northern Ireland.

Along the margin of Frau Both's letter, in which she further explained that her husband was no longer permitted to practise as a barrister, a civil servant had written just one word, 'regret'. The *Zionistische Rundschau* had been mistaken: the Government was not about to make Northern Ireland a haven for the persecuted Jews of the Third Reich. Altogether 244 letters seem to have been rejected – including all those referred to above – after only brief consideration and then marked in blue pencil with such curt comments as 'no reply', 'no opportunity', 'no opening', and 'not written to'. Dr Leo Adler's letter merited the remark 'chemicals, good firm' but still received the verdict, 'no reply'. Sandor Blau manufactured between three and four million buckles a year, with an export market in many countries, including the United States; his final letter of 25 October is inscribed in blue, 'regret – samples returned'.[245] A further twenty applications were obviously considered more carefully and some of these may have been accepted, but those refugees who did make it to Northern Ireland usually needed the active assistance of Belfast's Jewish community or of the Society of Friends.[246]

Jews had already made a remarkable contribution to Ulster's economic development – a contribution out of all proportion to their numbers. Northern Ireland lost the opportunity to offer help to fellow humans and draw on the genius and enterprise of a remarkable people. As it was, industries that had languished for nearly two decades were now called on to make a vital contribution to Britain's survival but at the same time they were to provide tempting targets for the Third Reich's Luftwaffe.

On the last night of peace, 2 September 1939, the blackout came into force all over Northern Ireland and in Pettigo the curtains on the Co. Fermanagh side of the border were drawn together, while in the Co. Donegal part of the village, lamps continued to cast their lights into the streets.[1] De Valera's decision to keep Éire neutral ensured that the period of the Second World War was a starkly contrasted experience for people living in the same historic province but divided by a political frontier into citizens of two distinct states.

'Ulster is ready when we get the word and always will be,' Craigavon had boasted.[2] Nevertheless, it was widely believed that Northern Ireland was too far away to merit German attack. Edmond Warnock, parliamentary secretary at the Ministry of Home Affairs, said to the Northern Ireland cabinet on 19 June 1939:

> An attack on Northern Ireland would involve a flight of over 1,000 miles. For aeroplanes of the bombing type, loaded, this is a very big undertaking . . . the enemy aeroplanes must twice pass through the active gun, searchlight and aeroplane defences of Great Britain . . . it is possible that we might escape attack.[3]

In May 1940 Warnock resigned in disgust because his government 'has been slack, dilatory and apathetic'.[4] By then the German panzer divisions were surging through the Ardennes, bypassing the Maginot line en route to Paris, and soon the United Kingdom itself was in peril. On a fine Saturday afternoon, 30 November 1940, a single, unobserved German plane flew high across the Ards towards Belfast. The crew brought back photographs of suitable targets, identified by the Luftwaffe's Section 5 photo-reconnaissance unit, including, 'die Werft Harland & Wolff Ltd, die Tankstelle Conns Water, das Flugzeugwerk Short & Harland, das Kraftwerk Belfast, die Grossmühle Rank & Co, das Wasserwerk

Belfast, die Kasernenanlagen Victoria Barracks'.[5] The entire city of Belfast, the Germans discovered, was defended by only seven anti-aircraft batteries. Craigavon had been buried two days before and it was left to his successor John Andrews to face the fact that Ulster was not ready when the complacency of the Government was mercilessly exposed during the German air raids of April and May 1941.

Sir Basil Brooke was fortunate in being able to oust Andrews from office in 1943, just as the corner was being turned. Northern Ireland for a time became the principal base for American forces prior to the assault on Hitler's fortress Europe, the most forward position in the counter-attack on U-boat wolf packs operating in the Western Approaches, and a key supplier of food, aircraft, ships, armaments and other vital equipment for the Allied war effort.

Neutral Éire was spared the horrors of sustained aerial bombard-ment, unrestricted submarine warfare and other terrors of total war. Thanks largely to the protective shield provided by the Royal Navy and the Royal Air Force and, later, by the United States forces, the Dublin government could view the world conflict as no more than an 'Emer-gency'. De Valera's attempts to ignore the war were not wholly success-ful, however: as the people of Co. Donegal watched and listened to the Battle of the Atlantic raging so close to their coasts, the Dublin govern-ment came under strong pressure to join the Allied cause. The taoiseach's diplomatic success in fending off all threats and inducements left Éire both insulated and isolated by 1945.

Snubbed by de Valera, British governments were eventually to show their gratitude to the Stormont government with practical financial assistance. During the first year of the war, however, Craigavon pro-claimed the unyielding support of the people of Northern Ireland with-out having the slightest idea of what that might involve.

'WE MUST SHARE AND SHARE ALIKE WITH OUR FELLOW CITIZENS
ACROSS THE WATER'

Along with other and greater anxieties, early in 1939 the people of Britain were given brutal reminders that for some the enduring Ulster problem was a burning issue. On 16 January explosions damaged telephone exchanges, factories and power stations in London, Man-chester and Birmingham. In further attacks the following day a fish porter was killed in Manchester. This new IRA campaign of violence had been launched after governments in Belfast, London, Berlin, Rome and other capitals had failed to respond to ultimatums demanding an immediate British withdrawal from Northern Ireland. One ultimatum had been written by Joe McGarrity of Philadelphia. Like other militant republicans, he was bitter that his former associate de Valera, having called the bluff of the Blueshirts, had then shunned and attempted to suppress the IRA and, in the Anglo-Éire Agreement of 1938, had in effect accepted partition for the present. By the end of July 1939 there had been 127 explosions in England which resulted in Westminster legislation to register all Irish people in Britain and give the authorities power to deport suspects. The IRA responded with a bomb in King's Cross station in London, which killed one person and wounded fifteen others. On 25 August a bomb in Coventry killed five people and injured more than fifty others. Thereafter, lacking support from the Irish community in Britain, the campaign slowly fizzled out.[6] Far from altering British policy on partition, the IRA violence strengthened Westminster's resolve to support the Government in Belfast, particularly now that Northern Ireland would have a key strategic role in the coming war.

'Is it credible', the *Daily Mirror* asked in May 1939, 'that the British government can even dream of repeating in 1939 the hideous blunder of 1918, and of enforcing conscription in any part of Ireland?'[7] Freshly returned from a long Pacific cruise, Craigavon announced in the spring that he wanted his people to make an equal sacrifice in defence of the realm. De Valera was outraged and declared that as his constitution claimed all Ireland to be part of Éire's territory, conscription in Ulster would be nothing short of 'an act of aggression'. 'I have just read a speech by de Valera, the Irish Taoiseach,' Hitler told the Reichstag, 'in which . . . he reproaches England with subjecting Ireland to continuous aggression.' Next day the *Manchester Guardian* reminded its readers 'that Herr Hitler, as he sarcastically reminded us yesterday, keeps a close eye on this rather vulnerable spot in our heel'.[8] Determined to show that his people were prepared to accept the burdens as well as the benefits of the Union, Craigavon travelled to London in May in a high state of agitation. There Chamberlain gently and skilfully forced the premier to back down, as Lady Craigavon records in her diary:

> The British Government were frightened of the issue being complicated by de Valera kicking up a dust, though Ulster affairs have *nothing* to do with him . . . J. was asked flat out by Chamberlain, 'Is Ulster out to help Britain in her war effort?' to which, of course, he answered, 'You know we are . . .' Chamberlain then said, 'If you really want to help us, *don't* press for conscription. It will only be an embarrassment.' What else could J. do than say, 'Very well, I won't!'[9]

Craigavon faced sharp criticism from his cabinet colleagues when he returned and Brooke recalled that the premier felt 'resentment, anger and hurt pride'. Craigavon's response was that, in compensation, he had pressed strongly for an increased share in rearmament work. Over the first seven months of 1939 Northern Ireland received government contracts worth more than £6 million for equipment such as battledress, bedding, service dress, and electrical wiring. In August the 10,000-ton cruiser HMS *Belfast* left the lough ready for service; work was well under way on the 28,000-ton aircraft carrier HMS *Formidable*; and Harland and Wolff was also busy converting and arming seven passenger liners, two auxiliaries and twenty-four trawlers. By the beginning of September 1939 Short and Harland had built eleven Bristol Bombays and four Hereford bombers, and design work had begun on the first of the heavy bombers, the four-engined Stirling. Since the beginning of the year the region's unemployment register had fallen by over thirty thousand. Yet the growing importance of Belfast as a source of vital war material was certain to increase the city's vulnerability.

When on Sunday 3 September Chamberlain broadcast to the nation that Britain was now at war with Germany, Police Constable Billy McNeill cycled immediately to Mountpottinger RUC station in Belfast and there he and his comrades sat 'waiting for the sirens to go and the bombers to come over anytime'. Next day at Stormont Tommy Henderson asked if the Government realised 'that these fast bombers can come to Northern Ireland in 2¾ hours'.[10] In the same debate Craigavon said:

> We here today are in a state of war and we are prepared with the rest of the United Kingdom and Empire to face all the responsibilities that imposes on the Ulster people. There is no slackening in our loyalty.

A month later he declared: 'We must share and share alike with our fellow citizens across the water.'[11] Already, however, there was mounting evidence that the Northern Ireland government was incapable of sharing the burdens of the war on an equal basis with the rest of the United Kingdom.

'I AM AFRAID NO M.P. REALISES THERE IS A WAR ON'

On the first night of the war Rodney Green, then a Queen's University student, could see lights gleaming over much of west Belfast as the blackout order was being defied. During the first two days of the war, the RUC logged twelve anti-war incidents, including: the lighting of bonfires and gas street lamps; the burning of gas masks; two soldiers stripped of their uniforms; the shooting of an army reservist in the abdomen; and the painting of hostile slogans, one of which declared 'ARP for English slaves, IRA for the Irish'.[12] Clearly the people of Northern Ireland were not united in common defence as the war got under way.

'Senor Mussolini and Ataturk are his only rivals in the post-war record of continuous office', the *Sunday Times* had observed of Craigavon after his 1938 election victory.[13] Sir Wilfrid Spender, however, thought that he was a premier whom 'true friends would advise to retire now', for he was 'too unwell to carry on' and incapable of doing 'more than one hour's constructive work' in a day.[14] Lady Londonderry confided to Sir Samuel Hoare, the home secretary, that Craigavon had become 'gaga'.[15] According to Spender, Dawson Bates was 'more ill than is generally known' and 'incapable of giving his responsible officers coherent directions on policy'. Bates's parliamentary secretary, Edmond Warnock, for all his righteous indignation later, showed little sense of urgency in preparing the people for civil defence. Altogether, Spender concluded, the ministers' 'disregarding of their responsibilities' presented a 'grave danger to the system of democratic government'.[16] In short, the Unionist government seemed utterly unfit to face the challenge of the war. The only exception was Sir Basil Brooke, the minister of agriculture, who threw himself into the task of making the region a major supplier of food to Britain in her time of danger.

Asked by Westminster to extend the ploughed area of Northern Ireland by 150,000 acres, Brooke immediately raised the target to 250,000 acres. Then, finding the initial response disappointing, he sent a personal letter to every single farmer and, in a hired tobacco van fitted with loudspeakers, he drove out across the northern countryside urging men at numerous markets and fairs to plough up the sward. Spender disapproved, remarking that 'it savours rather of a political campaign'. Undeterred, Brooke followed up by giving a radio talk entitled *The Plough Versus the Submarine*; ordering that potatoes, carrots and cabbage be grown in lazy beds on the Stormont estate; getting golf clubs to plant corn on their fairways; and persuading Queen's University to cultivate its front lawn. In his diary he described as 'a fine show' a farm where nearly three quarters of the land had been ploughed up with a pair of donkeys.[17] During 1939–40 Northern Ireland was the only United Kingdom region to exceed its quota and this rate was sustained the following year. The additional 270,000 acres ploughed was a 40 per cent increase on prewar levels and twice the comparable figure for England and Wales. Under Brooke's direction the number of tractors in the region was raised to four and a half times the prewar figure by the beginning of 1941 and the control of dairy production was so successful that in wintertime up to seventeen thousand gallons of milk were shipped across the Irish Sea every day. There were disappointments, however: home flax cultivation did not achieve its target until 1943–4; lack of fertiliser caused a drop in crop yields; and acute shortages of imported feed so reduced the pig population that Brooke noted in his diary 'chaos if things go on' and 'if no relief must kill pigs'.[18] Nevertheless, his overall achievement was striking and he deplored his colleagues' lack of drive. In particular, Brooke was disgusted by his party's unsuccessful opposition to food rationing: 'I am afraid no M.P. realises there is a war on. If Ulster stands out on this she is doomed. Her loyalty is skin deep.'[19]

During the summer of 1940 the loyalty of the Northern Ireland government was put to a very severe test.

'THE MACKEREL ARE FAT – ON THE FLESH OF YOUR KIN'

On the very first night of the war the liner *Athenia* was torpedoed by U-30 off the north-west coast of Co. Donegal and sank with the loss of 112 lives. German submarines were spotted off Larne, Dundrum Bay and the Ards on 10–11 September; a week later another was seen near Tory Island; and on 18–19 September three more were reported close to the Ards and Rathlin. On 26 September four U-boats were sighted near the coasts of Northern Ireland, two of them venturing into the mouth of Belfast Lough. During the first fortnight of the conflict, 28 ships totalling 147,000 tons were lost.[20] Churchill, now first lord of the Admiralty, urged his cabinet colleagues that 'we should coerce Southern Ireland both about coast watching and the use of Berehaven, etc'.[21]

'A more feckless act can hardly be imagined' was Churchill's view of 'the gratuitous surrender of our right to use the Irish ports in war'.[22] Certainly the Royal Navy felt the loss keenly and the Ulster poet, Louis MacNeice, commented bitterly in 'Neutrality' on the fate of British crews inadequately protected:

> But then look eastward from your heart, there bulks
> A continent, close, dark, as archetypal sin,
> While to the west off your own shores the mackerel
> Are fat – on the flesh of your kin.[23]

De Valera was unmoved and he did not shift from the policy of neutrality announced in the spring of 1939, which he confirmed in his Radio Éireann broadcast on the evening of Sunday 3 September:

> With our history, with our experience of the last war, and with part of our country still severed from us, we felt that no other decision and no other policy was possible.[24]

Almost the entire population of Éire supported neutrality and de Valera rebuffed numerous approaches from the British government seeking the use of Lough Swilly, Berehaven and Cobh.

In the spring of 1940 the vortex of total war suddenly swung west-wards: the Germans overran Denmark and Norway at the beginning of April; a month later they swept over the Netherlands and Belgium; and then the Wehrmacht forged through the Ardennes, reaching Paris in June. As the shattered remains of the British Army gathered on the Dunkirk beaches Churchill, who had just replaced Chamberlain as prime minister, is said to have remarked gloomily in his map room that the only properly armed and disciplined force left in the United King-dom was the Ulster Special Constabulary. Then, as the Battle of Britain got under way, the Battle of the Atlantic intensified. The fall of France enabled U-boats to operate from Brest and Lorient, and long-range Focke-Wulf Condor bombers flew out from French air bases in search of British shipping off the west coast of Ireland to land eventually at Stavanger in Norway. After attending a defence conference in Dublin as a representative of Fine Gael, General Richard Mulcahy reported that 'a large number of sinkings are taking place close up around Malin Head', but that German aircraft were able to save fuel by flying close to Éire's coastline further south. 'Nests for [Allied] fighters jumping off the West Coast of Ireland could be very destructive, and could practically stop any great volume of this,' he admitted.[25] As Britain's plight became even more desperate Churchill sought drastic political solutions.

On 24 May 1940 Lord Halifax, the foreign secretary, wrote to Churchill asking him to give

> further thought to the possibilities of securing any improvement in Eire on the political side by any *démarche* in the direction of Northern Ireland. I see James Craig has just been over . . . The whole matter would seem to be one of the utmost urgency.[26]

Churchill agreed and asked Malcolm MacDonald – though he regarded him 'as rat-poison on account of his connexion with the Eire ports' – to approach de Valera.[27] In effect MacDonald, until recently dominions secretary, offered a declaration in favour of the reunification of Ireland in return for British use of the treaty ports. Churchill's cabinet discussed these negotiations on 20 June, the day before France signed an armistice with Germany, and agreed to make this offer:

> That there should be a declaration of a United Ireland in principle, the practical details of the union to be worked out in due course; this United Ireland to become at once a belligerent on the side of the Allies.[28]

One Foreign Office official noted in his diary that this 'looked like coercion of Northern Ireland'. 'I do not believe,' Chamberlain said at the next cabinet meeting, 'that the Ulster Government would refuse to play their part in bringing about so favourable a development.'[29] When next day and for the first time, on 26 June, Craigavon was told about the offer he fired off this cypher telegram:

AM PROFOUNDLY SHOCKED AND DISGUSTED BY YOUR LETTER MAKING SUGGESTIONS SO FAR REACHING BEHIND MY BACK AND WITHOUT ANY PRE-CONSULTATION WITH ME FULL STOP TO SUCH TREACHERY TO LOYAL ULSTER I WILL NEVER BE A PARTY.

Chamberlain was stung and ended his cypher riposte: 'PLEASE REMEMBER THE SERIOUS NATURE OF THE SITUATION WHICH REQUIRES THAT EVERY EFFORT BE MADE TO MEET IT.'[30] The Westminster government refused to be deflected by Craigavon and added this clause to its proposal: 'This declaration would take the form of a solemn undertaking that the Union is to become at an early date an accomplished fact from which there shall be no turning back.'[31]

Thus Churchill, impelled by the gravity of Britain's position in the summer of 1940, seemed prepared to abandon the northern loyalists and make plans to withdraw completely from every part of Ireland. The Northern Ireland cabinet was appalled and only Brooke felt that the menace of Nazi Germany was so imminent that Westminster's offer to Dublin should be seriously considered. Craigavon telegraphed to express his conviction that

DE VALERA IS UNDER GERMAN DICTATION AND FAR PAST REASONING WITH FULL STOP HE MAY PURPOSELY PROTRACT NEGOTIATIONS TILL ENEMY HAS LANDED FULL STOP STRONGLY ADVOCATE IMMEDIATE NAVAL OCCUPATION OF HARBOURS AND MILITARY ADVANCE SOUTH.[32]

Suddenly the crisis was over: on 7 July de Valera rejected the offer of Irish unity, 'which we note is purely tentative and has not been submitted to Lord Craigavon and his colleagues'.[33] In fact the British government had not made the agreement of the Northern Ireland cabinet a condition in their proposals.

The German occupation of France forced Britain to divert its convoys around the headlands of Co. Donegal and into the North Channel – a decision strengthened by Churchill's failure to get Éire to abandon its neutrality. Northern Ireland now had a crucial role to play as U-boats continued to wreak havoc on merchant shipping in the Western Approaches. 'All had to come in around Northern Ireland,' Churchill said later; 'Here by the grace of God, Ulster stood a faithful sentinel.'[34]

The neutral waters off Co. Donegal were being used both as refuges and as bases for German submarines. A British intelligence report observed that U-boats 'get sanctuary in the rocky isles off the extreme

West coast from Bloody Foreland to Donegal Bay, but principally in the vicinity of Gola and Aran islands'.[35] Sir Charles Tegart, former chief of the Bombay Police, visited Bunbeg and concluded that 'local Irishmen accept the visits of U-Boats with as common place an air as they accept the sun rise on a fine day'.[36] He was particularly suspicious of Wilhelm Hemersbach,

> who runs the hotel at Inver and who is openly hostile to Britain, having had his property at Donaghadee, County Down, confiscated during the Great War. His hotel is the meeting place of many of the Germans in Eire and members of the German Consulate in Dublin frequent there, ostensibly for recreation.[37]

This was true, but there is no evidence to support Tegart's allegation that Hemersbach supplied submarine crews with 'large quantities of eggs and butter'.[38] In any case this hotel at the same time was a popular venue for Major-General Bernard Montgomery's mother, Maud, and for British officers taking their leave to go duck shooting on Lough Eske – including Lieutenant Philip Mountbatten, later Prince Philip, Duke of Edinburgh. There is little doubt, however, that Co. Donegal fishermen at sea were selling their catch to U-boat crews.

People in Glenties recalled that the walls of their homes shook every night during the autumn of 1940 with the blast of great explosions out in the Atlantic, where Royal Navy convoy escorts were attempting to hold U-boat wolf packs at bay. Admiral Raeder reported to Hitler in September: 'The main operational area at present is the western part of the North Channel and the waters west of Scotland. It is very remunerative.'[39] Obsolete Ansons flew out from Sydenham, Aldergrove and Newtownards in all weathers, but their elusive targets continued to inflict devastating losses. Ulster was the first landfall for convoys coming in from the Atlantic and frantic efforts were made to make Northern Ireland the principal base for the counter-attack against German submarines. Derry became the principal port for fuelling destroyers and other escorts, and the city that had experienced nothing but unremitting depression since the end of the First World War now became the focus of feverish activity as the old graving dock was lengthened, a motor launch slipway was built, a forty-seven-acre ammunition depot was prepared and a repair shop was put up by Harland and Wolff. In June 1940 a team of experts began looking for suitable sites for new airfields and eventually seven were chosen: Long Kesh, Nutt's Corner, Maghaberry, Eglinton, Kirkistown, Ballykelly and Castle Archdale – this last was a seaplane base on lower Lough Erne. While the work of construction went on, however, British losses at sea continued to mount: Northern Ireland's largest shipping firms, the Head Line and John

Kelly Limited, suffered more than half their total wartime losses between January and June 1941.

At the same time the Third Reich's western advance brought Northern Ireland well within range of German bombers, now inflicting devastating attacks on British cities.

'THE PERIOD OF THE NEXT MOON . . . MAY WELL BRING OUR TURN'

'I have heard speeches about Ulster pulling her weight but they have never carried conviction,' Edmond Warnock said, announcing his resignation from the Northern Ireland government in May 1940.[40] A fortnight later Lieutenant-Colonel Alexander R.G. Gordon, parliamentary secretary at the Ministry of Finance, also resigned, explaining to the Commons that the Government was

> by nature of its personnel, its lack of drive and initiative and utter lack of what war means . . . quite unfitted to sustain the people in the ordeal we have to face . . . It should resign and be reconstituted immediately.[41]

Speaking on a motion condemning the high level of unemployment, Jack Beattie described the prime minister as having reached his 'doting stage'. It is likely that several Unionist backbenchers agreed with him. The cabinet secretary was understandably irritated that his valuable time was used to telephone London to order marmalade from Fortnum and Mason for Lady Craigavon or to run out to buy tobacco and cigarettes. In September Warnock introduced a vote of censure, calling for a complete change in the Government's composition. He described Milne Barbour's direction at the Ministry of Commerce as 'wrong, inept and palsied', and remarked that when a person became a member of the Northern Ireland government 'he becomes a tenant for life . . . Nothing but death, illness or promotion ever removes anybody.' Craigavon's simple response to the call to revamp his government was: 'My answer is that I am not going to do it.'[42]

On Sunday 24 November 1940, just after listening to the six o'clock news on the wireless, Craigavon died peacefully in his armchair. The grief at his death was widely and deeply felt amongst loyalists. With skill and energy he had led the Ulster Unionists in their successful campaign to prevent Westminster imposing Home Rule on all of Ireland; as the man more responsible than any other for the partition of his country, he had established the United Kingdom's first devolved government and prevented it from lapsing into anarchy in 1921–2; but thereafter he had allowed matters to drift and showed a fatal complacency and narrowness of vision in permitting the grievances of the nationalist minority to suppurate over two decades. Admittedly he faced immense difficulties: de Valera's irredentism; economic decline;

almost unworkable devolutionary arrangements; and a bitterly divided society.[43]

Andrews had often deputised for Craigavon and there was no dispute when he was chosen to succeed him as prime minister. 'For psychological reasons if for no other, we must make cabinet changes,' Brooke urged Andrews, but the only new face in the Government was Lord Glentoran.[44] The old guard, therefore, remained in office and under the direction of Andrews it was no more capable than before of coping with the exigencies of war.

When Harold Wilson came to Belfast in December 1940 on behalf of the Manpower Requirements Committee, he was appalled by Northern Ireland's poor performance. He reported that after 'fifteen months of war, far from being an important centre of munitions, the province had become a depressed area' which had 'not seen the construction of a single new factory'.[45] Apart from orders placed with Harland and Wolff, those given to existing firms had been on an 'extremely meagre scale', despite freedom from air attack, uncongested ports and railways, and a large pool of skilled labour. Over a period when unemployment in Britain had almost halved it had risen steadily in Northern Ireland to almost seventy-two thousand by November 1940, even though over the previous year some fourteen thousand workers had crossed the Irish Sea to get jobs in Britain. Milne Barbour had done almost nothing to encourage the suspension of restrictive practices in the workplace to speed the completion of orders, and Short and Harland's record of stoppages was a cause of great concern.

The Northern Ireland government had done almost nothing to unite the people of the region in common cause against Hitler's Germany. Without even consulting his colleagues, Craigavon decided that the B Specials should form the nucleus of the Home Guard and, not surprisingly, opposition MPs condemned this as 'creating a sectarian and political force', making 'political loyalty' a condition of recruitment.[46] The appointment of Brooke – notorious for his partisan remarks in 1933 – to head a drive for recruits for the armed forces was unlikely to appeal to the minority. Though he spoke at sixteen rallies across the region from mid-July 1940 onwards, he was afraid to appear at Derry city. He used the Unionist Party headquarters in Glengall Street as his base and amongst those who appeared on platforms with him was Lord Londonderry, noted for his prewar sympathy for the Nazi leaders and for entertaining Joachim von Ribbentrop, Hitler's foreign minister, at Mount Stewart. Recruitment levels in Northern Ireland remained embarrassingly low and in 1941–2 enlistment only exceeded one thousand per month on three occasions.[47]

Above all, the Northern Ireland government failed to make adequate preparations to protect its citizens. Major Frank Eastwood, appointed air-raid precautions officer in Belfast during the Munich crisis of 1938, had predicted that 'thousands of fire bombs will be thrown from planes like apples out of a basket', causing fires 'beyond the control of our regular fire brigade'. Craigavon, however, preferred to listen to Major-General Sir Hastings-Ismay, deputy secretary of the Committee of Imperial Defence, who, according to Spender, 'considered that there was very little likelihood of any attack being made upon us'.[48] Much vital time was lost while the Northern Ireland government argued that civil defence in the region was Westminster's financial responsibility. Warnock considered that since Belfast would 'not be subject to frequent attack or to attack by large concentrations of enemy aircraft', it would be 'illogical for the Government to provide Anderson shelters for private houses' and announced that the Ministry of Home Affairs had 'no plans for the direct protection of the people'.[49]

'All sorts of rot going on here', Lady Londonderry wrote to her husband soon after the outbreak of war; 'Air raid warnings and blackouts! As if anyone cared or wished to bomb Belfast.'[50] After a brief flurry of activity, the regional government's attitude to civil defence soon lapsed back to being as soporific as before. Dawson Bates simply refused to reply to army correspondence, and it was little wonder that when the Ministry of Home Affairs was informed by imperial defence experts that Belfast was a certain Luftwaffe target, nothing was done.[51] The city had no fighter squadrons, no balloon barrage and only twenty anti-aircraft guns when the war began; only around two thousand civil defence volunteers had been trained; and there were only four public air-raid shelters made of sandbags round the city hall, together with underground toilets at Shaftesbury Square and Donegall Square North.[52] Only some houses in the harbour area had domestic shelters and not a single one had been provided anywhere else in Northern Ireland. So complacent was the Government that by November 1939, on Warnock's orders, most of Belfast's searchlights had been sent back to England, along with the brigades that manned them. It was therefore not surprising that the general public refused to take precautions seriously. Before the war it was planned to evacuate seventy thousand children; it was not until July 1940 that a scheme was adopted to take seventeen thousand out of the city. Only 7,000 children turned up, followed by 1,800 six weeks later, and more than half of those evacuated had returned by the spring of 1941. The Belfast Corporation was so lacking in any real sense of urgency that vital pipe fittings for fire-fighting appliances and building materials for shelters were not available when Hitler turned his forces westward in 1940. Andrews, almost seventy and just one year younger than the man he replaced, had neither the health nor the vision to provide the leadership now desperately required. Spender confided to his diary that the new prime minister had 'no idea of the war situation', and that it was 'very difficult for a man of his upbringing and outlook to realise ... the relative importance of matters of local interest and those of European concern'.[53]

To fend off criticism, Craigavon had appointed John MacDermott as minister of public security in June 1940. It did not take the new minister long to appreciate the fearfully inadequate defences in the region but again and again his efforts were frustrated by public apathy and lack of support from his colleagues. As the bombing of British cities got under way it was clear that Belfast was the most unprotected city in the United Kingdom. On 24 March 1941 MacDermott expressed his anxiety in a letter to Andrews: anti-aircraft cover was less than half the approved strength in Belfast; the city did not possess a single searchlight; and no other town in Northern Ireland had any defence at all. He concluded:

> Up to now we have escaped attack. So had Clydeside until recently. Clydeside got its blitz during the period of the last moon. There are certain technical reasons which probably give us some ground for thinking that at present the enemy could not easily reach Belfast *in force* except during a period of moonlight. The period of the next moon from, say, the 7th to the 16th of April, may well bring our turn.[54]

On the night of 7–8 April a small squadron of German bombers, led by a pathfinder Heinkel 111 from Kampfgruppe 26, raided Belfast, and completely destroyed the four-and-a-half-acre Harland and Wolff fuselage factory, reduced a major timber yard to ashes, and delivered damaging blows to the docks. Compared with the horrifying assault on London, Liverpool, Glasgow, Bristol and Great Yarmouth the same night, the attack was a small one. After returning to their bases in northern France, Luftwaffe bomber crews reported that Belfast's defences were 'inferior in quality, scanty and insufficient'.[55] Sirens had sounded only after the first bombs had fallen. The people of Northern Ireland now knew they were vulnerable after all.

THE BELFAST BLITZ: THE EASTER RAID, 1941

Easter Tuesday, 15 April 1941, had been a dull oppressive day but the sky was clearing that evening as 180 German bombers, predominantly Junkers 88s and Heinkel 111s, flew in formation over the Irish Sea. As the raiders approached the Ards they dropped to seven thousand feet.

On the Castlereagh Hills ground crews manned anti-aircraft guns; Hawker Hurricane Mark IIs sped down the runway at Aldergrove aerodrome; and at 10.40 p.m. sirens wailed in Belfast.[56]

Casting intense light, hundreds of flares drifted down, then incendiaries, high-explosive bombs and parachute mines rained on the city. It was not the industrial heartland but the congested housing north of the city centre that received the full force of the attack. This may not have been the German intention: perhaps the Belfast Waterworks at the Cave Hill was mistaken for the harbour; perhaps a hastily contrived smoke screen at the shipyards confused the pilots; or perhaps the instruction to take a bearing on the twin spires of St Peter's on the Falls caused the Germans to overshoot their targets. The result was a fearful carnage in the New Lodge, the lower Shankill and the Antrim Road. Suspended from green artificial silk parachutes, seventy-six landmines slowly drifted down; designed to rend apart the reinforced concrete and steel of factories and workshops – their existence not acknowledged by the British government until 1944 – more than half of these fell on decaying terraced houses. In Veryan Gardens and Vandyck Gardens 130 homes were destroyed and in one house eight members of the Danby family were killed. York Street Spinning Mill, the largest of its kind in Europe, was sliced in two; the collapsing six storeys obliterated forty-two houses, and damaged twenty-one, in Sussex Street and Vere Street. A bomb struck one house in Ballynure Street and nine people were killed.

Still the bombers kept coming 'for all the world like some gigantic swarm of insects whose drone was only ineffectually interrupted by bangs and crashes', Moya Woodside recorded in south Belfast.[57] After the raid a Luftwaffe pilot gave this description on German radio:

> We were in exceptional good humour knowing that we were going for a new target, one of England's last hiding places. Wherever Churchill is hiding his war material we will go ... Belfast is as worthy a target as Coventry, Birmingham, Bristol or Glasgow.[58]

In the Ulster Hall Delia Murphy, the popular singer and wife of the Irish ambassador to Australia, kept singing through the raid. Some of her audience were later forced to take refuge in a shelter in Percy Street; when a parachute mine fell next to it, thirty people were killed. HMS *Furious* was the only vessel in port to add to the anti-aircraft barrage but she sheared loose from the recoil of her guns.

At 1.45 a.m. a bomb fell at the corner of Oxford Street and East Bridge Street, wrecking the city's central telephone exchange. All contact with Britain and the anti-aircraft operations control room was cut off. The guns on the ground fell silent for fear of shooting down the Hurricane fighters, which, with cruel irony, had been withdrawn shortly before by

Fighter Command. For another two hours the Luftwaffe attacked Belfast completely unopposed. Altogether 203 metric tons of bombs and 800 firebomb canisters were dropped on the city.

Around 140 fires now raged in Belfast and several of these spread into conflagrations. Just as the Auxiliary Fire Service arrived to fight the great inferno sweeping across the Antrim Road, the water pressure fell away – the mains had been cracked in thirty places. In east Belfast Mary Wallace looked out from her home near the ropeworks: 'The sky was red, pure red,' she recalled; 'You would have thought that someone had set fire to the world.'[59] The Ministry of Public Security requested help from civil defence regions throughout Northern Ireland and the War Office responded promptly to a call for aid, sending a total of forty-two pumps and four hundred firemen from Glasgow, Liverpool and Preston. From his house near Stormont, MacDermott watched the flames enveloping the city. As he heard the crash of his windows shattering he crawled under his desk and at 4.15 a.m. he telephoned Brooke who was staying nearby. The line was still working. MacDermott asked for permission to request fire engines from Éire. 'I gave him authority as it is obviously a question of expediency', Brooke noted in his diary.[60] At 4.35 a.m. a telegram was sent by railway telegraph, because the telephone lines to Dublin had been cut. De Valera was awakened and agreed without hesitation to send help. Soon after, Major Comerford, Dublin's chief fire superintendent, was enlisting thirty volunteers at the Tara Street station. Altogether seventy men and thirteen fire engines from Dublin, Dún Laoghaire, Drogheda and Dundalk sped northwards. 'I had to sit on my hands to keep them from getting numb,' one volunteer remembered; 'There were no landmarks on the way up; we reached our destination by following the telephone lines.'[61]

As they approached the city outskirts the southern firemen saw smoke and flames rising hundreds of feet into the air. Horrified at the carnage, John Smith, Belfast's chief fire officer, was found beneath a table in Chichester Street fire station, weeping and refusing to come out. There was little the firemen could do to fight the flames – hoses were cut by falling buildings, fittings were often the incorrect diameter, and the water pressure had fallen too far. Ewart's weaving mill on the Crumlin Road was still burning twenty-four hours later. There were numerous individual acts of heroism but Spender felt that the city fire brigade 'made a poor showing' and MacDermott admitted that some civil defence workers had 'sloped off'. An American, seconded to Short and Harland by the Lockheed Aircraft Corporation, was not impressed by his fellow workers; in a letter to his parents in California he wrote:

You have heard about how tough the Irish are – well all I can say is that the tough Irish must come from S. Ireland because the boys up in N. Ireland are a bunch of chicken shit yellow bastards – 90% of them left everything and ran like hell. Short and Harlands the Aircraft factory that builds Stirlings here had 300 Volunteer fire fighters in the plant, after the raid they were lucky to get 90 of them.[62]

Outside of Belfast the Germans struck at targets that lay within their flight path. Around midnight two large parachute mines were dropped near the Buncrana Road in Derry: one fell in a field, causing some blast damage to houses and railway carriages; but the other devastated ex-servicemen's homes in Messines Park, completely demolishing 5 houses, killing 15 people and leaving 150 homeless. It is likely that the bomber was attempting to block the River Foyle at a narrow point nearby to disrupt Derry's capacity as a base for guarding the Western Approaches. About an hour later, on the other side of Northern Ireland, Newtownards aerodrome was struck by explosives and incendiaries and ten guards were killed. At the same time fourteen bombs were dropped on Bangor, killing five people and injuring thirty-five others.[63]

At dawn on Wednesday 16 April a thick yellow pall covered Belfast. Exhausted air-raid wardens, firemen and ambulance men tore at the smouldering rubble to bring the trapped, dead and injured to the surface. 'We wrestled with street doors blown halfway down hallways', Sam Hanna Bell remembered. 'From under the stairs of a house we extracted an old woman still clutching a miniature Union Jack.' The Reverend Eric Gallagher, then minister of Woodvale Methodist Church, helped to dig out the bodies of fourteen members of his congregation from the ruins of houses in Ohio Street. The previous evening he had called at a house there and he remembered a five-year-old boy. 'He sat sitting on my knee for some time, and we were playing while I talked to the family', he recalled; 'I helped to dig him out of the rubble the next morning.'[64]

On the Crumlin Road army lorries were piled high with corpses and severed limbs. Many of the dead were brought into the Falls Road Public Baths. As more arrived the pool had to be emptied in order to lay out over 150 corpses; an attendant remembered:

One coffin contained – all open – a young mother with her two dead children, one in each arm. One lovely girl of sixteen lay in a coffin in her white confirmation robe with blue silk ribbon and black hair.[65]

There the bodies lay for three days as relatives attempted, often in vain, to identify them. Two hundred and fifty-five corpses were laid out in St George's Market. Here Emma Duffin was one of the nurses on duty. 'A man watered the floor with disinfectant from a watering pail', she recorded in her diary: 'a wise precaution as the place smelt. It was a hideous nightmare.' She had seen 'death in many forms, young men dying of ghastly wounds' during the First World War but while Death in hospital beds in France had been 'solemn, tragic, dignified . . . here it was grotesque, repulsive, horrible'. She continued:

No attendant nurse had soothed the last moments of these victims, no gently reverent hand had closed their eyes or crossed their hands. With tangled hair, staring eyes, contorted limbs, their grey-green faces covered with dust, they lay bundled into the coffins, half-shrouded in rugs or blankets or an occasional sheet, still wearing their dirty, torn, twisted garments. Death should be dignified, peaceful, Hitler had made death grotesque. I felt outraged. I should have felt sympathy, grief, but instead feelings of revulsion and disgust assailed me.[66]

Of the bodies taken here, 151 were identified and only 92 taken away by relatives and friends for burial. On Monday 21 April the unclaimed dead were buried in mass graves: Protestants at the city cemetery and Catholics (identified by rosaries and emblems) in the Milltown cemetery close by. T.J. Campbell, leader of the Nationalist Party, rightly observed in the Commons that the 'toll was greatest in the narrow streets, where life crowds thick and fast and where the struggle for existence never ends from the cradle to the grave'.[67] The official figures were 745 people dead and 430 seriously injured. The actual total was at least nine hundred dead. No other city, except London, had lost so many lives in one air raid.[68]

Journalists discovered that their descriptions of panic and low civilian morale were censored out of their reports. Some six thousand people arrived in Dublin from Belfast, including an air-raid warden still wearing his helmet. Tens of thousands left the city for the countryside. 'Children clutched their favourite toys,' the Belfast Telegraph reported, 'little girls carrying dollies . . . Many brought with them their pets, from budgerigars to tabbies.'[69] Of those who remained, forty thousand had to be put up in rest centres and seventy thousand had to be given meals every day in emergency feeding centres. The military authorities were deeply unimpressed by uncoordinated rescue work and attempts to restore normal life. Troops who spent 10,500 working days in providing help were disgusted by widespread looting and the 'attitude of large numbers of able-bodied young men, who spent their time sight-seeing and refused to lend a hand'.[70] Apart from urgently requesting more defence equipment from Britain, neither the Government nor the Belfast Corporation were able to do a great deal to improve the protection of citizens. One response by the Ministry of Public Security to the desperate situation was to issue this order on 19 April: 'Destroy all dangerous animals at the zoo immediately.' Two RUC marksmen were sent to Bellevue Zoo and, the *Belfast Telegraph* recorded, Head Keeper Dick Foster 'stood by with tears streaming down his face, as the executioners proceeded from cage to cage and despatched the animals 33 in number, and a vulture'. The animals included, unbelievably, two raccoons.[71]

Moya Woodside noted that everyone seemed to be quoting Lord Haw Haw. 'He will give us time to bury our dead before the next attack'; 'Tuesday was only a sample'; 'People living in such and such an area will have their turn'.[72] Belfast was to have its turn again – before its defences could be significantly strengthened.

'A SEA OF FLAMES SUCH AS NONE OF US HAD SEEN BEFORE':
4–5 MAY 1941

At 9.45 p.m. on Sunday 4 May 1941 the first squadrons of German bombers took off from northern France and about an hour after midnight the attack on Belfast began. In the words of one pilot, 'visibility was wonderful. I could make out my targets perfectly.'[73] Until 1.55 a.m. the pathfinders of Kampfgruppe 100 dropped six thousand incendiaries almost exclusively on the harbour, the aircraft factory and the shipyards; then the rest of the bombers were led in by the rapidly spreading conflagration. Most of the Luftwaffe flew between 7,000 and 9,000 feet, but the defences were so weak that some aircraft with specific targets were able to fly as low as 2,500 feet below the balloon barrage. Three corvettes nearing completion were totally destroyed; another was badly burned; transport ship *Fair Head* sank at her moorings; three ships received direct hits in the Abercorn yard; and altogether Harland and Wolff suffered the devastation of two thirds of its premises. Much of the densely inhabited area about the Newtownards Road was burning fiercely.

The German crews reported a 'picture of destruction none of us will forget'.[74] A war correspondent, Ernst von Kuhren, flying with one squadron, broadcast his impressions afterwards:

> I can really say that I could not believe my eyes. When we approached the target at half-past two we stared silently into a sea of flames such as none of us had seen before ... In Belfast there was not a large number of conflagrations, but just one enormous conflagration which spread over the entire harbour and industrial area ... Here the English had concentrated an important part of their war industries because they felt themselves safe, far up in the North, safe from the blows of the German airforce. This has come to an end.[75]

Jimmy Mackey, a regular fireman, recalled:

> At the larger fires, there were firestorms. As the flames took hold, there was a great in-rush of air; they sucked it in creating a shortage of oxygen and making breathing difficult.

After fighting an uneven battle with the flames for a night and a day, Mackey fell asleep with exhaustion, his head resting against a lamppost in Donegall Street.[76] Charlie Gallagher was with one of six fire crews which drove from Derry; he stopped to let his engine cool at the top of the Glenshane Pass and there, forty-five miles from Belfast, the fires in the city were clearly visible and appeared to 'pulsate up and down'. Once again thirteen fire appliances came up from Éire but their efforts were to little avail: the water mains had been cracked in sixty-seven places and when the tide went out the fire hoses could not reach the river water. This time much damage was inflicted on the city centre: the area around St Anne's Cathedral burned intensely; almost the whole northern side of High Street was ablaze down to the Albert Memorial; and Arnott's store, the Bank Buildings, the Athletic Stores, the Ulster Arcade, the Water Office, Rosemary Street Presbyterian Church and the banqueting room of the city hall were either destroyed or severely damaged. That night almost three hundred people, many from the Shankill, took refuge in Clonard Monastery, whose 'Domestic Chronicles' record:

> The crypt under the sanctuary, also the cellar under the working sacristy has been fitted out and is opened to the people, women and children only, as an air-raid shelter. This act of ours is very much appreciated by all, Protestants included. Prayers are said and hymns sung by the occupants during the bombing.[77]

In less than three and a half hours the bombers had dropped 95,992 incendiaries and 237 tons of high explosives. Early on Monday morning a lone German aeroplane flew over Belfast to make a photographic record of the results of the raid. *Der Adler* published aerial views of the city and gave a full page to analysing the successful outcome of the attack. For the first and only time in the war, Northern Ireland made headline news in the German press. *Völkischer Beobachter* began its report 'Strong Air Fighter Units Bomb Belfast' and 'Back from Belfast: Fires Everywhere'. Radio listeners in Germany were told that the 'Belfast shipyard and industry have been completely destroyed'.[78] This was not entirely correct for Harland and Wolff's building slips, power station, Admiralty offices and pumping station were largely unscathed; nevertheless, the company's claim of £3 million for bomb damage was the largest single amount sought by any firm in the United Kingdom during the war. By now 53.5 per cent of Belfast's housing stock had been destroyed or badly damaged and the death toll for this May raid was 191 – a surprisingly low figure largely explained by two facts: that in this Sabbatarian city the centre was largely deserted when the attack began; and a very large number of people had already fled to the countryside.

The exodus from Belfast during and after the April and May air raids was on a huge scale and MacDermott was right to observe that more were leaving there 'in proportion to population than any other city in the United Kingdom'.[79] On 16 April Joseph McCann saw 'streams of people moving up the Falls, the women and children with mattresses and bedclothes strapped to prams and handcarts', and the following morning the *Northern Whig* reported that the scenes 'were like the pictures of American pioneers'. Moya Woodside watched

> an exodus on foot, trams, lorries, trailers, cattle floats, bicycles, delivery vans, anything that would move was utilized. Private cars streamed past . . . all sorts of paraphernalia roped on behind. Hundreds were waiting at bus-stops. Anxiety on every face . . . [80]

By 17 April there were two thousand evacuees in Dromara, a village normally with a population of five hundred. Towns close to Belfast were overwhelmed. In Lisburn, one member of the Women's Voluntary Service reported, all needed to be 'fed, housed, deloused, marshalled, bathed, clothed, pacified and brought back to normal'.[81]

This mass migration from Belfast brought into the open the extreme deprivation of those now bombed out of congested streets who had endured two decades of unemployment and neglect. Emma Duffin's middle-class sensibilities were offended by 'the incredible dirt of the people, of children crawling with lice, not even house trained, who destroyed mattresses and stuffed clothes down W.C.s in order to get new ones'. Moya Woodside recorded that the eleven evacuees staying with her mother were 'all filthy, the smell of the room is terrible, they refuse all food except tea and bread, the children have made puddles all over the floor, etc.'. Several had tuberculosis and two had severe scalp infections. Her sister, living thirty miles from Belfast, complained of

> the appalling influx from the slums the day after the raid. They were totally unprepared for such numbers and the type of people arriving. The whole town is horrified by the filth of these evacuees and by their filthy habits and take-it-for-granted attitude . . . The smell is awful . . . They don't even use the lavatory, they just do it on the floor, grown-ups and children.[82]

By 3 May Spender estimated that one hundred thousand people – around one quarter of the population of Belfast – had fled to the Ulster countryside. The city was so deserted, Sarah Nelson remembered, 'it was like the plague had come'.[83] Yet well over half those killed on the night 4–5 May were women and children, and next morning, as railway and bus stations were once again besieged, a fresh exodus began.

Emma Duffin told how a colleague on board a train thronged with evacuees noticed a woman who 'had a dead baby in her arms and was asking for a bottle for it from everyone she met'.[84] By the end of May some 220,000 had left the city, thus creating acute congestion in the farmhouses and rural towns. On 15 May Dawson Bates had written a memorandum to the Northern Ireland cabinet urging that the governor turn over his Hillsborough residence to refugees and requesting the use of 'large houses, institutions or camps for respectable families who are at present billeted at the rate of 30 to small houses'. As for the families he did not consider respectable, those his ministry had done so little to protect, he concluded:

> There are in the country probably about 5,000 absolutely unbilletable persons. They are unbilletable owing to personal habits which are sub-human. Camps or institutions under suitable supervision must be instituted for these.[85]

Meanwhile, the really prosperous could leave Northern Ireland altogether. Moya Woodside described a Co. Donegal hotel, which was

> almost the last place in Europe where the lights are still alight . . . Last year it was only half-full and those wearing evening dress were in a minority. This year it is crowded out mainly with Belfast's wealthier citizens and about 75 per cent are in evening wear. In fact the display of jewellery and furs is terrific. I am amused to note that a man's economic status is indicated by the number and size of the precious stones which adorn his wife's person and by the comparative length of her silver fur and mink shoulder cape.

For the great majority of those who had left Belfast, evacuation involved hardship and inconvenience. Nellie Bell, married the day before the Easter raid, shared a cottage with a family in Donaghcloney. She recalled how difficult it was for her husband to get to work in Belfast each day:

> Bob was working shifts 6.00 to 2.00 and 2.00 till 10.00. Well, to get to work on early shifts, Bob and me both had to get up about 3.00 or 3.30 a.m. Though this is 1941, the cottage had no gas or electric. I had to light a fire with bellows to make him a cup of tea or boil an egg or something. He walked the 4 or 5 miles to Lurgan to get a train to leave him into Belfast. After a couple of weeks he got a bicycle which helped a bit but after a puncture or two, it didn't work very well either.

Many evacuated children also had to work. A welfare officer in Cookstown was 'deeply ashamed' by the exploitation of orphans from Dr Barnardo's and other homes used as cheap labour on farms in Co. Armagh and around Ballymena and Ballycastle.[86] In Belfast itself there were still 150,000 people in target areas without access to shelters.

Radio Paris, under German direction, informed its listeners in the middle of May: 'Fearing air raids, 20,000 women and children escape every evening from Belfast to the outskirts of the city.' This was a considerable underestimate. Jim McConville remembers:

> The exodus began around 10 p.m. Hundreds went as far as the Falls Park; thousands felt safer another mile out of the city. Parents and children 'well happed up' against the cold night air would sit around on folding stools, or lie on ground sheets; some could and would sleep; most of us talked, joked and bantered as only the Belfast working man can; someone would light a cigarette and immediately from all around would come: 'Put out that match! Do you want Jerry to see us!'

Though rumours circulated in Protestant areas that Catholics had helped to guide German bombers by shining torches from the rooftops, the shared experiences of fear, hardship and bereavement did reduce intercommunal tensions for a time. 'This nightly journey "up the road" to the safety of the countryside, and the return in the early hours of the morning,' Jim McConville wrote, 'helped intensify the feeling of togetherness that had grown up as the war progressed . . . New friendships were forged; old acquaintances and long-time neighbours were seen in a new light; kindness and a helping hand appeared from the most unexpected quarters.'[87] Protestants and Catholics were also united in their contempt for the Government's ineptitude and complacency. 'I broke down after the things I saw,' Tommy Henderson said bitterly at Stormont on 13 May, 'I broke down when I saw lying dead men I had been reared beside. When I saw the whole district where I roamed in my bare feet razed to the ground.' Then looking angrily towards the prime minister, he asked:

> Will the Right Hon member come with me to the hills and to Divis mountain? Will he go to the barns and sheughs throughout Northern Ireland to see the people of Belfast, some of them lying on damp ground? Will he come to Hannahstown and the Falls Road? The Catholics and Protestants are going up there mixed and they are talking to one another. They are sleeping in the same sheugh, below the same tree or in the same barn. They all say the same thing, that the government is no good.[88]

Henderson's fury would have been all the more intense had he known how much time the Northern Ireland government had devoted to arranging camouflage for the Stormont parliament buildings and to debating at length how to protect the bronze statue of Carson in its grounds from bomb damage. Andrews consulted Carson's widow about the statue and two months later put its safety as the first item on the cabinet agenda, where it was agreed to form a committee to make recommendations. This was during a period when tens of thousands of

Belfast citizens were still without the protection of air-raid shelters.

Fortunately for the people of Northern Ireland the Germans did not again return in force. By a strange irony, the last Luftwaffe raid in Ireland was not on Belfast but on Dublin. During the first hour of Saturday 31 May 1941 air-raid precautions wardens went to their posts as sirens warned of approaching German aircraft. Then around 1.30 a.m. bombs fell on North Circular Road, Summerhill Parade and Phoenix Park, and half an hour later North Strand was hit, killing or mortally injuring thirty-four – over half the dead were women and children. Twenty-five houses were destroyed and another 345 were left unfit for habitation. Were the Germans punishing Éire for treating stranded Allied air crews more leniently than German ones? Did the Germans fail to see the flares sent up to signal that they were flying over a neutral state? No clear answer can be given.

On 26 June 1941 the Wehrmacht crossed the borders of the Soviet Union, thus ending the isolation of the United Kingdom. By the end of the year the general European war had become a worldwide conflict and Hitler sealed his fate, shortly after the Japanese assault on Pearl Harbour, by casually declaring war on the richest nation on earth – the United States.

'THE TRAMP OF MARCHING YANKS'

In January 1941, almost a year before the United States entered the war, plans were laid to set up US Army Corps bases in Northern Ireland and to develop Derry as the terminal for convoys crossing the Atlantic to Britain. On 30 June 1941, 362 'civilian technicians' arrived at Derry and their numbers more than doubled over the next five months as they built a new quay at Lisahally, a ship repair base, a radio station, personnel camps, an administrative headquarters and ammunition and storage depots.[89] Then, on 26 January 1942, the first American troops stepped ashore at Belfast's Dufferin Quay under the command of the youngest major-general in the US Army. Sir Basil Brooke had been summoned to London a few days before and told by his uncle, Alan Brooke, chief of imperial general staff, that Churchill wanted him 'to see personally that the hospitality accorded to the Americans was of the very highest order'.[90] It was, and the band of the Royal Ulster Rifles played the 'Star-Spangled Banner' to give what the *Belfast Telegraph* called 'a hearty Ulster welcome'.[91] This newspaper continued:

> Over the Province prowling enemy planes received a hot reception from ground defences, and for a time the thudding of distant heavy gunfire synchronised with the tramp of marching Yanks as they clattered down

the gangways and on to the square-setts of the landing stage . . . Many of the Americans had thought that at the beginning in camp they would have to live 'rough', and they were pleasantly surprised . . . The inevitable dog mascot has made its appearance, an American soldier somehow managing to bring along a mongrel known as 'Jitterbug'.

At Stormont Andrews admitted that an 'event so historic and so significant' had given him 'a thrill of emotion', and he added:

> Between the United States and Ulster there are many bonds that cannot be broken, bonds created by kinship and language, identity of outlook and a common faith in democracy.[92]

In February the US Naval Operating Base in Derry was officially commissioned and by May 1942 the number of Americans in Northern Ireland had reached thirty-seven thousand. On the eastern shores of Lough Neagh a new town sprang up at Langford Lodge; here the Lockheed Overseas Corporation, on behalf of the American government, repaired and maintained aircraft. United States airmen were also stationed at airfields at Eglinton, Maydown and Mullaghmore in Co. Londonderry; Toome and Maghaberry in Co. Antrim; Cluntoe in Co. Tyrone; and Greencastle in Co. Down. During the autumn of 1942 the first contingents of American troops had moved on to North Africa in preparation for the invasion of Italy. A year later greater numbers arrived in readiness for the Normandy landings and for a time there were 120,000 Americans in the North. The United States spent seventy-five million US dollars developing its facilities in Derry, particularly for the repair, maintenance and refuelling of convoy escorts. The Americans made their headquarters at Talbot House, near Magee College, and constructed a massive underground bunker there. Here, too, was the most important naval radio station in the European theatre of operations. At one stage 149 vessels were based in Derry to patrol the Western Approaches, together with some 20,000 sailors. By 1943, the official historian John W. Blake has written, Derry

> held the key to victory in the Atlantic . . . By that critical Spring when the battle for the security of our Atlantic lifelines finally turned our way, Londonderry was the most important escort base in the North-Western approaches. Everybody at Londonderry co-operated in this supreme effort.

For a while outsiders – Americans, Canadians, the free forces of occupied states, and refugees from Gibraltar – seemed as numerous as the citizens themselves.[93]

During the second half of 1943, when units of the XV (US) Army Corps disembarked to prepare for the D-day landings, the numbers were so great that they had to be spread across Northern Ireland. The first arrivals went to the Newry–Armagh area and later contingents were based at Newcastle, Cookstown, Omagh, Lurgan and at several points in Co. Fermanagh.[94] Watching them marching through Bangor, David Davidson concluded: 'You could not help but like them.'[95] Training films led Americans to expect a much more backward society in the North than they found. Nevertheless, the contrast in living standards was striking. As one woman in Newry remembers:

> Food and luxuries were very short in Newry, but I can tell you that Yanks did not go short. They were a great attraction to all the kids and their families. If you had a Yank visiting your house, you never went short. We all learned to chew gum and smoke Camel cigarettes.[96]

From the outset the Americans were great favourites with the children. In Derry Jim Girr recalled

> when they took over the picture houses. Every child of school age was marched over to the pictures. You got a big bag of sweets going up to the picture show which lasted three or four hours. It was a great treat as sweets were scarce. The American 'technicians' paid for everything.[97]

Local men, however, resented the competition for the attention of young women. Charlie Gallagher, an air-raid precautions officer in Derry, recollected: 'We were getting our eyes wiped left, right and centre . . . The British used to say of the Americans that they were "over-fed, over-paid, over-sexed and over here". The Americans' reply was that the British were "under-paid, under-fed, under-sexed and under Eisenhower".'[98] A Mass Observation reporter in Northern Ireland summed up the Americans' off-duty activities as 'pubs and pickups'. Young women from the Shankill who consorted with Americans, according to Rita McKittrick, were seen as 'brash and had a fast reputation. You were sort of blacklisted if you went out with them', and her mother told her to have 'nothing to do with them' or she would 'get killed'.[99] At best such women were subjected to scoffs and sneers:

> Coming in with a Yank on a jeep,
> All the girls in Derry thinks its cheap.
> With their clothes up to their bums
> And their chewing Yankee gum,
> Coming in with a Yank on a jeep.[100]

At times the American presence led to severe friction. Jimmy Penton remembers that in Protestant east Belfast Americans were 'warned off' Dee Street and 'never came near it'. On the Falls Joseph McCann recalled:

> Girls who had gone out with them were likely to get their hair cut off. It was a common occurrence. Fights were sometimes sparked off by troops asking for girls.

In October 1942 a black GI was killed in a fight between local men and American troops in Antrim town. A few weeks earlier an American quartermaster had predicted 'bloodshed in the near future', observing that white soldiers were irked by the popularity of blacks: 'The girls really go for them in preference to white boys.'[101]

Most people, however, were flattered by the attention Americans gave to Northern Ireland. The 2nd Infantry Division made Narrow Water Castle its headquarters and local people watched in fascination as troops practised hand-to-hand combat, dug trenches and put up fortifications around Newry, and were taught how to drive tanks over the south Down countryside – Ballymacdermot cairn had to be repaired hastily when a tank drove into it. Generals Eisenhower and Patton inspected their troops and amongst those who came to entertain the men were Larry Adler, George Formby, and Glenn Miller and his orchestra.[102]

All the excitement aroused by the American presence, however, could not hide widespread dissatisfaction with the performance of the Northern Ireland government.

ANDREWS OVERTHROWN: APRIL 1943

An air-raid alert at two o'clock in the morning of 25 July 1941 caused some thirty thousand people to flee from Belfast, though not a single bomb was dropped. Such was citizens' lack of confidence in the ability of the Northern Ireland government to protect them. Andrews seemed impervious to criticism from his own supporters and blithely observed in October 1941 that 'the position of the government was stronger than it had been for many years'. Then in December Harry Midgley, the colourful Northern Ireland Labour Party candidate, won Willowfield in east Belfast in a by-election. The loss of this fervently loyalist seat left Andrews severely shaken: he later confided to Spender by telephone that 'if there was a general election now the government would cease to have a majority'.[103]

Andrews proved incapable of making the adjustments necessary to silence his critics. He was easily diverted by trivialities and continued to be obsessed by the infiltration of 'Free Staters'. He asked Spender to investigate how many Catholics there were in the higher ranks of the civil service, commenting that the Government could only take 'those who are loyal'.[104] Andrews steadfastly refused to revamp his cabinet. Milne Barbour was ever more ineffectual but Dawson Bates was the minister attracting most odium. Bates continued to live seventy miles from Belfast at Portrush and during a period of acute petrol shortage ran up over thirty thousand miles each year in his large official motor-car. As minister of home affairs, he was dilatory and timorous in dealing with the Belfast Corporation, found guilty of gross corruption and blatant abuse of patronage in an inquiry reporting in June 1941. Only pressure from the backbenchers forced the Government to suspend the corporation and on 1 October 1942 city commissioners were appointed, a situation which lasted for three and a half years. Andrews himself showed no resolution in dealing with mounting labour disputes and the refusal of skilled trade unionists to accept dilution, that is, the bringing in of semi-skilled and unskilled workers to hasten the completion of urgent war work. Ernest Bevin, the minister responsible at Westminster, found the Northern Ireland government 'weak and complaisant' and, during an extensive wave of strikes in the autumn of 1942, Churchill sent a telegram to Andrews declaring that he was 'shocked at what was happening'.[105] Junior ministers – Wilson Hungerford, Brian Maginess and Mayne Sinclair, in particular – urged Andrews to prepare plans for the postwar period and to announce them as 'publicly and speedily as possible'.[106] The prime minister responded with only a woolly declaration of intent. Perhaps the most damning criticism came from the newly returned MP for Queen's University, Dr William Lyle, who called in vain for the setting up of a department of health: he said that by its callous neglect in 'the slaughter of innocents . . . the Ulster government had out-Heroded Herod'. As Lyle quietly pressed home his attack on the home affairs minister, Spender noticed that MPs were listening in 'tense silence'.[107]

Urged to change his team at a full party meeting on 19 January 1943, Andrews temporised and then told backbenchers they could expect no new faces in the Government until after Easter. The Government's standing continued to fall when the IRA made successful gaol breaks in Derry and Belfast and wartime output was again paralysed by a new bout of unofficial strikes. Andrews made no move when on 19 March the Unionist Party voted unanimously to ask him to 'reconsider the question of changes in his cabinet'.[108] A rebellion of backbenchers and junior ministers slowly matured and on 28 April, having boxed himself in by rejecting compromise proposals made by Brooke and others, Andrews was forced to resign. He seems to have recommended Lord Glentoran as his replacement, but the governor, realising Glentoran was not the party's choice, asked Brooke to form a government on 1 May.

Brooke made a clean sweep. Apart from himself, the only member of the previous government to be retained was John MacDermott, now the attorney-general. The former shipwright, William Grant, was made minister of labour, and Harry Midgley was given the office of minister of

public security for the duration of the war. Unlike Churchill's administration, however, this was no all-party government: no Nationalist or
Catholic was invited to join. Both the minister of education, the Reverend
Professor Robert Corkey, and the new leader of the senate, Sir Joseph
Davison, were noted for their virulent anti-Catholicism. The bitterness
arising from the ousting of the old guard took a long time before it was
purged from the Unionist Party and it was with difficulty that Brooke
strove to establish his authority and improve the public's opinion of his
government. In mid-1944 a Mass Observation report noted:

> The long domination of the Unionist Party is being threatened . . . and the
> present Prime Minister diplomatic, intelligent, lively Basil Brooke is con-
> sidered by some of his party too advanced and too liberal. There have
> been considerable background movements to replace him, and the soli-
> darity of the Unionist caucus shows, for the first time in twenty years,
> signs of a crater.[109]

By then the Americans had left Northern Ireland and were advancing
from their bridgeheads in northern France; fitted with ASV radar, Whitley
aircraft flew out from Limavady aerodrome and located U-boats with
increasing success; and escort vessels from Derry, now returned to
Admiralty control, co-operated closely with Short Sunderlands, American Consolidated Catalinas and Supermarine Stranraers taking off from
lower Lough Erne to close the 'Atlantic gap' and bring the German
submarine campaign to an end. As Allied forces rolled back the frontiers of the Third Reich, Northern Ireland was no longer in danger of
attack and, once again, was becoming an arsenal of victory.

'AN HOUR LOST IN THE FACTORIES OF NORTHERN IRELAND IS
AN HOUR GAINED FOR HITLER'

A report published on 12 June 1941 summed up how far the German air
raids had set back production: 45 per cent of shipbuilding capacity had
been lost; the making of aircraft components had not yet resumed; and
it would take another three months to recondition the Short and Harland
electrical department. Another six months were to pass before shipbuilding returned to normal production and another year before night
work began again in the Short and Harland machine shop.[110] Nevertheless, Northern Ireland made a valuable contribution to wartime output.

At Harland and Wolff the workforce in Belfast rose steadily to reach a
peak of 30,801 in December 1944.[111] Altogether Queen's Island launched
almost 170 Admiralty and merchant ships between 1939 and 1945,
including 40 'Flower'-class and 'Castle'-class corvettes for convoy escort; 27 'Algerine'-class minesweepers; 11 'Bay'-class and 'Loch'-class

frigates; 3 aircraft carriers; 11 landing craft; 8 tank-landing craft; 3 tank-carrying ships; and submarine and aircraft support vessels. In addition the firm launched from its Glasgow yards at Govan and Pointhouse 84 ships; reopened Swan Hunter's yard in Derry; repaired or converted around 30,000 vessels at Belfast, Liverpool, London, Derry and the Clyde; and manufactured over 13 million aircraft parts, over 500 tanks, thousands of field and anti-aircraft guns, and hundreds of searchlights. Short and Harland dispersed as many of its processes as possible in case of further attacks from the air. Fuselages and components were made at the King's Hall in south Belfast; a linen mill at Lambeg converted to the manufacture of tail planes, flaps, fins and rudders; at Newtownards a machine shop was set up in the Glen Print Works and sheet-metal pressings were made at Hawlmark; at Lisburn fuselage sections were manufactured at Altona and Stirling wings in a converted furniture factory at Largymore; and motor garages and farm outbuildings were pressed into service as makeshift stores. The workforce rose to 23,000 and by the end of the war had completed almost 1,200 Stirling bombers and 125 Sunderland flying boats.[112] Mackie's overcame male trade-union opposition to female labour with more success than any other firm and, after the 1941 blitz, took over space in linen mills and facto-ries, including Dickson's of Dungannon, John Allen's of Lurgan and Herdman's of Sion Mills. Not only did Mackie's undertake substantial fuselage assembly and undercarriage component manufacture for Short and Harland, but it also made seventy-five million shells and sixty-five million parts for bombs. The Sirocco Works in Belfast produced gre-nades, radar equipment and gun-mountings, and the ropeworks made one third of the cordage and ropes required by the War Office.[113] The linen industry was severely dislocated when the Germans overran its principal sources of flax in Russia, Belgium and France. Nevertheless, two million flax fabric parachutes were made, mainly in Carrickfergus; other centres produced great quantities of machine-gun belts, canvas and wagon covers, tent duck and heavy linen 'blitz cloth' for reroofing damaged buildings; and hundreds of thousands of uniforms were made, particularly in Derry.[114] Northern Ireland always had a higher propor-tion of female members of the workforce than the United Kingdom as a whole but the war brought large numbers of women into traditional male preserves for the first time, notably the aircraft, rope and engineer-ing industries. In engineering, for example, there were only 250 women employed in 1939 but by 1943 the number had risen to 12,300.

Despite Northern Ireland's impressive wartime output, production levels were consistently lower in the region than in any other part of the United Kingdom. In 1942 a Mass Observation reporter found that 'the slackness in the atmosphere is unmistakeable' and the following year an official of the Ministry of Aircraft Production estimated that Short and Harland was not working at more than 65 per cent efficiency and claimed that 'any amount of people are drawing pay for loafing about'.[115] There was abundant evidence of incompetent and high-handed management and low worker morale resulting in defective work, high absenteeism and poor time-keeping. Absenteeism at Harland and Wolff was estimated to be twice as high as in the worst yards in Britain – this, according to Bevin in 1943, was 'due as much to bad management as workmen slacking'.[116] Strikes were illegal from 1940 onwards but Northern Ireland was nevertheless affected by 270 strikes during the war. In March 1942 trade unions and employers formed joint production committees but their authority was consistently undermined by militant shop stewards seeking better wages and conditions. 'An hour lost in the factories of Northern Ireland is an hour gained for Hitler,' a Communist trade-union leader declared in vain when all the engineering workers walked out of Short and Harland in October 1942 after the sacking of two shop stewards.[117] Workers in other firms joined the strike, which ended only when the employers capitulated. Trolley-bus drivers, carters and dockers struck early in 1943 and were forced back to work only by the imposition of fines and the use of troops. By far the worst outbreak of industrial unrest began in February 1944 and lasted to the end of April, despite the opposition of trade-union officials, the Communist Party, newspapers and Church leaders. Some twenty thousand stopped work and thousands more came out when five shop stewards were sentenced to three months' hard labour. Only when the stewards appealed successfully against their sentences and wage increases were agreed did work resume.

The authorities did all they could to keep publicity about industrial unrest to a minimum but they were much less constrained in proclaiming their success in containing the IRA.

THE SUPPRESSION OF THE IRA

'We are King's Men and we shall be with you to the end,' Craigavon said in a broadcast to the British people early in 1940. Not all were king's men, he knew perfectly well, but by that time he was satisfied most IRA activists were behind bars or held on board the hulk *Al Rawdah*, anchored off Killyleagh, Co. Down. A few militant republicans remained at large, however, distributing issues of *War News* and broadcasting anti-British propaganda from a transmitter never found by the RUC. In December 1939 Sean McCaughey, a Belfast sheet-metal worker,

581

came back from internment in the South to become the commanding officer of the IRA northern command. For a time the IRA was more active in Northern Ireland than in Éire, but McCaughey was drawn into a sordid witch-hunt against his southern superior, Sean Hayes, and merely divided his movement.[118]

The arrival of the Americans, which drew a protest from de Valera at the occupation of Irish soil, galvanised the IRA to launch a fresh campaign. Reorganised by its new commander, Hugh McAteer from Derry, and by its intelligence officer and publicity director, John Graham, on 25 March 1942 the northern command resolved to take action 'by sabotage of war industries and enemy military objectives by a semi-military force'. On 3 April IRA men in Dungannon killed an RUC constable and wounded another, and two days later, on Easter Sunday, a policeman was seriously wounded in Strabane, and following a furious gun battle in Belfast, six IRA volunteers were captured in Cawnpore Street after shooting dead a constable. All six men were condemned to death. Reprieve committees north and south gathered around two hundred thousand signatures for a petition calling for mercy. Eventually, four days before the executions were due to take place, the sentences of all but one were commuted.[119] Tom Williams was hanged at 8 a.m. on 2 September 1942 in the Crumlin Road gaol. The *Belfast News-Letter* reported:

> Police had to intervene at the corner of the Old Lodge Road and Florence Place which runs alongside the county court house. Here on the stroke of eight a crowd of about 200 women and girls burst into 'God Save the King' while on the other side of the street a score of women were kneeling. Cheers followed the national anthem and then the crowd sang 'Land of Hope and Glory' and 'There'll always be an England', the praying women meanwhile remaining on their knees.[120]

The execution prompted a new burst of IRA action: on 2 September volunteers attacked from Co. Monaghan across the border and wounded a constable at Culloville; the following day Randalstown RUC station was bombed; on 4 September Belleek RUC barracks was attacked; two days later an RUC constable and a B Special were shot dead in Co. Tyrone at Clady; and there were numerous shooting incidents in west Belfast throughout the month.

The Northern Ireland government swiftly gained the upper hand. Some 200 men were rounded up in border areas and another 120 suspects in Belfast and all were duly interned. On 10 September the RUC arrested Graham after an exchange of fire and seized a radio transmitter, hand guns and five thousand copies of *Republican News*. Hugh McAteer was taken a month later. A curfew was imposed in the Falls and, in

582

effect, the IRA had shot its bolt. The escape of McAteer and another volunteer from Crumlin Road gaol in January 1943, and of twenty-one internees through a tunnel from Derry gaol in March, was deeply embarrassing to Andrews and Dawson Bates but it did not signal a revival of IRA activity. McAteer made a spectacular appearance at the Falls Road Broadway cinema on Holy Saturday 1943. While the staff was held at gunpoint, the audience was forced to take part in an Easter commemoration for 'the dead who died for Ireland'.[121] McAteer was subsequently recaptured, and the steady attrition of arrests reduced the IRA in the North to a few hunted men seeking refuge rather than action.

Most of the men who escaped from Derry gaol were captured by the Irish Army in Co. Donegal and thereafter interned at the Curragh in Co. Kildare. De Valera consistently interned more IRA suspects than the Northern Ireland authorities: by hangings, street gunfights and incarceration in bleak camps, his government had shattered its former associates north and south. Gerry Boland, Éire's minister for justice, claimed with much truth that the IRA was dead. That Northern Ireland was entirely free of IRA activity by the end of the war was in large measure due to the unwavering repression administered by the Dublin government – a fact Stormont ministers certainly could not acknowledge in public.

On the afternoon of 30 April 1945 Hitler took his own life in his Berlin bunker and on 2 May, when the Führer's death was announced in the Éire newspapers, de Valera called at the German Legation in Dublin 'to express condolence'.[122] To many this was an appalling act, particularly at a time when the ghastly horrors of the Nazi death camps were being revealed to the world. Sir John Maffey, the United Kingdom representative in Éire, reported to the Dominions Office that in the public mind the taoiseach's 'condolences took on a smear of turpitude', and that in Dublin there was 'a growing feeling that Mr de Valera had blundered into a clash with the ideals of decency and right'.[123] The wave of disgust that swept across the majority in Northern Ireland served as a reminder of how far the war had widened the gulf between north and south.

Soon after, on the evening of 7 May, news spread that the Germans would surrender at midnight. The *Belfast News-Letter* described how people poured into the capital to celebrate:

Along Donegall Place and Royal Avenue, long lines of revellers joined in snake-like formation, dancing in and out among rows of tramcars immobilised by the crowds. Songs were in the air everywhere. They ranged from 'Tipperary' and the favourites of 1918 to a completely new 'number' composed for the occasion which began: 'Hitler thought he had us with a Ya, Ya, Ya.'[124]

Flames leaped up from dozens of bonfires and, as bunting was hung out, the beating of drums and the clanging of dustbin lids added to the din of rejoicing. In east Belfast Mary Wallace and her sisters were woken by their mother and they dashed out into Bloomfield Avenue, where 'everyone was on the street', some still in their pyjamas, shouting and yelling. She was swept down the Newtownards Road over the Albert Bridge and by the time she got home it was 'as bright as day . . . freezing but so happy'.[125]

At noon next day the Ulster United Prayer Movement held a victory thanksgiving service in the grounds of Belfast City Hall and soon afterwards a huge crowd of citizens and service men and women – the biggest, it was thought, since Covenant Day, 1912 – gathered in Donegall Square and Donegall Place. Then a great hush fell as Churchill's broadcast, outlining the terms of Germany's capitulation, was relayed from loudspeakers. At the end of the broadcast servicemen in the city Young Men's Christian Association rose to their feet and sang the Doxology. 'We must not slack,' Sir Crawford McCullagh, the lord mayor, told the crowds: 'Celebrate the victory and go back to work.' No one seems to have followed the advice of this discredited leader of a corporation still in commission, and, indeed, all workers were given two days' holiday with pay. For the vast majority of people VE Day was the end of the war as far as they were concerned. As crowds surged through the streets, kerbs and air-raid shelters in Protestant districts were painted in loyal colours, and the city YMCA – which had served 3.25 million meals and given beds to 330,000 during the war – provided 4,000 free meals.[126] That evening, as the *Belfast Telegraph* reported,

> for the first time in six years the City Hall was flood-lit. As the illumination was switched on at 10.40 p.m. there was a tremendous cheer from thousands of people, among them many Allied Service men, who were much impressed by the majesty of the building silhouetted against the darkening sky. The Albert Memorial was also flood-lit, and here also large and excited crowds assembled. Huge bonfires blazed in many parts of the city and around them bands of young people danced in jubilant mood right into the early hours of the morning.[127]

Dozens of effigies of Hitler burned on lamp standards. On the Shore Road a bugle band led a procession of youngsters in the midst of whom was carried an effigy of the Führer, wearing his swastika and hanging from the gallows.

David Davidson remembered an 'explosion of joy' in Bangor as great numbers collected around the McKee Clock at the sea front and publicans served free beer from their bars.[128] In Derry, Charlie Gallagher recalled, the celebrations were more subdued, but it was here, on

14 May, that solemn tribute was paid to Northern Ireland's crucial part in the Battle of the Atlantic. U-boats had been instructed to surface and make their way to Lisahally, and the formal surrender of the first eight to arrive was accepted by Admiral Sir Maxwell Horton, commander-in-chief of the Western Approaches.[129] Standing beside him was Sir Basil Brooke and mingling in the watching crowds in civilian clothes was Colonel Dan Bryan. He had fought the British during the Anglo-Irish War and had been appointed head of G2, the Irish Army's intelligence service, in 1941, and now he had come from Dublin to witness this historic occasion. Eventually twenty-eight U-boats were towed into the Atlantic from Derry port and scuttled close to Rockall.

In Dublin VE Day had been marked by an ugly incident. Protestant students ran up Allied flags over the entrance of Trinity College and threw a burning tricolour into the street. In retaliation two students from the National University – one was Charles J. Haughey, the future taoiseach – set a Union flag ablaze. Only baton charges by *gardaí* in College Green prevented an angry crowd from invading the college. Some of the mob ran off to smash windows in the American Legation, Maffey's office and restaurants favoured by Trinity students.[130] Five days later, on 13 May, Anglo-Irish relations were strained further when Churchill's victory speech, heard across the world, not only paid tribute to Northern Ireland but also bitterly referred to the consequences of Éire's neutrality during the Battle of the Atlantic:

> This was indeed a deadly moment in our life and if it had not been for the loyalty and friendship of Northern Ireland we should have been forced to come to close quarters with Mr de Valera or perish for ever from the earth. However, with a restraint and poise to which, I say, history will find few parallels, His Majesty's Government never laid a violent hand upon them though at times it would have been quite easy and quite natural, and we left the Dublin Government to frolic with the Germans and later with the Japanese representatives to their hearts' content.[131]

On 17 May de Valera made a dignified and restrained response. Though in public his neutrality had been even-handed, and though the blazing lights of Dublin and the refusal to make the treaty ports available had helped the Germans to some degree, de Valera in practice leaned toward the Allies. With his full knowledge, British aircraft had been able to fly across Co. Donegal in search of U-boats; servicemen were often helped to make their way to Northern Ireland; and Allied internees were treated more favourably than Germans and certainly less harshly than IRA suspects. The aid sent during the Belfast blitz was widely appreciated. MacDermott expressed his gratitude at Stormont and one of his officials, Eric Scales, observed:

Perhaps the most spectacular feature of each of these raids was the immediate dispatch on each occasion of these voluntary firemen from a neutral state, racing through the night, with their peacetime headlamps blazing, to fires that none of them could ever previously have imagined. Such transcends the ordinary business of regional reinforcement.

Moya Woodside wrote that 'an action like this does more for Irish unity than the words of politicians', while Emma Duffin made this entry in her diary: 'Perhaps, this will draw North and South closer together. I wonder.'[132]

In the event north and south were to be pushed further apart in the postwar years, and the reduction of sectarian animosity in Northern Ireland, brought about by a common fear and a shared experience of the horrors of aerial bombardment, proved ephemeral. Nevertheless, Ulster was on the threshold of the most peaceful, hopeful and progressive period the province was to enjoy in the twentieth century.

13

THE QUIET YEARS

1945–1963

On 2 June 1941 the Reverend Dr J.B. Woodburn, the retiring moderator of the Presbyterian Assembly, gave this warning in his sermon:

> After the big Blitz of a few weeks ago I was inexpressibly shocked by the sight of people I saw walking in the streets. I have been working 19 years in Belfast and I never saw the like of them before – wretched people, very undersized and underfed down-and-out looking men and women. They had been bombed out of their homes and were wandering the streets. Is it creditable to us that there should be such people in a Christian country?
> . . . We have got to see that there is more talk of justice; we have got to see it enacted, and the work will have to begin immediately. If something is not done now to remedy this rank inequality there will be revolution after the war.[1]

There was no revolution. As reconstruction got under way and the region responded to the urgent demands of the Allied war machine, unemployment all but disappeared and even the great strikes of 1944 had no revolutionary purpose. Income per head of population, which had been three fifths of that in Britain in 1939, stood at three quarters by 1945.[2] The postwar boom was carefully controlled and, until the end of the 1950s, the traditional export industries displayed remarkable vigour. At the same time the dramatic reforms brought in by Clement Attlee's Labour governments at Westminster were largely applied to Northern Ireland and, as the 'imperial contribution' became a legal fiction, London underwrote the cost. The outcome was a more striking increase in living standards than at any other time in the century.

Never did the Unionist governments feel more secure. Not only had Northern Ireland been promised parity with Britain in its social services, and with the support of the central exchequer, but also successive Westminster administrations expressed in practical ways their gratitude to Stormont for standing by the Allies in their hour of need. Just after he resigned in 1943, John Andrews received this letter of appreciation from Churchill:

> But for the loyalty of Northern Ireland and its devotion to what has now become the cause of thirty governments or nations we should have been confronted with slavery and death and the light which now shines so brightly throughout the world would have been quenched ... During your premiership the bonds of affection between Great Britain and the people of Northern Ireland have been tempered by fire and are now, I believe, unbreakable.[3]

Attlee proved just as grateful and when Éire became a republic in 1948, he guaranteed to uphold Northern Ireland's constitutional position. Fearing neither insolvency nor abandonment by Westminster, Sir Basil Brooke presided over the most peaceful and progressive era in Northern Ireland's history.

Until towards the end of the 1950s the twenty-six counties drew still further apart from the six north-eastern counties. Éire's wartime isolation did not dissolve immediately in 1945: it was maintained by censorship, a high tariff wall and continued neutrality, which, as the Cold War set in, gave Northern Ireland an apparently important strategic role in NATO. As in Portugal, but unlike Switzerland and Sweden, wartime neutrality appeared to have an enervating effect on Éire. The South experienced arrested development until by the 1950s its society seemed caught in a 'thirties' time warp. The failure of new issues to emerge and the lack of social and economic progress was particularly evident in the border counties of Cavan, Monaghan and Donegal.

In Northern Ireland the advance of modernisation was, nevertheless, extremely uneven. Brooke often pointed to the superior welfare and educational services north of the border, yet he and his government remained complacently unwilling to alter political attitudes and structures, and there was no pressure from London to do so. The ancient divisions in the region had survived the war intact and were older and more profound than the political frontier weaving its erratic way through the province of Ulster. Any modernisation that ensued after 1945 was due not to Stormont governments but to powerful transformations elsewhere. No advantage was taken of the long period of internal peace and the isolation of the IRA to remedy obvious wrongs and soothe intercommunal resentment still stubbornly alive, especially where pockets of disadvantage were dangerously concentrated.

'CREEPING SOCIALISM'

Eager to show the loyalty of the majority in Northern Ireland before the British electorate went to the polls, Brooke called a general election for

15 June 1945. Political opinion in the region had not been put to the test for seven years and the Marquess of Donegall somewhat excitably remarked that the Government was 'hanging on by its eye-lashes and could be put out of office any time'.[4] It was not a leap in anti-partitionist support that the Ulster Unionist Party feared but disaffection in the Protestant camp, particularly in Belfast.

In spite of frequent and embarrassing splits – including the expulsion of Jack Beattie and the departure of Harry Midgley to form his own Commonwealth Labour Party – the Labour movement in Belfast had acquired confidence, solidarity and militancy during the war years. There seemed a real possibility of a significant shift in the voters' usual loyalties in the city, even though it was clear from the outset that the election would be fought on traditional lines in rural constituencies. However, the *Belfast News-Letter* declared that 'the Constitutional question emerges as the governing issue', and so it proved.[5] With thirty-four seats the Unionists were still impregnable and the Nationalists held ten. Nevertheless, Labour candidates had done well in the city considering that the assorted parties had split each other's votes in several constituencies: Midgley won Willowfield for Commonwealth Labour; Harry Diamond as a Socialist Republican ousted the Nationalist in the Falls; Beattie was elected as Independent Labour MP for Pottinger; the Northern Ireland Labour Party won Dock, Oldpark and, in a 1946 by-election, Belfast Central; and the irrepressible Tommy Henderson, elected again as an Independent Unionist for Shankill, was arguably as much a representative of Labour as the others. However, the constitutional issue – less significant in this than in any previous election since 1921 – was the prime cause of Labour's divisions and progressive parties were perpetually in danger of being squeezed out altogether when the border question was paramount.

In the Westminster elections in July 1945 the only Labour candidate returned was Jack Beattie. In Britain the Labour Party won the most overwhelming victory in its history and Attlee's new government began at once to implement its radical programme which ultimately would do much to transform the lives of the people of Northern Ireland. Even if the tidal wave sweeping Labour to power at Westminster had petered out to a gentle ripple by the time it had crossed the Irish Sea to Stormont, the cascade of ameliorating reforms originating in London had a profound effect on the citizens of a region who had lived under the shadow of the Poor Law long after it had been dismantled in the rest of the United Kingdom.

At first the deeply conservative Unionist government was horrified at the prospect of interference and high taxation likely to accompany this deep draught of socialism. Fearing confrontation between the Westminster and Stormont governments, Brooke consulted his colleagues on 15 November 1945, anxiously wondering 'whether any changes could be made to avert such a situation. Two possibilities were dominion status for Northern Ireland and a return to Westminster.'[6] The debate resumed on 29 November when Sir Roland Nugent, minister of commerce, and Brian Maginess, minister of labour, pressed strongly for further devolution leading to dominion status. Nugent argued that the Stormont government, with no mandate to implement Attlee's reform programme, would be reduced to the status of a department of the imperial government. It would be better to be

> masters of our own house . . . Without having to go to the Treasury practically all the time we would be in a better position to carry out our own programme. We would no longer be able to confess our inability to control our own destinies and we would be relieved from the constant anxiety as to what an unfriendly British government might be tempted to do in the way of pressing us to end partition.

The following April, the minister of agriculture, the Reverend Robert Moore, pointed out that Northern Ireland was getting farming subsidies of £13 million a year and suggested that a dominion-status state might 'well be sacrificing the substance of economic security on the British level for a shadowy independence which might carry the seeds of its own destruction through a deterioration in our economic prosperity'.[7] Though renewed fears of 'creeping socialism' revived the campaign for greater autonomy in 1947, Brooke was convinced by Moore's argument. In any case, as Nugent himself admitted, ministers of the Labour government were 'practical and experienced men who are personally friendly to Ulster'.[8] Even better, as it turned out, Attlee was prepared to foot the bill for his socialist programme.

When Sir William Beveridge sketched out his ground plan for a welfare state in 1942, Brooke had considered it impractical, and after 1945 Unionists at Westminster vigorously opposed one welfare measure after another. Yet bills that had been criticised stage by stage in London were shortly afterwards proposed, often with enthusiasm, by government ministers in Belfast. The explanation for this apparent contradiction was that Britain was prepared to pay most of the very large sums of money needed to finance welfare legislation in Northern Ireland. Drawing on Westminster's wartime promises and Britain's gratitude, Stormont extracted three agreements from the British government. The first, concluded in 1946, ensured that Northern Ireland would enjoy the same standards of social services as those prevailing in the rest of the United Kingdom, provided parity of taxation and treasury scrutiny were maintained. The Social Services Agreement and the amalgamation of the Unemployment Funds of Britain and Northern Ireland, both in force from July 1948, relieved the Stormont government of most of the expense of national assistance, health provision, family allowances, pensions and national insurance, including payments during sickness, unemployment, after retirement and at death.[9] The result was a striking advance in the material welfare of the people of Northern Ireland.

'HOUSES TO MEET THE NEEDS OF ITS WORKING PEOPLE'

The Reverend Dr J.B. Woodburn, having gone 'around some of the devastated places' after the Belfast blitz,[10] wrote to the minister of public security:

> I hope and trust that they will never be rebuilt again . . . A minister said to me, whose congregation had been bombed . . . if he could get the people entirely out of the way, he would be happy if the Germans would come and bomb the place flat.[11]

The miserably low quality of decayed terraced housing, particularly just north of the city centre, had in part been responsible for the very high death toll of the Easter 1941 raid. Luftwaffe bombs had demolished 3,200 houses and damaged 56,600, nearly 4,000 of them left completely uninhabitable. The proportion of Belfast's housing stock affected – 53.3 per cent – was higher than the average for blitz damage in British cities. Altogether 100,000 people in the city were temporarily without homes and 15,000 had no homes at all. Dr Thomas Carnwath, who published an official report in December 1941, stated that the typical number of inhabitants of terraced houses in 'bad areas' was fifteen, even though at least twenty-six thousand had evacuated from Belfast.[12]

The first-ever housing survey in the region was made in 1943; as Lucius O'Brien, then the Belfast city welfare officer, recalled: 'The results were pretty shocking and we sent the report to Mr Harry Midgley who was then Minister of Security. It seems that it aroused great feeling in the Cabinet.' The Government was forced to see that some one hundred thousand new houses were needed straight away throughout Northern Ireland and another one hundred thousand would have to be built if overcrowding and slums were to be eradicated. The survey revealed the low quality of much of the region's rural housing, entirely untouched by the blitz. Another 'Interim Report' the following year showed, however, that the problem was most acute in the inner-city area of Belfast: in Smithfield, for example, 65.9 per cent of houses were classed as totally unfit or grossly overcrowded.[13] The situation was so severe that exceptional measures would have to be taken. William Grant, the minister of health and local government, threw himself into the task with remarkable vigour. John Oliver, first appointed his private secretary and then his principal officer, wrote later:

> But Billy Grant was unique. He was a huge, rugged man, a football fan; a strong teetotaller . . . an Orangeman; a Labour-Unionist; a man of immense courage. He used to tell the story against himself of a trade union comrade bursting out 'Billy, it's a blessing that you're a teetotaller for you're coarse enough when you're sober.' He was one of those ministers who attract business.[14]

In 1945 Grant set up the Northern Ireland Housing Trust, modelled on the Scottish Special Housing Association, with power to borrow from the Government to build houses and pay back the capital with interest over sixty years. Beyond this state assistance, the trust had to pay its own way and fix its rents in relation to the cost of construction. These stringent conditions were imposed on Grant by colleagues deeply suspicious of state involvement. Maynard Sinclair, the minister of finance, insisted that as it was intended rents 'should be as low as possible, a strict degree of economy in the Trust's finances will be necessary'.[15] Lucius O'Brien, the trust's chairman from 1945 to 1969, recalled:

> On February 14th 1945, the very day the act was finally passed, vacant premises were handed over to us in Donegall Square South. Without furniture or even a telephone and two civil servants on loan the only staff, the five of us started from there to set the Trust in action.[16]

O'Brien, and those who served with him, such as Herbert Bryson and John G. Calvert, set a new high standard of probity and dedication in public life, but they could not build houses for those most acutely in need.[17] In 1946-7 they were forced to fix the rents at fourteen shillings a week; O'Brien observed later: 'This was a great shock and disappointment to us. The 14s. seemed a lot in those days and was much higher than we had hoped for.'[18] There was no shortage of applicants, however, and those capable of paying the rents did much to relieve the housing shortage. Houses were allocated with strict fairness, but this could not be said of many local authorities expected to carry the main burden of providing dwellings with the help of government subsidies. Grant frankly admitted past neglect and urged councils to action:

> It is the statutory duty of every local authority in Northern Ireland to provide houses to meet the needs of its working people . . . the fact that these requirements have in the past been more honoured in the breach than the observance does not mean that they should not be revived to meet our present needs.

With difficulty the minister had persuaded his party that subsidy was essential, for 'without a very substantial measure of Government aid, not a brick can be laid of houses which ordinary people can afford to rent'.[19] Subsidies were also given to private house builders and the Ministry of Agriculture provided grants for replacing or reconditioning agricultural labourers' dwellings and farmhouses. The Ministry of Agriculture rebuilt or replaced 9,500 houses and the Housing Trust completed 48,500 dwellings between 1945 and 1972.[20] Grant's target of one hundred thousand local authority houses was not reached until the early 1960s, but, disappointing though this was, the achievement was vastly more impressive than that of the interwar years. Yet the greatly increased public spending on housing was to set a time bomb ticking which would eventually explode in 1968–9. Most of the new dwellings were provided by local authorities and no steps were taken to ensure the even-handed allocation of council houses. The modernising welfare legislation was allowed to entrench and augment the petty parochialism of the past with grave consequences for the stability of Northern Ireland.

EDUCATIONAL REFORM AND WRANGLING

The resentment fuelled by the local administration of public housing expansion was slow in accumulating. By contrast, plans to extend the education system provoked an immediate storm. The Presbyterian General Assembly had applauded the revolutionising Butler Act in 1944, resolving that 'any less a measure of reform in Northern Ireland than that now secured for England would be disastrous to the well-being of the people'.[21] Lieutenant-Colonel Samuel Hall-Thompson, the minister of education, duly published his proposals in December 1944 but three long and rancorous years were to pass before the main elements of the Butler Act were applied to Northern Ireland.

'One aim of the White Paper is further to ostracise the Catholic voluntary schools,' T.J. Campbell declared at Stormont. All the Catholic bishops in Northern Ireland denounced the proposals in their Lenten pastorals, Cardinal MacRory condemning the spending of so much public money and 'the utterly unjust treatment of a large portion of the population on account of their religious convictions', and Dr Mageean observing that 'from bitter experience' he knew 'what had happened in other countries when the state took control of youth'.[22] Hall-Thompson proposed to increase capital grants to voluntary (mainly Catholic) schools from 50 to 65 per cent, to provide books to these schools free of charge and milk and meals for necessitous children. Far from being satisfied by

593

these plans, Catholic leaders condemned them as putting their schools under severe pressure to join the state system, particularly as the expansion of secondary education would require a great increase in expenditure. Expense could be saved by placing Catholic schools under 'four-and-two' committees, but the bishops rejected this option because it was 'but an instalment to the complete transfer of our schools'. They demanded 100 per cent funding on the grounds that state schools were in effect Protestant schools.[23]

It was Protestant opposition, however, which caused Hall-Thompson most trouble when his Education Bill was published in September 1946. The bill set out to scrap the 1930 act's insistence on Bible instruction, seeking only compulsory collective worship and religious instruction in state schools, and it also included a conscience clause for teachers not wishing to give religious instruction. Campaigners, organised by the United Education Committee of the Protestant Churches, wheeled into action with packed and angry protest meetings in Belfast, Bangor, Newtownards, Portadown and Derry. In particular, they opposed concessions to Catholics and while refusing to admit that state schools were denominational, demanded that these schools keep their Protestant ethos.

'There are no sacrifices we will not make, in order that our Protestant form of inheritance will be made secure,' declared the dean of Belfast while making an appeal for a £20,000 fighting fund at the Wellington Hall on 8 November 1946. The next day Hall-Thompson was howled down at a meeting of the Ulster Women's Unionist Council when he said that 'in the State schools the religious instruction must be undenominational'. So great was the uproar that Lady Clark asked to be excused from the chair, the minister left early, and members of the audience sang 'Derry's Walls' to mark their triumph. All over Northern Ireland the protest campaign continued. At St Jude's church hall in Belfast, for example, the Reverend Professor Robert Corkey asserted that state schools would be thrown open to 'Jews, Agnostics, Roman Catholics and Atheists'. A former education minister dismissed for inattention to his duties in 1944, Corkey was interrupted by some crying 'Nonsense!' and 'Tommy-rot' but most warmly applauded him, one person accusing the hecklers of being Communists.[24]

The standard of debate was not much better at Stormont. Midgley vituperatively opposed increased funding for Catholic schools and Herbert Quin, Unionist MP for Queen's University, declared: 'I feel there has been a betrayal of Protestantism.' In the senate William Wilton argued that under the conscience clause 'the education authority will have to appoint a teacher without regard to his religious views. He may be a Jew – although I am not saying anything against Jews – he may be a Roman Catholic, or even a member of the IRA.' 'The trouble about us here in Ulster,' Lord Glentoran remarked ruefully during the debate, 'is that we get excited by religion and drink.'[25] Despite all the opposition, Hall-Thompson had his way and his bill became law in 1947. But the traditionalists had their revenge two years later: Hall-Thompson proposed to pay Catholic teachers' national insurance and superannuation but the prime minister – just raised to the peerage as Lord Brookeborough – cut the ground from under him by attending a Grand Orange Lodge protest meeting in Sandy Row and promising to amend the scheme. Not surprisingly, Hall-Thompson resigned. According to Patrick Shea, the announcement that Midgley was to be the new minister of education 'brought dismay and shocked surprise in the Ministry's offices in Massey Avenue . . . People asked if Brookeborough was mad.'[26] Midgley had abandoned his Commonwealth Labour Party to cross to the Government benches in 1947, no longer the radical socialist of his early career, but now a Protestant populist virulently opposed to the Catholic Church. In fact permanent officials were able to exploit his lack of executive ability and Hall-Thompson's scheme was only slightly modified.

During the education debates at Stormont very little had been said about the major features of the reform. The principal task was to convert elementary schools into the new primary and secondary schools. Pupils would leave the first level at eleven years old; selected by a qualifying examination, the most able 20 per cent would proceed to grammar school and the remaining 80 per cent were to go on to 'intermediate' or 'technical' secondary school. The traditional grammar schools successfully resisted direct control and preserved their identity largely intact. All continued to charge fees and to take in a proportion of pupils who had not passed the examination; yet all obtained direct grants from the state and were not therefore 'public schools' in the British sense. The middle classes preferred to pay fees for their sons and daughters to attend grammar schools if they failed to pass the qualifying test. As a result, they did not concern themselves with the shortcomings of the intermediate and technical schools – often overcrowded and characterised by a regime of regular physical punishment – and the 1947 act did less to break down social barriers in the region than might have been expected.

The educational reforms, already delayed by such unedifying wrangles, took time to be implemented. Even the Belfast Education Committee, incomparably more energetic and enlightened than the Belfast Corporation itself, spent two years devising a scheme to put the 120

provisions of the 1947 act into effect. The Ministry of Education estimated that 100 county intermediate schools and 90 voluntary intermediate schools were required but by the end of the academic year 1950–1
only 10 county and 2 voluntary schools were in operation, with 6,696
pupils out of a total school population of 39,660 in the region. The
counties of Armagh and Tyrone did not have a single intermediate
school until 1954 and Fermanagh had none until 1955.[27] The raising of
the school leaving age to fifteen was deferred again and again until
finally put into operation in 1957. It is therefore not surprising that the
full social and political impact of educational advance was not felt until
the mid-1960s. Educational reform had a modernising effect in Northern Ireland only within the limits of a strictly segregated system. Children now were longer at school and therefore officially separated on
religious lines longer than before. Apart from Queen's University, it
was only in the growing further education sector – quietly and unobtrusively – that young people of all creeds were being educated together.

THE NEW HEALTH SERVICE

School children were the first to benefit from the region's vastly improved health services. The Belfast Education Committee provided
milk to needy children from October 1942 and a general school meals
service from January 1943. The blitz had revealed to public gaze, in a
way that cold statistics could not, the appallingly low standards of
health of the working classes. Those in the countryside who had thrown
open their homes to evacuees were horrified to find so many children
from Belfast infested with lice and wasting away from tuberculosis – as
the 1946 health report put it: 'The shock to householders who granted
them sanctuary was second only to the shock they had received on
learning of the disaster which had befallen Belfast.'[28]

Tuberculosis was responsible for almost half the deaths in the 15–25
age group, and in this field Stormont did not wait to take a lead from
Westminster. In 1941 the Tuberculosis Authority was set up with a
mission to find and treat victims and eventually to extirpate the disease
altogether. An impressive screening programme was launched to track
down what the public health posters described as 'The White Death',
and a special section was established to wage an unrelenting war on
Koch's bacillus, the most killing variety of tuberculosis. With the aid of
the drugs BCG and streptomycin, the campaign was so determined and
effective that by 1954 the death rate was reduced to the same level as
that in England and Wales. So well had the authority done its work that
it was dissolved in 1959.

Health report after report had forced Brooke to act before the war was over. 'Some of the evidence was so bad,' one member of a select committee remarked, 'that we had to stop it and ask the Minister of Home Affairs to take action.'[29] The result was the setting up of the Ministry of Health and Local Government in 1944. William Grant, the first minister, showed the same energy in the field of health as he had in housing. Then, in July 1948, the National Health Service, open to all, totally free and almost completely comprehensive, came into operation in Britain. In the same year an almost identical act passed through Stormont but, because of past neglect, the impact of this new service was more profoundly felt in Northern Ireland than in any other region of the United Kingdom. The dispensary system, separate hospital administrations and the Poor Law were swept away to be supplanted by the Northern Ireland General Health Service Board, providing general medical services, and the Hospitals Authority, appointed by the minister.

Only in one confined area was this progress delayed by religious controversy. The Mater Hospital in Belfast would not come into the state system because the Government insisted on complete control by the Hospitals Authority and refused to preserve its Catholic ethos. Unlike similar hospitals in England, the Mater was not allowed to claim payment for its outpatient services, though it continued its free service to people of all creeds. Since the great majority of patients paid national insurance, the Mater was in effect subsidising the Hospitals Authority, as it received no public funding whatsoever. Bitter sectarian debates ensued at Stormont when the Government refused to change its mind and the Mater was forced to finance itself by 'YP' football pools. Otherwise the new health service rapidly reversed the trends of the interwar years: deaths of mothers during childbirth fell to the same level as for England and Wales by 1954; and by the 1960s general mortality rates for Northern Ireland were the lowest for any region in the United Kingdom.

Contrasting welfare provision widened the gulf between the North and the South still further. The Fianna Fáil government introduced mass radiography but by the time it was forced out of office in 1948 building had not even begun on three regional sanatoriums authorised by the Dáil three years earlier. The infant mortality rate had risen alarmingly during the war years but a modest Health Act of 1947 – including provision for compulsory health inspection in schools and for the education of women 'in regard to motherhood' – was the subject of considerable controversy when the Catholic hierarchy denounced it as 'bureaucratic' and 'entirely and directly contrary to Catholic teaching on the rights of the family'.[30] Ulster Protestants were thus convinced that clerical obscurantism reigned supreme in a state they were ever more determined not to join. On the other hand, northern Catholics, though they benefited from improved welfare and educational services, did not abandon their aspirations. For a time, indeed, they believed the prospect of reunification was now clearly on the horizon with the advent of a Labour government at Westminster.

'ULSTER IS NOT FOR SALE'

On 15 November 1945 all the Nationalist MPs and senators, together with many priests and around five hundred other delegates, met in Dungannon. There the convention unanimously agreed to set up the Irish Anti-Partition League, 'with the object of uniting all those opposed to partition into a solid block'.[31] The Nationalists abandoned the erratic abstentionism of the war years in the hope of eliciting support for their cause from Attlee's new government. James McSparran, Stormont MP for Mourne and the league's chairman, ensured that branches were spread rapidly across the province and soon had the enthusiastic backing of support organisations in the rest of Ireland and amongst Irish communities in Britain and America.

The league's formation had been prompted in part by northern Catholic dissatisfaction with de Valera's inability to make progress on the issue of Irish reunification. The taoiseach, indeed, disapproved of this new Ulster campaign and tended to agree with his deputy, Belfast-born Seán MacEntee, that the Dublin government should keep silent on the North as 'the only way' to make progress on partition. The Iron Curtain was descending in central Europe and western statesmen remained acutely aware of Northern Ireland's strategic value. Herbert Morrison, a member of Attlee's government, remarked to de Valera that 'to expect us to coerce Ulster was expecting too much, especially in view of the troubled world in which we all lived'. When Brooke considered visiting the United States, the Foreign Office thought the proposal 'disastrous', observing that emphasis on 'Ulster particularism would therefore awaken sleeping dogs, which we had every reason to hope were not merely somnolent but lethargic'.[32] Sir John Maffey, Britain's representative in Dublin, did worry that the Anti-Partition League would win support abroad, explaining in a confidential memorandum that 'for the outside world Dark Rosaleen has a sex appeal, whereas Britannia is regarded as a maiden aunt'.[33] In fact the United States government was determined to remain aloof: Alger Hiss, director of the Office of Special Political Affairs (not yet known to be a Soviet spy), advised President Harry S. Truman that Irish partition was not an issue in which his government 'might properly intervene'.[34]

Though the time was distinctly unpropitious for an international campaign against the political division of Ireland, de Valera's hand was forced by domestic developments. Seán MacBride, a former IRA chief of staff, launched Clann na Poblachta as a new radical republican party in July 1946. The party won over many Fianna Fáil supporters and achieved two by-election victories the following year. De Valera now had no choice but to revive the old rallying cries and fight to retain his leadership of the mainstream national cause. In any case he himself was stirred by the devotion of a new generation to an issue so close to his own heart. In May 1946 he remarked to a startled Maffey that 'if he were a young man in Northern Ireland, he felt that he would be giving his life to fight the existing order of things'.[35] He eagerly contemplated new solutions, privately proposing to David Gray, the United States minister to Ireland, that the northern unionists could be sent to the British mainland and that the Irish in Britain be returned to a reunited Ireland. Concealing his loathing of de Valera only with difficulty, Gray considered this suggested enforced transfer of loyalists to be 'about as practicable as expelling the New Englanders from Massachusetts'.[36]

De Valera's new propaganda drive against partition failed to save him at the polls in February 1948. For the first time in sixteen years Fianna Fáil was out of power and de Valera, no longer constrained by office, threw himself into an international campaign to restore Irish unity by embarking on extensive speaking tours. The new coalition government, a bewildering array of interest groups led by John A. Costello of Fine Gael and with MacBride as the external affairs minister, competed stridently with Fianna Fáil for leadership of constitutional republicanism and irredentism. In the words of Maffey, now Lord Rugby, 'each party must now outdo its rivals in a passionate crusade for Irish unity'. The coalition announced that it was ready to give Unionists 'any reasonable constitutional guarantees' if they would accept reunification. 'They may bid as high as they please,' Brooke responded, 'but our answer remains the same – "Ulster is not for sale."'[37]

THE CHAPEL GATE ELECTION AND THE IRELAND ACT, 1949

On 7 September 1948 during a visit to Canada Costello announced that his government would repeal de Valera's External Relations Act and that Éire would become a republic. Completely unmoved by the anti-partitionist campaign, on 28 October Attlee gave this assurance at Westminster: 'The view of his Majesty's government in the United Kingdom has always been that no change should be made in the constitutional status of Northern Ireland without Northern Ireland's free agreement.'[38] At the end of the year, when the Dáil duly passed the Republic of Ireland Bill, the Labour government prepared to give Brooke the legislative guarantees he demanded. The Cold War was now reaching its climax as Stalin blockaded West Berlin and Britain played a leading role in the formation of NATO. In the defence of the North Atlantic, Northern Ireland held a key strategic position in view of the Irish Republic's policy of strict neutrality: according to Sir Norman Brook, secretary to the Westminster cabinet, this was 'self-evident' and for this reason Unionists should be given 'a rather more sympathetic hearing than they might be thought to deserve on their strict merits' and he was certain that any party at Westminster would be 'compelled to take a positive line' in support of Northern Ireland.[39] Attlee agreed with this advice and gave Brooke further reassurances at a meeting in London in January 1949. Brooke promptly called a general election to demonstrate once more that Northern Ireland was British.

The Anti-Partition League called on its southern allies for help and on 27 January 1949 representatives of political parties on both sides in the Dáil met in the Dublin Mansion House and there agreed to set up 'an anti-partition fund to be created by subscriptions and the holding of a national collection in all parishes on Sunday next'.[40] The issue of the *Belfast Telegraph* for 31 January bore the banner headline: 'The Chapel Gate Collections. Dublin. Limerick. Donnybrook lead . . .' Thus the northern poll was quickly dubbed 'the chapel gate election'.[41] The Unionist Party could hardly have asked for more favourable circumstances – the evidence of southern interference and clerical manipulation seemed incontrovertible. 'Our country is in danger', Brooke declared in his manifesto; '. . . today we fight to defend our very existence and the heritage of our Ulster children . . . "No Surrender, We are King's men"', and before the voters went to the polls on 10 February 1949 his final message was: 'I ask you to cross the Boyne . . . with me as your leader and to fight for the same cause as King William fought for in days gone by.'[42]

Representatives of the Mansion House fund came north to seek one agreed anti-partitionist candidate in each constituency. In Belfast especially, the Northern Ireland Labour Party was squeezed by both sides. It was extremely difficult for the party to argue now that the constitutional issue was irrelevant, yet it tried. When canvassing in the Oldpark, Bob Getgood was asked 'What about the Border?'; his reply that voters should refer to his party's manifesto was not likely to inspire confidence.[43] The election was the most violent since 1921. At Garvagh in Co. Londonderry loyalists, led by three Orange bands, converged on a Nationalist rally and broke it up with the aid of smoke bombs and fireworks, forcing the candidate and his agent to seek sanctuary in the police barracks. Jack Beattie, who accepted money from the fund, wore a steel helmet while campaigning in east Belfast.[44] After his election meeting in Templemore Avenue had been broken up, Beattie sent a telegram of protest to Downing Street: 'Stoned by official Unionist mobs and denied the right of free speech in my election campaign tonight. Armed Stormont police took no action.' The following night his Unionist opponent, Dr Sam Rodgers, said:

> It is a strange thing to see a big six-footer like him going to a wee man like Mr Attlee to seek protection. Why does he not do his crying to Mr Costello, the man he really supports? (Cheers).[45]

Opposition candidates in the Belfast constituencies of Cromac and Dock were also stoned and mobs struggled with each other every evening in the darkness; and, after being driven violently from several platforms, the Labour candidate in Antrim abandoned all public meetings. Hall-Thompson, though not a member of the Orange Order, rode round his constituency, like King William, on a white horse and brandished a blackthorn stick presented by Carson's son Ned, a Conservative MP who beat a Lambeg drum at the final Unionist rally in the Ulster Hall. A motion signed by some two hundred Labour MPs at Westminster calling for the suspension of elections until order could be restored was not debated, though Attlee did admit 'that elections there are not conducted on quite the same lines as we have over here'.[46]

The Northern Ireland Labour Party was eliminated, Beattie was defeated in Pottinger and the only surviving Labour MPs were two antipartitionists. For the first time the opposition at Stormont was entirely Catholic, a matter of much satisfaction to Brooke. The most serious casualty in this election was the modest advance in reconciliation made during the war and immediately after. Attlee duly carried out his earlier promise and his Ireland Act of June 1949 included the unequivocal guarantee that

> in no event will Northern Ireland or any part thereof cease to be a part of his Majesty's dominions and of the United Kingdom without the consent of the parliament of Northern Ireland.

Costello had not consulted Britain before announcing the repeal of the External Relations Act and so Attlee felt quite justified in shoring up the Unionist position. De Valera was in despair, saying that 'it makes one desperate' to see border nationalists being forced to 'lie under the heel of the Ascendancy in the neighbourhood of Belfast'.[47] He would have preferred to retain the tenuous link with the Commonwealth for, according to his friend Frank Gallagher, 'he believed harm would come to the cause of unity from the bridge to the North being destroyed'.[48] In fact there is no evidence that Ulster loyalists had drawn any comfort from the External Relations Act. Unionists wanted nothing to do with the South and the whole episode had left them in a position more impregnable than ever before in the twentieth century. While Northern Ireland remained the most disadvantaged region in the United Kingdom, the standard of living and the quality of public services were patently superior to those in the republic. Indeed, a new drive by the coalition government in Dublin to extend welfare provision only served to reinforce the northern Protestant conviction that reunification would lead inevitably to Rome rule.

Dr Noël Browne of Clann na Poblachta was the youngest, most radical and most charismatic member of Costello's coalition government. He had lost his eldest sister and both his parents from tuberculosis, and he himself had almost died from this disease still killing about one person in every eight hundred in Éire in 1947. Now, as minister for health, Browne worked with astonishing speed and energy. 'It was tough going', one health manager recalled; 'I lost half a stone in weight in the process, but it was a labour of love, because . . . he was so enthusiastic and appreciative.'[49] The death rate fell dramatically and it could be argued that the unremitting drive to eradicate Ireland's most notorious killer disease was the most heartening development of the postwar years. The style in which Browne had cut through red tape to get things done ruffled the feathers of members of the medical profession, who then reacted angrily to the minister's 'Mother and Child' scheme already sanctioned by the 1947 Health Act. It was when the Catholic bishops added their protests to those of the doctors that the plans to provide free treatment for mothers, and children up to the age of sixteen, were put in serious jeopardy. Since 1922 the Church had already had a powerful influence on legislation relating to censorship, constitutional reform, adoption and state welfare provision but the letter sent by the hierarchy on 10 October 1950 was unquestionably the most forthright ever delivered by the Church to the head of an Irish government. In the opinion of the bishops, 'the powers taken by the State in the proposed Mother and Child Health Service are in direct opposition to the rights of the family . . . If adopted in law they would constitute a ready-made instrument for totalitarian aggression.' Browne was undeterred and published his scheme on 6 March 1951. The bishops' objections had not been met and the minister then received a letter from the archbishop of Dublin which stated bluntly: 'I may not approve of the Mother and Child Service, as it is proposed by you to implement the Scheme.'[50]

Costello retreated before this episcopal onslaught and agreed to amend the scheme but when Browne refused to alter his position it was

MacBride, his party leader, who compelled him to resign on 11 April. Next morning the *Irish Times* declared 'that the Roman Catholic Church would seem to be the effective Government of this country'.[51] Northern loyalists heartily concurred. When Browne published all the correspondence available to him, the Unionists dined out on the unedifying revelations for years to come – even though Hall-Thompson had been forced to resign also as a result of clerical criticism and lack of support from his premier. The ensuing general election in the South on 30 May 1951 brought Fianna Fáil back into power, with de Valera as taoiseach.

The prospect of Irish reunification never seemed so distant as it did in 1951. In that year the writer Sean O'Faolain observed that Ireland had been 'snoring gently behind the Green Curtain that we have been rigging up for the last thirty years – Thought-proof, World-proof, Life-proof'.[52] Catholics on the European mainland were abandoning the vocationalism of the interwar years to join other denominations in Christian Democrat parties and to support state-financed social services; yet in 1951 John D'Alton, archbishop of Armagh, described the welfare state as 'a milder form of totalitarianism'. During the war Sir Wilfrid Spender was convinced that it was de Valera's intention to keep the South 'as remote from the world's affairs as Mars'.[53] Certainly southern politicians on both sides of the Dáil showed themselves remarkably out of touch with international developments in their genuine conviction that Britain could be persuaded or forced to abandon the government of Northern Ireland and accede to the demands of the Anti-Partition League. Realising the hopelessness of its position, the league dissolved itself in 1951. It had aimed to bring the Stormont regime to an end and at the same time draw attention to specific grievances within Northern Ireland, such as the manipulation of local government boundaries, and, had it concentrated on the second objective, it might have had more success with the assistance of sympathetic Labour MPs at Westminster. As it turned out, the league's campaign not only gave the Stormont government constitutional reinforcement but also discouraged London from investigating how it ran its affairs.

Sir John Maffey had drafted a paper for his masters entitled 'The Irish Question in 1945', in which he predicted that partition was such a burning issue that it would result in violence:

> It will cause guns to go off in Ireland once again. The Catholics of the North will call out to the Catholics of the South, saying: 'We are only doing what you did in 1916. Are you going to leave us in the lurch?'[54]

Nationalists had tried peaceful constitutional agitation, which had resulted in nothing but humiliation. Brookeborough was coarsely triumphalist and showed no inclination to foster constitutionalism amongst his opponents. Almost inevitably some northern Catholics decided that the only answer to loyalist intransigence was a new resort to arms.

For planning an armed operation in Derry without official approval, Liam Kelly of Pomeroy, Co. Tyrone, was expelled from the IRA in October 1951. Kelly thereupon set up his own militant organisation, Saor Uladh (Free Ulster), and won the support of a new generation of northern republicans impatient at IRA inaction and contemptuous of the Anti-Partition League's constitutional campaign. During Easter 1952 Saor Uladh seized control of Pomeroy for several hours to commemorate the 1916 Rising and in October 1953 Kelly put himself forward as an abstentionist in Mid-Tyrone during a Stormont general election. Kelly made his position clear to voters:

> I will not take the Oath of Allegiance to a foreign Queen . . . I do not believe in constitutional methods. I believe in the use of force; the more the better, the sooner the better.[55]

He won the seat, defeating the sitting Nationalist by a comfortable margin. Charged soon after for making a seditious speech, and refusing to give an undertaking to keep the peace, Kelly was gaoled. Seán MacBride, a member of Costello's coalition which put de Valera out of office in May 1954, used his influence to have Kelly elected a member of the Irish senate. MacBride was present when around ten thousand gathered in Pomeroy to welcome Kelly on his release from prison on 19 August 1954. The attempt by police to prevent the tricolour being paraded down the main street led to protracted rioting – the first major test for the Flags and Emblems Act passed that year, which not only made it an offence to interfere with the display of the Union flag but also gave the police power to remove the tricolour where it might lead to a breach of the peace. Kelly lost no time in revitalising Saor Uladh and, fearing that they would be upstaged by breakaway northern militants, the IRA leaders in Dublin brought forward their long-maturing preparations to renew the armed conflict.

Leo McCormack, a former British commando and a full-time IRA organiser, noticed one day that the sentry at the gate of Gough barracks, headquarters of the Royal Irish Fusiliers in Armagh, had no ammunition in his Sten gun. Hearing of this, the IRA leaders planned an elaborate operation: Seán Garland was sent from Dublin to enlist in the fusiliers, and a steady flow of photographs, maps and training schedules soon began to accumulate at IRA headquarters. Attending the weekly dance at the barracks as 'guests', other volunteers carried out a detailed reconnoitre, and on 10 June 1954 a party of armed IRA men drove across the border in a stolen cattle lorry and parked beside the barracks.[56] The sentry was tied up and during the raid was joined in the guardroom by eighteen other soldiers and an inquisitive civilian without an alarm being raised. After fumbling through a bunch of two hundred keys, the raiders found the correct one for the armoury. In less than half an hour the lorry had been loaded up with 250 rifles, 37 Sten guns, 9 Bren guns and 40 training rifles, and soon after it was driven back over the border, where the arms were quickly dispersed and hidden. According to a speaker at the annual commemoration by the grave of Wolfe Tone at Bodenstown, the IRA was now ready to launch Operation Harvest, a new campaign to drive British troops out of Northern Ireland:

Let there be no doubt in the mind of any man or woman in Ireland on this matter. These arms were captured by the Republican forces for use against the British occupation forces still in Ireland and they will be used against them, please God, in due course.[57]

In fact it took two more years to open the offensive, as the IRA was constantly dislocated by infighting and witch-hunts, and as the older men in Dublin vainly attempted to bring Saor Uladh under their control. Another major raid, at Omagh barracks in October 1954, failed completely and eight men involved were captured. Nevertheless, the militants were pushing constitutional Nationalists aside in Northern Ireland and in the May 1955 Westminster general election Republican Party candidates were elected for the two constituencies of Fermanagh–South Tyrone and Mid-Ulster. Northern activists west of the Bann set the pace: Saor Uladh launched an unsuccessful but dramatic raid on Rosslea RUC barracks just before dawn on 26 November 1955, organised training courses in the Sperrins, and attacked six border customs posts on 11 November 1956. The IRA could wait no longer. Operation Harvest began at midnight on 11 December 1956: action was to be strictly limited to Northern Ireland; Belfast was to be left alone; volunteers could fire at B Specials but not at the RUC; and 'flying columns' from all over the republic were to be taken into the North for active service.

Driving sleet gave convenient cover for the initial assault. In Derry a British Broadcasting Corporation transmitter was destroyed at Rosemount; the Magherafelt courthouse was burned to the ground; the Territorial Army building in Enniskillen was ruined; and in Newry a B Special hut was set on fire. It was a poor achievement for an operation involving around 150 volunteers. Mines placed on bridges surrounding lower Lough Erne failed to inflict permanent damage; men from Cork were arrested by the RUC before they could blow up a radar station on Torr Head; and another attempt on Gough barracks was frustrated by a vigilant defence. Undeterred, the IRA announced on 12 December that the campaign would continue in order to achieve

> an independent, united, democratic Irish Republic. For this we shall fight until the invader is driven from our soil and victory is ours.[58]

At Westminster Sir Anthony Eden, the prime minister, momentarily turned aside from the Suez crisis and the anxieties of the Hungarian uprising to pledge that his government would see to the 'safety of Northern Ireland and its inhabitants'. Brookeborough ordered the cratering or spiking of border roads, leaving only seventeen open; police patrols were augmented by a full call-up of B Specials and strengthened by British Army scout cars; and large numbers of IRA volunteers and Saor Uladh men were arrested and interned.

Over the next few years the IRA campaign continued fitfully without ever seriously disrupting the life of people in Northern Ireland. The high points of Operation Harvest were usually glorious failures, the most remembered being an attack on Brookeborough RUC barracks on New Year's Eve, 1956. Led by Seán Garland, twelve men drove in to this unfamiliar loyalist town and parked their stolen quarry dump truck too close to the barracks. Firing constantly, the volunteers placed a mine which failed to go off; Sergeant Kenneth Cordner, still under heavy fire, shot twenty-five rounds in a continuous burst; and, by the time the volunteers had fled to the Slieve Beagh Mountains on the border, Fergal O'Hanlon of Monaghan and Sean South of Garryowen in Co. Limerick had died of their wounds. The crowds turning up for the funerals of the two latest recruits to the republican pantheon of martyrs were enormous. Seán MacBride, critical of Costello's hostility to the IRA, brought down the coalition government in February 1957 and in the ensuing general election in the republic four Sinn Féin candidates were returned, including Fergal O'Hanlon's brother Einachan in Co. Monaghan and Ruairí Ó Brádaigh – destined to play a crucial role in the formation of the Provisional IRA twelve years later – elected for the constituency of Longford–Westmeath. The Sinn Féin deputies, refusing to take their seats in the Dáil, exerted no political influence and, in any case, de Valera returned to power. Though he told a meeting in Bandon, Co. Cork, that 'there was no single day he was in office that the idea of a united Ireland was not fully before his mind', de Valera said on BBC television:

> You always have people who think that force ought to be used. My own view is that the peaceful line of approach is best, in fact, the only one.[59]

The *Northern Whig* welcomed his return because he was certain to be 'master in his own house', and it was proved right: when the IRA killed Constable Cecil Gregg in an ambush at Forkhill, Co. Armagh, on 4 July 1957, de Valera reintroduced internment with devastating effect.[60] The fact that a Dublin government could not tolerate a paramilitary movement that refused to recognise its authority did not enter into the minds of the IRA leaders. While key men were being rounded up in the republic, 256 men and one woman were interned in Northern Ireland. As the number of activists was never very large, the RUC and B Specials became extremely well informed; 'safe houses' were in very short supply; and the great majority of Catholics in Northern Ireland remained largely indifferent to a campaign mostly carried out in rural areas during the hours of darkness. The IRA was literally driven underground and volunteers – suffering from vermin, from lack of food and from the cold – operated only with extreme difficulty from dugouts excavated in remote mountain sides. Nevertheless, the IRA offensive carried on in a series of often squalid incidents. On 17 August 1957 RUC Sergeant A.J. Ovens was killed by a booby-trap mine in a deserted farmhouse near Coalisland; on 11 November five men blew themselves up preparing a bomb on the Armagh–Louth border; a Saor Uladh volunteer was shot dead by police near Newtownbutler on 2 July 1958; thirteen days later the IRA commander in Co. Fermanagh, Pat McManus, killed himself with his own explosives; and in south Armagh an RUC constable and an IRA man were killed soon afterwards. The campaign, which had been responsible for 366 incidents by the end of 1957, rapidly ran down, and by the autumn of 1958 nearly all the leading activists were either interned or in gaol or dead. There were only twenty-seven incidents in 1959 and twenty-six in 1960. The Curragh internment camp was closed down in March 1959 and the Northern Ireland government released its last internee in April 1961. The murder of an RUC constable at Flurry Bridge near Jonesborough, Co. Armagh, on 12 November 1961 led Sean Lemass, elected taoiseach in 1959, to introduce military tribunals, which had been so effective against the IRA during the war. A few days later Brian Faulkner, Northern Ireland minister of home affairs, threatened to introduce the death penalty. Squeezed north and south, the IRA army council and executive council felt that they had no choice but to call off the campaign; Ruairí Ó Brádaigh, on their behalf, made an official statement on 26 February 1962 announcing the withdrawal of 'all full-time active service Volunteers', while at the same time renewing the IRA 'pledge of eternal hostility to the British Forces of Occupation in Ireland'.[61]

The final toll was twelve militant republicans and six RUC men killed; thirty-two members of the security forces injured; over two hundred convicted and sentenced for their role in the campaign, apart from other hundreds interned; an additional cost to the republic of £350,000 a year; and an extra cost of £500,000 to Northern Ireland per year, together with damage estimated at £700,000. The IRA had not brought the reunification of Ireland any closer and, indeed, support for republican abstentionist candidates ebbed rapidly away as the campaign drew to a close. It remained to be seen if the failure of the traditional republican campaign of violence would lead to a softening of traditional attitudes amongst the great majority of Protestants and Catholics in Northern Ireland.

'TO SHED OUR PAROCHIALISM IS NOT TO DENY OUR INHERITANCE'

When the IRA called its men off active service in February 1962, the *New York Times* made these observations:

> The original I.R.A. and Sinn Fein came in like lions . . . and now they go out like lambs . . . the Irish Republican Army belongs to history, and it belongs to better men in times that are gone. So does Sinn Fein. Let us put a wreath of red roses on their grave and move on.[62]

Throughout the 1950s the Catholic minority in Northern Ireland remained faithful to political aspirations constantly expressed in previous decades. During the coronation of Elizabeth II in 1953, for example, all the Nationalist representatives issued a proclamation, declaring that they

> hereby repudiate all claims now made or to be made in the future by or on behalf of the British Crown and Government to jurisdiction over any portion of the land of Ireland or of her territorial seas.[63]

Yet northern Catholics had very largely withheld their support from the IRA and even the impressive electoral support given for a time to abstentionist republican candidates west of the Bann could be interpreted as no more than votes of protest against Unionist inflexibility. The nationalist minority overwhelmingly endorsed constitutional political action rather than methods of violence, and the Brookeborough government enjoyed a greater security than any of its predecessors. Never had there been a more opportune moment for the Northern Ireland government to attempt to draw Catholics into the institutions of state and into a fuller participation in the public affairs of the region. Any real progress along this road would require tact, patience and political acumen of the highest order, but not even an attempt was made.

Throughout the 1950s and during the final years of Brookeborough's premiership, the Unionist government was given constant reminders that it risked alienating its traditional support if it strayed from the traditional path. A very sizeable proportion of loyalists looked on nationalists as traitors who could not be entrusted with political influence. Many felt it necessary to remind Catholics of Protestant supremacy and to bring pressure to bear on government ministers who stood in their way. This was clearly evident in the long-running dispute over Orange marches at Longstone Hill in Co. Down. When the Orange Lodge based in Annalong declared in June 1952 that its brethren would march along the Longstone Road on 12 July, Minister of Home Affairs Brian Maginess imposed a ban: this was not a traditional route; a detour would have to be made to pass through this Catholic district; and, in any case, he had recently prevented nationalists from marching into the centres of Enniskillen and Derry.[64] So great was the loyalist outcry, however, that the ban was lifted on 3 July. Ministers showing liberal tendencies often found their political futures endangered: in the Stormont general election of 1954 Hall-Thompson was ousted from his Belfast seat by Norman Porter, secretary of the evangelical National Union of Protestants, who stood as an Independent Unionist; and another Independent Unionist came close to defeating Maginess. In the same year Brookeborough moved Maginess to finance but the new home affairs minister, George B. Hanna, who reimposed the ban on the Longstone Road march, was forced to lift it again in 1955 – on that occasion Brian Faulkner, MP for East Down, joined Porter in leading the Twelfth parade over the controversial route. Locals blew holes in the road with three bombs the day before and three hundred RUC men had to be brought in to oversee the fifteen thousand Orangemen who marched that day. W.W.B. Topping, appointed minister of home affairs in 1956, allowed later Longstone Road parades only with the greatest reluctance but he faced intense criticism when he banned an Orange procession through Dungiven in 1959. The Bovevagh Orange Lodge had made its first march through the centre of this largely Catholic town in 1953 and trouble ensued every July thereafter. Topping was jeered during the main Twelfth parade in Belfast in 1959 for his decision, and before the year was out he had agreed to step down as minister to become the recorder of Belfast.[65]

Petty disputation over parading routes demonstrated how uneven and slow the progressive process was in Northern Ireland. Yet these years are rightly remembered as a time when intercommunal tensions eased to some degree. Government ministers were less prone than before to make provocative public declarations, though Midgley, still minister of education, said in Portadown in 1957: 'All the minority are traitors and have always been traitors to the government of Northern Ireland.'[66] A more usual slight to the minority by members of the

Government was simply to ignore Catholic opinion altogether and to equate the Protestants of Northern Ireland with the entire population of the region. A social studies conference held at Garron Tower in Co. Antrim in 1958 gave some indication of a shift in Catholic middle-class opinion: there Gerard Newe – later to become the first Catholic in the Stormont cabinet – condemned the futility of depending on the republic's claim to be the *de jure* government of the six north-eastern counties and declared that Catholics had a duty to 'co-operate with the *de facto* authority that controls . . . life and welfare'.[67]

Addressing Young Unionists at Portstewart, Co. Londonderry, in 1959, Sir Clarence Graham, chairman of the Ulster Unionist Party Standing Committee, said that Catholics should be allowed to join the Unionist Party and be selected as its candidates. Brian Maginess, now attorney-general, agreed:

> To shed our parochialism is not to deny our inheritance. To broaden our outlook means no weakening of our faith. Toleration is not a sign of weakness, but proof of strength. This will require . . . considered words instead of clichés, reasoned arguments instead of slogans.

Sir George Clark, grand master of the Grand Orange Lodge of Ireland, was alarmed and replied at Scarva, Co. Down:

> It is difficult to see how a Catholic, with the vast differences in our religious outlook, could be either acceptable within the Unionist Party as a member or, for that matter, bring himself unconditionally to support its ideals.[68]

Brookeborough did not hesitate to endorse this view, telling Young Unionists it would be difficult for Catholics 'to discard the political conceptions, the influence and impressions acquired from religious and educational instruction by those whose aims are openly declared to be an all-Ireland republic'. He continued:

> There is no change in the fundamental character of the Unionist Party or in the loyalties it observes and preserves. If that is called intolerance, I say at once it is not the fault of the Unionist Party. If it is called inflexible then it shows that our principles are not elastic.[69]

Brookeborough may have used all the security forces and special powers available to his government during the IRA campaign of violence but otherwise he showed considerable skill in restraining the hotheads on his own side from taking provocative retaliatory action. The prime minister had imbibed his political certainties, however, in the countryside of the loyalist marchlands and, for all his affable courtesy, was more inflexible in his views than Craigavon had ever been. He never seems to have entertained even the possibility that Catholics could become full participating citizens of Northern Ireland. Brookeborough believed that at best the minority should be tolerated and never ceased to regard all Catholics as potential traitors. He shamelessly reiterated the old rallying cries and made no attempt to steer his party towards a less divisive stand. Admittedly, apart from occasional protests made by Labour backbenchers, Westminster applied no pressure on the Stormont regime to adopt a more flexible and liberal approach. Thus the inattention of central government in London, the complacency of Brookeborough's government and the tired rhetoric of southern political leaders and northern Nationalists combined to let a unique opportunity slip: that of enfolding the majority of northern Catholics, repelled by the squalid violence of republican militants, into the political system. No doubt a sizeable proportion of Catholics would never have been reconciled to the political status quo but the tragedy was that Brookeborough seemed incapable of recognising the benefits of reconciling any of the minority to the regime.

Belfast was all but unaffected by the IRA campaign and it was in this city, more than anywhere else in Northern Ireland, that local politics showed some signs of conforming to the western European pattern. The Northern Ireland Labour Party, which had long remained neutral on the issue of partition, had been forced to make up its mind after Costello's announcement that Éire would become a republic. On 31 January 1949 the party accepted 'the constitutional position of Northern Ireland and the close association with Britain and the Commonwealth' and this was confirmed by a special delegate conference on 8 April when the executive was instructed to 'take all necessary steps to seek the closest possible means of co-operation with the British Labour Party'.[70] At first those who refused to accept this decision fared best: they joined the Irish Labour Party, now organising in the North, and won all seven seats in the Smithfield and Falls wards in Belfast, and full control in the Newry and Warrenpoint councils in local government elections. The Northern Ireland Labour Party failed to win any seats at Stormont in 1953 but its strength was growing and in the next general election, in 1958, it was spectacularly successful in Belfast: David Bleakley won Victoria; Billy Boyd, Woodvale; Vivian Simpson, Oldpark; and Tom Boyd, Pottinger. The first two had captured seats in overwhelmingly Protestant constituencies, causing much alarm at Unionist headquarters. For the first time the Northern Ireland parliament had an official opposition – though Brookeborough refused to accord this opposition privileges normally given at Westminster – and the level of debate was at once enhanced at Stormont, where bread-and-butter issues were at last discussed in greater depth. The four Labour MPs

611

were all Protestant and did not hesitate to support the Government's measures against the IRA, yet two of them – Vivian Simpson and Tom Boyd – were as much dependent on Catholic votes as on Protestant ones.

The support for the Northern Ireland Labour Party continued to grow in Belfast and hopes were high when Brookeborough called an election on 31 May 1962. The IRA campaign had been called off, domestic issues commanded most attention, and on the eve of the poll the *Belfast Telegraph* observed that the four Labour MPs had 'given the House of Commons an added validity and purpose'.[71] Fourteen Labour candidates succeeded in obtaining 26 per cent of votes cast in the region, though this did no more than increase the majorities for its four Belfast MPs. Never had a political party obtained so much cross-community support and its members abandoned their previous reluctance to raise such issues as discrimination in housing allocation and electoral practice. This was not the dawn of a new era, however, for the Unionist Party remained invulnerable and many voters had polled for Labour candidates not out of a zeal for socialism but simply in protest in constituencies where Unionists were often returned without a contest.

The relative success of the Northern Ireland Labour Party at this time owed much to an atmosphere of exceptional political calm in which the constitutional issue was pushed to the background and, in Belfast in particular, to deep anxieties about unemployment and an obviously faltering economy.

'ACTIVITY AT THE QUEEN'S ISLAND CONTINUES AT A VERY HIGH LEVEL'

On 8 October 1951, after reporting that Harland and Wolff had won an order from the Alfred Holt line for a cargo liner – the eighth since the war – the *Belfast Telegraph* gave readers a general account of work in progress:

> Activity at the Queen's Island continues at a very high level. Already the yards have launched eight ships of more than 10,000 tons, and at least two more are likely to reach the water before the end of the year. Sixteen slipways are now occupied and preparations are being made for the laying of keels in the remaining two. One of the ships concerned is the 28,000 ton passenger liner for the Peninsular and Orient Steam Navigation Co. Ltd. and the other is expected to be an oil tanker of 32,000 tons d.w. for the British Tanker Co. Ltd. Both the Abercorn and Victoria Yards are fully engaged.[72]

Seven cargo liners were on the slips in the Abercorn and Victoria yards; two refrigerated cargo ships for the Shaw Savill line were being built in the Queen's yard; four oil tankers were rising up in the Musgrave yard, including the 18,000-ton *British Skill*; the previous Saturday the Union-Castle liner *Rhodesia Castle* had left Belfast and a sister ship was being built; and Harland and Wolff had orders for fifteen other vessels. Later that month the company delivered the aircraft carrier HMS *Eagle*, the largest vessel in the Royal Navy, and *Juan Peron*, the world's biggest whale factory ship, during the building of which eighteen men were killed and fifty-nine seriously injured when a gangway collapsed. Never before and never again were the yards of Harland and Wolff so occupied; at one point in 1951 sixty-eight vessels were either being built or on order, and twenty-one thousand men were fully employed on Queen's Island.[73]

The expected postwar slump in shipbuilding had not materialised, averted in part by the devastation of German and Japanese yards, the maintenance of state controls, and the unprecedented aid given by the United States to western Europe under the Marshall Plan. Because Belfast had never concentrated on Admiralty work, Harland and Wolff was exceptionally well-placed to meet the high demand for merchant vessels and oil tankers, and to reconvert passenger liners commandeered for war work back to civilian service. In addition, Queen's Island built up a brisk business in manufacturing land engines, including a 40,000 kw steam turbine for Blackburn power station and a 30,000 kw turbine for Finland, and between May and November 1951 the company received orders for fourteen generating sets for locations as far apart as Nigeria, Zanzibar and Singapore. A drop in ship orders in 1948–9 had been swiftly brought to an end by the outbreak of the Korean War in June 1950 but what of the future when this conflict was over? The *Belfast Telegraph* gave this warning early in 1952:

> In the future British shipbuilders may be faced with intense competition from Germany and Japan. Allied controls on shipbuilding in Germany were lifted in April, and strenuous efforts are being made to restore the industry in that country to its former prosperity. Japan may eventually be an even more formidable rival than Germany, because she is able to draw upon large reserves of cheap labour.[74]

A year later Sir Frederick Rebbeck referred to 'very deadly competition' and said: 'I would not be in the least surprised if this year Germany does not head the output for the world and that is a dangerous signal.'[75] Indeed, from now on the United Kingdom shipbuilding industry faced severe competition but, while international demand for vessels continued to grow throughout the 1950s, the decline was not absolute. Between 1946 and 1955 world output of merchant tonnage rose by almost 100 per cent, but the United Kingdom's output increased only slightly. By world standards Harland and Wolff suffered relative decline but it outperformed other yards in the United Kingdom during the 1950s and Queen's Island gave every appearance of continuing prosperity throughout the decade. In the period 1946–61 annual launchings averaged around 129,000 tons, the workforce at Queen's Island rarely falling below twenty thousand. Notable vessels included the twin-screw turbine steamer *Iberia*, completed for P & O in 1954, the largest passenger liner launched by the company since the war; large oil tankers for Shell and BP, four of them over 750 feet long and each costing over £2 million; and Shaw Savill's *Southern Cross*, named by Elizabeth II in 1954, the first merchant vessel to have been launched by a reigning British monarch.[76]

On 16 March 1960 Dame Pattie Menzies, wife of the Australian prime minister, was welcomed at the launching platform on the Musgrave yard by Rebbeck; Brookeborough; the Northern Ireland governor, Lord Wakehurst; and the RUC band playing 'Waltzing Matilda'. Some twenty thousand spectators cheered vociferously when Dame Pattie broke a bottle of Australian red wine on the bows of *Canberra* and the 45,270-ton P & O liner entered Belfast Lough.[77] It was the last great launching of its kind in Belfast. The ship was the largest liner built in Britain since the *Queen Elizabeth*, with a revolutionary design still looking modern thirty years later. Yet Harland and Wolff lost £1.2 million on what was the most valuable contract ever awarded to the company.[78]

The launch of the *Canberra* marked the end of an era, and owing to a lack of orders, by 1962 the workforce in Belfast was reduced to 12,582.[79] Queen's Island was best equipped to build large passenger liners, now being confined to the luxury cruise market by the growing attractions of jet air transport; and general-purpose, dry-cargo vessels, now being supplanted by bulk carriers or by heavy vehicles on motorways. In retrospect the later 1950s were years of lost opportunity to adapt and modernise. Though the Belfast yard was still the largest shipbuilding unit in the world, it was not equipped to meet the rapidly growing international demand for large oil tankers and bulk carriers. Leading competitors overseas – particularly in Japan, Germany and Sweden – had abandoned the traditional 'keel up' assembly with labour-intensive prefabrication and large-scale welding.[80] But Rebbeck had a conservative distrust of the new techniques and failed to recognise the damaging effect of traditional management practices, demarcation disputes and late deliveries. By 1961 the condition of this leviathan – with a pivotal position in Northern Ireland's economy – was a matter of acute concern. Sir Frederick retired in March 1962 and the *Sunday Times* remarked that the new management faced the 'impossible task of floating a stranded whale'.[81]

Not all Harland and Wolff's difficulties were due to poor management. Westminster governments persisted in the belief that there was a free-market economy in world shipbuilding. As early as 1947, the Japanese Development Bank was subsidising its country's shipbuilders and shipowners. As Rebbeck himself pointed out in 1953, the credit terms offered by the Westminster government to shipowners wanting to buy British were far less generous than those offered by the Japanese, German and Swedish governments to their own national companies. Rebbeck had called on the Northern Ireland government to build a new large dry dock in Belfast the following year: this essential requirement for building the new generation of vessels was rejected because 'it would not be economic and is not desired by the Admiralty for strategic reasons'.[82]

LINEN: BOOM AND COLLAPSE

For most of the 1940s the only brake on Northern Ireland's linen industry seemed to be shortage of raw material. During the war some 150,000 acres had been set aside to grow flax in the region, but thereafter, farmers found the labour costs too high. Russia, which had grown nearly 70 per cent of the world's flax between the wars, now kept most of her crop for her own needs and ceased to export after 1950. Belgium and France at first found it impossible to meet demand. In spite of a special deal with McCleery's Clonard Mills in Belfast to supply one hundred thousand bundles of yarn, Clark's of Upperlands could only run three weeks out of every five. Trading conditions in 1947, Wallace Clark recalls, 'were in extraordinary contrast to those before the war. In a seller's market, price was of little importance. Yarn was booked on open contract to be invoiced at time of delivery.'[83] As flax supplies increased the industry flourished as it had not done for more than a quarter of a century. By 1948 Clark's of Upperlands employed seven hundred people, started up the Moneycarrie Upper House after a twelve-year break, had a hundred beetling engines working along the Clady river and produced thirty thousand webs over twelve months. A downswing in the industry in 1949 was swiftly reversed by the outbreak of the Korean War, particularly as the production of rayon – by now a serious rival to linen – was curtailed by a shortage of sulphur needed to process it.[84] By 1951 around seventy-six thousand workers in Northern Ireland were employed in textiles, the great majority in linen. Then in July 1953 the war came to an end and prices all but collapsed. At Upperlands a three-day week was imposed and the firm which had orders for thirty-three thousand webs in January had only three thousand on order by December.

This was no temporary downturn and from now on the industry was in a state of near-terminal decline. Many great Ulster linen houses closed, including: the Victoria Weaving Company in Belfast with 350 damask looms, the Inver Factory in Larne, Gunning's of Cookstown, and Clark's of Castledawson. Indeed, in an attempt to rationalise the trade, the Government subsidised closures and amalgamations. Over a seven-year period twenty-five thousand jobs were lost in textiles until by 1958 only fifty-one thousand were employed.[85] 'Loving is lovelier on linen' was a slogan used by one Ulster firm in a sales drive in Italy, but the fall in demand could not be stemmed.[86] Much contemporary criticism of the industry's inefficiency, cut-throat competition and conservatism was misplaced. Technical advance was actually quite rapid; the real problem was that linen, except for certain specialist purposes, was becoming outdated. Rayon had taken over much of linen's traditional garment trade during the postwar years and in the 1950s and 1960s nylon, Terylene and other synthetic fibres dominated the textile market. In addition dry-cleaning solvents and modern detergents could be damaging to linen; damask table cloths went out of fashion; and better-heated homes and motorcars led consumers to demand lighter and softer clothing and underwear. The linen industry had always been labour intensive and it could be argued that as soon as mill workers began to get a living wage the competition from other textiles produced in poorer regions of the world became overwhelming. By the end of the 1950s further closures included Kirk's of Keady, weavers; Hale Martin, flax spinners in Balnamore; the Lambeg Weaving and Finishing Company; and Nicholson and Templeton of Springfield in Belfast.[87] In the years that followed, two of the three largest concerns in Belfast – York Street (with 1,000 looms and 60,000 spindles) and Brookfield (1,400 looms and 35,000 spindles) – closed down altogether, and the third, Ewarts, survived only by greatly reducing output.[88]

The inexorable decline of linen occurred during a period of unparalleled and sustained economic growth in the western world. Could Northern Ireland take advantage of this boom to start up enough new enterprises to replace the jobs being lost in the region's traditional export industries?

'WE HAVE HELD THE LINE WHILE OLD INDUSTRIES HAVE FALTERED. BUT IT IS NOT ENOUGH'

Agriculture continued to be Northern Ireland's largest industry and, sustained by guaranteed prices and subsidies, it was well-placed to carve out a good share of Britain's lucrative market. Aided by the heavy importation of foreign feedstuffs, the production of eggs, poultry and pigs, in particular, made a spectacular recovery. Overall, the region's agricultural output increased by a comfortable average of 2 per cent per annum in the 1950s. The problem for the Government was that technical progress had the effect of reducing employment opportunities on the land. Labour-saving tractors, only numbering 850 in 1939, rose to 16,000 by 1950 and the numbers doubled again by the end of the decade. In addition, tillage declined from a ratio of three acres of pasture to one of tillage in 1950 to five to one by 1959. Not surprisingly, male employment in farming fell by 27 per cent in the 1950s. The Northern Ireland government therefore faced the problem of making up the shortfall in rural employment and compensating for the job losses in the declining industries at a time when the region's population increased from 1,370,921 in 1951 to 1,425,042 in 1959. In short, Northern Ireland's main economic hope was to attract in enough new manufacturing to keep the region's population at work.[89]

Aircraft manufacture in Belfast failed to maintain the wartime levels of production. Immediately after the peace, Short and Harland concentrated on converting Halifax bombers, Sunderlands, and Junkers (captured from the Germans) to civilian passenger aircraft and even made thousands of ten-gallon milk cans to meet a desperate postwar shortage. The Rochester plant was closed down in 1948 and all production was transferred to the Belfast works, now called Short Brothers, but the Government's majority stake in the company – 70 per cent in 1954 – did not guarantee regular employment. The success of Britain's Vickers Armstrong prevented Short Brothers from becoming a major manufacturer of military aircraft and the numbers employed at Sydenham, which had been 10,500 during the last years of the war, fell to a plateau of around 6,000. For a time the firm developed a market for passenger flying boats: the first Solent was named in May 1949 by Princess Elizabeth and the first Sealand was sold to Christian and Missionary Alliance of New York for use in Indonesia. The company developed the first tailless aircraft, the Sherpa, in 1951, and pioneered the vertical take-off SC1 in 1955, but much of its highly advanced research and development failed to yield a significant commercial return until the 1960s.[90]

The report by K.S. Isles and Norman Cuthbert, *An Economic Survey of Northern Ireland*, was published in 1957; it was the most penetrating and comprehensive study of its kind so far. The authors detailed the difficulties facing the region at a time of major structural change in the economy; natural resources were meagre and, apart from agriculture, there was a dearth of raw material and fuel for industry; most finished goods had only a small provincial market; and, above all, the range of industries that could prosper was restricted by the high cost of fuel and cross-channel transport. Indeed, Isles and Cuthbert effectively exposed a coal ring in Belfast and recommended investigation by the Monopolies Commission. Brookeborough's government sought further economic guidance from a working party under the direction of Sir Robert Hall, which published its report in October 1962. The Hall report underlined conclusions made by Isles and Cuthbert and, in particular, the difficulty of reducing unemployment from its level of some thirty thousand when the population's natural increase was about fifteen thousand per year. The main recommendation was that the Government should cease its efforts to support declining industries and concentrate on bringing dynamic outsiders to Northern Ireland:

> The introduction into the Northern Irish industrial community of the energetic executives and technicians of new industry helps to establish an attractive atmosphere for the newcomer.[91]

At the time the Hall report caused much gloom in government circles but a close examination of the evidence marshalled in its pages shows that the people of Northern Ireland had been enjoying the most sustained improvement in living standards since the setting up of the regional administration in 1921. Personal income per head had risen from £168 a year in 1950–1 to £284 by 1959–60. Between 1950 and 1960 industrial production increased by 40 per cent compared with 35 per cent for the United Kingdom as a whole. Brookeborough's government had largely succeeded in funding alternative employment for those who lost their jobs in the linen industry and in farming. State assistance was provided by the Industries Development Acts, 1945–53, the Re-equipment of Industry Act, 1951, and the Capital Grants to Industry Act, 1954. It is difficult to know whether the £4 million given to aid the linen industry between 1956 and 1961 was squandered when in those years another ten thousand textile workers lost their jobs.[92] However, forty-two thousand jobs had been created in new industries between 1945 and 1962, including: Courtaulds viscose rayon plant in Carrickfergus in 1950; AEI turbine factory in Larne in 1956; Chemstrand's Acrilan plant at Coleraine in 1959; Du Pont's synthetic rubber factory in Co. Londonderry in 1960; and Standard Telephones and Cables in south Antrim in 1962.[93] In addition, the volume of output per head of Northern Ireland industrial workers was reckoned to have gone up by 23 per cent between 1958 and 1963.

Though gross domestic product rose by a respectable 2.6 per cent per annum in the 1950s, Northern Ireland remained consistently the most disadvantaged region in the United Kingdom. At a time when unemployment levels were very low in almost all areas of Britain, Northern Ireland's annual rate was averaging 7 per cent. In this decade increase in industrial output averaged only 2.1 per cent compared with 3.5 per cent in Denmark, 8.5 per cent in Spain and 9.3 per cent in West Germany. Part of the problem was that growth was slow in the United Kingdom, now painfully adjusting to the loss of captive imperial markets. Northern Ireland had been able to do little more than hold the line during a period of remarkable economic growth in the West.[94]

If Northern Ireland missed out on the first part of the sustained expansion of western economies in the 1950s and 1960s, at least Unionists could console themselves that their government's record was far better than that in the South. During the Emergency the cost of living had risen by 70 per cent, while industrial wages had only increased by 27 per cent; 130,000 had emigrated between 1941 and 1946; unemployment was estimated to be 14 per cent in 1945; and it was not until 1947 that the output level of the late 1930s was surpassed. Industries sheltering behind the high tariff wall were inefficient and incapable of finding export markets and not only did Dublin governments restrict foreign investment but they also responded to crises by excessively deflationary budgets. National income in the republic expanded at a miserable rate of less than one per cent per year between 1951 and 1959 and forty thousand emigrated annually during the same period. Drastic measures were clearly necessary. In 1958 T.K. Whitaker, secretary to the Department of Finance, proposed a complete change of direction in his *Economic Development*: a dismantling of tariffs; encouragement of foreign investment; removal of controls on foreign ownership of manufacturing concerns; economic *rapprochement* with the United Kingdom; and co-ordinated planning to reduce unemployment and emigration.[95]

A new age seemed about to dawn. After winning a resounding victory in the 1957 general election, de Valera let his pragmatic deputy Sean Lemass begin the implementation of the Whitaker plan, even though it meant the abandonment of the ideal of self-sufficiency which had been so close to his heart. In 1959 de Valera was elected president of the republic and Lemass replaced him as taoiseach. In Northern Ireland, too, a younger generation of politicians was impatient for change. One of these was Captain Terence O'Neill, minister of finance since 1956, who said to the Pottinger Unionist Association in November 1962:

We have held the line while old industries have faltered. But it is not enough. We must do more. We intend to do more.[96]

A few months later O'Neill was given the opportunity to do more for the people of Northern Ireland.

From the beginning of 1962 the Belfast County Grand Orange Lodge made elaborate preparations to celebrate the fiftieth anniversary of the Solemn League and Covenant. Brookeborough and other leading members of the Government promised their full support without giving any indication that the event could not be a festive occasion for one third of the citizens of Northern Ireland. Bob Cooper, then treasurer of the Young Unionist Council, gave this warning to his party in February:

> The man at the bench, the man at the office, the man in the University, have an image of a party which will brook no criticism from its members and a government of ageing tired men who cannot look forward with hope and who are forced to look back with nostalgia; who prefer to celebrate an event of fifty years ago rather than to plan for the next fifty years.[97]

Government ministers seemed to take no heed of this caution and when the prime minister called a press conference to announce a general election in May, he was asked if the Unionist Party would make history by not making the border an issue. Brian Faulkner, the minister of home affairs, pointed to a poster bearing the Union flag and the slogan 'This We Will Maintain'.[98] Though the Government's majority was never in doubt, worries about the region's economic future helped to reduce the Unionist vote. Still Brookeborough refused to change course and duly reiterated the traditional rallying cries at the Covenant celebrations in September.

A month later, on 30 October 1962, Brookeborough faced furious criticism when the Hall report was presented at Stormont. In just two years unemployment had risen from 6.7 per cent to 7.5, and protests and demonstrations had recently been organised by the trade unions. Desmond Boal, Unionist MP for Shankill, voted with the Northern Ireland Labour Party on a motion condemning unemployment and called on Brookeborough to retire, and Vivian Simpson, Labour MP for Oldpark, condemned the failure to set up a regional planning unit and to give official recognition to the Northern Committee of the Irish Congress of Trade Unions: 'How can the trade unions give of their best if the Government refuses to recognise them?' he asked.[99]

The Irish Congress of Trade Unions was one of the few cross-border bodies commanding substantial support from both Catholics and Protestants, and Brookeborough's hostility to it epitomised his political inflexibility. His government seemed tired and uninspired even to his closest supporters. 'I want to say perfectly frankly and straightly that I have no intention of resigning as your Prime Minister,' Brookeborough announced in February 1963, but the following month his colleagues forced him to stand down.[100] The parliamentary Unionist Party probably would have chosen Brian Faulkner as his successor but the inner circle chose Captain O'Neill, who, after being handed a whiskey and soda by the governor, was informed of his appointment on 25 March.

In 1963 it seemed that the only major question facing both O'Neill and Lemass was how best to achieve social and economic betterment for the people they governed. A more relaxed political atmosphere apparently prevailed and a slow but steady easing of intercommunal tensions in Northern Ireland was anticipated by many. Others recognised that deep-rooted problems still festered beneath the surface. *The Indivisible Island*, written by Frank Gallagher and published in 1957, was a traditional nationalist tract against partition, but it presented a closely argued critique, supported by a mass of evidence, of the Northern Ireland government's inequitable treatment of the Catholic minority. Gallagher was a close friend of de Valera's, a former editor of the *Irish Press* and director of the Dublin government's information bureau between 1939 and 1948; thus Unionists could dismiss his charges as propagandist.[101] *The Northern Ireland Problem: A Study in Group Relations*, published in 1962, was a different matter: the authors, Denis P. Barritt and Charles F. Carter, were Quakers who accepted partition without question and worked closely with government agencies, and yet they produced damning evidence of ancient enmity still in full vigour and of widespread discriminatory practice both in public life and in the community.[102] Brookeborough had seen no reason for political reform and the certainty that he would never make a serious attempt to consider a redress of minority grievances was in part responsible for his long-standing popularity with the majority. Writing in 1969, Captain O'Neill observed:

> As I see it the tragedy of his premiership was that he did not use his tremendous charm, and his deep Orange roots to try and persuade his devoted followers to accept some reforms.[103]

O'Neill clearly believed some reforms were needed: would they be enough to satisfy Catholic demands and would he be able to carry the majority of his traditional supporters with him?

14

THE O'NEILL ERA

1963–1972

OVERVIEW

'Our task will be literally to transform Ulster,' O'Neill said to the Ulster Unionist Council a few days after being appointed prime minister in 1963; 'To achieve it will demand bold and imaginative measures.'[1] The following year he stated at Stormont that his principal aims were 'to make Northern Ireland economically stronger and prosperous . . . and to build bridges between the two traditions within our community'.[2] Dedicated though he was to the constitutional status quo and continued Unionist rule, O'Neill was the first Northern Ireland prime minister to state clearly that reconciliation was a central part of his programme. He sought to bring the benefits of modernisation to everyone in the region and not just to the Protestant majority, and, aged forty-eight in 1963, O'Neill represented a new liberal Unionist generation prepared to move away from the siege mentality of those involved in the turbulent events surrounding the formation of Northern Ireland. Their privileged backgrounds notwithstanding, Craigavon, Andrews and Brookeborough had more of the common touch than O'Neill, but when they said 'we here in Ulster', as they often did, they were not including the Catholic minority. Drawn from the old Ascendancy, with the blood of both the Chichesters and the Clandeboye O'Neills flowing in his veins, the new prime minister was further distanced from the people he governed by his Eton and Irish Guards background. After a long and friendly interview with O'Neill in 1969, Lord Longford recalled: 'The very fact that he felt apparently so much kinship with me made me realize how difficult it must be for him to feel completely at home as Prime Minister of Northern Ireland.'[3]

O'Neill was fortunate in being able to launch his programme at a time when world trading conditions were buoyant and when the Republic of Ireland was not only transforming its economy but also seeking friendlier co-operation with the United Kingdom. At the same time this was an era of rapidly rising expectations and vastly improved international communications. Despite his mould-breaking gestures of conciliation, O'Neill eventually created intense frustration within the minority by his inability to deliver thoroughgoing reform, while more and more loyalists were convinced that he was conceding too much, and turned against him. In less than two years Northern Ireland moved from a promising period of co-operation to violence so intense that in news coverage across the world it vied with reports of the Vietnam War. Many, not only in America and on the European mainland but also in Britain, who previously were unaware that Ireland was politically divided and who would have had difficulty in locating Ulster on the map, soon became familiar with places such as the Bogside, Divis Flats, the Creggan, the Shankill and the Falls.

By 1969 Northern Ireland was in a state of near-revolutionary crisis, leading to the fall first of O'Neill, then of his successor James Chichester-Clark, and finally of the whole system of devolved government. Ancient hatreds welled to the surface in bitter violence that soon surpassed that of 1920–2 and, as the Westminster government imposed direct rule on the region, Northern Ireland became the most continuously disturbed part of Europe since the ending of the Second World War. Such an outcome was not envisaged by anyone when Captain O'Neill first set out in an optimistic spirit to regenerate the economy of Northern Ireland.

PLANNING AN ECONOMIC REVOLUTION

Before becoming prime minister, O'Neill had served as minister of finance for seven years and much of the credit for attracting new firms to Northern Ireland was due to his professional approach. He had established contact with financial civil servants from the Irish Republic at World Bank meetings and had been deeply impressed by the implementation of Whitaker's report, which was opening up the South's economic development and dismantling tariffs. However, as O'Neill recalled later, Brookeborough 'condemned planning . . . as a socialist menace' and it was not until 1963 that this constraint was removed.[4] In his opening speech as premier O'Neill sketched out his vision of the future:

It is a new motorway driving deeper into the province. It is a new airport which will match our position as the busiest air centre in Britain outside

London. It is a new hospital in Londonderry – the most modern in the British Isles. It is new laboratories and research facilities at Queen's to carry us to the frontiers of existing knowledge and beyond. It is replacement of derelict slums by modern housing estates.[5]

This peroration was inspired by Sir Robert Matthew's *Belfast Regional Survey and Plan 1962*, commissioned by Brookeborough, which recommended a restriction of further growth in the regional capital and a grandiose scheme to create a new city between Portadown and Lurgan. O'Neill wanted comprehensive planning for the whole of Northern Ireland but failed to find a Whitaker equivalent amongst public servants on the Stormont estate – perhaps because, as John Oliver wrote later, 'appointments to senior positions in the civil service were timid, mediocre men were being encouraged, grey figures were beginning to predominate'.[6] Instead, O'Neill appointed Tom Wilson, an Ulsterman and Adam Smith professor of political economy at the University of Glasgow, as economic consultant to the Northern Ireland government in October 1963. Two months earlier an Economic Council had been set up under the chairmanship of Brian Faulkner, recently appointed minister of commerce. To work successfully this council needed the backing of the trade unions and it took O'Neill another twelve months to surmount 'one of the most difficult hurdles', that is, to convince the cabinet to recognise the Northern Committee of the Irish Congress of Trade Unions; the party meeting that endorsed this decision was, O'Neill recalled, 'a small gathering – many MPs were too frightened to attend it'.[7]

By the end of 1964 the prime minister had Wilson's report on his desk and on 1 January 1965 a Ministry of Development was set up under William Craig, previously the government chief whip, to direct the regional plans and put into effect the recommendations of the Economic Council. The Wilson plan, published in February 1965, largely endorsed Matthew's proposals but also called for further growth points at Derry, Larne, Bangor–Newtownards, Carrickfergus–Carnmoney, and Antrim–Ballymena. Not since the plantation had such a grand design been drawn up to direct Ulster's future: the scheme included a ring road for Belfast; a new city in the centre of the province; four motorways; a second university; a major manpower training programme; and the building of sixty-four thousand houses by 1970. The overall cost was put at £900 million, half of it to be provided by the Government. Above all, Wilson sought a more vigorous drive to import new firms to Northern Ireland, to be enticed by tax allowances, investment grants and employment premiums. This was the era when planning was much in vogue in western democracies: Westminster was reluctant to give further subsidies to declining industries and there is more than a suspicion that the enthusiastic adoption of the Wilson plan had behind it a carefully laid scheme by the Stormont government to extract more funds from Whitehall.[8]

There is little doubt now that the Wilson plan was seriously flawed, though perhaps no more so than other regional development schemes in the United Kingdom. The Matthew recommendations, subsequently endorsed by Wilson, were strongly criticised in August 1964 by the design-team head, Geoffrey Copcutt:

> The prosperity of the province is at present keyed to Belfast, and it is likely that any brake on the expansion of the port and city will produce, not consolidation, but decline . . . it is optimistic to restrict the one proven growth point in an increasingly competitive world, on the assumption that potential industrial customers can be steered elsewhere for charitable purposes.[9]

More ominously for the future, the regional plan took little heed of political sensitivities, particularly in its implementation. Nationalists were outraged when William Craig announced that the name of the new city between Lurgan and Portadown was to be Craigavon, after Northern Ireland's first prime minister. They also argued that the predominantly Protestant east was being favoured over the Catholic west. While admitting that the section on Derry in his plan was brief and hastily written, Wilson wrote the following in his defence in 1989:

> In preparing the economic plan, we endorsed the proposal to have growth centres and extended its application beyond the Belfast region. In doing so, we were asking for trouble, although that was not so obvious at the time. For a growth-centre policy must favour some areas rather than others, and it is a well-established law of public affairs that the indignation of the losers will be far stronger than the gratitude of the gainers.[10]

None the less, with the exception of Derry, all the growth centres were in the Protestant heartlands.

A further example of insensitivity to minority feeling was the recommendation of the 1965 report of the committee on higher education, under the chairmanship of Sir John Lockwood, that Northern Ireland's second university should be sited at Coleraine. Derry had high expectations of being chosen: Magee University College there had a long-established academic reputation and, though it had been a Presbyterian theological college, it now had full cross-community enrolment and support. Coleraine, thirty miles to the east of the city, was small but prosperous by comparison with Derry, and its population was overwhelmingly Protestant. In addition, the Lockwood committee had not a single Catholic member. John Hume, then a teacher at St Columb's in

Derry, organised the University for Derry Campaign and won support from both Unionists and Nationalists in the city at a packed meeting in the Guildhall. Mayor Albert Anderson, later a Unionist MP, and Eddie McAteer, the Nationalist leader, led an impressive motorcade in protest to Stormont; nevertheless, the Government endorsed the choice of Coleraine.[11]

For the present, such controversies seemed but small dark clouds on a far horizon. O'Neill's new economic strategy seemed to be working as multinational firms, including Grundig, British Enkalon, ICI, Michelin and Goodyear, were induced to set up in Northern Ireland. Flamboyant, articulate and energetic, Brian Faulkner appeared to possess the businesslike flair required, though his association with the incoming companies could be rather too close, as he ingenuously recorded in his memoirs:

> Goodyear was another 'blue chip' American firm which came to Ulster in 1966 after long negotiations . . . I was led to understand at the conclusion of these . . . that if ever I decided to get out of politics the Chairman of Goodyear would have a job waiting for me.[12]

The times favoured the influx of outside firms: the doubling of the United Kingdom's economic growth rate between 1959 and 1963 encouraged foreign businesses seeking unhindered access to the British market; international trade was so buoyant that capital came in search of labour; and the region's abundant supply of water, together with a large pool of workers with experience in textiles, favoured synthetic fibre multinationals in a period of cheap oil. Northern Ireland had other attractions for multinational executives: apparent political stability; familiar social institutions; English spoken everywhere; and inexpensive access to golf courses, beautiful countryside, and uncrowded angling and boating centres.[13] The manufacturing growth rate in the 1960s was 5.7 per cent, well ahead of the rest of the United Kingdom. Momentum faltered somewhat in 1966 but by 1974 projects sponsored under the Industrial Development Acts accounted for seventy-one thousand jobs, or 43 per cent of employment in manufacturing.[14] The incentives offered by the Ministry of Commerce were crucial in encouraging firms to set up in Northern Ireland rather than elsewhere, but the costs were high: by 1970 it was reckoned that the cost of each new job in the region was about twice that for Wales and Scotland.[15] The overall increase in employment was marginal because the older industries continued to decline, as a review of the implementation of the Wilson plan pointed out in 1969:

> In manufacturing industry a total of almost 29,000 jobs had been created by the end of 1969 compared with the target of 30,000. However, the

run-down in employment opportunities in the older industries was sufficiently large to offset this, and the net improvement in manufacturing employment was only 5,000 jobs.[16]

Linen mills and factories continued to shed workers or close down altogether, until by the beginning of the 1970s only twenty firms survived out of the two hundred in production in the early 1950s. Older clothing companies, tobacco firms, food processing plants, and aerated water factories contracted. Short Brothers encountered mixed fortunes: the *Belfast*, the largest freighter of its type, was not a commercial success and the Royal Air Force bought only ten; Seacat close-range, anti-aircraft missiles enjoyed modest success, having been ordered by eight foreign navies by 1965; and the real success was the versatile light freighter, the Skyvan – sixty-seven orders had been won by 1967.[17]

In spite of outward signs of success, the 1960s were years of traumatic decline for Harland and Wolff. Having closed the Victoria shipyard and three slips in the Abercorn yard, the company then abandoned its Clydeside commitments in 1963, including the Govan and Finnieston works, and the Clyde Foundry, once the largest in Europe. After launching the frigate HMNZS *Waikato* in February 1965, Harland and Wolff closed the Abercorn yard altogether, leaving only the Musgrave yard in operation.[18] *Sea Quest*, an oil rig of American design, entered Belfast Lough in January 1966, the first time such a structure had been launched complete, but there were no further orders and in June the accountants Price Waterhouse ominously reported that the company was 'unable to put its financial house in order from its own internal resources'.[19] The completion of the *Myrina* – the first 'very large crude carrier' built in the United Kingdom and the largest vessel launched in Europe in 1967 – was an impressive achievement, but Harland and Wolff was now paying the price for failing to modernise the Queen's Island works ten years earlier. A building dock capable of floating a tanker of a million tons was belatedly begun in 1968 but not completed until 1970. Soon afterwards the new Conservative prime minister, Edward Heath, announced that his government would no longer support 'lame ducks'; and Nicholas Ridley, joint parliamentary secretary at the Ministry of Technology, warned 'that it was not the Government's intention to continue to support British shipbuilding and assistance offered to Harland & Wolff must therefore be regarded as temporary'. Such a policy was very much at variance with that of other shipbuilding states which provided lavish support. Harland and Wolff fared no worse than other major British yards, but the United Kingdom was fast losing its role as a major shipbuilder: Britain's share of world output of merchant-ship tonnage fell from 40 per cent to 16 per cent in the 1950s and, by

1979, to just over 6 per cent. Meanwhile, bulk-carrier shipments of oil rose from 73 million tonnes in 1960 to 508 million tonnes in 1979, but the modern yards in Sweden, Japan and West Germany – with facilities for the rapid production of large vessels – took the lion's share of this expanding market.[20]

Despite a striking improvement in living standards, Northern Ireland was by far the most economically disadvantaged part of the United Kingdom. Household incomes in 1968–9 were 89 per cent of the United Kingdom average and the percentage of households with a total weekly income of below £20 was 36 in Northern Ireland compared with 29 in the kingdom as a whole. In 1970 the United Kingdom unemployment rate was 2.7 per cent; in Northern Ireland it was 7 per cent and the worst affected areas – Derry, Strabane, west Tyrone, south Armagh, and west Belfast – suffered a rate of 18 per cent.[21] In short, the dramatic decline of Ulster's traditional export industries (and the collapse of others, including the Belfast Ropeworks, the largest in the world, in 1966) meant that the regional government had to run to make sure the economy stood still. In such circumstances the achievement of O'Neill's administration in creating so many new jobs to replace those lost was impressive enough.

Meanwhile, the economic gap between north and south, which had yawned so wide in the 1950s, was rapidly narrowing, as under the direction of Taoiseach Sean Lemass the republic experienced its first industrial revolution.

'A ROAD BLOCK HAS BEEN REMOVED': O'NEILL MEETS LEMASS, 1965

Sean Lemass had served as minister for industry and commerce in every de Valera government and it was he who had directed the erection of tariff walls in the quest for economic self-sufficiency. Now as taoiseach between 1959 and 1966, he threw that whole policy – originally Arthur Griffith's brainchild – into reverse. Whitaker's recommendations were incorporated in a five-year plan, the *First Programme for Economic Expansion*. There was to be an orderly retreat from tariff protection, while at the same time a new dynamic drive was launched to draw foreign firms into the republic. The results were startling by comparison with the state's miserable performance over the previous decade. Manufacturing output increased by 5 per cent per annum between 1959 and 1972; employment in manufacturing leaped from 169,000 to 212,000; and industrial goods rose from one third to well over one half of the republic's exports. The agricultural annual growth rate only averaged one per cent, but the economy's overall growth was 4 per cent a year. By 1973 new foreign-owned firms employed forty thousand workers and exported a high proportion of their output.[22]

Lemass also abandoned the overt irredentism of previous governments. On the whole, the taoiseach preferred to say nothing about Northern Ireland at all and his simplistic view was that the best way to end partition was to raise living standards in the South so markedly that northern Protestants would be eager to reunite the country. He succeeded in stemming the emigration tide: 4 out of 5 children born in the twenty-six counties between 1931 and 1941 had left the country and now average net emigration fell from 43,000 per annum between 1956 and 1961, to 16,000 between 1961 and 1966, and down to 11,000 between 1966 and 1971.[23] Economic planning was probably far less important than the international boom in promoting the new prosperity, but the republic's agencies – the Industrial Development Authority, in particular – were especially adept at using the twin inducements of capital grants and tax relief on export earnings to draw in mobile capital from overseas.[24] Lemass knew that better relations with Britain were vital to the success of his economic strategy. That must include a *rapprochement* with Northern Ireland, but Brookeborough flatly refused to touch the hand of friendship Lemass had offered on several occasions. O'Neill was so entirely different from his predecessor that it was he – and probably he alone – who took the initiative and invited Lemass to Stormont.[25] Jim Malley, O'Neill's private secretary, was sent to Dublin in January 1965 with the invitation. For a week there was silence: in nervous agitation Whitaker's secretary had addressed the reply to 'Stormont Castle, Dublin', and it failed to appear – in fact Lemass had accepted without hesitation.

On the night of 13–14 January 1965 gale force winds, gusting to eighty miles an hour and accompanied by torrential rain, swept Northern Ireland. In Belfast, St Brendan's church collapsed and two vessels collided in the lough. O'Neill lay awake for other reasons: he had not informed his cabinet colleagues about the taoiseach's visit – how would they react?

'Welcome to the North,' O'Neill said as Lemass stepped out of his Mercedes shortly after midday. There was no reply. Finally breaking his silence in the lavatory of Stormont House, Lemass said: 'I shall get into terrible trouble for this.' He had, after all, fought in the General Post Office in the 1916 Easter Rising and had been interned by the British and imprisoned by the first Irish Free State government as a republican diehard. The taoiseach then relaxed and became more garrulous over a splendid lunch. Whitaker, who accompanied Lemass, remembered:

Our hosts thought the occasion worthy of champagne. The atmosphere was most friendly. I imagine Dr Paisley's worst fears would be confirmed if I were to say that the red wine we drank was Châteauneuf-du-Pape!

Summoned only that morning, O'Neill's colleagues smiled bravely for the cameras. Faulkner was the only northern minister who had met Lemass before:

> The first thing Lemass said to me was 'I hear you had a great day with the Westmeaths a few weeks ago.' I said, 'That's right indeed, I didn't realise you knew.' 'Ah,' he said, 'the boys told me.' He said, 'Have you had a day with Charlie lately?'

Faulkner's regular hunting with Charles Haughey, the taoiseach's son-in-law and minister for agriculture, helped to break the ice. After discussions on possible north–south economic co-operation, Lemass then left for Dublin, saying to waiting reporters when he returned: 'I think I can say a road block has been removed.' That evening on television O'Neill justified the meeting, observing that north and south 'share the same rivers, the same mountains, and some of the same problems'.[26]

No widespread hostile reaction greeted the O'Neill–Lemass meeting. Nevertheless, some members of the Northern Ireland government did not easily forgive O'Neill's willingness to discuss the visit with senior civil servants without mentioning it in cabinet. It is difficult, however, to disagree with O'Neill's view that his ministers would not have been able to agree and the meeting would therefore not have taken place. In the event, only Harry West, the minister of agriculture, refused to meet Lemass at Stormont. The following afternoon a car, trailing a very large Ulster flag, drove to Stormont to display placards which read: 'No Mass, no Lemass'; 'Down with the Lundys'; and 'IRA murderer welcomed at Stormont'. Two Protestant Unionist councillors and the Reverend Ian Paisley, moderator of the Free Presbyterian Church, then handed in a letter of protest:

> By acting without consulting the elected representatives of the Protestants of our country, you have adopted the tactics of a dictator and forfeited your right to be Prime Minister. We challenge you to go to the country on this issue.[27]

O'Neill did go to the electorate that year in November. Though he had returned the taoiseach's visit by going to Dublin, he increased the Unionist vote substantially. He campaigned strongly against the Northern Ireland Labour Party, which lost two seats, partly because the party was fatally divided on the issue of opening public parks and unlocking children's swings on Sundays, but mainly because O'Neill had adopted much of its programme and reduced unemployment. For the present, Paisley was little more than a gadfly, but as traditional loyalism reawakened, his support would grow with formidable speed until it made O'Neill's position untenable four years later.

Born in Armagh city in 1926 and brought up in Ballymena and its vicinity, Ian Paisley, the son of an independent Baptist pastor, acquired a reputation as a compelling preacher even when still in his teens. Soon after being appointed minister of the Ravenhill Evangelical Mission Church in Belfast at the age of twenty, Paisley became active in the right-wing National Union of Protestants, an organisation campaigning for the return of fundamentalists in local and Stormont elections; dedicated to upholding traditional values, including strict Sunday observance; buying Catholic property in marginal wards and constituencies; and denouncing mixed marriages, the allocation of council houses to Catholics and the appointment of Catholics to the staff of state schools. After splitting a congregation in Crossgar, Paisley formed the Free Presbyterian Church in 1951, with himself as moderator. In his struggle to acquire adherents, he quarrelled most often with fellow fundamentalists but it was his denunciation of ecumenical trends in the principal Christian Churches that brought him into public prominence.

Even before Captain O'Neill became prime minister there had been signs of reconciliation: the Catholic bishop of Down and Connor, William Philbin, had accepted an invitation to a reception in Belfast City Hall; Eddie McAteer addressed Young Unionists at Queen's University; and in 1963 Young Unionists went to Dublin for talks with a branch of Fine Gael. When Pope John XXIII died on 3 June 1963 the condolences of the people of Northern Ireland were sent to Rome by Lord Wakehurst, the governor, and O'Neill declared that the pope 'had won widespread acclaim throughout the world because of his qualities of kindness and humanity'. Next day the Union flag was flown at half-mast over the city hall. Paisley had already denounced the Queen Mother and Princess Margaret for 'committing spiritual fornication and adultery with the Anti-Christ' when they had visited Pope John in 1958, and now he held a rally at the Ulster Hall to excoriate 'the Iscariots of Ulster' who had expressed sympathy to the Vatican and he assured his packed audience: 'This Romish man of sin is now in Hell.'[28] Then he led a protest of some five hundred of his followers to the city hall and was subsequently fined £10 for leading an illegal procession – he avoided imprisonment only when an English businessman paid his fine. Paisley's tall commanding presence and pugnacious oratory delivered in a rich mid-Antrim accent ensured gathering support from those Protestant fundamentalists with the liveliest fear of Catholicism; but he was beginning to widen his appeal to greater numbers of loyalists, who were apprehensive that O'Neill's bridge-building gestures to the nationalist minority were weakening the bulwarks of unionism. The general election in 1964 called by Sir Alec Douglas-Home, the British prime minister, gave Paisley the opportunity to present his credentials as a political activist.

Interest in Northern Ireland was concentrated on marginal constituencies and on West Belfast, in particular, where there were four candidates: Harry Diamond, Republican Labour; Jim Kilfedder, Unionist; Billy Boyd, Northern Ireland Labour; and Liam McMillen, Republican. The Unionist Party feared a Labour victory at Westminster – Harold Wilson promised action against discrimination if he became prime minister – and was anxious that Boyd could attract enough Protestant votes to ensure the election of Diamond. Then Paisley learned that a small Irish tricolour was on display in the window of the Republican headquarters in Divis Street and on 27 September he threatened to take his supporters there to remove it if the authorities did not act. Next day the RUC, using their discretionary powers under the Flags and Emblems Act, removed the flag but clashed that night with local people. Another tricolour appeared in the Republican headquarters' window on 1 October and this time the police smashed into the premises with pickaxes and removed it. The ensuing rioting was intense: police were driven back by a barrage of stones, scrap metal and bottles; some petrol bombs were thrown; a corporation bus burned furiously; armoured cars looked menacing in the narrow streets and, with their headlights and searchlights, picked out the dense mass of struggling rioters and police; water cannon – in use for the first time in more than forty years – sprayed the crowds somewhat ineffectively; and throughout there was a cacophony of wailing sirens, yells, shouted party songs, and the crash of breaking glass. It was remarkable that no lives were lost, for such sectarian rioting had not been seen in Belfast since 1935 and no doubt it was a bemused audience in Britain that watched on television an updated re-enactment of intercommunal conflict that had blighted Ulster for generations.[29]

Kilfedder was returned for West Belfast and for his victory he thanked Paisley, without whom it would not have been possible. Paisley himself said soon after in the Ulster Hall:

> Protestantism has faced many serious crises in its history. We are facing a crisis now and the province is heading for even greater crises.

Though this election campaign saw other ugly clashes in Dungannon, Coleraine and Enniskillen, the violence was limited to confined locations and was quickly over. Most mainstream unionists still regarded Paisley as fanatical and provocative and supported O'Neill in his conciliatory moves towards the Catholic minority and the republic, giving him an enhanced majority in the Stormont elections of 1965.

O'Neill wrote of Brookeborough that in 'twenty years as Prime Minister he never crossed the border, never visited a Catholic school, and never received or sought a civic reception from a Catholic town'.[30] Indeed, Brookeborough had said in April 1958: 'We can never relax and if we do, Ulster is doomed.'[31] O'Neill was prepared to lower the Unionist guard and he was the first prime minister to make reconciliation of the two traditions official policy. He met Cardinal William Conway, archbishop of Armagh, and visited Catholic schools and hospitals, making sure where possible that he was photographed in the company of nuns. On Good Friday, 1966, he expressed the hope that Catholic and Protestant children could be educated together but, recognising that this was a long-term prospect, he added, 'let us at least be united in working together – in a Christian spirit – to create better opportunities for our children, whether they come from the Falls Road or from Finaghy'.[32] He was rewarded by a warm response from leaders of the minority and in February 1965 the Nationalist Party for the first time agreed to become the official opposition. Harold Wilson recalled a meeting he had with O'Neill in May 1965:

> I was anxious that the Ulster Unionist government under Captain O'Neill should be encouraged to press on with their programme of ending discrimination in housing allocations and generally improving the lot of the minority of Northern Ireland. Since coming into office he had by Northern Ireland standards carried through a remarkable programme of easement.[33]

O'Neill certainly worked hard to improve community relations, but Wilson's assumption that real progress had been made in ending discriminatory practices was false. Wilson, indeed, made no thorough attempt to see what changes were being made and between 1965 and August 1969 the only Labour government minister to visit Northern Ireland was Home Secretary Sir Frank Soskice, and then it was only for an afternoon.[34] The Unionist government's White Paper *The Re-Shaping of Local Government: Statement of Aims*, published in 1967, was largely concerned with administrative change and though the 1968 Electoral Law Amendment Act abolished university and business votes, it still denied universal suffrage in local government elections and did nothing to rectify boundary manipulations of earlier decades. Catholics benefited from the increase in building grants to voluntary schools from 65 to 80 per cent in 1968 but otherwise the structure left by Craigavon, Andrews and Brookeborough had been very little altered. Improved relations between Belfast and Dublin led to solid agreements on co-ordination of tourism promotion and a linking of electrical grids; and the Anglo-Irish Trade Treaty, which came into force in July 1966, promised greater economic interdependence between north and south. However, if O'Neill was to carry through real reform within Northern Ireland, he needed the full co-operation of his colleagues and complete domestic calm: in the years following, neither of these conditions were fulfilled.

'THE PARTY WOULD NEVER STAND FOR CHANGE'

The year 1966 proved a difficult one for O'Neill. Queen Elizabeth was due to visit Northern Ireland in July; and when, on 14 February, the ruling Unionists in Belfast Corporation chose 'Carson' as the name for a new bridge across the Lagan, Lord Erskine telephoned the town clerk, saying he was 'perturbed at the effect on Her Majesty of possible controversy over the name of the bridge' and suggested 'Queen Elizabeth II' instead, which was accepted.[35] Both Brookeborough and Kilfedder expressed outrage at the governor's interference but Paisley went further: he organised rallies and protests and brought over Ned Carson to review the recently formed Ulster Protestant Volunteers. During the Easter Rising commemorations in April, O'Neill found it difficult to resist Paisley's demands for special security measures. Republican ceremonies were being prepared in all the principal Catholic districts of the region – the largest, a procession from near the centre of Belfast to Andersonstown, a suburb south-west of the city. Paisley announced a counter-demonstration and it was only by mobilising 10,500 B Specials, sending army helicopters to the border, stopping trains from Dublin and arming the RUC with machine guns mounted at road checkpoints that the Government prevented serious trouble.

Paisley continued to grab the headlines. On 6 June he led several hundred supporters from his Ravenhill church in east Belfast across the Albert Bridge to protest at the Presbyterian Church's 'Romanising tendencies'. The route passed the Catholic Markets area and as the marchers approached Cromac Square singing 'Onward Christian Soldiers' local people, though they were pushed aside by the police, threw bricks and other missiles at the protesters. The marchers paraded three times round the city hall until the Presbyterian moderator and his guests, including Lord and Lady Erskine, emerged from the Presbyterian General Assembly in Church House – these Paisley and his followers vilified with cries of 'Popehead', 'Romanist', and 'Lundy'. Meanwhile, the police fought an intense battle in the Markets until midnight.[36] Subsequently Paisley and six others were convicted, fined and bound over to keep the peace for two years. Paisley refused to enter into the bail bond and on 20 July he was lodged in Crumlin Road gaol. The following weekend the police failed to quell rioting Protestants in the Shankill with baton charges, and water cannon had to be brought in to stop the looting of Catholic-owned public houses.

The year 1966 was also the fiftieth anniversary of the Somme and for that reason loyalist militants, meeting in the Standard Bar on the Shankill, named the group they formed there the Ulster Volunteer Force. This new terrorist UVF aimed to topple O'Neill and to combat the IRA: a petrol bomb thrown into Unionist Party headquarters in February was part of its campaign, as was the killing of Catholics suspected of being republicans. On 7 May a UVF member attempted to set fire to a Catholic-owned public house in the Shankill but instead his petrol bomb crashed into the home of Martha Gould, an elderly Protestant, who was burned to death. On 21 May Belfast newspapers received a UVF statement: 'From this day we declare war against the IRA and its splinter groups. Known IRA men will be executed mercilessly and without hesitation.'[37] On 27 May the UVF mortally wounded John Scullion, a Catholic but not a known IRA man, in Clonard Street. On 26 June three Catholics were shot in Malvern Street in the Shankill and one, Peter Ward, died of his wounds. Three men who had been drinking in the Malvern Arms were arrested soon after and convicted; one of them, Hugh McClean, said to the police: 'I am terribly sorry I ever heard of that man Paisley or decided to follow him.'[38]

On hearing of the murders, O'Neill returned to Northern Ireland from France, where he had been visiting the Thiepval Memorial to Ulstermen who had died at the Somme, and proscribed the UVF. In September he discovered that not only did he face the opposition of a vociferous loyalist minority in the streets but also members of his own government were turning against him. Desmond Boal, Unionist MP for Shankill who had defended Paisley's right to march on the Presbyterian General Assembly, passed round a petition criticising O'Neill's policies, and secret meetings followed in the home of Brian Faulkner, who clearly hoped the time had come for him to be prime minister. O'Neill was able to scotch the revolt but his position had been gravely weakened. On his release from prison in October, Paisley told supporters welcoming him home: 'O'Neill must go – O'Neill will go!'[39] At Stormont the prime minister described how extremists that year had opposed his policies:

From one side came the extreme Republicans, who sought to flaunt before our people the emblems of a cause which a majority of us abhor, and who once again refused to renounce violence as a political weapon.

From the other side came those self-appointed and self-styled 'loyalists' who see moderation as treason and decency as a weakness.[40]

Nineteen sixty-seven was the last year of peace but Protestant anger at O'Neill's moderation became ever more evident. Again and again the Government used the Special Powers Act to ban loyalist marches and protests. During the 12 July demonstrations that year the usual resolution paying tribute to the prime minister was either ignored or shouted down at many venues – George Forrest, Westminster MP for Mid-Ulster, was dragged from the platform at Coagh, Co. Tyrone, when he defended the resolution and was kicked unconscious. Co. Fermanagh was particularly hostile: following a dispute over a land deal in the county, O'Neill had dismissed Harry West as minister of agriculture. The RUC uncovered a UVF plot to assassinate the prime minister, who was dogged at almost every public appearance by Paisley and his followers calling for his resignation. Jack Lynch, who had become taoiseach in 1966 when Lemass retired, paid an official visit to Stormont in December 1967 only to have his car snowballed by Paisley and his supporters. Paisley posed for the photographers behind three placards: 'O'Neill the Lundy'; 'Keep Ulster Protestant'; and 'O'Neill the Ally of Popery'.[41]

O'Neill explained his dilemma in his autobiography: 'As the Party would never stand for change, I was really reduced to trying to improve relations between North and South; and in the North itself between the two sections of the community. In this respect I think I can truthfully say that I succeeded.'[42] There was ample evidence that he had done much to ease tensions between the majority and the minority, despite the strident criticism of loyalist conservatives. O'Neill, however, had raised Catholic expectations but found himself unable to deliver more than gestures of friendship: thoroughgoing reform did not follow and the result was acute frustration.

'THESE ARRANGEMENTS WERE DELIBERATELY MADE AND MAINTAINED'

During the morning of 28 August 1963 seventeen Catholic families occupied prefabricated bungalows due for demolition at Fairmount Park in Dungannon. In retaliation the urban district council cut off electricity and water but it restored supplies when newspaper reporters and television crews began to arrive. As more families moved in, bringing the number of squatters to 120, the Government restrained the Unionist council chairman from instituting ejectment proceedings and invited a delegation to meet William Morgan, the minister of health and local government, at Stormont. Faced with a leader in the *Belfast*

Telegraph supporting the families, Morgan agreed not to evict the squatters and promised to speed up the completion of a council housing estate in the Nationalist-held ward of the town. It seemed that a notable victory had been won by the Homeless Citizens' League, formed earlier in the year under the leadership of Patricia McCluskey. Nevertheless, by January 1967 only 34 Catholic families, compared with 264 Protestant ones, had been allocated council houses in Dungannon since 1945.[43]

Dungannon in 1963 had a population of about seven thousand, around half of whom were Catholics. Middle-class Protestants and Catholics mixed without difficulty in the local golf club and both sects were well represented amongst the teachers, lawyers and doctors in the town. All the accountants were Protestants, however, and Protestants dominated the banks, the hospital, the health services, the post office, the Electricity Board, the offices of the Ministry of Labour, and the skilled and managerial posts in the two textile firms in the locality.[44] Much of this imbalance can be explained by examining the historical evolution of the town, but the Homeless Citizens' League put together convincing evidence that local structures and practices were perpetuating inequality. The drawing of local boundaries after the abolition of proportional representation in 1922 had been completed without Nationalist co-operation, thus giving Unionists a free hand to maximise their vote. Though Dungannon's population was evenly divided, the urban district council was sectioned into three wards, two of them with small but safe Protestant majorities and one with an overwhelming Catholic majority. Thus the town had a perpetual Unionist administration. Local authority housing was intimately connected with political power: no points system operated; houses were allocated by councillors in their own wards; and since only ratepayers – in effect, householders – had a vote in local elections, the ruling Unionists had a strong political motive not to build houses for Catholic families, particularly in the two Unionist wards. Indeed, since 1945 not a single new house had been built in the Nationalist ward when the Homeless Citizens' League was founded. The league's first public protest had been to picket the urban district council offices when Catholic families were refused any of the 142 houses just completed in the Unionist wards. As no Catholic family had been given a permanent council house in the town for thirty-four years, Nationalist councillors could exercise their patronage only in allocating relets. Dr Conn McCluskey described the inevitable result:

> Young newly-weds were compelled to move in with in-laws and keep their wedding presents under the bed. This usually worked until the second child arrived, when family tensions began to mount . . . The strain on young mothers trying to maintain order and a degree of quiet, where

most facilities were shared, was very great. Men on night shift found it impossible to sleep . . . Something had to be done.[45]

Many other families all over the United Kingdom experienced similar conditions but in Dungannon the unequal allocation of council houses ensured that Catholics were far less likely than Protestants to acquire a dwelling of their own. Dungannon was not unique: as a member of the league's delegation to Stormont, Dr McCluskey left an imposing dossier on the minister's desk, showing that housing discrimination was widespread in Northern Ireland, particularly west of the Bann.

The Cameron Commission, appointed by O'Neill's government in 1969 to inquire into the disturbances of the previous year, concluded that in certain areas, notably Dungannon, Armagh and Derry,

> the arrangement of ward boundaries for local government purposes has produced in the local authority a permanent Unionist majority which bears little or no resemblance to the relative numerical strength of Unionists and non-Unionists in the area . . . there is very good reason to believe the allegation that these arrangements were deliberately made and maintained . . . to favour Protestant or Unionist supporters in making public appointments – particularly those of senior officials – and in manipulating housing allocations for political and sectarian ends.[46]

The most striking example of gerrymandering was Londonderry City – Unionist-controlled, though, as the Cameron report pointed out, the adult population was composed of 20,102 Catholics and 10,274 Protestants in 1966. The restriction of the franchise to ratepayers gave 14,429 Catholics and 8,781 Protestants the right to vote. The careful manipulation of boundaries ensured Unionist control: in the South ward 10,047 Catholics and 1,138 Protestants elected 8 Nationalist councillors; in the North ward 3,946 Protestants and 2,530 Catholics elected 8 Unionist councillors; and in the Waterside ward 3,697 Protestants and 1,852 Catholics returned 4 Unionist councillors.[47] Such gerrymandering was not restricted to the 1920s: boundaries were redrawn to Unionist advantage in Omagh in 1935, Derry in 1936, Armagh in 1946, and Co. Fermanagh in 1967.[48]

Until 1945 the local government franchise in the United Kingdom was restricted to owners or tenants of a dwelling, and their spouses. Thus lodgers and grown-up children still living with their parents had no vote. In addition, some large property owners had more than one vote. Brookeborough's government had refused to follow Britain step-by-step when Westminster removed these anomalies between 1945 and 1948 and, indeed, Warnock's Election and Franchise Act of 1946 actually restricted the local government franchise still further. The majority of those deprived of the vote were Protestants; but Catholics, being poorer and more overcrowded on average, were overrepresented among the disfranchised. Manipulation of local government boundaries was a potent means of retaining Unionist control but the Unionist majority was so substantial in most councils that the concession of universal suffrage would not have made a great deal of difference: the journalist Barry White, writing in the *Belfast Telegraph* at the end of January 1969, concluded that Unionists would lose their majority only in Armagh. Nevertheless, Unionist refusal to abolish qualifications laid the party open to the charge of resisting democracy and gave civil rights activists a powerful slogan, first coined by the Northern Ireland Labour Party: 'One Man, One Vote'.[49]

Control of local government automatically conferred power to make appointments. In 1957 Frank Gallagher showed that 31.5 per cent of local authority workers were Catholic, a figure near to the proportion of Catholics in the region's adult population. Protestants, however, dominated the higher grades: in 1951 only 11.8 per cent of senior posts – 130 out of 1,095 – were held by Catholics. In 1969 the Campaign for Social Justice in Northern Ireland, the Dungannon-based organisation launched in 1964, arrived at a similar percentage, and in the same year the Cameron Commission, after investigating five Unionist authorities, concluded:

> We are satisfied that all these Unionist controlled councils have used and use their power to make appointments in a way which benefited Protestants. In the figures available for October 1968 only thirty per cent of Londonderry Corporation's administrative, clerical and technical employees were Catholic. In Dungannon Urban District none of the Council's administrative, clerical and technical employees was a Catholic. In County Fermanagh no senior council posts (and relatively few others) were held by Catholics ... Armagh Urban District employed very few Catholics in salaried posts ... we have seen what would appear to be undoubted evidence of employment discrimination by Tyrone County Council.[50]

Favouritism in appointments was, and remains, endemic in Ireland, north and south. It had been entrenched by the 1898 Local Government Act, which, though set aside long since, continued to exercise its baleful influence. Except for a few celebrated cases, the enthusiastic application of patronage rarely had sectarian implications in the twenty-six counties, but in Northern Ireland favouritism was inevitably applied along religious lines. The most brazen examples were to be found west of the Bann but patronage was ubiquitous. In Belfast, for example, there were by comparison fewer cases of outright discrimination but there the patronage game was played by opposition councillors with as much vigour as the Unionists. A newly elected councillor was liable to be asked what binmen he wanted to appoint; if he refused to give names, he was likely to be told that his share of jobs in the city would be distributed evenly amongst the other fifty-nine councillors. Contracts, houses and even the most insignificant jobs were therefore given out as favours to supporters of all parties represented. The period after the Second World War did see a more professional approach and more open competition for some contracts and jobs but overall, patronage increased with the spectacular rise in local government spending.

In response to accusations that Catholics were taking over the civil service, an internal inquiry had been made in 1943 by the Ministry of Finance: it found that there were no Catholics in the 55 most senior posts and only 37 out of 634 in the higher grades.[51] The growth of the Welfare State after the war led to a corresponding increase in the number of civil servants but the religious imbalance remained. In 1957 there were still no Catholics amongst the 40 most senior officers; in 1959, according to Barritt and Carter, 94 per cent of the 740 most senior civil servants were Protestants; and in 1969 the Campaign for Social Justice found that 92.8 per cent of the higher ranks down to deputy principal were Protestants. Catholics may have had lower educational qualifications, forming only one quarter of the grammar school and university population in 1962, but even so, they did not obtain one quarter of the higher posts.[52] In part this was due to nationalist hostility to the regime. Patrick Shea remembered:

> It was my experience that some Catholics, and especially those in Belfast where, I had been told, the Bishop had advised them against seeking Government employment, looked with suspicion on Catholic civil servants. We had joined the enemy; we were lost souls.[53]

Shea himself several times encountered a bar placed on his promotion because of his religion. Sir Wilfrid Spender recommended his appointment as private secretary to the financial secretary to the Ministry of Finance, Major Maynard Sinclair. After consulting 'political advisers', Sinclair rejected Shea. 'I thought it only right that I should tell you about this,' Spender explained. 'I can only say that I am surprised and disappointed and very sorry.'[54] Later, in 1958, Shea was told by Reginald Brownell, permanent secretary to the Ministry of Education: 'Because you are a Roman Catholic you may never get any further promotion. I'm sorry.'[55] O'Neill recorded in his memoirs that when he was minister of finance he had to face opposition in the cabinet because he was suspected of bringing too many Catholics into the civil service.

Catholics were also underrepresented in other parts of the establishment. Between 1925 and 1949 no Catholic was appointed to the

Supreme Court and as late as 1969 Catholics held only six senior judicial posts out of a total of sixty-eight. In 1957 there was no Catholic on the Civil Service Commission, the Promotion Board for the Postal Service, the Unemployment Assistance Board, or the Fire Authority. There were 22 public boards by 1969, with 332 members in all, but only 49 were Catholics, and only 15.4 per cent of 8,122 employed in the publicly owned water, gas and electricity industries were Catholics.[56]

It is much more difficult to assess levels of discrimination in private employment, particularly as hard evidence is available only for the 1970s onwards. The lower socio-economic status and educational attainment of Catholics in Ulster were evident long before the creation of Northern Ireland. Protestants had always dominated the skilled trades and the long tradition of 'speaking for' sons, cousins, nephews and neighbours as a method of recruitment made it difficult for Catholics to find work in, for example, shipbuilding and engineering, except in time of war. Small family firms played an exceptionally important role in Northern Ireland's economy and generally employed people from one side of the community; if they expanded they were usually very wary of beginning the process of mixing Catholics and Protestants. Barritt and Carter often heard from managers the remark: 'Of course, we wouldn't mind having a Catholic in the office [or the factory]; but the workers would never stand for it.' Without naming the businesses, they gave examples of complete discrimination in 1962:

1 Large food firm employing only Protestants
2 Two food firms employing only Catholics (except that one has a Protestant manager)
3 Medium-sized engineering firm employing only Protestants: 'We have never had a Catholic, and we do not know how he would get on with the other workers.'
4 Large garage – same attitude . . .[57]

Discrimination in employment was a natural product of a divided community and Catholics and Protestants discriminated with equal zeal, but for historical reasons Catholics were bound to be at a disadvantage in the game. In the main, the traditional employers were Protestant and not all the newly arrived multinational firms were able to resist labour pressure to favour one religion in recruitment. Though Harland and Wolff was adjacent to the Catholic Short Strand, the company employed only four hundred Catholics out of a total workforce of ten thousand in 1970, and though the Sirocco Works and Mackie's foundry were sited in largely Catholic districts, the numbers of Catholics employed there were insignificant. On the other hand, because most public houses in the region were owned by Catholics most bar staff were Catholic.[58]

Allegations of discrimination in the allocation of council houses were rarely made until the 1950s. In part this was because the region's housing provision was lamentable until after the Second World War but it was also because Nationalist councillors collaborated with Unionists in a 'gentleman's agreement' to give out local authority houses to their own supporters. In any case, outright discrimination in public housing was not universal and Cahir Healy with much justification praised councils in Belfast and the counties of Antrim and Down for handling cases of need with fairness. In 1971 Richard Rose, the political analyst, concluded that 'the proportion of Catholics in subsidised housing is slightly *higher* than that of Protestants', though this was more than offset if family size was taken into account.[59]

The blatant cases of unfair treatment were to be found west of the Bann, where provision of local authority housing was made only where it would not upset the electoral balance. The most usual misuse of Unionist local government power was not to refuse to build council houses for Catholics but to build them where they would not endanger Unionist majorities. To a considerable extent this was helped by the ghettoisation of Catholics and Protestants in virtually every provincial town. The most striking example of highly localised provision was in Derry, where public housing for Catholics was provided only in the South ward. There were, however, some obvious cases of councils clearly discriminating in favour of Protestants. Asked by a senior official of the Housing Trust 'How many Roman Catholics do you have in your council houses?', the mayor of Portadown replied, 'One – and that's too bloody many.'[60] In 1964 the Northern Ireland senate was told that of 231 council houses put up in Enniskillen, only 22 had been given out to Catholic families. The Government was embarrassed by cases of biased allocation in Lisnaskea, but not to the extent of intervening. 'Would they not take the man off the bog bank and do what he was asking for once?' a Nationalist councillor asked in November 1963 when a dwelling was given to a Protestant 'in a fairly good house', while a more needy Catholic was refused. Three further cases in 1965 attracted public attention: a three-bedroomed house was given to an unmarried Protestant man in preference to a widow and her sons living in a condemned hovel; a request from the Fermanagh Welfare Committee to allocate a house to a father of four about to be evicted was ignored; and a Catholic on the waiting list for ten years was turned down in favour of a Protestant waiting only two years.[61] William Morgan did 'deplore' a remark by the housing committee chairman in Enniskillen in 1963 that houses should only be given out to the 'right' people; but the Government would not overrule councils clearly discriminating in, for example, Caledon, Cookstown, Dungannon, and Fintona (a town which provided ample material for a propaganda film made for the Dublin government in the late 1950s).

Dungannon's Homeless Citizens' League was significant because it advocated direct action and criticised Nationalists' participation in 'gentlemen's agreements' with Unionists. It drew inspiration from the black civil rights campaign in the United States. 'What's not acceptable in South Africa or Birmingham, Alabama, is surely not going to be acceptable as applicable on a religious basis in Dungannon, Co. Tyrone?' asked the writer of a letter in the *Dungannon Observer* on 21 September 1963. The first picket outside the council offices included people carrying placards that stated: 'If our religion is against us, ship us to Little Rock' and 'Racial discrimination in Alabama hits Dungannon'.[62] The McCluskeys made no issue of partition and appealed not to Dublin but to Stormont and Westminster. As Conn McCluskey wrote later:

> We began a search amongst our 'own kind', gaining experience all the time. Many were too nationalist to be of use. Fifty years of the same sort of agitation by the Nationalists had achieved nothing. Heated discussions about the 'border' would be a waste of time and energy. Our idea was, since we lived in a part of the United Kingdom where the British remit ran, we should seek the ordinary rights of British citizens which were so obviously denied us.[63]

In the house of Peter Gormley, a surgeon in the Mater Hospital, the McCluskeys formed the Campaign for Social Justice in Northern Ireland and launched the new organisation on 14 January 1964 in the Wellington Park Hotel, Belfast. Their press release explained that they planned to oppose policies of discrimination, 'collect comprehensive and accurate data on all injustices done against all creeds and political opinions', enlist the support of any political party prepared to help them, and seek 'equality for all'.[64] In effect they had launched the civil rights movement in Northern Ireland.

THE CIVIL RIGHTS MOVEMENT BEGINS

In most divided societies there is a tendency for the dominant group to regard the other as lazy, improvident and feckless. In Northern Ireland this view seems to have been most strongly held by middle-class Protestants. Even Tom Wilson, a liberal critic of the Government's treatment of Catholics, wrote in 1955 that 'as for business life, Presbyterians and Jews are probably endowed with more business acumen than Irish Catholics', adding that Ulster Catholics 'were made to feel inferior, and to make matters worse they often *were* inferior, if *only* in those personal qualities that make for success in competitive economic life'.[65] The attitude that Catholics were work-shy could be found also amongst working-class Protestants, as this verse from a loyalist ballad indicates:

And when their babies learn to talk
They shout 'discrimination',
Their dad just lies in bed all day
And lives upon the nation.[66]

However, a more commonly held view in Protestant enclaves was not that Catholics were lazy but that, under the influence of their Church and the IRA, they simply could not be trusted. Only a minority of Protestants seem to have accepted that Catholics had genuine grounds for seeking a redress of their grievances. A handful of Unionist MPs and a key group of senior civil servants urged O'Neill to press forward with reform. Some middle-class Protestants, including Charles Brett, Brian Garrett and Erskine Holmes, strove through the Northern Ireland Labour Party to see British standards of fair treatment applied in the region. Perhaps a greater number of educated Protestants, repelled by traditional loyalties and taking the attitude 'a plague on both your houses', simply avoided politics altogether. In 'The Coasters' the poet John Hewitt memorably recalled those who opted out:

You coasted along.
And all the time, though you never noticed,
the old lies festered;
the ignorant became more thoroughly infected;
there were gains, of course;
you never saw any go barefoot.[67]

In 1969 the Cameron Commission concluded that the emergence of a civil rights movement owed much to the expansion of the Catholic middle class, largely as a result of the 1947 Education Act, 'less ready to acquiesce in the situation of assumed (or established) inferiority and discrimination than was the case in the past'.[68] Clearly there is much truth in this assertion but it needs qualification. The extension of secondary and higher education took time to make an impact and social economist A.E. Aunger's examination of the census results of 1961 and 1971 showed that between those dates there was hardly any change in the social structure of the male Catholic population. A tabulation of occupation by religious affiliation for both men and women had been made in the 1911 census but was not repeated until 1971. Between these dates the percentage of Catholics classified as professional and managerial had risen from 5 to 12, and of Protestants from 8 to 15. Otherwise the relative position of Catholics in the six north-eastern counties had slipped over this sixty-year period: lower-grade non-manual from 23 to 19 per cent; skilled manual from 24 to 17; semi-skilled manual from 28 to 27; but the percentage of unskilled rose from 20 to 25.[69] In short, the proportion of Catholics in the lowest-paid jobs had risen considerably.

The Nationalist Party certainly did not play a central role in getting the civil rights movement under way. This conservative and clericalist survival of the Irish Parliamentary Party had failed to adopt a coherent policy on the issue of discrimination largely because it sought, not a reformed administration in Belfast, but an end to the partition of Ireland. When the party became an official opposition after the O'Neill–Lemass meeting in 1965, it failed to formulate a policy of constructive criticism. O'Neill was heartened by the Nationalist MPs' response to his overtures of friendship but Unionists must have been astonished when, early in 1968, they accepted a supplementary estimate of £29,000 for the B Specials and when a White Paper on local government was debated at Stormont, Eddie McAteer observed: 'I want to say frankly that our party's view has not yet fully crystallised on this subject.'[70]

The drive to force the Unionist government into thoroughgoing reform was not the work of a single organisation. 'Ulster Labour and the Sixties', the Northern Ireland Labour Party's 1962 election programme, could be regarded as the opening salvo of the civil rights movement. Unequivocal in its support of the Union, the party pressed hard for the application of British standards in local government and public housing, and in a series of conference resolutions and detailed policy documents called for an end to discrimination on religious or political grounds. It was hampered by its inability to win a seat at Westminster and it suffered the loss of two Stormont seats in 1965. Nevertheless, the party remained vigorous in Belfast, attracting cross-community support, and other activists were to draw heavily on its resource of arguments and evidence.

Anti-partition politics remained confused in Belfast, where the 'Green Tories' of the Nationalist Party had lost ground in the Catholic working-class districts. Gerry Fitt, the Republican Labour MP for Dock since 1962, demonstrated formidable skill in mobilising support by getting himself elected for West Belfast in 1966 and the impact he made at Westminster was immediate. This colourful, fast-talking ex-sailor, whose pithy style contrasted with that of the somewhat sedate upper-middle-class Unionists, explained Catholic grievances in terms everyone could understand. In particular, he galvanised a group of Labour MPs at

Westminster who were concerned at the lack of reform in Northern Ireland: launched in the House of Commons on 3 June 1965, the Campaign for Democracy in Ulster aimed to amend the Race Relations Act 'to include discrimination on religious grounds'; to bring electoral law into line with the rest of the United Kingdom and 'to examine electoral boundaries with a view to providing fair representation for all sections of the community'; and to set up a royal commission to inquire 'into the administration of Government in Northern Ireland, with particular reference to allegations of discrimination'.[71] Sixty MPs sponsored the campaign but the number rose the following year and in April 1967 Fitt organised a visit to Northern Ireland by three Labour MPs. Paul Rose, MP for a Manchester constituency and president of the movement, remembered that

> in some areas we were met by bands and led to the rostrum set up in the middle of the town like conquering heroes. Even the pubs closed. In Strabane virtually the whole town turned out at eleven at night, and television cameras were thrust upon us at one in the morning.[72]

The campaign, however, failed to stir up much interest even amongst Irish exiles in Britain. At the outset Rose said that the movement's main hope was to overturn the convention at Westminster that MPs could not discuss matters relating to Northern Ireland. It failed in this also: Alice Bacon, minister of state at the Home Office, refused to breach the convention, saying in August 1966 that to do so would harm relations between the London and Belfast governments.[73] Harold Wilson confirmed this view the following month:

> The constitutional relationship of the Northern Ireland Government cannot, and should not, be ignored and it is a fact that under the Government of Ireland Act 1920, the matters you have raised fall clearly within the competence of the authorities in Northern Ireland.[74]

In fact the 1920 act did allow for Westminster intervention and, indeed, the application of prices and incomes legislation could be seen as interference in areas normally under Stormont's sphere of influence.

Outside interest in Northern Ireland's affairs was slow to emerge. Even two Irish national dailies, the *Irish Press* and the *Irish Independent*, were unwilling to publicise material provided by the Campaign for Social Justice on the grounds that their readers would not find it newsworthy. However, a small minority in Britain were concerned. The National Council for Civil Liberties held a conference on Northern Ireland in March 1965; Charles Brett, chairman of the Northern Ireland Labour Party, spoke first on religious discrimination in housing and in employment, and on the manipulation of local government boundaries. On 3 July 1966 a much wider audience was alerted to anomalies in Northern Ireland when the *Sunday Times* published journalist Cal McCrystal's article, 'John Bull's Political Slum'.[75] The Labour government, nevertheless, retained its faith that O'Neill could put the region's house in order. The initiative still lay with the people of Northern Ireland themselves.

Nell McCafferty, the journalist and writer, remembered family prayers during her childhood in Derry in the 1950s:

> God send John a job; God send Jackie and Rosaleen a house; Holy Mother of God look down on Peggy in America and Leo in England; Jesus and his Blessed Mother protect Mary that's going with a sailor.[76]

On the United Kingdom's periphery, the city remained depressed even during years of economic expansion. Ian Nairn, author of a book on British cities, described Derry in 1961:

> This is one of the most unexpected and paradoxical of our cities. It is one of the remotest places in the British Isles . . . For forty years it has been the victim of a real topographical tragedy . . . a manufacturing town of 60,000 people where a rural centre of 20,000 would have been sufficient . . . whenever a recession or squeeze begins, Derry is likely to feel it first. It is like being attached to the free end of a rope; a gentle pull at one end means a vicious kick at the other.[77]

In March 1966, 5.9 per cent in the region were unemployed but in Derry 23.3 per cent of males and 4.8 per cent of females were out of work. Du Pont's synthetic rubber factory provided vitally needed jobs but few other multinationals were attracted here and the BSR gramophone factory opened in 1967 only to close seven months later with the loss of 1,800 jobs. Deprivation was general in the city but most acutely felt in the Catholic districts: the percentage of people living at densities of more than two per room in 1961 was 21.1 per cent in the largely Catholic South ward, 5.7 per cent in the North ward, and 7.9 per cent in the Waterside.[78] The refusal of the Lockwood committee to recommend Derry as the site for the region's second university united citizens there for a time, as Major Gerald Glover of the Unionist Party recalled: 'Ninety per cent of the population was bitterly disappointed, and this became a tremendous grievance shared by both Protestants and Roman Catholics.'[79] Traditional political allegiances soon re-emerged, however.

In October 1962 left-wing veteran John Sharkey wrote to a friend: 'Labour in Derry has become a dirty joke. It is an actual fact that eventually membership whittled down to about three or four.'[80] Stephen McGonagle, a trade-union organiser, made valiant attempts to get elected under various Labour labels, but essentially he was a one-man band. A Londonderry branch of the Northern Ireland Labour Party was set up in April 1965 and Ivan Cooper, deserting the Bond's Glen and Claudy Young Unionist Association, was its candidate in the Stormont general election later that year. His achievement was remarkable even though he was not elected: he obtained 32 per cent of the vote and the cross-community nature of his support was demonstrated when he stood for the council elections of May 1967: he received 34.5 per cent of the vote in South ward and 30 per cent and 27.5 per cent respectively in North ward and in Waterside.

The McCluskeys and the Homeless Citizens' League in Dungannon had been the first to take their protest to the streets but more sustained direct action followed in Derry. Some thirty out-of-work men set up the Derry Unemployed Action Committee in January 1965; members interrupted a corporation meeting, calling for united action to bring new industries to the city; and they picketed a dinner in the Guildhall addressed by Brian Faulkner. In October 1966 an organisation calling itself the Derry Young Republican Association held an open-air protest following the eviction of a family from the Creggan housing estate and soon after barricaded themselves in a house in Harvey Street in a successful attempt to prevent another family being made homeless. A more spectacular effort to prevent another eviction in Harvey Street in July 1967 was defeated only after the police, assailed by crockery, broke down a barricade to force in the door. Housing rapidly was becoming the central issue in Derry, where local Unionists were resisting an unanswerable case for extending the city boundary for fear that the electoral balance would be tipped enough to lose them control of the corporation. Between 1946 and 1967 Derry had built only 70 new houses per 1,000 of population compared with 144 for Newry, 109 for Coleraine and 140 for Larne. In the year ending May 1967 only seven corporation houses had been completed and the executive sanitary officer reported soon after that over one thousand homes in the city were occupied by more than one family; and in 1968 only four corporation houses had been built before the corporation was wound up in November.[81]

'Only two children?' a Londonderry Corporation official, looking over his spectacles, said to Paddy Doherty, who had asked for a council house; 'Come back in nine years and I'll take your name.'[82] Instead Doherty bought an inexpensive plot in Westland Road and set about building his own house with his own hands in his spare time. Doherty – later known as Paddy 'Bogside' – was one of an energetic group of Derry Catholics who put their faith in self-help. Doherty joined with Father Anthony Mulvey and John Hume to found the first Northern

Ireland branch of the Credit Union in 1960: the total invested at the inaugural meeting in Rossville Hall was £7 10s.0d.[83] Hume, a graduate of Maynooth College and a teacher at his old school, St Columb's, threw himself into this movement to free the poor from bondage to money-lenders and this co-operative bank (which did not achieve full legal status until 1969) developed rapidly until by 1973 its share capital exceeded £1 million. Achieving prominence as an organiser and speaker in the campaign to bring Northern Ireland's second university to Derry, Hume represented the new generation of Catholics benefiting from postwar education reform. Like men such as Ben Caraher, John Duffy and Ciaran McKeown in Belfast, Hume despaired of the inadequacies and inconsistencies of the Nationalists. In articles published in the *Irish Times* in May 1964, he wrote:

> Weak opposition leads to corrupt government. Nationalists in opposition have been in no way constructive. They have – quite rightly – been loud in their demands for rights, but they have remained silent and inactive about their duties. In 40 years of opposition they have not produced one constructive contribution on either the social or economic plane to the development of Northern Ireland . . . leadership has been the comfortable leadership of flags and slogans. Easy no doubt, but irresponsible . . . It is this lack of positive contribution and the apparent lack of interest in the general welfare of Northern Ireland that has led many Protestants to believe that the Northern Catholic is politically irresponsible and there-fore unfit to rule.[84]

He dismissed the Nationalist argument that the only obstacle to the reunification of Ireland was Britain and called on northern Catholics to face 'the realistic fact that a united Ireland, if it is to come, and if violence rightly is to be discounted, must come about by evolution, ie by the will of the Northern majority'.[85]

Hume and his associates also applied the principle of self-help to the housing problem in their native city. Founded in October 1965, mainly on the initiative of Father Mulvey, the Derry Housing Association bought large houses, divided them into flats for young couples, and returned half the rent after two years for use as deposits to building societies. In the first year the association housed a hundred families, twenty-seven of them in Farren Park, a green-field site on Buncrana Road. A more ambitious scheme to build seven hundred houses in Duncreggan Road on the north side of the city was turned down by the corporation. Hume represented the association at a two-day hearing in the Guildhall, producing nearly 150 pages to document the city's hous-ing crisis, but the appeal failed.[86]

Eamonn McCann, like Hume a Bogside eleven-plus success and a former pupil of St Columb's, was impatient with the Derry Housing

Association's measured and legalistic approach. A student of psychology at Queen's University in the early 1960s, where he proved himself a witty and at times an electrifying orator, McCann moved to London and became editor of the socialist *Irish Militant*. On a return visit to Derry he took part in a housing demonstration and decided to stay; there he joined the Northern Ireland Labour Party and steered it leftwards, and soon he was at the head of the most sustained direct-action protests over housing policy the region had seen so far. The Derry Housing Action Committee, formed in September 1967, made its first demonstration in March 1968 by invading the Guildhall and, as the Unionists withdrew, a statement was read out demanding

> that the Corporation immediately extend the city boundary and embark on a crash housing programme . . . The formation of this committee marks the beginning of a mass movement away from the false political leaders and against the exploiting capitalist class who have left in their wake a trail of human misery, degradation and decay.

The group interrupted corporation business again in May 1968 when one representative shouted out that the councillors 'filled him with nauseation'.[87] Discovering that John Wilson, his wife and two children (one of them suffering from tuberculosis) were living in a caravan in the Brandywell, the Derry Housing Action Committee made another protest, as McCann recalled:

> On 22 June, a Saturday, about ten of us manhandled the Wilson's caravan on to the Lecky Road, the main artery through the Bogside, and parked it broadside in the middle of the road, stopping all the traffic. We distributed leaflets in the surrounding streets explaining that we intended to keep the caravan there for twenty-four hours as a protest against the Wilsons' living conditions and calling for support. We then phoned the police, the mayor and the newspapers, inviting each to come and see.[88]

Other demonstrations that summer included: a sit-down protest on Craigavon Bridge when the mayor opened a new carriageway on 3 July; a protest at the allocation of a house to a prison officer on the housing list for only a few weeks; a public meeting in the Diamond; a rally in Foyle Street; and a large protest meeting in the Guildhall foyer at the end of August when Ivan Cooper called on people to fight for their rights, 'as the Blacks in America were fighting'.[89]

By now the age of television had come into its own. Popular action could attract immediate worldwide attention and the year 1968 provided numerous examples, such as: the peaceful defiance of Prague as the Soviet tanks rolled in; demonstrations against the Vietnam War;

the continuing campaign for black civil rights in America; and the students' violent revolt in Paris. The housing protests in Derry failed to stimulate interest beyond Northern Ireland but before the end of the year this apparently quiet backwater of the United Kingdom would be catapulted by the media into a position of global prominence and the region's age-old problems would be exposed to examination by an audience of a size not thought possible just a few months previously.

In June 1968 Miss Emily Beattie was allocated a council house in the Co. Tyrone village of Caledon. As the Cameron Commission reported the following year:

> She was 19 years old, a Protestant, and secretary to the local Councillor's solicitor, who was also a Unionist Parliamentary candidate living in Armagh . . . In concentrated form the situation expressed the objections felt by many non-Unionists to the prevailing system of house allocation in Dungannon Rural District Council. By no stretch of the imagination could Miss Beattie be regarded as a priority tenant.[90]

The local Republican Club had been encouraging Catholic families to squat in newly built houses and one of these was evicted before Miss Beattie could take possession. Austin Currie, the Nationalist MP for East Tyrone, raised the issue at Stormont on 19 June and then squatted in the house himself before being removed by a policeman, who happened to be Miss Beattie's brother. The proceedings were fully covered by the region's television stations.

A protest meeting followed in Dungannon on Saturday, 22 June, under the auspices of the Northern Ireland Civil Rights Association. This organisation was by no means as all-embracing as its title suggested or as it, briefly, later became. Loyalists who argued that it was a front for the IRA had a point: ever since the collapse of the 1956–62 campaign, republicans had been seeking peaceful means of advancing their cause. Cathal Goulding, the IRA chief of staff in Dublin, was present at a conference of Wolfe Tone Societies in Maghera on 13–14 August 1966 and there it was agreed to join with those who sought reform within the region, including the Northern Ireland Labour Party and the trade unions. The outcome was a seminar on civil rights in Belfast on 28 November 1966 and the formation of the Northern Ireland Civil Rights Association at the International Hotel in Donegall Square South on 29 January 1967. Over one hundred delegates from a wide range of organisations were present – including all the Northern Ireland political parties – and though Nelson Elder, a Unionist senator, walked out during the meeting, Young Unionist Robin Cole agreed to become a member of the executive committee.[91] The association made very little impact until after the Caledon episode. In July 1968 Austin Currie telephoned the committee and at a meeting in Maghera proposed a march from Coalisland to Dungannon to draw attention to the misallocation of public housing in Co. Tyrone. Betty Sinclair, a veteran Communist and chairwoman of the association, was opposed to protest marches but eventually the committee – persuaded by the Campaign for Social Justice in particular – agreed to Currie's proposal. Units of the Ulster Protestant Volunteers from the counties of Tyrone and Londonderry saw the plan to bring marchers to Market Square in the centre of Dungannon as nothing short of a nationalist invasion of loyalist territory. With Paisley's support they organised a counter-demonstration in Market Square; the Unionist chairman of the urban district council called on the authorities to reroute the civil rights march; and John Taylor, Unionist MP for South Tyrone, after failing to persuade Paisley to abandon the counter-demonstration, asked the minister of home affairs, William Craig, to redirect the march to the Catholic district of the town.[92]

On 24 August 1968 some 2,500 people assembled in Coalisland, outnumbering the town's population by two to one. They represented, among others, organisations as diverse as the Northern Ireland Labour Party, the Young Socialists, the Irish National Foresters, the Campaign for Social Justice, the Gaelic Athletic Association, the Derry Housing Action Committee and the Wolfe Tone Societies. Only as the march was about to begin were they told that they would not be allowed into the centre of Dungannon. The five miles between the two towns were covered without incident until at the outskirts of Dungannon the marchers found around four hundred police with dogs barring the way, and a rope slung between three RUC tenders close to the local hospital entrance.[93] Marchers sat down on the road in front of the police as their organisers put up a microphone on a lorry. Behind the police barricade, about 1,500 loyalists sang party songs, jeered and brandished clubs and staves, and an attempt by some Young Socialists to break through was driven back by a police baton charge. Then Betty Sinclair successfully persuaded the marchers to listen to the speakers, arguing that 'what we have done today will go down in history and in this way we will be more effective in showing the world that we are a peaceful people asking for our civil rights in an orderly manner'.[94] Erskine Holmes, a member of the executives of both the Northern Ireland Labour Party and of the Civil Rights Association, read out a statement condemning Craig and the RUC for stopping a non-sectarian demonstration from entering Dungannon. Others were more defiant: Currie compared the police cordon to the Berlin Wall and declared that the campaigners would continue with their disobedience until their aims were achieved, and Gerry Fitt, after shouting out, 'My blood is boiling – only that there is a danger to women and children I would lead the men past that barricade', went on to declare that he would not stop until full civil rights had been won.[95]

To many of those who took part, the Coalisland–Dungannon march was similar in character to demonstrations elsewhere against nuclear weapons or participation in the Vietnam War. Ulster's history dictated that this could not be so, for the province, except for middle-class suburbia, was divided by invisible lines into Protestant and Catholic areas. Given, as the historian Joseph Lee has pointed out, the 'dearth of major atheist settlements',[96] parades and demonstrations were bound to be regarded as assertions of, or challenges to, the territorial imperative of one side or the other. Certainly a high proportion of those present at Dungannon had never made any formal study of the province's past and they were unprepared for what was to come. Bernadette Devlin, a Queen's University student who attended the march, recalled: 'I do believe that then for the first time it dawned on people that Northern Ireland was a series of Catholic and Protestant ghettoes.'[97] The counter-demonstration had been a feature of Ulster's history for almost two centuries. Loyalists refused to see the civil rights movement as non-sectarian: the protesters, they believed, were nationalists and republicans intent on invading Protestant territory and, under the cover of demanding civil rights, seeking to undermine the status quo and draw Northern Ireland into a thirty-two-county republic.

Soon after the march, Eamonn McCann and Eamonn Melaugh of the Derry Housing Action Committee asked that the next civil rights demonstration be held in their city. Members of the Civil Rights Association executive, determined to show their movement was not sectarian, agreed to a traditional Protestant route from the Waterside on the east side of the Foyle, over Craigavon Bridge to the Diamond in the heart of the walled city. The date fixed was 5 October: the Middle Liberties Young Unionist Association threatened a counter-demonstration but it was the Apprentice Boys of Derry who announced a procession over the same route, on the same day and at the same time – 'this proposed procession was not a genuine "annual" event,' the Cameron Commission reported later, 'and we regard the proposal to hold it at the precise time indicated as merely a threat to counter demonstrate'.[98]

On the evening of 4 October Conn McCluskey, Fred Heatley and Frank Gogarty met the organisers of the march in Derry. As members of

653

the Civil Rights Association's executive, they had come to persuade McCann and Melaugh not to defy the ban on the march within the city imposed the previous day by William Craig. In a tempestuous meeting members of the Derry Housing Action Committee declared their intention of going ahead.[99] Reluctantly, the Civil Rights Association gave its approval. Moderates agreed to take part only with the deepest misgivings for they feared that the young radicals intended to invite trouble – indeed, McCann recorded later that 'our conscious if unspoken strategy was to provoke the police into over-reaction and thus spark off a mass reaction against the authorities'.[100]

THE DERRY CIVIL RIGHTS MARCH: 5 OCTOBER 1968

Only about four hundred demonstrators turned up at Waterside station. McAteer was there only because Fred Heatley and Betty Sinclair had called at his home to ask for his support and even then he told them he did not like the company they were keeping. Hume took no part in the march preparations but, because he had been outraged by Craig's ban, he took his place behind a blue banner bearing the words 'Civil Rights March'. Fitt arrived with three Westminster MPs, brought directly from the Labour Party Conference then in session. The Protestant residents of the Waterside made no attempt to interfere as placards were held aloft with slogans including 'Class not Creed', 'The Proper Place for Politics is in the Streets', and 'Police State Here'. When the march seemed prepared to move off, RUC County Inspector William Meharg warned the demonstrators that he could not allow a march in 'this part of the Maiden City'.[101]

Finding the planned route barred, the marchers moved into Duke Street only to find that the police had swiftly formed up there. Heatley, kneed in the groin by a constable, was the first arrested; McAteer, Currie and Fitt were struck by batons, Fitt so badly that he was taken, with blood streaming from his head, to an ambulance; marchers behind sat down and an impromptu meeting was attempted, with short speeches given by Betty Sinclair and Michael Farrell, the Young Socialist leader; an effort was made to sing 'We Shall Overcome'; some tried to throw their placards at the police; and then constables with drawn batons advanced from both ends of the street. For several minutes the marchers were batoned until Meharg, using a loud-hailer, ordered: 'The police will hold their hands, please.' The *Irish Times* journalist, Fergus Pyle, reported:

> Instead of a pause, this announcement was the prelude to a methodical and efficient movement forward by the police, hitting everything in front of them. Some people in the crowd tackled them back and poles from

placards were flying through the air. From my vantage point I saw nothing in the few seconds between the County Inspector's announcement to have incited what appeared to be a concerted start by the police.[102]

As parties of police chased after fleeing demonstrators, some passers-by fell victim to their batons: one British Labour MP saw a constable lift a pair of spectacles off a woman aged about sixty and then strike her on the head. Water cannon arrived to spray not only marchers but also bystanders and an Ulster Television crew filming from a flat in Duke Street.

In twos and threes some demonstrators took McAteer's advice to take a 'wee walk' to the Diamond. As they arrived unfurling a Campaign for Nuclear Disarmament banner an angry jeering crowd of local people gathered to taunt the police. Repeated baton charges followed as the RUC pushed Catholic youths down to Butcher Gate and the Bogside. A barricade across Fahan Street halted the police advance and, as it was set on fire, a furious stone-throwing battle ensued, constables returning the missiles flung at them. Catholics from the Bogside, almost none of whom had taken part in the march, were able to thrust their way back to the Diamond around 10.30 p.m. and a chaotic conflict with the police resumed. More violent disorder, including the throwing of petrol bombs and the looting of shops, erupted the following afternoon and evening.[103]

A few hundred feet of film, captured by Radio Telefís Éireann cameraman Gay O'Brien, changed the course of Ulster's history.[104] Images of unrestrained police batoning unarmed demonstrators, including MPs, 'without justification or excuse' as the Cameron Commission judged later, flashed across the world. William Craig's unrepentant bluster on television and radio that the RUC had not used undue force and that the civil rights march was 'in fact, a Republican front' and associated 'with the IRA and Communism' only served to convince the British media that a reactionary regime had been caught in the act of suppressing free speech within the United Kingdom.[105] At a stroke the television coverage of the events of 5 October 1968 destabilised Northern Ireland, and as the sectarian dragon was fully reawakened, the region was plunged into a near-revolutionary crisis, characterised by bitter intercommunal conflict and protracted violence and destruction.

'ULSTER STANDS AT THE CROSSROADS': OCTOBER–DECEMBER 1968

On Sunday 6 October ten students picketed William Craig's east Belfast home. He dismissed them as 'a crowd of bloody fools'.[106] The following Tuesday the Queen's University Students' Union agreed on a march

655

from Elmwood Avenue to the city hall next day. Stressing the non-violent and non-sectarian character of their protest, the demonstrators – numbering about three thousand and including twenty academic staff and a large proportion of Protestants – accepted police redirection when Paisley held a meeting on their route at Shaftesbury Square, provided they could proceed to the front of the city hall. Some loyalist counter-demonstrators got to the city centre before them, however; the police, making no attempt to remove them, stopped the legal march in Linenhall Street and there, for three hours, the students held a peaceful sit-down protest. On their return to the university the students reassembled for an emotional mass meeting, later described by one of them as 'a cross between a Quaker meeting and a Pentecostalist service'.[107] There they agreed to call themselves the People's Democracy; elected a 'faceless committee' composed of undergraduates and graduates of unknown political affiliation; and accepted a six-point programme:

> One man, one vote; fair boundaries; houses on need; jobs on merit; free speech; repeal of the Special Powers Act.[108]

As the movement's historian, Paul Arthur, pointed out, until now 'there was very little indication that Belfast undergraduates were part of the world-wide wave of student protest'.[109] In the early 1960s easily the most persistent and acerbic critic of the establishment was Bowes Egan, a law student from Belleek. Commanding a large personal following, he dissected the Lockwood report with brilliant effect and more than anyone else encouraged undergraduates to question authority. In those years the most important radical organisation was the Queen's University of Belfast Labour Group, dominated by highly articulate products of the 1947 Education Act, including Erskine Holmes, Michael Farrell and Eamonn McCann. Until October 1968, however, the great majority of students demonstrated a high level of political apathy. Now the People's Democracy was a potent addition to the great wave of protest surging forward in the wake of the Derry civil rights march.

During most of October and November Northern Ireland was in ferment. The Civil Rights Association, hitherto no more than a small band of activists, burgeoned as branches sprang up across the region, particularly in towns with significant Catholic populations, and support was pledged by sympathetic organisations on the European mainland and throughout the English-speaking world. Yet the association was only one part of a mass movement demanding change. Excitement was intense in Derry, where the newly formed Derry Citizens' Action Committee seized the initiative by launching a major programme of civil disobedience, including an illegal sit-down protest in Guildhall

Square on 19 October.[110] The climax came on 16 November when almost twenty thousand citizens, shepherded by dozens of stewards under the direction of Dr Raymond McClean, industrial medical officer at Du Pont, set out to establish their claim to carry their protest into the heart of Derry. All 'non-traditional' parades had been banned and a disastrous confrontation was prevented only by the good sense of the police and the strict discipline imposed by the organisers. The RUC blocked the march only at the west end of Craigavon Bridge and allowed the action committee to make a token breach, one embarrassed constable actually helping Michael Canavan over the waist-high steel barriers, and then the demonstrators dispersed to make their way to the Guildhall by side streets and footpaths.[111] Over the next few days several impromptu parades were made to the city centre in defiance of the government ban. Meanwhile, in Belfast the People's Democracy applied steady pressure in a variety of demonstrations, including the occupation of the Great Hall at Stormont on 24 October.

The mounting crisis in Northern Ireland forced Harold Wilson's administration to confront the region's problems, perhaps for the first time. O'Neill, Craig and Faulkner were summoned to Downing Street and there a package of reforms was insisted on. Several difficult cabinet meetings followed at Stormont before O'Neill was able to announce a five-point programme on 22 November – Londonderry Corporation was to be replaced by an appointed development commission; local councils were to adopt a fair points system of housing allocation; sections of the Special Powers Act would be repealed; an ombudsman would investigate citizens' grievances; and universal suffrage in local government elections would be considered. In just forty-eight days since 5 October 1968 the Catholic minority had won more political concessions than it had over the previous forty-seven years. O'Neill observed later that 'the civil rights movement brought about reforms which would otherwise have taken years to wring from a reluctant Government'.[112] This very fact galvanised many loyalists now convinced that a Wilson–O'Neill–Lynch conspiracy was afoot to undermine their position. The Ulster Protestant Volunteers made an appeal beseeching 'our loyal brethren, for the sake of God, our country and our children, to forget all petty quarrels and jealousies and defend our constitution and liberty. He that would be free must strike the first blow.'[113]

The juggernaut of the mass civil rights movement could not be halted at once by O'Neill's announcement. A march planned for 30 November in Armagh was to go ahead. Paisley warned police that 'appropriate action' would be taken if the march was not banned and posters were put up a couple of days beforehand:

For God and Ulster. S.O.S. To all Protestant religions. Don't let the Republicans, IRA and CRA make Armagh another Londonderry. Assemble in Armagh on Saturday 30 November.[114]

Hearing of plans to ring the city with road blocks, Paisley led a convoy of 30 cars into Armagh in the middle of the night but the police seized 2 revolvers and 220 other weapons including scythes, bill hooks and pipes with sharpened ends from supporters driving in next morning. Around two thousand loyalists occupied the city centre by midday and when told this was an unlawful assembly, Paisley refused to leave, saying that he intended holding a religious service. The five thousand civil rights marchers avoided confrontation but a loyalist wielding a lead-filled sock knocked an Independent Television News cameraman unconscious.[115]

Captain O'Neill decided to appeal directly to the people of Northern Ireland by making a television broadcast on 9 December. The prime minister began with the words 'Ulster stands at the crossroads', and asked:

What kind of Ulster do you want? A happy respected province . . . or a place continually torn apart by riots and demonstrations, and regarded by the rest of Britain as a political outcast?

To the civil rights leaders he said: 'Your voice has been heard, and clearly heard. Your duty now is to take the heat out of the situation.'[116] O'Neill's impassioned appeal, sonorously delivered, was heard by the leaders, and the Derry Citizens' Action Committee, the Civil Rights Association and the Nationalist Party called off further street protests to give the Government time to introduce reforms. Craig made a virulent attack on O'Neill's speech and was promptly sacked. As the year 1968 drew to a close the prime minister's standing in the region seemed high. The *Belfast Telegraph* printed coupons with the words 'I back O'Neill' to be posted to the premier by readers; tens of thousands did so and altogether he received at least 150,000 letters and telegrams of support. In addition, O'Neill got an overwhelming vote of confidence from the parliamentary Unionist Party; he was voted 'man of the year' by Dublin's *Sunday Independent;* and even the Co. Donegal Sinn Féin leader Seamus Rodgers declared that a peaceful civil rights movement had done more in a few weeks 'than decades of IRA activities'.[117]

Northern Ireland was at peace but only a few days into the new year action taken by the People's Democracy and its opponents bleakly demonstrated how ephemeral that peace was to be.

Just before 9 a.m. on New Year's Day, 1969, around forty young people gathered beside Belfast City Hall ready to walk seventy-five miles from there to Derry. According to a statement put out the night before, it was to be a march modelled on that led by Martin Luther King in 1965 between Selma and Montgomery. This was Ulster not America, however: McAteer said it was 'not good marching weather – in more senses than one'; and Hume counselled the People's Democracy against it, assuring the leaders that 'the march would lead to sectarian violence'.[118] Even the People's Democracy, at a large meeting in December, had voted against the march, but the Young Socialist Alliance declared its intention of going ahead. Michael Farrell feared that without direct action the civil rights movement would expire as 'O'Neill's miserable reforms' would be found acceptable, and Bernadette Devlin explained afterwards:

> Our function in marching from Belfast to Derry was to break the truce, to relaunch the civil rights movement as a mass movement and to show people that O'Neill was, in fact, offering them nothing.[119]

And so the fateful decision was made by the People's Democracy militants to traverse the Ulster countryside. Much of the route would be through Protestant territory and already, as the marchers set out, about seventy loyalists pulled at their banners, hurled invective and chanted 'One Taig, no vote' and 'Paisley, Paisley, Paisley'. At their head was Major Ronald Bunting, Paisley's right-hand man at the Armagh counter-demonstration who had promised to 'harry and harass' the march all the way to Derry.[120]

On a railway bridge just outside Antrim a man summoned fellow Protestants to action by beating vigorously on a Lambeg drum and there Bunting reappeared with his supporters. A dangerous confrontation was prevented only by the transport of marchers round the town in police tenders on the proposal of Nat Minford, the local Unionist MP. They stopped overnight in Whitehall, where they were disturbed by a bomb scare. As the students resumed their walk towards Randalstown next day loyalists along the route made it plain that to them the march was a brazen republican invasion of their territory. They had to detour Randalstown in local supporters' cars. O'Neill had refused to ban the march and so the RUC was obliged to protect it – a task which, despite the presence of journalists and television crews, most of the men made clear they found utterly distasteful and they did not hide their contempt for the students.[121] Indeed, the People's Democracy leaders faced growing evidence of police collusion with Bunting.

The marchers passed through Toome, which was well-disposed towards them. Then the RUC, invoking the Public Order Act, redirected the march via Bellaghy to Maghera but, hearing of trouble ahead, halted it in the village of Gulladuff. In Maghera loyalists openly prepared an attack. Inez McCormack, wife of one of the marchers, drove ahead to the town, where she found young men carrying cudgels and smashing up furniture to make weapons:

> Then a single constable came slowly down the street. I was relieved, knowing that now the police would learn of the danger and take action. To my astonishment he joined with a crowd carrying broken chair legs, apparently in amiable conversation.[122]

To avoid confrontation the marchers bypassed the town in supporters' cars and stopped for the night in Brackaghreilly. Denied their intended victims, the counter-demonstrators wrecked and looted twenty shops in Maghera and laid siege to Walsh's Hotel, where many reporters were staying, hurling bottles and stones through the windows. Next day the marchers crossed the Sperrins over the Glenshane Pass and that night, outside a hall in Claudy, where they attempted to rest, loyalists yelled threats. Meanwhile, opponents of the People's Democracy laid an elaborate ambush on the Derry–Claudy road near the junction of the Ardmore Road: several truck loads of new-quarried stones were brought in and crates of empty bottles were taken there by bus.

Police warned the marchers next day of danger ahead but did not suggest any of the several alternative routes available. The People's Democracy and its supporters were led into the ambush: stones and bottles cascaded down; when marchers tried to escape into the fields, police officers drew batons and forced them back on the road; in and around Burntollet Bridge men swarmed down, armed with crowbars, chair legs, lead piping and other weapons; and police offered little protection, some mingling with the attackers in a friendly way. The attack was unrelenting, though the marchers did not resist. Dozens were injured: one young woman was beaten unconscious and left lying face down in a stream, and Judith McGuffin, a Belfast teacher, recalled:

> Showers of rocks crashed round us . . . a middle-aged man in a tweed coat, brandishing what seemed to be a chair leg, dashed from the left-hand side of the road, hit me on the back, then pulled down the hood of my anorak and struck me on the head. I then tried to crawl away, but, teeth bared, he hit me again on the spot on my skull . . . I fell, and a fellow marcher picked me up and dragged me up the road; I passed out, and came round in the ambulance on the way to Altnagelvin Hospital.[123]

Many of the assailants were later identified from photographs as being local members of the B Special Constabulary.

Those marchers still on their feet struggled on to Derry, where again they were subjected to showers of stones and bottles. In Spencer Road a journalist, after seeing a marcher fall 'like a log at my feet', noticed that adults urged their children on to the attack. 'How do you explain the attitude of a mother,' he asked, 'who encourages her son to keep on?' In Irish Street, Seamus Murphy recalled, 'we were met with an avalanche of stones, sticks and petrol bombs. The police, like good guardians of law and order, immediately got into their tenders and disappeared' – a description verified by photographs of the scene.[124] Trouble continued after the People's Democracy had been given a rapturous reception by the Derry Citizens' Action Committee at the Guildhall. As darkness fell police discipline collapsed: twenty constables burst into Wellworths supermarket, smashed glass counters and batoned customers; and a large Reserve RUC force invaded the Bogside, threw bricks through windows, smashed down doors, pelted people with stones and sang sectarian songs into the early hours of Sunday morning.

Northern Ireland had been given a vicious push towards the precipice. O'Neill's announcement of reforms the previous November and the consequent truce called by the civil rights movement had held out the real prospect of a peaceful settlement. Now that prospect vanished. The march had inflamed sectarian passions to a level not seen since 1922, and Protestant fury at the People's Democracy 'invasion' of their territory was matched by Catholic bitterness at the savagery of the assault on the march and the partisan and undisciplined behaviour of the police. O'Neill's political survival was now seriously in question.

'NOW HE IS REAPING THE WHIRLWIND': THE FALL OF O'NEILL

'The march to Londonderry planned by the so-called People's Democracy was, from the outset, a foolhardy and irresponsible undertaking,' O'Neill declared at the start of a television broadcast on Sunday 5 January. He continued:

> At best, those who planned it were careless of the effects which it would have . . . Some of the marchers and those who supported them in Londonderry itself have shown themselves to be mere hooligans, ready to attack the police and others . . . Enough is enough. We have heard sufficient for now about civil rights; let us hear a little about civic responsibility.

It was a confused and ill-considered speech, recorded after a hasty return from England. Nearly all the prime minister's criticism was directed at the marchers and the 'extremism of the Republicans, radical Socialists and anarchists'. His analysis was sharply at variance with the assessment of leading British newspapers and television commentators. Catholics were aghast at O'Neill's proposal to call up the B Specials when so many off-duty constables had been photographed amongst the attackers at Burntollet. O'Neill said that the RUC had 'handled this most difficult situation as fairly and as firmly as they could': television footage and eyewitness accounts indicated otherwise.[125] This, indeed, was one of the disastrous consequences of the march: over the years the police had been remarkably successful in winning acceptance in all areas of Northern Ireland, but now the RUC's reputation collapsed in Catholic districts. Over the ensuing months the whole region became even more polarised along sectarian lines.

'You are now entering Free Derry' appeared in large painted letters on a gable end at the edge of the Bogside. Several of the roads leading into the main Catholic districts of the city were barricaded; vigilante patrols emerged armed with clubs; and for a time a transmitter broadcast as 'Radio Free Derry, the Voice of Liberation'. After five days, Hume, Cooper and Canavan persuaded the Bogsiders to take down their barricades but the hands of the moderate leaders had been forced by events: they, too, ended their moratorium on street demonstrations.[126] On Saturday 11 January a civil rights march in Newry quickly went out of control. This time the police showed restraint as militants – some of them youths from Dundalk – disobeyed the organisers, dashed a microphone from John Hume's hand, made an assault on the RUC and overturned seven of their vehicles, setting some on fire and pushing others into the canal. Most Protestants and many Catholics who had been campaigning for civil rights now withdrew from the movement in disgust. Republicans gained increasing control of demonstrations which erupted in the weeks that followed and it would not be long before O'Neill's prediction in his broadcast that 'it is a short step from the throwing of paving stones to the laying of tombstones' would be proved correct.[127]

With increasing desperation, O'Neill attempted to steer a middle course. On 15 January he announced an official inquiry into the recent disturbances under the chairmanship of Lord Cameron, a Scottish judge. Soon afterwards Faulkner and Morgan resigned from the cabinet in protest and on 3 February twelve Unionist MPs met in Portadown and there called for O'Neill's resignation. On the same day the prime minister decided to appeal over the heads of his critics and called a general election for 24 February. The traditional parties faced an unprecedented challenge. O'Neill found himself opposed by Unionists from the 'Portadown parliament' and by Paisley's Protestant Unionists, while the Nationalists had to compete with a wide range of civil rights activists. Paddy Devlin won Falls for the Northern Ireland Labour

Party, and as Independents, John Hume, Ivan Cooper and Paddy O'Hanlon replaced Nationalists, including Eddie McAteer. Paisley, released from prison when he appealed his sentence for his part in organising the Armagh counter-demonstration, attracted most media attention during his colourful, rumbustious campaign in O'Neill's Bannside constituency. The People's Democracy made a strong bid for cross-community support in nine constituencies but though, on average, its candidates won 26.4 per cent of the vote none was elected and none seems to have attracted significant Protestant support. Farrell once observed: 'We're not concerned in the least justifying ourselves to people who have proved by their theory and action that they are not socialists'; but the 2,310 votes he acquired in Bannside were undoubtedly cast because he was a civil rights militant and not because of his socialism.[128]

In this most confused election in Northern Ireland's history, O'Neill had, in retrospect, performed rather well. Of the 39 Unionists returned, 27 were pro-O'Neill, 10 were anti-O'Neill and 2 were unclear about where their loyalties lay. No Protestant Unionist was elected, though Paisley obtained only 1,414 fewer votes than O'Neill. However, the prime minister had sought an overwhelming mandate for his reform programme and evidence of substantial Catholic support. He had got neither of these and, above all, his position was weak because he could not trust those MPs who in theory were on his side. In the following weeks the ground was slowly cut from beneath his feet. A by-election for the Westminster constituency of Mid-Ulster on 17 April resulted in victory for Bernadette Devlin, twenty-one years old and the youngest woman ever to have been elected to Westminster. Despite her firm socialist stand, the massive vote was a traditional Catholic anti-Unionist one. Her dramatic appearance in the House of Commons undoubtedly led the British government to urge O'Neill to implement further reforms. On 22 April O'Neill agreed to 'one man, one vote' – universal suffrage in local elections. Next day his cousin, Major James Chichester-Clark, resigned from the Government in protest and this was but one outward and visible sign of the growing revolt against the prime minister. The parliamentary Unionist Party accepted this reform by twenty-eight votes to twenty-two on 24 April, but O'Neill was all too aware that his support was slipping away as Northern Ireland lapsed into further turbulence during the spring of 1969.

The resignation of Betty Sinclair, Fred Heatley and Dr Conn McCluskey from the executive of the Civil Rights Association in March 1969 indicated that the militants – the People's Democracy and republicans – had gained control of the movement. The organisers of the numerous protests in the streets seemed to seek confrontation, retaliation from the police, and the destabilisation of the region. The growing anger of the Protestant majority that resulted strengthened the position of O'Neill's Unionist critics and raised the standing of Paisley, who had lost his appeal and returned to Crumlin Road gaol on 25 March. The final push was given by a series of explosions which, O'Neill wrote later, 'quite literally blew me out of office'.[129] At 3.55 in the morning of 30 March a large explosion destroyed an electricity substation at Castlereagh; on 20 April a bomb smashed the main water pipeline between the Silent Valley reservoir in the Mourne Mountains and Belfast, and an electricity pylon was wrecked in Co. Armagh. Four days later another device fractured the water pipeline feeding the city's supply from Lough Neagh; and on 25 April an explosion damaged a pipeline at Annalong. The RUC announced that the bombings 'were caused by people working to an IRA plan', and believing this to be true, O'Neill mobilised one thousand B Specials and ordered all police officers, other than those on traffic duty, to carry arms.[130] Eileen Paisley, campaigning for her husband's release from prison, said the explosions were a natural outcome of O'Neill's reforming programme: 'Captain O'Neill has sown the wind, now he is reaping the whirlwind.'[131] The IRA had carried out some attacks on post offices but in fact – as the police proved later in the year – all the major bombings had been the work of loyalist extremists intent on implicating militant republicans, hardening Unionist opinion against further concessions, and thereby forcing O'Neill out of office. This plot succeeded perfectly: convinced that the civil rights protests were turning into a terrorist campaign, several Unionist MPs threatened to desert O'Neill and join his critics; and on 28 April 1969 the prime minister resigned. That evening he said on television:

> I have tried to break the chains of ancient hatreds. I have been unable to realise during my period of office all that I had sought to achieve. Whether now it can be achieved in my life-time I do not know. But one day these things will be and must be achieved.[132]

Just the day before, the *Sunday Times* Insight Team had made its own grim assessment:

> The monster of sectarian violence is well out of its cage. The issue now is no longer Civil Rights or even houses and jobs. The issue is now whether the state should exist and who should have the power, and how it should be defended; and this is an issue on which the wild men on both sides have sworn for 40 years, frequently in blood, that they will never back down.[133]

The night O'Neill resigned bonfires blazed up in celebration on the Shankill Road, where the people were convinced that the appeasement of Catholic agitators had been brought to an end. O'Neill was replaced by neither the man who had done most to pull him down, William Craig, nor by Brian Faulkner, the man who could have done most to save him. The parliamentary Unionist Party, by a margin of one vote, chose a safe, compromise candidate as prime minister, Major James Chichester-Clark. He declared his intention of going ahead with the reform programme but bought himself time by announcing an amnesty on 6 May, which allowed the rapid release of Paisley and Bunting from prison. Militant civil rights activists continued to protest on the street, however, and this inevitably heightened sectarian tensions, as Eamonn McCann admitted in an interview in the May–June issue of *New Left Review:*

> The cry 'get the Protestants' is still very much on the lips of the Catholic working class. Everyone applauds loudly when one says in a speech that we are not sectarian, we are fighting for the rights of all Irish workers, but really that's because they see this as the new way of getting at the Protestants.[134]

During the latter part of May the worst violence was confined to Hooker Street on the sensitive frontier zone between densely inhabited Catholic and Protestant districts in Belfast, but trouble spread as the traditional marching season approached and serious rioting was directed against the hard-pressed police, particularly along the Crumlin Road and in Ardoyne. Numbering only 3,200 men for the whole region, the RUC was already at full stretch: every weekend and several nights a week it had to deploy in massed strength; even those with severe injuries turned out (one officer with a fractured ankle in plaster looked after a busy Belfast station for an entire night without assistance, while his colleagues helped elsewhere); it was not uncommon for men to be on duty without a break for three consecutive days; and protective equipment was in short supply.[135] A suggestion from Scotland Yard that horses be used against demonstrators was given the reply: 'They might eat them.'[136] A battalion of more than five hundred soldiers had been brought into Northern Ireland in April but the RUC inspector-general, Anthony Peacocke, insisted that the civil authorities could cope. It shortly became evident they could not.

On 12 July protracted rioting ensued in Belfast when Orange bands were pelted with bottles from Unity Flats, a Catholic enclave at the foot of Peter's Hill. In Derry, Catholic youths stoned the Twelfth parade and fierce street violence continued in the city through the night and all next day. In Dungiven on 13 July police launched repeated baton charges at Catholics attempting to storm an Orange hall and B Specials fired shots over the heads of people leaving a dance hall. Early in August a Protestant mob made a sustained attack on Unity Flats, smashing most of the windows before police reinforcements drove them back up the Shankill with baton charges; RUC men attempting to keep rioters apart on the Crumlin Road were stoned by Protestants and petrol-bombed by Catholics; and when water cannon were used to repel fresh attacks on Unity Flats, the Shankill Defence Association put out this statement: 'We make it clear the police are no longer our friends and can never expect the help of Ulster loyalists again.'[137] There was mounting anxiety in official circles about the imminent Apprentice Boys parade in Derry. Robert Porter, the home affairs minister, was reluctant to impose a ban, and when Hume travelled to London to express his fears at the Home Office, he was considered unduly alarmist.[138] Since most of its demands had been met, the Derry Citizens' Action Committee was in abeyance but it was supplanted by the more militant Derry Citizens' Defence Association which, though it promised it would do nothing to provoke trouble, was led by Sean Keenan, widely understood to be a former IRA activist. With memories of the police invasion after Burntollet still fresh in their minds, the people of the Bogside prepared for a siege and, as arsenals of petrol bombs were prepared, the main roads into the district were barricaded with scaffolding, paving stones, planks and furniture.

THE BATTLE OF THE BOGSIDE: 12–14 AUGUST 1969

On Tuesday 12 August 1969 fifteen thousand Apprentice Boys came into Derry from all over Northern Ireland for the annual celebration of their ancestors' defiance in 1689. To the accompaniment of fifes, accordians, pipes and drums, they marched for most of the day through the city without incident, much to the relief of seven hundred RUC officers on duty. Then as the parade wound past the perimeter of the Bogside loyalist supporters on the walls threw down some pennies on the Catholics below, and Harold Jackson, reporting for the *Guardian*, saw a middle-aged Catholic fire a marble from a catapult.[139] From behind a barbed-wire barrier Catholic youths threw nails and stones at the loyalists and in moments an intense battle developed. After enduring showers of missiles, the police rattled their batons on their riot shields and charged to separate the rioters below the walls. Hume, Cooper and McAteer linked arms in an attempt to hold back the people of the Bogside but they were swept aside and, struck by a flying brick, Cooper was knocked unconscious. Bernadette Devlin, carrying a loud-hailer, urged Catholics to strengthen the barricades and to prepare for resistance. In an attempt to reduce pressure on police battling with mobs in William Street, a party of RUC tried to take down the barricade in Rossville Street – this not only convinced Catholics that their homes were about to be attacked but also created a gap through which Protestants now surged. From the high roof of the Rossville Flats, between fifteen and twenty youths threw down a deadly rain of petrol bombs and the advance was halted. Again and again, while hundreds of Derry citizens were still locked in combat with each other, police vainly attempted to break their way into the Bogside. Radio messages being passed between units registered their frustration:

> Green Two: We are getting it fierce tight here but we'll have to win this war.
>
> Black Five: We're on fire! . . . They are right on top of us.
>
> Green Two to Sierra: Come on! Send all available armour to the junction of Rossville Street and let's have a go if we break through here. Over.
>
> Sierra to Green One: Watch! There are some trenches dug on those roads . . . let's have all support in Lecky Road and let's finish them off. Come on!
>
> Green One: You are on fire! Consolidate. Consolidate what you have there . . . can we get more foot people in there? Over . . . come on armour! come on armour![140]

As night fell Deputy Inspector-General Graham Shillington watched the violence rage at the corner of Sackville Street and Little James Street. While several buildings burned furiously nearby, he saw 'very tired policemen who were doing their best to keep two opposing groups apart'.[141] The officers had been on their feet for sixteen hours and some had dropped with exhaustion onto the footpath, even while mobs several hundred strong on either side kept up a relentless fusillade of stones and petrol bombs. Shillington dashed back to Victoria barracks and got permission from the minister of home affairs to use CS gas, officially described as 'tear smoke'. Desperate police radio messages indicated a fast-deteriorating situation:

> Two to One: This is Little Diamond, the barrier, just for your information. Over.
>
> Green One to Green Two: I know bloody fine where it is but I'm not going to stick me head in a noose. We go in, smash up and get out toute bloody suite. Out.[142]

Sometime after midnight the first canisters of CS gas were fired, driving back the rioters for a time; but the wind blew the gas towards the police, causing some to choke, while those with respirators almost asphyxiated because they had not removed the cardboard packing stuffed between the vents.

Shillington walked along the city wall at dawn and saw the crowds reassemble to pelt his weary men with stones and bottles. Hearing reports of other disturbances erupting all over the region, he was now certain the army would have to be called in. By mid-morning the fighting in Derry had become general and intense. Reporting for *The Times*, John Clare watched the Bogside defenders on the roof of Rossville Flats:

> It was a ten-storey block lined by about forty teenagers, many girls. I counted eighteen milk crates, each containing twenty bottles half-full of petrol and with a piece of rag rammed down the neck. Girls aged 14 or 15 toiled up the stairs carrying crates of stones and bottles. After ten minutes I could hardly see with the tears running out of my eyes. In the courtyard behind the flats young people leant against the walls, weeping and choking. In a corner small boys aged 8 or 9 decanted petrol from a tin drum into milk bottles.[143]

Bernadette Devlin, followed by a camera crew, broke up paving stones and, swimming goggles on her forehead, attempted to inspire further resistance with her rhetoric; some journalists, however, noted that she was considered an outsider and ignored for much of the time. John Hume worked tirelessly to halt the violence by walking the streets for two days and nights, remonstrating with petrol-bombers and arranging a truce which at best lasted a few hours. Rosemount RUC station was set on fire and while other buildings blazed up, mobs resumed their sectarian warfare. When a Protestant street was barricaded at both ends, the inhabitants were forced to scramble for safety over back walls; and after midnight a Methodist hostel for down-and-outs, five of them Protestant and twenty-nine Catholic, was petrol-bombed.[144]

'The Irish Army's coming! The Irish Army's coming!' Hume heard people shout when it was announced that the taoiseach was about to make a broadcast. It was with mounting gloom that Hume listened to Lynch's words:

> It is evident that the Stormont Government is no longer in control of the situation. Indeed the present situation is the inevitable outcome of the policies pursued for decades by successive Stormont Governments. It is clear, also, that the Irish Government can no longer stand by and see innocent people injured and perhaps worse.[145]

Lynch was not about to send troops over the border, however, but he did call for a United Nations peacekeeping force because the RUC was 'no longer accepted as an impartial force' and the use of British troops he described as 'unacceptable'.[146] Reunification was, he believed, the only long-term solution. Lynch's broadcast did nothing to calm the violence and the conflict raged on all through a second night. Dr Raymond McClean set up a makeshift casualty station in the Candy Corner shop in Westland Street; by now, with the help of first-aid volunteers, he had treated – without anaesthetic or the availability of running water – nearly a thousand patients, some with lacerations and others afflicted by CS gas and 'showing alarming respiratory symptoms'.[147]

During an emergency session at Stormont the following day, Gerry Fitt told the Commons that the government of Northern Ireland had become irrelevant in the affairs of the Irish people. All opposition MPs, save one, had walked out before the home affairs minister told the House that troops had been sent to Derry. At Westminster, Home Secretary James Callaghan said that the general officer commanding had been instructed

> to take all necessary steps, acting impartially between citizen and citizen, to restore law and order. Troops will be withdrawn as soon as this is accomplished. This is a limited operation.[148]

He also pledged that Northern Ireland would remain in the United Kingdom 'so long as the people of Northern Ireland wish'. At 4.15 p.m., 14 August, eighty men of the Prince of Wales Own Regiment set out for Derry's Waterloo Place and replaced the RUC. Eddie McAteer spoke to people who had just been in combat with the police and successfully urged them to welcome the troops. Eamonn McCann recalled the scene:

> The police pulled out quite suddenly and the troops, armed with machine guns, stood in a line at the mouth of William Street. Their appearance was clear proof we had won the battle, that the RUC was beaten . . . Bernadette Devlin, her voice croaking, urged, 'Don't make them welcome. They have not come here to help us', and went on a bit about British imperialism, Cyprus and Aden. It did not go down very well.[149]

The Battle of the Bogside was over and an uncertain calm settled on the city of Derry. Violence, meanwhile, had spread elsewhere and was about to reach a fearful climax in Belfast.

BELFAST: 12–16 AUGUST 1969

Hearing news of dramatic conflict in Derry, on the evening of 12 August Catholics took to the streets in many provincial towns, and RUC stations in Coalisland, Strabane and Newry came under attack. The following night, in response to a Civil Rights Association appeal to take pressure off the Bogside by stretching police resources, Catholics duly rioted in Dungannon, Dungiven, Armagh, and again in Newry. Trouble flared up in Belfast, too. Here the very size of the city ensured that there were numerous potential flashpoints, often widely separated.

On Thursday 14 August tension steadily increased in several parts of Belfast. The police, who had been under virtual siege in Hastings Street barracks the previous night, were strained and fearful. The force in the city was so undermanned and short of equipment that frantic but unsuccessful attempts were made to put Lancia cage cars – last used in the 1935 riots – on the road. News came in that a civilian, John Gallagher, had been shot dead when B Specials fired into a crowd following a riot after a Civil Rights Association meeting in Armagh – the first violent death of the present Troubles. Protestants were angry that whole areas of the region had apparently slipped out of government control and that the victory of the Bogside over the RUC was a deadly blow directed at the integrity of Northern Ireland – a feeling strengthened by Lynch's broadcast. Catholics in turn were exultant that the regime so many of them loathed was now thrown on the defensive. Fear was at its most intense along the Falls–Shankill divide. Those most in peril lived in one narrow, mixed area – Cupar Street and its vicinity – where the two territories met.[150] That evening as Protestants were gathering under the direction of John McKeague on the Shankill Road, Catholic youths assembled in strength in front of Divis Flats.

Police armoured personnel carriers, failing to disperse the rioters, merely became targets for volleys of stones and petrol bombs. As darkness fell police and Special constables on foot attempted to close in from the side streets, and behind them the Protestants mobilised. Suddenly shots rang out, from which side it will never be known for certain. Within minutes gunfire became general. Police Shorlands – armoured cars made on Queen's Island – fired bursts of heavy-calibre bullets from their Browning machine guns, fitted as a desperate measure earlier in the day; many shots hit Divis Flats and a nine-year-old boy was killed as he took refuge in a back room. Protestants surged down the narrow streets interconnecting the Shankill and the Falls, tossing petrol bombs into houses as they went, and as they emerged into Divis Street the mobs clashed repeatedly. There was evidence later that fully armed B Specials had lent their support to the loyalist incursion. Fierce fighting also erupted at Ardoyne. Shots could still be heard as the dawn came on Friday 15 August. Including those who later died of their wounds, 6 people had been killed in Belfast; at least 12 factories had been destroyed; and over 100 houses had been wrecked and another 300 damaged by petrol bombs.[151] Most of those who had lost their homes were Catholics and they crowded into church halls in the heart of the

670

Falls with what belongings they had been able to take with them. Some took the train at Great Victoria Street for Dublin. Isolated Protestant and Catholic families moved out to make their way hurriedly to relatives and friends. Huge barricades sprang up, particularly in the Falls: telegraph poles, trees, thousands of paving stones, vans, trucks, cars and sixty corporation buses were used to construct them.[152]

The decision to bring troops into Belfast was only taken at midday on Friday 15 August and it was not until the late afternoon that the 2nd Battalion the Queen's Regiment moved into the city, followed by men of the Royal Regiment of Wales. Watching a great pall of smoke rising from a burning linen mill, one officer thought it all looked like a Second World War newsreel.[153] Residents on the Falls Road, preferring soldiers to armed police, plied them with cups of tea. Virtually no preparation had been made for sending the troops into the city and, with only a few exhausted and demoralised police officers to guide them, they took time to get their bearings. In any case not enough soldiers had been brought in to prevent further violence that night: virtually all the houses in Bombay Street in Clonard were destroyed; other houses in Brookfield Street were set on fire; and a Protestant rioter was killed in Ardoyne. Protestants – ignoring army warnings given on loud-hailers and the firing of CS gas canisters – made further determined petrol-bombing raids on Saturday night. Though one soldier was slightly injured by gunfire, the army kept to its instructions to use minimum force and did not fire a single round.

The violence of July and August had resulted in 10 deaths in the region; 154 people suffering gunshot wounds; 745 injured in other ways; around 300 treated at first-aid posts for the effects of CS gas; 16 factories gutted by fire; 170 homes destroyed and another 417 damaged; 60 Catholic-owned public houses attacked and 24 of them left in ruins; and in Derry one dairy alone losing 43,000 milk bottles during the three-day battle in the Bogside. Catholic-owned or occupied premises accounted for 83.5 per cent of the damage, estimated at £8 million.[154] These figures take no account of the rapid spread of fear and intimidation. The Scarman Tribunal, set up to investigate the disturbances of the summer of 1969, reported that in Belfast alone 1,820 families fled their homes during and immediately after these riots; 1,505 of these families were Catholic, making up more than 3 per cent of all Catholic households in the city.

Except for the middle-class suburbs, Belfast had become a war zone. Soldiers first blocked off streets with knife-rests and concertina wire; later, sensitive areas were separated by walls of corrugated iron bristling with barbed wire. By sending troops for active duty in Northern

Ireland, the Westminster government had made one of its most crucial military decisions since Suez.

'The honeymoon period between troops and local people is likely to be short lived. Indeed, it is probably at its height right now.'[155] The GOC, Lieutenant-General Sir Ian Freeland, gave this warning before television cameras soon after his men had moved into Belfast. Martial law had not been declared – the army was there to 'aid the civil power' by curbing violence, but otherwise it was up to the politicians to decide what to do next. Chichester-Clark met Wilson in London on 19 August and the two governments agreed to issue the 'Downing Street Declaration'. It affirmed that 'every citizen of Northern Ireland is entitled to the same equality of treatment and freedom from discrimination as obtains in the rest of the United Kingdom irrespective of political views or religion'; and, to reassure unionists, it reaffirmed 'that Northern Ireland should not cease to be part of the United Kingdom without the consent of the people of Northern Ireland ... The border is not an issue.'[156] No major political changes were envisaged, however, and no serious thought seems to have been given to invoking the 1920 Government of Ireland Act and restoring the functions of Stormont to Westminster.

The army had been put on active service in Northern Ireland as a last desperate measure; the number of soldiers deployed was strictly limited, and already the Westminster government was wondering how military disengagement might take place. Soldiers had been sent into the streets only because Chichester-Clark's request could not be refused: Richard Crossman, a member of Wilson's government, had gone 'through all the papers' to confirm that 'it was impossible to evade British responsibility if there was a civil war or widespread rioting'.[157] Accustomed to insulating itself from Northern Ireland's domestic problems, London was ill-prepared for the crisis that had broken in the summer of 1969. The Home Office had responsibility for overseeing the region's affairs but, with more than enough delicate issues to cope with in Britain, its ministers had shown extreme reluctance even to keep themselves informed. Crossman observed that the chancellor of the exchequer himself did not know 'the formula by which Northern Ireland gets its money ... I am longing to see whether now we shall get to the bottom of this very large and expensive secret.'[158] The memoirs of Crossman and others close to Wilson indicate that cabinet discussion on Northern Ireland was brief and often poorly informed. Wilson himself seems to have been most in favour of action. In May 1969 the defence minister, Denis Healey, reported in alarm to Crossman:

The P.M. was always demanding active intervention early on, with this crazy desire to go over there and take things over, that we side with the R.C.s and the Civil Rights movement against the government, though we know nothing at all about it.[159]

Wilson was clearly overruled by his colleagues and Healey's view that 'they must push Chichester-Clark only as far as he wanted to go' seems to have prevailed. Once the troops were sent in, few conditions were laid down in return for their use, as there was every intention of pulling them out as soon as possible. In public, nevertheless, the Westminster government gave the appearance of dealing with the crisis in a confident and energetic manner.

James Callaghan made up his mind to visit Northern Ireland to reassure the people there of his government's determination to tackle their problems. Some parts of the region were still in a state of virtual rebellion; these were known as 'no-go' areas, where the security forces did not dare to enter. 'Free Derry' and much of west Belfast behaved like revolutionary communes, with local people appointing their own law-and-order force and kangaroo courts.[160] Assuring politicians that soldiers could take over these areas in three hours but that it would take three years to get them out again, army officers patiently persuaded local defence committees to take down the barricades. In Derry, for example, the army convinced the Bogside Defence Association that burned-out vehicles were a hazard to traffic. There, the barricades were replaced by white lines, painted in person by Michael Canavan, and the troops took care not to cross them. Having toured troubled parts of Belfast on 27 August, Callaghan arrived in Derry the following day, where he left his army escort behind, crossed the white lines, and with difficulty made his way through the press of jostling people, some chanting protests about prison conditions. 'I can't stand this much longer,' Callaghan confided and Hume took him into a tiny house near Free Derry Corner. After drinking a cup of tea with the woman of the house, he climbed the narrow stairs and through a small bedroom window delivered a compelling speech by megaphone, recognising past wrongs and promising justice in the future.[161] His words were rapturously received and broadcast widely across the world. Callaghan was respectfully but more cautiously welcomed in Protestant districts and there the people were assured that the Union was safe in his government's hands. The home secretary's jaunty, avuncular tone exuded optimism and confidence, but in private he had forebodings about the future, as Crossman noted in his diary on 11 September: Callaghan said to him that

> life was very bleak ... there was no prospect of a solution. He had anticipated the honeymoon wouldn't last very long and it hadn't. The British troops were tired and were no longer popular and the terrible thing was that the only solutions would take ten years, if they would ever work at all.[162]

Callaghan's gloom may have been prompted by the realisation that he had been more successful in pleasing Catholics – who were now removing the last of the barricades – than Protestants. The Cameron report, the most authoritative condemnation of discrimination written up to then, was published on 12 September and, probably for the first time ever, long queues of eager purchasers formed outside Her Majesty's Stationery Office in Chichester Street, Belfast. Loyalist apprehension that the old system had gone for ever was sharply increased when Lord Hunt's recommendations on the policing of Northern Ireland were made public on Friday 10 October: the Ulster Special Constabulary was to be disbanded; the RUC was to be disarmed; and a new part-time force – later named the Ulster Defence Regiment – would be under the control of the GOC. Anthony Peacocke was replaced by Sir Arthur Young, then commissioner of the City of London police, under the new rank of chief constable.

For activists on the Shankill Road this was too much. On Saturday around 10 p.m. about three thousand loyalists advanced towards Unity Flats and fired upon police attempting to halt them, mortally wounding Constable Victor Arbuckle – the first policeman to be killed in the present Troubles. The 3rd Battalion the Light Infantry moved in and as the troops came under protracted rifle and automatic fire and showers of petrol bombs, the conflict almost matched that of 14 August in intensity; yet the army fired only twenty-six shots, killing two rioters with cool deliberation.[163] Next day, when Chichester-Clark made a television appeal for calm, he was expressing the view of most Protestants that the Shankill rioters had gone too far in opposing the Crown forces. The 'honeymoon period' had not yet come to an end: arms searches were carried out in the Shankill without retaliation and military police, followed soon after by unarmed RUC patrols, were able to enter the Falls and the Bogside without opposition. As the year 1969 drew to a close the region was at peace and many observers expressed high hopes about the future. On 29 December, however, the *Irish Press* reported a split within the IRA, in which dissidents had broken with the leadership and set up a new command: the Provisional IRA was born.

Immediately after the troops had been called in, Chichester-Clark stated that the disorders were brought on by the IRA and 'others determined to overthrow the state'. The RUC Special Branch did not agree:

> It would be absurd to say that the present situation has been brought about solely by the machinations of the Movement . . . the present condition in the streets has caught the IRA largely unprepared in the military sense . . . Reliable sources report a shortage of arms.

In a confidential document Scotland Yard confirmed that the IRA 'is not organised or equipped to play a significant independent role' within the Civil Rights Association.[164] In Belfast fewer than sixty men regarded themselves as IRA members and most of these were 'drop-outs after the border campaign for whom republicanism was now mainly a social event . . . providing the opportunity for drink and reminiscence'.[165] No arms training had taken place for years and in May 1969 the IRA's total arsenal in the city was a machine gun, a pistol, and some ammunition. A few more firearms were unearthed on the night of 14 August and IRA volunteers did fire shots into Cupar Street, Conway Street and Dover Street. Nevertheless, as Father Marcellus Gillespie informed the Scarman Tribunal, angry residents in Ardoyne at a meeting on Sunday 17 August had demanded guns for their defence and castigated the IRA as the 'I Ran Away'.[166]

Cathal Goulding had been steering his movement towards quasi-Marxist political activity and away from violence. Conservative traditionalists, particularly in Belfast, had no liking for this sophisticated radicalism: one such was Joe Cahill who said, when he saw the welcome given to British soldiers on the Falls Road, 'It brought tears to my eyes. Here was the enemy, the instigators of what had just happened in the country and the people were collaborating with them.'[167] Seán Mac Stiofáin agreed. This British-born hardliner, who had been imprisoned after a failed arms raid in Essex in 1951 and was now the IRA director of intelligence, led the coup that split the movement in December 1969. The breakaway group, as an interim arrangement, elected a provisional executive just before Christmas, with Mac Stiofáin as chief of staff of the Provisional IRA and Ruairí Ó Brádaigh as president of Provisional Sinn Féin, its political counterpart. Ten months later they stated that this temporary period was over, but the names Provisional Sinn Féin and Provisional IRA have remained with them ever since.[168]

The Provisionals swiftly established themselves in Catholic housing estates in Belfast, though for the present the old organisation – now

675

known as the Official IRA – kept its hold in the lower Falls and in the Markets area of the city. As yet, support for both wings of the movement was on a small scale and it took time for the Provisionals to extend their organisation outside Belfast. In some respects the Provisional IRA harked back to the old Ribbon traditions: it was frankly sectarian; its tactics were violent; and it was conservative – Mac Stiofáin, for example, refused to smuggle condoms south of the border for making bomb detonators because he considered them immoral objects. The Provisionals' hostility to Marxist socialism appealed strongly to some southern businessmen keen to help fellow Catholics in the North and some of their cash was to help solve the organisation's most immediate problem: shortage of arms.

Dublin had been even more unprepared than London for the events of August 1969. Lynch's broadcast – widely interpreted by both Catholics and Protestants in Northern Ireland as the prelude to intervention – was in reality a coded message to the British government that it was time to send in its troops. The taoiseach knew perfectly well that the republic's armed forces were incapable of defending national territory, let alone sending armed columns to Catholic enclaves in Derry and Belfast. He correctly assessed southern public opinion: the republic should stay out of the North's imbroglio and yet something ought to be done to bring relief to northern Catholics. Irish Army field hospitals and refugee camps were set up along the border and the Dáil agreed to establish a fund of £100,000, principally to help Catholics driven out of their homes. Lynch's position was a difficult one: he had just fought a general election in June and faced attempts by two of his ministers, Charles Haughey and Neil Blaney, to oust him. Both Haughey and Blaney dominated a Dáil cabinet committee monitoring the northern crisis and, together with Kevin Boland, minister for local government, they formed a powerful caucus of northern men with connections eager for intervention. Haughey had not forgotten how his parents had been forced out of Swatragh, Co. Londonderry, in the 1920s. In the recent election Blaney had topped the poll in the three-member constituency of North East Donegal and he was a formidable figure in Fianna Fáil. In the *Observer* Mary Holland described his campaigning style:

In the sleepy country towns of County Donegal the Minister of Agriculture, Neil Blaney, roars at his constituents. Wearing dark glasses and chewing gum, he blazes into town on a trail of bonfires, the prototype of every Irish mother's son who crossed the Atlantic to help build Tammany Hall.[169]

During the violence of August 1969, Blaney pressed hard in cabinet to send the Irish Army across the border, though it was not until December that he stated in Letterkenny that 'no one has the right to assert that force is ruled out' as a way of ending partition.

On 6 May 1970 Lynch dismissed Blaney and Haughey from his government and on 28 May both men were charged with conspiracy to smuggle arms. Blaney was discharged in July on the grounds that there was no case to answer and a jury found Haughey not guilty in October. In the course of the 'arms scandal' the Provisional IRA leader in Belfast, John Kelly, declared: 'We did not ask for blankets or feeding bottles. We asked for guns – and no one from Lynch down refused that request or told us that this was contrary to Government policy.'[170] Controversy still rages over the extent to which the Fianna Fáil government was embroiled, but there is no doubt that southern money played a crucial role in putting the Provisionals on their feet. Haughey authorised a grant of £100,000 to the Irish Red Cross, but since that organisation had no standing in Northern Ireland, the money was placed in the Clones branch of the Bank of Ireland and more than £30,000 vanished to import arms for the Provisional IRA.[171] Irish-Americans also supplied cash and arms, including Armalite rifles capable, when folded, of being carried about in breakfast cereal packets.

During the first months of 1970 the Provisionals operated with caution, knowing that the great majority of Catholics still welcomed the presence of British troops and openly fraternised with them. If anything, the army encountered more difficulty with Protestants, resentful over reforms forced on Stormont by Westminster. Paratroopers dealt harshly with Shankill rioters during four nights in January when they attempted to break through to Catholic streets. Troops were equally tough when confronted by Catholic mobs. On Easter Tuesday, 31 March 1970, the Junior Orangemen had permission to march in Belfast. On their way out they marched along the Springfield Road without incident, but on their return that evening Catholic youths began to throw bottles at the bands and when about seventy soldiers of the Royal Scots Regiment arrived they were attacked with stones and petrol bombs. When rioting erupted in the Ballymurphy estate the following night, six hundred troops swept in with five Saracen armoured cars. Pelted with missiles, the army fired 104 canisters of CS gas and soldiers – with blackened faces and beating a tattoo on their riot shields – charged in, smashed doors, yelled abuse and seized as many youths as they could. The rioting continued for another two nights, during which shots were fired and Protestants invaded behind the soldiers. The Provisionals, who had actually tried to restrain the youths at first, steadily gained recruits after these riots and recognised the value of deliberately provoking confrontation with the army.[172]

'Grown men! Pathetic! Ridiculous!' Freeland once remarked on seeing traditional parades.[173] His pleas, and those of Sir Arthur Young, to ban all marches were ignored at Stormont. Yet interference with traditional parades also threatened to provoke trouble: when troops diverted Orange bands away from the Catholic enclave of Ardoyne in Belfast on 2 June, the response in the Shankill was two nights of severe rioting. When Orangemen did parade past Ardoyne on 27 June, rioting deteriorated into a gun battle in which three Protestants were killed. That same day across the Lagan loyalists converged on the isolated Catholic Short Strand district. The army said it did not have enough men to move in and made matters worse by sealing off bridges. The Provisionals opened fire from St Matthew's Church and killed or mortally wounded four Protestants, and lost one of their own men.[174] This episode convinced loyalists that the British Army was allowing armed republicans to operate with impunity and at the same time lent powerful weight to the Provisionals' argument that Catholics should look to their organisation for their defence.

The incident that did more than any other in 1970 to bring recruits to both factions of the IRA was the lower Falls curfew. On 3 July information was received at Springfield Road RUC station that a cache of arms could be found at 24 Balkan Street. Here police and troops quickly uncovered fifteen pistols, a rifle, a sub-machine-gun, explosives and ammunition. As a furious local protest developed, the order to use CS gas was given. At 10 p.m. Freeland imposed 'a movement restriction' on the lower Falls, sealed the area off for thirty-five hours, and set his men on a rigorous house-to-house search. The Official IRA now joined the war against the British Army and when its volunteers began shooting, troops fired 1,500 rounds and killed 3 people, including a press photographer. Another person was crushed to death by an armoured car. Though over a hundred weapons were found, the curfew was a political blunder, as the *Sunday Times* Insight Team concluded:

> 3–5 July 1970 did convert what was perhaps only an increasingly sullen Catholic acceptance of the Army into outright communal hostility . . . In the months that followed, recruitment to the Provisionals was dizzily fast: the movement grew from fewer than a hundred activists to nearly 800 by December.[175]

That summer the Provisionals launched a bombing campaign. Targets in July and August included the Elsinore Hotel in Belfast, the homes of Lord Justice Curran and the Reverend Martin Smyth MP, a customs station in Armagh, the Newcastle telephone exchange, the Newry bus depot, several electricity substations over the region, and a number of public houses. There had been a hundred explosions by mid-September but these were on a small scale, merely a foretaste of what was to come.

'WHAT A BLOODY AWFUL COUNTRY'

Nineteen seventy was a year of political realignment. The break-up of the Unionist Party was underlined on 17 April by Paisley's victory in Bannside in a by-election following O'Neill's elevation to the peerage. Liberal unionists, opposed to violence and dedicated to reform and reconciliation, formed the nucleus of the Alliance Party launched four days later. It took more protracted negotiation – much of it in the Co. Donegal village of Bunbeg – before the Social Democratic and Labour Party came into being on 21 August. Though it did have a few Protestant members, the SDLP at once became the principal voice of the Catholic minority. From the outset it had to resolve the tension between the socialism of its Belfast representatives, Paddy Devlin and its leader Gerry Fitt, and the liberal conservatism of the rest led by John Hume.

The Westminster general election on 18 June not only gave Paisley a new audience in London but also put the Conservatives in office, with Edward Heath as prime minister and Reginald Maudling as home secretary. Maudling was distinctly ill at ease in carrying out his Northern Ireland duties, as a senior army officer recalled:

> Reggie Maudling had no idea. He would never go out. We would get people to meet him and he would wander round and say things like 'Are you going to Ascot?' He was hopeless talking to community leaders on the streets. After his first visit here he sat in my office with his head in his hands and said, 'Oh, these bloody people! How are you going to deal with them?'[176]

He is infamous for the remark he made on his flight back to London after his first visit on 1 July, one version of which runs: 'For God's sake bring me a large Scotch. What a bloody awful country.'[177] Maudling once observed that the Government could do little more than make sure that there was no more than 'an acceptable level of violence' – a comment that drew indignant protest at the time, but seemed more realistic to many with the passing of every violent year.

Heath's government had no better idea than its Labour predecessor what should be done with Northern Ireland. The army was expected to continue its policing role under the direction of Chichester-Clark's government, but its freedom of action was increased by allowing it the power to veto proposals put by the Stormont-dominated Joint Security Committee.[178] The troops were having little success in curbing the activities of the Official and the Provisional IRA and yet were failing to win the support of loyalist militants: at the end of September 1970, for example, rioters on the Shankill Road besieged an army post for three days. Catholics, in turn, were in conflict with soldiers in Derry in October and in Ardoyne in November. Unionists at Stormont criticised Chichester-Clark for his willingness to accept reforms proposed by Westminster and for his unwillingness to adopt more rigorous action against the IRA. Paisley denounced Chichester-Clark's 'pussy-footing, fence-straddling' government and on 25 January 1971, 170 delegates to the Ulster Unionist Council called for their prime minister's resignation.[179]

Certainly the violence continued to grow. At the beginning of the year, while the disarmed RUC policed Protestant areas, troops on patrol in Ballymurphy were locked in conflict with Catholics during four days of furious rioting: buses were hijacked and burned; youths threw petrol bombs, grenades and nail bombs; and as soldiers and police searched house after house for arms with a heavy hand, they were assailed by missiles, which now included darts projected from catapults, steel ball bearings and bolts shot from crossbows.[180] Further riots broke out in the New Lodge Road, where, on 6 February 1971, Gunner Robert Curtis of the 94th Locating Regiment was killed by machine-gun fire – the first British soldier to die in Northern Ireland since the army had come 'in aid of the civil power'. Most of the communal violence in the early months was concentrated in Belfast but as the Provisionals' bombing campaign gathered pace it was spread across the region: a BBC transmitter was destroyed on Brougher Mountain near Enniskillen; a new bus station was wrecked in Newry; and in Holywood nine people were injured when a public house was blown up. On 10 March the Provisional IRA lured three Royal Highland Fusiliers to their deaths, each soldier shot in the back of the head at Ligoniel, overlooking Belfast.

The newly appointed GOC, Lieutenant-General Harry Tuzo, told his officers that there was nothing to be gained by 'pussy-footing around' and said that the army should be 'even-handed, resolute and tough'.[181] It was not tough enough for Unionists at Stormont who wanted more direct control over security. 'Just as bloody well they didn't! My God!' a senior officer remarked later to Desmond Hamill, ITN journalist and writer; 'They had no broad political ideas. They just wanted to smash the Catholics.'[182] Following a protest march by loyalist shipyard workers, Chichester-Clark sought stronger security measures in London, but he was turned down. On 20 March 1971 he resigned because, he said, there was 'no other way of bringing home to all concerned the realities of the present constitutional, political and security situation'.[183] Three days later, Brian Faulkner achieved his long-sought ambition by being elected prime minister. The most articulate of all Northern Ireland premiers, Faulkner had an air of professionalism which seemed to promise that the Government could curb the escalating violence.

That hope was not realised. Catholics remembered Faulkner's inflexible loyalism and participation in the provocative Longstone Road marches in the 1950s, and intensified their opposition to the Stormont regime. Bonfires were made of census forms and collectors were attacked.[184] By 7 May 1971 there had been 314 gelignite explosions in the region since 1969, 136 since the beginning of the year, and 33 since Easter Tuesday, 13 April. Incidents became more vicious. In a sectarian attack just before midday on Monday 24 May a bomb was thrown at the Mountainview Tavern on the Shankill Road; the explosion wrecked the building and injured several people severely. Next day a suitcase of gelignite was thrown into the reception area of the Springfield Road RUC–army command post in Belfast; twenty-two were injured, including a two-year-old child whose skull was fractured and a sergeant of the Parachute Regiment was killed as he attempted to protect children.[185] Once again the approach of the marching season raised political temperatures, though the Ancient Order of Hibernians called off its August parades to ease the burden placed on the security forces. While the tempo of the Provisional IRA bombings increased, rioting broke out all over Northern Ireland: on Sunday 13 June troops fought a fierce hand-to-hand battle with Orangemen in Dungiven and the Reverend William McCrea, Free Presbyterian minister of Magherafelt, was arrested; Protestant youths clashed with the police in Lisburn on 3 July; two young men were shot dead by soldiers in Derry on 8 July, where riots raged through most of the month; intercommunal violence broke out towards the end of the month in Newry and a few days later in Lurgan also; on Saturday 7 August, after a van driver had been shot dead and his passenger beaten by soldiers when his vehicle backfired outside Springfield Road command post, rioting erupted over much of west Belfast; and as the fighting spread to Ardoyne on Sunday 8 August, one soldier was shot dead and six others were injured by gunfire.[186] Next morning internment was imposed.

INTERNMENT

Just after 4 a.m. on Monday 9 August 1971 thousands of soldiers across Northern Ireland set out in arrest squads, each accompanied by an RUC

Special Branch officer to identify suspects. Even during those early hours women in many city enclaves were vigilant and banged dustbin lids on the pavements and blew whistles to warn of the approach of troops. Altogether 342 men were seized, formally rearrested at police stations and then taken to holding centres at Magilligan, Girdwood and Ballykinler. The operation was completed by 7.30 a.m. and, after two days, 104 men were released and the remainder of the suspects were transferred either to Crumlin Road gaol or the *Maidstone*, a prison ship moored at Belfast docks.[187]

Terrible violence followed. Even at breakfast time that fateful Monday columns of smoke rose up from burning barricades and gun battles had broken out in several places. Two soldiers and eight civilians were killed; in Belfast Protestant families fled from Ardoyne, some setting fire to about one hundred evacuated houses; Catholics fled from their homes in streets near the Crumlin Road. Rioting and shooting continued almost without ceasing and spread to Derry, Strabane, Armagh and Newry, where shops and factories were burned. Faulkner announced at 11.15 a.m. that his government was 'quite simply at war with the terrorist'.[188] A month earlier the SDLP had withdrawn from Stormont when it was refused an inquiry into the shooting dead of the two young men by soldiers in Derry on 8 July. Now it joined with Nationalists and Republican Labour representatives at a meeting later that day in Dungannon and called for the withholding of all rent and rates as a protest against internment. In Belfast, while a pall of smoke hung over the city from barricades of burning buses, trucks and cars, the Provisional IRA presented some of their best-known leaders at a secret press conference.[189]

Internment was entirely one-sided. No attempt was made to arrest loyalist suspects despite the UVF's record of violence. A very few Protestants were arrested, including John McGuffin and Major Bunting's son Ronald, but they were civil rights activists. There was not a single person on the army's list of 452 names who was not an anti-partitionist. Internment was a major blunder if only because it failed to bring about the seizure of the leading members of the Provisional IRA. The army, which had advised Faulkner not to take this drastic step, simply lacked the necessary information. The RUC, still demoralised since August 1969, had failed to recognise the rise of a completely new generation of republican militants. Police intelligence was clearly out of date: most of those taken were members of the Official IRA, many of them inactive; and several included on the list were merely non-violent critics of Faulkner's government. John McGuffin reckoned that of 160 men held in Crumlin Road gaol, no more than

80 'had anything to do with the IRA, and of these only four were senior officers (none of them the top men)'. One of those interned was Liam Mulholland, aged seventy-seven, who had been previously imprisoned in 1929.[190]

By electing Faulkner prime minister the Unionist Party had signalled its determination to have internment but it could not be imposed until the Westminster government had given its assent. Heath became known for his 'U-turns', notably on incomes policy, and now – with the approval of his advisers Sir John Hunt, the newspaper proprietor Cecil King, and even James Callaghan – he decided to allow Faulkner to make his gamble. From the very first day it became clear that the gamble had failed. The second day, Tuesday 10 August 1971, was the most violent since August 1969: 11 people were killed in Belfast alone, including Father Hugh Mullan, shot while administering the last rites to an injured man at Ballymurphy; about 240 houses at Farringdon Gardens, Velsheda Park and Cranbrook Park in Ardoyne were destroyed by fire; a member of the Ulster Defence Regiment was shot dead on the Tyrone–Donegal border; and Derry experienced protracted rioting as more than 30 barricades were put up in the Creggan and the Bogside. During the month of August there were thirty-five violent deaths and around one hundred explosions. About seven thousand Catholics sought refuge in Dublin and in Irish Army camps and several hundred Protestants moved to Liverpool for safety.

As violence intensified, fear spread like a plague. Richard Black, Francis Pinter and Bob Ovary made a study of residential displacement in Belfast during the first three weeks following the introduction of internment. 'The total number of movements for which we could account for both origin and destination was 2,100', they concluded in their report (entitled *Flight*), though they added that 'new information is still coming in'. The report observed:

> The nature of the movement of population this August has differed greatly from the major upheaval which unsettled the Belfast community in August 1969 . . . On this occasion the Army 'Peace Line' dividing the strongly segregated areas appears to have been effective at least in preventing further significant dislocation of population, and the major upheaval has transferred to the mixed areas which were formerly thought to serve as 'buffer zones' guaranteeing stability.

It added that this 're-sorting of mixed areas into segregated areas . . . is an extremely ominous development and shows no sign of being arrested in the immediate future'.[191] In this three-week period more than one in every hundred families in Belfast were forced to move – intimidation, fear of intimidation, and the destruction of homes were the reasons given for moving. Other families left to get away from constant street gun battles and an uncounted number of families had burned or wrecked their homes as they left to prevent 'the other side' moving in. About 2 per cent of the 45,000 Catholic households in Belfast and 0.5 per cent of 135,000 Protestant households were displaced. Altogether 60 per cent of the movements were made by Catholic families and 40 per cent by Protestant families. In short, this was the biggest enforced movement of population in Europe since 1945.

Catholic fury, maintained by continuing arrests, was inflamed further by reports of the ill-treatment of suspects. In apparently well-authenticated accounts the public learned that internees had been punched, beaten with batons and forced to run over broken glass; that eleven men had been hooded, deprived of food, drink, sleep and toilet facilities, and beaten; that others had been blindfolded and thrown out of helicopters hovering just above the ground; and that at least one man had a cigarette stubbed out on the back of his neck. The report of a government inquiry, led by Sir Edmund Compton, was widely viewed as cover-up when it appeared on 16 November 1971. Its bland conclusions contrasted sharply with the mass of evidence gathered by the BBC programme *24 Hours*, the Association for Legal Justice, Amnesty International, and the *Sunday Times* Insight Team – a group of journalists who made further charges the following March that internees had also been subjected to electric shock treatment, sensory deprivation and hallucinogenic drugs. In addition, not enough time had been available to prepare adequate prisons for such a large number of suspects: conditions on the *Maidstone* and in the Second World War armed services camps of Magilligan and Long Kesh were extremely harsh by comparison with those in gaols in Britain, where inmates had been tried and convicted in open court. By mid-December 1971, 1,500 suspects had been arrested but nearly 1,000 had been released – a strong indication that internment was failing in its principal objective of locking up the leading activists of the IRA.[192] A serving officer in the 45 Commando Group Royal Marines went further by deploring the political impact of internment in an article he wrote for his regimental magazine:

> The British Army, as the instrument of internment, has become the object of Catholic animosity. Since that day the street battles, countless explosions, migrations from mixed areas and cold-blooded killings have done little to reassure us that internment would, by the removal of the gunner, provide a return to a semblance of law and order, a basis for a political solution to Ulster's problems. Ironically it appears to have produced the opposite effect . . .

It has, in fact, increased terrorist activity, perhaps boosted IRA recruitment, polarised further the Catholic and Protestant communities and reduced the ranks of the much needed Catholic moderates. In a worsening situation it is difficult to imagine a solution.[193]

Angered by the Provisional IRA's ability to wage its bloody and destructive campaign, loyalists demanded stronger measures. At a huge meeting in Victoria Park in Belfast on 6 September 1971, Paisley called for the formation of a 'third force' – similar in character to the Special Constabulary – to supplement the efforts of the army and the RUC. At the end of the month he launched the Democratic Unionist Party to represent those Protestants dissatisfied with what he considered to be the weakness of the Unionist government. During the same month, the Ulster Defence Association was formed as a loyalist paramilitary organisation in Protestant working-class districts. The turmoil of these years produced a bewildering array of organisations and parties, with a confusing clutch of acronyms and abbreviations to match; many were ephemeral, but the DUP and the UDA proved to be enduring.

The Provisionals lashed out against internment with a ruthless offensive, particularly in Belfast. Every night the city reverberated to sharp sounds of rifle and automatic fire, and even in the suburbs windows rattled with the shock waves of explosions. During August 1971 there were 131 bomb attacks, 196 in September and 117 in October. It seemed that the Provisional IRA was making a concerted attempt to destroy Northern Ireland's economy, with the short-term aim of drawing the security forces away from Catholic enclaves and the long-term objective of forcing Britain to abandon the region. Victorian buildings, near to the end of their life span, collapsed easily and burned fiercely but the glass of new office blocks could be replaced. Even when carried on over several years, the bombing campaign did not cause devastation equal to that brought about by the 1941 blitz. The Provisionals gathered growing support in the ghettoes, but that did not mean they won the backing of a majority of Catholics, alienated though most of them were. Many agreed with Cardinal William Conway when he asked on 12 September: 'Who wanted to bomb a million Protestants into a United Ireland?'[194] The loss of innocent lives caused widespread revulsion, even amongst those who sympathised with the Provisionals' political aims. Atrocities included a bomb on 25 August at the Electricity Board's central office, which killed one person and maimed sixteen others; an explosion at the Four Step Inn on the Shankill Road on 29 September which killed two and injured twenty; and the bombing of the Red Lion restaurant on the Ormeau Road in Belfast on 2 November, which killed three people and left thirty-six injured.

The violence showed no sign of abating as 1971 drew to a close. During the four months before internment four soldiers and four civilians had been killed; but over the four months that followed seventy-three civilians, thirty soldiers and eleven policemen had lost their lives in the ensuing violence.[195] The explosion in McGurk's public house in Belfast on 4 December was the most horrific single incident of the year. Fifteen people were killed. By the light of arc lamps surgeons treated the injured in the open; gas escaping from fractured pipes flamed in the rubble as all through the night the dead and mutilated were uncovered brick by brick; and rescue operations were hampered as nearby the army came under fire and rival crowds fought in the darkness. The bomb had been placed by loyalist paramilitaries. On 11 December an explosion at a Shankill Road furniture store, placed by republican paramilitaries, killed two children and two adults; the surgeon who certified the deaths of the children recalled the scene in the mortuary: 'I remember standing there with two policemen. And we cried our eyes out.'[196]

The prospects for 1972 looked bleak indeed.

'THE ARMY RAN AMOK THAT DAY': BLOODY SUNDAY, 30 JANUARY 1972

'If it is true that the darkest hour precedes the dawn,' a *Belfast Telegraph* editorial observed on 1 January, 'then Northern Ireland may hope for streaks of light in the sky in 1972.' It continued:

> At times the year past could hardly have seemed worse. The turning-point must come soon . . . This is the year of decision, when Ulster must decide if it is to be peace or war, a hope of progress or the prospect of a steep descent into the morass.[197]

Nearly six months had passed since the imposition of internment and in the wake of the violence following it feelings were running too high to give Northern Ireland the respite it desperately needed. 'I say to Maudling: Why the hell should we talk to you?' Austin Currie declared at an anti-internment rally in Belfast on 2 January, adding: 'We are winning and you are not.' Two days later in an interview in *The Times* Faulkner predicted a Protestant backlash 'the like of which has never been seen or envisaged'.[198] On Saturday 22 January a fleet of hired buses picked up civil rights demonstrators behind the Guildhall in Derry and left them off at the Oasis Ballroom at Magilligan. From there they walked over the dunes and along the strand to the internment camp, and after Hume had argued with a senior army officer about the right to demonstrate, troops in full view of the television cameras drove back the protesters with baton charges and canisters of CS gas.[199] The soldiers were men of the 1st Battalion the

Parachute Regiment, recently drafted in to strengthen units already in Derry – an ominous sign of a more pugnacious approach being adopted by the army.

On Sunday 30 January troops on Derry's walls watched with mounting anxiety several hundred people gather in the Creggan estate. In defiance of a government ban the Civil Rights Association was about to lead a mass protest against internment into Guildhall Square. Over the past fortnight the Provisional IRA had fired 319 rounds at the security forces, killing two soldiers and wounding two others, in 80 shooting incidents in the city; 84 nail bombs had been thrown; and for months riot-hardened youths had been battling nightly with troops. District Inspector Frank Lagan, one of the most senior Catholics in the RUC, had his own anxieties that afternoon: for long he had persuaded the army to avoid provocation as far as possible in an attempt to prevent the alienation of the vast majority in the city; and now Major-General Robert Ford, commander land forces Northern Ireland, planned to teach a lesson to the 'YDHs' – Young Derry Hooligans – by sending in a snatch unit of paratroopers at the close of the march.[200]

By the time the marchers had passed the Bogside they numbered at least fifteen thousand and soon the sprawling phalanx was funnelled into the route to the city centre. At the bottom of William Street the army sealed off the approach to the Guildhall and the organisers began to implement their contingency plan to lead the marchers to Free Derry Corner. With growing ferocity Catholic youths pelted the soldiers at the army's barricade with a continuous rain of missiles. 'The Paras want to go in,' an officer reported to Brigadier Pat MacLellan. 'For Heaven's sake!' Lagan interrupted, 'hold them until we're satisfied that the marchers and rioters are well dispersed.' MacLellan took Lagan's advice and did not give the order. Soldiers fired CS canisters and rubber bullets at the youths. A few minutes after 4 p.m. MacLellan said gently to Lagan: 'I'm sorry, but the Paras have gone in.' Clearly he had been overruled by Ford.[201]

Then the killing began. People on the march were certain the first shots were fired by the army; troops, on the other hand, said they came under fire as they moved forward to make arrests. Whatever the truth of the matter, there is no doubt that men of the Parachute Regiment continued shooting, firing 108 rounds, injuring thirteen, including one woman, and killing thirteen men, seven of them under nineteen years of age. 'My God, these soldiers are going to shoot us all,' Dr Raymond McClean thought as he moved from one casualty to the next, most of whom were dead or dying.[202] Father Edward Daly, a priest from the Bogside who later became bishop of Derry, was running when he saw 'a young boy laughing at me. I'm not a very graceful runner.' Then, he continued:

> The next thing he suddenly gasped and threw his hands up in the air and fell on his face . . . He asked me, 'Am I going to die?' and I said 'No', but I administered the last rites. The gunfire started up again and a bullet struck quite close to me . . . I can remember him holding my hand and squeezing it. We all wept . . . We got him to the top of the street. I kneeled beside him and told him, 'Look son, we've got you out.' But he was dead. He was very youthful looking, just in his seventeenth year but he only looked about twelve . . . He had a baby face.[203]

Lord Widgery, who headed the official inquiry, concluded that some of the shooting 'had bordered on the reckless'. One army officer recalled that a section of the Parachute Regiment 'quite frankly, lost control. For goodness sake, you could hear their CO bellowing at them to cease firing, and only to fire aimed shots at actual targets.' The Derry coroner, Hubert O'Neill, noted that many of the victims were shot in the back and made this condemnation at the close of the official inquest:

> It strikes me that the Army ran amok that day and shot without thinking. They were shooting innocent people . . . I say it without reservation – it was sheer, unadulterated murder.[204]

The Catholics of Derry and people all over Ireland had already come to the same conclusion before the day was over. Next day there were angry and violent protests throughout Northern Ireland; in the Commons Bernadette Devlin pulled Maudling's hair and slapped his face; the taoiseach announced a national day of mourning, saying that the shootings were 'unbelievably savage and inhuman'; and Hume said on RTE that many 'feel now it's a united Ireland or nothing. Alienation is pretty total.'[205] On 2 February thirty thousand people in Dublin marched to the British Embassy and burned it down.

The Official IRA carried its war to England on 22 February by bombing the officers' mess of the Parachute Regiment at Aldershot: five women working in the canteen, a Catholic padre and a gardener were killed. In Belfast the Abercorn restaurant was bombed without warning when it was crowded with shoppers on Saturday 4 March. Janet Bereen and Anne Owens were sitting almost on top of the bomb when it exploded. They were killed. Four people – Rosaleen and Jennifer McNern, Irene Arnold, and Jimmy Stewart – lost both legs. Rosaleen McNern's right arm was ripped off as well. At least 130 people were injured.[206] Ulster Vanguard, a new loyalist pressure group, expressed the anger of Protestants exasperated by the inability of the security forces to check republican terrorism. Some seventy thousand attended its rally in Belfast's Ormeau Park on 18 March, where its leader, William Craig, declared:

> We must build up a dossier of the men and women who are a menace to this country, because if and when the politicians fail us, it may be our job, to liquidate the enemy.[207]

Two days later a bomb exploded without warning in Donegall Street; it killed 2 policemen and 4 civilians, and more than 100 people were injured, 19 seriously.

'Look, let's face it,' a Stormont minister said in February to a *News Letter* journalist, 'Ted Heath regards us as his doorstep Cyprus. Don't be surprised by anything that happens – I won't.'[208] From the previous August the British prime minister had let Faulkner take control of security policy. Now he was convinced that Stormont was incapable of containing a situation rapidly going out of control. On 24 March Faulkner and his ministers were summoned to London where Heath bluntly told them of his plans to transfer control of security to Westminster, to appoint a Northern Ireland secretary of state and to end internment. As the Northern Ireland prime minister recalled:

> After some time it was becoming clear that Heath had not been making an opening bid to soften us up, but had made up his mind before he met us, and was presenting what amounted to an ultimatum.[209]

The Unionist government ministers were outraged at the transfer of the control of security and in particular of the RUC. On his return to Belfast Faulkner conferred with the rest of his cabinet and, as Heath expected, he telephoned immediately afterwards to tell him they were resigning. The British prime minister thereupon prorogued Stormont for a year and appointed William Whitelaw as secretary of state for Northern Ireland.

For just over fifty years Northern Ireland had been a self-governing part of the United Kingdom. Except for a violent beginning, nearly all of those years until 1969 had been so peaceful that Westminster felt able to leave the devolved administration largely to its own devices. Now after three years, during which Northern Ireland had been convulsed by violence, the British government found Unionist rule wanting. Heath suspended Stormont, but the twelve months of direct rule from Westminster extended to two decades and more as peace eluded Conservative and Labour governments alike.

15

DIRECT RULE

1972–1992

OVERVIEW

The parliament of Northern Ireland met for the last time on Tuesday 28 March 1972. Just after 2.35 p.m. in the Commons the adjournment motion was proposed by Nat Minford, the leader of the House. The public gallery was closed but members of the Press were there in force, including Henry Kelly, reporting for the *Irish Times*:

> For the Prime Minister, Mr Faulkner, the MPs stayed attentive, then they drifted off to restaurant or bar, room or lobby . . . Souvenir hunts took on a remarkable intensity. The day's order paper and the order paper that would have been taken, had direct rule not been imposed, were being passed round from MP to MP for signature. Even journalists were putting their names as mementoes on the turquoise-blue papers – such a familiar sight all over Stormont . . . But Stormont ended, quietly almost in anti-climax. In the restaurant a Unionist Senator looked towards a table of MPs and Ministers, 'Captains and Kings,' he muttered. Then he added, 'My foot.'[1]

A huge column of loyalists with their bands had converged on the majestic drive before Stormont. This was the second day of a protest strike that was interrupting power supplies, closing down businesses and stopping public transport all over the region. Tempestuous cheers greeted Faulkner and Craig, so recently estranged, when they appeared together on the balcony of the parliament buildings. The fear some had that Craig would announce a Vanguard coup was not realised and Faulkner urged restrained, dignified protest. Then the immense crowd of some one hundred thousand – a tenth of Northern Ireland's Protestant population – dispersed with banners and Ulster flags flying.

The imposition of direct rule failed to stem the violence and year after year the population endured a wretched cycle of bombings, assassinations and shootings. Regiments that had arrived fresh from Aden and Cyprus in 1969 were still on active service in Northern Ireland twenty-three years later. Successive British administrations, rejecting the full integration of Northern Ireland into the rest of the United Kingdom, sought community government composed of both Protestant and Catholic elected representatives, but this search for agreement on power-sharing was in vain. In time London and Dublin learned to work in closer co-operation, a process which culminated in the Anglo-Irish Agreement of 1985. This, in turn, aroused intense Protestant indignation and in consequence a new loyalist coalition embarked on a course of non-cooperation with the British government. Unionists were furious that the Irish Republic had been given a consultative role for the first time in the region's affairs; militant republicans, however, were incensed that Dublin had given its clearest approval so far of Britain's right to govern in Northern Ireland, and therefore carried on their armed struggle.

Violence bred all too easily and fed upon itself in those Catholic and Protestant enclaves characterised by run-down housing, inadequate facilities, poor education and a lack of jobs. Almost at a stroke the international oil crisis of 1973–4 dealt a savage blow to the region's economy and set off a protracted decline, itself hastened by political instability and disorder. Economic collapse was averted only by Westminster's massive financial support. Though the gap between the poor and the well-off yawned dangerously wide in the 1980s, government aid ensured a continued rise in living standards and public housing of such a high quality that it was primarily responsible for impressive urban renewal. The border largely sealed off the counties of Donegal, Cavan and Monaghan from Northern Ireland's Troubles. The Irish Republic's economic revolution, which had begun during the premiership of Lemass, maintained its momentum well into the 1980s, and previously sleepy agricultural market centres such as Ballybofey, Carrickmacross and Killashandra became manufacturing and processing centres of some importance. Protestants just south and west of the border lived in far greater safety than those holding out on isolated farms in south Armagh, west Tyrone and much of Co. Fermanagh – an indication that, regardless of changing economic conditions, society in Northern Ireland remained dangerously polarised.

Until the end of the 1980s there was a widespread tendency to regard the Ulster 'problem' as being a curious and unique historical survival. The disintegration of the Soviet bloc at the other end of Europe indicated otherwise. There, the new-found freedom not only cleared the way for an open society and representative democracy but also allowed long-dormant ethnic rivalries to gush to the surface. As Armenians and Azeris, and Serbs and Croats, slaughtered each other it was plain they were impelled by atavistic urges remarkably parallel to those fuelling the Troubles in Northern Ireland. Indeed, as the civil conflicts of Yugoslavia and Nagorno-Karabakh extended in 1991–2, the bombings and sectarian killings in Northern Ireland ominously increased in tempo. Many despaired of ever finding a compromise solution capable of restoring peace to Ulster, a despair which brings to mind the words of an adviser to Henry VIII in the sixteenth century:

> It is a proverbe of old date, 'The pryde of Fraunce, the treason of Inglande, and the warre of Ireland, shalle never have ende.' Whiche proverbe, twycheing the warre of Irland, is lyke allwaye to contynue, withoute Godd sett in mennes brestes to fynde some newe remedye, that never was founde before. [2]

'THE WAR GOES ON': MARCH–JULY 1972

'Well it's such a new thing, it might just work,' Faulkner said of direct rule the day after his resignation.[3] The secretary of state, William Whitelaw, had already arrived, his previous experience of Northern Ireland being limited to a brief social visit and a golf outing. He was to face the most intractable problems with energy, great charm and seemingly inexhaustible patience. Catholics welcomed the fall of Stormont, and to build on that, Whitelaw planned to restrain the army, phase out internment and put out feelers to the IRA to negotiate an end to its campaign. To recover Protestant support he had to stop the violence and end Catholic no-go areas, where republican paramilitaries seemed in control. In addition to this daunting programme, he had to put in place a new government structure and prepare a fresh constitutional arrangement for the region.

Following the fall of Stormont, Provisional IRA leaders met in a seaside resort south of the border. Their conference ended 'on a note of complete unity' and they announced that 'the war goes on'.[4] The Provisionals' campaign gathered devastating momentum now that activists had gained more expertise and the deadly effectiveness of the car bomb was demonstrated. This destruction reached a climax on 14 April 1972 when thirty bombs were exploded all over Northern Ireland; on 1 May explosions at the Courtaulds plant in Carrickfergus killed one person and injured fifteen others; and on 10 May a bomb started a fire which destroyed the Belfast Co-operative store, the largest in the region. The Provisionals spread fear and anger as they stepped up their ruthless onslaught, and almost every parked vehicle became an object of suspicion.[5] The army recorded 1,223 engagements and shooting incidents and forty deaths during May 1972 – a death toll that was the highest for any month since the Troubles had begun three years before. Republican militants were running the risk of alienating their own ghetto strongholds, however – too many innocent people were being maimed and killed. In April, after the death of a local woman killed in a gun battle in Andersonstown started by the Provisionals, women approached Seán Mac Stiofáin and asked him to stop the violence; but the following day he told the Easter republican parade in Derry that a truce would mean that 'the fight of this generation will be lost and the suffering you have seen over the last three years will have to be endured again'. A meeting of the peace group Women Together was disrupted by the vice president of Provisional Sinn Féin, Maire Drumm, and her supporters. Nevertheless, in Belfast the Central Citizens' Defence Committee collected fifty thousand signatures for a petition calling on both wings of the IRA to stop the war, and on 14 April – a day of widespread destruction – a hundred women in Derry marched into the Creggan after a £30,000 payroll was seized from a shirt factory;[6] however, both the Provisionals and the Officials denied responsibility for the robbery.

The call for peace was ignored and during May further incidents increased revulsion. In particular, on 14 May a girl of thirteen was killed by crossfire in Ballymurphy; on 18 May a woman was hit by a sniper in Andersonstown and as she was being helped into an ambulance by troops, eight more shots were fired; on 26 May an explosion in Oxford Street killed a sixty-four-year-old woman; and on 29 May, in two separate incidents, a seventy-year-old woman was injured and a twelve-year-old girl on holiday from Liverpool was mortally wounded when the Provisional IRA shot at police in the Oldpark area. On 22 May Ranger William Best, a Catholic who had never served in Northern Ireland, was murdered in Derry when he was home on leave; next day a rally of some 1,500 met to call for an end to the violence.

On 29 May the Official IRA announced a ceasefire. Could Whitelaw persuade the Provisionals also to lay down their arms? He had removed the ban on marches, asked Lord Justice Diplock to recommend a new system of trying those charged with political offences, and released hundreds of internees. And in June, after a prolonged hunger strike in Belfast prison, Whitelaw granted 'special category status' to internees – a decision he later bitterly regretted – which absolved them from prison work, allowed them to wear their own clothes and to have extra visits and food parcels.[7] The problem was that this apparent appeasement of republicans stoked the fires of loyalist anger. Seeing that the army's 'softly, softly' approach allowed republican paramilitaries to create extensive no-go areas, the UDA erected barricades in Protestant districts of

Belfast and Derry and patrolled them with their hooded and armed volunteers. Loyalist militants responded to IRA terror with their own brand of terror: assassination. Murder gangs roamed the streets with the intention of killing Catholics, whether or not they were republican activists. This assassination campaign got under way in April and the random nature of the murders spread fear across the region. As so many lived in dread of a knock on the door in certain districts, more people again moved their homes. Sometimes Catholics were killed in a ritualistic practice known as 'rompering', in which victims were beaten up and tortured in a back room or garage before being shot. Virtually all of those murdered had no connections with the IRA. Thomas Madden, for example, was a middle-aged night watchman found dead with at least 150 stab wounds in his body.[8] The Provisionals, less fastidious than the Official IRA about sectarian murder, attempted to respond with their own campaign to kill Protestants. By the end of 1972 eighty-one Catholics and forty Protestants had been assassinated.

'I am in a public dialogue,' John Hume said to a BBC interviewer when asked if he was negotiating with the Provisionals. 'They hear what I'm saying.' With the apparent knowledge of Whitelaw, Hume met Provisional IRA leaders in the Creggan and in a Donegal town public house.[9] After protracted negotiation Gerry Adams and Dáithí Ó Conaill met the secretary of state's representatives on 20 June and two days later the Provisional IRA announced a ceasefire beginning at midnight on 26 June. Whitelaw was so delighted he 'literally jumped for joy, embracing Hume in a bear hug'.[10] The Provisionals fought on right up to the deadline: shooting continued for three days in the Suffolk area of Belfast; three soldiers were killed by mines in the Glenshane Pass on 24 June; and in the hours approaching midnight on 26 June, the Provisionals carried out armed robberies, detonated explosions all over the region and killed a policeman and two soldiers.

In Derry the Brandywell army post was dismantled and three barricades were taken down in the Bogside. Other barricades remained, however, and the UDA erected more of their own. On the first day of the ceasefire William Craig had announced that loyalists had no option but to go into Catholic no-go areas and 'clean out the IRA terrorists'.[11] Belfast, in particular, witnessed menacing parades of uniformed UDA men wearing hoods and carrying iron bars and clubs. Troops, including men of the Parachute Regiment, clashed repeatedly with Protestant youths organised in Tartan gangs in east Belfast. A dangerous confrontation was narrowly avoided on Monday 3 July when the UDA attempted to put up a permanent shield round Woodvale, close to the Shankill in west Belfast; vigilantes wearing masks used mechanical drills to break up the road surface before driving in steel girders. About fifty Catholic families would have been marooned inside this barricaded Protestant enclave and the army refused to allow the creation of this no-go area. Some eight thousand UDA men drew up in formation to defy the soldiers in Ainsworth Avenue. For hours they stood in the rain, and only after making a compromise arrangement with Major-General Robert Ford did they withdraw.[12] Both the security forces and unarmed UDA men would patrol the area.

On Friday 7 July a team of Provisional IRA negotiators was flown by helicopter from Derry to Aldergrove and from there in a Royal Air Force aircraft to London. Talks with Whitelaw took place in Cheyne Row, at the home of his junior minister, Paul Channon. While the secretary of state could accept some short-term demands, he could not agree to the Provisionals' insistence on an amnesty for all 'prisoners of war' and a British declaration that all troops would be pulled out of Northern Ireland within three years. Adams, in particular, seems to have felt duped by the British and he may have engineered the collapse of the ceasefire two days later.[13]

Protestant families had pulled out in fear from the mixed estate of Lenadoon near Andersonstown in west Belfast. The Northern Ireland Housing Executive, a new government agency, allocated the vacated houses to Catholic families. The UDA threatened to burn them down, and after several days of confrontation, the Provisionals gave the army an ultimatum to move in the Catholic families by 4 p.m. on Sunday 9 July. Very large angry crowds faced each other as the deadline approached, kept apart with difficulty by the army. As the UDA stood impassive behind the troops some three thousand Catholics hurled stones at the soldiers, who responded with rubber bullets and CS gas. Then the army rammed a furniture van when it refused to stop and very soon afterwards Provisional IRA snipers opened fire. The ceasefire had ended.

That weekend in Belfast ten people were killed, including a thirteen-year-old girl and a Catholic priest. The fighting was furious and on 18 July the hundredth British soldier to die on active service in Northern Ireland since 1969 was killed in Belfast. This new onslaught by the Provisionals was to reach a horrific climax on Friday 21 July.

'THERE WERE THE LACERATIONS. THERE WERE THE LIMBLESS. AND THERE WERE THE DEAD': BLOODY FRIDAY

In the first hour of Friday 21 July 1972 a twenty-one-year-old Catholic, Anthony Davidson of Clovelly Street in the Springfield area of

Belfast, answered a knock on his door. He was shot several times through the chest at point-blank range. He was the first to die that day, bringing the death toll from violence in Northern Ireland since 1969 to 454.

That morning, newspapers carried large public announcements detailing the introduction of traffic restrictions in Belfast city centre 'to afford greater security protection to all concerned'.[14] Before lunch time armed youths raided the Ballyhackamore post office and the York Street branch of the Bank of Ireland. The weather had been perfect since dawn, helping to draw people into the city centre to shop for the weekend. A succession of bomb scares started the confusion of the afternoon, with office workers, shop assistants and customers pouring into the streets. Two children ran into the Smithfield bus station and shouted that a bomb had been planted and that they had been told to give the warning. The depot had just been cleared when, at 2.10 p.m., a large bomb exploded in an enclosed yard there: over thirty buses were destroyed or damaged; part of the corrugated iron roof was thrown into the street; heavy metal doors, placed across the depot entrance after the last attack, were lifted off their hinges and hurled into the street; and houses in Samuel Street nearby suffered blast damage, some doors being blown in.

At 2.16 p.m. three men armed with sub-machine-guns carried a suitcase bomb into the Brookvale Hotel, off the Antrim Road; the building was completely destroyed. Seven minutes later a bomb placed on the platform of the York Road railway station blew off the roof – a passenger had spotted a suspect suitcase just in time to give the alert. At 2.45 p.m. a car bomb at Star Taxis on the Crumlin Road wrecked nearby tax offices and damaged prison warders' houses. So far the bombs had caused only a few slight injuries.

At 2.48 p.m. a bomb in a Volkswagen driven into the rear of Oxford Street bus station exploded. Two soldiers, who had just jumped out of their Land-Rover, were killed instantly. This explosion caused frightful carnage; in addition to the soldiers, four people, including a bus driver, were killed. The wrecked cafeteria and adjacent buildings blazed fiercely and firemen ignored warnings of other bombs close by to recover the bodies of the dead.[15] 'Police and troops carried plastic bags', the *Belfast Telegraph* reported, 'as they went about the gruesome task of collecting the mutilated bodies, parts of which were flung up to 30 yards away from the blast.'

Between 2.48 p.m. and 3.12 p.m. twelve more explosions reverberated in and around Belfast. At 3.15 p.m. a bomb in a hijacked vehicle exploded at the Cavehill Road shopping centre. No warning had been given. Maureen Walker described the horror of that moment to a *Belfast Telegraph* reporter

Oh God, there was flames, and then when they seemed to have died away there was nothing but only glass and blood. The people all around were confused and they screamed for their children. Somebody in the hairdressers was blown clean through the window.

Another woman who helped the injured saw 'people lying all over the pavements. There was blood everywhere. It seemed that all those injured were women and children.'[16] Three people were killed, one a mother of seven children. Another casualty was Stephen Parker, aged fourteen; his father, the Reverend Joseph Parker, rushed down to help the injured, not knowing that his own son had died in the blast.

Nine had been killed and at least 130 maimed by blasts that day in Belfast. Twenty bombs had been detonated in sixty-five minutes. As smoke, flames and debris shot up from each successive explosion, ambulances, fire engines and police Land-Rovers roared through the city streets, with sirens blaring. The ambulance and fire-control rooms were overwhelmed and, with buses destroyed, the railway lines blocked and several streets cut off, all routes out of the city centre were filled with people rushing homewards on foot. On that still, but now overcast, afternoon exhaust fumes from vehicles caught in traffic jams added to the pall hanging over many parts of Belfast. Only the hard-won experience of the city's hospitals prevented the death toll rising higher than it did.[17] At the Royal Victoria Hospital a *Belfast Telegraph* reporter saw the fleets of ambulances come in:

There were the lacerations. There were the limbless. And there were the dead – men, women and children, their faces covered in blood, with others mutilated beyond recognition.[18]

Many watching the television news reports were reduced to tears by horrifying pictures of firemen and rescue workers, as Alf McCreary wrote in *Survivors*, 'scraping up the remains of human beings into plastic bags, like lumps of red, jellied meat from the pavement'.[19]

That day of violence was not yet over. Three large bombs were detonated in Derry and by midnight there had been thirty-nine explosions in Northern Ireland. In Belfast there was much shooting as the army intensified its search for arms and explosives in the vicinity of Shaw's Road. At Ardoyne over nine hundred shots were fired at troops between 11.30 p.m. and 1.15 a.m., and soldiers claimed to have seen a total of twelve gunmen. In a fierce gun battle between troops and the Provisionals in the Markets area four people were hit by stray bullets and one gunman was killed. In a stolen car at Forth River Road a man and a woman were found both shot through the head. At Cliftonpark Avenue a man was shot from a passing car, and at first light a man's body was discovered on waste ground at Liffey Street in the Oldpark area.[20]

During the final hours of what already was being called Bloody Friday, Whitelaw was in conference with his security chiefs at Stormont. Senior army officers insisted that now was the time to get rid of no-go areas. At 1 a.m. Whitelaw, head in hand, agreed that this must be done and that he would ask the cabinet for approval. On 23 July the Dublin newspaper the *Sunday Independent* made this judgement in an editorial:

> There is a black sin in the face of Irish Republicanism today that will never be erased. Murder now lies at the feet of the Irish nation and there is no gainsaying that fact.[21]

The wave of horror and disgust running through Catholic Ireland, north and south, offered the British government the unique opportunity to implement a plan long-prepared by army chiefs: Operation Motorman.

OPERATION MOTORMAN AND AFTER

For thirty-six hours during Saturday and Sunday 29 and 30 July 1972 huge C130 transport aircraft touched down at Aldergrove every five minutes. From them seven additional battalions with their support units climbed out to bring the army's strength in Northern Ireland to twenty-two thousand, the highest since 1922. A VC10 jet arrived on a special flight from Hong Kong with a cargo of riot helmets and shields. During the first hours of Monday 31 July there was some anxious swearing as the low tide in Lough Foyle temporarily delayed the landing of AVREs, specialist tanks originally designed to deal with German pillboxes in Normandy in 1944. About one hundred armoured personnel carriers, including Saracens and Humbers, had already been brought in. The biggest British military operation since the 1956 Suez crisis was about to begin.

At first light, twenty-six companies surrounded the Bogside and the Creggan estate. Heath had anticipated a thousand casualties, but Major-General Ford expected only 'as many as 100'. The leading AVRE demolished the first barricade without difficulty but then took a wrong turn and ruined someone's front garden in turning round. Virtually no resistance was offered and by breakfast time people found the army occupying blocks of flats, parish halls, schools and football grounds.[22] The secretary of state gave a broadcast to explain that Operation

Motorman was designed to 'remove the capacity of the IRA to create terror and violence'.[23] In fact, the army was careful to tear down barricades in Protestant no-go areas as well – the lesson of internment had been learned – and the Parachute Regiment spearheaded the occupation of loyalist enclaves. Catholic no-go areas were taken over in Belfast with as much ease as in Derry. Two people had died in shooting incidents in Derry but otherwise army commanders could congratulate themselves that Operation Motorman had been an untrammelled success.

While these traumatic events had been unfolding in urban areas, there was tragedy in the village of Claudy in Co. Londonderry. Three large car bombs sent in by the Provisional IRA devastated the main street and left ten people dead or mortally wounded, bringing the number killed in Northern Ireland during the month of July 1972 to a total of ninety-five, the highest in any month of the current Troubles.[24] The widespread condemnation following the atrocity in Claudy helped to ensure little or no resistance as the army settled in. This time the troops prepared to stay for some time: in Andersonstown and the surrounding area, for example, there were no fewer than sixteen fortified army posts and work began on four large forts, soon given names such as 'Silver City' and 'Fort Apache' by local people – loyalists, in turn, described the occupied enclaves as 'Apache country'.[25] No longer able to store explosives, patrol with firearms or prime bombs with such impunity as before, the Provisionals had suffered a severe military reverse. They were not extinguished, however, and – like loyalist paramilitaries – kept their organisation going in a network of shebeens that had replaced public houses destroyed in 1969. But for the present the Provisionals were eclipsed by the constitutional politicians as they moved towards a unique compromise experiment: a power-sharing devolutionary government.

IN SEARCH OF A POLITICAL SOLUTION

By breaking their ceasefire the Provisionals lost their best opportunity in two decades to negotiate terms for the people they claimed to protect, and their ruthless bombing campaign gave the SDLP the opportunity to climb down from its unproductive abstentionist position. Whitelaw was now searching in earnest for a constitutional settlement. Unionists, the Northern Ireland Labour Party and the Alliance Party attended the secretary of state's first attempt at round-table talks in Darlington, Co. Durham, at the end of September 1972. The SDLP, keeping to its position of 'no talks while internment lasts', refused to go, but soon afterwards

Hume told his party that 'the time has come for us to come out and say frankly that we are prepared to talk to anyone and to talk now'.[26] The British government's discussion paper on the future of Northern Ireland agreeably surprised both the SDLP and the Irish premier, Jack Lynch: it did reaffirm Attlee's guarantee that the region would remain part of the United Kingdom as long as the majority there wished it but it also stated that

> any new arrangements for Northern Ireland should, whilst meeting the wishes of Northern Ireland and Great Britain, be, so far as possible, acceptable to and accepted by the Republic of Ireland.[27]

The SDLP had already broken the ice by meeting Heath at Chequers and on 24 November Lynch met the prime minister in London to signal his approval.

During Operation Motorman, army chiefs had been furious with Whitelaw for making his explanatory broadcast early enough to tip off IRA leaders, most of whom managed to slip across the border to avoid arrest. The republic remained an invaluable refuge but very soon it was no longer the haven for paramilitary republicans it had been since 1969. On 6 October the Fianna Fáil government closed down the Dublin headquarters of Provisional Sinn Féin; Maire Drumm was arrested on 5 November; on 19 November Mac Stiofáin was sentenced to six months' imprisonment; the governing body of RTE was dissolved on 24 November for defying a government directive not to interview Mac Stiofáin; and on 1 December, when two bombs planted by loyalists in Dublin killed two people and injured at least eighty others, the Dáil voted to give the Government special emergency powers: from now on suspected terrorists could be convicted on the evidence of a senior police officer given before three judges in a court without a jury.[28] Ruairí Ó Brádaigh, president of Provisional Sinn Féin, was arrested on 29 December and held under this legislation. Martin McGuinness, the Derry Provisional IRA commander, was captured near Ballybofey by gardaí on the last day of 1972.

The final months of 1972 seemed to be fulfilling Faulkner's prophecy of a Protestant backlash. The authorities were incapable of halting the spate of gruesome sectarian murders, particularly in Belfast, and talk of political compromise helped to provoke clashes between loyalists and the security forces. Incidents included a gun battle in the Shankill on 7 September, during which paratroopers shot dead two civilians; the shooting dead of a UVF man on 16 September in Larne by the RUC, again permitted to carry arms; Tartan gang attacks on Catholic property in east Belfast on 11 October, followed by fierce rioting there next day when a man and a fifteen-year-old boy were run down and killed by army Saracens; and protracted violence and shooting at troops in several parts of Belfast on 17 October. Occasionally militant loyalists carried their campaign over the border, killing two teenagers with a bomb in Co. Cavan on 28 December, for example, and murdering a young engaged couple in Co. Donegal on 31 December. In Northern Ireland the death toll for the year remains the worst in two decades of violence: 103 soldiers, 41 police and UDR and 323 civilians, 121 of whom were classed as sectarian assassinations. A further wave of murders in January 1973 led to the internment of loyalists for the first time in fifty years on 3 February. That weekend thirteen people were shot or assassinated during savage rioting over much of Belfast, and a loyalist strike on 7 February was accompanied by another seven deaths, including a fireman killed by a UDA sniper.[29] Meanwhile, the Provisional IRA, in spite of serious reverses, remained a formidable terrorist force. The need for decisive political action by the Government had rarely seemed more urgent.

The implementation of the Conservative government's political solution began on 8 March when the citizens of Northern Ireland voted in a referendum to decide whether or not the region should remain in the United Kingdom. On the advice of their political representatives, nearly all Catholics chose to boycott this 'border poll'. Altogether 97.8 per cent of voters – 57 per cent of the electorate – gave a decisive verdict in favour of maintaining the Union.[30] Twelve days later the new constitutional arrangements were published in a White Paper. Northern Ireland was to have a form of self-government restored to it: an assembly elected by proportional representation, with an executive having the power to legislate on transferred matters. As before, Westminster would remain responsible for excepted matters but would hand over minimum reserved matters later if the experiment was judged a success. This devolutionary scheme was dependent on two conditions: the secretary of state had to be satisfied that the executive had widespread support throughout the community, that is, power had to be shared between Protestant and Catholic representatives; and arrangements had to be made for a Council of Ireland, linking Belfast, London and Dublin on matters of common interest to both parts of the country. The bipartisan approach at Westminster, by which government and opposition co-operated to adopt a common policy on Northern Ireland, ensured that this constitutional package rapidly became law.[31]

'We neither reject it totally nor do we accept it totally,' Faulkner observed cautiously of the devolutionary arrangements.[32] Demanding the restoration in full of the old Stormont regime, Craig, Paisley, the Grand Orange Lodge, the UDA and other traditional loyalists rejected the scheme outright. The first test came in the local government elections of 30 May 1973, in which the O'Neill reforms were combined with the reintroduction of proportional representation. In spite of a confusing kaleidoscope of party labels, Unionist candidates (particularly those opposed to power-sharing) performed impressively, leaving anti-partitionists in full control in only one council, Newry and Mourne. The second test followed in the assembly elections on 28 June 1973. Whitelaw's hope that the cross-community parties would do well was completely dashed: out of a total of seventy-eight seats the Alliance captured eight and the Northern Ireland Labour Party only one. Unionists opposed to power-sharing – principally Unofficial Unionists, Vanguard and DUP – numbered twenty-six, leaving the Official Unionists under Faulkner's leadership with twenty-four seats.[33] To what extent the Official Unionists backed Whitelaw's scheme and were prepared to remain loyal to Faulkner was decidedly uncertain. Altogether the moderate centre won 12 per cent of the vote, Official Unionists 29 per cent, anti-White Paper candidates 31 per cent and the SDLP 22 per cent.[34] Whitelaw seized on the outstanding performance of the SDLP, which, with nineteen members elected, was now without question the voice of Northern Ireland's Catholics. He saw here the opportunity to isolate IRA activists in the minority community by attempting to meet the demands of the SDLP, a party unequivocally opposed to violent remedies. In doing so, the secretary of state gravely underestimated the strength and determination of those assembly deputies who were hostile to his constitutional solution. In particular, he and the staff in the Northern Ireland Office assumed that divisions in the loyalist camp signalled weakness and misinterpreted the anti-British stand of some Unionist deputies as a sign that they could be won over to co-operation with the SDLP in time.

In February 1973 Fianna Fáil was defeated in a general election for the first time since 1954 and the formation of a Fine Gael–Labour coalition augured well for the success of Whitelaw's plans. In its election manifesto Fine Gael had stressed the need 'to promote a peaceful solution in the north' by encouraging power-sharing and irredentist claims would certainly not be pressed by the new taoiseach, Liam Cosgrave, son of the Free State pro-treaty premier.[35] Garret FitzGerald was the perfect foil to the aggressively uncharismatic and near-monosyllabic Cosgrave. Appointed foreign affairs minister and soon known to British and Irish journalists alike as 'Garret the Good' and 'Garrulous FitzGerald', he quickly won the respect of Westminster politicians by his tireless concern for the welfare of everyone in Northern Ireland, helped by the fact that his mother was a Co. Down Presbyterian. The most prominent Labour member of the Government was Conor Cruise O'Brien, descended on both sides of his family from the Irish Parliamentary Party establishment; 'the Cruiser' was an internationally respected intellectual heavyweight who was to ruffle many a nationalist feather by warning of the dire consequences of ignoring loyalist susceptibilities.

Early in July 1973 Cosgrave flew to London and urged Heath to move forward with caution. In an address to Conservatives he even went so far as to say that any pressure for movement on the issue of partition 'would dangerously exacerbate tension and fears' and 'double the problem at a stroke'. Such a view caused consternation in the SDLP, a party largely funded by Fianna Fáil, Fine Gael and Labour in its first years. Gerry Fitt and Paddy Devlin, despite their republican backgrounds, had by now become convinced of the need to respect Protestant fears; but the SDLP's 'country members', led by John Hume, were traditional nationalists who, in any agreement, wanted to see real progress towards the political reunification of Ireland. Over the summer and early autumn of 1973 – largely as a result of repeated SDLP deputations to Dublin – a profound shift occurred in the Cosgrave government's position. The Council of Ireland was originally assigned a very minor role, co-operation being envisaged on such matters as tourism and transport and going little further than the agreement made by O'Neill and Lemass in 1965. By September 1973 the coalition government sought an enhanced status for the council and stressed the importance of the 'Irish Dimension' in any agreement. Desperately concerned to marginalise the Provisional IRA and to get the SDLP to accept his security and detention measures, Whitelaw felt compelled to comply. What was originally intended to be an internal constitutional rearrangement in Northern Ireland had now been given a much wider scope, gravely imperilling the chances of Protestant co-operation.[36] That a power-sharing government was formed at all was in itself historic in importance.

'DUBLIN IS JUST A SUNNINGDALE AWAY'

When Whitelaw appeared on the steps of Stormont Castle on Wednesday 21 November 1973, journalists saw tears of emotion welling up in his eyes.[37] Agreement in principle on the formation of a power-sharing executive had been reached more than a month before and now, after ten hours of continuous negotiation, his patient diplomacy had been crowned with success. The eleven members of the government-designate – six Unionist ministers, four SDLP and one Alliance – appeared for a photo call the following day. The formation of the executive was an extraordinary achievement: Faulkner, the man who had led provocative marches over the Longstone Road, who helped to pull down O'Neill and who introduced internment, was to be chief executive; and his deputy was to be Fitt, the leader of the SDLP, a party that had promised no talks while internment continued. 'We are on the road to peace now,' Cosgrave said, but DUP assembly member the Reverend William Beattie called the agreement 'the greatest betrayal since Lundy' and the Provisional IRA, describing the SDLP as 'arch-collaborators', announced that the armed struggle would be 'pursued and intensified'.[38] So fierce was the anger of many loyalist politicians that the assembly had to be adjourned on 28 November and again a few days later when Vanguard and DUP members assaulted Unionists in the chamber who supported the executive.

On 2 December, in an act of startling insensitivity, Heath reassigned Whitelaw and appointed Francis Pym secretary of state. It gave an inauspicious start to the tripartite talks beginning on 6 December at Sunningdale, the civil service staff college in Berkshire. Cosgrave insisted on being present and so Heath, to his credit, attended throughout and worked tirelessly for agreement, even though it meant postponing a scheduled meeting with the Italian premier Mariano Rumor. 'We must understand that we are asking a lot of the Protestant people of the North,' Hume had said just a few days earlier at his party conference. 'The Anglo-Irish problem can be solved only when the fears of the Protestant community are stilled.'[39] Hume was in a strong position: the loyalist opposition in the assembly, much to Paisley's indignation, had not been invited to the talks; Hume's view had the unequivocal support of Cosgrave and FitzGerald; and he was held in high regard by Heath, who saw Faulkner as a reactionary representative of the old Stormont regime. Fitt and Devlin wanted to be certain power-sharing would be secured and were therefore willing to play down the role of the Council of Ireland to retain the support of the Unionists. Faulkner, in return for Dublin's co-operation against terrorism, was 'prepared to go along with a limited amount of nonsense from the nationalists' on the council.[40] For Hume, however, the key issue was the council, which he and the Irish government wanted to invest with real executive powers to bring north and south closer together. Alone of the republic's representatives, Cruise O'Brien felt that Dublin should be content to settle for the 'miracle' of power-sharing without pressing for a strong Council of Ireland, but he was under pressure to abide by his own government's policy agreed in cabinet. In the end it may have been Paddy Devlin who limited the executive functions of the council. Garret FitzGerald recalled how Devlin reduced the list of functions from thirteen to the eight finally agreed:

> With some pride I showed him the list of functions that might be devolved to the Council. 'Out of the question,' he asserted after a quick glance at the piece of paper on which I had noted the results of our meeting. He was not going to have his friends – gesturing towards the somewhat bemused Unionists – hung from lamp-posts on their return to Belfast, as they assuredly would be if the list of executive functions we had agreed were published. And he attacked the list vigorously.[41]

It took fifty hours' negotiation over four days to reach agreement. On the evening of Friday 7 December delegates were invited to dinner at 10 Downing Street, where Devlin attempted without success to get Heath to join him in singing the Orange ballad, 'The Sash'; but they all sang without restraint on the bus back to Sunningdale, Faulkner contributing 'Galway Bay'. Hume firmly took charge of the key to the SDLP's drinks cabinet until agreement was certain.[42] Faulkner and Cosgrave often walked the grounds together, talking of hunts and horses and, on one occasion, the taoiseach waited to watch the end of a race on television before responding to the prime minister's urgent request to see him. FitzGerald later recorded some other recollections:

> I assumed Pym was in bed, but at one stage his head popped around the door. Seeing us he immediately said 'Sorry', and withdrew – which, considering we were sitting in *his* office, was distinctly odd . . . Pym was like a fish out of water at Sunningdale, tending to buttonhole other participants to ask anxiously: 'What's happening?' . . . As the night wore on . . . Gerry Fitt was unambiguously asleep on a couch; indeed, I seem to recall him performing the impressively athletic feat of sleeping perched along the top edge of a couch.[43]

Faulkner pressed for the deletion of Articles 2 and 3 of the 1937 constitution but to no avail. Cruise O'Brien, in favour of such a step, pointed out that it would require a referendum which he felt certain would fail.

There were cheers all round when final agreement was announced on the evening of Sunday 9 December but as the Unionist and Alliance delegates returned to Belfast in an unheated Royal Air Force aircraft they were not at all convinced they could persuade enough Protestants to accept the settlement to make it work – indeed, the house of Unionist Peter McLachlan was stoned in protest that night. The following day the main loyalist paramilitary groups announced the formation of a new Ulster Army Council to resist a Council of Ireland. The Provisional IRA signalled its view by detonating three bombs in London on 18 December, injuring sixty-three people, and another three explosions followed there two days later. The death toll for 1973 in Northern

Ireland was 171 civilians, 58 soldiers and 21 police and UDR men, and there were few signs that the Northern Ireland executive, formally installed on New Year's Eve, would be able to ensure that 1974 would be the 'year of reconciliation'.[44]

On Friday 4 January at a crucial meeting of the Ulster Unionist Council, a motion to reject the 'proposed all-Ireland Council settlement' was carried by eighty votes. The ground cut from beneath his feet, Faulkner had no choice but to resign as Unionist leader and withdraw, with his assembly Unionist group, from the party's headquarters in Glengall Street. Even during their first month in office, the ministers of the power-sharing executive found it almost impossible to govern. Not only did the vicious cycle of murders, shootings and bombings maintain its momentum but also demonstrations and protest riots greeted every public attempt to set the Council of Ireland in motion. On Tuesday 22 January, during the first meeting of the assembly that year, loyalist members created uproar by occupying frontbench seats; they were forcibly removed by the RUC and it took eight police officers to carry Paisley to the front steps of Stormont.

The hammer blow fell when Heath called a general election for 28 February. Loyalist parties opposed to the December settlement – the DUP, Vanguard and the Official Unionists now led by Harry West – formed a common front named the United Ulster Unionist Council. Faulkner had not yet been able to create an effective party machine and, to make matters worse, the parties represented in the executive campaigned against each other. With the powerful slogan 'Dublin is just a Sunningdale away', the loyalist pact candidates won 366,703 votes and 11 of Northern Ireland's 12 Westminster seats,[45] and Fitt retained his West Belfast seat for the SDLP. Unionists who stayed loyal to Faulkner failed to win a single seat and managed to attract only 94,301 votes. Paisley increased his majority in North Antrim to an overwhelming 27,631 – a personal triumph, which strengthened his claim to be the voice of the Protestant majority.[46] The February election was in effect a referendum on the Sunningdale Agreement, now decisively rejected by 51 per cent of the electorate. It was quite clear that the assembly, where the executive could still command a majority, no longer reflected the wishes of most people in Northern Ireland.

The same election swept the Conservatives out of office and the new Labour prime minister, Harold Wilson, appointed Merlyn Rees secretary of state. Constantly required in London because of Labour's slender majority, Rees had little time to master the intricacies of the fast-changing political scene in Northern Ireland. If the executive was to have any chance of survival, it needed his wholehearted support, which it did not always get. In any case, the executive constantly threatened to implode: while Faulkner desperately tried to get the Council of Ireland watered down, his SDLP colleagues – allocated the ministries of housing, health and commerce – risked the loss of their own support by halting the rents and rates strike they themselves had begun. Wilson visited Northern Ireland on 18 April and declared that there could be no alternative to the Sunningdale Agreement, but the initiative had passed to the executive's loyalist opponents. Loyalist politicians talked of ways of toppling the executive but they could come to no agreement on whether a strike or a boycott should be attempted, or at what point extra-parliamentary pressure should be applied. In the end their hands were forced by a group of Protestant workers calling themselves the Ulster Workers' Council.

On Monday 13 May four assembly members – Ian Paisley, John Taylor, Ernest Baird and Austin Ardill – met the UWC and were told bluntly: 'We've got the strike organised – it begins tomorrow at six when the vote is taken in the Assembly.'[47]

'THE POINT OF NO RETURN': THE UWC STRIKE, MAY 1974

On Tuesday 14 May 1974 the assembly passed an amendment expressing faith in power-sharing by forty-four votes to twenty-eight. At 6.08 p.m. Harry Murray and Bob Pagels, representing the UWC, informed journalists at Stormont that a strike would begin in protest against ratification of the Sunningdale Agreement. After stating that electricity output would be reduced from 725 megawatts to 400, Murray concluded:

> It is a grave responsibility but it is not ours. It is Brian Faulkner's. He and his friends are ignoring the wishes of 400,000 people who voted against them in the General Election and in doing so they must take the responsibility for this strike.[48]

Tracing its origins back to groups of loyalist workers in the shipyards from 1969 onwards, the UWC by the spring of 1974 had become a twenty-one-man committee drawn from Harland and Wolff, Short Brothers, the power stations, engineering works and the new industrial estates. Paisley, West and Craig had been co-opted on to the committee under the chairmanship of Glenn Barr, a Vanguard assembly member and UDA officer from Derry.

At first the loyalist strike seemed to fail: by 9 a.m. on Wednesday the roads were still open and most firms reported that 90 per cent of their employees had turned up for work. That morning at the Vanguard headquarters in Hawthornden Road in suburban east Belfast the UWC sought the help of the city's UDA, led by Andy Tyrie. Squads of UDA men and Tartan youths called on businesses all over Belfast. Robert Fisk, a reporter for *The Times*, recalled:

> Driving along the Newtownards Road with a colleague that morning, I saw several groups of Tartans lounging outside public houses and found that some of the local shopkeepers had closed down so quickly that they had forgotten to change the 'Open' signs on their front doors . . . In the Belfast suburb of Dunmurry I came across a small firm whose manager had been threatened by twelve youths who had instructed him to send his employees – all of them women – back to their homes . . . By midday, intimidation was beginning to reach epic proportions.[49]

At Larne masked UDA men in camouflage jackets prevented the ferry from sailing and toured the streets carrying wooden clubs to close down shops, and the town was sealed off with barricades constructed of hijacked vehicles. During the morning, workers streamed home from the ICI and Courtaulds synthetic fibre plants in Carrickfergus; men in Harland and Wolff were told that any cars remaining in the employees' car park at 2 p.m. would be set on fire; and Mackie's in west Belfast was one of the last firms to close, stopping work at 4 p.m. That afternoon much of Northern Ireland experienced four-hour power cuts and three quarters of Derry was without electricity. Faulkner denounced the 'irresponsible extremists' in a short statement and asked of the UWC: 'Where do they come from? Who elected them? What is their authority?' Tempers frayed that evening at Stormont when Stan Orme, Rees's deputy, wagged his finger at Paisley, Craig and UWC delegates. 'You're nothing but a civil righter – you started all this,' Harry Murray said to Orme.[50]

The strike slowly gained momentum during the rest of the week. Farm vehicles shut off roads all over north Down; at Mackie's those who turned up for work were ordered out by a group of men brandishing guns; Catholic women leaving Michelin's Mallusk factory at the end of their shift were attacked by about one hundred UDA men; and so many of Citybus's vehicles were seized to make barricades in Belfast that it withdrew its service. Paddy Devlin was about to resign as health and social services minister – which might well have brought down the executive – when news came through of dreadful bloodshed, which caused him to stay his hand. Car bombs, probably driven in and planted by the UVF, had exploded without warning in Monaghan, killing five, and in central Dublin, where twenty-two people died and at least another hundred were injured; the death toll eventually reached thirty-two. 'I am very happy about the bombings in Dublin,' said Sammy

Smyth of the UWC; 'There is a war with the Free State and now we are laughing at them.'

By Saturday 18 May Northern Ireland was experiencing blackouts lasting up to six hours at a time; tilley lamps hissed on the counters of large department stores; dairies and bakeries had been forced to shut down; and Dr Garth McClure, a paediatrician at Belfast's Royal Victoria Hospital, expressed fears for the lives of babies in his care if incubators were cut off through power cuts and lack of fuel for emergency generators.[51] On Sunday night the UWC ordered the erection of almost one hundred road blocks to encircle central Belfast and the following morning gangs of youths hijacked lorries and cars to seal off most of the main routes into the city. For a time, only Andersonstown, south Belfast and the Falls had unimpeded contact with the rest of Ulster. On Tuesday 21 May, Len Murray, general secretary of the Trades Union Congress, joined with Billy Blease, Andy Barr and some other trade-union leaders to lead a return-to-work march at the shipyard; only around two hundred turned up and, though they were protected by troops and police, they were showered with insults and rotten tomatoes.

Just before dawn next day a convoy of Bedford trucks, full of soldiers, moved out of Thiepval barracks in Lisburn and converged in Belfast with hundreds more troops of the 1st Battalion the Light Infantry from the Hastings Street post. As the men, with blackened faces, leaped purposefully out of their vehicles in Shaftesbury Square women in nearby Sandy Row banged dustbin lids on pavements. A bloody confrontation between the army and loyalist strikers seemed certain. As it turned out, the soldiers patiently negotiated with the local UDA and together they dismantled the barricades. 'We couldn't oppose our own British Army,' Harry Patterson of the UWC said later. 'This is the army that I joined up in in 1939–45. How could I oppose the British Army?'[52] There were some, however, who thought the relationship between the strikers and the security forces altogether too cosy.

Lieutenant-General Sir Frank King, GOC Northern Ireland, now had 17,500 soldiers in the region under his command. His daily helicopter flights over Belfast convinced him, however, that the strike was too extensive to be broken by the number of men he had at his disposal. 'If you get a very large section of the population which is bent on a particular course,' King said, 'then it is a difficult thing to stop them taking that course.'[53] Some journalists to this day are convinced that the army chiefs came close to taking matters into their own hands. In any case, Wilson, Rees and even most members of the executive hesitated to send the troops in and, even though two hundred technical experts were brought in from as far away as Hong Kong and billeted in secrecy at Aldergrove, army chiefs feared that strikers would remove vital switches and other critical pieces of machinery if soldiers took over the power stations.[54]

The prime minister, however, was becoming convinced of the need for army intervention of some kind, seemingly signalled by his notorious broadcast on Saturday 25 May denouncing the strike:

> It is a deliberate and calculated attempt to use every undemocratic and unparliamentary means for the purpose of bringing down the whole constitution of Northern Ireland so as to set up there a sectarian and undemocratic state . . . British taxpayers have seen the taxes they have poured out, almost without regard to cost . . . Yet people who benefit from all this now viciously defy Westminster, purporting to act as though they were an elected government; people who spend their lives sponging on Westminster and British democracy and then systematically assault democratic methods. Who do these people think they are?[55]

This ill-advised and self-indulgent speech rallied Protestant feeling behind the strikers to such an extent that Glenn Barr said they thought of making Wilson an honorary member of the UWC. Nell McCafferty was in Derry with her mother, a Catholic, during the broadcast, as she reported to *Irish Times* readers two days later:

> 'What?' my mother sat up. 'Spongers? Is he calling us "spongers"? In the name of God . . . is he telling us we're spongers?' She made for the radio.[56]

The UDA and UWC fully expected dramatic action on the scale of Operation Motorman. In the event, army intervention was limited to a takeover of fuel supplies and the distribution of petrol from a limited number of stations. Civil servants who were supposed to deal with cash and the appropriate number of Green Shield stamps failed to appear. 'We found ourselves doing this,' one army officer remembered. 'We handled the cash and pumped the petrol. I don't expect they ever squared the books since then. But we did the chore they asked us to do!'[57] In response the UWC ordered a reduction in electricity to 10 per cent of capacity and a withdrawal of workers in essential services. The strike was by now more effective than ever: Derry was without a gas supply; food supplies ran low following a wave of panic buying; livestock in air-conditioned units were starting to suffocate; chickens were slaughtered in thousands due to shortage of feed; every day around forty thousand gallons of milk were being poured away; the postal service was breaking down; and the power supply had become so weak that the telephone system was failing.

On Monday morning, 27 May, Hugo Patterson, the official spokesman for the Northern Ireland Electricity Service, was interviewed for the BBC by Barry Cowan:

Patterson:	Let's be clear about this; this shutdown is on, it's complete, it's final, it's irrevocable. I don't think there's any going back on this one now.
Cowan:	In other words, as of two minutes ago, nine-thirty, the complete shutdown of power in Northern Ireland has begun and cannot now be stopped.
Patterson:	... you're right ... We are past the point of no return.[58]

Patterson's hourly broadcasts had a profound effect on Faulkner, who now wanted to negotiate with the strikers. The SDLP executive ministers could not agree to negotiation and called instead for the army to occupy the power stations. At 1.20 p.m. that Monday Faulkner resigned and a loyalist demonstration at Stormont became a massive victory rally. Brian Garrett, chairman of the Northern Ireland Labour Party, went to the Vanguard headquarters to implore the UWC to order a return to work; there he found power workers and loyalist politicians singing 'Oh God, our help in ages past' by candlelight. Meanwhile, flames leaped up from bonfires in Protestant districts to celebrate the end of one of the most successful general strikes in Europe since 1945.[59]

STALEMATE: THE CONVENTION

During fifteen days a self-appointed junta in league with loyalist paramilitaries had made an entire region of the United Kingdom ungovernable. For much of this period most of the people of Northern Ireland had been deprived of electricity, gas, transport, fresh food, piped water, employment and other facilities taken for granted in any western European state.[60] The willingness of the middle classes to apply to strike leaders for travel permits and petrol coupons demonstrated the extent to which the UWC had been able to effect its claim to be a provisional government of Ulster. Glenn Barr later said that decisive action by the army could have broken the UWC on the first day but as the strike gained momentum it left the security forces, civil servants, public services, trade-union leaders, moderate politicians and the Westminster government ever more impotent. The *Daily Mail* described the state to which Belfast had been reduced during the second week:

> You can't have a breakfast egg or bacon – the shelves are bare. You can't make a hot drink because there's no electricity. You can't catch a bus because there aren't any. You can't post a letter because it won't arrive. Petrol is so scarce that some people are trying to run their cars on paint fillers.[61]

Only the toppling of the democratically elected power-sharing executive prevented the region from sliding into further chaos.

711

A curious feature of the strike was that it led nationalist politicians north and south to demand the suppression of popular industrial action by the British Army. Cruise O'Brien was almost alone in the Dáil when he said he did not see how Rees could have acted otherwise without dire consequences. Even the moderate *Irish Times* concluded: 'In all the shame that Britain has suffered at the hands of her departing colonials this lying down to the bigots of Belfast ranks high in infamy.' Certainly intimidation played an important role but it was patchy in its applica-tion.[62] Robert Orr, a further education teacher, was stopped at Cloughfern in south Antrim by men wielding clubs. 'I'm going to Belfast to work,' he told them. The men looked embarrassed and replied, 'All right – on you go.' Schools remained open and many a teacher was waved through a road block with the cheery cry, 'Morning, sir!' Office workers and commuters, sharing cars to conserve petrol, travelling by train, or walk-ing, continued to work if they wanted to, in Belfast, Derry and the main provincial towns. Above all, as the strike progressed it won the support of the vast majority of Protestants, including the middle classes – to a considerable extent as a result of Wilson's speech.

The creation of the power-sharing executive has been the most suc-cessful of the British political initiatives in Northern Ireland in more than twenty years of the Troubles. Having wrecked Whitelaw's handi-work, the loyalists concluded that they had the power to destroy any political arrangement made by the British government which did not suit them. Successive Westminster administrations attempted thereaf-ter to square the circle of meeting some nationalist aspirations without completely alienating the unionists at the same time.[63] The failure of these efforts led to a protracted political stalemate.

'The initiatives taken at Darlington and Sunningdale, the policies of the Heath Government and of our own had reached a dead end', Harold Wilson wrote later. 'No solution could be imposed from across the water. From now on we had to throw the task clearly to the North-ern Ireland people themselves.'[64] Like Heath before him, Wilson had the complete support of the opposition at Westminster in attempting new solutions; for example, the bill legalising elaborate new machinery to extend direct rule went through the Commons in a single day in mid-July 1974 without a division. There was all-party backing, too, for legislation winding up the Northern Ireland assembly and replacing it with an elected Constitutional Convention 'to consider what provisions for the government of Northern Ireland would be likely to command the most widespread acceptance throughout the community there'.[65] The 'Irish Dimension' was quietly sidelined but Westminster remained wedded to power-sharing as the only acceptable outcome. Once again

British politicians hoped that a silent majority in Northern Ireland would yield a moderate centre strong enough to deliver community government. Rees waited for ten months before calling the convention, probably to give Faulkner time to get his Unionist Party of Northern Ireland, formed in September 1974 and committed to power-sharing, organised in the constituencies.

London was whistling in the wind. In the Westminster general election of October 1974 (when Enoch Powell, after his break with the Conservative Party, was elected as an Official Unionist in South Down) the United Ulster Unionist Council captured 58 per cent of the vote and neither of the two Faulknerite candidates were elected. The results of the convention election, held on 1 May 1975, were for Rees just as cheerless. Out of the 78 seats, the Unionist Party of Northern Ireland won only 5 (Faulkner himself barely scraped home on the last count); Alliance held steady at 8, and only one candidate, David Bleakley, was returned for the Northern Ireland Labour Party. The SDLP was reduced to 17 but the Craig–West–Paisley loyalist coalition won 54.8 per cent of the vote and 47 seats.[66] 'Doesn't it mean that the Protestants have won?' Cosgrave asked Cruise O'Brien, who not only agreed but also, to the taoiseach's consternation, made a public statement that loyalists could not be obliged to accept power-sharing against their will.[67]

The majority Unionists in the convention had no intention of accepting power-sharing. For a time Rees was hopeful as comparatively orderly debates on procedure got under way and interparty talks were held behind closed doors over the summer of 1975. Craig began to bend somewhat and suggested a temporary acceptance of power-sharing while the security crisis persisted. For his heresy he was castigated by Paisley, expelled from the United Ulster Unionist Council, and propelled rapidly into political oblivion. This was an outward and visible sign of a bitter leadership struggle that did much to fracture the loyalist coalition, already divided and confused by conflicting arguments for total integration with the rest of the United Kingdom and for an independent Northern Ireland. On 7 November 1975 the intransigents held together sufficiently, nevertheless, to endorse the convention report by forty-three votes to thirty-one; this recommended a return to majority rule, the only variation from the former Stormont regime being proposals to allow parliamentary committees to have opposition – that is, Catholic – chairmen. This was unacceptable to Westminster, the power-sharing parties and even to some Vanguard members, including Glenn Barr, who resigned from the United Ulster Unionist Council in support of Craig.

Rees still nursed hopes that the deadlock could be broken. Informal talks continued into February 1976, when the convention reconvened.

713

Further debate proved futile and after unseemly uproar on 3 March, when the convention reaffirmed its call for the return of majority rule, the Labour government lost patience and wound up the constitutional discussions. The convention report was never debated at Westminster. The bipartisan view now was that direct rule must be made to work. Curbing the continuing violence remained the Government's top priority, but other concerns – which normally preoccupy the administration of a peaceful western European state – demanded attention. Of these, by far the most urgent task facing Westminster's representatives on the Stormont estate was to see that the citizens of Northern Ireland were properly housed.

'THE LARGEST SLUM LANDLORD IN EUROPE'

Morale had been remarkably high over most of Northern Ireland during the UWC strike. Loyalists sensed victory, while militant republicans, sure that the strikers inadvertently were doing their work for them, had rising expectations of British withdrawal from Ulster. Meanwhile, Churches, voluntary groups and relief organisations had thrown themselves into the task of providing social services where the official ones had been paralysed. Operating a twenty-four-hour service, agencies all over Belfast had stored food, bottled gas, paraffin and other essentials, and attempted to organise transport for those most in need. Louis Boyle, in his account of the impact of the strike on the social services, observed:

> Few areas were left uncovered; never before had so much community activity been seen in Belfast; public meetings when held were packed, volunteers were numerous and it seemed in some areas that everyone was involved in some way.[68]

For example, in an estate of five hundred households, two meetings were held on 26 May: four hundred women attended one at 4 p.m. and five hundred men were present at the other at 5 p.m. The following evening a public meeting in a small Catholic community in central Belfast attracted an attendance of eight hundred people.

Voluntary action had been swift and effective in response to an unprecedented crisis, but it was the local authority and government agencies that had to cope with the more enduring problem of social need in Northern Ireland. In contrast with the welfare departments of the counties of Antrim and Down, that of the Belfast Corporation did not provide an exceptional service following the eruption of violence in 1969 until forced to do so by the Government. The upheavals that eventually brought about the imposition of direct rule also precipitated drastic changes in the structure of local government. The Cameron report had levelled the charge of maladministration at local councils, particularly those west of the Bann. The first step was taken on 19 August 1969 when the Westminster and Stormont governments agreed, in the so-called Downing Street Declaration, to strip all control of public housing away from local councils and transfer it to a regional authority, the Northern Ireland Housing Executive. Soon afterwards the Stormont government – nudged no doubt by London – appointed Sir Patrick Macrory, a former member of the Development Council and noted historian, to chair a review body to produce a plan for local government reform.[69]

The Macrory report delighted the civil rights movement and out-raged Unionists when it was published in 1970, but it was accepted by Chichester-Clark and duly implemented by Whitelaw in 1973. The twenty-six district councils which replaced the former complex local authority structure found their responsibilities drastically limited by comparison with their predecessors and their counterparts in England, Scotland and Wales. Their functions were reduced to little more than the emptying of dustbins, the burying of the dead, and the administra-tion of community and leisure centres.[70] The provision of social services, health care, and education and library services became the responsibility of boards. Most board members were appointed by the Northern Ireland Office, which ensured those councillors who were elected on to the boards could never exercise a controlling influence. The secretary of state, given much latitude because his job was consid-ered such an unenviable one, seemed to have acquired powers falling not far short of those possessed by the governor of Hong Kong.[71] Outside the control of locally elected persons and beyond direct public influence though they were, these new bodies faced daunting tasks ahead. Intimidation, intercommunal violence and enforced population movement ensured that the most urgent of those tasks was to attend to the housing needs of the people.

Sixteen months dragged by between the Downing Street Declaration and the giving of royal assent to the Housing Executive Bill in February 1971. While Faulkner, then minister of development, made unconvinc-ing claims that he had intended 'having a central authority for building houses' before the British government intervened, Craig, West, Paisley and other backbenchers fought the bill's provisions all the way.[72] The Housing Executive held its first meeting at Stormont on 4 March 1971 and the remainder of the year was taken up with setting up the new structure and absorbing the functions of the Housing Trust, the Development Commissions and the housing departments of Belfast Corporation and other local councils.

The situation, meanwhile, had been deteriorating week by week. In Belfast alone, 3,570 families had moved as a direct result of the violence during the summer of 1969 and a further 2,100 households had been forced to move after the imposition of internment had thrown so many parts of the city into a state of extreme turmoil. Whole streets had been burned down; intimidation was widespread; and rioting, petrol-bombings and shootings were most intense in the very areas most acutely in need of housing action. Even firemen were attacked when called to blazing buildings and the hazards of carrying out emergency repairs were demonstrated when two slaters, mistaken for snipers, were shot by the army. Illegal squatting, much of it perfectly understandable at first, was swiftly taken over by armed paramilitaries on both sides. The site foreman on Belfast Corporation's Westland Road estate was forced by the UDA to hand over keys for new houses and in Beechmount notices were stuck up in windows, stating to whom the houses had been allocated by the Provisionals.[73] *Flight*, the report published three weeks after the introduction of internment, concluded: 'Spontaneous and organised squatting is re-segregating housing in such a way as to undermine the credibility for the community of non-sectarian housing policies.'[74]

Immense problems therefore faced the Housing Executive from the outset. During 1971–2 there were 22,000 tenants in the public sector on rent-and-rates strike as part of the civil disobedience campaign in protest at the introduction of internment, and there were still over 17,000 refusing such payments in 1973, and nearly 4,000 in March 1975. In Belfast 14,000 houses were damaged by explosions in 1972–3 and altogether the total number in the city destroyed or damaged in the violence reached 25,000 by 1976.[75] The fact that most bricklayers were Protestant and the majority of tilers and slaters were Catholic made swift remedial action in troubled areas virtually impossible.[76] In any case, many contractors refused to tender for work in disturbed districts and others who did found it difficult to fend off paramilitary racketeering. To make matters worse, some £15,000 were stolen in forty-four armed robberies of rent collectors in just one year, April 1972 to March 1973.[77] On 9 November 1972 a 300-pound car bomb wrecked the Housing Executive headquarters and between 1972 and 1984 a total of forty-nine attacks on executive property caused damage assessed at £2,788,485.[78] As the first comprehensive housing authority in the United Kingdom, it had also inherited all the problems created by decades of neglect and mismanagement before the Troubles had begun. The Housing Executive began its task, in the words of a government minister, as 'the largest slum landlord in Europe'.

A House Condition Survey carried out in 1974 revealed the scale of the problem. In Northern Ireland as a whole 19.6 per cent of the total dwelling stock was statutorily unfit, compared with 7.3 per cent in England and Wales. In the Belfast urban area at least half the houses required repairs costing £250 or more and 24.2 per cent of all dwellings – 29,750 out of a total stock of 123,120 – were statutorily unfit. Even more alarming was the revelation that in the inner city west of the Lagan half the houses, excluding bricked-up houses, caravans and shacks, were classed as unfit. In this area 34.3 per cent had no washbasin, 32.4 per cent had no inside toilet, 29.8 per cent were without a fixed bath in a bathroom and 23.2 per cent had been built before 1870.[79]

Having created a great bureaucratic machine, the governments in Westminster showed a growing reluctance to pay for the new dwellings Northern Ireland so desperately needed. Unfit houses were being demolished faster than new dwellings were being built and in 1973 the Housing Executive put up only 435 houses in Belfast. Like the Housing Trust before it, the Housing Executive was supposed to be self-financing and it was fortunate that it embarked on a course of deficit-financing. Under severe political pressure to make progress, the executive was forced to let design and layout standards slip somewhat. In 1977, 7,676 new dwellings were completed in the region but this was the best figure of the decade and a second House Condition Survey in 1979 showed that the demolition of old housing stock was advancing faster than the building of new homes. The corner was being turned, however, and in Belfast unfitness levels had dropped from over 24 per cent in 1974 to 15 per cent by 1979.[80]

The work of the Housing Executive was complicated and frequently hampered by the grandiose schemes of the 1960s – it was during this time of cheap energy, economic expansion and optimism that the M1 and M2 motorways, the new city of Craigavon, the Matthew plan and the Belfast Urban Motorway had been conceived. Craigavon failed to become the great manufacturing heartland O'Neill's government had hoped it could be but at least there was no shortage of public housing in the area. The Building Design Partnership had estimated that 74,500 new homes would be needed in the Belfast urban area by 1981 but that there were sites for only 47,500 within the Matthew stop line; 27,000 families, therefore, would have to move to the new growth centres, such as Antrim. Few in power then thought to ask the opinion of the people who were to have their homes demolished and be sent out beyond the city boundary.

The road-building programme was well advanced by 1969 and though they gashed through some of the richest agricultural land in Ulster, the motorways were widely welcomed. The building of the approach to the M2 motorway, however, required the break-up of the densely inhabited dockland area of Sailorstown: some of the population there were rehoused in high-rise flats nearby and the rest were dispersed to growth centres. The urban motorway was due to engulf three hundred acres of land, on which stood seven thousand homes; even if most of these were due for demolition, the very publication of the plans spread inner-city blight more rapidly, as property owners let buildings decay in the projected path of the new road. Feelings ran high particularly in the Shankill: here blight had been given fourteen years to spread in the period between the time when the plans were first mooted and in January 1974, when the area was finally vested.[81] The Protestant community there felt threatened with extinction: only a small number of those families displaced could be rehoused in the same area; competition for completed dwellings was intense; and illegal squatting added to the tension. Popular opposition forced the abandonment of plans for fifteen-storey blocks of flats, but the medium-rise 'Weetabix' blocks – ugly and badly designed – provoked equally furious local criticism. Ron Wiener, in his study *The Rape and Plunder of the Shankill*, recorded one resident's feeling of loss:

> It was one of the best roads for shopping and kindness and people were so friendly and happy. What a pity to watch it just dying away fast. It would break your heart because we loved this road. To me the old Shankill was heaven.[82]

The Housing Executive quickly set its face against high-rise flats and opted for dwellings of a more traditional style, built strictly to minimum standards of space, design and lay-out, as recommended in the Parker-Morris report for London. The new housing authority, however, had inherited high-rise flats and had no option but to complete those already partly built. These included the Rossville Flats, built by Londonderry Corporation, and Unity Flats in Belfast, both storm centres during the early stages of the Troubles.[83] By far the largest headache was the Divis Flats complex, started by Belfast Corporation in 1966 on the site of the Pound Loney in the lower Falls. The Housing Executive completed the scheme in 1972: it consisted of twelve medium-rise blocks and one multistorey tower, and provided a total of 795 dwelling units. The decision to build the complex had been a popular one with local people who wanted to stay in the area and with the Catholic Church because it retained the local community within St Peter's parish. Even before building work was finished, however, the flats were beset by problems all too familiar in high-rise developments for low-income groups in London, Glasgow, Liverpool and Dublin, such as degradation, damp and vandalism. Population pressure was already acute in Catholic west Belfast and the stop line left the housing authority with only the option of building upwards if it was to reduce waiting lists in the area. The complete failure of 'streets in the sky' forced a radical reappraisal in the late 1970s and it was not until the 1980s and early 1990s that the Housing Executive was able to provide dwellings of a character and on a scale to meet the needs of the people.

The reduction of unfitness levels required financial subventions from Westminster on an unprecedented scale: the region simply could not generate the funds needed. Indeed, the Northern Ireland economy sustained a series of damaging blows, which made it ever more dependent on assistance from the central exchequer.

'IF NO MEASURES ARE TAKEN, THE OUTLOOK IS GRIM': THE ECONOMY

The UWC strike succeeded only because the great majority of adult male Protestants were in work and were confident that their jobs were secure. That confidence was misplaced and men standing by their barricades were not aware of the profound effect the international oil crisis would have on Northern Ireland's economy. By 1974 the region had become more dependent on cheap oil than any other part of the United Kingdom and the blow delivered by the quadrupling of energy prices, therefore, was acutely felt.

The rapid growth of synthetic fibre production had been Northern Ireland's best success story. Encouraged by government incentives, there had been two great surges of inward investment in the industry, in the early and late 1960s: synthetic fibre production in the region, negligible before 1958, accounted for one third of the United Kingdom's output by 1973. The industry was concentrated in the Protestant heartland of south Co. Antrim and, when it reached its peak in 1974, it provided over one third of all manufacturing jobs in Antrim town and nearly three quarters of those in Carrickfergus.[84] Prodigious quantities of oil were consumed both as a raw material and in the manufacturing process. Suddenly the whole industry in Northern Ireland became imperilled. The United States, pursuing a cheap energy policy, and states such as Portugal with lower labour costs, posed intense competition and penetrated Northern Ireland's markets, particularly in the rest of the United Kingdom. The leap in oil prices threatened those economies all over the world which did not have access to cheap domestic supplies of energy but Northern Ireland suffered more than any other part of the United Kingdom because it was furthest from the commercial

719

hub of the European Community. Many firms were pushed towards the edge by the sudden rise in transport costs, as well as the leap in the price of electricity, nearly all of it generated in Northern Ireland from imported oil.

The dislocating impact of intercommunal violence and political uncertainty was not immediate. Projects agreed and contracts signed before the Troubles got under way were still having a beneficial effect. Potential investors, however, were frightened off. The Provisionals, by 'attacking the soft underbelly of British investment' in their bombing campaign, hoped in time to force British withdrawal from Northern Ireland: they failed but their organisation and other paramilitaries certainly succeeded in diverting outside capital away from the region.[85]

Despite more difficult international trading conditions, the Irish Republic's economy expanded almost as rapidly between 1973 and 1979 as it had done in the period 1959–72. The state's industrial exports grew by 11 per cent per annum, manufacturing output by 5.9 per cent and the gross domestic product by 3.8 per cent. By contrast, Northern Ireland's gross domestic product between 1973 and 1979 only grew by 1.9 per cent annually and this expansion was almost wholly accounted for by subsidies from Westminster.[86] Between 1961 and 1970 manufacturing employment in Northern Ireland had increased relative to the United Kingdom as a whole and over the longer period 1956 to 1979 manufacturing output in the region had risen by 96 per cent by comparison with 65 per cent in all of the United Kingdom. These figures, however, do not show the sharp contraction in manufacturing after the peak of 1973: between then and 1979 production in Northern Ireland dropped by 9 per cent compared with a United Kingdom fall of 4 per cent.[87] During those six years Northern Ireland's manufacturing output suffered a dramatic decline of 5 per cent annually. In that period jobs in the region's manufacturing sector were being lost at the rate of 3 per cent per annum. Much of this was due to the reluctance of outsiders to invest in such a violent and unsettled area.

During the middle 1960s the Department of Commerce had been able to announce an average of seven thousand new industrial jobs per annum but in 1976 only three thousand jobs were promoted.[88] Even if Northern Ireland had managed to continue to increase industrial production at three quarters of the rate in the republic (as was the case in the 1960s) then production would have been 39 per cent higher at the end of the 1970s – the equivalent of fifty thousand jobs. 'Even if this is an optimistic overstatement', the economist John Simpson concluded, 'a loss of over 30/35,000 industrial jobs' due directly to the violence he thought to be 'a conservative estimate'.[89] In their report of 1976,

W.G.H. Quigley and his review team summarised the economic condition of the region:

> The Northern Ireland economy is in serious difficulty and, if no measures are taken, the outlook is grim. Unemployment is 10% and, on present policies, it is unlikely to fall below that level, whatever upturn there may be in the national economy.[90]

On his appointment as secretary of state in 1976, Roy Mason declared his intention of taking decisive action to revive Northern Ireland's economy and that the Quigley report would be his guide. Quigley recommended that more should be done to attract in multinational firms but that alone could not avert a major crisis: in the medium term there was no alternative to a 'heavily subsidised Northern Ireland economy, with the state playing a much greater role, both direct and supportive'.[91] Mason and his junior minister, Don Concannon, achieved far less than they hoped. Their main success was in shielding Northern Ireland from some of the most damaging effects of the Callaghan government's deflationary policies – policies in effect imposed by the International Monetary Fund. Employment in the public services in Northern Ireland was not cut back as it was across the Irish Sea and, indeed, taking the 1970s as a whole, jobs in the public sector in the region increased by 52 per cent as compared with 22 per cent in the United Kingdom as a whole. Lord Melchett, another junior minister, inaugurated programmes to increase government spending in deprived areas by assisting community groups and building a large number of leisure centres. His aim, he said later, was to make direct rule more palatable by presenting it as 'compassionate and caring'.[92]

In the 1960s the problem had been that the old industries had been shedding labour almost as fast as the newly arrived firms were creating employment. After 1973, jobs were being lost even faster in the multinationals than in the traditional export industries. Harland and Wolff, making losses every year since 1964, ran into acute financial difficulties: the company was saved from closure only when the Stormont government took shares and wrote off losses in 1971. Westminster took over these responsibilities when direct rule was imposed and provided more subsidies: altogether Harland and Wolff received £174 million from public funds between 1966 and 1974.[93] The erection of two great cranes, Goliath and Sampson, gave every indication that all was well and that modernisation was surging ahead. Vessels of impressive size were floated out into Belfast Lough between 1970 and 1974: there were six supertankers ranging between 126,535 and 138,037 tons, including *Olympic Banner* and *Olympic Brilliance* for two Onassis companies and *Lotorium* for Shell Tankers; and nine bulk carriers, the 65,135-ton *Canadian Bridge* being the largest. The future looked bleak, however, and orders were slow to come in even though the market for tankers worldwide was buoyant for most of 1973.[94] The company's position became desperate with the market collapse in the wake of the oil crisis. Contracts expected to bring in a profit of £10 million suddenly became unprofitable and the 'negative net worth' of Harland and Wolff was approaching £32 million. During the greatest boom in world shipbuilding history, the company had its largest-ever losses. In July 1974 Harland and Wolff was about to go into receivership when, at the eleventh hour, the Government stepped in and the following year became the sole shareholder.[95]

Henceforth successive governments gave assistance in the full knowledge that it would bring no financial return. Other shipbuilding states were doing the same. For the present, the Troubles ensured that Westminster did not feel able to cope with the political consequences of allowing such a key industry to go under. Harland and Wolff's labour force was still around ten thousand in 1974 and work continued on contracts signed before the oil crisis. In 1976 tonnage reached a record high with the floating out of three Shell supertankers – *Lepeta, Leonia* and *Lima* – totalling 954,000 deadweight tons, more than a third of the United Kingdom's output. In addition, the engine works completed sixteen sets of machinery, nine of them for export and a record for United Kingdom marine engine builders in that year. No ships were ordered at all in 1975 and 1976 and Harland and Wolff suffered a steady decline for the remainder of the decade.[96]

Greater government intervention and assistance in the region's economic affairs was prompted to a considerable extent by the need to make direct rule work, given the failure of political initiatives designed to restore stability. The inability of consitutional politicians to find common ground could only encourage the Provisional IRA to sustain and widen its campaign.

THE PROVISIONAL IRA CAMPAIGN IN BRITAIN

Constitutional initiatives, both when they appeared to be succeeding and when they most certainly were failing, made little impression on the Provisional IRA. The British showed no sign of getting out of Northern Ireland and for this reason the Provisionals planned to take their campaign of violence to Britain – the hope was that public opinion there, already showing growing support for a 'troops out' movement, would become so exasperated that withdrawal would become a major issue. As early as June 1972, at a Provisional IRA army council meeting in Blackrock, Co. Dublin, Seán Mac Stiofáin had concluded that 'sooner or later there would have to be a drift to another area to take the heat off Belfast and Derry'. The bombing of Aldershot had been the work of the Official IRA and it was not until 1973 that the Provisionals took their war across the Irish Sea. Their intention, Dáithí Ó Conaill said later, was to 'strike at economic, military, political and judicial targets'.[97]

Members of the Provisionals' Belfast brigade hijacked four cars in the city, resprayed them, attached false number plates, packed them full of explosives, drove them to Dublin and took them by ferry to England. The explosions in London on the day of the border poll, 8 March 1973, which killed one man and injured 180 others, were the consequence. Seven men and three women, including Dolours and Marion Price, were charged following a tip-off by a highly placed informant. Over the summer, incendiaries and bombs were detonated around the Midlands and in London stores, stations and stock exchanges.[98] The Provisionals denied planting explosives on a coach taking army families from Manchester to Catterick on 4 February 1974, which blew up on the M62, killing nine soldiers, a woman and two children; there is little doubt, however, that they were responsible.[99] Other horrific incidents followed in the autumn: on 5 October two soldiers and three civilians were killed and fifty-four people were injured by 'no-warning' bombs in two public houses in Guildford, Surrey; on 7 November a public house frequented by soldiers in Woolwich was bombed, leaving one soldier and one civilian dead and twenty people injured; and on 21 November bombs detonated in two Birmingham public houses killed 21 people and injured more than 180 others, many of whom were left horribly scarred.[100] The Labour government, sharing the general public's revulsion, rushed through the Prevention of Terrorism (Temporary Provisions) Bill, which became law on 29 November and enabled the authorities to exclude suspects from any part of Ireland from entering England, Scotland and Wales and allowed British police to hold those suspected of terrorist activities without a charge for forty-eight hours or up to seven days on higher authority.[101]

The Provisionals gained nothing from their atrocities in Britain. Their bombing campaign attracted widespread condemnation even from those on both sides of the Irish Sea who sympathised with their objectives. They discovered they could not depend on the support of Britain's extensive Irish community, where many were prepared to inform the police and where Special Branch officers could operate effectively. Nevertheless, a fresh Provisional IRA offensive in England was launched during the autumn of 1975. Explosives were planted in London's West

End; Professor Gordon Hamilton Fairley was killed by a bomb intended for a Conservative MP; Captain Roger Goad, a bomb-disposal expert, was murdered; and on 27 November Ross McWhirter, co-compiler of *The Guinness Book of Records* and a supporter of a campaign for stronger measures against terrorists, was shot dead. Towards the end of the year, however, Scotland Yard scored a notable success. On the evening of Saturday 6 December four Provisional IRA activists were cornered in a block of flats in Balcombe Street in London, where they took Sheila and John Matthews hostage. Armed police surrounded the area, cut the telephone line and monitored the men's conversation with sophisticated listening devices; and after 138 hours the siege ended on Friday 12 December when the four Provisionals gave themselves up.[102] This campaign in Britain fell far short of its objectives. Papers seized by police showed that the intention was to assassinate fifty-eight MPs, thirty judges, leading businessmen and military chiefs. Operations there proved costly and counter-productive for the Provisional IRA and, while they were not abandoned altogether, the violent campaign to drive out the British was therefore very largely confined to Northern Ireland.[103]

Long before the collapse of the convention, the Westminster government was revising its tactics for containing the continuing violence in the North. The Provisionals – facing a sharp drop in support in the wake of the Birmingham bombings and more sophisticated pressure from the security forces – agreed to secret peace talks with Protestant clergy, held at Feakle, Co. Clare, on 9–11 December 1974. A ceasefire was arranged on 22 December and though broken for a time in the new year it was resumed on 11 February. To sustain the ceasefire, Rees set up 'incident centres' in Catholic districts and speeded up the phasing out of internment, the last detainee being released in December 1975. Only one soldier was killed between January and June of 1975 but otherwise the deaths increased: during the first nine months of the truce 196 were killed, 37 more than in the same period in 1974.[104] Sectarian murder, particularly of Catholics, accounted for a rising proportion of those being killed; but many local Provisional commanders – particularly in south Armagh, Belfast and Derry – did not share the enthusiasm of their 'armchair' Dublin superiors for the ceasefire and fought on.

Kenneth Newman, a commander in the London Metropolitan Police Force, had surprised many of his colleagues by applying for and obtaining the post of senior deputy chief constable of the RUC in 1973. A veteran of the Palestine police, Newman had dealt with violence arising out of religious hatred at close quarters, seeing, for example, the men of a village crucified to the doors of their houses; and doctors, nurses and patients massacred in a hospital convoy. He was certain that the army's 'high profile' in Northern Ireland was ultimately counter-productive in a society with such a seriously alienated Catholic population.[105] The answer was to restore the flagging morale of the RUC, establish for it a reputation for professionalism and impartiality, and steadily replace troops with police officers and local people enlisted as part-time members of the UDR. Under pressure to reduce army commitment in Northern Ireland, Rees enthusiastically supported Newman's proposals. Cabinet approval was given in London and so the policy of 'Ulsterisation' was born – a strategy still in place sixteen years later.

'THE FUNERAL DIRGE GETS GROUND INTO YOUR SOUL'

On 1 May 1976 Newman replaced Jamie Flanagan as chief constable of the RUC. Newman 'was completely down to earth, oozing with common sense,' an officer recalled. 'In no time respect for his ability was sky-high.'[106] The 'Wee Man' faced the formidable task of restoring the self-respect of a force in a state of near-disarray since 1969 and under constant threat of disbandment as government officials contemplated the creation of a new civilian force acceptable in Catholic districts. Now a new era opened with the implementation of Ulsterisation: the RUC establishment was to be doubled to ten thousand at the rate of around five hundred officers a year; the annual budget was to be increased from £49 million to £60 million; the RUC Reserve, numbering 4,790 at the time, was to be expanded; new fleets of armoured civilian patrol cars and Hotspur armoured Land-Rovers were ordered; and regular officers were to be armed with standard NATO 7.62 mm rifles, M1 carbines, handguns and Federal riot guns to fire plastic baton rounds. Only in the most difficult areas would the army stay in strength; elsewhere the police would have responsibility for law and order and, if military aid was needed, it would be supplied as far as possible by part-time soldiers of the UDR. Newman said at a conference at Hillsborough on 13 May: 'The RUC would be hard but sensitive.'[107] On the same day *Republican News* announced that the Provisional IRA promised a 'long hot summer' as its response to the RUC's new 'high risk profile'.[108] On 15 May three police officers were killed by a booby-trap bomb at Belcoo and another RUC man was shot dead in a gun battle in Warrenpoint.[109] During his first month as chief constable, Newman attended funerals of seven murdered officers and he was to say, 'The funeral dirge gets ground into your soul.'[110]

'The price of human life is now so cheap in Belfast,' one policeman observed, 'that you can have old scores settled for the price of a few bottles of Guinness.'[111] Newman found that there were five hundred unsolved murders in the RUC's files, one for every detective in the force.[112] The annual toll of deaths from political violence had been rising since 1974, when 216 had been killed. The death toll for 1975 was 217 civilians, 14 soldiers and 16 RUC and UDR. That year had been characterised by 'tit-for-tat' sectarian killings and murders arising from paramilitary feuding. Several incidents had been particularly cold-blooded. On Saturday 5 April two Catholics were killed when a bomb was thrown into McLaughlin's bar in north Belfast; three hours later, five Protestants died when a bomb was thrown into the Mountainview Tavern on the Shankill Road; seventy people were injured in the two incidents; and an eighteen-year-old man died in a republican feud in Ballymurphy. On 31 July three members of the popular Miami Showband were shot dead when members of the UVF flagged down their van near Newry; and two UVF men were killed when a bomb they were putting in the van blew up prematurely. Five Protestants died and forty others were injured on 13 August when the Bayardo bar was bombed on the Shankill Road. On Thursday 2 October twelve people were killed in bombings and shootings all over the region. The year 1976 had begun with the fire-bombing of Belfast city-centre stores, causing several million pounds worth of damage. On Sunday 4 January five Catholics were murdered by masked gunmen at Whitecross, Co. Armagh, and at Ballydugan, Co. Down. In revenge, the following day a bus carrying Protestant workers was stopped at Kingsmills, Co. Armagh; the Catholic bus driver was told to stand aside and ten Protestants were then machine-gunned to death. In just one twenty-four-hour period, on 5 June, eight died in tit-for-tat killings.[113]

Christopher Ewart-Biggs was appointed British ambassador to the Irish Republic in 1976; a writer of thrillers which had been banned by the Irish censors, who had worn a tinted monocle since he lost an eye at the Battle of El Alamein, he was particularly well-informed about Irish affairs. On the morning of Wednesday 21 July he was setting out from the ambassador's residence in Sandyford, Co. Dublin, when a landmine placed by the Provisionals exploded under his car: he and Judith Cooke, a Stormont civil servant, were killed; and Brian Cubbon, the permanent secretary to the Northern Ireland Office, and the driver were seriously injured.[114] Garret FitzGerald, due to receive the ambassador at 10 a.m., recalled: 'I was filled with horror at the atrocity, with shame that Irishmen had murdered the envoy of a neighbouring country, and with shock at our failure to protect him.' Jane Ewart-Biggs heard of the explosion on her car radio in London. In her grief she did not turn against the Irish but, as FitzGerald rightly observed, 'instead she took to her heart the country that had deprived her of her husband, and has worked ever since for reconciliation amongst Irish people and between Ireland and Britain'.[115] Very shortly afterwards, indeed, she was deeply involved in a new movement to end the violence: the Peace People.

PEACE PEOPLE, THE SHANKILL BUTCHERS AND WAR IN 'BANDIT COUNTRY'

On Tuesday 10 August 1976 Anne Maguire and her four children were walking near their home at Finaghy in south Belfast when a wounded gunman's getaway car crashed into them. Mrs Maguire was badly injured, two of her children were killed and a third child died the following day. Next day her sister, Mairead Corrigan, and Betty Williams, who had witnessed the tragedy, founded the Peace People.[116] For many years teachers, community workers, and groups such as Women Together and Protestant and Catholic Encounter had been working hard to promote reconciliation, but this new movement captured the imagination of Northern Ireland people to an extent that others previously had not. On 12 August over a thousand women gathered at Finaghy Road North where the children had died, and six thousand people signed a peace petition organised by women in Andersonstown. Two days later several bus loads of women from the Shankill joined another peace rally at the same place; twenty thousand attended a peace rally in Belfast's Ormeau Park on 21 August; a similar number marched up the Shankill Road a week later; and some twenty-five thousand gathered for a Peace People rally in Derry on 4 September.[117] In the following weeks peace rallies were held all over Northern Ireland, in many places south of the border, and in London.

Residents of the Shankill warmly shook hands with nuns and priests during the peace march there but the Peace People walked up the Falls in torrential rain to a more hostile reception of abuse and stones. The DUP declared on 14 September that the movement was 'counter-productive' and there were several ugly incidents in which Peace People workers were attacked by loyalists and republicans alike. Largely directed by the journalist Ciaran McKeown, the movement won acclaim across the world for the undoubted courage of its members. However, in such a deeply divided society, embittered by nearly seven years of violence, the Peace People found it difficult to sustain widespread support.

Violence had become a way of life, particularly in congested working-class districts characterised by dilapidated housing, poor job opportunities, high levels of deprivation and inadequate leisure facilities. Large parts of Belfast and Derry remained under the control of paramilitaries and gangs. Rent collectors, milkmen and bread roundsmen were robbed repeatedly; bars were held up at gunpoint before closing time; small shops, sub-post offices and bookmakers were particularly vulnerable; and the stealing and hijacking of vehicles seemed an everyday event. Public houses and illegal drinking clubs were the focus of both paramilitary and freelance criminal activity. Extortion and protection racketeering were operating on such a vast scale that the police hardly dared to estimate the annual cost to the community. Control of employment on building sites, in drinking clubs and in taxi services extended the authority and increased the income of paramilitaries on both sides of the sectarian divide. Those who broke the paramilitary code – for example, by taking money for themselves rather than for the organisation – were brutally beaten, shot in the knee or 'executed'.[118] In such circumstances and with so many weapons of death available, horrific murders were all too possible. In 1976 there were 121 sectarian killings, only one fewer than in 1972.[119]

During the winter 1975–6, much of north and west Belfast lived in fear while a gang of UVF murderers roamed the streets. Because of the way they mutilated their victims they were known as the Shankill Butchers. Their leader was Lennie Murphy who, though from a staunch Protestant family, was known as 'Murphy the Mick' at primary school because of his 'Catholic' surname. He had acquired a criminal record at the age of twelve.[120] The group would drive into a Catholic area, seize a victim, subject him to torture of appalling barbarity and then slit his throat. Murphy was as much feared in Protestant districts because he killed those who quarrelled with him. On Sunday 30 November 1975, for example, Noel Shaw, an eighteen-year-old UVF man, was forcibly taken to the Lawnbrook Social Club on the Shankill Road; there he was strapped to a chair on a stage, kicked, beaten, pistol-whipped and finally shot dead before an approving company of drinkers, and his body was dumped in a laundry basket. The gang continued their killings through 1976 and into 1977.[121] Chief Inspector Jimmy Nesbitt, whose C Division had solved 101 out of 132 murders since 1974, led Operation Knife Edge to catch the Shankill Butchers. Nesbitt actually arrested Murphy but failed to persuade the court to convict.[122] Later Murphy was convicted of arms possession but carried out another murder shortly after his release in August 1981. In November he was shot dead by the Provisionals, almost certainly with the assistance of information supplied by the UVF. There were eighty-seven death notices for Murphy in the *Belfast Telegraph* and masked UVF men, led by a piper playing 'Abide with me', fired shots in tribute at his funeral. His gravestone in Carnmoney cemetery bears the inscription: 'UVF. For God and Ulster. Here lies a soldier. Murphy.'[123]

In the attractive countryside of south Armagh the policy of Ulsterisation did not lead to military withdrawal. Known to the army as 'Bandit Country', this area had never observed any Provisional IRA ceasefire and troops regarded the salient of Northern Ireland jutting into the republic about Crossmaglen as the most dangerous posting of all. Thirty soldiers had been killed there by the end of 1975, over half in and about the large market square of the town. Gun and bomb attacks were frequently launched by the Provisionals from just across the border. A larger region, taking in Co. Armagh and part of Co. Tyrone, was referred to as the 'Murder Triangle' because so many soldiers and Provisionals had been killed there and because this was the principal rural district for tit-for-tat sectarian murders – during the 1975 ceasefire the Provisionals had killed twenty-six people in the area. The small but antiquated Irish Army could only hope to hinder but not prevent Provisional IRA activists from slipping over the border and back again unnoticed – the frontier between south Armagh and the republic had no fewer than 169 officially recognised crossing places and the Dublin government estimated that it would take two million men to seal off the South from the North.[124] The wildness of the south Armagh uplands provided excellent cover for insurgents and made continuous surveillance almost impossible.[125] Patrolling the area was a nerve-racking task, as paratrooper Captain A.F.N. Clarke recalled:

I check my equipment for the fiftieth time. Map, compass, belt and pouches, codes, personality check-list, stolen car list, ammunition, rifle and lastly my radio operator to see whether he has everything . . . within a few seconds we are airborne and moving tactically along at low level, swinging round trees and hills, dropping into little gullies, dodging power lines and telephone wires.
    We are moving down towards Cullaville right on the border with the Republic. The Wessex swings round in a tight turn, drops, flares, and touches on the soggy turf. As soon as the wheels touch we are off and running. Guns into fire positions, my section commanders and I showing the route. There's no time to notice the tight feeling in your stomach or the nervous playing with the safety catch . . .
    'Right lads, let's go.'
    We follow, fight our way through the blackthorn hedge and position ourselves on the road. It's an eerie feeling standing there knowing that there are hidden pairs of eyes watching us and logging every move we make for future reference.[126]

It was in 1976, under the direction of a new secretary of state, Roy Mason, that decisive measures were taken to suppress insurgency along the borderlands.

Fog shrouded Aldergrove airport the day Mason arrived in September 1976 and he had to travel by car rather than helicopter to Stormont – a slow journey, for the UDA hijacked vehicles, erected road blocks and organised twenty-six bomb hoaxes in protest at the treatment of loyalist prisoners. He surprised journalists by saying that as the IRA was 'reeling', his first concern was the poor state of Northern Ireland's economy: 'Unemployment, little new investment, too many businesses closing down, these are the questions which must receive priority.'[127] Merlyn Rees revealed his concern by his constantly furrowed brow, by his characteristic hand-wringing and by his frequent appearance drawing anxiously on a cheroot; and he was well-read in Irish history, frequently consulting J.L. Hammond's *Gladstone and the Irish Nation*, which he kept on his desk. To visitors he would read extracts from official security papers for 1916–22 and say: 'When you see the Cabinet papers for the 1970s, you'll see that nothing has changed!'[128] Roy Mason, by contrast, was bombastic and pugnacious, theatrically affecting the style of a paternalistic colonial governor, appearing for photo-opportunities clad in a tweed safari suit made for him in Belfast and smoking a pipe resolutely clenched between his teeth. 'He is an anti-Irish wee get,' Gerry Fitt said to journalists and, indeed, Mason showed his contempt for local politicians of all parties by refusing for some time to see them at Stormont.[129] The army welcomed his appointment: as defence secretary he had successfully resisted cuts in military spending and persuaded his cabinet colleagues of the need for a more robust approach to terrorism. Officers often referred to this former miner as 'Pitprop Mason', partly in admiration and partly for fear he would give way suddenly under the weight of his gung-ho verbiage.[130]

In fact the contrast between Rees and Mason was largely one of style. Rees had already abandoned hope of a constitutional arrangement acceptable to London and Dublin, and he had overseen the first use of the Special Air Service in south Armagh. The process of Ulsterisation would continue, Mason explained in June 1977: the police would enforce law and order; the army would specialise in undercover work; starting in North Queen Street in Belfast, soldiers and police officers would run joint operations; sentences for terrorist crime would be increased; and the use of Diplock courts – with one judge and no jury – would be extended for trying those accused of offences related to political violence.[131]

A more vigorous army presence was soon felt in south Armagh. The fort there had been attacked by home-made mortar bombs launched from a truck. In response the army built a concrete sangar to overlook the town square, brought in by a fleet of helicopters and erected in a day. The Special Air Service – known to all as the SAS – was deployed from 1976 onwards in 'Bandit Country' to deadly effect. Operating generally in four-man patrols, the SAS penetrated deep into the countryside, ambushing the Provisionals on several occasions with considerable success, and its reputation for ruthless efficiency may well have had a strong constraining influence. Such was the enthusiasm of units engaged in these covert operations that in many instances they pursued their foe into the republic – eight SAS men were arrested by *gardaí* in Co. Louth and charged with firearms offences in Dublin, but the explanation that the incursion had arisen out of a 'map-reading error' was accepted.[132] Indeed, co-operation between security forces north and south of the border steadily improved in these years. Border police stations fitted with telephone scramblers made the sharing of information more secure, and senior officers and specialists from the two jurisdictions met more often and more constructively than before.

Just before his departure, Rees had told the Commons that the situation was at its worst since 1972. A Northern Ireland Office announcement in August 1976 reported that since January the security forces had had 13 members killed and 111 injured; had come under attack on 230 occasions; had dealt with 180 explosions and made safe 81 bombs; had seized 4,864 pounds of explosives; and had charged 264 suspects with serious terrorist crimes.[133] Soon after, the army reported: 'The RUC and the UDR have been specifically singled out by the Provisionals. The death toll here is: RUC, 15; UDR, 7; Army, 6.'[134] The price of Ulsterisation was that more local recruits would pay for it with their lives. Nevertheless, from the summer of 1976 the Provisional IRA was thrown on the defensive. One reason was that arms were becoming far more difficult to obtain from the United States. During the early days of the Troubles, the IRA enjoyed much American sympathy, even from the establishment – Senator Edward Kennedy on 20 October 1971 had demanded the 'immediate withdrawal of British troops from Northern Ireland and the immediate convening of all parties for the purpose of establishing a united Ireland'. Atrocities carried out by the Provisionals soon caused Irish-American spokespersons to change their view, Senator Daniel Moynihan denouncing the Provisional IRA as 'a band of sadistic murderers'. The Irish Northern Aid Committee – better known as Noraid – at first succeeded in smuggling arms in suitcases, containers and furniture to Ireland, but the Federal Bureau of Investigation and the Central Intelligence Agency were now closing in on the organisation. During the first years of the Troubles, Noraid sent 600,000 US dollars to Ireland but in the mid-seventies this dropped to 160,000 US dollars. Colonel Gaddafi of Libya claimed to have given £5 million to the Provisionals by 1974 but the steady flow of arms was severely interrupted when the *Claudia*, containing five tons of weapons, was seized off the republic's coast in March 1973.[135]

During the latter part of 1976 and throughout 1977 there was a dramatic drop in incidents of political violence: civilian deaths had fallen to 69 in 1977 from 245 in 1976; shootings were down by 33 per cent; explosions by 52 per cent; and there had been no sectarian murders since May 1976.[136] In part this was due to the Government's success in curbing loyalist violence. After Northern Ireland's longest and costliest trial so far, on 11 March 1977 twenty-six men were given sentences amounting in total to some seven hundred years – a blow from which the UVF took much time to recover.[137] Two months later Mason was able to give a triumphant rebuff to a fresh loyalist challenge to the maintenance of the law.

Paisley headed an organisation calling itself the United Unionist Action Council. On 23 April it gave 'notice to Mr Roy Mason that he has seven days to begin a powerful and effective offensive against the IRA and announce steps to implement the Convention Report'.[138] Mason used the time given him to bring over the Scots Guards emergency Spearhead Battalion, together with technical experts and specialist vehicles. Newman was determined to be firm, as one of his subdivisional commanders recalled:

> I told him that if we moved against the Protestants the whole place would go up in flames . . . that there would be the most fantastic backlash. He just said, 'You have no discretion in the matter. If there is a barricade it will be removed. If you feel you can't do it, I shall want to know why – personally.' My God! I was terrified.[139]

When the 'constitutional stoppage' began on the night of Monday 2 May, Newman called in journalists and television crews to observe the police sweep away a large barricade in east Belfast. Paisley had made a grave miscalculation. This time the trade-union leaders persuaded their members to stay at work and on Tuesday the rock-'n'-roll veteran, Chuck Berry, was able to go ahead with his concert that evening in Belfast.[140] The power workers failed to join the strike and by the following weekend Paisley was reduced to making a last stand in Ballymena. Farm vehicles and barricades sealed off the streets, but on the morning of 9 May troops and police encircled the town, army bulldozers swept aside the tractors and trailers, and Paisley and several of his supporters were arrested. The strike swiftly collapsed and Mason glowed with pride at this demonstration of what he saw as even-handed treatment of Protestants and Catholics alike.

'Stonemason will not break us,' the Provisionals had claimed, but by December Newman was able to report to the secretary of state that the year 1977 had been the least violent for six years.[141] Mason declared that 'the tide has turned against the terrorists and the message for 1978 is one of real hope', and he told the *Daily Express*:

> We are squeezing the terrorists like rolling up a toothpaste tube. We are squeezing them out of their safe havens. We are squeezing them away from their money supplies. We are squeezing them out of society and into prison.[142]

Alan Wright, chairman of the Northern Ireland Police Federation, warned: 'Words can be as lethal as bullets in the unfortunate circumstances in which we work.'[143] Mairead Corrigan and Betty Williams, even as they received the Nobel Peace Prize in Oslo on 10 December, realised the damaging effect of Mason's bravado on their attempts to woo Catholics from violence; as it was, the Unionist-dominated Belfast City Council had decided against giving the Peace People leaders a civic reception.[144] In any case, Mason's triumphalist utterances were premature.

'THE IRISH WILL HAVE TO BE LEFT TO SWEAT IT OUT FOR A WHILE'

Just before 9 p.m. on Friday 17 February 1978 three experienced Provisionals hooked two firebombs on to window security grilles of La Mon House. This large hotel, midway between Belfast and Comber, was packed with more than three hundred people attending a variety of functions, including annual prize distributions by the Northern Ireland Collie Club and the Northern Ireland Junior Motor Cycle Club. The devices were of a new type made of recrystallised ammonium nitrate mixed with aluminium filings and attached to gallon tins of petrol. The warning was telephoned too late and the blasts threw sheets of blazing petrol across a crowded function room and sent a fireball through the hotel, engulfing it in minutes. Twelve people died and twenty-three were horribly injured. Some victims had been so badly burned that pathologists had to depend on dental records to identify them.[145] The following day the RUC issued ten thousand copies of a poster showing one of the charred bodies, and many institutions and businesses displayed them for months afterwards to mark the widespread abhorrence felt on both sides of the community.

The La Mon atrocity was the culmination of a new bombing campaign begun in the previous December, when, during a fortnight, the

Provisionals had detonated twenty devices all over the region in an attempt to kill off the ailing tourist industry. Clearly the organisation had lost none of its ruthlessness and was regaining some of its strengths. Mason was right to say that there were fewer explosions, but the average size of each bomb detonated was much larger than before. The movement was reorganising: Dublin-based 'armchair' leaders were sidelined by activists in Ulster, who set up a separate northern command in November 1976, in which volunteers were divided into companies and active service units.[146] Those in the large companies collected and hid firearms, gathered intelligence, drove cars and imposed the Provisionals' rough justice in the Catholic enclaves by, for example, knee-capping burglars, drug pushers and persistent joyriders. The small active service units were more tightly disciplined than before; each composed of only three or four members using aliases, they did not – in theory, at any rate – know the identities of those who controlled them. This reorganisation had been forced on the Provisionals by the vastly improved system of army and police intelligence.[147] The Prevention of Terrorism Act permitted suspects to be held for up to seven days without being charged. During that time, many of those brought to Castlereagh police headquarters broke down under interrogation and yielded much valuable information; as a senior detective recalled:

> The fact that we were able to interview them for hours on end and through the night was what broke them. On the journey down in the car, once Castlereagh was mentioned they were talking freely.[148]

The Provisionals countered this with some success by training their volunteers to say nothing at all, rather than, as before, providing them with alibis, which were so often proved false. The UDA adopted a similar approach: a captured training document ordered its men to 'make no statement no matter if someone else does. The organization will not accept any reason even should you only involve yourself, 48% planning + 1% operating + 1% escape and evasion + 50% silence = 100% success.'[149]

The interrogation techniques used at Castlereagh provoked a flood of complaints against the police and a report by Keith Kyle on BBC television's *Tonight* programme on 2 March 1977 eventually led to an investigation by Amnesty International. In June 1978 Mason failed in his attempt to dissuade Amnesty from publishing its report, which accused the interrogators of inhumane treatment of suspects. He therefore announced a government inquiry led by the English Crown Court judge Harry Bennett. The Bennett report of March 1979 strongly criticised the regime at Castlereagh and at the new interrogation centre at Gough barracks in Armagh. It was the failure of the Government to act decisively on the report's recommendations for the introduction of a wide range of safeguards that caused Gerry Fitt to withdraw his support in the Commons.[150] A fortnight later, at Westminster, James Callaghan, the prime minister since April 1976, lost a motion of confidence by one vote.

The Callaghan government's constant struggle to retain a majority in the Commons precluded careful consideration of new political initiatives in Northern Ireland. The *New Statesman* reported in January 1977 the prime minister's view that 'the Irish will have to be left to sweat it out for a while if they are ever to come to their senses'.[151] Mason's indifference to complaints about the security forces reinforced the isolation of the SDLP but, at the same time, Labour's evaporating majority encouraged attempts to come to informal terms with the Unionists. Northern Ireland was promised more seats at Westminster – where it was underrepresented in relation to its population – in the hope that the Unionists would keep Labour in office.[152] This unedifying deal, with all the hallmarks of expediency, soon fell through. Having delayed fatally during 'the winter of discontent', marked by widespread industrial unrest, Callaghan was forced to go to the polls in May 1979. The Conservatives were swept to power and talk of British withdrawal from Northern Ireland – frequently heard even at the most senior level – quickly dried up. For the next eleven years direct rule would continue under the supervision of just one prime minister – Margaret Thatcher.

THE CONSERVATIVES RETURN TO THE PROBLEM

Margaret Thatcher, when leader of the opposition, had visited Belfast in 1977. There, on one of her celebrated 'shop-abouts', she bought some Galway cut glass. It was a small but significant gaffe: she could have chosen a piece made by Tyrone Crystal, a firm created by cross-community action in Dungannon and, with government help, succeeding so well that it was now seeking an export market.[153] Clearly she had much to learn about the Irish imbroglio, as Garret FitzGerald recalled after a meeting with her in the same year:

> Margaret Thatcher then asked me why politicians in Northern Ireland could not reach agreement with each other. As I tried to explain the depth of the differences between them it became clear that she was labouring under the illusion that the majority Convention report had involved a proposal for emergency power-sharing over a five-year period. I endeavoured to put her right on this . . . I felt torn between dismay at the fact that even after eighteen months of party leadership she was still so poorly

briefed on Northern Ireland and a measure of hope that I might have made sufficient impact to reverse the drift in Conservative policy under Neave's spokesmanship.[154]

Airey Neave had caused alarm in both the SDLP and the Dáil by demanding a tougher security policy in which the army would once more take the lead and by moving the Conservatives away from the bipartisan commitment to power-sharing at Westminster. Best-known for his daring escape from Colditz prison camp during the Second World War, Neave was a close personal friend of Margaret Thatcher's and he had worked hard to secure her election as party leader.

A succession of atrocities was to hasten the political education of Margaret Thatcher on Northern Ireland affairs. In The Hague on Thursday 22 March 1979 the Provisional IRA shot dead Sir Richard Sykes, the British ambassador to the Netherlands, and on the same day it detonated twenty-four explosions across Northern Ireland.[155] A week later Airey Neave was driving his car out of the House of Commons underground car park when a bomb strapped underneath the driver's seat exploded: he died soon afterwards in hospital. This murder was claimed by the Irish National Liberation Army, a breakaway paramilitary group, which stated Neave had been chosen for assassination because of his 'rabid militarist call for more repression against the Irish people'.[156] That day Callaghan had called a general election and, as the opinion polls clearly signalled a Conservative victory, Neave had been expected to be appointed the next Northern Ireland secretary of state. Following the Labour defeat, Margaret Thatcher as prime minister chose Humphrey Atkins to take on the task intended for Neave. 'Humphrey Who?' asked a headline in the *Sunday News* and, indeed, Atkins was comparatively unknown – so, too, were the policies he would pursue.[157]

The Provisional IRA once again had been intensifying its campaign of violence. On Tuesday 17 April, just before the election, four police officers were killed when a 1,000-pound bomb in a van parked near Bessbrook in Co. Armagh exploded as they drove past, and during the month eight soldiers and three UDR men had died in several violent incidents.[158] The Provisionals published a secret British Army report they had obtained, which had been written by a senior intelligence officer, Brigadier James Glover. Entitled *Future Terrorist Trends*, the Glover report gloomily concluded that the Provisional IRA campaign would continue as long as the British remained in Northern Ireland: there was no shortage of recruits, who were well trained; active service units were composed of men with up to ten years' operational experience; the Provisional IRA had as its source of income each year about £550,000 from armed robbery, £250,000 from racketeering, and £120,000 from overseas donations; and attacks on the security forces were becoming more effective.[159] Glover expected the Provisionals to possess more sophisticated weapons in future:

We expect the main development in the next five years to be better sights, including possibly a laser sighting aid and night vision aids. Weapon handling and tactics used, particularly in rural areas, will probably improve. The Provisionals may well attempt to step up their use of mortars. They may readapt the Mk 6 or similar weapons for ranges up to 1,200 metres and the Mk 9 for ranges under 300 metres . . . some anti-aircraft missiles may well be in their hands before the end of the period.[160]

Certainly the Provisionals were beginning to imitate the SAS along the border, sleeping by day and operating at night, laying mines and drawing the security forces into traps. There were three Provisional IRA commando units, each with ten men specially trained to operate along the border and each volunteer issued with a rifle, a magnum pistol and a knife.[161] The south Armagh commando unit carried out two operations on Monday 27 August, making it the bloodiest day of 1979. During that morning in the little harbour of Mullaghmore in Co. Sligo, Earl Mountbatten and five members of his family boarded *Shadow V*, a twenty-eight-foot cruiser, to set out on the last fishing expedition of their holiday. When the boat had cleared the harbour entrance it was blown to pieces by a radio-triggered bomb. Earl Mountbatten, aged seventy-nine; his grandson Nicholas, aged fourteen; and a fifteen-year-old crew member from Enniskillen, Paul Maxwell, died almost immediately. Dowager Lady Brabourne died of her injuries the following day, and Lord and Lady Brabourne were seriously hurt. Tommy McMahon, a carpenter from Carrickmacross who was explosives officer in the south Armagh Provisional IRA commando unit, was arrested very soon afterwards.[162]

On the same day other members of the south Armagh unit prepared a trap on the dual carriageway running along the northern shore of Carlingford Lough between Warrenpoint and Newry. Operating from the southern shore, on the Cooley peninsula in the republic, and using a model aircraft radio control device, the Provisional IRA team detonated a bomb in a hay wagon as a convoy of vehicles carrying a platoon of the 2nd Parachute Regiment passed by. Six men were killed and the survivors took shelter by the stone gateway to Narrow Water Castle. Reinforcements arrived by air and as a Wessex helicopter lifted off with some of the wounded on board another explosion erupted. The Provisionals had expected the soldiers to take refuge here and had planted 500 pounds of explosives several days beforehand under the granite archway. Another twelve men died. The Provisionals fired

737

some shots which were returned by troops, who killed an Englishman on holiday – as it happened, one of the queen's coachmen – on the south side of the lough. For the Parachute Regiment this was the worst loss since the Arnhem campaign of 1944 and for the prime minister it was an awful demonstration of the destructive power of the Provisional IRA.[163]

'ON MY KNEES I BEG YOU TO TURN AWAY FROM THE PATHS OF VIOLENCE'

'Come along! Let's get on with this,' Margaret Thatcher said at brigade headquarters in Portadown, cutting short officers' small talk. Two days after the Warrenpoint massacre, the prime minister had flown into Northern Ireland to view the situation for herself. Brigadier David Thorne produced a single epaulette from the uniform of Lieutenant-Colonel David Blair, commanding officer of the Queen's Own Highlanders, killed at Warrenpoint. 'Madam Prime Minister,' he said, 'this is all I have left of a very brave officer.' The army chiefs demanded the right to hot pursuit across the border, the introduction of selective detention and a return to full control of security under the direction of one supremo. Donning a combat jacket, Margaret Thatcher asked to be taken to the Crossmaglen post and as she talked to soldiers there they showed her where twenty men had died not a hundred yards from where she was standing.[164]

It was widely expected that the prime minister would accede to army demands, but the only concession was the appointment of Sir Maurice Oldfield, former head of MI6, as chief security co-ordinator. Ulsterisation would continue: more troops would be withdrawn and the RUC would again be augmented. Speaking to Margaret Thatcher at Gough barracks during her visit, Newman had been able to convince her that – despite recent disasters – the police were overseeing a steady improvement in security.[165]

The Provisional IRA's popularity seemed to slump in Catholic areas, particularly after the killings of 27 August. The murder of Earl Mountbatten – the viceroy who supervised the end of British rule in India – was inexplicable and few would have been convinced by the limp justification given by Bobby Sands, the Twinbrook Provisional IRA leader: 'He knew the problem and did nothing about it. He did nothing except to exploit Ireland and its natural resources.'[166] The daily lives of ordinary citizens became more 'normal' than at any time since the start of the Troubles. Tens of thousands of Ulster's Catholic population were present at Drogheda on Saturday 29 September 1979 when Pope John Paul II addressed 'all men and women engaged in violence' and said:

'On my knees I beg you to turn away from the paths of violence and return to the ways of peace.'[167] Though promptly rejected by the Provisionals, it was an appeal that had the support of the vast majority of the Irish people.

Margaret Thatcher, while reinforcing her reputation for intransigence in other spheres, was nevertheless showing greater flexibility than before in her treatment of the Northern Ireland problem. In part this was due to the value she placed on the 'special relationship' between Britain and the United States. Tip O'Neill, Speaker of the United States House of Representatives, led a successful lobby to bring pressure on Westminster and in August 1979 the American State Department caused much alarm by suspending the sale of handguns to the RUC. Soon afterwards Atkins announced a new political initiative: a round-table conference of all constitutional parties would be called to find a new devolutionary solution. A consultative document followed in November, which offered six models of government for the region and ruled out of order discussion on Irish unity or the constitutional status of Northern Ireland. Because there would be no debate on the 'Irish Dimension', the majority in the SDLP opposed the White Paper.[168] As a result, Fitt resigned from leadership of the party, giving this explanation:

> Nationalism has been a political concept in Ireland over many, many years but I suggest that it has never brought peace to the people of the six counties. I for one have never been a nationalist to the total exclusion of my socialist ideals.[169]

John Hume was elected the new leader – a position, in reality, he had been holding for some time – and under his direction the party's commitment to peaceful tactics remained as firm as ever. Nevertheless, with Hume at the helm, the SDLP was adopting a more traditional nationalist stand which threatened to frustrate the Atkins initiative. The loyalists, in turn, ensured that the round-table conference was doomed. James Molyneaux, leader of the Official Unionists since 1979, flatly rejected the White Paper on the grounds that its implementation would mean Northern Ireland's inevitable absorption into the Irish Republic.[170] For a time it looked as if Paisley might agree to compromise. He and his party had recovered remarkably since the collapse of the 'constitutional stoppage': in the 1977 local government elections the DUP had more than doubled its number of councillors to seventy-four; and in the European elections in 1979 when he attacked the EC as a threat to Protestantism, Paisley easily headed the poll with just under 30 per cent of first-preference votes.[171] In February 1980 *The Economist* observed:

'Mr Paisley seems to be becoming more moderate now that he sees the possibility of becoming top dog in the province.' He described Atkins as an 'engaging mannerly Tory' and his 'friend', but it soon emerged that he still opposed sharing power with Catholics and simply sought the return of majority Protestant rule.[172]

It was November before the Conservative government admitted the complete failure of its constitutional initiative and now, like the SDLP, Margaret Thatcher turned to Dublin for a way out of the impasse. The prospects looked poor enough. Jack Lynch had been replaced as taoiseach in December 1979, largely because Fianna Fáil objected to his agreement to exchange police information with the British and allow British Army helicopters to fly up to five miles into the republic's airspace in pursuit of fleeing gunmen and bombers.[173] Lynch's successor was Charles Haughey, a man still tainted with the 1970 arms scandal and whose father had been second in command of the northern division of the IRA in the 1920s. Haughey had been concerned to establish his republican credentials and pointedly refused to condemn IRA front organisations in America. Nevertheless, preliminary talks in London between the taoiseach and the prime minister seemed promising and on 8 December 1980 Margaret Thatcher flew to Dublin – the first visit to the city by a British premier since partition. The conference appeared to be a diplomatic triumph: the joint communiqué issued later referred to 'further development of the unique relationship between the two countries' and announced another meeting to consider 'the totality of relationships within these islands' and joint studies to find ways of setting up 'possible new institutional structures'.[174]

Paisley was appalled. On 19 December Margaret Thatcher agreed to discuss her Dublin summit with the DUP leader in her House of Commons office. The prime minister was repelled by his hectoring tone as he accused her of giving Dublin 'direct involvement' in Northern Ireland's affairs. Referring to her promise that the region would remain part of the United Kingdom until a majority there voted otherwise, she furiously repeated 'I stand by the guarantee' again and again, striking her chair for emphasis. Paisley returned to Northern Ireland to launch a new campaign, with the cry: 'Stop the joint studies.' A bombastic claim by Brian Lenihan, the Irish foreign minister, that Ireland would be reunited within ten years helped to rally Protestants to the new cause. In February 1981 Paisley brought journalists to see five hundred men in combat jackets drawn up in military formation on a hill near Ballymena. Soon after, in imitation of the Covenant, he produced an 'Ulster Declaration' for loyalists to sign in protest at the Thatcher–Haughey initiative, and he announced eleven rallies across Northern Ireland, which he termed the 'Carson Trail'.[175] At Omagh he declared:

Our ancestors cut a civilisation out of the bogs and meadows of this country while Mr Haughey's ancestors were wearing pig-skins and living in caves . . . When our forefathers donned the British uniform and fought for their King and Country, Mr Haughey's fellow countrymen used their lights to guide enemy bombers to their targets in Northern Ireland.[176]

At Newtownards Paisley vilified the Official Unionists, even accusing them of plotting his assassination, and described Haughey as a man with 'a green baton dripping with blood' in the one hand and 'a noose specially prepared for the Protestants of Ulster in the other'. In fact the Carson Trail slowly fizzled out but Paisley had firmly established his claim to be the principal defender of loyalist interests: in the local government elections of May 1981 the DUP vote for the first time surpassed that of the Official Unionists, albeit by the slenderest of margins.[177] By this time, however, relations between Dublin and London had cooled almost to freezing point as the result of a new and grave crisis: the hunger strike in the Maze prison.

'WE ACCEPT THE TRAGIC CONSEQUENCES THAT MOST CERTAINLY AWAITS US':
THE H-BLOCK HUNGER STRIKE

Little notice was taken by journalists on 1 March 1981 when Bobby Sands, the Provisional IRA prisoners' officer commanding, began refusing food in the Maze prison. Hunger strikes had been attempted before in Northern Ireland's gaols but none had been taken to the point of death. Warders nevertheless warned that Sands was likely to see it through and a fellow prisoner, Pat McGeown, observed that he was 'withdrawn . . . you got the impression you were talking to someone who was one step removed from life already'.[178] The Sands family, burned out of its home in the north Belfast estate of Rathcoole in 1972, had moved to Twinbrook in west Belfast, and there Sands had joined the Provisionals at the age of eighteen. Found soon afterwards in possession of a gun, he spent three years in custody and then returned to lead the Provisional IRA active service unit in Twinbrook. As he wrote in a 'comm' – a secret communication written on toilet paper and generally hidden in the rectum or beneath the foreskin – he

was snared again on 14.10.76, six months later, outside a furniture showroom in Dunmurry in which were four ticking bombs. You'll get all the crack on that somewhere, it was pretty fierce – two or three comrades were shot, I was caught in a car with three others and a gun. Anyway I

741

was took to Castlereagh and got very bad time . . . I got sentenced to 14 years for possession with intent.[179]

In the Maze he took a lead in the prisoners' campaign for the restoration of political status.

'You must be joking me,' Ciaran Nugent said when he was asked what size he took in clothes before being given a prison uniform.[180] He was the first IRA man convicted of a terrorist offence and sent to gaol after the cut-off date for special category status. Nugent refused to wear prison clothes and, for breach of discipline, was confined to his cell twenty-four hours a day and lost his entitlement to 50 per cent remission of sentence for good behaviour. Others joined Nugent and – after furniture had been broken up – their lives were restricted to concrete rooms, each with only another cell mate, a Bible, a mattress and three blankets. That was in 1976: the 'blanket protest' had begun.

'Criminalisation', an essential feature of Ulsterisation, was anathema to Provisional IRA volunteers who saw themselves as freedom fighters in a noble cause. Mason and Atkins saw them as common law-breakers and killers, and both were determined that they should have no more privileges than other convicted criminals. Special category prisoners, internees dwindling in number as they were speedily released, were held in Nissen huts at Long Kesh; but the new inmates were put into a complex of eight single-storey brick units whose shape led them to be named H-blocks. Each H-block had cost over £1 million to build and the Government was almost certainly right to assert that the new prison – now known as the Maze after the adjacent racecourse – was the most modern and luxurious in Europe. Mason would not yield to the demand for political status and so the 'blanketmen' refused to wash and finally resorted to a 'dirty protest' – following brawls with warders in 1978 over the emptying of chamber pots, prisoners smeared their excrement over their cell walls. Towards the end of 1980 there were 1,365 prisoners in the Maze, 837 republicans, of whom 341 were taking part in the dirty protest.[181] Atkins, like Mason before him, refused to give way and the Provisional IRA launched a campaign to assassinate prison warders: nineteen, including a female warder, had been murdered by January 1980.

The propaganda value of the hunger strike had been vividly demonstrated by Terence MacSwiney in 1920 and it had been a form of protest practised in Ireland in ancient times. The Provisional IRA army council, however, feared that a major hunger strike would divert resources and that failure would bring ridicule on the movement. At first, the Provisional leaders seemed proved right when a strike in 1980 collapsed in December. Some prisoners were determined to resume and Sands replied to an army council appeal to hold back with this comm:

Comrade, find enclosed confirmation of hunger strike. We need that hunger strike statement that fast comrade. The delay is damaging us . . . We accept the tragic consequences that most certainly awaits us and the overshadowing fact that death may not secure a principled settlement.[182]

In March 1981 Sands wrote his last comm, a birthday request to 'get me one miserly book and try to leave it in: the Poems of Ethna Carberry – cissy. That's really all I want, last request as they say. Some ask for cigarettes, others for blindfolds, yer man asks for Poetry.'[183] The by-election in April, resulting from the death of Frank Maguire, Independent MP for Fermanagh–South Tyrone, presented a unique opportunity as other selected prisoners joined Sands in refusing all food. Bernadette Devlin (now Bernadette McAliskey) threatened to stand if a hunger striker was not chosen as a candidate. She had survived a UDA gun attack in January, when she had been shot nine times – this the Provisionals had avenged five days later by killing Sir Norman Stronge, aged eighty-six and a former Speaker of the Northern Ireland Commons, and his son James, a former Unionist MP, and by burning down their home of Tynan Abbey.[184] The SDLP accepted an agreed anti-unionist candidate, Frank Maguire's brother Noel, but he withdrew at the last moment in favour of Bobby Sands. There was intense international attention on the day of the election, Thursday 9 April. Catholics largely ignored the SDLP advice not to vote and in an 87 per cent poll only 3,280 ballot papers were spoiled; the Official Unionist Harry West was defeated by a margin of 1,446 votes; and Sands was elected to Westminster. That victory came on the fortieth consecutive day that Sands had refused food.

The unnerved British government did not refuse the dying man's request for a visit by members of the Dáil. The three who came were also members of the European parliament: Síle de Valera, granddaughter of the statesman; Neil Blaney; and Dr John O'Connell, editor of the *Irish Medical Times*. They found Sands sleeping on a sheepskin rug spread over a water bed, his sight almost gone. Dr O'Connell attempted to persuade Sands to end his hunger strike. Haughey, Hume and several Catholic bishops called on the European Commission of Human Rights to intervene – the commission had already acknowledged that the prisoners had no right to political status but condemned 'the inflexible approach of the State authorities'.[185] At the request of Cardinal Tomás Ó Fiaich, the archbishop of Armagh, Pope John Paul II sent his secretary, the Newry-born Monsignor John Magee, to visit

743

Sands and attempt mediation. Neither the republican prisoners nor the secretary of state would give way. Then, at 1.17 a.m. on Tuesday 5 May 1981, Sands died on the sixty-sixth day of his hunger strike.

The American government issued a statement expressing deep regret. In Belgium students invaded the British consulate at Ghent. In France the Le Mans city council named a street after Sands, and in Paris thousands marched behind a portrait of Sands, chanting 'The IRA will conquer.' Opposition members of the Indian Upper House stood for a minute's silence. In Rome Amintore Fanfani, president of the Italian senate, expressed condolences and in the Soviet Union *Pravda* described the episode as 'another tragic page in the grim chronicle of oppression, discrimination, terror and violence' in Ireland. Bombs were thrown at British property in Milan, Lisbon and Toulouse.[186] On the day of the funeral at least one hundred thousand people – nearly one fifth of the entire Catholic population of Northern Ireland – crowded the route from St Luke's Church in Twinbrook to Milltown cemetery. Fearing trouble, the army put up huge screens in front of a Protestant estate near its Lenadoon post. There was no violence: indeed, journalists present found the silence, broken only by a lone piper, awesome in so vast a throng of mourners.

The hunger strike went on. Francis Hughes died on 12 May; Raymond McCreesh and Patsy O'Hara on 21 May; Joe McDonnell on 8 July; Martin Hurson on 13 July; Kevin Lynch on 1 August; Kieran Doherty on 2 August; Tom McElwee on 8 August; and Mickey Devine on 20 August. Riots reminiscent of those a decade earlier erupted after every death. Amongst those who died were Carol-Anne Kelly, aged eleven, and fourteen-year-old Julie Livingstone, both killed by plastic bullets; and a milkman and his fifteen-year-old son, fatally injured when the float was pelted by bricks in Belfast. Meanwhile, the Provisionals stepped up their relentless war on the security forces – in the worst incident five soldiers were killed by a landmine near Bessbrook on 19 May.[187]

Father Denis Faul, the Dungannon priest best known for his documentation of army and police brutality, did more than anyone else to break the deadlock. Towards the end of July he persuaded families of some of the hunger strikers to call on Gerry Adams, vice president of Provisional Sinn Féin, to end the protest. The Provisional IRA denounced Faul as a 'treacherous, conniving man', but he responded that in choosing a prisoner who was ill with an ulcer to join the hunger strike the Provisionals were 'scraping the bottom of the barrel'.[188] By 9 September five hunger strikers were being given medical attention at the request of their families. Five days later, in a cabinet reshuffle, James Prior replaced Atkins as secretary of state. Widely believed to have been assigned this bed of nails as punishment for his 'wet' opposition to the prime minister's right-wing radicalism, Prior bravely declared that it was his 'duty to the nation' to go to Belfast – a city for which he had warm feelings, he told reporters on his arrival, because he had kissed his first girl there.[189] Prior had a well-established reputation as a patient, flexible and yet formidable negotiator with the trade unions, avoiding the head-on confrontation so desired by his leader. During his period of office he was to shield Northern Ireland from some of the most doctrinaire features of Thatcherism.

During late July Atkins had repeated that there could be no negotiations on the Maze prison dispute. On 17 September Prior visited the hunger strikers and spoke to them for three hours. The Government's approach to the issue was attracting widespread criticism. The French foreign minister, Claude Cheysson, spoke of the hunger strikers' 'supreme sacrifice', saying that their courage demanded 'respect'; he offered to refuse to attend the wedding of Prince Charles and Lady Diana Spencer but Dublin discouraged this protest gesture. In New York the British consulate did not fly the Union flag for fear it would be torn down.[190] In a two-hour speech in Havana to representatives from a hundred states Fidel Castro described the IRA as heroes and likened the regime at the Maze to the Spanish Inquisition, thus prompting the British ambassador, David Thomas, to walk out. In Stormont at the end of September Prior talked at length to Father Faul and Cardinal Ó Fiaich. Concessions were hinted at, and on Saturday 3 October 1981 the Provisional IRA called off the hunger strike. During 217 days of protest, 10 prisoners had starved themselves to death and 61 people had been killed, 30 of them members of the security forces. The *Daily Mail* commended Margaret Thatcher's 'magnificent obstinacy'; the *Sunday Express* applauded the victory for 'firm moral purpose, over the confused, tortured mentality of appeasement'; and the *Guardian* observed that the 'Government has overcome the hunger strikes by a show of resolute determination not to be bullied'.[191] The Foreign Office privately held a very different view: the handling of the whole affair had been an unmitigated diplomatic disaster which was to add to Britain's difficulties during the Falklands War.

Three days after the ending of the hunger strike, the secretary of state announced that henceforth Maze prisoners could wear their own clothes, half of the lost remission would be restored and visiting and mail facilities would be improved. The granting of the first concession alone would have ended the hunger strike in the initial stages. Prison work was still demanded until Sunday 25 September 1983, when thirty-eight

Provisional IRA prisoners got out of the Maze in the biggest escape in United Kingdom prison history; even though nineteen were rapidly recaptured, the workshops at the Maze were closed because they presented too great a security risk.[192] Formal recognition of political status was never given, but the Provisionals were discovering the new attractions of the ballot box.

THE BALLOT BOX, THE ARMALITE AND ROLLING DEVOLUTION

On 1 November 1981 Provisional Sinn Féin met for its annual conference, or ard fheis, in Dublin's Mansion House. There Danny Morrison, the party's director of publicity, asked rhetorically:

> Who here really believes that we can win the war through the ballot box? But will anyone here object if with a ballot box in this hand and an Armalite in this hand we take power in Ireland?[193]

The delegates did not object and endorsed the movement's new strategy of contesting elections while at the same time continuing its campaign of violence. The victory of Sands in Fermanagh–South Tyrone had been repeated in August 1981, when Owen Carron, his election agent, won the seat. Adams, in particular, was certain the republican cause could be advanced by harnessing the surge of sympathy for the hunger strikers in Catholic areas.

The mass turnouts at the funerals of prisoners who had starved themselves to death did not necessarily mean a comparable number supported the Provisional IRA or the demands for political status, or would be prepared to vote for Provisional Sinn Féin. People essentially had been paying their respect to men of their own class and creed, and had been signalling their belief that the British government had been callous and inflexible.[194] Nevertheless, the standing of the Provisionals in Catholic enclaves had risen spectacularly and members of the organisation's active service units felt themselves to be freedom fighters more surely than at any time since the imposition of direct rule.

On the morning of Saturday 14 November 1981 five members of the Provisionals' Belfast brigade walked into a community centre in Finaghy and shot dead the Reverend Robert Bradford and a caretaker who tried to stop them. Bradford, the Official Unionist MP for South Belfast, had been meeting his constituents at his regular weekly surgery. Coming only a fortnight after Morrison's speech, this murder was a brutal reminder that the Armalite was not being muzzled for the sake of the ballot box. Yet intervention in the electoral arena forced the Provisionals to cultivate Catholic support: their violence for the next few years was more carefully targeted at members of the security forces and at their

746

political enemies; and, for a time, the destructive assault on commercial premises and offices – which, after all, generally employed Catholics as well as Protestants – was almost completely brought to a halt. Provisional Sinn Féin was shortly to get an opportunity to test the political waters when James Prior launched a fresh scheme to find an acceptable constitutional arrangement for Northern Ireland.

At Bradford's funeral only swift action by bodyguards prevented the secretary of state from being assaulted by loyalist mourners. On 23 November Protestants took part in a 'day of action' to protest against inadequate security and Paisley organised demonstrations across the region calling for a 'third force' – officially recognised paramilitaries similar to the B Specials – to suppress republican violence. Prior, however, was more concerned with the large-scale alienation of the Catholic minority in the wake of the hunger strike. The complete integration of Northern Ireland into the rest of the United Kingdom – then the majority view in the Official Unionist Party – he ruled out largely because it was totally unacceptable to the SDLP. Garret FitzGerald, taoiseach since June, encouraged the British government to attempt an internal constitutional arrangement. In February 1982 Prior unveiled his plan for 'rolling devolution': a new assembly would be elected, this time with only an advisory and consultative role, executive power being transferred in stages only if cross-community support for a devolutionary government could be achieved.[195]

The spring of 1982 proved to be a bleak one for the hapless secretary of state. The Official Unionists demanded either full integration or the implementation of the convention report; the DUP sought devolution without power-sharing; the SDLP, disappointed by the lack of reference to an 'Irish Dimension', pronounced the proposals 'unworkable'; and Haughey, who had ousted FitzGerald in February, defiantly rejected an internal solution and called for eventual British withdrawal. Prior doggedly pressed ahead and drafted a White Paper explaining the bill: it stated that direct rule had 'served Ulster well' and that Northern Ireland politicians had an 'inescapable responsibility' to devise a scheme of regional government likely to command 'widespread acceptance' throughout the community.[196] The cabinet gave its tepid approval, Prior recalling later that Margaret Thatcher was distinctly chilly in her reception of his plans.

The Falklands War was raging when the bill was debated at Westminster but, even so, interest there was so flaccid that it gave a very strong indication of British boredom with the seemingly insoluble and interminable crisis in the region. No major party leader spoke and all five of the former Northern Ireland secretaries of state remained silent.

Gerry Fitt remarked that he was the only MP from Northern Ireland who was completely in favour of the bill. The Unionists and a group of dissident Conservatives kept the debate going by denouncing the bill's provisions.[197] Enoch Powell, who after his break with the Conservatives had represented South Down as an Official Unionist, opposed any form of devolution:

> The ultimate truth is that within the United Kingdom political purpose can only be dissolved and held in equilibrium, deprived of its dangers and given beneficence, force and the power of improvement, within the single parliamentary legislative structure of the United Kingdom.'[198]

Prior recalled that Margaret Thatcher thought it 'a rotten Bill' and that Ian Gow, her parliamentary private secretary, was 'tipping the wink to the Official Unionists that the Prime Minister was not in favour of it'. Nevertheless, with Labour's support the bill became law and the Conservative MP, Teddy Taylor, summed up the general view at Westminster by observing: 'It will do no great good and certainly no great harm.'[199]

As early as 14 July Prior announced that the assembly elections would be held on 20 October 1982. Long before voting took place it was all too apparent that the secretary of state's initiative was stillborn. The loyalist camp was divided between the integrationist Official Unionists and the DUP still determined to have the old Stormont regime restored. The SDLP was split on whether or not the party should have anything to do with the assembly at all: Currie opposed abstention as an old-fashioned and discredited tactic, but in the end, as a compromise, it was agreed to fight the election but otherwise to boycott the proceedings. Provisional Sinn Féin seized the opportunity to demonstrate its electoral muscle, which it did by winning five of the seventy-eight seats and by obtaining 10.1 per cent of first-preference votes, largely at the expense of the SDLP, which dropped to fourteen seats. Alliance – the only party to welcome rolling devolution wholeheartedly – was rewarded with ten seats, while the DUP got twenty-one, the Official Unionists twenty-six, and the only representatives of the kaleidoscope of loyalist factions that had sprung to life a decade before were James Kilfedder of the Ulster Popular Unionist Party and Frank Millar, Independent Unionist.[200]

With no representatives of the nationalist minority taking part in its proceedings, the assembly simply became a Unionist talking shop. Nevertheless, some of Prior's hopes were realised as the assembly committees – infected by the enthusiasm of Alliance members – carried out much useful work in education and economic development and

748

loyalist areas in the region became more peaceful than at any time since the Troubles had begun.

The regular Monday-night Razzamatazz disco at the Droppin' Well public house in Ballykelly, on the road between Coleraine and Derry, was packed with about 150 young people on 6 December 1982. Many were men of the Cheshire Regiment, which had moved into the Shackleton barracks nearby during the spring. As the evening's entertainment was drawing to a close a strategically placed bomb blew out one wall and brought the concrete roof collapsing down. In a freezing wind the desperate search for those caught beneath the rubble continued all through the night into the dawn. The final toll was twelve soldiers and five civilians killed, and sixty-six injured, some very seriously.[201] Though this atrocity had been perpetrated by members of the Irish National Liberation Army, it was a chilling reminder that more than 10 per cent of Northern Ireland's electorate had voted for Provisional Sinn Féin representatives who justified and promoted acts of violence such as this.

Even more alarming to James Prior was the Provisional Sinn Féin triumph in the Westminster general election of June 1983, which returned the Conservatives to power. In West Belfast Fitt was defeated by Gerry Adams, now president of Provisional Sinn Féin, and in a 73 per cent turnout 13.4 per cent of the electorate voted for Provisional Sinn Féin candidates.[202] Margaret Thatcher's new government faced the real possibility that the party which was the political wing of the Provisional IRA would supplant the SDLP as the principal representative of Northern Ireland's Catholic minority. The SDLP's share of the vote had fallen to 17.9 per cent, and only one candidate, John Hume, had been elected to Westminster. Many analysts considered the continuing rise of Provisional Sinn Féin's electoral support to be irresistible and suggested that Hume could lose his European seat in 1984.

Ever since Mason had replaced Rees as secretary of state the SDLP had felt isolated and undermined. Given no share in the administration of Northern Ireland since the fall of the executive, the party saw itself becoming an ever more impotent voice of the minority, in danger of being upstaged by republican paramilitaries. Hume and his followers turned with increased desperation to Dublin but the republic could do little for them while relations with London remained frosty. It was the electoral success of Provisional Sinn Féin that helped to concentrate minds in both capitals. The slow *rapprochement* between the two governments got under way and the first step in breaking the deadlock was the meeting of a multi-party conference in May 1983: the New Ireland Forum.

By the end of 1982, Garret FitzGerald recalled, 'the state of Anglo-Irish relations was little short of disastrous'.[203] FitzGerald described himself as a 'revolving-door Taoiseach' in these years, leading a coalition government for short spells and facing Fianna Fáil administrations under Haughey during others. No matter who held the reins of power in Leinster House, the wave of intense hostility in the republic towards Margaret Thatcher during the Maze hunger strike precluded any meaningful discussions with London on the Ulster question. Relations between the two governments deteriorated further during the Falklands War, when Haughey seemed to enjoy snubbing the British at every opportunity. Following a phone-tapping scandal implicating Haughey, FitzGerald revolved back into office early in 1983 with a comfortable majority. Now was his opportunity to seek a way out of the impasse: 'I had come to the conclusion', he wrote later, 'that I must now give priority to heading off the growth of support for the IRA in Northern Ireland by seeking a new understanding with the British government.'[204] He began by implementing Hume's proposal for a forum 'where all constitutional politicians committed to a new Ireland would together define what we really wish this new Ireland to be'.[205] Hume had asked parties in the republic to

> join with us in abandoning rhetoric and, by placing their cards on the table, show what sort of role there will be for the Protestant community, what share of power, what safeguards, what sort of economic situation and what would be the relations between Church and State.[206]

The taoiseach's insistence that all participants renounce violence ensured the exclusion of Provisional Sinn Féin, but the refusal of Unionist parties to have anything to do with the New Ireland Forum meant that it was essentially a conference representing 90 per cent of nationalists on the island.

On 30 May the forum held its inaugural meeting in the splendour of St Patrick's Hall in Dublin Castle, once the heart of British government in Ireland. In his opening speech FitzGerald declared:

> We represent a powerful collective rejection of murder, bombing and all the other cruelties that are being inflicted on the population of Northern Ireland in an attempt to secure political change by force. Let the men of violence take note of this unambiguous message from the nationalist people of Ireland: the future of the island will be built by the ballot box, and by the ballot box alone.[207]

Thereafter, the forum met in closed sessions in the castle's St George's Hall. Real work did not begin until towards the end of September to leave time for the preparation of submissions. The volume of paper received almost overwhelmed representatives and it was not until May 1984 that a report was produced. The process itself ensured that the forum became a powerful educative force in the republic, revealing to many people for the first time the deep complexity of the situation north of the border. This in itself was an important achievement, for a 1978 survey had shown that only 10 per cent of southerners had gone to Northern Ireland in the previous year, that only 10 per cent more had been there at any time in the preceding ten years and that a majority had never set foot in the region.[208] One submission, when expanded and published under the title *Ireland: A Positive Proposal*, was to exert a wide influence. Written by Kevin Boyle, a Newry-born civil rights leader who was now professor of law in Galway, and Tom Hadden, a Portadown-born law lecturer in Queen's University and founding editor of *Fortnight*, the respected independent review, this submission demonstrated how unhelpful the old-fashioned nationalist rhetoric had become with chapters such as 'The simple solutions: why they will not work' and 'Direct rule: why it has not helped'. RTE viewers were treated to the remarkable sight of Catholic bishops being cross-examined by politicians in a public session on Thursday 9 February 1984. Cahal Daly, bishop of Down and Connor, began with this statement:

> The Catholic Church in Ireland totally rejects the concept of a confessional state. We have not sought and we do not seek a Catholic state for a Catholic people. We believe that the alliance of Church and State is harmful for the Church and harmful for the state.

The bishops insisted that there could be no diminution of the civil and religious rights of Northern Ireland Protestants if Ireland was to be united. When asked if there was not a case for allowing divorce in the twenty-six-county republic, if it was to be permitted in a thirty-two-county one, Bishop Daly said that that was 'a political question which is not appropriate for us to answer'.[209]

After almost a year of discussions, twenty-eight private sessions, thirteen public sessions and fifty-six meetings of the Fianna Fáil, Fine Gael, Irish Labour and SDLP party leaders, the New Ireland Forum issued a report of its findings at the beginning of May 1984.[210] It criticised British policy since the onset of the Troubles as being one of 'crisis management', and commented that Westminster had not given northern Catholics constructive ways of expressing their nationalism, thus imperilling constitutional politics. The forum offered three options: 'a unitary state, achieved by agreement and consent'; a federal arrangement; and a joint-authority solution under which 'the London and Dublin governments would have equal responsibility for all aspects of the government of Northern Ireland', giving 'equal validity to the two traditions in Northern Ireland'.[211]

Almost immediately Haughey began wrecking what had been agreed. At the press conference following the report's official release he said: 'The only solution is as stated in the report: a unitary state with a new constitution . . . the natural unity is unification of Ireland.'[212] FitzGerald was aghast: Haughey had extracted concession after concession during the deliberations (including omission of a willingness to modify Articles 2 and 3 of the constitution) and now he had plumped for only one of three options and rejected the whole concept of majority consent in Northern Ireland being a precondition of Irish reunification. The taoiseach rejected Haughey's interpretation and later made it clear that his preferred option was a move towards joint authority.[213]

The forum discussions were of little more than academic interest unless the British government could be persuaded to listen. The ice had been broken when FitzGerald met Margaret Thatcher at Chequers in November 1983; there the taoiseach reminded her that Provisional Sinn Féin had won 43 per cent of the Catholic vote in the June election and that a further rise in support would undermine constitutional politics, with grave consequences for both the republic and Britain. Though the taoiseach left for home thinking he had achieved nothing, Margaret Thatcher was clearly moved by his arguments. The Anglo-Irish Intergovernmental Council, set up in November 1981, met regularly from November 1983 onwards and Sir Robert Armstrong, secretary to the cabinet, came to Dublin in March 1984 to begin informal talks with the Irish government, talks which became formal a year later.

Parties representing the Protestant majority in Northern Ireland were quick to condemn the forum report. In *Opportunity Lost*, the Official Unionist response written by Peter Smith, the proposed introduction of joint authority was described as 'an idiotic scheme':

> Unionists would see it as a first step to a united Ireland. The sight of Irish policemen on Northern Irish streets would inevitably produce a tremendous reaction. The direct involvement of Irish officials in governing Northern Ireland would be a source of great resentment.

The DUP document, *The Forum Report Answered*, judged the nationalist argument that joint authority would strengthen Britain's guarantee to Northern Ireland as 'a palpable lie and deceit' and claimed that it would deliver the region 'out of the United Kingdom irretrievably half-way to an all-Ireland Republic'.[214]

In a Commons debate on 2 July 1984, Prior welcomed the positive tone of the forum report and warned that 'the dangers for the people of Northern Ireland of sitting back and doing nothing are greater than the obvious risks of seeking to make some political advance'. Some backbench Conservatives did not agree: according to Ivor Stanbrook, the report was 'a humbug, a deceit, a snare, and a delusion' which was designed 'to expand the frontiers of the Irish Republic'.[215] Much of the debate centred on the question of security. Hume recalled the day in June of the European election in Derry, where he 'saw a group of youths in masks filling bottles with petrol'. He continued:

> Such occurrences are not unusual in front of my house. There are 650 members in the House. If I ventured to ask them what they would do in such circumstances, 649 of them would tell me that they would pick up the telephone and ring the police. I did not do that. I knew that had I done so I would simply have made a bad situation worse. That is a stark reality of life in areas of Northern Ireland that do not give their allegiance to the Union.[216]

The forum, in short, was attempting to change the political atmosphere to ensure community backing for the forces of law and order. Paisley was certain that the report intended to put Northern Ireland 'into some all-Ireland settlement'. 'That is anathema to the people who sent me to the House,' he continued. 'They want no part or lot in it, and they will not have it.' Then he reminded members of the reality of continuing violence in Northern Ireland:

> I have followed too many funeral processions, I have held too many widows' hands and I have patted too many orphans' heads not to know the agony my people have gone through. They are not only Protestant but Roman Catholic bereaved ones. I have received a lot of stick from Union- ists for even going to their homes . . . There is a desire for peace. That peace can only come within Northern Ireland.[217]

Not long afterwards, MPs who thought they were far removed from such ongoing tragedy were themselves brought face to face with the violence generated by the Troubles.

THE ANGLO-IRISH AGREEMENT, NOVEMBER 1985

During the middle of September 1984 Patrick Magee booked into the Grand Hotel in Brighton for three days. Magee – who had already planted sixteen bombs for the Provisionals in London, Manchester, Liverpool, Coventry and Southampton – unscrewed a panel in the bathroom of room 629 and placed explosives (wrapped in layers of cellophane to hide the smell) with a timer, similar to those used in video recorders, set to go off in twenty-four days' time. At 2.54 a.m. on Friday

12 October, the last day of the Conservative Party annual conference, the bomb exploded killing Jeanne Shattock instantaneously and sending the central chimney stack crashing down through twenty-eight rooms. Five people were killed, including Roberta Wakeham, wife of the chief whip, and Sir Anthony Berry, MP for Enfield-Southgate. Many were horribly wounded, including Norman Tebbit, the Conservative Party chairman, and his wife, both buried for hours under the debris. The Provisionals claimed responsibility, regretting their failure to kill the prime minister. 'Today we were unlucky, but remember, we have only to be lucky once.'[218]

Margaret Thatcher refused to allow this cruel attack to divert her from the developing formal talks between the London and Dublin governments. It was FitzGerald who proposed that the summit meeting between the two premiers be transferred to England.[219] The negotiations at Chequers, a week after the Brighton bombing, proved difficult. Douglas Hurd, who had replaced Prior as the Northern Ireland secretary of state, seemed eager to confine discussion to co-operation on security. FitzGerald felt the talks were going backwards, as he recalled:

> Margaret Thatcher then asked me to open the discussion, saying I looked depressed. I said that, frankly, I was very worried . . . Unless a political solution was found that would enable the minority to identify with the system of government in Northern Ireland it would be impossible to solve the security problem. We were clearly having difficulty in getting our British colleagues to accept this . . . Yes, I was depressed.[220]

Margaret Thatcher resisted any move towards joint authority and pressed the taoiseach to agree to an advisory security commission. Even though little progress seemed to be made, she said to FitzGerald, 'We like you', remarking later, 'Garret, you look depressed. Is it that bad? I am not depressed. We're now tackling the problem in detail for the first time.'[221]

In the press conference she gave at the end of the summit meeting, the prime minister described it as 'the fullest, frankest and most realistic bilateral meeting I have ever had with the Taoiseach'.[222] Her replies to journalists' questions showed sensitivity to the republic's concerns until she was asked about the forum's recommendations:

> I have made it quite clear – and so did Mr Prior when he was Secretary of State for Northern Ireland – that a unified Ireland was one solution that is out. A second solution was confederation of two states. That is out. A third solution was joint authority. That is out. That is a derogation from sovereignty. We made that quite clear when the Report was published.[223]

Fianna Fáil was jubilant and Haughey accused the taoiseach of being responsible for the republic's 'greatest humiliation in recent history' in his 'abject capitulation to a new British intransigence'. The *Irish Times* said of the prime minister: 'She is as offhand and patronising as she is callous and imperious.'[224] FitzGerald was restrained in the Dáil but his observation that Margaret Thatcher had been 'gratuitously offensive', made in a closed Fine Gael party meeting, was leaked to the press.[225] Nevertheless, the rift between Dublin and London, so heartening to Unionists in the assembly, was soon healed: both premiers felt compelled to come to agreement because there was not the slightest indication of political compromise in Northern Ireland.

The northern impasse was the natural outcome of a profoundly polarised society – representatives risked electoral annihilation if they moved too far from the position their voters expected them to take. Paralysis was ensured by a double veto: the SDLP, looking over its shoulder at Provisional Sinn Féin, refused to consider devolved government without the 'Irish Dimension' being given a place of prominence; and the Official Unionists and the DUP, competing with each other to be the authentic voice of loyalism, refused to accept power-sharing or any concessions to the republic.[226]

Of the two standpoints, the Conservative government seemed to find the loyalist one the more exasperating. Had Unionists been prepared to accept some form of power-sharing with nationalists when Prior had launched his rolling devolution initiative, the SDLP would have found it impossible to stay out of the assembly and Margaret Thatcher would probably have been deaf to Dublin's blandishments. Provisional Sinn Féin's success in the polls had changed all that. The prime minister, herself the lady who was 'not for turning', grew impatient with the rigid non-negotiable stance of both the Official Unionists and the DUP. Unionist complacency was reinforced by Attlee's guarantee – updated by the 1973 Northern Ireland Constitution Act – and by the lack of a nationalist opposition in the assembly. The prime minister's 'out . . . out . . . out' press-conference reply seemed to signal an unbridgeable chasm between London and Dublin, and in June 1985 the *News-Letter* interpreted a speech by Hurd as meaning: 'Dublin's influence is likely to be almost totally excluded from the affairs of Northern Ireland.'[227] In fact Margaret Thatcher and Garret FitzGerald were swiftly moving towards an elaborate arrangement that was designed to be immune to loyalist protest. The Protestants of Northern Ireland were almost completely unprepared for the historic settlement, made without any consultation with them or their representatives, due to be signed by FitzGerald and Thatcher in Hillsborough Castle on Friday 15 November 1985.

An angry loyalist demonstration outside the castle gates the previous evening seemed to justify the massive security operation when helicopters flew in the two premiers and their ministers from Aldergrove to

Hillsborough. Before facing the world press and television cameras, Sir Robert Armstrong and Dermot Nally posed the most difficult questions they could anticipate to rehearse FitzGerald and Margaret Thatcher.[228] The ceremonial signing and question-and-answer session followed. FitzGerald began with a statement, momentarily and uncharacteristically faltering, intended to reassure unionists:

> The agreement affirms clearly that any change in the status of Northern Ireland would only come about with the consent of the majority of the people in Northern Ireland. The agreement thus makes provision for the nationalist aspiration to unity in the only conditions in which the nationalist people of Ireland – the constitutional nationalists – seek or would accept its fulfilment without violence and with the consent of a majority in Northern Ireland. The corollary of this is that the northern unionist community have for the first time a commitment, in the form of an international agreement, that a change in the status of Northern Ireland, such as would be involved in a move to Irish political unity, would not take place without the consent of the majority in Northern Ireland.[229]

The 1985 Anglo-Irish Agreement was an elaborate document of twelve clauses. The most striking innovation was the Intergovernmental Conference, headed by the secretary of state and the Irish foreign minister, which would meet regularly to promote cross-border co-operation and deal with security, legal and political matters – political concerns were to be of particular interest to the Catholic minority and included discrimination, electoral arrangements, the status of the Irish language and the use of flags and emblems.[230] The conference was to be serviced by a permanent secretariat of northern and southern civil servants, which had already been set up at Maryfield just outside Holywood, east of Belfast. Article 4 stated that both governments supported devolution 'on a basis which would secure widespread acceptance throughout the community' – in short, powers exercised by the secretary of state would be devolved only if there was agreement on power-sharing.[231]

Though *The Times* and the *Daily Telegraph* had some reservations, the agreement won enthusiastic praise from the British press, the *Daily Mail* commending this 'brave attempt to bury an ancient conflict'. FitzGerald fully expected the condemnation of Fianna Fáil, not only because he had succeeded where Haughey had failed but also because it was a 'sad day for Irish nationalism', for a Dublin government had given its complete support to British presence in Ulster. It was no surprise that Provisional Sinn Féin described the agreement as a 'disaster' which copper-fastened partition. More worrying for the prime minister was the resignation of her trusted confidant, Ian Gow, because in his view it would 'prolong Ulster's agony'. Equally unsettling for the taoiseach was the resignation of Senator Mary Robinson of the Irish Labour Party.

756

The most tenacious advocate of liberal change in the republic, she condemned the Anglo-Irish Agreement as being 'unacceptable to all sections of unionist opinion'.[232]

The agreement *was* unacceptable to all sections of unionist opinion, with the sole exception of the Alliance Party. The *News-Letter* spoke for a clear majority in Northern Ireland in rejecting the agreement outright and on 16 November its editorial went so far as to say:

> At Hillsborough yesterday the ghosts of Cromwell and Lundy walked hand in hand to produce a recipe for bloodshed and conflict which has few parallels in modern history.[233]

The first loyalist reaction was one of shock – such a far-reaching change had not been expected while Margaret Thatcher was prime minister. Second, Protestants were appalled that Dublin would have a say in the affairs of a region they regarded as being irretrievably British. Maryfield was a Trojan horse and certain evidence to them that Westminster eventually intended to abandon them to the mercies of the republic, despite repeated assurances to the contrary. Third, loyalist anger was stoked by the complete lack of consultation and aggravated by clear evidence that the SDLP had been asked for its opinion and kept informed. Official Unionists and the DUP had been treated like pariahs and their repeated requests for some enlightenment on the progress of the London–Dublin talks had been met with silence. This sense of hurt was expressed poignantly by the Official Unionist Harold McCusker in a speech he made in the Commons twelve days after the agreement had been signed:

> I went to Hillsborough on the Friday morning . . . I stood outside Hillsborough, not waving a Union flag – I doubt whether I will ever wave one again – not singing hymns, saying prayers or protesting, but like a dog and asked the Government to put in my hand the document that sold my birthright. They told me that they would give it to me as soon as possible. Having never consulted me, never sought my opinion or asked my advice, they told the rest of the world what was in store for me.
> I stood in the cold outside the gates of Hillsborough castle and waited for them to come out and give me the agreement second hand . . . A senior police officer went into Hillsborough castle, asked for the document and brought it out to me.
> I felt desolate because as I stood in the cold outside Hillsborough castle everything that I held dear turned to ashes in my mouth.[234]

In 1912 the loyalists of Ulster could count on the support of a great body of British opinion in their resistance to Home Rule. Now they felt more isolated and friendless than at any time in centuries. Only by calling on their own resources could they resist the Anglo-Irish

Agreement. A formidable and protracted campaign of protest and non-cooperation began.

'Let it be said loudly and clearly that this is not the battle of Jim Molyneaux or Ian Paisley, the battle of the unionist family. This is the battle of the loyalist people of the *whole* of Ulster.'[235] Applause thundered round Belfast City Hall as Paisley finished speaking these words and then he seized the right hand of Molyneaux – who winced perceptibly – to symbolise the reunification of the unionist parties making common cause in resistance to the agreement. The number of loyalists who had gathered in Belfast city centre to make their protest on Saturday 23 November 1985 was immense. All morning, coaches, trains and motorcars had poured into the city, and middle-class residents of the leafy southern suburbs returning from their morning shopping were startled to find no room left to park in front of their own homes. Many Protestants from the country had arrived in family groups smartly dressed in their Sunday best. Nothing like it had been seen since 1912. The world press and television networks had been caught unprepared and were poorly represented – the best still photograph of the occasion appeared in the local sports newspaper, *Ireland's Saturday Night*. Estimates of the numbers present varied wildly but they may have reached two hundred thousand or possibly even more.[236] 'IRON LADY be warned. Your iron WILL MELT from the HEAT OF ULSTER', one placard proclaimed and thousands of others carried the message 'ULSTER SAYS NO'.[237]

'Never! Never! Never!' Paisley shouted to the multitude before him, signalling the pledge of the DUP and the Official Unionists to undo the agreement.[238] Already councillors had assaulted Tom King, who had taken over as secretary of state from Douglas Hurd in September 1985, while visiting Belfast City Hall and Unionist MPs had agreed to resign from Westminster and force by-elections if a referendum on the accord was refused. Now loyalist leaders faced the challenge of sustaining morale and of preventing protest from dissipating itself in uncoordinated action.

The obstacles lying in the path of unionist opposition were formidable indeed. Westminster governments, as the forum report had sourly observed, had learned much in their 'crisis management' of Northern Ireland: this time no regional institution had been constructed which would have been capable of being torn down by loyalist resistance and the operation of the Intergovernmental Conference could not be wrecked by Unionist non-cooperation.[239] In addition, the Anglo-Irish accord was rapidly winning international approval. Abroad, Ulster loyalists could easily be represented – along with Provisional Sinn Féin, the Provisional IRA and Fianna Fáil, their bedfellows in opposing the agreement – as political dinosaurs incapable of enlightened compromise. Haughey recognised this as opinion polls in the republic began to report overwhelming support for FitzGerald's diplomatic triumph. Certainly Fianna Fáil vigorously opposed the accord in the Dáil because it reinforced partition, gave Dublin approval to Northern Ireland's institutions and seemed to flout Articles 2 and 3 of the constitution.[240] Nevertheless, Haughey was careful to say that he would do nothing to interrupt the work of the Intergovernmental Conference in Maryfield.

The Dáil approved the agreement by eighty-eight votes to seventy-five on 21 November 1985. A few days later the House of Commons debated the issue. Unionist MPs found themselves isolated there, save for the support of a rump of Conservative backbenchers led by Ian Gow. Bipartisan co-operation across the floor of the House was reinforced by the warm approval given by Heath, Prior, Atkins and Mason, and Neil Kinnock, leader of the opposition, declared that the agreement

> is the reward that the gunmen got for their violence. They have engendered such revulsion against insecurity, fear and brutality that they have made Nationalists seek change even at the cost of indefinitely postponing their own Nationalist aspirations.

Ian Gow disagreed: the accord 'would never have been signed unless there had been a prolonged campaign of violence'.[241] Enoch Powell concluded that the prime minister had been 'bombed into submission' by the IRA and Ivor Stanbrook described the accord as

> a bad agreement, conceived in desperation, born out of fear of violence and foreign pressure, and confirmed in folly. It will make matters worse, not better in Northern Ireland.[242]

'The agreement,' Margaret Thatcher said, 'does not set us on some imagined slippery slope to Irish unity, and it is nonsense to claim that it might.'[243] For that reason Tony Benn and a few other left-wing Labour MPs opposed it on the grounds that it did not point the way to a united Ireland. None the less, the Anglo-Irish Agreement was approved by 473 votes to 47 on 27 November – one of the biggest majorities on a division in the history of the House of Commons.[244] Soon afterwards the accord was formally registered as an international treaty with the United Nations.

There was no doubting the historic importance of the agreement. For the first time since the partition of 1920–1 a Westminster government had unequivocally recognised that the republic had a role to play in the governing of Northern Ireland. The accord did force the South to acknowledge that reunification was at best a long-term aspiration, which must have the approval of a majority in the North: nevertheless, it came close to stating that partition had not been a success.[245] All too aware that the Union as they knew it had been signed away at Hillsborough, Ulster loyalists were firm in their resolution to 'derail' the 'sell out'.[246] Their problem, however, was how to achieve this without imperilling the Union they held so dear.

Margaret Thatcher, more than any other prime minister in the latter half of the twentieth century, was unlikely to cave in before extra-parliamentary protest. When her own prestige was at stake, she would defy loyalist resistance with the same inflexible determination she had displayed to General Galtieri, the miners and the print unions. If loyalists – as some suggested – sought independence for Northern Ireland, international approval, particularly in London and in Dublin, could not be expected. A unilateral declaration of independence would require a level of military and economic strength which the region simply did not possess. The loyalist strike of 1974 had pulled down the power-sharing executive but the British government had learned from the mistakes it made then. The 1977 'constitutional stoppage' had proved an embarrassing failure and in the grim economic conditions of the 1980s few Protestants were likely to withdraw their labour for long enough to bring Northern Ireland to its knees. Most Unionists believed that the 'Dublin diktat' could be opposed only by a programme of restrained defiance and non-cooperation.[247]

On 2 December 1985 Sir John Hermon, the RUC chief constable, and Larry Wren, the Garda commissioner, met for the first time in three years at police headquarters in Dublin. The provisions of the Hillsborough agreement were being implemented. The time for loyalist action had arrived.

'THERE WILL BE NO CAPITULATION TO DUBLIN, NO BOWING TO THE IRA'

On Wednesday 11 December 1985 thousands of loyalist aircraft and shipyard workers downed tools and marched on Maryfield to protest against the first meeting of the Anglo-Irish Intergovernmental Conference due to take place that day. For several hours they battled with the police in an attempt to tear down the gates. Meanwhile, the Irish foreign minister, Peter Barry, was flown in by helicopter to Stormont Castle, where crowds pulled at the newly erected cordon of barbed wire. During these disturbances thirty-eight police officers were injured and the RUC gained the upper hand only after firing plastic bullets. On the last day of 1985 a loyalist anti-agreement march set out from Derry and after five days converged on Maryfield during the afternoon of Saturday 4 January 1986. Reinforced by local people, the protesters this time pulled down the gates and during protracted clashes with the RUC, overturned and burned a police car.[248]

Loyalist leaders now faced a dilemma: how far could they push their 'backlash' against the agreement in the streets, when their own police, overwhelmingly Protestant, were in the front line? 'Politics is not the business of the RUC, our business is policing,' Hermon stated in a message to the force. 'I believe our future lies in our abiding dedication to serving all the people of Northern Ireland impartially and justly, without fear or favour, without regard to religion, class or creed.'[249] To a very considerable extent the fate of the new Anglo-Irish relationship hinged on how far Hermon could implement his ideal. So far, the RUC, now fighting again on two fronts, was withstanding the test exceptionally well.

The constitutional protest was put to the test on 23 January 1986, when by-elections were held in the fifteen constituencies where Unionist MPs had resigned their seats. The SDLP and Provisional Sinn Féin fielded candidates in four constituencies, and in another four constituencies, to ensure a contest, the Unionists put up dummy candidates all bearing the name of the Irish foreign minister, Peter Barry. The overwhelming referendum against the agreement did not quite materialise: Seamus Mallon, for the SDLP, captured Newry and Armagh from the Official Unionist, Jim Nicholson; overall Unionist support fell short of the 500,000-vote target by over 80,000; and the fall in Provisional Sinn Féin's share of the nationalist vote from 41.9 per cent to 35.4 indicated that the Anglo-Irish accord was producing the beneficial result desired by both Dublin and London.

A month later Molyneaux and Paisley flew to London to see the prime minister, but apart from promising that she would apply the agreement 'sensitively', Margaret Thatcher conceded nothing.[250] Hardline loyalists demanded more direct action. A 'day of action' was called for 3 March, but many Unionists feared their cause would be discredited: Frank Millar, general secretary of the Official Unionist Party, put out a press release on 20 February stating that 'violence has no part to play in our campaign against the Agreement'.[251]

At first light on the day of action oil and nails were thrown onto the M1 motorway, making it impassable. All over Northern Ireland roads

761

were blocked by tractors, trailers and other farm vehicles and in Belfast masked pickets manned barricades. Intimidation was widespread as public services were disrupted, much of industry was closed down and there were extensive power cuts. Energetic police action kept the Foyle Bridge open in Derry, but on the main Belfast–Dublin road adjacent to Dromore the RUC let a huge barricade stand for more than seven hours. A gang of loyalist youths rampaged through Belfast city centre inflicting much damage to property and that night police were stoned and shot at in Protestant enclaves.[252]

The violence and disorder of 3 March were acutely embarrassing for both Molyneaux and Paisley. Dignified and effective direct action was proving difficult to deliver. Giving evidence before an assembly committee, Noel Stewart, senior partner with Coopers and Lybrand, expressed his fear that the region's businesses were in danger of losing customer loyalty:

> My personal concern is that if, in fact, the commercial life of this province is brought to a standstill it won't be a simple issue of turning on the taps and everything will flow again. Business won't just drift back to us.[253]

Molyneaux could not risk losing middle-class backing by sanctioning further political strikes. Paisley, widely expected to become the man of the hour in leading loyalist resistance, had become more cautious with experience. He agreed with Peter Robinson, the thirty-seven-year-old deputy leader of the DUP, that Northern Ireland was on the 'window-ledge' of the Union; he also agreed with him that loyalists should not jump off that ledge into independence and that his party's aim was 'the Union, the whole Union and nothing but the Union'.[254] The Unionist leaders continued to walk the narrow line between acceptable extraparliamentary direct action and outright lawbreaking. Too often that spring their supporters overstepped the mark and besmirched the campaign with violence and intimidation.

On Easter Monday, 31 March 1986, some two thousand loyalists showed up for an Apprentice Boys' parade in Portadown, though it had been banned by the secretary of state. As the marchers forged their way through the Catholic Garvaghy district of the town they were confronted by a phalanx of police and vicious fighting followed. During the rioting that erupted there the next day, the RUC fired 148 plastic bullets, mortally wounding a twenty-year-old Protestant.[255]

The RUC had become a special object of hatred because it was apparent that the Anglo-Irish Agreement could not work without its co-operation. Frustrated by their inability to influence Westminster's policies towards Northern Ireland, loyalists accused the police of being at the beck and call of the Irish foreign minister. At first they had been content to taunt officers with cries of 'Barry's Boys' and 'Judas', throwing silver coins at their feet, but soon the RUC was subjected to a sustained campaign of intimidation. On the evening of the day of action fifteen police homes had been attacked, eight of them in Portadown. Within a few days of the Easter riots in Portadown there were forty-five attacks on police, their families and their homes. After their door had been smashed down and a petrol bomb had been thrown into their living room, a part-time woman reservist and her mother escaped from their house with their clothes on fire only to be greeted by a jeering crowd outside.[256] Paul Johnson, reporting for the *Guardian*, described a typical attack:

> The Protestant gunman made his move at just after three o'clock in the morning. Manoeuvring round the back of the comfortable red-and-white-painted detached house, he aimed up at the first-floor bedroom window. Three shots smashed through the glass and thumped into the far wall, above the bed where a teenage boy lay asleep. His brother, a policeman, rushed into the room – just in time to see flames from a petrol bomb lighting up the back garden.
>
> The incident on Tuesday – off Antrim Road in Belfast – had its desired result: the family is getting out.

Johnson noted police resentment 'at the part played by some Unionist politicians in creating the conditions for the violence to erupt'. Molyneaux and Paisley 'tried to destabilise the force early last month with a newspaper advertisement in which they told officers that they had to make up their minds over the Agreement'.[257] Other loyalists were less circumspect and daubed on gable walls: 'Join the RUC and come home to a real fire.' On houses abandoned by the police the graffito 'Buy and die' was often to be found.[258]

The Reverend Martin Smyth, Official Unionist MP for South Belfast, declared that the RUC had not buckled under after seventeen years of continuous pressure from the Provisional IRA and they were hardly likely to succumb now to petrol-bomb attacks and shooting incidents perpetrated by loyalists. Unionist political leaders hastened to distance themselves from these attacks, causing Eddie McGrady, the SDLP chief whip, to comment of Paisley: 'It is the height of contradiction for the man to bring the mobs out on the streets and the Third Force on to the hilltops and then to condemn their violence.'[259] Paisley strove to maintain morale, saying at the DUP annual conference:

> Moderates in this land are coming to me in droves and saying, 'Big Man, keep it up, keep it up' . . . God almighty is a god of justice. The world court of public opinion has passed a verdict on Mrs Thatcher. It is a verdict in favour of the ordinary Ulsterman, the Loyalist . . . Trusting in

the God of our fathers and confident that our cause is just, we will never surrender our heritage. There will be no capitulation to Dublin, no bowing to the IRA and no sell out of our hard won victories. Let God defend the right.[260]

Privately, Paisley and the other loyalist leaders were growing anxious that their campaign was at times counter-productive and in danger of running out of steam.

On 23 April 1986 Molyneaux and Paisley unveiled a twelve-point plan of civil disobedience. Unionist MPs would continue to boycott Westminster; the people would be asked to withhold their rates; in councils where Unionists were in control – eighteen of the twenty-six – public business was to be disrupted; and, amongst other points in the 'battle plan', government representatives were to be shunned and there was to be a day of prayer for deliverance from the agreement on 3 May.[261] In one important respect the loyalists' prayers were answered: a referendum in the republic on 26 June seemed to confirm long-held fears that Protestant liberties would be imperilled in a reunited Ireland. In his campaign to liberalise the Irish constitution, FitzGerald had put an amendment to the people to allow divorce in certain limited circumstances. Forgetting protestations about Protestant civil and religious rights made before television cameras when making their submission to the New Ireland Forum, the Catholic bishops overtly threw their weight against the amendment, which was defeated by 63.5 per cent to 36.5 on a turnout of 63 per cent.[262] The *Irish Times*, in despair, concluded: 'We have two countries.'[263] Paisley was exultant:

> In the providence of God, this has brought us back from the brink. If the referendum had been a success the British government would have pushed us with more vigour down the United Ireland road. The civil war, which I believed was at hand, had receded because of that.[264]

In most respects the Unionist plan was a miserable failure. The absence of Unionist MPs at Westminster was hardly noticed and, in any case, Powell defied the boycott. Reforms in the early 1970s had ensured that local authorities in Northern Ireland exercised very limited powers and so the repeated adjournments and other disruptive measures did not cause as much dislocation as might have been expected. When a Unionist-held council refused to strike a rate, the Northern Ireland Office simply sent in a commissioner to do so. Many Unionists were uncomfortable with abstention tactics, which seemed rather too similar to those applied by Sinn Féin for decades. One consequence of the Troubles was that in Belfast the long run of embarrassingly unprepossessing and cabalistic lord mayors had been broken: David Cook, the first and only Alliance councillor to hold the office, brought with him a longed-for rush of fresh air; Tommy Patton, a former shipyard worker, was indefatigably courteous to everyone and, as a result, did much to promote better community relations; and John Carson won admiration from all sides for the skill and diplomatic flair with which he represented the city. Carson, for all his dislike of the Anglo-Irish Agreement, felt that the battle plan was too negative and made the local community the chief victim; he played a leading role in persuading the city council to vote twenty-seven to twenty-three in favour of ending adjournment protests on 6 May 1986.[265] The health and education area boards, responsible for the lion's share of local government spending, were dominated by appointed rather than elected representatives: many Unionists were reluctant to withdraw from them as this would not prevent them functioning – one councillor said that such action was like 'shooting yourself in the foot'.[266]

Negative action by the DUP in particular simply ensured the demise of the assembly. A 'Committee on Victimisation in Employment', with Paisley as chairman, was set up to report on allegations that some employers had prevented their workers from joining the day of action on 3 March. Insufficient information was found to justify further action.[267] On 15 May fourteen DUP members took over the Stormont switchboard and harangued all callers about the injustice of the Anglo-Irish Agreement. Tom King told the Commons on 12 June that the assembly was failing to carry out its two principal functions – scrutiny of legislation and administration of devolved powers. He moved the dissolution order. In anticipation the assembly members televised their last proceedings and made long speeches denouncing the agreement, government ministers, the 'dishonourable' policy of placating the SDLP, the 'insulting disregard' for their positive proposals, and King's refusal to attend their debates. When the assembly was dissolved on 23 June, eighteen DUP members and three other Unionists stayed on to discuss the motion 'that the Assembly still says "No"'. At two o'clock next morning they were forcibly removed by the RUC, which had been much vilified in the final days of debate. Paisley was carried, head first, out of the chamber by four strong policemen.[268] As he scrambled to his feet on the steps of Parliament Buildings he shouted at the officers in front of television cameras: 'Don't come crying to me the next time your houses are attacked. You'll reap what you sow.'[269]

Such antics did nothing to win friends and influence people across the Irish Sea, particularly in Westminster. On 24 June Paisley declared that Northern Ireland was on the verge of civil war and called on Protestants to mobilise: wild talk of this kind made him a reviled figure in the British press, on a par with the miners' leader, Arthur Scargill.[270]

Two days later the *Daily Mail* denounced him as a 'hate-filled rabble-rouser' and *The Times* headed a critical leading article on the DUP leader with the words 'The Uncivil Warrior'.[271] 'Ulster *still* says NO', posters proclaimed all over Northern Ireland, but there was not the slightest indication that the Government was taking any notice. The campaign of protest was acquiring an air of desperation. Some Unionists suggested that loyalists refuse to pay their television licence fees and one proposed a dog licence boycott on the grounds that 'it's a dog's life under the Anglo-Irish Agreement'. A plan to put up Unionist candidates in marginal English and Scottish seats, in the hope of ousting Conservatives, got off to a bad start in the Fulham by-election that year when the Unionist candidate got fewer votes than Screaming Lord Sutch of the Monster Raving Looney Party. 'Unionism today is immersed in the politics of protest', David McKittrick wrote in the *Listener* on 10 July. He continued:

> Yet Unionists have a strong self-image of themselves as a respectable and law-abiding community, and one part of the Protestant mind is uneasy with all this. Besides, things can easily get out of hand ... there is widespread Protestant apprehension that the medicine (Mr Paisley's protests) is more dangerous than the disease (the agreement). If someone could think of a non-hazardous and essentially peaceful means of destroying the accord, then most Protestants would swing behind it; but no one can ... In the meantime, the marching season is upon us.[272]

'PREPARED TO TAKE DIRECT ACTION AS AND WHEN REQUIRED'

During the marching season of 1986, attention was focused on Portadown, a town convulsed by fierce battles between loyalists and the police in the spring and during the previous summer. The Orange marchers insisted on going by their traditional route from the town centre, along Obins Street and through The Tunnel, a Catholic enclave of some seventy families. In July 1985 the RUC had altered the route to avoid provocation and had thus drawn upon themselves the fury of the Protestant mob. This time, on the advice of the secretary of state, an Orange church parade was allowed to follow this route on 6 July, but hand-to-hand fighting erupted when George Seawright, the DUP activist, attempted to join in with his supporters.[273] The marches of 12 and 13 July were banned from The Tunnel but John Hume protested that the authorities had given in to the bully boys since the alternative route was through the predominantly Catholic Garvaghy Road. Though there had been ugly incidents and rioting for six nights in succession in Belfast and Portadown, the chief constable was relieved that the violence had not been on a larger scale: he reported that of the 1,950 marches (170 fewer than in 1985) only 67 had been accompanied by disorder.

Peter Robinson told his supporters that politics was dead in Ulster. As Barry White wrote in a *Belfast Telegraph* profile, 'He has been seen as the real mastermind of the opposition, prompting Paisley, who in turn prompts Molyneaux.'[274] Robinson had called Margaret Thatcher 'a political prostitute' in the Commons and on another occasion suggested she should be electrocuted; he paraded his contacts with the paramilitaries, and he believed that God walked beside him in his mission to save Ulster. Catholics, the *Observer* reported, saw him as 'cold, ruthless and intransigent without the humorous warmth and bull-like echoes of the mellowing Paisley'. 'Paisley had led his followers up and down the hill many times,' David Bleakley had said. 'Robinson is capable of taking them over the abyss.'[275] On the night of Thursday 7 August 1986 Robinson led five hundred loyalists across the border into Co. Monaghan and after they had beaten up two *gardaí* they marched through the village of Clontibret to the Garda barracks, where they daubed anti-agreement slogans. Robinson was arrested and a week later in a Dundalk court he was remanded to appear at Ballybay. After a week-long trial in January 1987 he pleaded guilty to unlawful assembly and was freed after paying £17,500 in fines and compensation.[276] While on bail before his trial, Robinson was free to throw himself into a new campaign to apply paramilitary pressure on the British government.

The Ulster Clubs had been formed in the summer of 1985 to protest at the re-routing of traditional Orange marches in Portadown. Once the Anglo-Irish Agreement had been signed, members were to be found hurling bricks at police defending Maryfield, enforcing the day of action, protesting in Portadown and joining flying pickets to harass government ministers and Northern Ireland Office officials. The clubs caused great alarm in the Press but much of their initial energy had been dissipated in talk. The formation of Ulster Resistance was an attempt to revive and discipline those loyalists seeking direct action. Paisley presided over the inaugural meeting in the Ulster Hall on 10 November 1986 and after a closed session issued a statement that Ulster Resistance would 'embark upon a province-wide recruitment of men willing and prepared to take direct action as and when required. Such action will be strictly disciplined, calculated and controlled.'[277] Next day more than two thousand men, many wearing military jackets and red berets, paraded in a show of strength in Kilkeel, Co. Down. The RUC warned that anyone wearing paramilitary uniform could face prosecution but Robinson defiantly headed a colour party in Portadown on 17 November.[278] Even the leaders of the new movement, however, were uncertain what should be done next.

The first anniversary of the Anglo-Irish Agreement was marked by a huge demonstration at Belfast City Hall on Saturday 15 November 1986, but the protest was marred by violence and disorder during which some seventy shops were looted or damaged. Within sight of the platform party, gangs of youths broke into a wine shop, a jewellery store, and a sports outfitters, from where they pelted the police with golf balls. The Official Unionist MP Ken Maginnis bravely tried to disperse them with his umbrella, but the RUC had to fire plastic bullets to put them to flight.[279] As it was, few of the tens of thousands of peaceful demonstrators present were confident their protest could succeed.

Paisley was as defiant and truculent as ever: on 9 December, for example, he had been expelled from the debating chamber of the European parliament after constantly interrupting an address by Margaret Thatcher.[280] Nevertheless, he remained cautious and held back the militants of Ulster Resistance; as *New Society* observed the same month: 'This man will lead a protest, but will have no truck with a revolt.'[281] Staying on the constitutional path, the Unionist leaders launched a petition at the city hall on 1 January 1987, to be presented to the queen, calling for a referendum on the Anglo-Irish Agreement. By February the petition had four hundred thousand signatures but the Government simply ignored it.

New public order regulations proved highly effective in controlling parades and paramilitary displays. Despite the vote the previous May to end adjournment protests, Belfast City Council had not resumed normal business in full: a fine of £25,000, imposed in February by the High Court for failing to strike a rate, swiftly punctured the Unionist campaign of non-cooperation in local government.[282] Dr John Thompson, the outgoing Presbyterian moderator, described the tactics used against the agreement as 'counter-productive and morally questionable', while Frank Millar bleakly concluded that the protest campaign was now a 'shambles'.[283]

Unionist leaders could console themselves with the undeniable fact that their movement had held together remarkably well. London, however, saw only an arrogant and intransigent unionism flirting dangerously with violence. The Government felt certain that to yield to Protestant pressure would drive more northern Catholics into the arms of Provisional Sinn Féin, and this view was reinforced by the alarming escalation of attacks on Catholics since the agreement had been signed.

'We are living on our nerves. My wife could not sleep and the children were terrified. At night I sat up downstairs with the electric fire on, keeping a watch just in case.' A forty-three-year-old father of six recounted his family's experiences for Paul Johnson of the *Guardian* in May 1986. His home was in New Buildings, an estate of several hundred houses on the road between Strabane and Derry, whose overwhelmingly Protestant composition was signalled by red, white and blue kerbstones, the words 'No Surrender' painted on the tarmac, and 'PAF' (Protestant Action Force) daubed in front of the Catholic primary school. On 3 March, the day of action, masked men climbed over the hedge and pressed their faces against the front window, and while the family crouched in terror together on the living room floor, bricks and bottles were thrown at the back of the house. The following Saturday a letter arrived: it read, 'Get out you Fenian bastards'; a week later another letter carried the message, 'Bottles today, bullets tomorrow'.

The family decided to move across the Foyle to an exclusively Catholic district but the Housing Executive took five weeks to complete the transfer. During that time the eldest boy began suffering epileptic fits after a break of almost ten years; people previously keen to chat in the shops simply turned their backs; and a Protestant friend of one of the sons was told he would be knee-capped if he persisted in keeping company with Catholics. The father described the day of departure:

> What I cannot get over is that after living there for 16 years no one said goodbye. On the day we moved out, some even closed their curtains. Why? I don't really know. I don't think it has much to do with the Anglo-Irish agreement.

Four families had moved out of the estate and seven more were waiting to go, all of them Catholic. There had been no television cameras, no dramatic petrol-bombings or shootings, just – in Johnson's words – 'a gradual but incessant build up of a more insidious pressure'.[284]

Since 1969 thousands of families had suffered in a similar way to those in New Buildings. Intimidation was a grim aspect of the Troubles, largely unseen by visiting journalists. In a detailed study published in 1986 John Darby, director of the Centre for the Study of Conflict at the University of Ulster, Coleraine, pointed out that intimidation was a characteristic of ethnic conflicts developing along predictable lines. Unlike conditions in international wars, he wrote, 'the combatants permanently inhabit the same battlefield'. He continued:

It is not possible to terminate hostilities by withdrawal behind national frontiers. Even during tranquil periods their lives are often intermeshed with those of their enemies. As a consequence, inter-community conflict is often characterised by internecine viciousness rather than by the more impassive slaughter of wars.[285]

Incidents of intimidation had been declining steadily since the peak of August 1971, but the period following the signing of the Anglo-Irish accord witnessed a new upsurge. Protestants marooned in predominantly Catholic streets and estates were just as liable to be intimidated out of their homes, as the evacuations of 1969 and 1971 had demonstrated. Nevertheless, Catholic families had suffered more than Protestant ones in proportion to their numbers and in 1986–7 they were almost exclusively the victims of housing intimidation. On 31 March 1986 loyalist gangs petrol-bombed eleven Catholic homes in Lisburn; further attacks followed, particularly in Belfast on 6 and 8 April; and the RUC reported seventy-nine sectarian attacks by loyalists on Catholic homes and dozens of petrol-bombings of Catholic schools, shops, churches and businesses in less than a month, between 1 and 26 April 1986.[286] The marching season brought a new wave of violence and on 14 July a loyalist gang, numbering around fifty and armed with hatchets and cudgels, attacked twenty Catholic houses in Rasharkin, a village between Ballymena and Ballymoney; the secretary of state described these attacks as some of the nastiest and most vicious throughout 'the emergency'.[287]

At the same time there was a fresh spate of sectarian killings of Catholics in north Belfast. On Christmas Eve 1986 the *News-Letter* reported that the 'terrible toll of death and injuries' had gone up 'by more than 50 per cent since the introduction of the Anglo-Eire agreement, bringing the total killed during the 17 years of violence in Northern Ireland to 2,524, and leaving nearly 30,000 injured'.[288] Certainly the number of violent deaths was rising again: 54 in 1985; 61 in 1986; and 93 in 1987. The violence was by no means one-sided: 71 of those killed over these three years were police or members of the UDR – sure evidence that militant republicans had stepped up their war against the security forces since the signing of the Anglo-Irish pact.

'A DECLARATION OF MURDEROUS VIOLENCE AGAINST THE COMMUNITY ITSELF'

'In the final analysis the agreement is about stabilising British interests,' Adams observed after the Anglo-Irish accord had been signed. 'British army intelligence could do nothing about the structures and organisation of the IRA in the 26 counties; only "security" harmonisation with Dublin could remedy this lack.'[289] He did not add that his principal anxiety was the threat the agreement posed to Provisional Sinn Féin's political support – like the loyalists he believed that the pact had been made possible only by Provisional IRA violence, but he feared the main beneficiaries would be John Hume and the SDLP. The agreement, indeed, inaugurated a period of acute difficulty for the militant republican movement, which was exactly what it was primarily intended to do.

The fifteen by-elections of 23 January 1986 gave an early indication of decline with a 5 per cent swing of the nationalist vote away from Provisional Sinn Féin. At the annual conference on 1 November in Dublin's Mansion House a large majority of delegates voted that Provisional Sinn Féin candidates, if elected in the republic, should take their seats in the Dáil. This was too much for Ó Brádaigh and Ó Conaill, who stalked out leaving Adams and Morrison in complete control. The new policy was put to the test during the republic's general election on 19 February 1987. Provisional Sinn Féin put up twenty-seven candidates in twenty-four multi-member constituencies and fought a vigorous campaign. The result was an unmitigated humiliation – not one seat was captured and the party received a mere 1.85 per cent of the total votes cast.[290] Clearly the citizens of the republic, once the initial wave of sympathy for the hunger strikers had passed, wanted no truck with the men of violence. To make matters worse the Progressive Democrats – a breakaway party from Fianna Fáil unreservedly in support of the Anglo-Irish Agreement – had done well. After a three-week delay Haughey was elected taoiseach. Now dependent on the Progressive Democrats' backing, he abruptly announced his support for the accord, while American approval was signalled by President Ronald Reagan's authorisation of the first 50 million US dollar grant to the International Fund for Ireland, set up in conjunction with the agreement.[291]

The British general election on 11 June 1987 delivered another hammer blow to the republican movement: the only comfort was the re-election of Adams for West Belfast; the Provisional Sinn Féin share of the vote, 13.4 per cent in 1983, dropped to 11.4 per cent; and Hume and Mallon were joined by Eddie McGrady, who defeated Powell in South Down, to raise SDLP representation in the Commons.[292] One of the main unspoken objectives of the Anglo-Irish Agreement had been to turn the northern Catholic vote away from the militant republicans towards the constitutional nationalists of the SDLP; and although there was still a solid bedrock of support for Provisional Sinn Féin, the SDLP had unequivocally recovered its position as the principal voice of the minority in Northern Ireland. The Provisionals did not abandon electoral politics but they felt justified in concentrating their energies in the field where they had most experience: the campaign of death and destruction.

'Britain's imperialist history is littered with wreckage and corpses', Gerry Adams declared in an article he wrote for the *Guardian* in March 1987. He continued:

> Its involvement in Ireland is one inglorious, shameful record, which continues until this day ... British interference in Ireland is undemocratic, immoral and imperialist. It costs the British public £1.5 billion annually in subventions. But no price can be put on the damage to Britain's reputation and prestige abroad due to its dirty war in Ireland ... Republicans have a vested interest in peace.[293]

At the time there was little evidence that the Provisionals had an interest in peace. Indeed, the fact that so much of the wreckage and so many of the corpses in Northern Ireland were the result of Provisional IRA violence was doing much to turn the Catholic electorate towards the SDLP. The continuing programme of Ulsterisation ensured that the RUC and the UDR were in the front line. Many were murdered when off-duty: they included Detective Constable Derek Breen shot dead while drinking in a Maguiresbridge public house; Inspector James Hazlett, who had been awarded the British Empire Medal for throwing himself on top of a civilian during a bomb blast, killed when taking his dog for a walk; and Constable John McVitty, murdered when working his Rosslea farm with his twelve-year-old son.[294] Twelve police officers were killed in 1986 and another sixteen had been murdered by the end of April 1987.[295] Eight members of the UDR died in 1986 and another eight were killed the following year: several were victims of the Provisional IRA under-car, booby-trap bomb.[296]

Republican sympathisers might well be prepared to accept that police and part-time soldiers were 'legitimate targets', but many were dismayed as the Provisionals widened their net of violence to include anyone who had dealings with the security forces. On 19 August 1985 Seamus McAvoy was seized by armed men outside his bungalow in Dublin, taken inside and shot dead. He was the proprietor of a Coalisland firm making portable buildings, many of which were sold to the army and the RUC. This was the beginning of a new onslaught which included the murder in Derry of the German, Kurt Koenig, shot on 21 November 1985 because he had previously been a catering manager for the police. Provisional IRA threats were usually enough to discourage contractors from repairing damaged stations and barracks, and Royal Engineers, protected by the Spearhead Battalion, had to be called in to do the work. Speaking at Tone's grave on 22 June 1986, Provisional leader Martin McGuinness declared that killing contractors 'posed serious problems for the British government' – this was true but it also increased revulsion in the community.[297] Further threats to civilians considered to be collaborators, 'whether pushing pens or pushing brooms', caused the (largely Catholic) Workers' Party to denounce the Provisionals: 'They are fascists and must be rejected totally by all decent people in this country.'

On 5 August 1986 the Provisional IRA issued a detailed statement listing all those who were now to be 'treated as collaborators': included were civil servants; food and cleaning contractors; vending machine suppliers; British Telecom; and Standard Telephones. Seamus Mallon responded that this was nothing less than 'a declaration of murderous violence against the community itself'.[298] Unquestionably this campaign caused the security forces much inconvenience, as a large advertisement in the *Irish News* on 14 August indicated:

> To whom it may concern. I, Francis O'Kane of Garvagh Co. Derry, have stopped working for the security forces. I and men employed by me have not done any work for the security forces for the past three months. Signed – Francis O'Kane.[299]

The Provisionals, however, paid a high price in further erosion of popular support, particularly as Catholics depended heavily on the building and catering trades for employment. The blanket threat was also an indication of growing desperation and 1987 was to be a year of severe military reverse for the organisation.

Early in the evening of 8 May eight heavily armed Provisional IRA volunteers launched a carefully planned attack on Loughgall RUC station, in Co. Armagh. A mechanical digger, hijacked from a farm, crashed through the perimeter fencing with a large bomb in its bucket. The explosion wrecked the building but immediately afterwards SAS soldiers, tipped off and lying in wait, attacked the Provisionals, who had begun shooting into the station. The army fired an estimated 1,200 rounds and killed all eight volunteers and an innocent passer-by driving in his car.[300] All the Provisional IRA members had been leading activists and included James Lynagh, a veteran of the commando unit operating along the Co. Monaghan border. Superintendent Harry Breen put their weapons on display the following day: they included two Belgian .223 rifles; an SLR rifle; three Heckler and Koch sub-machine-guns; a Spaz 12-bore shotgun; and a .357 Ruger revolver.[301] Ballistics tests later showed that these weapons had been used in thirty-three raids or murders – the Ruger revolver, taken from the body of Reserve Constable William Clements, shot dead in December 1985, had killed two contractors and a part-time member of the UDR.[302]

This was the biggest loss of life the IRA had suffered in a single incident since 1921 and its spokesmen admitted that it was a devastating setback.[303] The news triggered off the worst rioting seen in west Belfast for many years: between 150 and 200 petrol bombs were thrown at the security forces; firemen fighting a blaze at Mackie's foundry were forced by rioters to withdraw; and dozens of shots were fired at police in the Oldpark area and at Broadway. In Derry, youths threw stones at police in the Bogside and petrol and acid bombs at Shipquay Street, Castle Gate and Waterloo Place. Flames leaped up from barricades in Coalisland, where the police station was stoned and hijacked vehicles were burned. Such demonstrations of support were of little comfort to the Provisionals, however.

The IRA came to kill, they did not care who they killed, and they were killed themselves: what can they expect?' Canon Christopher Lowry, rector of Loughgall, expressed the view of an overwhelming majority – and certainly that of Tom King, who looked exceptionally pleased with himself next morning as he spoke to new recruits at a UDR passing-out parade at Ballykinler. More significant for the Provisionals was the condemnation of the republic's foreign minister, Brian Lenihan, who said: 'It was the IRA leadership who are responsible for putting those young lives at risk.'[304] To make matters worse the militant republican cause was being lowered in the estimation of its natural supporters by a savage feud between factions of the Irish National Liberation Army, which by the middle of 1987 had left sixteen members dead, including the leader of its army council.[305] For the Provisionals, hopes of escalating their war were badly dented as their delegates met for their annual conference in Dublin that autumn.

On 31 October 1987 the *Eksund*, an old freighter loaded with 150 tons of arms and explosives, was intercepted off the French coast. All members of the crew were Irish and it became apparent, after investigation by the French police, that this huge arsenal had been supplied by Colonel Gaddafi of Libya for the exclusive use of the Provisional IRA. The ship's hold contained enough war material to keep the Provisionals well supplied for years to come, including 20 Sam-7 ground-to-air missiles, rocket-propelled grenades, 1,000 Kalashnikov rifles, mortars, recoilless rifles and 2 tons of Semtex. Semtex, made in Czechoslovakia, was perfectly suited for terrorist use, being odourless and twice as powerful as other plastic explosives used previously by the Provisional IRA.[306]

The relief of the London and Dublin governments at the *Eksund's* seizure was short-lived. The French authorities reported accumulating evidence that the freighter's consignment was the fifth to be delivered to the Provisionals by Libya, as retaliation against Britain for letting the United States use her air bases for the attack on Tripoli on 14 April 1986. The machinery created by the Anglo-Irish accord was rapidly put in motion as police on both sides of the border launched a concerted search operation. Some very large underground concrete bunkers were found in the counties of Galway, Wicklow and Limerick, but nothing of consequence was seized. Then, at the end of January 1988, a substantial arms cache was discovered in bunkers under Five Fingers Strand at Malin Head, Co. Donegal: the weapons, for the most part manufactured in eastern Europe, were clearly part of an earlier Libyan consignment. Fearing that the Provisional IRA now had ground-to-air missiles, the army fitted deflecting devices to helicopters sent out on patrol.[307] The days when commanders and politicians confidently claimed that the Provisionals were close to defeat were now over, but at least they had the comfort of knowing that the standing of the organisation in the community had plunged to an all-time low. This was the direct outcome of the Remembrance Day Massacre in Enniskillen.

'I HAVE LOST MY DAUGHTER . . . BUT I BEAR NO ILL WILL'

Along with many others, Gordon Wilson and his twenty-year-old daughter Marie gathered at the war memorial in Enniskillen on Sunday 8 November 1987 for the annual wreath-laying. Just before 11 a.m., when the ceremony was to begin, a bomb exploded behind them. The three-storey gable end of St Michael's Reading Rooms crashed down.[308] After 'a sinister hush, a terrible quietness,' Gordon Wilson recalled, 'there was shouting and moaning, and screaming, and yells of agony'. Buried beneath several feet of rubble, his shoulder dislocated, he attempted to find his glasses. His daughter lay buried beside him:

> She held my hand tightly, and gripped me as hard as she could. She said, 'Daddy, I love you very much.' Those were her exact words to me, and those were the last words I ever heard her say.[309]

Like so many others, a member of the Boys' Brigade dropped his wreath and ran to help. 'People were crawling around crying for help,' he said later. 'They were all crushed . . . We should have been remembering the dead, not digging them out.' Pat O'Doherty was drinking tea in bed when the bomb went off, and he dashed out to do what he could:

> I was clawing around with a member of the UDR who realised that the woman we were digging out was his mother, but by the time we got her out she was dead.[310]

Dr Robin Eames, the Church of Ireland primate of all Ireland, was to have preached at St MacCartan's Cathedral. He was speaking to a woman in UDR uniform at the door of the cathedral who told him that her husband was at the cenotaph. Half an hour later he had to tell her that her husband had been killed. 'I won't forget her face,' he recalled in an interview he gave to Peter Beaumont of the *Observer* in April 1992. Instead of giving his sermon, the archbishop rushed to visit the injured and dying in Erne Hospital. 'A look of pain crossed his face, remembering the moment that brought him closest to complete despair', Beaumont wrote, and the report continues:

> 'I saw the . . .' He paused at the unquiet memory. 'The faces in the hospital. They will never leave me. I *see*,' he said with emphasis, 'the faces of the little children who have lost a father as they walk behind the coffin with roses in their hands. I see the faces of good, honest, decent people who have never done wrong to anyone else, who have lost a loved one, blown to bits by a terrorist bomb. And of course I weep.'[311]

Altogether eleven people were killed and sixty-three injured, nineteen of them very seriously.[312] Marie Wilson died in hospital and her father that evening gave an interview to Mike Gaston for the BBC. He described in a tone of quiet anguish his last conversation with Marie as they lay beneath the rubble, and he went on to say:

> The hospital was magnificent, truly impressive, and our friends have been great, but I have lost my daughter, and we shall miss her. But I bear no ill will. I bear no grudge. Dirty sort of talk is not going to bring her back to life. She was a great wee lassie. She loved her profession. She was a pet. She's dead. She's in Heaven, and we'll meet again. Don't ask me, please, for a purpose. I don't have a purpose. I don't have an answer. But I know there has to be a plan. If I didn't think that, I would commit suicide. It's part of a greater plan, and God is good. And we shall meet again.[313]

No words uttered in more than twenty years of violence in Northern Ireland have had such a powerful, emotional impact. In a few sentences he had spoken for all the bereaved and injured, and over the next few days millions across the world were to share his grief. Charlie Warmington, a friend from the BBC, telephoned to tell him that he saw apparently hardened reporters in tears when they heard the broadcast.[314]

President Reagan expressed his 'revulsion'; Pope John Paul II told of his 'profound shock'; the Soviet news agency TASS described the bombing as 'barbaric'; and Charles Haughey spoke 'for every decent Irish man and Irish woman in expressing the anger and revulsion we feel towards those who planned and executed this criminal act of carnage against the innocent people gathered to commemorate their dead'.[315] In Dublin thousands filed through the door of the Mansion House to sign a book of condolences. On the following Sunday a minute's silence was observed across the republic in memory of the victims and a memorial service in Dublin's St Patrick's Cathedral was televised nationwide. After delivering a heart-touching sermon, the Reverend Brian Hannon, the Church of Ireland bishop of Clogher, walked back from the pulpit in tears.[316] That day Carmencita Hederman, the lord mayor of Dublin, presented a Book of Condolences to Enniskillen. 'She tried to make a speech which she had carefully prepared,' Gordon Wilson remembered, 'but she broke down, and that very act of breaking down told us more of her heartfelt sympathy and solidarity, and that of the many people she represented, than a thousand well-turned phrases.'[317]

'Mr Wilson, for one, has generated much hope that good may yet come from Marie's brutal and untimely death', the *Sunday Times* concluded on 15 November. Loyalist paramilitaries admitted later that they were planning retaliation within hours of the Enniskillen bombing but were halted by the broadcast; and the *Daily Mirror* was justified in observing six months later: 'Christian compassion saved a bloodbath of revenge killings from angry loyalists.'[318] The world-famous Dublin rock group U2 was about to go on stage in America when news came through of the bombing. During the number 'Sunday Bloody Sunday', the group's vocalist, Bono, proclaimed above the backing music to the audience:

> I've had enough of Irish-Americans, who haven't been back to their country in twenty or thirty years, come up to me and talk about the resistance, the revolution back home and the *glory* of the revolution, and the *glory* of dying for the revolution. Fuck the revolution! They don't talk about the glory of *killing* for the revolution ... Where's the glory in bombing a Remembrance Day parade of old-age pensioners, the medals taken out and polished up for the day? Where's the glory in that? that leave them dying or crippled for life or dead under the rubble of the revolution, that the majority of the people in my country don't want. *No more!*

Subsequently included in *Rattle and Hum*, the film of U2's *Joshua Tree* tour across the United States, these words were heard by millions and may have done more to discourage Irish-American financial support for the Provisional IRA than all the politicians' appeals put together.[319]

In the Dáil fresh legislation to expedite the extradition of terrorists was pushed through and came into force on the last day of November. This, together with closer co-operation north and south of the border in the drive against the Provisionals, seemed to indicate that the Anglo-Irish Agreement was yielding practical results. The accord remained firmly in place, but over the next two years a succession of crises and revelations severely strained relations between London and Dublin.

'There was blood everywhere,' Derek Luise told Simon de Bruxelles of the *Observer*. 'My brother and I laughed because we thought it was just a film. There was no shouting, just shots, about five or eight, one after the other.' Luise, a motor mechanic, had just witnessed the killing of Mairead Farrell and Sean Savage beside a petrol station on the main street leading out of Gibraltar to the Spanish frontier on Sunday 6 March 1988. Seconds later there were more shots as Daniel McCann was put to death. All three were Provisionals intent, it seems certain, on car-bombing a parade of the Royal Anglian Regiment due to take place forty-eight hours later. At first public reaction was profound relief that a bloody outrage had been averted by the swift response of an SAS team. Soon after, there was deep disquiet when it emerged that the Provisionals had no bomb in Gibraltar, and that they were unarmed. Clearly the SAS gave them no opportunity to surrender and was determined to kill them outright: Luise saw two men in jeans and casual jackets firing at a range of four feet at two of their victims, who were lying on the pavement; and Peti Celicia, who had been watching from her bedroom window, said there 'were five or six shots, very quick. A man was standing over them firing down. I never heard any shouting.'[320]

To many, not just in Ireland, this incident confirmed the conviction that the Government was pursuing a 'shoot-to-kill' policy against the Provisional IRA, without the sanction of parliament. Dr David Owen, the Social Democrat leader at Westminster, said soon afterwards: 'In a democracy no one – the SAS, the Special Branch, the police, or the armed services – can take the law into their own hands.'[321] Margaret Thatcher set her face against any form of judicial inquiry and, as further disturbing revelations emerged, controversy raged in the media and in parliament, placing the Anglo-Irish Agreement under acute pressure. Then, as a major diplomatic row developed, the scene swung back dramatically to Northern Ireland.

The bodies of the three Provisionals killed in Gibraltar were flown to Dublin and taken north in a cortège. Great numbers of sympathisers were present at the funerals in Belfast's Milltown cemetery on Wednesday 16 March. Suddenly Michael Stone, a lone loyalist who had infiltrated the crowd, threw three home-made hand grenades and fired shots killing three people and injuring several others before being overpowered by police.[322] For the first time in a long while the security forces had kept well to the periphery of a republican funeral and wild rumours flew about west Belfast that Stone had been tipped off by the RUC.[323] This violent attack had been filmed as it happened and was widely shown on television. One of those killed by Stone was Kevin Brady, a Provisional IRA activist; his funeral on Saturday 19 March in Andersonstown was an occasion when feelings were running high, and Provisional Sinn Féin stewards, fearful of another loyalist attack, assiduously checked cars and frisked mourners. Robert Howes and Derek Wood, two corporals from the Royal Corps of Signals in civilian clothes, strayed into the gathering mourners in a car. When a steward motioned them to turn round, they panicked, brandished a gun, mounted the pavement and reversed in desperation. 'The crowd thought it was another loyalist attack and moved in on them,' one man, not an IRA supporter, said later.[324]

The full, chilling horror of what followed was recorded by television cameras: a furious crowd closed in on the vehicle and dragged the men away. Later, the two corporals were stripped, beaten and shot dead beside the Andersonstown Leisure Centre. Mary Holland, reporting for the *Observer*, heard the shots and found a priest 'kneeling beside the body of a man who was naked except for underpants and shoes and socks. His head was covered with blood from gunshot wounds. At this stage he was still breathing and trying to move his head.' After attempting mouth-to-mouth resuscitation, she ran to call an ambulance on a bookmaker's telephone:

> When I came out, there were two bodies and the Army and police had arrived. Both bodies were now covered with tarpaulins and the blood was seeping away from them onto the pavement. As I went towards the first body in the car park, a youth walking away from it said to me: 'Short and sweet anyway.'[325]

'The younger element think it's a great coup,' one man told David McKittrick of the *Independent*. 'They think it's great. They're rejoicing in the fact that they got two Brits.' A woman who had been trying to stop her sons joining republican groups said to McKittrick, 'It was barbaric, utterly barbaric. It was animal – they were like monkeys in cages. They were on that car like lunatics. It was utterly and totally revolting. Watching it on TV just made me sick.'[326] This was the opinion of the vast majority on seeing the televised report that evening.

The Gibraltar killings and the violent episodes ensuing in Belfast came at a time of mounting disquiet in Dublin about the operation of British justice and security policies in Northern Ireland. While the Anglo-Irish Agreement was the first step towards unity in loyalists' eyes, it was to southerners a clear admission that partition was there to stay for a long time to come. As McKittrick put it in February 1988: 'The Republic expects someday to inherit the north – but not yet, Lord, not yet.'[327] Instead of indulging in empty rhetoric about removing the border, the Dublin government sought through the agreement to ensure fair treatment and justice for the Catholic minority in Northern Ireland. Though much was being achieved, there was also much cause for concern.

Southern anxieties arose from incidents long predating the agreement. On 11 November 1982 three members of the Provisional IRA were shot dead by police at a checkpoint outside Lurgan. The RUC admitted later in the day that the victims were unarmed. Thirteen days later Michael Tighe, a youth without paramilitary connections, was killed at a farm in Ballyneery, near Lurgan, during an RUC stakeout of an arms find. No firearms were recovered on 12 December 1982 when police shot dead two Irish National Liberation Army volunteers in a housing estate on the outskirts of Armagh. Accusations that the Government had adopted a shoot-to-kill policy seemed to be dramatically confirmed two years later. Sir Barry Shaw, the Director of Public Prosecutions for Northern Ireland, refused to accept Hermon's recommendations that no charges should be brought against police officers involved in the 1982 incidents. During his trial in 1984, Constable John Robinson said that he and others had been instructed by senior police officers to tell lies to maintain the confidentiality of covert operations. It was later revealed that RUC units, such as E4A, had been specially trained in counter-insurgency by the SAS, had illegally crossed the border, and had laid elaborate traps for some of their victims. To defuse the mounting controversy, the British government appointed John Stalker, the deputy chief constable of Greater Manchester, to conduct an inquiry.[328]

From the moment he arrived in Belfast in May 1984 Stalker was sure he was being obstructed by senior officers in the RUC. Crucial files were discovered to be 'out' and key officers not available for interview. Hermon dismissed an interim report in September 1985 as 'voluminous' and, as the inquiry continued, he even returned letters from Stalker unopened. The chief constable argued that Stalker was straying into areas beyond his remit, where he might wreck covert operations and put police officers' lives at risk.[329] Then, on 5 June 1986, Stalker was removed from the inquiry and replaced by the West Yorkshire chief constable, Colin Sampson. Sampson was also to investigate allegations against Stalker, including one that he had a financially corrupt friendship with Kevin Taylor, a Manchester property developer.[330] It was eventually shown that there was no substance in the allegations and the view was widely held on both sides of the Irish Sea that they had been trumped up to prevent Stalker producing embarrassing evidence about the activities of the security forces in Northern Ireland.[331]

Stalker published his memoirs in 1987. He concluded that there was 'a policy inclination, if not a policy, to shoot suspects dead without warning rather than to arrest them'; that all three shooting incidents in November–December 1982 might have constituted unlawful killing or murder; that a cover-up was employed against him; and that he was removed from the inquiry through a conspiracy. He had recommended the prosecution of eleven police officers, including a chief superintendent, and was contemplating recommending charges against more senior men when his inquiry was suddenly stopped. While Stalker was being 'welcomed in Dublin as a hero and an honest cop' during the launch of his book, the Director of Public Prosecutions in Belfast was still pressing for charges to be brought against certain police officers.[332] Then, on 25 January 1988, the attorney-general, Sir Patrick Mayhew, announced that the eleven officers investigated both by Stalker and by Sampson would not be prosecuted for reasons of 'national security'. The Dublin government was appalled and officially expressed 'deep dismay'. Three days later the Court of Appeal in London rejected a new appeal by the six people convicted of the Birmingham bombings in November 1974, despite growing evidence that the convictions were unsafe.[333]

For nationalists north and south of the border the sheen had long since disappeared from the Anglo-Irish Agreement. The general feeling that the British establishment had closed ranks to place its own interests before the course of justice in Ireland was strengthened by the Gibraltar killings, denounced by sixty Labour MPs at Westminster as 'an act of terrorism . . . tantamount to capital punishment without trial'.[334] Leading British newspapers and senior public figures were clearly troubled by the marked secrecy of the Government, exposed, for example, by the Thames Television *This Week* programme on the Gibraltar killings, *Death on the Rock*. In Ireland, McKittrick reported: 'Britannia, they are saying bitterly, still waives the rules.'[335] Yet these signs of strain between Dublin and London actually pointed up the practical value of the Anglo-Irish Agreement. Communications were kept open and co-operation on security measures was both maintained and strengthened.

After much delay and frustration, the republic began to extradite republican suspects. Gerard Harte was extradited north on Tuesday 23 August 1988 and, four days later, the Maze prison escaper, Robert Russell, was handed over to the RUC at the Killeen border crossing near Newry, Co. Down.[336] 'It was like Beirut around here on Saturday,' the *Independent* reported a west Belfast resident as saying. 'From the Whiterock right down the Falls Road was just one burning lorry after another.' In a protest closely co-ordinated by the Provisionals, lorries were rammed through loading-bay gates in Mackie's and set alight; heavy machine-gun fire was directed at the New Barnsley army base; and rioting and shootings were reported on a large scale in Newry, Strabane and Derry.[337] Despite the Enniskillen bombing, despite closer cross-border security co-operation, and despite frequent 'mistakes' in which the 'wrong' people were killed, the Provisional IRA remained the most successful guerrilla movement in western Europe.

The Anglo-Irish Agreement had given the Irish Republic a unique consultative role in Northern Ireland's affairs but the weight of responsibility for governing the region remained with the Westminster government and this seemed likely to continue for a long time to come. Counter-insurgency measures preoccupied the media and still were the principal source of anxiety in London, but as a charge on the public purse, they were dwarfed by the costs of propping up the region's ever-weakening economy.

'THE INDEPENDENT KEYNESIAN REPUBLIC OF NORTHERN IRELAND'

In 1979 the economy of the western world, and that of the United Kingdom in particular, took a downward plunge and by the second quarter of 1980 this depression was leaving a trail of devastation in Northern Ireland. Between 1979 and the autumn of 1981 no fewer than 110 substantial manufacturing firms in the region closed down. When Grundig finally shut the doors of its prestigious Dunmurry plant in October 1980, one of the reasons given by the management for doing so was the existence of 'disturbances of a political nature'.[338] The continuing violence, and the international attention paid to Northern Ireland during the 1981 hunger strikes in particular, continued to frighten off overseas investment. Inducements offered to outside firms remained generous but they were no longer unique: other states faced with recession were holding out equally tempting grants and the region had long since lost the special attraction for industrialists it once had.

It was not violence, however, that was mainly responsible for turning economic decline into a crisis. This depression, the worst since the 1930s, was precipitated by another leap in oil prices and in Northern Ireland this sealed the fate of most of the remaining synthetic fibre plants. Courtaulds shut down their Carrickfergus works in 1979 and British Enkalon closed in Antrim in 1981. The severe downswing coincided with the implementation of a tight monetary policy by Margaret Thatcher's Conservative administration. As cuts in public expenditure began to have effect the construction industry quickly ran into severe difficulties: between 1979 and the autumn of 1981 unemployment amongst those previously employed in construction rose by over

75 per cent, reducing employment in the industry to the lowest level recorded since the Second World War.[339] For the first time since 1945 employment in services, which had grown every year without exception, dropped in 1981. As almost every firm which did not go under shed labour, redundancies tripled and unemployment doubled to 21.1 per cent of the insured working population by July 1982.[340]

Northern Ireland's fragile economic base was in danger of cracking apart and nothing demonstrated this more than the foundering of the Government's flagship project, the De Lorean sports car factory in Dunmurry, on 31 May 1982. David Beresford of the *Guardian* described its passing:

> The funeral, such as it was, passed off uneventfully. The obsequies were performed by the 1,500 workers and the Department of Health and Social Security who kept open two social security offices on the Bank Holiday, so the workers could sign on the dole. The factory resembled a well kept graveyard . . . The presses, huge extractor fans, ovens and jigs were silent; about 1,000 cars sat motionless on the assembly line, vainly waiting for the engineers and fitters to transform them into status symbols for American roads. The tragedy attendant on all funerals was in the pride with which Mr Brendan Mackin, a shop steward and the former De Lorean production foreman, guided me through the factory. As he demonstrated a gull-wing door, it squeaked and he said: 'Don't be put off by the noise: it's just the new hinges.'[341]

The failure was a double blow not only because it was such a high-profile venture but it was also the most energetic attempt yet made by Westminster to bring industrial regeneration to west Belfast. Though £80 million of taxpayers' money had been made available to the firm, De Lorean was undercapitalised and, as scandal dogged the flamboyant proprietor and the American automobile market slumped, it had lurched from one financial crisis to another since it opened in 1978.[342] The 1985 Robert Zemeckis Hollywood film *Back to the Future* made the De Lorean sports car a cult object by portraying it as a time machine, but it appeared on the screens three years too late. Lear Fan, the American corporation making aircraft with carbon fibre fuselages, was enticed to Northern Ireland but it failed too with a similar loss to the exchequer.

The sharp drop in manufacturing output between 1979 and 1981 proceeded at the same rate – just over 14 per cent – in Northern Ireland as in the United Kingdom as a whole.[343] This, indeed, was part of the problem: Northern Ireland was on the periphery of a state which had the poorest growth record of any advanced industrialised state since 1945. The region was also the weakest in the United Kingdom, suffering most severely in any downswing and recovering very tardily in any ensuing revival. Manufacturing employment fell by a quarter in the

United Kingdom in the period 1979–86 but by a third in Northern Ireland: this disparity is explained by the economic recovery across the Irish Sea after the middle of 1982, which simply failed to benefit manufacturing in Northern Ireland.[344] Barry White, reporting the gloomy prognostications of the government-funded Economic Council in May 1983, came to this conclusion:

> No serious economist pretends that the employment levels of 1979 will ever be reached again, whatever the strength of the recovery. Too many large factories have closed, never to re-open . . . The erosion of manufacturing employment has been little short of catastrophic, falling by almost half from 177,000 in 1970 to 95,000 today – a figure which is certain to drop to 90,000 by the end of this year.[345]

White's prediction proved all too correct: on Monday 25 July one of Faulkner's 'blue-chip' companies, Goodyear, announced that it would close its Craigavon factory in October with the loss of 773 jobs. 'Despite the signs,' the *Belfast Telegraph* commented, 'the finality of today's announcement is a traumatic shock for the people of Craigavon, which was intrinsically developed around the big Goodyear plant.' Opened in 1967 for the production of conveyor belting, fan belts and other industrial rubber items, Goodyear had at one time employed 1,800; now the recession and Far East competition had made its Ulster operation completely uneconomic and the company had lost £4.5 million in the first seven months of 1983.[346]

In the December 1983 issue of the *Irish Banking Review*, Professor William Black of Queen's University observed that while 'evidence of an upward movement in the UK economy is beginning to accumulate', not even 'a very vigorous acceleration' could 'reverse the upward movement of unemployment' in Northern Ireland. He predicted only a slight 'improvement on the catastrophic experience of the past four years', during which thirty-six thousand manufacturing jobs had been lost in the region.[347] The industrial decline seemed inexorable and even during the 'Lawson boom' of 1987–8, unemployment continued to grow. Altogether forty thousand manufacturing jobs disappeared in the decade between 1979 and 1989. The firm of Dun and Bradstreet recorded that the business failure rate in 1989 was 22 per cent in Northern Ireland compared with 9.7 per cent in England and Wales.[348] This protracted shake-out removed most of the branch factories of British and overseas multinationals, thus leaving the industrial sector once again dominated by the older indigenous firms.

'Flax is back' was the headline over Michael Drake's *Belfast Telegraph* article on 8 March 1985, reporting the progress of the Industrial Development Board's Linen Task Force in promoting the domestic cultivation of the crop from 100 acres to nearly 1,000. The linen industry's decline had been steep since 1959 when forty-four mills across Northern Ireland had kept forty-five thousand in employment. Even at its lowest point, 1983, the region still had 32 mills giving work to 6,000 and producing 3,300 tons of yarn worth £24.7 million; and by 1986 yarn output increased by 20 per cent to 4,050 tons valued at £33.6 million. With the assistance of advanced wet-spinning machinery made in Mackie's, high-quality yarn was spun for the fine-textured high fashion cloth most in demand. This quality, together with belated improvements in design, helped linen to find favour as a material for Italian shirts and dresses for high society women in New York; and the renowned fashion designer, Paul Costelloe, made a particular point of using Ulster linen in his creations. 'It is a light fabric with enormous capacity to absorb moisture which makes it very cool to wear,' Bruce Robinson of the Industrial Development Board explained. 'In addition, people will tell you that it is a very sensuous fabric ideally suited to the more casual dress of the 1980s.' By 1988 Northern Ireland's linen products, including yarn, were worth an estimated £140 million annually; the depression of 1990–2 caused more closures and contraction, but the industry retained a significant, if precarious, niche in a specialised international market.[349]

The severe downswing of 1979–82, together with the Government's monetarist policy, almost finished off shipbuilding in Belfast. Harland and Wolff found it possible to complete only one main propelling engine and two British Rail ferry vessels – their gross tonnage of 14,000 was the smallest output from Belfast since the 1930s. The Conservative government, however, could not face the closure which the continued application of its free enterprise philosophy would inevitably begin. Adam Butler, a junior minister, and Jim Prior between them persuaded their colleagues to throw the struggling shipyard a vital financial lifeline. With this help Harland and Wolff won orders for a floating harbour in the Falklands, bulk carriers for British Steel and four refrigerated vessels for the Blue Star line.[350] John Parker, appointed chairman in November 1982, admitted that the Blue Star ships would be built at a loss but observed that the contract 'provides a degree of stability at a time when a storm of uncertainty is rocking the whole of European shipbuilding'. Prior announced an additional £37.5 million subsidy in April 1984, saying that he looked forward 'to the company securing more new orders and further reducing its future requirement for public funds'.[351] A valuable and prestigious order, worth £110 million, was won four months later: Harland and Wolff was chosen out of seventeen world shipbuilders, including the short-listed Mitsubishi of Japan and

Chantier de l'Atlantique of France, to build a Single Well Oil Production System ship for British Petroleum – a vessel designed to extract oil from marginal offshore fields particularly in the North Sea. This success, together with Ministry of Defence contracts for support vessels, left Harland and Wolff in a more secure position than most other British yards. The company still had the largest construction yard in Europe but the workforce – 7,542 in 1979 falling to 5,163 by 1985 – was only a fraction of what it had been a quarter of a century earlier.[352]

In the early 1980s Short Brothers bypassed Harland and Wolff to become Ulster's biggest manufacturing concern. The securing of an order worth £460 million – the largest single contract so far in the history of the firm – for Sherpa freighters from the United States Air Force in March 1984 provided work for around 6,600 at the Sydenham factory.[353] The most profitable division in Short Brothers manufactured armaments, such as Seacat and Blowpipe missiles, and Boeing and Rolls Royce provided subcontract work; most employees, however, were engaged in making small civil aircraft. The successful outback transporter of the 1960s, the Skyvan, had been modernised to provide a choice of three models: the Sherpa freighter; the Shorts 330, carrying thirty-three passengers; and the Shorts 360, taking thirty-six seats. All three could use a runway of only 4,000 feet, were easy to maintain and could be flown over built-up areas because of their comparatively quiet turbo-prop engines. *Flight* magazine observed: 'The ugly duckling Shorts 330, and particularly, the bigger 360 – which is still no swan – are rapidly assuming the mantle of the aircraft to beat in today's commuter airliner battle.' By the end of 1983 twelve airlines, including Mississippi Valley Airlines and the Australian Murray Valley Airlines, operated the 360; and by the spring of the following year the company had orders and options for a total of 180 of its aircraft. The Shorts 360 sold at between 20 and 30 per cent below the price of its nearest rival but its box-shaped cabin could not be pressurised: in an era when passengers were demanding greater comfort this shortcoming placed strict limits on the aircraft's future sales potential.[354]

In 1983 Short Brothers announced an operating profit for the first time since 1975 but interest payments on bank loans still produced an overall loss of £19 million on a turnover of £202 million.[355] Official statisticians generally placed both Harland and Wolff and Short Brothers in the private sector but both were wholly owned by the Government and utterly dependent on massive subventions from the exchequer. These two concerns, accounting for around 10 per cent of all manufacturing employment, received about one third of all public resources going to industrial support. In 1989 the Government, in line with its policy in Britain, privatised both companies: this did not mean that it had abandoned them to free market forces; the Public Accounts Committee revealed that the sale of Short Brothers to the Canadian aerospace company Bombardier had cost the taxpayer £986 million; and the management–employee buy out of Harland and Wolff required £500 million of public money.[356] The shipyard managed to stay in profit in its first years of trading as a private company but the announcement of three hundred redundancies in November 1991 ensured that the workforce there would be reduced to below two thousand in the following year.[357]

The decline of manufacturing did not stop the steady migration from rural to urban areas but there was widespread evidence that many stayed in farming, despite low incomes in many places, because of the dearth of employment opportunities. Agriculture was the region's most important industry, employing 8 per cent of Northern Ireland's civilian workforce and another 3 per cent in related industries. It accounted for between 4 and 5 per cent of Northern Ireland's gross domestic product in 1988 compared with 2 per cent of that of the United Kingdom as a whole and 3.5 per cent of that of the European Community. Average farm size was low: 43.7 hectares as against 272 in Scotland and 106.3 in all of the United Kingdom; and 71 per cent of Northern Ireland's land was designated as being in Severely Disadvantaged Areas. Ulster farmers had the advantage that nearly all owned their holdings (only 59 per cent in England and Wales were wholly owner-occupied in 1988) and many had the opportunity to let or rent land by the traditional conacre system.[358]

Both the Irish Republic and the United Kingdom joined the European Community in January 1973 and enjoyed the protection of the common agricultural policy. Not all farmers appreciated that protection and regulation. Intensive pig and poultry production was hard hit by the high price of grain (nearly all of it imported) and the imposition of milk quotas created acute difficulties in a region heavily dependent on dairying. Agriculture proved as sensitive to energy prices as urban industries: farmers' incomes dropped severely in 1974–5, in 1980 and in the late 1980s. The larger holdings were as technically efficient as those in Britain and there was a steady rise in mechanisation – the percentage of farms with milking parlours increased from 29 in 1978 to 53.6 in 1986, for example. Despite high transport costs, the poultry meat sector survived remarkably well; intensive egg and pig production declined; and natural climatic advantages ensured that pasture farming dominated more than ever – 71.5 per cent of Northern Ireland's agricultural output came from cattle, milk and sheep in 1986 compared with 57.5 per cent in 1972.[359]

Agriculture was subsidised and protected across the whole European Community, and Northern Ireland benefited no more than other disadvantaged regions. Other sectors of the region's economy, however, received financial support from Westminster on an unprecedented scale. Harland and Wolff obtained £350 million from the exchequer between 1977 and 1986, for example.[360] 'More money for these people?' Margaret Thatcher said to Garret FitzGerald when he suggested seeking European contributions for the International Fund. 'Why should they have more money? I need that money for my people in England.'[361] In fact the prime minister drew back from the consequences of applying undiluted Thatcherism to Northern Ireland, and Ian Aitken, writing in the *Guardian* on 26 July 1989, referred to the region as 'the Independent Keynesian Republic of Northern Ireland, where monetarism remains unknown'.[362] In the same year the Economic Council summed up the disparity:

Public expenditure in Northern Ireland (excluding social security) has grown by about 1.3 per cent per annum in real terms over the past five years. This compares with an average annual decrease nationally of approximately 0.5 per cent.[363]

Exceptional efforts were made both to attract new investment and to stimulate industry within the region, particularly through the Industrial Development Board and the Local Enterprise Development Unit. Much was achieved by these two agencies in the 1980s but the economic climate became so harsh that in 1990–1 the Industrial Development Board only managed to get 1,294 new jobs, most of them arising from public sector 'back office' relocations from Britain.[364] This new recession brought more depressing news: 260 were made redundant at Mackie's in June 1991 and the remaining employees were put on short time; and on 6 April 1992 more than 500 textile workers faced life on the dole when Coats Viyella (which had recently shut down its Welch Margetson plant in Belfast with the loss of 350 jobs) closed its Magherafelt factory.[365] In short, by the beginning of the 1990s Northern Ireland had all but ceased to be a manufacturing region. By 1989 government employment schemes, providing 25,600 places, accounted for a quarter of all jobs in industry and the employment of the remainder in manufacturing was heavily dependent on public subsidy.[366] The region's economy had in effect become a service economy. The public sector gross domestic product had risen from 33 per cent of the whole in

1974 to 44 per cent in 1986, compared with 29 per cent and 34 per cent in those years in all of the United Kingdom.[367] This was made possible only by the British subvention – money transferred by Westminster over and above the sum raised in taxation in Northern Ireland – which increased from less than £100 million in 1972 to £1.6 billion in 1988–9 (or £1.9 billion if expenditure on the British Army and European Community grants are included).[368] One way of looking at the subvention is that Northern Ireland is part of the United Kingdom and is simply getting the extra help that other ailing regions are entitled to receive – that help is greater per head of population in Northern Ireland than in any other region but by almost every yardstick that can be applied Northern Ireland *is* the most deprived area, with the weakest economy in all of the United Kingdom.[369] Another way of viewing the subvention is that Northern Ireland has one of the most dependent economies in the world.[370]

The bulk of the subvention was spent neither on direct aid to industry nor on the security forces. The overwhelming share was assigned to the public services and the most visible sign of this expenditure was the transformation of the region's public housing – not only a vital stimulus to the economy but also a major attempt to ease intercommunal tensions.

'ENTITLED TO ASPIRE TO PARITY OF MINIMUM HOUSING STANDARDS'

There are thirteen 'peace lines' in Belfast, their location decided on by the security forces and the Northern Ireland Office. The earliest one to be put up was at Cupar Street, a grim and formidable barrier of concrete reminiscent of the Berlin Wall marking the volatile divide between the Protestant Shankill and the Catholic Falls. The line at Manor Street is a high corrugated iron fence, but the most recently erected, made of curving brick walls surrounded with shrubs, are almost architecturally pleasing. Altogether 1.2 per cent of houses in the city are separated by peace lines.[371] Wide strips of no-man's-land and planted parks were useless as alternatives since they provided battle grounds and cover for paramilitaries, and only the Westlink, part of the urban motorway, fortuitously made an effective barrier to possible sectarian confrontation.[372]

The peace lines are a visible sign that housing a divided community presents exceptional problems requiring exceptional measures. Despite furious criticisms from some local councillors, the Housing Executive has succeeded in maintaining its reputation for impartiality ever since it adopted and published a single standard points system in April 1973.[373] The Housing Trust had made valiant attempts to create integrated estates, particularly in Twinbrook, and the Housing Executive for a time tried to follow in its footsteps.[374] This policy collapsed following the burning of whole streets in August 1971 and the events surrounding the breakdown of the Provisionals' ceasefire in Lenadoon during July 1972. Henceforth, save for middle-class residential suburbs, segregation seemed the only recipe for stability in urban areas and in not a few rural ones as well.

The most acute housing problems were in Belfast but for a time those in Derry were as bad in proportion to the city's population. The Housing Executive inherited a waiting list of some two thousand families, accounting for around one seventh of Derry's inhabitants. The local authorities there discriminated blatantly to the eleventh hour: Londonderry Corporation refused to allow building at Shantallow on the bogus grounds that proper drainage was impossible there; and Londonderry Rural District Council, with unedifying haste, allocated virtually all the Ballynagard estate off the Culmore Road to Protestants just before the Development Commission took over. Until then many small terraced dwellings housed two or three families each and no Catholic on the waiting list for less than five years had any hope of being allocated a new home. Faced with repeated riots and gun battles, squatting, intimidation of contractors, the rents-and-rates strike and no-go barricades, the commission and then the Housing Executive strove to make up for past neglect starting with new schemes at Shantallow and Gobnascale. Gradually over the ensuing twenty years the Foyle itself became a peace line: on the west bank, save for a diminishing Protestant enclave within the old city walls, the population became almost wholly Catholic; while across the river, the Waterside reinforced its position as the largest Protestant stronghold in the north-west. A similar process occurred in Newry, which began in the summer of 1969 when Protestant families fled Derrybeg, a congested estate of 350 houses put up in the 1960s which became an IRA bastion, and continued with a spate of sectarian murders reaching a horrific climax with the massacre of ten Protestants at Kingsmills on 5 January 1976. Here the line of segregation was the Carnlough Road, Protestants migrating to the north and Catholics to the south.[375]

The Labour government, shocked by the evidence of the 1974 House Condition Survey, more than doubled the resources available to the Housing Executive in real terms between 1974 and 1977. Then the International Monetary Fund intervened to curb government spending and the region's housing budget was cut by 15 per cent.[376] The return of a Conservative government in 1979, which made council housing its particular target, brought further swingeing cuts. Charles Brett, chairman of the Housing Executive, made impassioned appeals for clemency. 'The figures for overcrowding are just double those in Manchester, one of the worst housed cities in England', he declared in October 1980. 'Over the past year the Board of the Executive has searched with increasing desperation for additional sources of funds.'[377] In July 1981 he observed that over 'the past two years we have had a succession of cuts, moratoriums, and shifts in budget allocation, which have left the Board of the Executive reeling', and he asked of the Government, 'Do they or do they not accept the principle that different parts of the United Kingdom are entitled to aspire to parity of minimum housing standards?'[378]

Salvation was at hand. Brett's case was reinforced by a report published in May 1981 by the Northern Ireland Economic Council, which argued that spending money on housing would do more than anything else to put life into the region's ailing economy because construction was labour intensive and used local materials. Chris Patten, the housing minister in the Northern Ireland Office, was impressed and said that he had 'no doubt at all that the housing statistics demonstrate the intensity of the problems in Northern Ireland'.[379] Before the end of 1981 the Government had agreed to make housing its first social priority in Northern Ireland. By the mid-1980s the Housing Executive was able to spend around £100 million a year on its capital programme and for a time the organisation had around five thousand on its payroll. In 1986–7 public spending on housing per head in the region was nearly three times that of England and Wales.[380] In line with government policy more emphasis was placed on rehabilitation, designed to give older dwellings another thirty years of use, and on 'enveloping' to renovate external fabric. By March 1992 nearly eight thousand dwellings had been 'enveloped' in Belfast alone at a cost of £21 million.[381]

The continuing Troubles caused both Protestants and Catholics to seek safety in numbers. In Belfast this produced particular problems. Protestants found it attractive to move to estates on the fringe, such as Monkstown and Newtownabbey, and growth centres such as Antrim and Newtownards. This outward movement could create difficulties, for many of these migrants had been in the eye of the storm and their arrival could upset previously good community relations in rural towns. Houses were most plentiful in Craigavon because industry had failed to burgeon there as expected: sandwiched between Lurgan, with a large Catholic population, and overwhelmingly Protestant Portadown, the new city became a new battleground as more families arrived from

Belfast. Eventually degradation there was so severe that some streets had to be demolished.[382] Meanwhile, Catholics clustered in older housing in north and west Belfast, creating acute pressure there. To move into the by now underinhabited Shankill would have been a completely reckless challenge to the loyalist territorial imperative. The only answer was to breach the stop line and build in the green belt. Protestant Lisburn clamoured against the southward advance of a Catholic tidal wave through Protestant farmland, but the Government gave way before the entreaties of the Housing Executive. Lessons from the past had been learned: particular attention was paid to good planning and design to promote a sense of community; and careful steps were taken to prevent squatting. The first thirty families moved during November 1980 into the new development, named Poleglass, which would eventually provide two thousand new homes.[383]

Poleglass was built just in time, for the public pressure to demolish the Divis complex was becoming intense. In 1986, after its first major 'investment appraisal', the Housing Executive concluded that the most cost-effective, long-term answer was to pull down the twelve medium-rise blocks and replace them with 260 new houses. The nineteen-storey Divis Tower, still popular with tenants, was to remain. This decision was followed by consultation on an unprecedented scale, local residents being involved in decisions ranging from street layout to the variety of brick to be used. The Weetabix blocks in the Shankill had been demolished and a programme was launched to redevelop Unity Flats.[384]

By 1992 it could be said that Northern Ireland's housing crisis was over. In 1987 the unfitness level had fallen to 8.4 per cent, though this was unevenly distributed: in Castlereagh it was only 1.4 per cent, while in Co. Fermanagh it was still 27 per cent, due to the need to upgrade facilities in farmhouses. Between 1982 and 1991 the Housing Executive had spent £2.4 billion on new dwellings, maintenance, grants and renovation.[385] The face of the region had been transformed by the programme and the quality of construction, layout and design of recent schemes had attracted well-warranted praise from housing experts in Britain and further afield. Examples of imaginative and harmonious design include: the harbour front, Killyleagh; Ellis Street, Carrickfergus; Creggan Street, Derry; River Road, Dunmurry; Derrin Park, Enniskillen; Poleglass; and Donegall Pass, Lord Street, Lancaster Street, St George's Gardens, and the new Divis in Belfast. Often these put to shame the vulgar 'Tudor' and 'Georgian' private middle-class developments and certainly the tasteless 'Irish hacienda' style so prevalent in Co. Donegal and much of the west of Ireland. In addition, the vigorous drive to upgrade Northern Ireland's housing may have contributed significantly to the notable fall in levels of violence in the region in the 1980s by comparison with the 1970s. Paramilitary strongholds tended to be in the remaining rundown and congested enclaves and in the more soulless estates put up in the 1960s and early 1970s. In the 1850s and 1860s, Napoleon III encouraged his Prefect of the Seine, Baron Haussmann, to sweep away narrow streets and build broad boulevards in Paris to make it difficult for the revolutionary mob to erect effective barricades. It is impossible to say whether or not the Government funded massive housing redevelopment in Northern Ireland with a similar purpose in mind, but certainly the new courts and cul-de-sacs made rioting difficult to organise, not to speak of the determination of residents not to have their newly acquired 'wee palaces' damaged or destroyed.

It is likely that, pound for pound, government spending on housing did as much to improve the quality of life for citizens as public money earmarked for any other purpose in Northern Ireland. Government policies which widened the gap between the rich and poor all over the United Kingdom, together with the region's persistent economic frailty, nevertheless ensured that poverty remained widespread in Northern Ireland.

'EVIDENT POVERTY IN CATHOLIC AND PROTESTANT AREAS ALIKE'

Peter Townsend, author of *Poverty in the United Kingdom*, paid his first visit to Belfast in 1968:

> I was struck not only by the evident poverty in Catholic and Protestant areas alike, but by scenes which seemed to belong more to the 1930s – of red-haired boys using scales on a cart drawn by an emaciated pony to sell coal by the pound, teenage girls in a second-hand clothing shop buying underslips and skirts, and some of the smallest 'joints' of meat in butchers' windows that I have ever seen.[386]

In his survey, 44.3 per cent of Northern Ireland's households were classified as in poverty.[387] Since then there has been a marked rise in the region's living standards but the gap between the rich and the poor remained wide in an area which continues to be the most disadvantaged in the United Kingdom. Townsend, in his research published in 1979, ranked the degree of poverty in regions using eight different criteria: Northern Ireland came first on six of these and was second and third on the other two – indeed, he reckoned that the only advantage the poor had there was relative freedom from pollution.[388]

Westminster made vigorous attempts to improve the situation and, in spite of the rapid decline of manufacturing employment, succeeded in raising household incomes in both real and relative terms. In 1974 households in Northern Ireland had been on average 50 per cent worse off than those in the poorest British region. Not much had changed by 1979 when Northern Ireland households on average were £10 a week worse off than those in the poorest region across the Irish Sea. By the end of the 1980s the gap between Northern Ireland and the poorest British regions had been closed and personal incomes were on a par with those in Wales and the north of England. In part this was due to the 'Thatcher revolution', which had widened the gulf between the social classes and between the most prosperous and most deprived areas in the United Kingdom. In part it was the result of exceptional measures being taken in Northern Ireland – here Conservative ministers applied the principles of Thatcherism with less fervour than in any other part of the state.[389] The decision to make housing a social priority in the early 1980s launched a programme of regeneration which vastly improved the quality of life across the region and did much to stave off economic collapse. In March 1988 *The Economist* made this claim about one of the Northern Ireland Office ministers:

> Mr Needham, who used to escort parties of English MPs round the province to show them its problems, found them so envious of his baili-wick's housing and health that he stopped inviting them.

By 1990, 10 per cent of Northern Ireland's gross domestic product was being assigned to healthcare compared with 6 per cent in England; and the region had eleven hospital beds per ten thousand of the population while England had only seven.[390] In education there was mounting criticism in England, Scotland and Wales during the 1980s of the Conservative governments' penny-pinching approach. In Northern Ireland, in contrast, total real expenditure by the education and library boards fell only slightly until 1986 when it began to rise significantly.[391]

Improvements notwithstanding, Northern Ireland still had an acute poverty problem by western European standards. No region in the United Kingdom was without that problem, but in proportion to its population poverty was more deep-rooted and widespread in Northern Ireland than in any area in Britain. The central cause of poverty was unemployment. Comparing the statistics is difficult because since 1979 there have been twenty-nine changes in the official definition of the unemployed and in the calculation of the unemployment rate: most of these alterations reduce the size of the category of unemployment but, above all, the major change has been to count only those unemployed persons actually claiming benefit.[392] Thus 18.6 per cent were classed as unemployed in Northern Ireland in June 1986 but 21.5 per cent were out of work by the methods of computation used prior to October 1982. In June 1986 there were nearly eleven thousand adults in employment and training schemes and over nine thousand young people in the Youth Training Programme who were not classed as unemployed. The jobless figures would have been higher had not many left Northern Ireland to seek employment in Britain or further afield. The two years of intense violence following the introduction of internment prompted many to quit the region mainly for their own safety: the Registrar General estimated a 'net outward migration' of 44,100 in 1971–3. Thereafter the annual outflow averaged around 8,000 a year, dropping to 5,300 in 1979–80 and rising to 9,900 in 1981–2.[393] Even during the unrest accompanying the H-block hunger strikes, the main cause of emigration throughout the 1980s and into the 1990s was lack of work.

Unemployment was consistently higher in Northern Ireland than in any other region: in 1979 it was 9.1 per cent and the worst region across the Irish Sea was the North with a rate of 7.9 per cent. In 1986, when 11.8 per cent were out of work in the United Kingdom as a whole, the hardest-hit areas were: Northern Ireland, 18.6 per cent; the North, 16.3; the North West, 14.9; and Wales, 14.9. Northern Ireland was by no means the only or the worst unemployment black spot in the European Community. In 1986 13.3 per cent were out of work in Bremen, West Germany; 14.2 in Hainaut, Belgium; 19.3 in Sardinia, Italy; and 30.2 per cent in Andalucia, Spain.[394] Northern Ireland certainly would have been on a par with Andalucia but for the large subventions from London. Identifiable public expenditure per head in Northern Ireland was £2,511, compared with £1,740 in Great Britain in 1983–4, and in 1987–8 the figures were £3,174 and £2,154. Excluding the extra cost of the army, this transfer was equivalent to 26 per cent of Northern Ireland's gross domestic product in 1976–7 and 21.8 per cent in 1986–7.[395]

Poverty remained a persistent problem in spite of these subventions and, in the United Kingdom, Northern Ireland usually was at the top of the list of regions in the accepted indicators of deprivation. In the 1970s about twenty out of every thousand babies were dying before they reached their first birthday. By the late 1980s the rate had dropped to 10.5 per thousand but was still high when the United Kingdom average was 6.6. In 1985 the average weekly income in Northern Ireland was £108.75 compared with £216.63 in the United Kingdom as a whole – two out of five households, or 37 per cent, had an income below the 'living wage' of £100 a week in 1984–5 compared with 29 per cent in the United

Kingdom. Families in Northern Ireland spent a higher proportion of their incomes on food (23.4 per cent), fuel and power (9.4 per cent), and clothing (9.4 per cent) than the United Kingdom averages of 20.3, 6.2 and 7.4 per cent for these items. Contrary to the popular view, the spending on alcohol, 3.5 per cent of the household budget, was lower than the United Kingdom average of 4.9 per cent.[396]

With the exception of old-age pensions, there was a much higher dependence on state benefits in Northern Ireland than in any other region of the United Kingdom: in 1983, 23 per cent of households were living on supplementary benefit and by 1987 this had risen to 26 per cent.[397] Then, in April 1988, the 1986 Social Security Act was applied to Northern Ireland: this replaced supplementary benefit with income support and substituted the social fund, which offered loans, for single payment grants. The impact on families dependent on benefit was immediate. The social fund budget for 1988–9 was only just over half the value of single payments made in 1986 and, furthermore, every single social security office in Northern Ireland underspent its social fund allocation. This legislation – along with a rise in indirect taxation, a reduction in direct taxation on the well-off, and more rigid tests of availability for employment prescribed by the 1989 Social Security Act – widened the gap between the prosperous and the poor all over the United Kingdom. Despite special action taken to bring help to unemployment blackspots in Northern Ireland, the high level of benefits dependency in the region ensured that the impact of social security reform was more severe than in any other area of the state.[398] In December 1989 the regional director of St Vincent de Paul said:

> Since the government's single payments for the needy were changed into loans, demand for our services has increased dramatically . . . people who managed to cope in the past are now turning to us in desperation.[399]

St Vincent de Paul is a Catholic charity and it was amongst Catholics that unemployment, low-paid employment and deprivation were most prevalent.

'RELATIVE CATHOLIC DISADVANTAGE IN THE JOB MARKET IS A COMPLEX MATTER'

In 1971 Catholic males were 2.6 times as likely to be unemployed as Protestant males in Northern Ireland. This differential dropped to 2.4 times in 1981, to just below 2.4 times in 1983–4, and rose again to 2.5 times in 1985–7.[400] The imbalance thus proved stable over many years and even the economic crisis of 1979–82, which led to the loss of so many jobs held by Protestants in engineering and the artificial fibres industry, hit Catholics just as hard, owing to severe contraction in construction and in the clothing industry: 17.3 per cent of Catholic males were unemployed in 1971 compared with 6.6 per cent of Protestant males; in 1981 the percentages were 30.2 as against 12.4; and they were 35.0 as against 15.0 in 1983–4. No matter where they lived, Catholics were more likely to be out of work. In 1981 the percentages of men unemployed in this selection of local government districts were as follows: Ards, 21.2 Catholics and 9.8 other denominations; Ballymena, 22.1 and 11.1; Cookstown, 43.3 and 14.4; Craigavon, 30.4 and 11.0; Larne, 24.4 and 13.1; and Strabane, 39.0 and 21.9. Altogether 30.2 per cent of Catholic men were out of work that year compared with 12.4 per cent of Protestants and other non-Catholics and 19.1 per cent of men in Britain's worst-affected region, Merseyside. Even the most deprived Protestant district, the Shankill, with 27.6 per cent of men out of work, had a lower level of male unemployment than the Catholic average for the whole region. By comparison the percentages for Whiterock and the Falls in Catholic west Belfast were 56.4 and 52.6 respectively in 1981.[401]

For many the disparity in Protestant and Catholic rates of unemployment is simply explained in one word: discrimination. However, evidence seems to point to the truth of the observation of Paul Compton, professor of geosciences at Queen's University, that 'the reason for relative Catholic disadvantage in the job market is a complex matter and is not amenable to simple explanation'. In a study he helped to carry out in 1987, Compton showed that Catholics who had emigrated overseas were still twice as likely to be unemployed as Protestants going abroad.[402] Catholics, indeed, were not as inclined to leave Northern Ireland as they had been from the late 1970s onwards, due mainly to the international decline of job opportunities. Protestants, particularly those with special skills and good educational qualifications, showed an increased tendency to emigrate: by 1987–8, 2,872 A level students – more than 40 per cent of the total – were leaving to take up higher education places in Britain or in the Irish Republic. A great majority were Protestants and a high proportion did not return. In addition, just over 17 per cent of graduates from Northern Ireland's two universities found employment outside the region.[403] This largely Protestant 'brain drain' did not affect the statistics as much as the greater natural increase of the Catholic labour force which, ranging between 12 to 15 per cent in the period 1971–81, was double that of the Protestant workforce, between 4 and 6 per cent. Unemployment tends to be concentrated among the younger and newer entrants to the workforce and Catholics were therefore more strongly affected. Catholic families, larger than

Protestant ones, tended to fall more easily into the poverty trap, in which social security payments exceed the likely take-home pay from poorly rewarded employment. Catholics were disadvantaged, too, by the greater emphasis given to the teaching of science and technology in Protestant schools, which reduced the range of occupations available to those leaving Catholic schools.[404] Employment opportunities were far better in the counties of Antrim and Down than west of the Bann, where Catholics predominated.

A major factor in making it difficult for the Government to redress Catholic disadvantage in the job market was the reluctance of Catholics to join the police and the UDR. The policy of Ulsterisation ensured that nearly one in ten of all Protestant men were in paid employment in the security forces in some capacity by the late 1980s.[405] In 1992 the average pay of police officers was £30,000 a year, and since virtually all had their homes east of the Bann, their combined spending power largely benefited the prosperous Protestant areas of north Down and south and mid-Antrim.

Some progress was made in reducing the differential. Between 1971 and 1981 the number of Catholic 'managers of large establishments' more than doubled, while the Protestant figure increased by just over one half: but in 1981 Catholics still made up only 18.5 per cent of the total in this category. The civil service raised the percentage of Catholics in post from 35.5 in 1981 to 41.0 in 1985 but at the most senior levels – senior principal or above – Protestants predominated at just above 90 per cent.[406] The BBC in Northern Ireland employed hardly any Catholics except in menial positions until the mid-1960s, but redressed the balance rapidly thereafter. The Queen's University of Belfast, in contrast, was very slow in taking action: its academic, administrative and ancillary staff remained overwhelmingly Protestant. The Westminster government decided that more vigorous measures were needed to counter long-entrenched practices, such as employees 'speaking for' relatives and friends seeking employment.

In 1986 the management of Short Brothers was deeply concerned when some of its Catholic employees were attacked by Protestant workers who insisted on decorating the premises with bunting during the marching season. All loyalist flags and decorations were removed and as a result about two thousand employees went on strike – a dispute resolved only when the management agreed to keep the Union flag flying permanently over its Sydenham factory. The largest industrial concern in Northern Ireland, with over 90 per cent of its employees Protestant in 1988, Short Brothers had secured valuable contracts in the United States for its Sherpa and 30-3 aircraft and for the manufacture of parts for the Boeing 7J7 airliner. Public opinion in America had forced disinvestment in South Africa and now a powerful lobby there sought the implementation of the 'MacBride principles', guidelines approved by the Nobel prize winner Sean MacBride to boycott Ulster firms thought to be discriminating against Catholics. Though the MacBride principles were condemned by John Hume and the United States government, the threat was enough to encourage the British government to take more decisive action. A new code of practice was issued in September 1987: it recommended that preferential treatment should not be given to existing employees' relatives; that conditions of employment not job-related, such as service in the armed forces, be removed; and that employers advertise widely, rather than rely on word-of-mouth recruitment. The code was voluntary but the Government pledged to refuse to do business with those who would not comply with the code – a powerful incentive, as it was by far the largest employer in the region.[407]

In 1989 the Fair Employment Agency was replaced by the Fair Employment Commission with stronger teeth and the code of practice was now given the force of law. The new act was thus explained by the Department of Economic Development:

> Employers must register, monitor their workforces and regularly review their recruitment, training and promotion practices. They must take affirmative action measures and set goals and timetables where necessary. There are both nominal fines and economic sanctions – involving loss of business and grants – for those guilty of bad practice.[408]

As it had done so often in the nineteenth century, the British government was prepared to experiment and intervene in Ireland to an extent not contemplated on its mainland. Attempts by Labour-controlled local authorities to enforce 'contract compliance' in order to improve the employment prospects of black people were outlawed, for example. While the Northern Committee of the Irish Congress of Trade Unions felt the fair employment legislation did not go far enough, others believed the Government was yielding to American pressure. Paul Compton challenged the thinking behind the act and the findings of the Policy Studies Institute which partly inspired it: he argued that the legislation 'is based on a mistaken analysis of the problem and does not address the real causes of Catholic disadvantage in the work place'.[409]

The legislation began to have some effect. On 25 October 1991 the Fair Employment Commission announced that Dunellen Limited of Belfast had been disqualified from receipt of government contracts for failure to complete workforce monitoring returns – the first such case. A month later a labour-force survey commissioned by the Northern

Ireland Office found that the unemployment differential between Catholic and Protestant men had fallen from two and a half times to two times.[410] Catholics nevertheless remained underrepresented at the top level. Announcing the results of a survey into senior staff positions in eighty-seven public bodies on 19 May 1992, Bob Cooper, chairman of the Fair Employment Commission, said he was 'particularly concerned that the Roman Catholic proportion among the highest paid staff is only 20.5 per cent'.[411] Tackling the problem of Catholic disadvantage was both difficult and controversial during a period of deep recession, for the limited employment available meant that any gain by one part of the community ensured a corresponding loss by the other part.

Catholics felt themselves to be at a disadvantage not only in seeking work and promotion but also in education provision. The Government would not fund Catholic schools to the same extent as those schools prepared to accept full state control, and the Catholic Church steadfastly declined to give up its own control. Thus the vast majority of children were educated separately. Surveys indicated that young people in Northern Ireland were much more likely to adopt the assumptions and values of their parents than those elsewhere in the United Kingdom: separate schooling undoubtedly reinforced this tendency. A minority of parents refused to accept this situation and sought to establish integrated schools. It was not until the late 1980s that the Northern Ireland Office supported this movement and strove to harmonise the education provided for children of all creeds in the region.

PROMOTING MUTUAL UNDERSTANDING

On 25 October 1991 the movement for integrated education in Northern Ireland came of age: at Lisnabreeny on the Castlereagh Hills the first purpose-built permanent post-primary school to educate young people 'of all religions and no religion together' was formally opened. People had come from as far afield as the United States, Italy, Switzerland and France; the three men who had been education ministers since 1981 – Nicholas Scott, Dr Brian Mawhinney and Lord Belstead – were there not to make speeches but simply to be present at a historic ceremony, along with many of those who had striven for years against formidable odds to make this dream come true – prominent amongst them was Sister Anna, a Church of England nun who had raised large sums for the school and acquired many of the musical instruments which so enhanced this joyful and emotional occasion. The climax of the day was the unveiling ceremony carried out by two former pupils: Anna Toner recalled how the school had begun in 1981 in a scout hut near Shaw's

Bridge, with twenty-eight pupils and two full-time teachers in two classrooms separated by a curtain, and how art classes were conducted in a garage amongst canoes; and Jonathan McBride remembered how he was one of four eleven-year-olds in uniform being stoned by Catholic youths at Finaghy Road railway station – he was certain the assailants did not know that two of them were Catholic and two were Protestant. For ten years Lagan College had subsisted in huts and mobile classrooms: now 750 pupils and 47 teaching staff were brought together on one site in perhaps the most architecturally pleasing school buildings erected in the region for more than a century.

Interviewed by pupils after the ceremony, Dr Brian Mawhinney said with evident sincerity that the decision to build Lagan College was the 'single most rewarding hour of my six years as Minister of Education'.[412] It was during the administration of this Ulsterman, who represented Peterborough, that the Government gave its wholehearted support to integrated education where parents showed sufficient determination. By 1992 there were sixteen schools educating Protestants and Catholics together in roughly even numbers, but they accounted for a mere one per cent of pupils in the region: the Catholic Church was determined that Catholic children should be educated in Catholic schools, and stood aloof; the DUP was hostile. However, some Official Unionists were openly sympathetic, and leading clergy from the 'main' Protestant denominations cautiously welcomed the development of integrated schooling. Protestant schools – most of them fully funded by the state – regarded themselves as being open to young people of all beliefs. Several prestigious grammar schools did, indeed, attract significant numbers of Catholics; it was undeniable, however, that they and the great majority of state schools retained a distinctly Protestant ethos.

In 1982 the Department of Education issued a circular which stressed that education for mutual understanding was both a duty and a responsibility for everyone in education. This signalled the Government's intention to build on pioneering work by John Malone and others, in particular by funding cross-community school contact schemes. The preparations for the introduction of the national curriculum from 1989 onwards provided a unique opportunity to bridge the gulf dividing Protestant and Catholic schools: henceforth, all pupils during the compulsory years of schooling would be following the same programmes of study. The Northern Ireland Office did not wait to follow England and Wales and work began on cross-curricular themes to be incorporated within the main curriculum subjects. Two of these themes, cultural heritage and education for mutual understanding, were unique to the region: they included encouragement of joint work between schools of both main traditions; the study of cultural traditions within the pupils' locality, region and further afield, and the extent to which their heritage was shared, diverse and distinctive; and sought to ensure that by the age of sixteen 'pupils should have investigated the origins of our present discontents'.[413] It would no longer be possible, for example, for some schools to avoid the study of Irish history and others the study of British history. The DUP condemned these proposals, incorporated into the Education Reform Order (Northern Ireland) of 1990, as an insidious form of social engineering.[414]

The violence and tensions that inspired the most experimental aspects of the common curriculum in the 1990s had discouraged Labour administrations from introducing comprehensive schooling in the 1970s. The eleven-plus tests were scrapped but selection in various guises was in effect retained by the Conservatives: the special favour shown to grammar schools did much to explain why Northern Ireland's A level results were consistently better per head of the school population than anywhere else in the United Kingdom and why the proportion leaving school without any qualifications whatsoever was higher than in any other region. The low Protestant birth rate, together with the power given to grammar schools to maintain their numbers, ensured that the most demoralised sector in the whole system was that containing state secondary schools, constantly affected by staff redundancies and threat of closure. Access to higher education was greatly improved, particularly for mature students, and the amalgamation of the Ulster Polytechnic and the New University to form the University of Ulster in 1984 banished the last trace of bad taste lingering since the Lockwood report. By far the largest integrated sector was further education – which had been bringing Protestants and Catholics unobtrusively together since 1947 – and when the three Belfast colleges were amalgamated in 1991 as the Belfast Institute of Further and Higher Education, it was the biggest of its kind in the United Kingdom. Teacher training was integrated only in Queen's University and the University of Ulster: proposals to merge Belfast's colleges of education in 1981–2 were strenuously and successfully baulked by the Catholic Church.

Adults are in as much need of mutual understanding as their children: that certainly was Dr Mawhinney's view. A government agency, the Central Community Relations Unit, was set up in 1987 to ensure that all statutory bodies promoted such understanding in their policies and programmes. With the help of this unit, the Cultural Traditions Group was formed the following year to encourage a more general public awareness of, and sensitivity to, local cultural diversity. Over more than twenty years of violence much valuable reconciliation work had been done by organisations such as Women Together, Co-operation North, Protestant and Catholic Encounter, the Ulster Quaker Peace Education Project and the Corrymeela Community. In 1990 the Government – recognising that such activities were often underresourced and insufficiently analysed – provided funds to allow the establishment of the Community Relations Council: it aimed to encourage greater understanding between the two sides of Northern Ireland's community and, in particular, was concerned with the building of trust and the reduction of prejudice. In Co. Tyrone the village of Castlederg every year had two Christmas trees, one Protestant and the other Catholic: it was a graphic indication of how far some parts of the region had to go to build up that trust.

Lack of trust provided fertile ground for paramilitary organisations to flourish in the community, particularly where deprivation was most acute. The Provisional IRA – undeterred by its losses and the receding prospect of victory – remained as determined as ever to fight on: the movement now had two decades of campaign experience on which to draw in prosecuting its long war.

'THE LONG WAR': 1988–91

At 12.20 a.m. on Saturday 20 August 1988 in the open countryside, on the main road midway between Ballygawley and Omagh, the Provisionals detonated a large bomb placed on a parked trailer. An unmarked military bus travelling from Aldergrove airport was blown off the road, eight soldiers were killed and twenty-eight others were injured.[415] Alan Rainey, a dairy farmer, was one of the first on the scene; he told Noel McAdam of the *Belfast Telegraph*:

> There were bodies strewn all over the road and others were caught inside the bus and under it. There were people running around stunned, screaming and bleeding and shouting for someone to come to their aid . . . one of the soldiers – he was no more than a youngster – had somehow crawled into a calf-shed, six inches deep in muck, and as we arrived he gasped his last, bent over a bale of hay.

Ken Maginnis, MP for the area, also saw that young soldier die. Fighting back his own tears, he said: 'I have seen grown men crying here tonight. It is an appalling act of callousness.' Later that day he flew to London to ask the prime minister to reintroduce internment. Paddy Ashdown, leader of the Social and Liberal Democrats, spoke for the great majority of Westminster MPs, however, when he said that calls for internment should be resisted; 'I have no doubt that the IRA's intention is to provoke such a reaction,' he added.[416] No more than a security review was promised by the Government.

So far that year twenty-one soldiers had been killed in Northern Ireland. Two months earlier six off-duty soldiers had died when a Provisional IRA bomb exploded under their minibus after they had taken part in a charity fun run in Lisburn; and a few days later the Provisionals had shot down their first army helicopter near Crossmaglen.[417] In general, however, the locally recruited RUC and members of the UDR were pushed into the front line and suffered accordingly. On 20 March 1989 the RUC suffered the loss of its most senior officer so far: Chief Superintendent Harry Breen, commander of H Division; he and Superintendent Bob Buchanan, the officer responsible for border liaison, were returning from a conference with senior *gardaí* in Dundalk when they were ambushed and killed by heavily armed men near Jonesborough, Co. Armagh.[418] In another incident, a 1,000-pound Provisional IRA bomb killed three RUC constables in a car outside Armagh on 24 July 1990. It also killed a nun, Sister Catherine Dunne, in a passing car.

Towards the end of the year the Provisionals deployed a new form of attack – the 'human' or 'proxy' bomb. The strategy was first put into effect on 24 October 1990: Patsy Gillespie, who the Provisional IRA claimed had worked for the security forces, was seized in Shantallow in Derry and his family there was held hostage. Strapped into a van loaded with explosives, he was forced to drive into the Buncrana Road checkpoint, and there the bomb killed him together with five soldiers. Simultaneously two almost identical attacks were made at checkpoints in Omagh and at Cloghoge, near Newry: the first proxy bomb failed to explode but the second killed a soldier. The biggest-ever Provisional IRA bomb to date, containing 3,500 pounds of explosives, was driven into an army checkpoint near Rosslea on 23 November by the same tactic but it failed to detonate.[419] Margaret Thatcher had visited the area just a week before, where she said, 'We must never, never, give in to terrorism, never.'[420]

While there was no sign that the Provisional IRA would be brought to complete defeat, the movement had faced an ever more sophisticated response from the security forces. It had also faced growing media indifference, outside the region, to their campaign inside Northern Ireland. For this reason militant republicans made new attempts to extend their war abroad. They resumed with attacks on the RAF on 1 May 1988, killing three men on leave in the Netherlands; an army sergeant major was shot dead in Ostend on 12 August 1988; Heidi Hazel, the German wife of a British soldier, was murdered in Dortmund on 7 September 1989; an RAF corporal and his six-month-old daughter were killed by Provisional gunmen near Wildenrath in West

Germany on 26 October 1989; and two Australian lawyers, mistaken for British soldiers, were shot dead in front of their partners in Roermund in the Netherlands on 27 May 1990.[421]

For the first time since 1982 the Provisionals managed to kill a serviceman in Britain when they bombed Inglis barracks in north London on 1 August 1988. An attempt on Tern Hill barracks in Shropshire was foiled by a sentry the following February, but on Friday 22 September 1989 they attacked an unexpected target: the Royal Marines School of Music at Deal in Kent. A band was playing moments before a bomb in the recreation centre exploded at 8.26 a.m., causing the three-storey building to collapse and killing eleven young bandsmen. Claiming responsibility, the Provisionals issued a statement that they had 'visited the Royal Marines in Kent, but we still want peace and we want the British government to leave our country'. 'I wonder what the minds who think up these outrages believe that they contribute to the future of Northern Ireland?' John Hume asked. 'They contribute nothing except bitterness and pain.' David Hearst, the *Guardian*'s Northern Ireland correspondent, believed that these attacks on 'soft targets' indicated that the Provisional IRA was on the defensive 'since it lost eight men in the SAS trap at Loughgall police station in May, 1987'. He continued:

> Each year, as the security net north and south of the border by the RUC and the Garda Siochana tightens, the IRA has to risk more to achieve less. With nearly eight months of this year passed the security forces have captured 8½ tons of explosive, double the quantity seized last year. The 52 attacks on RUC stations and the 153 explosions are both down on last year, but the arrest rate remains the same. Some 263 people, the majority of them Republicans, have appeared on terrorist charges . . . the leadership of the IRA knows better than anyone else how quickly the business of keeping the long war going reverts to a long, hard slog.[422]

On Monday 30 July 1990 the Conservative MP for Eastbourne, Ian Gow, was killed by a bomb attached to his car outside his home in Sussex. For the Provisionals the murder of one of their most notable critics was a welcome propaganda coup, drawing attention away from the funeral of Sister Catherine Dunne just three days earlier. 'Who, reading this article', Mary Holland asked in the *Observer*, 'can remember the names of the five other people murdered by the IRA in Northern Ireland during the week that preceded Mr Gow's death? How many international television crews rushed to the scene to film the grief of *their* families and friends?'[423] At the end of the year Mark Brennock, northern editor of the *Irish Times*, pointed out:

> The IRA killed just six people outside Northern Ireland during the year, but the amount of British media coverage received by IRA activities in

Britain and continental Europe came close to rivalling the coverage given to the 75 deaths in the Troubles in the North.[424]

Shortly after the murder of Ian Gow, two Provisional IRA death lists, one uncovered in Clapham and the other in west Belfast, contained the names of 253 leading British figures, including judges, generals, politicians and other prominent critics of its cause.[425] Early in 1991, when the eyes of the world were on the conflict in the Persian Gulf, the Provisionals did not allow the British government to forget its Ulster imbroglio. On Thursday 7 February they fired mortars from a van at 10 Downing Street: two of the bombs overshot the target but one exploded a mere fifteen yards from the room where the war cabinet was meeting. This was indeed, as John Major, the prime minister, pointed out, 'a deliberate attempt to kill the Cabinet', and the Provisionals issued a statement afterwards that 'while the nationalist people of the six counties are forced to live under British rule then the British cabinet will be forced to meet in bunkers'.[426] Ten days later a Provisional IRA bomb killed one person at Victoria station in London. However, the Provisionals found Britain – for all the publicity value of their occasional successes there – too hostile an environment in which to sustain their war.

Sporadic acts of violence by militant republicans in Britain were, in time, to reveal deeply disquieting evidence of police corruption and maladministration of justice. The horrific no-warning bombings of English public houses in 1974 had killed twenty-eight people and maimed scores of others; with anti-Irish feeling running high and the public demanding action, the British police overreacted. In spite of evidence that the suspects had been ill-treated in custody, unsubstantiated confessions were a key element in their conviction. Champions of civil liberty and investigative journalists argued that there had been a gross miscarriage of justice. Such forensic evidence as was presented at the trials was discredited but it was not until a police inquiry revealed that police notebooks had been tampered with that the courts bowed to pressure for a review. In October 1989 the four who had been convicted of the bombings in Guildford were freed and, on 14 March 1991, the six men imprisoned for seventeen years after the Birmingham bombings at last won their appeal. Almost immediately afterwards the home secretary, Kenneth Baker, announced the setting up of a royal commission on criminal justice – British justice had been seriously discredited, however, and the whole deplorable affair was a propaganda coup for the Provisionals in their principal killing field: Northern Ireland.

Albert Graham, a former B Special and a labourer who lived in a railway cottage near Lisnaskea, Co. Fermanagh, joined the UDR when it was formed in 1970. Three of his sons and one of his daughters, Hilary, also became members soon afterwards. Hilary was knocked down by a car which crashed through a checkpoint and, after months in hospital, died of her injuries. Ronnie was the first of the brothers to be murdered: while he was making a delivery of groceries on 5 June 1981 to an isolated farmhouse, where the Provisional IRA held a woman and her daughter hostage, he was shot dead by masked gunmen. One of those involved in the killing was a thirteen-year-old, allegedly sworn into the organisation a month earlier. Five months later another brother, Cecil Graham, was mortally wounded by sixteen high-velocity Armalite bullets while visiting his Catholic wife's parents at Donagh. On 1 February 1985 a third brother, Jimmy Graham, died from fifteen gunshot wounds: he was waiting in a bus outside Derrylin primary school, having agreed at short notice to take a party of children for a swimming lesson.[427]

Ken Maginnis, who reached the rank of major in the UDR before being elected a Unionist MP, kept a computerised record of all the deaths and injuries suffered by members of the regiment. His findings led him to conclude that Provisional IRA attacks on the UDR were not only sectarian but also genocidal: because so many eldest sons and wage earners had been targeted, he became convinced the aim was to drive Protestants from their farms and jobs west of the Bann.[428] Certainly many Protestants had fled their farms in Co. Fermanagh, leaving them unworked, and a good number had emigrated to Canada. Since it had been formed, the regiment had by the end of 1990 suffered on average the loss of one member every thirty-nine days – 188 killed in all – and another seriously injured every nineteen days.[429] Particularly in rural areas a very high proportion of adult male Protestants had joined the UDR and because most served part-time and lived in the community they were dreadfully vulnerable. Even long after they had left the regiment, they remained legitimate targets in the eyes of the Provisionals: this ensured that a very large number were at risk – by the end of 1990 more than forty thousand men and women had enlisted and served for a time with the UDR. The strain on members was intense and at least forty-five of them took their own lives.[430]

To the vast majority of northern Catholics, the UDR was simply the Special Constabulary in a new guise and therefore a sectarian force. In July 1980 Michael Canavan, the SDLP spokesman on law and order, presented a paper to the secretary of state stating that his party had campaigned in vain 'for every UDR man to be security rescreened in order to root out the paramilitary elements. Until this is done the Regiment will be identified amongst the minority community more as a menace to than a support for law and order.' The document continued:

Former members of the Regiment have been convicted in the courts of (inter-alia) sectarian multiple murder; sectarian murder; sectarian attempted murder; sectarian pub bombing in Northern Ireland, England, the Republic of Ireland; sectarian arson; sectarian assault; sectarian intimidation; arms theft of their own weapons.[431]

This catalogue was one the Government could not deny and, indeed, senior RUC officers were alarmed to discover that – though 44 per cent of all applicants to the regiment had been rejected – people given an adverse vetting report were regularly recruited.[432] Though forming only a small proportion of the UDR, there continued to be enough 'bad apples' in the regiment to cause acute concern. Between 1985 and 1989 twenty-nine members were convicted of 'scheduled offences', compared with only six policemen and eight regular soldiers. In May 1985 Garret FitzGerald observed that 'the force in its present form, in its composition, its discipline and performance, is a force which Nationalists must and do fear . . . their record is one which I don't think any government should be satisfied with'.[433] Lord Hunt, whose 1969 report had led to the formation of the UDR, agreed: in a letter to the *Independent* on 22 February 1990, he argued that because serious crimes 'had tended to discredit the whole Regiment – however unfairly', because hopes of substantial Catholic recruitment 'had not been realised', and because of 'the changed constitutional situation of the mid-Eighties', the UDR 'should be phased out' and its duties transferred to an augmented RUC.[434]

Shortly after Hugh Annesley had replaced Hermon as chief constable in May 1989, he faced mounting evidence that loyalist paramilitaries had access to classified security information about republican suspects, and that it was being used in their search for victims of their assassination campaign. John Stevens, deputy chief constable of Cambridgeshire, was appointed in September to make an inquiry. His report absolved the RUC but led to eight members of the UDR being charged with criminal offences in 1990. The fate of the regiment was sealed and in his far-reaching 'peace dividend' arms reduction scheme, Defence Secretary Tom King planned to end part-time membership and amalgamate the full-time regiment with the Royal Irish Rangers, and his successor amalgamated the UDR with the Royal Irish Rangers on 1 July 1992 to form the Royal Irish Regiment.[435]

If constitutional nationalists were openly hostile to the UDR, they were ambivalent in their attitude to the RUC. Not more than 2 per cent of the UDR had been Catholic in the 1980s, but the proportion of recruits from the minority to the police had been rising perceptibly. On 28 February 1991 the RUC announced that Catholics now formed 8 per cent of the force. Brian Feeney of the SDLP remarked that the police had a 'long way to go' before nationalists could perceive 'equality of status' in the RUC.[436] This may well have been true, but the SDLP, despite its strong support for the rule of law, had been distinctly coy in calling on Catholics to join the force. The Gaelic Athletic Association continues to attract a huge following amongst northern Catholics; its decision, therefore, made on 7 April 1991, to continue its ban on members of the RUC taking part in its games was profoundly depressing for those who sought to make the police fully acceptable to all in the community. [437] Acceptability of the police remains crucial in the search for peace in Northern Ireland. The RUC was not responsible for the absence of political consensus in Northern Ireland, but the force has had to carry much of the burden of dealing with that lack of basic agreement. Like Lloyd George's coalition administration seventy years earlier, British governments have tended to emphasise that they are coping with terrorism and, correspondingly, to play down the fact that they are attempting to rule a profoundly divided people. The RUC has therefore been given a pivotal role and, in the circumstances, it has managed remarkably well; that is the view of Adrian Guelke, a South African politics lecturer at Queen's University and a specialist on the politics of policing, who wrote in 1992:

> The existence of a reformed police force able, through its commitment to professionalism, to stand above the province's sectarian divisions, despite being drawn predominantly from one community, has played an important role in sustaining the effectiveness of direct rule. Without it, it would have been extremely difficult for the government in Northern Ireland to have maintained its own independence from sectarian pressures to the extent that it has, except at a very high cost. That is a measure of the importance of policing in Northern Ireland.[438]

The pressures of serving in the RUC are severe. By the spring of 1991 nearly 270 members of the force had been killed since 1968 and well over 8,000 had been injured – in that period one in every sixteen had been killed or injured. John Brewer, a professor of social studies, found that members of the RUC 'score heavily on all the indices of stress: marital breakdown and divorce, alcohol addiction, even suicide'. Yet Michael Morgan observed in the March 1991 issue of *Fortnight* that 'the RUC now finds itself in the unenviable position of the vulnerable first line against a much stronger IRA, better armed than ever before'.[439]

'They really ought to know after all these years that we are not going to be pushed around by terrorist acts,' Prime Minister John Major declared on 22 February 1991 during a visit to Northern Ireland, severely curtailed by the demands of the Gulf War. Both the Provisionals and militant loyalist groups had been increasing the tempo of violence since the beginning of the year. The Crossmaglen army post had come under mortar attack on 18 January; fifty homes were damaged by a 500-pound Provisional IRA van bomb driven to the UDR base near Magherafelt on 3 February; and there was a grim succession of tit-for-tat sectarian murders. Cecil Walker, Official Unionist MP for North Belfast, said that loyalist prisoners he talked to wanted an end to 'this ruthless sectarian slaughter', but his words did not prevent four Catholic men from being shot dead in a public house in Cappagh, Co. Tyrone, by the UVF on 3 March.[440] A Catholic storeman, aged seventeen, was beaten and stabbed to death by loyalist youths in Lisburn on 18 March and ten days later three people at a mobile shop on the Catholic Drumbeg estate in Craigavon were shot dead by a UVF gunman. Belfast taxi drivers – operating one of the most courteous, inexpensive and efficient services available in any western European city – became fatally vulnerable in this sectarian war. Samuel Bell, a convert to Catholicism who was found dead beside his car on 3 April, was the sixth taxi driver to be murdered in Belfast in fifteen months. Loyalist paramilitaries crossed the border to shoot dead Eddie Fullerton, a Provisional Sinn Féin councillor, at his home in Buncrana, Co. Donegal, on 25 May. The Provisionals meanwhile continued murdering members of the security forces and detonated several large bombs: a van bomb in Cookstown, Co. Tyrone, on 26 May injured thirteen people and damaged more than a hundred houses; and a lorry containing 4,000 pounds of explosives was driven to the UDR base at Glennane in Co. Armagh, where three members of the regiment were killed and eighteen others were injured on 31 May. In a carefully planned covert operation, soldiers trapped and killed three Provisional IRA members on 'active service' at Coagh, Co. Tyrone, on 3 June – more than two hundred bullets were fired into their stolen car, which reopened the shoot-to-kill controversy.

Westminster once more began the search for the elusive constitutional formula which might stem the violence. Peter Brooke, latest in the line of secretaries of state to make this attempt, began what the media universally described as 'talks about talks'. It was a grindingly slow, uphill process. When in frustration Brooke remarked on 5 February that he might have to 'put up the shutters for the time being' on his talks initiative, Haughey said in alarm the following day that if that occurred it would be 'catastrophic', adding on 3 March that it would be 'tragic' if nothing emerged.[441] In the *Observer* on 31 March Mary Holland wrote:

A few weeks ago there was a joke doing the rounds in political circles in Belfast. Question: What do you get when you cross Peter Brooke with Don Corleone? Answer: An offer you don't understand but can't refuse.

Certainly all the politicians had heaped praise on Brooke on 26 March and Paisley thanked the secretary of state for the 'honesty', uprightness and great openness' with which he had conducted the preliminary negotiations.[442] 'What is still missing', Fionnuala O Connor observed of Paisley in *Fortnight*, 'is evidence that he can stomach sharing any restored administration at Stormont with the "republicans" of the SDLP.' She continued:

Whatever the true motives of all those involved, the process so far has been more a mechanical operation, a crude business in the shunting yard, than any battle for hearts and minds. That still seems some way off.[443]

So it proved: despite patent goodwill on all sides and what Archbishop Cahal Daly described as the 'tremendous desire' that the politicians keep talking, the negotiations ran into the sands and were abandoned.[444]

Loyalist paramilitaries had begun a ceasefire at midnight on 30 April when the Brooke talks began, but militant republicans failed to respond and the killing went on. When the talks broke down on 3 July, the ceasefire was formally ended the following day. For several years republicans had been responsible for most violent deaths in Northern Ireland but, particularly in the second half of 1991 and the first months of 1992, the UVF and the Ulster Freedom Fighters (a cover name for the UDA) reaped as bloody a harvest, targeting known members of Provisional Sinn Féin when possible but continuing also to kill Catholics at random as before. Francis Crawford was just one of many innocent victims: a Catholic father of five and retired joiner, he agreed to help out a friend by making deliveries from the Weo Ping Chinese takeaway in north Belfast and was lured by a telephone call to his death on 31 August. 'There were three delivery drivers on that night', Owen Bowcott of the *Guardian* was told, 'it could have been anyone that took that order.' The gunmen's stolen car was found in the Shankill near to a slogan daubed on a wall: 'Kill all Taigs'.[445] When Larry Murchan, a Catholic shopkeeper in west Belfast, was shot dead on 28 September, he became the two-thousandth civilian victim of the Troubles: the 'Loyalist Retaliation and Defence Group' claimed responsibility and said the murder was in retaliation for the killing of John Haldane, a director of a timber company shot by the Provisional IRA nine days before. When the

Provisionals murdered four men in Belfast on 13 November, a loyalist gang the following evening donned combat jackets and balaclava helmets, stopped traffic outside Lurgan and shot three men dead – in a statement admitting responsibility, the UVF 'deeply regretted' that one of their victims, John Lavery, was a Protestant. By the end of November loyalist paramilitaries had killed thirty-nine people since the beginning of the year.[446]

Between April and the end of November 1991, the Provisional IRA murdered twelve Protestants – the organisation clearly was more prepared than before to become involved in tit-for-tat killings. On the evening of the Lurgan murders, Provisionals assassinated three men in Belfast, and five-month-old Terri White, struck by two of their bullets, was fortunate to survive. The Provisionals' principal aim, however, remained the campaign to force a British withdrawal from Northern Ireland. Security chiefs became all too aware that, while the organisation was far from this objective, its military strength was growing; one of them said:

> The IRA terrorists are better equipped, better resourced, better led, bolder and more secure against our penetration than ever before. They are absolutely a formidable enemy. The essential attributes of their leaders are better than ever before. Some of their operations are brilliant, in terrorist terms.

'The continuing menace is clear', David McKittrick observed. 'The IRA has an experienced leadership, a very substantial, Libyan-supplied armoury and a conveyor-belt of recruits undeterred by the near certainty of ending up in jail. It is, in short, a killing machine which shows no sign of flagging.'[447]

On Wednesday 4 September the security forces were given chilling evidence of the Provisionals' new capacity to maim and destroy. A bomb containing 8,000 pounds of explosives, intended for an attack on the Annaghmartin army checkpoint in Co. Fermanagh, was found close to the border on a trailer abandoned after it had sunk to its axle in a field. This find signalled the start of a new and sustained bombing onslaught. The Provisionals' bombs were bigger than before, based on easily available chemical fertiliser and incorporating Semtex as primer and set off by advanced electronic timing devices and sophisticated detonators. It could take a team of two dozen to put together a single bomb. Two soldiers were killed and eighteen people were injured when the Provisionals bombed the corridor linking the military and civilian wings of Musgrave Park Hospital in Belfast on 2 November – an attack which prompted the *Irish Independent* to observe that they had 'once again found new depths of depravity to plumb'. Two large bombs, one near the

Belfast Law Courts and another beside the Plaza Hotel, caused extensive damage and injured seven people on 28 November. At the same time the Provisionals inflicted further destruction with firebombs and incendiaries – by the beginning of December they had planted more than a hundred firebombs alone in Northern Ireland since the start of the year and the *Independent on Sunday* estimated that the bill for bomb damage to homes in the region had reached £2 million during the same period.[448]

The campaign gained momentum in the run-up to Christmas 1991. On Wednesday 4 December a very large van bomb, containing 1,200 pounds of explosives, was set off in Glengall Street in Belfast: the shock waves shattered several hundred windows in office blocks in adjacent Great Victoria Street, inflicted severe damage on the Europa Hotel – the most frequently bombed hotel in Europe – and destroyed part of the Grand Opera House where the annual pantomime was in rehearsal. Jeremy Hanley, the Northern Ireland Office junior minister, stood beside the ruins and said to television reporters:

> I'd ask what exactly the IRA and Sinn Féin are doing bombing Christmas out of Belfast . . . The only benefit is to the people trying to build the dole queues. The IRA are giving out UB40s, they are giving out P45s this Christmas. They are ruining this beautiful country.[449]

An even larger bomb, made up of some 2,000 pounds of explosives, not only wrecked part of the Craigavon RUC station on Thursday 12 December, but also devastated a large area surrounding it, inflicting severe damage to a church, a school and many houses. Dr Brian Mawhinney, the Northern Ireland Office minister, described this attack as 'the latest Christmas message from the IRA'. Six days later another large bomb near the Law Courts left another part of Belfast city centre with a huge task of clearing up and repair. After a seventy-two-hour truce over Christmas, the Provisionals resumed their shootings, fire attacks and bombings. The last large explosion of the year was at the Aughnacloy army checkpoint in Co. Tyrone on 29 December. The *Belfast Telegraph* summed up the 'Ulster Toll of Terror' for 1991: a total of 230 explosions (50 more than in 1990); the largest-ever IRA bombs; 142 incendiary attacks, compared with 26 in 1990; the busiest year for bomb disposal teams since 1978; 73 attacks with a new home-made device, the 'coffee-jar bomb'; and what the army described as a 'significant increase' in grenade and mortar attacks.[450]

'STILL THEY REFUSE TO COME TO THE TABLE. WHAT IF 50 DIED, OR 150?'

During the first months of 1992, Northern Ireland seemed to be marking the twentieth anniversary of direct rule by sinking back into violence and sectarian warfare reminiscent of the worst days of the 1970s. Having begun the new year by destroying the Suites Direct shop in Newtownards, Co. Down, burning the Top Man store in Belfast and attacking Pomeroy RUC station in Co. Tyrone, the Provisional IRA declared the following day that it possessed 'the means and the will, not only to continue with this struggle but to intensify it'.[451] On Saturday 4 January an 800-pound van bomb in Bedford Street inflicted many millions of pounds worth of damage in the heart of Belfast and two days later another large bomb devastated offices in the city's High Street. Derry was attacked on 9 January when a van bomb exploded close to the RUC station in Strand Road. The discovery of massive arms caches in the middle of the month at Westrock and Beechmount in Belfast – including ammunition, 78 firebombs and 1,500 pounds of explosives – seemed to indicate that the Provisionals still had substantial reserves from the Libyan shipments of the mid-1980s. Eamonn Mallie and John Merritt, in their report in the *Observer* on 12 January, described 'the continuing chaos caused by the IRA's latest push which has placed Belfast under virtual siege':

Approaches to Belfast and roads to the city centre are now cordoned by vehicle checkpoints, operating around the clock. Hundreds of part-time members of the Ulster Defence Regiment are on full-time duty patrolling the city . . . However often Belfast's resilient residents and businessmen reassure themselves and outsiders that 'life goes on as normal', it is not normal to find street after street brought to a dead-end with white security tape; to pass so many 'business as usual' signs on window-boarded premises, or to feel yourself viewed through the sight of a soldier's rifle scanning the populace from a hole in the top of an armoured car.[452]

On Friday 17 January a minibus carrying employees of Karl Construction travelled a country road near Cookstown; at Teebane Cross the headlights triggered an elaborately prepared bomb trap, and the resulting explosion killed seven men, mortally wounded the driver, and injured six others. All were Protestants, attacked because their employer carried out work for the security forces. The killings raised to twenty-six the number of people murdered by the Provisional IRA for working on army and police projects since 1985, and brought the total murdered within a twenty-mile radius of Cookstown since March 1989 to thirty in the bitter war between the Provisionals and loyalist paramilitaries in the area. That bitterness was reflected in the comment made by Jean Caldwell, whose husband was killed at Teebane: 'I am angry and bitter and feel nothing but hatred. I can't just sit here and forgive them.' Protestant anger intensified when Peter Brooke, in response to a request by the *Late Late Show* host Gay Byrne, sang two verses of 'My Darling Clementine' on Irish television just a few hours after the Teebane massacre.[453] 'A less nice man would probably have refused', Mary Holland observed, but it was unquestionably 'a gross error of judgment', as the *Belfast Telegraph* put it, and the *Irish Press* acknowledged that 'a serious misjudgment' had been made by 'a decent man'.[454]

Brooke had been in Dublin to explain to Gerry Collins, the Irish foreign minister, that his latest attempt to get agreement between representatives of the constitutional parties in Northern Ireland had got nowhere – as he put it himself, 'I have to say that the prospects of advance recede.'[455] Fionnuala O Connor, in the February issue of *Fortnight*, concluded that the January talks 'have produced more mutual mistrust than new understanding': the Unionist leaders maintained a 'standfast' position, while the SDLP, convinced that the only interest Molyneaux and Paisley had in the talks was to damage the Anglo-Irish process, thought Brooke 'a bungler, and an innately unionist bungler from the start'. In the same issue of the magazine Emily O'Reilly expressed the growing frustration of many at the politicians' inability to talk to each other:

Eight died in Tyrone. The level of outrage rises so high. Still they refuse to come to the table. What if 50 died, or 150? What then? Do Messrs Paisley and Hume and Robinson and Mallon, the whole damn lot of them, have a body count in their heads above which they will definitely begin to move heaven and earth to do something about it and get the talks started again? Pick a number lads. Any number.[456]

Adrian Guelke, in a case of mistaken identity, had been shot by members of the Ulster Freedom Fighters the previous September. He survived this assassination attempt and expressed his conviction that there was a close link between the talks and the escalation of violence: 'What comfort there is to be drawn from the course of events over the last year is the Provisionals' evident fear of agreement among the constitutional parties.' The Anglo-Irish Agreement had contained the conflict by reducing its international significance, he wrote, and the prospect of a new political settlement 'rattled Gerry Adams and Co, by shaking their confidence that they had all the time in the world to wear successive British governments down. A wider settlement threatened to sideline the Provisionals still further.' The collapse of the Brooke initiative 'saved the Provisionals from this fate and the apparent government confusion over security policy encouraged them to step up their campaign of violence and destruction.[457]

The nature of the conflict had changed. The Provisional IRA had found it more difficult to kill members of the security forces – fewer soldiers and police died in the violence during 1991 than in any year since 1970 – and it turned to 'soft targets' such as commercial premises and people providing goods and services to the RUC and the army.[458] Meanwhile, loyalist paramilitary groups, strengthened by a shipment of arms from South Africa in 1988, had acquired a new set of hardline leaders. In addition, the Stevens inquiry had exposed undercover agents and closed off crucial sources of intelligence for the security forces. Loyalist violence was often reactive and the UVF, the Ulster Freedom Fighters and other Protestant paramilitaries responded to the Provisionals' campaign with counter-assassinations: this was fearfully demonstrated early in February 1992.

'HOW CAN THEY GO TO BED AND SLEEP?'

On Wednesday 5 February 1992 Sean Graham's betting shop on the Ormeau Road in south Belfast was crowded at the beginning of the afternoon racing. Just after 2 p.m. two men, wearing masks and boiler suits, burst through the door with an automatic rifle and a pistol and fired indiscriminately at close range. An elderly man at the back of the shop described the scene to Owen Bowcott of the *Guardian*:

> I saw 15 or 16 people standing up and the next thing they were all lying on the ground. I just froze. I tried to help the injured. One guy – a pal – was gone. His face hacked away . . . It was just like a meat plant, everyone piled one on top of another.[459]

Five Catholics were killed and seven more were wounded. As he lay dying the fifteen-year-old schoolboy, James Hamilton, said to his friends, 'Tell my mummy I love her' and his aunt told reporters soon afterwards: 'The people who did this must not have any feelings at all. How can they go to bed and sleep?'[460] The Ulster Freedom Fighters claimed responsibility and declared 'Remember Teebane'. 'It was only a matter of time after Teebane,' a community worker in the Shankill said to Alan Murray of the *Guardian* the following day. Murray continued:

> Sadly you will not find much sympathy for the victims of yesterday's shootings. It took the politicians 17 years to get round the table. When they stopped talking they were saying to the gunmen, 'Go ahead, it's your show now.' The politicians bear a heavy responsibility.[461]

The betting shop murders brought the death toll from violence since the beginning of the year to 27 and the overall total of victims since 1969 to 2,969. Civilian deaths had risen sharply: more had died in 1991 than in any year since 1976; and the toll for 1992 had reached thirty-one by the end of February. The record for the period preceding the Ormeau Road killings showed how widespread was the threat to ordinary people going about their business: one Catholic shot dead and his brother mortally wounded in their butcher's shop in the Moy on 3 January; a Catholic shot dead in his chip van at Moira on 9 January; a Protestant stoned to death in Belfast on 11 January; a Catholic killed by an under-car bomb the following day (the Provisional IRA said his death was a mistake); a Protestant shot dead by the Ulster Freedom Fighters, who alleged he was an RUC Special Branch informer, in Dundonald the next day; eight Protestants murdered at Teebane on 17 January; a Catholic stabbed to death in an east Belfast club on 26 January; a Catholic shot dead by loyalists in Lisburn on 30 January; a Catholic taxi driver murdered in north Belfast on 2 February; a Protestant shot dead while delivering bread in Dungannon the following day; the next day an off-duty policeman, thought to be suffering from depression after the death of a friend, entered Provisional Sinn Féin headquarters on the Falls Road and shot dead three Catholics and then committed suicide at Ballinderry; and on the day of the betting-shop massacre, an off-duty member of the UDR shot dead his Provisional IRA assailant near Belleek.[462]

The approach of the Westminster general election saw the Provisionals determined to keep the Ulster question high on the political agenda. On 5 March a 1,000-pound bomb wrecked the commercial heart of Lurgan and another very large explosion once again extensively damaged offices in the centre of Belfast. Nineteen days later a bomb next to Donegall Pass RUC station injured five policemen and eight civilians, including a two-month-old baby, and devastated homes, shops, restaurants and offices over a wide area just south of Belfast city centre.[463] On 9 April the election in Northern Ireland did seem to bring a slight shift to the centre, punishing the extremists: John Hume, Eddie McGrady and Seamus Mallon all increased their majorities; the Official Unionists improved their lead over the DUP; and Laurence Kennedy of the Conservative Party (a liberal in Northern Ireland terms) won 32 per cent of the vote in North Down. In West Belfast Joe Hendron of the SDLP ousted Gerry Adams – tactical voting by Protestants had given him a marginal majority. Adams's hopes of being brought into constitutional discussions were dashed by his defeat. The following day the Provisional IRA expressed its own opinion in customary fashion in London.

At 9.25 p.m. on Friday 10 April a bomb in a Ford Transit van, containing 100 pounds of Semtex, with twice the explosive force of the Brighton device, blew up inside London's financial 'square mile'. Three people, including fifteen-year-old Danielle Carter, were killed; seventy-five others were injured; the Baltic Exchange and the Chamber of Shipping in St Mary Axe were damaged beyond repair; every window in the Commercial Union's twenty-three-storey building was shattered; and twenty-four other buildings would require extensive renovation. A bomb of the same size at Staples Corner caused traffic chaos for weeks to come and the cost of the damage inflicted in the capital was estimated at several hundred million pounds.[464] London's determination that there should be business as usual was the same as that so often witnessed in Northern Ireland in similar circumstances. The *Daily Telegraph* reporter, Eric Bailey, found Stuart Michael, a commercial manager, directing operations with his walkie-talkie amidst the wreckage early on Monday 13 April:

> 'We're live. We're running,' hollered Mr Michael. 'They can't get us out of business. We've got the traders up there working. They're suited and booted and they're dealing.'[465]

The Provisional IRA, accepting responsibility for the bombings, declared that the destruction was a 'direct consequence of Britain's illegal occupation of Irish territory'.[466] The explosions had been in the constituency which had re-elected Peter Brooke, but he was now replaced as secretary of state by Sir Patrick Mayhew, the former attorney-general. When Mayhew reopened the interparty talks on 29 April at Stormont he said that there was a 'strength of feeling' in Northern Ireland that the political impasse must be brought to an end.[467] Few can have doubted, however, that London would still be coping with western Europe's longest-running conflict since 1945 well after the destruction in its financial heart had been fully repaired.

'GROWN USED TO PICKING ITSELF UP AFTER EACH EXPLOSION AND
REBUILDING ITS LIFE'

Early in 1983 Padraig O'Malley, a political scientist at the University of Massachusetts, described Belfast as 'ugly and sore to the eye, the will to go on gone . . . a modern wasteland . . . Only the ghettoes have their own vitality. By early evening Belfast is abandoned.'[468] Patrick Bishop, who covered Ireland for the *Observer* between 1979 and 1982, went so far as to compare the provincial capital to 'Berlin after a thousand bomber raid'. He continued:

> The poverty is ancient and ingrained. The buildings seem to be suffering from a contagion that has covered them with boils and scabs. Single terraces stand in isolation in rubble lakes where bonfires perpetually burn, watched by tough, ragged little boys and skinny dogs. Every surface is etched minutely and obsessively with graffiti.[469]

Yet even as these impressions were being written, the transformation of Belfast had begun. The relentless Provisional IRA bombing campaign had all but ceased and paramilitary crime had been reduced: between 1972 and 1979 there had been 1,289 civilian deaths, 25,127 shooting incidents and 5,123 explosions; while during the years 1980–7 there had been 372 civilian deaths, 4,392 shooting incidents and 1,912 explosions.[470] 'The startling fact is that the average, uninvolved Northern Ireland civilian is roughly 10 times more likely to be killed by a car than by a bomb or a bullet', the journalist Simon Hoggart observed in August 1984. 'If he lives outside the Catholic ghettoes of West Belfast, the rural border country, and the streets of Derry, then his chances are overwhelmingly better than that.'[471] Northern Ireland had become incomparably safer than large American cities: in 1987 there were five violent deaths in the region per one hundred thousand inhabitants, whereas the figure for San Francisco was eighteen.[472] In such improved conditions, Belfast sprang back to life.

'An outsider who had not visited the city for two or three years would notice the difference right away', Billy Simpson wrote in the *Belfast Telegraph*. 'A new buzz and bustle about a Belfast that suddenly looks better, smells better and smiles easier. A city on its way back.'[473] No longer subjected to body searches, citizens were able to pour in and out of the security gates at will. Bright shops and boutiques blossomed, and flower tubs, thousands of trees, new paving and modern lamp standards adorned the main streets. Between 1982 and 1985 forty-one restaurants, thirty-eight cafes and fifty-five hot-food bars opened there. Around £86 million were invested in commercial development in the inner city between 1983 and 1985 and it was estimated that in 1984 alone day-trippers from the republic spent £120 million in Northern Ireland, much of it in Belfast.[474] A great deal of this regeneration was heavily subsidised by the Government and before the end of the decade a succession of tall postmodernist commercial premises and office blocks began to dominate the skyline. The showpiece of the 1989 Belfast Urban Plan was the Laganside scheme to transform around three hundred acres of the port's waterfront into a tourist and leisure complex, which was to include the city council's Laganbank development, a centre containing a concert hall, an ice rink and a hotel; a harbour village; a marina; and a business village.[475]

By June 1992, when the Canary Wharf development in London was declared bankrupt, it seemed likely that private enterprise might not be prepared to commit all of the investment expected of it and that some of the more grandiose elements of the Laganside project would have to be dropped. Certainly investors had tended to overreach themselves in speculative office building, particularly in Great Victoria Street, where by the spring of 1992 a great deal of floorspace remained unlet. As elsewhere, the recession of the early 1990s weakened business activity but the revival of the previous decade remained substantially intact: even the Provisionals' renewed bombing campaign in 1991–2 failed to drive out shoppers and those seeking entertainment. The show went on, certainly for the Grand Opera House: after the van bomb of 4 December 1991, the performances of the Christmas pantomime were transferred to La Mon House; the damage was repaired in just a few months; and the theatre reopened on 21 April 1992 with, appropriately enough, *Les Liaisons Dangereuses*. 'Over the years', Owen Bowcott of the *Guardian* observed, 'Belfast has grown used to picking itself up after each explosion and rebuilding its life.'[476]

Paddy Doherty, the man who had struck a deal with the army which allowed the Bogside to run its own affairs for nine weeks in 1969, remembered conditions in Derry in 1981 when 'one in ten buildings within the city centre had been wiped out, either bombed or simply left derelict'. In that year he played a leading role in setting up the Inner City Trust, a cross-community organisation to revive the heart of Derry which subsequently secured close government co-operation and financial support. A ten-year regeneration programme culminated in Impact '92, a marketing campaign to bring funds and jobs to the city; an attractive craft village opened inside the city walls, with an impressive new museum beneath; and a genealogy centre was scheduled for 1993. Like Belfast, Derry continued to suffer acute deprivation caused by severe unemployment and low pay, only partially cushioned by high-quality public housing and inner-city regeneration. In spite of free mingling in and about the city walls, Derry had become more segregated than ever, the Foyle serving as a broad frontier dividing Catholics and Protestants. Perhaps this rigid separation in a curious way helped to foster a new spirit of cross-community collaboration. In an upbeat *Guardian* report in January 1992, John Mullin observed: 'Terrorism in Derry is now negligible, the result, say locals, of a council which works together across the political spectrum.'[477]

A few councils were learning of the rich rewards to be gained from sharing the responsibility of providing services to a deeply divided community. However, most of Northern Ireland's political representatives continued to reject power-sharing and this stand was reflected in many local authorities.

'A BITTER FROZEN LITTLE TABLEAU, A MICROCOSM OF POLITICAL LIFE IN NORTHERN IRELAND'

'I would like,' the Sinn Féin councillor said, 'to raise item B572 of the minutes.' All 30 Unionist councillors immediately rose to their feet and headed for the door. 'We object to the proposed closure of St George's Market,' the Sinn Féin man said. One of the Unionists, Alderman Sammy Wilson, turned and shouted: 'Gunman, gunman, that's what he is.' His colleagues joined in: 'Gangsters, IRA men, get them out.' Some banged desks. A councillor, on a point of order, asked: 'Is it in order to appeal to keep the market open when his party blew it up?' Alex Maskey, the most outspoken of the Sinn Féin people, retorted: 'You never know, it could be bombed again.'

So began David McKittrick's report of a Belfast City Council debate in June 1988. Maskey had been shot in the stomach by loyalists the previous year and he stood just twenty feet away from Elizabeth Seawright, whose husband George – notorious for his remark that Catholics should be incinerated – had been murdered by republican assassins. Later that evening a Provisional Sinn Féin councillor spoke a few words in Irish. 'It is not in order to speak in a foreign language in this chamber,' said the lord mayor, Nigel Dodds of the DUP, who from the chair would only refer to any of the Provisional Sinn Féin representatives as 'You'. Rhonda Paisley, councillor and daughter of the DUP leader, remarked that the Irish language 'drips with their bloodthirsty saliva' and an SDLP councillor, failing to stifle Alderman Wilson's taunts about the 'leprechaun language', wearily said: 'For heaven's sake grow up. Show a bit of political maturity.'[478]

Political maturity seemed a scarce commodity in Belfast City Council, where citizens were then represented by nine Provisional Sinn Féin councillors, six SDLP, six Alliance, one Workers' Party and thirty Unionist. The disruption and disorder had begun when the political wing of the Provisional IRA decided – against the usual policy of abstention – to take an active part in local government: with the exception of the Alliance Party, unionists refused to debate with or have any dealings with Provisional Sinn Féin councillors; and business was repeatedly halted by the protracted campaign of non-cooperation following the Anglo-Irish Agreement. Nearly all Unionist-dominated local authorities were dislocated in this way but the prospect of constructive co-operation seemed more distant in Belfast than anywhere else. McKittrick concluded:

> The sides sit, implacable and irreconcilable, just feet away from each other, each regarding compromise as defeat. Together they make up a bitter frozen little tableau, a microcosm of political life in Northern Ireland.[479]

The pettiness of the city's local politics was demonstrated when Nigel Dodds, lord mayor again in 1992, refused to meet Mary Robinson, president of the Irish republic, in Belfast on 3 February – this in spite of her criticism of the Hillsborough accord and her attempts in the Irish senate to remove Articles 2 and 3 from the 1937 constitution. The *Belfast*

Telegraph described this snub as an 'insult' and said that the lord mayor should have 'put his personal political dogma aside and welcomed her officially'.[480] West of the Bann, however, there were more hopeful signs of progress and enlightenment.

In 1986 Michael McLoughlin was ejected from the chamber of Dungannon District Council by the police after making a tempestuous protest against Unionist domination of an area where Protestants and Catholics were almost equal in number. A year later he put forward a motion to 'seek ways and means of bringing together in greater under-standing the two major traditions in the council's area'. The somewhat sceptical councillors on all sides gave their approval but nothing was done until the Remembrance Day massacre in Enniskillen concentrated minds: 'An active committee to pursue mutual understanding developed,' McLoughlin recalled, 'and peace began to break out in a chamber that had seen bitterness and acrimony since the council's inception in 1973.' The outcome was a 'responsibility-sharing' motion that the chair be rotated every six months between 'constitutional' councillors from the two main traditions. In an act of very considerable political courage three Unionists – Ken Maginnis MP, Ralph Brown and Jim Brady – voted for the motion in 1988 and the experiment began. Aware of the risk Maginnis and his supporters had taken, the moderate nationalists took scrupulous care to foster Unionist trust. In the 1989 local government elections voters demonstrated their approval by giv-ing increased support to those candidates who had promoted the new consensus politics. 'Over these four experimental years', McLoughlin wrote in May 1992, 'there has been a steady marginalisation of the extreme voices on both sides of the chamber' – two months earlier, for example, fourteen of the nineteen councillors voted to declare Dungannon District Council a 'violence-free zone', in order to 'further improve community trust and harmony, and at the same time . . . advance discussions towards a political agreement on the totality of relationships within these islands'.[481]

Responsibility-sharing was not in prospect in those councils with large unionist or nationalist majorities, much less in Northern Ireland as a whole. Over much of the region, however, councils were very evenly balanced and there were signs that some of these were prepared to follow Dungannon's example. Down District Council rotated its major posts 'between the two traditions' and, though it had an SDLP majority, it unanimously elected Official Unionist Sam Osborne as chairman on 1 June 1992. On the same day Derry City Council elected its first DUP mayor, Alderman William Hay – the sixth Unionist to be chosen for that office since the council had been restructured in 1973.

An attempt to adopt a similar policy of rotation in Fermanagh District Council failed by a margin of one vote, and in Belfast City Council, the DUP and Official Unionists rejected all compromise: Unionists retained their majority on all eight committees and rejected Alliance and Provisional Sinn Féin proposals to restructure them.[482] Local authorities, in any case, had very limited powers and their activities were of only marginal interest to citizens going about their daily lives.

'PEOPLE PRESERVE AND PROTECT WHAT BITS OF NORMALITY
    REMAIN TO THEM'

'The spirit of the Blitz has been institutionalised so that people preserve and protect what bits of normality remain to them. This is one reason why Ulster folk are so keen on *going out'*, Patrick Bishop observed in 1984. He continued:

> There is something brave and encouraging about the indefatigable diners and the denizens of the discos. They, at least, are staying . . . The province has a staggering number of night clubs, often stuck at the side of roads in the middle of nowhere. It seems impossible that they can make a living, yet night after night the cars arrive disgorging ladies done up like the women-folk of 'Dallas' and their stout escorts, steadfastly determined to enjoy themselves.[483]

'Over on the mainland', Simon Hoggart wrote in the same year, 'we tend to assume that Ulster is a horrible place to live, where violent death faces everyone every day. Far from it.'[484] Even during the worst periods of violence, the King's Hall in south Belfast, for example, attracted capacity audiences to see entertainers of international repute. Carrickmore, a village nestling on the southern slopes of the Sperrins, was host to the Mid-Ulster Festival of amateur drama every spring throughout the Troubles: entrants were drawn from all over the province and beyond to an area the security forces believed required exceptional vigilance, often being put up by local people who asked for no payment. In short, a vigorous cultural life cutting across the sectarian divide continued and blossomed: local writers – some who have achieved international recognition – experienced a new stimulus with the emergence of successful publishing houses; the Belfast Festival at Queen's annually attracted top performers of international theatre and music; and the Ulster Orchestra matured into one of the finest in the United Kingdom.

Those who attended the Ulster Orchestra's regular Friday evening concerts were overwhelmingly middle class. After being driven along the road from Belfast and past Holywood, Helen's Bay, Crawfordsburn and Bangor – an area of north Down widely known as the 'gold coast' –

Margaret Thatcher wondered if Northern Ireland suffered any deprivation at all. The middle classes enjoyed salaries on the same scales as those in Britain; low mortgages for housing which was by far the cheapest in the United Kingdom; good uncongested roads, giving easy access not only to beautiful countryside and unspoilt beaches but also to inexpensive boating, angling, golfing and other recreations; and high-quality education for their children in grammar schools, involving none of the costs required of their counterparts in Britain paying fees to public schools. 'There are more BMWs sold here than anywhere else in the UK and five per cent of all new cars are Mercedes', David Hearst reported in the *Guardian* in April 1987.[485] He could have added that more new cars were bought per head of the population in Northern Ireland than in any other region of the United Kingdom. Such purchasers were part of what the economist John Kenneth Galbraith in 1992 called the 'constituency of contentment', benefiting from income tax cuts which had widened the gap still further between the comparatively prosperous and the 'underclass'.[486]

The absence of a Northern Ireland equivalent to London's cardboard city is largely explained by the high quality of public housing and the peril of being picked out for assassination by paramilitaries. Though the underclass was less immediately visible to visitors than in Dublin or cities of comparable size across the Irish Sea, there remained major areas of acute deprivation – of special significance in the region, since they were paramilitary strongholds. By far the most important of these was west Belfast, described in March 1988 by David McKittrick:

> Many parts of west Belfast have always been one huge poverty trap. The area has the worst unemployment, the worst housing, the worst health, of any place in Northern Ireland. It holds around 90,000 people. The 1981 census put unemployment at 32 per cent for males, with some notable blackspots: the jobless figure in Whiterock ward, for example, was 56 per cent. Since then things have not improved. It is a huge ghetto, almost totally Catholic, bounded by mountains, swamp, a motorway, and hostile loyalist districts.[487]

The Government launched the 'Making Belfast Work' scheme in July 1988 largely with the intention of providing special aid to west Belfast. Les Allamby of the Belfast Law Centre reckoned, however, that alterations in social benefits resulted in an annual total loss of over £7 million to the area – more than 70 per cent of the sum spent by the scheme in its first year of operation.[488]

In Britain similar areas generated crime, drug pushing, joyriding, muggings and sporadic baiting of the police. In Northern Ireland deprivation produced fewer 'ordinary decent criminals' (as the police term them) but generated support and justification for paramilitary activity. McKittrick observed, however, that in west Belfast the Troubles 'have created an anarchic underclass of young men who regard the IRA as just another form of authority'.[489] Candida Crewe interviewed Protestant youths in north-west Belfast for a report in the 2 May 1992 issue of the *Guardian*. They all described themselves as 'rejects' and all had 'a deep loathing of Catholics who, they said, "live in filth"'. She continued:

> In his spare time Stuart sniffs glue, 'but only in the summer because you can go into a big field and you get better dreams that way'; he nicks about two cars a week to go joyriding; and he beats up and throws petrol bombs at Catholics, 'because it's a good laugh fighting people you don't like' . . . 'Joyriding's brilliant,' Lee, 17, from Springmartin said. 'Nothing's better. It's even a wee bit better than sex.'

Stuart and Lee, their Protestant 'reject' friends and their Catholic counterparts probably suffered no more psychological damage than did young people growing up in Britain's inner cities. 'Research studies never evidenced a direct link between the Troubles and a propensity to social dysfunction and violence', John Growcott, a senior social worker, observed. The dangers of straying from one enclave to another were similar to those encountered in the various ethnic areas of Birmingham and London. 'There aren't many who go about hitting wee girls, but, on the whole, strangers will be done,' a teenage girl told Candida Crewe. 'It's like what happens to animals when they go into another's territory.'

Law-breaking youths in Belfast and Derry, however, ran far greater risks than their counterparts in Britain's cities. Lee's joyriding career was ended when 'I got beaten with baseball bats by the UDA', and his friend Dexter said: 'I beat up this fellah on the estate the other day . . . so five members of the UFF came round my house with balaclavas on and beat me up with truncheons. I had to go to hospital.'[490] Teenagers who had become persistent petty criminals were liable to be shot in the legs by paramilitaries who were anxious to keep the police out of their enclaves and be seen as capable of maintaining order there. In effect the Provisional IRA, the UDA and other paramilitaries operated a form of alternative policing in deprived areas, often with the tacit approval of their communities.

Given a significant social role, the men of violence were able to continue their killing. The countryside was not exempt:

> In Tyrone's green fields men mutter darkly of vendetta, unconsciously plunging between the centuries in mid-sentence. Mortal enemies stalk each other from a distance of five miles. Hatred burns so bright that vengeful young killers smirk and boast of their murders to strangers. It is

an enclosed world of bowel-shaking fear, cold joyous revenge, dark paranoia and venomous suspicion. And the fields are watered with the blood of men.[491]

This grim account by the journalist Kevin Toolis was prompted by a succession of murders in a rural part of east Tyrone, only ten miles in radius: twenty-three men there had died violently between 26 April 1988 and 16 September 1991. Toolis's article was published in December 1991. With the alteration of one word only, the extract above could have been applied at the same time and with equal truth to the disintegrating state of Yugoslavia.

'IN CONTRAST WITH THESE UNCONTROLLABLE TIDES, ULSTER'S CRISIS SEEMS QUITE PETTY'

Sarajevo and Belfast have several features in common: both are provincial capitals; both are about the same size and are surrounded by hills; both have populations united by a common language but divided by religion; and both have suffered bitter and bloody intercommunal conflict in the last decades of the twentieth century. During the late spring and early summer of 1992 Sarajevo was in the eye of the Balkan storm. A power-sharing Bosnian government had failed in its attempts to seek peaceful accommodation with Belgrade and, in reprisal for a Muslim ambush, the Serbs closed in on Sarajevo and subjected it to a protracted bombardment. 'It was as if', Ian Traynor wrote in the *Observer*, '. . . the British army surrounded West Belfast and started shelling it randomly because the IRA had killed a few soldiers.'[492] Between March and the third week of May 1992 an estimated 2,225 had been killed in Bosnia alone. Over the previous year 1,300,000 had been made homeless during the civil war in Yugoslavia, 700,000 of them in Bosnia during the first seven weeks of fighting.[493] In just a few months the people of Bosnia had suffered as much and more as the people of Northern Ireland over twenty-three years of violence.

The liberalisation of Communist rule under Gorbachev, followed by the fall of oppressive regimes, the pulling down of the Berlin Wall and the disintegration of the Soviet Union, prompted waves of justified rejoicing as the peoples of central and eastern Europe took charge of their own destinies. From the outset, however, the successful popular movements were characterised by reawakened ethnic antagonisms. 'As in Ulster,' William Millinship reported from Azerbaijan in March 1992, 'neither side welcomes objective observers, only unqualified sympathy and support.'[494] The physical differences between Azeris and Armenians were apparent to western journalists but the peoples of Yugoslavia had intermarried for centuries – a fact which did nothing to suppress the bitterness of ethnic conflict, as Ed Vulliamy pointed out in the *Guardian*:

> The sheer hate is terrifying. The mutually shared venom that divides the Croatians and the Serbs is something like that which has inspired the slaughter in Northern Ireland for so long; but it is even more acrid and intense, even more deeply steeped in its bloody past – and much better supported by force of arms.[495]

In short, the inhabitants of Northern Ireland were learning from 1988 onwards that their problems were not unique and some were induced to put their divisions into a global perspective – Hugo Young, the author and columnist, urged them to do so in November 1991:

> The condition of Ulster defeats every liberal device. It nullifies language, repudiates politics. To some extent, however, Ulster wallows in this state. An irresolvable conflict is what gives the place its uniqueness, we hear. But how long can this self-glorying, this claim on our awe, survive events elsewhere: in Yugoslavia, for example?

He saw 'no imaginable blueprint for any peaceful future' in the Balkans, where 'History leaves such a massive disjunction between people and territory'. 'In contrast with these uncontrollable tides, Ulster's crisis seems quite petty,' he continued. 'To the extent that history once justified it, time has done much to liquidate the historic problems that stood in the way of coexistence.' Referring to the Brooke talks, Young was convinced that compared 'with what Lord Carrington and Cyrus Vance have attempted, they should have been a breeze'.[496]

Since the Second World War several European governments had been successful in containing or reducing ethnic tensions by fresh constitutional arrangements. Examples include: autonomy for South Tyrol in 1972; devolved governments in Catalonia and the Basque country after Franco's death in 1975; the creation of the canton of Jura in Switzerland in 1978; a measure of self-government for Corsica in 1982; and the evolution of Belgium into a federal state by 1988.[497] In Northern Ireland the passage of time was eroding many of the problems that fuelled its conflict, but lingering uncertainty about the territorial destiny of the region undoubtedly worked against efforts to bring about lasting peace. Despite the firm assurances given in the 1985 Anglo-Irish Agreement, unionists felt sure that Westminster was distinctly unenthusiastic about maintaining the Union; that the aim of even the most moderate representatives of the Catholic minority was to draw them into a united Ireland; and that the Protestant religion and way of life would not be properly respected or protected in an all-Ireland republic.

Nationalists for their part still had hopes of unification, even if that prospect was receding, and in the meantime did not feel themselves treated with complete fairness within Northern Ireland.

Hugo Young was right to point out that many of the historic problems standing in the way of coexistence were being dissolved. The unwillingness of Dublin governments to incorporate the six north-eastern counties into the republic became more evident with the passing of every year. The removal of Articles 2 and 3 of the 1937 constitution – indeed the abandonment of the entire document – seemed to some not far round the corner. In 1992 unedifying court cases over the availability of contraceptives and the right to travel abroad for abortions showed that the old certainties were under threat; and the scandal surrounding Bishop Eamonn Casey's alleged use of diocesan funds to support his son and former mistress signalled what seemed to be an inexorable decline in the moral authority of the Catholic hierarchy. Above all, the election of Mary Robinson as president of the republic in November 1990, and the subsequent further growth of her popularity, demonstrated that a sea change was taking place in the modernisation of southern Irish society.

On Friday 20 March 1992, during the Westminster general election campaign, Gerry Adams was interviewed by James Naughtie on BBC Radio Ulster. As a spokesman for Provisional Sinn Féin, by law he could only be broadcast while defending his West Belfast seat and he took this rare opportunity to speak volubly about his solution to Northern Ireland's problems. The only barrier to peace, he believed, was the continued British military occupation of the six counties. John Hume shared the studio with Adams and again and again, while being repeatedly interrupted, he intoned quietly into the microphone: 'But we are a deeply divided people.'[498] There was a growing recognition in all constitutional parties at Westminster, in Dáil Éireann and in Northern Ireland itself that, as Padraig O'Malley put it, 'the relationship between the two communities within Northern Ireland must be addressed before the North–South relationship can be resolved'.[499] The Catholic minority continued to harbour deep misgivings about security policies and the administration of justice, but much more was being done to tackle disadvantage in employment and education, to give Catholic cultural interests their rightful place, and to promote better community relations.

Ever since it was created in 1921, the political border has made a striking difference to the destinies of the people of Ulster living each side of it. Since partition the history of the inhabitants of Cavan,

Donegal and Monaghan has been remarkably uneventful – mercifully so, many would say. Though the people living in those three counties suffered several decades of economic stagnation, the long haemorrhage of emigration and inferior social services by comparison with those in the remaining six counties, they enjoyed unbroken peace, and the Protestant minority, admittedly dwindling, was integrated in time. From the premiership of Lemass onwards, Cavan, Donegal and Monaghan benefited from the republic's explosive economic growth and the belated introduction of the welfare state. So buoyant was the economy that many emigrants – known as 'new-come-homes' – returned to their native townlands. Above all, the political frontier largely sealed off the three counties from the violence tearing at Northern Ireland for almost a quarter of a century.

Despite the marked increase in the republic's prosperity, governments in Dublin became ever more alarmed at the prospect of taking full responsibility for all of Ulster, largely because the economic burden would be intolerable. As it was, by the early 1990s the security cost imposed by the northern Troubles was three times as much per head in the republic as it was in Britain. If the republic, with a population of only three and a half million, had to take over the annual subsidy from the United Kingdom exchequer to Northern Ireland, it would cost every citizen there on average £570 – more than fifteen times the present sum for every person in Britain. In short, it was in the interest of both the London and Dublin governments to work more closely together than ever before in harmonising their policies towards Northern Ireland. Some saw this collaboration as a perfect recipe for political stalemate but for others it was a heartening advance in international relations. The need to break the political deadlock within Northern Ireland in 1992 became more urgent not only because of the upsurge in violence early in the year but also because the acute difficulties brought on by the economic recession increased the burden of the annual subvention from Westminster, set to rise to £2,500 million in 1993.

Historians looking at Germany in 1945 could not have prophesied that by the 1990s that country would be reunited, a bulwark of democracy with the strongest economy in Europe. Few, also, predicted the rapid break-up of the Soviet monolith in eastern Europe. It is unlikely, too, that leading Unionist politicians could have foreseen a time when they would sit willingly round a table at Stormont with representatives of the Dublin government; yet that is what they did in July 1992. This conference did not produce a dramatic breakthrough and an examination of previous talks is not encouraging. Perhaps the most remarkable feature of these talks, tentatively offering a hope for the future, was that they took place during the marching season – traditionally a time of heightened political tension – and yet they provoked no significant popular opposition. There has been a perceptible shift in attitude, however slight, and while a widely accepted solution still seems remote, it is no longer quite so inconceivable.

MAPS

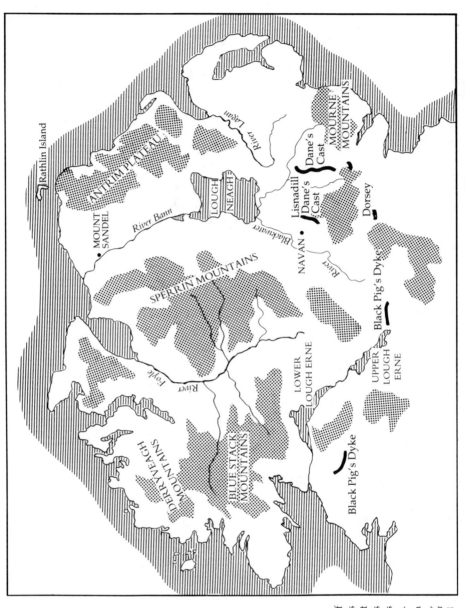

Physical features map of
Ulster which includes
Mount Sandel, Navan Fort
and linear earthworks
defending routeways
through the drumlin belt.

Based in part on map in
J.P. Mallory and T.E. McNeill,
*The Archaeology of Ulster: From
Colonisation to Plantation*, p. 151

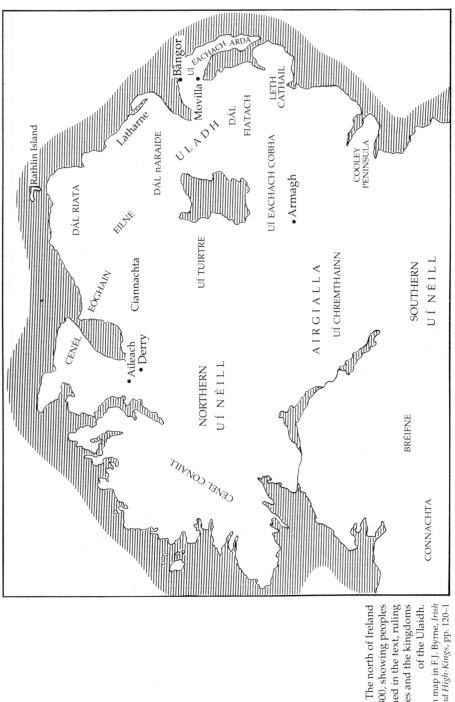

The north of Ireland
c. AD 800, showing peoples
mentioned in the text, ruling
families and the kingdoms
of the Ulaidh.

Based on map in F.J. Byrne, *Irish
Kings and High-Kings*, pp. 120–1

Rathlin Island

Bangor

Uí EACHACH ARDA

Movilla

LETH
CATHAIL

Latharne

DÁL
FIATACH

U L A D H

DÁL RIATA

EILNE

DÁL nARAIDE

COOLEY
PENINSULA

Uí EACHACH COBHA

Armagh

Cíannachta

Uí TUIRTRE

EÓGHAIN

CENÉL

Aileach

Derry

NORTHERN
UÍ NÉILL

AIRGIALLA

Uí CHREMTHAINN

SOUTHERN
UÍ NÉILL

CENÉL CONAILL

BRÉIFNE

CONNACHTA

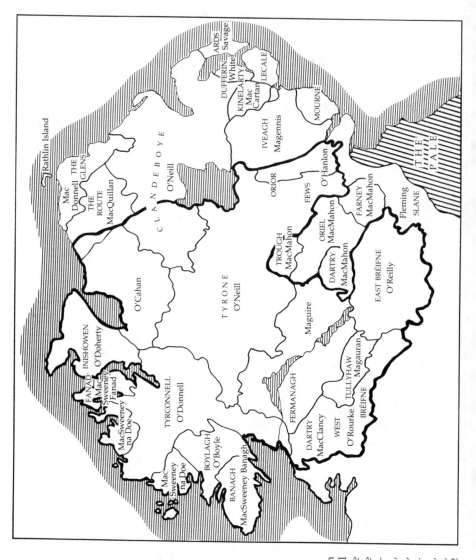

Ulster in the early sixteenth century, showing the principal lordships. The heavy black line encloses the six counties of the plantation of Ulster in 1610 – Tyrconnell (Donegal), Coleraine, Tyrone, Armagh, Fermanagh and Cavan.

Based on map 1 in T.W. Moody, F.X. Martin and F.J. Byrne, *A New History of Ireland*, vol. 3, p. 2

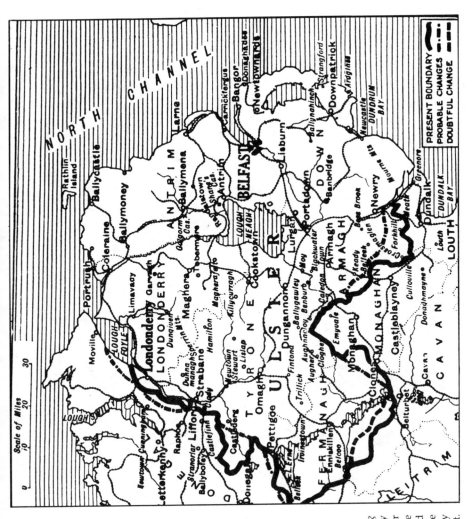

Map published in the *Morning Post* on 7 November 1925. By revealing that only minor adjustments to the frontier were intended, this map precipitated the crisis which led to the suppression of the Boundary Commission report.

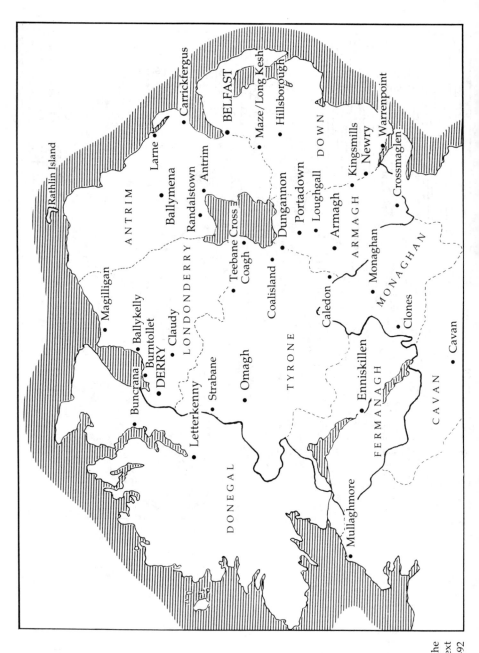

Map showing some of the places referred to in the text covering the period 1968–92

Where the title of a book, article or pamphlet is not given, the complete reference will be found in the bibliography.

ABBREVIATIONS

BNHPS Proceedings and Reports of the Belfast Natural History and Philosophical Society
IHS Irish Historical Studies
NHI A New History of Ireland
OSM Ordnance Survey Memoirs
PRONI Public Record Office of Northern Ireland
RSAI Jn Journal of the Proceedings of the Royal Society of Antiquaries of Ireland
SPO State Paper Office of Ireland, Dublin Castle

CHAPTER 1
1 Woodman, 1981, p. 92
2 Evans, 1981, p. 27
3 Quoted in Gillespie and O'Sullivan, 1989, p. 11
4 Harbison, 1988, p. 25
5 Gailey, 1984, p. 15; Mallory and McNeill, 1991, pp. 31–2
6 Hamlin and Lynn, 1988, p. 8
7 Quoted in Loughrey, 1988, p. 25
8 Harbison, 1988, p. 114
9 Hamlin and Lynn, 1988, p. 21
10 Harbison, 1988, p. 153
11 Mallory and McNeill, 1991, p. 156
12 Cary and Warmington, 1929, p. 43
13 Carson, 1983, p. 10
14 Hamlin and Lynn, 1988, p. 21
15 Kinsella, 1970, p. 7
16 Gantz, 1981, p. 1
17 Byrne, 1973, p. 36
18 Marsh, 1966, pp. 23, 29
19 Ibid., p. 44
20 Ó Laoghaire in McNally (ed.), 1965, p. 29
21 Mac Niocaill, 1972, p. 77
22 Bieler, 1963, p. 37
23 McNally (ed.), 1965, p. 126; de Paor, 1964, p. 67
24 Adamson, 1979, p. 19
25 Ibid., pp. 74–5
26 Bardon, 1970, p. 40
27 Hamlin and Lynn, 1988, p. 44
28 Ó Corráin, 1972, p. 52
29 Ibid., p. 84
30 Ibid., p. 88

CHAPTER 2
1 Todd, 1867, p. 3
2 de Paor, 1964, p. 132

3 Todd, 1867, p. 51
4 Annals of Ulster, AD 811
5 Todd, 1867, p. 7
6 Annals of Ulster, AD 832–40
7 Ibid., AD 866
8 Todd, 1867, p. 41
9 Ibid., p. 52
10 Annals of Ulster, AD 919
11 Todd, 1867, p. 135
12 Dasent, 1911, p. 327
13 Martin in NHI, vol. 2, 1987, p. 64
14 Ibid., p. 57
15 Ibid., p. 60
16 Giraldus, 1978, p. 175
17 Ibid., p. 177
18 Annals of the Four Masters, AD 1177
19 Giraldus, 1978, p. 181
20 O'Meara, 1982, p. 101
21 Giraldus, 1978, p. 179
22 Hamlin and Lynn, 1988, p. 38
23 McNeill, 1980, pp. 7–9
24 Giraldus, 1978, p. 185; Orpen, 1968, vol. 2, p. 23
25 Orpen, 1968, vol. 2, p. 23
26 Giraldus, 1978, p. 181
27 Orpen, 1968, vol. 2, pp. 139–42; Martin in NHI, vol. 2, 1987, p. 136
28 Roger of Wendover in Orpen, 1968, vol. 2, p. 236
29 Annals of the Four Masters, AD 1210
30 Sweetman and Handcock, 1886, pp. 59–62
31 Ibid., pp. 63–4; Orpen, 1968, vol. 2, pp. 253–5
32 McNeill, 1980, p. 16; Lydon in NHI, vol. 2, 1987, p. 158
33 Sweetman and Handcock, 1886, p. 169
34 Annals of Connacht, AD 1224; Orpen, 1968, vol. 3, p. 38

35 McNeill, 1980, p. 22
36 Orpen, 1968, vol. 3, p. 276
37 *Ibid.*, pp. 284–5
38 Orpen, 1968, vol. 4, pp. 139–40, 145; McNeill, 1980, p. 73
39 Orpen in RSAI Jn., part 1, vol. 43 (March 1913), p. 31
40 McNeill, 1980, pp. 69–70
41 Orpen in RSAI Jn., part 3, vol. 44 (March 1914), pp. 61–5; McNeill, 1980, pp. 79–81
42 Orpen in RSAI Jn., part 2, vol. 43 (June 1913), p. 139
43 McNeill, 1980, pp. 40–1; Orpen in RSAI Jn., part 2, vol. 43 (June 1913), p. 138 and part 3, vol. 14 (March 1914), p. 66
44 McNeill, 1980, pp. 92–3; Orpen in RSAI Jn., part 3, vol. 44 (March 1914), p. 62
45 McNeill, 1980, pp. 41, 45, 53

CHAPTER 3

1 Lydon in NHI, vol. 2, 1987, p. 284
2 Annals of Connacht, AD 1315
3 *Ibid.*
4 Orpen, 1968, vol. 4, p. 167
5 Annals of Connacht, AD 1315
6 Gilbert, 1886, vol. 2, p. 297
7 *Ibid.*, p. 345
8 Annals of Connacht, AD 1318
9 Watt in NHI, vol. 2, 1987, p. 353
10 Orpen, 1968, vol. 4, pp. 234, 245; McNeill, 1980, p. 33
11 McNeill, 1980, pp. 122–3
12 Watt in NHI, vol. 2, 1987, p. 367
13 *Ibid.*, pp. 387–8
14 Annals of Connacht, AD 1317–63
15 Down in NHI, vol. 2, 1987, p. 449; *Calendar of State Papers*, Henry VIII, Correspondence, vol. 3, p. 11
16 Hayes-McCoy, 1937, p. 32
17 *Calendar of State Papers*, Henry VIII, Correspondence, vol. 3, p. 44
18 Nicholls, 1972, pp. 130–7
19 Lydon in RSAI Jn., vol. 93 (1963), pp. 135–49; Otway-Ruthven, 1980, p. 334
20 Lydon, 1973, p. 120
21 Simms in *Clogher Record*, vol. 9 (1977), p. 135
22 *Ibid.*, p. 137
23 *Ibid.*, p. 140
24 Ellis, 1985, p. 187
25 Carpenter in Haren and de Pontfarcy (eds), 1988, p. 106
26 *Ibid.*, p. 108
27 *Ibid.*, p. 110

28 *Ibid.*, p. 114
29 *Ibid.*, p. 117
30 *Ibid.*, pp. 110–11
31 Allingham, 1897, p. 61
32 Quinn, 1966, pp. 64–7, 79
33 Carpenter in Haren and de Pontfarcy (eds), 1988, p. 110
34 Quinn, 1966, pp. 69–71
35 Carpenter in Haren and de Pontfarcy (eds), 1988, p. 111
36 Nicholls in NHI, vol. 2, 1987, pp. 412–17
37 Gailey, 1984, p. 21; Hamlin and Lynn, 1988, p. 70
38 Carson, 1977, pp. 22–3; Barry, 1987, p. 186
39 Cosgrove in NHI, vol. 2, 1987, pp. 531–2
40 Simms in Lydon (ed.), 1981, pp. 230–1
41 Hill, 1873, p. 37
42 *Ibid.*
43 Simms in Lydon (ed.), 1981, p. 217
44 *Ibid.*, p. 228
45 Annals of Ulster, AD 1498
46 *Calendar of State Papers*, Henry VIII, Correspondence, vol. 3, pp. 28, 24, 31
47 *Ibid.*, p. 3
48 *Ibid.*, p. 155
49 *Ibid.*, p. 478
50 *Calendar of the Carew Mss*, vol. 3, p. 421
51 *Ibid.*, p. 199; Ellis, 1985, pp. 138–41
52 Watt in Lydon (ed.), 1981, p. 209
53 *Calendar of State Papers*, Henry VIII, Correspondence, vol. 3, p. 15
54 Hill, 1873, p. 40
55 de Breffny and Mott, 1976, p. 99
56 Ellis, 1981, p. 205
57 *Ibid.*, p. 206

CHAPTER 4

1 Bagwell, 1885, vol. 2, p. 8
2 Falls, 1950, p. 87
3 Hogan in Pender (ed.), 1947, pp. 154–70
4 Bagwell, 1885, vol. 2, p. 55
5 *Ibid.*, p. 56
6 *Ibid.*, p. 54
7 Hill, 1873, p. 134
8 Bagwell, 1885, vol. 2, p. 103
9 Hayes-McCoy in NHI, vol. 3, 1978, p. 85
10 Annals of the Four Masters, AD 1567
11 *Calendar of State Papers*, vol. 21, p. 8; Hill, 1873, p. 141

12 Canny, 1976, p. 75
13 *Ibid.*, p. 73
14 *Ibid.*, p. 76
15 Quinn, 1966, p. 108
16 Bagwell, 1885, vol. 2, p. 244
17 *Ibid.*, p. 258
18 Annals of the Four Masters, AD 1574; Bagwell, 1885, vol. 2, p. 289
19 Clark, 1971, p. 90
20 Bagwell, 1885, vol. 2, p. 302
21 *Ibid.*,
22 *Ibid.*
23 *Ibid.*, p. 324
24 Clark, 1971, p. 99
25 Bagwell, 1885, vol. 2, p. 305
26 Bardon, 1982, p. 7
27 Canny, 1976, p. 91
28 *Ibid.*, p. 90
29 Hill, 1873, p. 158
30 Bagwell, 1890, vol. 3, p. 128
31 *Ibid.*, p. 137
32 Hill, 1873, p. 166
33 Bagwell, 1890, vol. 3, p. 150
34 *Ibid.*
35 *Ibid.*, p. 151
36 Fallon, 1978, p. 129
37 *Ibid.*, p. 136
38 *Ibid.*, p. 80
39 *Ibid.*, p. 90
40 *Ibid.*
41 *Ibid.*, p. 105
42 Allingham, 1897, p. 48
43 Bagwell, 1890, vol. 3, p. 189
44 Allingham, 1897, p. 63
45 *Ibid.*, p. 66
46 Bagwell, 1890, vol. 3, p. 186
47 *Ibid.*, p. 202
48 Annals of the Four Masters, AD 1591; Bagwell, 1890, vol. 3, p. 226
49 Annals of the Four Masters, AD 1591
50 Bagwell, 1890, vol. 3, p. 224
51 *Ibid.*, p. 244
52 Hayes-McCoy, 1969, p. 101
53 *Ibid.*, p. 100
54 *Ibid.*, p. 103
55 *Ibid.*, p. 100
56 *Ibid.*, pp. 107–11
57 Bagwell, 1890, vol. 3, p. 254
58 Falls, 1950, p. 195
59 Silke, 1970, pp. 29–32
60 Falls, 1950, p. 203
61 Hayes-McCoy, 1969, p. 114
62 Bagwell, 1890, vol. 3, p. 282
63 Benn, 1877, p. 69
64 Hill, 1873, p. 188
65 *Ibid.*, p. 189
66 Hill, 1873, p. 188
67 Bagwell, 1890, vol. 3, p. 296

68 Hayes-McCoy, 1969, p. 116; Falls, 1950, p. 214
69 Hayes-McCoy, 1969, p. 119
70 Falls, 1950, p. 228
71 *Ibid.*, p. 239
72 *Ibid.*, p. 241
73 Bagwell, 1890, vol. 3, p. 343
74 Falls, 1950, p. 252
75 *Ibid.*, p. 254
76 Docwra, 1849, p. 237
77 *Ibid.*, p. 238
78 *Ibid.*, p. 239
79 *Ibid.*, p. 240
80 *Ibid.*, p. 241
81 *Ibid.*, p. 242
82 *Ibid.*, p. 244
83 *Ibid.*, p. 245
84 Moryson, 1617, Book 1, p. 186
85 Hayes-McCoy, 1969, p. 136
86 Moryson, 1617, Book 2, p. 137
87 *Ibid.*; Hayes-McCoy, 1969, p. 139
88 Hayes-McCoy, 1969, p. 140
89 *Ibid.*
90 Moryson, 1617, Book 1, p. 186
91 *Ibid.*, p. 188
92 Silke, 1970, p. 78
93 *Ibid.*, pp. 69–74
94 *Ibid.*, p. 79
95 Docwra, 1849, p. 247
96 *Ibid.*, p. 249
97 *Ibid.*, p. 250
98 Moryson, 1617, Book 3, p. 141
99 Moryson, 1617, Book 2, pp. 223–4
100 Falls, 1950, p. 277
101 Moryson, 1617, Book 2, pp. 252, 266
102 Silke, 1970, pp. 108–15
103 Annals of the Four Masters, AD 1601
104 *Calendar of the Carew Mss*, vol. 4 (1601–3), p. 195
105 *Ibid.*, p. 196
106 *Calendar of State Papers Ireland*, 1601–3, p. 185
107 Annals of the Four Masters, AD 1601
108 Moryson, 1617, Book 3, p. 177
109 *Ibid.*
110 Docwra, 1849, p. 258
111 *Ibid.*, p. 260
112 Moryson, 1617, Book 3, p. 197
113 *Ibid.*, p. 199
114 *Ibid.*, p. 283
115 *Ibid.*, p. 285
116 *Ibid.*
117 *Ibid.*, p. 225

CHAPTER 5

1 Falls, 1950, p. 337
2 Robinson, 1984, p. 38
3 Benn, 1877, p. 79

4 Walsh, 1986, p. 37
5 *Ibid.*, pp. 52–3
6 Moody, 1939, p. 193
7 Canny, 1976, p. 386
8 *Calendar of State Papers Ireland,*
   1606–8, p. 270
9 Walsh, 1986, p. 46
10 *Calendar of State Papers Ireland,*
   1606–8, p. 270
11 Annals of the Four Masters, AD 1608
12 *Calendar of State Papers Ireland,*
   1606–8, p. 281
13 *Ibid.*, p. 273
14 *Ibid.*, p. 276
15 Hill, 1877, p. 34
16 *Calendar of State Papers Ireland,*
   1606–8, pp. 504–6
17 *Calendar of State Papers Ireland,*
   1608–10, p. 7
18 *Ibid.*, pp. 15, 17
19 *Ibid.*, p. 27
20 *Ibid.*, p. 34
21 *Calendar of State Papers Ireland,*
   1606–8, p. 275
22 *Calendar of State Papers Ireland,*
   1608–10, p. 17
23 Hill, 1869, pp. 13, 27; Perceval-
   Maxwell, 1973, pp. 49–50
24 McCall, 1983, p. 75
25 *Ibid.*, p. 82
26 *Ibid.*, p. 65
27 Perceval-Maxwell, 1973, p. 63
28 *Ibid.*, p. 232
29 *Ibid.*, p. 47
30 Hill, 1869, p. 66
31 *Ibid.*
32 Report of the Plantation Commissioners, 1611, typescript copy,
   Lambeth Palace Library cod. 630
   fol. 144
33 *Calendar of State Papers Ireland,*
   1606–8, p. 512
34 Curl, 1986, p. 21
35 Moody, 1939, p. 31
36 *Ibid.*, p. 36
37 Robinson, 1984, p. 63
38 Livingstone, 1969, p. 74
39 Gilbert, 1879, vol. 1, pp. 317, 324
40 Gillespie, 1985, p. 34
41 Perceval-Maxwell, 1973, p. 29
42 *Ibid.*, p. 326
43 *Ibid.*, p. 27
44 *Ibid.*, p. 26
45 Gillespie, 1985, p. 31
46 Perceval-Maxwell, 1973, p. 46
47 Gilbert, 1879, vol. 1, pp. 324, 319
48 Moody, 1939, p. 64
49 *Ibid.*, p. 369

50 *Ibid.*, p. 70
51 *Ibid.*, p. 137
52 Curl, 1986, pp. 33–5
53 Moody, 1939, p. 113
54 *Ibid.*, p. 108
55 Curl, 1986, p. 45
56 Moody, 1939, p. 150
57 Curl, 1986, p. 62
58 *Ibid.*, p. 63; Moody, 1939, pp. 160–1
59 Moody, 1939, pp. 164–6
60 *Ibid.*, p. 229
61 Edwards, 1938, p. 40
62 Brady in Brady and Gillespie (eds),
   1986, p. 162
63 *Ibid.*, p. 197; Reid, 1867, vol. 1, p. 149
64 Moody, 1939, p. 330
65 Reid, 1867, vol. 1, pp. 180–2
66 *Ibid.*, p. 189
67 Gillespie, 1985, pp. 68–72
68 Stevenson, 1981, p. 13
69 Reid, 1867, vol. 1, p. 237
70 *Ibid.*, p. 253
71 Gilbert, 1879, vol. 1, p. 374
72 Gillespie in Brady and Gillespie
   (eds), 1986, p. 195
73 Gilbert, 1879, vol. 1, part 1, p. 364
74 Perceval-Maxwell in IHS, vol. 21
   (1978–9), pp. 149–50
75 Gilbert, 1879, vol. 1, p. 363
76 Perceval-Maxwell in IHS, vol. 21
   (1978–9), p. 161
77 Gilbert, 1879, vol. 1, p. 363
78 Reid, 1867, pp. 315–18
79 Livingstone, 1969, p. 84
80 Lecky, 1892, vol. 1, p. 85; Hickson,
   1884, vol. 1, p. 308
81 Hickson, 1884, vol. 2, p. 20
82 *Ibid.*, p. 324
83 Perceval-Maxwell in IHS, vol. 21
   (1978–9), p. 161
84 Curl, 1986, p. 91
85 Stevenson, 1981, pp. 53–4
86 *Ibid.*, pp. 104–6
87 *Ibid.*, p. 112
88 Hayes-McCoy, 1969, p. 179
89 *Ibid.*, p. 193
90 Stevenson, 1981, p. 233
91 Ranelagh, 1981, p. 106
92 Stevenson, 1981, pp. 276–7
93 Bagwell, 1890, vol. 3, pp. 300–301
94 Corish in NHI, vol. 3, 1978, p. 358
   (map)
95 Bardon, 1982, p. 18
96 Bagwell, 1890, vol. 3, p. 335
97 Moody in BNHPS, 2nd series, vol. 1
   (1937), pp. 23–4
98 *Ibid.*, p. 27
99 *Ibid.*, p. 21

100 Corish in NHI, vol. 3, 1978, p. 385
101 Camblin, 1951, p. 48
102 Simms in NHI, vol. 3, 1978, p. 443;
Foster, 1988, p. 128
103 Robinson, 1984, p. 156
104 Bardon, 1982, pp. 18–19
105 Curl, 1986, p. 97; Simms in NHI,
vol. 3, 1978, p. 447

CHAPTER 6

1 Young, 1898, pp. 240–1
2 Quinn, 1972, pp. 39, 41
3 Hill, 1873, p. 381
4 Young, 1898, p. 241; Hill, 1873,
p. 382
5 Macrory, 1980, p. 114
6 Simms in NHI, vol. 3, 1978, p. 480
7 Gibbs in Maguire (ed.), 1990,
pp. 10–16
8 Ibid., p. 17
9 McGuire in Maguire (ed.), 1990,
p. 43
10 Macrory, 1980, p. 124
11 Parkhill and Speers (eds), 1990, p. 14
12 Macrory, 1980, p. 124
13 Ibid., p. 145
14 Gilbert, 1892, p. 45
15 Ibid., p. 171
16 Parkhill and Speers (eds), 1990, p. 16
17 Macrory, 1980, p. 214
18 Ibid., p. 224
19 Ibid., p. 212
20 Gilbert, 1892, p. 75
21 Macrory, 1980, p. 214
22 Ibid., p. 236
23 Ibid., p. 253
24 Ibid., p. 238
25 Ibid., p. 291
26 Ibid., p. 215
27 Ibid.
28 Ibid., p. 286
29 Ibid., p. 298
30 Gilbert, 1892, p. 84
31 Macrory, 1980, p. 313
32 Ibid., p. 314
33 Ibid., p. 315, Witherow, 1913,
pp. 266–70
34 Bardon, 1985, p. 10
35 Ibid.
36 Parkhill and Speers (eds), 1990, p. 27
37 Story, 1691, p. 52
38 Tyrconnell, 1932, p. 100
39 Story, 1691, p. 56
40 Parkhill and Speers (eds), 1990, p. 31
41 Tyrconnell, 1932, p. 108
42 Parkhill and Speers (eds), 1990, p. 32
43 Bardon, 1985, p. 10
44 Ibid.

45 Ellis, 1976, p. 23
46 Bardon, 1985, p. 10
47 Southwell, PRONI, T 440 Letter IX,
Belfast 18 June 1690, p. 18
48 Danaher and Simms, 1962, p. 64
49 Ellis, 1976, p. 36
50 Parkhill and Speers (eds), 1990, p. 43
51 Southwell, PRONI, T 440 Letter XIV,
Duleek 2 July 1690, p. 38
52 Ibid., p. 40
53 Ibid., p. 37
54 Ellis, 1976, p. v
55 Simms in NHI, vol. 3, 1978, p. 498
56 PRONI, D 638/12
57 Murtagh in Hayes-McCoy (ed.),
1964, p. 66
58 Ibid., p. 67
59 Foster, 1988, p. 151; Simms in NHI,
vol. 3, 1978, p. 506
60 Simms in NHI, vol. 3, 1978, p. 507
61 Livingstone, 1980, p. 136
62 Ibid., p. 137
63 Ibid., p. 135
64 Ibid., p. 137
65 Ibid., p. 135
66 Bardon, 1982, p. 26
67 Beckett, 1966, p. 150
68 Ranelagh, 1981, p. 116
69 Livingstone, 1980, p. 147
70 Ibid., p. 144
71 Lecky, 1892, vol. 1, p. 170
72 Ibid.
73 Fitzpatrick, 1989, p. 44
74 Simms in NHI, vol. 4, 1978, p. 23;
Dickson, 1966, p. 2
75 Livingstone, 1980, p. 132
76 Beckett, 1948, p. 37
77 Reid, 1867, vol. 3, p. 3
78 Beckett, 1948, p. 46
79 Reid, 1867, vol. 3, p. 30
80 Bardon, 1982, p. 26
81 PRONI, T 781/1, p. 50
82 Ibid., p. 2
83 Beckett, 1948, p. 60
84 Ibid., p. 49
85 Ibid., p. 86
86 Ibid., p. 87
87 Livingstone, 1980, p. 132
88 McCracken in NHI, vol. 4, 1986, p. 33
89 Boulter, 1770, vol. 1, p. 178
90 McCracken in NHI, vol. 4, 1986, p. 33
91 Ibid., p. 34
92 Livingstone, 1980, p. 134
93 Dickson, 1966, p. 33
94 Ibid., p. 22; Fitzpatrick, 1989, p. 55
95 PRONI T.S.P.I. T 659/1352
96 Boulter, 1770, vol. 1, pp. 209–10
97 Ibid., p. 224

98 PRONI T.S.P.I. T 659/1352
99 Dickson, 1966, p. 28 (footnote 1)
100 Dickson, 1966, pp. 41, 29
101 PRONI T.S.P.I. T 659/Bundle 391
102 Boulter, 1770, vol. 1, p. 209
103 Crawford in Gillespie and
     O'Sullivan (eds), 1989, p. 96
104 Gribbon in Cullen and Smout (eds),
     1977, p. 85
105 *Ibid.*, p. 77
106 *Ibid.*, p. 82
107 Murnane and Murnane in *Clogher
     Record*, vol. 12, no. 3 (1987), p. 362
108 Crawford, 1972, p. 31
109 Murnane and Murnane in *Clogher
     Record*, vol. 12, no. 3 (1987), p. 335

CHAPTER 7

1 Harris, 1744, p. 112
2 McCutcheon, 1980, p. 89
3 Harris, 1744, p. 118
4 Crawford, 1972, p. 27
5 *Ibid.*, p. 28
6 Hutton, 1892, vol. 1, p. 128
7 McCutcheon, 1980, p. 252
8 Crawford, 1972, p. 19
9 McCutcheon, 1980, p. 292
10 Gribbon, 1969, p. 83
11 Hutton, 1892, vol. 1, p. 131
12 McCutcheon, 1980, p. 248
13 Crawford, 1972, p. 75
14 Crawford in *Irish Economic and Social
    History*, vol. 15 (1988), p. 37
15 McCutcheon, 1980, pp. 292, 251;
    Clark, 1982, p. 12
16 Clark, 1982, p. 16
17 McDonnell, 1990, p. 9
18 Crawford in *Irish Economic and Social
    History*, vol. 15 (1988), p. 42
19 Crawford, 1972, p. 17
20 Hutton, 1892, vol. 1, p. 123
21 *Ibid.*, p. 128
22 Crawford, 1972, p. 12
23 *Ibid.*, p. 77
24 Hutton, 1892, vol. 1, pp. 116, 127,
    148, 149
25 Crawford in Brady, O'Dowd and
    Walker (eds), 1989, p. 40
26 McCracken, 1971, p. 29
27 *Ibid.*, pp. 93, 83, 84
28 *Ibid.*, p. 78
29 *Ibid.*, pp. 73, 80, 137, 118
30 Bell and Watson, 1986, p. 112
31 *Ibid.*, pp. 45, 27, 28
32 Harris, 1744, p. 13
33 Bell and Watson, 1986, p. 30
34 Harris, 1744, p. 98
35 *Ibid.*, p. 15

36 Hutton, 1892, vol. 1, p. 136
37 Evans, 1978, p. 145
38 Harris, 1744, p. 43
39 Kirkham in Roebuck (ed.), 1981,
    p. 67
40 *Ibid.*, p. 72
41 *Ibid.*, p. 78
42 *Ibid.*, p. 77
43 *Ibid.*, p. 76
44 *Ibid.*, p. 77
45 Harris, 1744, pp. 81, 70
46 Hutton, 1892, vol. 1, p. 137
47 *Ibid.*, pp. 169, 181
48 Hutton, 1892, vol. 1, p. 181; de
    Latocnaye, 1796–7, p. 191
49 Hutton, 1892, vol. 1, p. 183
50 Harris, 1744, pp. 236–7
51 Hutton, 1892, vol. 1, pp. 190, 164,
    187
52 Maxwell, 1949, p. 23
53 Malins and Glin, 1976, p. 81
54 Crawford in Cullen and Smout
    (eds), 1976, p. 196
55 Roebuck in Roebuck (ed.), 1981,
    pp. 95–6
56 Maxwell, 1949, p. 79; Malins and
    Glin, 1976, p. 79
57 Maxwell, 1949, p. 79; de Latocnaye,
    1796–7, p. 187
58 Maxwell, 1949, p. 88
59 Malins and Glin, 1976, p. 153
60 *Ibid.*, pp. 151–2
61 de Latocnaye, 1796–7, p. 201
62 Maxwell, 1949, p. 99
63 Malins and Glin, 1976, p. 46
64 *Ibid.*, p. 44
65 Hutton, 1892, vol. 1, pp. 191, 195
66 *Ibid.*, p. 127
67 Maxwell, 1949, p. 176
68 Crawford in Roebuck (ed.), 1981,
    p. 141; Clarkson and Crawford,
    1985, p. 11
69 Camblin, 1951, p. 81; Crawford in
    Roebuck (ed.), 1981, p. 145
70 Harris, 1744, p. 33
71 *Ibid.*, p. 58; Camblin, 1951, pp. 81–2,
    78; Crawford in Roebuck (ed.), 1981,
    pp. 145–6
72 Crawford in Roebuck (ed.), 1981,
    p. 141
73 Camblin, 1951, p. 88
74 *Ibid.*, p. 92
75 Maxwell, 1949, pp. 335–6
76 Clarkson and Crawford, 1985,
    pp. 12–22
77 Camblin, 1951, p. 87
78 Bowden, 1791, p. 227
79 Maxwell, 1949, p. 231

80 Crawford and Trainor (eds), 1969, p. 88; de Latocnaye, 1796–7, p. 200
81 Canavan, 1989, pp. 72–3, 93; Hutton, 1892, vol. 1, p. 116
82 Canavan, 1989, p. 90
83 Brett, 1967, p. 2
84 Bardon, 1982, pp. 36–45; Brett, 1967, pp. 1–8
85 McCutcheon, 1980, p. 329
86 *Ibid.*, p. 52
87 *Ibid.*, p. 49; Canavan, 1989, p. 83
88 McCutcheon, 1980, p. 332
89 *Ibid.*, p. 89
90 *Ibid.*, pp. 1–4
91 Crawford, 1989, pp. 6–7
92 Bardon, 1982, p. 34
93 Dickson, 1966, p. 74
94 *Ibid.*, p. 75
95 Crawford and Trainor (eds), 1969, p. 38
96 *Ibid.*, p. 39
97 Dickson, 1966, p. 69
98 *Ibid.*, p. 79
99 Lammey, 1984, p. 160
100 PRONI Educational Facsimile, *Emigration*, p. 133
101 Kirkham in Roebuck (ed.), 1981, p. 79
102 Dickson, 1966, p. 208
103 *Ibid.*, p. 289
104 PRONI Educational Facsimile, *Emigration*, p. 134
105 Dickson, 1966, pp. 64, 86
106 PRONI Educational Facsimile, *Emigration*, p. 132
107 Fitzpatrick, 1989, p. 68
108 Crawford and Trainor (eds), 1969, p. 53
109 Joy, 1817, p. 138
110 PRONI Educational Facsimile, *Volunteers*, p. 141
111 Joy, 1817, p. 140
112 O'Connell, 1965, p. 28
113 *Ibid.*, p. 63
114 Lammey, 1984, p. 164
115 PRONI Educational Facsimile, *Volunteers*, p. 141
116 *Ibid.*, p. 143
117 Smyth in Bartlett and Hayton (eds), 1979, p. 114
118 PRONI Educational Facsimile, *Volunteers*, p. 144
119 O'Connell, 1965, p. 186
120 PRONI Educational Facsimile, *Volunteers*, p. 148
121 Joy, 1817, p. 165
122 PRONI Educational Facsimile, *Volunteers*, p. 152
123 O'Connell, 1965, p. 325
124 Malcolmson in Bartlett and Hayton (eds), 1979, pp. 145, 153
125 Wright, 1870, vol. 2, p. 474
126 Joy, 1817, p. 183
127 Kelly in O'Brien (ed.), 1989, p. 98
128 O'Connell, 1965, p. 354
129 Joy, 1817, p. 282
130 Foster, 1988, p. 170; Bardon, 1982, p. 50
131 Joy, 1817, p. 348
132 Zimmermann, 1967, p. 125
133 Joy, 1817, pp. 349–53
134 Elliott, 1989, p. 134
135 Joy, 1817, p. 358
136 Elliott, 1982, p. 28
137 Joy, 1817, p. 358
138 McNeill, 1988, pp. 82–3, 91
139 Lecky, 1892, vol. 3, p. 283
140 *Belfast News-Letter*, 28 March 1795
141 Joy, 1817, p. 433
142 Lecky, 1892, vol. 3, p. 338
143 *Ibid.*, p. 326
144 MacDermot, 1969, p. 145
145 Miller, 1990, p. 34; Miller in Clark and Donnelly (eds), 1983, pp. 165–73
146 Miller, 1990, p. 49
147 *Ibid.*, p. 30
148 *Ibid.*, pp. 71, 80
149 *Ibid.*, p. 89
150 *Ibid.*, p. 103
151 *Ibid.*, pp. 88, 94
152 *Ibid.*, p. 132
153 Bartlett in IHS, vol. 24, no. 95 (May 1985), p. 388
154 Miller, 1990, p. 113
155 *Ibid.*, p. 121
156 *Ibid.*, p. 125
157 *Ibid.*, p. 129
158 Heatley, 1967, p. 16
159 Emmet, MacNeven and O'Connor, 1978, p. 9
160 Elliott, 1982, pp. 72, 97
161 Zimmermann, 1967, p. 127
162 de Latocnaye, 1796–7, p. 211
163 Canavan, 1989, p. 112
164 Elliott, 1982, pp. 104–5, 111
165 Zimmermann, 1967, p. 133
166 MacDermot, 1969, p. 198
167 Dickson, 1960, p. 106
168 Bartlett; copy to author from Thomas Bartlett
169 Joy, 1817, p. 443
170 Dickson, 1960, p. 111
171 *Ibid.*, p. 119
172 *Ibid.*, p. 109
173 *Ibid.*, p. 112

174 Ibid., p. 180
175 Ibid., p. 110
176 Elliott, 1982, p. 205; Dickson, 1960, pp. 127–8
177 Dickson, 1960, p. 138
178 Akenson and Crawford, 1977, p. 42
179 Dickson, 1960, p. 135
180 Ibid., p. 142
181 Ibid., p. 143
182 Ibid., p. 147
183 Ibid., p. 228
184 Maxwell, 1880, p. 213
185 Dickson, 1960, p. 152
186 Zimmermann, 1967, p. 156
187 Maxwell, 1880, p. 215
188 Dickson, 1960, p. 156
189 Maxwell, 1880, p. 217
190 Zimmermann, 1967, p. 168
191 Elliott, 1989, p. 387
192 Elliott, 1982, p. 237
193 Lammey, 1984, p. 301
194 Bolton, 1966, p. 156
195 PRONI, D 1606/1/206
196 PRONI, D 561/1/74, 2 April 1800

CHAPTER 8

1 Elliott, 1982, p. 312
2 PRONI, OSM Connor
3 O'Farrell, 1971, p. 110
4 Steven Watson, 1960, p. 401
5 O'Farrell, 1971, p. 74
6 Connolly in NHI, vol. 5, 1989, pp. 26–33
7 Senior, 1966, p. 126
8 Douglas Carson, 'The Battle of Garvagh', BBC Radio Ulster, 1976
9 Connolly in NHI, vol. 5, 1989, p. 80
10 Connolly in Roebuck (ed.), 1981, p. 169
11 Senior, 1966, pp. 187, 145–6
12 O'Farrell, 1971, p. 73
13 Connolly in NHI, vol. 5, 1989, p. 99
14 Northern Whig, 2 October 1828
15 Ibid.
16 Ibid., 9 October 1828
17 Ibid., 16 July 1829
18 Connolly, 1982, p. 164
19 Connolly in Roebuck (ed.), 1981, p. 158
20 Connolly, 1982, p. 77
21 Ibid., p. 149
22 Ibid., pp. 162, 150; Maxwell, 1949, p. 154
23 Connolly, 1982, p. 168
24 Holmes, 1981, p. 8
25 Ibid., p. 23
26 Ibid., p. 12
27 Ibid., p. 31

28 Ibid., p. 66
29 Bowen, 1978, p. 44
30 PRONI, OSM Tamlaght O'Crilly, Doagh, Drummaul
31 PRONI, OSM Islandmagee
32 Bowen, 1978, pp. 85, 94; Connolly in NHI, vol. 5, 1989, p. 78; Connolly in Roebuck (ed.), 1981, p. 161
33 O'Neill, 1984, p. 38
34 Senior, 1966, pp. 243–7
35 Holmes, 1981, pp. 115–16
36 Senior, 1966, p. 252
37 Ibid., p. 273
38 Repealer Repulsed, 1841, p. 12 (pamphlet held in Linen Hall Library)
39 Ibid., p. 27
40 Ibid., p. 38
41 Bardon, 1982, p. 93
42 Northern Whig, 22 January 1841
43 Repealer Repulsed, 1841, p. 110 (pamphlet held in Linen Hall Library)
44 Chambers, 1983, pp. 121–49
45 Dubourdieu, 1812, pp. 410, 515, 519
46 Bardon, 1982, p. 67
47 Dubourdieu, 1812, p. 406; Kennedy in Kennedy and Ollerenshaw (eds), 1985, p. 66
48 McCall, 1865, pp. 380–2
49 McCutcheon, 1980, p. 293
50 McCall, 1865, p. 287; Ollerenshaw in Kennedy and Ollerenshaw (eds), 1985, p. 69
51 McCall, 1865, p. 390
52 Ibid., p. 287; Ollerenshaw in Kennedy and Ollerenshaw (eds), 1985, pp. 70–1
53 McCutcheon, 1980, p. 67
54 Ibid., p. 104
55 Belfast News-Letter, 13 August 1839
56 McCutcheon, 1980, p. 190 (footnote 26)
57 Ibid., p. 107
58 Ibid., p. 140
59 Ibid., p. 108
60 Thackeray, 1842 [1985], pp. 313–16
61 Hill, 1845, p. 18
62 Ibid., p. 19
63 Crawford, 1972, p. 87
64 McCutcheon, 1980, p. 293
65 Crawford, 1972, p. 63
66 Ibid., p. 84
67 Ibid., p. 51
68 Ibid., p. 46
69 PRONI, OSM Drummaul, Laragh, Dunsfort, Pomeroy, Currin
70 McEvoy, 1802, p. 69

71 Ó Gráda in NHI, vol. 5, 1989, p. 133; O'Neill, 1984, pp. 35, 54; Maguire, 1972, pp. 8, 29; Roebuck in Roebuck (ed.), 1981, p. 97
72 Sampson, 1814, p. 295
73 Coote, 1804, pp. 245, 250, 73; Sampson, 1814, p. 302
74 McEvoy, 1802, p. 33
75 Dubourdieu, 1812, p. 223; McParlan, 1802, pp. 61, 34
76 Dubourdieu, 1812, p. 354
77 McEvoy, 1802, p. 33
78 Ibid., p. 34
79 Ó Gráda in NHI, vol. 5, 1989, p. 117
80 Coote, 1804, p. 136
81 McCall, 1865, p. 385
82 PRONI, OSM Cumber
83 McCloskey, 1983, p. 19
84 O'Neill, 1984, pp. 76, 29; Clarkson in Kennedy and Ollerenshaw (eds), 1985, pp. 137–41
85 O'Neill, 1984, pp. 76, 55, 81
86 McCloskey, 1983, p. 17
87 Ibid., p. 18
88 Ó Gráda in NHI, vol. 5, 1989, p. 109
89 Andrews, 1985, pp. 390–1; Freeman in NHI, vol. 5, 1989, pp. 244–5
90 PRONI, OSM Currin, Aghalurcher
91 Ibid., Drummaul
92 O'Neill, 1984, p. 49
93 PRONI, OSM Ballybay, Aghabog
94 Sampson, 1814, p. 224; McEvoy, 1802, pp. 125, 188
95 O'Neill, 1984, p. 104
96 PRONI, OSM Bovevagh, Galloon, Trory, Drumlomman
97 O'Neill, 1984, p. 117
98 PRONI, OSM Drumachose, Currin, Urney, Ardstraw, Aghaderg
99 Hill, 1845, p. 8
100 McParlan, 1802, pp. 67, 91
101 Hill, 1845, p. 21; McParlan, 1802, p. 73
102 Hill, 1845, p. 20
103 Ibid., p. 9; Evans, 1981, p. 91; PRONI, OSM Tamlaght O'Crilly
104 Hill, 1845, p. 13; Evans, 1981, p. 91
105 PRONI Educational Facsimile, Famine, p. 1
106 Woodham-Smith, 1989, p. 48; Donnelly in NHI, vol. 5, 1989, p. 273
107 PRONI Educational Facsimile, Famine, pp. 1, 15
108 Woodham-Smith, 1989, p. 53
109 Donnelly in NHI, vol. 5, 1989, pp. 282, 295
110 Commissariat, August 1846, p. 29 (H.C. 1847, LI)
111 Ibid., August–September 1846, p. 61
112 Ibid., p. 29
113 Woodham-Smith, 1989, p. 116
114 Commissariat, October 1846, p. 146 (H.C. 1847, LI)
115 Ibid., pp. 147, 212
116 Ibid., November 1846, p. 314; Donnelly in NHI, vol. 5, 1989, p. 298
117 Donnelly in NHI, vol. 5, 1989, p. 299
118 Board of Works, November 1846, p. 255 (pt 1 [764], H.C. 1847, L)
119 Ibid., October 1846, pp. 140–1, 154, 158, 384
120 Ibid., November 1846, p. 286
121 Ibid., p. 287
122 Ibid., December 1846, p. 325
123 Ibid., pp. 384, 414, 423, 440
124 Ibid., p. 382
125 Woodham-Smith, 1989, p. 158
126 Ibid., pp. 158–9
127 Northern Whig, 19 November 1846
128 Northern Whig, 19 and 29 December 1846
129 Northern Whig, 3 December 1846
130 As reprinted in Northern Whig, 22 December 1846
131 Board of Works, December 1846, p. 451 (pt 1 [764], H.C. 1847, L)
132 PRONI Educational Facsimile, Famine, p. 3
133 Northern Whig, 26 November and 22 December 1846
134 The Times, 16 November 1846
135 Northern Whig, 17 December 1846
136 PRONI Educational Facsimile, Famine, p. 5
137 Board of Works, Letters vol. 2, 9 January 1847, p. 91 (pt 1 [764], H.C. 1847, L)
138 Woodham-Smith, 1989, p. 143
139 PRONI BG 92/A/1, p. 229
140 Board of Works, Letters vol. 2, 31 January 1847, p. 93 (pt 1 [764], H.C. 1847, L)
141 Ibid., p. 25
142 Ibid., p. 92
143 PRONI Educational Facsimile, Famine, p. 6
144 Board of Works, Distress, Letters vol. 2, 13 February 1847, p. 238 and 16 February 1847, p. 152 (H.C. 1847–8)
145 Ibid., 20 February 1847, p. 153
146 PRONI Educational Facsimile, Famine, p. 7
147 PRONI, BG 22/A, pp. 55, 426
148 PRONI Educational Facsimile, Famine, p. 7

149 PRONI, BG 92/A/1, pp. 229, 235, 278
150 PRONI, BG 109/A/2, pp. 54–7
151 *Ibid.*, pp. 61–3
152 Board of Works, Distress, February 1847, pp. 239, 67 (H.C. 1847–8)
153 *Ibid.*, p. 187
154 *Ibid.*, p. 156
155 Woodham-Smith, 1989, p. 172
156 Donnelly in NHI, 1989, vol. 5, pp. 307–9
157 Woodham-Smith, 1989, pp. 188–94
158 Bardon, 1982, p. 97
159 *Ibid.*, pp. 98–9
160 *Belfast News-Letter*, 30 April 1847
161 Brooke (ed.), 1973, p. 152
162 *Belfast News-Letter*, 30 July 1847
163 Woodham-Smith, 1989, pp. 203, 285
164 *Ibid.*, p. 299; Donnelly in NHI, vol. 5, 1989, p. 310
165 Donnelly in NHI, vol. 5, 1989, p. 288
166 Board of Works, Distress, 6 February 1847, p. 236 (H.C. 1847–8)
167 *Ibid.*, July 1847, p. 108
168 *Ibid.*, September 1847, pp. 108, 223
169 *Ibid.*, November 1847, p. 222
170 *Ibid.*, p. 97
171 PRONI Educational Facsimile, *Famine*, p. 14
172 Board of Works, Distress, March 1848, p. 356 (H.C. 1847–8)
173 *Ibid.*, 7 February 1848, p. 73 (H.C. 1847–8)
174 *Ibid.*, 16 April 1848, p. 75 (H.C. 1847–8)
175 *Ibid.*, January 1848, p. 642 (H.C. 1847–8)
176 *Ibid.*, February 1848, pp. 644–5 (H.C. 1847–8)
177 *Ibid.*, 21 March 1848, p. 649 (H.C. 1847–8)
178 *Ibid.*, January 1848, pp. 107–8 (H.C. 1847–8)
179 *Belfast News-Letter*, 9 March 1847
180 Donnelly in NHI, vol. 5, 1989, p. 318
181 Board of Works, Distress, January and February 1848, pp. 78, 347, 601 (H.C. 1847–8)
182 *Ibid.*, 7 February 1848, p. 73
183 *Ibid.*, 14 January 1848 and 15 February 1848, p. 911
184 PRONI, BG 109/A/3 f. 6
185 Woodham-Smith, 1989, p. 335
186 Donnelly in NHI, vol. 5, 1989, p. 288
187 PRONI Educational Facsimile, *Famine*, p. 16
188 PRONI, 2 March 1849, BG 109/A/3 f. 71 V
189 Donnelly in NHI, vol. 5, 1989, p. 320
190 Farrell, 1971, p. 112
191 Donnelly in NHI, vol. 5, 1989, pp. 328–9
192 *Belfast News-Letter*, 13 July 1849
193 *Ibid.*
194 Bardon, 1982, pp. 100–101
195 Zimmermann, 1967, p. 311
196 *Newry Telegraph* report reprinted in *Belfast News-Letter*, 20 July 1849
197 *Ibid.*
198 Zimmermann, 1967, p. 313; *Newry Telegraph* report reprinted in *Belfast News-Letter*, 20 July 1849
199 Taylor, 1967, p. 91

CHAPTER 9

1 Boyd, 1969, p. 12
2 Frankfort Moore, 1914, p. 48
3 Clarkson in Kennedy and Ollerenshaw (eds), 1985, p. 138
4 Donnelly in NHI, vol. 5, 1989, pp. 351–2
5 Clarkson in Kennedy and Ollerenshaw (eds), 1985, pp 138–44
6 Speed, 1976, p. 63
7 Daly, 1986, p. 108
8 Donnelly in NHI, vol. 5, 1989, p. 355
9 Fitzpatrick in NHI, vol. 5, 1989, p. 563
10 *Ibid.*, p. 582
11 PRONI, T 2046/1, 1 November 1852
12 PRONI, T 2046/4, 27 May 1853
13 PRONI, T 2046/7, 30 May 1859
14 Handley, 1947, p. 25
15 *Ibid.*, p. 26
16 *Ibid.*, p. 31
17 Fitzpatrick in NHI, vol. 5, 1989, p. 650
18 Livingstone, 1980, p. 228
19 O Lochlainn, 1984, p. 203
20 Handley, 1947, p. 7
21 Donnelly in NHI, vol. 5, 1989, p. 337; Daly, 1986, p. 110
22 PRONI, D 1606/5/3, 23 March 1847
23 Livingstone, 1980, p. 294
24 Donnelly in NHI, vol. 5, 1989, p. 337
25 Livingstone, 1980, p. 232
26 Kennedy in Kennedy and Ollerenshaw (eds), 1985, pp. 38–40
27 Livingstone, 1980, p. 225
28 Bew and Wright in Clark and Donnelly (eds), 1983, pp. 194–5
29 Lee, 1973, p. 39
30 Pearl, 1979, p. 135
31 Livingstone, 1980, p. 226
32 *Ibid.*, p. 227
33 Whyte, 1972, pp. 8–18
34 Foster, 1988, p. 311
35 Maguire, 1984, p. 97

36 Donnelly, 1973, p. 51
37 Walker, 1981, pp. 121–3
38 Bell and Watson, 1986, pp. 138–49
39 Walker, 1981, p. 95
40 Bell and Watson, 1986, pp. 69–80
41 *Ibid.*, pp. 118–24
42 *Ibid.*, p. 128
43 Vaughan in Cullen and Smout (eds), 1976, p. 222
44 Walker, 1981, p. 102
45 Vaughan in Cullen and Smout (eds), 1976, pp. 216–17; Vaughan, 1984, pp. 18–23
46 Walker, 1989, pp. 2, 74; Vaughan, 1984, pp. 5–6
47 Dolan, 1980, p. 110
48 Vaughan, 1983, pp. 21, 43
49 Dolan, 1980, p. 108
50 Reprinted in *Freeman's Journal*, 12 April 1861
51 *Ibid.*
52 SPO, R.P. 1861/7273
53 Dolan, 1980, p. 138
54 Vaughan, 1983, p. 50
55 Bardon, 1985, p. 16; Bardon, 1982, pp. 101–3
56 Bardon, 1982, p. 103
57 Froggatt in Harkness and O'Dowd (eds), 1981, p. 173
58 Brooke (ed.), 1973, p. 157
59 PRONI, T 2046/5
60 *Ibid.*, T 2046/9–12
61 Crawford, 1972, pp. 54–5
62 Ollerenshaw in Kennedy and Ollerenshaw (eds), 1985, p. 77
63 *Ibid.*, pp. 77–8; Bardon, 1982, p. 117
64 Macneice in Roebuck (ed.), 1981, pp. 176–90
65 Brooke (ed.), 1973, p. 176
66 Purdon, 1877, pp. 12–13; Brooke (ed.), 1973, p. 177
67 Purdon, 1877, pp. 7, 14–15
68 Brooke, 1973, p. 177
69 Purdon, 1877, p. 9
70 *Ibid.*, p. 8
71 Messenger, 1980, p. 131
72 Armstrong in IHS, vol. 7 (1951), p. 256
73 *Ibid.*, p. 243
74 Purdon, 1877, p. 37
75 Patterson in Kennedy and Ollerenshaw (eds), 1985, pp. 165–6
76 Crawford, 1972, pp. 88–9
77 Purdon, 1877, Appendix, pp. 47–8
78 Ollerenshaw in Kennedy and Ollerenshaw (eds.), 1985, pp. 80–1
79 Moss and Hume, 1986, pp. 11–12
80 *Ibid.*, pp. 12–16
81 *Ibid.*, p. 19
82 Bardon, 1982, p. 128
83 Moss and Hume, 1986, p. 28
84 *Ibid.*, p. 31; Bardon, 1982, p. 129
85 Bardon, 1982, pp. 130, 133
86 Moss and Hume, 1986, p. 47
87 *Ibid.*, p. 59
88 *Ibid.*, pp. 65–6
89 Ollerenshaw in Kennedy and Ollerenshaw (eds), 1985, pp. 94, 67–8
90 Carson, 1958, p. 11
91 *Ibid.*, p. 20
92 *Ibid.*, pp. 23–5, 28
93 *Ibid.*, pp. 32–6
94 *Ibid.*, p. 80
95 Connell, 1966, p. 93
96 *Ibid.*, p. 102
97 *Ibid.*, p. 109
98 *Ibid.*, p. 111
99 *Ibid.*, p. 105
100 Carson, 1958, pp. 102–5
101 Connolly, 1985, p. 46
102 Carson, 1958, p. 68
103 *Ibid.*, p. 59
104 *Ibid.*, p. 66
105 *Ibid.*, p. 79
106 Comerford in NHI, vol. 5, 1989, pp. 396-7; Connolly, 1985, pp. 26–7
107 Lee, 1973, p. 47
108 Vaughan in NHI, vol. 5, 1989, p. 738
109 Walker, 1989, pp. 15–19
110 Vaughan in NHI, vol. 5, 1989, p. 740
111 Bardon, 1982, p. 83
112 Vaughan in NHI, vol. 5, 1989, p. 739
113 Macaulay, 1987, pp. 117–30
114 Connolly, 1985, p. 49
115 *Ibid.*, pp. 49, 54, 57; Macaulay, 1987, p. 373
116 Livingstone, 1980, pp. 252–3
117 Weatherup, 1990, pp. 28–9
118 Brett, 1967, p. 36
119 Lee, 1973, pp. 48–9
120 Boyd, 1969, p. 33
121 PRONI, MIC 327/Reel 1
122 Frankfort Moore, 1914, p. 20
123 *Daily News*, 11 September 1857
124 Frankfort Moore, 1914, p. 28
125 *Belfast News-Letter*, 13 August 1864
126 Bardon, 1982, pp. 111–14; Bardon, 1985, p. 18
127 *Northern Whig*, 19 August 1864
128 Bardon, 1985, p. 134; Boyd, 1969, pp. 84–8
129 Frankfort Moore, 1914, p. 33
130 Larkin, 1987, p. 10
131 *Ibid.*, pp. 13–23
132 Kee, 1989, vol. 2, pp. 17–18

133 Macaulay, 1987, p. 184
134 *Ibid.*, p. 185
135 Kee, 1989, vol. 2, pp. 45–50
136 Patterson, 1980, p. 1
137 *Belfast News-Letter*, 13 July 1867
138 Patterson, 1980, p. 3
139 Walker, 1989, p. 71
140 *Ibid.*, pp. 57–8
141 *Ibid.*, p. 76
142 Boyd, 1969, p. 116
143 Vaughan in NHI, vol. 5, 1989,
     pp. 744–5
144 *Ibid.*, p. 727
145 Walker, 1989, p. 67
146 Vaughan in NHI, vol. 5, 1989, p. 749
147 *Ibid.*, pp. 746–7
148 *Ibid.*, p. 736
149 John Cole in *Down Your Way*, BBC
     Radio 4, 2 December 1990
150 Lyons, 1971, p. 139
151 Walker, 1989, p. 93
152 *Ibid.*, p. 111
153 *Ibid.*, p. 92
154 *Ibid.*, p. 88
155 Kee, 1989, vol. 2, p. 67
156 PRONI, T 2046/18 and T 2046/21
157 Moss and Hume, 1986, p. 46
158 Moody, 1981, pp. 209, 328
159 Tuke, 1880, pp. 10–11
160 *Ibid.*, p. 12
161 *Ibid.*, pp. 25–8
162 Murphy, 1981, p. 140
163 Tuke, 1880, p. 12
164 Dolan, 1978, p. 29
165 *Ibid.*, p. 37
166 *Ibid.*, p. 76
167 Walker, 1989, p. 129
168 *Ibid.*, p. 135
169 *Ibid.*, p. 149
170 Marlow, 1973, p. 175
171 *Ibid.*, p. 201
172 Lloyd, 1892, pp. 6–8
173 *Ibid.*, p. 10
174 Moody, 1981, p. 446
175 Lloyd, 1892, pp. 9–11
176 Bew and Wright in Clark and
     Donnelly (eds), 1983, p. 215
177 Walker in Clark and Donnelly (eds),
     1983, p. 248
178 *Ibid.*, p. 247
179 Moody, 1981, p. 448
180 Abels, 1966, p. 106
181 *Ibid.*, p. 107
182 *Ibid.*, p. 106
183 Moody, 1981, p. 455
184 Abels, 1966, p. 117
185 Livingstone, 1980, p. 340
186 Walker, 1989, p. 161

187 *Ibid.*, p. 162
188 Walker in Clark and Donnelly (eds),
     1983, p. 250
189 Abels, 1966, p. 195
190 Bew and Wright in Clark and
     Donnelly (eds), 1983, p. 219
191 *Ibid.*, p. 200
192 Loughlin, 1986, p. 125
193 MacKnight, 1896, vol. 2, p. 44
194 Buckland, 1973, p. 3
195 MacKnight, 1896, vol. 2, p. 44
196 Abels, 1966, pp. 217–18
197 Walker, 1989, p. 176
198 *Ibid.*, p. 214
199 *Ibid.*, p. 185
200 Abels, 1966, p. 235
201 MacKnight, 1896, vol. 2, p. 116
202 Abels, 1966, p. 237
203 Buckland, 1973, p. 9
204 Stewart, 1967, p. 21
205 *Belfast News-Letter*, 23 February 1886
206 Walker, 1989, p. 230
207 Buckland (ed.), *Documents*, p. 105
208 Abels, 1966, p. 242
209 MacKnight, 1896, vol. 2, p. 127
210 Abels, 1966, p. 243
211 MacKnight, 1896, vol. 2, pp. 128–9
212 Walker, 1989, p. 236
213 Abels, 1966, p. 244
214 MacKnight, 1896, vol. 2, p. 140
215 Abels, 1966, p. 245
216 MacKnight, 1896, vol. 2, p. 148
217 Frankfort Moore, 1914, p. 58
218 Inquiry Belfast riots of 1886, 1887, p. 4
219 *Ibid.*, pp. 4–5
220 Boyd, 1969, p. 127
221 Inquiry Belfast riots 1886, 1887, p. 7
222 *Belfast News-Letter*, 10 June 1886
223 *Ibid.*, 14 June 1886
224 Frankfort Moore, 1914, pp. 62–3
225 MacKnight, 1896, vol. 2, p. 146
226 Walker, 1989, p. 249
227 Jackson, 1989, pp. 125–8
228 MacKnight, 1896, vol. 2, p. 145
229 Walker, 1989, p. 235
230 MacKnight, 1896, vol. 2, p. 202
231 *Ibid.*, p. 205

CHAPTER 10

1 *Belfast News-Letter*, 15 October 1888
2 *Ibid.*
3 *Ibid.*
4 *Ibid.*; *Pictorial World*,
   14 February 1889
5 *Industries of Ireland*, 1891, p. 40
6 *Belfast Directory*, 1887; Clarkson in
   Kennedy and Ollerenshaw (eds),
   1985, p. 155

7   *Belfast Directory*, 1887
8   Bardon, 1982, p. 141
9   *Belfast Directory*, 1896
10 *Industries of Ireland*, 1891, p. 97
11 Bardon, 1982, pp. 132–3
12 *Belfast Directory*, 1887
13 *Industries of Ireland*, 1891, p. 96
14 *Ibid.*, p. 62
15 Bardon, 1985, p. 20
16 Moss and Hume, 1986, p. 67
17 *Ibid.*, p. 77
18 *Belfast Evening Telegraph*, 14 January 1899
19 *Ibid.*
20 Bardon, 1985, p. 20
21 *Industries of Ireland*, 1891, p. 149
22 Mullin, 1986, p. 136
23 Lacy, 1990, p. 196
24 *Ibid.*, pp. 189–92
25 Mitchell, 1989, p. 10
26 Clarkson in Kennedy and Ollerenshaw (eds), 1985, p. 137
27 *Ibid.*, p. 141
28 *Ibid.*, p. 152
29 Dunlop, 1983, pp. 15–25
30 *Industries of Ireland*, 1891, p. 157
31 *Ibid.*, p. 52
32 *Pictorial World*, 1888–9, p. 29
33 Clarkson in Kennedy and Ollerenshaw (eds), 1985, p. 153
34 Lowe, 1880, p. 79
35 Ó Cléirigh, 1990, pp. 9–19
36 McCaughan and Appleby (eds), 1989, p. 121
37 *Ibid.*, p. 127
38 Loughlin, 1986, p. 160
39 *Ibid.*, p. 160
40 Bell, 1988, pp. 202–3, 114, 92, 32, 174, 31–2, 122, 112, 25–6, 103–5, 55, 32, 163–4
41 Loughlin, 1986, p. 146
42 *Ibid.*, p. 126
43 *Ibid.*, pp. 127, 129
44 *Ibid.*, p. 145
45 *Ibid.*, p. 224
46 *Ibid.*, p. 133
47 *Ibid.*, p. 235
48 *Ibid.*, p. 175
49 *Ibid.*, p. 230
50 *Ibid.*, p. 132
51 MacKnight, 1896, vol. 2, pp. 152–3
52 Moss and Hume, 1986, p. 73
53 Boyce, 1990, p. 203
54 Buckland, *Irish Unionism: Two*, 1973, p. xxx
55 Boyce, 1990, p. 204
56 Laffan, 1983, p. 5
57 Loughlin, 1986, p. 163
58 *Ibid.*, p. 164
59 *Ibid.*, p. 147
60 Laffan, 1983, p. 6
61 Abels, 1966, p. 332
62 Kee, 1989, vol. 2, p. 114
63 Abels, 1966, p. 317
64 Loughlin, 1986, p. 242
65 *Ibid.*, p. 246
66 *Belfast News-Letter*, 17 June 1892
67 *The Times*, 18 June 1892
68 *Freeman's Journal*, 18 June 1892
69 *Northern Whig*, 18 June 1892
70 *The Times*, 18 June 1892
71 *Belfast News-Letter*, 18 June 1892
72 *The Times*, 18 June 1892
73 *Northern Whig*, 18 June 1892
74 *Belfast News-Letter* 18 June 1892
75 *Northern Whig*, 18 June 1892
76 Loughlin, 1986, p. 247
77 *Ibid.*, p. 249
78 *Ibid.*
79 *Ibid.*, p. 268
80 MacKnight, 1896, vol. 2, p. 322
81 Buckland (ed.), *Documents*, 1973, p. 273
82 MacKnight, 1896, vol. 2, p. 329
83 Buckland (ed.), *Documents*, 1973, p. 276
84 Buckland, *Irish Unionism: Two*, 1973, p. 19
85 Loughlin, 1986, pp. 252, 273
86 *Ibid.*, p. 268
87 Boyce, 1990, p. 213
88 Jackson, 1989, p. 130
89 Lee, 1973, p. 123
90 Jackson, 1989, p. 80
91 *Ibid.*, p. 58
92 *Ibid.*, p. 59
93 Lyons, 1968, p. 182
94 Murphy, 1981, p. 192
95 Jackson, 1989, pp. 269–70
96 Patterson, 1980, p. 44
97 *Ibid.*, pp. 52–60
98 *Ibid.*, p. 60
99 Jackson, 1989, pp. 161–4
100 *Ibid.*, p. 243
101 *Ibid.*, pp. 128, 139
102 *Ibid.*, p. 128
103 Campbell, 1991, p. 375
104 *Ibid.*, pp. 363–81
105 *Ibid.*, p. 373
106 *Ibid.*, pp. 334–5
107 Boyce, 1990, p. 231
108 O'Farrell, 1971, p. 229
109 *Ibid.*, p. 269
110 *Ibid.*, p. 243
111 *Ibid.*, p. 245
112 Gray, 1985, p. 54

113 Killen, 1985, p. 19
114 Lyons, 1971, p. 260
115 Lyons, 1968, p. 275
116 *Ibid.*, p. 294
117 *Ibid.*, p. 288
118 Buckland, *Irish Unionism: Two*, 1973, p. 42
119 Jackson, 1989, p. 289
120 *Ibid.*, p. 286
121 *Ibid.*, p. 296
122 Buckland (ed.), *Documents*, 1973, p. 204
123 Gray, 1985, p. 62
124 *Ibid.*, p. 56
125 *Ibid.*, p. 72
126 *Ibid.*, pp. 81–2
127 *Ibid.*, pp. 90, 63, 91
128 *Ibid.*, p. 92
129 *Ibid.*, p. 85
130 *Ibid.*, p. 118
131 *Ibid.*, p. 54
132 *Ibid.*, p. 156
133 *Ibid.*, p. 158
134 Larkin, 1965, p. 31
135 Lyons, 1968, p. 308
136 *Ibid.*, p. 309
137 *Ibid.*, p. 311
138 Stewart, 1967, p. 90
139 Jackson, 1989, p. 315
140 *Ibid.*, p. 317
141 *Ibid.*, p. 313
142 *Ibid.*, p. 316
143 *Ibid.*, p. 319
144 Stewart, 1967, p. 48
145 Buckland, 1980, p. 14
146 Stewart, 1967, p. 49
147 Lee, 1989, p. 15
148 Stewart, 1967, p. 49
149 *Ibid.*, p. 53
150 *Ibid.*, p. 56
151 *Ibid.*, p. 55
152 *Ibid.*, p. 56
153 Lee, 1989, p. 13
154 Stewart, 1967, p. 58
155 Kee, 1989, vol. 2, p. 175
156 Laffan, 1983, p. 24
157 Buckland, *Irish Unionism: Two*, 1973, p. 85
158 *Belfast News-Letter*, 30 September 1912
159 *Ibid.*
160 Stewart, 1967, p. 62
161 Bardon, 1985, p. 22
162 Stewart, 1967, p. 66
163 *Irish News, Freeman's Journal* and *Manchester Guardian*, 30 September 1912; Stewart, 1967, p. 65
164 Stewart, 1967, p. 67
165 Murphy, 1981, p. 197
166 *Ibid.*, p. 196
167 McMinn, 1985, p. xli
168 *Ibid.*, pp. li–lii
169 *Ibid.*, p. lvi
170 Stewart, 1967, p. 59
171 Kee, 1989, vol. 2, p. 183
172 Stewart, 1967, p. 107
173 *Ibid.*, pp. 141, 150–1
174 Buckland, *Irish Unionism: Two*, 1973, p. 52
175 Martin in Martin and Byrne (eds), 1973, p. 121
176 Laffan, 1983, p. 31
177 Livingstone, 1969, p. 272
178 Martin in Martin and Byrne (eds), 1973, p. 171
179 *Ibid.*, p. 174
180 Stewart, 1967, p. 177
181 *Ibid.*, pp. 176–95
182 Buckland (ed.), *Documents*, 1973, p. 249
183 *Ibid.*, p. 252
184 *Ibid.*, p. 257
185 *Ibid.*, p. 259
186 Livingstone, 1980, p. 367
187 *Irish News*, 12 November 1913
188 Murphy, 1981, p. 210
189 Brett, 1967, p. 63
190 Buckland, *Irish Unionism: Two*, 1973, p. 99
191 Stewart, 1967, p. 229
192 *Ibid.*, p. 223
193 *Ibid.*, p. 227
194 Bardon, 1982, p. 183
195 Laffan, 1983, p. 46
196 *Irish News*, 6 August 1914
197 *Ibid.*
198 *Ibid.*, 10 August 1914
199 Stewart, 1981, p. 94
200 *Ibid.*, pp. 99, 94
201 *Ibid.*, p. 95
202 Lyons, 1971, p. 328
203 PRONI, D 1231/K/10/1–16
204 Stewart, 1981, p. 95
205 Laffan, 1983, p. 47
206 Martin in *Clogher Record*, vol. 12, no. 2 (1986), p. 201
207 *Ibid.*, p. 199
208 *Ibid.*, p. 194
209 *Ibid.*, p. 208
210 Buckland, *Irish Unionism: Two*, 1973, p. 105
211 Martin in *Clogher Record*, vol. 12, no. 2 (1986), p. 208
212 Lee, 1989, p. 30
213 Beckett, 1966, p. 441
214 Buckland, *Irish Unionism: Two*, 1973, p. 106

215 Buckland (ed.), *Documents*, 1973, p. 406
216 Orr, 1987, p. 164
217 *Ibid.*, p. 178
218 *Ibid.*, p. 171
219 Bardon, 1982, p. 186, letter lent to author by Kathleen Page
220 PRONI, D 2109/13
221 Mitchell, 1989, p. 37
222 Moss and Hume, 1986, pp. 175–205; Johnson in Kennedy and Ollerenshaw (eds), 1985, pp. 186–7
223 Johnson in Kennedy and Ollerenshaw (eds), 1985, pp. 185–6
224 Moss and Hume, 1986, p. 207
225 Buckland, *Irish Unionism: Two*, 1973, p. 109
226 Buckland (ed.), *Documents*, 1973, p. 423
227 Buckland, *Irish Unionism: Two*, 1973, p. 110
228 Farrell, 1971, p. 10
229 Bowman, 1982, p. 35
230 Kee, 1989, vol. 3, p. 47
231 Barton, 1988, p. 26
232 *Belfast News-Letter*, 12 November 1918; *Irish News*, 12 November 1918; *Belfast Telegraph*, 11 November 1918
233 Boyce, 1990, p. 261
234 Barton, 1988, p. 30
235 Farrell, 1971, p. 50
236 *Ibid.*, p. 51
237 Johnson in Kennedy and Ollerenshaw (eds), 1985, pp. 186–8
238 Moss and Hume, 1986, p. 206
239 Patterson, 1980, p. 105
240 Moss and Hume, 1986, pp. 210–24; Johnson in Kennedy and Ollerenshaw (eds), 1985, p. 188
241 de Paor, 1970, p. 101

CHAPTER 11

1 Marwick, 1970, p. 145
2 Kee, 1989, vol. 3, p. 70
3 Barton, 1988, p. 28
4 Murphy, 1981, p. 253
5 Lacy, 1990, pp. 227–8
6 *Ibid.*, p. 228
7 Farrell, 1983, pp. 19–20; Murphy, 1981, p. 255
8 Barton, 1988, p. 32
9 Farrell, 1983, pp. 16–17
10 *Ibid.*, p. 19; Hezlet, 1972, p. 12
11 Barton, 1988, p. 32
12 Farrell, 1976, p. 27
13 *Ibid.*, p. 28
14 Buckland (ed.), *Documents*, 1973, pp. 444–5

15 Bardon, 1985, p. 24
16 *Ibid.*
17 *Ibid.*
18 Buckland, *Irish Unionism: Two*, 1973, p. 123; Farrell, 1976, p. 31
19 Middlemas, 1971, p. 38
20 Farrell, 1983, p. 15
21 *Ibid.*, p. 21
22 *Ibid.*, p. 23
23 *Ibid.*
24 *Ibid.*, pp. 32–3
25 *Ibid.*, p. 49
26 *Ibid.*, p. 48
27 Laffan, 1983, p. 64
28 *Ibid.*
29 Buckland, *Irish Unionism: Two*, 1973, p. 114
30 *Ibid.*, p. 117; Laffan, 1983, p. 65
31 Buckland, *Irish Unionism: Two*, 1973, pp. 118–21
32 Laffan, 1983, p. 64
33 Buckland, *Irish Unionism: Two*, 1973, p. 129
34 *Ibid.*, pp. 130–1
35 Farrell, 1976, p. 37
36 Buckland, *Irish Unionism: Two*, 1973, p. 129
37 Bowman, 1982, p. 47
38 Taylor, 1965, p. 155
39 Longford, 1962, p. 61
40 Middlemas, 1971, p. 78
41 Buckland (ed.), *Documents*, 1973, p. 455
42 Middlemas, 1971, p. 78
43 Buckland (ed.), *Documents*, 1973, p. 456
44 Farrell, 1976, p. 41
45 Buckland, *Irish Unionism: Two*, 1973, p. 146
46 Middlemas, 1971, p. 90
47 Buckland, *Irish Unionism: Two*, 1973, p. 147
48 Middlemas, 1971, p. xxiii
49 *Ibid.*, p. 137
50 Buckland, *Irish Unionism: Two*, 1973, p. 148
51 Middlemas, 1971, p. 154
52 Buckland, *Irish Unionism: Two*, 1973, p. 149
53 *Ibid.*
54 Pakenham, 1962 [1st edition 1935], p. 230; Churchill, 1929, p. 305
55 Pakenham, 1962 [1st edition 1935], p. 241
56 Middlemas, 1971, p. 187
57 *Ibid.*, p. 190
58 Farrell, 1976, p. 44
59 Churchill, 1929, p. 318

60   Farrell, 1976, p. 45
61   *Ibid.*, p. 44
62   Bowman, 1982, p. 69
63   Farrell, 1976, p. 48
64   Kennedy, 1988, pp. 73–4; Farrell, 1983, p. 92
65   Shea, 1981, pp. 78–9
66   Bardon, 1982, p. 199
67   Buckland, *Irish Unionism: Two*, 1973, p. 167
68   Farrell, 1976, p. 51; Kennedy, 1988, p. 76
69   Farrell, 1983, pp. 109–10
70   *Ibid.*, p. 114
71   *Parliamentary Debates* (Northern Ireland House of Commons), vol. 2, col. 101 on 21 March 1922 and vol. 2, col. 359 on 5 April 1922
72   Bardon, 1982, p. 201
73   Farrell, 1976, p. 50
74   *Parliamentary Debates* (Northern Ireland House of Commons), vol. 2, col. 91 on 21 March 1922
75   Buckland, *Irish Unionism: Two*, 1973, p. 167
76   Farrell, 1976, p. 57
77   Kennedy, 1988, p. 81
78   *Ibid.*, p. 76
79   Farrell, 1983, pp. 132–3
80   Middlemas, 1971, p. 210
81   *Ibid.*, p. 212
82   Bew, Gibbon and Patterson, 1979, p. 66
83   Neeson, 1969, pp. 204, 323
84   Longford and O'Neill, 1970, p. 222
85   Farrell, 1976, p. 62
86   de Vere White, 1948, p. 83
87   Middlemas, 1971, p. 186
88   Buckland, *Irish Unionism: Two*, 1973, p. 146
89   Middlemas, 1971, p. 195
90   Chambers, 1983, p. 239
91   Buckland, 1979, p. 13; Middlemas, 1971, p. 159
92   Bew, Gibbon and Patterson, 1979, p. 77
93   Buckland, 1979, p. 23
94   *Ibid.*
95   Farrell, 1976, p. 90
96   Bew, Gibbon and Patterson, 1979, p. 77
97   Buckland, 1979, p. 22
98   Buckland (ed.), *Documents*, 1973, p. 205
99   Shea, 1981, p. 113
100 Buckland, 1979, p. 21
101 Buckland, *Irish Unionism: Two*, 1973, p. 152
102 Farrell, 1976, p. 82
103 Buckland, 1979, p. 232
104 *Ibid.*, p. 268
105 *Ibid.*, p. 269
106 *Ibid.*, p. 226
107 Akenson, 1973, p. 41
108 *Ibid.*, p. 66
109 *Ibid.*, p. 52
110 Buckland, 1979, p. 250
111 Akenson, 1973, p. 76
112 *Ibid.*, pp. 79, 82
113 *Ibid.*, p. 108
114 *Ibid.*, p. 102
115 *Ibid.*, p. 114
116 Buckland, 1979, p. 267
117 Middlemas, 1971, p. 221
118 *Ibid.*, p. 226
119 Farrell, 1983, pp. 222–4
120 Laffan, 1983, p. 102
121 Shea, 1981, p. 95
122 Hand, 1969, p. 201
123 *Ibid.*, p. 231
124 Farrell, 1983, p. 239
125 Farrell, 1976, p. 103
126 Hand in Martin and Byrne (eds), 1973, pp. 237–8
127 Middlemas, 1971, p. 236
128 Hand, 1969, p. xix
129 *Ibid.*, p. xviii
130 Hand in Martin and Byrne (eds), 1973, p. 274; Farrell, 1983, p. 243
131 Laffan, 1983, p. 101
132 *Evening Herald* (Dublin), 19 November 1925
133 Buckland, *Irish Unionism: Two*, 1973, p. 174
134 Laffan, 1983, p. 105; Farrell, 1983, p. 249
135 Mansergh, 1936, p. 248
136 Buckland, 1979, p. 231
137 *Ibid.*, p. 235
138 *Ibid.*
139 Mansergh, 1936, p. 134; Farrell, 1976, p. 110
140 Farrell, 1976, p. 118
141 Moore, 1987, p. 36
142 Buckland, 1979, p. 17
143 Ervine, 1949, p. 526
144 Bardon, 1982, p. 225
145 Lyons, 1971, p. 682
146 Buckland, 1979, p. 3
147 *Ibid.*, pp. 37–8
148 Bardon, 1982, p. 192
149 Clark, 1982, p. 94
150 Buckland, 1979, p. 54
151 Johnson in Kennedy and Ollerenshaw (eds), 1985, p. 196
152 Moss and Hume, 1986, p. 243

153 Lacy, 1990, p. 188
154 Geary and Johnson in *Irish Economic and Social History*, vol. 16 (1989), p. 57
155 Moss and Hume, 1986, p. 266
156 Buckland, 1979, p. 130
157 *Ibid.*, p. 58
158 Johnson in Roebuck (ed.), 1981, p. 244
159 *Ibid.*, p. 241
160 *Ibid.*
161 Buckland, 1979, p. 124
162 *Ibid.*
163 *Ibid.*, p. 150
164 *Ibid.*, p. 153
165 Shea, 1981, p. 117
166 Devlin, 1981, p. 98
167 Buckland, 1979, p. 158
168 Devlin, 1981, p. 81
169 *Ibid.*, p. 112
170 Moss and Hume, 1986, p. 292
171 *Belfast News-Letter*, 2 October 1932
172 *Parliamentary Debates* (Northern Ireland House of Commons), vol. 14, col. 553 on 30 September 1932
173 Munck and Rolston, 1987, p. 22
174 *The Times*, 12 October 1932
175 *Belfast Telegraph*, 11 October 1932
176 Munck and Rolston, 1987, p. 31
177 *Ibid.*
178 Bardon, 1982, p. 220
179 Buckland, 1979, p. 53
180 Munck and Rolston, 1987, p. 64
181 *Ibid.*, p. 65
182 *Ibid.*
183 McAughtry, 1977, p. 26
184 Munck and Rolston, 1987, p. 71
185 Bardon, 1982, p. 222
186 Munck and Rolston, 1987, p. 70
187 *Ibid.*, p. 71
188 *Ibid.*, p. 74
189 *Ibid.*, p. 75
190 Barton, 1989, p. 12
191 Munck and Rolston, 1987, p. 71
192 Brett, 1986, p. 23
193 Bardon, 1982, p. 209
194 Munck and Rolston, 1987, p. 66
195 Barton, 1989, p. 8
196 Buckland, 1979, p. 164
197 Brett, 1986, p. 24
198 Buckland, 1979, p. 83
199 Mansergh, 1936, p. 207
200 Buckland, 1979, p. 97
201 *Ibid.*, pp. 87–8
202 *Ibid.*, p. 102
203 Longford and O'Neill, 1970, p. 275
204 Barton, 1988, p. 83
205 Kennedy, 1988, p. 164
206 *Ibid.*, p. 165
207 *Ibid.*, p. 191
208 Bowman, 1982, p. 109
209 Barton, 1988, p. 81
210 Campbell, 1941, p. 316
211 *Ibid.*, p. 317
212 Barton, 1988, p. 81
213 Kennedy, 1988, p. 165
214 Farrell, 1976, p. 136
215 *Ibid.*, p. 90; Barton, 1988, p. 98
216 Barton, 1988, p. 79
217 *Ibid.*, p. 80
218 *Ibid.*, p. 78
219 *Parliamentary Debates* (Northern Ireland House of Commons), vol. 16, cols 1091, 1095
220 Kennedy in MacManus (ed.), 1967, p. 145
221 Farrell, 1976, p. 138
222 Bardon, 1982, p. 228
223 *Northern Whig*, 13 July 1935
224 *Belfast News-Letter*, 13 July 1935
225 *Irish News*, 13 July 1935
226 *The Times*, 15 July 1935
227 Bardon, 1982, p. 230
228 Farrell, 1976, p. 142
229 Bowman, 1982, p. 155
230 *Ibid.*, p. 148
231 *Ibid.*, p. 151
232 Kennedy, 1988, p. 173
233 *Ibid.*, p. 174
234 Bowman, 1982, p. 160
235 *Daily Express*, 13 January 1938
236 Bardon, 1982, pp. 231–2
237 *Ibid.*, p. 232
238 Bowman, 1982, p. 181
239 Barton, 1988, p. 93
240 *Belfast News-Letter*, bicentenary supplement, 1 September 1937
241 *Ibid.*
242 Clark, 1982, p. 115
243 Moss and Hume, 1986, p. 313
244 Johnson in Roebuck (ed.), 1981, p. 201
245 PRONI, COM 17/3/1
246 PRONI, COM 17/3/2

CHAPTER 12

1 Fisk, 1983, p. 101
2 Barton, 1989, p. 27
3 Fisk, 1983, p. 447
4 Barton, 1988, p. 149
5 Fisk, 1983, p. 476
6 Farrell, 1976, pp. 152–4
7 Fisk, 1983, p. 94
8 *Ibid.*
9 *Ibid.*, p. 96
10 Barton, 1989, p. 42

11   *Ibid.*, p. 43
12   Fisk, 1983, pp. 102–3
13   *Ibid.*, p. 57
14   Barton, 1989, p. 40
15   Bowman, 1982, p. 180
16   Barton, 1989, p. 40
17   Barton, 1988, p. 141
18   *Ibid.*, p. 137
19   *Ibid.*, p. 148
20   Fisk, 1983, pp. 112–16
21   *Ibid.*, p. 116
22   Carroll, 1975, p. 26
23   *Ibid.*, p. 24
24   *Ibid.*, p. 12
25   Fisk, 1983, p. 301
26   *Ibid.*, p. 185
27   *Ibid.*, p. 193
28   *Ibid.*, p. 198
29   *Ibid.*, p. 195
30   *Ibid.*, p. 207
31   *Ibid.*, p. 208
32   *Ibid.*, p. 210
33   *Ibid.*, p. 212
34   Bardon, 1982, p. 237
35   Fisk, 1983, p. 150
36   *Ibid.*, p. 142
37   *Ibid.*, p. 144
38   *Ibid.*, p. 145
39   Blake, 1956, p. 311
40   Farrell, 1976, p. 158
41   Barton, 1988, p. 152
42   *Ibid.*, p. 153
43   Buckland, 1980, pp. 123–5
44   Barton, 1988, p. 168
45   *Ibid.*, p. 172
46   *Ibid.*, p. 156
47   *Ibid.*, pp. 158–9
48   Barton, 1989, p. 31
49   *Ibid.*, p. 36
50   Fisk, 1983, p. 478
51   Barton, 1989, p. 28
52   *Ibid.*, p. 29
53   *Ibid.*, p. 55
54   Blake, 1956, p. 168
55   Barton, 1989, p. 81
56   Bardon, 1985, p. 26
57   Barton, 1989, p. 126
58   *Ibid.*, p. 107
59   *Ibid.*, p. 120
60   *Ibid.*, p. 129
61   Bardon, 1982, p. 239
62   Fisk, 1983, p. 495
63   Barton, 1989, pp. 170–2
64   Bardon, 1985, p. 26
65   *Ibid.*
66   Barton, 1989, p. 148
67   *Ibid.*, p. 139
68   *Ibid.*, p. 151
69   Bardon, 1985, p. 26
70   Barton, 1989, p. 141
71   Bardon, 1985, p. 26
72   Barton, 1989, p. 161
73   *Ibid.*, p. 178
74   *Ibid.*, p. 185
75   Fisk, 1983, p. 500
76   Barton, 1989, p. 206
77   *Ibid.*, p. 202
78   *Ibid.*, p. 212
79   *Ibid.*, p. 164
80   *Ibid.*, pp. 159–60
81   *Ibid.*, p. 166
82   *Ibid.*, pp. 166–7
83   *Ibid.*, p. 163
84   *Ibid.*, p. 232
85   Fisk, 1983, p. 507
86   Barton, 1989, p. 235
87   Bardon, 1982, p. 241
88   *Parliamentary Debates* (Northern Ireland House of Commons), vol. 24, col. 828
89   Lacy, 1990, pp. 238–9
90   Barton, 1989, p. 192
91   *Ibid.*, p. 272
92   *Belfast Telegraph*, 27 January 1942; Barton, 1989, p. 272
93   Lacy, 1990, pp. 240–1
94   Barton, 1989, pp. 274–5
95   *Ibid.*, p. 276
96   Canavan, 1989, p. 212
97   Lacy, 1990, p. 239
98   *Ibid.*, p. 241
99   Barton, 1989, p. 277
100 Lacy, 1990, p. 241
101 Barton, 1989, p. 277
102 Canavan, 1989, p. 212
103 Barton, 1988, pp. 199–200
104 *Ibid.*, p. 219
105 *Ibid.*, pp. 202–3
106 *Ibid.*, p. 205
107 *Ibid.*, p. 212
108 *Ibid.*, p. 218
109 *Ibid.*, p. 229
110 Moss and Hume, 1986, p. 336
111 *Ibid.*, p. 347
112 Barton, 1989, p. 258
113 *Ibid.*, p. 260
114 Clark, 1982, p. 124
115 Barton, 1989, pp. 283–4
116 *Ibid.*, p. 284
117 Farrell, 1976, p. 173
118 Bardon, 1982, p. 236; Bowyer Bell, 1972 [1st edition 1970], pp. 237–56
119 Farrell, 1976, p. 165
120 *Ibid.*, p. 166
121 *Ibid.*, p. 167
122 Carroll, 1975, p. 160

123 Fisk, 1983, p. 536
124 Barton, 1989, p. 294
125 *Ibid.*, p. 295
126 Bardon, 1982, p. 246
127 *Belfast Telegraph*, 9 May 1945
128 Barton, 1989, p. 296
129 Lacy, 1990, p. 242
130 Carroll, 1975, p. 161; Fisk, 1983, p. 537
131 Carroll, 1975, p. 163
132 Barton, 1989, p. 288

CHAPTER 13

1 *Belfast News-Letter*, 3 June 1941
2 Wichert, 1991, p. 41
3 Barton, 1989, p. 287
4 Bardon, 1982, p. 247
5 *Ibid.*
6 Harkness, 1983, p. 106
7 *Ibid.*, p. 107
8 *Ibid.*, p. 108
9 Buckland, 1981, p. 86
10 Wichert, 1991, p. 26
11 Barton, 1989, p. 157
12 *Ibid.*, p. 222
13 Buckland, 1981, p. 91
14 Oliver, 1978, p. 19
15 Brett, 1986, p. 26
16 Bardon, 1982, p. 249
17 Brett, 1986, p. 27
18 Bardon, 1982, p. 250
19 Brett, 1986, p. 26
20 *Ibid.*, p. 27
21 Bardon, 1982, p. 253
22 Akenson, 1973, p. 168
23 *Ibid.*, p. 170
24 *Belfast News-Letter*, 9 November 1946
25 Akenson, 1973, p. 178
26 Shea, 1981, p. 162
27 Akenson, 1973, pp. 184, 215
28 Bardon, 1982, p. 248
29 *Ibid.*, p. 251
30 Whyte, 1971, p. 143
31 Farrell, 1976, p. 179
32 Bowman, 1982, pp. 261–2
33 *Ibid.*, p. 259
34 *Ibid.*, p. 260
35 *Ibid.*, p. 262
36 *Ibid.*, p. 260
37 *Ibid.*, pp. 267, 269
38 Farrell, 1976, p. 183
39 Bowman, 1982, p. 270
40 Farrell, 1976, p. 184
41 *Belfast Telegraph*, 31 January 1949
42 Farrell, 1976, pp. 184, 187
43 Bardon, 1982, p. 257
44 Farrell, 1976, p. 186
45 Bardon, 1982, p. 258
46 Farrell, 1976, p. 187
47 Bowman, 1982, p. 271
48 *Ibid.*, p. 273
49 Whyte, 1971, p. 199
50 *Ibid.*, p. 218
51 *Ibid.*, p. 231
52 Bowman, 1982, p. 255
53 *Ibid.*
54 *Ibid.*, p. 256
55 Farrell, 1976, p. 205
56 Bowyer Bell, 1972 [1st edition 1970], p. 305
57 *Ibid.*, p. 309
58 *Ibid.*, p. 343
59 Bowman, 1982, p. 291
60 *Ibid.*, p. 292
61 Bowyer Bell, 1972 [1st edition 1970], p. 393
62 Buckland, 1981, p. 105
63 Farrell, 1976, p. 204
64 *Ibid.*, pp. 207–8
65 *Ibid.*, p. 222
66 *Ibid.*, p. 221
67 Buckland, 1981, p. 104
68 Harbinson, 1973, pp. 43–4
69 Buckland, 1981, p. 102
70 Farrell, 1976, p. 194
71 Harkness, 1983, p. 133
72 *Belfast Telegraph*, 8 October 1951
73 Bardon, 1982, pp. 259–60
74 *Belfast Telegraph*, 3 January 1952
75 Bardon, 1982, p. 261
76 Geary and Johnson in *Irish Economic and Social History*, vol. 16 (1989), pp. 59–60; Moss and Hume, 1986, pp. 373–5
77 Bardon, 1982, p. 261
78 Moss and Hume, 1986, p. 378
79 *Ibid.*, p. 445
80 Geary and Johnson in *Irish Economic and Social History*, vol. 16 (1989), pp. 60–1
81 Moss and Hume, 1986, p. 400
82 Geary and Johnson in *Irish Economic and Social History*, vol. 16 (1989), p. 61
83 Clark, 1982, p. 129
84 Kennedy, 1989, p. 11
85 *Ibid.*
86 Clark, 1982, p. 138
87 *Ibid.*, p. 140
88 Bardon, 1982, pp. 262–3
89 Wichert, 1991, pp. 58–9
90 Corlett, 1981, pp. 81–91
91 Wichert, 1991, p. 63
92 *Ibid.*, pp. 50, 60, 65
93 Harkness, 1983, p. 134
94 Kennedy, 1989, p. 9

95   *Ibid.*, pp. 6–10
96   O'Neill, 1969, p. 32
97   Purdie, 1990, p. 13
98   *Ibid.*, p. 10
99   *Ibid.*, p. 12
100 Lee, 1989, p. 414
101 Bowman, 1982, p. 76
102 Whyte in Gallagher and O'Connell (eds), 1983, p. 2
103 Lee, 1989, p. 414

CHAPTER 14

1   Buckland, 1981, p. 110
2   Wichert, 1991, p. 86
3   Longford and McHardy, 1981, p. 104
4   Harkness, 1983, p. 138
5   *Ibid.*, p. 140
6   Lee, 1989, p. 415
7   Longford and McHardy, 1981, p. 105
8   Bew, Gibbon and Patterson, 1979, p. 153
9   Bardon, 1982, p. 270
10   Wilson, 1989, p. 100
11   White, 1984, pp. 38–9
12   Buckland, 1981, p. 114
13   Kennedy, 1989, pp. 16–17
14   *Ibid.*, pp. 14–16
15   Buckland, 1981, p. 113
16   Wichert, 1991, p. 89
17   Bardon, 1982, p. 267
18   Moss and Hume, 1986, p. 438
19   *Ibid.*, p. 417
20   *Ibid.*, pp. 435–8
21   Buckland, 1981, p. 114
22   Kennedy, 1989, pp. 14–16
23   Lee, 1989, pp. 379, 359
24   Kennedy, 1989, p. 16
25   Lee, 1989, p. 367
26   Bardon, 1982, pp. 272–3. Author interviewed O'Neill and Faulkner in 1975 for *O'Neill Meets Lemass*, BBC Radio Ulster, 1976; also, correspondence between Douglas Carson and Whitaker lent to author.
27   Maloney and Pollak, 1986, p. 119
28   *Ibid.*, p. 111
29   Bardon, 1982, p. 271
30   Farrell, 1976, p. 240
31   Maloney and Pollak, 1986, p. 77
32   Wichert, 1991, pp. 91–2
33   Bew and Patterson, 1985, p. 11
34   *Ibid.*, p. 13
35   Bardon, 1982, p. 274
36   Maloney and Pollak, 1986, p. 132
37   Hall, 1988, p. 2
38   Farrell, 1976, p. 236

39   Maloney and Pollak, 1986, p. 144
40   Wichert, 1991, p. 91
41   Maloney and Pollak, 1986, photograph facing p. 121
42   Wichert, 1991, p. 91
43   McCluskey, 1989, pp. 9–13
44   *Ibid.*, p. 9
45   *Ibid.*, p. 10
46   Farrell, 1976, p. 89
47   *Ibid.*, p. 85
48   Whyte in Gallagher and O'Connell (eds), 1983, pp. 4–5
49   *Ibid.*, p. 5
50   *Ibid.*, p. 8
51   *Ibid.*, p. 9
52   Barritt and Carter, 1972, p. 96
53   Shea, 1981, p. 112
54   *Ibid.*, p. 142
55   *Ibid.*, p. 177
56   Whyte in Gallagher and O'Connell (eds), 1983, pp. 9–10
57   Barritt and Carter, 1972, p. 101
58   Bardon, 1982, p. 280
59   Whyte in Gallagher and O'Connell (eds), 1983, p. 20
60   *Ibid.*, p. 19
61   Purdie, 1990, pp. 84–5
62   *Ibid.*, p. 91
63   McCluskey, 1989, pp. 15–16
64   *Ibid.*, p. 17
65   Lee, 1989, p. 418
66   Nelson, 1984, p. 72
67   Quoted in Purdie, 1990, p. 9
68   Bew, Gibbon and Patterson, 1979, p. 165
69   *Ibid.*, pp. 166–7
70   *Ibid.*, p. 170
71   Purdie, 1990, p. 108
72   *Ibid.*, p. 111
73   *Ibid.*, p. 113
74   McCluskey, 1989, p. 32
75   *Ibid.*, p. 19
76   Purdie, 1990, p. 161
77   *Ibid.*, p. 160
78   *Ibid.*, p. 161
79   *Ibid.*, p. 165
80   *Ibid.*, p. 166
81   *Ibid.*, pp. 172–5
82   White, 1984, p. 29
83   *Ibid.*, p. 31
84   *Ibid.*, p. 43
85   *Ibid.*, p. 45
86   *Ibid.*, p. 51
87   Purdie, 1990, p. 181
88   *Ibid.*, p. 182
89   *Ibid.*, p. 186
90   de Paor, 1970, p. 166
91   McCluskey, 1989, pp. 104–5

92 Maloney and Pollak, 1986, p. 155
93 McCluskey, 1989, p. 107
94 Purdie, 1990, p. 136
95 Maloney and Pollak, 1986, p. 156
96 Lee, 1989, p. 420
97 Purdie, 1990, p. 138
98 de Paor, 1970, p. 172
99 McCluskey, 1989, pp. 110–11
100 Longford and McHardy, 1981, p. 113
101 Purdie, 1990, p. 140
102 *Ibid.*, p. 142
103 *Ibid.*, p. 143
104 White, 1984, p. 63
105 Purdie, 1990, pp. 147–8
106 Arthur, 1974, p. 29
107 Purdie, 1990, p. 207
108 Arthur, 1974, p. 30
109 *Ibid.*, p. 23
110 White, 1984, p. 65
111 *Ibid.*, p. 68
112 *Ibid.*
113 Maloney and Pollak, 1986, p. 162
114 *Ibid.*, p. 163
115 *Ibid.*, p. 164
116 O'Neill, 1969, pp. 140, 145
117 Hall, 1988, p. 8
118 Arthur, 1974, p. 38
119 *Ibid.*, p. 40
120 Egan and McCormack, 1969, p. 2
121 *Ibid.*, p. 3
122 *Ibid.*, p. 14
123 *Ibid.*, p. 33
124 *Ibid.*, p. 46
125 *Ibid.*, pp. 59–60
126 White, 1984, p. 70
127 Egan and McCormack, 1969, p. 60
128 Buckland, 1981, p. 123
129 Harkness, 1983, p. 155
130 Hall, 1988, p. 12
131 Maloney and Pollak, 1986, p. 179
132 O'Neill, 1969, p. 200
133 Hall, 1988, p. 12
134 Bew and Patterson, 1985, p. 19
135 Ryder, 1989, p. 107
136 *Ibid.*, p. 108
137 Hall, 1988, p. 15
138 White, 1984, p. 79
139 Longford and McHardy, 1981, p. 120
140 Hamill, 1985, p. 3
141 Ryder, 1989, p. 111
142 Hamill, 1985, p. 4
143 *Ibid.*, p. 5
144 White, 1984, p. 82
145 *Ibid.*, p. 84
146 *Ibid.*, p. 85
147 McClean, 1983, p. 76
148 Hamill, 1985, p. 7
149 *Ibid.*, p. 13
150 Bardon, 1982, p. 278
151 *Ibid.*, p. 282
152 *Ibid.*, p. 283
153 Hamill, 1985, p. 17
154 Ryder, 1989, pp. 113–14; Hamill, 1985, pp. 14, 20
155 Hamill, 1985, p. 21
156 Farrell, 1976, p. 264; Arthur and Jeffery, 1988, p. 11
157 Bew, Gibbon and Patterson, 1979, p. 181
158 *Ibid.*, p. 176
159 *Ibid.*, p. 180
160 White, 1984, p. 90
161 *Ibid.*, p. 91
162 Bew, Gibbon and Patterson, 1979, p. 182
163 Bardon, 1982, p. 283
164 Hamill, 1985, p. 20
165 Bishop and Mallie, 1989, p. 90
166 *Ibid.*, p. 117
167 *Ibid.*, p. 122
168 *Ibid.*, pp. 136–7
169 Sacks, 1976, p. 59
170 *Sunday Times* Insight Team, 1972, p. 187
171 *Ibid.*, p. 190
172 Bishop and Mallie, 1989, p. 149; *Sunday Times* Insight Team, 1972, pp. 203–4
173 *Sunday Times* Insight Team, 1972, p. 202
174 Hamill, 1985, p. 35
175 *Sunday Times* Insight Team, 1972, p. 221
176 Hamill, 1985, p. 36
177 Hall, 1988, p. 23
178 Bew, Gibbon and Patterson, 1979, p. 183
179 Maloney and Pollak, 1986, p. 201
180 Hamill, 1985, p. 44
181 *Ibid.*, p. 46
182 *Ibid.*, p. 50
183 Deutsch and Magowan, 1973, vol. 1, p. 98
184 *Ibid.*, p. 105
185 *Ibid.*, p. 107
186 *Ibid.*, pp. 110–18
187 McGuffin, 1973, pp. 86–7
188 Deutsch and Magowan, 1973, vol. 1, p. 118
189 Ryder, 1989, p. 122
190 McGuffin, 1973, p. 87
191 Bardon, 1982, p. 285
192 McGuffin, 1973, pp. 119–25
193 Hamill, 1985, p. 63

194 Hall, 1988, p. 29
195 Hamill, 1985, p. 65
196 Bardon, 1982, p. 287
197 Hall, 1988, p. 30
198 *Ibid.*, p. 31
199 McClean, 1983, p. 125
200 Hamill, 1985, pp. 87–9
201 *Ibid.*, p. 90
202 McClean, 1983, p. 133
203 Hall, 1988, p. 31
204 Hamill, 1985, p. 93
205 Bishop and Mallie, 1989, p. 209; White, 1984, p. 120
206 Bardon, 1982, p. 287
207 Hall, 1988, p. 33
208 Bew, Gibbon and Patterson, 1979, p. 183
209 Longford and McHardy, 1981, p. 149

CHAPTER 15

1 *Calendar of State Papers*, Henry VIII, Correspondence, vol. 3, p. 11
2 Teacher's Notes: BBC Radio *Modern Irish History*, autumn 1981, p. 15
3 White, 1984, p. 124
4 Bishop and Mallie, 1989, p. 219; White, 1984, p. 125
5 Bishop and Mallie, 1989, p. 220
6 *Ibid.*, pp. 222–3
7 Longford and McHardy, 1981, p. 152
8 Bishop and Mallie, 1989, p. 238
9 White, 1984, p. 129
10 *Ibid.*, p. 130
11 Hall, 1988, p. 37
12 Hamill, 1985, p. 109
13 White, 1984, p. 131; Bishop and Mallie, 1989, pp. 226–8
14 *Irish News*, 21 July 1972
15 Barzilay, 1973, vol. 1, p. 83
16 *Belfast Telegraph*, 22 July 1972
17 Bardon, 1985, p. 28
18 *Belfast Telegraph*, 22 July 1972
19 McCreary, 1976, p. 244
20 Bardon, 1985, p. 28
21 Hamill, 1985, p. 112
22 *Ibid.*, p. 115
23 Flackes, 1980, p. 103
24 Flackes and Elliott, 1988, p. 412
25 Farrell, 1976, p. 299
26 White, 1984, p. 136
27 Farrell, 1976, p. 300
28 *Ibid.*, p. 302
29 Bell in Bell, Johnstone and Wilson (eds), 1991, pp. 156–8; Farrell, 1976, pp. 304–5
30 White, 1984, p. 138
31 O'Leary, Elliott and Wilford, 1988, pp. 60–1
32 Farrell, 1976, p. 307
33 *Ibid.*, pp. 307–9
34 Bew and Patterson, 1985, p. 57
35 *Ibid.*
36 *Ibid.*, pp. 57–9
37 White, 1984, p. 133
38 Farrell, 1976, p. 310; Hall, 1988, p. 46; Bell in Bell, Johnstone and Wilson (eds), 1991, p. 161
39 White, 1984, p. 147
40 *Ibid.*, p. 145
41 FitzGerald, 1991, p. 215
42 White, 1984, p. 151
43 FitzGerald, 1991, p. 215
44 Bell in Bell, Johnstone and Wilson (eds), 1991, p. 161; Hall, 1988, p. 47
45 Farrell, 1976, p. 315
46 Maloney and Pollak, 1986, p. 355
47 Fisk, 1975, p. 48
48 *Ibid.*, p. 19
49 *Ibid.*, p. 58
50 *Ibid.*, p. 62
51 *Ibid.*, p. 84
52 *Ibid.*, p. 145
53 *Ibid.*
54 Hamill, 1985, p. 149
55 Buckland, 1981, p. 171
56 Fisk, 1975, p. 209
57 Hamill, 1985, p. 153
58 Fisk, 1975, p. 140
59 *Ibid.*, p. 224
60 *Ibid.*, p. 13
61 *Ibid.*, p. 221
62 *Ibid.*, p. 187
63 Arthur and Jeffery, 1988, pp. 12–14
64 O'Leary, Elliott and Wilford, 1988, p. 38
65 *Ibid.*, p. 39
66 *Ibid.*, pp. 41–2
67 White, 1984, p. 179
68 Boyle in Darby and Williamson (eds), 1978, p. 160
69 Flackes, 1980, pp. 85–6
70 Gaffikin and Morrissey, 1990, p. 39
71 Hadfield in Roche and Barton (eds), 1991, p. 140
72 Brett, 1986, p. 11
73 *Ibid.*, p. 66
74 *Ibid.*, p. 65
75 Brett, 1986, pp. 46, 50; Bardon, 1982, p. 294
76 Brett, 1986, p. 50
77 *Ibid.*, p. 41
78 *Ibid.*, caption to plate 29
79 Bardon, 1982, p. 295
80 Brett, 1986, pp. 47–9; Bardon, 1982, p. 298
81 Bardon, 1982, p. 296

82 *Ibid.*, p. 297
83 Brett, 1986, p. 43
84 Kennedy, 1989, p. 29
85 *Ibid.*, p. 28
86 *Ibid.*, pp. 21, 26
87 Simpson in Darby (ed.), 1983, p. 85
88 *Ibid.*, p. 86
89 *Ibid.*, p. 107
90 Bardon, 1982, p. 302
91 Bew and Patterson, 1985, p. 90
92 *Ibid.*, pp. 91–2
93 Geary and Johnson in *Irish Economic and Social History*, vol. 16 (1989), pp. 61–2
94 Moss and Hume, 1986, p. 560
95 Geary and Johnson in *Irish Economic and Social History*, vol. 16 (1989), p. 62; Moss and Hume, 1986, p. 458
96 Moss and Hume, 1986, pp. 560–1, 465
97 Bishop and Mallie, 1989, p. 250
98 *Ibid.*, pp. 253–4
99 Aughey in Jeffery (ed.), 1985, p. 76
100 Bell in Bell, Johnstone and Wilson (eds), 1991, p. 166
101 Hamill, 1985, p. 176
102 Aughey in Jeffery (ed.), 1985, p. 80
103 Bishop and Mallie, 1989, p. 256
104 Hamill, 1985, p. 180; Bew and Patterson, 1985, p. 83
105 Ryder, 1989, p. 137
106 *Ibid.*, p. 139
107 *Ibid.*, p. 141
108 Hamill, 1985, p. 192
109 Bell in Bell, Johnstone and Wilson (eds), 1991, p. 178
110 Ryder, 1989, p. 143
111 Hamill, 1985, p. 191
112 Ryder, 1989, p. 145
113 Bell in Bell, Johnstone and Wilson (eds), 1991, pp. 171–2, 175
114 Hamill, 1985, p. 197
115 FitzGerald, 1991, p. 282
116 Bardon, 1982, p. 300; Bell in Bell, Johnstone and Wilson (eds), 1991, p. 179
117 Hall, 1988, p. 63
118 Ryder, 1989, pp. 145, 126
119 White in Darby (ed.), 1983, p. 193
120 Dillon, 1990, p. 4
121 *Ibid.*, pp. 101–2
122 Ryder, 1989, pp. 176–9
123 Dillon, 1990, p. xv; Ryder, 1989, p. 185
124 Hamill, 1985, p. 187
125 Banyard in Jeffery (ed.), 1985, p. 105
126 *Ibid.*, p. 106
127 Bew and Patterson, 1985, pp. 93, 89
128 Hamill, 1985, p. 200
129 Longford and McHardy, 1981, p. 182
130 Hamill, 1985, p. 201
131 *Ibid.*, p. 217
132 Banyard in Jeffery (ed.), 1985, p. 104
133 Ryder, 1989, p. 145
134 Hamill, 1985, p. 200
135 Bishop and Mallie, 1989, pp. 297–305
136 Flackes and Elliott, 1988, p. 411
137 Ryder, 1989, p. 155
138 *Ibid.*, p. 160
139 Hamill, 1985, p. 218
140 Ryder, 1989, p. 164
141 Longford and McHardy, 1981, p. 181; Ryder, 1989, p. 172
142 Bew and Patterson, 1985, p. 93; Hamill, 1985, p. 226
143 Ryder, 1989, p. 172
144 Hall, 1988, p. 68
145 Ryder, 1989, pp. 174–5; Bishop and Mallie, 1989, p. 336
146 Bishop and Mallie, 1989, p. 311
147 *Ibid.*, p. 322
148 *Ibid.*, p. 321
149 Ryder, 1989, p. 191
150 Longford and McHardy, 1981, p. 201
151 Bew and Patterson, 1985, p. 77
152 *Ibid.*, pp. 93–4
153 Longford and McHardy, 1981, p. 203
154 FitzGerald, 1991, pp. 286–7
155 Bell in Bell, Johnstone and Wilson (eds), 1991, p. 185
156 Flackes, 1980, p. 72
157 Longford and McHardy, 1981, p. 205
158 Bell in Bell, Johnstone and Wilson (eds), 1991, p. 186
159 Hamill, 1985, p. 238
160 *Ibid.*, p. 240
161 Bishop and Mallie, 1989, p. 312
162 *Ibid.*, pp. 313–14
163 Hamill, 1985, pp. 249–50; Bishop and Mallie, 1989, p. 314
164 Hamill, 1985, pp. 251–2
165 *Ibid.*, p. 258
166 Bishop and Mallie, 1989, p. 313
167 Bell in Bell, Johnstone and Wilson (eds), 1991, p. 187
168 Bew and Patterson, 1985, pp. 112–13
169 *Ibid.*, p. 113
170 Longford and McHardy, 1981, p. 216
171 Flackes, 1980, p. 107
172 Bew and Patterson, 1985, p. 114
173 Longford and McHardy, 1981, p. 222
174 *Ibid.*, p. 223

175 Maloney and Pollak, 1986, pp. 380–2
176 *Ibid.*, p. 382
177 *Ibid.*, pp. 383–4
178 Bishop and Mallie, 1989, p. 365
179 Beresford, 1987, p. 55
180 *Ibid.*, p. 26
181 *Ibid.*, pp. 28, 31
182 *Ibid.*, p. 54
183 *Ibid.*, p. 88
184 Bell in Bell, Johnstone and Wilson (eds), 1991, p. 189
185 Beresford, 1987, p. 119
186 *Ibid.*, pp. 131–2
187 Bell in Bell, Johnstone and Wilson (eds), 1991, pp. 190–2
188 Bishop and Mallie, 1989, p. 373
189 Beresford, 1987, p. 415
190 *Ibid.*, pp. 131–3
191 *Ibid.*, pp. 428–9
192 Bell in Bell, Johnstone and Wilson (eds), 1991, p. 197
193 Bishop and Mallie, 1989, p. 378
194 *Ibid.*, p. 371
195 O'Leary, Elliott and Wilford, 1988, pp. 67–8
196 *Ibid.*, pp. 68–9
197 *Ibid.*, p. 72
198 *Ibid.*, p. 75
199 *Ibid.*, pp. 76, 79
200 Bishop and Mallie, 1989, p. 380; O'Leary, Elliott and Wilford, 1988, p. 82
201 Hamill, 1985, p. 269
202 Bell in Bell, Johnstone and Wilson (eds), 1991, p. 196
203 FitzGerald, 1991, p. 462
204 *Ibid.*
205 White, 1984, p. 243
206 *Ibid.*, p. 244
207 Kenny, 1986, p. 39
208 O'Malley, 1983, p. 75
209 Kenny, 1986, p. 40
210 O'Malley, 1990, p. 1
211 *Ibid.*, p. 2
212 FitzGerald, 1991, p. 492
213 O'Malley, 1990, p. 3
214 Kenny, 1986, p. 58
215 *Ibid.*, pp. 65–6
216 *Ibid.*, p. 67
217 *Ibid.*, p. 68
218 Bishop and Mallie, 1989, pp. 424–6
219 FitzGerald, 1991, p. 509
220 *Ibid.*, p. 519
221 *Ibid.*, p. 521
222 *Ibid.*, p. 522
223 Kenny, 1986, p. 82
224 Bell in Bell, Johnstone and Wilson (eds), 1991, p. 201
225 FitzGerald, 1991, p. 525
226 O'Malley, 1990, p. 5
227 Aughey, 1989, p. 67
228 FitzGerald, 1991, p. 568
229 *Understanding Northern Ireland,* UTV/Channel 4, 1992, programme 6
230 O'Leary, Elliott and Wilford, 1988, p. 189
231 Kenny, 1986, p. 99
232 O'Leary, Elliott and Wilford, 1988, p. 189; Bell in Bell, Johnstone and Wilson (eds), 1991, p. 203
233 O'Leary, Elliott and Wilford, 1988, p. 190
234 Kenny, 1986, p. 102
235 *Understanding Northern Ireland,* UTV/Channel 4, 1992, programme 6
236 Aughey, 1989, p. 86
237 *Understanding Northern Ireland,* UTV/Channel 4, 1992, programme 6
238 Aughey, 1989, p. 86
239 *Ibid.*, p. 71
240 Kenny, 1986, p. 108
241 *Ibid.*, p. 113
242 Aughey, 1989, p. 72; Kenny, 1986, p. 115
243 Kenny, 1986, p. 113
244 *Ibid.*, p. 117
245 O'Malley, 1990, pp. 13–14
246 Kenny, 1986, p. 103
247 Aughey, 1989, p. 72
248 Ryder, 1989, p. 326
249 *Ibid.*, p. 325
250 Kenny, 1986, pp. 120–1
251 Aughey, 1989, p. 77
252 Ryder, 1989, p. 327; Bell in Bell, Johnstone and Wilson (eds), 1991, p. 204
253 *Belfast Telegraph,* 10 April 1986
254 Aughey, 1989, p. 80
255 *Guardian,* 10 April 1986
256 Ryder, 1989, pp. 328–9
257 *Guardian,* 10 April 1986
258 Ryder, 1989, p. 329
259 *Belfast Telegraph,* 10 April 1986
260 *Guardian,* 21 April 1986
261 Aughey, 1989, p. 88
262 *Ibid.*, p. 95
263 *Ibid.*, p. 96
264 Hall, 1988, p. 107
265 Bell in Bell, Johnstone and Wilson (eds), 1991, p. 205
266 Aughey, 1989, p. 89
267 O'Leary, Elliott and Wilford, 1988, p. 193
268 *Ibid.*, pp. 193–4
269 McKittrick, 1989, p. 19

270 Bell in Bell, Johnstone and Wilson (eds) 1991, p. 205
271 O'Leary, Elliott and Wilford, 1988, p. 194
272 McKittrick, 1989, pp. 19–20
273 Bell in Bell, Johnstone and Wilson (eds), 1991, p. 205
274 *Belfast Telegraph*, 18 April 1986
275 *Observer*, 17 August 1986
276 Bell in Bell, Johnstone and Wilson (eds), 1991, pp. 206–7
277 Aughey, 1989, pp. 74–6
278 Bell in Bell, Johnstone and Wilson (eds), 1991, p. 206
279 Ryder, 1989, p. 331
280 Bell in Bell, Johnstone and Wilson (eds), 1991, p. 206
281 Aughey, 1989, p. 77
282 Bell in Bell, Johnstone and Wilson (eds), 1991, p. 207
283 *Belfast Telegraph*, 26 February 1987; Aughey, 1989, p. 89
284 *Guardian*, 3 May 1986
285 Darby, 1986, p. vii
286 *Guardian*, 3 May 1986; Bell in Bell, Johnstone and Wilson (eds), 1991, p. 205
287 Hall, 1988, p. 108
288 *News Letter*, 24 December 1986
289 Bishop and Mallie, 1989, p. 440
290 *Ibid.*, p. 451
291 Hall, 1988, p. 111
292 Flackes and Elliott, 1988, p. 355
293 *Guardian*, 9 March 1987
294 Ryder, 1989, p. 334
295 Flackes and Elliott, 1988, p. 411
296 Ryder, 1991, pp. 216–17
297 Ryder, 1989, pp. 335–7
298 Hall, 1988, pp. 108–9
299 Ryder, 1989, p. 337
300 *Ibid.*, p. 339
301 *Belfast Telegraph*, 9 May 1987
302 Ryder, 1989, p. 339
303 Bishop and Mallie, 1989, p. 455
304 *Belfast Telegraph*, 9 May 1987
305 Hall, 1988, p. 111
306 Ryder, 1989, p. 358; Bishop and Mallie, 1989, p. 462
307 Ryder, 1989, p. 359
308 *Guardian*, 9 November 1987
309 Wilson and McCreary, 1990, p. 34
310 *Guardian*, 9 November 1987
311 *Observer*, 12 April 1992
312 Bell in Bell, Johnstone and Wilson (eds), 1991, p. 209
313 Wilson and McCreary, 1990, p. 46
314 *Ibid.*, p. 49
315 Bishop and Mallie, 1989, p. 460;

316 Wilson and McCreary, 1990, p. 46
     Wilson and McCreary, 1990, p. 63
317 *Ibid.*, p. 58
318 *Ibid.*, p. xviii
319 U2, *Rattle and Hum*, Paramount Pictures, 1988, CIC Video
320 *Observer*, 13 March 1988
321 *Ibid.*
322 Bell in Bell, Johnstone and Wilson (eds), 1991, p. 210
323 *Sunday Tribune*, 20 March 1988
324 McKittrick, 1989, p. 108
325 *Observer*, 20 March 1988
326 McKittrick, 1989, pp. 107–8
327 *Ibid.*, p. 103
328 Guelke in Hadfield (ed.), 1992, pp. 102–4; Ryder, 1989, p. 345
329 Ryder, 1989, pp. 346–7
330 McKittrick, 1989, p. 101; Bell in Bell, Johnstone and Wilson (eds), 1991, p. 205
331 Ryder, 1989, pp. 348–9
332 McKittrick, 1989, p. 101
333 Bell in Bell, Johnstone and Wilson (eds), 1991, p. 210
334 McKittrick, 1989, p. 104; Bell in Bell, Johnstone and Wilson (eds), 1991, p. 210
335 McKittrick, 1989, p. 105
336 Bell in Bell, Johnstone and Wilson (eds), 1991, p. 212
337 McKittrick, 1989, pp. 110–11
338 Bardon, 1982, p. 303
339 *Ibid.*, p. 305
340 *Belfast Telegraph*, 20 July 1982; Gaffikin and Morrissey, 1990, p. 43
341 *Guardian*, 1 June 1982
342 Bardon, 1982, p. 304
343 Gaffikin and Morrissey, 1990, p. 78
344 *Ibid.*, p. 75
345 *Belfast Telegraph*, 9 May 1983
346 *Belfast Telegraph*, 25 July 1983
347 Black in *Irish Banking Review*, December 1983
348 Gaffikin and Morrissey, 1990, p. 82
349 *Belfast Telegraph*, 8 March 1985 and 9 February 1988
350 Moss and Hume, 1986, pp. 474–80
351 *Belfast Telegraph*, 4 August 1983 and 13 April 1984
352 Moss and Hume, 1986, p. 481; *Belfast Telegraph*, 9 August 1984
353 *Belfast Telegraph*, 3 March 1984
354 *Belfast Telegraph*, Christmas colour supplement 1983
355 *Belfast Telegraph*, 3 March 1984
356 Gaffikin and Morrissey, 1990, p. 88

357 *Fortnight*, July–August 1991 and January 1992
358 Spencer and Whittaker in Harris, Jefferson and Spencer (eds), 1990, pp. 21–5
359 *Ibid.*, pp. 32, 28
360 Geary and Johnson in *Irish Economic and Social History*, vol. 16 (1989), p. 63
361 *Fortnight*, November 1991
362 Gaffikin and Morrissey, 1990, p. 35
363 *Ibid.*, p. 44
364 *Fortnight*, July–August 1991
365 *Belfast Telegraph*, 6 April 1992
366 Gaffikin and Morrissey, 1990, p. 77
367 Hewitt in Harris, Jefferson and Spencer (eds), 1990, p. 357
368 Gaffikin and Morrissey, 1990, p. 49
369 *Ibid.*, p. 80
370 Bradley in Harris, Jefferson and Spencer (eds), 1990, p. 447
371 Shannon, 1991, p. 46
372 Brett, 1986, p. 77
373 *Ibid.*, p. 40
374 *Ibid.*, p. 70
375 *Ibid.*, pp. 67–8
376 Gaffikin and Morrissey, 1990, p. 157
377 Bardon, 1982, p. 298
378 Gaffikin and Morrissey, 1990, p. 157
379 *Ibid.*
380 *Ibid.*, p. 158
381 Shannon, 1991, p. 35
382 Brett, 1986, p. 68
383 *Ibid.*, p. 79
384 Shannon, 1991, pp. 58–9
385 Gaffikin and Morrissey, 1990, p. 161; Shannon, 1991, p. 65
386 Evason, 1985, p. 1
387 *Ibid.*, p. 2
388 Gaffikin and Morrissey, 1990, p. 107
389 *Ibid.*, pp. 50–3
390 *Ibid.*, p. 60
391 *Ibid.*, p. 167
392 Jefferson in Harris, Jefferson and Spencer (eds), 1990, p. 159; Gaffikin and Morrissey, 1990, p. 55
393 Jefferson in Harris, Jefferson and Spencer (eds), 1990, pp. 172–3
394 Hewitt in Harris, Jefferson and Spencer (eds), 1990, pp. 368–9
395 Bradley in Harris, Jefferson and Spencer (eds), 1990, p. 447
396 McWilliams in Hanna (ed.), 1988, pp. 7–8
397 Evason, 1985, p. 22; McWilliams in Hanna (ed.), 1988, p. 5
398 Gaffikin and Morrissey, 1990, p. 109
399 *Ibid.*, p. 111
400 Compton in Roche and Barton (eds), 1991, p. 48
401 Rowthorn and Wayne, 1988, pp. 111–14
402 Compton in Roche and Barton (eds), 1991, pp. 47, 75
403 *Fortnight*, October 1989
404 Compton in Roche and Barton (eds), 1991, pp. 56–9, 48
405 Rowthorn and Wayne, 1988, p. 112
406 Arthur and Jeffery, 1988, p. 31
407 *Ibid.*, pp. 28–31
408 Gaffikin and Morrissey, 1990, p. 92
409 Compton in Roche and Barton (eds), 1991, pp. 70–1
410 *Fortnight*, December 1991 and January 1992
411 *Belfast Telegraph*, 19 May 1992
412 'Lagan College: 10th Anniversary 1981–1991', video made by Lagan College, 1991
413 *Cultural Heritage: A Cross Curricular Theme* (report to Parliamentary Undersecretary of State for Education), Belfast, 1989, p. 6
414 Gaffikin and Morrissey, 1990, p. 176
415 Bell in Bell, Johnstone and Wilson (eds), 1991, p. 212
416 *Belfast Telegraph*, 20 August 1988
417 Bell in Bell, Johnstone and Wilson (eds), 1991, p. 211
418 Ryder, 1989, p. 372
419 *Irish Times*, 27 December 1990; Bell in Bell, Johnstone and Wilson (eds), 1991, pp. 219–20; Ryder, 1991, p. 242
420 Bell in Bell, Johnstone and Wilson (eds), 1991, p. 220
421 *Ibid.*, pp. 211–18
422 *Guardian*, 23 September 1989
423 *Observer*, 5 August 1990
424 *Irish Times*, 27 December 1990
425 *Guardian*, 4 August 1990
426 *Fortnight*, April 1991
427 Ryder, 1991, pp. 142–4
428 *Ibid.*, p. 123
429 *Ibid.*, pp. 118–19
430 *Ibid.*, pp. 134, 145
431 *Ibid.*, p. 199
432 *Ibid.*, p. 206
433 *Ibid.*, pp. 184, 205
434 *Ibid.*, p. 207
435 Guelke in Hadfield (ed.), 1992, pp. 106–7
436 *Fortnight*, April 1991
437 *Fortnight*, May 1991
438 Guelke in Hadfield (ed.), 1992, pp. 108–9
439 *Fortnight*, March 1991

440 *Fortnight*, April 1991
441 *Ibid.*
442 *Observer*, 31 March 1991
443 *Fortnight*, April 1991
444 *Fortnight*, July 1991
445 *Guardian*, 16 November 1991
446 *Fortnight*, December 1991
447 *Ibid.*
448 *Fortnight*, January 1991 and February 1991
449 *Understanding Northern Ireland*, UTV/Channel 4, 1992, programme 6
450 *Belfast Telegraph*, 23 January 1992
451 *Fortnight*, February 1992
452 *Observer*, 12 January 1992
453 *Observer*, 19 January 1992
454 *Fortnight*, March 1992; *Observer*, 19 January 1992
455 *Observer*, 19 January 1992
456 *Fortnight*, February 1992
457 *Ibid.*
458 *Ibid.*
459 *Guardian*, 6 February 1992
460 *Belfast Telegraph*, 6 February 1992
461 *Guardian*, 7 February 1992
462 *Belfast Telegraph*, 6 February 1992; *Fortnight*, February 1992 and March 1992
463 *Fortnight*, April 1992
464 *Guardian*, 13 April 1992
465 *Daily Telegraph*, 14 April 1992
466 *Observer*, 12 April 1992
467 *Belfast Telegraph*, 29 April 1992
468 O'Malley, 1983, p. 15
469 *Observer*, 19 February 1984
470 Gaffikin and Morrissey, 1990, p. 42
471 *Observer*, 12 August 1984
472 Gaffikin and Morrissey, 1990, p. 61
473 *Belfast Telegraph*, 13 May 1985
474 Bardon, 1985, p. 30
475 Gaffikin and Morrissey, 1990, pp. 120–1
476 *Guardian*, 22 April 1992
477 *Guardian*, 6 January 1992
478 McKittrick, 1989, pp. 134–5
479 *Ibid.*, p. 136
480 *Fortnight*, March 1992
481 *Fortnight*, May 1992; *Community Relations*, no. 8, May 1992
482 *Belfast Telegraph*, 2 June 1992
483 *Observer*, 19 February 1984
484 *Observer*, 12 August 1984
485 *Guardian*, 15 April 1987
486 *Observer*, 23 May 1992
487 McKittrick, 1989, p. 108
488 Gaffikin and Morrissey, 1990, p. 145
489 McKittrick, 1989, p. 108
490 *Guardian*, 2 May 1992
491 *Guardian*, 7 December 1991
492 *Observer*, 11 May 1992
493 *Guardian*, 21 May 1992
494 *Observer*, 8 March 1992
495 *Guardian*, 13 January 1992
496 *Guardian*, 19 November 1991
497 Alcock in Hadfield (ed.), 1992, pp. 149–50
498 BBC Radio Ulster News, 20 March 1992
499 O'Malley, 1990, p. 100

In her introduction to *Northern Ireland Since 1945*, Sabine Wichert points out that by 1987 there had been well over five thousand publications on Northern Ireland alone. *Belfast Before 1820*, a bibliography compiled by Noragh Stevenson for the Linen Hall Library in 1967, contains 618 entries and no estimate can be made of the number of books, pamphlets and articles directly relevant to the history of Ulster from earliest times to 1992. It follows that of necessity this bibliography must be highly selective.

Very helpful bibliographies can be found in the published volumes of *A New History of Ireland*; *The Archaeology of Ulster* by J.P. Mallory and T.E. McNeill; and *Ireland 1912–1985* by Joseph J. Lee. The Bibliographical Essay in R.F. Foster's *Modern Ireland 1600–1972* is particularly instructive, and by far the most lucid guide to publications on Northern Ireland between 1921 and 1990 is *Interpreting Northern Ireland* by John H. Whyte. The Political Collection at the Linen Hall Library, Belfast, and *Fortnight* magazine are indispensable for those seeking to make a detailed study of the Troubles in Northern Ireland since 1969.

Abels, Jules. *The Parnell Tragedy*, London, 1966
Adamson, Ian. *The Cruthin*, Bangor, 1974
   Bangor: Light of the World, Bangor, 1979
   The Battle of Moira, Newtownards, 1980
Akenson, Donald Harman. *Education and Enmity: The Control of Schooling in Northern Ireland 1920–50*, Newton Abbot and New York, 1973
Akenson, D.H. and W.H. Crawford. *James Orr: Bard of Ballycarry*, Belfast, 1977
Allingham, Hugh. *Narrative: Translation of Captain Cuellar's Narrative of the Spanish Armada and His Adventures in Ireland, by Robert Crawford*, London, 1897
Andrews, J.H. *Plantation Acres: An Historical Study of the Irish Land Surveyor*, Belfast, 1985
Annals of Connacht see Freeman
Annals of Ulster (to AD 1131): Annala Uladh, edited by Sean Mac Airt and Gearóid Mac Niocaill, Dublin, 1983
Annala Rioghachta Eirann: Annals of the Kingdom of Ireland by the Four Masters, from the Earliest Period to the Year 1616, edited by John O'Donovan, 2nd ed., Dublin, 1856
Armstrong, D.L. 'Social and economic conditions in the Belfast linen industry 1850–1900', *Irish Historical Studies*, vol. 7 (1951)
Armstrong, Olive. *Edward Bruce's Invasion of Ireland*, London, 1923
Arthur, Paul. *The People's Democracy 1968–73*, Belfast, 1974
   Government and Politics of Northern Ireland, 2nd ed., London and New York, 1987
Arthur, Paul and Keith Jeffery. *Northern Ireland Since 1968*, Oxford, 1988
Aughey, Arthur. *Under Siege: Ulster Unionism and the Anglo-Irish Agreement*, Belfast, 1989
Aunger, Edmund A. 'Religion and occupational class in Northern Ireland', *Economic and Social Studies*, vol. 7, no. 1 (1975)

Bagwell, Richard. *Ireland Under the Tudors: With a Succinct Account of the Earlier History*, 3 vols, London, 1885–90

Ireland Under the Stuarts and During the Interregnum, 3 vols, London, 1909–16

Bardon, Jonathan. *The Struggle for Ireland 400–1450 AD*, Dublin, 1970

Belfast: An Illustrated History, Belfast, 1982

Bardon, Jonathan and Stephen Conlin. *Belfast 1000 Years*, Belfast, 1985

Barritt, Denis P. and Charles F. Carter. *The Northern Ireland Problem: A Study in Group Relations*, 2nd ed., Oxford, 1972 (1st ed. 1962)

Barry, T.B. *The Archaeology of Medieval Ireland*, London and New York, 1987

Bartlett, Thomas. 'Select documents xxxviii: defenders and defenderism in 1795', *Irish Historical Studies*, vol. 24, no. 95 (May 1985)

Bartlett, Thomas and D.W. Hayton (eds). *Penal Era and Golden Age: Essays in Irish History, 1690–1800*, Belfast, 1979

Barton, Brian. *Brookeborough: The Making of a Prime Minister*, Belfast, 1988

The Blitz: Belfast in the War Years, Belfast, 1989

Barzilay, David. *The British Army in Ulster*, 4 vols, Belfast, 1973–81

Beckett, J.C. *Protestant Dissent in Ireland, 1687–1780*, London, 1948

The Making of Modern Ireland 1603–1923, London, 1966

Beckett, J.C. and T.W. Moody (eds). *Ulster Since 1800*: vol. 1, *A Political and Economic Survey*, London, 1955; vol. 2, *A Social Survey*, London, 1957

Bell, Jonathan and Mervyn Watson. *Irish Farming 1750–1900*, Edinburgh, 1986

Bell, Robert. *The Book of Ulster Surnames*, Belfast, 1988

Bell, Robert, Robert Johnstone and Robin Wilson (eds). *Troubled Times: Fortnight Magazine and the Troubles in Northern Ireland 1970–91*, Belfast, 1991

Benn, George. *A History of the Town of Belfast from the Earliest Times to the Close of the Eighteenth Century*, Belfast, 1877

Beresford, David. *Ten Men Dead: The Story of the 1981 Irish Hunger Strike*, London, 1987

Bew, Paul and Henry Patterson. *The British State and the Ulster Crisis: From Wilson to Thatcher*, London, 1985

Bew, Paul, Peter Gibbon and Henry Patterson. *The State in Northern Ireland 1921–72: Political Forces and Social Classes*, Manchester, 1979

Bieler, Ludwig. *Ireland: Harbinger of the Middle Ages*, Oxford, 1963

Bishop, Patrick and Eamonn Mallie. *The Provisional IRA*, London, 1989

Black, Eileen (ed.). *Kings in Conflict: Ireland in the 1690s*, Belfast, 1990

Black, R., F. Pinter and R. Overy. *Flight: A Report on Population Movement in Belfast, August 1971*, Belfast, 1975

Blake, J.W. *Northern Ireland in the Second World War*, Belfast, 1956

Blaney, Dr Roger. *Belfast: 100 Years of Public Health 1888–1988*, Belfast, 1988

Boal, F.W. 'Territoriality on the Shankill/Falls divide', *Irish Geography*, vol. 6, no. 1 (1969)

Board of Works. *Correspondence from July 1846 to January 1847 Relating to the Measures Adopted for the Relief of the Distress in Ireland, with Maps, Plans, and Appendices*, Board of Works Series, pt 1 [764], H.C. 1847, I

Board of Works: Distress. *Correspondence Explanatory of the Measures Adopted by Her Majesty's Government for the Relief of Distress Arising from the Failure of the Potato Crop in Ireland*, H.C. 1846, XXXVIII

Papers Relating to Proceedings for the Relief of Distress and State of the Unions and Workhouses in Ireland, fourth series, 1847, H.C. 1847–8

Bolton, G.C. *The Passing of the Irish Act of Union: A Study in Parliamentary Politics*, Oxford, 1966

Boulter, Hugh. *Letters*, 2 vols, Dublin, 1770

Bowden, C.T. *A Tour Through Ireland in 1790*, London, 1791
Bowen, D. *The Protestant Crusade in Ireland 1800–70*, Dublin, 1978
Bowman, John. *De Valera and the Ulster Question 1917–1973*, Oxford, 1982
Bowyer Bell, J. *The Secret Army: A History of the IRA*, Dublin, 1970
Boyce, D. George. *The Irish Question and British Politics 1868–1986*, London, 1988
   Nineteenth-Century Ireland: The Search for Stability, Dublin, 1990
Boyd, Andrew. *Holy War in Belfast*, Tralee, 1969
Boyle, Kevin and Tom Hadden. *Ireland: A Positive Proposal*, Harmondsworth, 1985
Brady, Ciaran and Raymond Gillespie (eds). *Natives and Newcomers: Essays on the Making of Irish Colonial Society 1534–1641*, Dublin, 1986
Brady, Ciaran, Mary O'Dowd and Brian Walker (eds). *Ulster: An Illustrated History*, London, 1989
Brett, Charles E.B. *Buildings of Belfast 1700–1914*, London, 1967
   Housing a Divided Community, Dublin and Belfast, 1986
Brooke, Peter (ed.). *Problems of a Growing City: Belfast 1780–1870*, Belfast, 1973
   'Robert McElborough: an autobiography of a Belfast working man', Belfast, 1974, typescript
Browne, Noël. *Against the Tide*, Dublin, 1986
Bruce, Steve. *God Save Ulster! The Religion and Politics of Paisleyism*, Oxford and New York, 1986
Buchanan, R.H. and B.M. Walker (eds). *Province, City and People*, Antrim, 1987
Buckland, Patrick. *Irish Unionism: Two: Ulster Unionism and the Origins of Northern Ireland, 1886–1922*, Dublin and New York, 1973
   The Factory of Grievances: Devolved Government in Northern Ireland 1921–39, Dublin and New York, 1979
   James Craig, Lord Craigavon, Dublin, 1980
   A History of Northern Ireland, Dublin, 1981
Buckland, Patrick (ed.). *Irish Unionism, 1885–1923: A Documentary History*, Belfast, 1973
Byrne, F.J. *Irish Kings and High-Kings*, London, 1973
Calendar of the Carew Manuscripts Preserved in the Archiepiscopal Library at Lambeth, 1515–74, 6 vols, London, 1867–73
Calendar of the State Papers Relating to Ireland, 24 vols, London, 1860–1911
Camblin, G. *The Town in Ulster*, Belfast, 1951
Cameron Report. *Disturbances in Northern Ireland: Report of the Commission Appointed by the Governor of Northern Ireland*, Belfast, Cmd 532, 1969
Campbell, Flann. *The Dissenting Voice: Protestant Democracy in Ulster from Plantation to Partition*, Belfast, 1991
Campbell, T.J. *Fifty Years of Ulster: 1890–1940*, Belfast, 1941
Canavan, Tony. *Frontier Town: An Illustrated History of Newry*, Belfast, 1989
Canny, Nicholas. 'The Flight of the Earls 1607', *Irish Historical Studies*, vol. 17, no. 67 (March 1971)
   The Elizabethan Conquest of Ireland: A Pattern Established 1565–1576, Hassocks, Sussex, 1976
Carroll, Joseph T. *Ireland in the War Years 1939–1945*, Newton Abbot and New York, 1975
Carson, Douglas. *Ulster Castles and Defensive Buildings*, London, 1977
Carson, John T. *God's River in Spate: The Story of the Religious Awakening of Ulster in 1859*, Belfast, 1958
Cary, M. and E.H. Warmington. *The Ancient Explorers*, London, 1929

Chambers, George. *Faces of Change: The Belfast and Northern Ireland Chambers of Commerce and Industry 1783–1983*, Belfast, 1983

Churchill, W.S. *The World Crisis: The Aftermath*, London, 1929

Clark, Samuel and James S. Donnelly, Jr (eds). *Irish Peasants: Violence and Political Unrest 1780–1914*, Manchester, 1983

Clark, Wallace. *Rathlin – Disputed Island*, Belfast, 1971

Linen on the Green: An Irish Mill Village 1730–1982, Belfast, 1982

Clarkson, L.A. and E.M. Crawford. *Ways to Wealth: The Cust Family of Eighteenth-Century Armagh*, Belfast, 1985

Cleary, P.G. 'Spatial Expansion and Urban Ecological Change in Belfast with Special Reference to the Role of Local Transportation, 1861–1917', Ph.D. thesis, Queen's University Belfast, 1979

Commissariat. *Correspondence of July 1846 to January 1847 Relating to the Measures Adopted for the Relief of the Distress in Ireland and Scotland*, Commissariat Series, H.C. 1847, LI

Correspondence from January to March, 1847, Relating to the Measures Adopted for the Relief of the Distress in Ireland, Commissariat Series, pt 2, H.C. 1847, LII

Connell, K.H. *Irish Peasant Society: Four Historical Essays*, Oxford, 1968

Connolly, Sean J. *Priests and People in Pre-Famine Ireland 1780–1845*, Dublin, 1982

Religion and Society in Nineteenth-Century Ireland, Dundalk, 1985

Coote, Charles. *Statistical Survey of the County of Armagh*, Dublin, 1804

Corlett, John. *Aviation in Ulster*, Belfast, 1981

Crawford, W.H. *Domestic Industry in Ireland: The Experience of the Linen Industry*, Dublin, 1972

'The evolution of the linen trade', *Irish Economic and Social History*, vol. 15 (1988)

'The construction of the Ulster road network 1700–1850', paper presented at symposium, 'The history of technology, science and society', University of Ulster, September 1989

Crawford, W.H. and B. Trainor (eds). *Aspects of Irish Social History 1750–1800*, Belfast, 1969

Cullen, L.M. and T.C. Smout (eds).*Comparative Aspects of Scottish and Irish Economic and Social History 1600–1900*, Edinburgh, 1976

Curl, James Steven. *The Londonderry Plantation 1609–1914*, Chichester, 1986

Daly, Mary E. *The Famine in Ireland*, Dundalk, 1986

Darby, John. *Conflict in Northern Ireland: The Development of a Polarised Community*, Dublin and New York, 1976

Intimidation and the Control of Conflict in Northern Ireland, Dublin, 1986

Darby, John (ed.). *Northern Ireland: The Background to the Conflict*, Belfast and New York, 1983

Darby, John and A. Williamson (eds). *Violence and the Social Services in Northern Ireland*, London, 1978

Dasent, G.W. *The Story of Burnt Njal from the Icelandic of the Njal's Saga*, London, 1911

Day, Angelique and Patrick Williams (eds). *The Ordnance Survey Memoirs of Ireland*, 13 vols, Belfast, 1990–2

de Breffny, Brian and George Mott. *The Churches and Abbeys of Ireland*, London, 1976

de Latocnaye, Le Chevalier. *A Frenchman's Walk Through Ireland 1796–7*, translated from the French by John Stevenson, 1917; reprinted, with an introduction by John A. Gamble, Belfast, 1984

de Paor, Liam. *Divided Ulster*, Harmondsworth, 1970
de Paor, Maire and Liam de Paor. *Early Christian Ireland*, London, 1958
de Vere White, Terence. *Kevin O'Higgins*, London, 1948
Department of the Environment for Northern Ireland. *Historic Monuments of Northern Ireland*, 6th ed., Belfast, 1983
Deutsch, Richard and Vivien Magowan. *Northern Ireland: A Chronology of Events 1968–74*, 3 vols, Belfast, 1973–5
Devlin, Bernadette. *The Price of My Soul*, London, 1969
Devlin, Paddy. *Yes, We Have No Bananas: Outdoor Relief in Belfast, 1920–39*, Belfast 1981
Dickson, Charles. *Revolt in the North: Antrim and Down in 1798*, Dublin and London, 1960
Dickson, R.J. *Ulster Emigration to Colonial America 1718–1775*, London, 1966
Dillon, Martin. *The Shankill Butchers: A Case Study of Mass Murder*, London, 1989
Dillon, M. and N. Chadwick. *The Celtic Realms*, London, 1967
Docwra, Henry. 'A narration of the services done by the army ymployed to Lough-Foyle', *Miscellany of the Celtic Society*, edited by John O'Donovan, Dublin, 1849
Dolan, Liam. *The Third Earl of Leitrim*, Fanad, 1978
Land War and Eviction in Derryveagh 1840–65, Dundalk, 1980
Donnelly, James S. *Landlord and Tenant in Nineteenth-Century Ireland*, Dublin, 1973
Doyle, David Noel. *Ireland, Irishmen and Revolutionary America 1760–1820*, Dublin and Cork, 1981
Dubourdieu, Revd J. *Statistical Survey of the County of Down*, Dublin, 1802
Statistical Survey of the County of Antrim, Dublin, 1812
Dunlop, Eull (ed.). *Mid-Antrim: Articles on the History of Ballymena and District*, Ballymena, 1983
Edwards, R.D. (ed.). 'Letter-book of Sir Arthur Chichester 1612–14', *Analecta Hibernica*, no. 8 (1938)
Egan, Bowes and Vincent McCormack. *Burntollet*, London, 1969
Elliott, Marianne. *Partners in Revolution: The United Irishmen and France*, London and New Haven, 1982
Wolfe Tone: Prophet of Irish Independence, London and New Haven, 1989
Ellis, Peter Berresford. *The Boyne Water: The Battle of the Boyne, 1690*, London, 1976; reprinted Belfast, 1989
Ellis, S.G. *Tudor Ireland: Crown, Community and the Conflict of Cultures, 1470–1603*, London and New York, 1985
Emmet, T.A., W.J. MacNeven and A. O'Connor. *The Origin and Progress of the Irish Union*, Dublin, 1798; reprinted Belfast, 1978
Evans, E. Estyn. *Mourne Country*, 3rd ed., Dundalk, 1978
The Personality of Ireland: Habitat, Heritage and History, Belfast, 1981
Evason, Eileen. *On the Edge: A Study of Poverty and Long-Term Unemployment in Northern Ireland*, London, 1985
Fallon, Niall. *The Armada in Ireland*, London, 1978
Falls, Cyril. *Elizabeth's Irish Wars*, London, 1950
Farrell, Brian. *The Founding of Dáil Éireann: Parliament and Nation-Building*, Dublin, 1971
Farrell, Michael. *Northern Ireland: The Orange State*, London, 1976
The Poor Law and the Workhouse in Belfast 1838–1948, Belfast, 1978
Arming the Protestants: The Formation of the Ulster Special Constabulary 1920–27, Dingle and London, 1983

Filip, Jan. *Celtic Civilization and Its Heritage*, Prague, 1960

Fisk, Robert. *The Point of No Return: The Strike Which Broke the British in Ulster*, London, 1975

In Time of War: Ireland, Ulster and the Price of Neutrality 1939–45, London, 1983

FitzGerald, Garret. *All in a Life: An Autobiography*, Dublin, 1991

Fitzpatrick, D. *Irish Emigration 1801–1921*, Dundalk, 1984

Fitzpatrick, Rory. *God's Frontiersmen: The Scots-Irish Epic*, London, 1989

Flackes, W.D. *Northern Ireland: A Political Directory, 1968–79*, Dublin and New York, 1980

Flackes, W.D. and Sydney Elliott. *Northern Ireland: A Political Directory 1968–88*, Belfast, 1989

Foster, R.F. 'History and the Irish Question', *Journal of the Royal Historical Society*, vol. 20 (1983)

Modern Ireland 1600–1972, London, 1988

Frame, Robin. 'The Bruces in Ireland, 1315–18', *Irish Historical Studies*, vol. 19, no. 73 (March 1974)

Frankfort Moore, F. *The Truth About Ulster*, London, 1914

Freeman, A. Martin (ed.). *Annala Connacht: The Annals of Connacht (AD 1224–1544)*, Dublin, 1983

A Full and True Account of the Besieging and Taking of Carrickfergus Castle by the Duke of Schomberg, London, 1689

Gaffikin, Frank and Mike Morrissey. *Northern Ireland: The Thatcher Years*, London and New Jersey, 1990

Gailey, Alan. *Rural Houses of the North of Ireland*, Edinburgh, 1984

Gallagher, Frank. *The Indivisible Island: The History of the Partition of Ireland*, London, 1957

Gallagher, Tom and James O'Connell (eds). *Contemporary Irish Studies*, Manchester, 1983

Gantz, Jeffrey. *Early Irish Myths and Sagas*, Harmondsworth, 1981

Geary, F. and D.S. Johnson 'Shipbuilding in Belfast, 1861–1986', *Irish Economic and Social History*, vol. 16 (1989)

Gilbert, J.T. (ed.). *Chartularies of St Mary's Abbey*, 2 vols, Dublin, 1884–6

A Contemporary History of Affairs in Ireland (1641–9), 3 vols, Dublin, 1879

'A Light to the Blind': A Jacobite Narrative of the War in Ireland, 1688–1691, Dublin, 1892; reprinted, with an introduction by J.G. Simms, Shannon, 1971

Gillespie, Raymond. *Colonial Ulster: The Settlement of East Ulster*, Cork, 1985

Gillespie, Raymond and Harold O'Sullivan. *The Borderlands: Essays on the History of the Ulster–Leinster Border*, Belfast, 1989

Giraldus Cambrensis. *Expugnatio Hibernica: The Conquest of Ireland*, edited by A.B. Scott and F.X. Martin, Dublin, 1978

Glassie, Henry. *Passing the Time: Folklore and History of an Ulster Community*, Dublin and Philadelphia, 1982

Goldring, Maurice. *Belfast: From Loyalty to Rebellion*, London, 1991

Gray, John. *City in Revolt: James Larkin and the Belfast Dock Strike of 1907*, Belfast, 1985

Gribbon, H.D. *The History of Water Power in Ulster*, Newton Abbot, 1969

Gribbon, Sybil. *Edwardian Belfast: A Social Profile*, Belfast, 1982

Hadfield, Brigid (ed.). *Northern Ireland: Politics and the Constitution*, Buckingham and Philadelphia, 1992

Hall, Michael. *20 Years: A Concise Chronology of Events in Ireland from 1968–1988*, Belfast, 1988

Hamill, Desmond. *Pig in the Middle: The Army in Northern Ireland 1969–1984*, London, 1985
Hamlin, Ann and Chris Lynn. *Pieces of the Past*, Belfast, 1988
Hammond, D. *Songs of Belfast*, Dublin, 1978
  Steelchest, Nail in the Boot and the Barking Dog: The Belfast Shipyard, Belfast, 1986
Hand, Geoffrey J. *see Report of the Irish Boundary Commission*
Handley, James E. *The Irish in Modern Scotland*, Cork, 1947
Hanna, Eamon (ed.). *Poverty in Ireland Social Study Conference*, Lurgan, 1988
Hanson, R.P.C. *Saint Patrick: His Origins and Career*, Oxford, 1968
Harbinson, John F. *The Ulster Unionist Party 1882–1973: Its Development and Organisation*, Belfast, 1973
Harbison, Peter. *Pre-Christian Ireland*, London, 1988
Haren, Michael and Yolande de Pontfarcy. *The Medieval Pilgrimage to St Patrick's Purgatory*, Enniskillen/Monaghan, 1988
Harkness, David. *Northern Ireland Since 1920*, Dublin, 1983
Harkness, David and Mary O'Dowd (eds). *The Town in Ireland*, Belfast, 1981
Harris, R.I.D., C.W. Jefferson and J.E. Spencer (eds). *The Northern Ireland Economy: A Comparative Study in the Economic Development of a Peripheral Region*, London and New York, 1990
Harris, Rosemary. *Prejudice and Tolerance in Ulster: A Study of Neighbours and 'Strangers' in a Border Community*, Manchester, 1972
Harris, Walter. *The Antient and Present State of the County of Down, Containing a Chorographical Description, with the Natural and Civil History of the Same*, Dublin, 1744
Hayes, Maurice. *Whither Cultural Diversity?*, Community Relations Council pamphlet no. 2, Belfast, 1990
Hayes-McCoy, G.A. *Scots Mercenary Forces in Ireland, 1565–1603*, Dublin and London, 1937
  Ulster and Other Irish Maps, c. 1600, Dublin, 1964
  Irish Battles: A Military History of Ireland, London, 1969
Hayes-McCoy. G.A. (ed.). *The Irish at War*, Cork, 1964
Heatley, Fred. *Henry Joy McCracken and His Times*, Belfast, 1967
Herdman, Rex. *They All Made Me*, Omagh, 1970
Hickson, Mary. *Ireland in the Seventeenth Century*, 2 vols, London, 1884
Hidden, A.E. and C.J. Latimer. *Science and Technology: Belfast and Its Region*, Belfast, 1987
Hill, Lord George. *Facts from Gweedore*, London, 1845
Hill, George. *An Historical Account of the MacDonnells of Antrim*, Belfast, 1873
  An Historical Account of the Plantation in Ulster 1608–20, Belfast, 1877
Hill, George (ed.). *The Montgomery Manuscripts*, Belfast, 1869
Holmes, R.F. *Henry Cooke*, Belfast, 1981
Holt, Edgar. *Protest in Arms: The Irish Troubles 1916–1926*, London, 1960
Hunter, R.J. 'Towns in the Ulster Plantation', *Studia Hibernica*, vol. 11 (1971)
Hutton, A.W. *see* Young
The Industries of Ireland. Part I. Belfast and Towns of the North. Business Men and Mercantile Interests. Wealth and Growth. Historical. Statistical. Biographical, London, 1891; reprinted, with an introduction by W.H. Crawford, Belfast, 1986
Isles, K.S. and N. Cuthbert. *An Economic Survey of Northern Ireland*, Belfast, 1957
Jackson, Alvin. *The Ulster Party: Irish Unionists in the House of Commons, 1884–1911*, Oxford, 1989

Jalland, Patricia. *The Liberals and Ireland: The Ulster Question in British Politics to 1914*, Brighton, 1980

Jeffery, Keith (ed.). *The Divided Province: The Troubles in Northern Ireland 1969–1985*, London, 1985

Johnson, David. *The Interwar Economy in Ireland*, Dundalk, 1985

Johnston, Dorothy. 'Richard II and the submissions of Gaelic Ireland', *Irish Historical Studies*, vol. 22, no. 85 (March 1980)

Joy, Henry, Jr. *Historical Collections Relative to the Town of Belfast: From the Earliest Period to the Union with Great Britain*, Belfast, 1817

Kee, Robert. *The Green Flag*, London, 1972; later published as three separate volumes: *The Most Distressful Country* (vol. 1), *The Bold Fenian Men* (vol. 2), and *Ourselves Alone* (vol. 3), London, 1989

Kennedy, Dennis. *The Widening Gulf: Northern Attitudes to the Independent Irish State 1919–49*, Belfast, 1988

Kennedy, Liam. *The Modern Industrialisation of Ireland 1940–1988*, Dundalk, 1989

Kennedy, Liam and Philip Ollerenshaw (eds). *An Economic History of Ulster 1820–1939*, Manchester, 1985

Kenny, Anthony. *The Road to Hillsborough: The Shaping of the Anglo-Irish Agreement*, Oxford, 1986

Kernohan, J.W. *The Parishes of Kilrea and Tamlaght O'Crilly*, Coleraine, 1912

Killen, John. *John Bull's Famous Circus: Ulster History Through the Postcard 1905–1985*, Dublin, 1985

Kinsella, Thomas (trans.). *The Táin: Translated From the Irish Epic 'Táin Bó Cuailnge'*, Oxford, 1970

Lacy, Brian. *Archaeological Survey of County Donegal*, Lifford, 1983
    Siege City: The Story of Derry and Londonderry, Belfast, 1990

Laffan, Michael. *The Partition of Ireland 1911–1925*, Dundalk, 1983

Lammey, D. 'A Study of Anglo-Irish Relations Between 1772 and 1782, with Particular Reference to the "Free Trade" Movement', Ph.D. thesis, Queen's University Belfast, 1984

Larkin, Emmet. *James Larkin: Irish Labour Leader 1876–1947*, London, 1965
    The Consolidation of the Roman Catholic Church in Ireland 1860–1870, Dublin, 1987

Lawrence, R.J. *The Government of Northern Ireland: Public Finance and Public Services 1921–1964*, Oxford, 1965

Lecky, W.E.H. *A History of Ireland in the Eighteenth Century*, 5 vols, London, 1892–6

Lee, Joseph J. *The Modernisation of Irish Society 1848–1918*, Dublin, 1973
    Ireland 1912–1985: Politics and Society, Cambridge, 1989

Letters and Papers, Foreign and Domestic, Henry VIII, 21 vols, London, 1862–1932

Livingstone, Peadar. *The Fermanagh Story*, Enniskillen, 1969
    The Monaghan Story, Enniskillen, 1980

Lloyd, C. *Ireland Under the Land League*, Oxford, 1892

Longford, Frank Pakenham, Earl of, and Anne McHardy. *Ulster*, London, 1981

Longford, Frank Pakenham, Earl of, and Thomas P. O'Neill. *Eamon de Valera*, Dublin, 1970

Loughlin, James. *Gladstone: Home Rule and the Ulster Question 1882–93*, Dublin, 1986

Loughrey, Patrick (ed.). *The People of Ireland*, Belfast, 1988

Lowe, Henry N. *Fermanagh Directory and Household Almanac for 1880*, Enniskillen, 1880; reprinted Belfast, 1990

Lubenow, W.C. *Parliamentary Politics and the Home Rule Crisis 1886*, Oxford, 1988
Lydon, James. 'Richard II's expeditions to Ireland', *Journal of the Royal Society of Antiquaries of Ireland*, vol. 93 (1963)
  Ireland in the Later Middle Ages, Dublin, 1973
Lydon, James (ed.). *England and Ireland in the Later Middle Ages*, Dublin, 1981
Lyons, F.S.L. *John Dillon: A Biography*, London, 1968
  Ireland Since the Famine, London, 1971
Mac Niocaill, Gearóid. *Ireland Before the Vikings*, Dublin, 1972
McAughtry, Sam. *The Sinking of the Kenbane Head*, Belfast, 1977
Macaulay, Revd Ambrose. *Patrick Dorrian, Bishop of Down and Connor, 1865–85*, Dublin, 1987
McCall, Hugh. *Ireland and Her Staple Manufactures*, 2nd ed., Belfast, 1865
McCall, Timothy P.J. 'The Gaelic Background to the Settlement of Antrim and Down, 1580–1641', MA thesis, Queen's University Belfast, 1983
McCana, Proinsias. *Celtic Mythology*, London, 1975
McCann, Eamonn. *War and an Irish Town*, Harmondsworth, 1974
McCaughan, Michael and John Appleby (eds). *The Irish Sea: Aspects of Maritime History*, Belfast, 1989
McClean, Dr Raymond. *The Road to Bloody Sunday*, Swords, 1983
McCloskey, J. *Statistical Representation of Ballinascreen, Kilcronan, Desertmartin, Banagher, Dungiven and Boveva in the County of Londonderry*, edited by D. O'Kane, Ballinascreen, 1983
McCluskey, Conn. *Up Off Their Knees: A Commentary on the Civil Rights Movement in Northern Ireland*, Galway, 1989
McCracken, Eileen. *The Irish Woods Since Tudor Times: Distribution and Exploitation*, Newton Abbot, 1971
McCracken, J.L. *The Irish Parliament in the Eighteenth Century*, Dundalk, 1971
McCreary, Alf. *Survivors*, Belfast, 1976
McCutcheon, W.A. *The Industrial Archaeology of Northern Ireland*, Belfast, 1980
MacDermot, Frank. *Theobald Wolfe Tone and His Times*, Tralee, 1969
McDonnell, Pat. *They Wrought Among the Tow: Flax and Linen in County Tyrone*, Belfast, 1990
McEvoy, James. *Statistical Survey of the County of Tyrone*, Dublin, 1802
McGuffin, John. *Internment*, Tralee, 1973
McKittrick, David. *Despatches from Belfast*, Belfast, 1989
MacKnight, Thomas. *Ulster As It Is*, 2 vols, London, 1896
MacManus, Francis (ed.). *The Years of the Great Test 1926–39*, Cork, 1967
McMinn, J.R.B. 'Liberalism in north Antrim, 1900–14', *Irish Historical Studies*, vol. 23, no. 89 (May 1982)
  Against the Tide: J.B. Armour, Irish Presbyterian Minister and Home Ruler, Belfast, 1985
McNally, Robert (ed.). *Old Ireland*, Dublin, 1965
McNeill, Mary. *The Life and Times of Mary Ann McCracken 1770–1866: A Belfast Panorama*, Dublin, 1960; reprinted Belfast, 1988
McNeill, T.E. *Anglo-Norman Ulster: The History and Archaeology of an Irish Barony 1177–1400*, Edinburgh, 1980
  Carrickfergus Castle, Belfast, 1981
McParlan, James. *Statistical Survey of the County of Donegal*, Dublin, 1802
Macrory, Patrick. *The Siege of Derry*, London, 1980
Maguire, W.A. *The Downshire Estates in Ireland, 1801–45*, Oxford, 1972
  Living Like a Lord: The Second Marquis of Donegall 1769–1844, Belfast, 1984

Maguire, W.A. (ed.). *Kings in Conflict: The Revolutionary War in Ireland and its Aftermath 1689–1750*, Belfast, 1990

Malins, Edward and The Knight of Glin. *Irish Landscape Gardening 1660–1845*, London, 1976

Mallory, J.P. and S. Conlin. *Navan Fort: The Ancient Capital of Ulster*, Belfast, 1985

Mallory, J.P. and T.E. McNeill. *The Archaeology of Ulster: From Colonisation to Plantation*, Belfast, 1991

Maloney, Ed and Andy Pollak. *Paisley*, Dublin, 1986

Mansergh, Nicholas. *The Government of Northern Ireland: A Study in Devolution*, Woking, 1936

Marlow, Joyce. *Captain Boycott and the Irish*, London, 1973

Marsh, Arnold. *Saint Patrick and His Writings*, Dublin, 1966

Martin, F.X. 'Easter 1916: an inside report on Ulster', *Clogher Record*, vol. 12, no. 2 (1986)

Martin, F.X. and F.J. Byrne (eds). *The Scholar Revolutionary: Eoin MacNeill and the Making of the New Ireland*, Shannon, 1973

Marwick, Arthur. *Britain in the Century of Total War: War, Peace and Social Change 1900–1967*, Harmondsworth, 1970

Mattingly, H. *Tacitus on Britain and Germany*, London, 1948

Maxwell, Constantia. *Irish History from Contemporary Sources (1509–1610)*, London, 1923

Country and Town in Ireland Under the Georges, Dundalk, 1949

Maxwell, W.H. *History of the Irish Rebellion in 1798*, London, 1880

Messenger, Betty. *Picking Up the Linen Threads: A Study in Industrial Folklore*, Belfast, 1980

Middlemas, Keith (ed.). *Thomas Jones: Whitehall Diary, vol. 3: Ireland 1918–1925*, Oxford, 1971

Miller, David W. *Queen's Rebels: Ulster Loyalism in Historical Perspective*, Dublin, 1978

Miller David W. (ed.). *Peep O' Day Boys and Defenders: Selected Documents on the County Armagh Disturbances*, Belfast, 1990

Mitchell, Brian. *On the Banks of the Foyle: Historic Photographs of Victorian and Edwardian Derry*, Belfast, 1989

Moody, T.W. 'Redmond O'Hanlon', *Proceedings and Reports of the Belfast Natural History and Philosophical Society*, 2nd series, vol. 1 (1937)

'The treatment of the native population under the scheme for the plantation in Ulster', *Irish Historical Studies*, vol. 1, no. 1 (March 1938)

The Londonderry Plantation, 1609–41: The City of London and the Plantation of Ulster, Belfast, 1939

'Sir Thomas Phillips of Limavady, servitor', *Irish Historical Studies*, vol. 1, no. 3 (March 1939)

Davitt and Irish Revolution 1846–82, Oxford, 1981

Moody, T.W. (ed.). 'Ulster plantation papers, 1608–13', *Analecta Hibernica*, no. 8 (1938)

Moore, Brian. *The Emperor of Ice-cream*, London, 1987

Morgan, Hiram. 'The end of Gaelic Ulster: a thematic interpretation of events between 1574 and 1610', *Irish Historical Studies*, vol. 26, no. 191 (May 1988)

Moryson, Fynes. *An History of Ireland, From the Year 1599 to 1603*, 2 vols, London, 1617; reprinted Dublin, 1735

Moss, Michael and John R. Hume. *Shipbuilders to the World: 125 Years of Harland and Wolff, Belfast, 1861–1986*, Belfast, 1986

Mullin, T.H. *Ulster's Historic City: Derry, Londonderry*, Coleraine, 1986
Munck, Ronnie and Bill Rolston. *Belfast in the Thirties: An Oral History*, Belfast, 1987
Murnane, Peadar and James H. Murnane. 'The linen industry in the parish of Aughnamullen, Co. Monaghan, and its impact on the town of Ballybay, 1740–1835', *Clogher Record*, vol. 12, no. 3 (1987)
Murphy, Desmond. *Derry, Donegal and Modern Ulster 1790–1921*, Derry, 1981
Nelson, Sarah. *Ulster's Uncertain Defenders: Protestant Political, Paramilitary and Community Groups and the Northern Ireland Conflict*, Belfast, 1984
A New History of Ireland
    Vol. 2: Cosgrove, Art (ed.). *Medieval Ireland 1169–1534*, Oxford, 1987
    Vol. 3: Moody, T.W., F.X. Martin and F.J. Byrne (eds). *Early Modern Ireland 1534–1691*, 2nd ed., Oxford, 1978
    Vol. 4: Vaughan, W.E. and T.W. Moody (eds). *Eighteenth-Century Ireland 1691–1800*, Oxford, 1986
    Vol. 5: Vaughan, W.E. (ed.). *Ireland Under the Union, 1: 1801–70*, Oxford, 1989
    Vol. 9: Moody, T.W., F.X. Martin and F.J. Byrne (eds). *Maps, Genealogies, Lists: A Companion to Irish History, Part 2*, Oxford, 1984
Nicholls, Kenneth. *Gaelic and Gaelicised Ireland in the Middle Ages*, Dublin, 1972
Ó Cléirigh, Nellie. *Carrickmacross Lace: A Survey and Manual with Full-Size Patterns*, Gerrards Cross, 1990
Ó Corráin, Donncha. *Ireland Before the Normans*, Dublin, 1972
O Domhnaill, Sean. 'Sir Niall Garbh O'Donnell and the rebellion of Sir Cahir O'Doherty', *Irish Historical Studies*, vol. 3, no. 9 (March 1942)
O Lochlainn, Colm (ed.). *The Complete Irish Street Ballads*, London, 1984
O'Brien, Conor Cruise. *States of Ireland*, St Albans, 1974
O'Brien, G. (ed.). *Parliament, Politics and People: Essays in 18th Century Irish History*, Dublin, 1989
O'Connell, Maurice R. *Irish Politics and Social Conflict in the Age of the American Revolution*, Philadelphia, 1965
O'Donovan, John (ed.). *The Banquet of Dun na nGedh and the Battle of Magh Rath*, Dublin, 1842
O'Dowd, Liam, Bill Rolston and Mike Tomlinson (eds). *Northern Ireland: Between Civil Rights and Civil War*, London, 1980
O'Farrell, P. *Ireland's English Question: Anglo-Irish Relations 1534–1970*, London, 1971
O'Leary, Cornelius, Sydney Elliott and R.A. Wilford. *The Northern Ireland Assembly 1982–1986: A Constitutional Experiment*, London and Belfast, 1988
Oliver, John Andrew. *Working at Stormont*, Dublin, 1978
O'Malley, Padraig. *The Uncivil Wars: Ireland Today*, Belfast, 1983
    Northern Ireland: Questions of Nuance, Belfast, 1990
O'Meara, John J. (trans.). *The History and Topography of Ireland: Gerald of Wales*, Harmondsworth, 1982
O'Neill, K. *Family and Farm in Pre-Famine Ireland: The Parish of Killashandra*, Wisconsin, 1984
O'Neill, Terence. *Ulster at the Crossroads*, with an introduction by John Cole, London, 1969
    The Autobiography of Terence O'Neill, Prime Minister of Northern Ireland 1963–1969, London, 1972
O'Rahilly, T.F. *Early Irish History and Mythology*, Dublin, 1946
Orpen, Goddard H. *Ireland Under the Normans, 1169–1333*, 4 vols, Oxford, 1911–20; reprinted Dublin, 1968

'The earldom of Ulster, part 1 – Introductory to the inquisitions of 1333', *Journal of the Proceedings of the Royal Society of Antiquaries of Ireland*, vol. 43 (March 1913)

'The earldom of Ulster, part 2 – Inquisitions touching Carrickfergus and Antrim', RSAI Jn, vol. 43 (June 1913)

'The earldom of Ulster, part 3 – Inquisitions touching Down and Newtownards', RSAI Jn, vol. 44 (March 1914)

'The earldom of Ulster, part 4 – Inquisitions touching Coleraine and military tenures', RSAI Jn, vol. 45 (June 1915)

'The Normans in Tirowen and Tirconnell', RSAI Jn, vol. 45 (June 1915)

Orr, Philip. *The Road to the Somme: Men of the Ulster Division Tell Their Story*, Belfast, 1987

Otway-Ruthven, A.J. *A History of Medieval Ireland*, London, 1968

Pakenham, Frank. *Peace by Ordeal: An Account, from First-Hand Sources, of the Negotiation and Signature of the Anglo-Irish Treaty 1921*, London, 1962; *see also* Longford

Parkhill, Trevor and Sheela Speers (eds). *Kings in Conflict: Ireland in the 1690s*, Educational Resource Pack, documentary research by Patricia Hill, Donald McBride and Patricia Pauley, Belfast, 1990

Patterson, Henry. *Class Conflict and Sectarianism: The Protestant Working Class and the Belfast Labour Movement 1868–1920*, Belfast, 1980

Pearl, Cyril. *The Three Lives of Gavan Duffy*, Kensington, New South Wales, 1979

Pender, Seamus. *Essays and Studies Presented to Professor Tadhg Ua Donnchadha*, Cork, 1947

Perceval-Maxwell, Michael. *The Scottish Migration to Ulster in the Reign of James I*, London and New York, 1973

'The Ulster rising of 1641 and the depositions', *Irish Historical Studies*, vol. 21 (1978–9)

The Pictorial World: Belfast and Its Industries, 29 December 1888, 24 January and 14 February 1889 – A Select Compilation, Belfast, 1986

Public Record Office of Northern Ireland. *The Act of Union; Eighteenth-Century Ulster: Emigration to North America; The Great Famine; The Penal Laws; The '98 Rebellion; The United Irishmen; The Volunteers, 1778–84*, all in the Education Facsimile Series, Belfast, n.d.

Purdie, Bob. *Politics in the Streets: The Origins of the Civil Rights Movement in Northern Ireland*, Belfast, 1990

Purdon, C.D. *The Sanitary State of the Belfast Factory District (1864 to 1873 Inclusive)*, Belfast, 1877

Quinn, D.B. *The Elizabethans and the Irish*, New York, 1966

'William Montgomery and the description of the Ards, 1683', *Irish Booklore*, vol. 2 (1972)

Raftery, J. (ed.). *The Celts*, Cork, 1964

Ranelagh, John. *Ireland: An Illustrated History*, London, 1981

Reeves, William. *Ecclesiastical Antiquities of Down, Connor and Dromore*, Dublin, 1847

Reid, J.S. *History of the Presbyterian Church in Ireland*, edited by W.D. Killen, 3 vols, Belfast, 1867

The Repealer Repulsed: A Correct Narrative of the Repeal Invasion of Ulster. Dr. Cooke's Challenge . . . Also, an Authentic Report of the Great Conservative Demonstrations in Belfast on the 21st and 23rd of January, 1841, Belfast, 1841

Report of the Commissioners of Inquiry Respecting the Origins and Circumstances of the Riots in Belfast in June, July, August and September 1886, Belfast, C. 4925, 1887

Report of the Irish Boundary Commission, with an introduction by Geoffrey J. Hand, Dublin, 1969

'Report of the Plantation Commissioners, 1611', Lambeth Palace Library cod. 630, fol. 144, (typescript copy, Linen Hall Library), Belfast, n.d.

Richter, Michael. *Medieval Ireland: The Enduring Tradition*, Dublin, 1988

Robinson, Philip S. *The Plantation of Ulster: British Settlement in an Irish Landscape, 1600–1670*, Dublin and New York, 1984

Roche, Patrick J. and Brian Barton (eds). *The Northern Ireland Question: Myth and Reality*, Aldershot, 1991

Roebuck, Peter (ed.). *Plantation to Partition: Essays in Ulster History in Honour of J.L. McCracken*, Belfast, 1981

Rose, Richard. *Governing Without Consensus: An Irish Perspective*, London, 1971

Rowthorn, Bob and Naomi Wayne. *Northern Ireland: The Political Economy of Conflict*, Oxford, 1988

Ryder, Chris. *The RUC: A Force Under Fire*, London, 1989
The Ulster Defence Regiment: An Instrument of Peace?, London, 1991

Sacks, Paul Martin. *The Donegal Mafia: An Irish Political Machine*, London and New Haven, 1976

Sampson, G. Vaughan. *Statistical Survey of the County of Londonderry*, Derry, 1814

Sayles, G.O. 'The siege of Carrickfergus Castle 1315–1316', *Irish Historical Studies*, vol. 10, no. 37 (1956)

Senior, H. *Orangeism in Ireland and Britain 1795–1836*, London, 1966

Shannon, Colm. *Building a Better Belfast*, Belfast, 1991

Shea, Patrick. *Voices and the Sound of Drums: An Irish Autobiography*, Belfast, 1981

Silke, John J. *Kinsale: The Spanish Intervention in Ireland at the End of the Elizabethan Wars*, Liverpool, 1970

Simms, Katharine. 'The medieval kingdom of Lough Erne', *Clogher Record*, vol. 9 (1977)
From Kings to Warlords: The Changing Political Structure of Gaelic Ireland in the Later Middle Ages, Woodbridge and Wolfboro, 1987

Speed, P.F. *The Potato Famine and the Irish Emigrants*, Then and There Series, London, 1976

Stalker, John. *Stalker*, London, 1988

Steven Watson, J. *The Reign of George III 1760–1815*, Oxford, 1960

Stevenson, David. *Scottish Covenanters and Irish Confederates: Scottish-Irish Relations in the Mid-Seventeenth Century*, Belfast, 1981

Stewart, A.T.Q. *The Ulster Crisis*, London, 1967
The Narrow Ground: Aspects of Ulster, 1609–1969, London, 1977
Edward Carson, Dublin, 1981

Story, George. *A True and Impartial History of the Most Material Occurrences in the Kingdom of Ireland During the Two Last Years*, London, 1691

Sunday Times Insight Team. *Ulster*, Harmondsworth, 1972

Sweetman, H.S. and G.F. Handcock (eds). *Calendar of Documents Relating to Ireland 1171–1307*, 5 vols, London, 1886

Taylor, A.J.P. *English History 1914–45*, Oxford, 1965
The Habsburg Monarchy 1809–1918: A History of the Austrian Empire and Austria-Hungary, Harmondsworth, 1967

Thackeray, William Makepeace. *The Irish Sketch Book 1842*, London, 1843; reprinted, with an introduction by John A. Gamble, Belfast, 1985

Todd, James Henthorn (ed. and trans.). *Cogadh Gaedhel re Gallaibh: The War of the Gaedhil with the Gaill, or The Invasions of Ireland by the Danes and Other Norsemen*, London, 1867

Tuke, James Hack. *Irish Distress and Its Remedies*, London, 1880

Tyrconnell, Richard Talbot, Earl of. 'Letter book of Richard Talbot, Earl of Tyrconnell', *Analecta Hibernica*, vol. 4 (October 1932)

Vaughan, W.E. *Sin, Sheep and Scotsmen: John George Adair and the Derryveagh Evictions, 1861*, Belfast, 1983

Landlords and Tenants in Ireland 1848–1904, Dundalk, 1984

Walker, Brian. *Faces of the Past*, Belfast, 1974

Sentry Hill: An Ulster Farm and Family, Belfast, 1981

Ulster Politics: The Formative Years 1868–86, Belfast, 1989

Walker, Graham. *The Politics of Frustration: Harry Midgley and the Failure of Labour in Northern Ireland*, Manchester, 1985

Wall, Maureen. *The Penal Laws, 1691–1970*, Dundalk, 1976

Walsh, Micheline Kerney. *Destruction by Peace: Hugh O'Neill After Kinsale: Glanconcadhain 1602–Rome 1616*, Armagh, 1986

Weatherup, Roger. *Armagh: Historical Photographs of the Primatial City*, Belfast, n.d.

Weir, Anthony. *Early Ireland: A Field Guide*, Belfast, 1980

White, Barry. *John Hume: Statesman of the Troubles*, Belfast, 1984

Whyte, John H. *The Independent Irish Party 1850–9*, Oxford, 1958

Church and State in Modern Ireland 1923–1970, Dublin, 1971

The Tenant League and Irish Politics in the Eighteen-Fifties, Dundalk, 1972

Interpreting Northern Ireland, Oxford, 1990

Wichert, Sabine. *Northern Ireland Since 1945*, Harlow, 1991

Wilson, Gordon with Alf McCreary. *Marie: A Story From Enniskillen*, London, 1990

Wilson, Tom. *Ulster: Conflict and Consent*, Oxford, 1989

Witherow, Thomas. *Derry and Enniskillen in the Year 1689: The Story of Some Famous Battle-Fields in Ulster*, Belfast, 1913

Woodham-Smith, Cecil. *The Great Hunger: Ireland 1845–1849*, London, 1989

Woodman, P.C. 'A Mesolithic camp in Ireland', *Scientific American*, vol. 245 (August 1981)

Excavations at Mount Sandel 1973–77, County Londonderry, Belfast, 1985

Wright, Frank. *Northern Ireland: A Comparative Analysis*, Dublin, 1987

Wright, Thomas. *The History of Ireland from the Earliest Period of the Irish Annals to the Present Time*, 2 vols, London and New York, 1870

Young, Arthur. *A Tour in Ireland 1776–1779*, 2 vols, edited by A.W. Hutton, London, 1892

Zimmermann, Georges-Denis. *Songs of Irish Rebellion: Political Street Ballads and Rebel Songs, 1780–1900*, Dublin, 1967

Ards, 21, 67, 73; bailiwick, 45; fisheries, 47, 194; description of, 148–9; unemployment, 797

Armagh, Co., 4, 11, 15, 124, 506; Christianised, 16; plantation exemptions, 126; Cromwellian confiscation, 142; planters in, 147; linen industry, 184–5, 187; farming, 188; agrarian agitation, 206, 207; sectarian violence, 223–7; opposition to Union, 239; wakes, 248; density of population, 269, 270; Great Famine, 283–4, 308; evictions, 312; Protestant percentage, 345; elections, 374, 377, 459, 508; excluded from Home Rule, 447; and Boundary Commission, 508; apple-growing, 520; evacuees as cheap labour, 572; education in, 596; unemployment rate, 628; explosions, 664, 679; Protestants vulnerable, 691; 'Bandit Country', 729, 730–1; Provisional IRA unit, 737–8

Armagh cathedral, 80, 348

Armagh city, 6, 43, 99, 101, 107, 179, 200; monastery, 24, 28, 30; Brian Boru in, 29; primacy recognised, 31; plundered by O'Neill, 58; relieved by Sussex, 77; taken by Shane O'Neill, 78; defended by Russell, 97; Mountjoy garrison in, 109; defended by Chichester, 110; falls to rebels (1641), 137; population of, 146; no Catholic archbishop, 169; improvements, 201; arms searches, 230; 'invasion' of Ulster, 246; sectarian riots, 247, 536; railway, 264; evangelical meetings, 341–2; Orange parades, 355; economic decline, 397; population decline, 397; Nationalists win control, 468; local authority dissolved, 499–500; gerrymandering, 638; civil rights march, 657–8; civil rights riots, 670; internment riots, 682

Armour, Revd James B., 440, 514

Armoy, Co. Antrim, 29

Armstrong, Sir Robert, 752, 756

Arnold-Foster, H.O., 411, 414

Arranmore Island, Co. Donegal, 285

Ascendancy see landlords

Ash, Captain Thomas, 152, 156, 158

Asquith, Herbert H., 425, 430–2, 434, 445, 454, 456, 477, 478; Home Rule Bill, 435–6, 439; and partition, 441, 446, 447; First World War, 448; Home Rule Bill postponed, 450–1; negotiations with Carson, 453–4; condemns Black and Tans, 480

Atkins, Humphrey, 736, 745, 759; round-table conference, 739–40; and hunger strikes, 742

Attlee, Clement, 587, 589–91, 598, 700, 755; Ireland Act, 599–602

Audleystown, Co. Down, 6

Augher, Co. Tyrone, 158, 216

Aughnacloy, Co. Tyrone, 813

Aughrim, Battle of, 164–5

Augustinian order, 32, 38, 72

Austin's department store (Derry), 396

Australia, 311–12, 324, 347

Austria, 20, 298, 300, 334, 352, 495, 526

Avaux, Jean-Antoine, de Mesmes, Comte d', 155, 159

axe factories, 5

B Specials, 475–6, 485, 487, 506, 545, 582, 634, 645, 747; strength increased, 488–9; Home Guard, 562; and Saor Uladh, 605–7; and civil rights marches, 660, 662, 666; O'Neill mobilises, 662, 664; Belfast riots, 670; see also Ulster Special Constabulary

Bachall Íosa, 35, 73

Bagenal, Sir Henry, 79, 86, 89, 94–5, 96, 101

Bagenal, Nicholas, 202

Bailieborough, Co. Cavan, 269, 272

Baillie, Michael G.L., 11–12

Bainbrigge, Major-General, 300

Baird, Ernest, 707

Baker, Major Henry, 154

Balcombe St siege (London), 724

Baldwin, Stanley, 506, 508, 509, 541, 549

Balfour, Arthur, 410, 412, 413, 433, 442, 477; chief secretary, 383–4; irritated by Unionists, 418–19, 426; resigns, 434

Balfour, Gerald, 413

Balkan states, 466, 495, 826–7

Ballast Board (Belfast), 301

Ballinaleck, Co. Fermanagh, 287–8

Ballinamallard, Co. Monaghan, 290

Ballinamore and Ballyconnell Navigation, 258, 262–3

Ballinascreen, Co. Londonderry, 273, 281

Ballybay, Co. Monaghan, 217, 276; 'invasion' of Ulster, 245–6; tenant-right meeting, 315

Ballybofey, Co. Donegal, 691

Ballycarry, Co. Antrim, 149

Ballycastle, Co. Antrim, 501, 572; taken by Shane O'Neill, 79; tannery, 189; United Irishmen, 228; mining, 269; Land League, 368

Ballyclare, Co. Antrim, 65, 189

Ballyconnell, Co. Cavan, 283

Ballygally, Co. Antrim, 137

Ballykelly, Co. Londonderry, 749

Ballykelly airfield, 560

Ballykinler camp, Co. Down, 451, 486, 774; internment, 682

Ballymacarrett, Co. Down, 260, 288

Ballymacdermot cairn, 577

Ballymaghan, Co. Down, 40

Ballymena, Co. Antrim, 340, 572, 740; 1798 rebellion, 232, 233; debating duel, 252; railway, 264, 397; linen industry, 328; evangelical revival, 343, 344; Paisley arrested, 732; unemployment, 797

Ballymoney, Co. Antrim, 197, 285, 397, 440–1

Ballymurphy (Belfast): riots, 677–8, 680; girl killed, 693; republican feud, 726

Ballynagilly, Co. Tyrone, 4–5, 6

Ballynahinch, Co. Down, 229; 1798 rebellion, 233, 234–5, 236

Ballynure, Co. Antrim, 45, 260

Ballyscullion, Co. Londonderry, 9, 198

Belfast Morning News, 387, 408
Belfast News-Letter, 203, 246, 366, 387; bicentenary edition, 533, 546
Belfast Poor Law Union, 293
Belfast Regional Survey and Plan (Matthew, 1962), 624
Belfast Ropeworks, 338, 457, 464, 497, 548; closed, 628
Belfast Shipping Federation, 427
Belfast Urban Plan, 819
Belgium, 300, 334, 615, 744, 795, 827
Bell, Nellie, 572
Bell, Sam Hanna, 567
Bellaghy, Co. Londonderry, 343
Belleek, Co. Fermanagh, 78, 95, 99, 817; break of, 158; Great Famine, 295; Pottery, 358, 399; A Specials ambushed, 492; barracks attacked, 582
Belmore, 1st Earl of, 197
Belturbet, Co. Cavan: Presbyterians meet, 173; population of, 272, 397; Great Famine, 289
Benburb, Co. Tyrone, 80; Battle of, 140
Bennett, Judge Harry: Bennett report, 734–5
Beresford, Lord Charles, 437
Beresford, David, 783
Beresford, Tristram, 129
Berwick, Duke of, 158, 202
Bessbrook, Co. Armagh, 260, 262, 329; bombing (1979), 736; landmine (1981), 744
Better Government of Ireland Act (1920), 465, 476–9, 503, 505, 521, 541, 646; superseded by treaty, 484; restrictions of, 514–15; not invoked, 672
Bibby, John, and Sons, 335–6
Big Wind, night of the (January 1839), 261
Biggar, Joseph, 359, 360, 367, 369
Bigger, Francis Joseph, 420–2
Birkenhead, Lord (Frederick Edwin Smith), 437
Birmingham, 553; pub bombs, 723, 724; pub bombs convictions appealed, 781; pub bombs convictions quashed, 806
Birmingham, George A. (Canon James O. Hannay), 420
Birrell, Augustine, 425, 426
Biscuits, Ford of the, 95
Bishop, Patrick, 818, 823
Bisset, Margery, 68
Black and Tans, 467, 487
Black Death, 55–6
Black Pig's Dyke, 11
Blacker, William, 225–6
Blackwater Fort, Co. Armagh, 83, 85; destroyed, 96; rebuilt by Burgh, 99; isolated, 100–1; Chichester recovers, 110
Blair, Colonel David, 738
Blaney, Captain Edward, 107, 109
Blaney, Neil, 676–7, 743
Bleakley, David, 611, 713, 767
Blease, Billy, 709
Blenerhasset, Thomas, 126–7, 128

Bloody Friday (1972), 695–8
Bloody Sunday (1972), 686–8
Blount, Charles see Mountjoy, Lord
Blue Star line, 785
Blueshirts, 535, 541, 542, 554
Boal, Desmond, 620, 635
Board of Works: road network, 265–6; Great Famine, 283, 284, 285, 287, 291, 293
Boards of Guardians, 299, 524
Bodley, Sir Josias, 63, 109, 130
Boer War, 418
Bogside Defence Association, 673
Boland, Kevin, 676
Bombardier (Canada), 787
bombings: Belfast (1921), 484–5; Belfast (1922), 487–8; (1939, IRA), 553–4; (1969), 664; (1970), 678–9, 680–1; (1971), 685–6; Aldershot and Abercorn, 688; (1972), 692–3; Bloody Friday, 695–8; Claudy, 699; Dublin and Monaghan (1974), 708; Britain (1973–4), 722–5; (1976), 725–6; (1978), 733–4; (1979), 736, 737–8; (1982), 749; (1984), 753–4; booby–trap bombs, 772; (1987), 775–7; (1988–91), 803–6; 'proxy' bombs, 804; (1991), 810, 812–13; (1992), 814, 817–19
Bompard, Contre-Amiral, 237
Bonamargy Abbey, Co. Antrim, 73, 86
Bonaparte, Napoleon, 198, 237, 240, 241, 247, 249, 258–9
Bonar Law, Andrew, 434–5, 436, 441, 448, 458–9; accepts partition, 446; attacks Home Rule Bill, 451; treaty talks, 483; replaces Lloyd George, 494–5; and Boundary Commission, 505; arbitration committee, 535
'bonnacht', 69
Bono (U2), 777
Book of Armagh, 15, 24, 29, 35, 420
border: Pettigo incident (1922), 492; cross-border trade, 520–3; economic war, 536; roads closed, 606; used by IRA, 729; 'map-reading errors', 731; 'hot pursuit', 740
Bosnia, 826–7
Boulter, Hugh, archbishop of Armagh, 174, 175, 177, 179
Boundary Commission, 484, 486, 494, 500, 505–9, 510; suggested, 478
Bovevagh, Co. Londonderry, 277
Bowcott, Owen, 811, 816, 820
Boycott, Captain Charles, 366
Boyd, Billy, 611, 632
Boyd, Tom, 611, 612
Boyle, Kevin, 751
Boyne, Battle of the, 162–4
Bradford, Revd Robert, 491, 746
Braidwater Spinning Mill (Ballymena), 397
Breen, Detective Constable Derek, 772
Breen, Chief Superintendent Harry, 773, 804
Bréifne, 30
Brennock, Mark, 805–6
Brereton, Captain, 287, 288
Brett, Charles, 644, 646–7, 791
Brian Boru, 26, 29–30

Brighton bombing, 753–4
Brigid, St, 16, 38
Britain: land links with, 3; Roman Empire, 10–11; Napoleonic Wars, 228, 241, 244; attitudes to Famine, 299–300; industrial revolution, 300, 305; emigration to, 310–11; socialism, 417; shipbuilding, 516, 518, 613–14, 627–8; lack of new industries, 548; rearmament, 549; financial support for NI, 588, 590–1, 625; Suez crisis, 606; unemployment, 618–19, 628, 795; and NI economic development, 625; improved relations with republic, 629; involvement with NI, 672–3; institutes direct rule, 689; housing, 717; oil crises, 719–20; deflation, 721; Provisional IRA bombing campaign, 722–5; depression (1980s), 783–4, 788–9; standard of living, 794
British Army, 690–1; Belfast riots (1886), 382; Belfast dock strike (1907), 429; Curragh mutiny, 442, 445; co-operation with UVF (1920), 469; and Belfast blitz, 568–9; sent to NI (1969), 668–9; into Belfast, 671–2; honeymoon period, 672–4; Ballymurphy riots, 677–8; Protestant reaction to, 677–8; increased attacks on, 680–1; and internment, 681–6; Bloody Sunday, 686–8; Provisional IRA attacks on, 692–3; attacked by loyalists, 694–5, 700–1; Operation Motorman, 698–9; and UWC strike, 709–12; bus blown up (Manchester), 723; and RUC, 725; 'Murder Triangle', 729; increasing vigour, 729–30; Bessbrook bomb, 736; 'hot pursuit', 740; plastic bullets, 744; Ballykelly bomb, 749; contractors targeted, 772–3; Gibraltar shootings, 778; 'shoot-to-kill' policy suspected, 778–81, 810; Aldergrove bus bombed, 803; attacked overseas, 804–6; see also Parachute Regiment and Special Air Service
British Broadcasting Corporation (BBC), 605, 680, 684
British Embassy (Dublin), 688
British Enkalon (Antrim), 626, 782
British Petroleum, 786
Broighter, Co. Londonderry, 9
Bronze Age, 7–10
Brooke, Sir Basil, 553, 554, 562, 585, 603, 614, 622; and UVF, 467, 470, 474; and special constabulary, 476; inflammatory speeches, 538–9; minister of agriculture, 546–7; and Second World War, 556–7; authorises help from Éire, 566; and US troops, 574; replaces Andrews, 577–9; calls election, 588–9; and Attlee government, 590–1; created Lord Brookeborough, 595; health service, 597; considers visiting US, 598; Chapel Gate election, 600–1; closes border roads, 606; attitude to Catholics, 608–12, 633; and economic planning, 618–19, 623, 624; resignation, 620–1; refuses Lemass overtures, 629; outraged by Erskine decision, 634; refuses local government reform, 638
Brooke, Sir Calisthenes, 101

Brooke, Peter, 810–11, 814–15, 818, 827
Brookeborough, Co. Fermanagh, 368
Brookeborough, Lord see Brooke, Sir Basil
Brookeborough barracks, 606
Brookfield Mill (Belfast), 390, 616
Broughshane, Co. Antrim, 260
Browne, Dr Noël, 601–2
Brownlow, William, 211–12, 216
Bruce, Edward, 2; see also Bruce invasion
Bruce, Robert, 56; see also Bruce invasion
Bruce, Dr William, 293
Bruce invasion, 47, 49–53, 55
Brunswick Clubs, 246–7
Bryson, Herbert, 592
Buckingham Palace conference, 447
Buckinghamshire, Earl of, 211, 212, 214
Bunbeg, Co. Donegal, 560, 679
Buncrana, Co. Donegal, 260, 810
Bundoran, Co. Donegal, 397, 398
Bunting, Edward, 221, 420
Bunting, Major Ronald, 659, 665
Burgh, Hussey, 214, 216
Burgh, Lord Thomas, 99, 100
Burke, Edmund, 170–1, 218–19
Burntollet Bridge, Co. Londonderry, 659–61
Burt Castle, Co. Donegal, 118–19
Burtonport, Co. Donegal, 284–5
Bushmills, Co. Antrim, 47
Butler, Adam, 785
Butt, Isaac, 358–9, 360
Butter Market (Belfast), 389

Cahill, Joe, 675
caiseals (cashels), 21–2
Caldwell, Sir James, 195, 199
Caldwell, Jean, 814
Caledon, Co. Tyrone, 643, 651
Caledon House, 198–9
Callaghan, James, 669, 683, 721, 735, 736; visits NI, 673–4
Camergi, Co. Tyrone, 43
Cameron Commission, 638–9, 644–5, 651, 662, 715; on Derry march, 653, 655; report published, 674
Campaign for Democracy in Ulster, 646
Campaign for Social Justice in Northern Ireland, 639, 640, 643, 646, 652
Campbell, John and Joseph, 421
Campbell, T.J., 450, 512, 537, 568, 593
Campbell-Bannerman, Sir Henry, 375, 425, 430
Campbells, 68, 83, 96
Canada, 309–10, 353, 807
canals, 183, 200, 202, 203–5, 258, 262–3
Canavan, Michael, 657, 662, 673, 807–8
Canberra, 614
Canning, George, 131, 242
Canning, George, of Garvagh, 152
Cantrell and Cochrane (Belfast), 391
Caol-uisce Castle, Co. Fermanagh, 43
Capital Grants to Industry Act (1954), 618
Cappagh, Co. Tyrone, 810

Carbery, Ethna (Anna Johnston), 421
Carew, Sir George, 106, 110, 111
Carey, barony of, 135
Carlingford Lough, 39–40, 42, 398
Carlow, Co., 232
Carlyle, Thomas, 280, 299
Carndonagh, Co. Donegal, 18
Carnmoney, Co. Antrim, 47
Carrick, Co. Donegal, 284
Carrickatee estate, Co. Monaghan, 370
Carrickfergus, Co. Antrim, 39, 54, 67, 81, 84, 102, 133, 201; foundation of, 37; de Courcy mint, 38; King John in, 40; besieged by de Lacy, 41; bailiwick, 45; county, 46; fishery, 47; Bruce siege of, 51–3; Castle, 65; isolated, 67; Essex in, 83; ravaged by MacDonnell, 85; Chichester in, 100, 109; Mac Néill escapes from, 120–1; Black Oath enforced, 134; rebellion (1641), 136–7; surrenders to Venables, 141; population of, 146; Williamite assault on, 152–3; surrenders to Schomberg, 160; deforestation, 189; attacked by French, 211, 214; free elections, 216; martial law, 230; Brunswick Club, 246; linen industry, 580; Courtaulds bombed, 692; UWC strike, 708; synthetic fibre industry, 719; building improvements, 792
Carrickmacross, Co. Monaghan, 71, 397, 691; rapparees, 167; Lawless in, 245; Great Famine, 289; lace-making, 399
Carrickmore, Co. Tyrone, 823
Carrigart, Co. Donegal, 288
Carrington, Lord, 827
Carron, Owen, 746
Carson, Sir Edward, 416, 418, 424, 440, 442, 446, 463, 474, 601; leads Ulster Unionists, 432–7; visits Enniskillen, 436–7; Solemn League and Covenant, 437–9; seeks partition, 441; and UVF, 443; calls Volunteers to war, 448; and First World War, 449; withdraws from Commons, 451; and Easter Rising, 453; invited to Dáil, 462; wins Duncairn, 462; warns government, 470–1; argues for four counties, 478; opposes devolution, 479; opposes Boundary Commission, 484; Fisher writes to, 508; protection of statue of, 573; name suggested for bridge, 634
Carson, John, 765
Carson, Ned, 601, 634
'Carson Trail', 741
Carter, Charles F., 621, 640, 641
Casement, Roger, 420, 424–5, 440, 452, 453
Cashelreagh, Co. Donegal, 22
Cassels, Richard, 197, 204
Castle Archdale, Co. Fermanagh, 560
Castle Caldwell, Co. Fermanagh, 198, 199
Castle Coole, Co. Fermanagh, 197
Castle Hume, Co. Fermanagh, 199, 440
Castle Leslie, Co. Monaghan, 293
Castle Roe, Co. Londonderry, 1
Castle Upton, Co. Antrim, 197, 437
Castleblayney, Co. Monaghan, 179, 397

Castledawson, Co. Londonderry, 436
Castlederg, Co. Tyrone, 803
Castlereagh (Belfast), 664, 792; detention centre, 734–5
Castlereagh, Lord (Robert Stewart), 238–9, 242, 271
Castlereagh Castle, 66
castles, 36–7; forbidden to betaghs, 46; erected by Gaelic lords, 65–6
Castleward, Co. Down, 45
Castlewellan, Co. Down, 200, 329
Cathach (Psalter) of Colmcille, 17, 18
Cathal Crobhdearg, King of Connacht, 39, 41
Catholic Association, 244
Catholic Church: English hierarchy restored, 316; spiritual revival (1850), 340–9; church attendance in Ulster, 345; devotional practices, 346–7; seen as international conspiracy, 406–7; and Gaelic revival, 422–3; opposed to Education Bill, 503–4; Mother and Child scheme, 602–3; New Ireland Forum, 751; and integrated education, 802
Catholic Committee, 222
Catholic emancipation movement, 223–7, 241–2, 245–7
Catholic Representation Association, 423
Catholics: recusancy fines, 135; massacres (1641), 137–9; and English Civil War, 139–40; landowners disappear after Cromwell, 141–2; Cromwellian persecution, 145; hopes raised by James II, 149, 150; promises in Treaty of Limerick, 165–6; proportion of Ulster population, 167–8; conversions of, 170; Volunteer support for, 216–18; relief acts, 217, 221–2; and Act of Union, 238–9; evangelicalism, 240; devotional revival, 247–9; literacy rates, 248; Mass attendance, 248; social status of, 345; spread of, 346; Liberal votes, 356; Home Rule vote, 374–5; Belfast churches, 387; seen as separate nation, 400–2; economic position of, 405–6; Protestant views of, 406–7; fear of partition, 446; and civil service, 497–9; position in NI state, 510–14; reaction to de Valera constitution, 543; seeking reunification, 598–9; opposed to terrorism, 608; ignored in economic plans, 625–6; UVF attacks on, 635; employment of, 639–42, 644–5, 796–800; reactions to violence, 685; boycott border poll, 701; Provisional IRA seeks support of, 746–7; intimidation of, 769–80; see also Penal Laws and sectarianism
cattle, 22, 46–7; movement of, 64–5; trade, 133, 258; export banned, 146; disease, 175; houghing, 207
Caulfield, Sir Toby, 112, 128, 130
Cavan, Co., 4, 11, 30, 135, 146, 158, 320, 366, 397, 538, 691, 701; belongs to king, 124; townland divisions, 125; rebellion (1641), 137–8; Williamite War, 153; Presbyterians in, 173; stately homes, 197; cess revolt, 206; Defenders, 225; election (1826), 245; Mass attendance, 248;

Cluntoe airfield, Co. Tyrone, 575
Clydeside, 335, 336, 535, 580; Harland and Wolff
    leave, 627
coach travel, 264–5
Coagh, Co. Tyrone, 636, 810
coal, 183, 202, 203–4, 522–3; imported, 259;
    Belfast coal ring, 618
Coalisland, Co. Tyrone, 203, 607, 772, 774;
    sectarianism, 247; mining (1923–4), 522–3; RUC
    barracks attacked, 669
Cogadh Gaedhel re Gaillaibh, 25–9
Cohaw, Co. Cavan, 6
Cole, Sir William, 135, 137, 138
Coleraine, Co. Londonderry, 1, 15, 42, 43, 50,
    120, 149, 648; importance of, 47; belongs to
    king, 124; planted, 128–31; rebellion (1641),
    138; population of, 146; attacked by Jacobites,
    153; Williamite War, 154; distilling, 193;
    fisheries, 195; electorate, 216; Orange parades,
    244; Presbyterian Synod, 250; Great Famine,
    280; linen industry, 328; evangelical meeting,
    341; Churchill speech, 384; industrial
    development, 397–8; election clashes, 632
Coleraine Foundry, 397
Collins, Michael, 469, 481, 483, 485, 500, 541;
    leads Free State government, 486; pact with
    Craig, 489; civil war, 492–3
Colmcille, St, 17, 19, 38, 420
Colton, John, archbishop of Armagh, 61, 72
Columbanus, St, 19–20
Colwyn, Lord Frederick, 535
Combe Barbour's (Belfast), 391, 428; Catholics
    driven out, 471
Comber, Co. Down, 45, 82, 152, 190, 329; linen
    industry, 260, 398
Comgall, St, 18, 19
Commerce, Ministry of (NI), 522, 550–1, 626, 720
Commonwealth Labour Party, 589, 595
Communist Party, 581, 652
Compton, Sir Edward, 684
Concannon, Don, 721
Confederation of Kilkenny, 139–40
Congal One Eye, King of Dál nAraide, 20
Congested Districts Board, 386, 413, 415, 426
Connacht, 14, 42, 92, 94, 106, 366; O'Donnells
    overrun, 102; economic status of, 146;
    emigration from, 308; agriculture, 320
Connachta, the, 14
Connolly, James, 442, 453
Connor, Co. Antrim, 48, 240; Battle of, 51
Conolly, Thomas, 216
Conolly, William, 166
Conor, King of Ulster, 12
conscription, 459–60, 554
Conservative and Unionist Party, 383, 386, 432,
    679, 713, 782; and Home Rule, 359–60, 379–80,
    413, 425–6; tensions within, 419; rallies to
    Unionist support, 434–7; border poll, 701;
    under Thatcher, 735–41, 794; rolling
    devolution, 747–8; Brighton bombing, 753–4;
    irritation with Unionists, 755; subventions to

NI, 785–9, 791; education policy, 802; NI
    candidate, 817; see also Conservative Party
Conservative Party (pre-1886), 354, 355–6, 366;
    1885 election, 374–5; see also Conservative and
    Unionist Party
constabulary (Irish), 45, 242, 244, 253, 307, 312;
    Dolly's Brae, 303–4; evictions, 322–3; see also
    Royal Irish Constabulary and Royal Ulster
    Constabulary
constitution see Irish constitution (1937)
Conway, Sir Fulke, 124, 127
Conway, Cardinal William, 633, 685
Conway estate, Co. Antrim, 189
Conyngham, Marquess of, 285, 290, 321
Cook, David, 764–5
Cooke, Revd Henry, 248, 250, 251, 254, 257;
    challenges O'Connell, 255
Cookstown, Co. Tyrone, 200, 342, 397, 513; Land
    League, 368; local authority dissolved, 500;
    evacuees as cheap labour, 572; US troops in,
    576; housing discrimination, 643;
    unemployment, 797; van bomb, 810
Coolcran, Co. Fermanagh, 23
Cooper, Bob, 620, 800
Cooper, Ivan, 648, 650, 662; wins seat, 663; Battle
    of the Bogside, 666–7
Co-operation North, 803
Coote, Sir Charles, 141, 189
Cootehill, Co. Cavan: tannery, 189; population
    of, 272, 397; Great Famine, 296
Corkey, Revd Professor Robert, 579, 594
Corkey, Revd Dr William, 503
Corn Laws, 272, 281
Cornwallis, Lord, 238, 239
Corrigan, Mairead, 727, 733
Corry, Captain H.W.L., 359–60
Corry, J.P., and Co., 339
Corrymeela Community, 803
Cosgrave, Liam, 702–3, 713; Sunningdale
    Agreement, 703–7
Cosgrave, W.T., 493, 500, 502, 512, 521, 535, 541;
    and Boundary Commission, 505, 509
Costello, John A., 599, 601, 606; declares
    republic, 599–600; Mother and Child scheme,
    602–3
cottiers, 189, 268–71, 272–4, 275–6; Great
    Famine, 295, 298
cotton industry, 257–60, 267, 334, 517, 526;
    Belfast mill, 203; protective duties, 238;
    American Civil War, 327, 328
Council of Ireland, 509, 701–7
Counter–Reformation, 74, 132, 135
county 'cess', 196, 205–6, 207
Courtaulds (Carrickfergus), 618, 692, 708, 782
Covenant, the National (Scotland, 1643), 133–4
Covenant, Solemn League and (Ulster, 1912),
    437–9; fiftieth anniversary, 620
Cowan, Barry, 710–11
Cowan, Sir Edward, 375–6
Craig, Captain Charles, 477–8, 505
Craig, Lady, 479, 481, 554, 561

Craig, Sir James, 441, 442, 463, 492, 552, 553, 581, 610, 622, 633; opposition to Home Rule, 426; and Carson, 432–3; Ulster Day, 437; and First World War, 448, 449; warns government, 474; formation of Ulster Special Constabulary, 476; suggests Boundary Commission, 478; succeeds Carson, 479; meets de Valera, 480; and treaty, 482–4; and Collins, 486, 489; and loyalist kidnappings, 486–7; expands Ulster Special Constabulary, 488–9; formation of NI state, 494–505; and Boundary Commission, 505–9; Stormont legislation, 510–14; created Viscount Craigavon, 513; presidential style of, 513; and unemployment, 523–5, 527; begging expeditions, 535; supports Brooke, 538–9; on de Valera constitution, 543; general election (1938), 544–5; and Second World War, 554–5, 563, 564; ill-health, 556; and offer on treaty ports, 557–8; death of, 561–2

Craig, William, 624, 652, 657, 665, 694; and Derry march, 654, 655; sacked, 658; leads Ulster Vanguard, 689, 690; rejects power-sharing, 702; UWC committee, 707, 708; expelled from UUUC, 713; fights Housing Executive Bill, 715

Craigavon, Co. Armagh, 625, 717, 784, 810; families flee to, 791–2; unemployment, 797; RUC station bombed, 813

Craigavon, Lady see Craig, Lady

Craigavon, Viscount see Craig, Sir James

Cratlagh, Co. Donegal, 364

Crawford, Lieutenant-Colonel Fred, 431, 443, 444, 472, 474–5, 485

Crawford, Lindsay, 416, 428, 432

Crawford, William Sharman, 297, 314, 315, 316

Crebilly Castle (Ballymena), 491

Credit Union, 649

Crimean War, 300, 318

Croagh Patrick, Co. Mayo, 15

Crolly, Dr, archbishop of Armagh, 348

Crom Castle, Co. Fermanagh, 159

Cromaghs, Co. Antrim, 8

Crommelin, Louis, 174, 180

Cromwell, Oliver, 149, 150; in Ireland, 140–1

Crossdall, Co. Monaghan, 96

Crossmaglen, Co. Armagh, 399, 729, 738, 804, 810

Crossman, Richard, 672–3, 674

Cruithne (Cruthin), the, 13, 14, 19, 20–1

Crumlin, Co. Antrim, 260

Crumlin Rd gaol (Belfast), 582, 583; Paisley in, 635, 664; internment, 682–3

Cuchulain, 12

Cuellar, Captain Francisco de, 63, 90–2

Culdaff Relief Committee, 283–4

Cullen, Paul, Cardinal, 316, 345, 346, 348, 352, 353

Culloville, Co. Armagh, 582

Cullyhanna, Co. Armagh, 522

Culmore Fort, Co. Donegal, 104, 118–19, 129, 155

Cultra, Co. Down, 37

Cultural Traditions Group, 802–3

Cumann na nGaedheal, 535

Cumber, Co. Londonderry, 272

Cunard line, 337, 393

Cunningham, Waddell, 205, 206

Curragh camp, Co. Kildare, 583, 607; mutiny, 442, 445

Currie, Austin, 651, 652–3, 686, 748; Derry march, 654

Currin, Co. Monaghan, 267, 268, 274, 277

Cushendall, Co. Antrim, 249, 260, 492

Cushendun, Co. Antrim, 79

Czechoslovakia, 495, 496, 650

Daghda, 16

Dáil Éireann, 469, 482, 493; established, 462; declared illegal, 465; Unionist distrust of, 477–8; 'Belfast Boycott', 485, 486, 521; treaty debate, 485–6; and NI councils, 499–500; and Boundary Commission, 509; de Valera enters, 510; NI fund, 676; emergency powers legislation, 700; TDs visit Sands, 743; approves Anglo-Irish Agreement, 759; Provisional Sinn Féin drops abstention, 771

Dál Fiatach, 13, 21, 34, 36, 38

Dál nAraide, 20–1

Dál Riata, 17, 21, 27

Dalrymple, General William, 225, 226

D'Alton, John, archbishop of Armagh, 603

Daly, Cahal, Archbishop, 751, 811

Daly, Commandant-General Charles, 493–4

Daly, Fr Edward, 687–8

Dane's Cast, 11

Darby, John, 769–70

d'Arcy, Inspector, 296–7, 298

Dartraige, the, 13

Dartry, Co. Monaghan, 13

Davidson, Anthony, 695–6

Davidson, David, 576, 584

Davidson's Sirocco Works see Sirocco Works

Davies, Sir John, 60, 115, 116, 118; plantation scheme, 120, 125

Davison, Sir Joseph, 539–40, 579

Davitt, Michael, 367, 368–9, 400, 408, 413

Dawson, George, 288–9, 294–5

de Braose, Matilda, 39, 40

de Braose, William, 39, 40, 41

de Bruxelles, Simon, 778

de Burgo, Elizabeth (Brown Earl's daughter), 44, 49, 52, 54, 59

de Burgo, Richard, 3rd Earl of Ulster (Red Earl), 2, 42, 44–5, 48, 49–52, 53

de Burgo, Walter, 43–4, 54

de Burgo, William, 4th Earl of Ulster (Brown Earl), 49, 53–4, 59

de Burgos: change of name, 54

de Clare, Richard fitzGilbert (Strongbow), 33

de Courcy, John, 26, 40; invasion of Ulster, 34–7; quarrel with king, 38–9

de Galloway (Scots), 41, 42

de Lacy, Hugh, 33, 38–40, 41–2

de Lacys, 35, 51

de Latocnaye see Latocnaye, Le Chevalier de

Dobbs, Richard, 149
Docwra, Sir Henry, 104–5, 107, 110, 112, 118; aid from O'Dohertys, 108–9; destroys harvest, 113
Dodds, Nigel, 821
Doe Castle, Co. Donegal, 66, 119–20, 139
Doherty, Paddy, 628–9, 820
Dolly's Brae, Co. Down, 302–4
dominion status, 590
Donaghadee, Co. Down, 46, 122, 127, 256, 398
Donaghcloney, Co. Down, 329, 333
Donaghmore, Co. Tyrone: Great Famine, 280; nationalist meeting, 446
Donal mac Aedo, King of Uí Néill, 21
Donard Park, Co. Down, 440
Donegal, Co., 11, 129, 150, 318, 321, 553, 572, 585, 691, 701, 792; early tribes, 14; caiseals, 22; Armada survivors, 88, 89; agriculture, 192; fisheries, 194; Mass attendance, 248; open-air Masses, 248; wakes, 248; roads, 265–6; survey (1802), 270; Ordnance Survey, 274; poverty of, 278–80; crop failures, 280; Great Famine, 282, 284–5, 295, 308; emigration, 309; Adair purchase, 317; Protestant percentage, 346; agricultural depression, 362–3; Lord Leitrim murder, 363–5; Land League, 366; elections, 375, 415; Congested Districts, 386, 413; shirt-making outworkers, 395; birth rate, 396; Irish language in, 421; Unionist associations, 426; excluded from partition, 454, 467; Sinn Féin in, 469–70; Unionists seek inclusion, 478; British Army in, 492; civil war in, 493–4; and Derry, 521; U-boats, 559–60; neglected, 588; peace and prosperity, 829
Donegal Abbey, 108, 109
Donegal Castle, 65
Donegal town, 73, 80, 297
Donegall, Arthur Chichester, 4th Earl of, 202
Donegall, Arthur Chichester, 5th Earl and 1st Marquess of, 203, 206–7, 208, 238
Donegall, George Augustus Chichester, 2nd Marquess of, 244, 258, 262, 317
Donegall, George Hamilton Chichester, 3rd Marquess of, 317
Donegore, Co. Antrim, 45, 251
Donnelly, Patrick, bishop of Dromore, 169
Doonbought, Co. Antrim, 48
Dorrian, Patrick, bishop of Down and Connor, 346–7, 353
Dorsey, the, 11, 12
Dortmund shooting, 804
Douglas-Home, Sir Alec, 632
Down, Co., 11, 45, 67, 82, 506, 642, 714, 798; early tribes, 13; Normans in, 26, 27, 36–8; plantation, 120–4, 133, 147; Cromwellian confiscation, 142; O'Hanlon in, 144; agriculture, 192; large estates, 195; agrarian agitation, 207; United Irishmen, 227–30; 1798 rebellion, 233–7; famine relief, 285; Great Famine, 288, 308; emigration, 309; Protestant majority, 345; Land League, 366–7; elections,

416; excluded from Home Rule, 447; de Valera election candidate, 479
Down District Council, 822
Downhill, Co. Londonderry, 3, 198
Downing St attack, 806
Downing St Declaration, 672, 715
Downpatrick, Co. Down, 15, 23, 34–5, 38, 43, 178, 344, 355; monastery, 25, 47; King John in, 40; walls of, 47; medieval kiln, 48; population of, 146; restored, 200; Volunteers, 215; 1798 rebellion, 234, 235; Russell hanged, 240; Orange parades, 244; Brunswick Club, 246; Land League, 368; economic decline, 398; local authority dissolved, 500; housing, 534
Downpatrick cathedral, 38
Downshire, Arthur Hill, 2nd Marquess of, 238
Downshire, Arthur Blundell Sandys Trumbull Hill, 3rd Marquess of, 262, 287
Downshire estate, 269
Doyle, Lynn C., 406–7
Drapers' Company, 130, 131
Draperstown, Co. Londonderry, 342
Drennan, Dr William, 220, 242, 249
Drew, Revd Thomas, 306
Drogheda, Co. Louth, 52, 61; Black Death, 55–6; besieged (1641), 138; Cromwellian massacre, 140–1, 150
Dromabest, Co. Antrim, 8
Dromara, Co. Down, 191
Dromore, Co. Down, 79, 398, 475; burned in 1641 rebellion, 137; break of, 152–4; neglect of, 200–1; opposition to O'Connell, 255; attacks on Catholics (1920), 471
Dromore, Co. Tyrone: nationalist demonstration, 373
Dromore Castle, Co. Down, 45
Dromsnat, Co. Monaghan: monastery, 12
Droppin' Well pub bombing, 749
Druim Cett (Derry), 17
Drumane (Ford of the Biscuits), 95
Drumaness, Co. Down, 329
Drumbo, Co. Down, 29
Drumglass, Co. Tyrone, 203
Drumlane, Co. Cavan, 29
Drumlomman, Co. Cavan, 277
Drumm, Maire, 693, 700
Drummaul, Co. Antrim, 267, 268, 275
Drummond, Thomas, 325
Du Pont (Derry), 618, 647, 657
Dublin, 30, 258, 718; Norse of, 26–9; taken by Normans, 33; King John in, 39; Bruce siege of, 52; Black Death, 55–6; 'Land of Peace', 57; Reformation in, 73–4; Essex dies in, 85; Williamite War, 160, 162; linen merchants, 180–1, 187; distilling, 193; imports of coal, 204; Ascendancy capital, 213; Whig Club, 220; United Irishmen, 227; Emmet rebellion, 240; railway, 264, 398; Fenian rising, 352–4; labour movement in, 430, 442; civilians shot by army, 447; Four Courts siege, 493; Eucharistic Congress, 537; refugees from Belfast blitz, 568;

blitzed, 574; Belfast refugees to (1969), 671; British Embassy burned down, 688; loyalist bomb (1972), 700; car bombs (1974), 708–9; *see also* Pale, the

Dublin Castle, 221; heads exposed over gate, 81, 87; Red Hugh O'Donnell imprisoned, 92, 93–4; attack foiled, 135; Emmet rebellion, 240

Dudley, Robert, Earl of Leicester, 79, 81

Dufferin, Co. Down, 67, 127

Dufferin and Ava, Marquess of, 450

Duffin, Adam, 377, 412, 453, 455, 458

Duffin, Emma, 455, 567–8, 571–2, 586

Dun, Thomas, 50, 53

Dunadry, Co. Antrim, 46, 355

Dunaverney, Co. Antrim, 9

Dunbar McMaster and Co., 262, 329

Dundalk, Co. Louth, 97, 145, 179, 441; razed by Bruce, 50; Edward Bruce crowned, 52; plundered by Shane O'Neill, 80; taken by rebels (1641), 138; Schomberg's camp, 160; Williamite War, 162

Dundonald, Co. Down, 40, 47, 54, 817

Dundrum, Co. Down, 37, 38, 39, 40, 42, 71

Duneane, Co. Antrim, 249

Dunfanaghy, Co. Donegal, 285

Dunfanaghy Union, 363

Dungannon, Co. Tyrone, 23, 71, 93, 109, 119, 343, 397, 580; Castle, 70, 97; Mountjoy in, 112; captured by rebels, 136; recovered by Monro, 139; linen industry, 187; building of, 201; Orange demonstrations, 254, 367; anti-Home Rule campaign launched, 376; police shot by IRA, 582; election clashes, 632; local authority discrimination, 636–8, 639, 643, 648; civil rights movement, 652–3, 670; Tyrone Crystal, 735

Dungannon Club (1905), 424

Dungannon Convention, 214–16, 223, 424

Dungannon District Council, 822

Dungiven, Co. Londonderry, 23, 129, 609; taken by MacMahon, 141; RUC charges crowd, 666; civil rights riots, 670; Orange riots, 681

Dunluce Castle, Co. Antrim, 79, 86–7, 91, 100

Dunmurry (Belfast), 460, 782, 783, 792

Dunne, Sister Catherine, 804, 805

duns, 23

Dunseverick, Co. Antrim, 23, 65, 79

Dunsilly, Co. Antrim, 37

Durham, Colonel James, 233

Eames, Dr Robin, archbishop of Armagh, 775–6

Earls, Flight of the, 115, 116–18

Easter Rising (1916), 443, 451–4, 459, 461, 629; amnesty, 458; fiftieth anniversary, 634

economic conditions: recovery (Restoration), 145–6; eighteenth century, 175–6, 208; effects of American Revolution, 211–12; slump (1815), 271–4; decline, early twentieth century, 396–9; during First World War, 456–7; post-First World War boom, 463–4; after partition, 467; depression, NI state, 515–35; oil crises,

691, 719–22; depression (1980s), 782–9; widespread poverty, 793–6; economic renewal, 818–20

Economic Survey of Northern Ireland, An (Isles and Cuthbert), 617–18

Edenduffcarrick, Co. Antrim, 67, 79; falls to Chichester, 100; Castle, 121; mansion, 197; *see also* O'Neills of Shane's Castle *and* Shane's Castle

education, 273, 426; higher education, 217, 345, 359; and proselytism, 252; National Schools, 254, 387; Londonderry Bill, 501–5; movement towards reform, 593–6; integrated, 596; higher education committee, 625; O'Neill's hopes, 633; discrimination in, 798, 800; moves for integration, 800–3

Education, Department of (Free State), 502

Education, Ministry of (NI), 515, 595–6, 640, 801

Education Act (1903), 504–5

Education Act (1947), 593–5, 644, 656

Education Reform Order (Northern Ireland) (1990), 802

Edward I, King of England, 43, 44, 45

Edward II, King of England: and Robert Bruce, 49; and Bruce invasion, 51, 53

Edward III, King of England, 53–4

Edward IV, King of England, 67, 69

Edward VI, King of England, 73

Edward VII, King of England, 388; Prince of Wales, 302, 345

Edward VIII: Prince of Wales, 513; abdication, 542

Egan, Bowes, 656

Eggs Marketing Act (1924), 521

Eglinton airfield, Co. Londonderry, 560, 575

Eilne, 13

Éire, 542–3; treaty ports, 545; neutrality of, 552–3; sends fire engines to Belfast, 566, 570, 585–6; suppression of IRA, 583; isolationism, 588, 603; health service, 597–8; *see also* Irish Free State *and* Republic of Ireland

Eksund gun-running, 774–5

Election and Franchise Act (1946), 638–9

elections: close boroughs, 216; (1826), 245; votes for artisans, 354; secret ballot, 358; labourers' vote, 374; along religious lines, 374–5; Nationalist victory (1886), 403; electorate doubled, 461; *see also* general elections

Electoral Law Amendment Act (1968), 633

Elizabeth I, Queen of England, 74; conquest of Ulster, 75–114; and Shane O'Neill, 77–80, 93, 102–3, 122; and Essex expeditions, 82–5; determined to defeat O'Neill, 102–3; refuses terms with O'Neill, 112; offers pardon, 113–14; debts of, 118

Elizabeth II, Queen of England, 608, 614, 617, 631; visits NI, 634

Ellison–Macartney, W.G., 360, 418

Emain Macha *see* Navan Fort

emigration, 208, 396, 795, 797, 807; Protestants to United States, 176–9; eighteenth century, 209–10; migrant labour, 276–7, 363; Great Famine, 308–12; coffin ships, 309–10; to

Britain, 310–11; transport, 336–7; remittances, 361; Derry port, 395; decline in, 629

Encumbered Estates Act (1849), 317

Engineering, 338–9

engineering industry, 390–1

England: emigration to United States, 115–16, 125; peace with Spain, 118; planters from, 126–7; deforestation, 127; civil war, 116, 133–4, 139–40; Restoration, 116, 142–3; prosperity, 146; labourers' revolt, 253; migrant labourers to, 277; Chartism, 297

Enlightenment, the, 170–1, 217–18

Enniskillen, Co. Fermanagh, 96, 141, 347, 441, 460, 538, 605; besieged (1593), 95; rebellion (1641), 137, 138; population of, 146; defended by Hamilton, 153; Williamite War, 153; Siege of, 158–9; tannery, 189; improvements, 201; Volunteers, 215; sectarian rioting, 247; Great Famine, 296–7; Orange parades, 355; Parnell visits, 372; population decline, 397; Carson visits, 436–7; Nationalists win control, 468; flag pulled down, 499; nationalist rally, 535; marches banned from centre, 609; election clashes, 632; housing discrimination, 642–3; Remembrance Day bomb, 775–7, 782, 822; building improvements, 792

Enniskillen Castle, 65

Enniskillen Dragoons, 255

Erenagh Abbey, Co. Down, 38

Erne, River, 4, 99

Erskine, Lord, 634

Ervine, St John, 513

Essex, 1st Earl of (Walter Devereux), 82–5, 92, 93, 94, 96

Essex, 2nd Earl of (Robert Devereux), 102–3

Established Church *see* Church of Ireland

ether-drinking, 342–3

Eucharistic Congress (1932), 537

Europa Hotel (Belfast), 813

European Community (EC), 720; entry to, 787–8; unemployment in, 795

European Parliament, 743, 749; elections, 739, 753; Paisley expelled from, 768

evangelicalism, 240; 1859 revival, 340–4

Evans, E. Estyn, 4

evictions, 206–8, 252–3, 275, 311, 312–14, 361–2; Derryveagh, 321–4; Lord Leitrim murder, 363–5

Ewart-Biggs, Christopher, 726

Ewart-Biggs, Jane, 726–7

Ewart's Mill (Belfast), 390, 547, 566, 616

External Relations Act (1936), 542, 599–600, 601–2

extortion, 728

extradition, 777, 781–2

Factory Act (1847), 332

Factory Act (1874), 332–3

Fahan, Co. Donegal, 18

Fair Employment Commission, 799–800

Fairley, Professor Gordon Hamilton, 724

Falklands War, 745, 747, 750, 760

Fallahogy, Co. Londonderry, 5

famines, 99; fourteenth century, 55, 62–3; after O'Neill rebellion, 113; after Cromwellian war, 141; early eighteenth century, 175–6; *see also* Great Famine

Fanad, Co. Donegal, 364

farmers *see* agriculture

Farney, Co. Monaghan, 92, 109

Farnham, 11th Baron, 478

Farrell, Michael, 654, 656, 659, 663

Faul, Fr Denis, 744, 745

Faulkner, Brian, 607, 609, 620, 621, 630, 648, 657, 665, 700, 715, 784; minister of commerce, 624, 626; revolts against O'Neill, 635; resigns, 662; succeeds Chichester-Clark, 681; internment, 681–6; resigns as prime minister, 689, 690, 692; Sunningdale Agreement, 703–7; resigns as Unionist leader, 706; denounces UWC, 708; resigns from Executive, 711; forms UPNI, 713

Feakle, Co. Clare: peace talks, 724

Feeney, Brian, 809

Feetham, Richard, 506–9

Fenian Brotherhood, 309, 352–4, 356, 359, 365; Lord Leitrim murder, 364–5

Fenton, Sir Geoffrey, 90, 106

Fergus Mór mac Erc, 17

Ferguson, Samuel, 420

Fermanagh, Co., 4, 11, 397, 506, 607; early tribes, 24; kingdom of Maguires, 59–60; Shane O'Neill in, 78, 80; O'Neill in hiding, 112; partitioned, 116; belongs to king, 124; townland divisions, 125; plantation exemptions, 126; Scots planters, 128; rebellion (1641), 137, 138; O'Hanlon in, 144; stately homes, 197, 199; cess revolt, 206; Great Famine, 280–1, 284, 295, 298, 307; emigration, 309; Protestant percentage, 345; Catholic majority, 346; peaceful co-existence, 357; elections, 411, 416; Congested Districts Board, 413; Irish Volunteers, 443; Sinn Féin candidate, 462; Sinn Féin in, 470; loyalists kidnapped, 486–7; county council dissolved, 499–500; and Boundary Commission, 508; housing, 532, 642, 792; proportion of Protestants, 538; US troops in, 576; education in, 596; hostility to O'Neill, 636; gerrymandering, 638, 639; housing discrimination, 642; Protestants vulnerable, 691; housing quality, 792; Protestants driven out, 807

Fermanagh District Council, 823

Fews, the, Co. Armagh: wasted by Mountjoy, 109; plantation exemptions, 126

Fianna Fáil, 510, 597, 603, 702–3, 754; economic war, 535–7; and IRA, 541–2, 700; loses power (1948), 599; arms crisis, 676–7; Haughey leads, 740; New Ireland Forum, 751–2; and Anglo-Irish Agreement, 756, 759

Finance, Ministry of (NI), 548, 640

Fine Gael, 543, 599, 631, 703, 755; in coalition, 702; New Ireland Forum, 751–2
Finner, Co. Donegal, 451
Fintona, Co. Tyrone, 643
Fir Lí, 36
Fir Manach, 59
fire brigades, 387
First World War, 386, 395, 446–8, 451, 466; volunteers from Ulster, 448–50; Battle of the Somme, 454–6; economic effects of, 456–7; conscription, 459–60; armistice, 460–2; increased employment for Catholics, 471; effects of, 516
fisheries, 1, 47, 63, 193–5, 279, 399; Derry salmon, 146
Fishmongers' Company, 128–9, 154, 272
Fisk, Robert, 708
Fitt, Gerry, 645–6, 653, 669, 679, 703, 748; Derry march, 654; Sunningdale Agreement, 703–7; on Mason, 730; withdraws support in Commons, 735; resigns as SDLP leader, 739; loses to Adams, 749
FitzGerald, Lord Edward, 417
FitzGerald, Garret, 726, 747, 788, 808; Sunningdale Agreement, 703–7; on Thatcher, 735–6; New Ireland Forum, 750–3; Anglo-Irish Agreement negotiations, 754–7
Fitzgerald, Garret Mór, 8th Earl of Kildare, 69–70
Fitzgerald, Garret Óg, 9th Earl of Kildare, 70
Fitzgerald, Silken Thomas, 70
FitzGilbert, Duncan, Earl of Carrick, 40
FitzWarin family, 40, 47
Fitzwilliam, Sir William, 76, 82, 88, 89, 91; divides MacMahons, 92
Five Fingers Strand, Co. Donegal, 775
Flags and Emblems Act (1954), 604, 632
Flanagan, Jamie, 725
Fleming, Patrick, 167
Flight of the Earls, 115, 116–18
flint, 3, 4, 5
Flood, Henry, 213, 215, 216
Florence Court, Co. Fermanagh, 198
folk religion, 345
food and drink, 62–3
Ford, Major-General Robert, 687, 695, 698
Forde, Lieutenant-Colonel W.B., 358
forestry: prehistoric forests, 3–6; British forests depleted, 127; planters' depredations, 129; deforestation, 146, 148–9, 189–90, 276; timber imports, 190
Forkhill, Co. Armagh: Defender outrage, 224
Forrest, George, 636
Forster, William, 285
Forster, William E., 366, 369
Fortnight, 751
Four Step Inn (Belfast), 685
Foyle, River, 175
Foyle College (Derry), 396
Foyle Shipyard, 395

France, 41, 98, 162, 166, 170, 300, 334, 352, 558, 615, 774, 800; English wars in, 45, 49; trade with, 47; English fear Irish alliance, 83; civil war, 112; trade with, 146; and American Revolution, 211, 212; and United Irishmen, 227, 228–9, 236–7; revolution (1830), 253; (1848), 298; Paris (1968), 651; reaction to Sands's death, 744
Franciscan order, 73, 132
Franco, General Francisco, 542, 544, 827
Frankfort Moore, F., 306, 349, 350, 352, 380, 382
Franz Josef, Emperor, 305, 352
Free Presbyterian Church, 630, 631
free trade, 214, 238
Freeland, Lieutenant-General Sir Ian, 672, 678
Freeman's Journal, 314, 453
French Revolution, 184, 218, 221
friars, 73
Fyn Castle, Co. Donegal, 65

Gaddafi, Colonel, 732, 774–5
Gaelic Athletic Association (GAA), 422, 652, 809
Gaelic Irish: society, 16–17, 20–4; surnames emerge, 30; kings with opposition, 30–1; weapons used, 35–6; and earldom, 46, 54, 56–7; 'The Great Irishry', 57–9; castles erected by, 65–6; outside the Pale, 66–8; Surrender and Regrant, 71–2; resist Elizabeth, 94; economic strength of, 99; devastated after O'Neill rebellion, 114; effects of plantation, 115–16; accept settlers, Antrim and Down, 121–2; exemptions from plantation, 126; response to plantations, 128, 130–3; unused to estate management, 135; rebellion (1641), 135–42; aristocracy wiped out, 142, 167
Gaelic League, 420, 421
Gaelic revival, 221, 386; twentieth century, 419–22; Catholic emphasis of, 422–3
Gage family, 192
Gall, St, 20
'Gall, the' (use of term), 56
Gallagh, Co. Londonderry: massacre of Spanish, 88
Gallagher, Charlie, 570, 576, 584–5
Gallagher, Frank, 601, 621, 639
Gallaher, Thomas, 427, 428
Gallaher's tobacco factory (Belfast), 391, 548
galloglaigh see gallowglasses
Galloon, Co. Fermanagh, 277
gallowglasses, 56–7, 97
Galt, John, 239
Garrett, Brian, 644, 711
Garrison, Co. Fermanagh, 137
Garron Tower, Co. Antrim, 491, 610
Gartan, Co. Donegal, 321
Garvagh, Co. Londonderry, 242–3, 600
Garvagh estate, 272; rents raised, 268–9
Gavan Duffy, Charles, 298, 347; tenant-right movement, 314–15, 316
Gavan Duffy, George, 465, 483
general elections: (1852), 316; (1868), 355–6;

892

(1874), 359; (1880), 365–6; (1885), 373–5; (1886), 383; (1892), 411; (1906), 425; (1910), 432; (1918), 461–2; (1938), 544–5; (1945), 588–9; Chapel Gate election (1949), 600–1; (1954), 609; (1962), 612; (1964), 632; called by O'Neill (1969), 662–3; (1974), 706–7, 713; (1987), 771–2; (1992), 817
geology, 4
Georg, Prince, of Daamstadt, 161
George I, King of England, 173
George III, King of England, 241
George IV, King of England: as Prince Regent, 241
George V, King of England, 446, 447; opens NI parliament, 481–2, 499; jubilee, 539
George's Market (Belfast), 389
Gerald of Wales, 34, 35–6, 38, 54
Geraldines, 33
'German Plot', 459–60
Germany, 300, 304, 336, 466, 476–7, 619, 829; (1848), 298; aid for Irish, 447–8, 452; Great Depression, 526; shipbuilding, 613, 614, 615, 627; unemployment, 795; Provisional IRA attacks in, 804–5
gerrymandering, 499–501, 511, 633, 638–9
Giant's Causeway, Co. Antrim, 170
Giant's Ring (Belfast), 8
Gibraltar shootings, 778, 781
Gilford, Co. Down, 329, 398
Ginkel, Baron, 161, 164–5
Girdwood, Co. Armagh, 682
Girona, 88–90, 100
Girr, Jim, 576
Gladstone, W.E., 354, 356, 382, 383, 405, 431, 514; and tenant right, 357–8, 366; and Home Rule, 358–60; 1881 Land Act, 369–70; 1885 election, 373–5; Home Rule Bill (1886), 375–80; attitude to Ulster, 404; and Parnell scandal, 407–8; Home Rule Bill (1893), 410–13; retires, 413
Glasgow, 310–11, 339, 394, 718; migrant labourers, 395; firemen sent from, 566
Glen Righe, Battle of, 36
Glenarm, Co. Antrim, 22, 46; Castle, 198
Glencolumbkille, Co. Donegal, 363
Glenconkeyne, Co. Londonderry, 119, 127; O'Neill in hiding, 112
Glenmona House, Cushendun, 491
Glennane, Co. Armagh, 810
Glens of Antrim, 68, 265, 383
Glenshane Pass, Co. Londonderry, 694
Glenshesk, Co. Antrim, 81
Glenties, Co. Donegal, 282, 362, 363; Great Famine, 287, 290, 293–4, 295, 297; U-boats, 560
Glentoran, Lord, 562, 578, 595
Glenveagh, Co. Donegal, 321, 324; Castle, 120
Glorious Revolution, 166
Glover, Major Gerald, 647
Glover, Brigadier James, 736–7
Gogarty, Frank, 653–4
Good, James Winder, 420
Goodland, Co. Antrim, 6

Goodyear (Craigavon), 626, 784
Gormley, Peter, 643
Gosford, Lord, 223, 227, 238
Gough barracks (Armagh), 604–5, 606, 734–5, 738
Goulding, Cathal, 651, 675
Government of Ireland Act *see* Better Government of Ireland Act
Gow, Ian, 748, 756, 759, 805
Graham family: and UDR, 807
Graham's betting shop (Belfast), 816
Grand Hotel (Brighton), 753–4
grand juries, 205, 215, 242; controlled by gentry, 196; roads, 265; Great Famine, 281, 283; abolished, 414
Grand Opera House (Belfast), 388, 813, 820
Gransha motte, 37
Grant, William, 510, 578, 592, 597
Grattan, Henry, 213, 215, 222, 241
Great European Famine (1315–17), 55
Great Famine, 176, 241, 264, 280–300; public works, 283–4, 287–91; relief committees, 285–6; disease, 291–4, 296–7; costs of, 299–300; effects of, 307–8; emigration, 308–12
'Great Irishry, The', 57–9
Greencastle, Co. Down, 42, 46, 47, 52, 575
Greencastle (Northburgh), 44
Greenlees, Andrew, 310, 327, 360–1
Greenwood, Sir Hamar, 474–5, 476, 481
Greer, Thomas, 187, 209, 210
Grey, Sir Edward, 425, 448
Greyabbey, Co. Down, 38, 46, 121, 122, 247
Grianan of Aileach, 14
Griffith, Arthur, 424, 436, 458–60, 482, 541, 628
Groomsport, Co. Down, 45
Grundig (Dunmurry), 626, 782
Guelke, Adrian, 809, 815
Guildford pub bombings, 723; prisoners freed, 806
Gulf War, 806, 810
Gulladuff, Co. Londonderry, 660
Gully Island, Co. Fermanagh, 199
gun-running, 443–5, 447
Gweedore, Co. Donegal, 191, 278–80, 321, 363

Hadden, Tom, 751
Haldane, John, 811
Hall, Sir Robert, 618, 620
Hall-Thompson, Lieutenant-Colonel Samuel, 593–4, 601, 603, 609
Hamill, Desmond, 680
Hamilton, Lord Claud, 356
Hamilton, Lord Ernest, 383
Hamilton, Gustavus, 153
Hamilton, Gustavus (2), 153, 158
Hamilton, James, 1st Viscount Clandeboye, 121, 122
Hamilton, Richard, 153, 154–9
Hamilton Rowan, Archibald, 220
Hanley, Jeremy, 813

Hanna, George, 480, 490
Hanna, Revd Hugh, 382
Hannahstown, Co. Antrim, 356
Hannay, Canon James O. (George A. Birmingham), 420
Hannon, Revd Brian, 777
Harland, Sir Edward J., 335, 336, 337–8, 380–1, 393
Harland and Wolff, 335, 336–9, 361, 388, 438, 518, 519, 548–9, 612–13, 627; *Oceanic* launched, 392–4; contingency plans for Home Rule, 404–5; First World War, 456–7; post-First World War, 464; Catholics driven out, 471; postwar slump, 518–20; Great Depression, 526; Second World War, 555; repair shop (Derry), 560; Second World War, 562, 579–80; blitzed, 564, 569, 570; absenteeism, 581; difficulties, 614–15; traumatic decline, 627–8; number of Catholics employed, 641; UWC strike, 707–8; Stormont takes shares, 721–2; government aid, 785–7, 788; *see also* Queen's Island
Harp Festival (Belfast), 221
Harris, Walter, 183, 190–2, 193–5, 200
Harry Avery's Castle, Co. Tyrone, 57
Haslett, James, 382, 383, 385, 417
Haughey, Charles J., 585, 630, 747, 750, 756; arms trial, 676–7; talks with Thatcher, 740–1; and hunger strikes, 743; New Ireland Forum, 752; and Anglo-Irish Agreement, 754–5, 759, 771; and Enniskillen bomb, 776; and Brooke talks, 811
Haughey's Fort, Co. Armagh, 8
Hay, William, 822
Hayes, Sean, 582
Hazlett, Inspector James, 772
H-block hunger strikes, 741–6, 750, 782, 795
Head Line, 560–1
Headfort estate, Co. Cavan, 252
Health Act (1947) (Éire), 597
Health and Local Government, Ministry of (NI), 597
health service, 596–8
Healy, Cahir, 510, 533, 537, 538, 642
Healy, T.M., 371–2, 414, 415, 423
Hearst, David, 805, 823
Hearts of Oak, 206, 207
Hearts of Steel, 206–8
Heath, Edward, 627, 689, 698, 712, 759; and NI, 679–80; and internment, 683; Cosgrave meets, 703; reassigns Whitelaw, 704; Sunningdale Agreement, 703–7; calls 1974 election, 706
Heatley, Fred, 653–4, 663
Hebrides, 56–7
Henderson, Tommy, 520, 527, 555, 573, 589
Hendron, Joe, 817
Henry, Paul, 389, 420
Henry, Professor Robert M., 420
Henry I, King of England, 33
Henry II, King of England, 31–3, 38
Henry III, King of England, 43, 44, 45
Henry III, King of England, 41

Henry VI, King of England, 66, 69
Henry VII, King of England, 49, 69
Henry VIII, King of England, 68, 70, 72, 75, 692; called King of Ireland, 71; Reformation, 72, 73
Herdman Channel (Belfast), 549
Herdman family, 262, 264
Herdman's (Sion Mills), 332, 580
Hermon, Sir John, 760, 761, 780, 808
Hertford, 4th Marquess of, 321, 356
Hervey, Frederick Augustus, bishop of Derry, Earl of Bristol, 197–8, 214–15, 216
Hewitt, John, 644
Hilden Mills (Lisburn), 329, 398
Hill, Lord George, 265–6, 279–80, 321
hill forts, 12, 14
Hillmount (Ballymena), 397
Hillsborough, Co. Down, 144, 200; plundered by Hamilton, 153; demonstration (1834), 254; opposition to O'Connell, 255; linen, 260; *see also* Anglo-Irish Agreement
Hitler, Adolf, 550, 554, 560, 574, 583
Hobson, Bulmer, 420–1, 424, 440, 443, 452
Hodson, Sir George, 252, 320
Hoggart, Simon, 819, 823
Holland, Mary, 676, 779, 805, 811, 815
Holmes, Erskine, 644, 652–3, 656
Holywood, Co. Down, 40, 47, 48, 123, 398, 680; railway, 264
Home Affairs, Ministry of (NI), 534, 563, 578; bans parades, 539–40
Home Government Association, 358–9
Home Rule movement, 365, 370–3; 1885 election, 373–5; reactions in Ulster, 373–84; first bill (1886), 375–80; Ulster crisis (1890–1920), 385–465; Unionist attitude misinterpreted, 402–4; growing Unionist opposition, 404–10; second bill (1893), 410–13; shelved, 413–15; third bill, 425–6; Carson's opposition to, 432–7; 1912 bill, 435–6; Asquith bill rejected, 439; partition considered, 441; 1914 bill passed for third time, 447; bill enacted and postponed, 450–1; six counties excluded, 453–4
Homeless Citizens' League, 637, 643, 648
Hope, Jemmy, 220, 233, 240
hospitals, 388–9, 597
House of Commons (Westminster): growing power of, 134; Irish Brigade, 316; evictions debated, 323; obstruction, 360, 369; electric light, 369–70; and NI Education Act, 504–5; relations with Stormont, 534–5; call for 1935 riots inquiry, 541; and NI, 646; Bernadette Devlin, 663; supports power-sharing, 712–14; Downing St Declaration, 715; Unionists hold balance of power, 735; approves Anglo-Irish Agreement, 759; boycotted by Unionists, 764; rejects internment option, 803
House of Lords (Westminster): defeats second Home Rule Bill, 412–13; constitutional crisis, 430–2; rejects Asquith bill, 439
housing, 426, 695, 717, 790, 823; prehistoric, 6;

894

post-and-wattle, 65; tower houses, 66; Belfast slums, 324–6, 532–3, 571–2, 591–2, 596, 716–17; inadequate, 532–4; survey (1943), 591–2; post-Second World War improvements, 591–3; local authority discrimination, 593, 636–8, 642–3; improvements, 714–19; high-rise flats, 718; intimidation of Catholics, 769–70; peace lines, 789–90; improvement progresses, 789–93, 794
Housing Act (1923), 533
Housing Act (1924) (UK), 533
Hughes, Francis, 744
Huguenots, 151, 165, 170, 174
Humbert, General Jean, 236
Hume, Sir Gustavus, 197
Hume, John, 662, 749, 766, 805, 828; University for Derry Campaign, 625–6; Credit Union, 648–9; Derry civil rights march, 654; wins seat, 663; Battle of the Bogside, 666–9; SDLP, 679; Bloody Sunday, 686, 688; and Provisional IRA, 694; Sunningdale Agreement, 703–7; SDLP leader, 739; and hunger strikes, 743; New Ireland Forum, 750–3; election results, 771, 817; condemns MacBride principles, 799
Hungary, 298, 304, 305, 334, 496
hunger strikes: H–blocks, 741–6, 795
Hungerford, Sir Wilson, 498, 578
Hunt, Sir John (later Lord Hunt), 674, 683, 808
Hurd, Douglas, 754, 755, 758
Hurson, Martin, 744
Hyde, Douglas, 421, 422

ICI (Carrickfergus), 626, 708
Impartial Reporter, 372
Inch Abbey, Co. Down, 38
Inch Island, Co. Donegal, 8
Independent Labour Party, 417
Independent Orange Order, 416, 417, 426, 428, 440
Independent Television News, 658
Indivisible Island, The (Gallagher), 621
industrial development, 203, 272, 300, 305; and linen industry, 185–6, 260–2, 266–8; dangers of linen mills, 329–3; new industries attracted, 626–7
Industrial Development Authority (IDA), 629
Industrial Development Board (IDB), 784–5, 788
Industries Development Acts, 618, 626
Industries of Ireland, The, 387, 391, 394, 398
Ineen Dubh (Fiona MacDonnell), 84, 93
Inishowen, Co. Donegal, 109, 170; ravaged, 50; granted to O'Doherty, 116; granted to Chichester, 120, 124; Great Famine, 283–4; migration to Derry, 396
Iniskeen, Co. Monaghan, 29
Inner City Trust (Derry), 820
Inniskeel, Co. Donegal, 282
inquisitions: (1226), 44–5; (1333), 47
insurance companies, 258
Insurrection Bill (1796), 228

Intergovernmental Conference, 756, 758–9, 760–1; *see also* Anglo-Irish Agreement *and* Maryfield Secretariat
International Fund for Ireland, 771, 788
International Monetary Fund, 721, 790
internment, 582–3, 607, 689, 699, 704, 795; (1922), 491; (1971), 681–6; ill-treatment of internees, 684; 'special category status' granted, 693; of loyalists, 701; civil disobedience, 716; final detainee released, 724; calls for reintroduction, 803
Iona, 17, 19, 20, 25
Ireland Act (1949), 601–2
Irish Anti-Partition League, 598
Irish Army, 585, 668–9; suppresses IRA, 583; and NI, 676–7; border patrols, 729
Irish Citizen Army, 442, 453
Irish Civil War (1922–3), 465, 466, 489–90, 492–4, 505
Irish Congress of Trade Unions (ICTU), 620; Northern Committee, 624, 799
Irish constitution (1937), 542–4; Articles 2 and 3, 705, 752, 759, 821, 828
Irish Convention, 458, 483
Irish Council, 68, 90, 128; report on rebellions, fifteenth century, 66; and O'Neill rebellion, 101
Irish Free State, 467; established, 484; election results, 492; and NI education, 502; army mutiny, 505; released from national debt payments, 509; farm size, 520; cross-border trade, 521–2; economic war, 535–7, 542; 1937 constitution, 542–4; *see also* Éire *and* Republic of Ireland
Irish Independent, 453, 646
Irish language, 406; link with Scotland, 57; surnames changed, 401; Gaelic revival, 421–2; in council chambers, 821
Irish Linen Board, 180–1
Irish Nation League, 459
Irish National Land League *see* Land League
Irish National Liberation Army (INLA), 736, 749, 774, 780
Irish News, 408, 453, 464, 504, 512
Irish Northern Aid Committee (Noraid), 731–2
Irish Parliamentary Party, 376, 383, 446, 451, 463, 645; obstruction, 360, 369; Parnell controls, 371–2; 1885 election, 373–5; first Home Rule Bill, 375–80; balance of power, 386; and Liberal Party, 402–4; Parnell split, 407–8, 411; second Home Rule Bill, 410–13; demoralised, 415; reunites, 415–16; and Gaelic revival, 422–3; third Home Rule Bill, 425–6; supports Asquith, 430–2; Home Rule Bill (1912), 435–6; resists use of force, 442; and Irish Volunteers, 445, 450; and Easter Rising, 453; outflanked by Sinn Féin, 458–60; election defeats (1918), 462; in Derry, 467; co-operation with Sinn Féin, 468, 470; *see also* Nationalist Party
Irish Press, 621, 646

Irish Protestant Home Rule Association, 379
Irish Republican Army (IRA), 466–7, 475, 535, 588, 644, 664; new name for Volunteers, 465; fighting in Derry (1920), 467–70; fighting in Belfast (1920), 473; Anglo-Irish War, 480–1; sends commandants north, 485; anti-treaty violence in NI, 486–95; Collins supplies arms to, 489; Irregulars, 489–90; attacks businesses, 491; civil war, 492–4; banned in Free State, 541–2; 1939 British campaign, 553–4; gaol breaks (1943), 578; suppression of, 581–3; Operation Harvest, 604–8, 610, 611; UVF attacks on, 635; and NICRA, 651; and civil rights movement, 662, 666; split, 674, 675; see also Official IRA and Provisional IRA
Irish Republican Brotherhood (IRB), 353, 360, 424–5, 442–3, 445, 451; Easter Rising, 452–3
Irish Society, 129–30, 133, 134, 146, 153, 394; schools, 341
Irish Temperance League, 387–8
Irish Tenant League, 314–15
Irish Trades Union Congress (ITUC), 417
Irish Transport and General Workers' Union (ITGWU), 430
Irish Volunteers, 443, 445, 459; gun-running, 447, 448; drilling, 447; split, 450; Easter Rising, 452–3; amnesty, 458; reorganise, 461
iron foundries, 146, 189
Ironmongers' Company, 130, 131
Irvinestown, Co. Fermanagh, 137, 501
Islandmagee, Co. Antrim, 68, 149, 251–2
Islay and Kintyre, Lords of, 68
Isle of Man, 36, 39, 399
Ismay, Thomas, 337, 393
Italy, 298, 300, 304, 466, 478, 744, 800, 827; nationalism, 352; unemployment, 795

Jackson, Harold, 666
Jacobites, 153, 166–7, 173
Jaffe, Daniel, 387
Jaffe, Sir Otto, 387
James I and VI, King of England and Scotland, 96, 100, 114, 117; receives O'Neill's submission, 115; plantation scheme, 118, 120, 121–2, 124–5; secret agents of, 121; turns to London Companies, 128–31
James II, King of England, 147, 149; war with William, 150–64
James IV, King of Scotland, 68
Japan, 518, 613, 614, 615, 628
Jesuit order, 73, 169, 247
Jews: applications to Northern Ireland, 550–1
John, King of England, 38, 39–40, 45
John Paul II, Pope, 738–9, 743–4, 776
Johnson, Paul, 763, 769
Johnston, Anna (Ethna Carbery), 421
Johnston, William, 354–6, 358, 383, 416
Johnston family, 127, 128
Joint Security Committee, 680
Jones, Paul, 210–11
Jones, Thomas, 475, 482–3, 484, 492, 496, 505, 508

Jonesborough, Co. Armagh, 607, 804
Joy, Robert, 203
Joy family, 203
joyriding, 825

Keady, Co. Armagh, 226, 500
Kellogg pact, 510
Kells, Co. Meath, 17, 25, 51, 158
Kelly, Henry, 690
Kelly, James, 529
Kelly, John, 677
Kelly, John, Ltd, 560–1
Kelly, Liam, 604
Kelly, Sir Samuel, 522
Kennedy, David, 539
Kennedy, Senator Edward, 731
Kennedy, Henry S., 540
Kennedy, Laurence, 817
Keynes, John Maynard, 466, 535–6
Kilcar, Co. Donegal, 362
Kilclief, Co. Down, 66
Kilclief House (Strangford), 491
Kildare, Co., 232
Kilfedder, James, 632, 634, 748
Kilkeel, Co. Down, 231, 399, 537; Ulster Resistance parade, 767
Kilkenny, Confederation of, 139–40
Kilkenny, Statutes of, 55
Killadeas, Co. Fermanagh, 18
Killala, Co. Mayo, 236
Killashandra, Co. Cavan, 275, 691; tannery, 189; population of, 272; poverty of, 277; Great Famine, 295–6
Killetra, Co. Londonderry, 127
Killevy, Co. Armagh, 18
Killinchy, Co. Down, 234
Killough, Co. Down, 285
Killowen Castle, Co. Londonderry, 43
Killultagh, Co. Antrim, 124, 127
Killybegs, Co. Donegal, 362, 363, 399, 413; Great Famine, 284, 290–1
Killylea, Co. Armagh, 286
Killyleagh, Co. Down, 45, 329, 581, 792; mansion, 197; 1798 rebellion, 234; Great Famine, 285
Killyleagh Castle, 440
Kilmainham Treaty (1882), 370
Kilnaleck, Co. Cavan, 293
Kilnasaggart, Co. Armagh, 18
Kilroot, Co. Antrim, 149, 171
Kiltooris Lough, Co. Donegal, 89
Kilwarlin Wood, Co. Antrim, 139
King, Lieutenant-General Sir Frank, 709
King, Tom, 758, 765, 774, 808
King, William, bishop of Derry, archbishop of Dublin, 168, 170, 173, 176
Kingscourt, Co. Cavan, 272
kingship, 21, 23–4; kings with opposition, 30–1
Kingsmills, Co. Armagh, 726, 790
Kinnegoe, Co. Armagh, 368–9
Kinsale, Battle of, 110–12, 122

431–2; threatened by Unionists, 441–2; resigned to partition, 446; Home Rule postponed, 450–1; Unionist distrust of, 478
Liberal Unionist Party, 379, 383
Liddell, Henry, 414
Liddle, Lieutenant-Colonel George, 470
Lifford, Co. Donegal, 80, 98, 106, 116; Williamite War, 159; rents, 197; borough sold, 216; Brunswick Club, 246
Lifford Castle, 65
lighthouses, 258
Limavady, Co. Londonderry, 44, 47, 129, 152, 397; aerodrome, 579
Limerick, siege of (1690–1), 164–5
Limerick, Treaty of (1691), 165
Limerick city, 26, 30, 146
liming, 190–1
linen industry, 148, 150, 179–82, 192, 224, 412, 428, 547, 627; eighteenth century, 184–8; health of workers, 187; farmer-weavers, 188–9; high rents for weavers, 196; slumps, 208, 211–12, 240; emigration of weavers, 209–10; and free trade, 238; Catholic weavers, 248; and industrial development, 260–2, 266–8, 272; crash, 271, 274; flax demand, 320; expansion of, 326–9; power looms, 327; health hazards, 329–34; wage levels, 333; First World War, 457; post-First World War, 463, 516–17; Great Depression, 526–7; Second World War, 580; collapse of, 615–16; Linen Task Force, 784–5
Linen Trade Circular, 328
Linfield Football Club, 436
Linfield Mill (Belfast), 390
Lisahally quay (Derry), 574, 585
Lisbellaw, Co. Fermanagh, 470, 487
Lisburn, Co. Antrim, 178, 500, 537, 810; rebellion (1641), 136–7; Venables victory, 141; population of, 146; plundered by Hamilton, 153; Quakers in, 174; weavers' colony, 180; weavers' riot, 187; rebuilt, 201; steam-driven mill, 203; Vitriol Island, 205; United Irishmen, 227; Brunswick Club, 246; opposition to O'Connell, 255; Great Famine, 285; elections, 356; industrial development, 398; sectarian riots, 472, 536; special constables, 475; Belfast evacuees, 571; aircraft manufacture, 580; Orange riots, 681; intimidation of Catholics, 770; soldiers' bus bombed, 804
Lisnafallen (Ballymena), 397
Lisnarick, Co. Fermanagh, 137
Lisnaskea, Co. Fermanagh, 22, 137, 470, 538, 807; Great Famine, 290; housing discrimination, 642
Lissane, Co. Londonderry, 8
Lissanoure (Ballymoney), 198
Litton, E.C., 370–1
Liverpool, 310, 311, 335, 336, 506, 580, 718, 797; firemen sent from, 566
Livestock Breeding Act (1922), 521
Lloyd George, David, 426, 430, 468, 479, 492, 500, 515, 809; negotiates partition, 453–4; prime minister, 456; 1916 amnesty, 458; and

partition, 463; Better Government of Ireland Bill, 465; and UVF, 474; establishes Ulster Special Constabulary, 475–6; and Anglo-Irish War, 480–2; treaty talks, 483–4; replaced by Bonar Law, 494–5
Llywelyn, of Wales, 41, 42, 43
local authorities: and housing, 532–4; NILP victories, 611; Cameron Commission, 638–9
Local Enterprise Development Unit (LEDU), 788
local government: elections (1920), 467–8; NI government reorganisation, 499–501; spending, 515; White Paper on, 633; universal suffrage agreed, 663; elections under PR, 702; under direct rule, 714–15; Macrory report, 715; elections (1981), 741; Unionist abstentionism, 764; loyalist abstentionism, 768; power-sharing in, 820–3
Local Government Act (1898), 414, 639
Local Optionists, 511
Locarno pact, 509, 510
Lockheed Aircraft Corporation, 566
Lockheed Overseas Corporation, 575
Lockwood, Sir John: Lockwood report, 625, 647, 656, 802
Logue, Cardinal Michael, 423, 436, 459, 462, 481
London, 580, 718: Derry restored to, 142; Earl of Antrim imprisoned, 142–3; Great Fire of, 146; bombs (IRA, 1939), 553, 554; blitz, 568; Provisonal IRA bombs, 705, 723–4, 805–6, 817–18; Balcombe St siege, 724
London Companies, 1, 133, 134, 197, 198; plantations by, 128–31; towns laid out by, 200–1
Londonderry, Co., 134, 250; Christianised, 16–17; plantation of, 128–30; Clothworkers' proportion, 178; linen industry, 186–7; deforestation, 189; distilling, 193; rents, 197; stately homes, 198; revolt at cess, 206; agrarian agitation, 207; United Irishmen, 228; open-air Masses, 248; survey (1802), 269; sea eagles, 276; rundale, 279; Great Famine, 280–1, 286, 294–5, 308; emigration, 309; ether-drinking, 342–3; Protestant majority, 345; elections, 360; shirt-making outworkers, 395; excluded from Home Rule, 447; attacks by IRA, 488
Londonderry, 6th Marquess of, 385–6, 388, 418–19, 426, 434
Londonderry, 7th Marquess of, 497, 562; Education Act, 501–3
Londonderry City (constituency), 374, 383, 403, 411, 439; gerrymandering, 638, 639; see also Derry city
Londonderry Corporation, 166, 499; replaced, 254, 657, 790; first Catholic mayor, 467–8; under Unionist control, 501; housing discrimination, 790; see also Derry City Council
Londonderry Rural District Council, 790
Londonderry Shipbuilding and Engineering Company, 395
Londonderry Standard, 314

898

899

defeated by James IV, 68; in Bonamargy, 73; Shane O'Neill flees to, 81; aid shipwrecked Spaniards, 88; change of weaponry, 97; allied with O'Neill and O'Donnell, 100
McElroy, Samuel C., 379, 383
McElwee, Tom, 744
MacEntee, Seán, 598
MacEoin, Sean, 485
McGarrity, Joe, 443, 452, 554
MacGill, Patrick, 319
McGonagle, Stephen, 647–8
McGrady, Eddie, 763, 771, 817
McGuffin, John, 682–3
McGuinness, Martin, 700, 772–3
McGurk's public house (Belfast), 686
McIlhenny, Henry, 324
MacIlwaine and Lewis (Ulster Iron Works), 339
McKeague, John, 670
McKelvey, Joe, 493
McKeown, Ciaran, 649, 727
McKinney, Thomas George, 317–19, 320
McKittrick, David, 766, 779, 781, 812, 821, 825
McKnight, Dr James, 314, 315
MacKnight, Thomas, 373, 375–6, 378–9, 383, 404–5, 412
McLachlan, Peter, 705
McLaughlin and Harvey, 389, 471
McLaughlin's bar (Belfast), 726
MacLellan, Brigadier Pat, 687
McLoughlin, Michael, 822
MacMahon, Brian MacHugh Oge, 111
MacMahon, Heber, bishop of Clogher, 141
MacMahon, Heber MacCooley, 92
MacMahon, Hugh, bishop of Clogher, 169, 171
MacMahon, Hugh Roe, 92
MacMahons, 43, 69, 70, 96; dispersed by Fitzwilliam, 92
MacManus, Cathal, archdeacon of Clogher, 60
MacManus, Terence Bellew, 352–3
McMillen, Liam, 632
MacMurrough, Dermot, King of Leinster, 31–3
MacNeice, Dr John, 539–40
MacNeice, Louis, 540, 557
MacNeill, Eoin, 421, 422, 443, 450, 452; on Boundary Commission, 506, 509
McNeill, Ronald, 406, 439
MacQuillans, 1, 67, 68, 121
Macready, General Sir Nevil, 470, 475, 492
MacRory, Cardinal, 471–2, 536, 538, 593
Macrory, Sir Patrick, 715
McSparran, James, 598
MacSweenys, 56–7, 66, 93; attack Shane O'Neill, 80–1; aid shipwrecked Spaniards, 89; Docwra attacks, 109
McTier, Martha, 221, 242, 249
McTier, Samuel, 220
McWhirter, Ross, 724
Mackie, James, 390–1
Mackie's (Belfast): Catholics driven out, 471; female labour, 580; Catholics employed, 641;

UWC strike, 708; burned, 774, 781–2; fashion linen, 785; redundancies, 788
Maffey, Sir John (later Lord Rugby), 583, 585, 598, 599, 603
Magee, Monsignor John, 743–4
Magee, Patrick, 753–4
Magee College (Derry), 396, 575, 625
Mageean, Dr Daniel, bishop of Down and Connor, 504, 541, 593
Magennis, Sir Conn, 136–7
Magennis, Glaisne, prior of Down, 67, 73
Magh Cobha Castle, Co. Down, 43, 45
Maghaberry airfield, Co. Antrim, 560, 575
Maghera, Co. Londonderry, 29, 343, 488, 651, 660
Magheracross, Co. Fermanagh, 357
Magherafelt, Co. Londonderry, 343, 500, 605, 788
Magherameenagh Castle, Co. Fermanagh, 492
Maghery, Co. Armagh, 253
Magilligan, Co. Londonderry, 192–3, 396, 682, 684
Maginess, Brian, 578, 590, 609, 610
Maginnis, Ken, 768, 803, 807, 822
Maguire, Amhlamh, 59
Maguire, Anne, 727
Maguire, Cuchonnacht, Lord of Fermanagh, 116–17
Maguire, Hugh, 95, 96, 104
Maguire, Sir Hugh, 101
Maguire, Hugh, Lord of Fermanagh, 78, 80
Maguire, Shane, Lord of Fermanagh, 80
Maguires, 59–60, 65, 70; attacked by Shane O'Neill, 78; rebellion (1641), 136, 138
Maguiresbridge, Co. Fermanagh, 470
Mahee Island (Strangford Lough), 18
Maidstone, 682, 684
Main, River, 48
Majestic, 338–9
Major, John, 806, 810
Malachy, St, 31, 32, 72
Malcolm, Dr Andrew, 292, 326
Mallie, Eamonn, 814
Mallon, Seamus, 761, 771, 773, 817
Malone, John, 801
Manchester bombings, 553
Manchester Martyrs, 354
Manpower Requirements Committee, 562
Mansion House fund, 600–1
Marketing of Fruit Act (1931), 547
Marketing of Potatoes Act (1928), 546–7
Markievicz, Countess Constance, 462
Mary, Queen of Scots, 79, 82, 83
Mary, wife of William III, 151
Mary I, Queen of England, 74, 87
Mary of Modena, wife of James II, 160, 161
Maryfield Secretariat, 756, 757, 759, 767; protests, 760–1; see also Anglo-Irish Agreement and Intergovernmental Conference
Mason, Roy, 721, 729, 730, 732–3, 742, 759; and interrogation techniques, 734–5
Mass Observation, 576, 579, 580–1
Mass rocks, 145, 169, 248

Massereene, Co. Antrim, 73, 83, 121, 124
Massereene, 10th Viscount of, 264
Mater Hospital (Belfast), 597
Matthew, Sir Robert, 624–5; Matthew plan, 717
Maudling, Reginald, 679, 686, 688
Mawhinney, Dr Brian, 800, 801, 813
Maxwell, Paul, 737
Maxwell, General Thomas, 159–60
Maydown airfield, Co. Londonderry, 575
Mayhew, Sir Patrick, 780, 818
Mayne, Rutherford (Samuel Waddell), 421
Mayo, Co., 227, 362
Maze prison, 355; hunger strikes, 741–6, 750, 782, 795; escape, 746; see also Long Kesh
Meath, Co., 14, 33, 52, 351
Meenacladdy, Co. Donegal, 362–3
megalithic tombs, 6–7, 8
Meharg, County Inspector William, 654
Melaugh, Eamonn, 653–4
Melchett, Lord, 721
Mellifont, Co. Louth, 31; Treaty of, 15, 113–14
mercenary soldiers, 68, 82, 86, 96
Merritt, John, 814
Messenger of the Sacred Heart, 423
metalworking: prehistoric, 7–9
Methodist Church: Temperance and Social Welfare Committee, 530
Methodist Times, 407
Methodists, 252, 416; evangelical revival, 340; and Land League, 368; Belfast churches, 387; condemn inadequate outdoor relief, 527
Miami Showband, 726
Michael, Stuart, 818
Michelin (Mallusk), 626, 708
Midgley, Harry, 480, 544, 545, 577, 589, 591; minister of public security, 578–9; education debate, 594; on Catholics, 609
Midland Bank, 518, 548, 549
Milford, Co. Donegal, 206, 331, 364
Milk and Milk Products Act (1934), 547
Milligan, Alice, 421
Millinship, William, 826
Minford, Nat, 659, 690
Mitchel, John, 241, 298–9, 312, 327
Mohill, Co. Donegal, 364
Moira, Co. Down, 198–9, 817; Battle of, 21
Molyneaux, James, 739, 758, 761–2, 763, 767; civil disobedience plan, 764; and Brooke talks, 815
Molyneux, Dr William, 148, 149, 201
Monaghan, Co., 4, 366, 397, 401, 691; native plantation of, 92, 94, 124; Williamite War, 153, 158; rapparees, 167; famine, 175; Massereene estate, 197; cess revolt, 206; opposition to Union, 239; election (1826), 245; poverty of, 278; Great Famine, 283–4, 286, 290, 295, 307; emigration, 309; evictions, 312; evangelical revival, 340; Protestant percentage, 346; chapel-building, 347; elections, 356; Land League, 368; new rents set, 370; Home Rule movement, 372; Irish language in, 421;

Unionist associations, 426; fear of exclusion from Ulster, 446; excluded from partition, 454, 467; raids from, 470; Unionists seek inclusion, 478; Boundary Commission, 509; sectarian aggression, 536; IRA, 582; neglected, 588; car bombs (1974), 708; peace and prosperity, 829
Monaghan Militia, 230, 231, 235
Monaghan town, 96, 201, 347–8, 397
monasteries, 17–20, 25–7, 30–1; political control of, 23–4; dissolution of, 73
Monck, General George, 142, 203
Moneymore, Co. Londonderry, 131, 136
Monro, Henry, 234–5
Monro, Major-General Robert, 139–40
Montgomery, George, bishop of Derry, Clogher and Raphoe, 116–17, 119, 121
Montgomery, Hugh, Laird of Braidstane, and later 1st Viscount of the Ards, 120–3, 190
Montgomery, Hugh de Fellenberg, 454
Montgomery, William, 148–9
Moore, John, 212, 223, 224
Moore, Dr John, 329–31
Moore, Revd S.J., 343–4
Morgan, Michael, 809
Morgan, William, 636–7, 642–3, 662
Morning Post, 508
Morrison, Danny, 746, 771
mortality rates, 531–2, 597, 795; Belfast, 326
Moryson, Fynes, 63, 64, 106, 110, 111, 113
Mother and Child scheme, 602–3
mottes, 36–7, 45, 46
Mount Sandel, Co. Londonderry, 1–3
Mountainview Tavern (Belfast), 681, 726
Mount-Alexander, Earl, 152–3
Mountbatten, Earl, 737, 738
Mountcashel, Viscount (Lieutenant-General Justin MacCarthy), 159
Mountjoy, 139
Mountjoy, Lord (Charles Blount), 103–4, 106–14, 116; destroys Tullahogue, 112–13; settles terms with O'Neill, 114; leaves Ireland, 115
Mountnorris, Co. Armagh, 107, 119
Movanagher, Co. Londonderry, 139
Movilla, Co. Down, 17, 26, 31, 48, 121
Moy, Co. Tyrone, 246–7
Moyry Pass: O'Neill's defence of, 106–7
Muckamore, Co. Antrim, 38, 124
Muckno Lake, 11
Muircertach, King of Uí Néill, 29
Mulholland, Thomas, 259, 261, 264, 302
Mullaghmore airfield, Co. Londonderry, 575
Mullan, Fr Hugh, 683
Mulvey, Fr Anthony, 648–9
Munster, 103, 106, 108, 272; rebellion in, 82; plantation disintegrates, 102
Murland, James and William, 261
Murphy, Edmund, 143–4, 145
Murphy, Lennie, 728
Murray, Adam, 154
Murray, Alan, 816
Murray, Harry, 707, 708

901

Murray, James, 321–2, 324
Musgrave Brothers (Belfast), 391, 471
Musgrave Park Hospital (Belfast), 812
Musgrave yard (Belfast), 627
Mussolini, Benito, 542, 556

Nally, Dermot, 756
Narrow Water Castle, Co. Down, 577, 737
Nation, 298, 315, 317
National Council for Civil Liberties, 646–7
National Health Service, 597
National Union of Dock Labourers, 427, 428, 430
National Union of Protestants, 609, 631
National University, 425
National Volunteers, 450
Nationalist Party, 371–2; election results, 383,
    439; Plan of Campaign, 384; split, 386; and
    Liberal Party, 402–4; in local government, 414;
    and 1903 Land Bill, 418; see also Irish
    Parliamentary Party
Nationalist Party (NI) 568, 603; election results,
    479–80, 544–5, 589, 662–3; refuse to meet
    Leech commission, 501; in Stormont, 507–8,
    510; abstentionism, 511–12; call for riots
    inquiry, 541; not in Brooke's cabinet, 579;
    Chapel Gate election, 600–1; opposed to
    terrorism, 608; agrees to be official opposition,
    633; and housing discrimination, 642; and civil
    rights movement, 645–6; calls off protests, 658;
    internment protest, 682
Navan Fort, Co. Armagh, 9, 10, 12–13, 14
Ne Temere decree, 406
Neave, Airey, 736
Needham, Richard, 794
Needham, Robert, 202
Neilson, Samuel, 222, 228, 230
Nelson, Revd Isaac, 343, 351
Nendrum, Co. Down, 29, 31
Netherlands, The, 112, 124, 150–1, 518;
    Provisional IRA attacks in, 804–5
neutrality, 545, 552, 553, 557, 585, 588, 600
New Industries (Development) Acts, 548
New Ireland Forum, 749, 750–3
New Ross, Co. Wexford, 48
New Theatre Royal (Belfast), 388
New University of Ulster (NUU), 625–6, 769,
    802; see also University of Ulster at Coleraine
New Zealand, 312, 347
Newcastle, Co. Down, 576, 679
Newe, Gerard, 610
Newman, Kenneth, 724–6, 732–3; and Thatcher,
    738
Newry, Co. Down, 76, 96–8, 102, 107, 113, 203,
    248, 397, 441; development of, 133, 398;
    attacked by rebels, 136; captives slaughtered,
    139; taken by Venables, 141; Williamite War,
    160; linen industry, 187, 328; distillery, 193;
    rebuilt, 202; Volunteers, 215; United Irishmen,
    228; Great Famine, 283, 299; Unionist
    organisations, 426; ships blacked, 430; Specials
    killed, 482; local authority dissolved, 499–500;

and Boundary Commission, 506–7; effects of
    border on, 521–2; Poor Law operation, 524;
    housing in, 534, 648; Cardinal Lauri visits, 537;
    US troops in, 576; B Specials attacked, 605;
    NILP controls council, 611; RUC barracks
    attacked, 669; civil rights riots, 670; bus depot
    bombed, 679, 680; intercommunal violence,
    681; internment riots, 682; SDLP wins seat, 761;
    extradition riots, 782; families displaced, 790
Newry and Mourne Council, 702
Newry Navigation, 183, 200, 202, 203–4
Newtownards, Co. Down, 45, 47, 82, 200, 398,
    814; sold to Montgomery, 121; successful
    colony, 122–3; 1798 rebellion, 234, 236;
    railway, 264; Great Famine, 297;
    aerodrome bombed, 567; aircraft manufacture,
    580; education protests, 594; 'Carson Trail',
    741
Newtownbarry, Co. Cavan, 253
Newtownbutler, Co. Fermanagh, 159, 470, 538,
    607
Newtownhamilton, Co. Armagh, 179
Niall Glúndubh, King of Uí Néill, 28, 30
Niall of the Nine Hostages, 13, 14
Nicolson, Bishop William, 175, 200
Nine Years War, 93–114; Yellow Ford, 101–2;
    Kinsale, 110–12
Nixon, J.W., 527
Noraid, 731–2
Normans, 1, 26, 31–3; military superiority of,
    35–6; mottes and castles, 36–7
Norris, Sir John, 97
North Atlantic Treaty Organisation (NATO),
    588, 600
Northburgh (Greencastle), 44, 52, 54
Northern Bank, 258
Northern Banking Company, 387
Northern Ireland: state established, 467, 476–9;
    elections (1921), 479–80; in treaty talks, 482–4;
    Special Powers Act, 490–1; on brink of
    anarchy, 491–5; death tolls, 494, 696, 701,
    705–6, 724, 726, 731, 770, 811, 816–17; early
    years of, 495–505; local government
    reorganised, 499–501; position of Catholics in,
    510–14; unemployment protests, 523–5; Wall
    Street Crash, 526–31; financial position of,
    534–5; and de Valera constitution, 543–4;
    economic improvement, 546–9; unprepared
    for war, 552–3, 555–7, 561–4, 573–4; US troops
    in, 553; rearmament industry, 555; Churchill's
    offer to de Valera, 558–9; government
    incompetence, 577–9; wartime production
    levels, 579–81; strategic significance of, 600;
    and Ireland Act, 600–2; report on industry,
    617–19; living standards improved, 618;
    economy under O'Neill, 623–8;
    institutionalised discrimination, 636–43;
    international image of, 646–7, 651, 655, 661–2;
    civil rights movement, 651–74; increasing
    violence, 675–81; internment, 681–6; statistics
    of violence, 686, 692–3, 695–8, 731, 732, 803–6,

902

O'Flynns, 37, 67
O'Gallagher, Redmond, bishop of Derry, 91, 92
O'Hanlon, Fergal, 606
O'Hanlon, Paddy, 663
O'Hanlon, Redmond, 143–4
O'Hanlon, Revd W.M., 324–5
O'Hanlons, 69, 78, 119
O'Hara, Patsy, 744

O'Higgins, Kevin, 494, 541
Old English, 132, 141; rebellion (1641), 138; and
    English Civil War, 139–40; Williamite War,
    164, 165; under pressure, 167
Oliver, John, 592, 624
Omagh, Co. Tyrone, 77, 397, 576; Williamite
    War, 159; Brunswick Club, 246; Great Famine,
    289; Nationalists win control, 468; Catholic
    teachers defiant, 502; barracks raided, 605;
    gerrymandering, 638; 'Carson Trail', 741;
    checkpoint attacked, 804
Omagh Castle, 66
Omagh Rural District Council, 501
O'Malley, Padraig, 818, 828
O'More, Rory, 135, 164
O'Mullans: conspiracy, 130
O'Neill, Lord, 197, 198; treatment of tenants, 275
O'Neill, Lord (1798), 233
O'Neill, Áed, King of Tír Eóghain, 40, 42–3
O'Neill, Áed Buidhe, King of Tír Eóghain, 43–4,
    67
O'Neill, Art, 70, 94, 105
O'Neill, Brian, 43, 45, 47, 76, 77, 93
O'Neill, Sir Brian MacPhelim, of Clandeboye,
    82, 83
O'Neill, Con Bacach, Earl of Tyrone, 67, 71–2,
    73, 75–6, 93
O'Neill, Sir Conn, 135
O'Neill, Conn Mac Néill, 120–2
O'Neill, Domnal, King of Tír Eóghain, 49, 50
O'Neill, Henrí Aimhréidh, 69
O'Neill, Henry (The Great O'Neill), 69
O'Neill, Hugh, Earl of Tyrone, 77–8, 88, 92, 122,
    128; turns against English, 93–5; rebels against
    Elizabeth, 96–100; Battle of Yellow Ford,
    101–2; Mountjoy's campaign against, 103–4,
    106–14; allies break away from, 105–6; appeals
    to Spain, 108; Battle of Kinsale, 110–12; terms
    of pardon, 113–14; submits to James I, 115;
    leaves Ireland, 116–18
O'Neill, Niall Mór, King of Tír Eóghain, 58–9,
    61–4
O'Neill, Niall Óg, King of Tír Eóghain, 58
O'Neill, Owen Roe, 139–41
O'Neill, Sir Phelim, 135, 136–7, 138, 141
O'Neill, Shane, 63, 97; sons of, 92, 93, 94
O'Neill, Sir Shane MacBrian, Lord of
    Clandeboye, 100, 121
O'Neill, Shane (The Proud), 75–81; submits to
    Elizabeth, 77–8; fall of, 79–81
O'Neill, Captain Terence, 619, 621, 640, 644, 645,
    679, 703, 704; economic progress, 622, 623–8;

meets Lemass, 628–30; opposition to, 631–6;
    reforms attempted, 657–8; TV broadcast, 658;
    forced to resign, 661–4
O'Neill, Turlough Luineach, 81–2, 83, 84, 85, 92,
    93–4, 105
Oneilland, Co. Armagh, 148, 206
O'Neills of Clandeboye, 66, 69, 70, 622; and
    Shane O'Neill, 76; allies of Shane O'Neill, 78;
    land threatened, 82; internal dissension, 92
O'Neills of Shane's Castle, 197, 198, 233, 251,
    275; see also Edenduffcarrick and Shane's
    Castle
O'Neills of Tír Eóghain, 1, 56; and Bruce
    invasion, 53; rivalry with O'Donnells, 57–8,
    69; Sliocht Henri and Sliocht Airt, 58;
    Maguires allies of, 59–60; castles of, 66;
    defeated by Grey, 71; conspiracy, 130
Operation Motorman, 698–9
Orange Order, 227, 406, 423, 426; founded, 226;
    not disarmed, 231; spread of, 237; opposes Act
    of Union, 238–9; conflict with Ribbonmen,
    242–5; banned, 244–5, 253–5; and 'invasion' of
    Ulster, 245–7; parliamentary report on, 254;
    Dolly's Brae, 302–4; riots, 306; defies Party
    Processions Act, 354–5; lifts Boycott's crop,
    366; and Land League, 367–8; and Home Rule,
    373; 1885 election, 374–5; and Conservatives,
    376–7; split, 416; complains of Catholic
    employment, 498; and Boundary Commission,
    506; and economic depression, 536; incensed
    by Eucharistic Congress, 537–9; criticism of,
    538–9; parades banned, 539–40; election
    conflicts, 600–1; disputes over marches, 609;
    and British Army, 677–8, 681; rejects power-
    sharing, 702; Anglo-Irish Agreement protests,
    766–8; see also Apprentice Boys of Derry,
    Independent Orange Order and loyalists
Ordnance Survey, 240, 248, 249, 251, 274–5; illegal
    distilling, 193; impact of mechanisation, 268
O'Reilly, Edmund, archbishop of Armagh, 139,
    145
O'Reillys, 69, 76, 78, 135; 1641 rebellion, 138
Orme, Stan, 708
Ormond, Duke of, 143, 144, 161
Ormond, 4th Earl of (White Earl), 69
Ormond, 10th Earl of, 77, 86, 101
O'Rourke, Sir Brian, 91, 92
O'Rourke, Tiernan, King of Bréifne, 31, 33
O'Rourkes, 30, 43, 103
Orr, Jacob, 266
Orrery, Lord, 198–9
Osborne, Sam, 822
O'Shiel, Kevin, 505, 507
Ostend shooting, 804
outdoor relief, 277, 297–8, 299, 363, 524–5; riots
    (1932), 527–9, 539
Ovary, Bob, 683
Ovens, Sergeant A.J., 607

Pagels, Bob, 707
Pain, Colonel G. Hacket, 445

Portugal, 124, 588, 719
Postal Service Promotion Board, 641
potatoes, 190, 192, 277, 280–1; reliance on, 270;
 harvesting of, 319
poteen, 193, 343
pottery: Neolithic, 6; medieval, 48
Powell, Enoch, 713, 748, 759, 764, 771
Poyning's Law (1494), 213, 214
Poyntzpass, Co. Armagh, 538
Presbyterian Church, 527, 634, 635; Social
 Services Committee, 530
Presbyterian General Assembly, 593
Presbyterians, 1, 173, 240, 345–6; as planters,
 132; and Wentworth, 133–4; *regium donum*,
 145, 162, 173, 357; emigration of, 150, 176–8;
 Penal Laws against, 171–5; Test Act, 172–4;
 rising middle class, 184; and United States,
 211; and Enlightenment, 217–18; renewed
 reform campaign, 218–19; and United
 Irishmen, 220–3, 229–31, 237; literacy rates,
 248; evangelicalism, 249–52; proselytism, 252;
 and repeal movement, 255; and tenant-right
 movement, 314–16, 354, 365–6, 384; and
 American Civil War, 327; evangelical revival,
 340–3; classless, 348; Liberal votes, 356; and
 Land League, 368, 370; Belfast churches, 387;
 Magee College, 396; and land reform, 416;
 support 1903 Land Bill, 418; and UVF, 440
Prevention of Terrorism Act (1974) (UK), 723, 734
Price, Dolours and Marion, 723
Prior, James, 744–5, 754, 759, 785; rolling
 devolution, 747–9, 755
Progressive Democrats, 771
Progressive Unionist Party, 544–5
proportional representation (PR), 468, 701;
 election (1921), 480; abolished in NI, 499–501;
 abolished for parliamentary elections, 510–11;
 local government elections (1973), 702
proselytism, 252
protection payments, 728
Protestant Action Force (PAF), 769
Protestant and Catholic Encounter, 727, 803
Protestant Imperial Federation, 417
Protestant Unionist Party, 662–3
Protestants, 73–4; planters, 131–2; opposition to
 nonconformism, 132–3; massacre of (1641),
 137–9; and English Civil War, 139–40;
 foundations of Ascendancy, 142; rally behind
 William, 152; Battle of the Boyne, 164;
 Ascendancy secured by William, 166;
 proselytism, 170; emigration to United States,
 176–9; atrocities against (1798), 236;
 evangelicalism, 240; reaction to Catholic
 emancipation, 247; Second Reformation,
 249–52; and repeal movement, 255–7; 1859
 revival, 340–4; compact community, 345–6;
 seen as separate nation, 400–2; blamed for
 bigotry, 404; economic domination of, 405–6;
 and Gaelic revival, 422–3; attitudes to
 Catholics, 643–4; reaction to army, 677–8;
 support for UWC strike, 712; *see also* sectarianism

Provisional IRA, 606, 680, 687, 701, 763; emerges,
 675–9; lure soldiers to Ligoniel, 680; response
 to internment, 682–3, 685; aim to wreck
 economy, 685; violence under direct rule,
 692–3; ceasefire (1972), 694–5; Bloody Friday,
 695–8; Irish Republic no longer haven, 700;
 and Sunningdale Agreement, 704; London
 bombs, 705; controls housing, 716; attacks
 economy, 720; British campaign, 722–5; Feakle
 talks, 724; further violence (1976), 725–6; shoot
 Lennie Murphy, 728; and SAS, 730–1; US
 support diminishes, 731–2; bombings (1978),
 733–4; Northern Command set up, 734; and
 interrogation, 734–5; increasing sophistication,
 736–7; drop in support, 738–9; hunger strikes,
 741–6; Armalite and ballot box, 746–7;
 Brighton bombing, 753–4; and Anglo-Irish
 Agreement, 759; loss of support, 771–2; target
 civilians, 772–3; Loughgall ambush, 773–4;
 Gibraltar deaths, 778; three shot at checkpoint,
 780; 'Long War' (1988–91), 803–6; 'proxy'
 bombs, 804; murders overseas, 804–6; death
 lists, 806; targeting police, 807–9; and Brooke
 talks, 810–11; tit-for-tat killings, 811–12;
 policing function, 825; *see also* Irish Republican
 Army *and* Official IRA
Provisional Sinn Féin, 693, 700, 744, 750, 752,
 768, 810, 828; election results, 748, 749, 755;
 and Anglo-Irish Agreement, 756, 759; by-
 elections, 761; and constitutional politics,
 770–2; targeted by UVF, 811; office attacked by
 RUC officer, 817; councillors, 820–3
public sector employment, 721; *see also* Northern
 Ireland Civil Service
Public Security, Ministry of (NI), 566, 568–9, 578–9
public works, 287–91, 299; Great Famine, 283–4
Purdon, Dr C.D., 329–32
Pyle, Fergus, 654–5
Pym, Francis, 704–7
Pytheas of Marseille, 10

Quakers, 174, 209, 285, 551, 621, 803
Queen's Colleges, 345
Queen's Island (Belfast), 302, 338, 456, 518, 519,
 548, 612–14; growth of shipyard, 334–9; strike,
 464; still working during Depression, 526;
 wartime production, 579–80; land engines,
 613; modernisation needed, 627; *see also*
 Harland and Wolff
Queen's University Belfast, 12, 530, 578, 631,
 650, 784, 797, 809; Gaelic in, 420; created, 425;
 integrated education, 596; Students' Union
 march, 655–6; Labour group, 656;
 employment of Catholics, 798; integrated
 teacher training, 802
Quigley, W.G.H., 721

racial divisions, 400–2
Radio Telefís Éireann, 655; governing body
 dissolved, 700

railways, 205, 258, 263–5, 285, 318, 328, 355, 385; and urban development, 397, 398
Ramelton, Co. Donegal, 260
Randalstown, Co. Antrim, 67, 275, 582, 659; 1798 rebellion, 232, 233; evangelical revival, 341
Raphoe, Co. Donegal: poverty of weavers, 267
rapparees, 164–7, 171
Rasharkin, Co. Antrim, 770
Rathcoole, Co. Antrim, 22
Rathfriland, Co. Down, 22, 213, 230, 288, 398
Rathlin Island, Co. Antrim, 5, 278; Essex massacre, 84–5; recovered by MacDonnells, 86; massacre, 94
Rathmore, Moylinny, Co. Antrim, 50
Rathmullan, Co. Down, 37
Rawdon, Sir Arthur, 153, 198–9
Rawdon, Sir George, 145–6
Rawros, Co. Donegal, 364
Reagan, Ronald, 771, 776
Rebbeck, Sir Frederick, 548–9, 613, 614
rebellions: Nine Years War, 93–114; (1641), 116, 135–42; Cahir O'Doherty, 118–20; (1798), 184, 232–7
Red Bay, Co. Antrim, 79, 86
Red Earl of Ulster see de Burgo, Richard
Red Lion restaurant (Belfast), 685
Redmond, John, 402–3, 414, 423, 433, 442, 446, 451, 458; reunites party, 415–16; third Home Rule Bill, 425, 426; supports Asquith, 430–2; convinced Unionists bluffing, 434; opposed to partition, 441; and Irish Volunteers, 445; commits Volunteers to war, 450; and Easter Rising, 453; death of, 459
Redmond, Revd John, 472–3
Redshanks, 68, 82, 96
Reede, Godard van, Baron Ginkel, 161
Re-equipment of Industry Act (1951), 618
Rees, Merlyn, 706–7, 709, 712, 724, 730, 731, 749; calls Convention, 713; 'Ulsterisation', 725
Reform Act (1832), 253, 300
Reform Act (1918), 461
rent-and-rates strike, 682, 707, 716
rents, 269, 272–3; conacre, 276–7; Great Famine, 286–7
repeal movement, 255–7
Representation of the People Act (1867), 354
Republic of Ireland: declared, 599–600; clerical domination, 601–2; military tribunals, 607; Whitaker plan, 619; economic progress, 622–3; growth under Lemass, 628–9; relations with NI, 633–4; and NI civil rights movement, 668–9; arms trial, 676–7; economic expansion, 691, 720; co-operation with Britain, 691; emergency powers legislation, 700; no longer terrorist haven, 700; coalition governments, 702–3; security forces co-operation, 731, 829; Thatcher–Haughey talks, 740–1; poor Anglo-Irish relations, 750; church and state, 751; role in NI recognised, 760; NI emigration to, 797; and Brooke talks, 811, 815; day-trippers to

Belfast, 819; liberalisation, 828; see also Éire and Irish Free State
Republic of Ireland Act (1948), 600
Republican Clubs, 651
Republican Labour Party, 632, 645–6, 682
Republican News, 582
Republican Party, 605, 632
Re-shaping of Local Government: Statement of Aims (White Paper), 633, 645
revolutions (1848), 298–9, 304–5
Ribbonmen, 253, 322, 353, 423, 676; Dolly's Brae, 303–4; Lord Leitrim murder, 364–5
Richard II, King of England, 58–9, 61
Richard III, King of England, 49, 69
Richardson, Lieutenant-General Sir George, 439
Richardson, Sons and Owden (Belfast), 389
ring-forts, 21–3
Ringhaddy Castle, Co. Down, 82
Ringneill Quay, Co. Down, 5
roads, 188, 265–6
Robinson, Bruce, 785
Robinson, Mary, 756–7, 821–2, 828
Robinson, Peter, 762, 767–8
Robinson, Richard, Baron Rokeby, 201
Robinson and Cleaver (Belfast), 389
Roden, Lord, 238, 250, 254, 303, 341
Roe, River, 47
Roermund shootings, 805
Roman Empire, 10–11, 13, 14–15, 19
rompering, 694
Roscommon, Co., 144, 458
Rosebery, 5th Earl of, 404, 413
Rosen, Lieutenant-General Conrad von, 154, 157, 160, 162
Rosslea, Co. Fermanagh, 7, 372–3, 605, 804
Rossmore, Lord, 262, 347, 373
Rossmore estate, Co. Monaghan, 370
Rossville Flats (Derry), 718
Rostrevor, Co. Down, 229, 249
round towers, 29
Route, the, Co. Antrim, 67, 68, 122, 440
Route Tenants' Defence Association, 379
Routh, Sir Randolph, 282, 283
Rowan Hamilton family, 197
Rowley, John, 129, 130, 131
Royal Air Force, 560, 574, 585, 627, 804–5
Royal Belfast Academical Institution see Belfast Academical Institution
Royal Irish Constabulary (RIC), 343, 364, 408, 440, 471, 499; and sectarian riots, 350–2; and Fenians, 353–4; Land League meetings, 367; Belfast riots (1886), 381–2; strike, 429; two shot dead (Soloheadbeg, 1919), 465, 485; Anglo-Irish War, 467; barracks evacuated, 468–9; and Ulster Special Constabulary, 476; casualties (1921), 482; attacked by IRA, 486–95; reprisals by, 489; RUC formed, 490; see also Black and Tans
Royal Irish Rangers, 808
Royal Irish Regiment, 808; see also Ulster Defence Regiment

Royal Mail Group, 520
Royal Marines School of Music (Deal), 805
Royal Navy, 456, 457, 557, 560
Royal School estates, 272
Royal Ulster Constabulary (RUC), 507, 634, 664,
680, 689, 733, 739; established, 490; Catholics
in, 497, 499, 687, 798; costs of, 515; outdoor
relief riots, 528–9; Second World War, 555;
shoot zoo animals, 569; and IRA, 581–2; and
Saor Uladh, 605–7; remove flag (Belfast), 632;
oppose UVF, 636; and civil rights
demonstrations, 652–5, 657, 662, 665–6;
Burntollet, 659–60; Bogside invasion, 661;
Battle of the Bogside, 666–9; resources
stretched, 669–71; Hunt's recommendations,
674; Special Branch, 675; and internment,
681–6; again permitted arms, 700; removes
loyalists from Stormont, 706; Newman in
charge, 724–6; Reserve expanded, 725;
Operation Knife Edge, 728; Castlereagh
interrogations, 734–5; loyalist intimidation of,
761–3; and Orange parades, 766–7; death toll,
770; Provisional IRA attacks on, 772, 804;
'shoot-to-kill' policy suspected, 778–81;
Catholic attitudes to, 809; officer attacks Sinn
Féin office, 817
Royal Victoria Hospital (Belfast), 388, 697, 709
Rugby, Lord see Maffey, Sir John
rundale, 279–80, 364
Russell, Lord John, 281, 283, 291, 314
Russell, Thomas, 222, 228, 240, 249
Russell, Thomas W., 416, 419
Russia, 334, 342, 417, 466, 476, 574, 615, 776;
Soviet bloc disintegrates, 691–2; reaction to
Sands's death, 744; break-up of, 826, 829
Rutland Island, Co. Donegal, 292

St Columb's College (Derry), 396, 469, 625–6, 649
St Leger, Sir Anthony, 57, 71
St Louis, Sisters of, 399
St Patrick's Cathedral (Armagh), 348
St Patrick's Purgatory, 61–3, 169; destroyed, 132
Saint-Ruth, Charles Chalmont, Marquis de,
164–5
St Vincent de Paul Society, 346, 525, 796
Saintfield, Co. Down: 1798 rebellion, 233–4
Salisbury, Robert Arthur Talbot Gascoyne Cecil,
3rd Marquess of, 368, 371, 374, 376, 379, 383,
407, 410, 437
Salisbury, Lord see Cecil, Sir Robert
Sampson, Colin, 780–1
Sampson, Revd Vaughan, 269, 276
Sands, Bobby, 738, 741–4, 746
Saor Uladh, 604–7
Sarajevo, 826–7; assassination (1914), 446–7
Sarsfield, Patrick, 164–5
Saul, Co. Down, 15
Saunderson, Major Edward J., 374, 379, 402, 411,
414, 418; and university question, 418
Savages, 45, 67
Scarman tribunal, 671, 675

Scarva, Co. Down, 610
Schomberg, Marshal, 157, 159–63, 202
Schwabe, Gustav C., 335, 336, 393
Scotch St (Armagh), 6
Scotland, 241, 522, 626; geology, 4; Roman
Empire, 10; Gaelic colonisation of, 17; political
alliances in Ulster, 20–1; Vikings, 26; Scots in
Ulster, 41; Scots awarded Antrim land, 42;
campaigns against, 44, 45; gallowglasses, 56–7;
Gaelic unity with Ulster, 57; Isles conquered
by, 67–8; Scots in O'Neill's service, 76; O'Neill
attacks MacDonnells, 79; English fears of
Scots-Irish alliance, 85–6; Spaniards try to
reach, 88, 89–90; Hamiltons and Montgomerys
plant settlers, 121; MacDonnell invites settlers,
122; deforestation, 127; planters from, 127–8;
Covenant, 133–4; and 1641 rebellion, 139;
refugees (1641), 139; famine, 171; Presbyterian
emigration from, 171; Presbyterian divisions,
173–4; migration to Ulster ceases, 177; migrant
labour, 277, 363; emigration to, 310–11;
Thatcherism, 794; see also Bruce invasion
Scott, Nicholas, 800
Scottish Isles, 29, 59, 75, 83; absorbed by
Scotland, 67–8; Scots retreat to, 86
Scrabo, Co. Down, 7, 48
Scullion, John, 635
Seawright, George, 766, 821
Second World War, 517, 544, 549–51, 552–86;
Dunkirk, 558; victory celebrations, 583–6
sectarianism, 419; housing; Peep o' Day Boys v.
Defenders, 223–7; growth in, 240; Ribbonmen
v. Orangemen, 242–5; Orange riots, 247;
Belfast riots, 247, 306, 349–52, 356–7, 380–2,
404, 539–41; Dolly's Brae, 302–4; Catholic
sections of Belfast, 346; Belfast, 348–9, 372, 403;
riots (1857), 349–50; riots (1864), 350–2; riots
(1872), 356–7; Derry, 396; Protestants blamed,
404; Belfast attacks (1912), 436; Derry fighting
(1920), 467–70; Belfast warfare (1920), 470–4;
families displaced, 482, 489, 491, 494, 683–6;
assassinations, 487–8, 700, 724, 790, 810–12,
816–17; in civil service, 497–9; and agricultural
depression, 535–6; increasing, 608–12;
institutionalised, 625–6, 636–43; election
campaigns, 632; aroused by civil rights
movement, 665–72; tit-for-tat killings, 726;
Shankill Butchers, 728; after Anglo-Irish
Agreement, 768, 769–70; and employment,
796–800; see also education and housing
seminaries, continental, 74, 132
Semtex explosive, 774, 812, 817
Sentry Hill farm, Co. Antrim, 317–19, 320
servitors, 115, 118, 125, 127; in Antrim and
Down, 121–2
Severely Disadvantaged Areas, 787
Sexton, Thomas, 383, 403
Shane's Castle, Co. Antrim, 67, 188, 195, 198,
251, 440; burned, 491; see also Edenduffcarrick
and O'Neills of Shane's Castle
Shankill Butchers, 728

908

incompetence, 573–4; debate on Education Bill, 594–5; opposition all Catholic, 601; first Catholic in cabinet, 610; first official opposition, 611–12; Nationalists official opposition, 633; prorogued, 689, 690; Convention, 712–14; Downing St Declaration, 715; support for Harland and Wolff, 721–2; Intergovernmental Conference, 761; North–South talks, 829

Story, George, 160, 163

Strabane, Co. Tyrone, 159, 397, 582; burned, 119; sectarianism, 247; Presbyterian Synod, 250; Nationalists win control, 468; local authority dissolved, 500; Catholic teachers defiant, 502; unemployment rate, 628, 797; RUC barracks attacked, 669; internment riots, 682; extradition riots, 782

Straits of Moyle, 57

Strangford, Co. Down, 82

Strangford Lough, 27, 29, 193–4, 344

Stranmillis (Belfast), 123

Stranorlar, Co. Donegal, 285

strikes see labour movement

Strongbow (Richard de Clare), 33

Stronge, Sir Norman, 743

Struell Wells, Co. Down, 249

suffragettes, 447

Sunday Times Insight Team, 664, 678, 684

Sunningdale Agreement, 703–7; UWC strike against, 707–11

surnames, 30, 401

Surrender and Regrant, 71–2

Sussex, Earl of, 76–7, 78, 80

Swan and Hunter (Derry), 395, 519, 580

Swanzy, District Inspector Oswald, 472

Swatragh, Co. Londonderry, 482, 676

Sweden, 125, 131, 518, 588, 614, 615, 628

Sweeney, Commandant-General Joe, 492, 493

Swift, Jonathan, 171, 172, 173

Switzerland, 588, 800, 827

Sydenham aerodrome, Belfast, 549

Sykes, Sir Richard, 736

synthetic fibre industry, 615–16, 626, 719, 782

Tablet, The, 314

Táin Bó Cuailgne, 12–13

Talbot, Richard, Earl of Tyrconnell, 150, 152, 160–1, 163, 164

Tamlaght O'Crilly, Co. Londonderry, 251, 279

Tandragee, Co. Armagh, 16, 246–7

tanneries, 189

Tartan gangs, 694, 700–1, 708

Taylor, John, 652, 707

Tedavnet, Co. Monaghan, 7

Teebane Cross, Co. Tyrone, 814–15, 816

temperance movements, 251, 534; evangelical revival, 342–3; Pioneer Association, 422–3

Templegowran, Co. Down, 260

Templepatrick estate, Co. Antrim, 15, 206

Templetown, Lord, Co. Antrim, 437–8

Templetown, 4th Viscount, 412

Templetown estate, Co. Monaghan, 313

Temporary Relief of Destitute Persons in Ireland Act (1847), 291

tenant-right movement, 178, 307, 313–16, 320, 354; Gladstone's bill, 357–8; election candidates, 360; smallholders unite, 365–6; boycott, 366; Wyndham's Land Bill, 418

Test Act (1704), 172–4, 177

Teutonic, 338–9

Thames Television, 781

Thatcher, Margaret, 767, 782, 788, 824; and NI problem, 735–41; and hunger strikes, 743, 745, 750; and rolling devolution, 747–8; Brighton bombing, 753–4; 'out, out, out' speech, 754–5; Anglo-Irish Agreement, 754–60; and Gibraltar shootings, 778; visits NI, 804

36th (Ulster) Division, 449, 450, 541; Battle of the Somme, 454–6

Thomas, David, 745

Thomson, James, 234–5

Thorne, Brigadier David, 738

Thurot, General François, 211, 214

Tievebulliagh, Co. Antrim, 5

Tighe, Michael, 780

Tipperary, Co., 299, 354, 465

Tír Conaill, 14, 28, 43, 46, 63, 93; Norman raids, 42; MacSweeny clan in, 57; raided by Shane O'Neill, 78; O'Donnell restored to power, 80; planned invasion of, 99

Tír Eóghain, 14, 22, 30, 40; O'Donnells of, 57–8; O'Neills of, 59; invaded by Earl of Kildare, 70; ravaged by Grey, 71

Titanic, 90, 438

Tithe War, 253

tithes, 242

Tobermore Baptists, 344

Toleration Act (1719), 173, 174

Tollymore, Co. Down, 198, 303

Tone, Theobald Wolfe, 220–3, 229, 237, 245; commemorations, 605, 772–3

Toolis, Kevin, 826

Toome, Co. Antrim, 9, 128, 195; tannery, 189; bridge, 205; bridge broken, 232; airfield, 575; civil rights march, 660

Topping, W.W.B., 609

tories, 143–4, 167

Tory Island, Co. Donegal, 16, 29, 120

tower houses, 66

town corporations, 196, 215

towns, 26, 200–3, 272; monasteries as, 18; earldom of Ulster, 47–8

Townsend, Peter, 793–4

trade, 48; with France, 47; decline, 133; export bans, 146; linen, 180–1; fluctuations, 206; transport developments, 399; First World War, 457; effects of First World War, 516

Trade Facilities Act (1921), 519

trade unions see labour movement

transport and communications, 183; roads, 188,

Ulster Protestant Volunteers, 634, 652, 657
Ulster Protestant Voters' Defence Association, 497
Ulster Quaker Peace Education Project, 803
Ulster Railway Company, 263–4
Ulster Resistance, 767–8
Ulster Special Constabulary, 474–6, 482, 499, 558, 685, 807; war against IRA, 486–90; test mobilisations, 506; dissolution recommended, 674; *see also* A Specials *and* B Specials
Ulster Television, 655
Ulster Tenant Right Association, 314
Ulster Unionist Convention (1892), 408–10
Ulster Unionist Council, 426, 436, 498, 622, 706; plans armed resistance, 431–2; and UVF, 439–41; and First World War, 449; accepts exclusion of six counties, 453–4; Irish Convention, 458–9; revives UVF, 474; accepts Ulster parliament, 477–8
Ulster Unionist Labour Association, 512
Ulster Unionist Party *see* Official Unionist Party *and* Unionist Party
Ulster Unionist Party Standing Committee, 610
Ulster United Prayer Movement, 584
Ulster Vanguard, 688–9, 690, 704; election results, 702, 706; UWC strike, 707–8, 711; supports Craig, 713
Ulster Volunteer Force (UVF) (1913–22), 439–42, 485, 522; gun-running, 443–5; drilling, 447; First World War, 448–50; revived, 467; Derry fighting (1920), 468–70; reorganises, 472, 474–5; in Liverpool, 506
Ulster Volunteer Force (UVF) (1966–), 635, 682, 700, 810; plot against O'Neill, 636; atrocities, 726; Shankill Butchers, 728; gaol sentences, 732; attacks by, 811–12
Ulster Women's Unionist Council, 446, 594
Ulster Workers' Council (UWC), 714; strike (1974), 707–11
Unbought Tenants' Association, 508
Unemployed Workers' Organisation, 524–5, 528–9
unemployment, 555, 587, 618–19, 620; (1922), 515; in NI state, 523–5; statistics, 529, 628; during Second World War, 562; during 1950s, 612–19; in agriculture, 617; impact of new industries, 626–7; and discrimination, 639–42; depression (1980s), 783–9; cause of poverty, 794–5; religious discrimination, 796–800; and paramilitaries, 824–5
Unemployment Assistance Board, 641
Unemployment Funds, 591
Union-Castle line, 526, 548
Unionist Clubs, 437
Unionist Clubs Council, 412
Unionist Party, 383, 665; strength of, 384; Convention (1892), 408–10; dissension within, 415–17, 679–80; end of constructive unionism, 417–19; and 1903 Land Bill, 418; and third Home Rule Bill, 425–6; plans violent action, 431–2; Carson as leader, 432–7; and Irish Convention, 458–9; increased seats, 462;

preparations for partition, 463–5; first NI government, 496–7; and Nationalists in Stormont, 510; Second World War incompetence, 552–3, 555–7, 561–4, 573–4, 577–9; Brooke takes over, 578–9; postwar government, 589–91; Chapel Gate election, 600–1; refuses to integrate Catholics, 608–12; criticism of Hall report, 620; opposition to O'Neill, 631–6; supports O'Neill, 658; election results (1969), 663; internment, 683; *see also* discrimination, housing, local government *and* Official Unionist Party
Unionist Party of Northern Ireland (UPNI), 713
United Education Committee of the Protestant Churches, 503–4
United Ireland, 403
United Irish League, 415–16, 417, 446
United Irishman, 298
United Irishmen, 220–3, 227, 240; French support, 227, 228–9, 236–7; martial law declared, 230–2; insurrection, 232–8; renewed efforts, 240
United Kingdom *see* Britain
United Nations, 668, 759
United States, 360–1, 362, 398, 465, 719, 744, 800; emigration to, 115–16, 125, 150, 184, 208–10, 308–10; Revolution, 210–14; War of Independence, 217, 224; Tone travels to, 222–3; Fenianism, 353; Irish-Americans and partition, 458–9; shipbuilding, 518; Wall Street Crash, 520, 525–6; troops in NI, 553, 574–7; and partition, 598–9; support for Provisional IRA, 677; less support for Provisional IRA, 731; pressure on Thatcher, 739; reaction to Enniskillen bomb, 776–7; MacBride principles, 798–9; *see also* American Civil War
United States Air Force, 786
United Ulster Unionist Council (UUUC), 713; strike, 732–3
Unity Flats (Belfast), 718
Universities Bill (1908), 425
University for Derry Campaign, 626
University of Ulster at Coleraine, 769, 802; *see also* New University of Ulster
university question, 418–19
Unlawful Societies Act (1825), 244
Upton family, 206
urbanisation *see* towns
USSR *see* Russia

Vanguard *see* Ulster Vanguard
Venables, Colonel Robert, 141
Versailles, Treaty of, 476–7
Victoria, Queen of England, 354, 357, 369, 376; visits Belfast, 302
Victoria Channel (Belfast), 300–2, 336, 549
Victoria locks (Newry), 398
Victoria Station bomb (London), 806
Victoria Weaving Company (Belfast), 616
Victoria yard (Belfast): closed, 627
Vikings, 2, 24, 25–30, 55

Vindicator, 256, 298
Volunteers (eighteenth century), 224, 404; formed in Belfast, 211, 212; strength of, 213–14; Dungannon Convention, 214–16; and Catholic emancipation, 216–18; renewed reform campaign, 218–20; suppressed, 221; attack Defenders, 223; Dungannon Convention, 223
Vulliamy, Ed, 827

Waddell, Helen, 421
Waddell, Samuel (Rutherford Mayne), 421
wage levels: linen industry, 333
Wakehurst, Lord, 614, 631
wakes, 248–9, 251
Wales, 41, 43, 72, 529, 535, 548, 626; housing, 717; Thatcherism, 794
Walker, Cecil, 810
Walker, Revd George, 154–5, 161–3
Walker, William, 417, 430
Wallace, Colonel R.H., 431
War News, 581
Ward, Peter, 635
Waring, Joseph, 460
Waring, Colonel Thomas, 400
Warnock, Edmond, 552, 556, 561, 563, 638
Warrenpoint, Co. Down, 200, 398, 430, 504, 507; NILP controls council, 611; RUC man shot, 725; soldiers bombed, 737–8
Wars of the Roses, 49, 59
Waterford, 48; taken by Normans, 33; King John in, 39; Richard II lands at, 58
Watt, A.A., Distillery, 395
weaponry: spread of muskets, 97
welfare state, 590–1
Wellington, Duke of, 247, 281
Wentworth, Thomas, 132–4; recusancy fines, 135
Wesley, John, 183, 201, 217, 249
West, Harry, 630, 636, 706, 707, 715; defeated by Sands, 743
Westenra, Henry, 245
Westlink (Belfast), 789
Westminster see House of Commons and House of Lords
Westminster Gazette, 474, 476
Wexford, Co., 26, 141, 232, 236
whaling, 194, 279
whiskey, 63, 193, 279, 280
Whitaker, T.K., 619, 623, 628, 629–30
White, Barry, 639, 767, 784
White, Captain Jack, 440
White Abbey, Co. Antrim, 38
White Island, Lough Erne, 18
White Linen Hall (Belfast), 389
White Star line, 336–8, 438, 519–20
Whiteabbey, Co. Antrim, 37
Whitecross, Co. Armagh, 726
Whitelaw, William, 689, 692, 712, 715; 'special category status', 693; and Provisional IRA, 694–5; Operation Motorman, 698–9; Sunningdale Agreement, 703–7

Whites of Dufferin, 67
Wickham, Lieutenant-Colonel Charles, 476, 485
Widgery, Lord, 688
Wild Geese, 166
Wilde, Oscar, 389, 432
Wildenrath shooting, 804–5
wildlife: red deer and wolf extinct, 189; rabbits, 192–3; pressure on land, 276
Willes, Edward, 183–4, 201
William III, of Orange, King of England, 149, 174, 255; war against James, 150–64; first Irish parliament, 165–6; and Penal Laws, 168
Williams, Betty, 727, 733
Wilson, Gordon, 775–7
Wilson, Harold, 562, 632, 633, 646, 709; insists on reforms, 657; Downing St Declaration, 672–3; appoints Rees, 706–7; visits NI, 707; 'spongers' speech, 710; Constitutional Convention, 712–14
Wilson, Field Marshal Sir Henry, 489
Wilson, John, 650
Wilson, Marie, 775–6
Wilson, Sammy, 821
Wilson, Tom, 643–4; Wilson plan, 624–5, 626–7
Wilson, Walter, 336, 337, 338
Wilson, Woodrow, 465, 477
Windsor Magazine, 393
Wingfield, Sir Richard, 119–20
Witness, 368, 374, 387
Wolfe Tone, Theobald see Tone, Theobald Wolfe
Wolfe Tone Societies, 651, 652
Wolff, Gustav, 335, 336, 338, 393
Wolfhill mills (Ligoniel), 390
women, employment of, 266–8, 332–3, 395, 580
Women Together, 693, 727, 803
Women's Voluntary Service, 571
Woodburn, Revd Dr J.B., 591
woodkerne, 97, 128, 131, 132, 167
Woods, Seamus, 493
Woodside, Moya, 565, 569, 571, 572, 586
Woolwich bombing, 723
Workers' Party, 773, 821
workhouses, 254, 277; Great Famine, 289–90; take full burden of relief, 293–4; growing strain on, 295–8; outdoor relief, 297–8; rate-in-aid, 299
Workman Clark and Co., 339, 361, 464, 523; First World War, 457; attacks 'disloyal' workers, 471; in difficulties, 519; closes down, 526
Worm Ditch, 11
Worthington-Evans, Sir Laming, 497, 506
Wright, Alan, 733
Wright, Thomas, 209, 210
Wright, William, 370
Würtemberg-Neustadt, Ferdinand Wilhelm, Duke of, 161, 162
Wyndham, George, 417–19
Wyndham Act (1903), 418

Yellow Ford, Battle of the, 101–2
yeomanry, 228, 230–1, 232, 233, 237, 243, 253;

913